Kim Viborg Andersen   John Debenham
Roland Wagner (Eds.)

Database and Expert Systems Applications

16th International Conference, DEXA 2005
Copenhagen, Denmark, August 22-26, 2005
Proceedings

Springer

Volume Editors

Kim Viborg Andersen
Copenhagen Business School
Njalsgade 80, 2300 Copenhagen S, Denmark
E-mail: kva.inf@cbs.dk

John Debenham
University of Technology, Sydney
P.O. Box 123, Broadway, NSW 2007, Australia
E-mail: debenham@it.uts.edu.au

Roland Wagner
University of Linz
Altenbergerstr. 69, 4040 Linz, Austria
E-mail: rrwagner@faw.uni-linz.ac.at

Library of Congress Control Number: 2005930886

CR Subject Classification (1998): H.2, H.4, H.3, H.5, I.2, J.1

ISSN   0302-9743
ISBN-10   3-540-28566-0 Springer Berlin Heidelberg New York
ISBN-13   978-3-540-28566-3 Springer Berlin Heidelberg New York

This work is subject to copyright. All rights are reserved, whether the whole or part of the material is concerned, specifically the rights of translation, reprinting, re-use of illustrations, recitation, broadcasting, reproduction on microfilms or in any other way, and storage in data banks. Duplication of this publication or parts thereof is permitted only under the provisions of the German Copyright Law of September 9, 1965, in its current version, and permission for use must always be obtained from Springer. Violations are liable to prosecution under the German Copyright Law.

Springer is a part of Springer Science+Business Media

springeronline.com

© Springer-Verlag Berlin Heidelberg 2005
Printed in Germany

Typesetting: Camera-ready by author, data conversion by Scientific Publishing Services, Chennai, India
Printed on acid-free paper   SPIN: 11546924   06/3142   5 4 3 2 1 0

Lecture Notes in Computer Science 3588

Commenced Publication in 1973
Founding and Former Series Editors:
Gerhard Goos, Juris Hartmanis, and Jan van Leeuwen

Editorial Board

David Hutchison
  Lancaster University, UK
Takeo Kanade
  Carnegie Mellon University, Pittsburgh, PA, USA
Josef Kittler
  University of Surrey, Guildford, UK
Jon M. Kleinberg
  Cornell University, Ithaca, NY, USA
Friedemann Mattern
  ETH Zurich, Switzerland
John C. Mitchell
  Stanford University, CA, USA
Moni Naor
  Weizmann Institute of Science, Rehovot, Israel
Oscar Nierstrasz
  University of Bern, Switzerland
C. Pandu Rangan
  Indian Institute of Technology, Madras, India
Bernhard Steffen
  University of Dortmund, Germany
Madhu Sudan
  Massachusetts Institute of Technology, MA, USA
Demetri Terzopoulos
  New York University, NY, USA
Doug Tygar
  University of California, Berkeley, CA, USA
Moshe Y. Vardi
  Rice University, Houston, TX, USA
Gerhard Weikum
  Max-Planck Institute of Computer Science, Saarbruecken, Germany

Preface

DEXA 2005, the 16th International Conference on Database and Expert Systems Applications, was held at the Copenhagen Business School, Copenhagen, Denmark, from August 22 to 26, 2005. The success of the DEXA series has partly been due to the way in which it has kept abreast of recent developments by spawning specialized workshops and conferences each with its own proceedings. In 2005 the DEXA programme was co-located with the 7th International Conference on Data Warehousing and Knowledge Discovery [DaWaK 2005], the 6th International Conference on Electronic Commerce and Web Technologies [EC-Web 2005], the 4th International Conference on Electronic Government [EGOV 2005], the 2nd International Conference on Trust, Privacy, and Security in Digital Business [TrustBus 2005], the 2nd International Conference on Industrial Applications of Holonic and Multi-agent Systems [HoloMAS 2005], as well as 19 specialized workshops.

These proceedings are the result of a considerable amount of hard work. Beginning with the preparation of submitted papers, the papers went through the reviewing process. This process was supported by online discussion between the reviewers to determine the final conference program. The authors of accepted papers revised their manuscripts to produce this fine collection. DEXA 2005 received 390 submissions, and from those the Program Committee selected the 92 papers in these proceedings. This year the reviewing process generated more than 1000 referee reports. The hard work of the authors, the referees and the Program Committee is gratefully acknowledged.

Profound thanks go to those institutions that actively supported this conference and made it possible. These are:

- Copenhagen Business School
- Danish Ministry of Science, Technology and Innovation
- DEXA Association
- Austrian Computer Society
- Research Institute for Applied Knowledge Processing (FAW)

The success and reputation of the DEXA series and DEXA 2005 would not have been possible without a high level of organization. Our thanks go to Andreas Dreiling (FAW, University of Linz) and Monika Neubauer (FAW, University of Linz). And our special thanks go to Gabriela Wagner, manager of the DEXA organization, and manager of the whole DEXA 2005 event. The editors express their great appreciation for her tireless dedication over the past 16 years which has established the high reputation that DEXA enjoys today, and made DEXA 2005 a major event.

June 2005

John Debenham
Roland R. Wagner

Program Committee

General Chairperson

Kim Viborg Andersen, Copenhagen Business School, Denmark

Conference Program Chairpersons

John Debenham, University of Technology, Sydney, Australia
Roland R. Wagner, FAW, University of Linz, Austria

Workshop Chairpersons

A Min Tjoa, Technical University of Vienna, Austria
Roland R. Wagner, FAW, University of Linz, Austria

Program Committee

Witold Abramowicz, Poznan University of Economics, Poland
Michel Adiba, IMAG — Laboratoire LSR, France
Hamideh Afsarmanesh, University of Amsterdam, The Netherlands
Ala Al-Zobaidie, University of Greenwich, UK
Walid G. Aref, Purdue University, USA
Ramazan S. Aygun, University of Alabama in Huntsville, USA
Leonard Barolli, Fukuoka Institute of Technology (FIT), Japan
Kurt Bauknecht, Universität Zürich, Switzerland
Trevor Bench-Capon, University of Liverpool, UK
Elisa Bertino, Università di Milano, Italy
Bishwaranjan Bhattacharjee, IBM TJ Watson Research Center, USA
Sourav S Bhowmick, Nanyang Technological University, Singapore
Christian Böhm, University of Munich, Germany
Omran Bukhres, Purdue University School of Science, USA
Luis Camarinah-Matos, New University of Lisbon, Portugal
Antonio Cammelli, CNR, Italy
Malu Castellanos, Hewlett-Packard Laboratories, USA
Tiziana Catarci, Università di Roma "La Sapienza", Italy
Aaron Ceglar, Flinders University of South Australia, Australia
Wojciech Cellary, University of Economics at Poznan, Poland
Elizabeth Chang, Curtin University, Australia
Sudarshan S. Chawathe, University of Maryland, USA
Ming-Syan Chen, National Taiwan University, Taiwan

Rosine Cicchetti, IUT, University of Marseille, France
Carlo Combi, Università degli Studi di Verona, Italy
Isabel Cruz, University of Illinois at Chicago, USA
Misbah Deen, University of Keele, UK
Elisabetta Di Nitto, Politecnico di Milano, Italy
Nina Edelweiss, Universidade Federal do Rio Grande do Sul, Brazil
Johann Eder, University of Klagenfurt, Austria
Amr El Abbadi, University of California, USA
Gregor Engels, University of Paderborn, Germany
Tomoya Enokido, Rissho University, Japan
Peter Fankhauser, Fraunhofer IPSI, Germany
Ling Feng, University of Twente, The Netherlands
Eduardo Fernandez, Florida Atlantic University, USA
Simon Field, Matching Systems Ltd., Switzerland
Burkhard Freitag, University of Passau, Germany
Mariagrazia Fugini, Politecnico di Milano, Italy
Antonio L. Furtado, University of Rio de Janeiro, Brazil
Manolo Garcia-Solaco, IS Consultant, USA
Georges Gardarin, University of Versailles, France
Alexander Gelbukh, CIC, Instituto Politecnico Nacional (IPN), Mexico
Parke Godfrey, York University, Toronto Canada
Paul Grefen, Eindhoven University of Technology, The Netherlands
William Grosky, University of Michigan, USA
Le Gruenwald, University of Oklahoma, USA
Abdelkader Hameurlain, University of Toulouse, France
Wook-Shin Han, Kyungpook National University, Korea
Igor T. Hawryszkiewycz, University of Technology, Sydney, Australia
Wynne Hsu, National University of Singapore, Singapore
Mohamed Ibrahim, University of Greenwich, UK
H.-Arno Jacobsen, University of Toronto, Canada
Gerti Kappel, Vienna University of Technology, Austria
Dimitris Karagiannis, University of Vienna, Austria
Randi Karlsen, University of Tromsø, Norway
Rudolf Keller, Zühlke Engineering AG, Switzerland
Latifur Khan, University of Texas at Dallas, USA
Myoung Ho Kim, KAIST, Korea
Masaru Kitsuregawa, Tokyo University, Japan
Gary J. Koehler, University of Florida, USA
John Krogstie, SINTEF, Norway
Petr Kroha, Technische Universität Chemnitz-Zwickau, Germany
Josef Küng, FAW, University of Linz, Austria
Lotfi Lakhal, University of Marseille, France
Christian Lang, IBM TJ Watson Research Center, USA
Jiri Lazansky, Czech Technical University, Czech Republic
Young-Koo Lee, University of Illinois, USA
Mong Li Lee, National University of Singapore, Singapore
Michel Leonard, Université de Genève, Switzerland

Tok Wang Ling, National University of Singapore, Singapore
Volker Linnemann, University of Luebeck, Germany
Mengchi Liu, Carleton University, Canada
Peri Loucopoulos, UMIST, UK
Sanjai Kumar Madria, University of Missouri-Rolla, USA
Akifumi Makinouchi, Kyushu University, Japan
Vladimir Marik, Czech Technical University, Czech Republic
Simone Marinai, University of Florence, Italy
Heinrich C. Mayr, University of Klagenfurt, Austria
Subhasish Mazumdar, New Mexico Tech, USA
Dennis McLeod, University of Southern California, USA
Elisabeth Metais, CNAM, France
Mukesh Mohania, IBM-IRL, India
Reagan Moore, San Diego Supercomputer Center, USA
Tadeusz Morzy, Poznan University of Technology, Poland
Noureddine Mouaddib, University of Nantes, France
Günter Müller, Universität Freiburg, Germany
Erich J. Neuhold, GMD-IPSI, Germany
Wilfred Ng, University of Science & Technology, Hong Kong, China
Matthias Nicola, IBM Silicon Valley Lab, USA
Shojiro Nishio, Osaka University, Japan
Gultekin Ozsoyoglu, Case Western Reserve University, USA
Georgios Pangalos, University of Thessaloniki, Greece
Dimitris Papadias, University of Science & Technology, Hong Kong, China
Stott Parker, University of California, Los Angeles, USA
Oscar Pastor, Universidad Politecnica de Valencia, Spain
Jignesh M. Patel, University of Michigan, USA
Verónika Peralta, Universidad de la Republica, Uruguay
Günter Pernul, University of Regensburg, Germany
Evaggelia Pitoura, University of Ioannina, Greece
Alexandra Poulovassilis, University of London, UK
Gerald Quirchmayr, Univ. of Vienna, Austria and Univ. of South Australia, Australia
Fausto Rabitti, CNUCE-CNR, Italy
Wenny Rahayu, La Trobe University, Australia
Isidro Ramos, Technical University of Valencia, Spain
P. Krishna Reddy, International Institute of Information Technology, India
Werner Retschitzegger, University of Linz, Austria
Norman Revell, Middlesex University, UK
Sally Rice, University of South Australia, Australia
Colette Rolland, University of Paris I, Sorbonne, France
Elke Rundensteiner, Worcester Polytechnic Institute, USA
Domenico Sacca, University of Calabria, Italy
Arnaud Sahuguet, Bell Laboratories, Lucent Technologies, USA
Simonas Saltenis, Aalborg University, Denmark
Marinette Savonnet, Université de Bourgogne, France
Erich Schweighofer, University of Vienna, Austria
Ming-Chien Shan, Hewlett-Packard Laboratories, USA

Keng Siau, University of Nebraska-Lincoln, USA
Giovanni Soda, University of Florence, Italy
Uma Srinivasan, CSIRO, Australia
Bala Srinivasan, Monash University, Australia
Olga Stepankova, Czech Technical University, Czech Republic
Zbigniew Struzik, University of Tokyo, Japan
Makoto Takizawa, Tokyo Denki University, Japan
Katsumi Tanaka, Kyoto University, Japan
Zahir Tari, University of Melbourne, Australia
Stephanie Teufel, University of Fribourg, Switzerland
Jukka Teuhola, University of Turku, Finland
Bernd Thalheim, Technical University of Cottbus, Germany
Jean-Marc Thevenin, University of Toulouse, France
Helmut Thoma, IBM Global Services, Basel, Switzerland
A Min Tjoa, Technical University of Vienna, Austria
Roland Traunmüller, University of Linz, Austria
Aphrodite Tsalgatidou, University of Athens, Greece
Susan Urban, Arizona State University, USA
Genoveva Vargas-Solar, LSR-IMAG, France
Krishnamurthy Vidyasankar, Memorial Univ. of Newfoundland, Canada
Pavel Vogel, TU München, Germany
Kyu-Young Whang, KAIST, Korea
Michael Wing, Middlesex University, UK
Vilas Wuwongse, Asian Institute of Technology, Thailand
Arkady Zaslavsky, Monash University, Australia

External Reviewers

Claudio Muscogiuri
Rodolfo Stecher
Patrick Lehti
Holger Kirchner
Aware Stewart
Predrag Knezevic
Bhaskar Mehta
Soloviev Sergei
Claudia Lucia Roncancio
Bruno Defude
Edgard Benitez
José Hilario Canós
Artur Boronat
José Carsí
Patricio Letelier
Wee Hyong Tok
Hanyu Li
Young-ho Park
Jung Hoon Lee
Ki Hoon Lee
Kyriakos Mouratidis
Hui Zhao
Xiang Lian
Ying Yang
Alexander Markowetz
Yiping Ke
James Cheng
An Lu
Lin Deng
Ho-Lam Lau
Woong-Kee Loh
Jae-Gil Lee
Jarogniew Rykowski
Krzysztof Walczak
Wojciech Wiza
Krzysztof Banaśkiewicz
Dariusz Ceglarek
Agata Filipowska
Tomasz Kaczmarek
Karol Wieloch

Marek Wiśniewski
Simon Msanjila
Irina Neaga
Pedro J. Valderas
Tsutomu Terada
Angela Bonifati
Eugenio Cesario
Alfredo Cuzzocrea
Filippo Furfaro
Andrea Gualtieri
Antonella Guzzo
Massimo Ruffolo
Cristina Sirangelo
Domenico Ursino
Sarita Bassil
Bo Xu
Huiyong Xiao
Feng Yaokai
Yi Ma
Noel Novelli
Choudur Lakshminarayan
Matthias Beck
Gerhard Bloch
Claus Dziarstek
Tobias Geis
Michael Guppenberger
Markus Lehmann
Petra Schwaiger
Wolfgang Völkl
Franz Weitl
Anna-Brith Jakobsen
Gianpaolo Cugola
Paolo Selvini
Jan Goossenaerts
Maurice van Keulen
Hajo Reijers
Pascal van Eck
Richard Brinkman
Alex Norta
Dimitre Kostadinov

Lydia Silva
Artur Boronat
José Hilario Canós
Pepe Carsí
Patricio Letelier
Diego Milano
Stephen Kimani
Enrico Bertini
Giuseppe Santucci
Monica Scannapieco
Silvia Gabrielli
Ling ChenQiankun Zhao
Erwin Leonardi
Yang Xiao
Ning Liao
Mamoun Awad
Ashraful Alam
Ping Wu
Shyam Anthony
Nagender Bandi
Fatih Emekci
Ahmed Metwally
Masatake Nakanishi
Changqing Li

Ioana Stanoi
Lipyeow Lim
Milind Naphade
Lars Rosenhainer
Jörg Gilberg
Wolfgang Dobmeier
Torsten Priebe
Christian Schläger
Norbert Meckl
Christos Ilioudis
Jacek Fraczek
Juliusz Jezierski
Robert Wrembel
Mikolaj Morzy
Jelena Tesic
Hiram Calvo-Castro
Hector Jimenez-Salazar
Sofia Galicia-Haro
Grigori Sidorov
George Athanasopoulos
Panagiotis Bouros
Eleni Koutrouli
George-Dimitrios Kapos
Thomi Pilioura

Table of Contents

How to Design a Loose Inter-organizational Workflow? An Illustrative Case Study
    Lotfi Bouzguenda 1

Recovering from Malicious Attacks in Workflow Systems
    Yajie Zhu, Tai Xin, Indrakshi Ray 14

Towards Mining Structural Workflow Patterns
    Walid Gaaloul, Karim Baïna, Claude Godart 24

Avoiding Error-Prone Reordering Optimization During Legal Systems Migration
    Youlin Fang, Heng Wang, Dongqing Yang 34

Automated SuperSQL Query Formulation Based on Statistical Characteristics of Data
    Jun Nemoto, Motomichi Toyama 44

Distribution Rules for Array Database Queries
    Alex van Ballegooij, Roberto Cornacchia, Arjen P. de Vries, Martin Kersten 55

Efficient Processing of Distributed Top-k Queries
    Hailing Yu, Hua-Gang Li, Ping Wu, Divyakant Agrawal, Amr El Abbadi 65

Evaluating Mid-(k, n) Queries Using B^+-Tree
    Dongseop Kwon, Taewon Lee, Sukho Lee 75

On Effective E-mail Classification via Neural Networks
    Bin Cui, Anirban Mondal, Jialie Shen, Gao Cong, Kian-Lee Tan 85

An Adaptive Spreading Activation Scheme for Performing More Effective Collaborative Recommendation
    Peng Han, Bo Xie, Fan Yang, Rui-Min Shen 95

Feature Selection by Ordered Rough Set Based Feature Weighting
    Qasem A. Al-Radaideh, Md Nasir Sulaiman, Mohd Hasan Selamat, Hamidah Ibrahim 105

A Full-Text Framework for the Image Retrieval Signal/Semantic Integration
Mohammed Belkhatir, Philippe Mulhem, Yves Chiaramella 113

A New Algorithm for Content-Based Region Query in Multimedia Databases
Dumitru Dan Burdescu, Liana Stanescu 124

SM3+: An XML Database Solution for the Management of MPEG-7 Descriptions
Yang Chu, Liang-Tien Chia, Sourav S. Bhowmick 134

LocalRank: Ranking Web Pages Considering Geographical Locality by Integrating Web and Databases
Jianwei Zhang, Yoshiharu Ishikawa, Sayumi Kurokawa, Hiroyuki Kitagawa 145

My Portal Viewer: Integration System Based on User Preferences for News Web Sites
Yukiko Kawai, Daisuke Kanjo, Katsumi Tanaka 156

Web Query Expansion by WordNet
Zhiguo Gong, Chan Wa Cheang, Leong Hou U 166

Webified Video: Media Conversion from TV Programs to Web Content for Cross-Media Information Integration
Hisashi Miyamori, Katsumi Tanaka 176

A Caching Model for Real-Time Databases in Mobile Ad-Hoc Networks
Yanhong Li, Le Gruenwald 186

Adaptive Query Processing in Point-Transformation Schemes
Byunggu Yu 197

On the General Signature Trees
Yangjun Chen 207

Optimizing I/O Costs of Multi-dimensional Queries Using Bitmap Indices
Doron Rotem, Kurt Stockinger, Kesheng Wu 220

Environmental Noise Classification for Multimedia Libraries
Stéphane Bressan, Tan Boon Tiang 230

Quality-Aware Replication of Multimedia Data
Yi-Cheng Tu, Jingfeng Yan, Sunil Prabhakar 240

Rotation and Gray-Scale Invariant Classification of Textures Improved by Spatial Distribution of Features
  Gouchol Pok, Keun Ho Ryu, Jyh-charn Lyu 250

Zooming Cross-Media: A Zooming Description Language Coding LOD Control and Media Transition
  Tadashi Araki, Hisashi Miyamori, Mitsuru Minakuchi,
  Ai Kato, Zoran Stejic, Yasushi Ogawa, Katsumi Tanaka 260

A Histogram-Based Selectivity Estimator for Skewed XML Data
  Hanyu Li, Mong Li Lee, Wynne Hsu 270

Accelerating XML Structural Join by Partitioning
  Nan Tang, Jeffrey Xu Yu, Kam-Fai Wong, Kevin Lü, Jianxin Li 280

Efficient Dissemination of Filtered Data in XML-Based SDI
  Jae-Ho Choi, Young-Jin Yoon, SangKeun Lee 290

Efficient Processing of Ordered XML Twig Pattern
  Jiaheng Lu, Tok Wang Ling, Tian Yu, Changqing Li, Wei Ni 300

A Flexible Role-Based Delegation Model Using Characteristics of Permissions
  Dong-Gue Park, You-Ri Lee 310

Provable Data Privacy
  Kilian Stoffel, Thomas Studer 324

Formalizing the XML Schema Matching Problem as a Constraint Optimization Problem
  Marko Smiljanić, Maurice van Keulen, Willem Jonker 333

Evolving XML Schemas and Documents Using UML Class Diagrams
  Eladio Domínguez, Jorge Lloret, Ángel L. Rubio, María A. Zapata ... 343

Building XML Documents and Schemas to Support Object Data Exchange and Communication
  Carlo Combi, Giuseppe Pozzi 353

Intensional Encapsulations of Database Subsets via Genetic Programming
  Aybar C. Acar, Amihai Motro 365

Preferred Skyline: A Hybrid Approach Between SQLf and Skyline
  Marlene Goncalves, María-Esther Vidal 375

Resolution of Semantic Queries on a Set of Web Services
Jordi Paraire, Rafael Berlanga, Dolores M. Llidó 385

Detecting Semantically Correct Changes to Relevant Unordered Hidden Web Data
Vladimir Kovalev, Sourav S. Bhowmick 395

Design for All in Information Technology: A Universal Concern
Jenny Darzentas, Klaus Miesenberger 406

An Efficient Scheme of Update Robust XML Numbering with XML to Relational Mapping
Hyunchul Kang, Young-Hyun Kim 421

On Maintaining XML Linking Integrity During Update
Eric Pardede, J. Wenny Rahayu, David Taniar 431

On the Midpoint of a Set of XML Documents
Alberto Abelló, Xavier de Palol, Mohand-Saïd Hacid 441

Full-Text and Structural XML Indexing on B^+-Tree
Toshiyuki Shimizu, Masatoshi Yoshikawa 451

XML-Based e-Barter System for Circular Supply Exchange
Shuichi Nishioka, Yuri Yaguchi, Takahiro Hamada, Makoto Onizuka, Masashi Yamamuro 461

Context-Sensitive Complementary Information Retrieval for Text Stream
Qiang Ma, Katsumi Tanaka 471

Detecting Changes to Hybrid XML Documents Using Relational Databases
Erwin Leonardi, Sri L. Budiman, Sourav S. Bhowmick 482

An Index-Based Method for Timestamped Event Sequence Matching
Sanghyun Park, Jung-Im Won, Jee-Hee Yoon, Sang-Wook Kim 493

Time Parameterized Interval R-Tree for Tracing Tags in RFID Systems
ChaeHoon Ban, BongHee Hong, DongHyun Kim 503

Efficient Algorithms for Constructing Time Decompositions of Time Stamped Documents
Parvathi Chundi, Rui Zhang, Daniel J. Rosenkrantz 514

Querying by Sketch Geographical Databases and Ambiguities
  Fernando Ferri, Patrizia Grifoni, Maurizio Rafanelli 524

Foundations for Automated Trading — It's the Information That Matters
  John Debenham 534

Intensional Query Answering to XQuery Expressions
  Simone Gasparini, Elisa Quintarelli 544

Optimizing Sorting and Duplicate Elimination in XQuery Path Expressions
  Mary Fernández, Jan Hidders, Philippe Michiels, Jérôme Siméon, Roel Vercammen 554

SIOUX: An Efficient Index for Processing Structural XQueries
  Georges Gardarin, Laurent Yeh 564

Searching Multi-hierarchical XML Documents: The Case of Fragmentation
  Alex Dekhtyar, Ionut E. Iacob, Srikanth Methuku 576

Semantic Storage: A Report on Performance and Flexibility
  Edgar R. Weippl, Markus Klemen, Manfred Linnert, Stefan Fenz, Gernot Goluch, A Min Tjoa 586

Towards Truly Extensible Database Systems
  Ralph Acker, Roland Pieringer, Rudolf Bayer 596

Transaction Management with Integrity Checking
  Davide Martinenghi, Henning Christiansen 606

An Optimal Skew-insensitive Join and Multi-join Algorithm for Distributed Architectures
  Mostafa Bamha 616

Evaluation and NLP
  Didier Nakache, Elisabeth Metais, Jean François Timsit 626

Movies Recommenders Systems: Automation of the Information and Evaluation Phases in a Multi-criteria Decision-Making Process
  Michel Plantié, Jacky Montmain, Gérard Dray 633

On Building a DyQE - A Medical Information System for Exploring Imprecise Queries
  Dennis Wollersheim, Wenny J. Rahayu 645

A Proposal for a Unified Process for Ontology Building: UPON
Antonio De Nicola, Michele Missikoff, Roberto Navigli 655

Transforming Software Package Classification Hierarchies into
Goal-Based Taxonomies
Claudia Ayala, Xavier Franch 665

Approximations of Concept Based on Multielement Bounds
Jianjiang Lu, Baowen Xu, Dazhou Kang, Yanhui Li, Peng Wang 676

Query Expansion Using Web Access Log Files
Yun Zhu, Le Gruenwald 686

An XML Approach to Semantically Extract Data from HTML Tables
Jixue Liu, Zhuoyun Ao, Ho-Hyun Park, Yongfeng Chen 696

Automatic Generation of Semantic Fields for Resource Discovery in the
Semantic Web
I. Navas, I. Sanz, J.F. Aldana, R. Berlanga 706

JeromeDL - Adding Semantic Web Technologies to Digital Libraries
Sebastian Ryszard Kruk, Stefan Decker, Lech Zieborak 716

Analysis and Visualization of the DX Community with Information
Extracted from the Web
F.T. de la Rosa, M.T. Gómez-López, R.M. Gasca 726

Learning Robust Web Wrappers
B. Fazzinga, S. Flesca, A. Tagarelli 736

Control-Based Quality Adaptation in Data Stream Management
Systems
*Yi-Cheng Tu, Mohamed Hefeeda, Yuni Xia, Sunil Prabhakar,
Song Liu* 746

Event Composition and Detection in Data Stream Management Systems
*Mukesh Mohania, Dhruv Swamini, Shyam Kumar Gupta,
Sourav Bhowmick, Tharam Dillon* 756

Automatic Parsing of Sports Videos with Grammars
Fei Wang, Kevin J. Lü, Jing-Tao Li, Jianping Fan 766

Improved Sequential Pattern Mining Using an Extended Bitmap
Representation
Chien-Liang Wu, Jia-Ling Koh, Pao-Ying An 776

Dimension Transform Based Efficient Event Filtering for Symmetric
Publish/Subscribe System
  Botao Wang, Masaru Kitsuregawa 786

Scalable Distributed Aggregate Computations Through Collaboration
  Leonidas Galanis, David J. DeWitt 797

Schemas and Queries over P2P
  Pedro Furtado 808

Threshold Based Declustering in High Dimensions
  Ali Şaman Tosun 818

XG: A Data-Driven Computation Grid for Enterprise-Scale Mining
  Radu Sion, Ramesh Natarajan, Inderpal Narang, Wen-Syan Li,
  Thomas Phan 828

A Rule System for Heterogeneous Spatial Reasoning in Geographic
Information System
  Haibin Sun, Wenhui Li 838

Querying a Polynomial Object-Relational Constraint Database in
Model-Based Diagnosis
  M.T. Gómez-López, R.M. Gasca, C. Del Valle, F.T. de la Rosa 848

A Three-Phase Knowledge Extraction Methodology Using Learning
Classifier System
  An-Pin Chen, Kuang-Ku Chen, Mu-Yen Chen 858

A Replica Allocation Method Adapting to Topology Changes in
Ad Hoc Networks
  Hideki Hayashi, Takahiro Hara, Shojiro Nishio 868

On a Collaborative Caching in a Peer-to-Peer Network for Push-Based
Broadcast
  Kazuhiko Maeda, Wataru Uchida, Takahiro Hara, Shojiro Nishio 879

An Efficient Location Encoding Method Based on Hierarchical
Administrative District
  SangYoon Lee, Sanghyun Park, Woo-Cheol Kim, Dongwon Lee 890

Personalized and Community Decision Support in eTourism
Intermediaries
  Chien-Chih Yu 900

Reengineering the Knowledge Component of a Data Warehouse-Based
Expert Diagnosis System
  *Jean-François Beaudoin, Sylvain Delisle, Mathieu Dugré,
  Josée St-Pierre* 910

A Model-Based Monitoring and Diagnosis System for a Space-Based
Astrometry Mission
  Aleksei Pavlov, Sven Helmer, Guido Moerkotte 920

An Effective Method for Locally Neighborhood Graphs Updating
  Hakim Hacid, Abdelkader Djamel Zighed 930

Efficient Searching in Large Inheritance Hierarchies
  Michal Krátký, Svatopluk Štolfa, Václav Snášel, Ivo Vondrák 940

Author Index 953

How to Design a Loose Inter-organizational Workflow? An Illustrative Case Study

Lotfi Bouzguenda

IRIT Laboratory, University Toulouse 1, Place Anatole France,
31042 Toulouse Cedex, France
lotfi.bouzguenda@univ-tlse1.fr

Abstract. This work deals with the design of Loose Inter-Organizational Workflow (IOW). Loose IOW refers to occasional cooperation, free of structural constraints, where the partners involved and their number are not pre defined. We show that the design of Loose IOW application is very complex due to three factors: (i) the heterogeneity and distribution of the component processes, the organizations and the information (ii) the autonomy of each partner, which must be preserved (iii) the need to integrate in a coherent framework the three dimensions of a workflow: process, information and organization. One possible way to deal with this complexity, and to ease loose IOW applications design, is to use a well known software engineering principle: *the separation of aspects*, which aims at decomposing a system in communicating sub systems, each one coping with a relevant abstraction that requires a model to be structured and described. Following this practice, a loose IOW application must be though as three communicating models: an informational model, an organizational model and a process model. The first two models are represented with UML class's diagram, while the last model is described with *Petri Nets with Objects* (PNO), which are a formal language, have a very adequate expressive power and make the glue between the three workflow dimensions. We illustrate our solution through the well-known "reviewing papers" case study.

1 Introduction

Inter-organizational Workflow Context. Inter-Organizational Workflow (IOW for short) is a current research problematic, which investigates the cooperation of several distributed, autonomous and heterogeneous business processes [1] [2]. We mean by cooperation the gathering of business processes and the sharing of resources (information, human and machine) between the component organizations in order to achieve a common global goal.

IOW can be studied in the context of two following distinctive scenarios: loose IOW and tight IOW [3]. In this work, we focus on loose IOW which refers to occasional cooperation between organizations, free of structural constraints, where the organizations involved and their number are not pre-defined but should be selected at run time in an opportunistic way.

The design of loose IOW application is very complex. This complexity is mainly due to three factors:

- The heterogeneity and distribution of the component processes, the organizations and the information since IOW supports the cooperation between business processes running in different organizations. Naturally, these organizations do not share the same information and do not have necessary the same capacities. Regarding the heterogeneity of processes, the same service can be provided by two different organizations according to processes which differ by their quality, their duration or the number of stages they require.
- The autonomy of each partner must be preserved. First, each partner participating in an IOW should be able to decide by itself, the conditions of the cooperation i.e. when, how and with whom it cooperates. Second, each partner may prefer publish the interface of its process rather than its detail (implementation).
- The need to integrate in a coherent framework the three related dimensions of a workflow (process, information and organization). Indeed, a workflow process is made of a set of coordinated tasks, each one uses and produces information and is performed by an actor (human or machine) of the organization.

Most of the works concerning IOW [1][2] only focus on the process dimension by providing interaction models to support distributed execution of component processes. These works do not make really the glue between the three-workflow dimensions.

The problem being addressed in this paper is *"how to design a loose IOW application considering the three main dimensions (organization, information and processes) in a coherent framework"*. One possible way to take into account these different dimensions and to deal with their complexity is to use a well known software engineering principle [4]: the *separation of aspects*, which aims at decomposing a system in communicating sub systems, each one coping with a relevant abstraction that requires a model to be structured and described. Following this practice, a loose IOW application must be though as three communicating models: an informational model, an organizational model and a process model. They are described below.

- The *informational model (IM)* describes the forms, documents, data that are used and produced by a workflow.
- The *organizational model (OM)* has two objectives. First, it structures actors in classes sharing the same features. A class is called *role* when it comprises actors having the same capabilities, and an *organizational unit* for actors belonging to a some organization structure. Second the organizational model attributes to each actor authorization to perform tasks. Roles and organizational Units are abstraction that can be used to define business processes without referring explicitly to the individual actors in a workflow, but rather to the capacity they must have.

The *process model (PM)* defines the component tasks, their coordination, and the information and actors involved in each task. This model refers to both the organizational model, which defines and organizes the set of potential actors, and the informational model, which allows access to the objects to be processed. To describe a process model we need a Process Description Language (PDL). Unfortunately, some PDLs define tasks at a low level detail, as the process to be executed, and do not provide abstractions to design and simulate the model. Conversely, other languages define tasks at a very high level, as a goal to be reached, and do not provide an operational semantics. The ideal language would be one with a very large expressive power to describe the three models (information, organization and process) in a uniform way, to provide an operational semantics and to define tasks at a very high level.

Our solution is based on the following principles:

- *The separation of aspects*, which introduces an original way to decompose a system in communicating sub systems, thus offering new reuse opportunities and easing software maintenance and evolution.
- *The use of PNO*, which is an appropriate PDL to formally describe processes referencing the organizational and informational models.

We illustrate our solution through the well-known "reviewing papers" case study (see table 1).

Table 1. The reviewing papers case study

We consider a distributed version of the well-known "reviewing papers" case study. The chairman receives papers from authors and then registers, codifies and classifies them by topics. According to this classification, he elaborates one or several call for reviewers in a public and well known electronic space. After receiving bids from potential reviewers, he selects some of them to constitute his Program Committee (PC). Then, he distributes the papers to be evaluated and the review form to the PC members. After receiving all the review reports from the PC members, the chairman synthesizes these reports and elaborates two lists, one for the accepted papers and the other one for the rejected papers and finally, he informs each author. This case study is inspired from the ACM Special Track on Coordination [5], and can be seen as a loose IOW since its actors (authors, chairman and reviewers) are distributed in different organizations (laboratories, enterprises or universities) and as we have described above, reviewers are recruited dynamically by the chairman. Moreover, each reviewer may have its own reviewing process. For example, some of them could delegate the reviewing to colleagues, while others will review all the papers by them self.

Organization of the paper. The remainder of this paper is organized as follows. Section 2 briefly introduces PNO formalism as an appropriate language for modeling processes and justifies why we use this formalism. Section 3 models the case study through three communicating models (OM, IM and PM). The IM is based on ontology to solve information heterogeneity. The OM is based on an original component "a Matchmaker" in charge of connecting dynamically partners. The PM is based on PNO formalism, which enable the description and the coordination of the component processes while referencing the two previous models. Section 4 briefly discuses the related works and concludes the paper.

2 Petri Nets with Objects

2.1 What Are Petri Nets with Objects?

Petri Nets with Objects (PNO) [6] are a formalism combining coherently Petri nets (PN) technology and Object-Oriented (OO) approach. While PN are very suitable to express the dynamic behavior of a system, OO approach enables the modeling and the structuring of its active (actor) and passive (information) entities. In a conventional PN, tokens are atomic and indissociable, whereas they are objects in a PNO. As any PN, a PNO is made up of places, arcs and transitions, but in PNO, they are labeled with inscriptions referring to the handled objects. More precisely, a PNO features the following additive characteristics:

- *Places* are typed. The type of a place is a (list of) type of some object-oriented sequential languages. A token is a value matching the type of a place such as a (list of) constant (e.g. 2 or 'hello'), an instance of an object class, or a reference towards such an instance. The value of a place is a set of tokens it contains. At any moment, the state of the net, or its marking is defined by the distribution of tokens onto places. A transition is connected to places by oriented arcs as it aims at changing the net state, i.e. the location and value of tokens.
- *Arcs are labeled with parameters*. Each arc is labeled with a (list of) variable of the same type, as the place the arc is connected to. The variables on the arcs surrounding a transition serve as formal parameters of that transition and define the flow of tokens from input to output places. *Arcs* from places to a transition determine the *enabling* condition of the transition: a transition *may occur* (or *is enabled*) if there exists a *binding* of its input variables with tokens lying in its input places. The *occurrence* of an enabled transition changes the marking of its surrounding places: tokens bound to input variables are removed from input places, and tokens are put into output places according to variables labeling output arcs.
- *Each Transition is a complex structure made up of three components*: a precondition, an action and emission rules. A transition may be guarded by a *precondition*, i.e. a side-effect free Boolean expression involving input variables. In this case, the transition is enabled by a binding only if this binding evaluates the precondition to true. Preconditions allow for the fact that the enabling of a transition depends on the location of tokens and also on their value. Most transitions also include *an action*, which consists in a piece of code in which transition's variables may appear and object methods be invoked. This action is executed at each occurrence of the transition and it processes the values of tokens. Finally, a transition may include a set of *emission rules* i.e. side-effect free Boolean expressions that determine the output arcs that are actually activated after the execution of the action.

Figure 1 gives an example of a PNO describing a simple task registering of paper, given the paper, call for paper, an available author and the Chairman in charge of registering the paper. This PNO is composed of a transition, four input places and two output places. Each place is typed with one of the four following object classes: <*Call for paper*>, <*Paper*>, <*Author*> and <*Chairman* >. Each input place contains a token

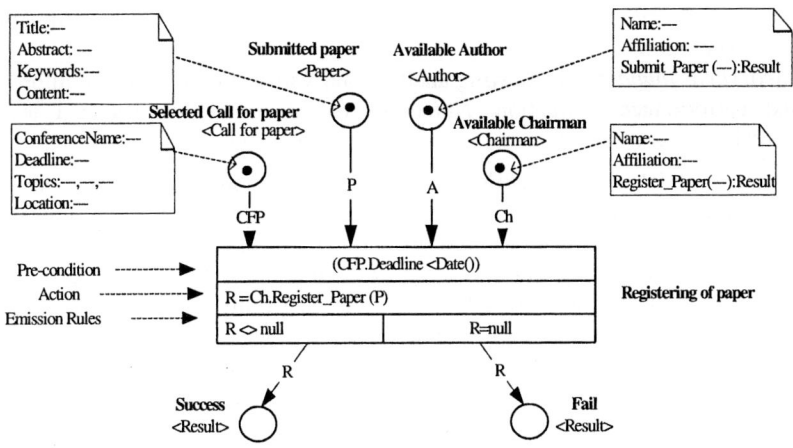

Fig. 1. Example of a PNO

whose value is indicated by a comment linked to it by an arrow. From left to right, the first two input places called *submitted paper* and *selected call for paper* contain one token corresponding respectively to a paper and a call for paper. The object class <Paper> has four attributes {Title, Abstract, Keywords, Content} and the object class <Call for paper> has four attributes {ConferenceName, Deadline, Topics, Location}. Let us also remark that the <Paper> and <Call for paper> object classes refer to informational model. The second two input places called *Available Chairman* and *Available Author* contain also one token corresponding respectively to a Chairman and an Author. The class object <Chairman> has two attributes {Name, Affiliation}, features a method {Register_Paper} and the <Author> object class, has two attributes {Name, Affiliation}, features a method {Submit_Paper}. Both object classes refer to organizational model. Now let us consider the transition registering of paper. It has a precondition *(CFP.Deadline<Date())* which indicates that the submission date must not exceed the actually date. If this precondition is satisfied, the action is executed and the Chairman is asked to execute the *Register_Paper* method. According to the result R, returned by this method, the emission rules will direct the process through one path or another. If the registering of paper is ok, the result R is not null and then a token is put in the *Success* output place. In the other case, a token is put in the *Fail* output place

2.2 Motivations for Using Petri Nets with Objects

Advantages of PN in Workflow Context. Petri Nets are widely used for workflow modeling [7]. Several good reasons justify their use:

- *An appropriate expressive power* that allows the clear and precise description of the different tasks involved in a process and their coordination. The main workflow control patterns [8] (e.g. sequence, parallel, split, join…) can be described by Petri Nets.
- *A graphical representation* that eases the process definition.

- *An operational semantics* enabling an easy mapping from specification to implementation.
- *Theoretical foundations* allowing analysis and verification of behavioral properties and performance evaluation. Numerous techniques with associated tools are available as varied as algebraic techniques, graph analysis and simulation.

Advantages of PNO in Workflow Context. Conventional Petri nets focus on the process definition and do not capture the organizational and the informational dimensions of a workflow. As we have mentioned it in the previous section, Petri nets with Objects extend classical Petri nets by integrating high-level data structure represented as objects and therefore provide the possibility to integrate in a coherent way the two dimensions missing in conventional Petri nets. Thus, using PNO, actors of the organizational model are directly represented as objects and they may be invoked through methods in the action part of a transition. In the same way, data and documents of the informational model are also represented by objects flowing in the PNO and transformed by transitions.

Advantages of PNO in IOW Context. PNO provides two mechanisms to support process interoperability. Interaction with other external processes can be modeled with additional (called connection) places. Input places can represent localizations where partners are asked to put typed information while output places represent localizations where typed information are made available for partners. This mechanism does not require to know the identity of the partner and the detail of their process. In this case, the autonomy of each partner is preserved. Regarding, the interaction with a priori known software components (matchmaker, ...), it can be modeled by directly invoking them in the action part of a transition. The use of a matchmaker is very useful in the context of loose IOW since it helps to dynamically connect distributed partners.

3 Modelization of the Case Study

The purpose of this section is to present our solution of the well-known "reviewing papers" case study. Our solution is made of three communicating models, namely the informational, organizational and process models.

3.1 The Informational Model

As we have mentioned in section 1, the loose IOW context corresponds to a situation where the identities of partners and their processes are not known a priori and consequently the informational model can not be described fully. To solve this problem, we propose the use of an ontology. This ontology describes the common vocabulary (or main concepts) of the domain being considered, and partners (reviewers and chairman in our case) are supposed to adhere to this common ontology in order to cooperate. As shown by [9], an ontology can be support for solving data semantic interoperability between partners.

Our informational model describes the structure of two types of information: documents and data. The documents can be classified in two great classes: *Manuscript* and *Electronic*.

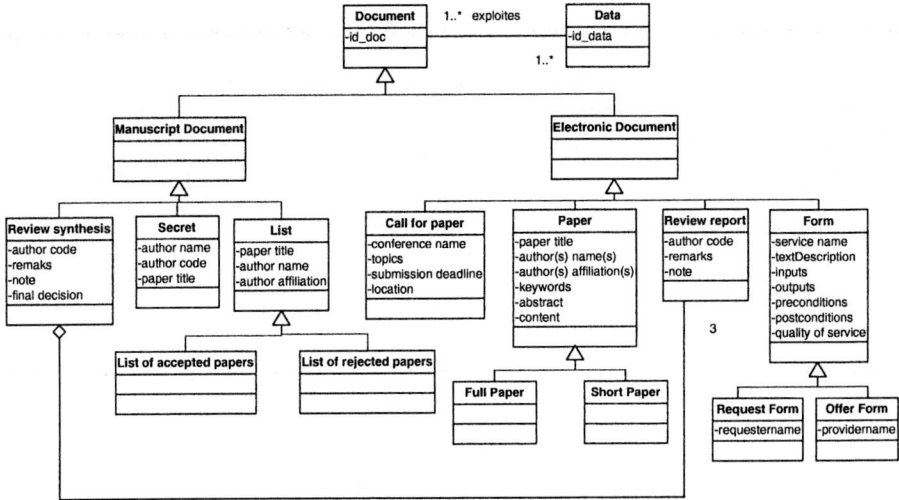

Fig. 2. Informational model: the ontology of the reviewing papers case study

The manuscripts documents are the following:

- *Secret*, which is produced by the chairman for codifying and decodifying papers when we consider anonymous authors;
- *List of accepted papers*, which is produced by the chairman for mentioning the accepted papers including the author's names and their affiliations.
- *List of rejected papers*, which is also produced by the chairman for mentioning the rejected papers including the author's names and their affiliations.
- *Review* synthesis, which is produced by the chairman and corresponds to an aggregation of a set of review reports.
- The electronics documents are the following:
- *Paper*, which is submitted by the author to the conference;
- *Review report*, which is filled by an anonymous reviewer containing his remarks and his evaluation note.
- *Call for paper*, which is produced by the Program Organization Chair and contains the necessary information about the conference such as submission deadline, categories of papers, topics and so on.
- *Request form (or call for reviewers)*, which is used by the chairman in order to express its needs for reviewer recruiting;
- *Offer form (or bid)*, which is used by the reviewer in order to describe its capabilities for reviewing papers.

These documents also exploit data which can be structured in information sources. The following figure gives an overview of our informational model described by means of UML class's diagram (see figure 2).

3.2 The Organizational Model

Our organizational model is based on the Agent-Group-Role Meta model (AGR for short) suggested by [10]. This meta model is one of the frameworks proposed to define the organizational dimension of a multi-agent system, and it is well appropriate to the IOW context. Several reasons justify the interest of this meta model: (i) it eases security: what happens in a group cannot be viewed from agents that do not belong to that group. (ii) adding dynamically a software component into the kernel of the application is easy because creating a new group or playing a new role may be seen as a plug-in process when a software component is integrated into an application. (iii) it supports coherent exchange because a role describes the constraints (obligations, requirements, skills) that an agent should satisfy to obtain a role. Moreover, our organizational model extends classical organizational models [11] by adding an original component called "Matchmaker" as it is presented in [12]. This component is very useful in the context of loose IOW since it helps to connect a requester (for instance chairman) to a provider one (for instance reviewer). More precisely, our organizational model is organized around the following components:

- Three types of groups: Program Committee, Authors and Matchmakers.
- Two types of agents: performer or non-performer.
- Four roles: Author (if the paper is co-authored, the corresponding author is the first in the list); Chairman; Reviewer and Matchmaker.

The following figure gives an overview of our organizational model by means of UML class's diagram (see figure 3).

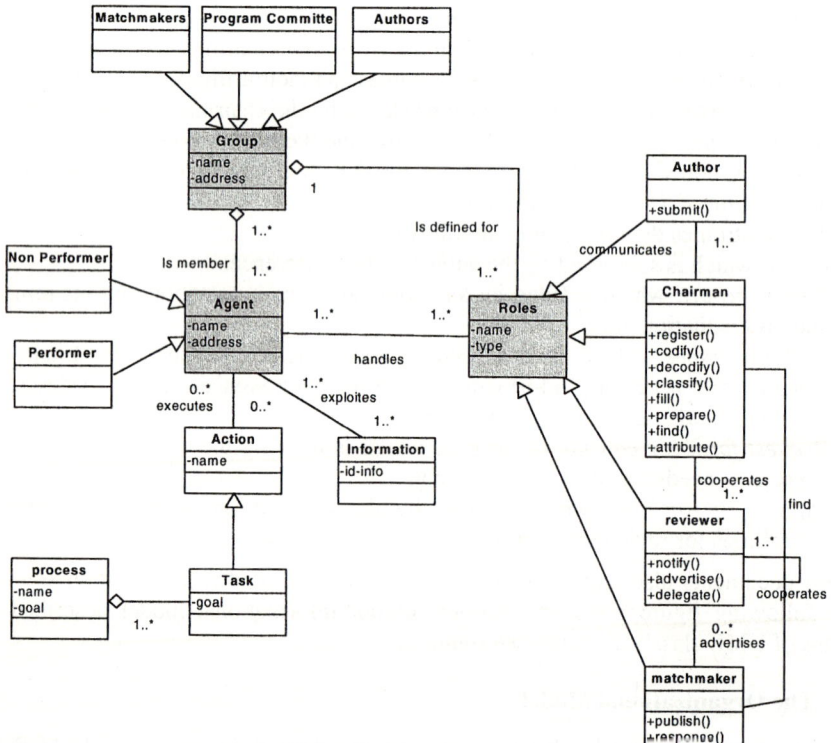

Fig. 3. Organizational model based on AGR meta model

Remark 1. Since we are in loose context, all potential partners are not known. To solve this difficulty, we propose the use of the notion of role seen as an abstraction that can be used without referring explicitly to the individual actors in a workflow but rather to the capacity they must have.

Remark 2. In our case study, we have only one matchmaker, which is specialized in the conference organization domain.

3.3 The Process Model

The reviewing papers process is made of several coordinated tasks and described with a PNO (see figure 4). In this figure, the left hand side net corresponds to the behavior of the chairman. In the middle, the transition in "grey" represents the behavior of the matchmaker, and on the right hand side net we have the behavior of a potential reviewer. Let us detail the tasks (transitions) composing the process:

1. *Registering of paper* by the chairman consists in entering and saving the different components of a paper (e.g. the author(s), received date, keywords etc) submitted by the author.
2. Codifying of paper by the chairman consists in deleting author (s) name (s) of already registered paper, and creating a secret document containing the attributed code for author(s), which helps the chairman after receiving review reports to decodify papers.
3. *Classifying of paper* by the chairman consists in gathering the anonymous paper by topic.
4. *Finding reviewers* consists in publishing requests (or call for reviewers) according to a precise and clear format. This publication by the chairman with destination for the matchmaker; each request form clearly describes the capabilities of the required reviewers. The role of the matchmaker is first to select the best partners and then to return the identities of partners to the chairman. We assume that the chairman and the reviewer share the same form (see the informational model in section 3.1) in order to facilitate the matching process.
5. *Attributing of paper* by the chairman consists in assigning a set of reviewers to a paper.
6. *Evaluating of papers* consists in judging papers by the assigned reviewers. Each evaluation is the review report filled by the corresponding reviewer. Moreover, each reviewer may have its own reviewing process as we have mentioned it in table 1. In this way, we represent the transition "Evaluating of papers" as a "black box" for the others partners.
7. *Collecting and summarizing review reports* by the chairman consists in erasing the anonymous mentioning off the review report and preparing a review synthesis.
8. *Preparing two lists* by the chairman consists in producing i) a document called "list of accepted papers" making appear the list of accepted papers as well as the authors and ii) a document called "list of rejected papers" containing the same information.

Remark 3. The places correspond to classes of the informational model and the organizational model.

Remark 4. To solve the distribution of component processes, we use two mechanisms: connection places (in black in the figure) and a Matchmaker in "grey".

Remark 5. For clarity reason, we do not give the detail of each transition.

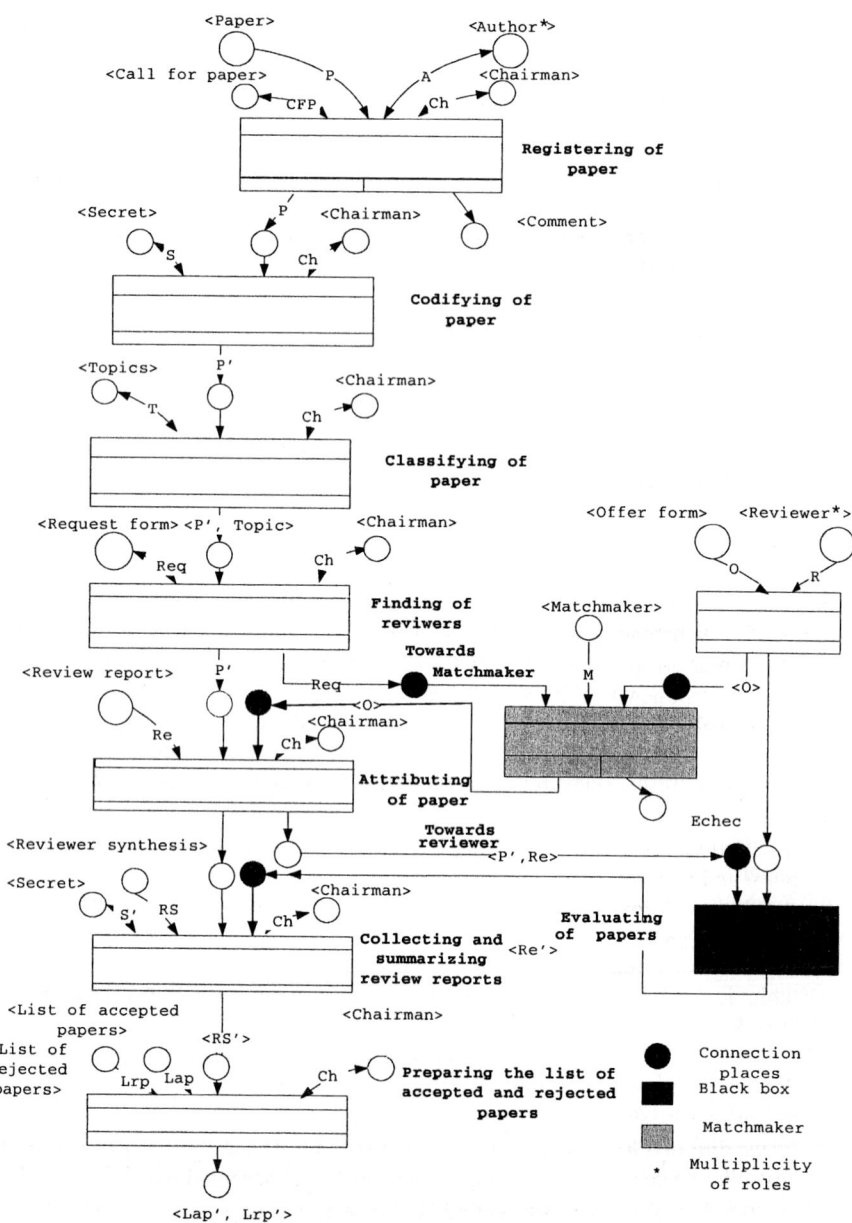

Fig. 4. Modelization of process model by means of Petri Nets with Objects

4 Discussion and Conclusion

The design of loose IOW remains insufficiently addressed. Existing propositions in the literature are rather dedicated to tight IOW ([13], [14] and [15]), and they do not really make the glue between the workflow dimensions i.e. information, organization and process. Theses works only focus on the process dimension by providing interaction models to support distributed execution of component processes. For instance, [13] only focuses on execution aspect of processes by proposing Web services based architecture to support dynamic inter-organizational business processes, and it does not concentrate on design aspect of processes. [14] only proposes a model supporting dynamic heterogeneous workflow process interconnection. Even if [15] deals with the design and execution aspects of processes, the resulting language "YAWL" -which extends Petri Nets with some additional patterns-, does not make the glue between the three-workflow dimensions. We believe our solution is currently unique in trying to take into account the three dimensions of a workflow in a coherent framework. This is made possible thanks to the use of Petri Nets with Objects formalism.

In this paper, we have presented a solution based on an approach the *separation of aspects,* and a formalism the *Petri Nets with Objects (PNO)* for the design of loose IOW. To better illustrate our solution, we have chosen the well-known "reviewing papers" case study. During the design of loose IOW, we have taken into account its three specifics features, namely the distribution, the autonomy and the heterogeneity. Regarding the *distribution*, we have integrated in the organizational and process models an original component called "Matchmaker" in charge of connecting dynamically distributed partners. Moreover, thanks to additional places (called connection places) provided by PNO formalism, it's possible to compose and coordinate components processes. Regarding the *autonomy*, we have added the concept of role in the organizational model, which can be considered as an abstraction, which does not refer explicitly to the individual actors but rather to the capacity they must have. Doing so, the workflow initiator does not have to know the potential partners and each partner can keep its internal structure private. Regarding the *heterogeneity*, we have used an ontology enabling the informational model description and data semantic conflict solving.

Our solution forms the basis of a method for the design of Loose IOW applications. It can be organized around three steps:

- Step1. *Creation of the informational model.* We must identify the universe of discourse i.e. the business domain. We use or we create an ontology of this domain to which the partner could adhere. Then the informational model can be built as it is a sub-set of this ontology.
- Step2. *Description of the organizational model.* We instantiate the AGR meta model which structures organizations participating in IOW in terms of Agents, Groups and Roles. To connect dynamically distributed partners, the organizational model must integrate mediator agents. The potential partners, not known at design time, are described through roles.
- Step3. *Description of the process model.* Once the informational and the organizational models are described, we describe the process model as a Petri-Net

with Objects. While some transitions correspond to local tasks, other transitions correspond to tasks to be sub-contracted. In this last case, the corresponding transitions must include an invocation method to call the mediator in charge of finding a partner, and input and output places to respectively provide information and receive result. The links with the two previous models are guaranteed by the two principles: i) The types of the places are classes of the informational or organizational models ii) actions inside transitions are methods of these classes. Once defined, the process model can be simulated, checked and validated. Our case study has been implemented in a simulator called MatchFlow [12] whose objective is to connect workflow service requesters (for instance chairman in our case) to workflow service providers (for instance reviewer in our case). MatchFlow implements the three-workflow dimensions. As future work, we plan to derive OWL-S specification [16] from PNO, which is considered as an appropriate language for Web Workflow Service description allowing providers to publish their capabilities and requesters to express their needs.

Acknowledgments

I would like to thank C. H. who made many suggestions and comments on the first draft of this paper.

References

1. Casati, F., Discenza, A.: Supporting Workflow Cooperation Within and Across Organizations. 15th Int. Symposium on Applied Computing (2000) Como (Italy) 196–202
2. van der Aalst, W.: Inter-Organizational Workflows: An Approach Based on Message Sequence Charts and Petri Nets. Int. Journal on SAMS, 34 (3) (1999) 335–367
3. Divitini, M., Hanachi, C., Sibertin-Blanc, C.: Inter Organizational Workflows for Enterprise Coordination. Chapter 15 of Coordination of Internet Agents, 2001: 369-398
4. 4 Hanachi, C., Sibertin-Blanc, C., Tout, H.: A Task Model for Cooperative Information Gathering. IEEE Int Conference on Systems, Man and Cybernitics, Hammamet, Tunisia, 2002
5. 19th ACM Symposium on Applied Computing, Special Track on Coordination Models, Languages and Applications, Web Site : http://www.cs.fit.edu/~rmenezes/sac04cm/
6. Sibertin-Blanc, C.: High Level Petri Nets with Data Structure. 6th Int. Workshop on PetriNets and Applications (1985) Espoo (Finland)
7. van der Aalst, W.: The application of Petri Nets to Workflow Management. Int. Journal on Circuits, Systems and Computers 8(1) (1998) 21–66
8. van der Aalst, W., ter Hofstede, A., Kiepuszewski, B., Barros, A.: Workflow Patterns. Int. Journal on Distributed and Parallel Databases 34(1) (2003) 5–51
9. Tatiana, A., Vieira, C., Marco Antonio, C., Luis Gustavo, F.: An Ontology-Driven Architecture for Flexible Workflow Execution. 10th Brazilian Symposium on Multimedia and the Web 2nd Latin American Web Congress (2004), Brazil, 70-77.
10. Ferber, J., Gutknecht, O., Michel, F.: From Agents to Organizations: an Organizational View of Multi-Agent Systems. AOSE 2003:214 -230
11. van der Aalst, W., Kumar, L., Verbeek, A.: Organizational Modeling in UML and XML in the Context of Workflow Systems. SAC 2003: 603-608

12. Andonoff, E., Bouzguenda, L., Hanachi, C., Sibertin-Blanc, C.: Finding Partners in the Coordination of Loose Inter-Organizational Workflow. COOP 2004: 147 -162
13. Schmidt. R.: Web Services Based Architectures to Support Dynamic Inter-organizational Business Processes. ICWS-Europe 2003: 123-136
14. Baïna, K., Benali, K., Godart. C.: Dynamic Interconnection of Heterogeneous Workflow Processes through Services. In CoopIS/DOA/ODBASE'03
15. van der Aalst, W., Alderd, L., Dumas, M., ter Hofstede., A.: Design and Implementation of the YAWL System. CAISE 2004: 142: 159
16. OWL Services Coalition: http://www.daml.org/services/owl-s/1.1/

Recovering from Malicious Attacks in Workflow Systems

Yajie Zhu, Tai Xin, and Indrakshi Ray

Department of Computer Science,
Colorado State University,
{zhuy, xin, iray}@cs.colostate.edu

Abstract. Workflow management systems (WFMS) coordinate execution of logically related multiple tasks in an organization. Such coordination is achieved through dependencies that are specified between the tasks of a workflow. Oftentimes preventive measures are not enough and a workflow may be subjected to malicious attacks. Traditional workflow recovery mechanisms do not address how to recover from malicious attacks. Database survivability techniques do not work for workflow because tasks in a workflow have dependencies that are not present in traditional transaction processing systems. In this paper, we present an algorithm that shows how we can assess and repair the effects of damage caused by malicious tasks. Our algorithm focuses not only on restoring the consistency of data items by removing the effects of malicious tasks but also takes appropriate actions to ensure the satisfaction of task dependencies among all the committed tasks.

1 Introduction

Workflow management systems (WFMS) are responsible for coordinating the execution of multiple logically related tasks performed by an organization. Since vulnerabilities cannot be completely removed from a system and preventive measures sometimes fail, a workflow may be subject to malicious attacks. A malicious attacker may create an illegal task or corrupt a task in a workflow to gain some personal benefits. This malicious task would possibly corrupt data items accessed by some benevolent tasks, or it may trigger some other tasks in this workflow due to the existence of intra-task dependencies in the workflow. Further, tasks that are dependent upon this malicious task can, in turn, corrupt other data items and affect other tasks. The process may continue and the damage can spread in a short span of time. In this paper we present an algorithm that shows how a workflow can detect and recover from such malicious attacks.

Recovering from malicious attacks have been investigated in the context of database systems. In such systems, a transaction executed by a malicious user might corrupt some data item. Other transactions reading from this data item and writing on other data items help spread the damage. Ammann et al. [1] have proposed techniques for assessing and repairing such damage. Their techniques involve parsing the database log to check which transactions were affected by malicious transaction and undoing and redoing the affected transactions. Panda et al. [7] have also proposed a number of algorithms on damage assessment and repair; some of these store the dependency information in separate structures so that the log does not have to be traversed for damage assessment and repair.

Techniques for damage assessment and recovery in database systems are not adequate for workflows. This is because transactions in a database are independent entities. The only way in which one transaction depends on another is through read-write dependencies. A workflow consists of tasks that have control-flow and data-flow dependencies specified among them, in addition to read-write dependencies. These dependencies ensure the proper co-ordination and execution of tasks in a workflow. The presence of these dependencies requires new techniques for damage assessment and recovery. In this paper, we propose one such technique.

A naive solution undoes the workflow with malicious tasks and the other workflows that have executed after it, and then re-executes these other workflows again. Our solution tries to improve upon this by minimizing the number of other workflows that need to be undone and re-executed. We take into account the nature of the dependencies that exist between the tasks of a workflow when we are doing damage assessment. The dependencies enable us to find out which specific tasks of the other workflows are affected. We undo these affected tasks only and re-execute them. Minimizing the number of tasks that are undone and re-executed speeds up the damage recovery process.

The remainder of the paper is organized as follows. Section 2 discusses related works in this area. Section 3 presents our definition of workflow and the various types of dependencies that exists in a workflow. Section 4 enumerates the information required and the assumptions in our recovery algorithm. Section 5 presents the workflow recovery algorithm. Section 6 concludes the paper with pointers to future works.

2 Related Works

Although a lot of research appears in workflow, we focus our attention to those discussing workflow dependencies, workflow recovery and workflow survivability. Eder and Liebhart [4] classify workflow as document-oriented workflow and process-oriented workflow, identify potential different types of failure, and discuss some possible recovery mechanisms. All these concepts are used to achieve one goal, which is to restore the most recent consistent process state after a failure, so that as little as possible long-duration work is lost and process execution can continue.

The FlowBack model [6] discusses the use of compensation for partial backward recovery of workflows. When user wants to abort the original process, the compensation process will be executed. The FlowBack prototype focuses on the flow control between tasks in the case of semantic failure but this flow control is ensured manually. The authors state that the compensation process can be very complex, because it must consider all the paths leading from each task in a workflow. Many tasks cannot be compensated due to the semantics of applications. Moreover, the compensation process is not transparent to the user.

Survivability has received attention in the database context. Ammann et al. propose a two pass repair algorithm for traditional database systems in their paper [1]. The static algorithm composes of two passes. Pass one scans the log forward from the entry where the first malicious task starts to locate every malicious and suspect tasks. Pass two goes backward from the end of the log to undo all malicious and suspect tasks. They also proposed a dynamic repair algorithm. Their paper focuses on the purely syntactic information about the interleaving of read and write operations. Their algorithms cannot be applied to workflow systems having control flow and data flow dependencies.

Gore and Ghosh [5] discuss the recovery and rollback problem in distributed extended transactions. They propose a solution to the recovery problem using partial rollbacks. In the proposed model, the transactions communicate and collaborate only by exchanging messages. These messages are stored in message logs and message tables which are used extensively during recovery. The drawback of this approach is that it is not general – it is based on specialized log structures. Moreover, the authors do not address the issue of transaction dependencies in this paper.

Yu, Liu and Zang [8] describe an algorithm for on-line attack recovery of workflows. The algorithm tries to build the list of redo and undo tasks, after an independent Intrusion Detection System reports malicious tasks. They also relax the restriction of executing order that exist in an attack recovery system; they introduced multi-version data objects to reduce unnecessary blocks in order to reduce degradation of performance in recovery. The authors in this paper treat all types of control-flow dependencies in the same manner. In our paper, we show that the different types of control-flow dependencies require different treatment for recovery. Our algorithm takes into account the type of dependencies in performing recovery from malicious attacks.

3 Our Workflow Model

In our model, a "workflow" is a set of tasks with dependencies specified among them that achieve some business objective. Formally, a *workflow* $W_i = <T, D, C>$ where T is the set of tasks in the workflow W_i, D is the set of dependencies, and C is the set of completion sets in T. A workflow W_i is said to be completed if all the tasks in anyone completion set are committed and all other tasks are either in an unscheduled or aborted state. We assume that each task in a workflow is a transaction as per the standard transaction processing model [2]. A task T_{ij}, which belongs to a specific workflow W_i, consists of a set of data operations (read or write) and task primitives; the begin, commit and abort primitives are denoted by b_{ij}, c_{ij}, and a_{ij} respectively. A task T_{ij} can be in any of the following *states: unscheduled (un_{ij}), initiation (in_{ij}), execution (ex_{ij}), prepare (pr_{ij})*(means prepare to commit), *committed (cm_{ij})* and *aborted (ab_{ij})*. Execution of task primitives causes a task to change its state. Detailed state transition diagrams are shown in 1.

In order to properly coordinate the different tasks in a workflow system, dependencies are specified on task primitives, task operations, and task input/outputs. We refer to these different kinds of dependencies as *task dependencies*. The only kind of inter-workflow dependency we consider is *read-write dependency*. Between tasks of the same workflow we can have read-write dependency as well as *control-flow dependencies*, and *data-flow dependencies*.

A *control-flow dependency* specified between a pair of tasks T_{ij} and T_{ik} expresses how the execution of primitives (begin, abort and commit) of task T_{ij} relates to the execution of the primitives (begin, abort and commit) of another task T_{ik}. we give some

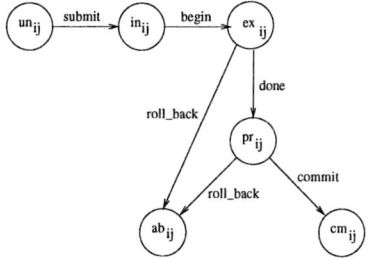

Fig. 1. States of Task T_{ij}

typical control-flow dependencies found in workflows. For a complete list of task dependencies, we refer the interested readers to the work by Chrysanthis 1991 [3].

[Commit dependency]$(T_{ij} \to_c T_{ik})$: If both T_{ij} and T_{ik} commit then the commitment of T_{ij} precedes the commitment of T_{ik}.
[Strong commit dependency]$(T_{ij} \to_{sc} T_{ik})$: If T_{ij} commits then T_{ik} must commits.
[Abort dependency]$(T_{ij} \to_a T_{ik})$: T_{ik} must abort if T_{ij} aborts.
[Termination dependency]$(T_{ij} \to_t T_{ik})$: T_{ik} cannot commit/abort until T_{ij} commits/aborts.
[Force-commit-on-abort dependency]$(T_{ij} \to_{fca} T_{ik})$: T_{ik} must commit if T_{ij} aborts.
[Exclusion Dependency]$(T_{ij} \to_{ex} T_{ik})$: if T_{ij} commits and T_{ik} has begun executing, then T_{ik} must abort.
[Begin dependency]$(T_{ij} \to_b T_{ik})$: T_{ik} cannot begin until T_{ij} has begun.
[Begin-on-commit/abort dependency]$(T_{ij} \to_{bc/ba} T_{ik})$: T_{ik} cannot begin until T_{ij} commits/aborts.
[Force begin-on-begin/commit/abort/terminate dependency] $(T_{ij} \to_{fbb/fbc/fba/fbt} T_{ik})$: T_{ik} must begin if T_{ij} begins/commits/aborts/terminates.

Task T_{ij} is *data-flow dependent upon* task T_{ik} in a workflow, denoted by $T_{ik} \to_{df} T_{ij}$. if there exists a data item x which is an input data item for task T_{ij} and an output data item of task T_{ik}, task T_{ij} accept x as an input from task T_{ik}, and both tasks belong to the same workflow. Note that if there is a data-flow dependency between task T_{ik} and T_{ij}, there will also be a control flow dependency of the form *begin-on-commit* between the two tasks. This is because for the output of T_{ik} to be available to T_{ij}, T_{ik} must commit before T_{ij} starts execution. So we do not consider data-flow dependencies separately while performing recovery.

A task T_{ij} is *read-write dependent upon* task T_{kl} if there exists a data item x such that: (i) T_{ij} reads x after T_{kl} has updated x, T_{kl} does not abort after T_{ij} reads x, and, (ii) if any T_{pq} updates x after T_{kl} has updated x but before T_{ij} reads it, then T_{pq} is aborted.

Example 1. Workflow W_1 consists of a set of tasks T = $\{T_{10}, T_{11}, T_{12}, T_{13}, T_{14}, T_{15}\}$. Each task performs a work: T_{10} – Make a car reservation from Company B; T_{11} – Reserve a ticket on Airlines A; T_{12} – Purchasing the Airlines A ticket; T_{13} – Canceling the reservation; T_{14} – Reserving a room in Resort C; T_{15} – Cancel the car reservation. The set of task dependencies D include: control-flow dependencies { $T_{14} \to_a T_{10}$,

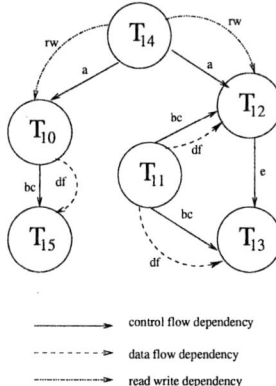

Fig. 2. Tasks and Dependencies in Workflow given in Example 1

$T_{11} \rightarrow_{bc} T_{12}, T_{11} \rightarrow_{bc} T_{13}, T_{12} \rightarrow_{ex} T_{13}, T_{14} \rightarrow_a T_{12}, T_{10} \rightarrow_{bc} T_{15}\}$, data Flow dependencies $\{ T_{10} \rightarrow_{df} T_{15}, T_{11} \rightarrow_{df} T_{12}, T_{11} \rightarrow_{df} T_{13}\}$, read-write Dependencies $\{ T_{14} \rightarrow_{rw} T_{10}, T_{14} \rightarrow_{rw} T_{12}\}$, As shown in this example, the three kinds of dependencies can co-exist in a workflow. The workflow can have several completion sets. Some possible completion sets are $\{T_{14}, T_{10}\}, \{T_{14}, T_{11}, T_{12}\}, \{T_{14}, T_{13}\}, \{T_{10}, T_{15}\}$ and $\{T_{14}, T_{11}, T_{13}\}$.

4 Information Needed by the Repair Algorithm

Workflow repair is much more complex than the recovery in traditional transaction processing system. The repair process will need to know the state of the workflow after some malicious attacks (damage assessment) and it will also need to know the actions needed to perform the recovery. The specific actions to be taken depends on the structure of the workflow, that is, the dependencies associated with the workflow. The structure of the workflow can be obtained from the workflow schema. A *workflow schema* defines the type of a workflow. The specification of a workflow schema includes: the specification of tasks, the dependencies between these tasks, and the set of completion sets for this type of workflows. Each workflow is actually an instance of a workflow schema. We denote the schema associated with workflow W_i as WS_i. The information about all the workflow schema is maintained in stable storage.

In order to recover from a workflow system failure and/or malicious attack, the state information of a workflow need to be logged onto some stable storage. We propose that such information be stored in the system log. Execution of a workflow primitive, a task primitive, or a task operation results in the insertion of log a record. Execution of a begin primitive in a workflow results in the insertion of the following log record. $< START\ W_i, WS_i >$ where W_i indicates the workflow id and WS_i indicates the schema id that corresponds to the workflow W_i. The completion of the workflow is indicated by a log record $< COMPLETE\ W_i >$. Execution of the primitive begin for task T_{ij} results in the following records being inserted in the log: $< START\ T_{ij} >$ where T_{ij} is the task id. Similarly, $< COMMIT\ T_{ij} >$ or $< ABORT\ T_{ij} >$ records the execution of the primitive commit or abort. Execution of operations also cause log records to be inserted: A read operation log record $< T_{ij}\ X, value >$ and a write operation log record $< T_{ij}\ X, v, w >$.

5 Workflow Repair Algorithm

We focus on those intrusions that inject malicious tasks into the workflow management systems. Under these intrusions, the attackers can forge or alter some tasks to corrupt the system or gain some personal benefit. We assume that there is an Intrusion Detection Manager (IDM) in the system. The IDM can identify the malicious attacks and report the malicious tasks periodically. But it cannot discover all the damage done to the system. The damage directly caused by the attacker can spread into the whole workflow system by executing normal tasks without being detected by the IDM.

We explain some of the terms that we use to explain the algorithm. A *malicious task* is a committed task which is submitted by an attacker. A *malicious workflow* is one which contains at least one malicious task in any completion set of it. A task T_{ij} is *control-flow dependent upon* another task T_{ik} if the execution of task T_{ij} depends upon the successful/unsuccessful execution of task T_{ik}. Note that not all tasks related by control-flow dependencies are control-flow dependent on each other. Some control-flow dependencies impose an execution order on the different tasks; these do not require one task to be executed because of the successful/unsuccessful execution of another. Such tasks are not control-flow depndent on the other. For example, the commit dependency $T_{wi} \rightarrow_c T_{wj}$ controls the order of two tasks entering the commit state. It does not require any task T_{wi} (T_{wj}) to be executed because of another T_{wj} (T_{wi}).

For any control-flow dependency $T_{wi} \rightarrow_{d_x} T_{wj}$ between T_{wi} and T_{wj}, either task T_{wi} or task T_{wj} may be malicious/affected after a malicious attack taken place. For each case, we analyze how the malicious/affected task affects the other task. The cases when T_{wj} is control-flow dependent on a malicious or affected task T_{wi} are enumerated in Table 1. This table also gives the repair actions that are needed for task T_{wj}. Only two control-flow dependencies can cause task T_{wj} to be control-flow dependent upon T_{wi}: abort dependency and begin-on-commit dependency. The abort dependency requires T_{wj} to abort if T_{wi} aborts. Since T_{wi} is a malicious/affected task it must be undone. This necessitates undoing T_{wj} if it has already been committed. The begin-on-commit dependency ensures that T_{wj} will not begin until T_{wi} commits. Thus undoing T_{wi} requires an undo of T_{wj} if T_{wj} has been commited.

Table 1. Is T_{wj} control-flow dependent upon the malicious or affected task T_{wi}?

Dependency	T_{wj} CF dependent upon T_{wi}?	Action in repair
$T_{wi} \rightarrow_{c/sc/t} T_{wj}$	No	No
$T_{wi} \rightarrow_a T_{wj}$	Yes	if T_{wj} commited, undo T_{wj}
$T_{wi} \rightarrow_{bc} T_{wj}$	Yes	if T_{wj} commited, undo T_{wj}
$T_{wi} \rightarrow_{b/ba} T_{wj}$	No	No
$T_{wi} \rightarrow_{fbb/fbc/fba/fbt} T_{wj}$	No	No
$T_{wi} \rightarrow_{fca/ex} T_{wj}$	No	No

Table 2. Is T_{wi} control-flow dependant upon the malicious or affected task T_{wj}?

Dependency	T_{wi} CF dependent upon T_{wj}?	Action in repair
$T_{wi} \to_{c/t/a} T_{wj}$	No	No
$T_{wi} \to_{sc} T_{wj}$	Yes	if T_{wi} commited, undo T_{wi}
$T_{wi} \to_{b/bc/ba} T_{wj}$	No	No
$T_{wi} \to_{fbb/fbc/fba/fbt} T_{wj}$	No	No
$T_{wi} \to_{fca/ex} T_{wj}$	No	No

If T_{wj} is a malicious or affected task, it must be undone. Table 2 shows whether T_{wi} is control-flow dependent upon task T_{wj} and the repair actions needed for T_{wi}. In this case only T_{wi} is control-flow dependent upon T_{wj} if there is a strong-commit dependency. This dependency will be violated if we undo T_{wj}. In such a case, if T_{wi} has committed, it must be undone.

Before presenting our algorithm, we state our assumptions. (i) We consider the effect of committed malicious tasks in repairing. (ii) We assume that the execution of different workflows can interleave with each other. (iii) Each task is executed as a transaction which means it has the properties of atomicity, consistency, isolation, and durability [2]. (iv) To ensure strict and serializable execution, we use the strict two phase-locking mechanism [2].

We denote the committed malicious tasks in a workflow system history by the set B, which are detected by IDM. Based on these malicious tasks, we can identify the corresponding malicious workflows as the set BW. The basic idea is that all malicious workflows must be undone. We must identify all affected task of other good workflows, and remove the effects of all malicious workflows.

Our algorithm proceeds in four phases. The first phase undoes all malicious workflows. It also collects the set of committed tasks for the good workflows. The second phase performs the damage assessment caused by malicious workflows by identifying all the set of affected tasks. In this we first identify the completed workflows that do not need any recovery action. We then identify all the tasks that were affected due to the presence of control-flow and read-write dependencies. The third phase undoes all the affected tasks. The fourth phase is responsible for re-execution and continuation of incomplete workflows.

Algorithm 1
Workflow Repair Algorithm
Input: (i) the log, (ii) workflow schemas, (iii) **BW** – set of malicious workflows
Output: a consistent workflow state in which the effects of all malicious and affected tasks are removed

Procedure WorkflowRepair
Phase 1: Undo malicious workflows and Identify the committed tasks sets of other workflows
$globalAborted = \{\}$ /* set holding aborted tasks of all workflows */
$committed[w] = \{\}$ /* set holding committed tasks of workflow W_w, which is not a malicious workflow */
$workflowList = \{\}$ /* set holding the committed tasks of all but malicious workflows */
begin

/* Scan backwards until we reach $<START\ W_i>$ where W_i is the earliest malicious workflow*/
do
    switch the last unscanned log record
    case the log record is $<ABORT\ T_{wi}>$
        $globalAborted = globalAborted \cup \{T_{wi}\}$
    case the log record is $<COMMIT\ T_{wi}>$
        if $W_w \notin \mathbf{BW} \wedge T_{wi} \notin globalAborted$
          for W_w, $committed[w] = committed[w] \cup \{T_{wi}\}$
    case the log record is update record $<T_{wi},x,v,w>$
        if $W_w \in \mathbf{BW} \wedge T_{wi} \notin globalAborted$
          change the value of x to v /*undo the task in the malicious workflow*/
    case the log record is $<START\ T_{wi}>$
        if $W_w \in \mathbf{BW} \wedge T_{wi} \notin globalAborted$
          write $<ABORT\ T_{wi}>$ log record
    case the log record is $<START\ W_w>$
        if $W_w \in \mathbf{BW}$
          write $<ABORT\ W_w>$ log record
        else
          $workflowList = workflowList \cup committed[w]$
end //phase 1
Phase 2: find all affected tasks
corrupted = {} //a set holds all corrupted data items
undo = {} //a set holds all affected tasks, which need to be undone
finished = {} //a set holds all completed workflows
begin
    /* Scan forward from $<START\ W_i>$ where W_i is the earliest malicious workflow */
    do
        while not end of log
          switch next log record
          case log record = $<COMPLETE\ W_i>$
              if there exists a completion set C_j of Workflow W_i such that $C_j \subseteq committed[i]$
                $finished = finished \cup \{i\}$
              else
                if $i \in finished$
                  $finished = finished - \{i\}$
          case log record = $<T_{ij},X,v,w>$ //write record
              /*find out the corrupted data item that is written by malicious or affected task*/
              if $(W_i \in \mathbf{BW} \wedge T_{ij} \notin globalAborted) \vee T_{ij} \in undo$
                $corrupted = corrupted \cup \{X\}$
          case log record = $<T_{ij},X,value>$ //read record
        /*find out the affected task which reads a corrupted data item*/
              if $X \in corrupted \wedge W_i \notin \mathbf{BW} \wedge T_{ij} \notin globalAborted \wedge T_{ij} \notin undo$
                $undo = undo \cup \{T_{ij}\}$
              /* get the set of control-flow affected tasks */
              $newSet = getControlflowAffected(T_{ij}, committed[i])$

```
                    if newSet ≠ NULL
                        undo = undo ∪ newSet
                        scan back to the earliest affected task in newSet
                 case log record = < COMMIT T_ij >
                    if T_ij ∈ undo
                        committed[i] = committed[i] − T_ij
end //phase 2
```
Phase 3: undo all the tasks in the undo set.
```
begin scan backwards from the end of the log and undo all tasks in undo list
    do
        switch the last unscanned log record
            case log record = < T_ij,X,u,v >
                if T_ij ∈ undo
                    restore the value of X to u //restoring before image
            case log record = < START T_ij >
                if T_ij ∈ undo
                    write < ABORT T_ij > log record
end //phase 3
```
Phase 4: resubmit the incomplete workflow to scheduler and continue the e execution.
```
begin
    for each committed[i] ∈ workflowList
        if i ∉ finished
            submit committed[i] to the scheduler
end //phase 4
```

6 Conclusions and Future Work

In this paper we have focussed on how to repair attacks caused by one or more malicious tasks in a workflow. In addition to the read-write dependencies that are present in the traditional transactions, workflows have control-flow and data-flow dependencies as well. These dependencies help spread the damage caused by malicious tasks and complicates the recovery process. Our algorithm removes the effects of workflows having malicious tasks and tries to minimize undoing the good tasks. Only good tasks that were affected are undone and re-executed.

We have given an algorithm that shows how the workflow can be repaired in the event of a malicious attack. A lot of work remains to be done. For instance, we need to formalize what we mean by a correct execution and correct repair of a workflow. Finally, we need to prove that our algorithm satisfies the correctness criteria. Workflow is an example of an extended transaction model. This work can be applied to other extended transaction processing models since read-write and control-flow dependencies also exist in these models. Specifically, we plan to propose how recovery from malicious transactions can occur in other kinds of extended transaction model.

Acknowledgement

This work was partially supported by NSF under Award No. IIS 0242258.

References

1. Paul Ammann, Sushil Jajodia, and Peng Liu. Recovery from malicious transactions. *IEEE Trans on Knowledge and Data Engineering*, 14:1167–1185, 2002.
2. P. A. Bernstein, V. Hadzilacos, and N. Goodman. *Concurrency Control and Recovery in Database Systems*. Addison-Wesley, Reading, MA, 1987.
3. P. Chrysanthis. *ACTA, A framework for modeling and reasoning aout extended transactions*. PhD thesis, University of Massachusetts, Amherst, Amherst, Massachusetts, 1991.
4. J. Eder and W. Liebhart. Workflow Recovery. In *Proceeding of Conference on Cooperative Information Systems*, pages 124–134, 1996.
5. M. M. Gore and R. K. Ghosh. Recovery in Distributed Extended Long-lived Transaction Models. In *In Proceedings of the 6th International Conference DataBase Systems for Advanced Applicationns*, pages 313–320, April 1999.
6. B. Kiepuszewski, R. Muhlberger, , and M. Orlowska. Flowback: Providing backward recovery for workflow systems. In *Proceeding of the ACM SIGMOD Inter-national Conference on Management of Data*, pages 555–557, 1998.
7. C. Lala and B. Panda. Evaluating damage from cyber attacks. *IEEE Transactions on Systems, Man and Cybernetics*, 31(4):300–310, July 2001.
8. Meng Yu, Peng Liu, and Wanyu Zang. Multi-Version Attack Recovery for Workflow Systems. In *19th Annual Computer Security Applications Conference*, pages 142–151, Dec 2003.

Towards Mining Structural Workflow Patterns

Walid Gaaloul[1], Karim Baïna[2], and Claude Godart[1]

[1] LORIA - INRIA - CNRS - UMR 7503,
BP 239, F-54506 Vandœuvre-lès-Nancy Cedex, France
[2] ENSIAS, Université Mohammed V - Souissi,
BP 713 Agdal - Rabat, Morocco
baina@ensias.ma, {gaaloul, godart}@loria.fr

Abstract. Collaborative information systems are becoming more and more complex, involving numerous interacting business objects within considerable processes. Analysing the interaction structure of those complex systems will enable them to be well understood and controlled. The work described in this paper is a contribution to these problems for workflow based process applications. In fact, we discover workflow patterns from traces of workflow events based on a workflow mining technique. Workflow mining proposes techniques to acquire a workflow model from a workflow log. Mining of workflow patterns is done by a statistical analysis of log-based event. Our approach is characterised by a "local" workflow patterns discovery that allows to cover partial results and a dynamic technique dealing with concurrency.

Keywords: workflow patterns, workflow mining, business process reengineering.

1 Introduction

With the technological improvements and the continuous increasing market pressures and requirements, collaborative information systems are becoming more and more complex, involving numerous interacting business objects. Analysing interactions of those complex systems will enable them to be well understood and controlled. Our paper is a contribution to this problem in a particular context : workflow application analysis and control by mining techniques (a.k.a. "reversing processes" [1]).

In our approach, we start by collecting log information from workflow processes instances as they took place. Then we build, through statistical techniques, a graphical intermediary representation modelling elementary dependencies over workflow activities executions. These dependencies are then refined to discover workflow patterns [2]. This paper is structured as follows. Section 2 explains our workflow log model. Section 3, we detail our structural workflow patterns mining algorithm. Section 4 discusses related work, and concludes.

2 Workflow Log Model

As shown in the UML class diagram in figure 1, WorkflowLog is composed of a set of EventStreams (definition 1). Each EventStream traces the execution of one case (instance). It consists of a set of events (Event) that captures the activities life cycle

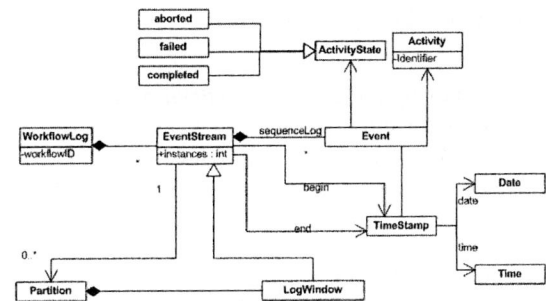

Fig. 1. Workflow Log Model

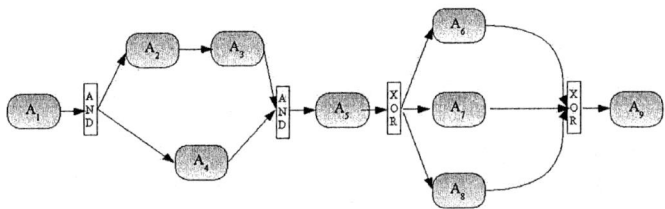

Fig. 2. Running example of workflow

performed in a particular workflow instance. An Event is described by the activity identifier that it concerns, the current activity state (aborted, failed and completed) and the time when it occurs (TimeStamp). A Window defines a set of Events over an EventStream. Finally, a Partition builds a set of partially overlapping Windows partition over an EventStream.

Definition 1. *(EventStream)*
An EventStream *represents the history of a worflow instance events as a tuple* stream= *(*begin, end, sequenceLog, isntances*) where:*
  ✓*(*begin:TimeStamp*) and (*end:TimeStamp*) are the log beginning and end time;*
  ✓sequenceLog : Event* *is an ordered* Event *set belonging to a workflow instance;*
  ✓instances : int *is the instance number.*
A WorkflowLog *is a set of* EventStreams. WorkflowLog=(workflowID, {EventStream$_i$, $0 \leq i \leq$ number of workflow instances}*) where* EventStream$_i$ *is the event stream of the ith workflow instance.*

Here is an example of an EventStream extracted from the workflow example of figure 2 in its 5th instantiation :

L = EventStream((13/5,5:42:12), (14/5, 14:01:54), [**Event**(Event("A_1", completed, (13/5, 5:42:12)), Event("A_2", completed, (13/5,11:11:12)), Event("A_4", completed, (13/5,14:01:54)), Event("A_3", completed, (14/5, 00:01:54)), Event("A_5", completed, (14/5,5:45:54)), Event("A_6", aborted, (14/5,10:32:55)), Event("A_7", completed, (14/5,10:32:55)), Event("A_9", completed, (14/5,14:01:54))],5)

3 Mining Structural Workflow Patterns

As we state before, we start by collecting WorkflowLog from workflow instances as they took place. Then we build, through statistical techniques, a graphical intermediary representation modelling **elementary dependencies** over workflow logs (see section 3.1). These dependencies are then refined by **advanced structural workflow patterns** (see section 3.2).

3.1 Discovering Elementary Dependencies

In order to discover direct dependencies from a WorkflowLog, we need an intermediary representation of this WorkflowLog through a statistical analysis. We call this intermediary representation : statistical dependency table (or SDT). SDT is built through a statistical calculus that extracts elementary dependencies between activities of a WorkflowLog that are executed without "exceptions" (*i.e.* they reached successfully their completed state). Then, we need to filter the analysed WorkflowLog and take only EventStreams of instances executed "correctly". We denote by WorkflowLog$_{completed}$ this workflow log projection. Thus, the unique necessary condition to discover elementary dependencies is to have workflow logs containing at least the completed event states. These features allow us to mine control flow from "poor" logs which contain only completed event state. By the way, any information system using transactional systems or workflow management systems offer this information in some form [1].

For each activity A, we extract from workflowLog$_{completed}$ the following information in the statistical dependency table (SDT): (i) The overall occurrence number of this activity (denoted $\#A$) and (ii) The elementary dependencies to previous activities B_i (denoted $P(A/B_i)$). The size of SDT is $N * N$, where N is the number of workflow activities. The (m,n) table entry (notation P(m/n)) is the frequency of the nth activity immediately preceding the mth activity. The initial SDT in table 1 represents a fraction of the SDT of our workflow example given in figure 2. For instance, in this table $P(A_3/A_2)=0.69$ expresses that if A_3 occurs then we have 69% of chance that A_2 occurs directly before A_3 in the workflow log. As it was calculated SDT presents some problems to express correctly activities dependencies relating to concurrent behaviour. In the following, we detail these issues and propose solutions to correct them.

Discarding errorneous dependencies : If we assume that each EventStream from WorkflowLog comes from a sequential (i.e no concurrent behaviour) workflow, a zero entry in SDT represents a causal independence and a non-zero entry means a causal dependency relation (*i.e.* sequential or conditional relation). But, in case of concurrent behaviour, as we can see in workflow patterns (like and-split, and-join, or-join, etc.) the EventStreams may contain interleaved events sequences from concurrent threads. As a consequence, some entries in initial SDT can indicate non-zero entries that do not correspond to dependencies. For example the events stream given in section 2 "suggests" erroneous causal dependencies between A_2 and A_4 in one side and A_4 and A_3 in another side. Indeed, A_2 comes immediately before A_4 and A_4 comes immediately before A_3 in this events stream. These erroneous entries are reported by $P(A_4/A_2)$ and $P(A_3/A_4)$ in initial SDT which are different to zero. These entries are erroneous be-

Table 1. Fraction of Statistical Dependencies Table ($P(x/y)$) and activities Frequencies (#)

Initial SDT							Final SDT						
$P(x/y)$	A_1	A_2	A_3	A_4	A_5	A_6	$P(x/y)$	A_1	A_2	A_3	A_4	A_5	A_6
A_1	0	0	0	0	0	0	A_1	0	0	0	0	0	0
A_2	**0.54**	0	0	0.46	0	0	A_2	1	0	0	-1	0	0
A_3	0	**0.69**	0	0.31	0	0	A_3	0	1	0	-1	0	0
A_4	**0.46**	**0.31**	**0.23**	0	0	0	A_4	1	-1	-1	0	0	0
A_5	0	0	**0.77**	**0.23**	0	0	A_5	0	0	1	1	0	0
A_6	0	0	0	0	1	0	A_6	0	0	0	0	1	0

$$\#A_1 = \#A_2 = \#A_3 = \#A_4 = \#A_5 = \#A_9 = 100,$$
$$\#A_6 = 23, \#A_7 = 42, \#A_8 = 35$$

cause there is no causal dependencies between these activities as suggested (i.e. noisy SDT). Underlined values in initial SDT report this behaviour for other similar cases.

Formally, two activities A and B are in concurrence *iff* $P(A/B)$ and $P(B/A)$ entries in SDT are different from zero with the assumption that WorkflowLog is complete. Indeed, a WorkflowLog is complete if it covers all possible cases (i.e. if a specific routing element can appear in the mined workflow model, the log should contain an example of this behaviour in at least one case). Based on this definition, we propose an algorithm to discover activities parallelism and then mark the erroneous entries in SDT. Through this marking, we can eliminate the confusion caused by the concurrence behaviour producing these erroneous non-zero entries. Our algorithm scans the initial **SDT** and marks concurrent activities dependencies by changing their values to (-1).

Discovering indirect dependencies: For concurrency reasons, an activity might not depend on its immediate predecessor in the events stream, but it might depend on another "indirectly" preceding activity. As an example of this behaviour, A_4 is logged between A_2 and A_3 in the events stream given in section 2. As consequence, A_2 does not occur always immediately before A_3 in the workflow log. Thus we have only $P(A_3/A_2) = 0.69$ that is an under evaluated dependency frequency. In fact, the right value is 1 because the execution of A_3 depends exclusively on A_2. Similarly, values in bold in initial SDT report this behaviour for other cases.

Definition 2. Window

*A log window defines a log slide over an events stream S : **stream** (bStream, eStream, sLog, workflowocc). Formally, we define a log window as a triplet **window**(wLog, bWin, eWin) :*

√ *(bWin : TimeStamp) and (eWin : TimeStamp) are the moment of the window beginning and end (with bStream ≤ bWin and eWin ≤ eStream)*

√ *wLog ⊂ sLog and ∀ e: **event** ∈ S.sLog where bWin ≤ e.TimeStamp ≤ eWin ⇒ e ∈ wLog.*

To discover these indirect dependencies, we introduce the notion of *activity concurrent window* (definition 2). An *activity concurrent window* (ACW) is related to the activity of its last event covering its directly and indirectly preceding activities. Initially, the width of ACW of an activity is equal to 2. Every time this activity is in concurrence with an other activity we add 1 to this width. If this activity is not in concurrence with other activities and has preceding concurrent activities, then we add their number to ACW width. For example the activity A_4 is in concurrence with A_2 and A_3 the width of its ACW is equal to 4. Based on this, we propose an algorithm that calculates for each activity the activity concurrent width regrouped in the ACW table. This algorithm scans the "marked" **SDT** calculated in last section and updates the ACW table.

Definition 3. Partition
A *partition* builds a set of partially overlapping Windows partition over an events stream. Partition : WorkflowLog $\rightarrow$ *(Window)**
$Partition(S$: EventStream($bStr$, $eStr$, $sLog$: $(Evt_i$ 1$\leq$i$\leq$n), $wocc$)) $= \{w_i$:Window; $1 \leq i \leq n\}$ where : Evt_i= the last event in w_i $\wedge$ width(w_i)= $ACWT[Evt_i.ActivityID]$.

After that, we proceed through an EventStreams partition (definition 3) that builds a set of partially overlapping windows over the EventStreams using the ACW table. Finally, we compute the final SDT. For each ACW, we compute for its last activity the frequencies of its preceding activities. The final SDT will be found by dividing each row entry by the frequency of the row's activity. Note that, our approach adjusts **dynamically**, through the width of ACW, the process calculating activities dependencies. Indeed, this width is sensible to concurrent behaviour : it increases in case of concurrence and is "neutral" in case of concurrent behaviour absence. Now, we can compute the final SDT (table 1) which will be used to discover workflow patterns.

3.2 Discovering Advanced Dependencies: Workflow Patterns

We have identified three kinds of statistical properties (sequential, conditional and concurrent) which describe the main behaviours of workflow patterns. Then, we have specified these properties using SDT's statistics. We use these properties to identify separately workflow patterns from workflow logs. We begin with the statistic exclusive dependency property which characterises, for instance, the sequence pattern.

Property 1. Mutual exclusive dependency property: *A **mutual** exclusive dependency relation between an activity A_i and its immediately preceding previous activity A_j specifies that the enactment of the activity A_i depends only on the completion of activity A_j and the completion of A_j enacts only the execution of A_i. It is expressed in terms of:*
  √ *activities frequencies :* $\#A_i = \#A_j$
  √ *activities dependencies :* $P(A_i/A_j) = 1 \wedge \forall k \neq j; P(A_i/A_k) = 0 \wedge \forall l \neq i; P(A_l/A_j) = 0.$

The next two statistic properties: concurrency property (property 2) and choice property (property 3) are used to insulate statistical patterns behaviour in terms of concurrence and choice after a "fork" or before a "join" point.

Property 2. Concurrency property: *A **concurrency** relation between a set of activities $\{A_i, 0 \leq i \leq n\}$ belonging to the same workflow specifies how, in terms of concurrency, the execution of these activities is performed. This set of activities is commonly found after a "fork" point or before a "join" point. We have distinguished three activities concurrency behaviours:*

✓ *Global concurrency where in the same instantiation the whole activities are performed simultaneously* : $\forall 0 \leq i, j \leq n; \#A_i = \#A_j \land P(A_i/A_j) = -1$

✓ *Partial concurrency where in the same instantiation we have at least a partial concurrent execution of activities* : $\exists 0 \leq i, j \leq n; P(A_i/A_j) = -1$

✓ *No concurrency where there is no concurrency between activities:* $\forall (0 \leq i, j \leq n; P(A_i/A_j) \geq 0)$

Property 3. Choice property: *A **choice** relation specifies which activities are executed after a "fork" point or before a "joint" point. The two actors of a "fork" point (respectively a "join" point) perform this relation are : (**actor 1**) an activity A from which comes (respectively to which) a single thread of control which splits (respectively converges) into (respectively from) (**actor 2**) multiple activities* $\{A_i, 1 \leq i \leq n\}$. *We have distinguished three activities choice behaviours* :

✓ *Free choice where a part of activities from the second actor are chosen. Expressed statistically, we have in terms of activities frequencies* ($\#A \leq \Sigma_{i=1}^{n}(\#A_i)) \land (\forall (1 \leq i, j \leq n; \#A_i \leq \#A)$ *and in terms of activities dependencies we have* :

 ✓ *In "fork" point* : $\forall 1 \leq i \leq n; P(A_i/A) = 1$
 ✓ *In "join" point* : $1 < \Sigma_{i=1}^{n} P(A/A_i) < n$

✓ *Single choice where only one activity is chosen from the second actor. Expressed statistically, we have in terms of activities frequencies* ($\#A = \Sigma_{i=1}^{n}(\#A_i))$) *and in terms of activities dependencies we have* :

 ✓ *In "fork" point* : $\forall 1 \leq i \leq n; P(A_i/A) = 1$
 ✓ *In "join" point* : $\Sigma_{i=1}^{n} P(A/A_i) = 1$

✓ *No choice where all activities in the second actor are executed. Expressed statistically, we have in terms of activities frequencies* $\forall 1 \leq i \leq n \; \#A = \#A_i$ *and in terms of activities dependencies we have* :

 ✓ *In "fork" point* : $\forall 1 \leq i \leq n; P(A/A_i) = 1$
 ✓ *In "join" point* : $\forall 1 \leq i \leq n; P(A_i/A) = 1$

Using these statistical specifications of sequential, conditional and concurrent properties, the last step is the identification of workflow patterns through a set of rules. In fact, each pattern has its own statistical features which abstract statistically its causal dependencies, and represent its unique identifier. These rules allow, if workflow log is completed, to mine the whole workflow patterns hidden in this workflow.

Our control flow mining rules are characterised by a "local" workflow patterns discovery. Indeed, these rules are context-free, they proceed through a **local log analysing** that allows us to **recover partial results** of mining workflow patterns. In fact, to discover a particular workflow pattern we need only events relating to pattern's elements. Thus, even using only fractions of workflow log, we can discover correctly corresponding workflow patterns (which their events belong to these fractions).

We divided the workflows patterns in three categories : sequence, fork and join patterns. In the following we present rules to discover the most interesting workflow patterns belonging to these three categories. Note that the rules formulas noted by : (P1) finger the Statistic exclusive dependency property, (P2) finger statistic concurrency property and (P3) finger statistic choice property.

Discovering sequence pattern: In this category we find only the sequence pattern (table 2). In this pattern, the enactment of the activity B depends only on the completion

Table 2. Rules of sequence workflow pattern

Rules	workflow patterns
(P1) ($\#B = \#A$)	Sequence pattern
(P1) ($P(B/A) = 1$)	A → B

Table 3. Rules of fork workflow patterns

Rules	workflow patterns
(P3)($\Sigma_{i=0}^{n} (\#B_i) = \#A$)	xor-split pattern
(P3)($\forall 0 \leq i \leq n; P(B_i/A) = 1$) ∧ (P2)($\forall 0 \leq i,j \leq n; P(B_i/B_j) = 0$)	A → XOR → $B_1, B_2, ..., B_n$
(P3)($\forall 0 \leq i \leq n; \#B_i = \#A$)	and-split pattern
(P3)($\forall 0 \leq i \leq n; P(B_i/A) = 1$) ∧ (P2)($\forall 0 \leq i,j \leq n\ P(B_i/B_j) = -1$)	A → AND → $B_1, B_2, ..., B_n$
(P3)($\#A \leq \Sigma_{i=0}^{n} (\#B_i)$) ∧ ($\forall 0 \leq i \leq n; \#B_i \leq \#A$)	or-split pattern
(P3)($\forall 0 \leq i \leq n; P(B_i/A) = 1$) ∧ (P2)($\exists 0 \leq i,j \leq n; P(B_i/B_j) = -1$)	A → OR → $B_1, B_2, ..., B_n$

of activity A. So we have used the statistical exclusive dependency property to ensure this relation linking B to A.

Discovering fork patterns: This category (table 3) has a "fork" point where a single thread of control splits into multiple threads of control which can be, according to the used pattern, executed or not. The dependency between the activities A and B_i before and after "fork" point differs in the three patterns of this category: and-split, or-split, xor-split. These dependencies are characterised by the statistic choice properties. The xor-split pattern, where one of several branches is chosen after "fork" point, adopts the single choice property. and-split and or-split patterns differentiate themselves through the no choice and free choice properties. Effectively, only a part of activities are executed in the or-split pattern after a "fork" point, while all the B_i activities are executed in the and-split pattern. The non-parallelism between B_i, in the xor-split pattern are ensured by the no concurrency property while the partial and the global parallelism in or-split and and-split is identified through the application of the statistical partial and global concurrency properties.

Table 4. Rules of join workflow patterns

Rules	workflow patterns
(P3)($\Sigma_{i=0}^{n}$ (#A_i)=#B)	xor-join pattern
(P3)($\Sigma_{i=0}^{n}$ P(B/A_i)=1) $\wedge$ (P2)($\forall 0 \leq i,j \leq n; P(A_i/A_j) = 0$)	
(P3)($\forall 0 \leq i \leq n; \#A_i$=#B)	and-join pattern
(P3)($\forall 0 \leq i \leq n; P(B/A_i) = 1$)$\wedge$ (P2)($\forall 0 \leq i,j \leq n \ P(A_i/A_j) = -1$)	
(P3)($m * \#B \leq \Sigma_{i=0}^{n}$ (#A_i)) $\wedge$ ($\forall 0 \leq i \leq n; \#A_i \leq \#B$) (P3)($m \leq \Sigma_{i=0}^{n} P(B/A_i) \leq n$) $\wedge$ (P2)($\exists 0 \leq i,j \leq n; P(A_i/A_j) = -1$)	M-out-of-N-Join pattern

Discovering join patterns: This category (table 4) has a "join" point where multiple threads of control merge in a single thread of control. The number of necessary branches for the causal of the activity B after the "join" point depends on the used pattern.

To identify the three patterns of this category: and-join pattern, xor-join pattern and M-out-of-N-Join pattern we have analysed dependencies between the activities A_i and B before and after "join". Thus the single choice and the no concurrency properties are used to identify the xor-join pattern where two or more alternative branches come together without synchronisation and none of the alternative branches is ever executed in parallel. As for the and-join pattern where multiple parallel activities converge into one single thread of control, the no choice and the global concurrency are both used to discover this pattern. In contrary of the M-out-of-N-Join pattern, where we need only the termination of M activities from the incoming N parallel paths to enact the B activity, The concurrency between A_i would be partial and the choice is free.

4 Discussion

The idea of applying process mining in the context of workflow management was first introduced in [3]. This work proposes methods for automatically deriving a formal model of a process from a log of events related to its executions and is based on workflow graphs. Cook and Wolf [4] investigated similar issues in the context of software engineering processes. They extended their work limited initially to sequential processes, to concurrent processes [5]. Herbst [6,7] presents an inductive learning component used to support the acquisition and adaptation of sequential process models, generalising execution traces from different workflow instances to a workflow model covering all traces. Starting from the same kind of process logs, van der Aalst et al. explore also proposes techniques to discover workflow models based on Petri nets. Beside analysing

Table 5. Comparing Process Mining Tools

	EMiT [12]	Little Thumb [13]	InWoLvE [14]	Process Miner [15]	WorkflowMiner
Structure	Graph	Graph	Graph	Block	**Patterns**
Local discovery	No	No	No	No	**Yes**
Parallelism	Yes	Yes	Yes	Yes	**Yes**
Non-free choice	No	No	No	No	**Yes**
Loops	Yes	Yes	Yes	Yes	**No**
Noise	No	Yes	Yes	No	**No**
Time	Yes	No	No	No	**No**

process structure, there exist related works dealing with process behaviour reporting, such as [8,9,10] that describe tools and case studies that discuss several features, such as analysing deadline expirations, predicting exceptions, process instances monitoring.

We have implemented our presented workflow patterns mining algorithms within our prototype WorkflowMiner [11]. WorkflowMiner is written in Java and based on Bonita Workflow Management System[1] and XProlog Java Prolog API[2]. Starting from executions of a workflow, (1) events streams are gathered into an XML log. In order to be processed, (2) these workflow log events are wrapped into a 1st order logic format, compliant with UML class diagrams shown in figure 1. (3) Mining rules are applied on resulted 1st order log events to discover workflow patterns. We use a Prolog-based presentation for log events, and mining rules. (4) Discovered patterns are given to the workflow designer so he/she will have a look on the analysis of his/her deployed workflow to restructure or redesign it either manually or semi-automatically.

Table 5 compares our WorkflowMiner prototype to workflow mining tools representing previous studied approches. We focus on seven aspects: **structure** of the target discovering language, **local discovery** dealing with incomplete parts of logs (opposed to global and complete log analysis), **parallelism** (a fork path beginning with and-split and ending with and-join), **non-free choice** (NFC processes mix synchronisation and choice in one construct), **loops** (cyclic workflow transitions, or paths), **noise** (situation where log is incomplete or contains errors or non-representative exceptional instances), and **time** (event time stamp information used to calculate performance indicators such as waiting/synchronisation times, flow times, load/utilisation rate, etc.).

WorkflowMiner can be distinguished by supporting **local discovery** through a set of control flow mining rules that are characterised by a "local" workflow patterns discovery enabling **partial results** to be discovered correctly. Moreover, even if non-free choice (NFC) construct is mentioned as an example of a workflow pattern that is difficult to mine, WorkflowMiner discovers M-out-of-N-Join pattern which can be seen as a generalisation of the basic Discriminator pattern that were proven to be inherently non free-choice. None of related works can deal with such constructs.

In our future works, we aim to discover more complex patterns by enriching our workflow log, and by using more metrics (e.g. entropy, periodicity, etc.). We are also interested in the modeling and the discovery of more complex transactional characteristics of cooperative workflows [16].

---

[1] Bonita, bonita.objectweb.org
[2] XProlog, www.iro.umontreal.ca/~vaucher/XProlog/

References

1. W. M. P. van der Aalst, B. F. van Dongen, J. Herbst, L. Maruster, G. Schimm, and A. J. M. M. Weijters. Workflow mining: a survey of issues and approaches. *Data Knowl. Eng.*, 47(2):237–267, 2003.
2. W. M. P. Van Der Aalst, A. H. M. Ter Hofstede, B. Kiepuszewski, and A. P. Barros. Workflow patterns. *Distrib. Parallel Databases*, 14(1):5–51, 2003.
3. Rakesh Agrawal, Dimitrios Gunopulos, and Frank Leymann. Mining process models from workflow logs. *Lecture Notes in Computer Science*, 1377:469–498, 1998.
4. Jonathan E. Cook and Alexander L. Wolf. Discovering models of software processes from event-based data. *ACM Transactions on Software Engineering and Methodology (TOSEM)*, 7(3):215–249, 1998.
5. Jonathan E. Cook and Alexander L. Wolf. Event-based detection of concurrency. In *Proceedings of the 6th ACM SIGSOFT international symposium on Foundations of software engineering*, pages 35–45. ACM Press, 1998.
6. Joachim Herbst. A machine learning approach to workflow management. In *Machine Learning: ECML 2000, 11th European Conference on Machine Learning, Barcelona, Catalonia, Spain*, volume 1810, pages 183–194. Springer, Berlin, May 2000.
7. Joachim Herbst and Dimitris Karagiannis. Integrating machine learning and workflow management to support acquisition and adaptation of workflow models. In *DEXA '98: Proceedings of the 9th International Workshop on Database and Expert Systems Applications*, page 745. IEEE Computer Society, 1998.
8. M. Sayal, F. Casati, M.C. Shan, and U. Dayal. Business process cockpit. *Proceedings of 28th International Conference on Very Large Data Bases (VLDB'02)*, pages 880–883, 2002.
9. Daniela Grigori, Fabio Casati, Malu Castellanos, Umeshwar Dayal, Mehmet Sayal, and Ming-Chien Shan. Business process intelligence. *Comput. Ind.*, 53(3):321–343, 2004.
10. K. Baïna, I. Berrada, and L. Kjiri. A Balanced Scoreboard Experiment for Business Process Performance Monitoring : Case study. In *1st International E-Business Conference (IEBC'05)*, Tunis, Tunisia, June 24-25, 2005.
11. W. Gaaloul, S. Alaoui, K. Baïna, and C. Godart. Mining Workflow Patterns through Event-data Analysis. In *The IEEE/IPSJ International Symposium on Applications and the Internet (SAINT'05). Workshop 6 Teamware: supporting scalable virtual teams in multi-organizational settings*. IEEE Computer Society Press, 2005.
12. Wil M. P. van der Aalst and B. F. van Dongen. Discovering workflow performance models from timed logs. In *Proceedings of the First International Conference on Engineering and Deployment of Cooperative Information Systems*, pages 45–63. Springer-Verlag, 2002.
13. A. J. M. M. Weijters and W. M. P. van der Aalst. Workflow mining: Discovering workflow models from event-based data. In Dousson, C., Hppner, F., and Quiniou, R., editors, *Proceedings of the ECAI Workshop on Knowledge Discovery and Spatial Data*, pages 78–84, 2002.
14. Joachim Herbst and Dimitris Karagiannis. Workflow mining with inwolve. *Comput. Ind.*, 53(3):245–264, 2004.
15. Guido Schimm. Process Miner - A Tool for Mining Process Schemes from Event-Based Data. In *Proceedings of the European Conference on Logics in Artificial Intelligence*, pages 525–528. Springer-Verlag, 2002.
16. W. Gaaloul, S. Bhiri, and C. Godart. Discovering workflow transactional behaviour event-based log. In *12th International Conference on Cooperative Information Systems (CoopIS'04)*, LNCS, Larnaca, Cyprus, October 25-29, 2004. Springer-Verlag.

Avoiding Error-Prone Reordering Optimization During Legal Systems Migration

Youlin Fang[1], Heng Wang[2], and Dongqing Yang[3]

[1] College of Computer Science, Bejing University of Technology,
Beijing 100022, P.R.China
ylfang@bjut.edu.cn
[2] School of Economics and Management, Tsinghua University,
Beijing 100084, P.R.China
wangh@em.tsinghua.edu.cn
[3] School of Electrical Engineering and Computer Science, Peking University,
Beijing 100871, P.R.China
dqyang@db.pku.edu.cn

Abstract. During Legal information systems migrations, one major problem is to handle attribute value cleaning. In the paper, we first show many data cleaning steps process on the values of the same data attributes and their derivations, and users may ignore or be puzzled by the data transforms that are defined to clean and transform the data sets, and such process can also be prone to error during process optimization. In this paper, we first define two major such problems as assignment conflict and range conflict,and giving problem definitions for such conflicts. Then we present two separate algorithms respectively to discover and solve the conflicts.

1 Introduction

As data extraction, transformation and loading(ETL) are being widely established to meet strategic business objectives, many organizations have found that ETL process, especially data cleaning and transformation is a complex, expensive, and bothersome process. Costly mistakes have been made in the designing stage of data cleaning[2][3][4][5].

In the design of data cleaning procedures, users may have to process the same property many times, e.g. substituting a code up to the specified business strategy, users usually do not know the error and potentially error in their cleaning process models. As asserted in [1], model checking is very important for such process, so users should be more careful to check whether their migration model is correct, and should avoiding making wrong migration optimization of the process model when executing. In this paper, we discuss the problem, and present algorithms to solve such conflict.

1.1 Outline of Paper

The remainder of the paper proceeds as follows. Section 2 gives a overview of the problem. Section 3 describes the equi-transformation conflict problem and containment-transformation conflict problem, and gives out typical types of these conflicts. In section 4,we first describe transformation algebraic properties, then present detecting algorithms for these two problem and propose methods to solve them . Section 5 concludes the paper.

1.2 Related Work

Erhard Rahm and Hong Hai Do[5]classify data quality problems that are addressed by data cleaning and provide an overview of the main solution approaches. They also discuss current tool support for data cleaning.

Serge Abiteboul and Sophie Cluet etc.[6] discuss a tool, namely ARKTOS, which they have developed capable of modeling and executing practical scenarios, to deal with the complexity and efficiency of the transformation and cleaning tasks by providing explicit primitives for the capturing of common tasks. ARKTOS provides three ways to describe such a scenario, including a graphical point-and-click front end and two declarative languages: XADL (an XML variant), which is more verbose and easy to read and SADL (an SQL-like language) which has a quite compact syntax and is, thus, easier for authoring.

Xiang Fu and Tevfik Bultan etc.[1] introduce the problem of automated verification of software systems that manipulate XML data. And it encourages us to rethink the data cleaning model in the data migration process.

Our contributions: The following are the major contributions of this paper:

- We present a overview of asssignment conflicts lying in data transformation modelling, then describe typical assignment conflicts of the modelling problem.
- We then present algorithms for effective finding and detecting potential conflict schedules, and present methods of determine the transformation schedule order by its partial order.

2 Problem Formulation

For a given data set S_1, we provide a sequence of data cleaning and transformation process and get the result S_2, that is $S_1\{T_1, \cdots, T_n\}S_2$, where $T_i(1 \leq i \leq n)$ is a mapping or a transformation procedure of a property in S_1 to a property in S_2. These transformation process are parallel, so that the designer do not give a order on which transform is processed.

2.1 Data Transformation

A transformation is a sequence of one and above transform in a given order. The process of data transformation is according to the right rule of transaction process in database,that is if a transaction is executed without other transactions or system errors, and the database is consistent at the beginning of the start, the database remains in consistence at the end of the transaction. The rule appears in transformation processing as:

- transformation process is atomic: A transformation must be executed as a single or no execution at all. If part of the transformation is executed, then the database is inconsistent under most of the circumstance.
- Parallel execution of transformation may lead to inconsistence in database. Otherwise we control the inter-affect between them.

2.2 Transformation Schedule

Definition 1. *(Transformation Schedule) A transformation schedule is a sequence of relation operations of multiple transformations according to execution order.*

When we discuss the transformation schedule, an important transformation is the operation which S_1 and S_2 have the common schema. As S_1 and S_2 have the same schema, if data are directly processed through copy at every step of transformation, the it need too much I/O cost.

2.3 Transformation Schedule Serialization

In data transformation schedule, one kind is serialized transformation schedule, that is if a transformation is finished after all of its operations are finished, the operations in the next transformation can then start and without operation mixed between two transformations, then we say such schedule is serial. More detailed, for any two arbitrary transformation T and T', if a operation in T is executed before a operation of T', then all the operations in T is executed before the execution of all the operations in T', a transformation schedule satisfying it is serial.

2.4 Transformation Modeling

In the modeling of data cleaning, designers may have two approaches to modeling data cleaning. One approach is directly writing scripts of cleaning, the other is achieved with the aid of cleaning modeling tools. Under both circumstance, the designer may not have a right process for the cleaning process, he can not assure the process is error-free in modeling. In fact, in the modeling of data cleaning process, there are many steps of transformation between two data sets, and the user know what he want when writing down these steps. But the problem arise when the steps and process are too many, these steps may process the data sets with the same schema, or with the same columns or properties.In process there are conflicts potentially. The users are not aware of such conflicts.

In the next section, we will discuss two typical conflicts in transformation modeling.

3 Semantic Conflicts in Data Transformation Modeling

In the previous section we considered the problem of semantic conflicts existing in transformation modeling. Now, we come to the typical conflicts a designer must face against.

3.1 Equi-transformation Conflict

Equi-transformation is the basic transformation with the following style:

```
Update   TableName
Set      ColumnName = Replace Value1 with Value2
Where    CharacterValueInColumnName = Value1
```

The CharacterValueInColumnName in the where-clause in Q1 maybe the column name or a positive position in the column, e.g., many primary key column is organized according to the specified length with different explanation, e.g., position n_1 to n_2 represents the country code and n_2 to n_3 represents the province code. With the replacement of column values, there may be conflicts among the replacements order.

Definition 2. *(Equi-transformation conflict) Let the result domain of Column-Name is S, the condition domain in transformation is S_1, $S_1 \subseteq S$, assignment domain is S_2, for the transformation T_1 and T_2 , we have*

1. *if $T_2.Value2 = T_1.Value2$, then T_1 is condition domain conflict with T_2.*
2. *if $T_1.Value1 = T_1.Value1$, then T_1 is assignment domain conflict with T_2.*
3. *if $T_2.Value1 = T_1.Value2$, then T_1 is loop domain conflict with T_2.*

What we mean of condition domain conflict is that if two transformation process the same object, there maybe conflict existing in the execution order of the two transformation. Different execution order may lead to different results. If we execute transformation T_1 and then execute T_2, then the last result of transformations is the results of execution of the transformation T_2; but if we execute transformation T_2 and then execute T_1, then the last result of transformations is the results of execution of the transformation T_1. An example is shown in Fig.1.

```
T1:     Update  Parts              T2:     Update  Parts
        Set     PartNo = 100543            Set     PartNo = 200543
        Where   PartNo = 130543            Where   PartNo = 130543
```

Fig. 1. Condition domain conflict among transformations

What we mean of assign domain conflict is that if the results of two transformation process are the same object, there maybe no conflict if there are only these two transformation process the object, but there are conflicts existing in the execution order of the two transformation if there are other transformations using the resulting object. An example is shown in Fig.2.

What we mean of loop domain conflict is that a definition value of a transformation is the assignment value of another transformation. Different execution order leads to different results. An example is shown in Fig.3. If we execute transformation T_1 and then execute T_2, then the last result of transformations is the results of execution of the transformation T_2, and no result would exist "PartNo="100543""; but if we execute transformation T_2 and then execute T_1, then the last result of transformations is the results of execution of the transformation T_1, there are still records "PartNo="100543"".

T1: Update Parts   T2: Update Parts
     Set   PartNo = 100543   Set   PartNo = 100543
     Where   PartNo = 130543   Where   PartNo = 190543

Fig. 2. Assignment domain conflict among transformations

T1: Update Parts   T2: Update Parts
     Set   PartNo = 100543   Set   PartNo = 160543
     Where   PartNo = 130543   Where   PartNo = 100543

Fig. 3. Loop domain conflict among transformations

3.2 Containment-Transformation Conflict

Containment transformation is the transformation whose where-clause have range comparison.

```
Update   TableName
Set      ColumnName = Func(ColumnName)
Where    ColumnName in Range (Value1, Value2)
```

The ColumnName in the where-clause in Q2 maybe the column name or a positive position in the column, e.g., many primary key column is organized according to the specified length with different explanation, e.g., position n_1 to n_2 represents the country code and n_2 to n_3 represents the province code. With the replacement of column values, there may be conflicts among the replacements order.

Definition 3. *(Containment-transformation conflict) Let the result domain of ColumnName is S, the condition domain in transformation is S_1, $S_1 \subseteq S$, assignment domain is S_2, for the transformation T_1 and T_2 , we have*

1. *if $T_1.(Value1, Value2) \cap T_2.(Value1, Value2) \neq \emptyset$, then T_1 is condition domain conflict with T_2.*
2. *if $T_1.Func(ColumnName) \cap T_2.Func(ColumnName) \neq \emptyset$, then T_1 is assignment domain conflict with T_2.*
3. *if $T_1.Func(ColumnName) \cap T_2.(Value1, Value2) \neq \emptyset$, then T_1 is loop domain conflict with T_2.*

What we mean of condition domain conflict is that if two transformation process the same object, there maybe conflict existing in the execution order of the two transformation. Different execution order may lead to different results. If we execute transformation T_1 and then execute T_2, then the last result of transformations is the results of execution of the transformation T_2; but if we execute transformation T_2 and then execute T_1, then the last result of transformations is the results of execution of the transformation T_1. An example is shown in Fig.4.

What we mean of assign domain conflict is that if the results of two transformation process are the same object, there maybe no conflict if there are only

```
T1:     Update  Parts
        Set     PartNo = PartNo+100
        Where   PartNo Between 130543 and 130546

T2:     Update  Parts
        Set     PartNo = PartNo+100
        Where   PartNo Between 130543 and 130546
```

Fig. 4. Condition domain conflict among transformations

```
T1:     Update  Parts
        Set     PartNo = PartNo+100
        Where   PartNo Between 130543 and 130546

T2:     Update  Parts
        Set     PartNo = PartNo+200
        Where   PartNo Between 130420 and 130480
```

Fig. 5. Assignment domain conflict among transformations

```
T1:     Update  Parts
        Set     PartNo = PartNo+100
        Where   PartNo Between 130543 and 130546

T2:     Update  Parts
        Set     PartNo = PartNo+100
        Where   PartNo Between 130420 and 130480
```

Fig. 6. Loop domain conflict among transformations

these two transformation process the object, but there are conflicts existing in the execution order of the two transformation if there are other transformations using the resulting object. An example is shown in Fig.5.

What we mean of loop domain conflict is that a definition value of a transformation is the assignment value of another transformation. Different execution order leads to different results. An example is shown in Fig.6. If we execute transformation T_1 and then execute T_2, then the last result of transformations is the results of execution of the transformation T_2, and no result would exist "PartNo="100543""; but if we execute transformation T_2 and then execute T_1, then the last result of transformations is the results of execution of the transformation T_1, there are still records "PartNo="100543"".

4 Serialization Conflict Resolution Algorithms

As there are two main conflict exist in modeling, there is a need for algorithms to find and resolve such conflict. In the following subsection, we first introduce the properties of transformation, and then present algorithms for resolution of equi-transformation conflict and of containment-transformation conflict.

4.1 Transformation Algebraic Properties

Definition 4. *(Commutative transformation) Two transformations T_1 and T_2 are commutative, if various execution of T_1 and T_2 have the same result.*

For two transformation with assignment conflict, if their execution results no side-effect, then they are commutative mutually.

Definition 5. *(Noncommutative transformation) Two transformations T_1 and T_2 are noncommutative, if various execution of T_1 and T_2 have the different results. T_1 and T_2 are mutually nonexchangeable.*

Noncommutative transformations can be the case that two transformations have different results according to different execution order, also can be the case with assignment conflict. In the case of assignment conflict, if we prescribe two transformations are nonexchangeable, then optimization of transformation schedule may result different status. And it lead to another concept, there is a certain priority among transformations.

Definition 6. *(Partial order of transformations) Two transformations T_1 and T_2 are partial order, if T_1 and T_2 have the different execution order. If T_1 is executed prior to T_2, then $T_1 \prec T_2$.*

With the definition of transformation partial order, we can easily extend to transformation set partial order.

Definition 7. *(Partial order of transformation sets) Two transformation sets TS_1 and TS_2 are partial order, if TS_1 and TS_2 have the different execution order, that is $\forall T_i \in TS_1, \forall T_j' \in TS_2$, $T_i \prec T_j'$ is true, and refer to $TS_1 \prec TS_2$.*

4.2 Algorithms for Equi-transformation Conflict

Our algorithm divides the process of finding equi-transformation conflict into three phase. In the first phase, we establish transformation list, condition domain list and assignment domain list. In the second phase, we detect whether there is condition domain conflict. Thus, in the third phase we detect whether there is loop domain conflict. We do not detect the assignment domain conflict, because if there is such a conflict, it take effect either in the condition domain conflict or in the loop domain conflict.

Algorithm 1: Equi-Transformation Conflict

```
// Establish transformation list, condition domain list
// and assignment domain list
For each transformation T_i
  If T_i is equi-transformation
  Then
    CondList.Add(T_i.ConditionValue, T_i);
    SetList.Add(T_i.SetValue, T_i);
    TransList.Add(T_i);
    EstablistLink(TransList, ConList,TransList);
```

```
// Detecting whether there is condition domain conflict
For each ConditionValue in CondList
  If a condition exists multiple link to TransList
  Then
    there are conflict and should be determine partial order.

// Detecting whether there is loop domain conflict
For each ConditionValue in CondList
  If ConditionValue is in SetList
  Then
    Transformation set which ConditionValue refer to is
    conflict with the transformation set which SetValue
    refer to, and there is a need to determine the
    partial order.
```

After having detecting all these equi-transformation conflicts, the designer can determine the partial order of transformation sets and serialize the transformation model. In processing, the users must first determine the partial order between different transformation set, and then determine the partial order among condition conflict transformations, last determine the partial order among assignment conflict transformations. After this, the users know the execution order the transformation must own and have a better result model.

4.3 Algorithm for Containment-Transformation Conflict Resolution

As to containment conflict, user can use the following algorithms to detecting the conflict, the basic idea is also to establish condition domain and assignment domain list, from which one can detect various conflict, but the algorithm is different from the algorithm above in that it must be reconstruct of the condition domain list and assignment domain list.

Algorithm 2: Containment Transformation Conflict

```
// Establish transformation list, condition domain list and
// assignment domain list
For each transformation T_i
  If T_i is containment-transformation
  Then
    CondList.Add(T_i.ConditionRange, T_i);
    SetList.Add(T_i.SetRange, T_i);
    TransList.Add(T_i);
    EstablistLink(TransList, ConList, TransList);

// Reconstruct condition domain list
For all ConditionValueRange in CondList
  Reconstruct the list according to the value range so that
  there is no intersect between neighborhood node.
```

Relink the transformations to the value range.

```
// Reconstruct condition domain list
For all SetValueRange in SetList
    Reconstruct the list according to the value range so that
    there is no intersect between neighborhood node.
    Relink the transformation to the value range.

// Detecting whether there is condition domain conflict
For each ConditionValueRange in CondList
    If a condition exists multiple link to TransList
    Then
        There are conflict and should be determine partial order.

// Detecting whether there is loop domain conflict
For each ConditionValue in CondList
```
    If $ConditionValue \cap SetValueRange_i \neq \emptyset$
```
    Then
        Transformation set which ConditionValue refer to is
        conflict with the transformation set which SetValue
        refer to, and there is a need to determine the partial
        order.
```

After having detecting all these containment conflicts, the designer can serialize the transformation model. In processing, the users must first remodeling the process according to the range after reconstruction, next determine the partial order between different transformation set, and then determine the partial order among condition conflict transformations, last determine the partial order among assignment conflict transformations. After this, the users know the order the transformation must obey and have a good result model.

5 Conclusions

Data cleaning is a key issue in legal system migration and data integration, and is a key process that guarantee the quality of data. Effective detecting and resolve potential problems lying in the process flow model of data cleaning is the precondition of enhancing data quality. In this paper, we studied the problem of detecting semantic serialization of data transformations. We first initiate the problem, and then present a detailed definition of the problem, and present the algebraic property of transformation, and then we present two kinds of conflicts in ETL modeling, and such process may be neglect in the modeling by most of the ETL tools, and present algorithms to detecting such problems and how to resolving it. Our approach can be used as a complement of ETL modeling tools, and also can guide the design of ETL process that enable error-free data loading.

References

1. Fu, X., Bultan, T., Su, J.: Model Checking XML Manipulating Software. In Proc. International Symposium on Software Testing and Analysis (ISSTA'04), July 2004.
2. Abiteboul, S., Cluet, S., Milo, T., Mogilevsky, P., Simeon, J., Zohar, S.: Tools for data translation and integration. IEEE Data Engineering Bulletin, 22(1):3-8, March 1999.
3. Chauhuri, S., Dayal, U.: An overview of data warehousing and OLAP technology. SIGMOD Record, 26(1):65-74, March 1997
4. Galhardas, H., Florescu, D., Shasha, D., Simon, E.: Ajax: An extensible Data Cleaning Tool. In Proc.2000 ACM SIGMOD Int. Conf. On Management of Data, Dallas, Texas,2000
5. Rahm, E., Do, H.-H.: Data Cleaning: Problems and Current Appoaches. In Bulletin of IEEE Computer Society Technical Committee on Data Engineering,2000
6. Vassiladis, P., Vagena, Z., Karayannids N., Sellis, T.: Arktos: Toward The Modeling, Design, Control and Execution of ETL Processes. In Information Systems,26(8):537-561, Elsevier Science Ltd.,2001

Automated SuperSQL Query Formulation Based on Statistical Characteristics of Data

Jun Nemoto and Motomichi Toyama

Keio University, Yokohama, Japan
{jun, toyama}@db.ics.keio.ac.jp
http://www.db.ics.keio.ac.jp/

Abstract. In this paper, we propose an automated SuperSQL query formulating method based on statistical characteristics of data so that the end-users can obtain the desired information more easily without burden of web application development side. SuperSQL is an extension of SQL to generate various kinds of structured presentations and documents. In our method, first, web producers prepare a provisional SQL query and send it to a relational database. Next, the automated algorithm formulates a SuperSQL query based on statistical information of the query result. Finally the resulting SuperSQL query is executed to return the categorized table to end-users. Experimental results demonstrate that the implemented system enables web producers to construct data-intensive web sites, which have better structure with respect to the recognition of the data by end-users.

1 Introduction

Data-intensive web sites such as shopping sites and news sites have become increasingly popular. Upon the presentation of database contents on these pages, it is common and popular to add a search box or sort key buttons to ease a user's effort.

In this paper, we introduce a mechanism to incorporate categorizing capability so that the users can obtain the desired information more easily. For example, in an online bookstore, you can quickly find the book you want if all the books are categorized by either authors, publishers, price ranges and so on. However, it is much more difficult for web producers to prepare categorized layouts, depending on the attribute in which users are interested. In this paper, in order to reduce such burden of web application development and to provide information using the dynamically arranged layout, we propose an automated SuperSQL query formulating method based on statistical characteristics of data. SuperSQL is an extension of SQL with the TFE which stands for Target Form Expression to generate various kinds of structured presentations and documents.

The outline of our processing flow is shown in Fig. 1. In our method, (1) web producers prepare a provisional SQL query and send it to a relational database to gather necessary information. (2) The automated algorithm formulates a SuperSQL query based on statistical information of the query results. Our current

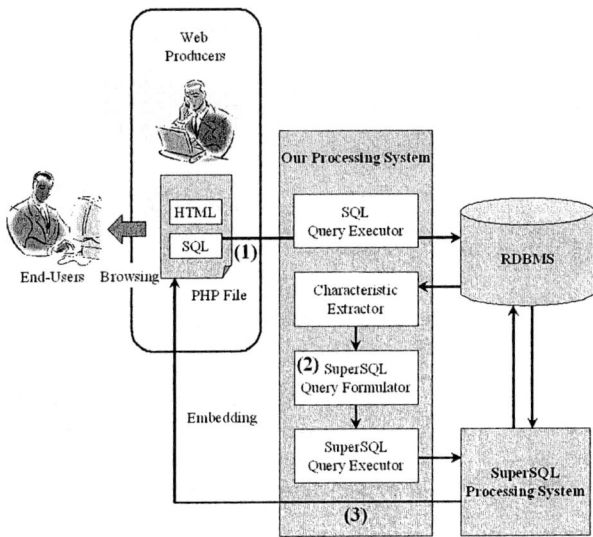

Fig. 1. Outline of System

implementation basically uses the number of distinct values. As for numeric type data, we use the coefficient of variation. (3) The resulting SuperSQL query is executed to return the categorized table to end-users.

The rest of the paper is organized as follows. An overview of SuperSQL is presented in Section 2. In Section 3, statistical characteristics of data which we assume are defined. Section 4 describes an automated SuperSQL query formulating method based on it. Section 5 shows implementation of our method and experimental evaluation. The related work is presented in Section 6 and the conclusion is given in Section 7.

2 SuperSQL

In this section, we briefly describe SuperSQL, which is the query language to return the final results to end-users.

2.1 An Overview of SuperSQL and TFE

SuperSQL is an extension of SQL with the TFE which stands for Target Form Expression to generate various kinds of structured presentation documents [5][6].

TFE is an extension of target list of SQL. Unlike an ordinary target list, which is a comma-separated list of attribute, TFE uses new operators, which are connectors and repeaters to specify the structure of the document generated as the final results of the query. Each connector and repeater is associated with a dimension: when generating a Web document, the first two dimensions are associated with the columns and rows of <table> structure of HTML and the third dimension is associated with hyper-links.

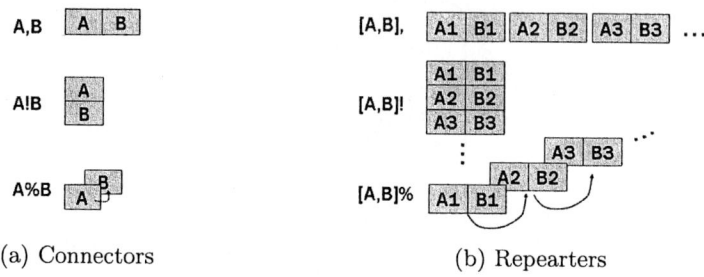

Fig. 2. Connectors and Repeaters in TFE

We have introduced the GENERATE <medium> <TFE> clause to SQL syntax to clarify the distinction with SELECT <target list> clause. Other target medium designations, which are allowed in the current implementation but not treated in this paper, include XML, Excel, LaTeX, PDF, etc.

2.2 Connectors and Repeaters

Binary operators represented by a comma (,), an exclamation point (!), and a percent (%) are used as the connectors of first three dimensions. Conceptually, they connect the objects generated as their operands horizontally, vertically, and in the depth direction respectively. Examples of connectors are in Fig. 2(a).

A pair of square brackets ([ ]) followed by any of the connectors is a repeater for each dimension. It will connect multiple instances in its associated dimension repeatedly. Example of repeaters are in Fig. 2(b).

2.3 Decorative Operators

Decorative operators are supported to designate decorative features of outputs, such as font size, table border, width, image directory, in the form of @ follows a TFE, and decorative specifications are in a pair of braces({}), which are separated by comma. Each decorative specification is in the form of "item = value". Decorative operators are described as below.

$$<TFE>@\{item_1 = value_1, item_2 = value_2, ..., item_n = value_n\}$$

3 Statistical Characteristics of Data

In order to formulate TFE, we use statistical characteristics of data. In this section, we describe two criteria, which we assume to use at present.

3.1 Instance Characteristics

Instance characteristics are measures to know how often distinct values appeared in an attribute. Let $A = \{a_1, a_2, \cdots, a_m\}$ denote the attribute set in the target list of SQL query. Then instance characteristics IC_i are defined as below.

$$IC_i = |distinct(V_i)|$$

Note that V_i is $\{v_{i1}, v_{i2}, \cdots, v_{in}\}$ where v_{ij} represents an instance that belongs to the attribute a_i in the query results. In addition, *distinct* is the function which eliminates duplicate values. Primarily, we assume that the smaller the instance characteristics, the much you want the table to be categorized.

However, this assumption may not always be true. For example, consider a student grade database, which has information of student's id, name, sex, department, subject, and grade. In this case, since the domain of the attribute sex is male and female, its instance characteristics must be at most two. Though this value is small one, most of end-users do not want the resulting table to be categorized by sex. Regarding these problem on the semantics of the attribute, we describe a countermeasure in Section 3.3.

3.2 Numeric Value Characteristics

If the data type of an attribute is numeric, the assumption in Section 3.1 may not be true. In case of numeric data type, end-users want the resulting table to be categorized when the attribute has many different values. Therefore, we define numeric value characteristics NC as follows.

$$NC_i = \frac{1}{\bar{v}_i} \sqrt{\frac{1}{n} \sum_{j=1}^{n} (v_{ij} - \bar{v}_i)^2}$$

This measure shows the coefficient of variation of v_i. The coefficient of variation can evaluate the practical dispersion without depending on the unit. If this value is higher than the threshold, we divide the interval $[min(V_i), max(V_i)]$ into equal ranges and provide the resulting table categorized by these intervals. As long as the threshold for the coefficient of variation is properly set, we can avoid unintentionally dividing the table which has many distinct values concentrated on a narrow interval.

3.3 User Interaction

End-users often would like to browse database query results from various points of view. However, the automated layout formulation depending on statistical characteristics of data cannot always generate the categorized table by which all end-users are satisfied. Therefore, we introduced interaction with end-users.

Primary Attribute. When end-users browse data-intensive web sites, the role and importance of each attribute is not equal. For example, consider an online shopping site. An end-user may want to select the item from the list of products ordered by makers, and another end-user may want to select the item from the list of products categorized by price ranges. We call the attribute given the highest precedence as the primary attribute for the user. The formulation of TFE is affected by the primary attribute.

Selecting History of Primary Attribute. The primary attribute varies from one user to another. If we can obtain the information about the primary attribute selection, the algorithm can narrow candidates of the attribute for categorization. For example, consider again the student grade database in Section 3.1. Suppose that departments and subjects are repeatedly selected as the primary attribute, and sex is rarely selected. Then, the history of selecting the primary attribute can prevent the algorithm from selecting sex as the grouping target in the default layout.

4 Formulating SuperSQL Query

In this section, we present an automated SuperSQL query formulating method. Since we choose the HTML as output media, we focus the formulation of TFE from now on. Regarding FROM clause and WHERE clause, we basically use the one in the original SQL query.

In formulating TFE, we start from choosing the attribute which is most suitable for grouping target. In order to choose the grouping target, we define the grouping priority GP as follows:

$$GP_i = \frac{n}{IC_i} \, g_i \, m \, h_i$$

Note that g_i is the weight given for the primary attribute. If a_i is the primary attribute, it takes the parameter α, otherwise it takes 1. In addition, h_i is the weight reflecting the selecting history of primary attribute and it is the ratio which measures how often is the attribute selected as the primary attribute among all the selections. We multiply m and n to prevent the criteria from being biased by the number of attributes and tuples in the query results. We choose the attributes which have a value of grouping priority greater than the threshold, as the grouping target.

The attribute selected as the grouping target is promoted the outermost so that other attributes are nested. For example, suppose that the SELECT clause of original SQL query is:

SELECT sid, department, subject, grade

and the attribute which have a value of grouping priority greater than threshold is department. In this case, the formulated TFE is:

[department , [sid , subject , grade]!]!

Moreover, in case that subject is also the grouping target, the resulting TFE is:

[department ! [subject , [sid , grade]!]!]!

The result of the SuperSQL query with above TFE is as follows.

	department1	
	sid1	grade1
subject1	sid2	grade2
	sid3	grade3
	department2	
	...	...

As the example shows, if there are more than one attributes for grouping, the attribute which has higher grouping priority is placed on outer side, so that it is treated as larger category. We connect the grouping target and other attributes horizontally, vertically, and in the depth direction in order from the inner connector.

Taking the numeric value characteristics into consideration, SuperSQL query formulation process is a bit different. First, in case that the data type of the primary attribute is numeric, we examine whether the numeric value characteristics are higher than the threshold. If it is higher than the threshold, we divide the domain of the primary attribute into equal ranges and the start value and the end value of each range is inserted into a temporary table. Then we join the temporary table and other tables and formulate the SuperSQL query, which makes the table grouped by each interval. On the other hand, if the numeric value characteristics are under the threshold, we enter into ordinary process, which calculates the grouping priority.

5 Implementation and Evaluation

5.1 Implementation

We have implemented a SuperSQL query formulating system based on statistical characteristics of data. In our current implementation, the above mentioned procedure is implemented as a PHP function. In this section, we describe the specification of the function using the running example.

Function Specification. The specification of implemented PHP function is as follows:

    int **dcssql** (string *sql*, boolean *style* [, string *primaryAttribute*])

The **dcssql** function inserts SuperSQL query results into the position where the function is called. A SuperSQL query is formulated using *sql* and *primaryAttribute*. Note that both arguments are string and *primaryAttribute* can be omitted.

The argument *style* is Boolean value to specify whether to add style information to the generated SuperSQL query. Style information is specified using decorative operators in Section 2.3.

```
1   /* sample.php */
2   <html>
3   <head>
4   <title>The List of Books</title>
5   <meta http-equiv="Content-Type" content="text/html;charset=EUC-JP"/>
6   </head>
7   <body>
8   <form method="get" action="sample.php">
9   <input type="radio" name="primary" value="name">Name
10  <input type="radio" name="primary" value="author">Authors
11  <input type="radio" name="primary" value="publisher">Publishers
12  <input type="radio" name="primary" value="category">Categories
13  <input type="radio" name="primary" value="price">Price Ranges
14  <input type="radio" name="primary" value="pdate">Published Date
15  <input type="submit" value="Choose!">
16  </form>
17  <?php
18      include("dcssql.inc");
19      $sql = "SELECT b.name, b.author, b.publisher,
             b.category, b.price, b.pdate FROM book b";

20      dcssql($sql, TRUE, "$_GET[primary]");
21  ?>
22  </body>
23  </html>
```

Fig. 3. An Example of a PHP File

Example. As defined above, once a web producer gives the **dcssql** function a standard SQL query, a style flag and a primary attribute, a SuperSQL query is formulated, executed, and the resulting HTML are returned. We suppose as usual that web producers provide it to end-users, together with other PHP and HTML codes. Notice that the web producer is expected to implement an interface to select a primary attribute and give it to the **dcssql** fuction. An example PHP file, which web producers prepare, is shown in Figure 3 and screenshots displayed when end-users access the sample PHP file are shown in Figure 4 and Figure 5. In two screenshots, the threshold of the GP is set to 2.0 and 1.5 respectively.

We explain the details of the PHP source in Figure 3. An interface to specify a primary attribute is described in Line 8-16. Though it is provided by radio buttons in this example, any HTML form interface is available as long as the primary attribute can be exclusively selected.

The include function in Line 18 includes the file, which has the entity of the **dcssql** function and others.

Line 19 sets the original SQL query. In this example, we assume a simple table of books which has isbn, name, authors, publishers, categories, price, and

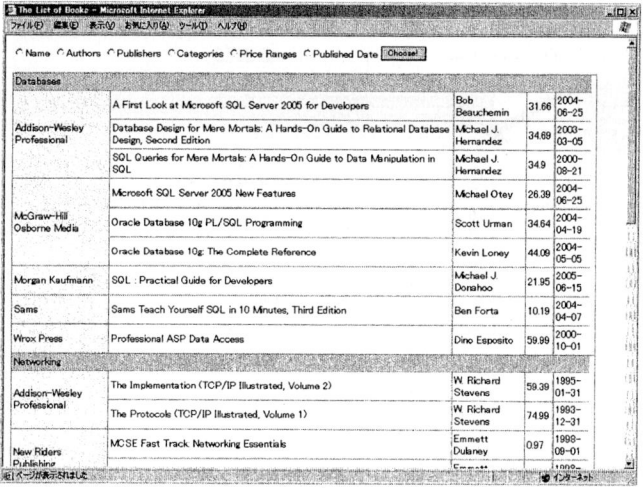

Fig. 4. The Result of sample.php ($\theta_{GP} = 2.0$)

published date as attributes. Note that price is numeric, published date is date type, and the others are string type. This table is assumed to contain one hundred records of books. In case that all the records in this table are returned to an end-user as query results, the instance characteristics of categories and publishers are higher than the others.

Line 20 receives form data about the primary attribute via the GET method and calls the **dcssql** function.

When end-users access the sample.php in Figure 3, the result without considering the primary attribute will be displayed. The result in Figure 4 is grouped by categories and publishers according to the grouping priority. In addtion to these attributes, the result in Figure 5 is grouped by authors. More remarkably, categories and other attirbutes are connected in the depth direction since the number of grouping targets are more than 3.

5.2 Experimental Evaluation

In this section, we present experimental evaluation of the implemented system.

We used databases of books, news, and geographic statistical information about Japan. To simplify queries, each database consists of only one table. The books table is the same database used in Section 5.1. The news table has ID, titles, text, sources, large categories, small categories, and arrival time as attributes. The text attribute is relatively large data so that the data size varies from 200 Bytes to 6000 Bytes. The statistical information table has ID, prefecture name, region name, the number of population, the area and so on. Except for the name of prefecture and region, all the attributes are numeric.

In this experiment, the threshold and other parameters are decided empirically. The threshold of the NC and the GP are set to 0.3 and 3 respectively. The parameter for the primary attribute is set to 5.

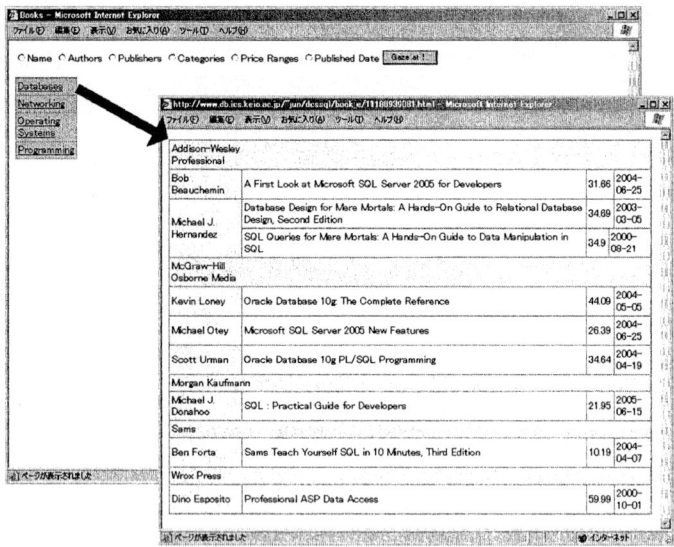

Fig. 5. The Result of sample.php ($\theta_{GP} = 1.5$)

Table 1. The Flat Table versus Generated Table

		Recognizability		Propriety of Structure	
		FLAT	NESTED	FLAT	NESTED
Books	avg.	1.50	3.75	2.38	4.25
	t-Statistic	-5.46		-6.05	
	t-Critical	1.81		1.77	
News	avg.	1.36	3.00	2.00	3.38
	t-Statistic	-3.87		-3.66	
	t-Critical	1.81		1.76	
Statistical Informaiton	avg.	2.75	3.00	3.38	3.50
	t-Statistic	-0.32		-0.18	
	t-Critical	1.77		1.77	

We got eight examinees to browse a normal flat table and the table generated by our system and then to give two scores to each table. The one score is about the recognizability and the other one is about the appropriateness of table structure. The appropriateness of structure does not mean prettiness but appropriateness for browsing the data such as books, news and statistical information. The score varies from 1 to 5, where 1 indicates the lowest level of recognizability or appropriateness and 5 indicates the highest one. Notice that all scores were given to each table as an absolute evaluation.

Then we compared the scores and performed t-tests. The null hypothesis was that there is no difference for the flat table and the categorized table generated by our system regarding the average score. The alternative hypothesis was that the average score for the categorized table is higher than that for the flat table. All the t-tests were performed as one-tail t-tests with significance level 5%.

The experimental results are in Table 1. FLAT means the flat table and NESTED means the table generated by our system. As the tables shows, except for the case of statistical information, the absolute value of t-Statistic is greater than t-Critical about both the recognizability and the appropriateness of table structure. Therefore the null hypothesis was rejected and the alternative hypothesis was accepted. In other words, the table generated by our system has better recognizability and structure for browsing books and news than the flat table. In contrast, the alternative hypothesis was not accepted in the data of statistical information. We consider this is because almost all the attributes in the statistical information table are numeric. In short, the algorithm often formulates the TFE producing a flat table. We got similar results in case of specifying the primary attribute. However they are omitted due to the space limit.

6 Related Work

An automatic categorization technique has been proposed by Chakrabarti et al. to present relational results that are devised to minimize users' efforts in browsing [2]. In contrast to our statistical characteristics based model, it is based on cost models that are defined to estimate information overload faced by users. In order to estimate the average cost, it uses the log of queries that users have asked int the past. There shall be no difficulties to incorporate the log-based cost models to work together with our statistical approach. The other differences between that work and ours are various presentation capabilities. We provide not only a simple group-by presentation but also an arbitrary one that a TFE in a SuperSQL query allows, for example, multi-page presentation in Figure 5.

There is a research studying a dynamic SuperSQL query formulation. ACTIVIEW is an adaptive data presentation system, which creates HTML pages dynamically adapting to the size of screen [3]. Though this work is similar to ours with respect to dynamic SuperSQL query formulation, it does not consider the statistical characteristics of data in determining layouts since its main purpose is adapting the outputs to the size of various screen such as a PDA and a mobile phone equipped with a web browser.

In the context of the generation of the reports, there are many researches. QURSED is a report generating system for XML documents [4]. Differing from our approach in giving developers discretionary power to generate reports, developers can prepare various queries and layouts using the QURSED system. The Oracle report tool offers a few fixed styles and does not consider data characteristics [7]. Table Presentation System TPS is a reporting system, which can represent various layouts by several table operations [1]. Its operations are easier than usual programming effort and the QURSED Editor. However, it only provides a static structured presentation and end-users have no way to provide their preferences to change the structure.

7 Conclusion

In this paper we defined the statistical characteristics of data in a SQL query result. Then we proposed an automated SuperSQL query formulating method based on it. Experimental results demonstrate that the implemented system enables web producers to construct data-intensive web sites, which have better structure for the recognition of the data by end-users, without burden of programming.

References

1. W. Chen, K. Chung, "A Table Presentation System for Database and Web Applications", *Proceedings of IEEE EEE '04 International Conference on e-Technology, e-Commerce and e-Service*, pp. 492-498, 2004.
2. K. Chakrabarti, S. Chaudhuri, S. Hwang, "Automatic Categorization of Query Results", *Proceedings of ACM SIGMOD '04 International Conference on Management of Data*, pp. 755-766, 2004.
3. Y. Maeda, M. Toyama, "ACTIVIEW: Adaptive data presentation using SuperSQL", *Proceedings of the VLDB '01*, pp.695-696, 2001.
4. Y. Papakonstantinou, M. Petropoulos, V .Vassalos, "QURSED: Querying and Reporting Semistructured Data", *Proceedings of ACM SIGMOD '02 International Conference of Management of Data*, pp. 192-203, 2002.
5. SuperSQL: http://ssql.db.ics.keio.ac.jp/
6. M. Toyama, "SuperSQL: An Extended SQL for Database Publishing and Presentation", *Proceedings of ACM SIGMOD '98 International Conference on Management of Data*, pp. 584-586, 1998.
7. P. Weckerle, "Enterprise Data Publishing with Oracle Reports: Any Data, Any Format, Anywhere", Oracle Technology Network Technology Information 2003, http://otn.oracle.com/technology/products/reports/

Distribution Rules for Array Database Queries

Alex van Ballegooij, Roberto Cornacchia, Arjen P. de Vries,
and Martin Kersten

CWI, INS1, Amsterdam, The Netherlands
{Alex.van.Ballegooij, R.Cornacchia, Arjen.de.Vries,
Martin.Kersten}@cwi.nl

Abstract. Non-trivial retrieval applications involve complex computations on large multi-dimensional datasets. These should, in principle, benefit from the use of relational database technology. However, expressing such problems in terms of relational queries is difficult and time-consuming. Even more discouraging is the efficiency issue: query optimization strategies successful in classical relational domains may not suffice when applied to the multi-dimensional array domain. The RAM (Relational Array Mapping) system hides these difficulties by providing a transparent mapping between the scientific problem specification and the underlying database system. In addition, its optimizer is specifically tuned to exploit the characteristics of the array paradigm and to allow for automatic balanced work-load distribution. Using an example taken from the multimedia domain, this paper shows how a distributed real-word application can be efficiently implemented, using the RAM system, without user intervention.

1 Introduction

Efficiently managing collections of e.g. images or scientific models, is beyond the capabilities of most database systems, since indexing and retrieval functionality are tuned to completely different workloads. Relational database systems do not support multidimensional arrays as a first class citizen. Maier and Vance have argued for long that the mismatch of data models is the major obstacle for the deployment of relational database technology in computation oriented domains (such as multimedia analysis) [1]. While storage of multidimensional objects in relations is possible, it makes data access awkward and provides little support for the abstractions of multidimensional data and coordinate systems. Support for the array data model is a prerequisite for an environment suitable for computation oriented applications.

The RAM (Relational Array Mapping) system bridges the gap caused by the mismatch in data-models between problems in ordered domains and relational databases, by providing a mapping layer between them. This approach has shown the potential to rival the performance of specialized solutions given an effective query optimizer [2]. This paper investigates how to improve performance by distributing the query over a cluster of machines. We hypothesize that the array paradigm allows RAM to automatically distribute the evaluation of complex queries. Extending the case study presented in [2], we detail how a non-trivial video retrieval application has been moved from a stand-alone application to a distributed database application, using the RAM system for automatic query-distribution. The execution time of the ranking process has been significantly improved without requiring manual optimizations of query processing.

2   The RAM Approach

The RAM system is a prototype array database system designed to make database technology useful for complex computational tasks [3]. Its innovation is the addition of multidimensional array structures to existing database systems by internally mapping the array structures to relations. Array operations are also mapped to the relational domain, by expressing them as relational queries. This contrasts with earlier array database systems; for example, array processing in RasDaMan was implemented as an extension module for an object oriented database system [4]. By storing array data as relations instead of a proprietary data structure, the full spectrum of relational operations can be performed on that array data. This indirectly guarantees complete query and data-management functionalities, and, since the array extensions naturally blend in with existing database functionalities, the RAM front-end can focus solely on problems inherent to the array domain.

The RAM system provides a comprehension based array-query language, to express array-specific queries concisely (comprehension syntax is explained in [5]). Array comprehensions allow users to specify a new array by declaring its dimensions and a function to compute the value for each of its cells. The RAM query language is inspired by the language described in the AQL proposal [6]. Due to space limitations we omit a detailed discussion of the RAM syntax, which can be found in [7], but its basic construct is the comprehension: $[f(x,y)|x < 2, y < 3]$. This defines an array of shape 2×3, with axes named x and y, where the value of each cell in the array is determined by an expression over its axes: $f(x,y)$. Support for this language is isolated in a front-end that communicates with the DBMS by issuing relational queries.

The RAM front-end translates the high level comprehension style queries into an intermediate array-algebra before the final transformation to the relational domain. This intermediate language is used by a traditional cost driven rule based optimizer specifically geared toward optimization of array queries. The RAM optimizer searches for an optimal query plan through the application of equivalence rules. A second translation step expresses the array algebra plan in the native query language of the database system. This can be not only a standard query language (SQL), but also a proprietary query language, such as the MonetDB Interface Language (MIL) for MonetDB [8], the database system used for the experiments in this paper.

3 Case Study

The case study used in this paper is a RAM based implementation of the probabilistic retrieval system that our research group developed for the search task of TRECVID 2002-2004 [9].

In this retrieval system, the relevance of a collection image m given a query image is approximated by the ability of its probabilistic model ω_m (a mixture of Gaussian distributions) to describe the regions $\mathcal{X} = (\boldsymbol{x_1}, \ldots, \boldsymbol{x_{N_s}})$ that compose the query image. Such a score $P(\mathcal{X}|\omega_m)$ is computed using the following formulas (the interested reader is referred to [10] for more details):

$$P(\boldsymbol{x_s}|\omega_m) = \sum_{c=1}^{N_c} P(C_{c,m}) \frac{1}{\sqrt{(2\pi)^{N_n} \prod_{n=1}^{N_n} \sigma_n^2}} e^{-\frac{1}{2}\sum_{n=1}^{N_n} \frac{(x_n - \mu_n)^2}{\sigma_n^2}}. \qquad (1)$$

$$P(\boldsymbol{x_s}) = \sum_{\omega_m=1}^{N_m} P(\omega_m) * P(\boldsymbol{x_s}|\omega_m). \qquad (2)$$

$$P(\mathcal{X}|\omega_m) = \sum_{s=1}^{N_s} log(\lambda P(\boldsymbol{x_s}|\omega_m) + (1-\lambda)P(\boldsymbol{x_s})). \qquad (3)$$

These mathematical formulas map nicely to concise RAM expressions:

Expression 1

```
p(s,m) = sum([P(c,m) * (1.0/(sqrt(pow(2*PI,Nn))*prod([S2(n,c,m)|n<Nn])))
         * exp(-0.5 * sum([pow(Q(n,s)-Mu(n,c,m),2)/S2(n,c,m)|n<Nn])) | c<Nc])
p(s)    = (1 / Nm) * sum([ p(s,m) | m<Nm ])
Scores  = [ sum( [ log( 1*p(s,m)+ (1-1)*p(s) ) | s<Ns ] ) | m<Nm ]
```

For a more in depth discussion of this implementation of the retrieval system in RAM, the interested reader is referred to [2].

Comparison between Equations 1, 2, 3, and RAM Expression 1 clearly shows that the mathematical description of the ranking problem maps almost 1-on-1 to RAM. We postulate that the RAM query language, thanks to its array based data model, remedies many of the *interfacing hurdles* encountered when implementing computation oriented algorithms in a database system. However, the retrieval problem inherently deals with complex computations and large volumes of data. This means that even though the efficiency of the RAM query evaluation is competitive with the native Matlab [11] implementation of the retrieval algorithm, the costly computations make it infeasible to use the system in an interactive setting.

4 Distributing Array Queries

The inherent parallelism of distributed systems may be exploited to overcome the computational limitations of a single machine. By distributing queries over multiple nodes, more complex queries than normally possible can be evaluated, having each node compute only part of the answer. Query distribution for relational databases is well studied and offers more than just efficiency (distributed database technology is discussed for example in [12] and [13]). In case of the RAM array database system however, the primary concern is to speed-up query evaluation.

This paper investigates the distribution of RAM queries over multiple computational nodes by discovering a suitable location in the query plan to split it into disjunct sub-queries. When simply using those opportunities readily available in an existing query plan it is hard to achieve a balanced query load across all nodes: it is rare to find sub-expressions that happen to be equally expensive to compute. Fortunately, the structured nature of array queries allows the creation of new, balanced opportunities to split the query for distribution.

4.1 Query Fragmentation Patterns for Array Queries

The straightforward approach to distribute an array query is to fragment the result space in disjunct segments and compute each of those parts individually. This approach is simply mimicked in RAM, generating a series of queries that each yield a specific fragment, and concatenating those resulting fragments to produce a single result, for example[1]:

$$[f(x)|x < n] \Rightarrow [f(x)|x < n/2] \mathbin{++} [f(x+n/2)|x < n/2]. \qquad (4)$$

Rewriting the query plan like this introduces an operator in the query, the array concatenation '++', which represents a new opportunity to split the query in balanced sub-queries.

It is possible to ensure that the new sub-queries are balanced thanks to the context knowledge that is available in the array domain. All the array operations are position-based rather than value-based. This absence of selective operations on values means that the size of all the intermediate results of a query plan is known in advance with no uncertainty.

Aggregations are also suitable for the creation of balanced sub-queries. Commutative and associative aggregates are equivalent to a series of binary operations, which means that such aggregates can be split into any number of parts, for example:

$$sum([f(x)|x < n]) \Rightarrow sum([f(x)|x < n/2]) + sum([f(x+n/2)|x < n/2]). \qquad (5)$$

Targeting distribution at aggregations specifically seems sensible since large aggregates are frequent in the typical query-load. This is reflected by distributed evaluation technology developed for information retrieval applications [14]. In many cases aggregation constitutes a large fraction of the total query cost.

---
[1] Note that the RAM system rewrites queries at the internal algebra level. However, we present the patterns denoted in RAMs high-level query language for readability.

4.2 Automatic Array Query Distribution

The RAM system is extended to include distribution of these fragmented queries by the introduction of a *distribute* pseudo-operator. The term pseudo-operator is used because it does not operate on the data, instead it manipulates the query execution itself: it distributes sub-queries over multiple computational nodes and collects the results. Notice that it performs a role similar to that of the *exchange* operator in the Volcano system [15].

This new pseudo-operator is introduced into query plans through the addition of tailored equivalence rules in the optimizer. These new rules implement the patterns identified in Section 4.1, Equations 4 and 5. For example, the pattern depicted in Equation 4 produces an expression formed by the concatenation of partial results: $E \Rightarrow concat(E_A, E_B)$, where *concat* is the algebra operator equivalent to the array concatenation, '++', in the RAM syntax. The rewriter includes the *distribute* pseudo-operator to indicate that the various query fragments should be distributed: $concat(distribute(E_A, E_B))$.

The query optimizer performs a top-down search for the best distribution plan. At each opportunity, uniform fragmentation of the query over all available nodes is attempted. The search is terminated as soon as the cost of non-distributed part of the next generated query plan surpasses the total cost of the best plan found earlier.

The RAM cost model is designed to steer the minimization of the data volume to be processed. Its cost function computes a score based on the total amount of data generated by a query. For normal operators the cost is recursively determined by assigning a cost for the operator itself to the sum of its children's costs:

$$cost(op(E_1 \ldots E_n)) = cost\_function(op) + \sum_{i=1}^{n} cost(E_i).$$

The *distribute* pseudo-operator is treated differently: it gets assigned only the maximum cost among its children, as they are evaluated in parallel, and a cost factor related to node-communication. Assuming data volume to be the dominant factor in data transfer leads to this cost estimate function:

$$cost(distribute(E_1 \ldots E_n)) = max(cost(E_1) \ldots cost(E_n)) + \sum_{i=1}^{n} c|E_i|, \quad (6)$$

where c is a constant tuned to the speed of the network connecting the nodes.

Although the current cost model may be further improved by taking more variables into account, it is shown to be reliable. The reason for this is not to be found in its complexity, but rather in the choice of the domain where the costs are estimated. Performing optimizations and deciding fragmentation strategies in the array domain allows for the exploitation of properties usually not available in the relational domain. Cost models tend to be complex and of limited reliability in the relational domain because the size of intermediate results can only be estimated. In the array domain, the exact knowledge on this factor justifies the usage of simple cost models and ensures more reliable results.

5 Experiments

This section presents experimental results aimed at verifying the effectiveness of the distribution strategies outlined in Section 4. The goal is to show that not only the query optimizer produces viable distribution plans, it also has the means to reliably select the most efficient strategy.

Figure 1 visualizes three possible strategies for the query derived from equation 3. These query plans are referred to as Query B, Query C, and Query D in the remainder of this paper. The original non-distributed query, as it is in Expression 1, is referred to as Query A.

These examples are just three of the many possible alternative distribution plans that are considered by the system. There is no need for users to study the formulas by hand to decide on a suitable query fragmentation strategy: the RAM system derives the most suitable strategy automatically. The experiments are focused on these three variants since they represent patterns that can be intuitively explained.

Query A, the original non-distributed query plan, is visualized in Figure 1(a).

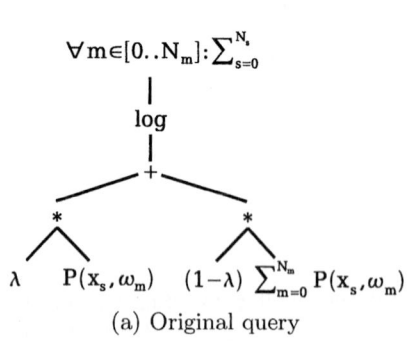
(a) Original query

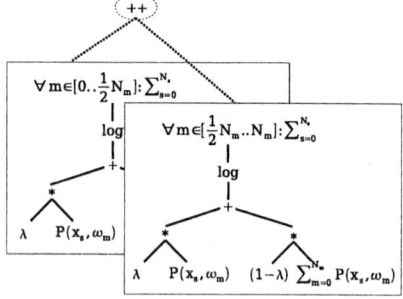
(b) Query on disjunct sub-collections

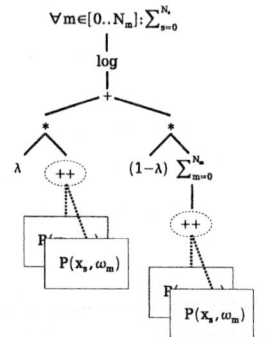
(c) Distribution pushed down in the query tree

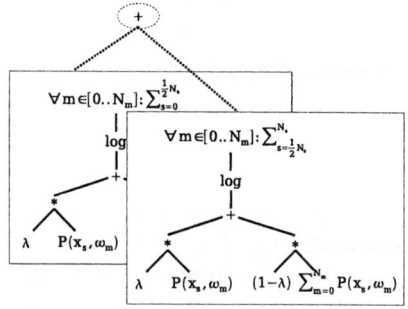
(d) Partial queries on the whole collection

Fig. 1. Query fragmentation strategies

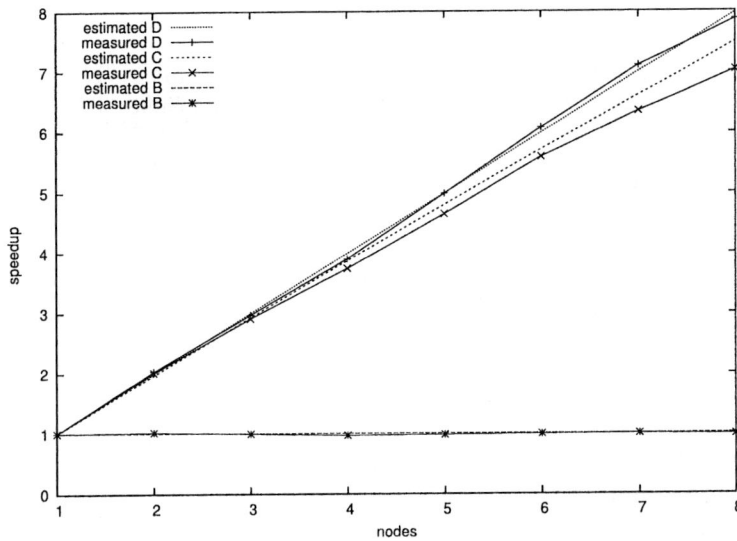

Fig. 2. Speed-up of Queries B, C, D when using an increasing number of nodes

Query B, depicted in Figure 1(b), represents the pattern where disjunct subsets of the collection are independently scored by different nodes. This approach is not effective in our case study, because of the aggregation over all documents that is part of the score for each individual document: when performed naively, this query-fragmentation strategy results in a situation where each node still needs to compute the values the entire collection.

One solution around this problem is to move fragmentation further down the query expression, as depicted in Figure 1(c) and implemented by Query C. In this case, the large intermediate matrix of individual sample probabilities per model is computed in fragments, assembled, and used to compute the final scores. This approach has two downsides however: this matrix has $N_s \times N_m$ elements which may result in considerable communication overhead, and a significant part of the computation is no longer performed in parallel as the collected data requires non-trivial post-processing.

Finally we consider Query D, as depicted in Figure 1(d), which fragments the query along another dimension of its problem space. The query is fragmented along the direction of the aggregation, each node computes a partial score for each document and these partial scores are subsequently combined into a single value. This approach results in a more manageable communication overhead compared to the previous solution, of N_s elements per node.

5.1 Measurements

Experiments have been conducted on a cluster composed of 8 slave nodes and one master node[2] Calibration tests have shown that, for this cluster of machines,

---

[2] Each configured with an Opteron 1.4GHz, 2GB of main memory, Gigabit network interface, and MonetDB [8] version 4.4.0.

Table 1. Execution statistics for query distribution over 8 nodes

Query	master % time	slave % time	network % time	network data volume
B	0.004	99.993	0.003	$c * Nm$
C	11.6	88.1	0.3	$c * Nm * Ns$
D	0.005	99.993	0.002	$c * Nm * \#nodes$

$c \approx 120$ is a suitable value for the constant c introduced in Equation 6. Query A has been executed on the single master node, and queries B, C, and D have been distributed over a number of nodes ranging from 2 to 8 slaves and a master-node.

Figure 2 summarizes the results in terms of speed-up with respect to the non-distributed Query A. For each of the three distributed variants, the estimated speed-up and the measured speed-up are shown.

The first observation is that in all cases the measured speed-up is in-line with the predicted values (Figure 2). This shows that, for these queries, the cost-model proposed in Section 4 reliably estimates the relative costs of alternative query plans.

The second observation is that Query D exhibits the best scalability, as predicted by the RAM optimizer and our intuitive expectations. Query C also exploits the increasing number of nodes, although not as effectively as Query D does, whereas Query B does not provide any significant speed-up. As shown in Table 1, for both queries B (worst) and D (best), nearly all time is spent computing the distributed part of the query. Here, time spent on communication and post-processing of the data on the master node is negligible. The reasons why Query C is less scalable than Query D are explained clearly by Table 1: first, since distribution is pushed down in the query tree, a significant fraction of the query (11%) is not parallelized, but executed sequentially by the master node; second, because Query C requires more data to be transferred than the other distributed queries, its communication overhead is more noticeable.

A final observation is that, in the experimental setting, communication costs are not really an issue. Only in the case of Query C, communication overhead is noticeable but still hardly significant for the overall cost. There are two apparent reasons for this: first, the workload represented by the query in our example case is large and by far the predominant factor in the overall execution costs; second, experiments were performed on a tightly coupled cluster of machines with a fast interconnecting network. While both aspects seem reasonable in light of our target domain – large scale scientific problems inherently bring costly computations and are usually processed on dedicated machinery – it remains to be seen how the results translate to different environments.

6 Discussion and Conclusions

The experimental results clearly indicate that distributed database technology is applicable to complex scientific queries, such as the ones issued by recent information retrieval research.

However, a correct reading of these results goes beyond a mere quantitative analysis of the problem at hand. Although the identification of the most efficient fragmentation strategy is an important issue for the practical usage of the system, we would like to emphasize that many strategies other than those presented are possible, and that it is not our intention to analyze their efficiency in this paper. The valuable information for the scope of our research is in the comparison between the estimated and the measured costs. Figure 2 shows that the RAM system is not only capable of fragmenting queries efficiently, but it appears to be particularly reliable in estimating the costs associated to different strategies.

In Section 4 we detail about the reasons of such an accuracy. Mapping array queries into the relational domain does not imply that all the optimization issues are also mapped to the new domain, where they could be effectively solved by the available solutions. We showed, for instance, how the size of intermediate results, that plays a crucial role in the optimization and in the distribution of a query, is known with no uncertainty in the array domain. The mapping process, however, results in an inevitable loss of such context information, which can then be only estimated by the target relational system. The novelty introduced by the RAM system is combining the exploitation of the context knowledge in the array domain with the usage of the advanced solutions available in the relational domain.

In this light, RAM appears to be an attractive solution for scientific computations on large data volumes. Its data model provides advantages at different levels: it drastically reduces user effort required to implement database-powered solutions by tackling problems within the array domain, and its structure allows a reduced complexity of the optimization process without sacrificing effectiveness. Likewise, query distribution benefits from its realization at the array level.

References

1. Maier, D., Vance, B.: A call to order. In: Proceedings of the 12th ACM SIGACT-SIGMOD-SIGART symposium on principles of database systems, ACM Press (1993) 1–16
2. Cornacchia, R., van Ballegooij, A., de Vries, A.: A case study on array query optimisation. In: First International Workshop on Computer Vision meets Databases (CVDB 2004), Maison de la Chimie, Paris, France, ACM Press (2004) 3–10 In cooperation with ACM SIGMOD.
3. van Ballegooij, A.: RAM: A Multidimensional Array DBMS. In: Proceedings of the ICDE/EDBT 2004 Joint Ph.D. Workshop. (2004) 169–174
4. Baumann, P.: A database array algebra for spatio-temporal data and beyond. In: Next Generation Information Technologies and Systems. (1999) 76–93
5. Buneman, P., Libkin, L., Suciu, D., Tannen, V., Wong, L.: Comprehension syntax. SIGMOD Record **23** (1994) 87–96
6. Libkin, L., Machlin, R., Wong, L.: A query language for multidimensional arrays: Design, implementation, and optimization techniques. In: ACM SIGMOD 1996, ACM Press (1996) 228–239

7. van Ballegooij, A., de Vries, A., Kersten, M.: Ram: Array processing over a relational dbms. Technical Report INS-R0301, CWI (2003)
8. Amsterdam, C., of Amsterdam, U.: Monetdb. (http://sourceforge.net/projects/monetdb/)
9. Ianeva, T., Boldareva, L., Westerveld, T., Cornacchia, R., de Vries, A., Hiemstra, D.: Probabilistic approaches to video retrieval. In: TREC Video Retrieval Evaluation Online Proceedings. (2004)
10. Westerveld, T.: Using generative probabilistic models for multimedia retrieval. PhD thesis, University of Twente (2004)
11. Inc., T.M.: Matlab. (http://www.mathworks.com)
12. Ceri, S., Pelagatti, G.: Distributed Databases. McGraw-Hill Book Company, (Singapore)
13. Ozsu, M.T., Valduriez, P.: Principles of distributed database systems (2nd ed.). Prentice-Hall, Inc., Upper Saddle River, NJ, USA (1999)
14. Dean, J., Ghemawat, S.: Mapreduce: Simplified data processing on large clusters. OSDI (2004)
15. Graefe, G.: Volcano - an extensible and parallel query evaluation system. IEEE Trans. Knowl. Data Eng. **6** (1994) 120–135

Efficient Processing of Distributed Top-k Queries*

Hailing Yu, Hua-Gang Li, Ping Wu, Divyakant Agrawal, and Amr El Abbadi

University of California, Santa Barbara, CA 93106, USA
{huagang, hailing, agrawal, amr}@cs.ucsb.edu

Abstract. Ranking-aware queries, or top-k queries, have received much attention recently in various contexts such as web, multimedia retrieval, relational databases, and distributed systems. Top-k queries play a critical role in many decision-making related activities such as, identifying interesting objects, network monitoring, load balancing, etc. In this paper, we study the ranking aggregation problem in distributed systems. Prior research addressing this problem did not take data distributions into account, simply assuming the uniform data distribution among nodes, which is not realistic for real data sets and is, in general, inefficient. In this paper, we propose three efficient algorithms that consider data distributions in different ways. Our extensive experiments demonstrate the advantages of our approaches in terms of bandwidth consumption.

1 Introduction

Ranking-aware queries have been studied in various contexts such as web, multimedia retrieval, relational databases, and distributed systems. This is mainly because they are needed for decision-making related activities such as identifying interesting objects, network monitoring, distributed denial-of-service attack detection and load balancing. For example, in a network monitoring setting, top ranking sources of data packets need to be identified to detect denial-of-service attacks. Fagin first introduced the ranking aggregation problem in the context of multimedia retrieval [6]. Assume there are m subsystems with each maintaining a list of objects together with their ranking scores. The score of an object can be any value that describes a certain characteristic of the object, e.g., its color, shape, etc. Top-k queries over the m subsystems return the objects with the k highest aggregated scores under a monotonic function. The best known algorithm solving this problem is the *Threshold Algorithm* (TA) which was independently discovered by several groups [8,11,7]. Based on Fagin's seminal work [6], many approaches have been proposed to solve the top-k query processing problem under various scenarios. In data streams, distributed top-k monitoring was studied in [1]. Supporting ranking query processing in relational databases from different perspectives has been studied in [3,5,9,10,15,14]. More recently, approximate top-k queries on multi-dimensional datasets with probabilistic guarantees were studied in [13]. A framework for distributed top-k retrieval in peer-to-peer networks was proposed in [2], which is mainly concerned with retrieving the top-k matching objects given the query object, but does not aggregate scores from all nodes in a distributed system.

---

* This research was supported by the NSF grants under IIS-02-23022, CNF-04-23336, and EIA-00-80134.

In this paper, we are concerned with answering top-k queries efficiently in distributed systems. In particular, we consider *Content Distribution Networks* (CDNs), which are deployed by many companies to avoid network congestion. CDNs typically consist of *cache servers* scattered around the globe for caching bandwidth-intensive objects from the *original server* such as images and video clips. This enables fast web and streaming media applications. When a request is sent to the original server, it is redirected to one of the cache servers which is closer to the client and/or can serve data faster. Effective monitoring of activities (by a *central manager*) over CDNs ensures successful content distribution. One such monitoring task is a top-k query, e.g., *"what are the top-k most popular URLs across the entire CDN?"*. A naïve approach to answer such a query is to have each cache server send the access statistics about all objects to the central manager. However, this incurs significant bandwidth consumption if the number of objects at each cache server is large. Hence bandwidth efficient algorithms for processing such top-k queries in a distributed environment are needed.

While the Threshold Algorithm (TA) is generally applicable in database applications, it is inefficient when applied to answer top-k queries in large distributed networks in terms of bandwidth consumption [4]. This is mainly because the number of rounds to finalize the answer to a top-k query under TA cannot be predetermined and it varies with different data distributions among the nodes. Hence, in [4] the first constant number of round algorithm for calculating top-k objects in distributed systems is proposed and referred to as the *Three-Phase Uniform-Threshold* algorithm (TPUT).

However, TPUT does not take data distributions into account and it simply assumes the uniform data distribution among all nodes, which is not realistic due to the heterogeneous nature of distributed systems. Thus, in this paper, we propose different algorithms to calculate top-k queries in constant number of rounds to further enhance the performance by accounting for varying data distributions. They are referred to as the *Three-Phase Adaptive-Threshold* algorithm (TPAT), the *Three-Phase Object-Ranking* based algorithm (TPOR) and the *Hybrid-Threshold* algorithm (HT). TPAT generalizes TPUT by utilizing summary statistics of the data. However, it could be very expensive to use summary statistics to accurately estimate data distributions. The main difficulty is for an algorithm to efficiently estimate data distributions, without *a-priori* knowledge. TPOR and HT are devised to overcome this difficulty. TPOR is fundamentally different from both TPUT and TPAT since it uses object rankings rather than object scores when estimating data distributions. TPOR is more bandwidth-efficient than TPUT when handling the case that object rankings are similar across all nodes. Nevertheless, TPOR performs worse than TPUT in the case when object rankings widely vary across all nodes. To remedy such a situation, HT is proposed to combine the advantages of both TPUT and TPOR, which is robust under different data distributions.

The rest of the paper is organized as follows. Section 2 formulates the problem. Section 3 presents our proposed algorithms. Section 4 evaluates the performance of our proposed algorithms. Section 5 concludes the paper and discusses the future work.

2 Problem Formulation and Performance Metric

We formalize the problem of top-k query processing in distributed systems by abstracting the above CDN example. Assume there are m nodes and one single *central manager* in a distributed system. Each node i is connected to the central manager and maintains a list of pairs $\langle O, S_i(O) \rangle$, where O is an object and $S_i(O)$ is the score of the object. Furthermore, we assume objects in each list are sorted in the descending order of their scores. Note that an object does not have to appear in all nodes. If an object does not appear in the list of a node, its score in that list is zero by default. The central manager initiates a top-k query which retrieves objects from the network with the k highest $f(S_1(O), \ldots, S_m(O))$ where f is a monotonic function such as the sum function SUM to compute the overall score of an object. For simplicity, we assume the sum function throughout this paper. In practice, this function could be a weighted sum to account for the relative importance of cache servers.

The goal of distributed top-k query algorithms is to achieve low bandwidth consumption. We assume that the computation cost in each node is negligible while the communication cost among nodes dominates the query response time. This is mainly due to the current trends in technology where the speed and bandwidth of the network is still a bottleneck. We take the number of $\langle object, score \rangle$ pairs transmitted across the network as our performance metric, which dominates the communication cost.

3 New Ranking Aggregation Algorithms

In this section, we propose three new algorithms for answering top-k queries in distributed systems. The first algorithm, the *Three-Phase Adaptive-Threshold* algorithm (TPAT), generalizes TPUT by exploiting data distributions using summary statistics to further enhance the pruning power of TPUT. The second algorithm, the *Three-Phase Object-Ranking* based algorithm (TPOR), prunes ineligible objects by their rankings (positions). In contrast, TPUT prunes ineligible objects based on their scores. The last algorithm, the *Hybrid-Threshold* algorithm (HT), combines the advantages of both TPUT and TPOR, and demonstrates that it is very robust to different data distributions.

3.1 Three-Phase Adaptive-Threshold Algorithm

In this subsection, we extend TPUT by relaxing the condition on how to divide the phase-1 bottom τ_1 among all nodes. Please refer to [4] for the details of TPUT due to the space limit. By dividing τ_1 uniformly among the nodes, TPUT assumes object scores are uniformly distributed among nodes in the network, i.e., each node contributes approximately the same to the result set. However this assumption does not consider the case in the real world where some nodes in the systems are hot spots for content-sharing. This results in non-uniformly distributed data among nodes. That is, some nodes may have objects with larger score distributions while other nodes may have objects with smaller score distributions. For convenience, they are referred to as *hot* and *cold* nodes respectively. The probability for a top-k object being from a hot node is much higher than being from a cold node. Intuitively, hot nodes usually contribute a larger portion of top-k objects than cold nodes do. Hence, we propose to divide τ_1 to m nodes adaptively according to their data distributions. In general a threshold lower than τ_1/m for a hot node allows more objects to be sent to the central manager, and vice versa.

We illustrate the adaptive division of τ_1 by using the example lists in Fig. 1. Assume that the central manager asks for a top 2 query. From Fig. 1., we observe that node 2 has

	node 1	node 2	node 3
1	<O_5, 21>	<O_4, 34>	<O_3, 30>
2	<O_2, 17>	<O_1, 29>	<O_4, 14>
3	<O_4, 11>	<O_0, 29>	<O_0, 9>
4	<O_3, 11>	<O_3, 26>	<O_5, 7>
5	<O_6, 10>	<O_5, 9>	<O_2, 1>
6	<O_7, 10>	<O_9, 7>	<O_8, 1>

Phase-1: TPUT/TPAT
PSUM
O4 : 48
O3 : 30
O1 : 29
O5 : 21
O2 : 17
← Phase-1 bottom

Phase-2 : TPUT
PSUM
O3 : 67
O4 : 59
O0 : 29
O1 : 29
O5 : 21
O2 : 17
O6 : 10
O7 : 10

Phase-2 : TPAT
PSUM
O3 : 56
O4 : 48
O5 : 30
O0 : 29
O1 : 29
O2 : 17

Fig. 1. Three example lists and the partial sum lists calculated in phase 1 & 2 of TPUT/TPAT

objects with a larger score distribution as compared to node 1 and node 3. Hence node 2 plays an important role to the final scores of top-k objects in the result set with higher probability than the other nodes. Thus more objects are expected to be sent from node 2 to the central manager and fewer objects from node 1 or node 3. If $\tau_1 = 30$ is non-uniformly divided into $T_1 = 12$, $T_2 = 8$, and $T_3 = 10$, which are assigned to nodes 1, 2, 3 respectively as the thresholds, then, in phase 2, node 1 sends $\langle object, score \rangle$ pairs up to position 2, node 2 up to position 5, and node 3 up to position 2. As compared with the uniform threshold $T = 30/3$, non-uniform thresholds send 3 fewer number of $\langle object, score \rangle$ pairs. TPAT algorithm is summarized as follows:

1. Phase 1: same as TPUT.
2. Phase 2: The central manager divides τ_1 non-uniformly into $T_1, \ldots, T_m$ according to some summary statistics sent from nodes. Then it sends T_i to node i as the threshold. The rest is the same as TPUT except that the upper bound of each object's aggregated score calculated by $U_{\text{sum}}(O) = S'_1(O) + \ldots + S'_m(0)$ where $S'_i(O) = S_i(O)$ if O has been reported by node i, and $S'_i(O) = T_i$ otherwise.
3. Phase 3: same as TPUT.

Theorem 1. *The TPAT algorithm correctly returns the exact top-k objects for any data distribution in each node of a two-tier distributed system.*[1]

The motivating example above only develops the general framework for an adaptive division of the phase-1 bottom τ_1 according to the data distribution in the network. The main challenge is how the data distribution can be captured approximately using summary statistics and how they are used to guide the adaptive division of τ_1. Since histograms have been widely used in various database problems and are the most commonly used form of statistics in practice, we now investigate them as a tool to guide the adaptive division of τ_1. In particular, *equi-depth histograms* [12] are used as an example to illustrate the framework of our proposed technique. Note that any kind of histograms can fit in our framework. Equi-depth histograms are constructed by dividing the domain into b buckets with roughly the same number of tuples in each bucket. This number and the bucket boundaries are stored. For notational convenience, the equi-depth histogram for the data in node i is represented by $H_i = \{B^i_1, \ldots, B^i_{b_i}\}$. $B^i_j (1 \leq j \leq b_i)$ is in the form of $([V^i_{min}, V^i_{max}], f)$, where $[V^i_{min}, V^i_{max}]$ is the boundary of bucket B^i_j and f is the total number of objects in the bucket. Hence, given a score predicate $s \geq p$, the total

---

[1] Note that all the proofs for theorems in this paper are omitted due to the space limit and please refer to [16] for complete proofs.

number of objects within the range can be approximated by examining the overlapped buckets by assuming a uniform distribution in each bucket.

In general, we need to divide the phase-1 bottom τ_1 among the histograms of the nodes so as to minimize the number of objects retrieved. This is a linear programming problem, whose complexity increases as the number of buckets in the histogram per node increases. To simplify the problem, we consider one-bucket histograms. Now the histogram for node i is represented by $H_i = \{B_1^i = ([V_{min}^i, V_{max}^i], f^i)\}$, i.e., each node returns the score range of its objects and the total number of objects at the node. Assume τ_1 is divided into $T_1, \ldots, T_m$ such that $\sum_{i=1}^{m} T_i = \tau_1$. Assuming uniform score distribution at each node, we can approximate the number of objects whose scores are no less than T_i by using the score range and the number of objects, i.e., $\frac{f^i}{V_{max}^i - V_{min}^i} * (V_{max}^i - T_i)$. Assume that this number is $f_i(T_i)$. Hence, the goal of adaptive division of τ_1 into $T_1, \ldots, T_m$ is to minimize $\sum_{i=1}^{m} f_i(T_i) = \sum_{i=1}^{m} \frac{f^i}{V_{max}^i - V_{min}^i} * (V_{max}^i - T_i)$ such that $\sum_{i=1}^{m} T_i = \tau_1$ and $V_{min}^i \leq T_i \leq V_{max}^i$.

When the score distribution in each node is non-uniform, the selectivity estimation accuracy using one-bucket histogram cannot be guaranteed. However, using more than one bucket for each histogram to summarize score distribution makes the optimization much more complex, which may incur infeasible computation cost. Hence, we introduce alternative techniques without using a *priori* knowledge on data distributions.

3.2 Three-Phase Object-Ranking Based Algorithm

We now propose a new algorithm, referred to as *Three-Phase Object-Ranking* based algorithm (TPOR), that is more likely to capture the heterogeneous nature of distributed networks without using any summary statistics. Its pruning of ineligible objects is based on object rankings instead of their scores. In particular, in the second phase of this new algorithm, instead of assigning a threshold for each node, the central manager sends the current top-k *object list* to each node. Upon receiving this list, each node examines its objects and passes all of its local objects that are ranked higher than any of the objects in the list to the central manager. In this way, the correlation between the object score and ranking is captured, which can avoid the case where an inappropriately small phase-1 bottom τ_1 is obtained by TPUT. The following example will show how TPOR works.

We again consider the example lists in Fig. 1. and the top-k query still requests the top 2 objects. As shown in Fig. 1., after the first phase, the objects with the two highest partial sums are O_4 and O_3. Hence in phase 2, the central manager sends the set of objects $\{O_4, O_3\}$ to each node. The lowest ranking of these two objects in node 1, 2, 3 are 4, 4 and 2 respectively. Therefore, node 1 sends $\{O_5, O_2, O_4, O_3\}$, node 2 sends $\{O_4, O_1, O_0, O_3\}$, and node 3 sends $\{O_3, O_4\}$. As compared with TPUT, 2 fewer objects are needed to be sent to the central manager. The rest processing is the same as TPUT and omitted here due to the space limit. TPOR algorithm is summarized as follows.

1. Phase 1: same as TPUT.
2. Phase 2: The central manager broadcasts the list L of the top-k object IDs from the partial sum list to all the nodes in the network. Upon receiving the list L, for each object O_j in L, node i finds its local score $V_{i,j}$ (if O_j does not occur in the local

list, $V_{i,j} = 0$) and determines the lowest local score T_i among all the k objects in L. Then node i sends the list of local objects whose values are $\geq T_i$ to the central manager. Now the central manager calculates the partial sums of all the objects seen so far, and identifies the objects with the k highest partial sums. Let us call the kth highest partial sum "phase-2 bottom" and denote it by τ_2. Then the central manager calculates the upper bounds of the objects seen so far using $U_{\text{sum}}(O) = S'_1(O) + \ldots + S'_m(0)$ where $S'_i(O) = S_i(O)$ if O has been reported by node i, and $S'_i(O) = T_i$ otherwise, and removes any object O_j from the candidate set whose upper bound is less than τ_2.
3. Phase 3: same as TPUT.

Theorem 2. *The TPOR algorithm correctly returns the exact top-k objects for any data distribution in each node of a two-tier distributed system.*

The difference between TPOR and TPUT lies in the fact that in TPOR, during phase 2, the central manager sends the entire top-k object ID list to all the nodes. We argue this will not incur much overhead since, in practice, the object ID can be hashed to integers, the value of k is in general not large and the object ID list can be multicast to all the nodes simultaneously. However, similar to TPUT, the performance of TPOR also depends on the data distribution. For example, in phase 2, if one node does not have any object in the object ID list, it will send all its local objects to the central manager.

3.3 Hybrid-Threshold Algorithm

In this subsection, we propose a hybrid algorithm, the *Hybrid-Threshold* algorithm (HT), which tries to combine the advantages of both TPOR and TPUT. In the second phase of HT, the central manager asks each node to send objects whose scores are no less than a hybrid threshold, which is calculated as the maximum of the uniform threshold $T = \tau_1/m$ from TPUT and the threshold obtained by TPOR. However, this cannot guarantee the correctness of the algorithm. It is possible that some objects in a node whose scores are between the uniform threshold by TPUT and the threshold by TPOR, are top-k objects. Thus, we devise to add a patch phase to make the algorithm correctly return the top-k objects. After phase 2, the central manager calculates the new partial sums for all the objects seen so far and identifies the objects with the k highest partial sums. Let the kth partial sum denote τ_2. Then the central manager calculates $T_{patch} = \tau_2/m$. Assume T_i is the lower bound of the object scores sent from node i in phase 2. If $T_{patch} \leq T_i$, the central manager sends T_{patch} to node i and asks node i to send the objects whose scores are no less than T_{patch}. Since T_{patch} is greater than T, the total number of objects sent by HT is no greater than that of TPUT. If $T_{patch} > T_i$ for every i, there is no need for this patch phase, i.e., all top-k object candidates have been considered. HT algorithm is summarized as follows:

1. Phase 1: same as TPUT.
2. Phase 2: The central manager broadcasts the list L to all the nodes in the network and $T = \tau_1/m$ as well. Upon receiving the list L, for each object O_j in L, node i finds its local score $V_{i,j}$ (if O_j does not occur in the local list, $V_{i,j} = 0$) and determines the lowest local score S^i_{lowest} among all the k objects in L. Then node

i sends the list of local objects whose values are $\geq T_i = \max(S^i_{lowest}, T)$ to the central manager. Now the central manager calculates the partial sums for all the objects seen so far, and identifies the objects with the k highest partial sums. Let us call the kth highest partial sum "phase-2 bottom" and denote it by τ_2.
3. Phase 3 (patch phase if necessary) : The central manager checks if the threshold from node i, T_i in phase 2 is greater than $T_{patch} = \tau_2/m$. If so, the central manager will send T_{patch} to node i as the threshold and ask it to send all the objects whose scores are no less than T_{patch}. Now the central manager calculates the partial sums for all the objects seen so far, and identifies the objects with the k highest partial sums. Let us call the kth highest partial sum "phase-3 bottom" and denote it by τ_3. Then the central manager calculates the upper bounds of the objects seen so far using $U_{\mathrm{sum}}(O) = S'_1(O) + \ldots + S'_m(0)$ where $S'_i(O) = S_i(O)$ if O has been reported by node i, and $S'_i(O) = \min(T_i, T_{patch})$ otherwise, and removes any object O_j from the candidate set whose upper bound is less than τ_3.
4. Phase 4: same as TPUT.

Theorem 3. *The HT algorithm correctly returns the exact top-k objects for any data distribution in each node of a two-tier distributed system.*

4 Experimental Evaluation

In this section, we experimentally evaluate the performance of our proposed algorithms TPOR and HT. Note that TPAT is not included here due to the computational overhead of using multi-bin histograms. However, TPAT is significant in that it provides us the basic framework which enables us to develop TPOR and HT. We implemented TPUT, TPOR, and HT in Java and compared their performance over various synthetic and real data sets. The performance metric we use for the algorithms is the bandwidth consumption. We are mainly concerned with the number of ⟨object, score⟩ pairs sent from nodes to the central manager since it is the dominant factor in bandwidth consumption. The control messages from the central manager to the nodes are broadcast through a broadcast media. Their size is very small and hence can be ignored.

4.1 Synthetic Data Sets

Various synthetic data sets were generated for performance evaluation as follows. Assume there are m nodes, node 0, ..., $m-1$, in the network and each node has n objects. Initially n values $v_1, \ldots, v_n$ are generated, which follow the Zipf's distribution [17] with a Zipf factor α. These n values are assigned to the n objects as their scores in node 0. The scores of an object O in other nodes are generated by using a random walk model: $S[i] = S[i-1] + s_i$. $S[i]$ represents the score of object O at node i and s_i is a random number in the range $[-r, +r]$. r is set to $c \times S[0]$ where c is a constant which is less than or equal to 10%. By varying α and c, we can simulate different scenarios such as the scenario in which the object rankings are similar in different nodes or the scenario in which the object rankings vary in different nodes.

The experimental results in this section are based on five synthetic data sets. Each of them has $m = 100$ nodes and each node has 10000 objects. These five data sets have

$\alpha = 0.1, 0.3, 0.5, 0.8, 1.0$ respectively. They are referred to as *Synthetic-α*. Synthetic-0.1 simulates a scenario where the rankings of objects in each node are quite different. Since $\alpha = 0.1$, the initial scores generated for objects are less skewed. Also the constant c of the random walk model is set to a larger value for those objects which have lower scores in node 0 and a smaller value for those objects which have higher scores in node 0. This ensures that some objects with higher initial rankings have lower rankings in other nodes and vice versa. With α increasing, the rankings of objects among all nodes tend to be similar. When $\alpha = 1$, the initial scores generated for objects are quite skewed. Moreover, since c is at most 10%, it is highly probable that the initial rankings of objects remain approximately the same for the other nodes. Thus, Synthetic-1.0 simulates a scenario in which object rankings are very similar in different nodes.

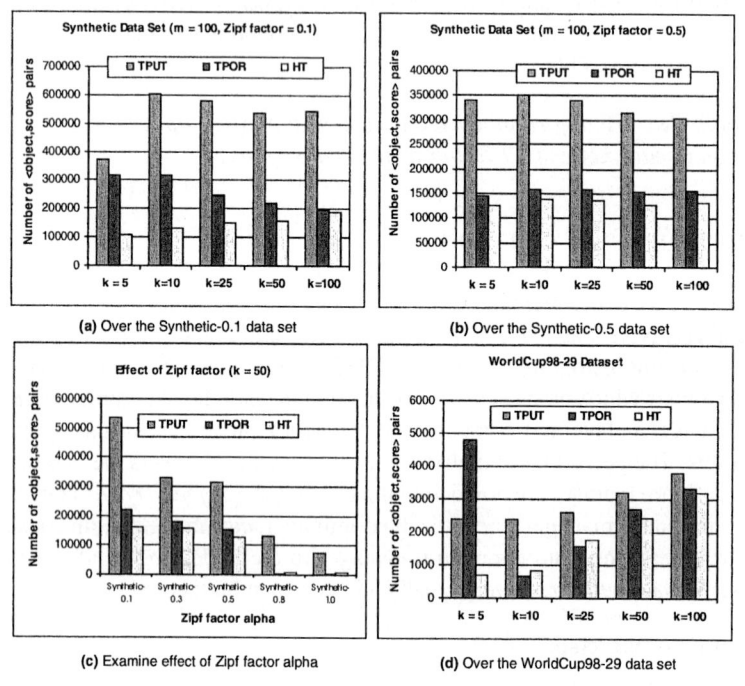

Fig. 2. Performance comparisons of TPUT, TPOR and HT

Fig. 2.(a) and 2.(b) show the performance comparisons of TPUT, TPOR, and HT over Synthetic-0.1 and Synthetic-0.5 data sets respectively. The queries are for the top-k referenced objects. From Fig. 2.(a) and 2.(b), we have the following observations: (1) TPOR and HT outperform TPUT, and the improvement of TPOR and HT is significant. On average TPUT sends 2 to 3 times more number of $\langle object, score \rangle$ pairs than TPOR and HT do; (2) When the object rankings among nodes become more similar, i.e., Fig. 2.(b) where $\alpha = 0.5$, the performance of TPOR and HT over them becomes relatively stable when k increases while this is not the case with TPUT. This is because, for such cases, TPOR and HT prune objects mainly based on their rankings, which is less sensitive to the score variations of objects; (3) For data sets in which the object rankings among nodes are less similar, i.e., Fig. 2.(a) where $\alpha = 0.1$, when k increases, the improvement of HT over TPOR decreases. This is because a higher k results in more objects sent to the central manager. Thus, the object ID list calculated for TPOR more accurately captures the true top-k objects. Then more nodes in HT use the thresholds calculated by the object rankings instead of the uniform threshold calculated by TPUT. Therefore, fewer $\langle object, score \rangle$ pairs are eliminated by using the uniform threshold; (4) The less the object rankings among nodes are similar, the more $\langle object, score \rangle$ pairs are eliminated by HT as compared with TPOR. The reason is that for data sets in which the object rankings are less similar, TPOR may calculate a less accurate object ID list and send more objects in the second phase. However, HT combines the advantages of both TPUT and TPOR, which can lead to significant gains.

Fig. 2.(c) examines the effect of the Zipf factor on the performance where k is set to 50. As α increases, the object rankings among nodes become more similar and the number of $\langle object, score \rangle$ pairs sent by TPUT, TPOR and HT decreases. This is because the objects collected from phase 1 provide more accurate information for pruning. Also, the improvement of TPOR and HT over TPUT becomes more pronounced. In Fig. 2.(c), for Synthetic-0.8 and Synthetic-1.0 data sets, TPOR outperforms HT. This is because these two datasets have very similar object rankings in different nodes and hence, most thresholds calculated in the second phase are actually greater than the threshold calculated by the TPUT method. Nevertheless, HT requires the patch phase which may have a lower threshold and thus more objects are sent during the patch phase.

4.2 Real Data Set

We studied the performance of the algorithms on a real data set containing the 2 hour URL access log from the 29 servers hosting the website for the 1998 World Cup Soccer on June 18, 1998. It is referred to as *WorldCup98-29*. The average number of referenced URLs in each server is about 6082. Fig. 2.(d) shows the performance comparisons of TPUT, TPOR, and HT over the real data set. The queries are for the top-k referenced URLs. From Fig. 2.(d), we observe that TPOR and HT outperform TPUT in most cases. The saving in bandwidth consumption for $k = 10$ is significant and up to 75%. The reason is that, for the WorldCup98-29 case, the final top 10 objects have very high rankings in all nodes. Thus, TPOR and HT can easily avoid returning ineligible objects, which are possibly returned by TPUT because of the lower value of τ_1. TPOR and HT perform approximately the same in most cases except for the top 5 case. This is because, in the first phase of TPOR, each node in the distributed system only returns its local top 5 objects to the central manager. The number of objects returned from all nodes is not sufficient to capture the final top-k objects. Alternatively, some objects which actually rank very low in some nodes are included in the object ID list which is calculated in the first phase. This in turn results in some nodes returning too many objects.

5 Conclusion and Future Work

In this paper, top-k query calculation in distributed networks is studied. Prior research on distributed top-k query calculation did not take into account data distributions when pruning ineligible objects. Non-uniformity of data distributions is likely to occur frequently due to the heterogeneous nature of distributed systems. In this paper, we proposed three different distributed top-k query algorithms that consider data distributions in different ways. We performed extensive experiments over both real and synthetic data sets to evaluate our proposed algorithms as compared with prior research. Our experimental results demonstrate that our final algorithm, HT, is more suitable for answering top-k queries in distributed systems when dealing with data with different distributions. So far, we only considered two-tier distributed systems. One natural step for our future work is to study the top-k query problem over distributed systems with hierarchical structures such as peer-to-peer systems.

References

1. B. Babcock and C. Olston. Distributed top-k monitoring. In *Proc. of Intl. Conf. on Managment of Data (SIGMOD)*, pages 563–574, 2003.
2. W-T. Balke, W. Nejdl, W. Siberski, and U. Thaden. Progressive distributed top-k retrieval in peer-to-peer networks. In *Proc. of Intl. Conf. on Data Engineering (ICDE)*, 2005, to appear.
3. N. Bruno, S. Chaudhuri, and L. Gravano. Top-k selection queries over relational databases: Mapping strategies and performance evaluation. *ACM Trans. on Database Systems*, 27(2):153–187, 2002.
4. P. Cao and Z. Wang. Efficient top-k query calculation in distributed networks. In *Proc. of Intl. Symposium on Principles Of Distributed Computing (PODC)*, pages 206–215, 2004.
5. S. Chaudhuri and L. Gravano. Evaluating top-k selection queries. In *Proc. of Intl. Conf. on Very Large Data Bases (VLDB)*, pages 397–410, 1999.
6. R. Fagin. Combining fuzzy information from multiple systems. In *Proc. of Intl. Symp. on Principles of Database Systems (PODS)*, pages 216–226, 1996.
7. R. Fagin, A. Lotem, and M. Naor. Optimal aggregation algorithms for middleware. In *Proc. of Intl. Symposium on Principles of Database Systems (PODS)*, pages 102–113, 2001.
8. U. Guntzer, W-T. Balke, and W. Kiessling. Optimizing multi-feature queries in image databases. In *Proc. of Intl. Conf. on Very Large Data Bases (VLDB)*, pages 419–428, 2000.
9. I. F. Ilyas, W. G. Aref, and A. K. Elmagarmid. Supporting top-k join queries in relational databases. In *Proc. of Intl. Conf. on Very Large Data Base (VLDB)*, pages 754–765, 2003.
10. I. F. Ilyas, R. Shah, W. G. Aref, J. S. Vitter, and A. K. Elmagarmi. Rank-aware query optimization. In *Proc. of Intl. Conf. on Managment of Data (SIGMOD)*, pages 203–214, 2004.
11. S. Nepal and M.V. Ramakrishna. Query processing issues in image (multimedia) databases. In *Proc. of Intl. Conf. on Data Engineering (ICDE)*, pages 22–31, 1999.
12. W. Poosala, P.J. Haas, Y.E. Ioannidis, and E.J. Shekita. Improved histograms for selectivity estimation of range predicates. In *Proc. of Intl. Conf. on Management of Data (SIGMOD)*, pages 294–305, 1996.
13. M. Theobald, G. Weikum, and R. Schenkel. Top-k query evaluation with probabilistic guarantees. In *Proc. of Intl. Conf. on Very Large Data Bases (VLDB)*, pages 648–659, 2004.
14. P. Tsaparas, T. Palpanas, Y. Kotidis, N. Koudas, and D. Srivastava. Ranked join indices. In *Proc. of Intl. Conf. on Data Engineering (ICDE)*, pages 277–288, 2003.
15. K. Yi, H. Yu, J. Yang, G. Xia, and Y. Chen. Efficient maintenance of materialized top-k views. In *Proc. of Intl. Conf. on Data Engineering (ICDE)*, pages 189–200, 2003.
16. H. Yu, H.-G. Li, P. Wu, D. Agrawal, and A. El Abbadi. Efficient processing of distributed top-k queries. Technical Report 2005-14, University of California at Santa Barbara, http://www.cs.ucsb.edu/research/trcs/docs/2005-14.pdf, 2005.
17. G. K. Zipf. *Human Behaviour and the Principle of Least Effort: an Introduction to Human Ecology.* Addison-Wesley, 1949.

Evaluating Mid-(k, n) Queries Using B$^+$-Tree*

Dongseop Kwon, Taewon Lee, and Sukho Lee

School of Electrical Engineering and Computer Science,
Seoul National University, Seoul 151-742, Korea
{dongseop, taewon}@gmail.com, shlee@snu.ac.kr

Abstract. Traditional database systems assume that clients always consume the results of queries from the beginning. In various new applications especially in WWW, however, clients frequently need a small part of the result from the middle, e.g. retrieving a page in a bulletin board in WWW. To process this partial retrieval, traditional database systems should find all the records and discard unnecessary ones. Although several algorithms for top-k queries have been proposed, there has been no research effort for partial retrieving from the middle of an ordered result. In this paper, we define a mid-(k,n) query, which retrieves n records from the kth record of an ordered result. We also propose an efficient algorithm for mid-(k,n) queries using a slightly modified B$^+$-Tree, named the B^{+c}-Tree. We provide the theoretical analysis and the experimental results that the proposed technique evaluates mid-(k,n) queries efficiently.

1 Introduction

In various new applications such as WWW, the results of users' queries are generally huge. It is because users in these applications do not prefer to specify appropriate predicates or they just want to look over all the data to find useful information.

For example, a lot of web sites provide online bulletin boards or archives of articles. In many cases, those bulletin boards are so huge that they have millions of articles which have been archived for years. Since they cannot display all articles in one web page, they display only several of the articles as a page, and provide links to access other pages. With these links, users can directly access any page they want. From the viewpoint of a server, all pages are randomly requested because there are numerous requests from users simultaneously and the WWW uses a connectionless protocol. Therefore, retrieving the kth record efficiently becomes important and essential especially in the WWW environments. Naïve or tricky solutions are commonly used for this problem at present, such as retrieving all and skipping unnecessary part, or using complicated subqueries.

Although there are several works on top-k queries, there has been no research effort for this partial retrieval from the middle of an ordered result, as far as we

---

* This work was supported in part by the Brain Korea 21 Project and in part by the Ministry of Information & Communications, Korea, under the Information Technology Research Center (ITRC) Support Program in 2005.

know. In this paper, we define a *mid-(k, n) query* as a query for retrieving n records from the kth record of an ordered result. In addition, we propose an efficient processing algorithm for mid-(k, n) queries using a slightly modified B$^+$-Tree[1], named the B^{+c}-Tree. Each pointer of an internal node of a B^{+c}-Tree keeps the number of leaf records in its subtree. Using this additional information, the B^{+c}-Tree evaluates mid-(k, n) queries efficiently. We present the theoretical analysis of the cost of the B^{+c}-Tree and the experimental results that the proposed technique outperforms the B$^+$-Tree.

The rest of this paper is organized as follows: In Section 2, we review related work. Section 3 defines mid-(k, n) queries and naïve solutions. In Section 4, we propose the B^{+c}-Tree for the efficient processing of mid-(k, n) queries. We analyze the cost of the B^{+c}-Tree in Section 5. Section 6 presents the experimental results to compare our technique with the B$^+$-Tree. Finally, Section 7 concludes the paper.

2 Related Work

As far as we know, there has been no research effort for mid-(k, n) queries. Top-k queries and quantile queries are possible candidates that can be available for processing mid-(k, n) queries. In this section, we review evaluation techniques for these two types of queries, and present the problems of these techniques for using mid-(k, n) queries.

2.1 Top-k Queries

There are several research work for top-k queries. Carey and Kossmann [2] present a method to limit the cardinality of a query result by adding the 'STOP AFTER' clause to a simple SQL, and propose efficient processing strategies for 'STOP AFTER' queries. Donjerkovic and Ramakrishnan [3] propose a probabilistic approach to optimize the top-k query processing. Chaudhuri and Gravano [4] propose a technique that translate a top-k query into a single range query using multi-dimensional histograms. Chen and Ling [5] propose a sampling-based method to translate a top-k query to a range query. However, all these techniques cannot be adopted for mid-(k, n) queries directly. The only naïve way is retrieving all the result of a top-k query which includes all the result of a mid-(k, n) query, and skipping all the unnecessary records from the beginning, which is greatly inefficient unless k is very small.

2.2 Quantile Queries

Theoretically, A quantile query, which is the problem of selecting selecting the ith order statistic from N elements, can be solved in $O(N)$ time bound in average case [6]. There are also several research works [7,8] for quantile queries for database systems. However, quantile queries are different from general mid-(k, n) queries, because mid-(k, n) queries have to retrieve a set of records from the kth to the $(k+n-1)^{th}$ instead of retrieving the kth record only. Of course, the algorithms for quantile queries can be used for mid-(k, n) queries with a little extension. However, the algorithms for quantile queries need to read all data at least once, since they are designed for the case of no-index. Therefore, they are not efficient for large volumes of data. Our proposed algorithm can evaluate mid-(k, n) queries more efficiently because it uses an index on the data.

3   Mid-(k, n) Queries

We define a **mid-(k, n) query** as a query that retrieves n records from the kth. The semantic of mid-(k, n) queries can be expressed by using the 'LIMIT n OFFSET k' clause, which are supported in PostgreSQL 7.4.7.

For example, the following query is for accessing *pageNo* page directly in an online bulletin board, where one page has *pageSize* articles.

```
SELECT * FROM BULLETIN1 ORDER BY wdate DESC
LIMIT pageSize OFFSET (pageNo-1) × pageSize
```

A naïve way to process mid-(k, n) queries is to sort all the records and to skip unnecessary records from the beginning until the kth. One possible alternative way is that a system executes a top-$(k + n)$ query instead of a mid-(k,n) query and discards the first $k - 1$ records. However, it is greatly inefficient unless k and n are small. In general cases, there is no efficient way to process mid-(k, n) queries.

In this paper, therefore, we propose an efficient algorithm for mid-(k, n) queries with some restrictions as follows: (1) There is an index on the columns which are used in the 'ORDER BY' clause. (2) Only the columns used in the 'ORDER BY' clause can appear in the 'WHERE' clause. As we mentioned in Section 1, many web applications often use only one sorting order. For this case, the first restriction is quite reasonable as a way of tuning the performance. In addition, the second restriction is also very common because users do not specify any search predicates in most cases. Therefore, our approach is useful for various applications especially in WWW.

4 B^{+c}-Tree

In this section, we give the detailed description about our proposed technique, the B^{+c}-Tree. The main difference between the B^{+c}-Tree and the B^{+}-Tree is that the B^{+c}-Tree keeps an additional count information with each pointer in the internal nodes. In the original B^{+}-Tree, an internal node has m child pointers and $m - 1$ keys. In the B^{+c}-Tree, as depicted in Figure 1, each pointer has the number of records in the leaf nodes of its subtree. For example, since the first leaf node has 2 records, the pointer pointing to the leaf node has a record count of 2. The first pointer of the root node has a record count of 7 because its subtree has 7 records in its leaf nodes. This record count can be maintained during an insertion and a deletion of a record. From now on, we will use PTR, KEY and

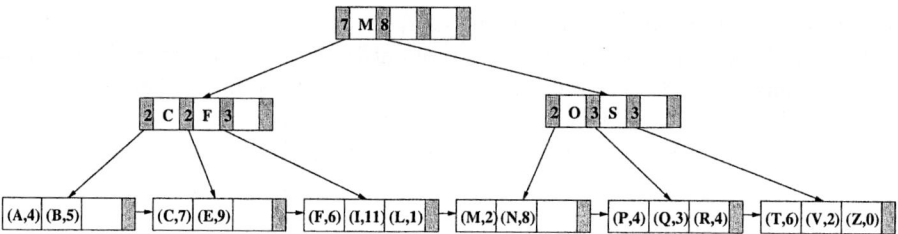

Fig. 1. An example of the B^{+c}-Tree

CNT to represent a pointer, a key and a record count, respectively. The range query is processed in the same way in both of the trees. By using the CNT values, the B^{+c}-Tree performs mid-(k, n) query more efficiently.

Now, we will present the algorithms for the mid-(k, n) query and the insertion and deletion of a record in the B^{+c}-Tree.

4.1 Algorithm for Mid-(k, n) Queries

For the convenience of the explanation, we divide mid-(k, n) queries into two classes.

- queries without search predicate
- queries with search predicates

For simplicity, we first describe two examples for each query class, and then present the detailed algorithm. Suppose there are the B^+-Tree and the B^{+c}-Tree with increasing order on the data records.

Example 1. Suppose a mid-$(9,1)$ query is given. To find out the 9th record from the ordered result, the B^+-Tree has to start to find from the first lead without any traversal from the root. Since the 9th record is located in the 4th leaf node, the B^+-Tree follows the pointers to a next leaf nodes until it reaches the 4th leaf node. Therefore, it needs 4 disk accesses.

The B^{+c}-Tree, as depicted in Figure 1, can utilize the CNT values to find the 9th record. By looking at the first entry of the root node, the B^{+c}-Tree can guess that there are 7 records in the first subtree of the root node. Therefore, there is no need to go to the first subtree. The B^{+c}-Tree follows the second pointer, and then examines the CNT values in that node. Since the CNT value for the first pointer is 2, the B^{+c}-Tree knows that the 9th record is in the first child of the node. Therefore, after following the first pointer to get to the leaf, The B^{+c}-Tree can find the 9th record. It requires 3 disk accesses. We can save 1 disk access in this case.

Example 2. Suppose there is a search predicate given with mid-$(5,1)$ query. Let the search predicate as 'D$\leq$ key $\leq$T'.

Since the query is to find the 5th record with a range predicate, we cannot use the CNT values in the B^{+c}-Tree directly. We first should know the position

Algorithm 1: Mid-(k, n) query

Function Mid-(k, n) $(range, start, limit)$
begin
    $pos \leftarrow$ GetPosition $(range)$
    $Result \leftarrow \emptyset, S \leftarrow 0, N \leftarrow$ the root node of the B^{+c}-Tree
    while N *is an internal node* **do**
        find the first entry e_i that satisfies $S + \sum_{n=0}^{i} CNT_n >= start - pos$
        $S \leftarrow S + \sum_{n=0}^{i-1} CNT_n$
        $N \leftarrow$ child node pointed to by PTR_i
    endw
    $R \leftarrow (start - pos - S)^{th}$ record of N
    while $|Result| < limit$ *and* R *in range* **do**
        $Result \leftarrow Result \cup R$
        $R \leftarrow$ next record
    endw
    return $Result$;
end

Algorithm 2: Getting the poisition of the lower bound predicate

Function GetPosition $(range)$
begin
    if *range has lower bound* **then**
        $R_f \leftarrow$ the smallest record in the range
        $pos \leftarrow$ position of R_f in the ordered result of all the records
    else
        $pos \leftarrow 0$
    endif
    return pos
end

of D. During the original key lookup process in the B^+-Tree, the B^{+c}-Tree can calculate the number of records whose key is less than D. In this example, we can find out that there is 3 records whose key is less than D. Therefore, in this case, we have to find 8th record as the same way as in Example 1.

The algorithm for mid-(k, n) queries is described in detail in Algorithm 1. Note that if there is no search predicate or no lower bound in a search predicate, we can directly go to the record at the desired position like Example 1. If there is a search predicate, first we have to find the position of the lower bound of the predicate.

If there is a search predicate and it has lower bound, the B^{+c}-Tree always have to traverse the tree twice from the root to a leaf. On the contrast, the B^+-Tree should retrieve not only all nodes in a path from the root to a leaf, but also all the leaf nodes from the leaf to the leaf node where the kth records is located.

Algorithm 2 is for finding the position of the lower bound record in this case.

Table 1. Notation

symbol	meaning
α	the average fill-factor of a node
h	the height of a tree
S_{page}, S_{header}, S_{record}, S_{key}, $S_{pointer}$, S_{count}	the size of a disk page, a header of a node, a record, a key (KEY), a pointer (PTR), and a record count (CNT), respectively
n_{record}	the number of records in a leaf node
M_{int}, M_{leaf}	the maximum number of pointers in an internal node, and records in a leaf node, respectively
C_{insert}, C_{delete}, C_{search}, C_{mid-k}	the number of disk access for an insert query (in case of no overflow), for a delete query (in case of no underflow), for an exact matching query, and for a mid-k query, respectively

4.2 Algorithm for Inserting and Deleting a Record

In this section, we describe the algorithms of the insertion and deletion for the B^{+c}-Tree.

To insert a record, we should choose a leaf node N where the search key value would appear. To keep correct CNT values, we should increase each CNT in the path from the root to N by one during the insertion. If a node is full, we should split it into two nodes. After the splitting, we should adjust the CNT value of each PTR in the parent node.

Deleting a record can be performed in the similar way of the insertion, except that we decrease each CNT values in the path from the root to the leaf where the deleted key exists by one. If we should merge two nodes, we can add up the CNT values of the pointers to the two nodes being merged.

5 Analysis

We now analyze the cost of the B^+-Tree and the B^{+c}-Tree in terms of the number of disk accesses. The notation used in this section is summarized in Table 1.

5.1 Cost of the B^+-Tree

Lemma 1. *The maximum cardinalities of an internal node and a leaf node of a B^+-Tree are as follows:*

$$M_{int} = \lfloor \frac{(S_{page} - S_{header} + S_{key})}{(S_{key} + S_{pointer})} \rfloor$$

$$M_{leaf} = \lfloor \frac{(S_{page} - S_{header} - S_{pointer})}{S_{record}} \rfloor$$

Proof. An internal node in a B^+-Tree consists of a header, M_{int} pointers, and $(M_{int} - 1)$ keys. If a node is to be stored in a disk page, the size of a node cannot be bigger than the size of a disk page. Therefore $S_{header} + (M_{int} -$

1) $\cdot S_{key} + M_{int} \cdot S_{pointer} \leq S_{page}$. From this, $M_{int} \leq \frac{(S_{page} - S_{header} + S_{key})}{(S_{key} + S_{pointer})}$. Since M_{int} is the maximum integer value that satisfy the previous equation, $M_{int} = \lfloor \frac{(S_{page} - S_{header} + S_{key})}{(S_{key} + S_{pointer})} \rfloor$.

A leaf node consists of a header, M_{leaf} records and a pointer to the following leaf node. Therefore, as the same manner, M_{leaf} is $\lfloor \frac{(S_{page} - S_{header} - S_{pointer})}{S_{record}} \rfloor$.

Lemma 2. *The height of a B^+-Tree is as follows:*

$$h = \log_{(\alpha \cdot M_{int})}(\lceil \frac{n_{record}}{\alpha \cdot M_{leaf}} \rceil)$$

Proof. If the average fill-factor of a node is α, a leaf node has the average $\alpha \cdot M_{leaf}$ data records. Therefore the B^+-Tree has $\lceil \frac{n_{record}}{\alpha \cdot M_{leaf}} \rceil$ leaf nodes. An internal node has the average $\alpha \cdot M_{int}$ pointers. Therefore, from these values, the height of a B^+-Tree is $\log_{(\alpha \cdot M_{int})}(\lceil \frac{n_{record}}{\alpha \cdot M_{leaf}} \rceil)$.

Theorem 1. *If there is no overflow during the insertion and no underflow during the deletion, cost of the B^+-Tree are as follows:*

$$C_{insert} = h + 1, \quad C_{delete} = h + 1, \quad C_{search} = h, \quad C_{mid-k} = h + \lceil \frac{k}{\alpha \cdot M_{leaf}} \rceil$$

Proof. To insert a record, we first find the leaf node that the inserted item can be stored. For this, it is necessary to read h disk pages. Then, it needs to 1 disk page for storing the item in the leaf. Therefore, C_{insert} is $h + 1$. C_{delete} is the same as C_{insert}. To process a exact matching query, it needs to read h disk pages from the root to a leaf. Therefore, C_{search} is h. Finally, to process a mid-(k, n) query, we first perform 1 exact matching query if a low bound is specified, and then read k records sequentially. Since k records is stored in $\lceil \frac{k}{\alpha \cdot M_{leaf}} \rceil$ disk pages, C_{mid-k} is $h + \lceil \frac{k}{\alpha \cdot M_{leaf}} \rceil$.

5.2 Cost of the B^{+c}-Tree

With the similar way to the B^+-Tree, cost of the B^{+c}-Tree is as follows:

Lemma 3. *The maximum cardinalities of an internal node and a leaf node of a B^{+c}-Tree are as follows:*

$$M_{int} = \lfloor \frac{(S_{page} - S_{header} + S_{key})}{(S_{key} + S_{pointer} + S_{count})} \rfloor$$

$$M_{leaf} = \lfloor \frac{(S_{page} - S_{header} - S_{pointer})}{S_{record}} \rfloor$$

Lemma 4. *The height of a B^{+c}-Tree is as follows:*

$$h = \log_{(\alpha \cdot M_{int})}(\lceil \frac{n_{record}}{\alpha \cdot M_{leaf}} \rceil)$$

Theorem 2. *If there is no overflow during the insertion and no underflow during the deletion, cost of the B^{+c}-Tree are as follows:*

$$C_{insert} = 2h, \quad C_{delete} = 2h, \quad C_{search} = h, \quad C_{mid-k} = 2h$$

Proof. For the insertion, the B^{+c}-Tree finds a leaf node and writes the inserted record into the leaf, same as the B^+-Tree. Then, since the counters in the internal nodes from the leaf to the root should be adjusted, it needs additional $h-1$ disk writes. Therefore, C_{insert} is $(h+1)+(h-1)=2h$. C_{delete} is the same as C_{insert}. The algorithm for exact matching queries of the B^{+c}-Tree is the same as that of the B^+-Tree. Therefore, C_{search} is h. Finally, to process a mid-(k,n) query, one traversal from the root to a leaf as same as the B^+-Tree is required if a lower bound is specified. Then, we need one more traversal from the root to a leaf in order to find the kth records. Therefore, C_{mid-k} is $h+h=2h$.

Note that the buffering effect of a disk cache is ignored in this analysis. If we ignore the buffering effect, we can say that the performance of the B^+-Tree for a mid-(k,n) query can be better than that of the B^{+c}-Tree when $\lceil \frac{k}{\alpha \cdot M_{leaf}} \rceil < h$, which means k is very small. With disk caches, however, the cost of the second traversal is ignorable because most of the accessed disk pages in the second traversal are the same as those in the first traversal. Therefore, the cost of the B^{+c}-Tree for mid-(k,n) queries is almost same as that of the B^+-Tree even in case of small k, like the experimental result shown in Section 6. For the same reason, the cost of insertions or deletions of the B^{+c}-Tree is almost same as that of the B^+-Tree when disk caches are used.

6 Experiments

In this section, we present the result of an experimental study to show the validity and the effectiveness of our approach. We have implemented a disk based B^+-Tree and B^{+c}-Tree on a 1GHz linux machine with 768MB main memory.

In the implementation, we directly managed the LRU buffer. We used 4KB disk pages for buffer cache. Each key and pointer occupy 4 bytes respectively. CNT size is 4 bytes. Therefore in the B^+-Tree, an internal node can contain about 510 pointers and in the B^{+c}-Tree, it can contain about 340 pointers.

Since the distribution of data does not affect our experiment, we used uniformly distributed data for the key values. We generated 1,000,000 data records for both of the trees. From now on, if there is no mention on the buffer cache size, we used 100 4KB-buffer pages which is about 5% of the total nodes in B^+-Tree.

6.1 Overheads of the B^{+c}-Tree

In this experiment, we inserted varying number of data records into both trees and compared the total disk I/Os. As shown in Figure 2(a), without the buffer cache, the B^{+c}-Tree requires about 1.5 times more disk accesses than B^+-Tree. However, as shown in Figure 2(b), if the buffer cache is used, there is almost

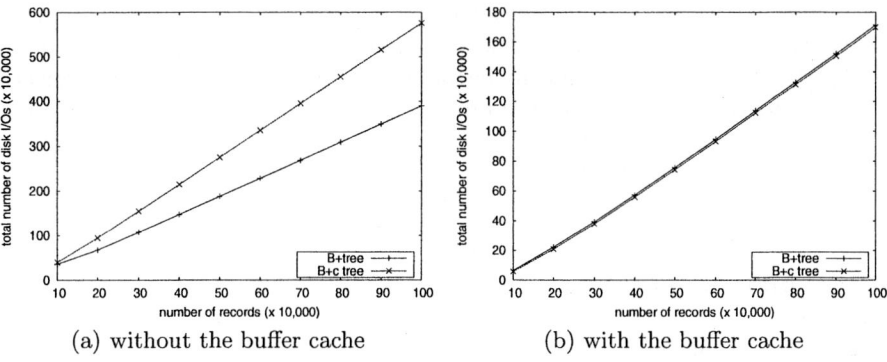

Fig. 2. Insertion cost with varying number of records

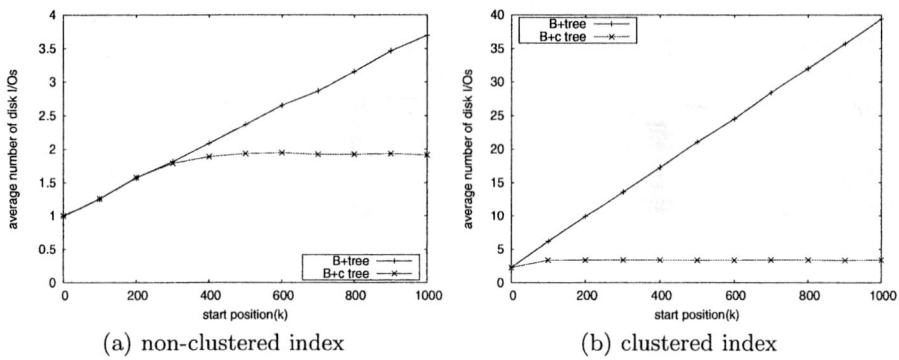

Fig. 3. Mid-(k, n) query cost with varying k

no difference between the two trees. It is because top level nodes are almost always in the cache which decreases the overhead of the B^{+c}-Tree as described in Section 5. Like the result of the insertion cost with the buffer cache, there is also no difference between the range query costs of the two trees. From these experimental results, we showed that the overhead of the B^{+c}-Tree is ignorable in spite of the additional record counts with the buffer cache.

6.2 Cost for Mid-(k, n) Queries

In this experiment, we performed mid-$(k, 20)$ queries with a non-clustered index and a clustered index. The reason why we used a clustered index here is that it is common to use a strong-clustered index in real applications as mentioned in Section 1. In the non-clustered index used in this experiment, a leaf node has 4-byte keys and 4-byte pointers. For the clustered index, we assumed a leaf node has a number of 4-byte keys and 100-byte sized tuples. We varied k from 0 to 1,000 in both experiments.

In Figure 3(a), the performance gap between the B^+-Tree and the B^{+c}-Tree grows larger from the point where k is about 300. Note that 300 is very small compared to the total number of records in the tree, which is 1,000,000 in this experiment. In the clustered index as in Figure 3(b), the performance of the B^{+c}-Tree is much better from the beginning. Since the B^{+c}-Tree is not affected by k as shown in Figure 3(b), the proposed technique is highly scalable so that it is appropriate for WWW applications.

Due to the buffering effect, the performance of the B^{+c}-Tree is almost same as that of the B^+-Tree in small k, as mentioned in Section 5.

7 Conclusion

Various new applications of database systems such as WWW have brought new needs of different kinds of queries which were not taken any notice in traditional database systems. One of those new kinds of queries is the mid-(k,n) query, which retrieves n records from the kth record of an ordered result. In this paper, we have addressed the problem of mid-(k, n) queries and have proposed an efficient algorithm for processing mid-(k, n) queries using a slightly modified B^+-Tree, named the B^{+c}-Tree. We also presented the theoretical analysis of the cost of the proposed method and provided experimental evidence that our approach outperforms the B^+-Tree. Future work includes extending this technique for supporting more complex cases of mid-(k, n) queries with several predicates.

References

1. Comer, D.: Ubiquitous b-tree. ACM Computing Surveys **11** (1979) 121–137
2. Carey, M.J., Kossmann, D.: Reducing the braking distance of an sql query engine. In: Proceedings of 24th Int'l. Conf. on Very Large Data Bases. (1998) 158–169
3. Donjerkovic, D., Ramakrishnan, R.: Probabilistic optimization of top n queries. In: Proceedings of 25th Int'l. Conf. on Very Large Data Bases. (1999) 411–422
4. Chaudhuri, S., Gravano, L.: Evaluating top-k selection queries. In: Proceedings of 25th Int'l. Conf. on Very Large Data Bases. (1999) 397–410
5. Chen, C.M., Ling, Y.: A sampling-based estimator for top-k query. In: Proceedings of the 18th Int'l. Conf. on Data Engineering. (2002) 617–627
6. Blum, M., Floyd, R.W., Pratt, V.R., Rivest, R.L., Tarjan, R.E.: Time bounds for selection. Journal of Computer and System Sciences **7** (1973) 448–461
7. Alsabti, K., Ranka, S., Singh, V.: A one-pass algorithm for accurately estimating quantiles for disk-resident data. In: Proceedings of 23rd Int'l. Conf. on Very Large Data Bases. (1997) 346–355
8. Manku, G.S., Rajagopalan, S., Lindsay, B.G.: Approximate medians and other quantiles in one pass and with limited memory. In: Proceedings of the 1998 ACM SIGMOD Int'l. Conf. on Management of Data. (1998) 426–435

On Effective E-mail Classification via Neural Networks

Bin Cui[1], Anirban Mondal[2], Jialie Shen[3], Gao Cong[4], and Kian-Lee Tan[1]

[1] Singapore-MIT Alliance, National University of Singapore
{cuibin, tankl}@comp.nus.edu.sg
[2] University of Tokyo Japan
anirban@tkl.iis.u-tokyo.ac.jp
[3] University of New South Wales Australia
jls@cse.unsw.edu.au
[4] The University of Edinburgh UK
gao.cong@ed.ac.uk

Abstract. For addressing the growing problem of junk E-mail on the Internet, this paper proposes an effective E-mail classifying and cleansing method in this paper. Incidentally, E-mail messages can be modelled as semi-structured documents consisting of a set of fields with pre-defined semantics and a number of variable length free-text fields. Our proposed method deals with both fields having pre-defined semantics as well as variable length free-text fields for obtaining higher accuracy. The main contributions of this work are two-fold. First, we present a new model based on the Neural Network (NN) for classifying personal E-mails. In particular, we treat E-mail files as a particular kind of plain text files, the implication being that our feature set is relatively large (since there are thousands of different terms in different E-mail files). Second, we propose the use of Principal Component Analysis (PCA) as a preprocessor of NN to reduce the data in terms of both size as well as dimensionality so that the input data become more classifiable and faster for the convergence of the training process used in the NN model. The results of our performance evaluation demonstrate that the proposed algorithm is indeed effective in performing filtering with reasonable accuracy.

1 Introduction

The ever-increasing number of Internet users coupled with the widespread proliferation of E-mail as one of the fastest and most economical forms of communication have resulted in dramatically increasing number of junk E-mails during the past few years. Consequently, users typically need to spend a non-trivial portion of their valuable time in order to delete junk E-mails. Additionally, junk E-mails can also fill up file server storage space quickly, especially at large sites with thousands of users, who may all be receiving duplicate copies of the same junk mail.

To address the problem of growing volumes of junk E-mails, automated methods for E-mail filtering are now beginning to be deployed in many commercial products, which typically allow users to define a set of logical rules for filtering junk E-mails. However, these solutions have two serious drawbacks. First, they require the users to be savvy enough to create a set of robust rules for E-mail filtering purposes. Second, they require the users to constantly tune and refine the filtering rules in response to the changes in junk E-mails over time. Understandably, the problem of filtering junk E-mails is challenging in practice due to the dynamically changing nature of junk E-mail and the tremendously large number of E-mails. In essence, an effective E-mail filter, which requires minimal manual work from the user, has now become a necessity.

The problem of dealing with junk E-mails has been extensively researched. Existing approaches to filtering junk E-mails involve the deployment of data mining techniques [6,7], the usage of E-mail addresses [9] and the application of text classification techniques [5,1]. In the realm of text classification, an E-mail message is viewed as a document and a judgement of its interestingness is viewed as a class label associated with the E-mail document. While text classification has been extensively researched [4,3,12], empirical study on the document type of E-mail and the features of building an effective personal E-mail filter within the framework of text classification has received relatively little attention. In this regard, the main contributions of this paper are two-fold:

1. We present a new model based on the Neural Network (NN) for classifying personal E-mails. In particular, we treat E-mail files as a specific kind of plain text files, the implication being that our feature set is relatively large (since there are thousands of different terms in different E-mail files).
2. We propose the use of Principle Component Analysis (PCA) as a preprocessor of NN to reduce the data in terms of both size and dimensionality so that the input data becomes more classifiable. This facilitates fast convergence of the training process used in the NN model. Notably, PCA only pre-processes the input to NN.

The results of our extensive performance evaluation on a *real* dataset of personal E-mails demonstrate that our proposed method is indeed effective in providing reasonable performance in terms of recall, precision and total accuracy rate, especially for *interesting* E-mails. To our knowledge, this is the first work on E-mail classification that uses a neural network-based strategy for classifying E-mails. The remainder of the paper is organized as follows. Section 2 discusses existing related works, while Section 3 provides the details of our design for the NN method to classify E-mails. Section 4 reports the results of our performance evaluation. Finally, we conclude in Section 5 with directions for future work.

2 Related Work

This section reviews related works in the area of junk E-mail filtering [2,5,13], Neural Networks [8] and Principle Component Analysis [10].

The Bayesian approach to filtering junk E-mail [13] considered domain specific features as well as the raw text of E-mail messages and enhanced the performance of a Bayesian classifier by hand-crafting and incorporating many features that are indicative of junk E-mail. Representing each individual message as a binary vector, the proposal in [13] detects junk mail in a straightforward manner using a given pre-classified set of training messages. In [2], the authors compare methods for learning text classifiers focussing on the kinds of classification problems that might arise in filtering personal E-mail messages. In [5], the E-mail documents to be classified are regarded as semi-structured textual documents comprising two parts. While one part is a set of structured fields with well-defined semantics, the other is a number of variable-length sections of free text. However, not many text classifiers take both portions into consideration. Additionally, conventional classification techniques may not be effective when dealing with variable-length free text. Notably, our work differs from the proposals in [2,5,13] in that these works focus on language processing, while we focus on general electronic text classification.

Neural networks [8,11] have been widely adopted in various fields of applications such as pattern recognition and identification. A neural network consists of simple elements i.e., the neurons operating in parallel and the connections between them. The training of a neural network is to adjust the weights of the connections for minimizing the difference between the output of the neural network and the target of the training data. We adopt the supervised back-propagation neural network in our E-mail classification system. The advantage of a neural network arises from its computing power (due to its massively parallel distributed structure), its ability to learn and more importantly, its capability to generalize. We only need to design the network structure and then input the training data. The results may be affected by the selection of the network structure and the input attributes, the training data and the stopping criteria.

PCA [10] is a widely used method for applications in signal/image filtering and pattern classification. It can transform data in the original space into another feature space, reduce the dimensionality of the input data, while keeping the most significant information. It examines the variance structure in the dataset and determines the directions along which the data exhibits high variance. The first principal component accounts for as much of the variability in the data as possible, and each succeeding component accounts for as much of the remaining variability as possible. Working as a pre-processor of neural networks, it can make the input data more classifiable and reduce the dimensionality of the training and validation dataset by using only the first several features, thereby speeding up the convergence of the training process.

3 System Design

This section discusses the design of our proposed system.

3.1 Model of NN for E-mail Classification

This section discusses how the NN method is used for E-mail filtering. The processing via the NN method involves three steps, namely *data pre-processing*, *training* and *testing*, as depicted in Figure 1. The $Feature\ Extraction$ refers to the data pre-processing, the details concerning which will be discussed shortly. For the training dataset, once we obtain the selected features, we feed them into the neural network and generate an E-mail classifier. For each test E-mail, we use the classifier to verify the efficiency of NN model. We adopt the error Back-propagation training algorithm in our model since it is one of the simplest as well as one of the most useful neural network algorithms.

Now let us discuss the method used for presenting data to the network for training as well as for testing. We employ cross-validation and early stopping. The available data is divided into the following three disjoint sets:

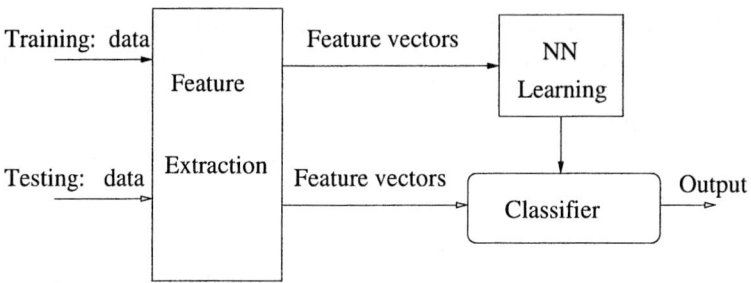

Fig. 1. The overview of NN method

1. Training set: This data is used to train the network.
2. Validation set: The error of the network averaged over this data is used to decide when the training algorithm has found the best approximation to the data without overfitting.
3. Testing set: The best network, determined by the validation test, is applied to the test set and the performance over the test set is given.

Training is accomplished by calculating the derivative of the network's error with respect to each weight in the network when presented a particular input pattern. This derivative indicates which direction each weight should be adjusted to reduce the error. Each weight is modified by taking a small step in this direction. With a nonzero momentum factor, a fraction of the previous weight change is added to the new weight value. Notably, this accelerates learning in some cases. The patterns in the training set are traversed one-by-one. A pass through all the training patterns is called an *epoch*. The training data is repetitively presented for multiple epochs, until a specified number of epochs have been reached. After each epoch, the error of the network applied to the validation set of patterns is calculated. If the current network scores the lowest error so far on the validation set, this network's weights are saved. At the conclusion of training, the network's best weights are used to calculate the network's error on the testing set.

Data Pre-processing. In general, E-mail messages are semi-structured documents that possess a set of structured fields with predefined semantics and a number of variable-length free text fields. The headers of E-mails are structured fields and usually contain information pertaining to the document, such as sender, date, domain etc. The major contents of the E-mail are variable-length free text fields, such as subject and the body. Understandably, both the structured fields and the free text portion could contain important information which could help in determining the class to which an E-mail belongs. Therefore, an effective classifier should be able to include features from both the structured fields and the free text. To make optimal use of the information in an E-mail message, we generate two kinds of features for each E-mail which we use in our NN model. The details are as follows.

Structured features: Features represented by structured fields in the header part of an E-mail document. In our model, seven structured features were generated.

- **Attachment:** Attachment occurs in the E-mail, true; else false.
- **Content type:** If the content type of E-mail is "plain text', true; else false.
- **Sender Domain:** We extract the sender domain from E-mail header, if it contains "edu", 1; contains "com" 2; else 3.
- **FW:** "Subject" of E-mail header starts with word "FW", true; else false.
- **Re:** "Subject" of E-mail header starts with word "Re", true; else false.
- **To group:** The E-mail is sent to a group, not a single person, true; else false.
- **CC.** The content of "CC" in the header of E-mails is not empty, true; else false.

Textual features: We use general text processing method for dealing with the textual features. The terms occurring in the body of a given E-mail and in the "Subject" of the E-mail are extracted and pre-processed, and are regarded as the features of the body of E-mails. We use Document Frequency Threshold to remove those features that have little influence on classification work. Finally, the feature values of the terms are the term weights calculated by the simple $idf.tf$ method. We also use Document Frequency Threshold to remove some features that have little influence on classification work. The threshold should not be too low since we should try to find fewer important features for NN according to the characteristic of NN itself.

Training of NN Model. With the results of data pre-processing, we can do the training and generate a classifier to filter the $uninteresting$ E-mail.

1. After processing both the header and body of all the training E-mail samples, a 2-D array of feature vector is obtained for $interesting$ and $uninteresting$ E-mails. The feature vector includes the features extracted from both the header as well as the body of the E-mails. The class labels of the E-mails are also recorded in a 2-D array. Class label is "1" for $interesting$ E-mails and "0" for $uninteresting$ E-mails.
2. Use the Error Back-propagation algorithm for generating a classifier from the feature vectors and then the classifier is returned as a file.

Testing of NN Model. In this stage, we will test the efficiency of our classifier.

1. Generate the feature vector for the header of each E-mail, group the feature vector of header and body together for each E-mail, and form a complete feature vector for each E-mail. The process is same as training part.
2. According to the feature vector generated for each new E-mail, use classifier, which has been built in training stage, to compute the output score for each E-mail. If the score > threshold (specified by the users), this E-mail can be regarded as the $interesting$ E-mail, or else $uninteresting$ E-mail.

3.2 Principal Component Analysis

Finding principal components (PCs) is basically a mathematical problem of finding the principal singular vectors of the input dataset using the well-known singular value decomposition method. The PCA transformation has two steps. First, we do principal component analysis of the training and validation data set. In this step, we transform the training and validation dataset into the singular vector space and get the eigenvectors and eigenvalues of each dimension. Second, we transform the testing data set into the same space as the training and validation data. This is done by simply multiplying it with the eigenvector matrix produced in the first step. In order to have some idea of the data after the PCA transformation, we plot the first two principal vectors of a training dataset with 747 features after transformation in Figure 2. The points are the vectors of the *interesting* E-mails, while the circles are the vectors of the *uninteresting* E-mails. From the figure, we observe that by using only the first *two* features, the vectors corresponding to the *interesting* and *uninteresting* E-mails can be distinguished relatively easily. Figure 3 depicts the eigenvalues of the principal components. It is clear that the first few eigenvalues are much more important than the later ones.

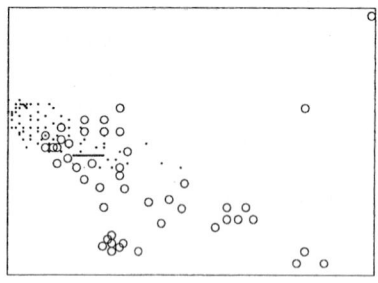

Fig. 2. Plotting of the first two *PC*s of the 747-features dataset

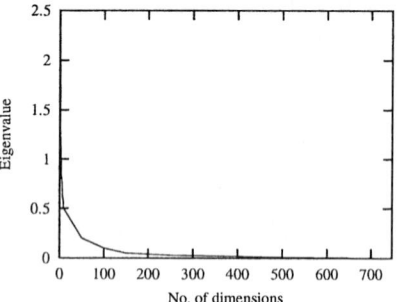

Fig. 3. Plotting of the eigenvalues of the 747-features dataset

4 Performance Evaluation

This section reports the performance evaluation of our proposed NN model for E-mail classification. All the experiments have been conducted on a SUN E450 machine with SUN OS 5.7. We have used a total of 2000 *real* personal E-mails as the dataset for our experiments. Notably, a dataset of 2K E-mails is considered large in our context primarily because of the difficulty associated with the collection of personal E-mails. We manually label each E-mail as *interesting* or *uninteresting* i.e., E-mails are divided into two classes for our experiments. For the dataset used in our experiments, the number of *interesting* E-mails and the number of *uninteresting* E-mails were 1500 and 500 respectively. During the experiments, the whole dataset was divided into three portions *randomly*, namely training data, validation data and testing data. While the training data is used to train a classifier, the validation data scores the error of training and provides the best model, which is then classified by the testing data.

We have used *precision* and *recall* as the metrics for evaluating the performance of our proposed E-mail classification approach because all the methods provide very fast response. Although the training stage of NN is time-consuming, the filtering stage of NN is extremely efficient and typically requires less than one second, hence we do not present response time as a metric in this paper. The definitions of recall and precision for *interesting* and *uninteresting* E-mails are quite similar. Here, we provide the definition for *interesting* E-mails only: $recall = \frac{N_{ii}}{N}$, $precision = \frac{N_{ii}}{N_i}$; where N is the number of total *interesting* E-mails, N_i is the number of E-mails classified as *interesting*, and N_{ii} is the number of *interesting* E-mails classified as *interesting*.

The output of neural network is a float from 0 to 1, and we classify an E-mail as *interesting* only when the output is greater than some pre-defined threshold. We label the *interesting* E-mail "1" and *uninteresting* E-mail "0", hence when we test the E-mail, the output of *interesting* E-mail approaches "1" and the output of *uninteresting* E-mail approaches "0" if we make a correct classification. Initially, we set the threshold as a default value "0.5". In all the experiments, we set a large epoch number in the training stage and only use the best weights in testing phase.

4.1 Effect of Neuron Number

First, we test the effect of neuron number of our neural network model on the classification performance. Basically, the neural network model has two hidden layers, and we can tune the number of neurons in the both of hidden layers of the network. The neuron number in the first layer must be larger than 1; while the neuron number of the second layer can be 0, in this case the neural network has only one layer. Denote neuron pair as $n1/n2$, where $n1$ is the number of first layer neuron and $n2$ is the number of second layer neuron.

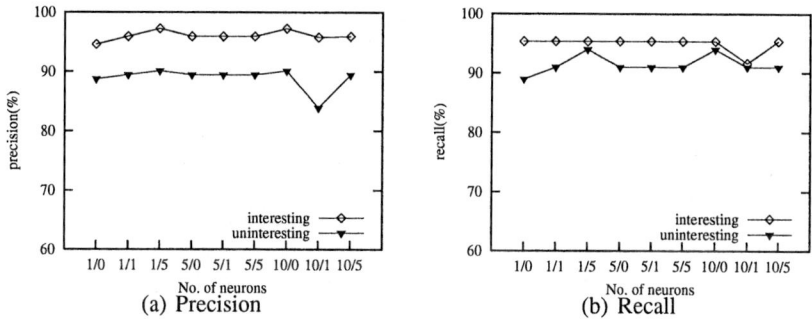

Fig. 4. Effect of neuron number on different layers

The first experiment aims at the performance of the classifier when different neuron pairs are used. The performance of NN of different neuron number is shown in Figure 4. 10 sets of features and 9 neuron pairs are used in our experiment to test which pair of neurons can perform well with high precision and high recall. For each neuron pair, Figure 4 (a) and (b) show the average precision and average recall of all these feature sets, respectively.

A few observations can be made from this experiment. First, the precision and recall curves of *interesting* E-mails are better than the ones of *uninteresting* E-mails no matter which neuron pair is used. Second, it is obvious that neuron pairs 1/5 and 10/0 can perform better than other neuron pairs for both the *interesting* E-mails and *uninteresting* E-mails. The average recall for both *interesting* and *uninteresting* E-mails is above 90%. Finally, it is easier for neural network to identify *interesting* E-mail files in our experiment. The reason could be that we select more *interesting* E-mail files than *uninteresting* ones. Hence they can be clearly characterized by some features.

In the following experiments, we will fix the structure of the NN model according to the performance shown in Figure 4. The NN has two hidden layers: the first layer has one neuron and the second layer has 5 neurons.

4.2 Effect of Feature Selection

As mentioned earlier, we extracted two kinds of features from E-mails, structured features and textual features. 8 structured features and up to 6000 textual features are generated for E-mail files. One question under exploration is how important these features are in E-mail classification. From the experiment, we can see how many features are better and enough to classify E-mails and how these features influence the recall, precision and accuracy rate of E-mail classification. The performance of NN for different feature selection is shown in Figure 5.

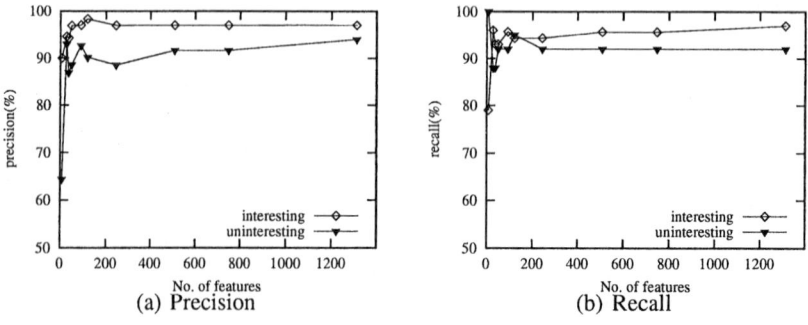

Fig. 5. Effect of feature selection

10 feature sets are selected to study the performance of NN classifier. The sizes of 10 feature sets are 8, 28, 37, 50, 92, 121, 243, 508, 747, and 1313 respectively. Each feature set consists of all 8 structured features and some textual features selected by $tf.idf$ formula. For example, 28 stands for 8 structured features plus 20 textual features.

Figure 5 presents the precision and recall of different features for *interesting* and *uninteresting* E-mails. The results show that the performance of classification is very unstable when the number of features we use is fewer than 200. Especially, when we only use structured features, the recall of *uninteresting* E-mails is surprisingly high, 100%; on the contrary, the recall of *interesting* E-mails is very low, 79%. However, the overall recall and precision for E-mail classification increase and become more stable when we use more features. With the number of features increasing, the accuracy rate increase gradually. From the figures, we can see that although 1313 features provide the best performance, the 508 features perform only a little worse and it can save more than half space to save the features and weights, and the execution time is less than half. So based on the figures, we select 508 features as an optimal strategy.

The results of the experiment show that the feature selection plays an important role in E-mail classification. We will use the PCA method to do the feature selection below and see how PCA influences the performance of classification more clearly.

4.3 Effect of PCA

The Performance of NN after PCA processing is shown in Figure 6. We use 1313 features of E-mail dataset, and do the principal component analysis and generate the new feature space with different dimensions (PCs).

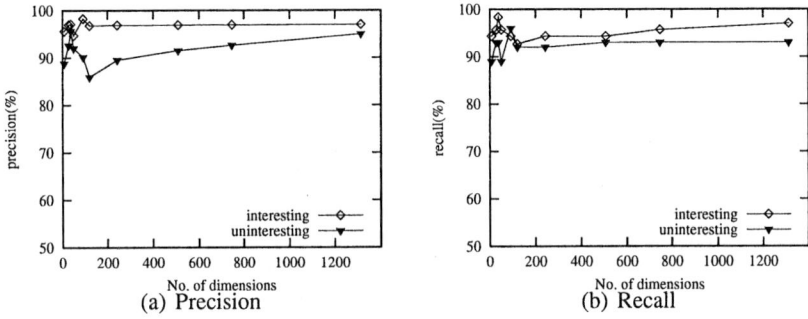

Fig. 6. Effect of PCA

Using PCA, most of the information in the original space is condensed into a few dimensions along which the variances in the data distribution are the largest. PCA method aims to transform the E-mail feature space into a new space there the first dimensions are more important, so we can easily select the more important features to do the classification effectively and efficiently. From the results, we can see that the average precision and recall rate is more than 93%, compared with about 85% when the PCA method is not used, for 8 features. Additionally, the number is low, say less than 200, the performance after PCA processing is more stable and better. Although in the second experiment, we select the most important words for each feature selection, the PCA can capture more information. When the number is 37, the performance is optimal and the space and time cost is only 10% of NN without PCA. Furthermore, we also find that fewer features selected by PCA can describe the characteristic of E-mails as well as the whole original features. It shows that adding many unimportant features does not necessarily enhance the performance of classification.

4.4 Comparison with other Schemes

We also compared our NN model with the decision tree and Naive Bayesian Classifier methods used in [5,13]. Because of different feature selections, we only compare the optimal performance for three methods. To simplify the comparison, we adopt the error rate, which is $\frac{number\ of\ false\ classification}{number\ of\ classfied\ messages}$. The error rate of proposed NN model is only 4%, which is more than 50% better than two competitive methods.

5 Conclusion

In examining the growing problem of dealing with junk E-mail, we provide NN model which embeds PCA as a preprocessor to eliminate junk E-mail from a user's mail stream. The efficiency of such filters can also be greatly enhanced by considering not only the full text of the E-mail messages, but also a set of structural features. Different ways of feature selection for the model were evaluated. Performance of the classifier was compared with respect to feature selection, parameter tuning and PCA processing. Our experiment results show that our models provide good performance in filtering junk E-mails. In the near future, we plan to incorporate other techniques (e.g., E-mail address analysis, real-time user feedback) into our proposed NN model. Moreover, we intend to examine the cost-effective integration of our E-mail classification scheme into existing E-mail systems.

References

1. X. Carreras and L. Marquez. Boosting trees for anti-spam email filtering. In Proc. Recent Advances in Natural Language Processing, 2001.
2. W. W. Cohen. Learning rules that classify e-mail. Proc. the AAAI Spring Symposium on Machine Learning in Information Access, 1996.
3. W.W. Cohen and Y. Singer. Context-sensitive learning methods for text categorization. Proc. SIGIR, 1996.
4. M. Craven, D. DiPasquo, D. Freitag, A. McCallum, T. Mitchell, K. Nigam, and S. Slattery. Learning to extract symbolic knowledge from the world wide web. Proc. the 15th National Conference on Artificial Intelligence, 1998.
5. Y. L. Diao, H. J. Lu, and D. K. Wu. A comparative study of classification based personal e-mail filtering. Proc. the 4th PAKDD, 2000.
6. T. Fawcett. in vivo spam filtering: A challenge problem for data mining. In KDD Explorations vol.5 no.2, 2003.
7. K. R. Gee. Using latent semantic indexing to filter spam. In ACM Symposium on Applied Computing, Data Mining Track, 2003.
8. S. Haykin. Neural networks: A comprehensive foundation. International Ed., Prentice-Hall, 2nd Ed, 1999.
9. J. Ioannidis. Fighting spam by encapsulating policy in email addresses. In Proc. Network and Distributed Systems Security Conference (NDSS), 2003.
10. I. T. Jolliffe. Principle Componet Analysis. Springer-Verlag, 1986.
11. S. Y. Kung. Digital neural networks. Prentice-Hall, 1993.
12. D. D. Lewis and M. Ringuette. A comparison of two learning algorithms for text categorization. Third Annual Symposium on Document Analysis and Information Retrieval,, 1994.
13. M. Sahami, S. Dumais, D. Heckerman, and E. Horvitz. A bayesian approach to filtering junk e-mail. Proc. AAAI Workshop Learning for Text Categorization, 1998.

An Adaptive Spreading Activation Scheme for Performing More Effective Collaborative Recommendation

Peng Han, Bo Xie, Fan Yang, and Rui-Min Shen

Department of Computer Science and Engineering, Shanghai Jiao Tong University,
Shanghai 200030, China
{phan, bxie, fyang, rmshen}@mail.sjtu.edu.cn

Abstract. While Spread Activation has shown its effectiveness in solving the problem of cold start and sparsity in collaborative recommendation, it will suffer a decay of performance (over activation) as the dataset grows denser. In this paper, we first introduce the concepts of Rating Similarity Matrix (RSM) and Rating Similarity Aggregation (RSA), based on which we then extend the existing spreading activation scheme to deal with both the binary (transaction) and the numeric ratings. After that, an iterative algorithm is proposed to learn RSM parameters from the observed ratings, which makes it automatically adaptive to the user similarity shown through their ratings on different items. Thus the similarity calculations tend to be more reasonable and effective. Finally, we test our method on the EachMovie dataset, the most typical benchmark for collaborative recommendation and show that our method succeeds in relieving the effect of over activation and outperforms the existing algorithms on both the sparse and dense dataset.

1 Introduction

Collaborative Filtering (CF) technique [2,6] has proved its ability of making good recommendations based on the opinions of people with similar interests. However, as most existing CF algorithms strongly depend on the user's ratings (explicit or implicit) on items to make recommendations, their performance will decay dramatically when the user has rated little items in the database which is called the new user or cold start problems in the CF area [12]. Furthermore, as the scale of web applications becomes larger and larger, the rating matrix tends to be very sparse. For example, EachMovie [9] and Movielens [8], two of the most popular datasets used in CF research, are respectively 97.6% and 95.8% sparse. So even the user seems to rate a relatively big number of items in the database, the overlap between him and other users may still be quite low, which consequently make the calculation of similarity difficult and less reliable.

Recently, there has been an increasingly effort to address the cold start and sparsity problem in CF related research. P. Massa [10] et al showed that by using trust propagation to infer an additional weight for other users, similar users are much reachable to each other than through correlated ratings. However, the problem is that the trust information itself is not easy to get. In fact, the user still needs to know other people's opinions (ratings) in order to establish a trust relationship between them. Z. Huang et al [7] made use of the transitive associations in user relationship to deal with the sparsity problem by introducing the concept of Spreading Activation (SA) into CF algorithms. They experimented with three spreading activation algorithms and found that the result significantly outperformed the current collaborative filtering approaches. However, their method only considers the binary (transaction) data, which prevents it from being applied to numeric ratings which is adopted in many popular applications such as Amazon [1]. Still, an "over activation" effect has also been observed in their methods which mean the performance of algorithm will decay when the dataset becomes dense.

In this paper, we present an adaptive spreading activation scheme which provides a more intuitive and effective framework for CF based recommendation. The contribution of this paper is twofold. First, we make an in-depth comparison and analysis between SA and existing similarity metrics and then introduce the concept of Rating Similarity Matrix (RSM) and Rating Similarity Aggregation (RSA) as a new user similarity metrics. Based on them, we provide a generalized similarity spreading scheme which could deal well with both the binary (transaction) and the numeric ratings. Second, we present an iterative algorithm to learn the RSM automatically from observed ratings. The experimental result on EachMovie dataset shows that our method succeeds in relieving the effect of over activation and outperforms the existing algorithms on both dealing with the sparse and dense dataset.

The remainder of the paper is organized as follows: In section 2, several related work has been discussed and an in-depth comparison and analysis between SA and existing similarity metrics has been made. In section 3, we introduce the basic algorithm framework of our similarity spreading scheme and present the iterative decay parameter algorithm in section 4. We conclude our work and present our consideration on future work in section 5

2 Related Work

2.1 Memory-Based Collaborative Filtering Algorithm

Memory-based Collaborative Filtering has first been proposed by P. Resnick and J. Riedl in GroupLens [11]. After that, it has become the most popular realization of CF for its simplicity and preferable performance. A memory-based CF algorithm uses a user×item rating matrix $\mathbf{V}$ as its input while each row of it represents a user record and each column represents a item. So each entry $v_{i,j}$ denotes the specific rating user i gives to item j. The key idea of it is to predict the active user's rating on certain item by calculating a weighted sum of other users' rating on that item as shown in eq. 1

$$P_{a,j} = \bar{v}_a + \kappa \sum_{i=1}^{N} \omega(a,i)(v_{i,j} - \bar{v}_i) \qquad (1)$$

Where $P_{a,j}$ denotes the prediction of the rating for active user a on item j and N is the number of users in user database. $\bar{v}_i$ is the mean rating of user i as calculated by eq. 2

$$\bar{v}_i = \frac{1}{|I_i|} \sum_{j \in I_i} v_{i,j} \qquad (2)$$

Where I_i is the set of items on which user i has voted. The weights $w(a,i)$ reflect the similarity between active user a and users i in the user database. κ is a normalizing factor to make the absolute values of the weights sum to unity. Two most used similarity metrics in CF are Pearson Correlation Coefficient and Vector Similarity displayed respectively as eq. 3 and eq. 4.

$$w(a,i) = \frac{\sum_j (v_{a,j} - \bar{v}_a)(v_{i,j} - \bar{v}_i)}{\sqrt{\sum_j (v_{a,j} - \bar{v}_a)^2 \sum_j (v_{i,j} - \bar{v}_i)^2}} \qquad (3)$$

$$w(a,i) = \sum_j \frac{v_{a,j}}{\sqrt{\sum_{k \in I_a} v_{a,k}^2}} \frac{v_{i,j}}{\sqrt{\sum_{k \in I_i} v_{i,k}^2}} \qquad (4)$$

2.2 Collaborative Filtering with Spreading Activation

Spreading Activation (SA) theory [4] has first been used in cognitive science and information processing. Huang [7] have tried to use SA on collaborative filtering. Its key idea is to describe the original user×item rating matrix through a graph model which represents each user and item as a node in the graph and uses edges to represent the relation between users and items. When making prediction for a specific user, the SA scheme first sets the node corresponding to that user as starting node and assigns it with an activation level. The scheme then spreads the activation level within the graph and activates other nodes iteratively. Finally, those item nodes with the highest activation level will be recommended to the active user. Here we use a simple example to illustrate the motivation of applying

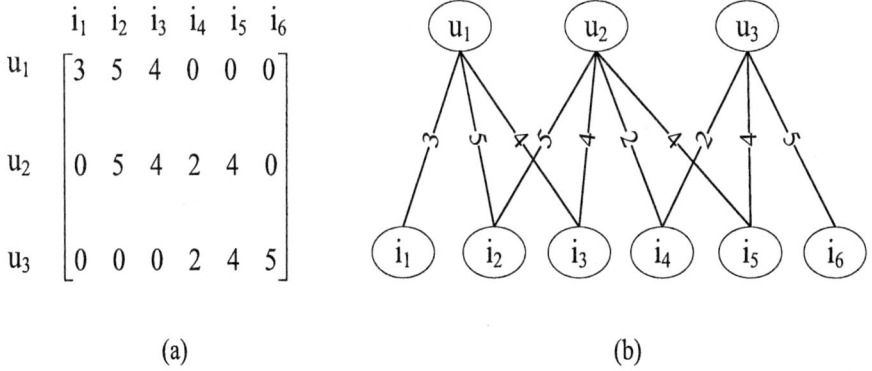

Fig. 1. (a) Original user × item rating matrix (b) Corresponding graph representation

SA to collaborative recommendation. Fig. 1-(a) and Fig. 1-(b) gives a rating matrix and its corresponding graph representation respectively.

Suppose we want to make recommendation for user u_1. Under the SA framework, the node representing u_1 will first be activated. After that, it will activate those item nodes which have direct relation with it such as i_1 and i_3 and these nodes will activate their adjacent nodes sequentially. This process will continue iteratively until certain constraint has been reached. For example relation between u_1 and i_6 can be found through path $u_1 - i_2 - u_2 - i_4 - u_3 - i_6$ which can not be discovered by standard memory-based CF algorithms since they only calculate the similarities between users who have common ratings. This ability makes SA framework especially effective in dealing with the cold start and sparsity problem in CF.

3 An Adaptive Spreading Activation Framework for Collaborative Recommendation

From the discussion above we can see that the key point of SA is a transitive activation process through which the similarity can spread within a graph model. In this section, we will present a more elaborate and adaptive spreading activation framework for collaborative recommendation to relieve the "over activation" effect.

3.1 A Unified SA Algorithm Framework for CF

Taking an in-depth look at the SA scheme we may find that the iterative activation is actually a similarity calculation process. For transaction dataset, the activation level a node can get from other node is the same as the common items they accessed multiplied by a certain decay factor. From this point of view, we give a more generalized similarity metrics for SA called Rating Similarity Aggregation (RSA) as eq. 5 shows:

$$\omega(a,i) = \sum_{j \in Co-Rated_{a,i}} RSM^j_{x,y} \qquad (5)$$

Here, $Co - Rated_{a,i}$ is the items rated by both user a and i while x and y is the ratings that they give to item j respectively. RSM^j is the Rating Similarity Matrix of item j and its entry $RSM^j_{x,y}$ denotes the similarity information we can get if we know two users gives ratings of x and y to item j respectively. For transaction dataset, each item's RSM is a 1×1 matrix which means if two users have both accessed (bought) a particular item, how much similarity information we can get. The semantic of RSA is that the similarity between two users should be the summation of their similarities shown on each common rated item. Compared with Pearson Correlation Coefficient and Vector Similarity, our new similarity metrics has the following two advantages:

1. Unlike other similarities, RSA differentiates each item through its own unique RSM which means ratings on different items will give unequal contributions

when calculation the similarity between users. For example, knowing two people both like the film "Matrix", which is a very popular film will not help us much to judge their similarity in tastes. A more exciting thing is RSM's ability in telling the meaning of different co_ratings patterns on the same item. Still taking the film "Matrix" for example, knowing two 1 point ratings from two users will have a totally different meaning from knowing a both 5 point ratings though they are both same rating patterns. As the two co_rating patterns will have different entries in "Matrix"'s RSM, we could differentiate them by assigning different value to it.
2. The calculation of RSA is an incremental process which means that the former result can be kept and reused. This makes the similarity updating much easier. Especially under those large scale and more dynamic environments, this characteristics will help to reduce a lot of calculation complexity. Still, the aggregation process helps to award those users who have more common ratings with the active users. On this point, RSA is more reasonable than traditional similarity metrics in which two users will be assigned a same similarity no matter they give one same rating with the active user or more.

Based on RSA, we present a unified SA algorithm framework for performing collaborative recommendation as follows which is based on a brand-and-bound architecture [3]:

Input:

User × Item Rating Matrix V : A $M \times N$ matrix, where M and N are the total number of users and items in the system respectively. $v_{i,j}$ is the rating user i gives to item j. For transaction dataset, $v_{i,j}$ equals one if user i has accessed (bought) item j, otherwise $v_{i,j}$ equals zero.

Rating Similarity Matrix, RSM : A unique symmetrical matrix for each item in the system, where $RSM^j_{x,y}$ denotes the similarity information we can get if we know two users give ratings of x and y to item j respectively.

Transitive Decay Factor, TDF : Used to decay the activation level during the spreading process in order to control the noise.

Activation Threshold, AT : Cease condition parameter. A node will stop spreading its similarity once its activation level is less than the AT value.

Algorithm Framework:

Initialization. Create an empty active node queue Q_{act}, temporary node queue Q_{temp} and output queue Q_{out}. Put the target user node into Q_{act} and assign it with an activation level value of 1. Set the current decay factor CDF to 1

Spreading Activation. Take out the nodes i in Q_{act} one by one, and calculate the similarity $\omega(i,j)$ between i and its neighbor nodes j through eq. 5. Here, the neighbor nodes mean those nodes which have common ratings with node *i*. Put node j in the Q_{temp} if it's not in it yet, otherwise, compare the current similarity value with the old one and use the bigger one as its new similarity value.

Normalization. Divide the similarities values of all the nodes in Q_{temp} by the highest one among them.

Decay. Multiply the similarities values of all the nodes in Q_{temp} by CDF.

Update. Empty the nodes in Q_{act}. For those nodes not in Q_{out}, insert them both into Q_{act} and Q_{out}. For those nodes already in Q_{out}, compare their similarity values in Q_{temp} and Q_{out} and use the bigger one as their current similarity values. At the same time, multiply the CDF by TDF.

Cease Control. Eliminate those nodes in current Q_{act} whose activation level is less than the AT value. If the Q_{act} is not empty, then go to the Spreading Activation step.

Prediction. Pick out the top 100 nodes in Q_{out} with the highest similarity value and predict the preference for target user using eq. 1

3.2 Iterative Rating Similarity Matrix Learning Algorithm

As we mentioned above, the introduction of RSM is the most important improvement we made on traditional similarity metrics. In this section, we will present an iterative algorithm which can learn the RSM for individual items from the observed ratings of users. Here, we use a very objective evaluation on the significance of common ratings on a certain item by calculating it as the average similarity between users who have these common ratings on that item. This idea can be formalized through eq.6

$$RSM_{x,y}^j = \frac{1}{\|R_x^j\|} \frac{1}{\|R_y^j\|} \sum_{s \in R_x^j} \sum_{t \in R_y^j} \omega(s,t) \qquad (6)$$

Where R_x^j and R_y^j denote the set of users who have give item j a rating of x and y, $\|R_x^j\|$ and $\|R_y^j\|$ is the size of them respectively.

As we can see from eq. 5 and eq. 6, the calculation of ω and RSM depend on each other. So this algorithm itself is iterative so that an initializing value should be assigned. In this paper, we deal with it by setting all the RSM to be an identity matrix at the beginning, which means that only the same ratings on certain item can contribute to similarity calculation. However, after several iterations, other entries can be learned automatically from the observed ratings of users and the initializing value can also be updated.

Based on the discussion above, the SA based CF algorithm framework can now be divided into two parts: RSM construction and similarity spreading activation. In the RSM construction phase, we will not consider the spreading effect and eq. 5 and eq. 6 will be used iteratively for certain times. As we can see from later experimental result, the RSM will converge and stabilize normally after 4-6 iterations. After the RSM has been constructed, we will then execute the algorithm framework presented in the previous section based on it.

4 Experimental Analysis

4.1 Data Set

In this paper, we use EachMovie data set [9], which is the most typical benchmark for collaborative recommendation, to evaluate the performance of our algorithm. The EachMovie data set is provided by the Compaq System Research Center, which ran the movie recommendation service for 18 months for experimenting collaborative filtering algorithms. The information they gathered during that period consists of 72,916 users, 1,628 movies, and 2,811,983 numeric ratings ranging from 0 to 5.

In order to test our SA algorithm framework in dense dataset, we pick out those users who have rated more than 60 items in the database which consists of near 6,000 user records. In our experiment, we name it as dense dataset and the original one as normal dataset respectively.

4.2 Metrics and Methodology

In our experiment, we use Mean Absolute Error (MAE), a statistical accuracy metrics which evaluates the accuracy of a predictor by comparing the predicted values with user-provided values, to compare the performance of our algorithms with traditional ones. The definition of MAE is given as eq. 7:

$$MAE = \frac{1}{\|A\|} \sum_{a \in A} \frac{\sum_{j \in T} |v_{a,j} - p_{a,j}|}{\|T\|} \quad (7)$$

Where $v_{a,j}$ is the actual rating user a gives to item j and $p_{a,j}$ is its predicted value. A and T is the active users set and test item set whose ratings are to be predicted while $\|A\|$ and $\|T\|$ is their size respectively. We select 500 users from the EachMovie as active users and pick out 500-5000 different user records as training set to predict the active users' rating step by step. We use both the Given-5 and All-But-One strategy [2] in our experiment. For Given-5 strategy, 5 ratings of each active user will be taken for granted as observed and other ratings will be put into T while for All-But-One strategy only one ratings will be put into T and all other ratings will be taken as already known. All the observed ratings and testing ratings has be drawn randomly.

4.3 Experimental Result and Analysis

In our first experiment, we use a same RSM generated by heuristic for every item in our SA based CF algorithm and compare its performance with standard CF algorithm thoroughly. The heuristic RSM is shown as follows:

$$\begin{pmatrix} 1.0 & 0.8 & 0.3 & 0.1 & 0 & 0 \\ 0.8 & 1.0 & 0.7 & 0.1 & 0 & 0 \\ 0.3 & 0.7 & 1.0 & 0.4 & 0.2 & 0.1 \\ 0.1 & 0.1 & 0.4 & 1.0 & 0.7 & 0.3 \\ 0 & 0 & 0.2 & 0.7 & 1.0 & 0.8 \\ 0 & 0 & 0.1 & 0.3 & 0.8 & 1.0 \end{pmatrix}$$

Fig. 4 and Fig. 5 show the result in normal dataset while applying Given-5 and All-But-One strategy respectively. Fig. 2 and Fig. 3 show the same result in dense dataset. From the result we can see that our SA based CF algorithm has outperformed the standard algorithm in all the four situations. Especially for the Given-5 strategy, which shows the performance of algorithm on new user situation, our algorithm shows a much better and stable performance as the size of training set increases. This illustrates the advantage of our SA based CF algorithm of exploring transitive relation between users compared with standard CF algorithm quite well.

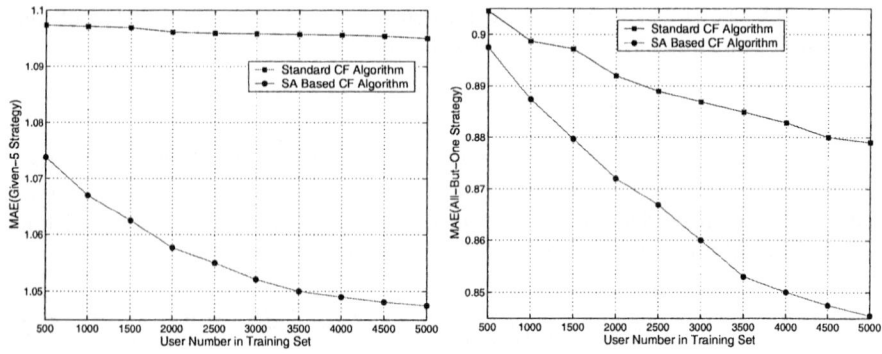

Fig. 2. Algorithm Prediction Accuracy Comparison(Dense Dataset)

Fig. 3. Algorithm Prediction Accuracy Comparison(Dense Dataset)

Still we can also find, our algorithm performs better than standard CF algorithm even under the dense dataset environment. This is caused by the difference between our algorithm and other SA scheme in the activation level updating phrase. Instead of summing up all the previous nodes' contribution, we only use the highest one which borrows its idea from the Maximum Capacity Paths [5] concept in social network theory. By doing so, we reduce the probability of introducing noise while keeping the most significant transitive association information.

Fig. 6 and Fig. 7 illustrate the effect of our iterative rating similarity matrix learning algorithm in both the normal and dense dataset under All-But-One strategy. From the result we could see that when the size of training dataset is small, the RSM learning algorithm does not even perform as good as a single

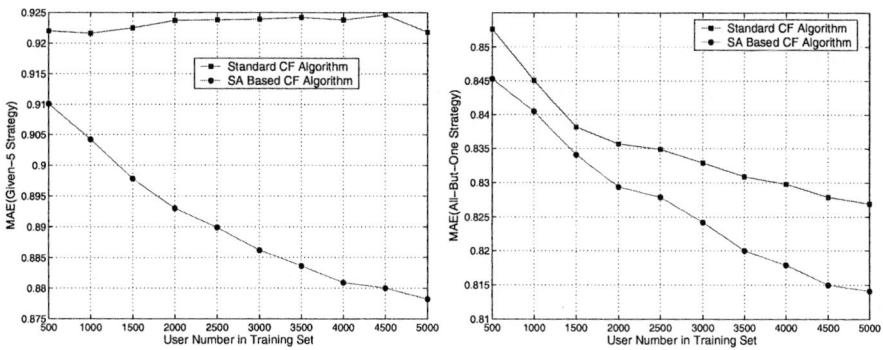

Fig. 4. Algorithm Prediction Accuracy Comparison(Normal Dataset)

Fig. 5. Algorithm Prediction Accuracy Comparison(Normal Dataset)

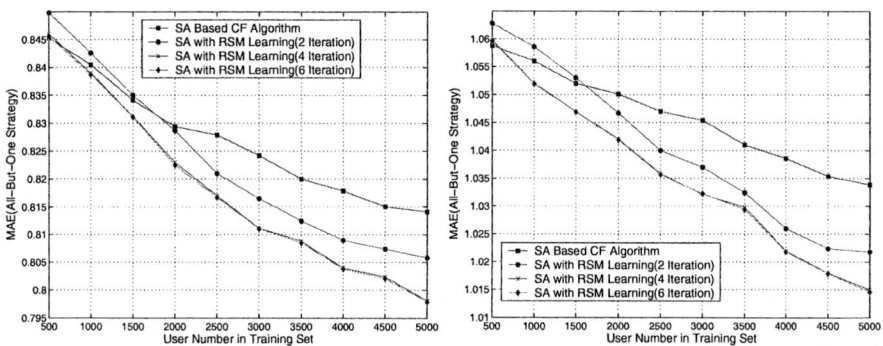

Fig. 6. Algorithm Prediction Accuracy Comparison(Normal Dataset)

Fig. 7. Algorithm Prediction Accuracy Comparison(Dense Dataset)

heuristic RSM. However, when the size of training dataset increased to around 1500 users, the RSM learning algorithm shows its advantage of differentiating each item's contribution to the user similarity calculation. From the experimental result we can also see that the RSM learning algorithm has a very high convergence speed. Only after 4-6 iteration, it will achieve the best performance.

5 Conclusion and Future Work

In this paper, we present an adaptive spreading activation scheme which provides a more intuitive and effective framework for CF based personalized recommendation. Based on this, we not only provide a generalized similarity spreading scheme which could deal with both the binary (transaction) and numeric ratings, but also present an iterative algorithm to learn the decay factor in spreading activation so as to relieve the effect of over activation in existing SA based CF scheme.

In the future work, we will focus on designing a more efficient RSM learning algorithm since though it proved to be effective on improving the prediction accuracy, it is a very time consuming process. We wish to find an incremental algorithm similar to the RSA calculation to deal with it.

References

1. Amazon homepage. In Http://www.amazon.com.
2. J.Breese,Heckerman D., and C. Kadie. Empirical analysis of predictive algorithms for collaborative filtering. In Proceedings of 14th Conference on Uncertainty in Artificial Intelligence, pages 43–52, 1998.
3. H. Chen. An algorithmic approach to concept exploration in a large knowledge network: Symbolic branch-and-bound search vs. connectionist hopeld net activation. Journal of the American Society for Information Science and Technology, 46(5):348–369, 1995.
4. A. M. Collins and E. F. Loftus. A spreading activation theory of semantic processing. Psychology Review, 82(6):407–428, 1975.
5. J. Golbeck, B. Parsia, and J. Hendler. Trust networks on the semantic web. In Proceedings of Cooperative Intelligent Agents 2003, 2003.
6. J. L. Herlocker, J. A. Konstan, A. Borchers, and J. Riedl. An algorithmic framework for performing collaborative filtering. In Proceedings of the 22nd annual international ACM SIGIR conference on Research and development in information retrieval, pages 230–237, 1999.
7. Z. Huang, H. C. Chen, and D. Zeng. Applying associative retrieval techniques to alleviate the sparsity problem in collaborative filtering. ACM Transactions on Information Systems, 22(1):116–142, 2004.
8. G. Nathaniel, J. B. Schafer, and J. A. Konstan. Combining collaborative ltering with personal agents for better recommendations. In Proceedings of the 1999 Conference of the American Association of Articial Intelligence, pages 439–446, 1999.
9. M. Paul and D. John. Each to each programmer's reference manual. In HP Labs Technical Reports (SRC-TN-1997-023). 1997.
10. P.Massa and B. Bhattacharjee. Using trust in recommender systems: an experimental analysis. In Proceeding of the iTrust2004 International Conference, 2004.
11. P. Resnick, N. Iacovou, M. Suchak, P. Bergstrom, and J. Riedl. Grouplens: An open architecture for collaborative filtering of netnews. In Proceedings of the 1994 ACM Conference on Computer Supported Cooperative Work, pages 175–186, 1994.
12. K. Yu, A. Schwaighofer, V. Tresp, and X Xu. Probabilistic memory-based collaborative filtering. IEEE Transaction on Knowledge and Data Engineering, 16(1):56–69, 2003.

Feature Selection by Ordered Rough Set Based Feature Weighting

Qasem A. Al-Radaideh, Md Nasir Sulaiman, Mohd Hasan Selamat,
and Hamidah Ibrahim

Faculty of Computer Science and Information Technology,
University Putra Malaysia, 43400 UPM, Serdang, Selangor, Malaysia
qradaideh@yahoo.com, {nasir, hasan, hamidah}@fsktm.upm.edu.my

Abstract. The aim of feature subset selection is to reduce the complexity of an induction system by eliminating irrelevant and redundant features. Selecting the right set of features for classification task is one of the most important problems in designing a good classifier. In this paper we propose a feature selection approach based on rough set based feature weighting. In the approach the features are weighted and ranked in descending order. An incremental forward interleaved selection process is used to determine the best feature set with highest possible classification accuracy. The approach is experimented and tested using some standard datasets. The experiments carried out are to evaluate the influence of the feature pre-selection on the prediction accuracy of the rough classifier. The results showed that the accuracy could be improved with an appropriate feature pre-selection phase.

1 Introduction

In data mining field, feature (attribute) selection techniques become increasingly essential for reducing the cost of computation and storage and for improving the accuracy of the predication [1]. Feature selection is the problem of choosing a small subset of features that are necessary and sufficient to describe the target concept. It plays an important role in data selection and preparation for data mining tasks. According to the authors of [1] and [2], the role of feature selection in data mining and machine learning is to: reduce the dimensionality of feature space, speed up and reduce the cost of a learning algorithm, improve the predictive accuracy of a classification algorithm, and to improve the visualization and the comprehensibility of the induced concepts. The authors of [1] have emphasized that not every feature selection method can serve all purposes.

For the data classification problem, one motivation for feature selection is to maximize the classification accuracy, since many irrelevant attributes may reduce the classification accuracy achieved by the induction algorithm [3]. Another motivation is to find smaller models for data resulting in better understanding and interpretations of data.

Rough set theory [4] was developed as a mathematical tool for knowledge discovery and data analysis, and concerns itself with the classificatory analysis of imprecise, uncertain or incomplete data acquired from experience. Rough set theory has several attractive features such as deriving rules from facts present in the data without preliminary or additional knowledge about data and finding a simpler representation of knowledge in the form of rules. Moreover, it has some features that help in determining the most relevant attributes to the target class.

In this paper we propose and evaluate a simple yet useful hybrid filter/wrapper feature selection approach that depends on a feature ranking method that uses some notions of rough set theory. The ranking mechanism is used as a heuristic for feature selection to measure the relevancy of attributes to the target class. The features are weighted and ranked as a filter process, and then a forward stepwise selection approach of features is used as a wrapper over the rough set based inducer. We use the rough set based classification to investigate the interactions between feature pre-selection and rough set classifiers. The results of the experiments showed that the proposed approach could be used to improve or at least preserve the classification accuracy for most of the tested datasets. To evaluate the performance of the proposed approach, the classification accuracy is used as measure to evaluate the feature selection approach.

2 The Problem of Feature Selection

Feature selection problem can best be viewed, from an algorithmic perspective, as a heuristic search, where each state in the search space represents a particular subset of the available features. In most cases, an exhaustive search of the state space is impractical, since it involves 2^n possible combinations, where n is the total number of available features. The time to search in the search space is bounded by $O(C2^n)$, where n is the number of features, and C is the computational cost required to evaluate each subset. Several approaches for feature selection have been proposed, ranging from simple greedy algorithms such as forward selection or backward elimination [1] to more complex methods such as genetic algorithms [5] and rough set theory [6]. A good comprehensive survey of the feature selection algorithms for data mining is found in [1].

Based on the relationship between feature selection and induction algorithms, feature selection methods are often divided into two generic approaches: filter and wrapper models [3]. Recently, Hybrid models are proposed to combine the advantages of both filter models and wrapper models [7]. The filter model assumes filtering the features before applying an induction algorithm, while the wrapper model uses the induction algorithm itself to evaluate the features. The authors of [1] suggested a unified model of the feature selection process. The model is depicted in Figure 1 where it includes four parts: feature generation, feature evaluation, stopping criteria, and testing. The outcome of the evaluation process in Phase 1 is a *value* which represents in the wrapper model the classification accuracy over the training dataset. For the filter model the value represents the result of the evaluation measure used to choose the best subset.

Feature selection search is often a greedy hill-climbing procedure. Two basic methods are usually used: Forward Selection (FS) and Backward Elimination (BE). FS starts with an empty set of features and iteratively selects one feature at a time until no improvement in classification accuracy can be achieved. BE starts with the full set of features and iteratively removes one feature at a time until no improvement in classification accuracy can be achieved. BE is more robust to interaction among features. However, FS can be more effective if there are few relevant features.

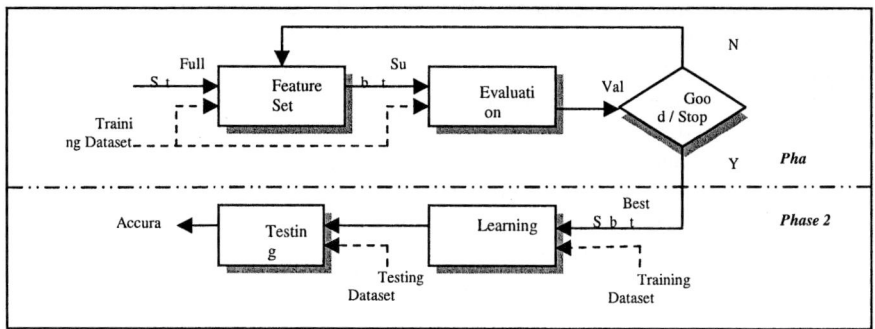

Fig. 1. The Unified Filter/Wrapper Approach of Feature Selection

3 Rough Sets Theory Preliminaries

This section provides some essential definitions from rough set theory that are used to extract the knowledge from the data and to rank the features set. More details and formal definitions about the rough set theory is found in [4] and [8].

In rough set theory, the structure of data is represented in the form of a Decision System (*DS*). The decision system is a pair of sets of the form $DS = (U, A \cup \{d\})$, where $U=\{x_1,...,x_m\}$ is a nonempty finite set of objects called the Universe, and $A=\{a_1,...,a_n\}$ is a nonempty finite set of attributes. Every attribute $a \in A$ is a total function $a:U \rightarrow V_a$, where V_a is the set of allowable values for the attribute a. In a practical rough set system V_a is a discrete and finite set of values. The attributes belonging to A are called conditional attributes and d is called decision attribute.

For each possible subset of attributes $B \subseteq A$, a decision system gives rise to an equivalence relation called an *Indiscernibility Relation IND(B)*, where two objects (x_i, x_j) are members of the same equivalence class if and only if they cannot be discerned from each other on the basis of the set of attributes B. The formal definition of *IND(B)* is expressed as: $IND(B)=\{(x_i, x_j) \in |U|\times|U| : a(x_i) = a(x_j) \; \forall \; a \in B\}$. The set of attributes that differentiate between two given objects x_i and x_j are stored in a *Discernibility Matrix (DM)*. The discernibility matrix of a decision system *DS* is a symmetric EC × EC matrix, where EC is the number of equivalent classes in the decision system, with entries $c_{ij} = \{ a \in A | a(x_i) \neq a(x_j)\}$ if $d(x_i) \neq d(x_j)$ and $\emptyset$ otherwise.

In rough set theory, the concept *reduct* of A refers to the minimal selection of attributes that preserves the indiscernibility relation computed on the basis of the full set of attributes. Preserving the indiscernibility relation preserves the equivalence classes. Formally, a *reduct* of a decision system *DS* is any subset $B \subseteq A \cup \{d\}$ such that $IND(B) = IND(A)$ and $IND(B - \{a\}) \neq IND(A)$ for every $a \in B$. Hence it is enough to consider only the attributes from the reduct to distinguish objects in *U*. The decision system may have several reducts and the core set of the decision system consists of the attributes that exist in all reducts (i.e., the intersection of the reducts).

4 Feature Weighting Using Discernibility Matrix

The feature ranking mechanism introduced by the authors of [9] makes use of attribute frequencies information in the discernibility matrix. The core concept of rough set has also influence the ranking method where if an entry of the DM consists of one attribute, it means that this single attribute must be a member of the core if the core is not empty. The attributes of the core have higher significance than other attributes of DM.

The mechanism derives from the definition of the Core, that the smaller the entry set of DM, the more chance the members of the set to be members of the Core. In this case shorter entries are more significant than longer ones. Based on this idea, to rank the feature, a weight w(ai) is assigned to every attribute ai. The weight is initialized to zero and recalculated when every entry cij of DM is added. The weight is computed according to the following formula.

$$w(a_i) = w(a_i) + |A| / |c_{ij}|, \forall a_i \in c_{ij} \tag{1}$$

In the formula |A| represent the cardinality of attribute set A of the decision system and |cij| is the cardinality of the discernibility matrix entry.

5 The Proposed Approach for Feature Selection

The approach proposed in this paper is a straightforward feature selection approach based on the evaluation of the relevancy of individual features. The approach is a simple yet useful hybrid filter/wrapper feature selection approach that depends on the concept of rough set based feature weighting. The weighting mechanism is used as a heuristic for feature selection to measure the relevancy of attributes to the target class. The features are weighted and ranked as a filter process, and then a foreword stepwise selection approach of features is used as a wrapper over the rough set based inducer.

Generally the approach passes two phases. In phase 1: it starts by generating the discernibility matrix for the decision system. At the same time all features are weighted using the ranking approach presented in section 4. The decision system is then rearranged with respect to the weights of features. The steps of feature ranking and rearrangement phase are presented in Figure 2.

```
Input:
     - A = Set of attributes {a₁,..,aₙ},
     - DS = Decision System (Dataset).
Output:
     - RA = List of ranked attributes.
     - RDS = Rearranged Decision System.
Steps
   - Initialize RA = {}
   - Initialize for i = 1 to n   w(aᵢ) = 0    /* n = number of attributes */
   - EQT = Build the Equivalence Classes table (DS).
   - DM = Build the Discernibility Matrix (EQT) and compute w(aᵢ) ∀ aᵢ ∈ cᵢⱼ
   - RA = Rank (Sort) feature set according to their weights (A)
   - RDS = Rearrange the Decision System according to the Ranked list of features
```

Fig. 2. Feature Ranking and Rearrangement Phase (1)

The main steps of phase 2 are presented in Figure 3 where the feature selection process starts by estimating the classification accuracy of the dataset using the complete feature set to be as a threshold that is used as a stopping criterion of the process. Then it starts by examining the first attribute of the ranked set of attributes (*AllSet*). Next, the attributes are added to the selected attribute set (*FSet*) by incremental interleaving factor. The factor starts by the value 1 up to the value 10 then it is reinitialized after each 10 moves towards the end of the attribute set. This option is suitable for large attribute set. This factor is used to accelerate the forward selection of attributes from the attribute set. After adding the attributes from the original ranked attribute set (*AllSet*) to the selected attribute set (*FSet*), the *FSet* is used by the rough set based inducer to estimate the classification accuracy. If the classification accuracy of the current set is less or higher than the accuracy of the original attribute set within a given range α (say +/- 5%), the acceleration stops and a tuning operation starts by removing one attribute at a time from *FSet* searching for a smaller subset with the same accuracy achieved.

```
Input:
       - RA = Ranked Set of attributes {b_1,..,b_n},
       - RDS = Ordered Decision System
Output:
       - Best Feature Set (FSet)
Steps
  - Threshold = Rough Set Inducer (A, DS)   /* estimate classification
                                               accuracy of original DS */
  - AllSet = RA
  - FSet = First attributes of AllSet
  - AllSet = AllSet - FSet
  - Repeat
-  FAccuracy = Rough Set Inducer (FSet, RDS)  /* estimate classification
   Accuracy */
-  Factor = [1..10]   /* reinitialized every 10 iterations */
-  If FAccuracy = Threshold +/- α  then loop (up to next or previous
   Factors)
-       k = k + 1
-  else k = k + Factor
-  FSet = FSet + the first k attributes of AllSet  /* append to FSet */
-  AllSet = AllSet - the first k attributes   /* remove from AllSet */
  - Stop when FAccuracy >= Threshold or No more attributes to added
```

Fig. 3. Feature Selection Phase (2)

In the classification process, if the accuracy is more important than the number of selected attributes, we can do forward tuning by adding more attributes to *FSet* one by one up to the next *factor*. The algorithm stops when a good accuracy is achieved comparing to the threshold accuracy or no more attributes to add to *FSet*.

6 Experimental Results and Discussion

The experiments reported here used 9 benchmark standard dataset. The datasets are obtained from UCI machine learning data repository [11]. The 9 data sets along with their characteristics are presented in Table 1 where **C.Attr** column refers to the number of the conditional attributes of the decision system. The last column **Class** refers to the number of range values of the decision attribute and the **Objs** column refers to the number of objects of the decision system.

Table 1. Datasets characteristics

Dataset	C. Attr	Objs	Class
Australian	14	690	2
Heart Disease	13	270	2
Hepatitis	19	155	2
Iris	4	150	3
Lymphography	18	148	4
Vehicle	18	856	4
Soya Bean	35	307	19
Zoo	16	101	7
Lung Cancer	56	32	2

For the evaluation purposes of the approach, we have adopted the *Before-After* evaluation approach commonly used in the machine learning community [1]. In the experiments we compare the classification accuracy for a given dataset *before* applying feature selection (i.e. using the full set of features) and the classification accuracy *after* applying the feature selection. The classification accuracy is measured using the 10-fold cross validation method, as recommended by Kohavi in [12] and the authors of [13].

In rough set based classification approach, generating reducts is an essential step to generate classification rules. To test the proposed approach we adopt the Johnson greedy algorithm [10] to generate the set of reducts. Sample of the experiments results are presented in Table 2. In the table, S_n means that the selected feature set (*FSet*) contains n attributes.

The final results are presented in Table 3. In the experiments, we compared the estimated classification accuracy of the reduced decision system that has only the selected relevant attributes with the estimated classification accuracy of the original decision system that includes the complete set of attributes which is presented in the (Full Acc) column of Table 3. The (Red Acc) column shows the classification accuracy using the proposed feature selection approach. The (Red #F) column is the number of the selected features and the (Full #F) column is the number of the full set features. The preliminary results show that the classification accuracy is improved for 7 datasets out of the tested 9 datasets and the same accuracy is resulted for 2 datasets.

It is noticed that the average accuracy using the reduced decision system is better than the accuracy over the original decision system with the full set of attributes.

Table 2. Feature Selection over Rough Inducer

DataSet	S_1	S_2	S_3	S_5	S_8	S_{11}	S_{15}	S_{18}
Australian	55.8	-	66.5	59.4	71.6	**76.1**	-	-
Heart Disease	55.6	-	68.9	**81.1**	80.4	80.4	-	-
Hepatitis	44.2	-	53.6	56.1	**60.4**	56.1	56.1	-
Iris	86.6	**94.0**	88.7	-	-	-	-	-
Lymphography	65.7	-	70.9	-	**82.0**	80.7	79.9	-
Soya Bean	17.9	-	47.2	-	69.0	**81.4**	81.1	78.8
Vehicle	25.5	-	42.3	-	46.9	50.3	**60.9**	-
Zoo	73.4	-	89.2	**95.0**	94.0	94.1	95.0	-

DataSet	S_5	S_8	S_{11}	S_{15}	S_{19}	S_{23}	S_{28}	S_{32}	S_{40}	S_{47}
Lung Cancer	**83.3**	74.6	69.3	71.3	72.7	72.7	72.7	72.7	69.3	78.0

Table 3. Final Results of Feature Selection for Rough Inducer

DataSet	Full #F	Full Acc%	Red #F	Red Acc%
Australian	14	74.9	11	**76.1**
Heart Disease	13	81.1	5	**81.1**
Hepatitis	19	59.2	8	**60.4**
Iris	4	84.7	2	**94.0**
Lymphography	18	77.6	8	**82.0**
Soya Bean	18	80.4	11	**81.4**
Vehicle	35	60.9	15	**60.9**
Zoo	16	94.0	5	**95.0**
Lung Cancer	56	76.0	5	**83.3**
Average	21.44	76.53	7.78	**79.36**

7 Conclusion

In this paper, we presented the feature selection problem and proposed an approach for feature subset selection based on feature ranking and greedy forward selection. The feature ranking approach used some notions of rough set theory, particularly discernibility matrix, reduct, and core. The results of the preliminary experiments using the approach over some standard datasets indicate that the proposed approach offers an attractive solution to the feature selection problem. The approach appears to work well for the rough set classifier. The experiments showed that the classification accuracy is improved for majority of the datasets and the average accuracy over the 9 datasets is higher using the reduced decision systems comparing to the average accuracy using the complete decision system. This indicates that the dataset includes some irrelevant and redundant attributes that are superfluous to the decision system.

References

[1] Liu H. and Motoda H. *Feature Selection for Knowledge Discovery and Data Mining.* Kluwer, Boston, 1998.

[2] Dash M. and Liu H. *Feature Selection for Classification.* Journal of Intelligent Data Analysis 1 (3), pp 131-156, 1997.

[3] John G. H., Kohavi R., Pfleger K. *Irrelevant Features and the Subset Selection Problem.* Proc. of the 11th International Conference on Machine Learning. pp. 121-129. 1994.

[4] Pawlak Z. *Rough Sets: Theoretical Aspects of Reasoning about Data.* Kluwer, Dordrecht. 1991.

[5] Yang J. and Honavar V. *Feature Selection Using A Genetic Algorithm.* Journal of IEEE Intelligent Systems, Vol 13, pp. 44-49, 1998.

[6] Boussouf M. and Quafafou M. *Scalable Feature Selection Using Rough Set Theory.* In Ziarko W. and Yao Y. (eds) : RSCTC 2000, LNAI 2001, pp. 131-138, Springer Verlag 2001.

[7] Sebban M. and Nock R.. *A Hybrid Filter/Wrapper Approach of Feature Selection using Information Theory.* Journal of Pattern Recognition, 35(4), pp. 835-846, 2002.

[8] Pawlak Z. *Rough Sets: Present State and the Future.* Foundation of Computing and Decision Sciences 18(3-4), pp 157-166, 1993.

[9] Hu K., Lu Y. and Shi C. *Feature Ranking in Rough Sets.* Journal of AI Communications. 16(1), pp 41-50. 2003.

[10] Nguyen, S. H. and Nguyen H. S. *Some Efficient Algorithms for Rough Set Methods.* In Proc. Conf. of Information Processing and Management of Uncertainty in Knowledge based system. Spain. pp. 1451-1456. 1996.

[11] Blake C., Keogh E., and Merz C. J. *UCI repository of machine learning databases.* University of California, Irvine, Department of Information and Computer Sciences. 1998.

[12] Kohavi R. *A Study of Cross Validation and Bootstrap for Accuracy Estimation and model Selection.* Proc. of the 15th International Conference on Artificial Intelligence. pp. 1137-1143. 1995.

[13] Al-Radaideh Q. A., Sulaiman M. N., Selamt M. H., and Ibrahim H. *Evaluation of Rough Sets Based Classifiers.* Proc. of Symposium of Intelligence Systems and Information Technology (ISITS04), Malaysia. pp. 205 - 210, Feb 2004.

A Full-Text Framework for the Image Retrieval Signal/Semantic Integration

Mohammed Belkhatir, Philippe Mulhem, and Yves Chiaramella

Laboratoire CLIPS-IMAG,
Université Joseph Fourier, Grenoble, France
{belkhatm, mulhem, chiara}@imag.fr

Abstract. This paper presents an approach for integrating perceptual signal features (i.e. color and texture) and semantic information within a coupled architecture for image indexing and retrieval. It relies on an expressive knowledge representation formalism handling high-level image descriptions and a full-text query framework. It consequently brings the level of image retrieval closer to users' needs by translating low-level signal features to high-level conceptual data and integrate them with semantic characterization within index and query structures. Experiments on a corpus of 2500 photographs validate our approach by considering recall-precision indicators over a set of 46 full-text queries coupling high-level semantic and signal features.

1 Introduction and Related Work

The democratization of digital image technology has led to the need to deal with a new generation of image retrieval frameworks enforcing expressivity, increased performance as far as retrieval results are concerned and computational efficiency.

After a first generation of systems known as content-based image retrieval (CBIR) systems [15] which have largely failed to relate low-level features to semantic characterization (also known as the **semantic gap**), keyword-based annotation frameworks dealing with the automatic extraction of the image semantic content have been proposed [7,9,12,17]. In [17], training sample regions of images are categorized into 11 clusters through a neural network mapping (e.g. *tree, fur, sand...*). To alleviate the restrained cardinality of the proposed previous sets of visual clusters, a richer index vocabulary consisting of 26 image labels called Visual Keywords (such as *sky, people, water...*) is specified in [9]. However, this solution relies on a query-by-example solution for querying and no language being able to manipulate the extracted semantics has been proposed. Also, relevance-based models for keyword annotation and retrieval are specified in [7]. The main disadvantage of this second class of frameworks relies on the specification of restrained and fixed sets of semantic classes, therefore severely limiting their expressivity. Regarding the fact that several artificial objects have high degrees of variability with respect to signal properties such as color and texture variations, an interesting solution is to extend the extracted visual semantics with signal characterizations in order to enrich the image indexing vocabulary and query language.

Therefore, a new generation of systems integrating semantics and signal descriptions has emerged and the first solutions [10,19] are based on the association of textual annotations with relevance feedback (RF). Prototypes such as iFind [19] offer loosely-coupled solutions based on textual annotations to characterize semantics and on a RF scheme operating on low-level signal features. These approaches present however two major drawbacks: first, they lack to exhibit a single framework unifying signal features and semantics, which penalizes the performance of the system in terms of retrieval efficiency and quality. Then, regarding the query process, the user is to query both textually in order to express high-level concepts and through several and time-consuming RF loops to complement his initial query.

As an extension to our previous work in [1,2,13], we propose a unified multi-facetted framework unifying visual semantics and signal (color and texture) features for automatic image retrieval that enforces expressivity, performance and computational efficiency. After specifying an automatized framework extracting the visual semantics, we enrich image description with processes establishing a correspondence between extracted low-level features and high-level signal concepts. E.g. with the visual semantics concept "sky" one might assign additional concepts such as "cyan", "grey" characterizing its color and "covered", "smooth" which feature its texture. Therefore, not only do we characterize visual semantics, but also relations linking them to high-level color or texture concepts. For this, we consider an efficient operational model that allows relational indexing and is adaptable to symbolic image retrieval: conceptual graphs [16]. We moreover extend its descriptive power to specify a rich query language consisting of several boolean and quantification operators. Indeed, we are interested in dealing with non-trivial queries combining multiple characterizations (such as proposed in the TRECVID multimedia retrieval task): visual semantics and high-level color concepts (e.g. "Find images with a **mostly grey** sky") or visual semantics and high-level texture concepts (e.g. "Find images with fields of **lined** flowers").

In the remainder, we first present the general organization of our model. We deal in sections 3, 4 and 5 with the descriptions of the visual semantics and signal characterizations. Section 6 specifies the query framework. We finally present validation experiments conducted on a test collection of 2500 photographs.

2 A Strongly-Integrated Model and Its Representation Formalism

As an extension of the work in [11], we propose the outline of an image model combining a set of interpretations, each considered as a particular **facet** of an image, to build the most exhaustive image description. At the core of the image model is the notion of **image objects (IOs)**, abstract structures representing visual entities within an image. Their specification is an attempt to operate image indexing and retrieval operations beyond simple low-level processes or region-based techniques [15] since IOs convey the visual semantics and signal color and texture information. Our image model is comprised of:

- The **visual semantics facet** which describes the image semantic content and is based on labeling IOs with a semantic concept. E.g., in fig 1, the first IO (Io1) is tagged by the semantic concept *Hut*. Its formal description will be dealt with in section 3.
- The **signal facet** which describes the image signal content in terms of symbolic perceptive features and consists in characterizing IOs with signal concepts. It itself con-

sists in two sub-facets. The *color subfacet* features the image signal content in terms of symbolic colors. E.g., the second IO (Io2) is associated with symbolic colors *Cyan* and *White*. The *texture subfacet* describes the signal content in terms of symbolic texture features. E.g. the second IO (Io2) is associated with texture keyword **lined**. The signal facet is detailed in section 4.

In order to instantiate this model within an image retrieval framework, we choose CGs which have proven to adapt to the symbolic approach of image retrieval [11,14]. CGs allow to represent components of our image retrieval architecture and to specify expressive index and query frameworks. Formally, a CG is a finite, bipartite, connex and oriented graph. It features 2 types of nodes: concept and relation nodes. In the example CG [DEXA2005]←(Name)←[Conference]→(Location)→[Copenhagen], concepts are between brackets and relations within parentheses. This graph is semantically interpreted as: the DEXA2005 conference is held in Copenhagen. Concepts and conceptual relations are organized within a lattice partially ordered by the IS-A ($\leq$) relation. For example, Building $\leq$ Construction denotes that the concept *Building* is a specialization of the concept *Construction*, and will therefore appear in the offspring of the latter within the lattice organizing these concepts. Within the scope of the model, CGs are used to represent the image content.

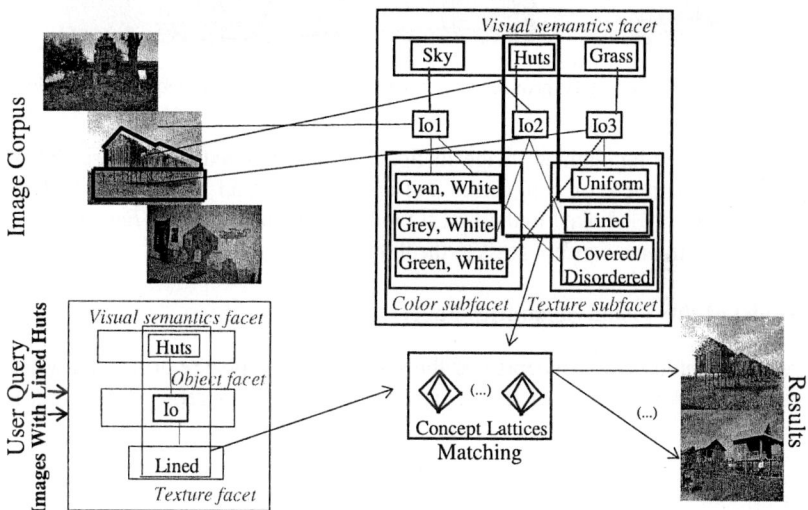

Fig. 1. System architecture and Image model

The index module provides a conceptual representation (called document index CG) of an image document with respect to the multi-facetted image model. Also, as far as the retrieval module is concerned, a user full-text query is translated into a conceptual representation (called image query graph) corresponding to the multi-facetted image description (such as the query "Find images with lined huts" in fig.1). The image query graph is then compared to all conceptual representations of image documents in the corpus. Lattices organizing semantic and signal concepts are processed and a relevance value, estimating the degree of similarity between image query and index graphs is computed in order to rank all image doc documents relevant to a query.

3 The Visual Semantics Facet

3.1 Extracting the Semantics

Several experimental studies presented in [12] have led to the specification of twenty categories or picture scenes describing the image content at a global level. Web-based image search engines (google, altavista) are queried by textual keywords corresponding to these picture scenes and 100 images are gathered for each query. These images are used to establish a list of semantic concepts characterizing objects that can be encountered in these scenes. A total of 72 semantic concepts to be learnt and automatically extracted are specified (further details regarding the architecture for semantic concept extraction can be found in [9]). Fig. 2 shows image samples taken from our corpus [1,2,9,13].

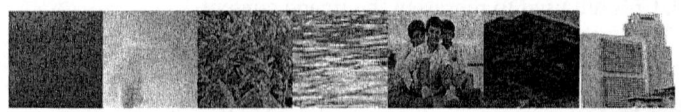

Fig. 2. Semantic concepts: ground, sky, vegetation, water, people, mountain, building

For instance, the highlighted image in fig. 1 is characterized by three semantic concepts, based respectively on top, center and bottom areas and linked to three IOs. The semantic concept *sky* is linked to the first IO *Io1*, the semantic concept *huts* to the second IO *Io2* and the semantic concept grass to the third IO *Io3*.

3.2 Model of the Visual Semantics Facet

IOs are represented by *Io* concepts and the semantic concepts are organized within the lattice in fig.3. An instance of the visual semantics facet is represented by a set of

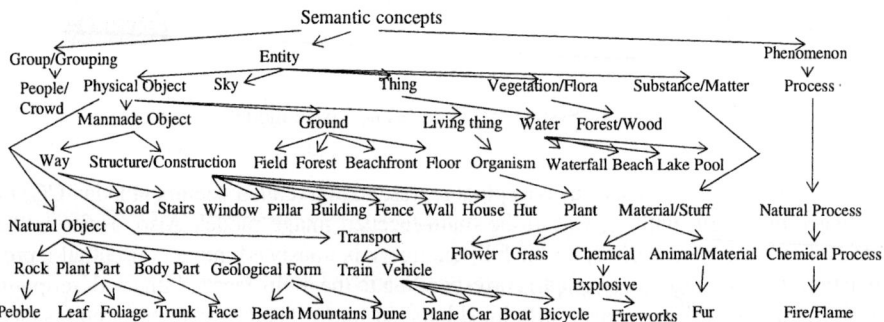

Fig. 3. Lattice organizing semantic concepts

CGs, each one containing an *Io* type linked through the conceptual relation *sct* to a semantic concept. The basic graph controlling the generation of all visual semantics facet graphs is: [Io]→(sct)→[SC]. E.g., graphs [Io1]→(sct)→[Sky], [Io2]→(sct)→[Huts] and [Io2]→(sct)→[Grass] are the representation of the visual semantics facet in figure 1 and can be translated as: the first, second and third IOs (Io1, Io2 and Io3) are respectively associated with the semantic concepts *huts*, *sky* and *grass*.

4 The Signal Facet

The integration of signal information within the conceptual level is crucial since it enriches the indexing framework and expands the query language with the possibility to query over both semantics and visual information. We now focus on the signal facet and deal with the integration of signal features within our multi-facetted conceptual model. This integration is not straightforward as we need to characterize signal features at the conceptual level, and therefore specify a rich framework for conceptual signal indexing and querying. We first propose conceptual structures for the color and texture subfacets and then thoroughly specify their representations in terms of CGs.

4.1 The Color Subfacet

Our symbolic representation of color information is guided by the research carried out in color naming and categorization [4] stressing a step of correspondence between color names and their stimuli. Within the scope of this paper, 11 color categories (C_1=cyan, C_2=white, C_3=green, C_4=grey, C_5=red, C_6=blue, C_7=yellow, C_8=purple, C_9=black, C_{10}=skin, C_{11}=orange) spotlighted in [11] are described in the HVC perceptually uniform space by a union of brightness, tonality and saturation intervals. Each IO is then indexed by two types of conceptual structures featuring its color distribution: boolean and quantified color concepts. Boolean concepts are detailed in [1]. We study next quantified color conceptual structures.

Index structures. Quantified color index concepts (*QCICs*) feature the color distribution of IOs by a conjunction of color categories and their corresponding integer pixel percentages. The second IO (Io2) corresponding to the semantic concept *sky* in figure 3 is characterized by the QCIC <C:59,W:41,Gn:0,G:0...>, interpreted as Io2 having 59% of cyan **and** 41% of white (cf. fig. 4).

Query structures. Our conceptual architecture is powerful enough to handle an expressive query language integrating visual semantics and color characterization through boolean and quantified operators. We propose here queries which associate visual semantics with quantifiers such as Q1: "Find images with a cloudy sky (*At Most* 25% of cyan)" and Q2: "Find images with lake water (*At Least* 25% of grey)" (queries involving boolean operators are thoroughly studied in [1]). Two types of conceptual structures are specified to support the previously defined query types: *At Most* color concepts (*AMCCs*) and *At Least* color concepts (*ALCCs*) represent the color distribution of an IO by a conjunction of color categories and respectively their associated maximum (translating the keyword *At Most* in a query) and minimum (translating the keyword *At Least*) pixel percentage. For instance, the AMCC <C:25,W:0,Gn:0,G:0...>$_{AM}$ and the ALCC <C:0,W:0,Gn:0,G:25...>$_{AL}$ respectively correspond to the color distributions expressed in queries Q1 and Q2.

A conceptual specification for the color subfacet. Color concepts are elements of partially-ordered lattices which are organized respectively to the type of the query processed [1]. There are 2 types of basic graphs controlling the generation of all color subfacet graphs. **Index color graphs** link an *Io* type through the conceptual relation q_c to a quantified color index concept: [Io]→(q_c)→[QCIC]. **Query color graphs** link an *Io* type through conceptual relations am_c or al_c to a quantified color query concept, respectively an *At Most* or *At Least* color concept: [Io]→(am_c)→[AMCC] and [Io]→(al_c)→[ALCC]. E.g., index graphs [Io1]→(q_c)→[<C:59,W:41,Gn:0,G:0...>], [Io2]→(q_c)→[<C:0,W:15,Gn:0,G:85...>] and [Io3]→(q_c)→[<C:0,W:25,Gn:75,G:0...>] are the index representation of the color subfacet in fig. 1 and are interpreted as the first IO (Io1) is associated with the CQIC <C:59,W:41,Gn:0,G:0...> (i.e. 59% of cyan and 41% of white), Io2 with the CQIC <C:0,W:15,Gn:0,G:85...> (i.e. 15% of white and 85% of grey) and Io3 with the CQIC <C:0,W:25,Gn:75,G:0...> (i.e. 25% of white and 75% of green).

4.2 The Texture Subfacet

From low-level texture features to symbolic characterization. For low-level texture extraction, in order to capture aspects related to human perception, we propose a solution inspired by the work in [6] where a computational framework for texture extraction which is the closest approximation of the human visual system is specified. The action of the visual cortex, where an object is decomposed into several primitives by the filtering of cortical neurons sensitive to several frequencies and orientations of the stimuli, is simulated by a bank of Gabor filters. However, as opposed to their work operating at a global level of an image, we will focus on computational texture extraction at the IO level. We will therefore characterize each IO by its Gabor energy distribution within 7 spatial frequencies covering the whole spectral domain and 7angular orientations. Each IO is then represented by a 49-dimensions vector, with each dimension corresponding to a Gabor energy.

Although several works have proposed the identification of low-level features and the development of algorithms and techniques for texture computation, few attempts have been made to propose a vocabulary for texture symbolic characterization. In [4], Bhushan et al. provide a texture lexicon, i.e. they highlight 11 high-level texture categories which constitute a basis for the symbolic classification of textures. In each of these categories, several texture words which best describe the nature of the characterized texture are proposed. We consider the following texture words as the representation of each of these categories: **bumpy, cracked, disordered, interlaced, lined, marbled, netlike, smeared, spotted, uniform** and **whirly**.

These 11 high-level texture words are then mapped to the 49-dimensions vectors of Gabor energies through support vector machines [18].

Conceptual structures for the texture facet. Texture index concepts are the index structures of the texture subfacet. They are supported by a vector structure **t** with eleven elements corresponding to texture words tw$_i$. Values t[i], i ∈ [1,11] are booleans stressing that the texture distribution of the considered IO is characterized by the texture word tw_i. E.g., the second IO (Io2) corresponding to the semantic concept *huts* in fig. 1 is characterized by the texture index concept <B:0,C:0...I:0,L:1,N:0...>, which is translated by Io2 being characterized by the texture word **lined**.

As far as query structures are concerned, our framework proposes an expressive query language which integrates visual semantics and symbolic texture characterization through boolean operators. A user shall be able to associate visual semantics with a boolean conjunction of texture words such as in Q3: "Find images displaying a road with both **bumpy** AND **cracked** textures", a boolean disjunction of texture words such as in Q4: "Find images with a **covered/disordered** OR **bright/uniform** sky" and a negation of texture words such as in Q5: "Find images with NON-**interlaced** flowers". Three types of conceptual structures are specified to support the previously defined query types. *And* texture concepts (ATCs) represent the signal distribution of an IO by a conjunction of texture words; *Or* texture concepts (OTCs) by a disjunction of texture words and *Not* texture concepts (NCCs) by a negation of texture words. The ATC <B:1,C:1...I:0,L:0,N:0...>$_{AND}$, the OTC <B:0,C:1...I:0,L:0,N:1...>$_{OR}$ and the NTC <B:0,C:0...I:1,L:0,N:0...>$_{NO}$ respectively correspond to the texture distributions expressed in queries Q3, Q4 and Q5.

In the conceptual specification of the texture subfacet, texture concepts are elements of partially-ordered lattices organized with respect to the type of the query processed [3]. There are 2 types of basic graphs controlling the generation of all the texture facet graphs. **Index texture graphs** link an *Io* type through the conceptual relation ind_tx to a texture index concept: **[Io]→(ind_tx)→[TIC]**. **Query texture graphs** link an *Io* type through conceptual relations and_tx, or_tx, or not_tx to a texture query concept, respectively an *And*, *Or* or *No* texture concept: **[Io]→(and_tx)→[ATC]**; **[Io]→(or_tx)→[OTC]** and **[Io]→(not_tx)→[NTC]**. Eg, index graphs [Io1]→(ind_tx)→[<B:0,C:0,D:1,I:0...>], [Io2]→(ind_tx)→ [<B:0,C:0...I:0,L:1,N:0...>] and [Io3]→(ind_tx)→[<B:0,C:0...U:1...>] are the index representation of the texture subfacet in figure 1 and are interpreted as: the first IO (Io1) is associated with the texture index concept <B:0,C:0,D:1,I:0 > (i.e **disordered/covered**), Io2 with the texture index concept <B:0,C:0...I:0,L:1,N:0...> (**i.e. lined**) and Io3 with the texture index concept <B:0,C:0...U:1...> (**i.e. uniform**).

5 The Query Module

Our conceptual architecture is based on a unified full-text framework allowing a user to query over both the visual semantics and the signal facets. This obviously enhances user interaction since the user becomes in charge of the query process by making his needs explicit to the system.

The representation of a user query in our model is, like image index representations, obtained through the combination (joint operation) of CGs over the visual semantics and signal facets (query color and texture graphs).

E.g., the Q3 query "Find images displaying a road with both **bumpy** and **cracked** textures" is represented by the graph: **[Io1]→(sct)→[Road]**
→ (and_tx)→[<B:1,C:1,D:0,I:0...>$_{AND}$]
The Q1 query is represented by the CG: **[Io1]→(sct)→[Sky]**
→(am_c)→[<C:25,W:0,Gn:0,G:0, ...>$_{AM}$]

An operational model of image retrieval based on the CG formalism uses the graph projection operation for the comparison of a query graph and a document graph. This operator allows to identify within a graph g_1 sub-graphs with the same structure as a given graph g_2, with nodes being possibly restricted, i.e. their types are specialization of g_2 node types. If a projection of a query graph Q within a document graph D exists then the document indexed by D is relevant for the query Q. However, brute-force implementations of the projection would result in exponential execution times. Based on the work in [14], we use an adaptation of the inverted file approach for image retrieval. We specify lookup tables associating visual semantics concepts to the set of image documents whose index contain it. Treatments that are part of the projection are performed during indexing following a specific organization of CGs which does not affect the expressiveness of the formalism. Moreover, lattices organizing signal color and texture concepts are defined by mathematical partial orders and not hard-coded, which allows to quickly process queries [1,2].

6 Validation Experiments: An Application to Home Photographs

The SIR prototype implements the theoretical framework exposed in this paper and validation experiments are carried out on a corpus of 2500 personal color photographs used as a validation corpus in several publications [1,2,9,13].

IOs within the 2500 photographs are automatically assigned a semantic concept as presented in section 3 and characterized with index signal structures presented in 4.

As opposed to state-of-the-art keyword-based frameworks allowing only single-word queries [7,9,12,17], we wish to retrieve photographs that represent elaborate image scenes and propose 46 queries and their ground truths involving semantic concepts with their color and texture characterizations such as *swimming-pool water*, *lined people*... The evaluation of our formalism is based on the notion of *image relevance* which consists in quantifying the correspondence between index and query images. We compare SIR with a keyword-based annotation framework: the *Visual Keyword* system [9,13] S_1 and a state-of-the-art loosely-coupled system S_2 combining a textual framework for querying on semantics and a RF process operating on low-level signal features.

For each proposed query in table 2, we construct relevant textual query terms using corresponding semantic and color concepts as input to SIR (e.g. 'Find images with at least 50% of cyan water' for *swimming-pool water*). Also, for each query proposed in table 3, relevant textual query terms using corresponding semantic and texture concepts are proposed as input to SIR (e.g. 'Find images with lined people' for *lined people*). S_1 processes 3 series of 3 random relevant photographs for each query (they correspond to swimming-pool water or lined people in our example queries). Also queries in table 2 and 3 are translated in relevant textual symbolic entities to be processed by the semantics framework of S_2 ('Find images with water' for *swimming-pool water* or 'Find images with people' for *lined people*). Then to refine the results, 3 random relevant photographs are selected as input to the RF framework.

Recall/precision curves of fig. 4 illustrate the average results obtained for queries in table 2 involving visual semantics and color characterizations: the curve associated with the *SIR* legend illustrates the results in recall and precision obtained by SIR, the curve associated with the *VK* legend by S_1 and the curve associated with the *SignSymb* legend by S_2. The average precision of SIR (0.455) is approximately 89,28% higher over the average precision of the VK system (0.2404) and approximately 37,9% higher over the average precision of the loosely-coupled state-of-the-art system (0.3165). Recall/precision curves of fig. 5 illustrate the average results obtained for queries in table 3 involving semantics and texture characterizations. The average precision of SIR (0.531) is here approximately 72,4% higher over the average precision of the VK system (0.308) and 61,89% over the average precision of the S_2 system (0.328). We notice that improvements of the precision values are significant at all recall values. The obtained results allow us to state that when dealing with elaborate queries which combine multiple sources of information (here visual semantics, color and texture features) and therefore require a higher level of abstraction, the use of an "intelligent" and expressive representation formalism (here the CG formalism within

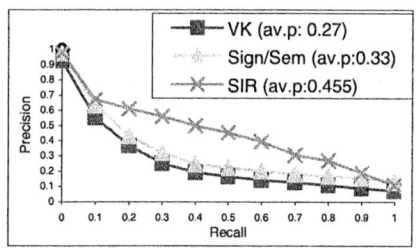

Fig. 4. Recall/Precision Curves (table 2)   **Fig. 5.** Recall/Precision Curves (table 3)

Table 2. Queries with Semantics & Textures

Bumpy Buildings/Walls	Field of Lined Flowers	Smeared Walls
Bumpy Roads	Lined Trees	Spotted Fur
Cracked Grounds	Marble Floor	Spotted Floors
Cracked Walls	Brick-like Ground	Uniform Crowd
Disordered/Covered Sky	Netlike Windows	Smooth Sky
Interlaced Foliage	Smeared Buildings	Uniform Floor
Lined Houses	Smeared Roads	Whirly Water
Lined People	Whirly Flowers	Chequered/Netlike Floor

Table 3. Queries with Semantics & Colors

Trees with Green Leaves	Green and White Walls	Lake Water
White Buildings	Night	River Water
Grey Buildings	Black and White Pics	Yellow Flowers
Yellow Buildings	Dirty Sand	Purple Flowers
Sandy Ground	Ground with Vegetation	Environment with Lights
Blue Sky	White and Red Towers	Grey Walls
Grey Sky	Green Vegetation	Swimming-Pool Water
Sunset Sky		

our framework) is crucial. As a matter of fact, our framework complements automatic keyword-based approaches through the enrichment of their single-word query frameworks with signal characterization (in this case the VKs). Moreover, it outperforms state-of-the-art loosely-coupled solutions by proposing a unified full-text framework optimizing user interaction and allowing to query with precision over visual semantics and high-level signal features.

7 Conclusion

We proposed within the scope of this paper the formal specification of a framework combining the two existing approaches in image retrieval, i.e. signal and semantic within a strongly-coupled architecture to achieve greater retrieval accuracy. Our work has contributed both theoretically and at the experimental level to the image retrieval research topic. We have considered IOs, abstract structures representing visual entities within an image in order to operate image indexing and retrieval operations at a higher level of abstraction than state-of-the-art frameworks. We have formally described the visual semantics and signal facets that define the conceptual information conveyed by IOs and have finally proposed a unified and rich framework for querying. At the experimental level, the obtained results allowed us to validate our approach and stress the relevance of integrating visual semantics and signal characterizations.

References

1. Belkhatir, M. & Mulhem, P. & Chiaramella Y.: Integrating Perceptual Signal Features within a Multi-facetted Conceptual Model for Automatic Image Retrieval. ECIR (2004) 267-282
2. Belkhatir, M.: Combining semantics and texture characterizations for precision-oriented automatic image retrieval. ECIR (2005) 457-474
3. Berlin, B. & Kay, P.: Basic Color Terms: Their universality and Evolution. UC Press (1991)
4. Bhushan, N. & al: The Texture Lexicon: Understanding the Categorization of Visual Texture Terms and Their Relationship to Texture Images. Cognitive Science 21(2) (1997) 219-246
5. Gong, Y. & Chuan, H. & Xiaoyi, G.: Image Indexing and Retrieval Based on Color Histograms. Multimedia Tools and Applications II (1996) 133-156
6. Guyader, N. & al. "Towards the introduction of human perception in a natural scene classification system". NNSP (2002)
7. Jeon, J. & al.: Automatic image annotation and retrieval using cross-media relevance models. SIGIR (2003) 119-126
8. Leow, W.K. & Lai, S.Y. "Invariant matching of texture for content-based image retrieval". MMM (1997) 53-68
9. Lim, J.H.: Explicit query formulation with visual keywords. ACM MM (2000) 407-412
10. Lu, Y. & al.: A unified framework for semantics and feature based relevance feedback in image retrieval systems. ACM Multimedia (2000) 31-37
11. Mechkour, M.: EMIR^2: An Extended Model for Image Representation and Retrieval. DEXA (1995) 395-404
12. Mojsilovic, A. & Rogowitz, B.: Capturing image semantics with low-level descriptors. ICIP (2001) 18-21

13. Mulhem, P. & Lim, J.H.: Symbolic photograph content-based retrieval. CIKM (2002) 94-101
14. Ounis, I. & Pasca, M.: RELIEF: Combining expressiveness and rapidity into a single system. SIGIR (1998) 266-274
15. Smeulders, A.W.M. & al.: Content-based image retrieval at the end of the early years. IEEE PAMI, 22(12) (2000) 1349-1380
16. Sowa, J.F. "Conceptual structures: information processing in mind and machine". Addison-Wesley publishing company (1984)
17. Town, C.P. & Sinclair, D. Content-based Image Retrieval Using Semantic Visual Categories. TR2000-14, AT&T Labs Cambridge (2000)
18. Vapnik, V.: Statistical Learning Theory. Wiley (1998)
19. Zhou, X.S. & Huang, T.S.: Unifying Keywords and Visual Contents in Image Retrieval. IEEE Multimedia 9(2) (2002) 23-33

A New Algorithm for Content-Based Region Query in Multimedia Databases

Dumitru Dan Burdescu[1] and Liana Stanescu[2]

[1] University of Craiova, Faculty of Automation, Computers and Electronics
burdescu@topedge.com
[2] University of Craiova, Faculty of Automation, Computers and Electronics
stanescu@software.ucv.ro

Abstract. This article presents an original method of implementation of the color set back-projection algorithm. This is one of the most efficient methods of automated detection of color regions from an image. The detected regions are then used in the content-based region query. The query is realized on one or more regions, taking into consideration the color feature, location, area and the minimal bounding rectangle of the regions. The efficiency of the method was studied by means of a number of experiments effectuated with the help of a software system realized for this purpose, on a collection of synthetic images. This method of implementation influences the content-based region query efficiency in a series of domains in which this technique is used, such as medicine, art, education.

1 Introduction

At present a real explosion of the multimedia information comes out. Unlike alphanumeric data, the multimedia data have no semantic structure. For a computer, an image is only a sequence of binary numbers or a bi-dimensional array. The image and object recognition with computer help, in such applications is a difficult problem. This is due to the fact that the information comprised in the multimedia data is not structured and so, the utilization of some attributes, which describe its content, is not possible. In conclusion, it is impossible to directly use a database management system for the administration of multimedia information. The database management systems have to hold a succession of additional properties compared to the traditional ones [1].

From that appears the big necessity of alternative methods for a quick and accurate retrieval, from a multimedia database of big dimensions, of multimedia information, which satisfies the user query. These techniques are very necessary in all the domains where the multimedia information, especially the visual information is used. There are some examples of possible utilizations of multimedia retrieval systems: medicine, security, education, journalism, divertissement, art and firmware register.

Since the images represent an important component in the multimedia domain, the problem of the content-based visual query has been subjected to the study. The content – based visual query may be realized either at the level of the entire image (content-based image query), or based on the color regions existing in images (content-based region query). In this article, the second direction, namely the content – based region query is presented. In its realization an automatic algorithm of big importance for the detection of color regions is used.

It is presented an original implementations of the color set back-projection algorithm introduced by J.R. Smith and Shih-Fu Chang at the Columbia University [3], [6]. The efficiency of this implementation is studied by means of some experiments effectuated on a collection of synthetic images. In order to establish the matching between the target and query regions several distances have been taken into computation: the distance that indicates the color similitude, the spatial distance between the centroids of the regions (location), the distance in area between the two regions and the distance in minimal bounding rectangles (MBR) between regions.

The implementation of the color set back-projection algorithm and the experiments were effectuated with the help of the IMTEST software system [8], created for the study of the content-based visual retrieval issue.

2 Problems Definitions

The objective of the content-based visual query is to search and retrieve in an efficient manner those images from the database that are most appropriate to the image considered by the user as query. The content-based visual query differs from the usual query by the fact that it implies the similitude search. Furthermore it is done the distinction between the two utilization ways of the content – based visual query, namely: content- based image query and content-based region query [3].

In a content-based region query, the images are compared based on their regions. In the first step of the query, content-based visual queries are effectuated on the regions, and not on the images. Then, in the final step of the query, there are determined the images corresponding to the regions and there is computed the total distance between the images by the weighting of the distances between regions.

The content – based visual query may be improved by adding the spatial information to the query. So, the total measure of the dissimilitude takes into consideration both the values of the features (color and texture), and the spatial values of the regions. There are two types of spatial indexing, namely: relative and absolute [3].

The most powerful images retrieval system is the one that allows queries in which are specified both the visual features and spatial properties for the desired images. Such query offers to the user the possibility to control the selection of regions and attributes which are the most important in the determination of the similitude. The visual and absolute spatial queries integrate the absolute spatial query and the content-based region query. The visual query and the relative spatial query integrate the relative spatial query and the content-based region query.

The color set back-projection algorithm is the technique implemented for the automated extraction of regions and representation of their color content. The extraction system for color regions has four steps [4], [5], [6], [7]:

1. the image transformation, quantization and filtering (the transformation from the RGB color space to HSV color space and the quantization of the HSV color space at 166 colors)
2. back-projection of binary color sets
3. the labeling of regions
4. the extraction of the region features

The algorithm follows the reduction of insignificant color information and makes evident the significant color regions, followed by the generation, in automatic way, of the regions of a single color, of the two colors, of three colors.

To conclude with the second step of the color set back-projection algorithm, is the following [6]:

1. Detection of single color regions
   1.1. Having the image histogram, $H[m]$, all the values $m'=m$ for which $H[m]>=p_0$ are detected.
   1.2. For each m' the color set c having the property $c[k]=1$ for $k=m$ and $c[k]=0$ in other cases is found. On the image $R[m,n]$ the back-projection algorithm for each color set c is applied and the color regions are found. For each region n the local histogram $L_n[m]$ is stored.
   1.3. The residue histogram $H_r[m]=H[m]- \sum_n L_n[m]$ is computed.
2. Detection of two colors regions
   2.1. The values $l'=l$ and $m'=m$, $l\#m$, $H[l]>=p_0$, $H[m]>=p_0$ and $H_r[l]>=p_1$, $H_r[m]>=p_1$ are found.
   2.2. For each set l', m' the color set c having the property $c[k]=1$ for $k=l'$ or $k=m'$ and $c[k]=0$ in other cases is found. On the image $R[m,n]$ the back-projection algorithm for each set c is applied and the color regions are found. For each region the local histogram $L_n[m]$ is recorded.
   2.3. The residue histogram $H_r[m]=H[m]- \sum_n L_n[m]$ is updated.
3. Detection of the three colors regions,...

For each detected regions the color set that generated it, the area and the localization are stored. All the information is necessary further on for the content-based region query with absolute or relative localization. The region localization is given by the minimal bounding rectangle. The region area is represented by the number of color pixels, and can be smaller than the minimum bounding rectangle.

3 A New Algorithm for Detecting Color Regions

In the first implementation of the color set back-projection algorithm (Method1), the image can be read in a .bmp format. Each pixel from the initial image is transformed in HSV format and quantized. At the end of this processing both the global histogram of the image, and the color set are available. On the matrix that memorizes only the quantized colors from 0 to 165 is applied a 5x5 median filter, which has the role of eliminating the isolated points. Having the HSV quantized matrix it is possible to begin the process of regions extraction presented above. In the first implementation (Method1), it may be observed that this process is in fact a depth – first traversal, described in pseudo-cod in the following way:

procedure FindRegions (Image I, colorset C)
```
InitStack(S)
Visited = Ø
 for *each node P in the I do
   if *color of P is in C then
     PUSH(P)
     Visited ← Visited ∪ {P}
     while not Empty(S) do
        CrtPoint <- POP()
        Visited ← Visited ∪ {CrtPoint}
        For *each unvisited neighbor S of CrtPoint do
          if *color of S is in C then
            Visited ← Visited ∪ {S}
            PUSH(S)
          //end if
        //end for
     //end while
     *Output detected region
   //end if
 //end for
```

Proposition 1
The total running time of a call of the procedure **FindRegions** (Image I, colorset C) is $O(m^2*n^2)$, where "m" is the width and "n" is the height of the image.

Proof
Recall that the number of pixels of the image is m*n, where "m" is the width and "n" is the height of the image. As it is observed next the first loop FOR of the algorithm is executed at most once for each pixel P in the image. Hence, the total time spent in this loop is $O(n*m)$. The WHILE loop processes the stack S for each pixel which has the same color of its neighbor. The inner loop FOR processes the pixels of unvisited neighbor. So, the total time spent in these loops is $O(m*n)$, because all pixels of the image are processed at most once. From previous statements it is inferred that the total running time of this procedure is $O(m^2*n^2)$ [2].

In the new algorithm (Method2), the image pixels are arranged into hexagons. The edge of a hexagon has a certain number of pixels (3, 4, 5). There are taken into consideration only the pixels which correspond to the vertices of the hexagons with an established edge. The image is viewed as a graph not as a pixel matrix. The vertices represent the pixels and the edges represent neighborhoods between pixels.
For each binary set is executed:
1. the graph is inspected until it is found the first vertex having the color from the color set
2. starting from this vertex, there are found all the adjacent vertices having the same color
3. the process will continue in the same manner for each neighbor, until there are not found vertices having the same color
4. it is verified if the detected region satisfies the imposed thresholds; in affirmative case, the region is labeled and introduced in the database

This process of regions extraction from a graph is in fact a breadth – first traversal, described in pseudo-cod in the following way:

```
procedure const_graph (Image I, Graph g,  Edge edge):
for * i->0,width/edge
   for * j->0;height/edge
      if (i mod 3==0)
            *if(jmod2==0)
               g[i][j]=I[edge*i][edge*j+edge-1]
            *if(jmod2==1)
               g[i][j]=I[edge*i][edge*j+edge+2]

      if (i mod 3==1)
          * if(j mod 2==0)
               g[i][j]=I[edge*i-1][edge*jedge]
          * if(j mod 2==1)
               g[i][j]=I[edge*i-1][edge*j+edge*2]

      if (i mod 3==2)
            *if(j mod 2==0)
               g[i][j]=I[edge*i-2][edge*j+edge-1]
            *if(j mod 2==1)
               g[i][j]=I[edge*i-2][edge*j+edge+2]

   //end for *j->0
   *output the graph g
//end for * i->0

procedure FindRegions (Graph G, colorset C) :
   InitQueue(Q)
   Visited = Ø
   for *each node P in the G do
      if *color of P is in C then
         PUSH(P)
         Visited ← Visited ∪ {P}
         while not Empty(q) do
            CrtPoint <- POP()
            Visited ← Visited ∪ {CrtPoint}
            for *each unvisited neighbor Q of CrtPoint do
               if *color of Q is in C then
                  Visited ← Visited ∪ {Q}
                  PUSH(Q)
               // end if
            //end for
         //end while
         *output-detected region
      //end if
   //end for
```

Proposition 2

The total running time of a call of the procedure **FindRegions** (Graph G, colorset C) is $O(n^2)$, where "n" is the number of nodes of graph attached to the image.

Proof

Observe that the first FOR loop of the algorithm is executed at most once for each node of the graph. Hence, the total time spent in this loop is $O(n)$. The WHILE loop processes the queue Q for each node which has the same color of its neighbor. The inner loop FOR processes the nodes of unvisited neighbor. So, the total time spent in these loops is $O(n)$, because are processed all nodes of the graph at most once.

From previous statements is inferred that the total running time of this procedure is $O(n^2)$ [2].

Taking into account that the color information of each region is stored as a color binary set, the color similitude between two regions may be computed either with the quadratic distance between color sets, or with Hamming distance between color sets. It was used the quadratic distance between binary sets s_q and s_t that is given by the following equation [3]:

$$d^f{}_{q,t} = \sum_{m_0=0}^{M-1} \sum_{m_1=0}^{M-1} (s_q[m_0] - s_t[m_0]) a_{m_0 m_1} (s_q[m_1] - s_t[m_1]) \tag{1}$$

Other three important distances are taken into consideration:

1. the spatial distance between the centroids of the regions [3]:

$$d^l_{q,t} = \sqrt{(x_q - x_t)^2 + (y_q - y_t)^2} \tag{2}$$

2. The distance in area between two regions q and t [3]:

$$d^a_{q,t} = |area_q - area_t| \tag{3}$$

3. The distance in MBR width (w) and height (h) between two regions q and t [3]:

$$d^s_{q,t} = \sqrt{(w_q - w_t)^2 + (h_q - h_t)^2} \tag{4}$$

The single region distance is given by the weighted sum of the color feature $d^f_{q,t}$, location $d^l_{q,t}$, area $d^a_{q,t}$ and spatial extent $d^s_{q,t}$ distances. The user may also assign a relative weight α to each attribute. For example, the user may weight the size parameter more heavily than feature value and location in the query. The overall single region query distance between regions q and t is given by [3]:

$$D_{tot} = \alpha_l \cdot d^l_{q,t} + \alpha_a \cdot d^a_{q,t} + \alpha_s \cdot d^s_{q,t} + \alpha_f \cdot d^f_{q,t} \tag{5}$$

For multiple regions query, the overall image query strategy consists of joining the queries on the individual regions in the query image. The join identifies the candidate target images.

4 Experiments and Results

In order to test the efficiency of the new method for a query on a single region or multiple regions with absolute spatial localization, several experiments have been made over the synthetic images collection.

For the new proposed algorithm (Method2) the hexagon edge equal to 3, respective 4 is considered. For each query, the images from the databases were inspected and relevance was assigned to them (1- relevant, 0 – irrelevant). In table 1, for each experiment the following information is given: the number of query regions, the weights for the distances (color, location, area and MBR) and the number of relevant images found in the first five retrieved images for Method1, Method2 with edge=3 and Method2 with edge=4.

Table 1. The experimental results

Nr. Of Query Reg.	Color	Loc.	Area	MBR	Met.1 Nr. of relevant images	Met.2 Edge=3 No. of relevant images	Met.2 Edge=4 No. of relevant images
1	100	0	0	0	5	5	5
1	100	100	0	0	5	4	3
1	100	100	100	0	1	1	1
1	100	100	100	100	1	1	1
2	100	0	0	0	5	5	5
2	100	100	0	0	4	3	3
2	100	100	0	0	4	3	3

If in the above table the results were synthetically presented, the effectuated experiments are much more detailed as follows.

In the first example query, the target is to retrieve the images that contain a red and a yellow shape. The values for the other three parameters are: location (100%), area (0%), minimum bounding rectangle (0%). Inspecting the 250 images from the database, it is remarked that 7 of them are relevant for this query. The graphic of the retrieving efficiency (precision vs. recall) in the case of the two presented algorithms (Method1 and Method2 with edge =3) is shown in Figure 1. It is important that the better is the search result, the farther from the origins is the curve precision vs. recall. In Figure 2 and Figure 3 are presented the retrieved images, using the Method2 with edge equal to 3 and respectively the Method1. The first image is the query image. The images are displayed in the ascending order of the distance D_{tot}. The "r" symbol indicates that the image was established as relevant, and "nr" like irrelevant. So, in this query the goal is to retrieve the images that contain a red and a yellow region, the red one in the right-upper corner of the image, and the yellow one in the right bottom side of the image.

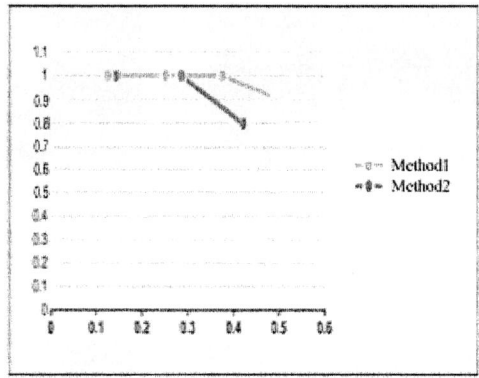

Fig. 1. Query 1: red and yellow shapes. The graphic of the retrieving efficiency for the Method1, and Method2 with the hexagon edge equal to 3.

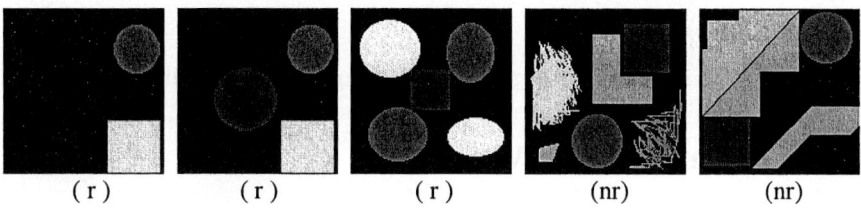

(r)　　　　(r)　　　　(r)　　　　(nr)　　　　(nr)

Fig. 2. The retrieved images using Method2 with hexagon edge equal to 3, for the query image from the first position

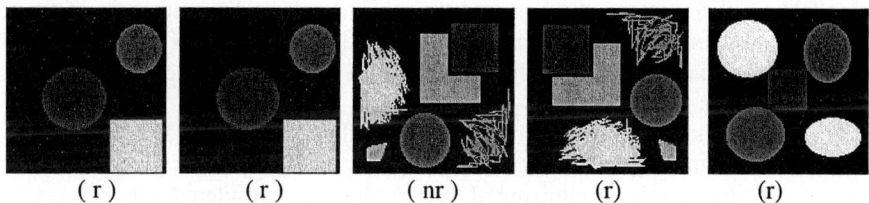

(r)　　　　(r)　　　　(nr)　　　　(r)　　　　(r)

Fig. 3. The retrieved images using Method1 for the query image from the first position

In the second query, the target is to retrieve the images that contain a shape having red color (100%). Also we take into consideration the location parameter (100%), the other two, namely area and minimum bounding rectangle are set to zero. The values of the four weights mean that the goal is the retrieval of the images that contain a red region in the center and bottom image side. Inspecting the images from the database, it is remarked that 7 of them are relevant for this query.

In Figure 4 and Figure 5 the retrieved images are presented, considering the Method2 with graph edge equal to 3 and the Method1. The first image is the query image.

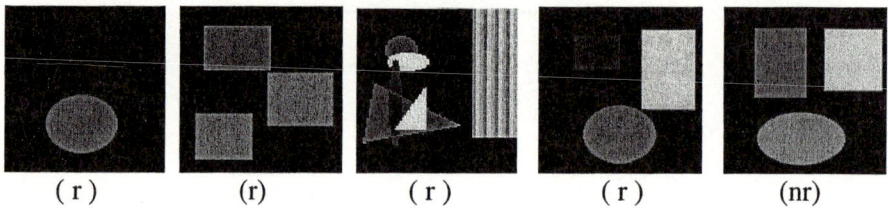

Fig. 4. The retrieved images using Method2 with hexagon edge equal to 3, for the query image from the first position

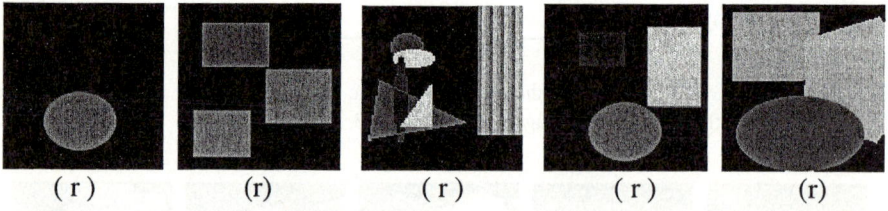

Fig. 5. The retrieved images using Method1 for the query image from the first position

5 Conclusion and Future Work

This article presents an original method of implementation of the color set back-projection algorithm, algorithm that allows the automated detection of the color regions from an image. The detected regions were then used in the content-based region query. The query was realized on one or more regions, taking into consideration the color feature, the location, the area and the minimum bounding rectangle of the regions. The efficiency of the two methods was studied by means of a number of experiments effectuated with the help of the IMTEST system, on a collection of synthetic images.

The experiments have been effectuated with Method2 and edge =2, 3, 4, 5, 6.

For Method2 and edge=2, the results were great, identical with those obtained with Method1. In this case the minimizing of the run time was considered to be too small.

Method2 with edge=5 or 6 caused a gradual quality reduction of the content-based region query, although it significantly minimizes the run time.

The effectuated experiments partially presented in table 1 show that in the great majority of the cases the results obtained with Method2 and edge=3 or edge=4 are as good as the ones obtained with Method1. There are few cases in which the number of relevant images retrieved by Method2 is smaller, and the difference was by only an image in the first five retrieved images. The conclusion is that Method2 with edge=3 or edge= 4 is the best solution not only from the point of view of quality, but also of the run time.

The very good results obtained in the effectuated experiments indicate the fact that each of the two implementations methods (Method1 and Method2) of the color set back-projection algorithm can be used in the processing of the content – based visual query. The advantage of the second method (Method 2 with edge equal to 3) is given by the fact that for detecting the color regions the pixel-by-pixel image traversal is not necessary, but only the pixels arranged in the vertices of a hexagon with edge equal to 3 pixels. So, the run time of the color region detection process using Method2 is more little than the run time of the first implementation method.

Minimizing the run time for the color set back-projection algorithm that automatically detects the color regions is an important objective, because there are some fields in which the number of color digital images that are stored is significant. For example, in the medical field, there are hospitals where only in a single department a number of 10000-12000 digital images is collected.

In the future the comparative study will be effectuated on diverse imagistic collections: synthetic images, image from nature and medical images with a bigger degree of diversity for the color hues.

References

1. Aslandogan, A., Yu, C.: Techniques and Systems for Image and Video Retrieval. In IEEE Transactions on Knowledge and data Engineering, Vol.11, No.1 (1999)
2. Burdescu, D.D.: Analiza complexitatii algoritmilor. Ed. Albastra Cluj-Napoca (1998)
3. Smith, J.R: Integrated Spatial and Feature Image Systems: Retrieval, Compression and Analysis, Ph.D. thesis, Graduate School of Arts and Sciences, Columbia University (1997)
4. Smith, J.R. , Chang, S.-F.: SaFe: A General Framework for Integrated Spatial and Feature Image Search. In: IEEE Signal Processing Society 1997 Workshop on Multimedia Signal Processing. June 23-25, Princetown, New Jersey, USA (1997)
5. Smith, J.R., Chang, S.-F.: Local Color and Texture Extraction and Spatial Query. In: IEEE Proc. International Conference on Image Processing. Laussane, Switzerland (1996)
6. Smith, J.R., Chang, S.-F.: Tools and Techniques for Color Image Retrieval, Symposium on Electronic Imaging. In: Science and Technology - Storage & Retrieval for Image and Video Databases IV, volume 2670, San Jose, CA, February 1996. IS&T/SPIE. (1996)
7. Smith, J.R., Chang, S.-F.: Automated Image retrieval Using Color and Texture. In: IEEE Transactions On Pattern Analysis and Machine Intelligence (1996)
8. Stanescu, L., Burdescu, D.: IMTEST-Software System For The Content-based Visual Retrieval Study. In: 14th International Conference On Control Systems And Computer Science. Bucuresti (2003)

SM3+: An XML Database Solution for the Management of MPEG-7 Descriptions

Yang Chu, Liang-Tien Chia, and Sourav S. Bhowmick

Center for Multimedia and Network Technology,
School of Computer Engineering,
Nanyang Technological University, Singapore 639798
{pg00815938, asltchia, assourav}@ntu.edu.sg

Abstract. MPEG-7 is a promising standard for the description of multimedia content. A lot of applications based on MPEG-7 media descriptions have been set up. Therefore, an efficient storage solution for large amounts of MPEG-7 descriptions are certainly desirable. MPEG-7 documents are also data-centric XML documents. Due to many advantages, the relational DBMS is the best choice for storing such XML documents. However, the existing RDBMS-based XML storage solutions can not reach all the critical requirements for MPEG-7 descriptions management. In this paper, we analyse the problems when using existing RDBMS-based XML storage approaches to store MPEG-7 documents and then present a new storage approach, called SM3+ that integrates the advantages of existing XML storage models and avoid the main drawbacks from them. Its features can reach the most critical requirements for MPEG-7 documents storage and management. Performance studies are conducted and the experimental results are encouraging.

1 Introduction

MPEG-7[1] is a standard for describing the content of different types of multimedia data. As the first standard of the Moving Picture Experts Group not dealing with coding exclusively, it offers richer semantics as compared with other existing XML based media description systems like Dublin Core and TV-anywhere. MPEG-7 documents can be defined and modified with the help of the Description Definition Language(DDL), which is based on XML Schema and extension to support additional data types. With MPEG-7, multimedia content can be exchanged between heterogeneous systems; plain text files can be used to store and share multimedia information; and multimedia data will be readily available to most users.

Since more and more applications are based on MPEG-7 descriptions, the amount of MPEG-7 descriptions is increasing considerably. Therefore, there will certainly be the need for adequate database support for the management of larger numbers of MPEG-7 descriptions. MPEG-7 descriptions are XML documents that conform to the XML Schema variant MPEG-7 DDL, therefor it is a self-suggesting idea to employ XML documents solutions for their management.

There are many XML storage solutions: Native XML database solutions, XML extensions of traditional database management systems and third-part middleware. Which one is suitable for MPEG-7 storage?

XML documents tend to be either data-centric or document-centric. Generally, for data-centric documents, we can use a traditional database, such as a relational, object oriented, or hierarchical database, to store them via third-party middleware or XMLEnabled database. Document-centric XML documents are often stored in a native XML database. MPEG-7 descriptions can be viewed as data-centric and we can use RDBMS-based XML storage solutions to manage them, since many advantages can be found in the relational database: widespread usage, proven underlying mathematical theory, query optimization techniques, advanced processing mechanism, etc. However, there exist a confusing variety of RDBMS-based XML storage solutions with different maturity and capabilities. Which one has sufficient abilities to support MPEG-7 documents management? In this regard, our paper will first analyze the problems in the existing RDBMS-based XML according to the main requirements of MPEG-7 documents storage solution; second, we propose a novel XML storage solution: SM3+, which can reach the most of requirements of MPEG-7 descriptions management.

2 Related Work

To store XML documents efficiently and effectively in a relational database, there is a need to map the XML DTD/Schema to the database schema. The schemas, which define how to map XML document into RDBMS can be categorized into two categories: structure-mapping (schema-conscious) approach and model-mapping (schema-oblivious) approach.

In structure-mapping, the design of the database schema is based on the understanding of DTD or XML Schema. It defines a relation or class for each element type and uses primary-key and foreign-key to describe the parent-child relationship between the elements in the XML documents. One advantage of this approach is that it supports querying documents efficiently because the mapped data can be indexed easily by built-in database indexes. Some examples of structure-mapping approach can be found in *Basic, Shared and Hybrid Inlining Technique*[2], *X-Ray*[3], *A Cost-Based Approach*[4].

In model-mapping, a fixed database schema is used to store the structure and data of any XML documents without the assistance of document schema. The complete structure of an XML document is stored with model-mapping. It will thus support complex XPath-based query and make it easy to reconstruct the data back into XML format. Some typical examples of model-mapping approach include *The Edge Approach*[5], *Monet*[6], *Xrel*[7], *XParent*[8], *SUCXENT++*[9], etc.

The database products provided with the leading database vendors are also the XML-enabled databases. Most of them introduce special datatypes to support XML storage, such as *XMLCLOB, XMLVARCHAR and XMLFile* in IBM DB2, *XML* in Microsoft SQL Server 2005 and *XMLType* in Oracle, and provide a number of XML specific methods to operate on those datatypes.

3 Analysis of MPEG-7 Descriptions Storage Solution

In[10], the authors present critical requirements for the management of MPEG-7 media descriptions and discuss current state-of-the-art database solutions for XML documents. In order to be suitable for the management of MPEG-7 descriptions, MPEG-7 storage solution should satisfy several critical requirements: fine-grained representation and access, typed representation and access, index structure and path indexing.

However, neither existing structure-mapping approaches nor model-mapping methods can achieve all the MPEG-7 storage requirements due to their intrinsic drawbacks. For structure-mapping, it provides weak support for hierarchical structure of the original XML documents. This drawback makes it impossible to support complex XPath-based query (i.e. recursive XML queries) efficiently. Furthermore, structure-mapping approaches cannot avoid the assistance of fixed DTD or XML Schema. Moreover, MPEG-7 cannot provide such fixed schema.

Due to the mapping process without the assistant of DTD or XML schema, model-mapping approach has to establish only a single value column that stores all values as strings, the most generic type. Such an approach, however, would make it impossible to reflect all kinds of datatypes and need an index in order to find all objects with the conditions based on the datatype other than string type. Considering the ability to describe data, model-mapping is a lot less flexible than structure-mapping. In MPEG-7 descriptions, there are many element types with list datatype, i.e. element *ColorValueIndex* in *DominantColor* descriptor, which would have following value: '216 23 43'. Model-mapping method would store this data as one string value in a single column. Such storage format makes the query inefficient when the users want to issue the query on each item in the list value. In other words, model-mapping approach cannot reach typed representation and access requirement for MPEG-7 description storage.

To a certain extent, the XML storage and management technology in the leading database systems can be viewed as a technology that integrates native XML database and relational database. Although these XML-enabled database systems provide powerful functions to satisfy most XML applications, they cannot reach fine-grained and typed representation requirements for MPEG-7 description storage. Furthermore, in these database systems, XPath operations are evaluated by constructing DOM from specific XML datatype and using functional evaluations. This can be very expensive when performing operations on large collections of documents. IBM DB2 and Oracle provide an alternative option for XML storage, which is called XML collection in IBM DB2 and structured storage in Oracle. Such alternative can support fine-grained and typed representation of XML documents, more powerful index structures and SQL constraints. However, they raise other critical problems. They have limited flexibility. Only documents that conform to the XML Schema can be stored with this technology. XPath operations are evaluated with the aid of XML Schema.

In order to resolve these problems, in this paper we introduce a novel XML storage method known as SM3+, abbreviated from "*combined Structure-mapping and Model-mapping*". The motivation of SM3+ is to integrate the advantages of structure-mapping and model-mapping, and avoid the main drawbacks from each of those methods. The following section introduces this new approach in details.

4 Our Approach: SM3+

4.1 Basic Idea

An XML document is often viewed as a tree graph. In XML tree, the internal nodes correspond to the element types with element content in XML document, while the leaf nodes correspond to the single-valued attributes and element types with PCDATA-only content in XML document. We also call the leaf nodes as evaluated nodes since they hold values.

The ideal of SM3+ is to use model-mapping approach to map all internal nodes and use structure-mapping approach to map all evaluated nodes. In an XML tree, the internal nodes depict the structure of the XML document and are only useful for document navigation. Storing them by using model-mapping method can keep complete structure information of XML tree and support efficient and easy document traverse. The evaluated node is the end point of each XPath and holds the data of XML document. It has little usage for XML tree navigation. Using structure-mapping approach to store them can better represent appropriate datatype of each evaluated node and provide a flexible storage schema to satisfy different storage requests.

In our previous version, SM3[11], we used XParent-like schema to store internal node. When storing large amount of XML data, it raises two drawbacks: much more space requirement and bad query performance due to more joins in corresponding SQL. We changed the storage schema for storing internal nodes in SM3+ and avoid drawbacks of previous version.

4.2 Database Schema

For Internal nodes. To efficiently store and query XML documents which have the tree-like node structure using a relational database system, the document order of XML file need to be captured in the relational data model. It can be accomplished by encoding each node's position in an XML document. Unlike pure model-mapping method, which encode all nodes' position, our approach only need to encode internal nodes.

There exist a variety of order encoding methods, but among them, *Dewey Order* performs reasonably well on both queries and updates. With *Dewey Order*, the ancestor-descendant relationship can be determined using only the *id* value, which is a sequence of numeric values separated by a dot that represents the path from the document's root to the node (as illustrated in Fig. 1). However, the *id* length depends on the tree depth and a string comparison of the *ids* may degrade the query performance and deliver wrong results with respect to the total node order, e.g. comparing 1.9 and 1.10. In[12], the authors provided a solution for these shortcomings and proposed a novel hierarchical labeling scheme called *ORDPATH*. *ORDPATH* provides a compressed binary representation of *Dewey*

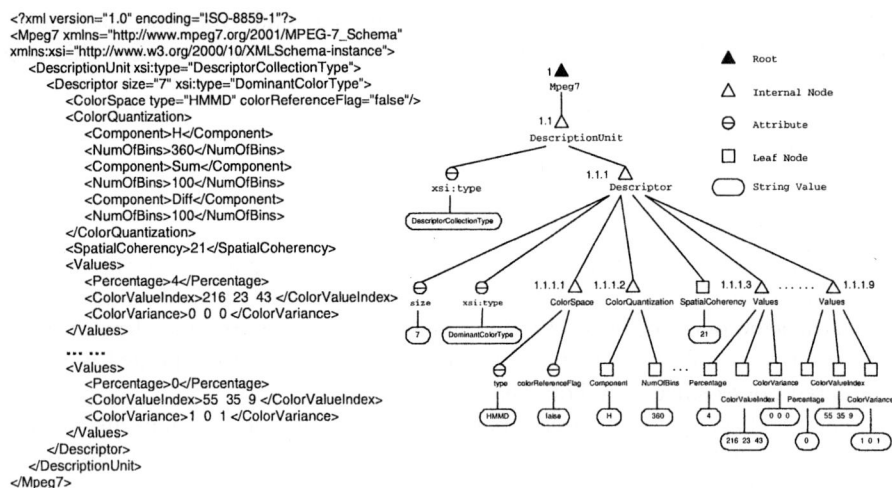

Fig. 1. An instance of MPEG-7 document and its tree graph

Order. It uses successive variable-length L_i/O_i bitstrings to represent *id* value of each node. Each L_i bitstring, which are represented using a form of prefix-free encoding, specifies the length in bits of the succeeding O_i bitstring. For example, if the L_i bitstring 01 is assigned length 3, this L_i will indicate a 3-bit O_i bitstring. The bitstrings (000, 001, ..., 111) can represent O_i values of the first eight integers, (0, 1, ..., 7). Thus 01101 is the bitstring for ordinal '5'[12]. With *ORDPATH*, *id* value of each node is constructed as binary string and document order can be preserved and yielded by simple bitstring comparison. The ancestor-descendent relationships between any two nodes X and Y can be also determined equally simply: X being a strict substring of Y or vice versa imply there is an ancestry relationship.

SM3+ uses *ORDPATH* to encode the position of each internal nodes and construct the document structure information in relational database model. Following are the table schemas to store internal nodes:

xpath (xpathid, length, xpathexp)

internalnode (uid, xpathid, nodename, ordpath, lid, oid, tablename, rtablename)

xpath table records the XPath information of XML tree. *internalnode* table represents the information of each internal node. *ordpath* is the *ORDPATH* value of the internal node. *uid* is used to identify the internal node. *lid* is the internal node local identifier that depicts the position of a node among sibling nodes. *oid* is useful for the queries that include index predicates. It is an index of the node that occurs more than once in the XML document. *tablename* and *rtablename* are used to indicate which table stores the value of this internal node's leaf nodes children and which table loads the value of repeatable leaf nodes children.

For Leaf Nodes. Relations will be created for each internal node whose children include leaf nodes and then these nodes are mapped into corresponding relation as attributes. It is similar to structure mapping, but it is not necessary to create foreign key for representing parent-child relationship between two internal nodes. In order to identify the datatype of each evaluated node and map them into database by using structure-mapping approach, a mapping schema is created for representing how to map them into database schema. The mapping schema is defined via mapping processing definition (MPD) file, which is also an XML file. In order to support the list datatype in MPEG-7 descriptions, we defined an attribute named *StringToMultiColumn* in MPD to enable the text value to be stored into several columns with proper datatype according to the users or applications requirements.

The database for a MPEG-7 descriptor shown in Fig. 1 is presented here in Fig. 2.

For internal nodes:

XPATHID	LENGTH	XPATHEXP
1	1	#/Mpeg7
2	2	#/Mpeg7#/DescriptionUnit
3	3	#/Mpeg7#/DescriptionUnit#/Descriptor
4	4	#/Mpeg7#/DescriptionUnit#/Descriptor#/ColorSpace
5	4	#/Mpeg7#/DescriptionUnit#/Descriptor#/ColorQuantization
6	4	#/Mpeg7#/DescriptionUnit#/Descriptor#/Values

(a) xpath table

UID	XPATHID	NODENAME	ORDPATH	LID	OID	TABLENAME	RTABLENAME
1	1	Mpeg7	x'48	1	1		
2	2	DescriptionUnit	x'4A40	1	1	descriptorcollection	
3	3	Descriptor	x'4A52	1	1	dominantcolor	
4	4	ColorSpace	x'4A5290	1	1	colorspace	
5	5	ColorQuantization	x'4A52B0	2	1		rtable
6	6	Values	x'4A52D0	4	1	values	
7	6	Values	x'4A52F0	5	2	values	
8	6	Values	x'4A5304	6	3	values	
9	6	Values	x'4A530C	7	4	values	
10	6	Values	x'4A5314	8	5	values	
11	6	Values	x'4A531C	9	6	values	
12	6	Values	x'4A5324	10	7	values	

(b) internalnode table

For evaluated nodes:

UID	XSITYPE
2	DescriptorCollectionType

(c) descriptorcollection table

UID	SIZE	XSITYPE
3	5	DominantColorType

(d) dominantcolor table

SPATIALCOHERENCY
0

UID	TYPE	COLORREFERENCEFLAG
4	HMMD	FALSE

(e) colorspace table

UID	LID	OID	NODENAME	VALUE
5	1	1	Component	H
5	2	1	NumOfBins	360
5	3	2	Component	Sum
5	4	2	NumOfBins	100
5	5	3	Component	Diff
5	6	3	NumOfBins	100

(f) rtable

UID	PERCENTAGE	COLORVALUEINDEX
6	4	216 23 43
7	10	44 67 30
8	2	210 33 39
9	6	150 80 2
10	4	209 60 15
11	3	206 42 22
12	0	55 35 9

(g) values table

Fig. 2. SM3+ database schema for the example of MPEG-7 document in Fig. 1

4.3 Extraction of Original XML Documents

There are two steps to implement the process of extracting data from RDBMS and reconstructing them into original XML documents: first, selecting all internal nodes data and leaf nodes data from database; second, with the aid of MPD file, reconstructing them into XML format document. The algorithm for reconstruction is presented in Fig. 3.

```
Input:    L₁ {l₁,l₂,...l_k} - list of internal nodes data ordered by
                UID, which is depth-first order of internal node
          L₂ - list of all leaf nodes data
Output:   𝒟 is the XML document to be returned.
1: n, p are instance of Class 'Node' which including
       XML node and level information.
2: s is a stack.
3: for all element in L₁ do
4:    if n=null then
5:       n.node = 𝒟.createElement(l_i.nodeName)
6:       n.level = l_i.level
7:       𝒟.appendChild(n.node)
8:       setLeafNodeChildren(n.node, L₂)
9:       p = n
10:   else if
11:      n.node = 𝒟.createElement(l_i.nodeName)
12:      n.level = l_i.level
13:      if n.level > p.level then
14:         s.push(p)
15:      else if n.level = p.level then
16:         p = s.peek()
17:      else if
18:         while n.level <= p.level do
19:            s.pop()
20:            p = s.peek()
21:         end while
22:      end if
23:      setLeafNodeChildren(n.node, L₂)
24:      p.node.appendChild(n.node)
25:      p = n
26:   end if
27: end for
```

Fig. 3. Extraction algorithm

4.4 SQL Translating

Although the data in XML documents has been stored in RDBMS, users or applications still view it modelled as XML trees, and issue queries against the XML trees. For supporting such requirement, our database system is required to have the function that allows high-level XPath-based queries to be mapped into efficient SQL queries against the underlying datasource. Due to space constraints we discuss the translation procedure briefly.

For example, the following XQuery:

for $b **in** doc('dominantcolor.xml')//Descriptor
where $b/Values/ColorValueIndex = '216 23 43' **return** $b/SpatialCoherency

would be translated into SQL as follows:

select d.spatialCoherency
from xpath xp1,xpath xp2,internalnode i1,internalnode i2,descriptor d,values v
where xp1.xpathexp like '#%/Descriptor' **and** xp2.xpathexp like '#%/Descriptor#/Values'
       and i1.xpathid=xp1.xpathid **and** i2.xpathid=xp2.xpathid **and** d.uid=i1.uid
       and   v.uid=i2.uid   **and**   v.colorvalueindex='216   23   43'   **and**   PARENT(i2.ordpath)=i1.ordpath

This query returns the *SpatialCoherency* of all *Descriptor* whose descendant *ColorValueIndex* has the value of '216 23 43'. The way to translate this query to SQL would be:

1. Obtain all internal nodes '*Values*' that have such XPath as '//Descriptor/Values' and their leaf node *ColorValueIndex* has the value of '216 23 43';
2. Get all internal nodes '*Descriptor*', which are the parent of internal nodes '*Values*', which are in the above result set. According to [12], we developed function *PARENT()* to determine the *ORDPATH* of the parent of the given internal node;
3. Retrieving the value of leaf node '*SpatialCoherency*' whose parents are these '*Descriptor*' nodes.

5 Experimental Results

In order to check the effectiveness of our method we have implemented SM3+ using Java language and carried out a series of performance experiments. In this

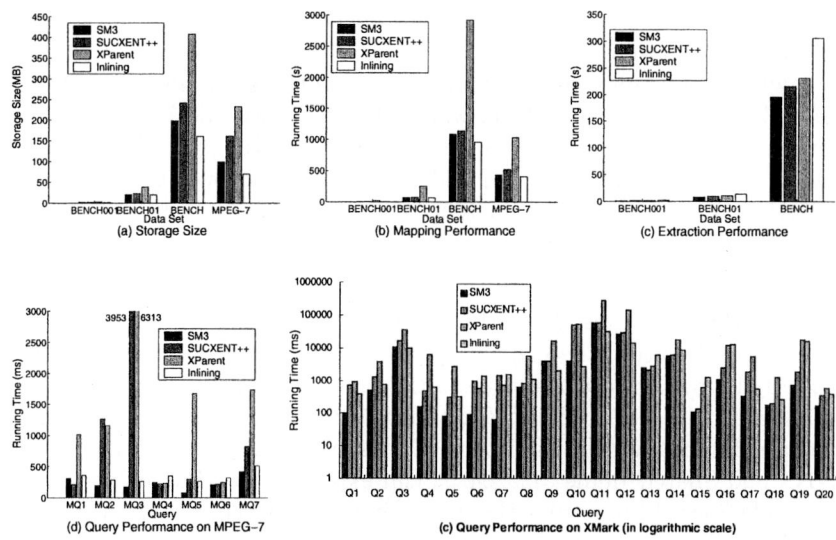

Fig. 4. Experimental Result: Storage size and Mapping performance

section, experimental results will be presented. We compared SM3+ to XParent and SUCXENT++, the pure model-mapping approach, and SM3+ to Shared Inline, a pure structure-mapping method.

The hardware platform used is a Dell PowerEdge 2650 with Xeon CPU 2.8GHz and 1.00GB RAM running Windows Server 2003 Enterprise Edition. The database system is IBM DB2. We used two experimental data sets: one from XMark project[13], a benchmark for XML data management, another from MPEG-7 descriptions. We generated the XMark benchmark data with different scale factors. Three different sizes of data are used: BENCH001 (which means 1% of the original BENCH) with 1.1MB size, BENCH01 with 11.3MB size and BENCH with 113MB size. The MPEG-7 description data set with the size of 85MB include one high-level descriptor: *UserDescriptionType* and eight low-level descriptors extracted from about 20,000 pictures: *ColorLayout, ColorStructure, ContourShape, DominantColor, EdgeHistogram, HomogeneousTexture, RegionShape* and *ScalableColor*.

Test queries need to be carefully selected for the performance study. XMark issues 20 benchmark queries that cover different aspects of XML queries for accessing XML data. We also issued seven common queries for testing query performance on MPEG-7 documents (note that low level descriptors are primarily useful for similarity searching. However, supporting similarity retrieval function in the MPEG-7 database system will be our future work. Corresponding performance experiment is not included current test). Due to the page limit, we do not list them here.

Storage Size. Fig.4.(a) describes the storage requirements of the four approaches. From this figure, XParent consumes much more storage space than the other approaches due to the additional space requirement to store ancestor-descendant relationship among all the nodes. SUCXENT++ stores all the leaf nodes, while SM3+ only stores the information of internal nodes and the relationship information among them, where the attributes and leaf nodes of each internal node will be stored in one row. For Shared Inline, it does not store the complete hierarchical structure of XML document and only uses primary-key and foreign-key to indicate the parent-child relationship. So the database size of Shared Inline is the smallest among the four approaches. According to the following table, we can observe how many rows each approach may insert.

Mapping Performance. Fig.4.(b) presents the mapping performance for different sample data set. The mapping performance depends on how many tuples are inserted into the database. Due to the different mapping schemas, the four methods load different tuples into database. Following data shows the rows inserted into database for each approach: SM3: 776715; Sucxent: 1127128; XParent: 2854179 and Shared Inline: 622204. It can explain why XParent performs the worst while Shared Inline runs the fastest in terms of mapping process.

Extraction Performance. Extraction performance depends on the time taken to extract the relevant data from database and the processing time to reconstruct the document. Fig.4.(c) shows SM3+, SUCXENT++ and XParent consume similar time to extract data and reconstruct them into XML format, while Shared Inline takes more time for such operation due to more SQL queries needed to fetch all data of subelements.

Query Performance. As one of structure-mapping methods, Shared Inline clusters elements corresponding to the same real world object and clusters the same kind of elements together. While SUCXENT and XParent map each element into one record in database and lose the benefit of clustering elements corresponding to the real world object. So Shared Inline performs better than SUCXENT and XParent when the query must apply predicates related to several sub-elements, for example, Q9, Q10, etc. However, structure-mapping methods cannot hold the whole hierarchical structure information of XML document. This results in much worse performance when issuing the queries with complex XPath expression, i.e. recursive queries. It is the reason for the bad performance of Shared Inline in terms of Q15, Q16, Q19, etc. SM3+ integrate the advantage of structure-mapping and model-mapping, meaning that SM3+ not only clusters elements of XML document corresponding to the same real world object, but also keeps the complete hierarchical structure information of XML document. It results in the good performance of SM3+ in terms of the most of testing queries.

6 Conclusions

In this paper, SM3+, a new approach to mapping, indexing and retrieving MPEG-7 documents and other data-centric XML documents using relational database system, has been described. SM3+ integrates the advantages of structure mapping and model mapping. Unlike structure-mapping method, SM3+ supports XPath-based query efficiently without involving many joins in SQL.

Compared with model-mapping, SM3+ solves the datatype problem in model-mapping without sacrificing the performance, and SM3+ even performs better than most model-mapping approach in the case of many XPath based queries. Furthermore, SM3+ provides a flexible storage schema for satisfying all kinds of storage requirements. Although SM3+ need mapping schema based on MPEG-7 schema, such mapping schema only represents which simple elements and attributes are included in the complex elements and datatype information. Since it is not necessary to provide the structure information of MPEG-7 documents when mapping MPEG-7 descriptions to RDBMS, it is possible to store an arbitrary MPEG-7 description conforming to existing MPEG-7 schema to RDBMS with SM3+. In summary, SM3+ matches the most critical requirements for MPEG-7 descriptions management, such as fine-grained and typed representation and access, index system and XPath-based query.

References

1. Josè M. Martìnez: MPEG-7 Overview (version 8). ISO/IECJTC1/SC29/WG11-N4980, Klangenfurt, July 2002. Available at http://www.mpegindustry.com/mp7a/w4980_mp7_Overview1.html.
2. Jayavel Shanmugasundaram, Kristin Tufte, Gang He, Chun Zhang, David DeWitt and Jeffrey Naughton: Relational Databases for Querying XML Documents: Limitations and Opportunities. The 25th VLDB Conference, Edinburgh, Scotland, 1999.
3. Gerti Kappel, Elisabeth Kapsammer and Werner Retschitzegger: X-Ray – Towards Integrating XML and Relational Database Systems. The International Conference on Conceptual Modeling, 2000.
4. Philip Bohannon, Juliana Freire, Prasan Roy, Jèrôme Simèon and Bell Laboratories: From XML Schema to Relations: A Cost-Based Approach to XML Storage. The 18th International Conference on Data Engineering (ICDE'02), 2002.
5. Daniela Florescu and Donald Kossmann: A Performance Evaluation of Alternative Mapping Schemes for Storing XML Data in a Relational Database. IEEE Data Engineering Bulletin 22(3), 1999.
6. Albrecht Schmidt, Martin Kersten, Menzo Windhouwer and Florian Waas: Efficient Relational Storage and Retrieval of XML Documents. In Proceedings of the Third International Workshop on the Web and Databases (WebDB 2000), Dallas, TX, 2000.
7. Masatoshi Yoshikawa and Toshiyuki Amagasa: XRel: A path-based approach to storage and retrieval of XML documents using relational databases. ACM Transactions on Internet Technology, 1(1). 2001.
8. Haifeng Jiang, Hongjun Lu, Wei Wang and Jeffrey Xu Yu: XParent: An Efficient RDBMSBased XML Database System. Proceedings of the 18th International Conference on Data Engineering (ICDE'02), 2002.
9. Sandeep Prakash, Sourav S. Bhowmick and Sanjay Madria: Efficient Recursive XML Query Processing in Relational Database Systems. 23rd International Conference on Conceptual Modeling(ER2004), Shanghai, China, 2004.
10. Utz Westermann and Wolfgang Klas: An Analysis of XML Database Solutions for the Management of MPEG-7 Media Descriptions. ACM Computing Surveys, Vol.35, No. 4, December 2003, pp. 331ÃÂ373.

11. Yang Chu, Liang-Tien Chia and Sourav S. Bhowmick: Looking at Mapping, Indexing & Querying of MPEG-7 Descriptors in RDBMS with SM3. MMDBÃÂ04, Washington, DC, USA, 2004.
12. Patrick OÃÂNeil, Elizabeth OÃÂNeil, Shankar Pal, Istvan Cseri, Gideon Schaller and Nigel Westbury: ORDPATHs: Insert-Friendly XML Node Labels. ACM SIGMOD Industrial Track, 2004.
13. Albrecht Schmidt, Florian Waas, Martin Kersten, Michael J. Carey, Ioana Manolescu and Ralph Busse: XMark: A Benchmark for XML Data Management. Proceedings of the 28th VLDB Conference, Hong Kong, China, 2002.

LocalRank: Ranking Web Pages Considering Geographical Locality by Integrating Web and Databases

Jianwei Zhang[1], Yoshiharu Ishikawa[1,2], Sayumi Kurokawa[1],
and Hiroyuki Kitagawa[1,2]

[1] Department of Computer Science, Graduate School of Systems and Information Engineering
[2] Center for Computational Sciences,
University of Tsukuba, 1-1-1 Tennodai, Tsukuba, Ibaraki, 305-8573, Japan
{zjw, saku39}@kde.cs.tsukuba.ac.jp
{ishikawa, kitagawa}@cs.tsukuba.ac.jp

Abstract. In this paper, we propose a method called LocalRank to rank web pages by integrating the web and a user database containing information on a specific geographical area. LocalRank is a rank value for a web page to assess its relevance degree to database entries considering geographical locality and its popularity on a local web space. In our method, we first construct a linked graph structure using entries contained in the database. The nodes of this graph consist of database entries and their related web pages. The edges in the graph are composed of semantic links including geographical links between these nodes, in addition to conventional hyperlinks. Then a link analysis is performed to compute a LocalRank value for each node. LocalRank can represent user's interest since this graph effectively integrates the web and the user database. Our experimental results for a local restaurant database shows that local web pages related to the database entries are highly ranked based on our method.

1 Introduction

Recently, *local search* [1,2], that provides information on a specific geographical area, has attracted a lot of research interests. For this purpose, gathering web pages related to a specific area becomes an essential task, but so far it is common that local web pages are collected manually. It is also difficult for a computer to determine whether a web page describes information on the area where a user is interested in. The reason is that vagueness often exists in geographical descriptions on web pages. Examples of vague descriptions are as follows: two or more locations may have a same place name, a person name appearing on a web page is mistaken for a place name, and so on.

We also notice another problem that a web page with high popularity on the global web may not be an important one for a specific geographical area. Conversely, an important web page for a specific geographical area may not be ranked to the top place by a conventional web mining method that considers reputation on the global web. Furthermore, for a specific geographical area, there are usually many web resources corresponding to entities existing in the real world (e.g., web pages of a certain organization in this area). They may have been known by a user or can be acquired easily from some web directories or by following the links of a portal web site about this area. For example, consider a user is interested in information about restaurants in Tsukuba city, Japan and he or she has a table shown in Fig. 1. Effective use of this known information to rank web pages is the main concern of this paper.

ID	Name	URL	Address	Phone	Zip Code
1	COCCOLINO	http://coccolino.jp/	3-1-5 Chikuho, Tsukuba, Ibaraki	029-864-4555	300-3257
2	GURUMAN	http://www.omisemall.com/goru/	3-7-17 Azuma, Tsukuba, Ibaraki	029-851-6107	305-0031
3	RANTEI	http://e-tsukuba.jp/rantei/index.htm/	1055-11 Shimohirooka, Tsukuba, Ibaraki	029-851-2603	305-0043
:	:	:	:	:	:

Fig. 1. Restaurants in Tsukuba city

Recently some researches [3,4] proposed to consider relationships between database entries as a kind of "links" and apply a link analysis to a database. We extend this idea to integrate the web and a user database and perform a link analysis to rank related web pages. In our method, we first construct a linked graph structure for the specific geographical area using entries contained in the database. The nodes of this graph consist of database entries and their related web pages. The edges in the graph are composed of semantic links including geographical connections between these nodes, in addition to conventional hyperlinks. Then a link analysis is performed based on this graph. This graph represents the information of the user provided database, its related web pages, and their relationships. Therefore, the results of the link analysis, called *LocalRank*, not only reflect web pages' popularity on the locally constructed web space (as opposed to the global web), but also take their relevance degrees to the user database into consideration. Hence, our method can be thought of as a ranking approach based on user's interest. Notice that we consider geographical locality by generating geographical links between database entries and between database entries and web pages, instead of directly judging which geographical area a web page intends to describe. In this paper, we also introduce a simple but effective method about how to collect web pages related to a user database.

The remaining part of this paper is organized as follows. Section 2 reviews the related work. The detailed proposed method is presented in Section 3. Section 4 shows the experimental results based on our method. Finally, we conclude this paper and discuss the future work in Section 5.

2 Related Work

Link Analysis. Currently, link analysis [5,6], that uses the hyperlinked structure of the web, is an important technology to identify high-quality web pages. Among existing approaches, Kleinberg's *HITS* [7] and Google's *PageRank* [8] are the most representative algorithms. HITS takes a subset of a web graph and generates hub and authority scores for each page in the subset. PageRank enforces that pages are important if important pages link to them. Our LocalRank calculation is similar to PageRank. However, we calculate ranks on an integrated space of the web and a database with additional consideration of semantic links, as opposed to the PageRank's approach. Recently, [3,4] consider relationships between database entries as a kind of links and apply a link analysis to a database. We extend this idea to perform a link analysis based on the integrated graph of the web and a user database.

Web and Its Geographical Locality. There exist many approaches for extracting pages related to a specific geographical area from the web. [9] proposes a notion of a *localness degree* to discover local information from the web. An *augmented web space* is presented in [10]. This augmented web space consists of web pages, hyperlinks and semantic links that represent geographical relationships between web pages. In contrast to these researches, we consider geographical locality of a web page by employing virtual geographical links to connect the web and a database and applying them a link analysis. The approach proposed in [11] is to determine *geographical scopes* of web resources. Based on the textual contents of a web resource, as well as the distribution of related hyperlinks, the scope of the resource is computed. In [12], a categorization method of queries to a search engine is proposed. Its feature is that the categorization is performed based on geographical locality. Some of these approaches may be helpful to extend our method.

Topic-Focused Crawling. Although it is not our emphasis to crawl web pages related to user database entries, our method is related to the web crawling technology. Recently, *topic-focused crawling* [13,14,15,16] is becoming a key technology for efficiently collecting web pages. [13] develops a framework to evaluate topic-focused crawling algorithms. The *PageRank crawler* [14] prefers accessing a web page with a high PageRank value. The *focused crawler* in [15] is based on a hypertext classifier. Its basic idea is to classify crawled pages with categories in a topic taxonomy. The *context focused crawler* in [16] guides its crawl using Bayesian classifiers trained to estimate the link distance between a crawled page and the relevant target pages. Our LocalRank values can be used to navigate a crawler to find highly relevant pages to a database, like a PageRank crawler. In this sense, our approach can be applied to a topic-focused crawling, where the "topic" is determined by database entries.

3 Proposed Method

In this section, we describe our method using the example table of restaurants in Tsukuba (Fig. 1). Subsection 3.1 presents the concept of an extended database. Subsection 3.2 shows a model for integrating the web and a database. Subsection 3.3 introduces how a graph structure is constructed and how LocalRank is calculated.

3.1 Extended Database

For a database of Fig. 1, we first consider its *extended database* shown in Fig. 2. This extended database, whose left and right parts denote the database and the web respectively, shows their relationships in the style of the entity-relationship diagram. The `restaurant` entity represents the set of the entries of Fig. 1. The `page` entity stands

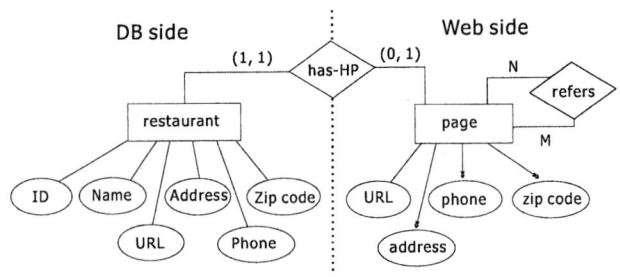

Fig. 2. Extended database

for the total set of all the web pages. The web pages' URLs, addresses, phone numbers and zip codes appearing on them are considered as the attributes of the page entity. The lines with two arrows show that an attribute may have zero to many values, because it is possible that zero to many addresses appear on a web page. The has-HP relationship connects the restaurant and page entities. The notations "(1, 1)" and "(0, 1)" mean that for a certain restaurant entry there must exist a corresponding homepage, while not all web pages must have a corresponding restaurant entry. The refers relationship represents hyperlink references between web pages.

Notice that for other databases, extended databases can similarly be constructed using additional attributes. Therefore attributes are not restricted to addresses, phone numbers, etc. They may be the ones that can be extracted from web pages with available tools according to user requirements.

3.2 Authority Transfer Graph

We describe next an *authority transfer graph* (Fig. 3), based on the idea of [3]. This graph is constructed based on the extended database explained in the previous subsection and reflects some relationships between its elements. For simplicity the attributes are omitted.

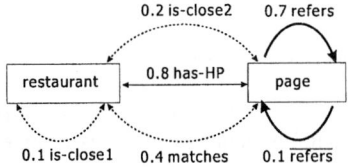

Fig. 3. An example of authority transfer graph

We call the solid lines and dotted lines in this graph *links*, since we extend the concept of hyperlinks between web pages to the integrated space of the web and a database. We also call the values between 0 and 1 assigned to links their *weights*. Actually, how to assign proper weights to links is a difficult task. It may be a trial process performed until the quality of results becomes satisfactory. In this paper we do not give more emphasis to the discussion on this problem. The solid lines correspond to the relationships has-HP and refers in the extended database (Fig. 2). The refers link means a reference from a web page to another page and the weight "0.7" means that a page's score is multiplied by 0.7 and then transferred to its linked page. The $\overline{\text{refers}}$ link represents a link in the opposite direction. In this example, the weight "0.1" means that the score of a link target page is multiplied by 0.1 and then transferred to the page linking to it. A kind of links, whose weights in both directions are equal, is represented by $\longleftrightarrow$. For example, we use the has-HP link to represent a correspondence relationship between a database entry and its homepage, and assume the weights from any side to another side are equal (i.e., they influence each other equally). In this case we use $\longleftrightarrow$ for has-HP.

The dotted lines show semantic relationships. The is-close1 link is generated between two restaurant entries when their addresses are close. The is-close2 link connects restaurant and page entities, and is generated when their geographical locations are close. The matches link is generated when it can be determined that the information a web page describes is about a restaurant entry. In general, there often exists flexibility in semantic links. Therefore, we assume that a user-defined predicate is given to define a semantic link. For example, is-close1 is generated when the distance between two restaurant addresses is below a certain threshold. We will later describe its sample implementation for the experiment. Although the is-close1 link in this example is based on a binary decision (i.e., an is-close1 link is generated or not), we may be able to assign more sophisticated weights to this kind of links, say, depending on their distance values. Such issues are our future challenges.

3.3 Link Analysis

In our method, we first construct a *data graph* (Fig. 4) in which the links defined in the authority transfer graph (Fig. 3) are realized. The data graph consists of database entries, their related pages, hyperlinks, and some semantic links. Then we perform a link analysis based on this data graph. The result of this link analysis, called *LocalRank*, combines the web pages' popularity on the local web space with their relevance degrees to the database entries. The LocalRank score is influenced by geographical locality because we integrate the web and a user database using semantic links including virtual geographical links (is-close1 and is-close2).

The following steps are what we have actually done in the experiment. This process may be able to be extended depending on the environment and the requirement when we apply our approach to a different context.

Constructing a Data Graph. First we describe how to generate the nodes of the data graph.
1. For each entry of the restaurant table, generate a corresponding node.
2. Download the homepage of each restaurant using the "URL" attribute of the table and let the set of pages be S_1.
3. Get the web pages that are reachable from the homepages in the same web site[1] and let the set be S_2.

---
[1] The decision is simply based on judging whether the URL string of a web page has a same prefix with that of a homepage.

4. For each homepage, retrieve its backlink pages using a search engine (Google is used in our experiment). These web pages compose a set S_3.
5. Perform keyword searches using the attribute values of each row of the `restaurant` table. In the experiment, we retrieve web pages using the "Name" and "Phone" attributes to create a query condition. The result set of web pages is called S_4.
6. For all the web pages in S_1, S_2, S_3 and S_4 acquired in Step 2, 3, 4 and 5, generate their corresponding nodes.
7. Extract URLs from the web pages in S_1, S_2, S_3 and S_4 and generate nodes for those whose corresponding pages have not been downloaded.

As shown above, the nodes of the data graph consist of the entries of the `restaurant` table and their related web pages including the downloaded and undownloaded ones.

Next the links between these nodes are generated as follows.

1. For the web pages in S_1, connect them to the corresponding `restaurant` entries with bidirectional `has-HP` links.
2. Based on the results of the URL extraction in Step 7 of the node generation, create `refers` and $\overline{\text{refers}}$ links between web pages (including the downloaded and undownloaded ones).
3. For the web pages in S_4 (obtained from a search engine using the "Name" and "Phone" attributes), connect them to the corresponding `restaurant` entries with bidirectional `matches` links.
4. Generate bidirectional `is-close1` links between database entries when the user-defined `is-close1` predicate is true. In the experiment, we implement the predicate by mapping the "Address" attributes of the database entries to coordinates and judging whether their distances, calculated using the coordinates, are below a given threshold or not.
5. Similarly, generate bidirectional `is-close2` links between the web pages in $S_1 \cup S_2 \cup S_3 \cup S_4$ and their corresponding database entries if the `is-close2` predicate is true.

We assign weights to the links based on the settings of the authority transfer graph. Notice that when two or more edges belonging to a same kind of links go out from a same node, the weight is divided by the number of outgoing edges. Let us see the example of Fig. 4. Since there are two `matches` links going out from the COCCOLINO entry, the weight "0.4" of the `matches` link in the authority transfer graph (Fig. 3) is divided by two and the weights of both outgoing edges become "0.2". Meanwhile the weight of the edge from a corresponding web page to the COCCOLINO entry remains "0.4". This weight setting approach is similar to that of PageRank [8].

As mentioned above, a graph structure called a *data graph* (Fig. 4) is constructed. In Fig. 4, the left oval nodes represent the entries of the `restaurant` table, while the middle square nodes and right circle nodes denote the downloaded web pages and the undownloaded URLs, respectively. The labels of the `refers` and $\overline{\text{refers}}$ links are omitted.

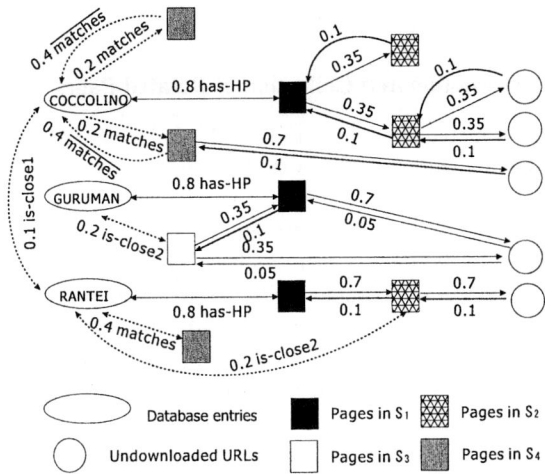

Fig. 4. An example of data graph

Score Calculation. We calculate next the score called *LocalRank* for each node[2] in the data graph constructed in the previous section. It can be calculated by the following equation.

$$r = d\mathbf{A}'r + \frac{(1-d)}{n}e \qquad (1)$$

where n is the number of the nodes in the data graph, d is a damping factor given by a user, $\mathbf{A}$ denotes an $n \times n$ matrix, the value of whose element (i, j) sums the weights of all edges from i to j, $\mathbf{A}'$ is the transposed matrix of $\mathbf{A}$, r denotes a column vector with n dimensions, whose element is the LocalRank value of each node, and e denotes an n-dimension column vector with all elements set to 1. All elements of r are initialized to 1 and the calculation terminates when r converges.

Notice that although the calculation equation is similar to PageRank, the sense of our LocalRank is different from PageRank. Since we calculate the scores based on the data graph which integrates the web and a user database, instead of the conventional web space, our LocalRank reflects how a web page is related to the database entries which the user provides, in addition to its popularity on the web space. Also notice that instead of the global web space, a local web space is used to perform a link analysis. Hence, our method ranks web pages considering their relevance degree to user's interest. Moreover, let us remind that we have used the geographical is-close1 and is-close2 links to connect the web and the database and applied them to the link analysis. Therefore, geographical locality is also infused into the rankings of web pages.

---

[2] Although we calculate scores for all nodes, we are much more interested in the ranks of web pages than those of database entries because we aim to effectively rank pages so as to find relevant ones according to user's interest.

4 Experiments

4.1 Database Construction and Collection of Related Pages

We select fifty-four homepages of restaurants in Tsukuba city from gourmet navigation pages (e.g., [17]) of some portal web sites about Tsukuba city. We also manually extract from these pages restaurants' names, URLs, and addresses and construct a database as shown in Fig. 1 using them as database attributes.

The pages related to the database are collected by the approach described in the previous section. They are 54 homepages (S_1), 1,409 web pages (S_2) reachable from the homepages, 166 backlink pages (S_3) of the homepages, and 285 web pages (S_4) acquired from Google using the "Name" and "Phone" attributes (e.g., "COCCOLINO" and "029-864-4555") as keywords. After the elimination of duplicate ones, 1,812 web pages can be obtained.

4.2 Information Extraction and Data Graph Construction

Then the useful information is extracted from the downloaded web pages by the following steps.

1. Link extraction: Extract all URLs except for those referring to media files or CGI files.
2. Zip code extraction: Extract zip codes, like "305-8573" (the hyphen can be omitted), from the web pages containing only one zip code. We do not use pages on which two or more zip codes appear because of their vagueness.
3. Address extraction: Extract full address descriptions, like "1-1-1 Tennodai, Tsukuba, Ibaraki" from a web page if it contains only one address. In this step, partial address descriptions (e.g., "Tsukuba, Ibaraki") are not used due to their vagueness.
4. Coordinate calculation: Calculate their corresponding latitudes and longitudes from the addresses acquired in Step 3 using Yahoo!JAPAN MAPS [18]. Given an address or zip code, this service returns a pair of latitude and longitude. For the "Address" attribute value of each row in Fig. 1, their coordinates are also calculated.

Then nodes and links of a data graph are generated. This data graph has 13,006 nodes consisting of 54 database entries and 12,952 web pages including 1,812 downloaded and 11,140 undownloaded ones. Additionally, 54 has-HP, 8,663 refers, 8,663 refers, 285 matches, 453 is-close1, and 1,407 is-close2 are generated, respectively. We connect two database entries with the is-close1 links when 1) the distance of their addresses is smaller than 2km, or 2) their zip codes are same. We calculate an accurate distance based on the system [19] serviced by Geographical Survey Institute, Japan. The is-close2 links are similarly generated between a web page and a database entry considering addresses or zip codes appearing on a web page.

4.3 Link Analysis Results

For the LocalRank calculation, we use a free scientific software "Scilab" [20], which has a sparse matrix handling facility, and let d in Equation (1) be 0.9. The information

Ranking	LocalRank	URL	Restaurant	Tsukuba
1	0.260874	e-tsukuba.jp/rantei/index.htm	Y	Y
2	0.021487	r.gnavi.co.jp/a275100/	Y	Y
3	0.018932	e-tsukuba.jp/rantei/link.htm	Y	Y
4	0.014155	www.geocities.jp/papy0164/syokuji/you.html	Y	B
5	0.012105	r.gnavi.co.jp/a275100/map1.htm	Y	Y
6	0.012086	www.collaborate-ibaraki.jp/dirsearch/kigyou/namediv/ni.asp	N	N
7	0.012056	www.joyoliving.co.jp/kurashi/data/thisweek.php?category=recruit	N	N
8	0.011492	www.joyo-net.com/mise/mise040408.html	Y	Y
9	0.011492	www.capital-group.co.jp/rantei.htm	Y	Y
10	0.011492	www.piazza.ne.jp/piazza/gourmet/index.asp?mode=detail&id=116	Y	Y
11	0.007308	e-tsukuba.jp/rantei/recruit.htm	Y	Y
12	0.007285	e-tsukuba.jp/rantei/company.htm	Y	Y
13	0.007185	e-tsukuba.jp/rantei/osusume.htm	Y	Y
14	0.007185	e-tsukuba.jp/rantei/email.htm	Y	Y
15	0.007185	e-tsukuba.jp/rantei/traffic.htm	Y	Y
16	0.002886	www.iki-iki.net/v7/townpage/a-you.htm	Y	B
17	0.002830	tarea.hp.infoseek.co.jp/lminami.html	Y	B
18	0.002737	www006.upp.so-net.ne.jp/puni/ibaraki-r-w1.htm	B	B
19	0.002670	www.h3.dion.ne.jp/ b-gakuji/syaon.html	N	N
20	0.002266	www.white-gyouza.co.jp/detail/detail18.htm	Y	Y

Fig. 5. 20 top-ranked downloaded pages

Ranking	LocalRank	URL	Restaurant	Tsukuba
1	0.019240	www.i-tsukuba.com/index.shtml	B	Y
2	0.002976	www.gnavi.co.jp	Y	N
3	0.002976	www.gnavi.co.jp/kanto/	Y	B
4	0.002924	my.gnavi.co.jp/Rating/regist.php?shopid=a275100&shopurl...	Y	N
5	0.002304	www.nilim.go.jp	N	N
6	0.002304	www.icube-t.co.jp	N	Y
7	0.002304	www.google.co.jp/custom	N	N
8	0.001833	www.tsukuba.ad.jp	B	Y
9	0.001817	www.i-tsukuba.com	B	Y
10	0.001815	www.ibarakiken.net	B	B
11	0.001813	www.e-tsukuba.jp	B	Y
12	0.000468	rm.gnavi.co.jp/Map/mc_view.php?dr=a275100&c=36...	B	B
13	0.000468	rm.gnavi.co.jp/Map/mc_view.php?dr=a275100&c=36...	B	B
14	0.000468	rm.gnavi.co.jp/Map/mc_view.php?dr=a275100&c=36...	B	B
15	0.000468	rm.gnavi.co.jp/Map/mc_view.php?dr=a275100&c=36...	B	B
16	0.000468	rm.gnavi.co.jp/Map/mc_view.php?dr=a275100&c=36...	B	B
17	0.000468	rm.gnavi.co.jp/Map/mc_view.php?dr=a275100&t=s	B	B
18	0.000468	rm.gnavi.co.jp/Map/mc_view.php?dr=a275100&c=36...	B	B
19	0.000468	rm.gnavi.co.jp/Map/mc_view.php?dr=a275100&c=36...	B	B
20	0.000468	rm.gnavi.co.jp/Map/mc_view.php?dr=a275100&c=36...	B	B

Fig. 6. 20 top-ranked undownloaded URLs

of the 20 top-ranked downloaded pages is shown in Fig. 5. We evaluate two features of a page by manually examining its content. The first one is whether a page describes information on restaurants or not. The second one is whether it presents information on the area of Tsukuba city or not. We mark a page with "Y" if it is highly relevant and "N" if completely unrelated. The symbol "B" denotes a border page (i.e., it is somewhat relevant). Pages 1-5, 8-15, 18 in Fig. 5 are the ones related to the "RANTEI" restaurant which is an entry of Fig. 1. Since this restaurant is linked from the major local portal sites and restaurant navigation sites, its related web pages are highly ranked. Page 20 is the homepage of the "WHITE-GYOUZA" restaurant that is also an entry of our sample database. Pages 16 and 17 are two link collections of restaurants in Tsukuba and its adjacent cities. Among the 20 pages, 17 pages describe the information on restaurants and/or the area of Tsukuba. Only three pages have neither of these two features. The web pages ranked after the top-20 ones are omitted here, but they have similar tendency.

Fig. 6 shows the 20 top-ranked undownloaded URLs. These web pages may be considered to be good candidates to begin the crawling to collect related web pages to the database. Pages 1, 8-11 are portal sites for Tsukuba which introduce general information including restaurant information on this city. Pages 2-4 are from a popular restaurant navigation site in Japan. In particular, page 3 focuses on the area of Ibaraki prefecture that includes Tsukuba city. In this sense, its mark of the "Tsukuba" column is denoted as "B". Pages 12-20 are the maps of some restaurants. Among the 20 pages, 17 pages either are related to restaurant information, or introduce the information on Tsukuba. Only three remaining pages (Pages 5, 6, and 7) are completely undesirable. The web pages corresponding to the URLs following this top-20 list also contain restaurant pages and local web pages, but their quality gradually goes down as ranks become lower. Based on this experiment, we can say that our LocalRank values are semantically meaningful since they reflect our intent to obtain highly related pages to the given local restaurant database. The rankings can serve as a reference when a user wants to select related pages to access from the undownloaded URLs.

5 Conclusion and Future Work

In this paper, we present a method called LocalRank to rank web pages by integrating the web and a local user database. The experimental results show that our framework is helpful. Notice that our method is flexible and may be applied to the collection and ranking of web pages for other user data, not restricted to the local restaurant information as mentioned in this paper, just by changing the type of semantic links and properly adjusting their weights.

We believe that there are still a number of interesting work that need to be carried out. First, we need to extend our experiment to a larger user database, and to different geographical areas. Moreover, it would be desirable to further investigate the influence of changing the weights of links. In addition, it is also necessary to pick up useful records from the collected web pages and complement the user database with them. We may be able to consider to use the LocalRank value as a reference to judge whether a page is useful for a database expansion.

Acknowledgement

This research is partly supported by the Grant-in-Aid for Scientific Research (16500048) from Japan Society for the Promotion of Science (JSPS), Japan and the Grant-in-Aid for Scientific Research on Priority Areas (16016205) from the Ministry of Education, Culture, Sports, Science and Technology (MEXT), Japan. In addition, this work is supported by the grants from the Asahi Glass Foundation and the Inamori Foundation.

References

1. Regional in the Yahoo! Directory. http://dir.yahoo.com/Regional/
2. goo TOWNPAGE. http://townpage.goo.ne.jp/
3. A. Balmin, V. Hristidis, and Y. Papakonstantinou, ObjectRank: Authority-Based Keyword Search in Databases. *Proc. VLDB 2004*, pp. 564-575, 2004.
4. F. Geerts, H. Mannila, and E. Terzi, Relational Link-Based Ranking. *Proc. VLDB 2004*, pp. 552-563, 2004.
5. P. Baldi, P. Frasconi, and P. Smyth, *Modeling the Internet and the Web: Probabilistic Methods and Algorithms*, Wiley, 2003.
6. S. Chakrabarti, *Mining the Web: Discovering Knowledge from Hypertext Data*, Morgan Kaufmann, 2002.
7. J.M. Kleinberg, Authoritative Sources in a Hyperlinked Environment. *JACM*, Vol. 46, No. 5, pp. 604-632, 1999.
8. S. Brin and L. Page, The Anatomy of a Large-scale Hypertexual Web Search Engine. *Computer Networks*, Vol. 30, No. 1-7, pp. 107-117, 1998.
9. C. Matsumoto, Q. Ma, and K. Tanaka, Web Information Retrieval Based on the Localness Degree, *Proc. DEXA 2002*, LNCS 2453, pp. 172-181, 2002.
10. K. Hiramatsu and T. Ishida, An Augmented Web Space for Digital Cities. *Proc. SAINT 2001*, pp. 105-112, 2001.
11. J. Ding, L. Gravano and N. Shivakumar, Computing Geographical Scopes of Web Resources. *Proc. VLDB 2000*, pp. 545-556, 2000.
12. L. Gravano, V. Hatzivassiloglou and R. Lichtenstein, Categorizing Web Queries According to Geographical Locality. *Proc. CIKM 2003*, pp. 325-333, 2003.
13. F. Menczer, G. Pant, and P. Srinivasan, Topical Web Crawlers: Evaluating Adaptive Algorithms. *ACM Trans. on Internet Technology*, Vol. 4, No. 4, pp. 378-419, 2004.
14. J. Cho, H. Garcia-Molina, and L. Page, Efficient Crawling through URL Ordering. *Computer Networks*, Vol. 30, No. 1-7, pp. 161-172, 1998.
15. S. Chakrabarti, M. van den Berg, and B. Dom, Focused Crawling: A New Approach to Topic-specific Web Resource Discovery. *Computer Networks*, Vol. 31, No. 11-16, pp. 1623-1640, 1999.
16. M. Diligenti, F. M. Coetzee, S. Lawrence, C.L. Giles, and M. Gori, Focused Crawling Using Context Graphs. *Proc. VLDB 2000*, pp. 527-534, 2000.
17. Gourmet navigation in Tsukuba city.
    http://www.i-tsukuba.com/yellow/gourmet/index.htm
18. Yahoo! JAPAN MAPS. http://map.yahoo.co.jp/
19. Measurement Calculation.
    http://vldb.gsi.go.jp/sokuchi/surveycalc/bl2stf.html
20. Scilab Home Page. http://scilabsoft.inria.fr/

My Portal Viewer: Integration System Based on User Preferences for News Web Sites

Yukiko Kawai[1], Daisuke Kanjo[1], and Katsumi Tanaka[1,2]

[1] National Institute of Information and Communications Technology,
3-5 Hikaridai,Seika-cho,Soraku-gun,Kyoto,619-0289 Japan
TEL: +81-774-98-6879, FAX: +81-774-98-6959
{yukiko, kanjo}@nict.go.jp
[2] Graduate School of Informatics, Kyoto University,
Yoshida-Honmachi, Sakyo-ku, Kyoto, 606-8501 Japan
TEL: +81-75-753-5969, FAX: +81-75-753-4957
ktanaka@i.kyoto-u.ac.jp

Abstract. We developed a novel web application called "My Portal Viewer (MPV)", which automatically categorizes and integrates metadata from many news pages based on the user's preferences after gathering these news pages from various news sites. Our unique approach is based on two points: one is an automatic categorization of collected information based on user's interests and knowledge, and the other is the look and feel of the MPV page, which is applied to the user's favorite news portal page, and part of the original content is replaced by the integrated content. Whenever a user accesses the MPV page after browsing news pages, he/she can obtain the desired content efficiently because the MPV presents pages refreshed based on the user's behavior through his/her favorite page layout, which reflects his/her interests and knowledge. In this paper, we describe the MPV framework, and methods that are based on the user's preferences for replacing and categorizing content have been developed using an HTML table model and a vector matching model.

1 Introduction

With the amount of Web content constantly increasing, users require novel applications that provide higher quality content. In particular, to help users retrieve information more efficiently applications that enable specific types of information to be selected from large amount of information gathered from the Web are needed. There is also a need for a system that effectively integrates high-quality content gathered from the Web according to individual user's requirements. We have developed an application called "My Portal Viewer" (MPV), which integrates information gathered from numerous Web pages on the basis of a user's preferences, interests, and knowledge.

Existing Web content integration systems categorize and integrate pages collected from several news Web sites[1][2][3]. For example, Google news[1] provide an integrated news portal site using a huge collection of pages from 4,500 news sites. With these systems, a user can look for news articles from the single screen of the integrated top page without having to search for and access several Web sites.However, existing integration systems have two problems:(1) each system has a different interface, and users have to adjust to browsing various interfaces; and (2) they only have a few defined categories, which means that users may have to repeat their search for the target articles from the many lists presented by each category. For example, the categories *world*, *business*, and *sports* are determined by the manager of the integration system. These broad categories make it difficult for the user to obtain specific information because to obtain a news article about, for example, *speech of president*, the user has to select the category *world* or *business* and look under several categories.

The proposed MPV efficiently provides users with their target information without the complexity associated with some conventional retrieval methods.The MPV collects and stores news Web pages by crawling through numerous relevant sites. It then generates an MPV page that integrates the stored pages. Our unique approach of information integration has two main functions:

- it categorizes content collected from news Web sites based on the user's preferences, and
- to provide and construct a friendly interface, it adopts the look and feel of the user's favorite existing top page.

The first point is that the categories are defined based on the user's interests and knowledge. The collected news articles are dynamically categorized based on the user's operating history. As this history changes over time, the content of the MPV page also changes dynamically, reflecting changes in the user's interests and knowledge. The user does not need to access several news Web sites or look for target information under various categories; in fact, the user can access information under the category of *president* directly by accessing the MPV page without having to access the categories *world* $\rightarrow$ *country* $\rightarrow$ *vote* $\rightarrow$ *president*.

The second point has the most impact in comparison with existing integration systems because individual integration systems don't need to prepare a top interface. First, users specify their favorite existing top page of a news Web site. The look and feel of this page is then applied to their own page, but only part of the content of the existing top page is mapped. Using the look and feel of their favorite top page makes it easier for users to browse for target information because they are familiar with location of information on that page. For instance, he/she knows where groups of information such as top news articles, categories, headlines and columns are arranged on the page they usually use.

In addition, there is synergy between the first and the second points in that the MPV maps the content of the original information on the existing top page to the integrated information based on the user's preferences. Users obtain targeted news articles from the integrated information immediately on opening the MPV page because the look and feel of the MPV page is the same as that of their favorite top page, except that the content is mapped to their personalized content. Personalized categorization and mapping integrated information makes it easy for users to locate the desired information from the information collect.

In this paper, we describe a novel browser, the MPV which changes dynamically based on user's news content preferences. In the next section, we describe related work on Web page integration, and in Section 3, we describe the concept of the MPV. In Sections 4 and 5, we describe a method for mapping the integrated content on to the user's favorite existing top page, and a method for categorizing and integrating collected meta-data based on the user's interests and knowledge. In Section 6, we show an MPV prototype and discuss our experimental results, and in Section 7, we outline the direction of future work.

2 Related Work

There has been considerable investigation of portal site technology for gathering, categorizing, personalizing and integrating information.

MSN NewsPot[2] uses not only collection and classification technology but also personalization technology. An individual preferred news articles are selected using personalized information based on his/her browsing history; the selected personalized articles are displayed on the right side of the originally developed interface. However, unfortunately the selected articles are not related or categorized.

MyYahoo! [4]makes it possible for the user to select and set various content categories. However, these categories are defined by the MyYahoo! system, and users cannot select categories based on their own interests and knowledge. Furthermore, although the look and feel of the integrated page can be modified, it is hard to reconstruct a more user-friendly layout.

Columbia's Newsblaster [5] is an online news summarization system in which collected news articles are categorized by event using a topic detection and tracking (TDT) method and TF · IDF. After each news article has been assigned to one of the six categories, each category is summarized using language technology. The user can then read a brief summary of an event based on several Web pages.

3 Concept of MPV

Figure 1 shows the concept of the MPV system. The MPV system consists of an MPV site on the server side and an MPV page and toolbar on the client side. First, the user inputs the URL of his/her favorite existing top page into the blank box in the MPV toolbar; in the example shown, the URL for the CNN home page in entered. When the user hits the enter key, the MPV toolbar sends the name of the entered URL to the MPV site. When the MPV site gets the URL, it extracts the layout of the entered URL page as well as the content of the page. If the MPV site does not have a specified page stored, it gets this page from the Web site of the specified URL. The MPV site then creates an MPV page that replaces some of the content of the specified page with content integrated from

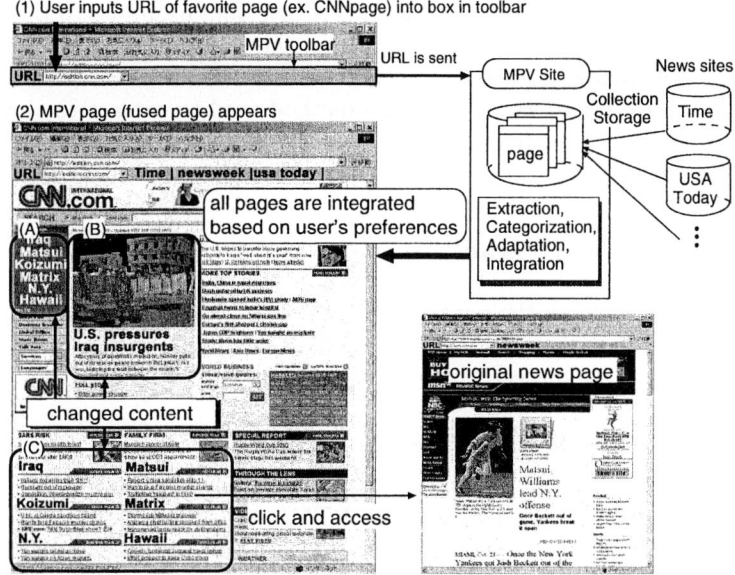

Fig. 1. Concept of MPV: Content on MPV page changes to display information that has been gathered and integrated

many stored pages. The integrated content is based on the user's preferences. As a result, the user can access the desired news articles through an interface has their preferred look and feel.

In figure 1, after the user enters the URL, an MPV page appears based on layout of the CNN top page transformed by the MPV site. The layout stays the same, but some of the content changes, including the categories, top news article with images, and the news headlines in each category. In this example, the original categories *world*, *worldbusiness*, and *technology* change to an Iraq-related news category, a baseball player-related news category, and a movie-related category because the user is interested in stories in these categories. The top news article with images and the news headlines in each category also change based on the user's preferences. In this example, the top news article with an image changes to an Iraq-related news article, and the original news headlines in each category change to headlines on *Iraq*, *baseball players*, and *movies*. The categories are modified dynamically based on the user's browsing history. If, for example, the user starts reading stories about football more often, the category of *football* is made into a new category and displayed to the category area of the MPV page, and displayed categories such as *Iraq*, *baseball players*, and *movies* that are no longer accessed on a regular basis are either demoted or deleted.

On the MPV site, the system collects news pages by crawling through Web sites and archiving the URLs and meta-data for all the news pages collected. When the MPV site receives a URL from the user, it analyzes the layout of the page specified by the user. It then changes the content of each area shown in the figure such as the category, a top news article, and headlines to the specified content after it categorizing and integrating the collected news page based on the user's preferences.

In the next section, we describe the method used to extract the layout and content from the original Web pages in order to change the categorized and integrated content.

4 Information Extraction

The MPV site replaces the content of only three areas on the user's specified existing top page with the integrated information. It does so by analyzing the original top page and detecting the layout and original content.

4.1 Original Layout Extraction

We analyzed the original top pages of six major news sites. The basic layout of these pages was used to construct an HTML table model. All the pages had five content articles: 1) site logo, 2) category keywords, 3) top news article with an image, 4) list of news headlines in each category, 5) advertisements. In this paper, we changed the second, third, and fourth articles above because each of these items is related to news articles.

We used the characteristics of the table model to change the content. In our method, the HTML table model is used to obtain the x-y coordinates for the existing top page layout. Using the HTML table model enables authors to arrange data consisting consists of text, images, links, other tables, etc., into rows and columns of cells [6]. The default directionality in a table is left-to-right (column 0 is on the left and row 0 is at the top). The TABLE element contains the instructions that specify the number of rows, columns, and other element. The number of rows in the table is equal to the number of TR tags in the TABLE element, and the rows are grouped according to the ROWSPAN values. The width of the table is equal to the WIDTH elements, and the number of columns is equal to the total number of TH or TD tags and COLSPAN values.

We derived the x-y coordinates in each table from the above definitions and calculate the table area based on the x-y coordinates. Figure 2 shows the layout obtained based on this HTML table model.

4.2 Content Detection

First, we describe the method we used to extract the table area from a news page. We then describe the content detection method we use to select three areas from the extracted area. The three areas are detected using the characteristics of each content type. These characteristics are as follows.

Area of category keywords: Each keyword has a regular array with a similar tag composition with repeating rows or columns. For example, a tag composition such as "<td><a href="*keyword*">*keyword*</a>" is repeated. Part of the keyword is the category keywords such as *world*, *sports*, *weather*, etc.

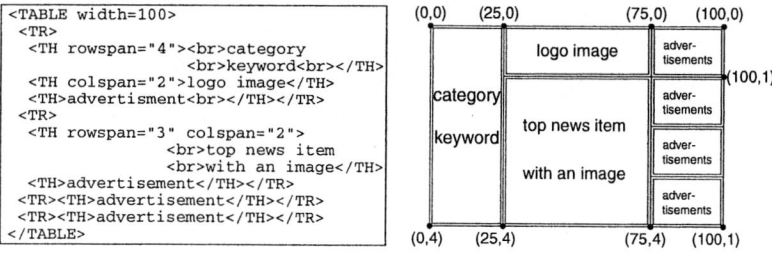

Fig. 2. HTML layout based on a sample table model

Area of top news article with an image: The top news article has a title and an image with a link. The table area of the top news article is arranged next to the category keyword area; for instance, the value of x or y is larger than that of the category area.
The title and image are linked to the news content on the same page.

Area of a list of news headlines for each category: Each list has a category keyword and the titles of the news articles. The table area for the headlines is arranged under the area for the top news article. The value of y is larger than that of the top news article area.
The keywords have the same links with the category keywords, and the titles are linked to the news content.

5 Categorization of News Article

The MPV site changes the content of three extracted areas in the user's favorite existing top page to categorized and integrated information based on the user's preferences.

The following process is used to categorize collected news articles.

1. The user's keywords are detected based on the user's browsing history using the user's table and the page table (these tables are described in the following section). The detected user's keywords are replaced with the keywords for the original category.
2. The top news article is chosen based on the weight of the user's keywords, the time that the news article was created, and the unread news articles.
3. Headlines matching the user's keywords are selected using the page table and a keyword tree.

5.1 Page Table and User's Table

The user's table contains the user's ID, and IDs of the pages browsed by the user. The page table contains information about the meta-data of collected Web pages including the time of their creation, the number of words on the pages, and the weight of each word. The words are proper nouns, general nouns, and verbs, and they are extracted by morphological analysis. The weight of each word is

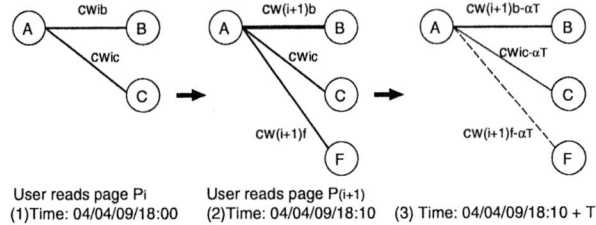

Fig. 3. Keyword tree for user's keyword A is constructed based on user's behavior

calculated using the term-frequency and weight of the three parts of speech as the following equation:

$$w_{ij} = tf = \frac{log(F_j + 1)}{log(F_{all})} \qquad (1)$$

where F_j is the frequency of the appearance of a word j in P_i, F_j is the frequency of appearance of all words in P_i. P_i is the page ID.

5.2 Detecting User's Keywords

To detect a user's keywords, we create and use a page table and a user's table based on the user's browsing history. Each user's keyword has a weight, which changes as the user browses different news articles. The detected user's keywords are replaced with the original category keywords in order of weight; in other words, the category keywords change dynamically as a result of the user's behavior.

This method of keyword detection is based on the summation of the weights of the appearance of the words on the pages browsed by the user, using the next equation: $I_j = \sum_{i=1}^{n} w_{ij}$ where $P_i (i = 1, \cdots, n)$ is the page browsed by the user, the j is the word on the page P_i, and w_{ij} is the weight of the word j. If the value of I_j is larger than a certain threshold, word j is detected as a user's keyword.

5.3 Headline Selection Using a Keyword Tree

Headlines corresponding to the user's keywords are selected from the meta-data of collected Web pages using a page table and a keyword tree. The meta-data are the titles, description, keywords and date of creation which that can be found on most news pages. The selected the titles are replaced with headlines.

A keyword tree is constructed based on the user's keywords. The root nodes of the keyword tree are the detected user's keywords, and the leaf nodes are the words of the same page browsed. Figure 3 shows the construction of a keyword tree. In this figure, after the user browses page P_i, which has keywords A, B, and C, keyword A is detected using equation (2), and keywords B and C (leaf nodes) are linked to keyword A (the root node). The constructed tree is shown on the left in Fig.3. Each link has a weight calculated using the co-occurrence relation value of the root and leaf nodes in the meta-data of all the collected pages. If the user browses another page, $P_{(i+1)}$, which has keywords A, B, and F, F is linked to A, and B's weight is updated. This is shown by the tree in the middle of Fig.3. If no value for the co-occurrence relation of the root and leaf nodes appears in the browsed page after T time, the weight is reduced by αT. This is shown by the tree on the right in Fig.3.

This method of headline selection uses the dot product of the vector of the weights of words of browsed pages and the tree links. First, pages containing the user's keywords are chosen using the page table, and a keyword tree containing the user's keywords is chosen. The weight of the keywords of the chosen page is defined as the vector $V_{pi} = (wa, wb, ..., wm)$, and the weight of the link of the chosen keyword tree t is defined as vector $V_t = (cw_a, cw_b, ...cw_m)$ (m is the number of all appearances of the words in V_{pi} and V_t). Then, the page vector $V_{pi}(i, \cdots, n)$ (n is the number of chosen pages) and the tree vector V_t are calculated by using equation $V_{pi} \cdot V_t$. When the value of $V_{pi} \cdot V_t$ is larger than the threshold, page P_i of V_{pi} is selected as matching the user's keyword t. Finally, the title of the chosen page P_i is represented as headlines that include the keyword t.

6 Prototype of MPV

We developed a prototype of the MPV toolbar and the MPV site. In this section, we show the experimental results obtained using the prototype system and discuss our methods for layout and content extraction, and user's keyword detection. Meta-data of Web pages from four news sites[1] were collected via crawling were stored on the MPV site. The MPV site categorized and integrated the meta-data based on the user's preferences at the same time that it extracted the layout and content of the three areas from the user's specified original top page.

Figure 4 shows how the MPV prototype was executed. Picture (1) in the figure shows the original top page and the MPV page. Only the content of the top news article with an image in the MPV page changes because the user's table and keyword tree have not yet been created when the user requests an MPV page for the first time. In (1), the top news article is the latest news article with an image that was selected from the four news sites.

Picture (2) shows how the MPV page changed with respect to the content of the three areas after the user browsed several news pages. The original category keyword area is mapped on to the user's interest keywords, and the headlines with the original keywords are replaced with headlines containing the user's keywords. The top news article with an image is selected based on the user's keywords, and the selected article is displayed as a headline that has not been read yet. As a result, the user can easily access and read the interesting news articles based on his/her preferences and does not need to access different news sites to look for target news article from various categories defined by site managers.

---

[1] http://www.cnn.com, http://news.yahoo.com, http://www.asahi.com/, http://www.time.com

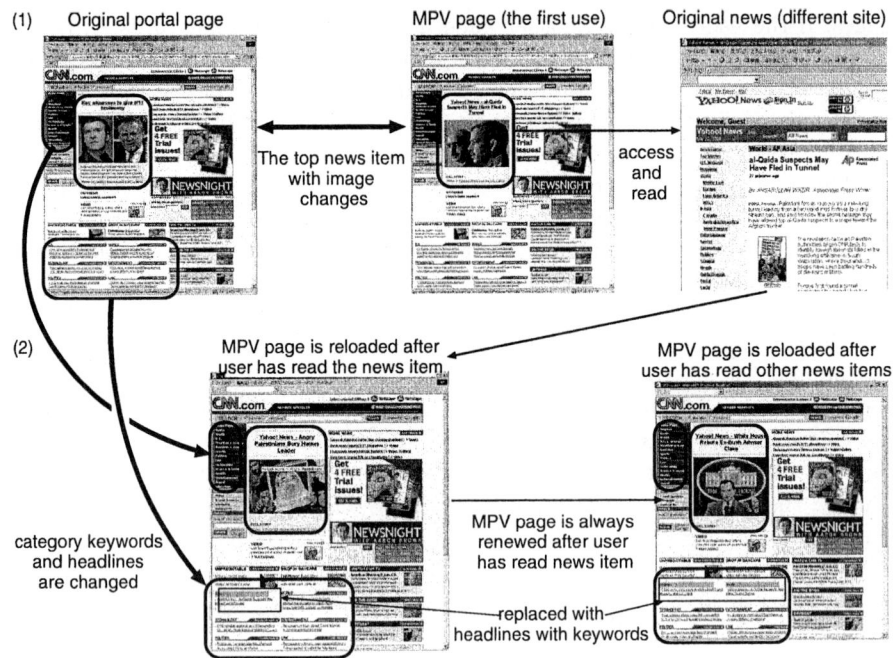

Fig. 4. Results of MPV page obtained using prototype system

Whenever the user reads a news article, the user's table and keyword tree are reconstructed. The right side in (2) shows an updated MPV page. A new keyword input by the user has been added, and the related headlines and top news article have been replaced using the reconstructed table and tree.

We were able to confirm that another MPV page was created by the top page of another news site when the same user specified that page after he/she read the article in Picture (2). The content of the three areas of this MPV page has changed because the user's table and keyword tree have been reconstructed.

6.1 Automatic Content Extraction

We developed an extraction method that automatically detects the layout and content of the three areas from the original top page.

Using the proposed method, we successfully extracted three areas using the original existing top pages of five news sites. We also extracted category keywords from four portal pages. The extracted keywords had a regular array, and the number of repetitions ranged from 7 to 11 in our experiment. However, we were unsuccessful in automatically extracting top news articles from the original portal pages of other Web sites because they contained advertisements with images between the category keywords and the top news articles.

We propose two methods of solving this problem: improving toolbar, and a new interface for user specifications. We improved toolbar. In this improved toolbar, the layouts of the top page of six Japanese web sites and for English Web sites are extracted by the MPV server before user specifies. Users can select only the selected web sites on the toolbar, but those sites are perfectly mapped and integrated. We are adapting other news sites to the toolbar. We will also adapt the new interface so that users can more easily specify the required areas of the top page. The specified areas are extracted by the MPV server, and then only those areas are mapped to the integrated content. The integration method must adapt to a variety of content for each area because the content may have different features such as the category, weather, top story, headlines, stock report, etc.

6.2 Automatic Detection of Articles

We conducted an experiment to evaluate the proposed method of detecting user's keyword. First, after the user frequently read news articles about the presidential race, the user's keywords such as the names of the candidates and the present president were extracted. On the MPV system, not all the content in the original top page changes. Some areas such as news flash, features, and columns remain. As a result, the user was able to access news articles of that were unrelated to the presidential race, and various user's keywords were detected.

7 Conclusion

We described a new application called "My Portal Viewer" (MPV), which enables users to obtain high-quality content from the Web based on their individual preferences. Several collected Web pages are integrated based on the user's preferences in the MPV site. The information is then integrated and displayed on the user's favorite existing top page, which reflects the user's categorization tree. Our prototype showed that users could easily access and read news articles that interested them by using an MPV page, and they did not need to access different news sites and look for target article in various categories defined by site managers. In the future, we plan to introduce a semantic Web technology to enable improved of the categorization, and will adapt the technology to other types of Web sites such as travel or conferences sites.

References

1. GoogleNews: (http://news.google.co.jp)
2. Newsbot: (http://uk.newsbot.msn.com)
3. Feed Demon: (http://www.bradsoft.com/feeddemon/index.asp)
4. MyYahoo!: (http://my.yahoo.co.jp/?myhome)
5. McKeown, K., Barzilay, R., Evans, D., Hatzivassiloglou, V., Klavans, J., Sable, C., Schiffman, B., Sigelman, S.: Tracking and summarizing news on a daily basis with columbia's newsblaster (2002)
6. W3C Recommendation: HTML 4.01 Specification, http://www.w3.org/TR/1999/REC-html401-19991224 (1999)

Web Query Expansion by WordNet

Zhiguo Gong, Chan Wa Cheang, and Leong Hou U

Faculty of Science and Technology, University of Macau,
P.O.Box 3001 Macao, PRC
{zggong, ma36600, ma36575}@umac.mo

Abstract. In this paper, we address a novel method of Web query expansion by using WordNet and TSN. WordNet is an online lexical dictionary which describes word relationships in three dimensions of Hypernym, Hyponym and Synonym. And their impacts to expansions are different. We provide quantitative descriptions of the query expansion impact along each dimension. However, WordNet may bring many noises for the expansion due to its collection independent characteristic. Furthermore, it may not catch current state of words and their relationships because of the explosive increase of the Web. To overcome those problems, collection-based TSN (Term Semantic Network) is created with respect to word co-occurrence in the collection. We use TSN both as a filter and a supplement for WordNet. We also provide a quantitatively study as what is the best way for the expansion with TSN. In our system, we combine the query expansions along each semantic dimension as our overall solution. Our experiments reveal that the combined expansion can provide a satisfied result for the Web query performance. The methodologies in this paper have been already employed in our Web image search engine system.

1 Introduction

In recent years, huge amount of information is posted on the Web and it continues to increase with an explosive speed. But we cannot access to the information or use it efficiently and effectively unless it is well organized and indexed. Many search engines have been created for this need in current years. Web users, however, usually submit only one single word as their queries on the Web [5], especially for a Web Image queries. It is even worse that the users' query words may be quite different to the ones used in the documents in describing the same semantics. That means a gap exists between user's query space and document representation space. This problem results in lower precisions and recalls of queries. The user may get an overwhelming but large percent of irrelevant documents in the result set. In fact, this is a tough problem in Web information retrieval. An effective method for solving the above problems is query expansion. In this paper, we provide a novel query expansion method based on the combination of WordNet [2], an online lexical system, and TSN, a term semantic network extracted from the collection. Our method has been employed in our Web image search system [4].

WordNet [2], like a standard dictionary, contains the definitions of words and their relationships. But it also differs from a standard dictionary in that, instead of being organized alphabetically, WordNet is organized conceptually. The basic unit in WordNet is a synonym set, or synset, which represents a lexicalized concept. For example, the noun "software" in WordNet 2.0 has the synsets {software, software system, software package, package} and also Nouns in WordNet are organized in a hierarchical tree structure based on hypernym/hyponymy. The hyponym of a noun is its subordinate, and the relation between a hyponym and its hypernym is an 'is a kind of' relation. As in Fig. 1, "freeware" is a hyponym of "software", or more intuitively, a "freeware" is a kind of "software". Hypernym (supername) and its inverse, hyponym (subname), are transitive semantic relations between synsets.

We use those various semantic relations between words in our query expansion. However, these three relations have different semantic relevances to the query word. The concept at the upper layers of the hierarchy has more general semantics and less similarity between them, while concepts at lower layers or at the same layer have more concrete semantics and stronger similarity [1]. To determine, in quantity, how to expand the query word along each direction, the average precision is used as the objective function for computing the optimal factor for each direction. On the other hand, some terms added to the query will bring some noises and the search may return large amount of irrelevant results, thus decrease the precision [3]. To solve this problem, we use TSN (Term Semantic Network) extracted from our collection to filter out the words with lower supports and confidences to the query word. By this way, noises can be well controlled.

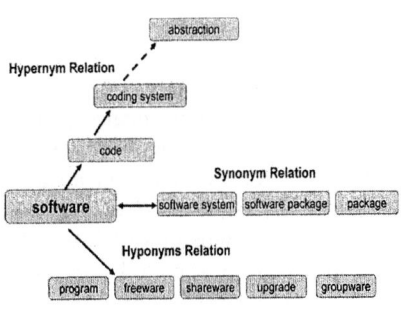

Fig. 1. Hierarchy relation of word "software" in WordNet

Besides noise controlling for WordNet expansion, TSN is also another important supplement for semantic describing between terms. WordNet is systematically created on the base of lexical analysis. It has two intrinsic weaknesses—poor current and collection independent. The first weakness may result in that newly created word semantic relations may not be used in the expansion, and the second one may generate some noise from the expansion. Since TSN is directly extracted from the collection, it can overcome the above shortages. To create TSN, we define association rule between two words in terms of 'Support' and 'Confidence' [12], then the semantic network is extracted with respect to the definition.

In reminder of this paper, we discuss related works in section 2. Section 3 provides our detail methodologies for query expansion with WordNet and TSN. The experiment results are illustrated in section 4. Finally, we conclude our work in section 5.

2 Related Work

As mentioned, query expansion is one of the promising approaches to deal with the word mismatch problem in information retrieval. It can be roughly classified into two groups: global analysis and local analysis.

The basic idea in global analysis is that the global context of a concept can be used to determine similarities between concepts. Context can be defined in a number of ways, as can concepts. The simplest definitions are that all words are concepts and that the context for a word is all the word that co-occurs in document. Similarity thesauri [6] and Phrase Finder [8] are used with those global techniques. Another related approach uses clustering to determine the context for document analysis [9]. Global analysis techniques are relatively robust. However, since the co-occurrence information for every pair of terms in the whole corpus are normally needed, the processing is generally rather computational resource consuming. Moreover, global analysis cannot handle ambiguous terms effectively. It did not show consistent positive retrieval results unless further strategies for term selection could be suggested.

Local technologies analyze only the information in some initial documents, which are retrieved for the original query. Terms are extracted from these documents for query expansion [7]. Local analysis can be further divided into two groups. The first one is called relevance feedback [10], which relies on user's relevance judgments of the retrieved documents. Relevance feedback can achieve great performance if users cooperate well. However, this method is seldom deployed in practice because users are not always willing or able to give sufficient and correct relevance judgment about documents. Local feedback methods [11] are developed to solve this problem. They work without user interaction by assuming the top ranked documents to be relevant. The drawback of these methods is: if the top-ranked documents happen to be irrelevant (this situation is very common in the Web query world), the suggested terms from these documents are also likely to be unrelated to the topic and the query expansion will fail.

Our approach in this paper belongs to the first category. But it is based on combination of the online dictionary WordNet and the collection related TSN. We use WordNet as the similarity thesaurus to expand the Web query. To solve the disadvantage of it, we use collection related TSN to filter out some noise words to improve the precisions of the queries. Furthermore, we provide a qualitative description on word expansion along different semantic dimensions.

3 System Design

In [4], we introduced our Web search system which include a crawler, a preprocessor, an indexer, a knowledge learner and query engine. Web document is gathered by crawler and loaded into the document database by document preprocessor. The indexer creates the inverted index for retrieval. In order to solve the problem of low precision of the query results, we design and implement a query expansion subsystem which performs functions such as keyword expansion, keyword filtering and keyword weighting. We will introduce each process in detail in the following.

3.1 Keyword Expansion

The query keyword used by users is the most significant but not always sufficient in the query phase. For example, if a user query with "computer", he only can get the object indexed by "computer". We use WordNet and TSN to expand the query. With

WordNet, we expand the query along three dimensions including hypernym, hyponymy and synonym relation [2]. The original query "computer", for instance, may be expanded to include "client, server, website, etc." In other words, with those expanded words together, the system could raise both the query precision and recall.

To extract TSN from the collection, we use a popular association mining algorithm – Apriori [12] — to mine out the association rules between words. Here, we only consider one-to-one term relationship. Two functions—*confidence* and *support*— are used in describing word relations. We define *confidence (conf)* and *support (sup)* of term association $t_i \rightarrow t_j$ as follows, let

$$D(t_i, t_j) = D(t_i) \cap D(t_j) \tag{1}$$

where $D(t_i)$ and $D(t_j)$ stand for the documents including term t_i and t_j respectively. Therefore, $D(t_i) \cap D(t_j)$ is the set of documents that include both t_i and t_j. We define

$$Conf_{ti->tj} = \frac{\| D(t_i, t_j) \|}{\| D(t_i) \|} \tag{2}$$

where $\| D(t_i, t_j) \|$ stands for the total number of documents that include both term t_i, and t_j; and $\| D(t_i) \|$ stands for the total number of documents that include t_i,

$$Sup_{ti->tj} = \frac{\| D(t_i, t_j) \|}{\|D\|} \tag{3}$$

where $\|D\|$ stands for the number of document in the database.

Those relationships are extracted and represented with two matrixes, we could use them to expand the query keywords. For example, the keyword "computer" has the highest confidence and support with the words "desktop, series, price, driver...etc" which are not described in WordNet but can be used to expand the original query.

3.2 Keyword Filtering

In the next step, we use TSN to eliminate some noise words in the keyword expansion of WordNet. Actually, the comprehensive WordNet often expands a query with too many words. And some of them are low-frequency and unusual words. They may bring in some noises and detract from retrieval performance, thus lead to precision decrease. So it is very important to avoid noises when expanding queries. We use the association rules to remove the expansion words that have lower support and confidence to the original word. In our system, we use the expanded words which have minimum confidence over 0.3 and support over 0.01 with the original query keyword into our query expansion. As the keyword "robot" in Fig 2, we filter out the words "golem, humanoid, mechanical man".

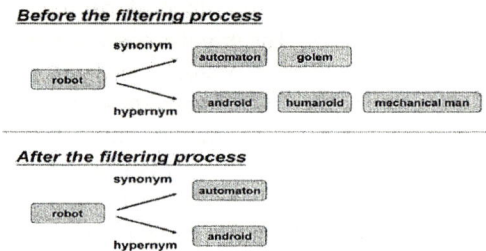

Fig. 2. Keyword filtering process of word "robot"

3.3 Keyword Weighting

In TFIDF model, term *t*'s semantic relevance to web page *p* is measured by *tf(t)*idf(t)*, where *tf(t)* is the frequency of *t* occurring in *p* and *idf(t)* is the inverted document frequency of term *t*. In this paper, we use terms (or concepts) in *p* to derive semantics of the Web image *i*. However, above TFIDF approach can not be directly applied to index the embedded image.

3.3.1 Semantic Relevance of Terms to the Embedded Images
In this paper, we modify TFIDF model regarding following two arguments:

(1) $idf(t_i)$ is used to enhance significances of the terms which appear in less documents, thus can discriminate the corresponding documents effectively. In our system, terms are used to derive the semantics of the embedded images other than discriminate images. Furthermore, image users only use one term or concept for image retrievals in most of the cases. As for those reasons, *idf* is not used in our system.

(2) As we mention in previous sections, we use WordNet and TSN to expand our original query keyword. If a Web page not only contains the original query keyword but also contains the words which expand by WordNet and TSN, it should be more relevant than the ones which only contain the original query keyword. With this observation, we define the total term weight over the whole *p* as

$$ttf(t) = tf(t) + \alpha \cdot tf(t_{Hypernyms}) + \beta \cdot tf(t_{Hyponyms}) + \gamma \cdot tf(t_{Synonyms}) + \delta \cdot tf(t_{LocalContext}) \quad (4)$$

where $t_{Hypernyms}$ is the term set which use WordNet hypernyms relation to expand words, $t_{Hyponyms}$ is the term set which use WordNet hyponyms relation to expand words, $t_{Synonyms}$ is the term set which use WordNet synonyms relation to expand words and $t_{LocalContext}$ is the term set which has top-rank TSN expansion words with our original keyword to expand our query. The factor α, β, γ and δ are used to indicate different effects from each expansion direction. And it is natural to suppose $0 < \alpha, \beta, \gamma, \delta < 1$.

In our approach, $ttf(t)|_p$ indicates the semantic relevant value of term *t* to the embedded image *i* embedded in *p*. Thus, the important and challenging task for using this measure is how to determine the values for the factors α, β, γ and δ.

3.3.2 Objective Function of Retrieval Performance

In the area of information retrieval, precision/recall is well accepted evaluation method for the performance of the systems [7, 13]. An ideal information retrieval system is trying to raise the values for both of the two objectives. Since the result of a retrieval is usually long list in size, especially in the World Wide Web environment, a figure of precision versus recall changing is commonly used as a performance measurement for a retrieval algorithm. However, this metric can not be used as an objective function in determining those factor values. Instead, in this study, we employ the single value summaries as our objective function in order to determine the values for the factors [7, 13]. The average precision is defined as

$$AP = \frac{1}{R} \sum_{k=1}^{R_t} \frac{k}{N_k} \qquad (5)$$

where R is the total number of all relevant results with respect to $ttf(q_i)|_p$ and N_k is the number of results up to the k-th relevant result in the result list. As a matter of the fact, AP is the single value metric which indicates the performance of querying q_k. In this paper, we assume that all expansion dimensions are independent, thus, we can determine them one by one. For example, the optimal values for α is determined when AP of queries with respect to rank function $ttf(t) = tf(t) + \alpha \cdot tf(t_{Hypernyms})$ reaches its maximum. And we also use the same way for determining other factor values.

Fig 3~6 show the curves of AP values via factor values for α, β, γ and δ respectively. Those figures indicate that query expansion along each dimension can always get some better performance than that without expansion (factor = 0). And the maximums for AP can be obtained with 0<factors<1. Table 1 shows optimal factor values with their corresponding AP values.

Table 1. Factor Values and Average Precision

Factor	Values	Average Precision
α (Hypernyms)	0.47	0.2406
β (Hyponyms)	0.84	0.3888
γ (Synonyms)	0.70	0.3404
δ (Local Context)	0.94	0.3559

From Table 1, it is clear that different semantic relations have different influences to the search results. Hypemyms relation has less significant impact than Hyponyms and Synonyms relations. With a close study, we find the reason may be due to the fact that Hypermyms relation (abstract concept expansion) may bring more noises than Hyponyms and Synonyms do. So its factor value is less than others. And Local Context (TSN) is closely semantic relevant to the original keyword. Thus, its factor value is very high.

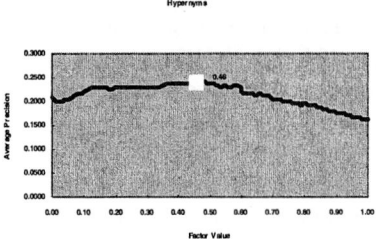
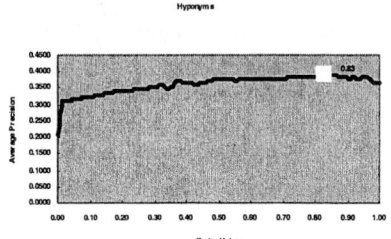

Fig. 3. Average precision versus Factor Values for Hyponyms relation

Fig. 4. Average precision versus Factor Values for Hypernyms relation

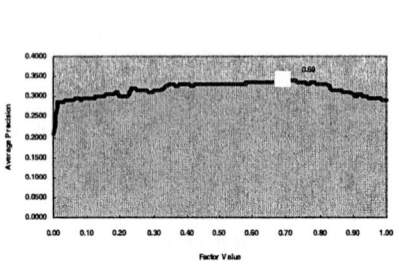
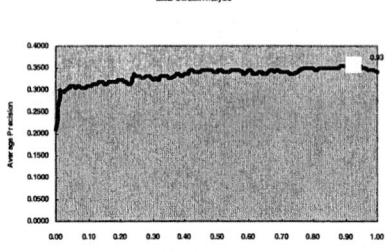

Fig. 5. Average precision versus Factor Values for Synonyms relation

Fig. 6. Average precision versus Factor Values for Local Context Analysis

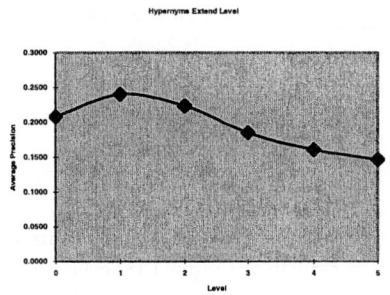
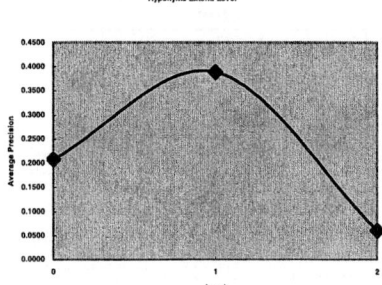

Fig. 7. Average precision versus Extend Level for Hypernyms relation

Fig. 8. Average precision versus Extend Level for Hyponyms relation

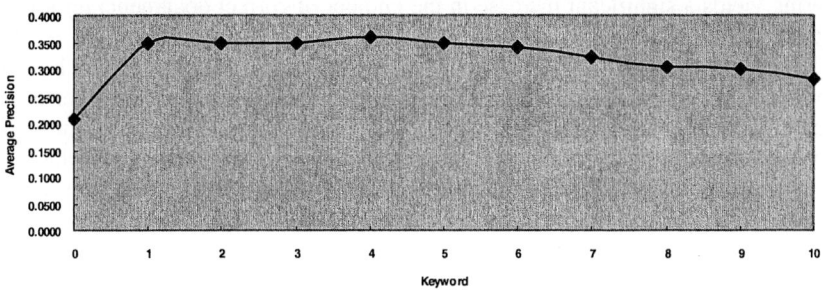

Fig. 9. Average precision versus Number of Keyword expand for Local Context

As a matter of the fact, we can get a word's hypernyms relations recursively up to the top root and hyponyms relations down to the bottom along WordNet. Therefore, it is interesting to know how many levels along hypernyms and hyponyms to expand the queries. For this objective, we use the same method as to calculate the factors by average precision. As in Fig 7~8, our experiments show that one level for expansion will get better results in both the situations. In fact, multiple hyponyms relations expand too many words which may diverge the original keyword meanings. That is, they will generate many noises in the results, thus reduce *AP* values. So in our system, we only use one level for both hypernyms and hyponyms expansions. In Fig 9, we also use the average precision method to calculate how many keywords are proper for expansions along TSN dimension. As the result, we find that using the first 4 top-rank words in TSN expansions can generate better performances.

4 Evaluation

Our experiments are carried out with our Web image search engine [4]. The crawler of our system gathered about 150,000 Web pages with a given set of seeds which are randomly selected from dot-com, dot-edu and dot-gov domains. After the noise images (icons, banners, logos, and any image with size less than 5k) are removed by the image extractor, about 12,000 web images embedded in the Web pages are left. Then, 5 human experts are assigned to define the subjects of the Web images manually. And sometimes, more than one subject is defined for the same images. For example, concepts 'Laptop', 'Notebook' and 'Computer' may be annotated to the same Web image. We select 30 concepts from the defined set as our query training set, and another 15 terms as our test samples. We measure the query performances with the precision-recall curves.

As shown in Fig 10, we compare the performances of original query, expanded query, keyword filtered query, *TSN* expanded query and the combined query in the experiments. Comparing with the original query, even though pure WordNet expansions can improve query recall dramatically, however, its precision improvement is limited. WordNet expansion with filtering by *TSN* is much better than both the original query and the pure WordNet expansion. It shows that WordNet with TSN filtering yields a significant increase in the number of correct documents retrieved and in the number of relevant results for the queries. The TSN expansion's recall and precision are both better than that of pure WordNet expansion, however, are lower than WordNet-TSN-Filtering expansion. The last curve in the figure shows the performance of combining WordNet-TSN-Filtering with TSN expansions. As the result, it is much-improved than any other alone. It combines advantages using the words which could not be expand in WordNet but are highly supported by TSN. Therefore, they can provide good retrieval performances for the web images search.

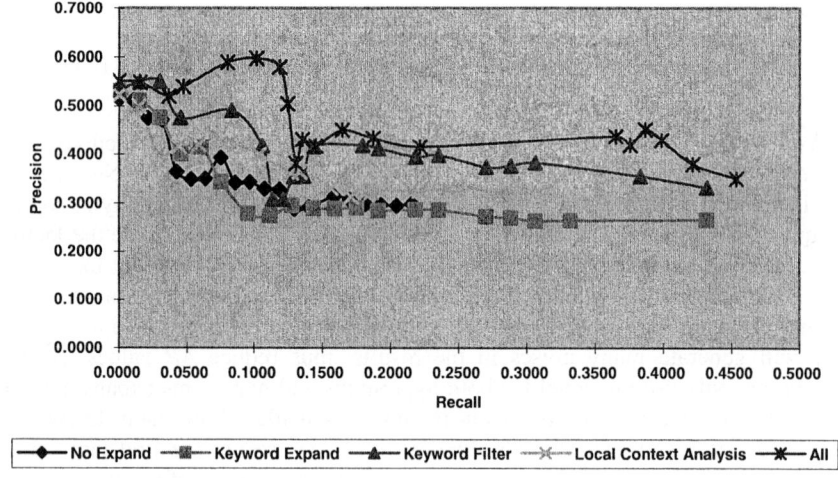

Fig. 10. Performance of Different Query Expansion Method

5 Conclusion and Future Work

In this paper, we propose a method for query expansions. We use WordNet nouns hypernym/hyponymy and synonym relation between words to expand the query words. And we use association rules to find collection dependent term relationships (TSN), and further to use TSN both as a filter and a supplement for WordNet expansion. In our approach, we use average precision (AP) as the objective function in calculating the optimal factor values and the expansion levels of hypernyms and hyponyms, and also use it to find the optima number of keywords to expand with TSN. The experiments show that the result of our combined query expansion is much better than only using WordNet or TSN along. The methodologies addressed in this paper are already exploited in our Web image search engine [4]. But some limitations also exist in the current work.

In our current work, we only assume the queries are single-word queries. Even though Web users often use only single words as their queries, multiple word queries can always dramatically reduce the search scope in the explosive Web document space. However, the words used in the same query may be semantically relevant with each other. That is, they are not independent. If we expand all the words in the same query independently as the overall expansion for the query, the performance may not be the ideal one. We plan to address this problem in our future work. That is, in query expansion, we will consider the semantic similarity between words and determine which word could be used for extension [14] to get a better result.

References

1. Yuhua Li, Zuhair A. Bandar, and David McLean, *An Approach for Measuring Semantic Similarity between Words Using Multiple Information Sources*, Knowledge and Data Engineering, IEEE Transactions on , Volume: 15 , Issue: 4 , July-Aug. 2003 Pages:871 - 882
2. Miller, G. A., Beckwith, R., Felbaum, C., Gross, D., and Miller, K., *Introduction to WordNet: An On-line Lexical Database,* Revised Version 1993.
3. Qianli Jin, Jun Zhao, and Bo Xu, *Query Expansion Based on Term Similarity Tree Model*, Natural Language Processing and Knowledge Engineering, 2003. Proceedings. 2003 International Conference on , 26-29 Oct. 2003 Pages:400 – 406
4. Zhiguo Gong, Leong Hou U and Chan Wa Cheang, *An Implementation of Web Image Search Engine*, Digital Libraries: International Collaboration and Cross-Fertilization: 7th International Conference on Asian Digital Libraries, ICADL 2004, Shanghai, China, December 13-17, 2004. Proceedings Pages:355 – 367
5. S. Lin, M.C. Chen, J. Ho and Y. Huang, *ACIRD: Intelligent Internet Document Organization and Retrieva*l, IEEE Transactions on Knowledge and Data Engineering, 14(3), 2002, pp. 599-614.
6. Qiu, Y. and Frei, H. P., *Concept based query expansion*, In Proceedings of ACM SIGIR International Conference on Research and Development in Information Retrieval, ACM Press, 160-170, 1993
7. R. Baeza-Yates and B. Ribeiro-Neto, *Modern Information Retrieval*, Addison Wesley, 1999
8. Jing, Y. F. and Croft, W. B., *An Association Thesaurus for Information Retrieval*, In RIAO 94 Conference Proceedings, p. 146-160, New York, Oct. 1994
9. Crouch, C. J., and Yang, B., *Experiments in automatic statistical thesaurus construction*, In Proceeding of ACM SIGIR International Conference on Research and Development in Information Retrieval, 1993, pp. 77-88
10. Rocchio, J.Y., *Relevance Feedback in Information Retrieval*, The SMART Retrieval System. Engelwood Cliff, N.J.: Prentice Hall, PP. 313-323, 1971
11. Buckley, C., Singhal, A., Mitra, M., and Salton, G., New Retrieval Approaches Using SMART: TREC 4, In Harman, D., editor, Proceedings of the TREC 4 Conference. National Institute of Standards and Technology Special Publication. 1996
12. R. Agrawaland R. Srikant, "Fast Algorithms for Mining Association Rules," *Proc. 20th Int'l Conf. Very Large Data Bases, (VLDB)*, Sept. 1994
13. R. K. Sriari, Z. Zhang and A. Rao, Intelligent indexing and semantic retrieval of multimodal documents, *Information Retrieval 2(2)*, Kluwer Academic Publishers, 2000, pp. 1-37.
14. Jun Yang; Liu Wenyin; Hongjiang Zhang; Yueting Zhuang; *Thesaurus-aided approach for image browsing and retrieval,* Multimedia and Expo, 2001. ICME 2001. IEEE International Conference on , 22-25 Aug. 2001 Pages:1135 – 1138.

Webified Video: Media Conversion from TV Programs to Web Content for Cross-Media Information Integration

Hisashi Miyamori[1] and Katsumi Tanaka[1,2]

[1] National Institute of Information and Communications Technology (NICT),
3–5, Hikari-dai, Seika-cho, Souraku-gun, Kyoto, 619–0289 Japan
[2] Kyoto University
Yoshida Honmachi, Sakyo, Kyoto, 606-8501 Japan
miya@nict.go.jp

Abstract. A method is proposed for viewing broadcast content that converts TV programs into Web content and integrates the results with related information, enabling one to flexibly browse the original content with value-added content and from various viewpoints. Even though the amount of information available via TV programs and the Web is increasing constantly, humans have a definite ceiling on their spare time for each media. To efficiently acquire information, they need a mechanism that can smoothly go back and forth across different media depending on situations and necessity. Our proposed method is a tool to achieve such cross-media information integration. Media conversion from TV programs to Web content enhances the browsability of the former, enabling one to skim a program's outline or to efficiently search for favorite scenes. Integration with related information enriches viewing of TV programs in different ways, such as value-added content and content based on particular viewpoints. Preliminary testing of a prototype system for next-generation storage TV validated the approach taken by the proposed method.

1 Introduction

The recent introduction of hard disk (HD) recorders for home use has greatly increased the amount of TV programming that can be recorded. The latest HD recorders have a capacity of 600 GB, enabling the recording of more than 1070 hours at a certain quality. Also, the recent spread of the high-speed internet environment has increased the amount of Web content available to general users. The amount of 20-50 TB estimated as surface Web in 2000 reportedly increased threefold to 167 TB in 2003[1].

However, a definite ceiling exists for humans to acquire information in a limited amount of time. For example, it is difficult to understand the particular details of a TV program by fast-forwarding in double or triple speed because, in the first place, TV programs are created to be viewed at normal speed. Also, it is not easy to find spare time for each media, such as TV or Web content. For example, when watching TV and wanting Web content related to the program, one needs to use a PC to open a search page and start an appropriate keyword search. It is often quite troublesome to find an appropriate page from the search results. Therefore, to acquire information efficiently, a mechanism is needed that smoothly goes back and forth across different media depending on situations and necessity.

This paper proposes Webified Video to achieve such cross-media information integration. Webified Video converts TV programs into Web content and integrates the results with related information, enabling flexible browsing of the original content with value-added content or from various viewpoints. Also, it enables one to efficiently acquire information by smoothly going back and forth across different media of TV programs and Web content. Preliminary testing of a prototype system for next-generation storage TV validated the approach of the proposed method.

The rest of the paper is organized as follows. In Section 2, an overview and the processing steps of Webified Video are presented. The implementation details of a prototype system generating Webified Video are explained in Section 3. Discussions and related works are shown in Sections 4 and 5, respectively. Finally, the paper is summarized in Section 6.

2 Webified Video Concept

Figure 1 shows Webified Video concept. First, TV programs and such metadata as closed caption texts are structured, followed by the retrieval of related information from the local and/or Internet content. Webified video is generated after associating the structured data and the retrieved related information with the original program via hyperlinks. By viewing the generated content with an appropriate browser, users can easily explore scenes in a program and efficiently access information with greater details or from multiple perspectives. User feedbacks are reflected in the webifying transformation that adaptively reorganizes the Webified Video.

The processing overview of the proposed method is shown in figure 2. First, a TV program is recorded and hierarchically segmented using information in the program's closed captions into different levels of details such as topics, subtopics, etc. Segmentation may be achieved using semantic analysis of the video, if necessary. Then, related information is retrieved from local and/or Internet content based on the obtained structured data. Finally, the related information and the original content are associated with each other via hyperlinks to generate integrated Web content.

Figure 3 shows a comparison of conventional and webified TV programs. Conventional TV programs are recorded as a single piece of data without any associations with related information, whereas webified TV programs are structured hierarchically at different levels of details and hyperlinked to various positions inside the program. Moreover, webified video is also linked to related informa-

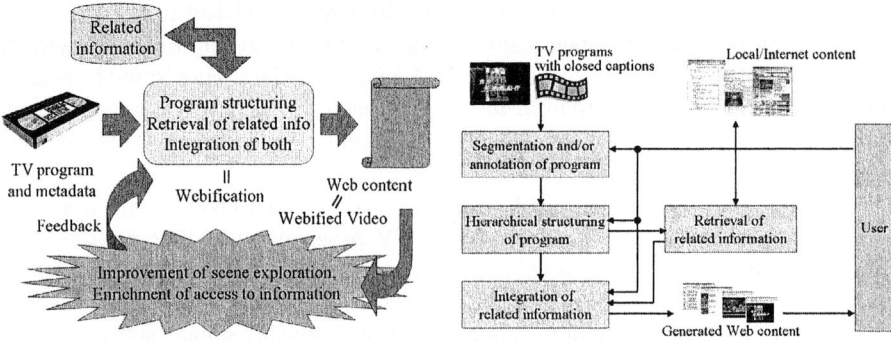

Fig. 1. Webified Video Concept **Fig. 2.** Processing steps of Webified Video

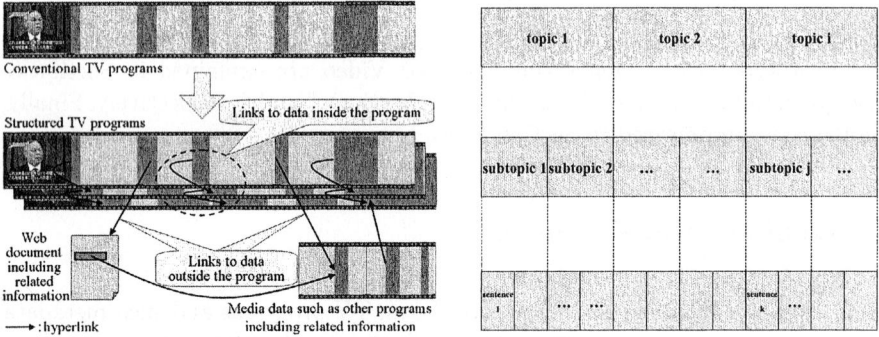

Fig. 3. Comparison of conventional and webified video

Fig. 4. Hierarchical structure of segmented data

tion outside the program, enabling the original program to be augmented with value-added content.

3 Implementation of Prototype Browser

A prototype browser based on Webified Video has been implemented.

Topic segmentation is performed hierarchically using closed captions recorded with TV programs. The segmented closed captions and corresponding video segments with different levels of details are structured as a pair and displayed vertically in the form of a storyboard on the screen. Related information obtained by complementary information retrieval and/or using live chats is located below the caption texts. Generated Web content can be viewed using a zooming feature so that the size of the displayed images of the segmented scenes can be changed smoothly, and that the storyboard can be switched from one to another with a different level of detail.

Users can thus seamlessly move back and forth between storyboard screens with different levels of details and the normal playback screen, enabling them to easily explore for specific scenes. Moreover, since hyperlinks to the related information are integrated in each storyboard, users can efficiently access related information at different levels of detail or from different perspectives depending on the situation.

The processing steps are explained in the following subsections.

3.1 Segmentation and/or Annotation of TV Program

As mentioned above, hierarchical segmentation uses the information in the closed captions, which are generally composed of a set of (t, s), where t denotes time and s denotes a single sentence representing speech content.

There are two main approaches to topic segmentation using closed captions. The first is based on learning, which is problematic because it limits domain, making it difficult to apply to general topics. Moreover, it needs sufficient training data. The other approach is based on statistical computation, such as the calculation of word distribution[2]. We chose the latter approach because it does not need training data and can be applied to any topic domain.

Topic segmentation using word distribution is based on three assumptions.

- A topic can be identified based on word distribution.
- Different topics have different word distributions statistically independent of each other.
- The words in a topic are statistically independent.

Let $W = w_1 w_2 ... w_n$ be a text consisting of n words, and let $S = S_1 S_2 ... S_m$ be a segmentation of W consisting of m segments. The probability of segmentation S is defined by $Pr(S|W) = Pr(W|S)Pr(S)/Pr(W)$. The most likely segmentation, $\hat{S}$, is given by $\hat{S} = argmax_S Pr(W|S)Pr(S)$ because $Pr(W)$ is a constant for a given text, W. $Pr(W|S)$ and $P(S)$ can be represented by the number of words in a temporary segment, the number of different words in W, etc.[2]. We define the cost of segmentation S as $C(S) \equiv -log Pr(W|S)Pr(S)$ and find $\hat{S}$ that minimizes $C(S)$. The most likely segmentation $\hat{S}$ can be obtained from a graph in which the nodes and edges are composed of segmentation gaps and segments, respectively, and from the identification of the path minimizing $C(S)$ using a dynamic programming algorithm.

Segmentation into topics is done by applying the above segmentation to $\{s_1, s_2, ..., s_l\}$, the set of closed caption sentences (primary segmentation). Similarly, segmentation into subtopics is obtained by applying it to $\{s_1, s_2, ..., s_l\}$, the set of closed caption sentences segmented into topics (secondary segmentation). The video data are then segmented based on the times for the segmented closed captions.

The original TV program is now segmented into data at three different levels of details, each having units of topics, subtopics, and sentences. The result is structured hierarchically, as shown in figure 4.

3.2 Retrieval of Related Information

Related information has been retrieved by complementary information retrieval and/or using live chats.

First, let's consider complementary information retrieval.

Complementary information retrieval[4] is a method of retrieving information in greater detail or from different perspectives that cannot be done using conventional similarity searches. It extracts data called topic structures from the information in closed captions, creates several structured queries based on these structures, and performs Web searches using a search engine[4].

A topic structure is composed of a pair of terms: subject and content. The subject term is dominant. Our method selects subject terms based on keywords that appear most frequently in the closed captions and that have the strongest co-occurrence relationship with other keywords. As content terms, it selects those terms that have a strong co-occurrence relationship with the subject terms. In other words, subject terms are the keywords that function as a title while content terms function as the body or content description.

By distinguishing terms as title words or content words, we can describe structured queries and search for information from various perspectives. Structured queries can be designed to search for greater details about the content titles or bodies or to search for details about the content titles or bodies from different perspectives. Therefore, this method can retrieve information that is similar but not the same, such as information whose subject is similar but not the content; it can also find information similar in terms of both subject and content.

In this paper, a group of structured queries having the following features is generated to perform Web searches using Google API.

1. Query focusing on greater details:
   − about the title
   − about the content
2. Query focusing on details from different perspective:
   − about the title
   − about the content

Secondly, let's consider using live chats.

Live chat communities on the Internet are virtual communities where viewers of a TV program congregate and post messages in real time about their impressions or the program itself. By enjoying chats in conjunction with a TV program, users feel a sense of unity by virtually sharing emotions with other viewers: a system that applies conventional TV viewing with a crowd in a physical space to a virtual space.

2ch, one of the biggest Japanese bulletin board sites on the Web, supports live chat on a large scale by providing a variety of bulletin boards for each TV channel and many threads in each bulletin board. A thread is a collection of messages posted on a particular topic and arranged in chronological order. Even for the same program, various chat communities have been created from different perspectives, such as different threads that support different baseball teams, because viewers have diverse interests and preferences.

Although dependent on settings, the message exchanged on a live chat is basically composed of three components: the time when the message was posted, the ID of the person who posted it, and its content, as shown in figure 5.

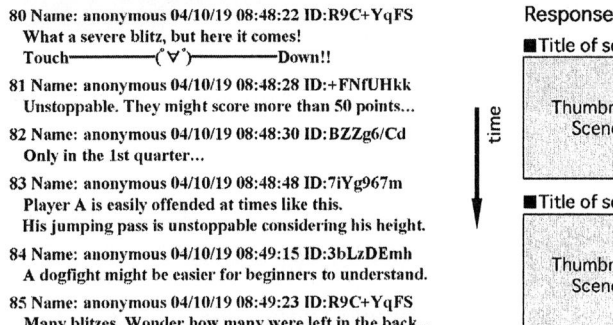
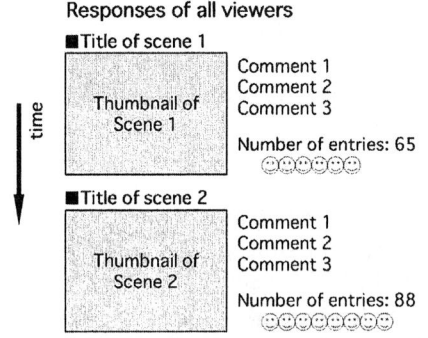

Fig. 5. Conversation in a live chat

Fig. 6. Chronological view

The authors previously proposed a method to obtain indices representing viewer's emotional changes while watching a TV program based on the number of posted messages and their content in live chats[5].

In this paper, the following group of indices, composed of sequences of values, is generated.

1. For total viewers:
   - measured time and measured unit of time
   - intensity of responses
     intensity of enjoyment/depression
2. For individual viewers:
   - ID of a person posting the message
   - measured time and measured unit of time
   - intensity of responses
   - intensity of enjoyment/depression

3.3 Generation of Web Content and UI

The structured program data (three layers: topics, subtopics, and sentences) are integrated with the retrieved related information into Web content for display. In this paper, the segmented caption texts and videos are displayed vertically in the form of a storyboard. As shown in figure 6, the thumbnail and the corresponding closed captions of a scene are arranged side by side as a pair, and pairs are arranged vertically in chronological order. When scene 1 in figure 6 corresponds to a video segment of topic 1, comments 1, 2, and 3 of scene 1 represent the closed captions of topic 1. A thumbnail of scene 1 is associated with video segments

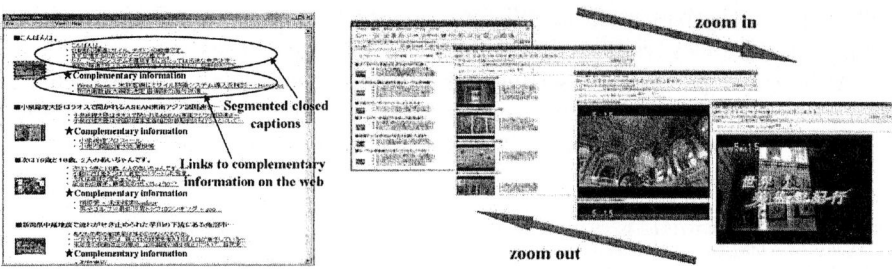

Fig. 7. Webified Video screen

Fig. 8. Transformation of screen appearance by Webified Video

of topic 1, whereas comments 1, 2, and 3 of scene 1 are associated with video segments of subtopics 1, 2, and 3 via hyperlinks, respectively. An example of Webified Video screen is shown in figure 7.

In figure 7, the results of complementary information retrieval are also embedded below the closed captions as hyperlinks. By clicking these anchors, users can easily access the related information for greater details or from multiple perspectives.

The transformation of screen appearance is illustrated in figure 8. A zooming feature can be used to smoothly change the size of the thumbnails as well as to switch from one storyboard to another with a different level of detail. For example, a zooming-in operation smoothly changes the size of the thumbnails on a storyboard representing topics 1, 2, ..., i in figure 4; when their size reaches a certain level, it switches to another storyboard that includes subtopics 1, 2, ..., j. An additional zooming-in operation smoothly changes the size of the thumbnails on the storyboard; when their size reaches another certain level, it switches to another storyboard that includes sentences. An additional zooming-in procedure finally switches it to the normal playback screen. A zooming-out operation has a completely opposite effect. As a result, users can seamlessly move back and forth between the storyboard and the normal playback screens, showing different levels of details, enabling them to easily explore for specific scenes.

4 Discussion

An important advantage of Webified Video is that it enables active browsing of TV programs, which are generally viewed passively, by converting them into Web content. Webified Video also facilitates access to sources of information by integrating hyperlinks at various positions in the program with ones to external related information for greater details or from different perspectives.

Particularly, a storyboard in chronological order, as shown in figure 6, can also be displayed in ranking order by utilizing characteristics of Web content. For example, the segmented scenes of a program can be listed in descending order with regard to responses from total viewers by sorting them according to the number of posted messages in live chats (figures 9 and 10). This display is useful when checking scenes with lots of viewer responses.

Also, the conversion of TV programs into Web content enables the integration of information for multiple programs. For example, a group of programs recorded on the same date can be summarized in a list, or a group of programs having the same title and/or the same topic can be summarized in chronological order. Such summaries can be displayed using video and/or audio, depending on the level of detail. Various types of summaries can be prepared in the proposed method's framework.

Meanwhile, in this paper, topic segmentation was adopted based on closed caption texts. However, they are currently not provided in sports-broadcasts. In such cases, cut detection of video, text extraction using video caption recognition, and event recognition techniques using domain knowledge are necessary[15].

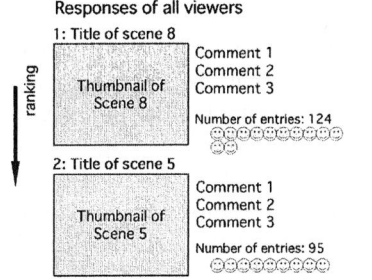

Fig. 9. Ranking view

Fig. 10. Ranking view reflecting viewers' responses from live chats

5 Related Work

Various researches have studied the conventional problem of displaying video overviews or creating video digests.

For example, an interface has been proposed that utilizes visual elements for exploring interesting shots from a video collection[6]. It enables efficient searches by combining a storyboard composed of several key frames representing video segments and filtering functions using visual characteristics.

Also, TV2Web[7] has been proposed in which video and its closed captions are structured after segmenting them into different units such as segments, scenes, and shots. Segmented units are then linked and displayed smoothly using zooming metaphors, providing a seamless user interface that is movable between TV screen and web pages.

Video Manga[8] has been proposed in which importance degrees of long and rare segments of video are calculated higher and in which selected images are displayed in a comic-book style by controlling the size of each key frame corresponding to the importance degrees.

A digest-generating system[9] has been proposed that adapts to personal preferences based on a significance test that uses manually prepared program indices and several rules.

These methods have been designed to improve browsability or comprehension of content in a limited time by spatially or temporally expanding key frames or video segments. They basically adopted approaches that curtailed the amount of information displayed to users. On the contrary, Webified Video takes an unique approach by augmenting information displayed to users via hyperlinks, although it adheres to the approach to improve browsability and content comporehension in a limited time.

Also, various researches have proposed video indexing as a fundamental technique to present content overview in a compact form or to provide only a digest of the content in a limited amount of time. Conventionally, several multimodal indexing methods have been proposed using such visual features as color[10], camera motion[11], human faces[12], texts obtained from closed captions[13], and classes and volumes of audio information[14].

However, because these methods are based on data provided by broadcast stations, the obtained indices basically reflect only the intentions of TV programmers and stations. Therefore, conventional methods cannot incorporate such factors as the viewpoints and responses of other viewers of a TV program into functions of scene search, summary presentation, and digest viewing.

The proposed method enables indexing so that the original content can be viewed with more detailed or broader information by utilizing complementary information retrieval. Also, it enables indexing that reflects viewpoints or responses from veiwers by utilizing live chats. By using these indices, Webified Video enables the original content to be viewed from various perspectives.

6 Conclusion

We have proposed Webified Video as a tool to achive cross-media information integration. We showed the validity of the proposed method by implementing a prototype system for next-generation storage TV. Webified Video segments and structures TV programs into different levels of details and generates hyperlinks to various positions in the program. It also retrieves related information outside the program and associates it with the original content via hyperlinks. Preliminary experiments showed that the proposed method simplifies scene exploration and facilitates access to information not provided by the program in detail or from various perspectives.

We plan to improve our prototype system by developing real-time webifying transformation, real-time browsing, and a better user interface. We plan to demonstrate that different styles of TV program viewing can be achieved by simplifying Webified Video implementation and conducting evaluation experiments using a larger number of participants.

References

1. Lyman, P., Varian, H.R., Swearingen, K., Charles, P., Good, N., Jordan, L.L., Pal, J.: How much information? 2003. http://www.sims.berkeley.edu/research/projects/how-much-info-2003/
2. Utiyama, M., Isahara, H.: A Statistical Model for Domain-Independent Text Segmentation. ACL/EACL-2001, pp. 491–498.
3. Manning, C.D., Shutze, H.: Foundations of statistical natural language processing. MIT Press, 1999.
4. Qiang, Ma., Tanaka, K.: Content Integration Based on Complementary Information Retrieval. IPSJ 2004-DBS-134, pp.337-343, 2004.
5. Miyamori, H., Nakamura S., Tanaka, K.: Automatic indexing of broadcast content using its live chat on the web. IEICE NLC2004-123, PRMU2004-205, pp.43-48, 2005.
6. Christel, M.G., Huang, C.: Enhanced access to digital video through visually rich interfaces. ICME, MD-L5.1, 2003.
7. Sumiya, K., Munisamy, M., Tanaka, K.: TV2Web: generating and browsing web with multiple LOD from video streams and their metadata, ICKS2004, pp.158-167, 2004.
8. Uchihashi, S., Foote, J., Girgensohn, A., Boreczky, J.: Video Manga: generating semantically meaningful video summaries. Proc. ACM Multimedia 99, 1999.
9. Hashimoto, T., Shirota, Y., Mano, H., Iizawa, A.: Prototype of Digest Viewing System for Television. IPSJ, Vol.41, No.SIG3(TOD6), pp.71-84, 2000.
10. Nagasaka, A., Tanaka, Y.: Automatic video indexing and full-video search for object appearances. IPSJ, Vol.33, No.4, pp.543-550, 1992.
11. Akutsu, A., Tonomura, Y., Hashimoto, H., Ohba, Y.: Video indexing using motion vectors. In SPIE Proc. VCIP '92, pp.522-530, 1992.
12. Smith, M., Kanade, T.: Video Skimming and Characterization through the Combination of Image and Language Understanding Techniques. CVPR, 1997.
13. Nakamura, Y., Kanade, T.: Semantic analysis for video contents extraction - spotting by association in news video. ACM Multimedia, pp.393-401, 1997.
14. Miyamori, H.: Automatic annotation of tennis action for content-based retrieval by integrated audio and visual information. CIVR2003, LNCS2728, Springer-Verlag, pp.331-341, 2003.
15. Miyamori, H., Tanaka, K.: Webification of TV program and its browsing method using extracted metadata and closed captions. FIT, D-036, 2004.

A Caching Model for Real-Time Databases in Mobile Ad-Hoc Networks

Yanhong Li and Le Gruenwald[*]

School of Computer Science, University of Oklahoma
Norman, OK 73072, USA
{yanhong.li-1, ggruenwald}@ou.edu
http://www.cs.ou.edu/~database

Abstract. Although caching has been shown to be an efficient technique to improve the performance of database systems, it also introduces the overhead and complexity in maintaining data consistency between the primary copies on servers and the cached copies on clients. Little research has been performed for data caching in the mobile ad-hoc network (MANET) environment where both servers and clients are nomadic. In this paper, a caching model called GMANET is designed to maintain both strong and weak cache consistency for distributed real-time database transaction systems in group-based MANETs, and at the same time, to incur as few update control messages as possible. GMANET is compared with the existing caching models by means of simulation. The experiment results show that the GMANET has the best performance in terms of percentage of transactions processed before their deadlines and is compatible with other caching models in terms of mobile hosts' energy consumption.

1 Introduction

With the advances in wireless networking technology and portable mobile devices, a new computing architecture called mobile ad hoc wireless networks (MANETs) is emerging. Applications in MANET are typically those that require the rapid deployment of mobile hosts and occur in a situation where a fixed infrastructure is not available. Example applications include military operations and disaster relief efforts.

Mobile hosts in MANETs are powered by short-lived batteries, communicate via an unreliable wireless link, and move in various speeds. As a result, these mobile hosts may experience severe network congestion, prolonged transaction execution, or even frequent abortion of the transactions. These additional restrictions plus the deadline constraints imposed on time-critical applications call for a new power-aware and communication-cost efficient caching technique for real-time MANET database system. Developing such a technique is the objective of our research.

Caching has been proven to be an essential technique for improving the performance of many computing environments, such as network file systems, wired distributed database systems, and web applications [3]. The purpose of caching is to bring the data source as close to clients as possible, and thus, save a round-trip when the re-

---
[*] This work was partially supported by the National Science Foundation grant No. IIS-0312746.

quested data are found in the local cache storage [1]. However, maintaining cache consistency is a challenging problem. Cache consistency can be categorized into two types: tight/strong cache consistency and loose/weak cache consistency [3, 14]. Strong cache consistency refers to the caching techniques that can always maintain consistency between the cached data and the original ones. Weak cache consistency refers to those that allow the data divergence between the cached data and the original ones.

The rest of this paper is organized as follows. Section 2 reviews the current caching techniques in mobile database systems. In Section 3, GMANET, a caching model for group-based MANETs, is proposed. Section 4 reports simulation results. Section 5 presents conclusions and future research work.

2 Literature Review

Several proposals have been made to solve the cache consistency problem in mobile databases. The invalidation report technique in which the servers broadcast the invalidation reports to their clients periodically was proposed to maintain strong cache consistency [2,7]. But, it incurs the query latency [2,7] and tremendous communication cost. The refresh time strategy aimed at maintaining weak cache consistency was proposed in [4]. However, it does not guarantee the freshness of the cached data so database transactions may access the dirty data.

Cooperative caching in MANET, which allows a client to access the cached data of its neighbors, was proposed in [13]. The Time-To-Live (TTL) mechanism in [13] is used to maintain the weak consistency level of the cache. Again, it is not applicable for transactions that need accurate data. Another caching model, called MANET caching, was proposed in [10]. The refresh time strategy was adopted from [4] and modified to maintain the weak cache consistency. However, the cached data can be only used for the read-only transactions that can tolerate out-dated data.

In reality, the mobile clients in many applications, such as battlefields, medical emergencies, and fire-fighting operations, are organized in groups and their movements follow pre-defined patterns [6] instead of total randomness of mobility like the mobility model used in [10]. Thus, a new caching model called GMANET for a group-based MANET is proposed in this paper and also takes power consumption, bandwidth, and real-time constraints into consideration.

3 The GMANET Caching Model

3.1 The GMANET Architecture

The GMANET architecture is illustrated in Fig. 1. Similar to the environment in the MANET caching model in [10], the proposed group-based MANET also consists of two representative devices, Large Mobile Hosts (LMHs) such as laptops, and Small Mobile Hosts (SMHs) such as PDAs. The group-based MANET has a number of groups. Each group logically has the following entities: group leader LMH (LMHg), ordinary LMH and group member SMH. The LMHgs and LMHs have the whole database management system and SMHs has a caching and query processing module.

The Location-Aided Routing protocol (LAR) [8] is assumed to carry out routing packets from the sending MH to the receiving MH. The groups, group leaders, and group members are defined by applications. If a group leader fails or needs to recharge its power, it will designate another LMH in its group as a deputy group leader until it recovers and then assumes the group leader role again.

Hereafter in this paper, clients refer to those SMHs that initialize transactions and send to servers, and servers refer to those LMHs that provide data service to other network members. When LMHs request data from other servers, they themselves become clients.

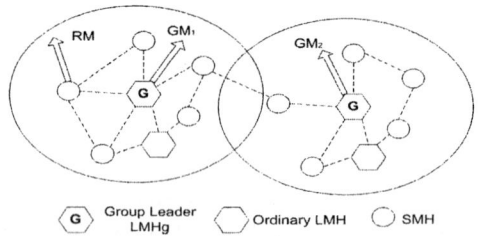

Fig. 1. The GMANET architecture modified from [6]

3.2 Data Access and Update Model

The data model proposed in [10] is adapted in this paper. According to the update characteristics, data are classified into the Periodically Updated data (PU) and Randomly Updated data (RU). The periodically updated data are the data that get updated at fixed update intervals that are specified by applications. Obviously, the periodically updated data are valid to use before their next updates. In battlefield applications, the information about logistics of all battalions is an example of a periodically updated data (PU). In contrast, the randomly updated data (RU) are updated anytime. An example of such data is the current number of refugees in the emergency and rescue operations. The purpose of this data update model is to support the different data freshness requirements of different transactions.

3.3 Transaction Type

In our real-time database system, transactions can be either firm or soft, which is defined by database applications. Firm transactions are aborted if they missed their deadlines while soft transactions continue execution unless they missed their second deadlines. Each transaction consists of a set of read and/or write operations. It has been observed that most of the applications in mobile environments generate more read operations than write operations [10]. All the write transactions are assumed to be executed on the servers; while the read-only transactions can be executed by accessing the cached data items. In some applications, some read transactions might not be as critical as the other read transactions with regard to data freshness. For example, from a driver's viewpoint, the weather information and the traffic information measured at noon is not much different than those measured at 12:05 PM. But, the information about the location, emergency medical care, or accident investigation should be as accurate as possible [9]. Therefore, the read-only transactions in [10] are further divided into two types: 1) Up-to-Date (UD) type read-only transactions that accept only fresh data (e.g. transactions querying data about locations of enemies) and 2) OD (Out-Dated) type read-only transactions that accept slightly stale data (e.g. transactions requesting data about logistics of battalions).

3.4 The Caching Process in GMANET

3.4.1 The Cache Consistency

In the MANET caching model [10], the caches on the servers and clients are both maintained at the weak consistency level by using the refresh time strategy, thus preventing all the UD type read transactions from using the cached copies. As a result, The UD type read transactions have to be sent and distributed to the original servers, lengthening the processing of these transactions. Therefore, the efficiency of the MANET caching model depends largely on the application requirements. I

In our proposed GMANET caching model, both the strong and weak cache consistency levels will be maintained. The cache on clients will be maintained at the weak consistency level by the refresh time strategy and the cache on group leaders will be maintained at the strong consistency level by an asynchronous invalidation strategy. GMANET with both cache types solves the above shortcoming of the MANET caching model. These two types of caching mechanism are discussed separately as follows.

3.4.1.1 Weak Cache Consistency on Clients

Clients are allowed to cache the previously accessed data items so that the subsequent requests may be satisfied by the cached data and thus avoid sending them to servers. The refresh time strategy in [4] is modified to keep the cached data consistent at the weak consistency level on the client side (SMHs and ordinary LMHs) in the GMANET caching model. Each cached data item is associated with a refresh time indicating how long this particular data item remains valid in the client's cache. In order to calculate the refresh time, the update log containing the statistics about the update pattern is maintained on each data server. The update log records the data id, the previous mean refresh time for this data item, and the latest update timestamp of all data residing on the server. Before servers return the transaction results to clients, they estimate a refresh time for each data item in the transaction result and the estimated refresh time will be sent along with the transaction result back to clients.

The refresh time calculation is modified as follows to fit the GMANET caching model: 1) $FRT_i = T_i + \overline{d_i} - T_{comm}$ for randomly updated data, 2) $PRT_i = T_i - P_i - T_{comm}$ for periodically updated data, 3) $T_{comm} = NoOfHops * PackageSize / Bandwidth$, where T_i is the current update timestamp of data item i, $\overline{d_i}$ is the mean update duration on data item i, P_i is the fixed update interval, T_{comm} is the transmission time between the sender and receiver, *NoOfHops* is the number of hops between the sender and the receiver, *PackageSize* is the transmission amount, and Bandwidth is the wireless bandwidth. The reason that the refresh time is subtracted by the communication cost is to reduce the effect of the communication time, and thus, reduce the staleness degree of the cached data when transmitting from servers to clients.

Through the refresh time strategy the clients are not relying on the servers' help to validate their cached data items because each cached data item has already been attached with the refresh time specifying how long it is valid in the future. It means that no additional communications between the clients and servers are needed. Unlike the invalidation strategy where the clients have to be connected and tuned in to receive the invalidation reports from servers periodically or asynchronously, this method allows clients to be free to move and disconnect (offline) and still be able to validate the cached data items when the clients access their cached data. However, the refresh time strategy cannot maintain strong cache consistency while the invalidation strategy does.

3.4.1.2 Strong Cache Consistency on Group Leaders

Group leaders are allowed to cache the passing-by data on behalf of their clients. This is because all the transactions initiated from clients are first sent to group leaders and, therefore, group leaders can see all the network traffic within their registered clients. Thus, LMHgs are selected as the locations where the cached data is maintained at the strong consistency level and valid for access anytime. This will improve the processing of UD type read-only transactions.

The caches on group leaders are kept fresh by relying on the combination of invalidation and refresh time techniques. From the review on strong cache consistency in Section 2, maintaining the cache at the strong consistency level is quite expensive since it requires all the updates made on the servers be propagated to the cache holders immediately. In GMANET, of all the LMHs we assume only group leaders are allowed to maintain their cache at the strong consistency level for their clients, thus cutting down the total number of sites that need invalidation messages. As a result, the communication overhead to maintain strong cache consistency is tolerable since the number of group leaders is much smaller than the number of LMHs in GMANET.

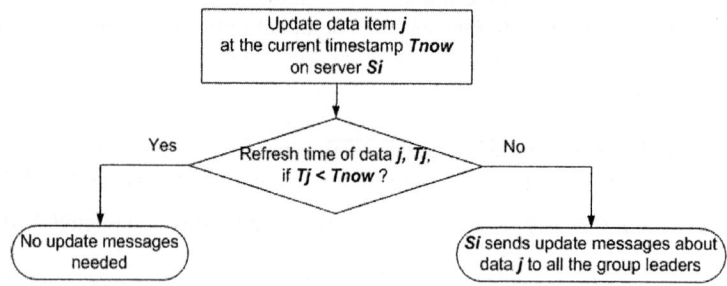

Fig. 2. The invalidation messages from LMHs to LMHgs

The communication overhead to maintain strong cache consistency by invalidation technique can be further reduced by making use of the refresh time for each cached data item. As discussed in the previous section, each data server maintains an update log, which is used to estimate refresh time for each accessed data item for its clients. The data servers also use the refresh time to reduce the update or invalidation message exchanges between them and the group leaders. As shown in Fig. 2, when data is updated on an data server, it first looks up its update log to see whether the refresh time of this updated data item is expired or not. If expired, then it is not necessary to send the update message to group leaders; if not expired, then the data server must send the update messages to each of the group leaders that have cached the updated data item. For example, if 50% of the cached data are associated with the correct refresh time, then the update messages will be cut down by 50%, compared with the cost of traditional invalidation methods to maintain strong cache consistency, where every update invokes a communication for propagating the updated value to all the cache holders.

It can also be seen that the tighter the estimated refresh time, the fewer update messages necessary to keep the cache consistent with the original servers. The tight estimation of the refresh time means that the refresh time tends to be small and expired before the actual update, and thus the data servers do not need to send out update messages, saving a lot of bandwidth and energy to transmit these control messages.

When a network partition occurs, the delayed update is assumed by the data servers. It means the data servers will wait to receive all acknowledgements of the group leaders before the actual updates are committed. If some group leaders are in a different partition, the data servers will delay the updates until the refresh time expires.

3.4.2 Cache Data by Clients and by Group Leaders

When a transaction result is returned to a client from its group leader, the client will check the transaction type since the client only caches the data requested by OD type read transactions; the data items accessed by UD type read transactions have already been cached by their group leaders. The reasons for this cache assignment are two folds. First, it is to reduce the cache storage burden on the client side since clients are much more limited in terms of memory and disk space. Second, it is to reduce the redundancy since it is not efficient if both clients and their group leaders cache the same data. For each data item marked with the refresh time in the transaction result, if it is already cached, the client updates its value and refresh time; if it is not cached and the cache storage is not full, the client inserts it into an empty space; otherwise, the client executes the replacement policy (Section 3.4.5) to select a slot for a newly arrived data item.

The group leaders will cache only data that are accessed by UD read-only transactions. When the results of all the sub transactions are sent back from all the participating servers (LMHps), the group leaders have a decision to make as to what kind of data they should cache. In order to reduce the overhead of the communication cost associated with the strong cache consistency policy, the group leaders only cache the data accessed by UD type read-only transactions instead of all the transactions. The accessed data by the OD type read-only transactions will be cached on the clients' side as discussed above. The cache on the group leaders will be used to satisfy all the subsequent UD read-only transactions sent from their group members.

3.4.3 Cache Access by Clients

In GMANET, the cache on the client side is only kept at the weak consistency level, and thus only OD type read transactions accepting slightly out-dated data can access it

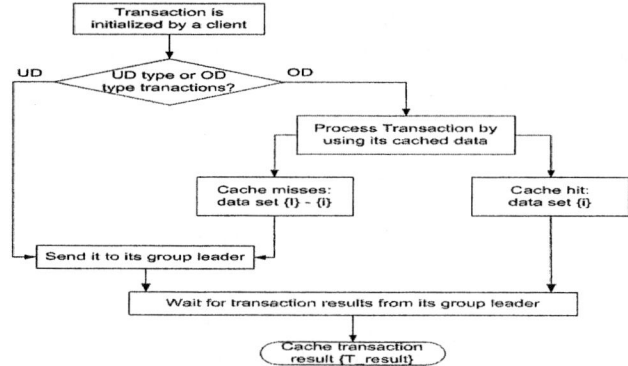

Fig. 3. The access of cached data items on the client side

(see Fig. 3); the cache on the group leaders is kept at the strong consistency level, and thus, read transactions, either OD or UD type, can access the cached data on LMHgs. All the write transactions have to be sent and processed at the group leaders LMHgs.

It is highly likely that the OD type read transactions are answered by using locally outdated cached data because the weak consistency protocol is used on the client's side. Even though the servers help estimate the refresh time based on the past update statistics of the clients, the refresh time of each cached data item is only the best effort estimation. Any updates happened on the servers may not reflect on the cached copies of the clients in a timely fashion, and thus, it is inevitable for OD type read transactions to access the stale cache.

The access of the cached data items by clients is shown in Fig. 3. If an initiated transaction is an OD type read transaction, the client checks its cache first and identifies all the cache misses and cache hits. It then sends the transaction requesting for cache misses to the group leader. If it is the UD type read-only or write transaction, the client sends it to its group leader for processing directly.

3.4.4 Cache Access by Group Leaders

When a transaction is initialized by an SMH and it is an OD read-only transaction, it is first processed by the SMH to identify the locally qualified cached data items called cache hit or cache miss otherwise. After processing, the SMH will package the cache misses and send them to its group leader. Since the cached data on LMHgs are always kept consistent with the original copies, all the read transactions, both UD and OD types, can access the cached data.

The cache access by group leaders is shown in Fig. 4. When a new transaction arrives, and it is the read transaction, it will be first processed by using the cached data maintained on the group leaders, and the cache hit data set, which is $\{i'\}$, and cache miss data set, which is $\{I\} - \{i\} - \{i'\}$ (note the $\{i\}$ is the local cache hit data set on the transaction initiator client), are identified. The group leader then distributes the cache misses to all the participating servers (LMHps). All the write transactions are distributed to the original servers for processing.

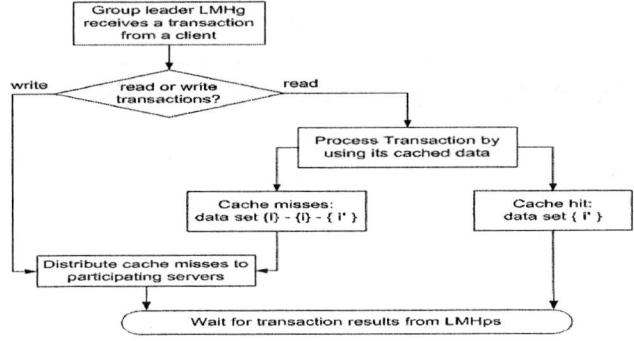

Fig. 4. The access of cached data on the group leader side

3.4.5 Cache Replacement

The cache replacement proposed in [10] is adapted in this research to make room for newly arrived data items when the cache storage is full. Both the group leaders and their group members use the same replacement policy. Initially, each mobile host (server or client) will check whether its storage is full or not. If it is not full, it inserts the newly arrived data into the empty entries in its cache. If it is full, it starts the replacement process by searching for expired data items in its cache. If an expired item is found, it just replaces it; otherwise it searches for the data items with the lowest access frequency accessed by soft transactions. If it is not found, then it searches for the data items with the lowest access frequency by firm transactions. The unique characteristic of this replacement policy is that it puts a higher caching priority on firm transactions than soft transactions, and thus, favors firm transactions over soft transactions since the firm transactions must be aborted if they missed their deadlines.

4 Simulation Experiments

Four simulation models using AweSim software [11] are built to compare the GMANET caching model, the MANET caching model, CHAN caching model and the baseline model without caching module. The performance metrics are 1) the percentage of transactions missing their deadlines, indicating how many transactions cannot be processed successfully within their transaction deadline requirements [10], 2) the total energy consumptions of all LMHs and all SMHs, 3) the average difference in energy consumption between two LMHs indicating how balance the system is in terms of energy consumption, and 4) the cache hit ratio, computed as the transactions fulfilled by the servers' or clients' caches over the total transactions initialized in the system. The parameters listed in Table 1 are the default parameter settings for the following simulation experiments.

4.1 Effect of Firm/Soft Ratio

The four models show different capacities of processing transactions before their deadlines in Fig. 5. The NO caching model performs the worst, followed by the

Table 1. The simulation parameters in the system

Parameter	Value Range	Default	Reference
Firm/Soft Ratio	0, 0.25, 0.5, 0.75, 1	0.5	
OD/UD Ratio	0, 0.25, 0.5, 0.75, 1	0.75	
Cache Size	0.2, 0.4, 0.6, 0.8	0.6	
Number of LMHs	-	20	
Number of SMHs	-	40	
Simulation Area	-	1000x1000	
Bandwidth	-	11 Mpbs	[12]
LMH Energy Dissipation Rate in Active Mode	-	15.4 w	[5,12]
LMH Energy Dissipation Rate in Doze Mode	-	7.97w	[5,12]
SMH Energy Dissipation Rate in Active Mode	-	2.178 w	[5,12]
LMH Energy Dissipation Rate in Doze Mode	-	1.4w	[5,12]

CHAN caching model and the MANET caching model; the best is the GMANET caching model. With more firm transactions in the system, the performance gaps among these four models become larger. It is obvious that the NO caching model is the worst because it does not equip with the caching component like the other three caching models. The better performance of the three caching models is contributed to the caching mechanism so that some transactions can reduce their transaction paths by going through shortcuts of the cached copies instead of the whole transaction path. Also, the shortened transaction path means a reduced amount of transmission, thus saving a lot of energy spent on transmission and computation. Among the three caching models, the GMANET has the best performance due to the fact that its caching system allows not only OD type read transactions but also UD type read transaction to access its cached data. Compared to GMANET, the MANET and CHAN Caching models allow only OD type read-only transactions to access their cached data, and require all the UD type read-only transactions to be processed by the original servers.

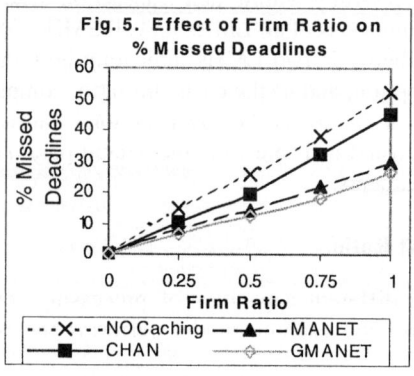

Fig. 5. Effect of Firm Ratio on % Missed Deadlines

4.2 Effect of OD Ratio

Fig. 6 shows that when the OD type transaction increases, the percentage of transactions missing deadlines decreases in both CHAN and MANET, but it remains more or less the same in the GMANET caching model, and does not exhibit as much sensitivity to the changes of OD type transactions as the other two caching models do. The above observed trend is expected. As all the caches in both the CHAN and MANET caching models are maintained at the weak consistent level, only OD type transactions are allowed to access the cached data and all the UD type transactions will be sent to the origin server to process. While the cache on the group leaders in GMANET is maintained at the strong consistency level and the cache on the clients is maintained at the weak consistency level, the OD type transactions can access the cached data on the clients and on the group leaders, and the UD type transaction can access the cached date on the group leaders. Thus, the performance gain in GMANET is contributed to its double cache types in the system. The performance in terms of percentage of transactions missing deadlines of GMANET is on average about 20% better than MANET, 50% better than CHAN, and 100% better than NO Caching.

4.3 Effect of Cache Size

The cache size on the clients and servers is varied to show its effect on the performance of the four models. The NO caching model does not change with the cache size in all the metrics studied because it has no caching mechanism. It can be seen in Fig. 7 that the percentage of the transactions missing deadlines decreases with the increase of the cache size in all the three caching models. With the increase of the cache size more data can be cached for the subsequent transactions, and thus, the probability of satisfying the transactions with the local cached data increases. Among the three caching models, the GMANET technique performs the best, followed by MANET and CHAN. The same analysis as that in the previous experiments holds true for the performance differences among the three caching models.

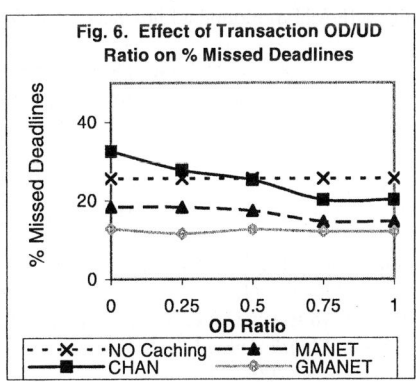

Fig. 6. Effect of Transaction OD/UD Ratio on % Missed Deadlines

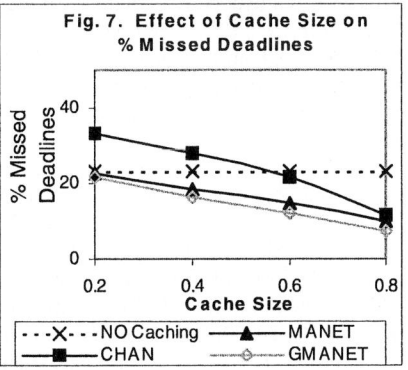

Fig. 7. Effect of Cache Size on % Missed Deadlines

5 Conclusions

Designing a caching technique in group-based MANETs is meaningful since, in practice, with most applications such as battlefields, medical emergencies, and firefighting, there are several logical units involved and their movements follow some pre-defined patterns instead of total randomness. A new caching model called GMANET has been proposed for group-based MANETs in this research, and the preliminary simulation results show that it performs the best in terms of its ability to complete transactions before their deadlines. However, a hand-off mechanism is needed to handle the scenario when the group leaders run out of energy and new group leaders are designated as their successors.

References

1. Baentsch, M., Baum, L., Molter, G., Rothkugel, S., and Sturm, P.: Enhancing the Web's infrastructure: from caching to replication. *IEEE Internet Computing.* 1 (1997) 18-27
2. Cao, G.: On Improving the Performance of Cache Invalidation in Mobile Environments. *Mobile Networks and Applications*, 7(2002) 291-303
3. Cao, L.Y., and OZSU, M.T.: Evaluation of Strong Consistency Web Caching Techniques. *World Wide Web: Internet and Web Information Systems*, 5 (2002) 95-123
4. Chan, B-Y., Si, A. and Leong, H-V.: A Framework for Cache management for Mobile Databases: Design and Evaluation. *Distributed and Parallel Databases*, 10 (2001) 23-57
5. Feeney, L. M., Nilsson, M.: Investigating the Energy Consumption of a Wireless Network Interface in an Ad Hoc Networking Environment. In *Proc. of IEEE INFOCOM.* Anchorage, Alaska, (April 2001) 1548-1557
6. Hong, X., Gerla, M., Pei, G., Chiang, C-C.: A Group Mobility Model for Ad Hoc Wireless Networks. In *Proc. of the 2nd ACM int'l workshop on Modeling, analysis and simulation of wireless and mobile systems.* Seattle, Washington (August 1999) 53-60
7. Jing, J., Elmagarmid, A., Helal, A. and Alonso, R.: Bit-sequences: An Adaptive cache invalidation method in mobile client/server environments. *Mobile Networks and Applications*, 2 (1997) 115-127
8. Ko, Y-B., Vaidya, N. H.: Location-Aided Routing (LAR) in mobile ad hoc networks. *Wireless Networks*, 6 (2000) 307-321
9. Lam, K-y., Chan, E., Yuen, Joe C-H.: Broadcast Strategies to Maintain Cached Data for Mobile Computing System. In *Proc. of the Workshops on Data Warehousing and Data Mining: Advances in Database Technologies.* Springer-Verlag, London, UK(1998) 193-204
10. Lau, C.: Handling Mobile Host Disconnection, Data Caching, and Data Replication in Managing Real-Time Transactions for Mobile Ad-Hoc Network (MANET) Databases. *Master Thesis, University of Oklahoma*, Norman, OK (2002)
11. Prisker, A. Alan B., O'Reilly, Jean J.: Simulation with Visual SLAM and AweSim. *Wiley System Publishing Corporation,* West Lafayette, Indiana (1999)
12. Shih, E., Bahl, P., Sinclair, M.J.: Wake on Wireless: An Event Driven Energy Saving Strategy for Battery Operated Devices. In *Proc. of the Eighth Annual Int'l Conf. on Mobile Computing and Networking.* Atlanta, Georgia (September 2002) 160-171
13. Yin, L. and Cao, G.: Supporting Cooperative Caching in Ad Hoc Networks. In *Proc. of the 5th ACM int'l workshop on Wireless Mobile Multimedia.* Atlanta, Georgia(Sep.2002) 56-63
14. Yu, H., Breslau, L., Shenker, S.: A Scalable Web Cache Consistency Architecture. In *ACM SIGCOMM Computer Comm. Rev., Proc. of the conf. on Applications, technologies, architectures, and protocols for computer communication.* Cambridge, MA (1999) 163-174

Adaptive Query Processing in Point-Transformation Schemes

Byunggu Yu

University of Wyoming, Department of Computer Science,
1000 E. University Avenue, Laramie,
Wyoming 82071, USA
yu@uwyo.edu

Abstract. Point-transformation schemes transform multidimensional points to one-dimensional values so that conventional access methods can be used to index multidimensional points, enabling convenient integration of multidimensional query facilities into complex transactional database management systems. However, in high-dimensional data spaces, the computational complexity of the required query transformation is prohibitive. This paper proposes a near-optimal solution based on our novel ideas of adaptive Z-ordering. The experimental results show that the proposed approach significantly improves the query performance of point-transformation schemes. The idea can easily be generalized to accommodate any hierarchical space-filling curve, not just the Z-curve.

1 Introduction

Many database applications, such as multimedia databases, on-line analytic processing, data ware-housing, data mining, and information retrieval, require a transactional Database Management System (DBMS) equipped with an efficient access method for multidimensional data objects. Although many multidimensional access methods have been developed, fully integrating a multidimensional access method into a transactional DBMS is difficult – the complexity of multidimensional access methods hinders the development of fine-grain (record-level) concurrency control and recovery [9]. *Transformation schemes* have been proposed as a convenient alternative. Transformation schemes can be categorized into two groups: *spatial transformation schemes (STS)* and *point-transformation schemes (PTS)*. STSs, such as r2G transformation schemes [9], map multidimensional regions onto higher dimensional points. PTSs, such as the pyramid-technique [3] and UB-trees [2,8], transform multidimensional points onto one-dimensional values. PTSs enable us to use a conventional access method (e.g., B+-trees [1]) of the underlying DBMS to index multidimensional point data.

The portability of an STS is maximized when it is combined with a PTS [9]. Considering the fact that most transactional DBMSs provide B+-trees [1], the importance of PTSs in the deployment of multidimensional access methods in transactional environments cannot be understated. The pyramid-technique [3] is a PTS mapping each multidimensional point onto a one-dimensional value (pyramid value). However, the mapping procedure does not preserve the uniqueness of the points (i.e., different data points can be mapped onto the same pyramid value). Thus, not only the pyramid values but also the original coordinates of the data points are stored in the underlying B+-tree [1].

Many popular PTSs are based on a space-filling curve (discussed in Section 2). A space-filling curve starts at the origin of the data space (universe) and visits all the locations in the universe. Since each unique location in the universe is visited only once, every data point on the curve has a unique distance from the origin. To process a range query, a set of the curve segments that intersect the given query is computed and each segment is processed by a one-dimensional range query (i.e., a fetch operation followed by zero or more get-next operations). That is, the given query range is transformed into a set of one-dimensional ranges. The query performance of this type PTSs is significantly influenced by several performance related factors (*performance parameters*) including the computation of the sub-query segments, the number of the sub-query segments, and the length of each segment. Our novel query processing technique proposed in this paper significantly improves the query performance of PTSs [2,4,8] by adaptively tuning these performance parameters on the fly.

The rest of this paper is organized as follows. Section 2 reviews point transformation schemes. Section 3 introduces the proposed query transformation technique. Section 4 presents our experimental results. Section 5 concludes this paper.

2 Point-Transformation Schemes

Most point-transformation schemes (PTSs) use the ubiquitous B+-tree [1] as the index structure. Spatial selection of points lying in a given query region is processed by using the standard search operations of the B+-tree: *fetch* and *get-next*. Given a search key value, the *fetch* operation starts with the root of the B$^+$-tree structure and propagates downward, traversing a single path in the tree. At each interior page, the entries are tested and the child page whose one-dimensional range encloses the given key value is selected. When the search reaches the leaf, the data entry whose key value is the same as the given key value is selected. In the case of unsuccessful search, the call returns the next data entry, if any, in the natural ordering of the entries' keys. The *get_next* operation simply returns the next data entry that immediately follows the current one at the leaf level of the structure (the data entries at the leaf level are sorted in an ascending order by their key values).

Many well-known PTSs use a space-filling curve (e.g., *Z-curve* [4,6,8] and *Hilbert-curve* [5]). Among these PTSs, UB-trees [2,8] have shown their portability and efficiency by being successfully implemented on some transactional DBMSs [8]. UB-trees (as well as DOT [4]) are based on the Z-curve.

One can think of the Z-curve as a hierarchical space-filling curve. A given d-dimensional hyper-square universe is first divided into 2^d d-dimensional subspaces of the same size by d $(d$-$1)$-dimensional division hyperplanes. Each $(d$-$1)$-dimensional division hyperplane is perpendicular to one of the axes. The subspaces are ordered as shown in Figure 1a. Then, as shown in Figures 1b and c, each subspace is recursively divided and ordered in the same way. This recursive division continues until every sub-space represents an exact location in the data space. To transform a d-dimensional point ($X_0, X_1, ..., X_{d-1}$) to a one-dimensional value (Z-*value*), the bit-interleaving shuffle function is used. The binary representations of the coordinates $X_0, X_1, ..., X_{d-1}$ are interleaved, beginning with the first bits. Thus, the ith bit of the Z-value is the i/d^{th} bit of $X_{i\%d}$ (note that the first bit is 0th bit).

There are three types of range queries for point data [9]: (1) *pEqual* (q, p), find every point p whose location is exactly the same as the given location q; (2) *pContains* (q', p), find every point p that is in the interior of the given range q'; (3) *pCovers* (q', p), find every point p that is in the interior or on the boundary of the given range q'. The exact match query (i.e., *pEqual* (q, p)) is processed as follows: first, the given query point q is mapped onto a Z-value z_q by the shuffle function; second, call the fetch function with the parameter z_q; third, repeatedly call the get-next function until the return data entry's key is greater than z_q.

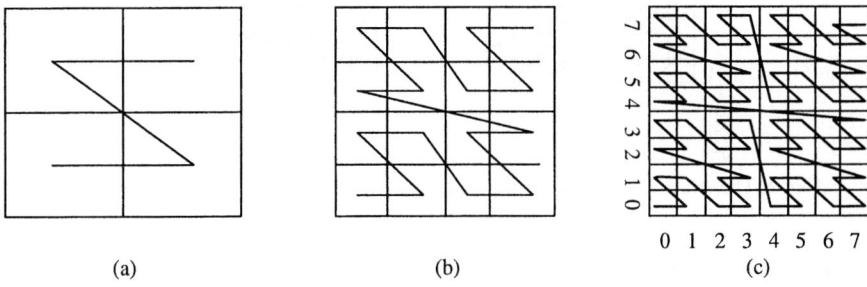

Fig. 1. Recursive Z-ordering: (a) one-level, (b) 2-level, and (c) 3-level (exact) Z-ordering of a normalized universe $[0, 7]^2$

The query range q' of *pContains* (q', p) and *pCovers* (q', p) is not a point, but the *minimal bounding rectangle* (*MBR*) of an arbitrary query region q [9]. To process a range query, one must find all data points that are contained by or covered by q'. The original UB-tree (i.e., UB/API [2,8]), as well as DOT [4], process a given range query as follows: (1) Compute every Z-curve segment (i.e., contiguous Z-values) that is covered by (for *pCovers*(q', p)) or contained by (for *pContains* (q', p)) the given query MBR q'; (2) Then each segment is processed by the underlying B+-tree. To process each segment, one fetch call and zero or more get-next calls are made.

As an example, suppose that a query *pCovers* (q', p) is given. Figure 2a shows a scenario with four Z-curve segments (bolded segments) inside q'. In this case, up to four fetch calls are required. In contrast, Figure 2b shows a case where many short segments (bolded segments and dots) are found. In this case, we need up to ten fetch calls for processing the query that covers 16 locations.

The problems of this approach are the significant computation overhead (Step (1)) and a large number of sub-queries (Step (2)). To attack these problems, Ramsak and his colleagues implemented UB-trees in a different fashion [8]. Instead of separated two steps (i.e., Steps (1) and (2)), they combined them. That is, the Z-curve segments are computed on the fly. In their *page-by-page* approach, the first Z-value intersecting q' is computed and an immediate fetch call is made. Then all matching data entries of the fetched leaf page of the B+-tree are found. Next intersecting leaf page can be found by computing the next nearest Z-value, which intersects q'. These steps are repeated until there is no more Z-value intersecting q'. In this implementation, the computation of the segments that belong to the same leaf page is not necessary. Consequently, the computation overhead is significantly reduced, and each involved leaf page of the B+-tree is read only once. Moreover, in the pipelined query evaluation, the first result data item is retrieved much faster. However, this *fully integrated UB-tree* requires some modification of the standard B+-tree interface functions (i.e., fetch and get-next).

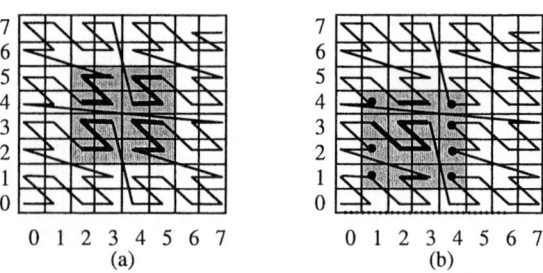

Fig. 2. The exact Z-ordering for the q's (a) [<2,2>, <5,5>] and (b) [<1,1>, <4,4>]

3 Adaptive Query Transformation

The solution that we propose in this section is restricting the level of recursive Z-ordering in the process of the range query. This restriction produces a smaller number of longer segments. For example, Figure 3 shows that a smaller number of segments (i.e., four segments) are produced when the 2-level Z-ordering is used to process the range query. By comparing Figures 2b and 3, one can easily find that each abstract Z-value (*Z-square*) in Figure 3 represents four exact locations. Note that the k-level Z-ordering produces $2^{d \times k}$ k-level Z-squares, each of which consists of 2^d contiguous (k+1)-level Z-squares, where d is the number of data dimensions. For example, the 1-level Z-ordering produces four Z-squares as shown in Figure 1. There are 16 2-level Z-squares in Figure 3.

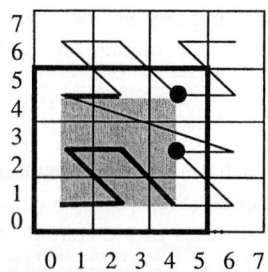

Fig. 3. Processing the range query in Figure 2b with the 2-level Z-ordering (every vertex on the curve corresponds to 4 coordinate pairs)

This restricted Z-ordering in the process of the range query incurs false drops. For example, in Figure 3, the bolded box is an abstract of q' (q' is the shaded region). The B+-tree searches will produce false drops, since the last two bits of the key values are not considered. Although we can easily find and discard these false drops[1], the k-level Z-ordering, with smaller k, comes at a larger number of additional page accesses to read in false drops. Therefore, to make this idea valuable, one must find the appropriate level of Z-ordering so that the performance gain with a smaller number of segments can overweigh the performance lose with the false drops.

3.1 Design

In Figures 1, 2, and 3, the universe is a hyper-square whose domain is $[0, 2^i-1]$, where i is an integer greater than or equal to 0, along all dimensions. However, in practice, different dimensions can have different domains. That is, the universe need not be represented by a single Z-curve. Consequently, the recursive Z-ordering becomes complicated. Fortunately, we can perform Z-ordering not on the data space but on a Z-square that fully encloses q'. We can calculate such *Bounding Z-square* (*BZ*) as follows: (1) the low-endpoint of BZ is set to 0 along every axis (i.e., $low_i(BZ) = 0$ for every dimension i)[2]; (2) find the smallest integer x such that $2^x - 1$ is greater than or equal to the high-endpoint of q' along every dimension. The high-endpoint of the BZ is $2^x - 1$ along every axis (i.e., $high_i(BZ) = 2^x - 1$ for every dimension i).

The Z-squares produced by a restricted Z-ordering are not necessarily covered by q' because they are not points. Instead, some (if not all) of them may overlap q' (compare Figures 2b and 3). Because of this, we need an additional post processing to find and discard false drops (data entries) from the result of the search before the actual data set is accessed.

In the process of the Z-squares that overlap q', one can reduce the number of get-next calls. If a point is covered by the given q', its exact Z-value z must be: $zlow(q') \leq z \leq zhigh(q')$, where $zlow(q')$ and $zhigh(q')$ are the Z-values of the low- and high-endpoints of q', respectively. Therefore, when a Z-square that overlaps q' is processed, we can bypass the Z-values that do not satisfy this condition by calculating the first key and the last key: (1) call the fetch function with the search key value calculated by Algorithm 1; (2) repeatedly call the get-next function until the return entry's key becomes greater than the key value calculated by Algorithm 2. An illustrated example is given in Figure 4.

```
Algorithm 1: FETCH_POINT              Algorithm 2: STOP_POINT
for(i=0; i<d; i++) {                  for(i=0; i<d; i++) {
  if(lowi(Z-square) < lowi(q'))         if(highi(Z-square) > highi(q'))
    fetch_pointi = lowi(q')               stop_pointi = highi(q')
  else                                  else
    fetch_pointi = lowi(Z-square)         stop_pointi = highi(Z-square)
}                                     }
return(Z_shuffle(fetch_point));       return(Z_shuffle(stop_point));
```

---

[1] These false drops can be filtered out before the actual data set is accesses because the Z-values of the data entries represent the exact location of the points. We can even re-generate the original coordinates by reversely applying the shuffle function.

[2] Here we assume that all data domains are positive and a negative coordinate value is not allowed.

Note that our query transformation processes Z-squares in the ordering of Z and makes a get-next call instead of a fetch call when the get-next function can certainly return an entry whose key is greater than or equal to the low-endpoint of the next Z-square (i.e., the Z-value of the low-endpoint of the Z-square is smaller than or equal to the current key). Therefore, contiguous Z-squares are naturally combined into a single segment and every empty Z-square covering no data point (i.e., the Z-value of the high-endpoint is smaller than or equal to the current key) is automatically discarded without unnecessary page accesses. Moreover, the portions of the BZ that are out of the universe are automatically clipped.

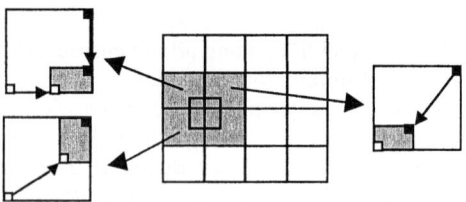

Fig. 4. Examples of the FETCH_POINT (white locations) and the STOP_POINT (black locations) algorithms

Given a query, determining the query transformation level k is the core of this proposed technique. When the length of the BZ along each axis is x, the $\log_2(x+1)$-level Z-ordering will produce exact locations of the universe. For example, the exact Z-ordering for the universe in Figure 1 is the 3-level (i.e., $\log_2(7+1)$-level) Z-ordering.

The exact Z-ordering in query processing requires a larger amount of CPU time and shows poor scalability to higher dimensional spaces. Because each level of Z-ordering divides each Z-square into 2^d (where, d is the number of dimensions) Z-squares, the number of fetch calls and the CPU overhead grow, exponentially, as the data dimensionality d increases. In contrast, a low-level Z-ordering requires a smaller number of fetch calls, but produces a greater number of get-next calls and false drops.

The above tradeoffs between high-level Z-ordering and low-level Z-ordering are balanced when the ratio (the number of page accesses for the fetch calls / the number of page accesses for the get-next calls) is 1. Since each fetch operation requires h page accesses (where h is the height of the B+-tree), a fetch operation is $ln2 \times c \times h$ (where c is the leaf-level page capacity of the B+-tree) times slower than a get-next operation on average.[3] The get-next operation does not necessarily return the next location on the Z-curve – the next entry often has a key that is several locations away from the current Z-value. For example, in Figure 2a, if there is no point at the locations (3,2) and (2,3), the get-next right after the fetch for (2,2) will return the point (3,3). That is, the get-next will pass several Z-values without incurring any page access (the number of Z-values passed is dependent on the spatial density of the data points). The average

---

[3] When the page capacity of the leaves is c, the expected number of entries in each leaf node of the B+-tree is $ln2 \cdot c$ [1,7].

ratio (the number of page accesses for the fetch calls / the number of page accesses for the get-next calls) is 1 when each fetch call is followed by $ln2 \times c \times h$ get-next calls. In other words, the tradeoffs are balanced when each of the Z-curve segments has $ln2 \times c \times h$ data points. This is ideal because an unsuccessful fetch is compensated by a sufficiently large number of following get-next operations that return data objects. That is, the wasted CPU time and fetch calls are minimized while a reasonable number of false drops being produced.

The k-level Z-ordering divides a d-dimensional BZ into $2^{d \times k}$ Z-squares. Therefore, the average number n_P of data points in a k-level Z-square that overlap the query region can be approximated as follows: $n_p \approx (1/2^{d \cdot k}) \cdot r \cdot n$, where, n is the total number of data points and $r = size(\text{BZ}) / size(\text{universe})$. Please recall that every search space is confined in the overlapping region of the BZ and the universe.

The ratio (the number of page accesses for the fetch operations / the number of page accesses for the get-next operations) of each Z-square is balanced when $n_P = ln2 \times c \times h$. With this, we approximate the appropriate level k of the Z-ordering using the following equation:

$$k \approx \max\left\{ \text{rint}\left(\frac{1}{d}\log_2\left(\frac{r \cdot n}{\ln 2 \cdot c \cdot h}\right)\right), 0 \right\} \quad (1)$$

In Equation 1, the level of the Z-ordering for a given range query can be adaptively restricted by the number d of dimensions, the size n of the data set, the page capacity c of the underlying index structure (B+-tree), and the parameter r, which is determined by the location and size of the given query range[4]. In addition, since we apply the Z-ordering to the BZ (Minimum Bounding Z-square), our query transformation can support non-square universe.

4 Experiments

We conducted a set of experiments to validate the effectiveness and efficiency of the proposed adaptive Z-ordering. For the experiments, we implemented a B+-tree library whose key-length can be initialized to a multiple of 4-byte unit. The page size was set to 2K-byte. Each d-dimensional test dataset consisted of 65,536 randomly generated d-dimensional data points each of which is represented by $<c_0, c_1, ..., c_{d-1}, tp>$, where tp is a 4-byte tuple pointer and c_i is a 4-byte coordinate value of the point, for $i=0, ..., d-1$. The extent of the data universe was confined to a random value in [8000, 12000] along every dimension, and duplicates (multiple points having the same position in the space) were allowed, and the position of each d-dimensional point was mapped onto a $d \times 4$-byte Z-value by the shuffle function.

For each test dataset, a B+-tree structure was built by inserting every point of the dataset. Then 500 range queries were processed both by the conventional query processing technique of PTSs (UB in Figure 5) and by the proposed adaptive query proc-

---

[4] In Equation 1, "rint" means rounded integer.

essing technique (AUB in Figure 5). Each range query was represented by two randomly generated end-points whose positions are in the interior of the data universe. The average number of page accesses and the average turn-around time (i.e., the average time interval between the time of query submission and the time of completion) of these 500 random queries were recorded. The experiments were performed on a Linux workstation equipped with a Pentium-1GHz processor and a SCSI hard-disk drive.

Our experimental results (Figure 5) show that the proposed query processing technique (AUB) is much superior to the conventional query processing technique (UB) in the tested cases. In the experiments, UB accessed a much larger number of pages because of a larger number of fetch calls.

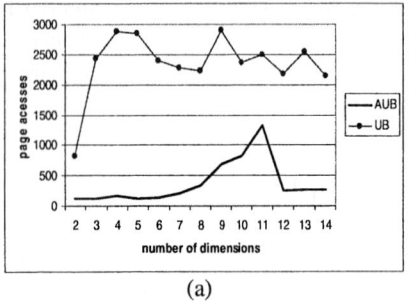
(a)

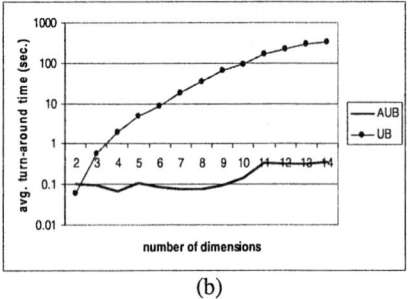
(b)

Fig. 5. The average number of page accesses (a) and the average turn-around time (b) of the UB-trees and the AUB-trees

To test the optimality of the Z-ordering level calculated by the proposed adaptive query processing technique (Equation 1), we have conducted another set of experiments. Figure 6 shows the average turn-around times of query processing with various levels of Z-ordering. While Figure 6a shows the scalability to higher-dimensional datasets, Figure 6b shows the scalability to larger datasets in 6-dimensional space. In the figure, 'UBx' denotes the query processing in which the level of Z-ordering is x and 'AUB' stands for the adaptive query processing based on Equation 1. UB is the conventional query processing. As revealed in Figure 6, although a few exceptional cases (e.g., the 5- and 6-dimensional cases in Figure 6a) exist, the proposed approach generally selects the optimum level of Z-ordering and very quickly and automatically adapts to the given environment.

The experimental results with skewed datasets in Figure 7 confirm this. In each skewed dataset, along every dimension, 80% of the points have the coordinates that are smaller than the mid-point of the confined data universe and 20% of the points have the coordinates that are greater than the mid-point of the universe. This represents two data clusters of different data densities.

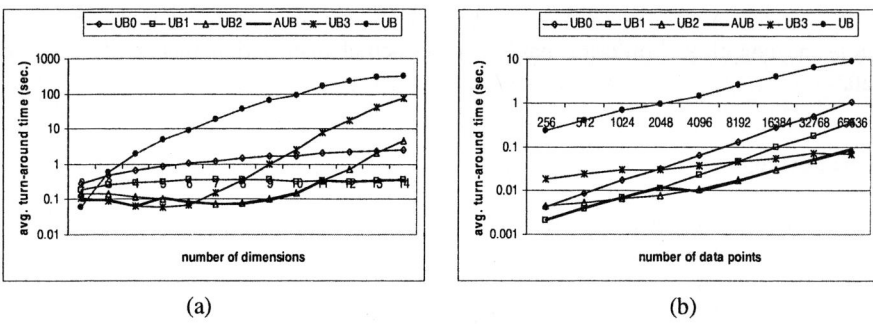

Fig. 6. The average turn-around time of UB, UB0, UB1, UB2, UB3, and AUB: uniformly distributed data

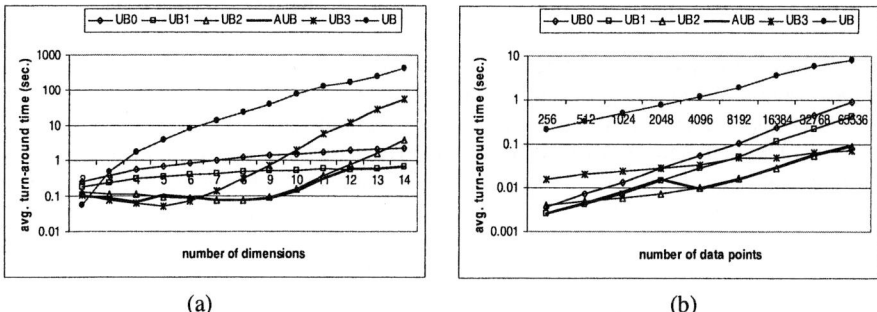

Fig. 7. The average turn-around time of UB, UB0, UB1, UB2, UB3, and AUB: skewed data

5 Conclusion

Multidimensional access methods are required by many database applications. Considering the fact that most DBMSs are equipped with the B+-tree, point-transformation schemes are very useful in supporting multidimensional database applications – one can integrate a point-transformation scheme into any DBMS without modifying the existing components of the DBMS.

In this paper, we proposed an adaptive query processing technique for point-transformation schemes. The proposed technique is based on the idea of restricted Z-ordering and significantly improves the query performance of point-transformation schemes for higher dimensional, larger data. Because the proposed query transformation creates a smaller number of longer sub-query segments, both the number of page accesses and the computational complexity can be dramatically reduced. Unlike some other variants of UB-trees, this approach requires no modification of the underlying DBMS, which enables a convenient integration of advanced multidimensional capabilities into complex transactional DBMSs. Our experimental results showed that the proposed query processing technique mostly selects the best level of Z-ordering that results in significant improvements in query performance.

A generalization of the proposed adaptive query processing technique can easily accommodate any hierarchical space-filling curve, not just the Z-curve. In our future work, we will investigate the idea of dynamically refining a basic parameter used to guide the adaptive Z-ordering based on the actual distribution of already accessed data.

References

1. R.A. Baeza-Yates, "Expected Behavior of B+-Trees under Random Insertions," Acta Informatica, 26:439--471, 1989.
2. R. Bayer, "The Universal B-Tree for Multidimensional Indexing: General Concepts," Proc. Int. Conf. on Worldwide Computing and Its Applications WWCA'97, 198--209, 1997.
3. S. Berchtold, C. Bohm and H.P. Kriegel, "The Pyramid-Technique: Towards Breaking the Curse of Dimensionality," Proc. ACM SIGMOD Int. Conf. on Management of Data, 142--153, 1998.
4. C. Faloutsos and Y. Rong, "DOT: A Spatial Access Method Using Fractals," Proc. 7th IEEE Int. Conf. on Data Engineering, 152--159, 1991.
5. I. Kamel and C. Faloutsos, "Hilbert R-tree: An Improved R-tree Using Fractals," Proc. 20th Int. Conf. on Very Large Data Bases, 500--509, 1994.
6. J.A. Orenstein and T.H. Merrett, "A Class of Data Structures for Associative Searching," Proc. ACM PODS Symposium on Principles of Database Systems, 181--190, 1984.
7. R. Orlandic and H. Mahmoud, "Storage Overhead of O-trees, B-trees and Prefix B-trees: A Comparative Analysis," Int. Journal of Foundations of Computer Science, 7(3):209--226, 1996.
8. F. Ramsak, V. Markl, R. Fenk, M. Zirkel, K. Elhardt and R. Bayer, "Integrating the UB-Tree into a Database System Kernel," Proc. 26th Int. Conf. on Very Large Data Bases, 263--272, 2000.
9. B. Yu and R. Orlandic, "Object and Query Transformation: Supporting Multi-Dimensional Queries through Code Reuse," Proc. ACM CIKM Int. Conf. on Information and Knowledge Management, 141--149, 2000.

On the General Signature Trees

Yangjun Chen[*]

Department of Applied Computer Science, University of Winnipeg,
Winnipeg, Manitoba, Canada R3B 2E9
ychen2@uwinnipeg.ca

Abstract. The signature file method is a popular indexing technique used in information retrieval and databases. It excels in efficient index maintenance and lower space overhead. Different approaches for organizing signature files have been proposed, such as sequential signature files, bit-slice files, S-trees, and its different variants, as well as signature trees. In this paper, we extends the structure of signature trees by introducing multiple-bit checkings. That is, during the searching of a signature tree against a query signature s_q, more than one bit in s_q will be checked each time when a node is encountered. This does not only reduce significantly the size of a signature tree, but also increases the filtering ability of the signature tree. We call such a structure a *general signature tree*. Experiments have been made, showing that the general signature tree uniformly outperforms the signature tree approach.

Keywords: index, signature file, signature identifier, signature tree, information retrieval.

1 Introduction

An important question in information retrieval is how to create a database index which can be searched efficiently for the data one seeks. Today, one or more of the following techniques have been frequently used: full text searching, B-trees [3], inversion [14, 23] and the signature file [11, 12, 17]. Full text searching imposes no space overhead, but requires long response time. In contrast, B-trees, inversion and the signature file work quickly, but need a large intermediary representation structure (index), which provides direct links to relevant data. In this paper, we concentrate on the techniques of signature files and discuss a new approach for organizing signature files.

The signature file method was originally introduced as a text indexing methodology [11, 12]. Nowadays, however, it is utilized in a wide range of applications, such as office filing [7], hypertext systems [13], relational and object-oriented databases [6, 15, 18, 22], as well as data mining [1]. In comparison with the other index structures, it has mainly the following advantages:

- it can be used to efficiently evaluate set-oriented queries;
- it can handle insertion and update operations easily.

---

[*] The author is supported by NSERC 239074-01 (242523) (Natural Sciences and Engineering Council of Canada).

A typical query processing with the signature file is as follows: when a query is given a query signature (a bit string) is formed from the query values. Then each signature in the signature file is examined over the query signature. If a signature in the file covers the query signature, the corresponding data object becomes a candidate that may satisfy the query. Such an object is called a drop. The next step of the query processing is the false drop resolution. Each drop is accessed and examined whether it actually satisfies the query condition. Drops that fail the test are called false drops while the qualified data objects are called actual drops.

Different approaches for organizing signature files have been proposed, such as sequential signature files, bit-slice files [15], S-trees [9], and its different variants [20, 21], as well as signature trees. In this paper, we introduce a new way to organize signature files by extending the structure of signature trees. Instead of checking only one bit in the query signature each time when a node is encountered during the searching of a signature tree, multiple bits will be checked. This enables us both to

(i)   decrease the size of a signature tree, and
(ii) increase the filtering ability of a signature tree.

Experiments are made, which show that the general signature tree is really beneficial in comparison with the signature tree approach.

The remainder of the paper is organized as follows. In Section 2, we show what is a signature file and what is a signature tree. In Section 3, we introduce the structure of general signature trees and discuss how they can be constructed. Section 4 is devoted to the maintenance of general signature trees. In Section 5, we report the experiment results. Finally, Section 6 is a short conclusion.

2   Signature Files and Signature Trees

Intuitively, a signature file can be considered as a set of bit strings, which are called signatures. Compared to the inverted index, the signature file is more efficient in handling new insertions and queries on parts of words; and especially suitable for set-oriented query evaluation. But the scheme introduces information loss. More specifically, its output usually involves a number of false drops, which may be identified only by means of a full text scanning on every text block short-listed in the output. Also, for each query processed, the entire signature file needs to be searched [11, 12]. Consequently, the signature file method involves high processing and I/O cost. This problem is mitigated by partitioning a signature file, by introducing an auxiliary data structure, as well as by exploiting parallel computer architectures [8].

2.1 Signature Files

Signature files are based on the inexact filter. They provide a quick test, which discards many of the nonqualifying elements. But the qualifying elements definitely pass the test although some elements which actually do not satisfy the search requirement may also pass it accidentally, *i.e.*, there may exist "false hits" or "false drops" [11, 12]. In an object-oriented database, for instance, an object is represented by a set of attribute values. The signature of an attribute value is a hash-coded bit string of length m with k bits set to "1". As an example, assume that we have an attribute value "professor". Its signature can be constructed as follows. In terms of [4], the letter triplets in a word (or an attribute value) are the best choice for information carrying text segments in the construction of the signature for that word. So we decompose "professor" into a series of triplets: "pro," "rof," "ofe," "fes," "ess," and "sor." Using a hash function *hash*, we will map a triplet to an integer p indicating that the pth bit in the string will be set to 1. For example, assume that we have *hash*(pro) = 2, *hash*(rof) = 4, *hash*(ofe) = 8, and *hash*(fes) = 9. Then, we will establish a bit string: 010 100 011 000 for "professor" as its word signature (see [10] for a detailed discussion.) An object signature is formed by superimposing the signatures for all its attribute values. (By 'superimposing', we mean a bit-wise OR operation.) Object signatures of a class will be stored sequentially in a file, called a *signature file*. Fig. 1 depicts the signature generation and comparison process of an object having three attribute values: "John", "12345678", and "professor".

```
object:      | John | 12345678 | professor |       queries:  query signatures:   matching results:
attribute signature:                                John      010 000 100 110    match with OS
         John       010 000 100 110                 Paul      011 000 100 100    no match with OS
         12345678   100 010 010 100                 11223344  110 100 100 000    false drop
         professor  ∨ 010 100 011 000
object signature (OS)  110 110 111 110             Fig. 1. Signature generation and comparison
```

When a query arrives, the object signatures are scanned and many nonqualifying objects are discarded. The rest are either checked (so that the "false drops" are discarded) or they are returned to the user as they are. Concretely, a query specifying certain values to be searched for will be transformed into a query signature s_q in the same way as for attribute values. The query signature is then compared to every object signature in the signature file. Three possible outcomes of the comparison are exemplified in Fig. 1: (1) the object matches the query; that is, for every bit set in s_q, the corresponding bit in the object signature s is also set (i.e., $s \wedge s_q = s_q$) and the object contains really the query word; (2) the object doesn't match the query (i.e., $s \wedge s_q \neq s_q$); and (3) the signature comparison indicates a match but the object in fact doesn't match the search criteria (false drop). In order to eliminate false drops, the object must be examined after the object signature signifies a successful match.

In addition, we can see that the signature matching is a kind of inexact matching. That is, s_q matches a signature s if for any bit set to 1 in s_q, the corresponding bit in s is also set to 1. However, for any bit set to 0 in s_q, it doesn't matter whether the corresponding bit in s is set to 1 or 0.

The purpose of using a signature file is to screen out most of the nonqualifying objects. A signature failing to match the query signature guarantees that the corresponding object can be ignored. Therefore, unnecessary object access is prevented.

To determine the size of a signature file, we use the following formula [4]:

$$m \times \ln 2 = k \times D,$$

where D is the average size of a block. (In a relational or an object-oriented database, D can be considered to be the average number of attributes in a tuple or in an object.).

In a signature file, a set of signatures is sequentially stored, which is easy to implement and requires low storage space and low update cost. However, when a query is given, a full scan of the signature file is required. Therefore, it is generally slow in retrieval. Fig. 2 is a quite simple signature file. If more than one objects share the same signature, that signature will be associated with the identifiers of all those objects.

signature file:

								OIDs
1	0	1	0	1	0	0	1	o_1
0	1	1	0	0	0	1	1	o_2
0	0	1	0	1	1	0	1	o_3
1	1	1	0	1	0	0	0	o_4
0	0	1	1	1	0	0	1	o_5
1	1	1	0	0	0	1	0	o_6
0	1	0	1	0	0	1	1	o_7
0	1	0	1	0	1	1	0	o_8

s_1. 010 100 110 100
s_2. 111 010 010 010
s_3. 001 001 001 001
s_4. 110 010 010 010
s_5. 000 010 001 001
s_6. 010 001 000 100
s_7. 100 000 110 010
s_8. 100 000 010 110

(a)

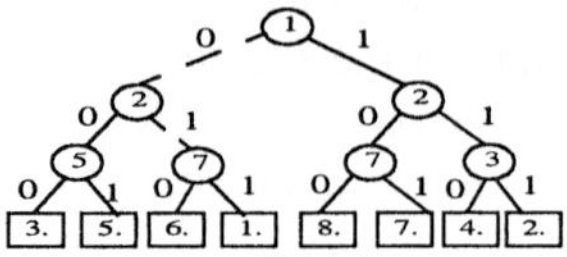

(b)

Fig. 2. Illustration of sequential

Fig. 3. A signature file and its signature tree

2.2 Signature Trees

In [5], a new method was proposed to organize signature files to speed up a signature file scanning. Using this method, a tree over a signature file S, called a signature tree, is constructed with the following properties.

(1) Each node v is associated with a number (denoted $skip(v)$) to tell which bit in s_q to check when v is encountered during the tree searching.
(2) For each node, its left outgoing edge is labeled with 0 and its right outgoing edge is labeled with 1.
(3) Each path from the root to a leaf represents a signature identifier that uniquely identifies a signature in S just as a *position identifier* used to identify a substring [2]. A signature identifier is defined as follows. Let $S = s_1.s_2 \ldots .s_n$ denote a signature file. Let $s_i[j]$ represent the jth bit in s_i. The signature identifier for an s_i is a sequence of pairs: $(j_1, s_i[j_1])(j_2, s_i[j_2])\ldots (j_h, s_i[j_h])$ $(1 \leq j_k \leq m;$ denoted $s_i(j_1, \ldots, j_h))$ such that for any $k \neq i$ $(1 \leq k \leq n)$ we have $s_i(j_1, \ldots, j_h) \neq s_k(j_1, \ldots, j_h)$.

For example, the tree shown in Fig. 3(b) is a signature tree for the signature file shown in Fig. 3(a).

In the tree shown in Fig. 3(b), each path represents an identifier for some signature. For instance, the path from the root to the leaf labeled with s_6 (see the dashed line) represents the signature identifier for s_6. It is because $s_6(1, 2, 7) = (1, 0)(2, 1)(7, 0)$ and for any $i \neq 6$ we have $s_i(1, 2, 7) \neq s_6(1, 2, 7)$.

In addition, we point out that this signature tree is constructed using an algorithm different from that discussed in [5], which generates a signature tree for a signature file like a *Pat-tree* for a long bit string [16, 19] and needs $O(n \cdot min(m, \log n))$ time. However, the algorithm used to generate the tree shown in Fig. 3(b) needs $O(n \cdot m \cdot \log n)$ time, worse than the algorithm proposed in [5]. But it can create a more balanced tree. Below is the formal description of this algorithm, in which we consider a signature file $S = s_1.s_2 \ldots .s_n$ as a boolean matrix and use $S[i]$ to represent the ith column of S.

Algorithm *balanced-tree-generation(file)*
input: a signature file.
output: a signature tree.
begin
let $S = file$; $n \leftarrow |S|$;
if $n > 1$ **then** { 1
   choose j such that $|w(S[j]) - n|$ is minimum;
   let $g_1 = \{s_{i_1}, s_{i_2}, \ldots, s_{i_k}\}$ with each $s_{i_l}[j] = 0 (l = 1, \ldots, k)$;
   let $g_2 = \{s_{i_{k+1}}, s_{i_{k+2}}, \ldots, s_{i_n}\}$ with each $s_{i_h}[j] = 1 (h = k+1, \ldots, n)$;

generate a tree containing a root *r* and two child nodes marked with g_1 and g_2, respectively;
$skip(r) \leftarrow j$;
replace the node marked g_1 with *balanced-tree-generation*(g_1);
replace the node marked g_2 with *balanced-tree-generation*(g_2);}
else return;
end

The idea of the algorithm is simple. First, we calculate the weight of each $S[i]$, *i.e.*, the number of 1s appearing in $S[i]$, denoted $w(S[i])$. This needs $O(n \cdot m)$ time. Then, we choose an *j* such that $|w(S[i]) - \frac{n}{2}|$ is minimum. Here, the tie is resolved arbitrarily. Using2 this *j*, we divide *S* into two groups $g_1 = \{s_{i_1}, s_{i_2}, ..., s_{i_k}\}$ with each $s_{i_l}[j] = 0$ ($l = 1, ..., k$) and $g_2 = \{s_{i_{k+1}}, s_{i_{k+2}}, ..., s_{i_n}\}$ with each $s_{i_h}[j] = 1$ ($h = k + 1, ..., n$); and generate a tree as shown in Fig. 4(a). In a next step, we consider each g_i ($i = 1, 2$) as a single signature file and perform the same operations as above, leading to two trees generated for g_1 and g_2, respectively. Replacing g_1 and g_2 with the corresponding trees, we get another tree as illustrated in Fig. 4(b). We repeat this process until the leaf nodes of a generated tree cannot be divided any more.

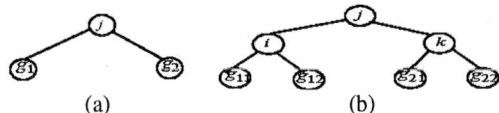

Fig. 4. Illustration of generation of balanced signature trees

(a)   (b)

The searching of a signature tree against a query signature can be done in the same way as discussed in [5], by means of which the behavior of a signature file as a filter is modeled as below. Let s_q be a query signature. The *i*th position of s_q is denoted as $s_q[i]$. During the traversal of a signature tree, the inexact matching is done as follows:

(i)   Let *v* be the node encountered and $s_q[i]$ be the position to be checked.
(ii) If $s_q[i] = 1$, we move to the right child of *v*.
(iii) If $s_q[i] = 0$, both the right and left child of *v* will be explored.

3 On the General Signature Trees

In this section, we extend the above signature tree structure by assigning each internal node *v* a sequence: $i_1, i_2, ..., i_l$ for some *l* to tell that the i_1th, i_2th, ..., and i_lth bits in s_q will be checked when *v* is encountered during the searching of a signature tree against s_q. In this way, the size of a signature tree can be significantly reduced.

3.1 Definition

Assume that $S = s_1.s_2 ... .s_n$ be a signature file. For each s_i, we denote it as $s_i = s_i[1]s_i[2] ... s_i[m]$, where each $s_i[j] \in \{0, 1\}$ ($j = 1, ..., m$).

Definition 1. (*general signature tree*) A general signature tree with respect to an integer *l* for a signature file $S = s_1.s_2 ... .s_n$, where $s_i \neq s_j$ for $i \neq j$ and $|s_k| = m$ for $k = 1, ..., n$, is a tree $T(l)$ such that

1. Each internal node v is associated with a sequence: $i_1, i_2, ..., i_l$ for some l, denoted $c(v)$, to tell that the i_1th, i_2th, ..., and i_lth bits in the query signature will be checked when v is encountered.
2. For each internal node of $T(l)$, the number of its outgoing edges is bounded by 2^l. Each edge e is labeled with a different bit string $b_1 b_2 ... b_l$, denoted $label(e)$.
3. $T(l)$ has n leaves labeled $1, 2, ..., n$, used as pointers to n different positions of $s_1, s_2 ...$ and s_n in S. Let v be a leaf node. Denote by $p(v)$ the pointer to the corresponding signature.
4. Let $v_1, ..., v_h$ be the nodes on a path from the root to a leaf v labeled i (then, this leaf node is a pointer to the ith signature in S, i.e., $p(v) = i$). Let $\{i_1^j, i_2^j, ..., i_l^j\}$ be the sequence associated with v_j ($1 \le j \le h-1$). Let $e_1, ..., e_{h-1}$ be the edges on the path and let $b_1^j b_2^j ... b_l^j$ be the bit string labeling e_j ($1 \le j \le h-1$). Then, $(i_1^1, b_1^1) ... (i_l^1, b_l^1) ... (i_1^{h-1}, b_1^{h-1}) ... (i_l^{h-1}, b_l^{h-1})$ makes up a signature identifier for s_i, $s_i(i_1^1, ..., i_l^1, ..., i_1^{h-1}, ..., i_l^{h-1})$.

Example 1. In Fig. 5(a), we show a general signature tree with $l = 2$, generated for the signature file shown in Fig. 3(a). It is easy to see that this tree contains less nodes than the tree shown in Fig. 3(b).

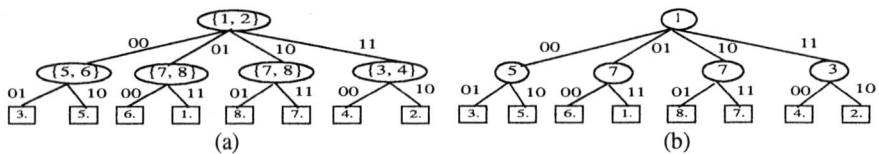

Fig. 5. Illustration for the construction of general signature trees

In addition, we notice that if the sequence associated with each node is contiguous, we need to store only one integer for a sequence. For example, the tree shown in Fig. 5(a) can be stored as shown in Fig. 5(b), in which a contiguous sequence is implicitly implemented.

The searching of a general signature tree against a query signature s_q can be done in away similar to that of a signature tree, but different in the label checkings as described below:

(i) Let v be the node encountered. Assume that the sequence associated with it is $i_1, i_2, ..., i_l$ for some l. Then, $s_q[i_1], ..., s_q[i_l]$ will be checked.
(ii) Let e be an edge outgoing from v and labeled with a bit string $b_1 b_2 ... b_l$. Then, if $b_1 b_2 ... b_l$ matches $s_q[i_1], ..., s_q[i_l]$, explore e. Recall that by "matching" we mean that for every j ($1 \le j \le l$) if $s_q[j] = 1$, we have $b_j = 1$; if $s_q[j] = 0$, b_j can be 1 or 0.

Example 2. Consider the signature file shown in Fig. 3(a) once again. The general signature tree for it is shown in Fig. 6(a). Assume $s_q = 100\ 110\ 010\ 000$. Then, only part of the signature tree (marked with thick edges in Fig. 6(a)) will be searched. On reaching a leaf node, the signature pointed to by the leaf node will be checked against s_q.

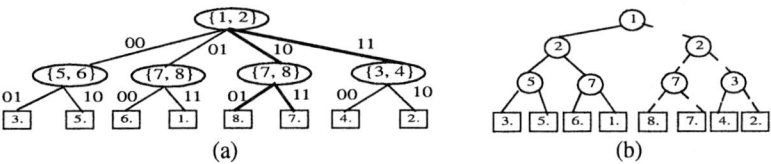

Fig. 6. Illustration for searching general signature trees and signature trees

We also notice that when we search the signature tree established for the same file, more edges will be accessed. (See the dashed edges in Fig. 6(b).) From the above example, we can see that in comparison with the signature trees, the general signature trees have the following two advantages:

(1) A general signature tree tends to have fewer nodes.
(2) When searching a general signature tree, fewer edges will be visited.

3.2 Construction of General Signature Trees

Now we discuss how a general signature tree is constructed for a given signature file S.

Given an integer l, we choose, from S, the i_1th, i_2th, ..., and i_lth columns to divide the whole S into j ($\leq 2^l$) groups: $g_1 = \{s_1^1, s_2^1, ..., s_{k_1}^1\}$, ..., $g_j = \{s_1^j, s_2^j, ..., s_{k_j}^j\}$ such that

1. In each g_k ($1 \leq k \leq j$), for any two signatures s_a^k and s_b^k we have $s_a^k[i_1] = s_b^k[i_1]$, ..., and $s_a^k[i_l] = s_b^k[i_l]$.
2. For any two different groups g_x and g_y, there exists at least an $i_z \in \{i_1, i_2, ..., i_l\}$ such that for any $s_1 \in g_x$ and $s_2 \in g_y$, we have $s_1[i_z] \neq s_2[i_z]$.
3. $\max\{|g_1|, ..., |g_j|\} - \min\{|g_1|, ..., |g_j|\}$ is minimized, which guarantees that S is divided as evenly as possible.

Then, we can generate a tree T_s of two levels with the root labeled with a sequence $\{i_1, i_2, ..., i_l\}$ and j leaf nodes with each labeled with a g_k. For instance, for the signature file shown in Fig. 3(a), we can generate a tree as shown in Fig. 7(a). In this tree, $g_1 = \{s_3, s_5\}$, $g_2 = \{s_1, s_6\}$, $g_3 = \{s_7, s_8\}$ and $g_2 = \{s_2, s_4\}$. In a next step, we consider each g_k ($k = 1, ..., j$) as a single signature file with i_1th, i_2th, ..., and i_lth columns removed, and perform the same operations as above. Assume that T_{g_k} ($k = 1, ..., j$) is the tree generated for g_k.

Replacing g_k with T_{g_k} for each k in T_s, we get another tree which is three levels high. For example, for the signature file shown Fig. 3(a), a tree as shown in Fig. 7(b) can be created, in which $g_{11} = \{s_3\}$, $g_{12} = \{s_1\}$, $g_{21} = \{s_6\}$, $g_{22} = \{s_1\}$, $g_{31} = \{s_8\}$, $g_{32} = \{s_7\}$, $g_{41} = \{s_4\}$, and $g_{42} = \{s_2\}$.

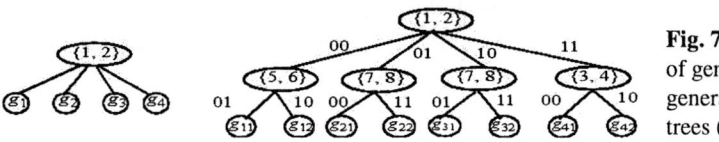

Fig. 7. Illustration of generation of general signature trees (a) (b)

This process will be repeated until the leaf nodes of a generated tree cannot be divided any more.

Below is a formal description of the above process.

Algorithm *general-tree-generation(file, l)*
input: *file* - a signature file; *l* - an integer.
output: a general signature tree.
begin
let $S = file$; $n \leftarrow |S|$;
if $n > 1$ **then** {
  choose the i_1th, i_2th, ..., and i_lth columns to divide the whole S into j ($\leq 2^l$) groups: $g_1 = \{s_1^1, s_2^1, ..., s_{k_1}^1\}$, ..., $g_j = \{s_1^j, s_2^j, ..., s_{k_j}^j\}$ as described above;
  generate a tree containing a root r and j child nodes marked with g_1, ..., g_j, respectively; $c(r) \leftarrow \{i_1, i_2, ..., i_l\}$; for ($i = 1$ to j) do
  {replace the node marked g_i with *general-tree-generation*(g_i, l);}
else return;
end

By applying this algorithm with $l = 2$ to the signature file shown in Fig. 3(a), a general signature tree as shown in Fig. 5(a) will be created. Since $O(\binom{m-l \cdot i}{l} \cdot l \cdot n)$ time is needed to generate the nodes at level i in the tree, the time complexity of the whole process is on the order of $\sum_{i=1}^{\frac{1}{l}\log N} \binom{m - l \cdot n}{l} \cdot l \cdot n$.

In the above discussion, a very important issue has not yet been addressed. That is, for a file containing n signatures, what l should be chosen?

In the following, we discuss a heuristics for this task.

Consider a complete balanced signature tree T with the outdegree of each internal node $k = 2^l$, constructed for a signature file containing n signatures. Let $v_1, v_2, ..., $ and v_k be the child nodes of a node v in T, and $e_1 = (v, v_1)$, $e_2 = (v, v_2)$, ..., and $e_k = (v, v_k)$ be the outgoing edges from v. If k is not so large, we can arrange an array A of size k to accommodate these edges in such a way that each entry $A[j]$ stores a link to a node v_i iff *label*$(e_i) = j$. So when we meet v during the searching of T against s_q, all those child nodes, which should be further explored, can be easily located. Assume that $c(v) = \{i_1, i_2, ..., i_l\}$ and $s_q[i_1] ... s_q[i_l] = b_1 ... b_l$. Then, any entry $A[j]$ with j equal to the value of a bit string $b_1' ... b_l'$ should be explored if for any i with $b_i = 1$ we have $b_i' = 1$. Then, it is easy to show that the average number of entries in A, which may be explored, is

$$\frac{1}{2^l}\left(2^l + \binom{l}{1}2^{l-1} + \binom{l}{2}2^{l-2} + \ldots + 1\right) = \left(\frac{3}{2}\right)^l.$$

Therefore, the average number of the nodes, which must be visited during the searching of T against a query signature, can be estimated by $O(.3^l$□□_—1□□2

However, if k is large, we can not store the children of a node in an array as above since it can be quite sparsely populated, leading to a high space overhead. In this case, we need to store them in a linked list to avoid wasting space. In this way, to locate the child nodes to be explored, the linked list has to be scanned and at average $O(2^{l-1})$ time is needed. So in this case the average number of the nodes to be checked is estimated by

$$O\left(2^{l-1} \cdot \frac{\left(\frac{3}{2}\right)^{\lceil \log_2 n \rceil} - 1}{\left(\frac{3}{2}\right)^l - 1}\right).$$

Assume that when $k \leq 2^{l_0}$ for some l_0, the child nodes are stored in arrays while when $k > 2^{l_0}$, they are stored in linked lists. Then, the average number of the nodes to be checked when searching a general signature tree is of the pattern shown in Fig. 8.

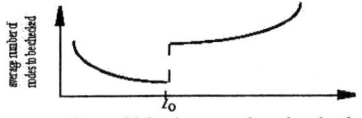

Fig. 8. Average number of the nodes to be checked

number of bits in *sq* to be checked

In practice, we can try different l's with the child nodes stored in arrays until the size of the general signature tree becomes larger than a given threshold. For instance, one of the goals of the general signature tree approach is to reduce the tree size. However, if, due to the sparse population of child links in the arrays, the size of a general signature tree with respect to an integer l becomes larger than the corresponding signature tree for the same signature file, we should set l_0 to be an integer smaller than l.

4 Maintenance of General Signature Trees

In this section, we consider the maintenance of general signature trees. Concretely, we discuss how a general signature tree is changed when a new signature is inserted into the signature file or when a signature is removed from it.

- *inserting a signature*

When a signature s is inserted into a signature file, we will first search the corresponding signature tree as described in 3.1. The searching stops when one of the following two conditions is satisfied:

(i) The searching meets a node v with $c(v) = \{i_1, i_2, \ldots, i_l\}$ and none of its outgoing edges matches $s[i_1]s[i_2]\ldots s[i_l]$.
(ii) The searching reaches a leaf node u with $p(u) = i$.

In case (i), we simply generate a new leaf node v' with $p(v')$ pointing to s and connect v and v' using an edge labeled with $s[i_1]s[i_2]...s[i_l]$. In case (ii), we will compare s and the signature s_i pointed to by $p(u)$ and find i_1', i_2', ..., i_l' such that $s[i_1']s[i_2']...s[i_l'] \neq s_i[i_1']s_i[i_2']...s_i[i_l']$. Then, we generate a new internal node v' with $c(v') = \{i_1', i_2', ..., i_l'\}$, and a new leaf node v'' with $p(v'')$ pointing to s. In addition, we *replace* u with v'. By "replace", we mean that the position of u in the tree is occupied by v' and u becomes one of its children. v'' is set to be another child node of v'. (See Fig. 9(a) for illustration.)

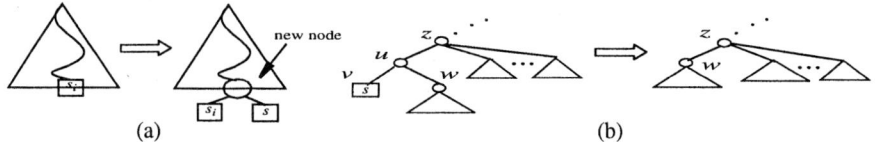

Fig. 9. Illustration for the maintenance of general signature trees

- *deleting a signature*

When a signature s is removed from a signature file, the corresponding signature tree may be changed in one of the following two ways:

(i) Let v be leaf node with $p(v)$ pointing to s. Let u be the parent of v. If u has more than two child nodes, v will be simply removed.

(ii) If u has exactly two child nodes v (to be removed) and w, replace u with the subtree rooted at w. (See Fig. 9(b) for illustration.)

After some insertions and deletions, a general signature tree may become unbalanced. So a tree should be reconstructed using the algorithm discussed in 3.2 periodically.

5 Experiments

We have implemented a test bed in C++, with our own buffer management (with first-infirst-out replacement policy). The computer was Intel Pentium III, running standalone. The capacity of the hard disk is 4.95 GB and the amount of the main memory available is 46 MB.

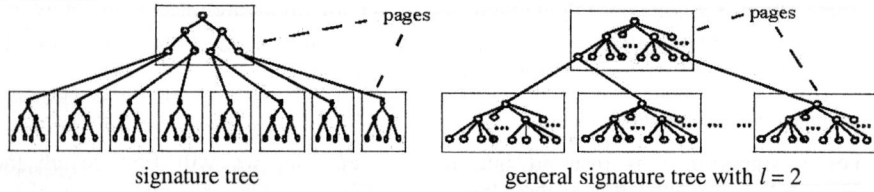

signature tree   general signature tree with $l = 2$

Fig. 10. Illustration for tree storage

We have tested the signature tree approach (ST) and the general signature tree approach (GST). For the GST, only two versions are tested: two contiguous bit checking (TwoCBC) and three contiguous bit checking (ThreeCBC). By the TwoCBC, each time when a node in encountered, two contiguous bits in the query signature will be checked, while by ThreeCBC, each time three contiguous bits in the query signature will be checked. They are applied to different signature queries against the signature files of different sizes. All the signatures are created randomly using a uniform distribution for the positions that will be set to 1. The performance measure was considered to be the number of page accesses required to satisfy a query. For each query, an average of 20 measurements was taken.

For the experiment purpose, all the trees are stored page-wise as illustrated in Fig. 10.

The considered parameters and the tested values for each parameter are given in Table 1.

Table 1:

parameters \ data	groupI	groupII	groupIII	groupIV
number of signatures (×1024)	100	200	100	200
signature size/weight (in bits)	64/32	64/16	128/64	128/32
page size (in KB)	1	2	1	2

For all the methods implemented, an entry in a signature file contains two fields: a signature and an object identifier as shown in Fig. 11(a). Each internal node structure for a signature tree contains three fields: an integer to indicate which bit of a query signature will be checked, and two pointers to the left and the right child of a node, respectively. (See Fig. 11(b) for illustration.) Similarly, each internal node of a general signature tree with $l = 2$ has an integer to indicate a contiguous bit string of length 2 to be checked, and 4 pointers to its child nodes. (See Fig. 11(c) for illustration.)

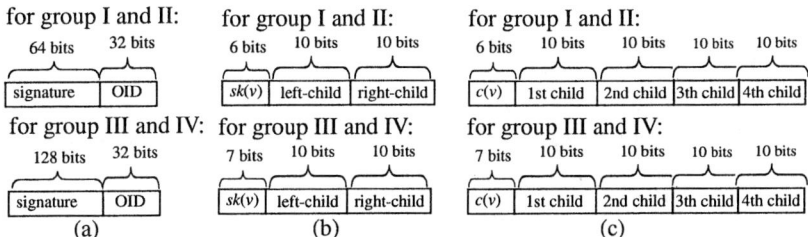

Fig. 11. Illustration for storing signature file entries and internal nodes in signature trees

Fig. 12 shows the test results for group I. The query signatures are generated randomly with all those positions to be set 1 uniformly distributed. Each of the queries is evaluated by different strategies.

From this figure, we can see that TwoCBC is much better than ST. But ThreeCBC is not much better than TwoCBC as we expect. It is because although the tree size of ThreeBCB is smaller than that of TwoCBC, a tree generated by ThreeCBC may not be so balanced as a tree generated by TwoCBC. However, as the length of signatures increases, we have more chance to find a balanced tree for ThreeCBC. So the discrepancy between ThreeCBC and TwoCBC increases as shown in Fig. 13.

In Fig. 14 and Fig. 15, we show the results of Group III and Group IV, respectively. These results also confirm the above analysis.

In addition, the weight of a query signature (*i.e.*, the percentage of 1-bits in a query signature) affects both signature trees and general signature trees greatly. Fig. 16 shows the number of page access when the three methods are used to search a signature file containing 100 × 1024 signatures to locate query signatures with different weights.

From this, we can see that as the weight of a query signature increases, the searching time of both the signature trees and the general signature trees reduces. It is because each bit set to 1 in the query signature may cut off a subtree. However, more bits set to 1 in a query signature impacts the general signature trees more than it does to the signature trees, which shows that the filtering ability of a general signature tree is stronger than a signature tree.

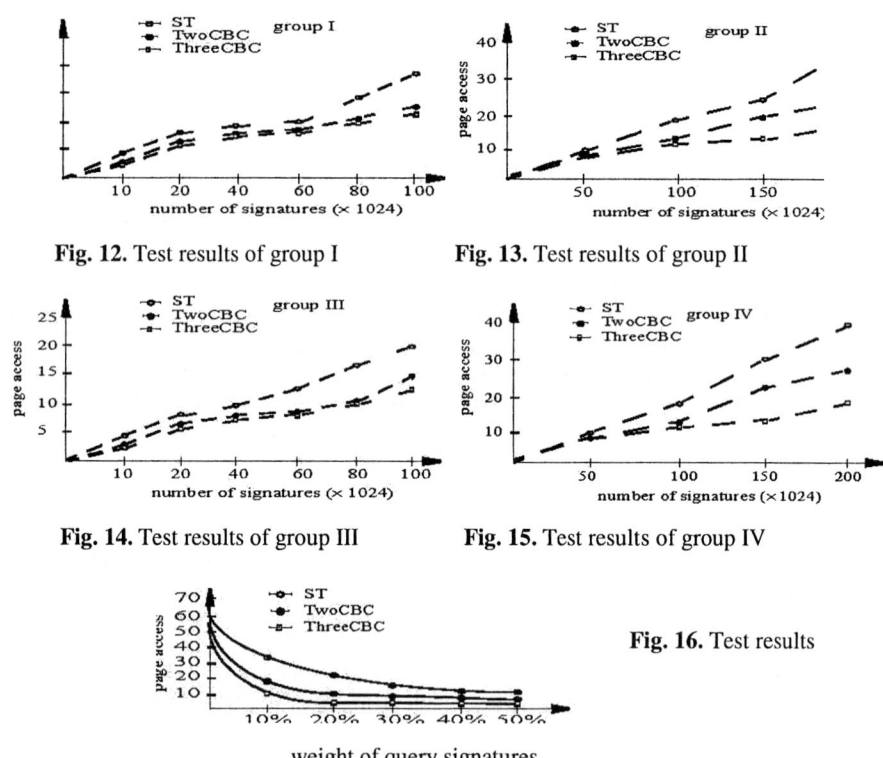

Fig. 12. Test results of group I

Fig. 13. Test results of group II

Fig. 14. Test results of group III

Fig. 15. Test results of group IV

Fig. 16. Test results

6 Conclusion

In this paper, we extend the structure of signature trees by checking more than one bits in a query signature s_q when encountering a node during the searching of a signature tree against s_q. In this way, we can not only reduce the size of a signature tree, but also increase its filtering ability. Experiments have been done, which shows that the general signature tree uniformly outperforms the signature tree approach.

References

[1] S. Abiteboul, S. Cluet, V. Christophides, T. Milo, G. Moerkotte and J. Simeon, "Querying documents in object databases," *Int. J. on Digital Libraries*, Vol. 1, No. 1, Jan. 1997, pp. 5-19.

[2] Aho, A.V., Hopcroft, J.E. and Ullman, J.D., *The Design and Analysis of Computer Algorithms*, Addison-Wesley Publishing Com., London, 1974.

[3] R. Bayer and K. Unterrauer, "Prefix B-tree," *ACM Transaction on Database Systems*, 2(1), 1977, pp. 11-26.
[4] S. Christodoulakis and C. Faloutsos, "Design consideration for a message file server," *IEEE Trans. Software Engineering*, 10(2) (1984) 201-210.
[5] Y. Chen, Signature Files and Signature Trees, *Information Processing Letters*, Vol. 82, No. 4, March 2002, pp. 213-221.
[6] W.W. Chang, H.J. Schek, A signature access method for the STARBURST database system, in: *Proc. 19th VLDB Conf.*, 1989, pp. 145-153.
[7] S. Christodoulakis, M. Theodoridou, F. Ho, M. Papa and A. Pathria, Multimedia document presentation, information extraction and document formation in MINOS - A model and a system, *ACM Trans. Office Inform. Systems*, 4 (4), 1986, pp. 345-386.
[8] P. Ciaccia and P. Zezula, Declustering of key-based partitioned signature files, *ACM Trans. Database Systems*, 21 (3), 1996, pp. 295-338.
[9] U. Deppisch, S-tree: A Dynamic Balanced Signature Index for Office Retrieval, ACM SIGIR Conf., Sept. 1986, pp. 77-87.
[10] D. Dervos, Y. Manolopulos and P. Linardis, "Comparison of signature file models with superimposed coding," *J. of Information Processing Letters* 65 (1998) 101 - 106.
[11] C. Faloutsos, "Access Methods for Text," *ACM Computing Surveys*, 17(1), 1985, pp. 49-74.
[12] C. Faloutsos, "Signature Files," in: *Information Retrieval: Data Structures & Algorithms*, edited by W.B. Frakes and R. Baeza-Yates, Prentice Hall, New Jersey, 1992, pp. 44-65.
[13] C. Faloutsos, R. Lee, C. Plaisant and B. Shneiderman, Incorporating string search in hypertext system: User interface and signature file design issues, *HyperMedia*, 2(3), 1990, pp. 183-200.
[14] D. Harman, E. Fox, R. and Baeza-Yates, "Inverted Files," in: *Information Retrieval: Data Structures & Algorithms*, edited by W.B. Frakes and R. Baeza-Yates, Prentice Hall, New Jersey, 1992, pp. 28-43.
[15] Y. Ishikawa, H. Kitagawa and N. Ohbo, Evaluation of signature files as set access facilities in OODBs, in *Proc. of ACM SIGMOD Int. Conf. on Management of Data*, Washington D.C., May 1993, pp. 247-256.
[16] D.E. Knuth, *The Art of Computer Programming: Sorting and Searching*, Addison-Wesley Pub. London, 1973.
[17] A.J. Kent, R. Sacks-Davis, and K. Ramamohanarao, "A signature file scheme based on multiple organizations for indexing very large text databases," *J. Am. Soc. Inf. Sci.* 41, 7, 508-534.
[18] W. Lee and D.L. Lee, "Signature File Methods for Indexing Object-Oriented Database Systems," *Proc. ICIC'92 - 2nd Int. Conf. on Data and Knowledge Engineering: Theory and Application*, Hongkong, Dec. 1992, pp. 616-622.
[19] Morrison, D.R., "PATRICIA - Practical Algorithm To Retrieve Information Coded in Alphanumeric," *Journal of Association for Computing Machinery*, Vol. 15, No. 4, Oct. 1968, pp. 514-534.
[20] E. Tousidou, A. Nanopoulos, Y. Manolopoulos, "Improved methods for signature-tree construction,"*Computer Journal*, 43(4):301-314, 2000.
[21] E. Tousidou, P. Bozanis, Y. Manolopoulos, "Signature-based structures for objects with set-values attributes," *Infromation Systems*, 27(2):93-121, 2002.
[22] H.S. Yong, S. Lee and H.J. Kim, "Applying Signatures for Forward Traversal Query Processing in Object-Oriented Databases," *Proc. of 10th Int. Conf. on Data Engineering*, Houston, Texas, Feb. 1994, pp. 518-525.
[23] J. Zobel, A. Moffat and K. Ramamohanarao, "Inverted Files Versus Signature Files for Text Indexing", *ACM Transaction on Database Systems*, Vol. 23, No. 4, Dec. 1998, pp. 453-490.

Optimizing I/O Costs of Multi-dimensional Queries Using Bitmap Indices

Doron Rotem, Kurt Stockinger, and Kesheng Wu

Lawrence Berkeley National Laboratory,
University of California, 1 Cyclotron Road, Berkeley, California 94720, USA
{D_Rotem, KStockinger, KWu}@lbl.gov

Abstract. Bitmap indices are efficient data structures for processing complex, multi-dimensional queries in data warehouse applications and scientific data analysis. For high-cardinality attributes, a common approach is to build bitmap indices with binning. This technique partitions the attribute values into a number of ranges, called bins, and uses bitmap vectors to represent bins (attribute ranges) rather than distinct values. In order to yield exact query answers, parts of the original data values have to be read from disk for checking against the query constraint. This process is referred to as *candidate check* and usually dominates the total query processing time.

In this paper we study several strategies for optimizing the *candidate check* cost for multi-dimensional queries. We present an efficient *candidate check* algorithm based on attribute value distribution, query distribution as well as query selectivity with respect to each dimension. We also show that re-ordering the dimensions during query evaluation can be used to reduce I/O costs. We tested our algorithm on data with various attribute value distributions and query distributions. Our approach shows a significant improvement over traditional binning strategies for bitmap indices.

1 Introduction

Large-scale data analysis of data warehouses and scientific applications requires efficient index data structures to cope with the increasing size and complexity of data. Bitmap indices are often used for querying large, multi-dimensional, read-only data stores. Due to its efficiency, this technique was also implemented by the major commercial database vendors.

The simplest form of bitmap indices works well for low-cardinality attributes, such as "gender", "types of cars sold per month", or "airplane models produced by Airbus and Boeing". However, for high-cardinality attributes such as "distinct temperature values in a supernova explosion", simple bitmap indices are impractical due to large storage and computational complexities. In this case, bitmap indices are built on attribute ranges (bins) rather than on distinct attribute values. The advantage of this approach is that a lower number of bitmap vectors is required. On the other hand, parts of the original data (candidates)

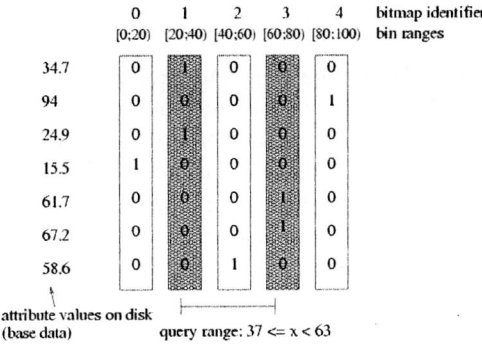

Fig. 1. Range query $37 \leq x < 63$ on a bitmap index with binning

have to be read from disk in order to get exact query answers. This process is called *candidate check*.

An example of a bitmap index with bins is given in Figure 1. Assume that we want to evaluate the query $37 \leq x < 63$. Bins 1, 2 and 3 contain the relevant data values. However, Bins 1 and 3 are edge bins since they contain also irrelevant values. Answering this query involves checking the values on disk corresponding to the four "1-bits" in these two columns. In this example only one of the four values qualifies, namely, 61.7. We call this additional step the *candidate check*. As we can see from this example, the cost of performing a *candidate check* on an edge bin is related to the number of "1-bits" in that bin.

In previous work we have shown that the *candidate check* is the major bottleneck of bitmap indices with binning. In this paper we use a dynamic programming algorithm, called *Dynamic-Bin*, for optimizing one-dimensional queries presented in [10] to achieve an efficient multi-attribute binning strategy. The key idea in *Dynamic-Bin* is to use query workload and data value distribution statistics in order to calculate the optimal location of bin boundaries. This is done by placing relatively more bins in regions of the data "heavily hit" by queries or containing a large fraction of the data.

The main contributions of this paper are:

- We study optimization issues related to multi-dimensional queries with bitmap indices. We show that the *candidate check* is the dominant part in query evaluation and introduce an optimization strategy based on attribute value distribution, query distribution as well as query selectivity with respect to each dimension.
- We show that re-ordering the dimensions during query evaluation can be used to further reduce I/O costs.
- We provide detailed experimental results on data with various attribute value distributions and query distributions. The results demonstrate a significant improvement over traditional binning strategies for bitmap indices.

2 Related Work

Bitmap indices are used for accelerating complex, multi-dimensional queries for On-Line Analytical Processing and data warehouses [2] as well as for scientific applications [11]. They were first implemented in a commercial DBMS called Model 204 [8]. Improvements on this approach were discussed in [9].

Various bitmap encoding strategies for low-cardinality attributes are presented in [1,14]. In order to overcome the storage complexity of bitmap indices, bitmap compression algorithms were evaluated in [4]. More recently a new compression scheme called Word-Aligned Hybrid (WAH) [12] was introduced. This compression algorithm significantly reduces the overall query processing time compared to existing algorithms.

A binning scheme for bitmap indices on high-cardinality attributes was discussed in [13]. This idea was extended and successfully applied for large-scale scientific data [11]. The authors demonstrated that bitmap indices with binning can significantly speed up multi-dimensional queries on high-cardinality attributes.

In [5] a methodology for building space efficient bitmap indices is introduced for high-cardinality attributes based on binning. The work in [5] focuses on point (equality) queries rather than range queries discussed in this paper. Similar to our approach, an optimal dynamic programming algorithm is used for efficiently choosing bin ranges. Our approach greatly reduces the complexity of the algorithm by proving that only query endpoints need to be considered as potential locations for bin boundaries rather than all possible values of the attribute as in [5].

The literature on histograms is partially related to bitmap indices. The optimal construction of range histograms is discussed in [6,3]. The main difference is that for bitmap indices precise answers are required and therefore the objective is to minimize disk access costs to edge bins. However, in the histogram case, some statistical techniques can be used to estimate errors without actual access to original data on disk.

3 Preliminaries

In order to make the paper self-contained, we summarize here our results for optimizing the candidate check for a single attribute. Detailed proofs can be found in [10]. Assume a dataset D has N records with a single attribute A. For simplicity we will assume that each value of the attribute is an integer in the range $[1, n]$. We are also given a collection of range queries Q such that each $q \in Q$ defines a range $q = [l_q, u_q)$ open on the right (i.e., it includes the points $l_q, l_q + 1, ..., u_q - 1$) and is associated with a probability p_q reflecting its relative popularity. The points $l_q \in [1, n]$ and $u_q \in [2, n+1]$ are called endpoints of query q. A bitmap index on A is built by partitioning the range $[1, n]$ into bins with one bitmap (consisting of N bits) associated with each bin as previously described. An integer constraint k, specifies the maximum number of bins allowed, i.e.,

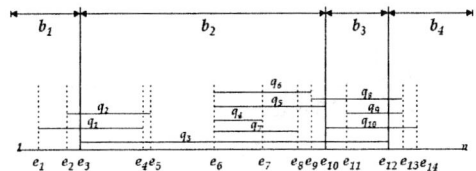

Fig. 2. Query endpoints and bin boundaries. Horizontal lines represent query ranges. Dotted vertical lines mark query endpoints.

it is required to partition the range $[1, n]$ into k successive sub-ranges (bins) $B = <b_1, b_2, ..., b_k>$. This is done by choosing $k-1$ integer bin boundary points x_i where $1 < x_1 < x_2 < ... < x_{k-1} < n + 1$. The sub-ranges associated with bins b_i are all open on the right and defined as follows:

$$b_1 = [1, x_1)$$
$$b_i = [x_{i-1}, x_i) \text{ for } 2 \leq i \leq k$$
$$b_k = [x_{k-1}, n+1)$$

A bin $b \in B$ is defined as an edge bin for query q if the range defined by the query q overlaps some part of the range defined by bin b but not its whole range i.e., $q \cap b \neq \emptyset$ and $q \cap b \neq b$. In general, a query may have 0, 1, or 2 edge bins.

In Figure 2 a set of 10 range queries and a binning into 4 bins is shown. In this example query q_3 has no edge bins since both its endpoints fall on bin boundaries. Each of the queries $q_4, q_5, q_6, q_7, q_{10}$ has 1 edge bin and each of the queries q_1, q_2, q_8, q_9 have 2 edge bins. As explained earlier, when query q is specified, a significant fraction of the I/O costs it incurs is related to the number of data pages we need to read in order to perform *candidate check* on each of its edge bins. For a given bin b, let $E(b)$ denote the set of queries that have bin b as an edge bin. For example, in Figure 2 $E(b_1) = \{q_1, q_2\}$; $E(b_2) = \{q_1, q_2, q_4, q_5, q_6, q_7, q_8\}$; $E(b_3) = \{q_9\}$; $E(b_4) = \{q_8, q_9, q_{10}\}$.

Let n_b denote the number of data values that fall into the range defined by b, this is also the number of "1-bits" in the bitmap corresponding to b. Based on the usual assumption that records are distributed uniformly across pages and assuming that the total number of pages occupied by attribute A is P, the expected number of disk pages that contain data values that fall in the range defined by bin b denoted by P_b, satisfies [9].

$$P_b = P(1 - (1 - \frac{1}{P})^{n_b}) \approx P(1 - e^{-\frac{n_b}{P}}) \qquad (1)$$

The expected I/O cost of answering the queries in Q when an attribute range is partitioned by the set of bins B is defined as

$$Cost(Q, B) = \sum_{b \in B} P_b \sum_{q \in E(b)} p_q \qquad (2)$$

The inner sum computes the total probability of all the queries that use a given bin b as an edge bin. This is then multiplied by the I/O cost of the bin (expected number of pages) and summed over all bins.

The problem we wish to solve, *OptBin* is defined as follows:

Given a dataset D with one attribute, a set of range queries Q and a constraint k on the number of bins, find a binning B_{opt}^k of the attribute range [1,n] into k bins that minimizes the total I/O cost of candidate check.

4 The Multi-attribute Candidate Check Problem

In this section we present results for the multi-attribute *candidate check* problem and its relationship to the single attribute case. We will start with some definitions. Let D be a dataset with N records defined over t attributes $A_1, A_2, ..., A_t$. Each record $R \in D$ has the form $R = v_1, v_2, ..., v_t$ where v_i represents its value with respect to attribute A_i. Let us assume that the range of possible values for each attribute A_i is $[1, n]$. A set Q of multi-attribute range queries is given where a query $q \in Q$ defines an intersection of t ranges and has the form $q = \bigcap_{i=1}^{t} r_i$ where $r_i = [l_q^i, u_q^i)$ defines the range of permissible values for attribute A_i (a range r_i is commonly omitted from q in the trivial case that it includes all permissible values of the attribute, i.e., $l_q^i = 1$ and $u_q^i = n$). A record $R = v_1, v_2, ..., v_t$ satisfies the range r_i if the value v_i falls in this range, i.e., $v_i \in [l_q^i, u_q^i)$. It satisfies the query q if it satisfies all its ranges, i.e., $v_i \in [l_q^i, u_q^i)$ for $1 \le i \le t$.

In order to get a handle on the issues involved with multi-attribute candidate check problem, let us first assume a bitmap index for each attribute was constructed according to some binning strategy. Given a query q and such a collection of bitmap indices, each range r_i defines 0, 1 or 2 edge bins in its respective bitmap index. A simple algorithm for answering a query q, which we call *Simple-CC*, is to perform an independent *candidate check* algorithm for each range $r_i = [l_q^i, u_q^i)$ using the bitmap index built for attribute A_i and present the result in a bitmap $b(r_i)$ with N entries. A "1-bit" in position j of $b(r_i)$ represents the fact that the jth record in D satisfies $[l_q^i, u_q^i)$. This is then followed by performing a Boolean AND operation on all the $b(r_i)$'s to obtain the final result. The algorithm *Simple-CC* will require accessing each value in the edge bins of all attributes. Note that the cost for *Simple-CC* is independent of the order in which the candidate checks are performed on the various attributes.

The *Simple-MultiOptBin* (SMOB) problem which generalizes *OptBin* is defined as follows:

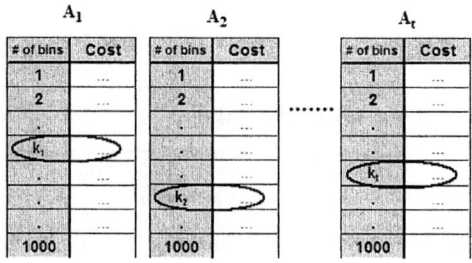

Fig. 3. Multi-attribute bin selection

Given a multi-dimensional dataset D, a set of range queries Q and a constraint k on the total number of bins, find t integers $k_1, k_2, ..., k_t$ where $k = \sum_{i=1}^{t} k_i$ and locations for bin boundaries such that k_i bins are allocated for the bitmap index for attribute A_i and the total expected I/O cost of candidate check using Simple-CC is minimized.

We can show that for each fixed selection of t integers $k_1, k_2, ..., k_t$ where $k = \sum_{i=1}^{t} k_i$ and k_i bins are allocated to attribute A_i, a solution in polynomial time $O(tkr^2)$ can be constructed by applying Dynamic-Bin algorithm separately for each attribute. This is done as follows:

Consider the set of queries q_i obtained from Q by taking from each query $q \in Q$ only its range relating to attribute A_i (i.e, $q_i = \bigcup_{q \in Q} [l_q^i, u_q^i]$). As the total amount of I/O cost in answering q is the sum of I/O costs incurred by answering each q_i, Dynamic-Bin algorithm is executed with constraint k_i on the number of bins and considering only queries in q_i.

The SMOB problem for $k = 1000$ is illustrated in Figure 3 where each table represents the output from applying the Dynamic-Bin algorithm on a single attribute and selecting some k_i for each attribute. The main problem is determining the values of the k_is. Unfortunately this turns out to be an NP-hard problem as shown in the next theorem.

Theorem 1. *The SMOB is NP-Hard even if all queries in Q have equal probability and each query includes a range for only one attribute.*

Proof. (Outline): The reduction is from a known NP-hard problem called "the multiple-choice knapsack problem" (MCKP) [7]. In the MCKP we are given t groups, each consisting of multiple items where item j in group i has value $v_{i,j}$ and cost $c_{i,j}$. It is required to select exactly one item from each group such that the total cost of selected items does not exceed a budget B and their total value is maximized. Given an instance of MCKP we can transform it to an instance of SMOB where each attribute represents a group with k members, each member represents a choice for the number of bins for that attribute. The values and costs in MCKP can be transformed to candidate check costs and the number of bins used respectively. Solving SMOB with total budget k represents a solution to the MCKP instance. □

Several effective heuristic strategies are known for obtaining sub-optimal solutions for the MCKP problem that are also applicable to the SMOB problem. In this paper we will not study this problem any further but rather focus on efficient strategies of evaluating queries for a given binning selection.

5 Query Evaluation with Attribute Reordering

An efficient query evaluation strategy is discussed in [11]. It attempts to reduce the amount of I/O costs by performing a *candidate check* algorithm in t phases. The idea is to reduce the I/O costs of accessing edge bins by only retrieving records that survived previous phases. In phase 1 we perform a *candidate check* for range r_1 and produce the bitmap $b(r_1)$. In phase 2 we first perform a Boolean AND between $b(r_1)$ and all potential bitmaps corresponding to the range r_2. We therefore reduce the number of "1-bits" in the edge bins corresponding to r_2. In general, in phase $i+1$ we perform edge bin access only on values corresponding to records that survived the *candidate check* in phase i. The next theorem shows that the I/O cost of this strategy depends on the order of performing the candidate check on the attributes.

Theorem 2. *Given a query $q = \bigcap_{i=1}^{t} r_i$ assume the I/O cost involved in candidate checking for range r_i is W_i and the fraction of records satisfying this range is s_i (selectivity).*

We assume that for all i, $0 < s_i < 1$ thus omitting the trivial cases where for some range r_i either $s_i = 0$ (the query has empty results) or $s_i = 1$ (no candidate check needed for r_i as all values qualify). Let $g_i = \frac{W_i}{1-s_i}$, then the optimal order of candidate check evaluation is in sorted non-decreasing order of g_is.

Proof. (Outline): We will use the notation $S_j = \prod_{i=1}^{j} s_i$. We show that any evaluation order that violates the above order cannot be optimal. Assume some optimal evaluation order has cost C_{opt} and renumber attributes according to that order. The cost of this evaluation is

$$C_{opt} = W_1 + W_2 S_1 + W_3 S_2 + ... W_j S_{j-1} + ... + W_t S_{t-1}$$

This cost expression assumes that in each phase the number of values in the edge bins that need to be checked are reduced by the product of the selectivities from previous phases and the number of disk accesses is approximately linear with the number of records in a bin. Assume that for two consecutive candidate checks in phases j and $j+1$ the sorting order is not obeyed, i.e., $g_j > g_{j+1}$. We will switch the evaluation order between these ranges to obtain another evaluation order with cost C^*, the difference in costs is

$$\begin{aligned} & C^* - C_{opt} \\ &= (W_{j+1} S_{j-1} + W_j s_{j+1} S_{j-1}) - (W_j S_{j-1} + W_{j+1} S_j) \\ &= W_{j+1} S_{j-1}(1 - s_j) - W_j S_{j-1}(1 - s_{j+1}) \\ &= S_{j-1}(1 - s_j)(1 - s_{j+1})(g_{j+1} - g_j) < 0 \end{aligned}$$

The inequality on the last line follows from the fact that each of the first three terms in the product is positive and the last term is negative due to the assumption that $g_j > g_{j+1}$. But this contradicts the optimality of C_{opt} as we found an order with a smaller cost. □

In Section 6 we compare the optimal order of evaluation (based on non-decreasing order of g_is) to three other orders: *alphabetic* which does not take into account any query or data characteristics (non-decreasing alphabetic order by name of attribute), *selectivity* based only on selectivity of each range (non-decreasing order of the s_is) and *candidates* based only on the I/O cost for candidate check (non-decreasing order of the W_is).

6 Experimental Results

In this section we present a representative subset of our experiments to evaluate the efficiency of our new binning and query evaluation strategies. We generated 100 million data points that follow a Zipf distribution with the parameters $z=0$, 0.5, 1 and 2. For all our experiments we used equality encoded bitmap indices and WAH compression [12]. We also generated 5,000 random range queries. The goal is to compare the following three different binning strategies: a) *Equi-width* binning: Each bin has the same width. b) *Equi-depth* binning: The bin boundaries are chosen in such a way that all bins have roughly the same number of entries. c) *Opt-binning*: The bin boundaries are chosen based on *Dynamic-Bin* introduced in Section 3.

Figure 4 shows the average number of candidates per attribute for the 5000 4-dimensional queries. Note that for each attribute the shape of the Zipf distribution is different. As we can see, in all cases, *Opt-binning* outperforms the other two binning strategies. In addition, the relative efficiency of *Opt-binning* increases with more skewness in the data.

The average number of candidates for all four attributes combined is given in Figure 5. We also show the impact of query reordering as discussed in Section 5. We can observe that ordering according to the number of candidates in the edge bins is quite competetive with the optimal reordering strategy for this data. Again we can observe that *Opt-binning* outperforms the other two binning

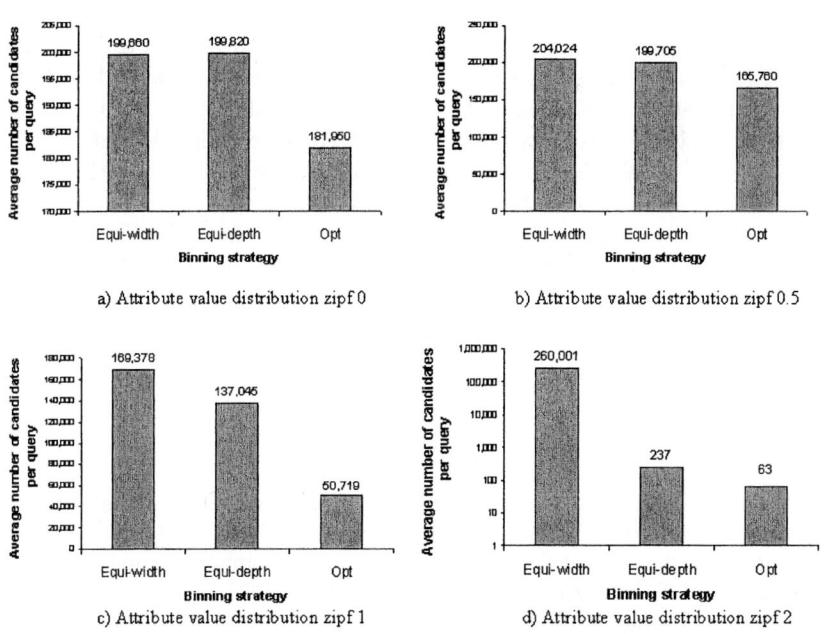

Fig. 4. I/O costs of candidate check per attribute

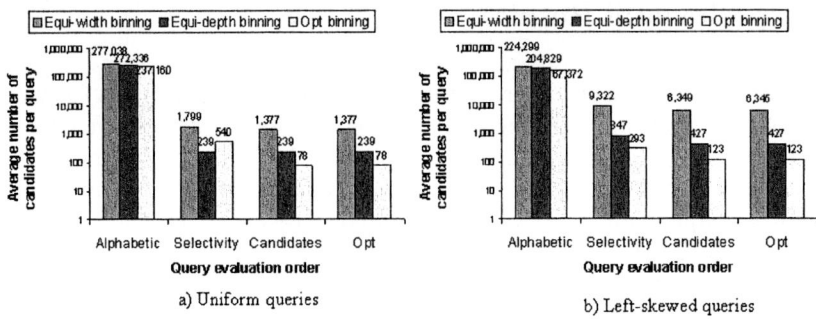

Fig. 5. Combined I/O costs of 4-dimensional queries with different distributions

strategies by a factor of 3 for uniform queries. For left-skewed queries the I/O costs are improved by nearly a factor of 4.

7 Conclusions and Future Work

For high-cardinality attributes bitmap indices with binning have a lower storage and computational complexity than simple bitmap indices. However, this advantage comes with an additional cost, the so-called *candidate check* costs for verifying parts of the data against the query constraints. In this paper we studied issues related to optimizing multi-dimensional queries on bitmap indices with bins. We introduced an optimization strategy based on attribute value distribution, query distribution as well as query selectivity with respect to each dimension. Our experimental results on data with various attribute value distributions and query distributions demonstrated that our new algorithm significantly improves the candidate check costs when compared to traditional strategies by at least a factor of 3. We also showed that the efficiency of our algorithm is more significant for highly-skewed data and queries.

In the future we plan to analyze several heuristics that efficiently determine the optimal number of bins for multiple attribute datasets. This problem is very important for multi-attribute queries where each attribute has different characteristics in terms of data distribution, selectivity and probability of occurring in a query expression.

References

1. C. Y. Chan and Y. E. Ioannidis. An Efficient Bitmap Encoding Scheme for Selection Queries. In *SIGMOD*, Philadelphia, Pennsylvania, USA, June 1999. ACM Press.
2. S. Chaudhuri and U. Dayal. An Overview of Data wharehousing and OLAP Technology. *ACM SIGMOD Record*, 26(1):65–74, March 1997.
3. S. Guha, N. Koudas, and D. Srivastava. Fast Algorithms For Hierarchical Range Histogram Construction. In *PODS 2002*, Madison, Wisconsin, USA, June 2002. ACM Press.

4. T. Johnson. Performance Measurements of Compressed Bitmap Indices. In *International Conference on Very Large Data Bases*, Edinburgh, Scotland, September 1999. Morgan Kaufmann.
5. N. Koudas. Space Efficient Bitmap Indexing. In *International Conference on Information and Knowledge Management*, McLean, Virginia, USA, November 2000. ACM Press.
6. N. Koudas, S. Muthukrishnan, and D. Srivastava. Optimal Histograms for Hierarchical Range Queries. In *PODS*, Dallas, Texas, USA, 2000. ACM Press.
7. A. E. Mohr. Bit Allocation in Sub-linear Time and the Multiple-Choice Knapsack Problem. In *Data Compression Conference*, Snao Bird, Utah, USA, March 2002. IEEE Computer Society Press.
8. P. O'Neil. Model 204 Architecture and Performance. In *2nd International Workshop in High Performance Transaction Systems*, Asilomar, California, USA, 1987. Springer-Verlag.
9. P. O'Neil and D. Quass. Improved Query Performance with Variant Indexes. In *Proceedings ACM SIGMOD International Conference on Management of Data*, Tucson, Arizona, USA, May 1997. ACM Press.
10. D. Rotem, K. Stockinger, and K. Wu. Efficient Binning for Bitmap Indices on High-Cardinality Attributes. Technical report, Berkeley Lab, November 2004.
11. K. Stockinger, K. Wu, and A. Shoshani. Evaluation Strategies for Bitmap Indices with Binning. In *International Conference on Database and Expert Systems Applications (DEXA)*, Zaragoza, Spain, September 2004. Springer-Verlag.
12. K. Wu, E. J. Otoo, and A. Shoshani. On the Performance of Bitmap Indices for High Cardinality Attributes. In *International Conference on Very Large Data Bases*, Toronto, Canada, September 2004. Morgan Kaufmann.
13. K.-L. Wu and P.S. Yu. Range-Based Bitmap Indexing for High-Cardinality Attributes with Skew. Technical report, IBM Watson Research Center, May 1996.
14. M.-C. Wu and A. P. Buchmann. Encoded Bitmap Indexing for Data Warehouses. In *International Conference on Data Engineering*, Orlando, Florida, USA, February 1998. IEEE Computer Society Press.

Environmental Noise Classification for Multimedia Libraries

Stéphane Bressan and Boon Tiang Tan

Department of Computer Science,
School of Computing,
National University of Singapore,
3 Science Drive 2, Singapore 117543
{steph, isc10161}@nus.edu.sg

Abstract. In the modern information society, multimedia libraries are increasingly essential core components of the information systems managing our digital assets. The effective and efficient management of large amounts of multimedia information involves the extraction of relevant features from unstructured multimedia documents, images, videos, and sound recordings, as well as the organization, classification, and retrieval of these multimedia documents. A particularly important aspect is the opportunity to combine a variety of diverse features. In this paper we are interested in a feature rarely considered in such systems: the environmental noise. We design, implement, present, and evaluate an experimental multimedia library system for video clips and sound recordings in which scenes are indexed, classified and retrieved according to their environmental noise. Namely, after adequate training, the system is able distinguish between such scenes as traffic scenes, canteen scenes, and gunfight scenes, for instance. We show how we improved existing techniques for the classification of sound to reach an accuracy of up to 90% in the recognition of environmental noise.

1 Introduction

For the past few years, there has been an increasing demand for multimedia libraries, especially with the explosion of the Internet and the increasing amount of bandwidth available to the end user. From online teaching courses to movie stores, we are entering a new age where multimedia data has become a part of our daily lives. With large amounts of data in the multimedia libraries, the effective and efficient management of this multimedia data will naturally become an issue. Inserting a piece of multimedia data into a correct collection in the library is easy if much information is known about it. The problem arises when an unknown piece of multimedia data is to be entered into the library. Of course, manual labeling of such data can be done but this solution becomes impractical if there are thousands of these unknown multimedia data. The situation is also true for the converse: given an unknown multimedia data, it is not easy to retrieve all the data in the library that is similar to it.

Environmental noise can be utilized to provide discriminatory information of an unknown piece of multimedia data and help in its classification. For example, given a movie clip, if gunfight noises occur in more than 20% of the clip, this clip can be classified as an action movie and inserted into its corresponding collection. In a wider context, the labels of the segments can also be used to write a descriptive summary of the movie or enable the user to fast forward to a desired scene. If one were to use images to classify the movie clip, he may end up with thousands of frames to consider – a problem neatly eliminated by using real-time sound from the multimedia data instead.

The objective of this paper is to propose an approach for the automated insertion and retrieval of data from multimedia libraries by extracting features from these data that identify environmental noise and to utilize known techniques for classification based on these features. Data selected for study in this paper include scenes taken from typical environments of our daily life, such as restaurants, traffic etc in addition to some recordings taken from multimedia data (video). This paper is organized as follows: In the next section, we shall review systems that allow classification and retrieval based on information content and related work done in the area of pattern classification. Section 3 describes feature extraction and classification techniques used. In Section 4, we present and also provide an analysis of the experimental results obtained on a set of test data. Design of a proposed multimedia video classifier and retrieval system is presented in Section 5. Conclusions and perspectives for future work are discussed in Section 6.

2 Related Work

The QBIC [2] (Query By Image Content) System is probably the best known image database system that is developed for the cataloguing of online image collections. Queries are done based on visual image content – properties such as color percentages, color layout, and textures occurring in the images. Such queries use the visual properties of images, so one can match colors, textures and their positions without describing them in words.

Most existing speech and noise recognizer applications uses the HMM (Hidden Markov Model) based approach. Ma et al. [3] implemented a hidden markov model based classifier using the HTK [6] toolkit to recognize several noise scenes for context aware applications and observed that the best results were obtained using a 15 state HMM model with 3 second duration segments. An overall recognition accuracy of 92.27% was obtained for 11 different scenes.

On the other hand, SVMs (Support Vector Machines) are the current state of the art in pattern classification, especially in the area of text classification. Thorsten [7] showed that SVMs consistently achieve good performance on text categorization tasks and outperforms existing methods substantially and significantly. This can be due to SVM's ability to generalize well in high dimensional feature spaces and this is especially important in text classification, where the number of features may exceed 10000. SVMs are also applicable in the field of image classification. Wu et al. [8] empirically compared the performance of the BPM and the SVM on an image dataset and concluded that the SVM is more attractive for the image classification task because it requires a much shorter training time for similar accuracy. Our paper is motivated by the work done by Ma et al. [3] and the emergence of SVMs as the new generation learning system based on the recent advances in statistical learning theory.

3 Feature Extraction and Classification Techniques

Time-signal information obtained from the initial recording of noise segments is not particularly useful since they are weakly discriminant. Moreover, it is inefficient to classify noise segments using all the samples in the recordings, e.g. a noise segment recorded at 22050Hz will have 22050 samples per second. Therefore, the extraction of useful information from the waveform and the representation in a compact format is required.

MFCC, also known as Mel Frequency Cepstral Coefficients, is the dominant format that is used to represent features extracted from speech and is widely used in speech recognition softwares. Empirical evidence also suggests that using MFCC vectors to represent noise segments improves recognition performance. Peltonen [4] had implemented a system for recognizing 17 sound events using 11 features individually and obtained the best results with MFCC vectors.

MFCC feature extraction begins by first obtaining the magnitude spectrum of the noise segment that is typically done using the Fast Fourier Transform. The magnitude spectrum is then non-linearly quantized using a mel-scale filterbank which models the psychoacoustic properties of the human ear. The MFCC vectors are then calculated from the log filterbank amplitudes using the Discrete Cosine Transform (DCT),

$$c_i = \sqrt{\frac{2}{N}} \sum_{j=1}^{N} m_j \cos\left(\frac{\pi i}{N}(j-0.5)\right)$$

where c_i is the ith MFCC, N is the number of filterbank channels and m_j is the output of the jth mel scale filterbank channel. This results in the MFCC feature vector.

3.1 Hidden Markov Models (HMM)

A HMM consist of an underlying Markov chain as shown in Fig 1. Each of the six circles represent a state of the model and at a discrete time t, corresponding to the frame time, the model is in one of the states and outputs a feature o_t, which is one part of the feature vector O.

$$O = o_1 + o_2 + \ldots + o_t + \ldots + o_T$$

At time $t+1$, the model moves to a new state, or stays in the same state and emits another feature O_{t+1}. This process is repeated until time T where the complete vector of features O is produced. Whether it stays in the same state or moves to another state is determined by the transition probability a_{ij}, where

a_{ij} = probability of moving from state i at time t to state j at time $t + 1$.

In any state, the production of a feature o_t is also governed by a set of output probabilities $b_j(o_t)$, where

$b_j(o_t)$ = probability of state j producing o_t

Finally, to find the probability that a HMM generates O, we need to define another variable $\alpha_j(t)$, where

$$\alpha_j(t) = P(o_1, \ldots o_t, x(t)=j | HMM)$$

$x(t)$ is the state of the HMM at time t. Therefore $\alpha_j(t)$ is defined as the joint probability of observing the first t features and being in state j at time t. So the probability that the HMM produces O is given by $\sum_{j=1}^{N} \alpha_j(T)$.

For classification of unknown feature vector O, we find the HMM model from a set of HMMs (one for each classification label) that generates O and gives the highest probability at the same time.

$$C_o = \arg\max_{M \in HMMs}(P(O|M))$$

where C_o is the determined class for vector O and $P(O|M)$ is the probability of HMM model M generating vector O. Training a HMM model for classification would require the parameters a_{ij} and $b_j(o_t)$ be found from a set of training feature vectors. This can be done using a maximum likelihood HMM estimation model which consist of using both the Viterbi and Baum-Welch algorithm, see [6] (although an initial estimate of these two parameters must be provided).

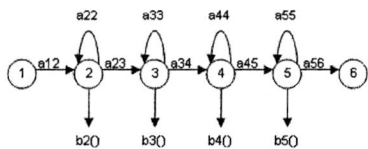

Fig. 1. A six state markov chain

3.2 Nearest Neighbor (NN)

Given a list of training feature vectors for a particular class, we could take the average of these vectors to give an approximate value for the centroid of these vectors in a feature space. Unknown test vectors are then classified based on some form of distance measure with the collection of centroids obtained, usually with the class of the centroid closest to it, hence Nearest-Neighbor. The determined class C_o of unknown vector O is thus given by

$$C_o = \arg\min_{cent \in centroids}(dist(cent, O))$$

where *dist(cent, O)* refers to distance between centroid *cent* and vector O. There are various forms of distance measures that can be used, such as the Euclidean distance, Cosine Similarity, Minkowski distance, etc.

3.3 Support Vector Machines (SVM)

For the purpose of visualization, consider the problem of binary classification in a two dimensional model space where feature vectors are classified into one of the two classes. Training vectors *x* and their labels *y* are given as

$$(x_1, y_1), (x_2, y_2), \ldots, (x_n, y_n) \quad\quad x \in \Re^2, y \in \{+1, -1\}$$

Fig 2 shows two possible separating lines for the same set of feature vectors that are linearly separable. How do we find the 'optimum' line that will separate these vectors? Furthermore, feature vectors often consist of large number of features and therefore would be projected into a higher dimensional space where the boundary separating the vectors would be hyperplanes instead. For the linearly separable case, the support vector algorithm simply looks for the separating hyperplane with the largest margin, where margin = 2d and d is the distance from the hyperplane to the nearest positive or negative example. It turns out that the margin is inversely proportional to the absolute value of hyperplane's normal |w|. This reduces the original problem to the following optimization problem

minimize |w|, subject to $y_i(w.x_i+b)-1 \geq 0$ for $\forall i = 1..n$

where (x_i, y_i) are the training examples and b is the bias term. In Fig 2, the dashed-line is the solution hyperplane, the margin is the distance between the two parallel solid lines and the vectors that fall on the two solid lines are called support vectors. Notice that the number of the support vectors is usually small compared to the size of the training set. It should be also obvious that the solution hyperplane is defined only by the support vectors.

The linearly non-separable case is handled via introduction of slack variables ξ_i to penalize training errors. The problem is rewritten as

$$\text{minimize } \frac{1}{2}|w|^2 + C\left(\sum_{i=1}^{n}\xi_i\right) \quad \text{for } \forall i = 1..n$$

subject to

$$w.x_i + b \geq 1 - \xi_i \quad \text{for } y_i = +1$$
$$w.x_i + b \leq -1 + \xi_i \quad \text{for } y_i = -1$$

where C is the value of the trade-off between training error and margin chosen by the user. Increasing the penalty on training errors will possibly cause the system to reject a hyperplane with a larger margin and choose one that minimizes the training errors instead.

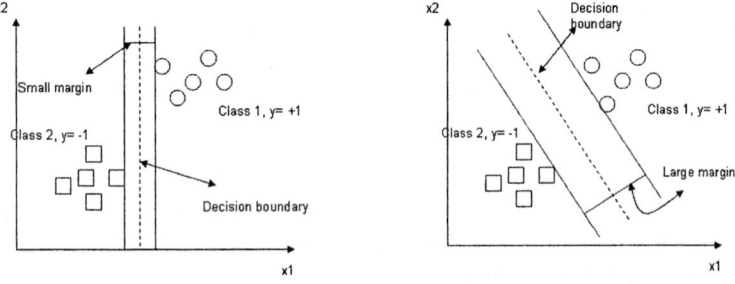

Fig. 2. Two possible separating lines for the hyperplane of the resulting SVM: left, a less acceptable one with a small margin, and right, a good one with a large margin

4 Performance Evaluation and Analysis

4.1 Data Collection and Feature Extraction

We used a unidirectional microphone, a laptop and Wavesurfer to record the auditory contexts from the various scenes. Table 1 shows the list of different scenes and their descriptions. For each scene, 4 different situations of the scene are obtained – 3 situations for each scene is used for training and the remaining situation is used for testing. Each situation would represent noise recordings taken from different locations but similar scenes. Digitization was achieved by sampling the analogue data at 22.050 kHz using 16bit quantization. For feature extraction of each noise segment, a 23-

channel mel-scale filterbank was applied to the magnitude spectrum and after the DCT, truncation resulted in a 12-feature MFCC vector. This was then augmented with the log energy term to give a 13-feature MFCC vector. Both the velocity and acceleration were computed and added to improve the performance. This results in a 39-feature MFCC vector for each noise segment which was used for the experiments.

Table 1. Description of the scenes

Scene	Description
Tennis Match	Noise recorded from video of different tennis matches
Canteen	Noise from different canteens in NUS
Laboratory	Noise from different PC laboratories in School of Computing, NUS
Traffic	Noise taken from various bus-stops in NUS
Gunfight	Noise from various movies depicting gunshots and explosions scenes
Disco	Noise from various movies depicting disco scenes
Silence	Makeshift soundproof room
Restaurant	Noise taken from various dinning restaurants in Orchard Road
Soccer Match	Noise recorded from video of different soccer matches
Lecture Theater	Noise taken from LT 33, 34, 27 and 25 in NUS, Science Faculty

4.2 Experimental Results

We implemented the HMM classifier for our experiments using the HTK [6] toolkit developed at the Speech, Vision and Robotics Group of the Cambridge University Engineering Department. The Nearest Neighbor classifier was implemented by us using cosine similarity as the distance metric. For the SVM classifier, we utilize the LIBSVM [1] integrated software developed by Chih-Chung Chang and Chih-Jen Lin. Linear SVMs with one-versus-all multiclassification strategy is used, with the trade-off value, C, between training error and margin equal to 1.

Table 2, 3 and 4 shows the classification results using 8 second duration segments for the HMM, SVM and NN classifier respectively. Each row sum adds up to 30 as we have 30 test segments for each scene. The reader can also visualize the table as a confusion matrix where each ij (row-column) entry represents the number of test segments from scene i that have been recognized as scene j.

From the confusion matrix of the HMM classifier, we can see that a few segments from the Laboratory scene were confused for the Lecture Theater scene. Similarly, we have some segments from the Tennis Match and Soccer Match scene confused with each other. This can be attributed to the fact that these scenarios contain scenes that have some similarities – periods of inactivity in Laboratory versus Lecture Theater and crowds cheering in Tennis versus Soccer Match. The results from the Disco scene are the worst among all the scenes, with only about 33% of the test segments being correctly classified. This may be acceptable since this scene is the most dynamic type, with fast interchanging periods of heavy noise and conversation. All other scenes have very good results. Looking at the confusion matrix for the NN classifier, we have the Disco and Lecture Theater scenes obtaining very poor results compared to other scenes. The NN classifier is unable to classify segments from the disco scene at all. This can again be due to the fast and dynamic changing nature of the disco scene. It is interesting to note that the NN classifier is also unable to classify segments from the Lecture Theater scenes, confusing it with the Traffic scene even though these two scenes do not seem to have any similar environmental noise events at all. Results from the SVM classifier are promising, as besides the Laboratory and Disco scenes, all other scenes have accuracy greater than 83%.

Table 2. Confusion matrix for the HMM classifier using 8 second time duration segments

Accuracy	Tennis	Canteen	Laboratory	Traffic	Gunfight	Disco	Silence	Restaurant	Soccer	Lecture
Tennis	11	0	0	0	0	0	0	0	19	0
Canteen	0	30	0	0	0	0	0	0	0	0
Laboratory	0	0	18	0	0	0	0	0	0	12
Traffic	0	6	0	22	0	0	0	2	0	0
Gunfight	0	0	0	0	30	0	0	0	0	0
Disco	0	0	0	0	7	10	0	13	0	0
Silence	0	0	0	0	0	0	30	0	0	0
Restaurant	0	0	0	0	1	0	0	29	0	0
Soccer	2	0	0	0	0	0	0	0	28	0
Lecture	0	0	0	0	0	0	0	0	0	30

Table 3. Confusion matrix for the NN classifier using 8 second time duration segments

Accuracy	Tennis	Canteen	Laboratory	Traffic	Gunfight	Disco	Silence	Restaurant	Soccer	Lecture
Tennis	25	0	0	0	0	0	0	0	5	0
Canteen	0	28	0	1	0	1	0	0	0	0
Laboratory	0	0	28	2	0	0	0	0	0	0
Traffic	0	0	0	30	0	0	0	0	0	0
Gunfight	0	0	0	3	22	3	0	2	0	0
Disco	0	0	2	5	2	0	0	20	0	1
Silence	0	0	0	0	0	0	30	0	0	0
Restaurant	0	0	0	0	2	0	0	28	0	0
Soccer	0	0	0	0	0	0	0	0	30	0
Lecture	0	3	0	20	0	0	0	0	0	7

Table 4. Confusion matrix for the SVM classifier using 8 second time duration segments

Accuracy	Tennis	Canteen	Laboratory	Traffic	Gunfight	Disco	Silence	Restaurant	Soccer	Lecture
Tennis	25	0	0	0	0	0	0	0	5	0
Canteen	0	28	0	0	0	2	0	0	0	0
Laboratory	0	0	6	24	0	0	0	0	0	0
Traffic	0	1	0	29	0	0	0	0	0	0
Gunfight	0	0	0	0	27	3	0	0	0	0
Disco	0	4	1	2	20	2	0	1	0	0
Silence	0	0	0	0	0	0	30	0	0	0
Restaurant	0	0	0	0	0	0	0	30	0	0
Soccer	0	0	0	0	0	0	0	0	30	0
Lecture	0	0	0	0	0	0	0	0	0	30

4.3 Analysis of the Experimental Results

From the experimental results obtained for the 8 second duration segments, we can see that there is no single classifier that works well for all scenes, although all three classifiers have difficulties recognizing segments from the Disco scene. The confusion matrix obtained for the HMM classifier is most logical as it has confused some test segments from the Tennis Match scene with the Soccer Match and some segments from the Laboratory scene with Lecture Theater. The NN classifier has confused the Lecture Theater scene with the Traffic scene even though these 2 scenes have hardly any environmental noise events in common. Furthermore, it is unable to classify any segments from the Disco scene. The SVM classifier is able to perform slightly better than the NN classifier in this aspect, classifying some Disco segments correctly and confusing the rest with the Gunfight scene.

Fig 3 shows the accuracy of the HMM, NN, SVM classifier with time durations of 1 to 30 seconds. These classifiers are trained with the following parameters – HMM with a 15 state model, NN using cosine similarity, SVM using linear classifier and one-versus-all multiclassification with penalty value $C = 1$. Maximum accuracy for the HMM classifier occurs when time duration equals to 2 seconds and decreases with increasing time duration of the segments. This contrasts with the results obtained for the NN and SVM, where we can see that classification accuracy generally increases as one increases the time duration of the segments. We obtained the best results from the SVM classifier, where it consistently outperforms the other 2 techniques after 8 second and obtaining the highest accuracy, 90% at 15 second.

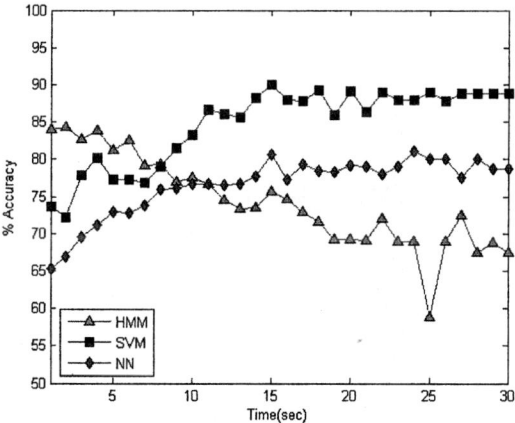

Fig. 3. Accuracy in percentage of the classification methods with 1-30 seconds segments

5 System Design for a Multimedia Video Classifier and Retrieval System

The proposed system design for a multimedia video classifier and retrieval system is shown in Figure 4. The system has 4 major components, namely the classification engine, the library, the query analyzer and the retrieval engine. The user is able to insert a new movie clip for classification or enter queries (retrieval) regarding movies or movie segments that have been previously classified and inserted into the library.

Classification of new movies are done in the classification engine, where it accepts segments of audio from the movie and classifies them based on a pre-trained model file. The obtained information and the movie are then inserted into the library. Depending on the classification results, the user may wish to correct some misclassification errors and use the altered results to optimize the model file.

The query analyzer parses the input query from the user into 3 categories, simple, complex and retrieval-by-example queries. Simple queries are defined as queries where information can be directly retrieved from the library and presented to the user, e.g. 'give me all segments of movie A that has gunfight noise' etc. Queries such as 'find me the segment in movie A where Arnold Schwarzenegger is involved in a gunfight and says I'LL BE BACK' is considered to be a complex query as other recognition systems is involved in the retrieval process. If the user presents an audio file as the input for a query, we define it as a retrieval-by-example query where we retrieve the top n matching video segments from the library and present it to the user.

We propose an incremental filtering of results to solve complex queries. For example, considering the complex query mentioned earlier, segments without gunfight labels will first be filtered out. A facial recognition system will then select segments where there are frames containing Arnold Schwarzenegger. The final results are then obtained using a speech recognition system where segments with 'I'LL BE BACK' are extracted from the previous results. Of course, other recognition systems could be also used but the general structure of the multimedia video classification and retrieval system is an incremental design where enhancement of the system can be done easily.

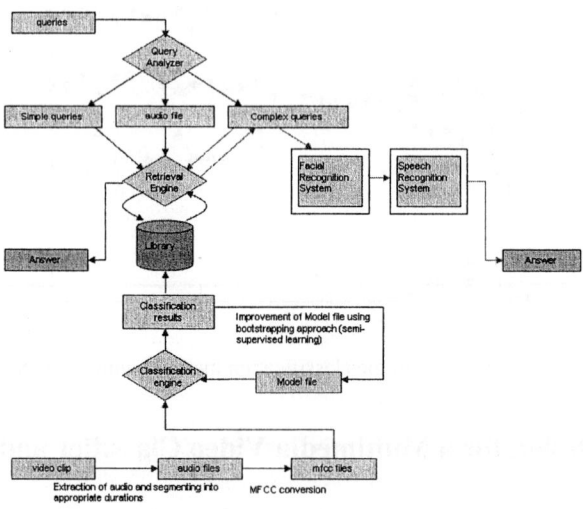

Fig. 4. System Design for proposed multimedia video classifier and retrieval system

6 Conclusions and Future Work

We have shown that environmental noise from multimedia data can be used for its classification as the experimental results obtained are very encouraging, especially the HMM and SVM classifier. With increasing time duration of segments, we find that the accuracy of the HMM classifier decreases in contrast with the NN and SVM classifier, where better results are generally obtained. However, the NN classifier is unable to classify certain types of scenes e.g. disco in our experiments regardless of the time duration. Although we did not show the total training time required for the different classifiers, we obtained the lowest training time for the SVM classifier (much lower than the HMM classifier). Therefore, we conclude that the SVM classifier is the best choice for classifying environmental noise for our data as it obtained the highest accuracy, 90% for our experiments, has a lower training time and consistently outperforms the HMM classifier in longer time duration segments.

In this paper, we have utilized the HMM, NN and SVM classification techniques for our experiments. Other techniques such as Bayesian networks etc can also be studied. Different feature extraction methods such as LPC can also be used to obtain the feature vectors for computation. Currently, we are developing the environmental noise classification part of the proposed system using SVMs and we have obtained encouraging results for entire movie clips – about 50-60% accuracy. Complex queries will require integration of other classification/recognition systems and challenges such as adapting the various systems for our specific needs will inevitably arise from the integration of such systems. We intend to integrate other systems into ours gradually and undertake further experiments using different features and classification techniques to improve on the classification accuracy of our system.

References

1. Chang C. C., Lin C. J., *LIBSVM – A Library for Support Vector Machines,* http://www.csie.ntu.edu.tw/cjlin/libsvm
2. Flickner M., Sawhney H., Niblack W., Ashley J., Huang Q., Dom B., Gorkani M., Hafner J., Lee D., Petkovic D.,Steele D., Yanker P., *Query by image content: The QBIC system.* IEEE Computer Magazine 28, pp.23-32, 1995.
3. Ma L., Smith D., Milner B., *Environmental Noise Classification for Context-Aware Application,* In Proc. Database and Expert Systems Applications, Prague, Czech Republic, 2003.
4. Peltonen V., Tuomi J., Klapuri A., Huopaniemi J. and Sorsa T., *Computational Auditory Scene Recognition,* In Proc. International Conference on Acoustic, Speech and Signal Processing, Orlando, Florida, 2002.
5. Rabiner L., R., *A Tutorial on Hidden Markov Models and Selected Applications in Speech Recognition,* In Proc. IEEE, Vol.77, No.2, pp.257–286, 1989.
6. Speech Vision and Robotics Group of the Cambridge University Engineering Department (CUED), *HTK ToolKit and Book,* http://htk.eng.cam.ac.uk/
7. Thorsten J., *Text Categorization with Support Vector Machines: Learning with Many Relevant Features,* In Proc. ECML-98, 10th European Conference on Machine Learning, 1997.
8. Wu G., Chang E., Li C., *BPMs versus SVMs for image classification,* In Proc. IEEE Intl. Conf. on Multimedia, pp. 505-508, 2002.

Quality-Aware Replication of Multimedia Data

Yi-Cheng Tu, Jingfeng Yan, and Sunil Prabhakar

Purdue University, West Lafayette, IN 47906, U.S.A.

Abstract. In contrast to alpha-numerical data, multimedia data can have a wide range of quality parameters such as spatial and temporal resolution, and compression format. Users can request data with a specific quality requirement due to the needs of their applications, or the limitations of their resources. On-the-fly conversion of multimedia data (such as video transcoding) is very CPU intensive and can limit the level of concurrent access supported by the database. Storing all possible replicas, on the other hand, requires unacceptable increases in storage requirements. Although replication has been well studied, to the best of our knowledge, the problem of multiple-quality replication has not been addressed. In this paper we address the problem of multiple-quality replica selection subject to an overall storage constraint.

We establish that the problem is NP-hard and provide heuristic solutions under a soft quality system model where users are willing to negotiate their quality needs. An important optimization goal under such a model is to minimize utility loss. We propose a powerful greedy algorithm to solve this optimization problem. Extensive simulations show that our algorithm finds near-optimal solutions. The algorithm is flexible in that it can be extended to deal with replica selection for multiple media objects and changes of query pattern. We also discuss an extended version of the algorithm with potentially better performance.

1 Introduction

Quality is an essential property for multimedia databases. In contrast to other database applications, multimedia data can have a wide range of quality parameters. Users can request data with specific quality requirements due to the needs of their applications, or the limitations of their resources. Quality-aware multimedia systems [1,2,3] allow users to specify the *quality* of the media to be delivered. The quality parameters of interest also differ by the type of media that we deal with. For digital videos, which we use as example throughout this paper, the quality parameters include resolution, frame rate, color depth, audio quality, compression format, security level, and so on [4]. For example, a video editor may request a video at very high resolution when editing it on a high-powered workstation, but request the video at low resolution and frame rate when viewing it using a PDA.

Generally, there are two approaches to satisfy user quality specifications: (i) *dynamic adaptation*: store only the highest resolution copy, and convert it to the quality format requested by the user as needed at run-time; or (ii) *static adaptation*: pre-compute each different quality that can be requested and store them on disk. When a user query is received, the appropriate copy is retrieved from disk and sent to the user. Dynamic adaptation suffers from a very high CPU overhead for transcoding from one quality to another [5,6]. Therefore, real-time adaptation is difficult in a multi-user environment. *Static adaptation* attempts to solve the problem of high CPU cost by storing precoded multiple quality copies of the original media on disk. By this, the heavy demand on CPU power at runtime is alleviated. We trade disk space for runtime CPU cycles, which is a cost-effective trade-off since disks are relatively cheap.

However, storage costs for static adaptation could be extremely high. This is because users vary widely in their quality needs and resource availability [5]. This leads to a large number of quality-specific copies of the same media content that need to be stored on disk. From a service provider's point of view, the storage requirements for static adaptation should not grow unboundedly as storage, although cheap, is not free. This is especially true for commercial media databases that must provide high reliability of disk resources. Our analysis [7] shows that the extra disk space needed to accommodate all possible qualities is $O(n^d)$ times of the original copy where n is the number of quality levels in one quality dimension and d is the number of quality dimensions. Therefore, it is infeasible to store all possible quality copies. On the other hand, the strategy of selecting few copies based on the bandwidth of user devices (T1, DSL, dial-up ...), as many media services do nowadays, ignores the diversity of user's quality needs. In this paper, we study the problem of quality selection under storage constraints for the purpose of satisfying user quality requirements.

We view the selection of media copies for storage as a data replication problem. Traditional data replication focuses on placement of copies of data in various nodes in a distributed environment [8]. Quality-aware replication deals with data placement in a metric space of quality values (termed as *quality space*). In the traditional replication scheme, data are replicated as exact or segmental copies of the original while the replicas in our problem are multiple quality copies generated via offline transcoding. In this paper, we assume user behavior can be described by a *soft quality* model where users are willing to negotiate when the original quality required is not available. Under this situation, users may accept a different quality with a decrease of satisfaction with the service. Our data replication algorithms are designed to achieve the highest user satisfaction under fixed resource (storage) capacities. Quality selection under a *hard quality* model where users have rigid quality requirements is discussed in our technical report [7]. There are two major contributions of this paper:

1. We formulate the replica selection problem as an optimization with the goal of maximizing user satisfaction. We propose a fast greedy algorithm with comparable performance to commercial optimizers. An improvement to the greedy algorithm is also discussed.
2. We extend the above algorithm to handle the situation of *dynamic replication* where changes of query pattern are expected. Our solution is fast and achieves the same level of optimality as the original algorithm.

2 Related Work

Quality adaptation in media delivery in response to heterogeneous client requests has attracted a lot of attention [2,6]. However, quality selection in static adaptation is not well addressed. A closely related work is [5] where quality selection (under storage constraint) is performed to achieve the smallest transcoding costs. In [9], the problem of optimal materialized view selection is studied. Both [5] and [9] address different data selection problems from ours. Furthermore, neither considers quality selection in response to dynamic changes of query pattern.

Efforts to build quality-aware media systems include [2,6,3,1]. In our previous work [1], we extend the query generation/optimization module of a multimedia DBMS to handle quality of queries as a core DBMS functionality. In [4], specification of quality parameters in multimedia databases is discussed. The traditional data replication problem has been studied extensively in the context of web [10,11], distributed databases [8], and multimedia systems [12,13]. The web caching and replication problem aims at higher availability of data and load balancing at the web servers. Similar goals are set for data replication in multimedia systems. What differs from web caching is that disk space and I/O bandwidth are the major concerns in multimedia systems. A number of algorithms are proposed to achieve high acceptance rate and resource utilization by balancing the use of different resources [13,14]. Unlike web and multimedia data, database contents are accessed by both read and write operations. This leads to high requirements for data consistency, which often conflict with data availability. Another important issue is dynamic data replication. As access rates to individual data items are likely to change, we need to make our replication strategy adapt to changes quickly and accurately to achieve optimal long-term performance. Wolfson et al. [15] introduced an algorithm that changes the location of replicas in response to changes of read-write patterns of data items.

3 System Model and Problem Statement

We assume that the database consists of a collection of servers that host the media content and service user queries. Servers have limited storage space S. For now, we consider only one media object and in Section 4 we extend our discussions to a system with V media objects. User requests identify (via a query) an object to be retrieved as well as the desired quality requirements on d quality dimensions. Each quality can thus be modeled as a point in a d-dimensional quality space. The domain of a quality parameter consists of finite number of values and we denote the total number of quality points as m. Each possible quality k is modeled by f_k and s_k where f_k represents the query rate for this version of the media and s_k is the byte size of this replica.

Utility is frequently used to quantify user satisfaction on a service [16] and is thus the primary optimization goal in quality-critical applications [17]. *Utility functions* serve the purpose of mapping quality to utility. For a request to a quality A, if A is replicated, the server retrieve that replica to serve the request and no utility is lost. Otherwise, the request is served by the closest replica B to A, and utility loss increases with the distance between A and B. Note that providing a higher quality than needed does cause utility loss because the client device may not have enough resources to handle it [7]. Techniques for generating utility functions can be found in [16].

Our problem is to pick a set L of replicas from the quality space that gives the largest total *utility* over time, which can be expressed as $U = \sum_{j \in J} f_j u(j, L)$ where J is the set of all quality points and $u(j, L)$ is the utility with which quality j is served by the closest replica in L. We set $u(j, L)$ to be an decreasing function (within the range of $[0, 1]$) of the distance between j and its nearest neighbor in L (see [7] for more details) and we have $u(j, L) = 1.0$ if $j \in L$. We weight the utility by the request rate f_j and the weighted utility is termed as *utility rate*. We name our problem the *fixed-storage replica selection* (FSRS) problem and it can be formulated as the following integer program:

$$\text{maximize} \quad \sum_{j \in J} \sum_{k \in J} f_j u(j,k) Y_{jk}, \quad (1)$$
$$\text{subject to} \quad \sum_{k \in J} X_k s_k \leq S, \quad (2)$$
$$\sum_{k \in J} Y_{jk} = 1, \quad (3)$$
$$Y_{jk} \leq X_k, \quad (4)$$
$$Y_{jk} \in \{0, 1\}, \quad (5)$$
$$X_k \in \{0, 1\}. \quad (6)$$

where $u(j, k)$ is the utility value when a request to point k is served by a replica in j, X_k is a binary variable representing whether k is replicated, Y_{jk} tells if j should be served by k. Equation (2) shows the storage constraint while Equations (3) and (4) mean that all requests from k should be served by one and only one replica. Here f_j, s_k, and S are inputs and X_k for all $k \in J$ is the solution.

A close match to FSRS is the so-called p-median problem with the same problem statements except Equation (2) becomes $\sum X_k = p$, meaning only p ($p < |J|$) points are to be selected. As the p-median problem is NP-hard [18], it is easy to see that FSRS is also NP-hard [7].

4 Replica Selection Algorithms

In dealing with the FSRS problem, we can use a benefit/cost model to analyze the value of a replica k: the cost is obviously the storage s_k, the benefit is the gain of utility rate by selecting k. A good heuristic would select the set of replicas with the highest benefit/cost ratios [7]. However, the benefit of one replica depends on the selection of other replicas. We propose an algorithm (Fig 1) that takes greedy guesses on such benefits. The main idea is to aggressively select replicas one by one. The first replica is assigned to a point k that yields the largest $\Delta U_k / s_k$ value as if only one replica is to be placed. We use $\Delta U_k / s_k$ to denote the *utility density* of replica k where ΔU_k is the marginal utility rate gained by replicating k. The following replicas are determined in the same way, i.e. the n-th replica maximizes $\Delta U_n / s_n$ based on the $n - 1$ replicas that are already selected.

Algorithm GREEDY	ADDREPLICA (s, P')
Inputs: f_k, s_k, S	1 $i \leftarrow$ NULL, $V_{max} \leftarrow 0$
Output: a set of selected replicas, P	2 **for** each quality point k **do**
	3 **if** $k \notin P'$ and $s_k \leq s$
1 $s' \leftarrow S$, $P \leftarrow \emptyset$, $k \leftarrow 0$	4 $U \leftarrow 0$
2 **while** $k \neq$ NULL **do**	5 **for** each quality point j
3 $k \leftarrow$ ADDREPLICA(s', P)	6 $U \leftarrow U +$ MAXUTIL(j, k, P')
4 $s' \leftarrow s' - s_k$	7 **if** $U/s_k > V_{max}$
5 append k to P	8 $V_{max} \leftarrow U/s_k$
6 **return** P	9 $i \leftarrow k$
	10 **return** i

Fig. 1. The *Greedy* algorithm

Algorithm *Greedy* (Fig 1) terminates when no more replicas can be added due to storage constraints. New replicas are selected via subroutine ADDREPLICA by trying all m points in the quality space to look for the one that yields the largest utility density. Note subroutine MAXUTIL (line 6 of ADDREPLICA) gives the utility from j to its nearest replica in $P' + k$, which can be done in constant time. As ADDREPLICA runs for $O(m^2)$ time, the time complexity for *Greedy* is $O(Im^2)$ where I is the total number of replicas selected.

The Iterative Greedy Algorithm. This algorithm attempts to improve the performance of *Greedy*. We notice that at each step of *Greedy*, some local optimization is achieved: the $(n+1)$-th replica chosen *is* the best given the first n replicas. The problem is: we do not know if the first n replicas are good choices. However, we believe the $(n+1)$-th replica added is more 'reliable' than its predecessors because more global information (existence of other selected replicas) is leveraged in its selection. Based on this conjecture, we develop the *Iterative Greedy* algorithm that iteratively improves the 'correctness' of the replicas chosen. Specifically, we repeatedly get rid of the most 'unreliable' selected replica and choose a new one. The operations in *Iterative Greedy* are shown in Fig 2. All replicas selected by *Greedy* are stored in a FIFO queue P'. In each iteration, we dequeue P' and find one replica (again, by ADDREPLICA) based on the remaining replicas. The newly identified replica is then added to the tail of P'. We record the set of replicas with the largest utility rate as the final output (P). The only problem here is how to set the number of iterations I. Since the primary goal of *Iterative Greedy* is to reconsider the selection of the first few 'unreliable' replicas, we can set I to be the number of replicas selected by *Greedy*. The time complexity of *Iterative Greedy* is thus $O(Im^2)$, which is the same as that of *Greedy*.

Handling Multiple Media Objects. With very few modifications, both *Greedy* and *Iterative Greedy* algorithms can handle multiple media objects. The idea is to view the collection of V physical media as replicas of one virtual media. The different content in the physical media can be modeled as a new quality

```
Algorithm ITERATIVEGREEDY
1    U_max ← 0, P ← ∅
2    for i ← 0 to I
3        do k ← dequeue P'
4            s' ← s' + s_k
5            l ← ADDREPLICA(s', P')
6            append l to P' and update s'
7            U ← total utility rate of P'
8            if U_max < U then
9                do U_max ← U
10                    copy P' to P
```

Fig. 2. The *Iterative greedy* algorithm. **Output:** P. **Inputs:** P' - a set of replicas selected, s' - available storage after P' is replicated.

dimension called *content*. A special feature of *content* is its lack of adaptability. For example, any replica of the movie *Matrix* cannot be used to serve a request to the movie *Shrek*. Assume the quality spaces of all physical media have m points, the FSRS problem with V media can thus be solved by simply running the *Greedy* algorithm for the virtual media with Vm points. Knowing that there is no utility gain between two replicas with different *content*, we only need to run the second loop (line 5) in ADDREPLICA for those with the same content. Thus, the time complexity of GREEDY is $O(IVm^2)$ rather than $O(IV^2m^2)$.

5 Dynamic Data Replication

In previous sections we deal with the problem of *static* replication, in which access rates of all qualities do not change over time. In this section, we discuss quality-aware data replication in an environment where access patterns change. A good dynamic replication algorithm needs to meet two requirements: quick response to changes and optimality of results. Dynamic replication in soft quality systems is a very challenging task. The difficulty comes from the fact that the access rate change of a single point could have cascading effects on the choices of many (if not all) replicas. We may have to rerun the static algorithms (e.g. *Greedy*) in response to such changes but these algorithms are too slow to make online decisions. In this section, we assume that runtime changes of access pattern only exist at the media object level. In other words, the relative popularities of different quality points for the same media object do not change. This assumption is found to be reasonable in many systems [12,13]. We understand that a solution for more general situation is also meaningful and we leave it as future work.

Let us first investigate how algorithm GREEDY selects replicas. The history of total utility rate gained and storage spent on each selected replica can be represented as a series of points in a 2D graph. We call the lines that connect these points in the order of their being selected a *Replication Roadmap* (RR). Fig 3 shows two examples of RRs plotted with the same scale. We can see that all replication roadmaps are convex. This is because: the slope of the line connecting any two consecutive points (e.g. $r1$ and $r2$ in Fig 3A) represents the ratio of ΔU_{r2} to s_{r2}. As *Greedy* always chooses a replica with the largest $\Delta U/s$ value, the slopes of the line segments along the RR are thus non-increasing.

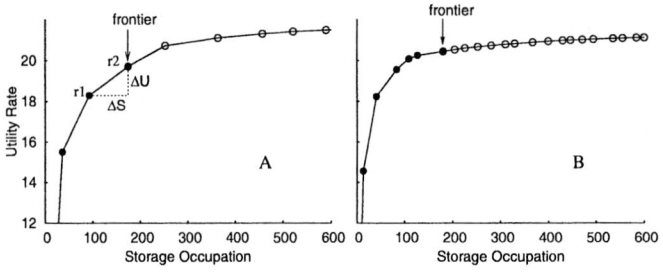

Fig. 3. Replication roadmaps

In dynamic replication, replicas need to be re-selected with respect to the new query rate of a media object. Suppose the query rate f_i of a media object i increases by a factor δ ($\delta > 0$). What happens now is that we may consider assigning extra storage to i as it reaches a position to use storage more profitably than before. As storage is limited, the extra chunk should come from another media object whose slope in the last piece of RR is small. Take Fig 3 as an example. Suppose we have fully extended RRs: all future replicas are precomputed (empty dots in Fig 3) and we call the last real replica the *frontier* of the RR. It buys us more utility to advance A's frontier (take storage) and move backwards on B's RR (give up storage). The beauty of this scheme is: we never need to pick up points far into or over the frontier to make storage exchanges. The convexity of RRs tells us that the frontier is always the most efficient point to acquire/release storage. Based on this idea, we design an online algorithm named SOFTDYNAREP for dynamic replication (see [7] for pseudocode).

The algorithm consists of two phases: the *Preprocess Phase* and *Online Phase*. In the first phase, we need to extend each RR formed by *Greedy* or *Iterative Greedy* by adding all m replicas. For all RRs, we put the immediate predecessor of the *frontier* in a list called *blist* and its immediate successor in a list called *flist*. Both lists are sorted by the slopes of the segments stored. The *Preprocess phase* runs at $O(Vm^3)$ time and it only needs to be executed once. The *Online Phase* is triggered once a change in query rate to an object i is detected. The idea is to iteratively take storage from the tail of *blist* and add that to the head of *flist* (we call this operation *storage exchange*) until a new equilibrium is reached. The running time of this phase is $O(I_e \log V)$ where I_e is the number of storage exchanges (obviously, $I_e = O(m)$). We claim that the online phase of SOFTDYNAREP achieves the same quality in the selected replicas as that by rerunning *Greedy*. A rigorous proof can be found in [7].

6 Experiments

We study the behavior of the proposed algorithms by extensive simulations. Due to space limitations, we only present the most important results. We use traces of 270 MPEG-1 videos extracted from a real video database[1] as experimental data. We simulate a 3D quality space with various number (100-500) of replicas. The s_k values for all replicas are generated from empirical equations [7]. As real-world

---

[1] http://www.cs.purdue.edu/vdbms

traffic traces for quality-aware systems are not available, we test various synthetic access patterns (i.e., f_k values) in our simulations. We run our experiments on a Sun Workstation with a UltraSparc 1.2GHz CPU.

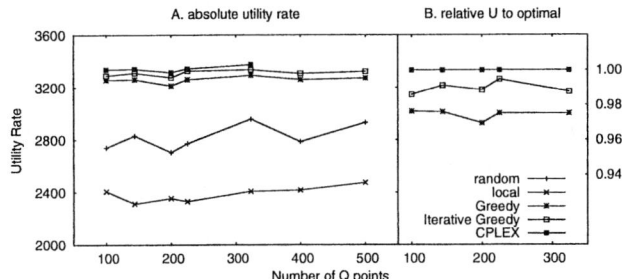

Fig. 4. Optimality of replica selection algorithms. Each data point represents the mean of four experiments.

Performance of Replica Selection Algorithms. We evaluate the performance of *Greedy* and *Iterative Greedy* algorithms in terms of optimality (Fig 4) and running time (Fig 5). In this experiment, we set f to 3600 requests/hour so the utility rate is bounded by 3600/hr. We compare our algorithms with three others: 1. the CPLEX mathematical programming package[2]; 2. a random algorithm; 3. a *local* algorithm that places replicas in the most frequently accessed areas in the quality space. CPLEX is a widely-used software for solving various optimization problems and is well-known for its efficiency. We tune CPLEX such that the results obtained are within a 0.01% gap to the optimal solution.

From Fig 4A, it is clear that our algorithms always find solutions that are very close to the optimal. More details can be found in Fig 4B where the relative U values obtained by our algorithms to those by CPLEX are plotted. Utility rates of solutions found by *Greedy* are only about 3% smaller than the optimal values. The *Iterative Greedy* cuts the gap by at least half in all cases: the solutions it finds always achieve more than 99% of the optimal utility rate. For both algorithms, the performance is insensitive to the number of quality points. Nor is it affected by access patterns or storage constraints. We tested different access patterns (e.g. Zipf, 20-80, and uniform) and S values (60-300GB) and obtained similar results (data not plotted here). The solutions given by *random* and *local* are far from optimal. The fact that the *local* algorithm performs even worse than the random algorithm shows that it is dangerous to consider only local or regional information in solving a combinatorial problem.

The running time of the above experiments are shown on a logarithmic scale in Figure 5. CPLEX is the slowest algorithm in all cases. This is what we expected as its target is the global optimal solution. Actually, we could only run CPLEX for the five smaller cases due to its long running time. Both *Greedy* and *Iterative Greedy* are 2-4 orders of magnitude faster than CPLEX. It takes them about 200 seconds to solve the selection of 30 videos in a quality space with 500 points.

---

[2] version 8.0.1, http://www.cplex.com

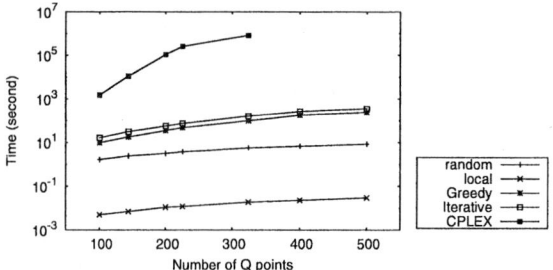

Fig. 5. Running time of different replica selection algorithms

Performance of dynamic replication algorithm. We also test our dynamic replication algorithm under the soft quality model for its optimality and speed. We simulate a system for a period of time during which events of query rate changes of media objects are randomly generated. We allow the query rate of videos to increase up to 20 times and to decrease down to 1/10 of the original rate. We first compare the total utility rate of the selected replicas between the online phase of SOFTDYNAREP and *Greedy*. For all events, the replicas selected by SOFTDYNAREP get utility rates that are consistently within 99.5% of that by rerunning the *Greedy* algorithm (Fig 6A). In this experiment of 270 videos and a 20×20 quality space, the running time of SOFTDYNAREP for each event is on the order of 10^{-4} seconds while GREEDY needs to run about half a hour to solve the same problems. The main reason for SOFTDYNAREP's efficiency is the small number of storage exchanges. In Fig 6B, we record such numbers for each execution of SOFTDYNAREP and very few of these readings exceed 15.

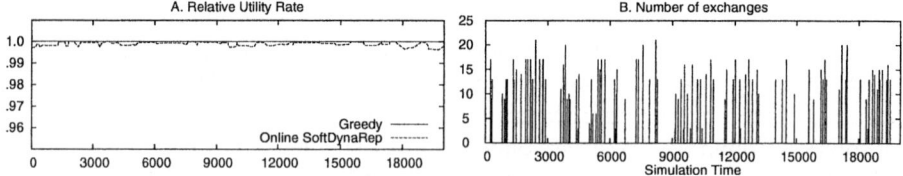

Fig. 6. Performance of SOFTDYNAREP

7 Conclusions

In this paper, we study the problem of selecting quality-specific replicas of media data. This problem is generally ignored in multimedia database research due to the oversimplified assumption that storage space is always abundant. We provide solutions to the problem under a soft quality model where users' quality needs are negotiable. We propose a greedy algorithm to solve the optimal replica selection problem heuristically. Experiments show that the total utility rates of the solutions found by our algorithm are over 97% of those of the optimal. An advanced version of this algorithm further increases that to 99%. A derived online algorithm provides an elegant solution to an important subproblem of dynamic data replication. While the greedy algorithm takes cubic time, the low time complexity of the online algorithm makes our solution scalable.

References

1. Tu, Y.C., Prabhakar, S., Elmagarmid, A., Sion, R.: QuaSAQ: An Approach to Enabling End-to-End QoS for Multimedia Databases. In: Proceedings of EDBT. (2004) 694–711
2. Nepal, S., Srinivasan, U.: DAVE: A System for Quality Driven Adaptive Video Delivery. (In: Proceedings of Intl. Workshop of Multimedia Information Retrieval (MIR04)) 224–230
3. HAfiD, A., Bochmann, G.: An Approach to Quality of Service Management in Distributed Multimedia Application: Design and Implementation. Multimedia Tools and Applications **9** (1999) 167–191
4. Bertino, E., Elmagarmid, A., Hacid, M.S.: A Database Approach to Quality of Service Specification in Video Databases. SIGMOD Record **32** (2003) 35–40
5. Lum, W.Y., Lau, F.C.M.: On Balancing Between Transcoding Overhead and Spatial Consumption in Content Adaptation. In: Proceedings of MOBICOM. (2002) 239–250
6. Mohan, R., Smith, J.R., Li, C.S.: Adapting Multimedia Internet Content for Universal Access. IEEE Transactions on Multimedia (**1**) 104–114
7. Tu, Y.C., Prabhakar, S.: Quality-Aware Replication of Multimedia Data. Technical Report CSD-TR-0423, Purdue University (2004)
8. Nicola, M., Jarke, M.: Performance Modeling of Distributed and Replicated Databases. IEEE Trans. Knowledge and Data Engineering **12** (2000) 645–672
9. Harinarayan, V., Rajaraman, A., Ullman, J.D.: Implementing Data Cubes Efficiently. In: Proceedings of SIGMOD. (1996) 205–216
10. Rabinovich, M.: Issues in Web Content Replication. Data Engineering Bulletin **21** (1998) 21–29
11. Qiu, L., Padmanabhan, V.N., Voelker, G.M.: On the Placement of Web Server Replicas. In: Proceedings of IEEE INFOCOM. (2001) 1587–1596
12. Little, T.D.C., Venkatesh, D.: Popularity-Based Assignment of Movies to Storage Devices in a Video-on-Demand System. Springer/ACM Multimedia Systems **2** (1995) 280–287
13. Wang, Y., Liu, J.C.L., Du, D.H.C., Hsieh, J.: Efficient Video File Allocation Schemes for Video-on-Demand Services. Springer/ACM Multimedia Systems **5** (1997) 282–296
14. Dan, A., Sitaram, D.: An Online Video Placement Policy Based on Bandwidth to Space (BSR). In: Proceedings of ACM SIGMOD. (1995) 376–385
15. Wolfson, O., Jajodia, S., Huang, Y.: An Adaptive Data Replication Algorithm. ACM Transactions on Database Systems **22** (1997) 255–314
16. Menges, G.: 2. In: Economic Decision Making: Basic Concepts and Models. Longman (1973) 21–48
17. Lee, C., Lehoczky, J., Siewiorek, D., Rajkumar, R., Hansen, J.: A Scalable Solution to the Multi-Resource QoS Problem. In: Proceedings of the IEEE Real-Time Systems Symposium. (1999)
18. Kariv, O., Hakimi, S.L.: An Algorithmic Approach to Network Location Problems. II: The p-Medians. SIAM Journal of Applied Mathematics (**37**) 539–560

Rotation and Gray-Scale Invariant Classification of Textures Improved by Spatial Distribution of Features

Gouchol Pok[1], Keun Ho Ryu[2], and Jyh-charn Lyu[3]

[1] Yanbian University of Science and Technology, Department of Computer Science,
Yanji, Jilin Province, China
gcpok@yahoo.co.kr
[2] Chungbuk National University, Department of Computer Science,
Cheongju, Chungbuk, Korea
khryu@dblab.chungbuk.ac.kr
[3] Texas A&M University, Department of Computer Science,
College Station, Texas, USA
jcliu@cs.tamu.edu

Abstract. In this paper, we present a framework for texture descriptors based on spatial distribution of textural features. Our approach is based on the observation that regional properties of textures are well captured by correlations among local texture patterns. The proposed method has been evaluated through experiments using real textures, and has shown significant improvements in recognition rates.

1 Introduction

Texture is one of the fundamental properties of natural images, and useful for various applications including remote sensing, medical image analysis, industrial surface inspection, and content-based image retrieval. Although texture analysis and classification have been widely studied in the literature, many existing approaches deal with limited problems that do not fully take into account the image variations with respect to orientation, intensity, and spatial scale [1] [2]. Over the years, a number of approaches to texture classification have been developed to address rotation invariance problems. Porter and Canagarajah [3] developed the rotation invariant texture classification schemes for three texture analysis models, i.e., wavelet transform, Gabor filters, and Gaussian Markov random fields (GMRFs). They achieved rotation invariance by discarding the orientation information or by averaging of the features over the circular neighborhoods. Hayley and Manjunath [4] used multichannel Gabor filters to extract rotation-invariant texture features. They decomposed Gabor elementary functions into amplitude and phase components, and, from these components, developed the texture model of micro-features that describe the amplitude, frequency, and directional characteristics of textures. Dimai [5] applied the framework of the general moment invariants to non-invariant Gabor features. Due to high computational complexity involved in extraction and classification of features, he employed sampling of filtering positions and a feature selection step. Fountain et al. [6] compared four different rotation texture analysis methods in retrieving texture images from the image database of the Brodatz album [7]. Other examples include the circular simultaneous autoregressive (CSAR) model by Kashiyap and Khotanzad [8], the multiresolution simultaneous autoregressive (MRSAR) model by Mao and Jain [9], the works by Pietikainen et al. [10], Fountain and Tan [11], and Greenspan et al. [12]. In addition to the rotation invariance problem, several recent works also addressed the scale invariance problem. Pun and Lee [1] proposed a scheme using the wavelet energy signatures and the log-polar transform. In their approach, rotation and scale variance of the input image were transformed to row shift variance by the log-polar transform, and then the row shift variance was eliminated by applying an adaptive wavelet packet transform. Experimental results reportedly showed the overall recognition accuracy of 90.8 percent using 96 energy features extracted from the 25 natural images of the Brodatz album [7]. Similarly, Leung and Peterson [14] used log-polar Gabor filters, and then estimated rotation and scale parameters using the mental transform. Cohen et al. [13] incorporated a likelihood function with the GMRF model to estimate rotation and scale parameters. Experiments were carried out with nine classes of the Brodatz album, which is rather a limited number of samples considering the wide variety of textures. Other works that address both the rotation and scale invariance problem include Wu and Yoshida [15], Tan [16], and Manian and Vasquez [17]. Gray-scale invariant texture classification, which has received little attention in the literature, is also important to deal with images of great intra-class variability usually caused by light reflectance and uneven illumination. Chen and Kundu [18] employed the histogram equalization technique to achieve gray-scale invariance. Notable drawback of this approach lies in that local intensity variability within an image can not be addressed generally by the global histogram equalization. Wu and Wei [19] proposed a similar approach. Both approaches assumed that the underlying function of gray-scale variation is liner, which could limit the usefulness of the methods. Ojala et al. [2] proposed a simple method using local binary patterns (LBP). They showed that uniform patterns, which refer to uniform occurrences of local binary patterns, are fundamental properties of local texture structures. More specifically, transition of gray levels in the circular neighborhood with respect to the gray level of the center pixel successfully capture primitive features such as edges, corners, and spots. Gray-scale invariance was achieved by using the relative measures of gray levels instead of directly using gray levels. However, gray levels are one of the essential properties of textures, as most feature-based and statistical approaches have been designed based on gray levels.

We propose that correct classification rate can be significantly increased by using co-occurrence relations of local textural features. The local textural features used in this study are the LBP and gray level intensities. The LBP operator [2] is excellent in capturing the spatial structure of local texture, but it discards, by definition, gray level information. Therefore, in general, the LBP per se is not appropriate for representing rotation invariance property. To compensate for this loss of gray level information, Ojala et al. [2] incorporated the variance of gray levels into the feature set for achieving rotation invariant classification of textures. In contrast, we have used co-occurrence of gray levels as well as that of the LBPs on a circular neighborhood system. The performance of the proposed approach has been evaluated using the same test sets of real texture images as those published in [2] [22]. The results have shown significant increase of correct classification rate compared to the ones obtained by Ojala et al..

The paper is organized as follows: Section 2 describes the framework to capture spatial distribution of local features, Section 3 presents experimental results, and Section 4 draws conclusion of this paper.

2 Rotation and Gray-Scale Invariant Texture Descriptors

2.1 Circular Neighborhood System

A circular neighborhood system N_r of radius r with respect to center pixel p_c is defined as the equally spaced P points, $p = 0, 1, \cdots, P-1$, on a circle of radius r, as illustrated in Fig. 1. Corresponding gray levels are denoted by $G_r^P = (g_0, g_1, \cdots, g_{P-1})$, and by g_c for a center pixel. Some points have non-integer coordinates, and their gray levels are computed by the linear interpolation of the four neighboring pixels as shown in Fig. 2 [20]. The gray level of point (x, y) is computed as,

$$g_{xy} = abg_{11} + a(1-b)g_{12} + (1-a)bg_{21} + (1-a)(1-b)g_{22}, \qquad (1)$$

where weights a and b are coordinate differences, $a = y_{22} - y$ and $b = x_{22} - x$, and g_{ij} are gray levels.

2.2 Local Binary Patterns

Ojala et al. [2] proposed a texture operator called local binary patterns (LBP) that use gray level differences between the pixels of a circular neighborhood and the center pixel. This section will review the procedure to compute the local

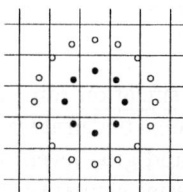

Fig. 1. Circular neighbor system. Black points constitute a neighborhood of (P=8,r=1.0), and white ones represent that of (P=16,r=2.0).

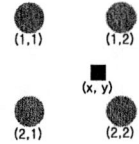

Fig. 2. Linear interpolation scheme

binary patterns as described in [2]. LBP with respect to the gray levels G_r^P in N_r is defined as,

$$LBP_r^P = (sgn(g_0 - g_c), sgn(g_1 - g_c), \cdots, sgn(g_{P-1} - g_c)), \quad (2)$$

where $sgn(x)$ is a sign function,

$$sgn(x) = \begin{cases} 1 \text{ if } x \geq 0; \\ 0 \text{ if } x < 0. \end{cases} \quad (3)$$

Thus, LBP_r^P is by definition a binary pattern in which bits of value 1 (value 0) correspond to pixels whose gray levels are greater than or equal to (less than) that of the center pixel. From the bit patterns of LBP_r^P, we compute the number of transitions from 1 to 0 and vice versa in the circular order,

$$U(LBP_r^P) = |sgn(g_{P-1} - g_c) - sgn(g_0 - g_c)| + \sum_{p=1}^{P-1} |sgn(g_p - g_c) - sgn(g_{p-1} - g_c)|. \quad (4)$$

Then, the pattern code of LBP is defined as,

$$LBP_{P,r}^{riu2} = \begin{cases} \sum_{p=0}^{P-1} sgn(g_p - g_c) & \text{if } U(LBP_r^P) \leq 2 \\ P+1 & \text{otherwise.} \end{cases} \quad (5)$$

Because signed differences $g_p - g_c$ are not affected by changes of luminance, gray-scale invariance property can be achieved by considering only the signs of the differences instead of their values. The distinct values of $uLBP_r^P$ is $P+2$ according to Eq. (5). For example, for $P = 24$, which is the number of pixels on the rectangular boundary of radius $r = 3$, the number of distinctive $uLBP$s is 26.

2.3 Improved Rotation Invariant Texture Descriptor

Once the $LBP_{P,r}^{riu2}$s for all pixels in the input image are computed, they are collected to form a histogram which is used as rotation-invariant texture features. Although the $LBP_{P,r}^{riu2}$ operator is excellent in capturing the textural structure in a local region of images, it does not consider the spatial relations of the textural features because the features are represented as a histogram. In

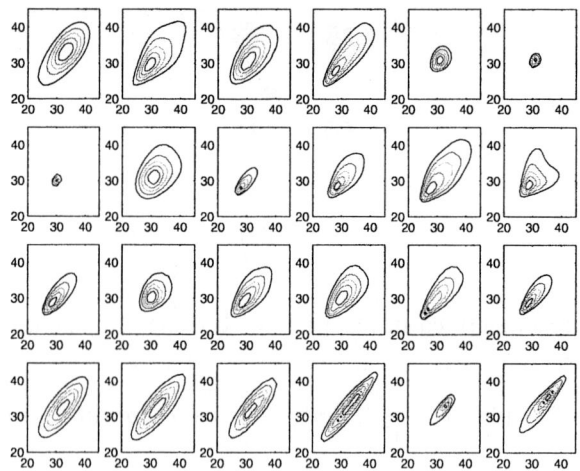

Fig. 3. Contour map of cooccurrence matrices obtained from gray levels quantized at 64 levels

contrast, we propose a method which considers spatial relations through a co-occurrence matrix of texture features. Let $COMAT(i,j)$ be the element of a co-occurrence matrix at i-th row and j-th column. The value of $COMAT(i,j)$ is computed by accumulating the number of pixels whose texture features have value j over the circular neighborhood around the center pixel of value i. The co-occurrence matrix obtained by relating $LBP_{P,r}^{riu2}$ and $LBP_{P',r'}^{riu2}$ is denoted by $COMAT_{P,R}^{P',R'}(i,j)$. It should be noted that $COMAT$ operator is different from the usual Gray Level Cooccurrence Matrix (GLCM) [23] in the sense that $COMAT$ does not consider the relative direction between two co-occurrences of features. Therefore, $COMAT_r^P(i,j)$ can achieve rotational inavariance property, whereas GLCM does not in general. Moreover, $COMAT$ operator can achieve higher rates of classification accuracy as the discriminant power is pictorially illustrated in Fig. 3 for 24 different texture classes whose details are described in Section 3.

2.4 Classification Measure

The similarity of two joint-histograms (generated from a test image and model images) is measured by a test of goodness-of-fit [2]. Given a test feature T and a model feature M, the G(log-likelihood ratio) is defined as,

$$G(T,M) = 2\sum_{h=1}^{H} T_h \log \frac{T_h}{M_h} = 2\sum_{h=1}^{H}[T_h \log T_h - T_h \log M_h], \quad (6)$$

where H is the number of joint-histogram bins and T_h and M_h are probabilities of T and M at bin h, respectively. Note that the term $T_h \log T_h$ in Equation 6 is constant, and therefore can be ignored without any effects on the classification

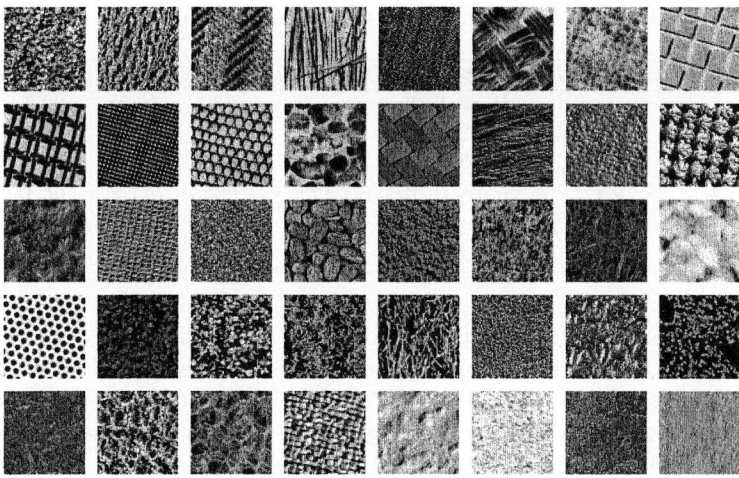

Fig. 4. Forty classes of textures from Bonn University image database

result. Therefore, a test sample S is assigned to the class of the model M that maximizes the log-likelihood statistic,

$$L(T, M) = \sum_{h=1}^{H} T_h \log \frac{T_h}{M_h}. \tag{7}$$

3 Experimental Results

The performance of the proposed algorithm was evaluated using two different sets of natural textures, one set provided by [21] and the other one replicated from the Outex texture database [22]. The Outex includes a large collection of natural textures and test suites for comparison of several types of texture analysis, together with the experimental results of published algorithms. We computed the average of cooccurrence matrices ($COMAT$) for each class, and used them as model features to which the testing image features are compared. This is in contrast to the scheme adopted by Ojala et al. [2] in which all sample instances are stored as references to be compared with the input image. This scheme is unrealistic for practical applications, even though high rate of correct classification can be achieved.

3.1 Experiment 1: Rotation Invariant Texture Classification

The objective of the experiment is to evaluate the performance for the rotation invariant texture classification. The test data include 40 classes of natural textures from the Bonn University [21], as shown in Fig 4. From each 512 × 512 texture image, 25 non-overlapping sample images of size 128×128 were extracted, and five images were used for training and 20 images for testing. The images in

Table 1. Classification Accuracies(%) for Experiment 1

Descriptor	P, R	Average	Descriptor	$(P, R), (P', R')$	Average
	8,1	88.4		(8,1), (16,2)	90.5
	16,2	92.5		(8,1), (24,3)	95.5
	24,3	93.9		(8,1), (34,4)	96.4
$LBP_{P,r}^{riu2}$	8,1 + 16,2	95.1	$COMAT_{P,R}^{P',R'}$	(16,2), (24,3)	96.1
	8,1 + 24,3	94.8		(16,2), (34,4)	95.1
	16,2 + 24,3	93.6		(24,3), (34,4)	93.2

the training set were rotated by eight different angles (0°, 15°, 50°, 85°, 110°, 125°, 140°, and 170°), while those in the testing set were rotated by another set of eight angles (5°, 20°, 45°, 80°, 100°, 130°, 150°, and 175°). Therefore, the training set include 1600 images (8 angles × 5 samples × 40 classes), and the testing set 6400 samples (8 angles × 20 samples × 40 classes).

The classification accuracies are summarized in Table 1. One can see that cooccurrence matrix-based $COMAT$ consistently outperform the $LBP_{P,r}^{riu2}$ operator for different values of P and r. This observations show that the textural properties over a local area are better represented by cooccurrence relations than $1-D$ histogram. As remarked by Ojala et al. [2]. $LBP_{P,r}^{riu2}$ have difficulties in disciminating strongly oriented textures because directional charateristics of textures appear over local area wider than radius r. This resulted in the performance degradation for recognizing *rattan*, *straw*, and *wood* textures. As expected, combining two $COMAT$ descriptors with different values of P and r and thus forming multiresolution scheme improved the classification performance. The superior results of our approach demonstrate its suitability for rotation invariant texture classification.

3.2 Experiment 2: Gray-Scale and Rotation Invariant Texture Classification

In this experiment, we evaluate the performance for gray-scale and rotation invariant texture classification using texture image set *Outex-TC-00010* from the Outex database [22]. The 24 classes of test images are illustrated in Fig. 5. Most of the texture images are canvases with strong directional structure. Some texture classes (e.g., *canvas025*, *canvas033*, and *canvas038*) show considerable local gray-scale distortions. Such characteristic of test data presents a challenging problem for gray-scale and rotation invariant texture analysis. From the texture image database, 480 images (24 classes × 20 images per class) of size 128 × 128 were randomly extracted and used as a training set, and 3840 images (24 classes × 160 images per class) of size 128 × 128 were extracted in such a manner that they were not overlapped with the training images, and used as a test set.

The experimental results are summarized in Table 2. These results are favorably compared with the results obtained by the LBP operators.

Fig. 5. Twenty-four classes of textures from *Outex-TC-00010*. Row 1: *Canvas001, Canvas002, Canvas003, Canvas005, Canvas006, Canvas009*. Row 2: *Canvas011, Canvas021, Canvas022, Canvas023, Canvas025, Canvas026*. Row 3: *Canvas031, Canvas032, Canvas033, Canvas035, Canvas038, Canvas039*. Row 4: *Tile 005, Tile 006, Carpet 002, Carpet 004, Carpet 005, Carpet 009*.

Table 2. Classification Accuracies(%) for Experiment 2

Descriptor	P,R	Average	Descriptor	$(P,R),(P',R')$	Average
$LBP_{P,r}^{riu2}$	8,1	80.1	$COMAT_{P,R}^{P',R'}$	(8,1), (16,2)	89.2
	16,2	82.5		(8,1), (24,3)	91.2
	24,3	88.2		(8,1), (34,4)	95.3
	8,1 + 16,2	91.6		(16,2), (24,3)	94.9
	8,1 + 24,3	93.1		(16,2), (34,4)	93.0
	16,2 + 24,3	92.6		(24,3), (34,4)	93.4
	8,1 + 16,2 + 24,3	92.2			

4 Conclusion

We have shown that gray-scale and rotational invariant texture classification can be improved by using cooccurrence information of local binary patterns. We developed a generalized gray-scale and rotation invariant texture descriptor *COMAT*, which allows for detecting local structures in a circular neighborhoods of any quantization of the angular space. The discriminative power of the proposed texture descriptor can be seen from pictorial illustration of *COMAT* shown in Fig. 6 Excellent experimental results obtained in the two experiments demonstrate that good discrimination can be achieved with the cooccurrence statistics of local binary patterns.

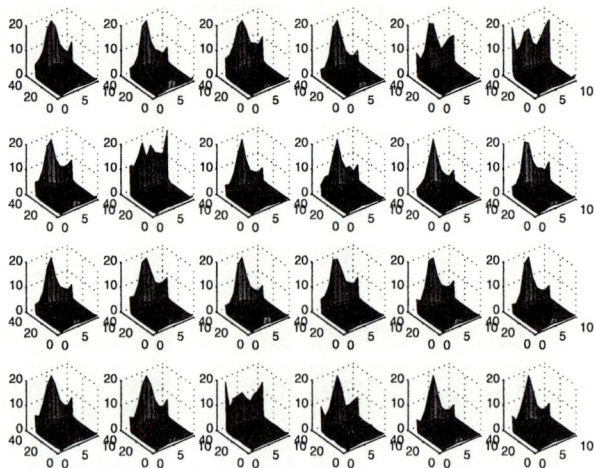

Fig. 6. Pictorial illustration of COMAT for textures in *Outex-TC-00010*

Acknowledgment

This work was supported by the Regional Research Centers Program.

References

1. C.-M. Pun and M.-C. Lee, "Log-Polar Wavelet Energy Signatures for Rotation and Scale Invariant Texture Classification," *IEEE Trans. Pattern Analysis and Machine Intelligence*, vol. 25, no. 5, pp.590-603, May 2003.
2. T. Ojala, M. Pietikainen, and T. Maenpaa, "Multiresolution Gray-Scale and Rotation Invariant Texture Classification with Local Binary Patterns," *IEEE Trans. Pattern Analysis and Machine Intelligence*, vol. 24, no. 7, pp.971-987, July 2002.
3. R. Porter and N. Canagarajah, "Robust Rotation-Invariant Texture Classification: Wavelet, Gabor Filter, and GMRF Based Schemes," *IEE Proc.-Vision Image Signal Processing*, vol. 144, no. 3, pp.180-188, June 1997.
4. G. M. Hayley and B. M. Manjunath, "Rotation Invariant Texture Classification Using Modified Gabor Filters," *Proc. Int'l Conf. Image Processing '95*, vol. 3, pp.262-265, 1995.
5. A. Dimai, "Rotation Invariant Texture Description using General Moment Invariants and Gabor Filters," *Proc. 11th Scandinavian Conf. Image Analysis '99*,pp.391-398, June 1999.
6. S. R. Fountain, T. N. Tan, and K. D. Baker, "A Comparative Study of Rotation Invariant Classification and Retrieval of Texture Images," *Proc. Ninth British Machine Vision Conf.*,pp.266-275, Sept. 1998.
7. P. Brodatz, *Textures:A Photographic Album for Artists and Designers*, Dover, 1966.
8. R. L. Kashiyap and A. Khotanzad, "A Moel-Based Methods for Rotation Invariant Texture Classification," *IEEE Trans. Pattern Analysis and Machine Intelligence*, vol. 8, pp.472-481, July 1986.

9. J. Mao and A. K. Jain, "Texture Classification and Segmentation Using Multiresolution Simultaneous Autoregressive Models," *Pattern Recognition*, vol. 25, pp.173-188, 1992.
10. M. Pietikainen, T. Ojala, and Z. Xu, "Rotation-Invariant Texture Classification Using Feature Distributions," *Pattern Recognition*, vol. 33, pp.43-52, 2000.
11. M. Pietikainen, T. Ojala, and Z. Xu, "Efficient Rotation Invariant Texture Features for Content-Based Imae Retrieval," *Pattern Recognition*, vol. 31, pp.1725-1732, 1998.
12. H. Greenspan, S. Belongie, R. Goodman, and P. Perona, "Rotation Invariant Texture Recognition Using a Steerable Pyramid," *Proc. 12th Int'l Conf. Pattern Recognition*, vol. 2, pp.162-167, 1994.
13. F. S. Cohen, Z. Fan, and M. A. Patel, "Classification of Rotated and Scaled Texture Images Using Gaussian Markov Random Field Models," *IEEE Trans. Pattern Analysis and Machine Intelligence*, vol. 13, no. 2, pp.192-202, Feb. 1991.
14. M. Leung and A. M. Peterson, "Scale and Rotation Invariant Texture Classification," *Proc. 26th Int'l Conf. Acoustics, Speech, and Signal Processing*, vol. 1, pp.461-465, 1992.
15. Y. Wu and Y. Yoshida, "An Efficient Method for Rotation and Scaling Invariant Texture Classification," *Proc. IEEE Int'l Conf. Acoustics, Speech, and Signal Processing*, vol. 4, pp. 2519-2522, 1995.
16. T. N. Tan, "Scale and Rotation Invariant Texture Classification," *IEE Colloquium Texture Classification: Theory and Applications*, 1994.
17. V. Manian and R. Vasquez, "Scaled and Rotated Texture Classification Using a Class of Basis Functions," *Pattern Recognition*, vol. 31, pp.1937-1948, 1998.
18. J.-L. Chen and A. Kundu, "Rotation and Gray Scale Transform Invariant Texture Identification Using Wavelet Decomposition and Hidden Markov Model," *IEEE Trans. Pattern Analysis and Machine Intelligence*, vol. 16, pp.208-214, 1994.
19. W. R. Wu and S. C. Wei, "Rotation and Gray-Scale Transform Invariant Texture Classification Using Spiral Resampling, Subband Decomposition, and Hidden Markov Model," *IEEE Trans. Image Processing*, vol. 5, pp.1423-1434, Oct. 1996.
20. D. Chetverykov, "Texture Analysis Using Feature Based Pairwise Interaction Maps," *Pattern Recognition*, vol. 32, no. 3, pp.487-502, 1999.
21. Collection of Microtextures, Computer Vision Group, University of Bonn, http://www-dbv.cs.uni-bonn.de/image/browse.
22. T. Ojala, T. Maenpaa, and M. Pietikainen, "Outex-A New Framework for Empirical Evaluation of Texture Analisis Algorithms," *Proc. 16th Int'l Conf. Pattern Recognition*, 2002.
23. R. M. Haralick, "Statistical and Structural Approaches to Texture," *Proceedings of the IEEE*, vol. 67, pp.786-804, 1979.

Zooming Cross-Media: A Zooming Description Language Coding LOD Control and Media Transition

Tadashi Araki[1], Hisashi Miyamori[2], Mitsuru Minakuchi[2],
Ai Kato[1], Zoran Stejic[1], Yasushi Ogawa[1], and Katsumi Tanaka[2,3]

[1] Software R&D Group, Ricoh Co., Ltd.,
1-1-17 Koishikawa, Bunkyo-ku, Tokyo, 112-0002 Japan
{araki-t, ai.katoh, zoran.stejic, yoga}@nts.ricoh.co.jp
[2] Interactive Comm. Media and Contents Group, NiCT,
3-5 Hikaridai, Seika-cho, Soraku-gun, Kyoto, 619-0289 Japan
{miya, mmina}@nict.go.jp
[3] Graduate School of Informatics, Kyoto University
Yoshida-Honmachi, Sakyo-ku, Kyoto, 606-8501 Japan
ktanaka@i.kyoto-u.ac.jp

Abstract. We propose a "Zooming Cross-Media" concept that uses zooming to achieve both changes in the level of detail and transitions between media, for contents containing varied media. Examples are text, images, video, and sound. As part of the concept, we propose a zooming description language (ZDL) based on XML. Unlike existing zooming interfaces, ZDL codes the zooming operation and behavior on the content side. Because ZDL adopts XML coding, we can locate "zooming" as the third interface in the Web document environment after "scrolling" and "anchor clicking." The zooming operation and behavior is independently coded from the content structure in ZDL. With ZDL, it is possible to (1) control the zooming of each "zoom object" making up the contents, (2) control the degree of zooming by introducing a "zoom rate" parameter, and (3) relate objects mutually and specify zooming propagation between related objects.

1 Introduction

Scrolling and *anchor clicking* are the basic browsing operations in the Web document environment. When we browse voluminous information by scrolling, we can display all the information on one page; but it is hard to overview it. With anchor clicking, the browsing context is likely to be lost because the information is divided across multiple pages.

With a zooming interface, the above problem can be solved to some extent because the zooming interface continuously controls the displayed image from the entire overview to the zoomed detail.

Various zoomable user interfaces (ZUIs) have been proposed [1, 2, 3]. Beyond a simple zooming interface, such as controlling the level of detail (LOD) of an image, a *semantic zooming* interface to realize semantic LOD control (for example, title→abstract→full text) and co-zooming between multiple objects etc. have been proposed.

The traditional ZUI, however, assumes existence of a specific viewer to achieve the zooming operation and behavior for each zoomable content. It is therefore impossible to browse such zoomable contents in a generic Web environment.

HTML, XML SMIL, etc. have been proposed as markup languages in the Web environment, but there is no language to code zooming operation and behavior.

To solve such problems, we propose the Zooming Description Language (ZDL). ZDL is a markup language based on XML and codes zooming operation and behavior on the content side (independently from a viewer). As ZDL is based on XML, zooming can be located as the third operation of the generic Web document environment against scrolling and anchor clicking. ZDL coexists with HTML or XML and adds the zooming operation and behavior coding except to the logical structure and the layout description of the content. The three basic concepts of ZDL are (1) zooming operation to each *zoom object* making up a content, (2) control of the degree of zooming by introducing a *zoom rate* parameter, (3) *zoom propagation* between zoom objects that are related mutually. ZDL can easily code LOD control of the media-objects (text, image, video and audio etc.) making up a zoom object. Beyond that, it can also control the display media transition.

We propose a new *Zooming Cross-Media* concept that includes (A) the zooming technique to achieve *LOD control* and *display media transitions*, and (B) a ZDL that codes such zooming operation and behavior.

Existing techniques and their problems are described in Chapter 2. Examples and significance of the Zooming Cross-Media are described in Chapter 3, details of ZDL and a concrete coding example are given in Chapter 4, discussions are in Chapter 5, and conclusions and future work are presented in Chapter 6.

2 Problems with Existing Interface

2.1 General Problems in Web document environment

It is desirable when browsing contents that the relationship between the whole abstract and every detail can be easily understood. A scroll bar is, however, needed and it is hard to overview all of the information when it is displayed on one page. On the other hand, if multiple pages are related by hyperlink and a browsing user moves from one page to another by anchor clicking, the browsing context is likely to be lost because the relationship between the start page and the current page become hard to remember when the user moves on multiple-stage links.

In browsing contents it is useful to achieve media transitions so that the browsing user can browse multiple information units that are related mutually in a favorite media or display balance. For example, it is useful for a browsing user to be able to browse news by video and audio, read it as text or use the two methods simultaneously. It is also useful to control the display balance between video and text when both media are used.

When we achieve such functions in a generic Web document environment, we have to make multiple pages of each page corresponding to the browsing user's taste or the browsing situation. The page structure, therefore, becomes complex. It is impossible to control the display balance between multiple media interactively and continuously. For example, it is impossible to control display balance between video size and quantity of text continuously in a generic Web document environment.

2.2 Traditional ZUIs and Their Problems

As zooming continuously changes display conditions of the information from the entire overview to zoomed detail, the possibility of losing browsing context lessens and the ease of overview is maintained to some extent.

Representative ZUI examples are Pad [1], Pad++ [2] and Jazz (currently Piccolo) [3]. These are zooming environments in which a two-dimensional image is continuously zoomed to a detailed image. Not only is the LOD changed, but also the "semantic zooming" concept is realized. For example, when a title is zoomed in, an abstract first appears and then the full text appears. Various other techniques have been proposed for ZUI [4, 5]. The first proposes the idea of multi-focus zooming and the second proposes cooperation between them.

These ZUI, however, assume the existence of a specific viewer (program) to achieve the zooming operation and behavior. The author must write a display program for each zoomable content. It is therefore impossible to browse such zoomable content in a generic Web environment. Beyond that, the idea of media transition is not proposed.

2.3 Markup Language on Web Environment and Zooming

Some markup languages, such as HTML, XML and SMIL, code the content structure, content layout or multiple object integration on a time line. No markup language, however, codes zooming operation and behavior.

3 Zooming Cross-Media

3.1 Abstract

The main two points of our Zooming Cross-Media are as follows:

(A) Achieve not only LOD control but display media transition
(B) Introduce Zooming Description Language (ZDL)

We also present examples that achieve what I proposed.

3.2 Examples That Realize Both LOD Control and Media Transition

TV2Web and Webified Video. TV2Web and Webified video [6, 7] structure a TV program as pairs of captions and separated video. There are LOD about them (segment, scene and shot etc.). Zooming operation not only changes video size but also produces the LOD transition and media transition (text → video) shown in Fig. 1.

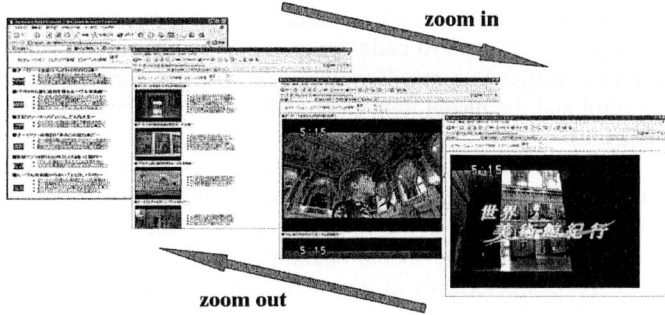

Fig. 1. Example of TV2Web

Business Trip Report (Meeting Minutes). Fig. 2 shows an example of a business trip report (meeting minutes) [8]. Fig. 2 (a) shows an initial state and the colored part is a selected text. Fig. 2 (b) and (c) show zoomed conditions. As the zooming operation proceeds, a detail text part (the lower part of the selected part) and a still/video image appear ((b) and (c) show the still and the video image, respectively). The still image and video image are a snapshot picture and a recorded video that were captured when the discussion corresponding to the selected text occurred.

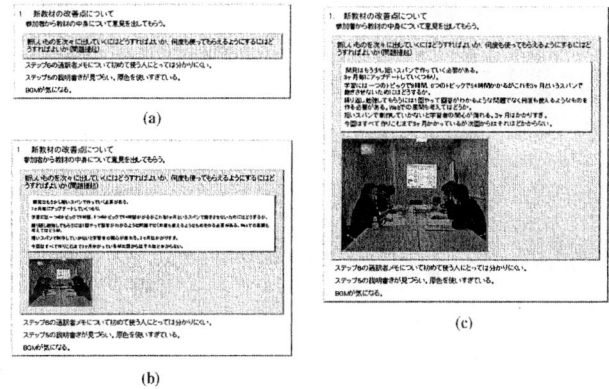

Fig. 2. Example of a Business Trip Report (Meeting Minutes)

3.3 The Novelty and Significance of Zooming Cross-Media

In the examples in Section 3.2, the object LOD control and the media transition between related objects is achieved by the zooming operation. The browsing user can control the media selection and the display balance according to personal preference. We achieve a new advantage in browsing content that is not possible in the traditional ZUI described in Section 2.2.

These examples, however, require specific display programs like the traditional ZUI. They cannot easily adapt the LOD control and the media transition adapted to various contents.

Our purpose is to integrate existing zooming techniques that were individually proposed and implemented, and to code the zooming operation and behavior generically. We therefore introduce a new *Zooming Cross-Media* concept, define zooming as the LOD control and the media transition, and propose a generic zooming description language (ZDL).

ZDL is a markup language based on XML and codes the zooming operation and behavior on the content side (independently from a viewer). As ZDL is based on XML, zooming can be located as the third operation of the generic Web document environment against scrolling and anchor clicking.

Fig. 3 shows the characteristics of zooming as the third operation comparing to scrolling and anchor clicking. In scrolling, the viewpoint moves continuously but the LOD and display media don't change. Change is discontinuous in anchor clicking. Conversely, the viewpoint doesn't change but the LOD and display media change continuously in Zooming Cross-Media. Fig. 3 conceptually shows these relationships.

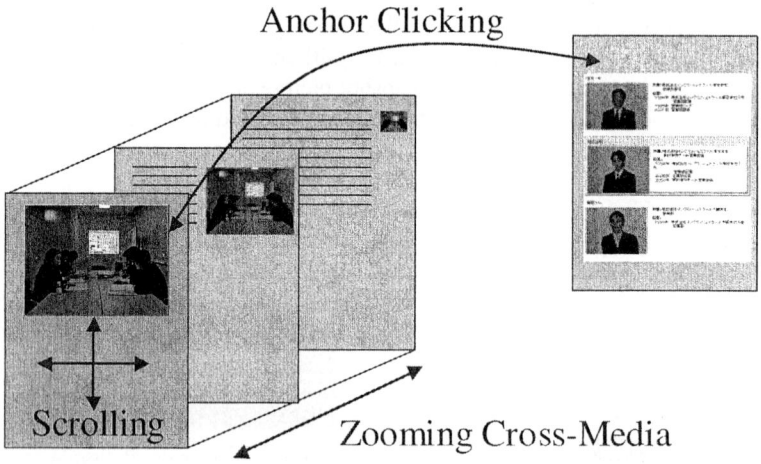

Fig. 3. Zooming Cross-Media, as Extension of the Web Browsing Environment, Compared to Scrolling and Anchor Clicking

4 Zooming Description Language (ZDL)

4.1 Position of ZDL and Requirements for ZDL

Our purpose is to introduce zooming operations to the existing Web document environment. HTML, XML, CSS, etc. code the content structure or layout in the Web environment. ZDL coexists with these languages and adds the zooming operation and behavior code.

To achieve the examples in Section 3.2, the zooming operation is needed not only to the entire content (entire page), but also to each object comprising the content. There may be a case where all objects except a specific object are not expected to be zoomed. The LOD control, the media transition, and the zoom propagation, for example, the propagation from the upper layer object to the lower object, need to be coded. Beyond that, it is desirable that a common zooming operation and behavior description be applied to all objects that have equivalent structures using a template description.

Following are requirements for ZDL based on the above discussion.

a. Code the zooming operation and behavior independently from the content structure
b. Code the zooming operation and behavior for each object comprising content
c. Distinguish the zoomable objects from unzoomable objects
d. Code LOD control and media transition
e. Code zoom propagation between mutually related objects
f. Use a template description

4.2 Basic Structure of the Zooming Description Language

Based on the requirements elaborated in the previous subsection, we define the basic elements of ZDL in the following way.

Zoom Object: the Basic Unit of Zooming Operation. *Zoom object* is a target of zooming operation, and consists of text, images, video, sound, and other *media-objects* making up the contents. A <template/> tag expresses a template of zoom objects. The "name" attribute specifies the template name and an attribute "match" specifies the base position of the contained media-objects in the content structure code. The media-objects are specified by <text/>, <video/>, etc. The "select" attribute specifies a relative position of each media-object, with respect to the base (reference) position specified through the "match" attribute. The user selects the desired zoom object and performs the zooming operation (e.g., by pointing to the zoom object by a mouse); however, ZDL does not deal concretely with how zoom object are selected.

Zoom Rate: Controlling the Degree of Zooming. A *zoom rate* is uniquely defined in a zoom object, and is a continuous value (from 0.0 to 1.0) that specifies the degree of zooming. An attribute "zoomFactor" specifies it. Using the <dispText/>, <dispVideo/> and similar tags, the display state of each zoom object with respect to a given zoom rate is coded. Based on this, it is possible to code the change in the LODs of media-objects, as well as the media transition (see Section 4.3). Further, the "initZoomFactor" attribute inside the <template/> tag represents the initial zoom rate used to initially display the contents. Zoom rate is determined by the zooming operation performed by the user (e.g., the relationship between the movement of the mouse and the zoom rate); however, the ZDL does not deal concretely with how zooming operations are performed.

Zoom Propagation between Related Objects. *Zoom propagation* means that when a zoom object (O) is zoomed, other related objects are also zoomed in conjunction with the object (O). For example, when an upper level object in the content structure is zoomed, lower level objects are also zoomed. A <propagation/> tag expresses this behavior. An attribute "destination" specifies a template name of destination objects and an attribute "select" specifies the position of their media-objects in the content structure. An attribute "relation" specifies the ratio between two changing rates of the zoom rate of the source and the destination objects. For example, when the ratio of zoom rates is 0.8, a change of 0.5 in the rate of the source object results in a 0.4 change in the rate of the destination object. Similarly, when the ratio of zoom rates is –0.5, a change of 0.6 in the rate of source object results in a –0.3 change in the rate of the destination object.

Using XPath to Establish Correspondence between the Document Structure and the Zooming Behavior. The "match" attribute inside the <template/> tag, the "select" attribute inside the <text/>, <video/> and similar tags, and the "select" attribute inside the <propagation/> tag all use the XPath to specify the corresponding location with the document structure.

4.3 Coding Example

A ZDL script coding the Fig. 1 example is shown in the following. The content structure is coded in usual XML and the zooming operation and behavior is coded in ZDL.

[Structure Description]
```
<program>
  <scene>
    <video href="scene1.mpg"/>
    <text href="scene1.txt"/>
  </scene>
  <scene>
    <video href="scene2.mpg"/>
    <text href="scene2.txt"/>
  </scene>
    ......
</program>
```
[Zooming Operation/Behavior Description]
```
<template name="Progarm" match="/program"
          initZoomFactor="0.0">
  <propagation destination="Scene" select="scene"
               relation="1.0"/>
</template>
<template name="Scene" match="/program/scene"
          initZoomFactor="0.0">
  <video select="video">
    <dispVideo zoomFactor="0.0" videoSize="5%"/>
    <dispVideo zoomFactor="1.0" videoSize="100%"/>
  </video>
  <text select="text">
    <dispText zoomFactor="0.0" fontSize="12pt"/>
    <dispText zoomFactor="0.5" fontSize="0pt"/>
  </text>
</template>
```

The structure code shows that each scene of a TV program consists of a video image and a caption in this example.

<template/> tags in the zooming operation/behavior code show that the whole program (name="Program") and each scene (name="Scene") are zoom objects and both initial zoom rates are 0.0 (initZoomFactor="0.0"). The <propagation/> tag shows that the zooming operation to the whole program is propagated to each scene. The zoom rate of each scene changes at the same change rate as that of the whole program (relation="1.0").

With each scene, the video image is displayed at 5% its original size and the caption is displayed in 12-point text when the zoom rate is 0.0 (zoomFactor="0.0"). When a zoom-in operation is done from this condition, video size increases. The caption disappears when the zoom rate reaches 0.5. Video size becomes 100% when the zoom rate is 1.0. This is an example of the media transition (from video and text to video only). Each scene can also be zoomed independently from the upper program.

5 Discussion

5.1 Logical Structure Zooming

In ZDL, objects that should become zoom objects are selected using the XPath, and the zooming behavior for those objects is specified. Consequently, it is possible to select all contents (the whole page) as the zoom object, or to select only specific objects as the zoom objects (it is also possible to select the whole page as well as the specific objects to be independent zoom objects).

5.2 Initial Zoom Rate Setting That Reflects User Preferences and/or Browsing Conditions

Browsing of various contents can be made even more effective by extending ZDL to allow the initial zoom rate to reflect user preferences, browsing conditions, or both. For example, for a business trip report, the person writing the report could display various parts of the report depending on the person the report is sent to – a meeting record for the bosses and travel expense details for administration. It is also possible to display certain information as images on a desktop PC, and as a textual summary on a mobile phone. (In the existing Web browsing requirement, this would require that multiple pages be created.)

5.3 Issues Concerning Zoom Propagation

When zoom propagation links several zoom objects to a certain zoom object, a mutual competition between different propagation paths could emerge, leading to a problem in zoom rate computation. A possible solution is to adopt the zoom rate corresponding to the shortest propagation path. (For example, where two propagation paths – e.g., "A→B→X" and "A→C→D→X" – exist, the zoom rate corresponding to the first, being shorter, would be adopted.). When there are several propagation paths with the same length, an appropriate rule could be introduced, e.g., adopting the average/minimum/maximum of the rates corresponding to the multiple paths.

Further, there are cases when the zoom rate resulting from the zoom propagation could not reflect the user's intention. For example, in Section 4.3, it is not possible to zoom in both video and text (since one becomes big as the other becomes little). A possible solution is to set each media-object as an independent zoom object and select both zoom objects at once and zoom them simultaneously. Then, applying the rule described in the previous paragraph, and assuming that the each propagation path is of length zero, the zoom rate of each object could be set independently.

5.4 Relationship to SMIL

SMIL (Synchronized Multimedia Integration Language) is used to integrate multiple media-objects along the temporal axis, and not for specifying browsing operations. Unlike SMIL, which uses time as parameter to control objects, ZDL uses the zoom rate. This makes SMIL and ZDL independent of each other, making their combination possible.

6 Conclusion and Future Work

We propose a Zooming Cross-Media concept that includes: (A) a zooming method that makes it possible to control both the *LOD of the displayed information*, and the *transition between the different media* being displayed; and (B) the Zooming Description Language (ZDL), which enables precise and flexible specification of the zooming behavior. With the objective to make Web browsing more effective, our intention is to introduce zooming as a third interface modality – in addition to scrolling and anchor clicking – for browsing the Web contents.

In the future, we plan to evaluate and verify efficiency of the proposed method and the description language by developing an editor and a viewer for zoomable contents and implementing a client-server environment for them.

References

1. K. Perlin and D. Fox: Pad: an alternative approach to the computer interface. *Proceedings of the 20th annual conference on Computer graphics and interactive techniques (SIGGRAPH'93)*, pp.57-64, 1993.
2. B. B. Bederson and J. D. Hollan: Pad++: A Zooming Graphical Interface for Exploring Alternate Interface Physics. *Proceedings of UIST'94*, pp. 17-26, 1994.
3. B. B. Bederson, J. Meyer and L. Good: Jazz: An Extensible Zoomable User Interface Graphics Toolkit in Java. *Proceedings of UIST'00*, pp. 171-180, 2000.
4. M. Sarkar, S. Snibbe, O. Tversky, and S. Reiss: Stretching the Rubber Sheet: a Metaphor for Viewing Large Layouts on Small Screens. *Proceedings of UIST'93*, pp. 81-91, 1993.
5. M. Toyoda and E. Shibayama: Hyper Mochi Sheet: A Predictive Focusing Interface for Navigating and Editing Nested Networks through a Multi-focus Distortion-Oriented View. *Proceedings of CHI'99*, pp. 504-511, 1999.

6. K. Sumiya, M. Munisamy, and K. Tanaka: TV2Web: Generating and Browsing Web with Multiple LOD from Video Streams and their Metadata. *ICKS2004 Proc.*, pp. 158-167, Mar. 2004.
7. H. Miyamori and K. Tanaka: Webified Video: Media Conversion from TV programs to Web content for Cross-media Information Integration. *DEXA2005*, Aug. 2005 (to appear).
8. T. Araki, H. Miyamori, A Kato, Y. Ogawa, A. Iizawa, and K. Tanaka: A Viewing Method for Multimedia Contents Using Zooming Metaphor. *Forum on Information Technology 2004*, D-007, Sep. 2004.

A Histogram-Based Selectivity Estimator for Skewed XML Data

Hanyu Li, Mong Li Lee, and Wynne Hsu

School of Computing, National University of Singapore,
3 Science Drive 2, Singapore 117543
{lihanyu, leeml, whsu}@comp.nus.edu.sg

Abstract. The optimization of XML queries requires an accurate and compact structure to capture the characteristics of the underlying data. A compact structure works well when the data is uniformly distributed and has many common paths. However, more detailed information needs to be maintained when the data is skewed. This work presents a histogram-based structure to capture the distribution of skewed XML data. It builds upon a statistical method to estimate the result size of XML queries. Experiment results indicate that the proposed method leads to a more accurate estimation.

1 Introduction

The growth of XML repositories on the World Wide Web has lead to much research on the storage, indexing and querying of XML data. High-level languages such as XPath and XQuery have been designed for users to formulate declarative queries over the data. Optimizing these queries requires data structures that facilitate accurate selectivity estimation [3,6,7,8,9].

Markov-based models [3,6] estimate linear path queries by using a Markov table to organize information on path frequencies. [9] designs a *position histogram* to capture the distribution of elements, and proposes a position histogram join to estimate the size of queries. [7,8] propose the *XSketch* framework that utilizes summarized graph structures to estimate linear and twig queries with value predicates. All these techniques utilize node or parent-child path frequencies to determine the result size of linear or twig queries.

[4] develops a statistical approach to estimate complex XML queries. The approach extracts highly summarized information, namely, *node ratio* and *node factor* from every distinct parent-child basic path. During the evaluation of an XML query, the statistical information is recursively aggregated to estimate the frequency of the target node. This approach requires a small memory footprint, and gives good accuracy when the underlying data is uniformly distributed.

In this work, we augment the statistical model with histograms to reduce estimation errors that occur when the data is skewed. We construct histograms for selected parent-child paths to capture the characteristics of underlying data distribution. The histograms are based on the interval-based numbering scheme that is widely used for structural joins. Experiment results demonstrate the effectiveness of this approach.

The rest of this paper is organized as follows. Section 2 gives the background knowledge. Section 3 describes the proposed histogram structure and its construction. Section 4 presents the experimental results, and we conclude in Section 5.

2 Preliminaries

[4] introduces a compact statistical XML query size estimator. The idea is that we capture the node ratio NR and the node factor NF of all the basic parent-child paths in the XML documents. An XML query is decomposed into a set of parent-child paths, and the NR and NF of these basic paths are aggregated to estimate the query selectivity.

The variable node ratio NR indicates the ratio of the occurrence of the root node in a path to the total occurrence of this node in an XML dataset. The node factor NF indicates the average number of nodes T for a given root node in a path. Formally, if P is a path and R is the root of the path, then the node ratio NR of R in P is given by

$$NR(R|P) = f(R|P)/f(R)$$

where $f(R)$ is the frequency of the node R in the dataset and $f(R|P)$ as the frequency of R with respect to the path P in the dataset. Further, if T is a target node in P, then the node factor NF of T in P is

$$NF(T|P) = f(T|P)/f(R|P)$$

Given the NF and NR of a path query P, we use the following equation to estimate the target node in an XML query.

$$f(R|P) = f(R) * NR(R|P)$$
$$f(T|P) = f(R) * NR(R|P) * NF(T|P)$$

Figure 1 shows an XML instances and the statistics maintained. The frequency of every distinct name node, the node ratio NR and node factor NF for every distinct basic parent-child path, are captured. For example, we have $f(B) = 4$ and $f(B|`A/B/C`) = 2$. Note that for parent-child paths, the root node R and the target node T are the parent and child nodes in the path respectively. Also, $NR \leq 1$ and $NF \geq 1$.

The key to this estimation method is the computation of NR' and NF' of a given query path from all basic parent-child paths. We use the symbol " ' " to distinguish the estimated result from the actual value. [4] develops two ways to aggregate these variables: serialization and parallelization, which we will illustrate with an example here. The formal definitions of these methods are given in APPENDIX.

Consider Figure 1 again. Suppose we want to retrieve all the nodes B which are parents of either C or D. If we assume that the data independence assumption holds, then we have $NR'(`B/C`\cup`B/D`) = NR(`B/C`) + NR(`B/D`) - NR(`B/C`) * NR(`B/D`) = 0.5 + 0.5 - 0.5 * 0.5 = 0.75$, where $`B/C`\cup`B/D`$ denotes the twig query. Thus, the selectivity of B is estimated to be $f(B) * NR' = 3$.

3 Histogram-Based Estimator

The compact statistical approach works well when the data is uniformly distributed. However, skewness in the data will reduce the accuracy of the estimation. For example, in Figure 1, the child nodes C and D are not uniformly distributed under all the B nodes. This skewness could be due to the correlation between C and D, that is, C and D tend to occur together under a same 'B' node. A query ('B/C'∪'B/D') will have an estimated frequency of 3 in this skewed XML instance. This relative error rate of 50% (the selectivity is 2) would be unacceptably high in larger datasets.

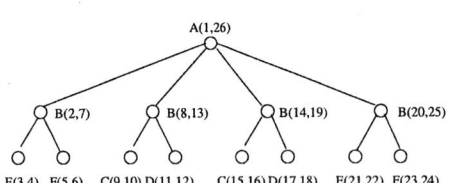

Node	Frequency
A	1
B	4
C	2
D	2
E	2
F	2

Parent–Child Paths	NR	NF
A/B	1	4
B/C	0.5	1
B/D	0.5	1
B/E	0.5	1
B/F	0.5	1

Fig. 1. Example of A Skewed XML Instance

In order to increase the accuracy of the selectivity estimation for skewed data, we design a histogram structure to capture the NR and NF of the basic parent-child paths.

3.1 Histogram Structure

The proposed histogram structure is based on the interval numbering scheme [5]. This scheme facilitates the quick determination of the ancestor-descendant relationship between any two nodes in an XML document. Figure 1 shows the intervals assigned to the nodes in the XML tree. The interval of a descendant node in the tree will be contained in the intervals of its ancestor nodes.

We construct a set of buckets, or a *bucket set*, on selected parent-child basic paths to capture the underlying skewed data. The histogram puts "similar" data into the same bucket to reduce the estimation error. A bucket stores the corresponding intra-bucket root node frequency, NR and NF values. Figure 2 shows the buckets that are built on the basic paths 'B/C', 'B/D' and 'B/E' for Figure 1.

In order to decide whether a histogram should be constructed on a basic parent-child path P, we design an algorithm to detect the distribution of NRs and NFs of P based on the interval ranges where P occurs (see Algorithm 1). For example, Figure 2 shows the distribution of NRs and NFs of path "B/E" on the range (2,25).

We introduce two parameters to guide the construction of buckets: *unit factor* (UF) and *variance factor* (VF). Unit factor UF controls the granularity of the buckets. Let the interval range of a path P be $(P(s), P(e))$. Then the granularity of the bucket range is defined as $(P(e) - P(s))/UF$, and the range of every bucket built on path P must be a multiple of this granularity.

The variance factor VF indicates the difference of $NR(NF)$ between a bucket and the overall data. That is, if $NR(NF)$ in a range is greater than $avg(NR) * VF$

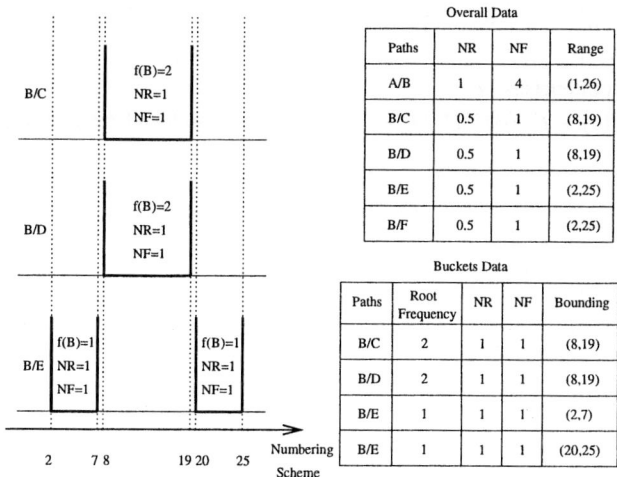

Fig. 2. Histograms of Paths

($avg(NF) * VF$) or less than $avg(NR)/VF$ ($avg(NF)/VF$), we consider the data in this range as being significantly different from the average value, and will trigger the construction of a bucket to cover this range.

Algorithm 1 constructs the histogram on a path P by scanning the all the interval information of the instances of P. The variables *unit_status* and *bucket_status* are represented by a 4-bit integer. Each bit indicates a status: high NR, high NF, low NR, low NF. In the procedure of scanning, if the status of a unit range is greater than 1, then this indicates that the data distribution in this unit is significantly different from the average value. If the data distribution in the next unit also differs significantly from the average value, then we check whether these two units have the same features, that is, both have high (low) NR or NF. This test can be carried out quickly by a bit AND operation. If the two units have common characteristics, then we can merge them into one bucket, and use the intersection of their status as the final bucket status. Otherwise, we simply output the first unit as a bucket and continue to process the next unit until we finish scanning the entire range of the path.

Note that the variables VF and UF actually control the bucket's depth and width respectively. Both of them have a direct influence on the memory usage, that is, when UF increases or VF decreases, more buckets will be constructed in memory.

3.2 Estimating XML Queries

[4] describes methods to aggregate the NR and NF of paths. However, if the paths are associated with histograms, which are sets of intra-bucket NR and NF values, then we need to generate a new set of bucket structure which is "compatible" to the histograms of the paths. Next, the histogram of each path is transformed to the structure of this "compatible" bucket set, and their intra-bucket NR and NF values can now be aggregated.

Algorithm 1 Tune Buckets in Histogram

Input: path P, VF, UF
Output: a set of buckets
1: $unit = (P(e) - P(s))/UF$ /*$P(s), P(e)$ denote the start and end points of P*/
2: $B(s) = P(s)$
3: $B(e) = P(s)$ /*$B(s), B(e)$ denote the start and end point of a bucket*/
4: $bucket\_status = 15$ (binary number '1111')
5: **while** $B(e) < P(e)$ **do**
6:     $unit\_status = getUnitStatus()$
7:     **if** $unit\_status > 0$ **then**
8:         **if** $unit\_status \cap bucket\_status > 0$ **then**
9:             $B(e) = B(e) + unit$
10:            $bucket\_status = unit\_status \cap bucket\_status$
11:         **else**
12:            output bucket $(B(s), B(e))$
13:            $B(s) = B(e) + 1, B(e) = B(e) + unit$
14:            $bucket\_status = unit\_status$
15:     **else**
16:         output bucket$(B(s), B(e))$
17:         $B(s) = B(e) + unit + 1, B(e) = B(e) + unit + 1$
18:         $bucket\_status = 15$

Compatible Bucket Set: Given a bucket set A built on a basic parent-child path P_A, a bucket set B is *compatible* with A if all the following conditions hold

1. Range covered by adjacent buckets in B must be consecutive;
2. Every bucket in B must either be totally contained in some bucket in A or totally outside the buckets of A;
3. Entire range covered by B contains the entire range of P_A.

Consider Figure 3(a) where a bucket set built on path P_2 is compatible with that built on path P_1. However, the bucket sets built on paths P_3 is not compatible with that built on P_1. Figure 3(b) shows two paths P_1, P_2 and a bucket set structure P_c that is compatible to both P_1 and P_2. Note that P_c has the minimum number of buckets and minimum total interval range.

Let us now examine how a bucket set can be converted into a compatible bucket set. Suppose the bucket set $B\{b_1, b_2, ...b_n\}$ has been built on some path P where R is the root node of P, and let $b_i(rf)$, $b_i(s)$ and $b_i(e)$ indicate the root frequency, start edge and end edge of bucket b_i respectively, while $P(s)$ and $P(e)$ denote the minimal and maximal value in the range covered by P. When bucket set B is converted to its compatible bucket set C, we compute the NR', NF' and root node frequency inside every bucket c_j. For each c_j, we check whether it is contained in some b_i. If it is, based on the assumption of uniform distribution of the intra-bucket data, we have NR' and NF' of c_j equal to that of b_i, and the $c_j(rf)$ is $b_i(rf) * (c_j(e) - c_j(s))/(b_i(e) - b_i(s))$. If c_j is not contained in any b_i, but is contained in the interval $(P(s), P(e))$, we assume that the data outside the buckets is uniformly distributed. Thus we have the following formulas to compute NR', NF' and root node frequency of c_j.

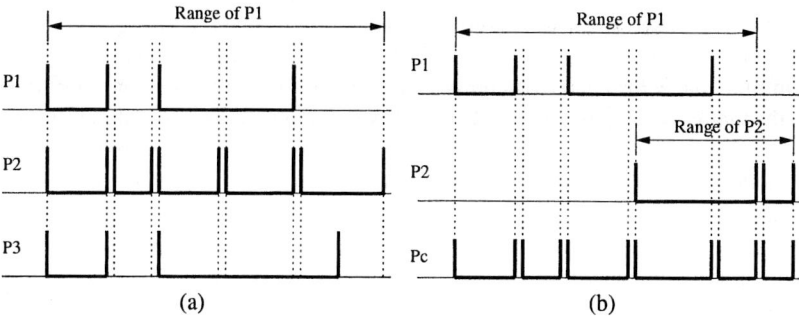

Fig. 3. Compatible Bucket Sets

$$c_j(rf) = \frac{[f(R) - \sum_{i=1}^{n} b_i(rf)] * [c_j(e) - c_j(s)]}{P(e) - P(s) - \sum_{i=1}^{n} [b_i(e) - b_i(s)]}$$

$$c_j(NR') = \frac{f(R) * NR - \sum_{i=1}^{n} b_i(rf) * b_i(NR)}{f(R) - \sum_{i=1}^{n} b_i(rf)}$$

$$c_j(NF') = \frac{f(R) * NR * NF - \sum_{i=1}^{n} b_i(rf) * b_i(NR) * b_i(NF)}{f(R) * NR - \sum_{i=1}^{n} b_i(rf) * b_i(NR)}$$

If c_j falls outside the range $(P(s), P(e))$, then we set the root frequency, NR and NF to be 0.

Algorithm 2 Estimate Query Result Size

Input: query Q, target node T;   **Output**: frequency count $f'(T|Q)$

1. Decompose Q into a set of parent-child paths, and retrieve their corresponding histogram data.
2. Aggregate the NR and NF values.

    (a) Traverse Q in bottom-up manner.
    (b) Convert the bucket set of current parent-child path into a new bucket that is compatible with the previous one.
    (c) Combine the NR and NF values of the current path with the NR and NF of the paths that have been processed

3. Calculate $f'(T|Q)$ in every bucket, output the summary.

Algorithm 2 shows the estimation algorithm. We first decompose a query Q into a set of parent-child paths and retrieve their corresponding histogram data. Next, we aggregate these NR and NF values. In this step, we traverse the Q in a bottom-up manner until the root node is reached. When a new parent-child path is encountered, we combine the NR and NF values of the new path with the NR and NF values of the paths that have been processed. Note that we only need the NR value if the subtree rooted at R (R is the parent node of current parent-child path) does not contain the target node T. Finally, we calculate the $f'(T|P)$ of every intra-bucket and output the summary.

Consider the twig query $Q = \text{'}//A/B[/C/E]/D\text{'}$, where C is the target node. We first decompose the query into a set of basic queries 'A/B', 'B/C', 'B/D' and 'C/E'. When aggregating the NR and NF values, we combine the paths 'C/E' and 'B/C' first, before aggregating the histogram data of '$B/C/E$' with that of 'B/D'. This procedure is repeated until we obtain $NR'(A|Q)$ and $NF'(C|Q)$ of every bucket. Finally, we summarize the estimated frequencies of C in all buckets and output the result.

4 Performance Study

We implement the proposed histogram solution in Java and carry out experiments to evaluate its effectiveness. The experiments are executed on a Pentium IV 1.6 GHz PC with 512 MB RAM running on Windows XP. We use both real world dataset (DBLP [1]) and synthetic dataset (XMark [2]). Table 1 gives the characteristics of datasets. Note that we generate five XMark files with different sizes.

Table 1. Characteristics of Datasets

Dataset	Size (MB)	#(Distinct Nodes)	#(Distinct Paths)
DBLP	22	26	35
XMark	20, 40, 60, 80, 100	83	114

4.1 Sensitivity Experiments

This set of experiments investigates the accuracy of the proposed histogram solution. We generate 50 positive queries on both DBLP and XMark datasets. These positive queries comprise of parent-child linear queries, ancestor-descendant linear queries, parent-child twigs and ancestor-descendant twigs. Each query involves 3 to 5 nodes.

Figure 4 shows the memory usage and accuracy for positive queries under varying UF and VF values. The same UF and VF values, e.g. 100 and 3 respectively, are used to scan every distinct path data, and buckets are constructed when data skewness is detected. Since the XMark datasets with different sizes give the similar curves, we only show the graph for X20 (file size is 20M).

As expected, the memory usage of our histogram structure grows as UF increases (Figures 4(a) and (c)) for both datasets, and there is a corresponding reduction in the relative error (Figures 4(b) and (d))). This is because the value of UF determines the unit width of the buckets. The larger the UF value (the smaller unit width) is, the larger the number of buckets is possibly obtained, thus leading to a more accurate estimation result. On the other hand, the VF parameter determines the "distance" between the

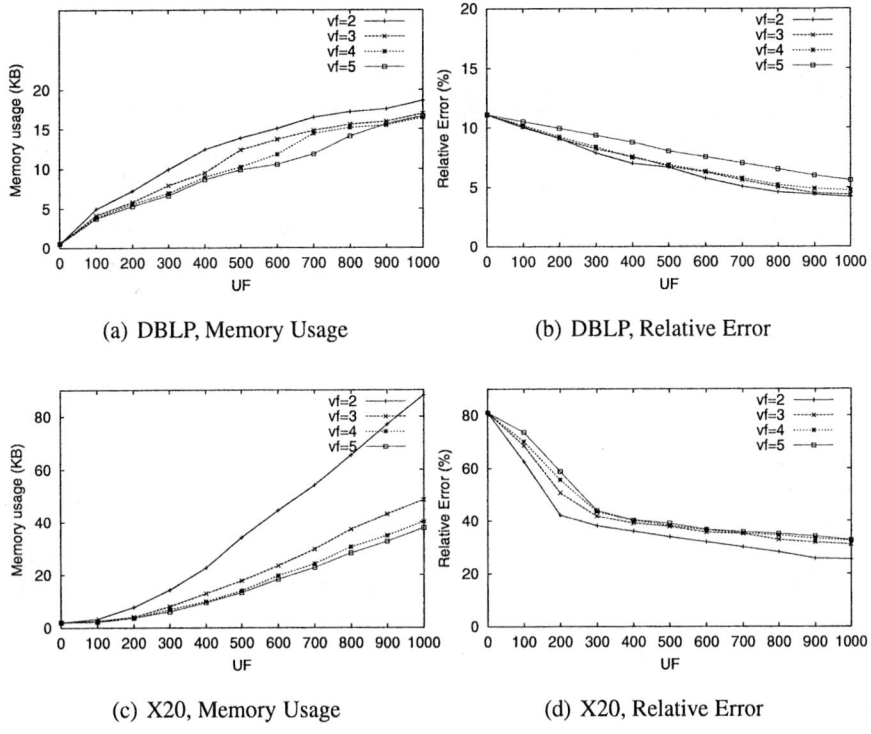

Fig. 4. Sensitivity Experiments (Positive Queries)

skewed data and overall data. That is, the lower the the value of VF is, the more data would be detected as "skewness" in the XML files. We observe that the UF value has a greater influence on the memory requirements compared to the VF value. This implies in this histogram structure, bucket width is the major factor to affect memory space consumption.

It can also be observed that our proposed technique utilizes a smaller amount of memory for DBLP dataset compared to that required by the XMark under the same UF and VF values. This is largely because of the relatively regular structure of the real-world dataset. This regular data distribution in the DBLP dataset also leads to a lower error rate (Figure 4(b) and (d)).

4.2 Comparative Experiments

We implement XSketch [7] using the f-stabilize method, and evaluate its accuracy with the proposed histogram method. 50 positive queries are generated for each XMark dataset using the template described in [7], i.e., queries with linear branches, and the target node is some leaf node. Only the parent-child relationship is used here. The length of the query path ranges from 3 to 12 nodes. Since the size of overall estimation information of our approach is much smaller than that of XSketch, we build histograms by

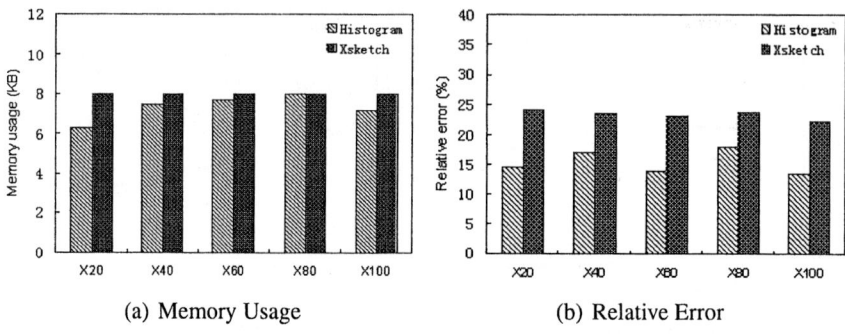

(a) Memory Usage (b) Relative Error

Fig. 5. Comparative Experiments

giving the same weight to all the distinct paths while the values of UF and VF used are 300 and 3 respectively.

Both our proposed method and XSketch have an accurate estimation result for real-world datasets, thus we only present the comparative experiments of synthetic datasets here. Figure 5 shows the memory usage and relative error of the two techniques for XMark datasets. We observe that, given approximately the same memory usage, the proposed estimation system has a smaller relative error compared to XSketch for XMark datasets. The XMark dataset is skewed and contains more irregularity in its structure. XSketch explicitly stores the graph structure of the XML data, and requires more memory space when the underlying data is irregular. In contrast, the proposed method captures two variables of basic parent-child paths, which are independent of the structural complexity of the XML graph. This leaves us additional memory space to build histograms to capture the data distribution, leading to greater accuracy. Note that the proposed histogram solution has a more accurate estimation result in this part compared with the result shown in Section 4.1, since only parent-child edges are used in the queries.

5 Conclusion

In this paper, we have presented a histogram-based XML query size estimator. This work extends our earlier statistical estimation approach to handle skewed data. We design an interval-based histogram to capture the data distribution. Experiments indicate that the proposed method is able to increase the estimation accuracy with minimal memory requirement.

References

1. http://www.informatik.uni-trier.de/~ley/db/.
2. http://monetdb.cwi.nl/.
3. A. Aboulnaga, A. R. Alameldeen, and J. F. Naughton. Estimating the Selectivity of XML Path Expressions for Internet Scale Applications. In *Proceedings of VLDB, Roma, Italy*, 2001.

4. M. Lee, H. Li, W. Hsu, and B. C. Ooi. A Statistical Approach for XML Query Size Estimation. In *EDBT workshop, dataX*, 2004.
5. Q. Li and B. Moon. Indexing and Querying XML Data for Regular Path Expressions. In *Proceedings of VLDB, Roma, Italy*, 2001.
6. L. Lim, M. Wang, S. Padmanabhan, J. S. Vitter, and R. Parr. XPathLearner: An On-Line Self-Tuning Markov Histogram for XML Path Selectivity Estimation. In *Proceedings of VLDB, Hong Kong, China*, 2002.
7. N. Polyzotis and M. Garofalakis. Statistical Synopses for Graph-Structured XML Database. In *Proceedings of the ACM SIGMOD, Madison, Wisconsin, USA*, 2002.
8. N. Polyzotis, M. Garofalakis, and Y. Ioannidis. Selectivity Estimation for XML Twigs. In *Proceedings of ICDE, Boston, Massachusetts, USA*, 2004.
9. Y. Wu, J. M. Patel, and H.V. Jagadish. Estimating Answer Sizes for XML Queries. In *Proceedings of EDBT, Prague, Czech Republic*, 2002.

Appendix

Serialized Linear Paths. Suppose we have two linear paths l_1, l_2 and their corresponding $NR(R_1|l_1)$, $NF(T_1|l_1)$, $NR(R_2|l_2)$ and $NF(T_2|l_2)$, where R_i and T_i are the first and last nodes in path l_i. If the target node T_1 has the same label as that of the node R_2, then we can connect these two paths l_1 and l_2 sequentially and remove R_2. The result is also a linear path, denoted as $l_1 \cdot l_2$. For example, if $l_1 = $ 'A/B', $l_2 = $ 'B/C', then $l_1 \cdot l_2 = $ '$A/B/C$'.

Given two paths l_1 and l_2 where $T_1 = R_2$, the following formula computes the NR and NF of the serialized path.

$$\begin{aligned}&NF'(T_1|l_1 \cdot l_2) = NF(T_1|l_1) * NR(T_1|l_2)\\&if\ (NF'(T_1|l_1 \cdot l_2) \geq 1)\\&\quad NR'(R_1|l_1 \cdot l_2) = NR'(R_1|l_1)\\&\quad NF'(T_2|l_1 \cdot l_2) = NF'(T_1|l_1 \cdot l_2) * NF(T_2|l_2)\\&else\\&\quad NR'(R_1|l_1 \cdot l_2) = NR'(R_1|l_1) * NF'(T_1|l_1 \cdot l_2)\\&\quad NF'(T_2|l_1 \cdot l_2) = NF(T_2|l_2)\end{aligned} \quad (1)$$

Parallelized Linear Paths. Given a set of linear paths $l_i, (1 \leq i \leq n)$ and the corresponding $NR(R_i|l_i)$, where R_i is the first node in path l_i, if $R_i = R_j (i \neq j; 1 \leq (i,j) \leq n)$, we can combine all the l_i into a twig where R is the root node and every l_i is a branch.

There are two possible relationships among the branches in the resulting path: intersection and union. In the case of intersection, we need to estimate the size of R that occurs in all of l_i. Otherwise, the path condition is satisfied if R is the root node of any one of the l_i. We denote the intersection and union associations in the paths as $l_1 \cap l_2 \ldots \cap l_n$ and $l_1 \cup l_2 \ldots \cup l_n$ respectively.

If P is given by $l_1 \cap l_2 \ldots \cap l_n$, then $NR'(R|P)$ is computed from the intersection of all l_i:

$$NR'(R|P) = \prod_{i=1}^{n} NR(R|l_i) \quad (2)$$

On the other hand, if P is given by $l_1 \cup l_2 \ldots \cup l_n$, based on set theory, we have

$$\begin{aligned}&NR'(R|P) = \sum_{i=1}^{n} NR(R|l_i) - \sum NR(R|l_{i_1})NR(R|l_{i_2}) + \ldots + \\&(-1)^{(k-1)} \sum NR(R|l_{i_1})NR(R|l_{i_2}) \ldots NR(R|l_{i_k})\\&(1 \leq (i_1, i_2 \ldots i_k) \leq n; i_a \neq i_b\ where\ a \neq b)\end{aligned} \quad (3)$$

Accelerating XML Structural Join by Partitioning

Nan Tang[†], Jeffrey Xu Yu[†], Kam-Fai Wong[†], Kevin Lü[‡], and Jianxin Li[§]

[†] Department of Systems Engineering & Engineering Management,
The Chinese University of Hong Kong, Hong Kong, China
[‡] Brunel University, London, UK
[§] College of Information Science and Engineering, Northeastern University, China
{ntang, yu, kfwong}@se.cuhk.edu.hk, kevin.lu@brunel.ac.uk

Abstract. Structural join is the core part of XML queries and has a significant impact on the performance of XML queries, several classical structural join algorithms have been proposed such as *Stack-tree* join and *XR-Tree* join. In this paper, we consider to answer the problem of structural join by partitioning. We first extend the relationships between nodes to the relationships between partitions in the plane and get some observations. We then propose a new partition-based method *P-Join* for structural join. Based on *P-Join*, moreover, we present an enhanced partitioned-based spatial structural join algorithm PSSJ.

1 Introduction

Structural join can be regarded as the core part of XML queries. A series of structural join algorithms were proposed in the literature. [10] proposed a merge-based join algorithm called *multi-predicate merge join*(MPMGJN). [6] proposed another merge-based join algorithm $\mathcal{EE}/\mathcal{EA}$. [1] proposed *Stack-Tree-Desc/Anc* algorithm which uses stack mechanism to efficiently improve the merge-based structural join algorithm. Then [2] utilized the B^+-*Tree* index on the *Stack-tree* algorithm to overleap the descendant nodes which do not participate in the join. [5] proposed *XR-Tree*, namely, XML Region Tree, to skip both ancestors and descendants nodes that do not participate in the join. In paper [7], an extent-based join algorithm was proposed to evaluate path expressions containing parent-children and ancestor-descendant operations. In order to further improve the query performance, two novel query optimization techniques, path-shortening and path-complementing were proposed in paper [9]. Path-shortening reduces the number of joins by shortening the path while path-complementing optimizes the path execution by using an equivalent complementary path expression to compute the original one.

Many numbering schemes have been utilized in previous algorithms because with them we could quickly determine the positional relationships between tree nodes. Previous strategies mainly focus to the relationship in 1-dimensional space while ignoring the relationships between partitions or subspaces in 2-dimensional space. Grust [4] answered the XPath queries in 2-dimensional space using Dietz numbering scheme. Distinct from structural join, however, [4] only aim at the set operation while structural join gives all the combination of ancestors and descendants, which is obvious more complex and practical.

The major contributions of this paper are summarized as follows:

- We extend the relationships between nodes to the relationships between partitions in a 2- dimensional space and get 9 observations.
- We present a partition-based structural join method, namely, *P-Join*. [2,5] skip ancestors and descendants nodes based on *Stack-tree* join algorithm. With *P-Join*, however, after filtering operation, the ancestor and descendant nodes are further classified into different areas using positional relationships on plane. Then some portions could directly output join results without actual join operation, other portions could also quickly produce join results utilizing spatial characters.
- We present an enhanced partition-based spatial structural join algorithm PSSJ based on *P-Join*.

The rest of this paper is organized as follows. In Section 2 we introduce the numbering scheme chosen and some concepts about partition relationships. Next, in Section 3 we present a partition-based structural join method *P-Join*. Section 4 presents an enhanced partition-based spatial structural join algorithm. Section 5 gives the performance evaluation. Finally Section 6 concludes this paper.

2 Numbering Scheme and Partition Relationships

There are many proposed numbering schemes to determine the positional relationships between any pair of tree nodes [3, 6, 1, 4]. In this paper, we use the Dietz numbering scheme [3] which uses *preorder* and *postorder* values, as a pair, to encode each tree node. Dietz numbering scheme expresses the positional relationship as follows: (i) For a node e_j and its ancestor e_i, $\text{PRE}(e_i) < \text{PRE}(e_j)$ and $\text{POST}(e_i) > \text{POST}(e_j)$. (ii) For two sibling nodes e_i and e_j, if e_i is the predecessor of e_j in preorder traversal, then $\text{PRE}(e_i) < \text{PRE}(e_j)$ and $\text{POST}(e_i) < \text{POST}(e_j)$. $\text{PRE}(e)$ and $\text{POST}(e)$ represent the *preorder* and *postorder* of e, respectively.

The tree nodes relationship can be clearly expressed on a space shown in Figure 1. Consider the node p in Figure 1. Any node e on the top left of p is the ancestor of p because $\text{PRE}(e) < \text{PRE}(p)$ and $\text{POST}(e) > \text{POST}(p)$; likewise, the

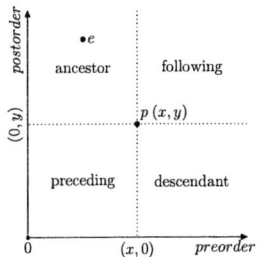
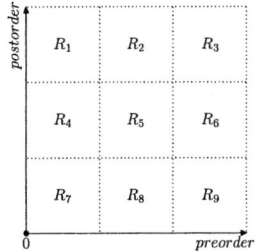

Fig. 1. Project Tree Nodes   **Fig. 2.** Partitions

node on the bottom right is the descendant of p; the node on the bottom left is the preceding node of p; the node on the top right is the following node of p.

The main reason of using the Dietz numbering scheme is simply explained below, in comparison with the region code, which uses a *start/end* position of an element to code its position [1]. nodes with the Dietz numbering scheme are distributed dispersedly, whereas the nodes with the region code are rather skewed and only in the upper triangle of a subspace. This dispersed distribution character of Dietz numbering scheme is more appropriate for our spatial-partitioning technique introduced in section 4, thus we choose Dietz numbering scheme. However, our algorithm could also work on region code.

In this paper, we extend the relationships between nodes as shown in Figure 1 to the relationships between partitions. As shown in Figure 2, the whole plane is partitioned into 9 disjoint rectangle partitions, $R_1, R_2, \cdots, R_9$. Here each R_i contains a subset of XML elements (or nodes in an XML tree). Consider the partition R_5 in the center of Figure 2. We made the following observations:

1. All nodes in R_1 are the ancestors of all nodes in R_5.
2. All nodes in R_3 are the "following" nodes of all nodes in R_5.
3. All nodes in R_7 are the "preceding" nodes of all nodes in R_5.
4. All nodes in R_9 are descendants of all nodes in R_5.
5. Some nodes in R_2 are ancestors or "following" nodes of some nodes in R_5.
6. Some nodes in R_4 are ancestors or "preceding" nodes of some nodes in R_5.
7. Some nodes in R_6 are descendants or "following" nodes of some nodes in R_5.
8. Some nodes in R_8 are descendants or "preceding" of some nodes in R_5.
9. Some nodes in R_5 may have any positional relationships with nodes in R_5.

The observation made above shows that we can process structural join using a partition-based approach. When users query the ancestors of nodes in R_5, i) we do not need to do structural join between R_5 and any of R_3, R_6, R_7, R_8 and R_9, because none of these partitions includes ancestors of any nodes in R_5; ii) we do not need to do structural join between R_1 and R_5, because all nodes in R_1 are the ancestors of all nodes in R_5; and iii) we only need to do structural join between R_2, R_4, R_5 and R_5 because some of nodes in R_2, R_4 and R_5 are the ancestors of some nodes in R_5. The similar techniques can be applied when users query the descendant or other XPath axes in the partition of R_5.

3 A New Partition-Based Structural Join Method

In this section, we propose a new partition-based method for structural join between ancestors and descendants. Our method can be easily extended to support other XPath axes including following, preceding, sibling, etc.

First, we show several cases in Figure 3, and then we outline our partition-based structural join method. Figure 3 (a) shows a general case where a 2-dimensional space is partitioned into 4 partitions, A_1, A_2, A_3 and A_4 according to D. Here, D is a minimum partition (rectangle) that contains all descendants. Note that D is always located the same as A_4 for any structural join based on ancestor/descendant relationships.

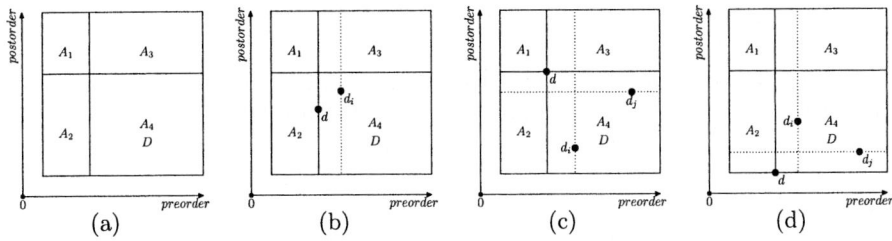

Fig. 3. Several Cases

One technique we use in our partition-based join is to dynamically adjust the partitions of A_1, A_2, A_3 and $A_4 (= D)$ when we attempt to find ancestors for every $d \in D$. In other words, the four partitions are conceptually redrawn for any $d \in D$. Two ascending B^+-Tree indices on the *preorder* and *postorder* value are created for A, respectively, to guarantee the efficent search operation. We only need to scan every $d \in D$ once. The details are given below. Assume that elements in partitions are sorted by their *preorder* values in ascending order. The adjustment of partitions has the following three cases for a node $d \in D$ with minimum *preorder* value. i) d is in the middle of the boundary between A_2 and D (Figure 3 (b)). ii) d is at the top of the boundary of A_2 and D (Figure 3 (c)). iii) d is at the bottom of the boundary between A_2 and D (Figure 3 (d)).

For the first case, we output d with all a in A_1, then traverse each a_i in A_2 in the reverse order and compare it with d, if a_i is not the ancestor of d, then all elements d_i after d cannot be the descendant of a_i, we do not need to join this a_i with any such $d_i \in D$. Otherwise, if a_i is an ancestor of d, all a_j before a_i are ancestors of d. Suppose, after processing d, we need to process the next descendant d_i in the sorted list (Figure 3 (b)). Because d is on the boundary between A_2 and D, the boundary between A_3 and $d_i \in D$ will remain unchanged. We can find those elements $a \in A_3$ such as $\text{PRE}(a) < \text{PRE}(d_i)$. Note when processing $d_i \in D$ in Figure 3 (b), those nodes a in A_4 such as $\text{PRE}(a) < \text{PRE}(d_i)$ are adjusted to A_2. It is important to note that the area of A_1 and A_2 are expanded while the area of A_3 and A_4 are shrunk. This adjustment process is shown in Figure 3 (b).

The second case is simple, because only all nodes in A_1 are the ancestors of d. All nodes in A_2 are the preceding nodes of d, all nodes in A_3 are the following nodes of d, and all nodes in A_4 are the descendants of d. We can simply output d with every $a \in A_1$ as join results. After processing d, we need to adjust the boundaries of D, when we process the next descendant d_i which has the smallest *preorder* value. In the first step, we identify a node $d_j \in D$ with the largest *postorder* value from the unprocessed descendants. In the second step, we adjust the following nodes a to the A_1: 1) $a \in A_2$ if $\text{PRE}(a) > \text{POST}(d_j)$, 2) $a \in A_4$ if $\text{PRE}(a) > \text{POST}(d_j)$, 3) $a \in A_3$ if $\text{PRE}(a) < \text{PRE}(d_i)$, and 4) $a \in A_4$ if $\text{PRE}(a) < \text{PRE}(d_i)$.

And in the third step of above case, we adjust those nodes $a \in A_4$ satisfying $\text{POST}(a) > post(d_j)$ to A_3; and $a \in A_4$ satisfying $post(a) < post(d_j) \& pre(a) < pre(d_i)$ to A_2. This adjustment process is shown in Figure 3 (c).

For the third case, all nodes in A_1 and A_2 are ancestors of d, and no nodes in A_3 and A_4 are ancestors of d. After processing d, we get the next element $d_i \in D$ following the sorted order. We can determine a node d_j which has the minimum *postorder* value from the remaining elements. Because d is at the bottom of the boundary between A_2 and D, the boundaries need to be adjusted. Here, we first remove those the elements a in A_2 and A_4 satisfying $\text{POST}(a) < \text{POST}(d_j)$, because these nodes a will not be ancestors of any descendants $d \in D$. Second, we adjust those elements $a \in A_3$ satisfying $\text{PRE}(a) < \text{PRE}(d_i)$ to A_1. Third, we adjust those elements $a \in A_4$ satisfying $\text{PRE}(a) < \text{PRE}(d_i)$ to A_2. This adjustment process is shown in Figure 3 (d). Above method is our partition-based structural join method, P-JOIN.

The main advantage of method *P-Join* is that it does not necessarily join every ancestors and descendants using a dynamic boundary adjustment technique. In fact, as a pre-processing technique, we can filter those nodes that cannot be matched before calling *P-Join*. Filter operation is extensively used in database system to save I/O cost, consequently improve the system performance. Traditional bit filter techniques in relational database utilize the equal relationship between attributes of two relations for filtering. For semistructured data like XML, however, bit filter techniques cannot be applied well, thus we filter nodes with their spatial positional characters.

Now we explain the filtering operation. First, we use the minimum rectangle containing all descendants d to filter A, all ancestors a in the area that cannot be the ancestor of any d are filtered. And then we use the minimum rectangle containing the remaining A to filter D, all nodes d in the area that will not be a descendant of any a will be filtered. It is easy to see that the filtering order of A and D is arbitrary and the results are the same. Moreover, one mutually filtering of A and D is enough and there is no need to recursively filter.

4 An Enhanced Partition-Based Spatial Structural Join Algorithm

In this section, we further investigate on how to partition A and D when querying the ancestor-descendant relationship $a/\!/d$. We will present a spatial partitioning approach. On top of the spatial partitioning approach, an enhanced partition-based spatial structural join algorithms is proposed.

4.1 Spatial-Partitioning

Partitioning A and D for minimization of structural join is challenging, and is itself complex and time consuming. To find an efficient partitioning method, we are now left with the challenge to find a method which considers the spatial characters of A or D first, and then partition the left D or A for structural join.

When the size of D is large, the nested level is high and the distribution is bad-proportioned, the partitioning methods that mainly consider D will get good performance. On the contrary, the methods which pay attention to A will be better. The partitioning order of A or D is symmetrical. In this section, we mainly discuss the partitioning method for D, the method for A can be applied in a similar manner.

Logically, an element node should be potentially distributed in any area of the 2-dimensional space. In practice, nevertheless, for a general XML data tree, element nodes are concentratively distributed near the area from the bottom left to top right of the 2-dimensional space. The root node will exist on the top left. Only when the whole XML data tree is a linear structure, the node will appear on the bottom right, which is obviously an abnormal case. Based on the characteristics of the general distribution of XML data trees, we propose an efficient spatial partitioning method, denoted SPATIAL-PARTITIONING.

The basic idea of SPATIAL-PARTITIONING is first to find two data marks that have the largest distance in D and search the nearest $\frac{|D|}{N}$ nodes of each data mark with a NEAREST method. Spatial-Partitioning will recursively call the NEAREST method until the size of a group is 1 or 2. The two data marks are chosen from the edges of the minimum rectangle containing all d. The selection of the $\frac{|D|}{N}$ nearest nodes is implemented as shown in Figure 4. The NEAREST() procedure is given below:

Nearest(x, n)
1. $nX \leftarrow x$'s nearest n points in x-axis
2. $e \leftarrow$ FURTHERMOST(x, nX)
3. $r \leftarrow$ DISTANCE(e, x)
4. $p \leftarrow minPreorder$ node in the left nodes
5. **while** X-DISTANCE$(p, x) < r$
6.   **do if** DISTANCE$(p, x) < r$
7.   **then** $nX \leftarrow nX - e + p$
8. $e \leftarrow$ FURTHERMOST(x, nX)
9. $r \leftarrow$ DISTANCE(e, x)
10. $p \leftarrow p.next$
11. **return** nX

In the NEAREST procedure, the FURTHERMOST(x, nX) searches the furthermost point of x in nX, the DISTANCE(e, x) is the $2D$ distance between e and x, the X-DISTANCE(p, x) is their horizontal distance.

We give an example for searching five nearest nodes of x including x in Figure 4. We first search five nearest nodes on the X-axis distance of x, which are x, e_1, e_2, e_3 and e_4. The furthermost node is e_1, and r_1 is the distance between x and e_1, any node whose horizontal distance with x is less than r_1 may be in the result. We choose node according to its preorder, so next we get e_4, which is nearer than e_1, so we remove e_1 and add e_4. Now the five nodes are x, e_2, e_3, e_4 and e_5. And then, we get e_6 and remove e_3, now the furthermost node is e_4 and the furthermost distance is r_3, other nodes' horizontal distance with x are all larger than r_3. Now we get $x's$ five nearest nodes x, e_2, e_4, e_5 and e_6.

Compared with computing all nodes to find their nearest n nodes, this partitioning method only need compute a small part of all nodes to get the results. Furthermore, along with the progress of partitioning, the nodes will be less and

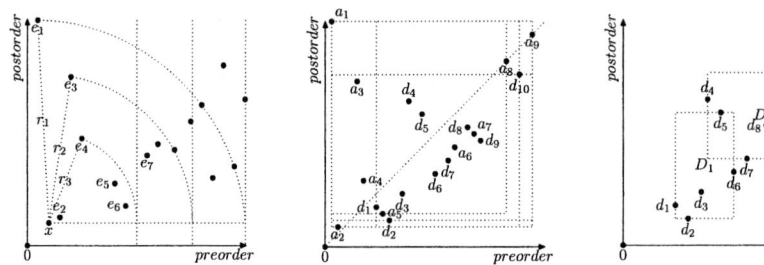

Fig. 4. Search n Nearest Nodes   **Fig. 5.** Node Distribution   **Fig. 6.** Partition D

the search speed will be quicker. The efficiency of NEAREST procedure profits from the particular plane distribution characters of tree nodes. With above example, we can easily see that our partitioning method could quickly partition D into N groups, each has $\frac{|D|}{N}$ nodes. We show SPATIAL-PARTITIONING algorithm below:

Spatial-Partitioning$(D, N, i = 1)$
1 switch
2   case $N = 1$:
3   return D_i
4   case $N = 2$:
5   choose p_1 and p_2 in D
6          $D_i \leftarrow$ NEAREST$(p_1, |D|/N)$; $D_{i+1} \leftarrow$ NEAREST$(p_2, |D|/N)$
7   return $D_i, D_i + 1$
8   case $N > 2$:
9   choose p_1 and p_2 in D
10         $D_i \leftarrow$ NEAREST$(p_1, |D|/N)$; $D_{i+1} \leftarrow$ NEAREST$(p_2, |D|/N)$
11         $D \leftarrow D - D_i - D_{i+1}$; $N \leftarrow N - 2$; $i \leftarrow i + 2$
12   GROUP(D, N, i)
13   return $D_1 \cdots D_N$

In our SPATIAL-PARTITIONING() method, if $N = 1$, we just distribute all D to one group. Otherwise, choose two enough remote datum marks on the edges of minimum rectangle containing all D, and search each datum mark's $\frac{|D|}{N}$ nearest points and distribute them to one group. And then, we recursively call the spatial partitioning method until all D are distributed to N groups. With this procedure, the number of d in each group is $\frac{|D|}{N}$.

To make the result simple and concrete, suppose partitioning number $N = 2$. We partition the D as shown in Figure 5, we first choose two enough remote points d_1 and d_{10}. Then choose d_1's $\frac{|D|}{N} = 5$ nearest points d_1, d_2, d_3, d_5, d_6 to first group D_1 and $d_4, d_7, d_8, d_9, d_{10}$ to the second group D_2. The partitioning result is shown in Figure 6. D_1 is the minimum rectangle containing all d nodes inside D_1, and D_2 is the minimum rectangle containing all d nodes inside D_2.

4.2 Partition-Based Spatial Structural Join Algorithm

Based on the SPATIAL-PARTITIONING method, we propose an enhanced partition-based spatial structural join algorithm, *PSSJ*.

PSSJ algorithm first filter most ancestors and descendants which will not be join results. Then use basic SPATIAL-PARTITIONING method to partition D. For each group in the spatial partition, we call *P-Join* method.

5 Performance Analysis

In this section, we present the experimental evaluation that yields a sense for the efficacy of our novel partition-based spatial structural join algorithm.

5.1 Experiment Setting

We ran experiments on a PC with Intel Pentium 2.0 GHz CPU, 512M RAM and 40G hard disk. The operating system is Windows XP. We employ an object-oriented XML management system XBase [8] for storage. The testing programs were written in INADA conformed to ODMG $C++$ binding. We have implemented PSSJ, *Stack-tree* join (STJ) and *XR-Tree* join algorithms.

We use synthetic data for all our experiments in order to control the structural and consequent join characteristics of the XML data. We use the IBM XML data generator to generate XML documents. The two DTDs adopted are department DTD and library DTD. Different sized documents that scale from 20M to 100M are generated with each DTD.

Experiments were performed to study the performance on our partition-based spatial structural join algorithm. Table 1 shows the set of queries for all data set on two DTDs. It also presents the nested case of our query set. The test query set contains all possible nested case of ancestor and descendant for thoroughly analyzing the performance of partition-based spatial structural join algorithm.

5.2 Varying Partitioning Number

The objective of this set of experiments is to test the query performance of PSSJ with varying partitioning number. We adopt one 100M document for each DTD. The performance curves of testing varying partitioning number are given in Figure 7.

Figure 7(a) shows the performance of Q_1 with partitioning number varying from 10 to 60. Figure 7(b) shows the performance of Q_2 with partitioning number

Table 1. Query Set and Nested Case

Query	Description	DTD	Anc Nested	Desc Nested
Q_1	department//employee	Department	highly	highly
Q_2	employee//name	Department	highly	less
Q_3	section//subsection	Library	less	highly
Q_4	section//title	Library	less	less

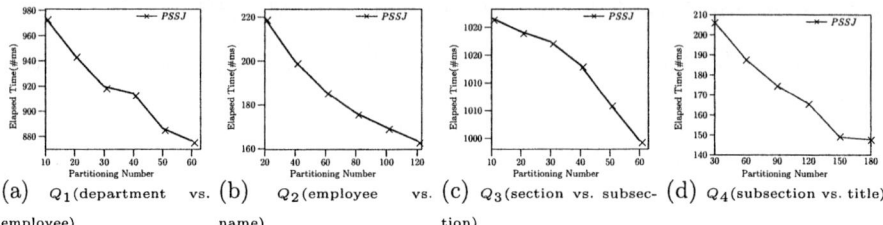

(a) Q_1(department vs. employee) (b) Q_2(employee vs. name) (c) Q_3(section vs. subsection) (d) Q_4(subsection vs. title)

Fig. 7. Varying Partitioning Number Test

from 10 to 60. Figure 7(c) shows the performance of Q_3 with partitioning number from 20 to 120. Figure 7(d) shows the performance of Q_4 with partitioning number from 30 to 180.

It can be seen from Figure 7 that PSSJ algorithm can get better performance along with the increase of the partitioning number, which demonstrates the effectiveness of our partitioning methods. We can also see that when the partitioning number gets to some value in some cases, the amplitude of performance will be slow. This value is closely relative to the number and the nested case of ancestors and descendants.

5.3 Varying Join Selectivity Test

In the second group of experiments, we study the capabilities of various algorithms to skip elements under different join selectivity. We keep the document size 100M and partitioning number unchanged for each query in this test. We test the case when the ancestor join selectivity and descendant join selectivity are varying. For this purpose, we change the document elements with dummy elements so that the desired selectivity on ancestors or descendants can be obtained. Figure 8 shows the performance of the three algorithms tested when varying join selectivity.

Figure 8(a) tests Q_1 and Figure 8(b) tests Q_2. The nested level of ancestors are high in both queries. We can clearly see from them that in this case, the join selectivity has great influence on *XR-Tree* algorithm, while has little influence on Stack-Tree join algorithm and our partition-based spatial join algorithm. And

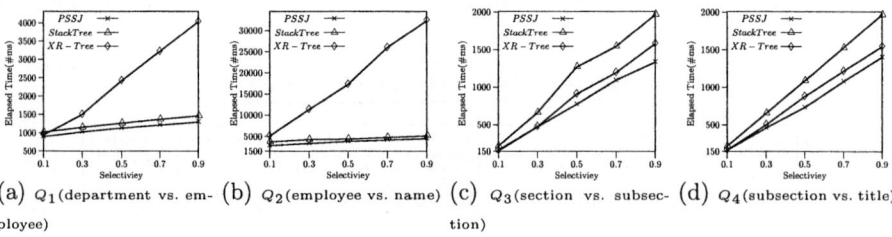

(a) Q_1(department vs. employee) (b) Q_2(employee vs. name) (c) Q_3(section vs. subsection) (d) Q_4(subsection vs. title)

Fig. 8. Varying Join Selectivity

in this case, *XR-Tree* has bad performance. Stack-Tree join algorithm has similar good performance as PSSJ.

Figure 8(c) tests Q_3 and (d) tests Q_4. The nested level of ancestors is low. We can see from (c)(d) that join selectivity has great influence on all tested algorithms. And in this case, *XR-Tree* is better than Stack-Tree join and a little worse than PSSJ.

6 Conclusions

In this paper, we extend the relationships between nodes to the relationships between partitions and get some observations about the relationships. We then propose a new partition-based structural join method *P-Join* for structural join between ancestors and descendants based on the observations. Moreover we present an enhanced partitioned-based spatial structural join algorithm PSSJ. Extensive experiments show the excellence of our new approach.

Acknowledgement

This work is partially supported by the CUHK strategic grant(numbered 4410001).

References

1. S. Al-Khalifa, H. V. Jagadish, N. Koudas, J. M. Patel, D. Srivastava, and Y. Wu. Structural joins: A primitive for efficient XML query pattern matching. In *Proceedings of ICDE '02*, 2002.
2. S.-Y. Chien, Z. Vagena, D. Zhang, V. J. Tsotras, and C. Zaniolo. Efficient structural joins on indexed XML documents. In *Proceedings of VLDB '02*, 2002.
3. P. F. Dietz. Maintaining order in a linked list. In *Proceedings of the Fourteenth Annual ACM Symposium on Theory of Computing*, 1982.
4. T. Grust. Accelerating XPath location steps. In *Proceedings of SIGMOD '02*, 2002.
5. H. Jiang, H. Lu, W. Wang, and B. C. Ooi. XR-Tree: Indexing XML data for efficient stuctural join. In *Proceedings of ICDE '03*, 2003.
6. Q. Li and B. Moon. Indexing and querying xml data for regular path expressions. In *Proceedings of VLDB '01*, 2001.
7. G. Wang and M. Liu. Query processing and optimization for regular path expressions. In *Proceedings of the 12th International Conference on Advanced Information Systems Engineering*, 2003.
8. G. Wang, H. Lu, G. Yu, and Y. Bao. managing very large document collections using semantics. *Journal of Comput. Sci. & Technol.*, 18(3):403–406, Jule, 2003.
9. G. Wang, B. Sun, J. Lv, and G. Yu. Rpe query processing and optimization techniques for xml databases. *Journal of Comput. Sci. & Technol.*, 19(2):224–237, March, 2004.
10. C. Zhang, J. Naughton, D. DeWitt, Q. Luo, and G. Lohman. On supporting containment queries in relational database management systems. In *Proceedings of SIGMOD '01*, 2001.

Efficient Dissemination of Filtered Data in XML-Based SDI*

Jae-Ho Choi, Young-Jin Yoon, and SangKeun Lee

Department of Computer Science and Engineering,
Korea University, Seoul, South Korea
{redcolor25, yoon333, yalphy}@korea.ac.kr

Abstract. With the increasing popularity of XML, there is a growing number of reports on the XML-based Selective Dissemination of Information (SDI) in the literature, in which many XML filtering systems have been proposed to support the efficient XML-based SDI. While previous research into XML filtering focused on efficient filtering algorithms, in this paper, we consider a novel XML dissemination problem, focusing on the efficient dissemination of filtered data. To this end, we describe a significant problem associated with the dissemination of XML documents and propose effective algorithms which allow for its resolution. Based on these effective algorithms, we developed an XML-based SDI system that can disseminate XML documents efficiently. The experimental results demonstrate that the proposed algorithms outperform earlier XML filtering systems in terms of the usage of network bandwidth.

1 Introduction

Extensible Markup Language (XML) [2] has recently become a standard information exchange language on the Internet. With the growing volume of XML information being exchanged over the Internet, much research is being done into XML Selective Dissemination of Information (SDI) systems [6], [8], [9], [11]. XML filtering systems rely upon user profiles that describe the information preferences of individual users to disseminate those documents that match the user profiles. XML filtering systems are particularly useful for the timely distribution of data to a large set of customers, in such applications as stock information systems and traffic information systems. In the case of stock information systems, the user registers the companies on the server. Afterwards, the server periodically delivers stock information that is filtered according to the user's profile. In the case of traffic information systems, the system either recognizes the client's location or obtains it from the client and then delivers appropriate filtered traffic information to the client. Many of these systems deploy XPath [3] as their query language.

---

* This work was done as a part of Information & Communication Fundamental Technology Research Program, supported by Ministry of Information & Communication in Republic of Korea.

So far, much of the research in this field has focused on the efficient matching of XML documents with the user's profile. In other words, the creation of an efficient matching engine has been a key research issue. In this paper, we describe the resolution of a novel XML dissemination problem, focusing on the efficient dissemination of the filtered data. To the best of our knowledge, this is the first report on the efficient delivery of filtered data. With the growing volume of data and increasing number of users on the Internet, the efficiency of dissemination and scalability are becoming key concerns, due to the limitations in the available bandwidth. The basic idea behind the algorithms proposed in this paper is to minimize the size of the data sent over the network, by removing any information that is not specifically requested by the client, since the size of the data may affect the performance, especially the response time. However, we first give an example describing the dissemination problem:

Example 1. *User **A** requests only those financial pages that contain information about company **C** from the newspaper located on the server. The server, which incorporates an XML filtering system, filters all of the newspapers and selects those newspapers which contain information about company **C**. Afterwards, the server sends the selected newspapers in their entirety, including the sports, political and financial pages.*

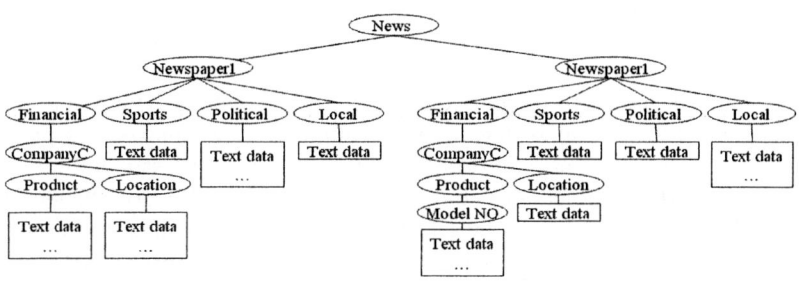

Fig. 1. The DOM tree of the sample XML document

The legacy XML filtering system results in an XML document comprising the entire newspaper, as shown in Figure 1, which is obviously inefficient, since the user requested the financial pages only. Therefore, the server should send only the financial pages. In this paper, we address this problem, by first analyzing the information that the user wants to obtain and then proposing efficient XML dissemination methods.

In the next section, we introduce previous studies related to XML filtering systems and XML optimization over networks. Section 3 discusses the XML dissemination problem in detail, and describes our methods of efficient XML dissemination. In Section 4, we present the experiment results which demonstrate the effectiveness of the proposed methods. We conclude this paper in Section 5.

2 Preliminaries

XPath, a standard language for addressing parts of an XML document, uses an XML document structure to formulate queries. Users can obtain parts of an XML document by describing an XPath expression. The XPath uses path expressions to select a node in an XML document [3]. In general, if a user formulates a query using XPath, the potential result should contain both data and structure information, because the meaning of the XML data is dependant on the structure information. In other words, a particular data, 'A', may have a different meaning depending on its structure information. From this perspective, one of the most critical tasks in XML indexing is to support document structure, and many different approaches [10], [13], [16] have been proposed for this purpose. This structure information deals with the special features of XML, which is a kind of semi-structured data [5], [7].

The XML filtering system exploits user profiles and XML documents as the input data. The system is centered on the matching engine and can be used in the SDI system. The filtering engine returns the matched data to the user. Many XML filtering systems use XPath for the definition of the profiles, because it provides a flexible way of specifying path expressions [6], [11]. It treats an XML document as a tree of nodes and uses the DOM [1] data model. Most previous studies on XML filtering focus on the issue of efficient user profile indexing. Frequently, the Finite State Machine (FSM) is used to find matched documents, with Deterministic Finite Automaton (DFA) being used as the FSM in [6], whereas Non-deterministic Finite Automaton (NFA) is adopted in [11], as it removes any duplication in the DFA.

Recently, the problem of redundancy in the answers to XPath queries has been addressed in several studies and the minimal view approach is proposed in [15]. A middleware that supports the efficient and robust streaming of XML documents across a wireless environment is proposed in [17]. An efficient XML transmission by using various data formats and compression techniques is examined in [12]. These problems and their solutions are complementary to our approach. In this paper, we examine the issue of minimal XML dissemination. In order to optimize the dissemination of the XML data, we seek to minimize the answer itself, rather than attempting to minimize the redundancy among the answer sets.

3 Proposed Methods

3.1 Definition of the XML Dissemination Problem

The XML data dissemination problem involves sending only the data that is requested by the user. As mentioned in Section 2, an XML document consists of data and its related structure information. We define the XML dissemination problem in terms of the dissemination of the appropriate data from a matched document resulting from a given query, as follows.

Definition 1. *The XML dissemination problem is to disseminate only the portion of D that is matched with a given query Q. The matched portion of D should contain both the data and the structure information, where*

- *The data information is a set of nodes that are pointed to by Q and its descendants, and*
- *The structure information of D is a set of routes from the root node of D to the nodes that are pointed to by Q.*

In the case of XML dissemination, the XML dissemination system should disseminate both the XML data and its structure information. When the server disseminates filtered data, the structure information may or may not be included in the disseminated document. In order to minimize the network cost, we need to optimize the result of the filtering operation itself, as explained in the following sections.

3.2 XML Dissemination Algorithms and Implementation

The XML dissemination problem is to send information that includes the structure information of the requested elements and the requested data information. To solve this problem, we propose two different methods. Firstly, we introduce two methods of presenting the structure information, viz. AS (All higher Structure) which presents the structure information and NAS (Non-duplicated All higher Structure) from which any duplication in the AS is removed. Secondly, we introduce two methods of presenting the data information, viz. AL (All lower Level) and FL (First lower Level). The former includes all of the descendants of the data information, while the latter includes only the children of the data information (i.e. the sibling data of the portion pointed to by XPath). The proposed algorithms can be classified into two different categories. The first category of algorithms consists of those used for the structure information, viz. AS and NAS. The second category consists of those algorithms used for the data information, viz. AL and FL. For efficient XML dissemination, these two categories of algorithm can be combined. Algorithms 1 and 2 show the pseudo code for the proposed NAS-AL and AS-FL algorithms, respectively. In these algorithms,

---

Algorithm 1 NAS_AL algorithm Pseudo code

01: **for** each node in an XML document **do**
02:   **if** print-flag is turned on **then** write the node; /* initially, print-flag=off */
03:   **if** the node is a start element node **then**
04:     push the node to the S and compare the node with N;
05:     **if** the node is same as N_f **then**
06:       makes and check H_i and compare S with H_i;
07:       write non-duplicated nodes using H_i and turn on the print-flag;
08:   **else if** the node is an end element node **then**
09:     pop the node from the S;
10:     **else if** popped node is a N_f **then** turn off the print-flag;

Algorithm 2 AS_FL algorithm Pseudo code

01: **for** each node in an XML document **do** /* initially, print-flag=off */
02:   **if** print-flag is turned on **then** write the node;
03:   **if** the node is a start element node **then**
04:     **if** finite-flag is turned on **then** /* initially, finite-flag=off */
05:       push the node to the S_t and check the depth of S_t;
06:       **if** the depth of $S_t > 1$ **then** turn off the print-flag;
07:       **else** turn on the print-flag;
08:     **else** push the node to the S and compare the node with N;
09:     **if** the node is same as N_f **then**
10:       make and check H_i and compare S with H_i;
11:       write duplicated nodes using H_i and B_i;
12:       turn on the print-flag and the finite-flag;
13:   **else if** the node is an end element node **then** pop the node from the S or S_t;
14:     **if** S_t is empty **then** turn off the finite-flag;

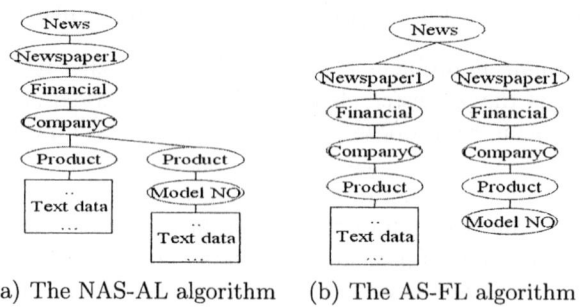

(a) The NAS-AL algorithm   (b) The AS-FL algorithm

Fig. 2. The application of our algorithms

two stacks are used : the stack to store the structure information and the stack to store the temporary structure, denoted as S and S_t. Also, the current state and finite state in the NFA are used for these algorithms, denoted as N_c, N_f, respectively. The history information of S and the information of branching position are used for our algorithm, denoted as H_i and B_i, respectively. The complete algorithm can be implemented using combinations of each category of algorithm. In other words, the following possibilities are open to us: AS-AL, AS-FL, NAS-AL, and NAS-FL. Herein, we show only two of these algorithms, since the description of the other two algorithms is straightforward.

Figure 2 shows the application of our algorithms to Example 1. The query that is used in this application corresponds to the selection: $Q:/news/newspaper1/financial/companyC/product$. With the NAS-AL algorithm, structure information is not duplicated and the data information is presented with all of the descendent nodes. With the AS-FL algorithm, on the other hand, the structure information is duplicated and the data information is presented as the children nodes only.

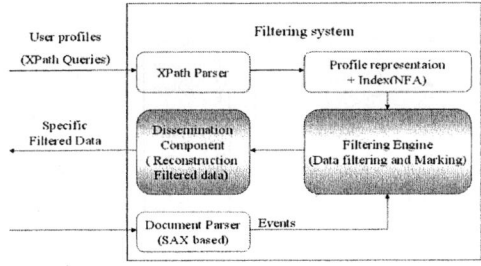

Fig. 3. The generic architecture of the XML-based SDI system

Based on the system available at [4], we implement our XML filtering engine and dissemination component. Figure 3 shows the generic architecture of our XML-based SDI system. In order to minimize the structure and data components in the query result, the proposed system uses flags for document parsing. The dissemination component uses these flags to reconstruct the output documents in such a way as to render their dissemination as efficient as possible. As in the case of legacy filtering systems, we used an event-based SAX parser for document parsing. Thus, the processing time incurred by our system is similar to that of other XML filtering systems. For the parsing of the user profiles, we implement the profile parser based on [11]. Therefore, our system generates an index using the NFA. We implement the system in JAVA language.

4 Performance Evaluation

4.1 Experimental Environments

As in [11], we conducted experiments using the NITF DTD and DBLP DTD. The NITF DTD is intended for news copy production, press releases, wire services, newspapers, and broadcast and Web-based news. The DBLP DTD is a bibliography DTD. We also used the XMark DTD [14] and Xbench DTD [18]. XMark and Xbench are benchmark systems designed to benchmark XML databases. In order to test the various document types, we use the DC/SD DTD and TC/SD DTD [18]. The DTD used in XMark is an Auction website DTD. The features of the other DTDs are listed in Table 1. We generated our documents using the IBM XML Generator. Two parameters are passed to the generator, viz. the maximum depth, D, and the maximum number of times that the element can

Table 1. The features of the DTDs

	NITF	XMark	DBLP
Number of elements name	123	77	36
Number of attributes	513	16	14
Maximum level of nested elements level	infinite	infinite	infinite

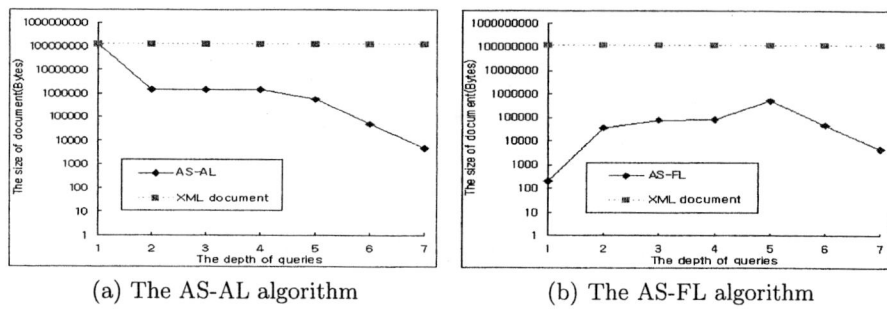

(a) The AS-AL algorithm (b) The AS-FL algorithm

Fig. 4. The size of the documents obtained with various depths of queries (DTD =Auction DTD, Source Document size =100MB)

be repeated under a single parent. By default, RP is limited to 5 and D is set to 10. In the case of the XMark DTD, we used xmlgen [14] to generate the XML document because it allows the data size to be set according to the user's wishes. In the experiment, we used queries that were generated by the query generator described in [11]. We selected queries that could be used to assess the various features of the XML documents. To measure the usage of network bandwidth, we adopted the size of the resulting data as a performance metric. The size of the XML documents is 1,522 KB in the case of the NITF DTD, 22KB for the DBLP DTD, and 100MB for the XMark DTD. The legacy filtering system returns the whole document that is matched with the user profile. Therefore, we used the default document size as the baseline for the performance test.

4.2 Experimental Results

The Effect of Varying The Depth of The Query. Figure 4(a) shows the size of the resulting documents for various queries. The proposed AS-AL algorithm gives a much smaller result set than the legacy system, which means that it uses the bandwidth resource more efficiently. The document that was used in this experiment is the Auction DTD and the queries are shown in Table 2. The Y axis represents the document size on a log scale, and the X axis represents the depth of the query. As shown in Table 2, the depth of the query grows as the query number increases.

Table 2. The Queries used in Auction DTD Experiment

Query number	The queries
10	/site/categories/category/description/text/bold/keyword/keyword/bold/emph
9	/site/categories/category/description/text/bold/keyword/keyword/bold
...	...
2	/site/categories
1	/site

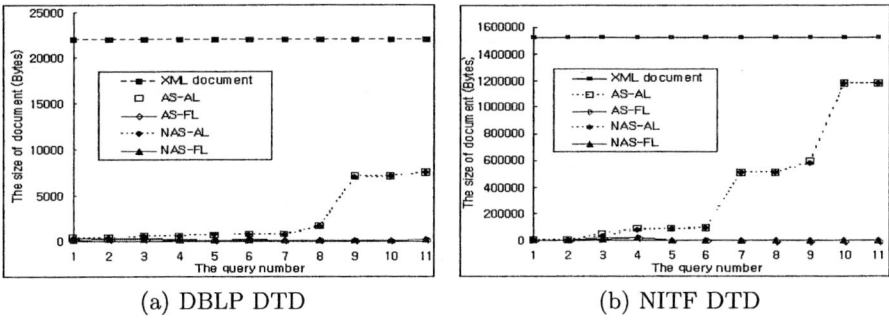

Fig. 5. The output size of the proposed algorithms

The auction DTD has a site element as its root element. Hence, in the case of query 1, all of the elements are selected by our algorithms. Then, our system generates the same result as the legacy system, however, in the other cases, our system performed much better than the legacy system. The result of the AS-AL algorithm contains all of the lower data, including the element nodes and text nodes. Therefore, the system performance improves as the depth of the query increases. Figure 4(b) shows the size of the resulting document in the case of the AS-FL algorithm. The queries that are used in this experiment are same as the previous experiment.

In this experiment, we used the same Auction DTD and the source XML document size is 100MB. Since this method outputs just one-level, the output data size can vary depending on the document features, regardless of the depth of the query. In the case of the Auction DTD, the first and last levels of the output of the queries are very small.

The Effect of Varying The DTD. Figure 5(a) shows the result in the case of the DBLP DTD which is used in our experiment. In the case of the DBLP DTD, most of the 'sup' elements include text element nodes. Therefore, if the query includes a 'sup' element, the output size of the document created by our system increases very sharply. The queries that are used in this experiment are similar to the previous queries in Table 2. The deepest query is /dblp/www/title/tt/sup/sub/tt/tt/sub/i/ref. For all of the queries, our system performs better than the legacy system. In the case of the AS-AL algorithm, our system reduces the network cost significantly, as compared to the legacy system.

Figure 5(b) shows the output document size of the proposed algorithms in the case of the NITF DTD. Consistent with the previous case, our system performs better than the legacy XML filtering system. The queries that are used in this experiment are similar to the previous queries in Table 2. The deepest query is /nitf/body/body.head/note/body.content/table/tbody/tr/th/body.content.

The Effect of Text Centric vs. Data Centric Documents. XML documents can be divided into text centric and data centric documents [18]. Figure

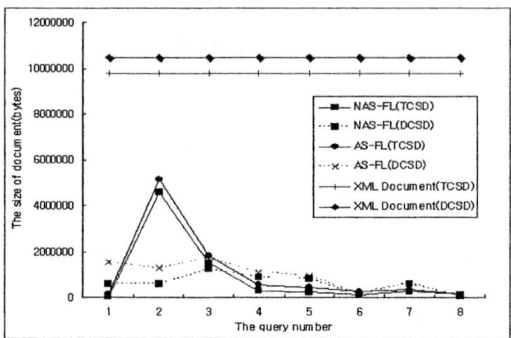

Fig. 6. The size of the output documents obtained with the TC/SD and DC/SD DTDs

6 shows the size of the output documents in the case of the DC/SD and TC/SD DTDs which are used in [18]. The DC/SD DTD is used for data centric documents, whereas the TC/SD DTD is used for text centric XML documents.

As expected, all of the proposed algorithms perform better than the baseline in Figure 6, however the difference between the AS and NAS algorithms is more visible for the data centric document than for the text centric one. This result shows that the NAS algorithm is more suitable for data centric applications. This can be explained as follows: in general, a data centric document contains more structure information than a text centric document of similar size. Since the NAS algorithm removes any duplicated structure information and the DC/SD DTD contains a greater amount of structure information, the NAS algorithm is more suitable for data centric XML documents. The queries that are used in this experiment are similar to the queries that are used in the previous experiment. The deepest queries are $/dictionary/e/ss/s/qp/q/qt/cr$ and $/catalog/item/authors/author/contact\_information/mailing\_address/street\_information/street\_address$, respectively.

5 Conclusion

So far, research into XML filtering systems has focused on the development of efficient filtering algorithms. In this paper, however, we focused on the efficient dissemination of filtered XML data which, to the best of our knowledge, is the first such attempt to be reported in the literature. Further, we developed efficient XML dissemination components for XML-based SDI systems. We proposed two categories of algorithms, which are used to present the higher and lower structure information, respectively. The experimental results show that the proposed algorithms decrease the size of the result document dramatically.

In the future, we plan to consider the XML dissemination problem in a wireless broadcast environment in which the efficient usage of bandwidth will have an even greater impact.

References

1. Document object model. http://www.w3.org/DOM.
2. Extensible markup language. http://www.w3.org/XML.
3. Xml path language. http://www.w3.org/TR/XPath.
4. Yfilter. http://yfilter.cs.berkeley.edu.
5. S. Abiteboul. Querying semi-structured data. In *Proceedings of International Conference on Database Theory*, pages 1–18, 1997.
6. M. Altinel and M. J. Franklin. Efficient filtering of xml documents for selective dissemination of information. In *Proceedings of International Conference on Very Large Data Bases*, pages 53–64, 2000.
7. P. Buneman, W. Fan, J. Simeon, and S. Weinstein. Constraints for semistructured data and xml. *ACM SIGMOD Record*, 30(1):47–54, 2001.
8. C. Y. Chan, P. Felber, M. N. Garofalakis, and R. Rastogi. Efficient filtering of XML documents with XPath expressions. In *Proceedings of International Conference on Data Engineering*, pages 235–244, 2002.
9. D. Chen and R. K. Wong. Optimizing the lazy DFA approach for XML stream processing. In *Proceedings of Conference on Australasian Database*, pages 131–140, 2004.
10. A. Deutsch, M. Fernandez, and D. Suciu. Storing semistructured data with STORED. In *Proceedings of ACM SIGMOD Conference on Management of Data*, pages 431–442, 1999.
11. Y. Diao, M. Altinel, M. J. Franklin, H. Zhang, and P. Fischer. Path sharing and predicate evaluation for high-performance xml filtering. *ACM Transactions on Database Systems*, 28(4):467–516, 2003.
12. Y. Diao, S. Rizvi, and M. J. Franklin. Towards an internet-scale xml dissemination service. In *Proceedings of International Conference on Very Large Data Bases*, pages 612–623, 2004.
13. R. Goldman and J. Widom. Dataguides: Enabling query formulation and optimization in semistructured databases. In *Proceedings of International Conference on Very Large Data Bases*, pages 436–445, 1997.
14. A. Schmidt, F. Waas, M. L. Kersten, M. J. Carey, I. Manolescu, and R. Busse. Xmark: A benchmark for xml data management. In *Proceedings of the International Conference on Very Large Data Bases*, pages 974–985, 2002.
15. K. Tajima and Y. Fukui. Answering xpath queries over networks by sending minimal views. In *Proceedings of the International Conference on Very Large Data Bases*, pages 48–59, 2004.
16. H. Wang, S. Park, W. Fan, and P. S. Yu. Vist: A dynamic index method for querying xml data by tree structures. In *Proceedings of ACM SIGMOD Conference on Management of Data*, pages 110–121, 2003.
17. E. Y. Wong, A. T. Chan, and H. V. Leong. Xstream: A middleware for streaming xml contents over wireless environments. *IEEE Transactions on Software Engineering*, 30(12):918–935, 2004.
18. B. B. Yao, M. T. Ozsu, and N. Khandelwal. Xbench benchmark and performance testing of xml dbmss. In *Proceedings of International Conference on Data Engineering*, pages 621–632, 2004.

Efficient Processing of Ordered XML Twig Pattern

Jiaheng Lu, Tok Wang Ling, Tian Yu, Changqing Li, and Wei Ni

School of computing, National University of Singapore
{lujiahen, lingtw, yutian, lichangq, niwei}@comp.nus.edu.sg

Abstract. Finding all the occurrences of a twig pattern in an XML database is a core operation for efficient evaluation of XML queries. Holistic twig join algorithm has showed its superiority over binary decompose based approach due to efficient reducing intermediate results. The existing holistic join algorithms, however, cannot deal with *ordered* twig queries. A straightforward approach that first matches the unordered twig queries and then prunes away the undesired answers is obviously not optimal in most cases. In this paper, we study a novel holistic-processing algorithm, called *OrderedTJ*, for ordered twig queries. We show that *OrderedTJ* can identify a large query class to guarantee the I/O optimality. Finally, our experiments show the effectiveness, scalability and efficiency of our proposed algorithm.

1 Introduction

With the rapidly increasing popularity of XML for data representation, there is a lot of interest in query processing over data that conforms to a tree-structured data model([1],[5]). Efficient finding all twig patterns in an XML database is a major concern of XML query processing. Recently, holistic twig join approach has been taken as an efficient way to match twig pattern since this approach can efficiently control the size of intermediate results([1],[2],[3],[4]). We observe that, however, the existing work on holistic twig query matching only considered *unordered* twig queries. But XPath defines four ordered axes: *following-sibling, preceding-sibling, following, preceding*. For example, XPath: *//book/text/following-sibling::chapter* is an ordered query, which finds all *chapters* in the dataset that are following siblings of *text* which should be a child of *book*.

We call a twig query which cares the order of the matching elements as an *ordered* twig query. On the other hand, we denote a twig query that does not consider the order of matching elements as an *unordered* query. In this paper, we research how to efficiently evaluate an *ordered* twig query.

To handle an ordered twig query, naively, we can use the existing algorithm (e.g. TwigStack[1]/TwigStackList[5]) to output the intermediate path solutions for each individual root-leaf query path, and then merge path solutions so that the final solutions are guaranteed to satisfy the order predicates of the query. Although existing algorithms are applied, such a post-processing approach has a serious disadvantage: many intermediate results may not contribute to final answers.

Motivated by the recent success in efficient processing unordered twig queries *holistically*, we present in this paper a novel holistic algorithm, called *OrderedTJ*, for *ordered* twig queries. The contribution of this paper can be summarized as follows:

1. We develop a new holistic ordered twig join algorithm, namely *OrderedTJ*, based on the new concept of *Ordered Children Extension (for short OCE)*. With OCE, an element contributes to final results only if the order of its children accords with the order of corresponding query nodes. Thus, efficient holistic algorithm for ordered-twigs can be leveraged.
2. If we call edges between branching nodes and their children as *branching edges* and denote the branching edge connecting to the n'th child as the n'th *branching edge*, we analytically demonstrate that when the ordered-twig contains only ancestor-descendant relationship from the 2nd branching edge, *OrderedTJ* is I/O optimal among all sequential algorithms that read the entire input. In other words, the optimality of *OrderedTJ* allows the existence of *parent-child* relationships in *non-branching* edges and the *first* branching edges.
3. Our experimental results show that the effectiveness, scalability and efficiency of our holistic twig algorithms for ordered twig pattern.

The remainder of the paper is organized as follows. Section 2 presented related work. The novel ordered twig join algorithm is described in Section 3. Section 4 is dedicated to our experimental results and we close this paper by conclusion and future work in Section 5.

2 Related Work

With the increasing popularity of XML data, query processing and optimization for XML databases have attracted a lot of research interest. There is a rich set of literature on matching twig queries efficiently. Below, we describe these literatures with the notice that the existing work deals with only *unordered* twig queries.

Zhang et al.([9]) proposed a multi-predicate merge join (MPMGJN) algorithm based on (*DocId, Start, End, Level*) labeling of XML elements. The later work by Al-Khalifa et al.([7]) gave a stack-based binary structural join algorithm. Different from binary structural join approaches, Bruno et al.([1]) proposed a holistic twig join algorithm, called *TwigStack*, to avoid producing a large intermediate result. However, the class of optimal queries in *TwigStack* is very small. When a twig query contains any *parent-child* edge, the size of *"useless"* intermediate results may be very large. Lu et al.([5]) propose a new algorithm called *TwigStackList*. They use *list* data structure to cache limited elements to identify a larger optimal query class. *TwigStackList* is I/O optimal for queries with only *ancestor-descendant* relationships in all branching edges. Recently, Jiang et al.([3]) researched the problem of efficient evaluation of twig queries with OR predicates. Chen et al.([2]) researched the relationship between different data partition strategies and the optimal query classes for holistic twig join. Lu et al.([6]) proposed a new labeling scheme called *extended Dewey* to efficiently process XML twig pattern.

3 Ordered Twig Join Algorithm

3.1 Data Model and Ordered Twig Pattern

We model XML documents as *ordered* trees. Figure 1(e) shows an example XML data tree. Each tree element is assigned a region code (*start, end, level*) based on its position. Each text is assigned a region code that has the same *start* and *end* values.

XML queries make use of twig patterns to match relevant portions of data in an XML database. The pattern edges are parent-child or ancestor-descendant relationships. Given an *ordered* twig pattern Q and an XML database D, a match of Q in D is identified by a mapping from the nodes in Q to the elements in D, such that: (i) the query node predicates are satisfied by the corresponding database elements; and (ii) the parent-child and ancestor-descendant relationships between query nodes are satisfied by the corresponding database elements; and (iii) the *orders* of query sibling nodes are satisfied by the corresponding database elements. In particular, with region encoding, given any node $q \in Q$ and its right-sibling $r \in Q$ (if any), their corresponding database elements, say e_q and e_r in D, must satisfy that $e_q.end < e_r.start$.

The answers to query Q with n nodes can be represented as a list of *n-ary* tuples, where each tuple $(t_1, t_2, ..., t_n)$ consists of the database elements that identify a distinct match of Q in D.

Figure 1(a) shows three sample XPath and Figure 1(b-d) shows the corresponding ordered twig patterns for the data of Fig 1(e). For each branching node, we use a symbol ">" in a box to mark its children ordered. Note that in Q3, we add *book* as the root of the ordered query, since it is the *root* of XML document tree. For example, the query solution for Q3 is only <$book_1$, $chpater_2$, $title_2$, "related work", $section_3$ >. But if Q3 were an *unordered* query, $section_1$, $section_2$ also would involve in answers.

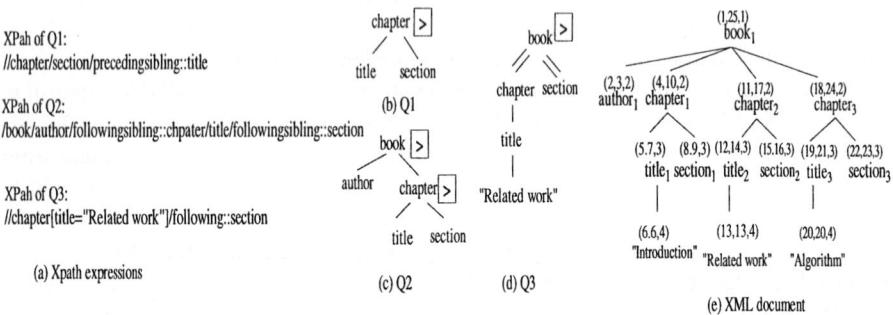

Fig. 1. (a) three XPaths (b)-(d) the corresponding ordered twig query (e) an XML tree

3.2 Algorithm

In this section, we present *OrderedTJ*, a novel holistic algorithm for finding all matches of an *ordered* twig pattern against an XML document. *OrderedTJ* makes the extension of *TwigStackList* algorithm in the previous work [5] to handle *ordered* twig pattern. We will first introduce data structures and notations to be used by *OrderedTJ*.

Notation and data structures. An ordered query is represented with an *ordered* tree. The function PCRchildren(n), ADRChildren(n) return child nodes which has parent-child or ancestor-descedant relationships with n, respectively. The self-explaining function rightSibling(n) returns the immediate right sibling node of n (if any).

There is a data stream T_n associated with each node n in the query twig. We use C_n to point to the current element in T_n. We can access the values of C_n by $C_n.\text{start}, C_n.\text{end}$ and $C_n.\text{level}$. The cursor can advance to the next element in T_n with the procedure advance(T_n). Initially, C_n points to the first element of T_n.

Our algorithm will use two types of data structures: *list* and *stack*. We associate a list L_n and a stack S_n for each node of queries. At every point during computation: the nodes in stack S_n are guaranteed to lie on a root-leaf path in the database. We use top(S_n) to denote the top element in stack S_n. Similarly, elements in each list L_n are also strictly nested from the first to the end, i.e. each element is an ancestor or parent of that following it. For each list L_n, we declare an integer variable, say p_n, as a cursor to point to an element in L_n. Initially, $p_n = 0$, which points to the first element of L_n.

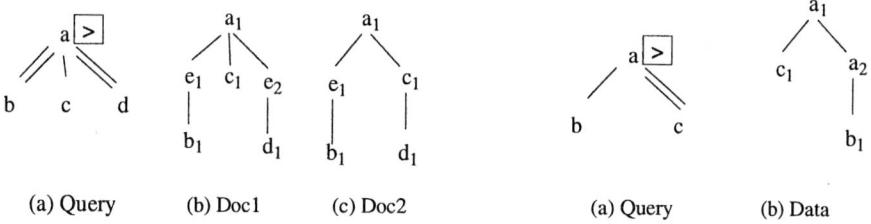

Fig. 2. Illustration to ordered child extension   **Fig. 3.** Optimality example

The challenge to ordered twig evaluation is that, even if an element satisfies the parent-child or ancestor-descendant relationship, it may not satisfy the order predicate. We introduce a new concept, namely *Ordered Children Extension* (for short, OCE), which is important to determine whether an element likely involves in ordered queries.

DEFINITION 1(**OCE**) *Given an ordered query Q and a dataset D, we say that an element e_n (with tag $n \in Q$) in D has an ordered children extension (for short OCE), if the following properties are satisfied:*

(i)   *for $n_i \in \text{ADRChildren}(n)$ in Q (if any), there is an element e_{n_i} (with tag n_i) in D such that e_{n_i} is a descendant of e_n and e_{n_i} also has OCE;*

(ii)   *for $n_i \in \text{PCRChildren}(n)$ in Q (if any), there is an element e' (with tag n) in the path e_n to e_{n_i} such that e' is the parent of e_{n_i} and e_{n_i} also has OCE;*

(iii)   *for each child n_i of n and $m_i = \text{rightSibling}(n_i)$ (if any), there are elements e_{n_i} and e_{m_i} such that $e_{n_i}.\text{end} < e_{m_i}.\text{start}$ and both e_{n_i} and e_{m_i} have OCE.* □

Properties (i) and (ii) discuss the ancestor-descendant and parent-child relationship respectively. Property (iii) manifests the order condition of queries. For example, see the ordered query in Fig 2(a), in Doc 1, a_1 has the OCE, since a_1 has descendants b_1,d_1, child c_1 and more importantly, b_1,c_1,d_1 appear in the correct order. In contrast, in Doc2, a_1 has **not** the OCE, since d_1 is the descendant of c_1, but not the *following* element of c_1(i.e. c_1.end $\not<$ d_1 .start).

```
Algorithm OrderedTJ ()
01While (¬end())
02      q_act= getNext(root);
03      if (isRoot(q_act) ∨ ¬empty(S_parent(q_act))) cleanStack(q_act, getEnd(q_act));
04      moveStreamToStack(q_act, S_q_act);
05      if (isLeaf(q_act))
06              showpathsolutions (S_q_act ,getElement(q_act));
07      else      proceed(T_q_act);
08 mergeALLPathsolutions;

Function end()
01 return    ∀n∈ subtreesNodes(root): isLeaf(n) ∧ eof(C_n);

Procedure cleanStack (n ,actEnd)
01 while (¬empty(S_n) and (topEnd(S_n)< actEnd)) do pop(S_n);

Procedure moveStreamToStack(n, S_n )
01 if((getEnd(n)< top(S_rightsibling(n)).start) //check order
02     push getElement(n) to stack S_n
06     proceed(n);

Procedure proceed(n)
01 if (empty(L_n))    advance(T_n);
02 else    L_n.delete(p_n);
03      p_n = 0; //move p_n to pint to the beginning of L_n

Procedure showpathsolutions(S_m, e)
01 index[m]=e
02 if (m == root ) //we are in root
03    Output(index[q_1],…,index[q_k]) //k is the length of path processed
04 else   //recursive call
05    for each element e_i in S_parent(m)
06         if  e_i satisfies the corresponding relationship with e
07                  showpathsolutions(S_parent(m), e_i)
```

Fig. 4. Rocedure OrderedTJ

Algorithm OrderedTJ. *OrderedTJ*, which computes answers to an ordered query twig, operates in two phases. In the first phase (line 1-7), the individual query root-leaf paths are output. In the second phase (line 8), these solutions are merged-joined to compute the answers to the whole query. Next, we first explain *getNext* algorithm which is a core function and then presents the main algorithm in details.

getNext(n)(See Fig 5) is a procedure called in the main algorithm of *OrderedTJ*. It identifies the next stream to be processed and advanced. At line 4-8, we check the condition (1) of OCE. Note that unlike the previous algorithm *TwigStackList[5]*, in line 8, we advance the **maximal** (not minimal) element that are not descendants of the current element in stream T_n, as we will use it to determine sibling order. Line 9-12 check the condition (iii) of OCE. Line 11 and 12 return the elements which violate the query sibling order. Finally, line 13-19 check the condition (ii) of OCE.

Now we discuss the main algorithm of *OrderedTJ*. First of all, Line 2 calls *getNext* algorithm to identify the next element to be processed. Line 3 removes partial answers that cannot be extended to total answer from the stack. In line 4, when we insert a new element to stack, we need to check whether it has the appropriate right sibling. If n is a leaf node, we output the whole path solution in line 6.

```
Algorithm getNext (n)
01  if (isLeaf(n))  return n;
02  for all n_i in children(n)  do
03        g_i = getNext(n_i);   if (g_i ≠ n_i ) return n_i ;
04  n_max = max arg_{n_i∈children(n)} getStart(n_i);
05  n_min = min arg_{n_i∈children(n)} getStart(n_i);
06  While (getEnd(n) < getStart(n_max))  proceed(n);
07  if (getStart(n) >getStart(n_min))
08        return  max arg_{n_i∈children(n)∧(getStart(n)>getStart(n_i))} getStart(n_i);
09  sort all n_i in children(n) by start values;
    // assume the new order are n'_1,n'_2, ...,n'_k
10  for each n'_i   (1 ≤ i ≤ n)  do   //check children order
11        if (n'_i ≠ n_i)  return  n'_i;
12        else if ((i>1) ∧ (getEnd(n'_{i-1})>getStart(n'_i))) return n'_{i-1}
13  MoveStreamToList(n, n_max);
14  for n_i in PCRchildren(n)   //check parent-child relationship
15        if (∃e'∈ L_n such that e' is the parent of  C_{n_i} )
16            if  (n_i is the first child of n)
17                Move the cursor of list L_q to point to e';
18            else  return n_i ;
19  return n;

Proceudre MoveStreamToList(n,g)
01 delete any element in L_n that is not an ancestor of getElement(n);
02 while C_n.start < getStart(g) do  if C_n.end>getEnd(g)   L_n.append(C_n);
03                                   advance(T_n)

Procedure getElement(n)
01  if (¬empty(L_n))       return L_n.elementAt(p_n);
02  else    return C_n;

Procedure getStart(n)
01 return the start attribute of getElement(n);

Procedure getEnd(n)
01 return the end attribute of getElement(n);
```

Fig. 5. Function GetNext in the main algorithm OrderedTJ

EXAMPLE 1. *Consider the ordered query and data in Fig 1(d) and (e) again. First of all, the five cursors are ($book_1$, $chapter_1$, $title_1$,"related work", $section_1$). After two calls of **getNext**(book), the cursors are forwarded to ($book_1$, $chapter_2$, $title_2$,"related work", $section_1$). Since $section_1.start=6<chapter_2.start=9$, we return section (in line 11 of getNext) and forward to $section_2$. Then $chapter_2.end=15> section_2.start=13$. We* return section again (in line 12 of getNext) and forward to $section_3$. Then $chapter_2.end=15 < section_3.start=17$. The following steps push $book_1$ to stack and output the individual two path solutions. Finally, in the second phase of main algorithm, two path solutions are merged to form one final answer □

3.3 Analysis of OrderedTJ

In the section, we show the correctness of *OrderedTJ* and analyze its efficiency. Some proofs are omitted here due to space limitation.

DEFINITION 2 (**head element** e_n) *In OrderedTJ, for each node in the ordered query, if List L_n is not empty, then we say that the element indicated by the cursor p_n of L_n is the head element of n, denoted by e_n. Otherwise, we say that element C_n in the stream T_n is the head element of n.* □

LEMMA 1. *Suppose that for an arbitrary node n in the ordered query we have getNext(n)=n'. Then the following properties hold:*

(1) n' has the OCE.
(2) Either (a) n=n' or (b) parent(n) does not have the OCE because of n' (and possibly a descendant of n').

LEMMA 2. *Suppose getNext(n)=n' returns a query node in the line 11 or 12 of Algorithm getNext. If the current stack is empty, the head element does not contribute to any final solution since it does not satisfy the order condition of query.*

LEMMA 3. *In Procedure moveStreamToStack any element e that is inserted to stack S_n satisfy the order requirement of the query. That is, if n has a right-sibling node n' in query, then there is an element $e_{n'}$ in stream $T_{n'}$ such that $e_{n'}.start > e_n.end$.*

LEMMA 4. *In OrderedTJ, when any element e is popped from stack , e is guaranteed not to participate a new solution any longer.*

THEOREM 1. *Given an ordered twig pattern Q and an XML database D. Algorithm OrderedTJ correctly returns all answers for Q on D.*

Proof:[sketch] Using Lemma 2, we know that when *getNext* returns a query node n in the line 11 and 12 of *getNext*, if the stack is empty, the head element e_n does not contribute to any final solutions. Thus, any element in the ancestors of n that use e_n in the OCE is returned by the *getNext* before e_n. By using lemma 3, we guarantee that each element in stack satisfy the order requirement in the query. Further. By using lemma 4, we can maintain that, for each node n in the query, the elements that involve in the root-leaf path solution in the stack S_n. Finally, each time that $n = getNext(root)$ is a leaf node, we output all solution for e_n (line 6 of *OrderedTJ*). □

Now we analyze the optimality of *OrderedTJ*. Recall that the unordered twig join algorithm *TwigStackList*([5]) is optimal for query with only ancestor-descendant in all branching edges, but our *OrderedTJ* can identify a little **larger** optimal class than *TwigStackList* for ordered query. In particular, the optimality of *OrderedTJ* allows the existence of parent-child relationship in the **first** branching edge, as illustrated below.

EXAMPLE 2. *Consider the ordered query and dataset in Fig 3. If the query were an unordered query, then TwigStackList([5]) would scan a_1, c_1 and b_1 and output one useless solution (a_1,c_1), since before we advance b_1 we could not decide whether a_1 has a child tagged with b. But since this is an ordered query, we immediately identify that c_1 does not contribute to any final answer since there is no element with name b before c_1. Thus, this example tells us that unlike algorithms for unordered query, OrderedTJ may guarantee the optimality for queries with parent-child relationship in the first branching edge.* □

THEOREM 2. *Consider an XML database D and an ordered twig query Q with only ancestor-descendant relationships in the n'th ($n \geq 2$) branching edge. The worst case I/O complexity of OrdereTJ is linear in the sum of the sizes of input and output lists. The worst-case space complexity of this algorithm is that the number of nodes in Q times the length of the longest path in D.* □

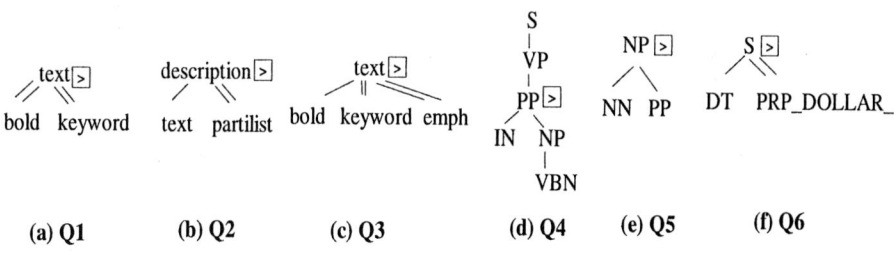

Fig. 6. Six tested ordered twig queries (Q1,2,3 in XMark; Q4,5,6 in TreeBank)

4 Experimental Evaluation

4.1 Experimental Setup

We implemented three ordered twig join algorithms: *straightforward -TwigStack (for short STW), straightforward-TwigStackList (STWL)* and *OrderedTJ*. The first two algorithms use the straightforward post-processing approach. By post-processing, we mean that the query is first matched as an unordered twig (by TwigStack[1] and TwigStackList[5], respectively) and then we merge all intermediate path solutions to get the answers for an ordered twig. We use JDK 1.4 with the file system as a simple storage engine. All experiments were run on a 1.7G Pentium IV processor with 768MB of main memory and 2GB quota of disk space, running windows XP system. We used two data sets for our experiments. The first is the well-known benchmark data: XMark. The size of file is 115M bytes with factor 1.0. The second is a real dataset: TreeBank[8]. The deep recursive structure of this data set makes this an interesting case for our experiments. The file size is 82M bytes with 2.4 million nodes.

For each data set, we tested three XML twig queries (see Fig 6). These queries have different structures and combinations of parent-child and ancestor-descendant edges. We choose these queries to give a comprehensive comparison of algorithms.

Evaluation metrics. We will use the following metrics to compare the performance of different algorithms. (i) **Number of intermediate path solutions** This metric measures the total number of intermediate path solutions, which reflects the ability of algorithms to control the size of intermediate results. (ii) **Total running time** This metric is obtained by averaging the total time elapsed to answer a query with six consecutive runs and the best and worst performance results discarded.

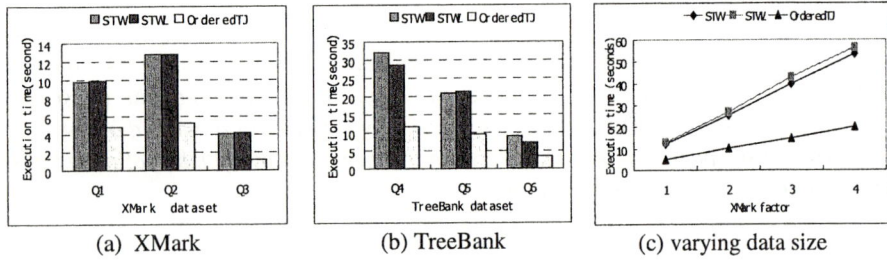

(a) XMark (b) TreeBank (c) varying data size

Fig. 7. Evaluation of ordered twig pattern on two datasets

Table 1. The number of intermediate path solutions

Query	Dataset	STW	STWL	OrderedTJ	Useful solutions
Q1	XMark	71956	71956	44382	44382
Q2	XMark	65940	65940	10679	10679
Q3	XMark	71522	71522	23959	23959
Q4	TreeBank	2237	1502	381	302
Q5	TreeBank	92705	92705	83635	79941
Q6	TreeBank	10663	11	5	5

4.2 Performance Analysis

Figure 7 shows the results on execution time. An immediate observation from the figure is that *OrderedTJ* is more efficient than STW and STWL for all queries. This can be explained that *OrderedTJ* output much less intermediate results. Table 1 shows the number of intermediate path solutions. The last column shows the number of path solutions that contribute to final solutions. For example, STW and STWL could output 500% more intermediate results than *OrderedTJ* (see XMark Q2).

Scalability. We tested queries XMark Q2 for scalability. We use XMark factor 1(115MB), 2(232MB), 3 (349M) and 4(465M). As shown in Fig 7(c), *OrderedTJ* scales linearly with the size of the database. With the increase of data size, the benefit of *OrderedTJ* over STW and STWL correspondingly increases.

Sub-optimality of OrderedTJ. As explained in Section 3, when there is any parent-child relationship in the n'th branching edges ($n \geq 2$), *OrderedTJ* is not optimal. As shown in Q4,Q5 of Table 1, none of algorithms is optimal, since all algorithms output some useless solutions. However, even in this case, *OrderedTJ* still outperforms STW and STWL by outputting **less** useless intermediate results.

Summary. According to the experimental results, we draw two conclusions. First, our new algorithm *OrderedTJ*, could be used to evaluate ordered twig pattern because they have obvious performance advantage over the straightforward approach: STW and STWL. Second, *OrderedTJ* guarantee the I/O optimality for a large query class.

5 Conclusion and Future Work

In this paper, we proposed a new holistic twig join algorithm, called *OrderedTJ*, for processing **ordered** twig query. Although the idea of *holistic* twig join has been proposed in unordered twig join, applying it for ordered twig matching is nontrivial. We developed a new concept *ordered child extension* to determine whether an element possibly involves in query answers. We also make the contribution by identifying a large query class to guarantee I/O optimal for *OrderedTJ*. Experimental results showed the effectiveness, scalability, and efficiency of our algorithm.

There is more to answer XPath query than is within the scope of this paper. Consider an XPath query: "//a/following-sibling::b", we cannot transform this query to an ordered twig pattern, since there is no *root* node in this query. Thus, algorithm *OrderedTJ* cannot be used to answer this XPath. In fact, based on region code (*start,end,level*), none of algorithms can answer this query by accessing the labels of *a* and *b* alone, since *a* and *b* may have *no common parent* even if they belong to the same level. We are currently designing a new labeling scheme to handle such case.

References

1. N. Bruno, N. Koudas, and D. Srivastava. Holistic Twig Joins: Optimal XML pattern matching. In *Proc. of the SIGMOD, pages 310-321 2002.*
2. T. Chen J. Lu , and T. W Ling On boosting holism in XML twig pattern matching using structural indexing techniques In *Proc. of the SIGMOD* 2005 To appear
3. H. Jiang, H. Lu, W. Wang, Efficient Processing of XML Twig Queries with OR-Predicates, In *Proc. of the SIGMOD pages 59-70 2004.*
4. H. Jiang, et al. Holistic twig joins on indexed XML documents. In *Proc. of the VLDB, pages 273-284, 2003.*
5. J. Lu , T. Chen and T. W. Ling Efficient Processing of XML Twig Patterns with Parent Child Edges: A Look-ahead Approach In *Proc. of CIKM, pages 533-542, 2004*
6. J. Lu et. al From Region Encoding To Extended Dewey: On Efficient Processing of XML Twig Pattern Matching In *Proc. of VLDB, 2005* To appear
7. S. Al-Khalifa et. al Structural joins: A primitive for efficient XML query pattern matching. In *Proc. of the ICDE, pages 141-152, 2002.*
8. Treebank http://www.cs.washington.edu/research/xmldatasets/www/repository.html
9. C. Zhang et. al. On supporting containment queries in relational database management systems. In *Proc. of the SIGMOD, 2001.*

A Flexible Role-Based Delegation Model Using Characteristics of Permissions*

Dong-Gue Park and You-Ri Lee

Department of Information and Technology Engineering, College of Engineering,
SoonChunHyang University,
San 53-1, Eupnae-ri, Shinchang-myun Asan-si Choongnam, Korea
{dgpark, thisglass}@sch.ac.kr

Abstract. Role-Based Access Control(RBAC) has recently received considerable attention as a promising alternative to traditional discretionary and mandatory access controls.[7] RBAC ensures that only authorized users are given access to protected data or resources. A successful marriage of Web and RBAC technology can support effective security in large scale enterprise-wide systems with various organization structures. Most large organizations have some business rules related to access control policy. Delegation of authority is an important one of these rules.[1] RBDM0, RDM2000 and PBDM models are recently published models for role-based delegation. RBDM0 and RDM2000 models deal with user-to-user delegation and total delegation. PBDM supports user-to-user and role-to-role delegations and also supports both role and permission level delegation, which provides great flexibility in authority management. But PBDM does not support constraints in RBAC delegation models, such as separation of duty in user-to-user and role to-role delegation. This paper proposes a new delegation model using characteristics of permissions, in which security administrator can easily perform partial delegation, permission level delegation and restricted inheritance. It supports flexible delegation by dividing a role into sub-roles according to characteristics of permissions assigned to the role and considering delegation and inheritance simultaneously. It provides flexibility in authority management such as multi-step delegation, multi-option revocation and controlled inheritance by including characteristics of PBDM and sub-role hierarchies concept. It also supports constraints such as separation of duty based on permission in user-to-user and role-to-role delegation.

1 Introduction

Access control is an important security issue in large organizations. Role-based access control (RBAC) has received considerable attention as an established alternative to traditional discretionary and mandatory access control for large organizations. [7,8] In RBAC, delegation means that a person gives all or part of his authority to somebody, which is an important one of some business rules related to access control policy. Delegation can take place in many situations such as backup of role, collaboration of

---

* "This work was supported by the Korea Research Foundation Grant."(KRF-2004-002-D00391).

work and decentralization of authority. [1] If an individual is on a business trip or long-term absence, the absent individual's job functions need to be delegated to somebody to be maintained by others. And when people need to collaborate with others in the same organization or other organizations, this requires to grant some access authority to share information. Finally, when an organization needs to setup initially or reorganize subsequently, job functions are distributed from higher job positions to lower job positions. While the third case needs durable delegation, the first and second cases need temporary delegation of authority, which means that the term of delegation is short; after the term ends, delegated authority is revoked or expired.[1]

Recently, a number of research activities dealing with various aspects of delegation have been published. [1-6] RBDM0, RDM2000, PBDM[1] and RBDM using sub-role hierarchies models[2] are recently published models for role-based delegation. RBDM0 and RDM2000 models deal with user-to-user delegation and total delegation. PBDM supports user-to-user and role-to-role delegations and also supports both role and permission level delegation, which provides great flexibility in authority management. [1] But PBDM does not support constraints in RBAC delegation models, such as separation of duty in user-to-user and role to-role delegation. RBDM using sub-role hierarchies supports various delegation types such as total/partial delegation user-to-user/role-to-role delegation. [2][3] But this model does not consider constraints such as multi-step delegation and temporal delegation. In this paper we propose a new flexible delegation model, which combines characteristics of PBDM and sub-role hierarchies concept. The proposed model supports restricted inheritance and permission level delegation simultaneously by dividing a role into several sub-roles according to characteristics of permissions assigned to the role. It also supports multi-step delegation, multi-option revocation and constraints such as separation of duty in user-to-user and role-to-role delegation. PBDM and RBDM model using sub-role hierarchies can be interpreted as special cases of the proposed delegation model in this paper. The advantages of these two models are thereby also available in the proposed model in this paper.

The rest of this paper is organized as follows. Next, in Section 2, we describe the previous technologies related in our approach. We briefly review RBDM0, RDM2000, PBDM and RBDM using sub-role hierarchies models. In Section 3, we present a new delegation model. In Section 4 we compare our model with previous works. This is followed by our conclusion in Section 5.

2 Related Works

RBDM0 model[5, 6] is the first attempt to model delegation involving user-to-user based on roles. It is a simple role-based delegation model and formalized the delegation model with total delegation. And it also deals with some issues including revocation, delegation with hierarchical roles and multi-step delegation. [4]

RDM2000, which is an extension of RBDM0, supports regular role delegation in role hierarchy and multi-step delegation. It has proposed a rule-based declarative language to specify and enforce policies. And it uses can_delegate condition to restrict the scope of delegation. But when delegator wants to delegate a piece of role, the RBDM0 or RDM2000 can not cover this case since the unit of delegation in RBDM0 or RDM2000 is "role".

PBDM supports flexible role and permission level delegation. A delegator delegates his/her entire or partial permissions to others by using it. It supports flexible delegation by separating delegation role from regular role and delegatable role and by separating temporal permissions delegated from other roles and its original delegatable permissions. RBDM0 and RDM2000 model can be interpreted as special cases of PBDM. The advantages of these two models are thereby also available in PBDM.[1] But PBDM does not support constraints such as separation of duty in user-to-user and role-to-role delegation and restricted inheritance.

RBDM model using sub-role hierarchies was proposed to support various delegation types such as total/partial delegation user-to-user/role-to-role delegation. It supports restricted inheritance functionally by using sub-role hierarchies. [2] But this model has problem that does not support constraints such as multi-step delegation and temporal delegation. And also it does not support permission level delegation.

3 A New Role-Based Delegation Model Using Characteristics of Permissions

3.1 Role Hierarchies Considering Characteristics of Permissions

3.1.1 Extended Sub-role Hierarchies

A role is a job function in the organization that describes the authority and responsibility conferred on a user assigned to the role. Administrators can create roles according to the job functions performed in their organization. This is very intuitive and efficient approach except unconditional permission inheritance. [2] In RBAC models, a senior role inherits the permissions of all its junior roles. This property may breach the least privilege principle, one of the main security principles which RBAC models support. In order to address this drawback, RBDM model using sub-role hierarchies

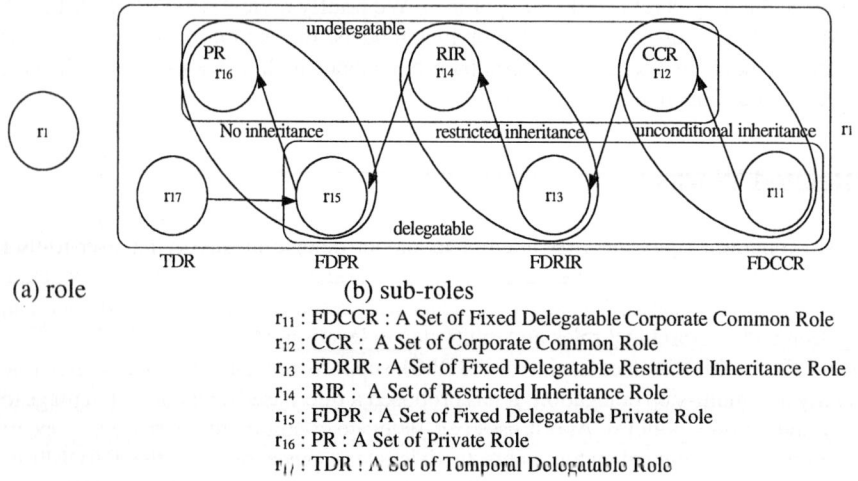

r_{11} : FDCCR : A Set of Fixed Delegatable Corporate Common Role
r_{12} : CCR : A Set of Corporate Common Role
r_{13} : FDRIR : A Set of Fixed Delegatable Restricted Inheritance Role
r_{14} : RIR : A Set of Restricted Inheritance Role
r_{15} : FDPR : A Set of Fixed Delegatable Private Role
r_{16} : PR : A Set of Private Role
r_{17} : TDR : A Set of Temporal Delegatable Role

Fig. 1. Extended Sub-role Hierarchies Concept Considering Characteristics of Permissions

divide a role into a number of sub-roles based on the characteristics of job functions and the degree of inheritance. [2] But it does not support constraints such as multi-step delegation, temporal delegation and permission level delegation. In order to solve these problems and to provide restricted permission inheritance and partial delegation simultaneously, we extend sub-role hierarchies concept. At first, we classify the sub-roles in sub-role hierarchies to two classes such as delegatable sub-roles and undelegatable sub-roles. And then each class sub-roles is divided into sub-roles considering corporation environment which consists of several departments and job positions such as corporate common roles and restricted inheritance roles which have restricted inheritance properties. Figure 1 shows a extended sub-role hierarchies concept compared with an original role. Also Table 1 represents the characteristics of permissions assigned to sub-roles in Figure 1.

Table 1. Categorization according to Characteristics of Permissions assigned to Sub-roles

Sub-role category	Degree of Inheritance	Degree of delegation	Characteristics of permissions assigned to sub-roles
PR	no inheritance	undelegatable	- permissions only allowed to directly assigned users - permissions can not be inherited to any other roles - permissions can not be delegated to any other roles or users
FDPR	no inheritance	delegatable	- permissions can not be inherited to any other roles - permissions can be delegated to any other roles or users
RIR	restricted inheritance	undelegatable	- permissions may or may not be inherited to its senior roles in RIR hierarchy - security administrator specify the roles to which permissions are restrictively inherited - permissions can not be delegated to any other roles or users
FDRIR	restricted inheritance	delegatable	- permissions may or may not be inherited to its senior roles in FDRIR hierarchy - security administrator specify the roles to which permissions are restrictively inherited - permissions can be delegated to any other roles or users
CCR	unconditional inheritance	undelegatable	- permissions allowed to all members in a corporation - includes junior roles' permissions in a CCR hierarchy - permissions can not be delegated to any other roles or users
FDCCR	unconditional inheritance	delegatable	- permissions allowed to all members in a corporation - includes junior roles' permissions in a FDCCR hierarchy - permissions can be delegated to any other roles or users
TDR	no inheritance	delegatable (multi-step delegation)	- permissions received from delegator with role-role assignment - permissions can be delegated by multi-step delegation.

3.1.2 User Assignment in Extended Sub-role Hierarchies

Figure 2 illustrates how users are assigned to roles in the extended sub-role hierarchies. Figure 2(a) shows a user-role assignment in a traditional role hierarchy and (b) depicts a user-role assignment in the proposed model. Solid lines in Figure 2 indicate permission inheritance, while a dotted line denotes restricted inheritance. For example, both $r_{11} \rightarrow r_{21}$ and $r_{12} \rightarrow r_{22}$ relations indicate that the permissions of the junior roles are unconditionally inherited to its seniors, respectively. But both $r_{13} \rightarrow r_{23}$ and $r_{14} \rightarrow r_{24}$ relations(a dotted line) shows restricted inheritance relation in which permissions of sub-role(r_{13}) and sub-role(r_{14}) are inherited only to designated its senior roles, in this example, r_{23} and r_{24}. The scope of restricted inheritance in the proposed model is determined by security administrator. Finally, r_{15} and r_{25} are fixed delegatable private sub-roles and no permission inheritance occurs between two fixed delegatable private sub-roles. Also r_{16} and r_{26} are private sub-roles and they are allowed to directly assigned users and permission inheritance is inhibited between them. Users can be assigned to private sub-roles. There are two kinds of sub-role hierarchies in Figure 2(b), which are horizontal hierarchy and vertical hierarchy. Horizontal hierarchy is a partially ordered relation between sub-roles, which are classified from the same original role, and there are unconditional permission inheritance between sub-roles in it. Vertical hierarchy is a partially ordered relation between sub-roles in the same sub-role category which can be inherited. (i.e., RIR, CCR, FDRIR and FDCCR). But there are both unconditional permission inheritance((i.e., CCR and FDCCR)and conditional permission inheritance(i.e., RIR and FDRIR) between sub-roles in it. Even though Figure 2(b) shows that there are six sub-roles at each role level and each user is allocated for all sub-roles by user-role assignment, a security administrator can assign some of them to user by security policy in real world .

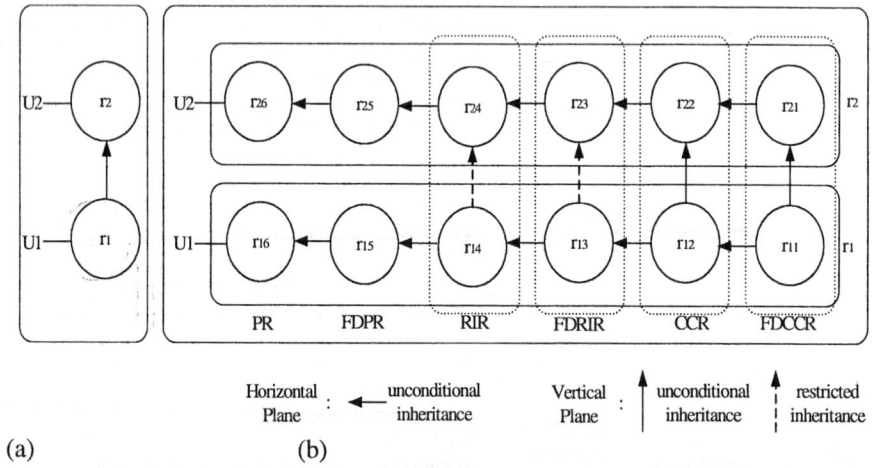

Fig. 2. Comparison of User-Role Assignment in the Extended Sub-role Hierarchies

3.2 Overview of Proposed Model

Figure 3 shows a brief of proposed model in this paper. In this model, there are six different layers of roles which are FDCCR, CCR, FDRIR, RIR, FDPR and PR. A role can be divided into six sub-roles by considering characteristics of permissions assign to it.

This partition induces a parallel partition of PA. PA is separated into seven partitions which are permission-fixed delegatable corporate common role assignment(PAFC), permission-corporate common role assignment(PACC), permission-fixed delegatable restricted inheritance role assignment (PAFR), permission-restricted Inheritance role assignment(PARI), permission-fixed delegatable private role assignment(PAFP), permission-private role assignment(PAPR) and permission-delegation role assignment (PADR) . But UA is not separated and a user is assigned to PR. PR is a top sub-role in horizontal hierarchy, which has all permissions in sub-roles consisted of horizontal hierarchy.

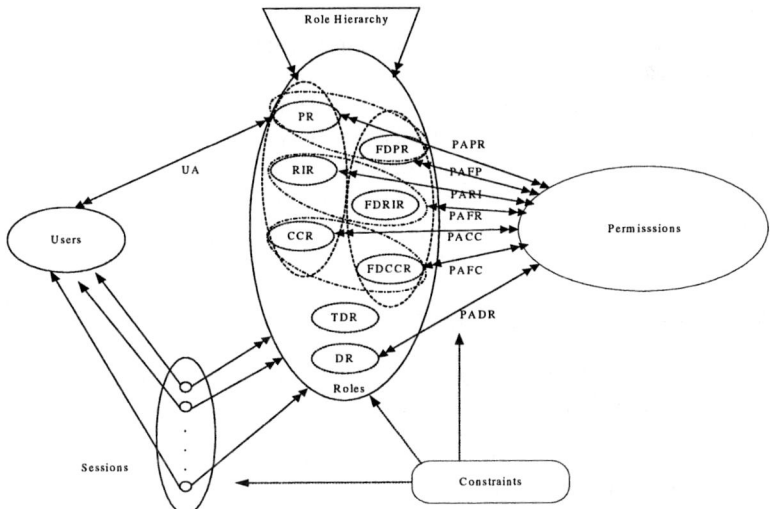

Fig. 3. A New Delegation Model Using Characteristics of Permissions

A security administrator can assign permissions to adequate sub-roles considering characteristics of permissions such as inheritance and delegation. In order to restrict junior's permission to senior role with degree of inheritance and business characteristics by using restricted inheritance hierarchy , we divide a role to two sub role classes about inheritance, one which has controlled inheritance characteristic and the other which has uncontrolled inheritance characteristic. [2] And we classify a role into two classes concerning delegation, one which has delegatable characteristic and the other which has undelegatable characteristic. The permissions, which have unique, private and undelegatable characteristic, are assigned to PR and the other permissions, which have unique, private and delegatable characteristic, are assigned to FDPR by a security administrator. As like this, the security administrator can control the permission flow by assigning different permissions to classes having different characteristic about delegation. Also, he can restrict junior's permission to senior role by using restricted inheritance hierarchy.

Permissions assigned to both RIR and CCR can not be delegated to other roles or users. But the permissions assigned to RIR are controlled inherited to senior roles with degree of inheritance and the permissions assigned to CCR are uncontrolled inherited to senior roles. By classifying a original role to two classes about inheritance, we can prevent that a role can be inherited all permissions of its junior roles and a role has unnecessarily too many permissions.

FDCCR and FDRIR are the roles whose permissions can be delegated to other roles or users by creating a delegation role. The difference between FDCCR and FDRIR is that the permissions, assigned to FDRIR like a RIR, are controlled inherited to senior roles and the permissions which are assigned to FDCCR like a CCR are uncontrolled inherited to senior roles. We divide a fixed delegatable role in PBDM[1] into three parts, such as FDPR, FDRIR and FDCCR to obtain fine-grained access control by considering simultaneously delegation and inheritance as characteristics of permissions.

A TDR has the permissions that it receives from a delegation role(DR) as delegator with role-role assignment. Since there is no role hierarchy for a TDR and its permissions are inherited to FDPR at the same horizontal plane even though multi-step delegations are occurred, invalid permission flow will not happen and then a role-to-role delegation can be achieved. In proposed model like PBDM2[1], delegator is FDPR, FDCCR and FDRIR and they are the owner of a delegation role. If multi-step delegation is occured, permissions assigned to TDR can be delegated to other users or roles.

3.3 Formal Description in Proposed Model

We define a set of components to formally describe the characteristics and behavior of the proposed model as follows:

- R : a set of roles($r1, r2, r3, ..., rn \in R$)
- P : a set of permissions($p1, p2, p3, ..., pn \in P$)
- POSR : sum of roles related to positions (vertical plane)
- JOBR : sum of roles related to jobs (horizontal plane)
  [JOBR = PR $\cup$ FDPR $\cup$ RIR $\cup$ FDRIR $\cup$ CCR $\cup$ FDCCR $\cup$ TDR]
- POSRi : a set of sub – roles in position i (where $1 \leq i \leq n$)
- $\geq$: a partial order on RH (if $r2 \geq r1$, then r2 is a senior to r1)
- RH : Role Hierarchy [RH $\subseteq$ R $\times$ R, partially ordered]
- RIRH : Hierarchy of RIRs [RIRH $\subseteq$ RIR $\times$ RIR, partially ordered]
- FDRIRH : Hierarchy of FDRIRs [FDRIRH $\subseteq$ FDRIR $\times$ FDRIR, partially ordered]
- CCRH : Hierarchy of CCRs [CCRH $\subseteq$ CCR $\times$ CCR, partially ordered]
- FDCCRH : Hierarchy of FDCCRs [FDCCRH $\subseteq$ FDCCR $\times$ FDCCR, partially ordered]
- DRH_r : Hierarchy of DRs owned by a role r [$DRH_r \subseteq DR \times DR$, partially ordered]

- POSRHi : Hierarchy of sub − roles [POSRHi ⊆ POSRi × POSRi, where $1 \leq i \leq n$, partially ordered]
- role_jobs(r) : a function to return which job a role r is related to,
  [R → PR ∪ FDPR ∪ RIR ∪ CCR ∪ FDRIR ∪ FDCCR ∪ TDR]
- role_positions(r) : a function to return which position a role r is related to,
  [R → POSRi, $1 \leq i \leq n$]
- UA ⊆ U × PR
- PA = PAPR ∪ PAFP ∪ PARI ∪ PAFR ∪ PACC ∪ PAFC ∪ PADR
  [PAPR ⊆ P × PR, PAFP ⊆ P × FDPR, PARI ⊆ P × RIR, PAFR ⊆ P × FDRIR, PACC ⊆ P × CCR, PAFC ⊆ P × FDCCR, PADR ⊆ P × DR, RAD = TDR × DR]
- user_pr(r) : a function mapping a PR to a set of users that are assigned to this role.
  [user_pr(r) : PR → 2^U]
- own_rp(r) : a function mapping each FDRIR to a FDPR at the same horizontal plane.
  [own_rp(r) : FDRIR → FDPR]
- own_cp(r) : a function mapping each FDCCR to a FDPR at the same horizontal plane.
  [own_cp(r) : FDCCR → FDPR]
- own_tp(r) : a function mapping each TDR to a single FDPR at the same horizontal plane.
  [own_tp(r) : TDR → FDPR]
- own_cd(r) : a function mapping a FDCCR to a set of DRs.
  [own_cd(r) : FDCCR → 2^{DR} and $\nexists$(fdccr$_1$, fdccr$_2$ ∈ FDCCR, dr ∈ DR) ·(fdccr$_1$ ≠ fdccr$_2$)
  ∧ (dr ∈ own_cd(fdccr$_1$) ∧ dr ∈ own_cd(fdccr$_2$))]
- own_rd(r) : a function mapping a FDRIR to a set of DRs.
  [own_rd(r) : FDRIR → 2^{DR} and $\nexists$(fdrir$_1$, fdrir$_2$ ∈ FDRIR, dr ∈ DR) ·(fdrir$_1$ ≠ fdrir$_2$)
  ∧ (dr ∈ own_rd(fdrir$_1$) ∧ dr ∈ own_rd(fdrir$_2$))]
- own_pd(r) : a function mapping a FDPR to a set of DRs.
  [own_pd(r) : FDPR → 2^{DR} and $\nexists$(fdpr$_1$, fdpr$_2$ ∈ FDPR, dr ∈ DR) ·(fdpr$_1$ ≠ fdpr$_2$)
  ∧ (dr ∈ own_pd(fdpr$_1$) ∧ dr ∈ own_pd(fdpr$_2$))]
- rad(r) : a function mapping a TDR to a set of DRs. [rad(r) : TDR → 2^{DR}]
- permissions_pr(r) : PR → 2^P, a function mapping a PR to a set of permissions.
  [permissions_pr(r) = {p : P | ∃ r' ≤ r·(r', p) ∈ PAPR}]
- permissions_fp(r) : FDPR → 2^P, a function mapping a FDPR to a set of permissions.
  [permissions_fp(r) = {p : P | ∃ r' ≤ r·(r', p) ∈ PAFP}]
- permissions_ri(r) : RIR → 2^P, a function mapping a RIR to a set of permissions.
  [permissions_ri(r) = {p : P | ∃ r' ≤ r·(r', p) ∈ PARI}]
- permission_cc(r) : CCR → 2^P, a function mapping CCR to a set of permissions.
  [permissions_cc(r) = {p : P | ∃ r' ≤ r·(r', p) ∈ PACC}]
- permission_fr(r) : FDRIR → 2^P, a function mapping a FDRIR to a set of permissions.
  [permissions_fr(r) = {p : P | ∃ r' ≤ r·(r', p) ∈ PAFR}]
- permission_fc(r) : FDCCR → 2^P, a function mapping a FDCCR to a set of permissions.
  [permissions_fc(r) = {p : P | ∃ r' ≤ r·(r', p) ∈ PAFC}]

- permissions_dr(r) : DR → 2^P, a function mapping a DR to a set of permissions.

  [permissions_dr(r) = {p : P | $\exists$ r' $\leq$ r·(r', p) $\in$ PADR}]
- permissions_t*(r) : TDR → 2^P, a function mapping a TDR to a set of permissions inherited from RAD.

  [permission_t*(r) = {p : P | $\exists$ r' $\in$ DR·(r', p) $\in$ PADR $\wedge$ r' $\in$ rad(r)}]
- permissions_f*(r) : FDPR → 2^P, a function mapping a FDPR to a set of delegatable permissions with PAFP, PAFR, PAFC and RAD (when multi-step delegation is allowed).

  [permissions_f*(r) = {p : P | (r, p) $\in$ PAFP} $\cup$

  {p : P | $\exists$ r' $\in$ FDRIR·(r', p) $\in$ PAFR $\wedge$ r = own_rp(r') } $\cup$

  {p : P | $\exists$ r" $\in$ FDCCR·(r", p) $\in$ PAFC $\wedge$ r = own_cp(r") } $\cup$

  {p : P | $\exists$ r'" $\in$ TDR·p $\in$ permissions_t*(r'") $\wedge$ r = own_tp(r'") }]
- $\forall$ dr $\in$ DR, $\exists$ fdpr $\in$ FDPR, $\exists$ fdrir $\in$ FDRIR, $\exists$ fdccr $\in$ FDCCR,

  Fdpr=own_rp(fdrir) $\wedge$ fdpr=own_cp(fdccr)·(dr $\in$ own_pd(fdpr) $\cup$ own_rd(fdrir) $\cup$ own_cd(fdccr)) $\wedge$ (permissions_dr(dr) $\subseteq$ permission_f*(fdpr)) :

  the permissions pool to create a delegation role owned by a role is the delegatable permissions that assigned to this role by PAFP, PAFR, PAFC and RAD. (when multi-step delegation is allowed).
- can_delegate $\subseteq$ FDPR × Pre_con × P_range × MD where Pre_con: prerequisite condition,

  P_range: delegation range,

  MD: maximum delegation depth : a relation to mapping a FDPR to its delegation range.

3.4 Permission Inheritance and Delegation in Proposed Model

Figure 4 depicts an example of role hierarchy. In Figure 4, we suppose that a security administrator wants that in each branch, the "review customer" permission of Branch Employer(BE) is inherited to Branch Buyer(BB) but is not inherited to Branch Accountant Manager (BAM), even though it is a senior role of BB. In the proposed model, this requirement is accomplished by assigning the "review customer" permission of BE to RI sub-role category of BE.

Figure 5 is the part of extended sub-role hierarchy of Figure 4. In Figure 5, even if B1AM role is a senior role of B1B, the permissions of r_{j4} in B1E role are not inherited to r_{i4} in B1AM. And if we suppose that a user, who is assigned to DM role, is on a business trip and so security administrator wants to delegate "review branch account" permission of DM role, which is partial permission assigned to DM role, to B1AM role, he can solve this requirement by performing the following three phases in the proposed model.

Phase1 : Create D1 as a DR.
Phase2 : Assign "review branch account" permission to D1.
Phase3 : Assign D1 to TDR in B1AM role by RAD.

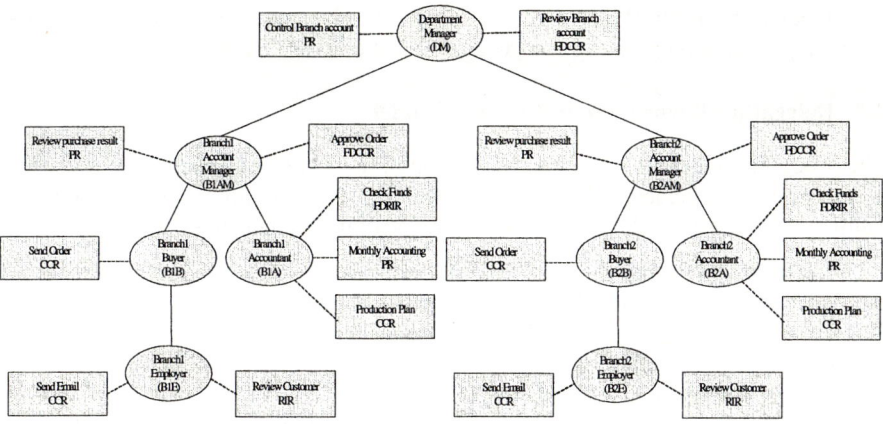

Fig. 4. Example of Role Hierarchy

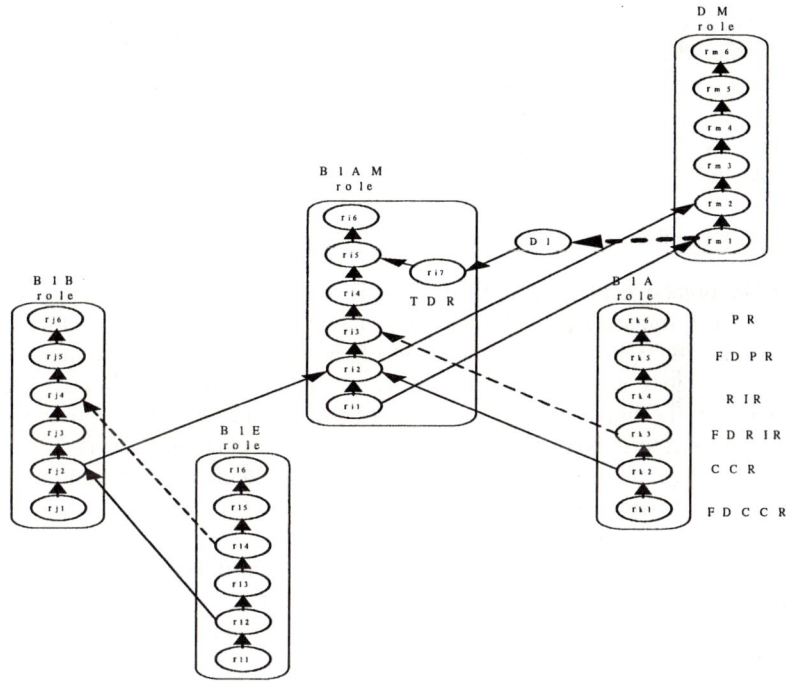

Fig. 5. Example of Permission Inheritance and Delegation in Proposed Model

The dotted line, which is from r_{m1} in DM role to D1 in Figure 5, shows that "review branch account" permission assigned to DM role is delegated to D1. The arrow line, which is from D1 in Figure 5, shows the TDR - DR assignment by RAD. Also, the proposed model supports multi-step delegation and multi-option revocation because it is extended from PBDM[1] and can have the advantage of PBDM. It provides multi-step delegation by using can_delegate function like PBDM.

3.5 Delegation Revocation in Proposed Model

The proposed model also supports multi-option revocation and multi-step revocation by extending the characteristics of PBDM, which provides multi-option revocation and multi-step revocation. Possible multi-step revocation mechanism is as follows.

1. Select lowest TDR (multi-step delegation case) which is delegated recursively one or more pieces of permissions from the DR which will be revoked.
2. Remove permissions, which should be revoked, from the TDR which was selected in step 1.
3. Select the DR which is owner of the TDR
4. If the DR selected in step3 is the DR which will be revoked, go to step 10 or go to step 5.
5. Remove permissions, which should be revoked, from the DR selected in step 3.
6. Find the FDPR which is owner of the DR selected in step 3.
7. If there are any other permissions in the DR, go to step 9 or go to step 8.
8. Remove the DR selected in step 3.
9. Find the TDR which is descendant of the FDPR in horizontal hierarchy. And go to step 2
10. Remove one or more pieces of permissions from the DR which will be revoked.
11. Remove the DR which will be revoked.

3.6 Separation of Duty in Permission Level Delegation

The primary objective of separation of duty is to prevent fraud and error, and is achieved by disseminating the roles and associated privileges for a specific business process among multiple users. Enforcement of the separation of duty requirements relies on an access control service that is sensitive to the separation of duty requirements.[9] It is important that separation of duty is studied in the proposed model in order to prevent to fraud and error, which are occurred in complex work processes such as controlled inheritance, partial delegation and temporal delegation . The proposed model provides Static Separation of Duty (SSoD) constraints and Dynamic Separation of Duty (DSoD) constraints based on role and permission. It prevents conflicts occurred from complex processes such as controlled inheritance, partial delegation and temporal delegation by supporting permission-based SSoD and DSoD .

We define a set of components to formally describe the characteristics and behavior of SSoD constraints and DSoD constraints of the proposed model. They are as follows:

• mutex_roles_set : a set of role pair with mutually static exclusive relation.
• mutex_permissions_set : a set of permission pair with mutually static exclusive relation.
• dynamic_mutex_roles_set : a set of role pair with mutually dynamic exclusive relation.
• dynamic_mutex_permissions_set : a set of permission pair with mutually dynamic exclusive relation.

SSoD constraints in the proposed model can satisfy as follows:
- user-assigned-roles(u) : a function to return roles which are assigned to user u
- user-delegated-roles(u) : a function to return roles which are delegated to roles which are assigned to user u
- role-assigned-permissions(r) : a function to return permissions which are assigned to role r
- role-delegated-permissions(r) : a function to return permissions which are delegated to role r

- $\forall$ r1, r2 $\in$ ROLES $\forall$ u $\in$ USERS $\forall$ p1, p2 $\in$ PERMISSIONS(r1 $\in$ user-assigned-roles(u) $\vee$

  r1 $\in$ user-delegated-roles(u)) $\wedge$ (r2 $\in$ user-assigned-roles(u) $\vee$ r2 $\in$ user-delegated- roles(u)) $\wedge$

  (p1 $\in$ role-assigned-permissions(r1) $\vee$ p1 $\in$ role-delegated-permissions(r1)) $\wedge$ (p2 $\in$ role-assigned- permissions(r2) $\vee$ p2 $\in$ role-delegated-permissions(r2)) $\rightarrow$

  (p1,p2) $\notin$ mutex_permissions _set

- $\forall$ r1, r2 $\in$ ROLES $\forall$ u $\in$ USERS (r1 $\in$ user-assigned-roles(u) $\vee$ r1 $\in$ user-delegated -roles(u)) $\wedge$

  (r2 $\in$ user-assigned-roles(u) $\vee$ r2 $\in$ user-delegated-roles(u)) $\rightarrow$ (r1,r2) $\notin$ mutex_roles_set

- $\forall$ r1, r2 $\in$ ROLES $\forall$ p1,p2 $\in$ PERMISSIONS (r1 $\geq$ r2) $\wedge$ (p1 $\in$ role-assigned-permissions(r1) $\vee$

  p1 $\in$ role-delegated-permissions(r1)) $\wedge$ (p2 $\in$ role-assigned-permissions(r2) $\vee$

  p2 $\in$ role-delegated-permissions(r2)) $\rightarrow$ (p1,p2) $\notin$ mutex_permissions_set

DSoD constraints in the proposed model can satisfy as follows:
- subject-user(s) : a function to return user who is subject of session s
- active-assigned-roles(s) : a function to return roles which are assigned to subject-user(s) and are active by session s
- active-delegated-roles(u) : a function to return roles which are delegated to roles which are assigned to subject-user(s) and are active by session s

- $\forall$ r1,r2 $\in$ ROLES $\forall$ s1,s2 $\in$ SESSIONS $\forall$ p1,p2 $\in$ PERMISSIONS (r1 $\in$ active-assigned-roles(s1) $\vee$

  r1 $\in$ active-delegated-roles(s1)) $\wedge$ (r2 $\in$ active-assigned-roles(s2) $\vee$ r2 $\in$ active-delegated-roles(s2)) $\wedge$

  subject-user(s1) = subject-user(s2) $\wedge$ (p1 $\in$ role-assigned- permissions(r1) $\vee$ p1 $\in$ role-delegated-permissions(r1)) $\wedge$ (p2 $\in$ role-assigned-permissions(r2) $\vee$

  p2 $\in$ role-delegated-permissions(r2)) $\rightarrow$ (p1,p2) $\notin$ dynamic_mutex_ permissions_set

- $\forall$ r1,r2 $\in$ ROLES $\forall$ s1,s2 $\in$ SESSIONS

  (r1 $\in$ active-assigned-roles(s1) $\vee$ r1 $\in$ active-delegated- roles(s1)) $\wedge$ (r2 $\in$ active-assigned-roles(s2) $\vee$ r2 $\in$ active-delegated-roles(s2)) $\wedge$

subject-user(s1) = subject-user(s2) → (r1,r2) ∉ dynamic_mutex_roles_set
- ∀ r1, r2 , r3 ∈ ROLES (r1 ≥ r2) ∨ (r3 ≥ r1 ∧ r3 ≥ r2)
→ (r1,r2) ∉ dynamic_mutex_roles_set
- ∀ r1, r2 , r3 ∈ ROLES (r1 ≥ r2) ∧ (r2, r3) ∈ dynamic mutex roles set
→ (r1,r3) ∈ dynamic_mutex_roles_set

4 Comparison of Proposed Model with Previous Works

Table 2 summarizes the characteristics of role-based delegation models, and compares the proposed model with previous works. The proposed model in this paper supports constraints such as separation of duty in user-to-user and role-to-role delegation and also supports restricted inheritance and permission level delegation simultaneously. And it supports multi-step delegation and multi-option revocation by extending PBDM. PBDM and RBDM model using sub-role hierarchies can be interpreted as special cases of the proposed delegation model in this paper. The advantages of these two models are thereby also available in the proposed model in this paper. By table 2, we explain effectiveness of the proposed model, which resolves the drawbacks of previous works.

Table 2. Comparison among Role-Based Delegation Models

Criteria / Delegation models		PBDM[1]	Sub-block model[2]	Proposed model
Delegation types	user-to-user	o	o	o
	role-to-role	o	o	o
Totality	total	o	o	o
	partial	o	o	o
Levels of delegation	single-step	o	o	o
	multi-step	o	x	o
SoD	role-based	x	o	o
	permission-based	x	x	o
temporal delegation		o	x	o
controlled inheritance		x	o	o

5 Conclusions

In this paper we propose a new delegation model, which combines PBDM and sub-role hierarchies concept. The proposed model supports temporary delegation situations, multi-step delegation and multi-option revocation like PBDM model and controlled inheritance like sub-role hierarchies model. It also supports constraints such as separation of duty in user-to-user and role-to-role delegation to provide more fine-grained access control.

Our further work is to extend our proposed model to support other delegation characteristics such as negative delegation and obligation delegation.

References

[1] Xinwen Zhang, Sejong Oh, and Ravi Sandhu, PBDM: A Flexible Delegation Model in RBAC, Proc. 8th ACM Symposium on Access Control Models and Technologies (SACMAT 2003), pp.149-157, June, 2003.
[2] HyungHyo Lee, YoungRok Lee and BongHam Noh, A new Role-Based Delegation Model Using Sub-role Hierarchies, International Symposium on Computer and Information Sciences (ISCIS 2003) LNCS 2869 pp.811-818 November, 2003
[3] YongHoon Yi, MyongJae Kim, YoungLok Lee, HyungHyo Lee and BongNam Noh, Applying RBAC Providing Restricted Permission Inheritance to a Corporate Web Environment, The Fifth Asia Pacfic Web Conference(APweb'03) LNCS 2642 pp. 287-292, September, 2003
[4] Longhua Zhang, Gail-Joon Ahn, and Bei-Tseng Chu, A rule-based Framework for Role-Based Delegation, Proc. 6th ACM Symposium on Access Control Models and Technologies (SACMAT 2001), May, 2001.
[5] Ezedin Barka and Ravi Sandhu, A Role-Based Delegation Model and Some Extensions, Proc. of 23rd National Information Systems Security Conference (NISSC 2000). December, 2000.
[6] Ezedin Barka and Ravi Sandhu, Framework for Role-Based Delegation Models, Proc of 16th Annual Computer Security Application Conference (ACSAC 2000). December, 2000.
[7] Ravi Sandhu, Edward Coyne, Hal Feinstein and Charles Youman, Role-Based Access Control Models, IEEE Computer, Volume 29, Number 2, February, 1996.
[8] Ravi Sandhu, Venkata Bhamidipati and Qamar Munawer, The ARBAC97 Model for Role-Based Administration of Roles, ACM Transactions on Information and System Security, Volume 2, Number 1, February, 1999.
[9] Jason Crampton, Specifying and Enforcing Constraints in Role-Based Access Control, Proc. 8th ACM Symposium on Access Control Models and Technologies (SACMAT 2003), pp.43-50,June, 2003.

Provable Data Privacy

Kilian Stoffel[1] and Thomas Studer[2]

[1] Université de Neuchâtel,
Pierre-à-Mazel 7, CH-2000 Neuchâtel, Switzerland
kilian.stoffel@unine.ch

[2] Institut für Informatik und angewandte Mathematik,
Universität Bern, Neubrückstrasse 10, CH-3012 Bern, Switzerland
tstuder@iam.unibe.ch

Abstract. In relational database systems a combination of privileges and views is employed to limit a user's access and to hide non-public data. The data privacy problem is to decide whether the views leak information about the underlying database instance. Or, to put it more formally, the question is whether there are certain answers of a database query with respect to the given view instance. In order to answer the problem of provable date privacy, we will make use of query answering techniques for data exchange. We also investigate the impact of database dependencies on the privacy problem. An example about health care statistics in Switzerland shows that we also have to consider dependencies which are inherent in the semantics of the data.

1 Introduction

Data privacy refers to the relationship between technology and the legal right to, or public expectation of privacy in the collection and sharing of data [16]. Although technology alone cannot address all privacy concerns, it is important that information systems take responsibility for the privacy of the data they manage [1]. The main challenge in data privacy is to share some data while protecting other personally identifiable information. Our aim is to formally prove that under certain circumstances none of the protected data can be logically inferred from the data which is made public.

We investigate this problem in the context of relational database systems. Assume we are given a database whose contents are supposed to be hidden and a view which is exposed to the public. We want to decide whether the view leaks information about the underlying database. Leaking of information means that the set of facts which can be inferred with certainty about the database is non-empty.

Data stored in a relational database system usually is protected from unauthorized access. Some database system users may be allowed to issue queries only to a limited portion of the database. This can be achieved by introducing views. A view can hide data a user does not need to see. Although, we can deny a user direct access to a relation, that user may be allowed to access part of that relation through a view. Thus the combination of privileges and views can limit a user's access to precisely the data that the user needs.

Silberschatz et al. [13] present the following banking example. Consider a clerk who needs to know the names of all customers who have a loan at each branch. This clerk is not authorized to see information regarding specific loans that the customers may have. Thus, the clerk must be denied access to the loan relation. But, if she is to have access to the information needed, the clerk must be granted access to a view that consists of only the names of customers and the branches at which they have a loan. For this example, we want to formally prove that the clerk cannot infer any information about specific loans from the view instances to which she has access.

Let us now study a simple example which shows how it can happen that private data may be derived from a published view instance. Consider a database schema that consist of a table A with two attributes and a table P with one attribute. We define two views by the following queries

$$V_1(x) \leftarrow A(x,y) \wedge P(y) \text{ and } V_2(x) \leftarrow A(x,x).$$

Assume that we have a view instance which contains $V_1(a), V_2(a)$. This view instance does not allow us to infer that a certain element belongs to P. The fact $V_1(a)$ might stem from entries $A(a,b)$ and $P(b)$ and we do not know what b is. Hence, there is no way to say something about P except that it is non-empty. This situation completely changes if we add a unique key constraint to A. Assume that the first attribute of A is a unique key for this table. Then $V_2(a)$ implies that $\forall y.(V(a,y) \to a = y)$. Therefore, by $V_1(a)$, we get that $P(a)$ must hold in any database instance which satisfies the key constraint and which yields the view instance. We see that equality generating dependencies may give rise to unwanted inferences of private data. Hence, in our setting, we have to take into account also the constraints of the database schema.

We formally model the problem of provable data privacy in the following framework: a data privacy setting consists of a database schema $\mathcal{R}$, a set of constraints Σ_r on $\mathcal{R}$, and a set of view definitions $\mathcal{V}$ over $\mathcal{R}$. In addition, assume we are given a view instance I over $\mathcal{V}$ and a query q over $\mathcal{R}$ which is asking for non-public information. In this setting, the data privacy problem consists of the following question: is there a tuple t of constants of I such that $t \in q(J)$ for every database instance J over $\mathcal{R}$ which satisfies the constraints in Σ_r and which yields the view instance I.

Making use of the notion of *certain answer*, we can state the question as: is there a tuple t of constants of I such that t is a certain answer of q with respect to I? That means, is there a tuple t such that $t \in q(J)$ for every 'possible' database instance J? The problem of answering queries against a set of 'possible' databases was first encountered in the context of incomplete databases [15]. Today, certain answer is a key notion in the theory about data integration [5,11,12] and data exchange [8,9,10].

We show that the techniques employed for query answering in the area of data exchange can be applied also to the data privacy problem. In a data exchange setting, we use a standard chase to produce a so-called universal database instance. The certain answers of a query are then computed by evaluating the query on this universal instance. We can make use of the same procedure to find certain answers in the context of data privacy which solves the data privacy problem. Certain answers in the presence of key constraints are also studied in [14]. There, we independently developed a method similar to, but less general than the one presented in [9] in order to solve the data privacy problem.

As we have seen, it is important to consider dependencies in a data privacy setting. This refers not only to constraints on the database schema; we may also encounter so-called *semantic dependencies* which are not explicitly stated but which are inherent in the semantics of the data. We study the following example: the Swiss Federal Statistical Office annually creates statistics about health care in Switzerland. The published data contains semantic dependencies which give rise to equality generating dependencies in the corresponding data privacy setting.

The rest of the paper is organized as follows. In Section 2, we present a formal definition of the data privacy problem. In Section 3, we summarize some results of [9] about query answering in the context of data exchange. We apply these data exchange techniques to solve the data privacy problem in Section 4. We also investigate the impact of dependencies on the privacy problem. This is illustrated in Section 5 with an example about semantic dependencies. Finally, Section 6 concludes the paper.

2 The Data Privacy Problem

In this section, we present the data privacy problem. We need some preliminary definitions in order to formally state the privacy problem.

Definition 1. 1. *A schema is a finite collection $\mathcal{R} = \{R_1, \ldots, R_k\}$ of relation symbols.*
2. *An* instance *I over $\mathcal{R}$ is a function that associates to each relation symbol R_i a relation $I(R_i)$.*
3. *A* view *over a schema $\mathcal{R}$ is a query of the form*

$$V_i(\boldsymbol{x}) \leftarrow \exists \boldsymbol{y} \phi_{\mathcal{R}}(\boldsymbol{x}, \boldsymbol{y})$$

  where $\phi_{\mathcal{R}}(\boldsymbol{x}, \boldsymbol{y})$ is a conjunction of atomic formulas over $\mathcal{R}$. We say that V_i belongs to a set of views $\mathcal{V}$ if $\mathcal{V}$ contains a view $V_i(\boldsymbol{x}) \leftarrow \exists \boldsymbol{y} \phi_{\mathcal{R}}(\boldsymbol{x}, \boldsymbol{y})$.
4. *A* view instance *over a set of views $\mathcal{V}$ is a finite collection of facts of the form $V_i(\boldsymbol{t})$ where V_i belongs to $\mathcal{V}$ and $\boldsymbol{t}$ is a tuple of constants.*
5. *We say a database instance J over $\mathcal{R}$ yields a view instance I over $\mathcal{V}$ if for all facts $V_i(\boldsymbol{t})$ in I, such that $V_i(\boldsymbol{x}) \leftarrow \exists \boldsymbol{y} \phi_{\mathcal{R}}(\boldsymbol{x}, \boldsymbol{y})$ belongs to $\mathcal{V}$, there exists a tuple $\boldsymbol{s}$ of constants of J such that each conjunct of $\phi_{\mathcal{R}}(\boldsymbol{t}, \boldsymbol{s})$ is an element of J.*

Consider the following setting for the data privacy problem:

Definition 2. *A data privacy setting* $(\mathcal{R}, \Sigma_r, \mathcal{V})$ *consists of*

1. *a schema $\mathcal{R}$,*
2. *a set of dependencies Σ_r on $\mathcal{R}$. Each element of Σ_r is either a tuple generating dependency [2] of the form*

$$\forall \boldsymbol{x}(\phi_{\mathcal{R}}(\boldsymbol{x}) \rightarrow \exists \boldsymbol{y} \psi_{\mathcal{R}}(\boldsymbol{x}, \boldsymbol{y}))$$

   or an equality generating dependency [2] of the form

$$\forall \boldsymbol{x}(\phi_{\mathcal{R}}(\boldsymbol{x}) \rightarrow (x_1 = x_2)),$$

   where $\phi_{\mathcal{R}}(\boldsymbol{x})$ and $\psi_{\mathcal{R}}(\boldsymbol{x}, \boldsymbol{y})$ are conjunctions of atomic formulas over $\mathcal{R}$, and x_1, x_2 are among the variables of $\boldsymbol{x}$,
3. *a set of views $\mathcal{V}$ over $\mathcal{R}$.*

The *data privacy problem* for this setting can be stated as: given a view instance I over $\mathcal{V}$ and a query q over $\mathcal{R}$, are there tuples $\boldsymbol{t}$ of constants such that $\boldsymbol{t} \in q(J)$ must hold for any instance J over $\mathcal{R}$ which respects Σ_r and which yields the view instance I? In that case, knowledge about $\mathcal{R}$, Σ_r, and $\mathcal{V}$ together with the data presented in I make it possible to infer non-public information. Hence, even if a user is denied to issue the query q, he can infer some of the answers of this query from the information which is presented to him in the view instance I.

To put this problem more formally, we introduce the notion of a certain answer in the context of the data privacy setting.

Definition 3. *Let $(\mathcal{R}, \Sigma_r, \mathcal{V})$ be a data privacy setting.*

- *If I is a view instance over $\mathcal{V}$, then a* possible database instance *for I is an instance J over $\mathcal{R}$ such that J respects Σ_r and J yields the view instance I.*
- *If I is a view instance over $\mathcal{V}$ and q is a query over $\mathcal{R}$, then a* certain answer *of q with respect to I, denoted by $\mathsf{certain}_\mathsf{p}(q, I)$, is the set of all tuples $\boldsymbol{t}$ of constants from I such that for every possible database instance J for I, we have $\boldsymbol{t} \in q(J)$.*
- *The* data privacy problem *for this setting is to compute $\mathsf{certain}_\mathsf{p}(q, I)$.*

Assume q is a query asking for non-public information. If $\mathsf{certain}_\mathsf{p}(q, I)$ is empty, that is if there are no certain answers, then it is not possible to infer any information about tuples in q from the view instance I and knowledge about the schema $\mathcal{R}$, the constraints Σ_r and the view definition $\mathcal{V}$. Conversely, if there is a tuple $\boldsymbol{t}$ in $\mathsf{certain}_\mathsf{p}(q, I)$, then some hidden information can be inferred.

3 Query Answering for Data Exchange

Fagin et al. [9] study query answering in the context of data exchange. We summarize some of their definitions and results which are relevant for the data privacy problem.

Let $\mathcal{S}$ and $\mathcal{T}$ be two disjoint schemata. We refer to $\mathcal{S}$ as *source* schema and to $\mathcal{T}$ as *target* schema. If I is an instance over $\mathcal{S}$ (a *source instance*) and J is an instance over $\mathcal{T}$ (a *target instance*), then $\langle I, J \rangle$ is the corresponding instance over $\mathcal{S} \cup \mathcal{T}$.

A *source-to-target dependency* is a tuple generating dependency of the form

$$\forall \boldsymbol{x}(\phi_\mathcal{S}(\boldsymbol{x}) \to \exists \boldsymbol{y} \psi_\mathcal{T}(\boldsymbol{x}, \boldsymbol{y})),$$

where $\phi_\mathcal{S}(\boldsymbol{x})$ is a conjunction of atomic formulas over $\mathcal{S}$ and $\psi_\mathcal{T}(\boldsymbol{x}, \boldsymbol{y})$ is a conjunction of atomic formulas over $\mathcal{T}$. A *target dependency* is a tuple generating dependency or an equality generating dependency:

$$\forall \boldsymbol{x}(\phi_\mathcal{T}(\boldsymbol{x}) \to \exists \boldsymbol{y} \psi_\mathcal{T}(\boldsymbol{x}, \boldsymbol{y})), \qquad \forall \boldsymbol{x}(\phi_\mathcal{T}(\boldsymbol{x}) \to (x_1 = x_2)).$$

Here, $\phi_\mathcal{T}(\boldsymbol{x})$ and $\psi_\mathcal{T}(\boldsymbol{x}, \boldsymbol{y})$ are conjunctions of atomic formulas over $\mathcal{T}$, and x_1, x_2 are among the variables of $\boldsymbol{x}$.

Definition 4. *[9, Def. 1] A* data exchange setting *$(\mathcal{S}, \mathcal{T}, \Sigma_{st}, \Sigma_t)$ consists of a source schema $\mathcal{S}$, a target schema $\mathcal{T}$, a set Σ_{st} of source-to-target dependencies, and a set Σ_t of target dependencies. The* data exchange problem *associated with this setting is the following: given a finite source instance I, find a finite target instance J such that $\langle I, J \rangle$ satisfies Σ_{st} and J satisfies Σ_t. Such a J is called a* solution *for I.*

Next, we specify the class of so-called universal solutions which have several 'good' properties. Before presenting its definition, we introduce some terminology and notation.

Let Const denote the set of all values, called *constants*, that occur in source instances. In addition, we assume an infinite set Var of values, called *labeled nulls*, such that Const $\cap$ Var $= \emptyset$. If K is an instance over a schema $\mathcal{R}$ with values in Const $\cup$ Var, then Var(K) denotes the set of labeled nulls occurring in relations in K.

Definition 5. *[9, Def. 2] Let K_1 and K_2 be two instances over a schema $\mathcal{R}$ with values in Const $\cup$ Var. A* homomorphism *$h : K_1 \to K_2$ is a mapping from Const $\cup$ Var(K_1) to Const $\cup$ Var(K_2) such that*

1. *$h(c) = c$, for every $c \in$ Const,*
2. *for every fact $R_i(\boldsymbol{t})$ of K_1, we have that $R_i(h(\boldsymbol{t}))$ is a fact of K_2, where, if $\boldsymbol{t} = (t_1, \ldots, t_n)$, then $h(\boldsymbol{t}) = (h(t_1), \ldots, h(t_n))$.*

Definition 6. *[9, Def. 3] Let $(\mathcal{S}, \mathcal{T}, \Sigma_{st}, \Sigma_t)$ be a data exchange setting. If I is a source instance, then a* universal solution *for I is a solution J for I such that for every solution J' for I, there exists a homomorphism $h : J \to J'$.*

Fagin et al. [9] show that the classical chase can be used to produce a universal solution: start with an instance $\langle I, \emptyset \rangle$ that consists of I, for the source schema, and of the empty instance, for the target schema; then chase $\langle I, \emptyset \rangle$ by applying the dependencies in Σ_{st} and Σ_t for as long as they are applicable. This process may fail (for instance, if an attempt to identify two constants is made) or it may not terminate. However, if it does terminate and if it does not fail, then the resulting instance is guaranteed to satisfy the dependencies and to be universal.

Theorem 1. *[9, Th. 1] Let $(S, T, \Sigma_{st}, \Sigma_t)$ be a data exchange setting. Let $\langle I, J \rangle$ be the result of some successful finite chase of $\langle I, \emptyset \rangle$ with $\Sigma_{st} \cup \Sigma_t$. Then J is a universal solution.*

Definition 7. *[9, Def. 7] Let $(S, T, \Sigma_{st}, \Sigma_t)$ be a data exchange setting. Let q be a k-ary query over the target schema T and I a source instance. The* certain answers *of q with respect to I, denoted by $\mathsf{certain}_e(q, I)$, is the set of all k-tuples t of constants from I such that for every solution J of this instance of the data exchange problem, we have $t \in q(J)$.*

There are situations in which the certain answers of a query q can be computed by evaluating q on a particular fixed solution and then keeping only the tuples that consist entirely of constants. If q is a query and J is a target instance, then $q(J)\!\downarrow$ is the set of all tuples t of constants such that $t \in q(J)$.

Theorem 2. *[9, Prop. 2] Let $(S, T, \Sigma_{st}, \Sigma_t)$ be a data exchange setting such that the dependencies in the sets Σ_{st} and Σ_t are arbitrary. Let q be a union of conjunctive queries over the target schema T. If I is a source instance and J is a universal solution, then $\mathsf{certain}_e(q, I) = q(J)\!\downarrow$.*

4 Proving Privacy

We can reduce the data privacy problem to the data exchange problem: starting from a data privacy setting $(\mathcal{R}, \Sigma_r, \mathcal{V})$, we create a corresponding data exchange setting $(S, T, \Sigma_{st}, \Sigma_t)$ such that $\mathcal{R} = T$, $\Sigma_r = \Sigma_t$, and $\mathcal{V}$ defines S and Σ_{st}. Hence, a query q over $\mathcal{R}$ may be issued to T. Moreover, a view instance I over $\mathcal{V}$ is a valid database instance over the schema S. We will show that the certain answers of q with respect to I under the data privacy setting will be the same as the certain answers of q with respect to I under the corresponding data exchange setting.

Definition 8. *The data exchange setting $(S, T, \Sigma_{st}, \Sigma_t)$ that corresponds to a data privacy setting $(\mathcal{R}, \Sigma_r, \mathcal{V})$ is given by:*

- *S consists of all relation symbols V_i which belong to $\mathcal{V}$,*
- *$\Sigma_t := \Sigma_r$,*
- *Σ_{st} contains $V_i(\boldsymbol{x}) \rightarrow \exists \boldsymbol{y} \phi(\boldsymbol{x}, \boldsymbol{y})$ if $V_i(\boldsymbol{x}) \leftarrow \exists \boldsymbol{y} \phi(\boldsymbol{x}, \boldsymbol{y})$ is an element of $\mathcal{V}$,*
- *$T := \mathcal{R}$.*

Obviously, if q is query over $\mathcal{R}$, then it is also a query over T; and if I is a view instance over $\mathcal{V}$, then it is also a database instance over S. The previous definition immediately leads to the following theorem:

Theorem 3. *Let $(\mathcal{R}, \Sigma_r, \mathcal{V})$ be a data privacy setting and $(\mathcal{S}, \mathcal{T}, \Sigma_{st}, \Sigma_t)$ its corresponding data exchange setting. Assume q is a query over $\mathcal{R}$ and I is a view instance over $\mathcal{V}$. The certain answers $\text{certain}_p(q, I)$ of q with respect to I for $(\mathcal{R}, \Sigma_r, \mathcal{V})$ are exactly the certain answers $\text{certain}_e(q, I)$ for $(\mathcal{S}, \mathcal{T}, \Sigma_{st}, \Sigma_t)$.*

This theorem, together with Theorem 2, provides a solution for the data privacy problem. Given a data privacy setting $(\mathcal{R}, \Sigma_r, \mathcal{V})$, a query q over $\mathcal{R}$, and a view instance I over $\mathcal{V}$. We can compute the certain answers of q with respect to I for $(\mathcal{R}, \Sigma_r, \mathcal{V})$ as follows:

1. compute the corresponding data exchange setting $(\mathcal{S}, \mathcal{T}, \Sigma_{st}, \Sigma_t)$,
2. construct a universal solution J for I with respect to $(\mathcal{S}, \mathcal{T}, \Sigma_{st}, \Sigma_t)$,
3. take $q(J)\downarrow$, that is evaluate q on J and keep only the tuples that consist entirely of constants.

5 Semantic Dependencies

A standard way to guarantee privacy while sharing data is to publish data only in the aggregate. However, this practice does not necessarily ensure data privacy. It is still possible that there are semantic dependencies which may lead to unwanted leaking of information.

If we only have view definitions, it is easy to see what information they reveal. However, if views can interact with dependencies, then it is less obvious what amount of information one may obtain. In a privacy setting, it is important to consider as many dependencies as possible: the more dependencies there are, the more data may be inferred. A dependency can be a constraint which is defined on a database schema. For example, as we have seen in the introduction, the presence of a unique key constraint can make it possible to derive private data. However, it is possible that a dependency is not explicitly stated; maybe it is inherent in the semantics of the data.

Let us investigate the following example of a semantic dependency. The Swiss Federal Statistical Office (SFSO) annually creates statistics on health care in Switzerland [3]. The collected data includes sociodemographic information about the patients (age, sex, region of residence, etc.) as well as administrative data (kind of insurance, length of stay in hospital, disease, etc.). Naturally, these data are highly sensitive and there are strict privacy policies about their treatment. For instance, only the year of birth and the region of residence of a patient are recorded; the date of birth and the precise place of residence are considered as too detailed.

The latest results about health care are from 2002. One of the published tables [4] contains information about the length of stay in hospital. The table has a row for each disease (encoded according to ICD-10 [17]); and basically three columns (the ICD-10 code, the number of inpatients with the corresponding disease, the average length of stay). In that table, we have 7644 rows with different ICD 10 codes. 903 of them are diseases which occurred only once, the corresponding number of inpatients is 1. Let us restrict the view to these rows.

Then the value of the attribute 'average length of stay' is the precise length of stay of the one patient with the corresponding disease. Hence, the length of stay depends on the ICD-10 code and is uniquely determined by it. This dependency may be used in a data privacy setting to infer more information.

On an abstract level, the situation is as follows: consider a relation R with two attributes A and B. Let V be the view defined by the query

```
select A, count(A), avg(B) from R group by A.
```

Assume we have a view instance I over V. We can restrict I to an instance I' which contains only those rows where the value of count(A) is 1. If we use I' instead of I to compute the possible instances of R, then each value of the A attribute determines a unique value for the B attribute. Hence, we can add the equality generating dependency

$$\forall x, y, z (\text{R}(x,y) \wedge \text{R}(x,z) \to y = z)$$

to the data privacy setting. It is possible that more data may be inferred by making use of this additional dependency.

Semantic dependencies are not easy to find. In the above example, the reason for their occurrence is that the view is defined by a query with small counts [6,7]. That means the grouping is too fine grained. There are many rows where the value of count(A) is 1. We can assign the average values of those rows as B values to the corresponding A values; and the A value uniquely determines the B value. It is important that we also consider this kind of semantic dependencies when we are studying data privacy settings.

6 Concluding Remarks

We have defined the data privacy problem to be the problem of deciding whether information about a database instance can be inferred from a given view instance. There is a related problem, namely to decide whether already the data privacy setting guarantees that there is no possible leaking of information. That is, whether $\text{certain}_\text{p}(q, I)$ is empty for every possible view instance I. In this case, we do have data privacy, no matter what the view instance is. Privacy follows already from the setting $(\mathcal{R}, \Sigma_r, \mathcal{V})$. We call such a setting *safe with respect to* q.

There is a trivial example of a data privacy setting which ensures privacy. Let $\mathcal{R}$ be a schema with a non-public relation symbol P. Further, let $\mathcal{V}$ be a set of views over $\mathcal{V}$ such that every view V in $\mathcal{V}$ satisfies: if $P(\boldsymbol{x})$ is an atom occurring in the definition of V, then each variable of $\boldsymbol{x}$ is existentially quantified in V. Let q be the query

$$q(\boldsymbol{x}) \leftarrow P(\boldsymbol{x}).$$

Given the data privacy setting $(\mathcal{R}, \emptyset, \mathcal{V})$, we find that $\text{certain}_\text{p}(q, I)$ must be empty for every view instance I. Hence, $(\mathcal{R}, \emptyset, \mathcal{V})$ is safe with respect to q. The reason for this is that the information stored in P is hidden by the existential quantifier in the view definitions and that there are no dependencies to infer that information.

We plan to further investigate safe data privacy settings. It would be nice to have a collection of patterns for safe privacy settings. Finally, an important direction is extending the data privacy problem to more complex view definitions and other forms of dependencies.

References

1. R. Agrawal, J. Kiernan, R. Srikant, and Y. Xu. Hippocratic databases. In *Proc. of 28th VLDB Conference*, 2002.
2. C. Beeri and M. Y. Vardi. A proof procedure for data dependencies. *Journal of the ACM*, 31(4):718–741, 1984.
3. Bundesamt für Statistik. Medizinische Statistik der Krankenhäuser.
4. Bundesamt für Statistik. Beilage ICD-10/2002, 2002. Available at http://www.bfs.admin.ch/bfs/portal/de/index/themen/gesundheit/ gesundheitsversorgung/behandlungen/analysen_berichte/stand/01.html.
5. A. Calì, D. Calvanese, G. D. Giacomo, and M. Lenzerini. Data integration under integrity constraints. In *Proc. of CAiSE 2002*, volume 2348 of *LNCS*, pages 262–279. Springer, 2002.
6. F. Y. Chin. Security in statistical databases for queries with small counts. *ACM Transactions on Database Systems*, 3(1):92–104, 1978.
7. L. Cox. Suppresion methodology and statistical disclosure control. *J. Am. Stat. Assoc.*, 75:377–395, 1980.
8. R. Fagin, P. G. Kolaitis, R. Miller, and L. Popa. Data exchange: Semantics and query answering. To appear in *Theoretical Computer Science*.
9. R. Fagin, P. G. Kolaitis, R. Miller, and L. Popa. Data exchange: Semantics and query answering. In *Proc. of ICDT'03*, pages 207–224, 2003.
10. R. Fagin, P. G. Kolaitis, and L. Popa. Data exchange: Getting to the core. In *ACM PODS'03*, pages 90–101, 2003.
11. A. Y. Halevy. Answering queries using views: A survey. *The VLDB Journal*, 10(4):270–294, 2001.
12. M. Lenzerini. Data integration: a theoretical perspective. In *ACM PODS '02*, pages 233–246. ACM Press, 2002.
13. A. Silberschatz, H. Korth, and S. Sudarshan. *Database System Concepts*. McGraw-Hill, fourth edition, 2002.
14. K. Stoffel and T. Studer. Canonical databases and certain answers under key constraints, 2004. Technical report IAM-04-009.
15. R. van der Meyden. Logical approaches to incomplete information: a survey. In *Logics for databases and information systems*, pages 307–356. Kluwer Academic Publishers, 1998.
16. Wikipedia The Free Encyclopedia. Data privacy. Available at http://en. wikipedia.org/wiki/Data_privacy.
17. World Health Organization WHO. International statistical classification of diseases and related health problems. 10th Revision.

Formalizing the XML Schema Matching Problem as a Constraint Optimization Problem

Marko Smiljanić[1], Maurice van Keulen[1], and Willem Jonker[1,2]

[1] University of Twente, P.O. Box 217, 7500 AE Enschede, The Netherlands
[2] Philips Research, Prof. Holstlaan 4, 5656 AA Eindhoven, The Netherlands
{m.smiljanic, m.vankeulen, w.jonker}@utwente.nl

Abstract. The first step in finding an efficient way to solve any difficult problem is making a complete, possibly formal, problem specification. This paper introduces a formal specification for the problem of *semantic XML schema matching*. Semantic schema matching has been extensively researched, and many matching systems have been developed. However, formal specifications of problems being solved by these systems do not exist, or are partial. In this paper, we analyze the problem of semantic schema matching, identify its main components and deliver a formal specification based on the constraint optimization problem formalism. Throughout the paper, we consider the schema matching problem as encountered in the context of a large scale XML schema matching application.

1 Introduction

Schema matching is a process of identifying semantically similar components within two schemas. Schemas, e.g., database schemas, are designed by humans; they are the product of human creativity. Therefore, it is said that a schema matching problem is an *AI-complete* problem [3], i.e., to solve this problem a system must implement human intelligence. The demand for schema matching is great in data exchange, and data analysis applications. Many semi-automatic schema matching systems have been developed [12] claiming various levels of usefulness [4]. These systems use heuristics to combine various syntactic features of schemas in order to estimate which schema components are similar. Machine learning, reuse of previous results, and user interaction, to name a few, are techniques used to improve the quality of matching.

In current schema matching systems, focus is placed on effectiveness. Heuristics are being used only to provide semantically relevant results. On the other hand, the efficiency of schema matching is mostly ignored. Systems are designed and tested on small scale problems in which efficiency is not an issue. New large scale schema matching applications emerge making the need for efficient schema matching imminent. Large scale schema matching approaches are being developed [13]. To understand and handle the complexity of the schema matching problem and to be able to devise an efficient algorithm to solve the matching problem, a *formal problem specification* must be acquired. To the best of our

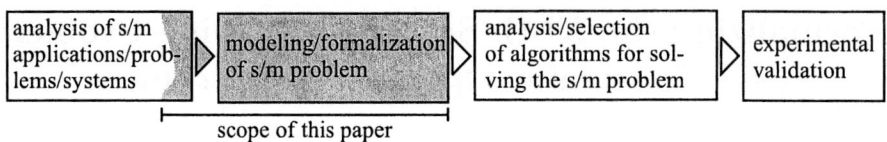

Fig. 1. The scope of this paper within the main line of schema matching (s/m) research

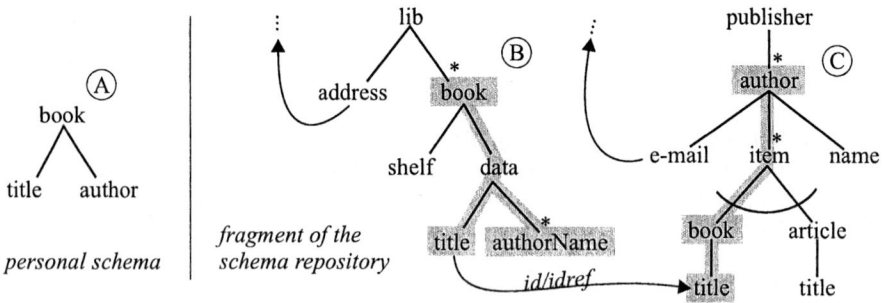

Fig. 2. Personal schema and a fragment of schema repository

knowledge, none of the existing schema matching system was built on the basis of a *complete formal specification* of the schema matching problem.

In this paper, we focus on understanding, modeling and formalizing the problem of semantic XML schema matching. The scope of this paper, within the main line of our research, is indicated in Fig. 1.

Our research is guided by a large scale schema matching application – a structured-data search engine called *Bellflower*. In Bellflower, the user defines his own XML schema called *personal schema*. A personal schema embodies the user's current information need and expectation with respect to the structure of the desired information. For example, a user looking for information on books would create a personal schema as the one shown in Fig. 2 (A). The task of Bellflower is to match the personal schema against a large *schema repository*, possibly containing all the XML schemas found on the Internet. A fragment of such a repository is shown in Fig. 2. Mappings that Bellflower retrieves are shown as shadowed subgraphs (B) and (C) in the repository. These mappings are presented to the user. The user then selects one mapping to be used by Bellflower to retrieve the actual data. Additionally, Bellflower allows the user to ask XPath queries over his personal schema, e.g., book[contains(author,"Verne")]/title, to filter the retrieved data.

The main contribution of this paper is a first thorough formal specification of the semantic XML schema matching problem. Another contribution is a comprehensive framework for the analysis and modeling of the semantic XML schema matching problem, which includes the description of the approximation of semantic matching that must be performed in order to build a system for schema matching.

The paper is organized as follows. Sec. 2 presents the model of semantic matching. Sec. 3 introduces the approximations of semantic matching in an XML schema matching system. Sec. 4 formalizes the matching problem using the constraint optimization problem formalism. Related research is discussed in Sec. 5 followed by the conclusion in Sec. 6.

2 Model of a Semantic Matching Problem

To come to a formal specification of a semantic XML schema matching problem, we devised a model of a *semantic matching problem* [14]. This section describes the main components of the model.

In a generic matching problem, a *template object* T is matched against a set of *target objects* $R = \{\tau_1, \ldots, \tau_k\}$. If a template object is related to a target object through some *desired relation*, i.e., $T \approx \tau_i$, it is said that they match and the (T, τ_i) pair forms one *mapping*. The *solution of a matching problem* is a list of mappings. In some matching problems, an objective function $\Delta(T, \tau_i)$ can be defined. The objective function evaluates to what extent the desired relation between the matching objects is met. In such problems, the objective function is used to rank, i.e., order, the mappings in the solution.

A semantic matching problem differs from the generic matching problem in that objects are matched based on their semantics. Semantics is commonly defined as the *meaning* of data. Therefore, in semantic matching the template and the target objects are matched based on their meanings. The desired semantic relation is a relation between meanings.

For example, in a semantic matching problem a person is looking for a book similar to Verne's book "20,000 Leagues Under the Sea". The person is matching its mental perception of Verne's book against a set of mental impressions about target books, e.g., books in his personal library. In this problem, the desired semantic relation is *similarity of mental impressions about books*.

The semantics, i.e., the ability to generate meanings about objects and to reason about these meanings, is the privilege of humans. Building a computer system that performs true semantic matching is in principle impossible. In practice, computer systems only *approximate* semantic matching [6].

The model of semantic matching that we are to show is a practical simplification of what is really happening in human mind. In our model of semantic matching, the desired relation is divided into a *semantic predicate function* and the *semantic objective function*.

Parts of the desired semantic relation that must necessarily be satisfied are captured within the semantic predicate function. For example, a person is looking for a book; it must be true that the target object is what this person thinks is a book. Further, the person might reason that books are similar if they have the same author; another predicate. The semantic objective function is a model of human's ability to establish ranking among meanings. E.g., the person will think that book A is more similar to Verne's book than book B if book A has a more similar topic; the person's opinion on topic similarity ranks the books.

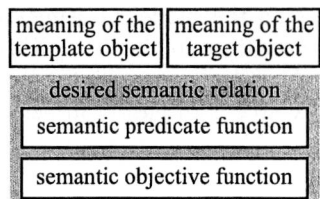

Fig. 3. Decl. components of a semantic matching problem

We have described a model of semantic matching in terms of four declarative components (rectangles in Fig. 3). In order to specify a semantic matching problem in a way that can be used by an automated computer system, all the components of the semantic model must be approximated. With approximation, semantic problem components are expressed using syntactic constructs. Sec. 3 describes these approximations in the context of a semantic XML schema matching problem.

3 Approximations in Semantic XML Schema Matching

The approximation of the components of the model of semantic matching is not a straightforward process. It is a design process burdened with trade-off decisions. In this section we describe approximations which are tailored to meet the needs of the XML schema matching encountered in the Bellflower system. Other schema matching systems would decide to approximate components differently. Nevertheless, the common point of all systems is that these semantic components are approximated.

3.1 Approximating the Meaning of Template and Target Objects

In *semantic XML schema matching*, the meanings of XML schemas are being matched against each other. XML schemas are created by humans in a design process. This design process creates a syntactic representation of some semantic concept. For example, a librarian designs an XML schema that models his understanding, i.e., semantics, of a library. This means that every XML schema is already an approximation, a model, of some meaning, i.e., *XML schemas are approximations of their own meaning*. Given an XML schema, no further approximation of its meaning is needed.

In practice, problems come from a different direction; from the heterogeneity of languages and techniques used by men to create schemas. To tame this syntactic diversity, schema matching systems always provide a generic, unified, data model. Different schema representations are then captured within this model. For XML schema matching in Bellflower, we use *directed graphs* enriched with *node and edge properties*; a model similar to ones used in other schema matching systems.

Definition 1. *A directed graph G with properties is a 4-tuple $G = (N, E, I, H)$ where*
- $N = \{n_1, n_2, ..., n_i\}$ *is a nonempty finite set of* nodes,
- $E = \{e_1, e_2, ..., e_j\}$ *is a finite set of* edges,
- $I : E \rightarrow N \times N$ *is an* incidence function *that associates each edge with a pair of nodes to which the edge is incident. For $e \in E$, we write $I(e) = (u, v)$ where u is called the* source node *and v the* target node.

- $H : \{N \cup E\} \times \mathcal{P} \to \mathcal{V}$ is a property set function where $\mathcal{P}$ is a set of properties, and $\mathcal{V}$ is a set of values including the null value. For $n \in \{N \cup E\}$, $\pi \in \mathcal{P}$, and $v \in \mathcal{V}$ we write $\pi(n) = v$ (e.g., $name(n_1) = $ 'book').

A *walk* p in a directed graph is any alternating sequence of nodes and edges, i.e., $p = (n_1, e_1, n_2, e_2, \ldots, e_{k-1}, n_k)$ such that an edge in p is incident to its neighboring nodes. Nodes n_1 and n_k are said to be the *source* and the *target* nodes of the walk p. In this paper, *path* and *walk* are synonyms.

A graph G' is a *partial subgraph* of graph G (i.e., $G' \sqsubset G$), if G' can be constructed by removing edges and nodes from graph G.

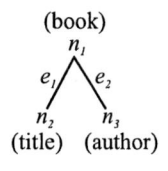

Fig. 4. Model of personal schema

The book personal schema from Fig. 2 is modeled as shown in Fig. 4.

- $N = \{n_1, n_2, n_3\}$
- $E = \{e_1, e_2\}$
- $I(e_1) = (n_1, n_2),\ I(e_2) = (n_1, n_3)$
- $name(n_1) = $ 'book', $name(n_2) = $ 'title', ...

We call a graph that models an XML schema a *schema graph*. In schema graphs, XML schema components are represented with either a *node*, an *edge*, or a node's or an edge's property. For example, relationships defined in XML schema by means of *id/idref* pairs, or similar mechanisms, are modeled as edges that we call *explicit edges* (edges with an arrow in Fig. 2). More details on how we represent an XML schema using a directed graph can be found in [14]. Schema graphs are a complete representation of an *XML schema*, i.e., the one can be converted into the other and vice versa without loss of information.

3.2 Approximating the Semantic Predicate Function

In semantic matching, the desired semantic relation is a relation between the meanings of a template and a target object. As shown in Sec. 3.1, schema graphs are used to approximate these meanings. Consequently, the desired semantic relation will be approximated as a relation between schema graphs.

We approximate the semantic predicate function with a predicate function $C(T, \tau)$, where T, τ are the template and the target schema graphs. C is a composition of a number predicates c_i, e.g., a conjunction.

$$C(T, \tau) = \bigwedge_{i=1}^{k} c_i(T, \tau)$$

Functions c_i specify various aspects of the relation between the template and the target schema graph that must be true in a mapping. We describe a few in the sequel.

Our schema repository comprises many XML schemas, or rather schema graphs, collected from the Internet. Such a repository can be treated in two different ways: as a set of independent schema graphs, or as one large schema graph. This distinction influences the definition of the target object in a matching task. The matching task is either:

1. for a template schema T, find the most similar target schema graph τ_i in the repository $R = \{\tau_1, \ldots, \tau_k\}$. The output of this matching approach is a list of concrete schemas from R, namely the ones most similar to T, or
2. for a template schema T, find the most similar partial subgraphs τ_i in R (i.e., $\tau_i \sqsubset R$, see Def. 1). The output of this matching approach is a list of subgraphs of the repository schema graph R. Such subgraphs can in general be composed of nodes and edges from different concrete schema graphs participating in R.

In our research, we adopt the second matching goal. This allows a personal schema to be matched to a target schema obtained by joining fragments of several distinct schemas, or to be matched to a fragment of only one schema, as well. A predicate function $c_1(T, \tau) := (\tau \sqsubset R)$, where R is the schema repository, can be used to specify this matching goal. Predicate c_1 is not very strict and does not consider the properties of the personal schema. For the book personal schema in Fig. 2, the c_1 predicate would be satisfied, for example, for τ being any single node of the repository. This seldom makes any sense. We therefore provide a stricter relation between the template and the target schema graph as follows.

The target schema graph $\tau = (N_\tau, E_\tau, I_\tau, H_\tau)$, where $\tau \sqsubset R$ for repository R, can form a mapping with a template schema graph $T = (N_T, E_T, I_T, H_T)$ if the following set of rules is satisfied.

1. for each node $n \in N_T$, there exists one and only one *match node* $n' \in N_\tau$, depicted as $n' = Match(n)$. E.g., in Fig. 2 the node 'authorName' in (B) is the match node for the node 'author' in (A).
2. for each edge $e \in E_T$, there exists one and only one match path $p' \in \tau$, depicted as $p' = Match(e)$, where $source(p') = Match(source(e))$, and $target(p') = Match(target(e))$. E.g., in Fig. 2 the path 'book-data-title' in (B) is the match path for the edge 'book-title' in (A).
3. the fact that schemas in a mapping (T, τ) meet the conditions 1 and 2 is depicted as $\tau = Match(T)$.

A new predicate can be defined as $c_2(T, \tau) := (\tau = Match(T))$.

Note that the first rule restricts node mappings to what is known as $1 : 1$ node mapping, i.e., each personal schema node is mapped to only one target node. Other systems [7] need different set of restrictions to be able to accommodate the $1 : N$ or $M : N$ node mappings.

In principle, the set of predicate functions is complete when it precisely defines the search space within which the match for the template object is to be found. For example, a schema matching system that does not handle cyclic data structures should include the predicate $c_3(T, \tau) := (T \text{ is non cyclic}) \wedge (\tau \text{ is non cyclic})$.

3.3 Approximating the Semantic Objective Function

The semantic objective function is approximated with an objective function $\Delta(T, \tau) \in \mathbb{R}$, where T is a template schema graph, τ is a target schema graph taken from the repository R. It is common to normalize the value of the objective function to the $[0, 1]$ range. Furthermore, $\Delta(T, \tau)$ is *undefined* if the predicate function $C(T, \tau) = false$.

It has been shown that a number of different heuristics have to be used in order to acquire higher matching quality [5, 12]. The heuristics exploit different schema properties as datatypes, structural relations, and documentation, to name a few. Each of the heuristics is implemented using a separate ranking function $\delta_i(T, \tau) \in \mathbb{R}$. These ranking functions are composed to define the objective function Δ. This composition can be algebraic, AI based, or hybrid, often involving additional heuristics. A comprehensive survey by Rahm and Bernstein [12] discusses different approaches for building the Δ function.

In this section, we have shown how to approximate declarative components of semantic XML schema matching problem. The result is a set of declarative syntactic components. In our research, we came to understand that these components are almost identical to components of a known class of problems called *constraint optimization problems (COP)* [1, 10]. In the sequel, we show one way to specify a schema matching problem in the COP framework. We also discuss benefits that schema matching can draw from being treated as a COP.

4 Formal Specification of the Problem

In this section, we first describe the formalism for representing constraint optimization problems. We then show one way to specify semantic XML schema matching problem using this formalism.

4.1 Constraint Optimization Problems

Constraint programming (i.e., CP) is a generic framework for problem description and solving [1, 10]. CP separates the declarative and operational aspects of problem solving. CP defines different classes of problems, of which we solely focus on the declarative aspects of *constraint optimization problems*.

Definition 2. *A constraint optimization problem (i.e., COP) P is a 4-tuple $P = (X, D, C, \Delta)$ where*
- $X = (x_1, \ldots, x_n)$ *is a list of variables,*
- $D = (D_1, \ldots, D_n)$ *is a list of finite domains, such that variable x_i takes values from domain D_i. D is called the* search space *for problem P.*
- $C = \{c_1, \ldots, c_k\}$ *is a set of constraints, where $c_i : D \rightarrow \{true, false\}$ are predicates over one or more variables in X, written as $c_i(X)$.*
- $\Delta : D \rightarrow \mathbb{R}$ *is a the objective function assigning a numerical quality value to a solution (solution is defined below).*

COP is defined in terms of *variables* X, taking values from search space D. A complete variable assignment is called *valuation*, written as Θ. Θ is a vector in D, thus assigning a value in D_i to each variable x_i, $i = \overline{1, n}$. A valuation Θ for which *constraints* $C(X)$ hold, i.e., $C(\Theta) = true$, is called a *solution*. The quality of a solution is determined by the value of the objective function, i.e., $\Delta(\Theta)$.

4.2 Semantic XML Schema Matching as COP

This section presents one possible way for specifying an XML schema matching problem as COP. The approach is based on rules defined as a part of the $c_2(T, \tau)$ predicate in Sec. 3.2. To support the explanation in this section, we will use the book personal schema, and the schema repository shown in Fig. 2, as well as the personal schema graph given in Fig. 4.

Definition 3. *A semantic XML schema matching problem with a template schema graph T, a repository $R = (N_R, E_R, I_R, H_R)$ of target schema graphs τ_i, where $\tau_i \sqsubseteq R$, a predicate function $C(T, \tau)$, and an objective function $\Delta(T, \tau)$ is formalized as a constraint optimization problem $P = (X, D, C, \Delta)$. The following four rules construct P in a stepwise manner.*

Rule-1. For a template schema graph $T = (N_T, E_T, I_T, H_T)$, the repository of target schema graphs R is formalized in a COP problem P, as follows:
1. for each node $n_i \in N_T$, a node variable x_{n_i} and a domain N_R are added to P (see section 3.2, rule 1),
2. for each edge $e_i \in E_T$, a path variable x_{p_i} and a domain $\mathcal{L}_R$ are added to P, where $\mathcal{L}_R$ is the set of all paths in repository R (see section 3.2, rule 2),
3. for each edge $e_k \in E_T$, where $I_T(e_k) = (n_i, n_j)$, a constraint $ic_k(X) := source(x_{p_i}) = Match(n_i) \wedge target(x_{p_i}) = Match(n_j)$ is added to P. We denote the conjunction of all such constraints as $IC(X)$ – the incidence constraint. This constraint ensures that target paths are connected in the same way as template edges are connected.

For the book example, P is, so far, defined as

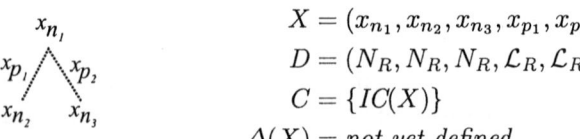

$$X = (x_{n_1}, x_{n_2}, x_{n_3}, x_{p_1}, x_{p_2})$$
$$D = (N_R, N_R, N_R, \mathcal{L}_R, \mathcal{L}_R)$$
$$C = \{IC(X)\}$$
$$\Delta(X) = \text{not yet defined}$$

Fig. 5. Target object variables

Fig. 5 illustrates *Rule-1*; node and edge variables are assigned based on the shape of the book template schema graph.

Rule-2. The predicate function $C(T, \tau)$ is formalized in P by adding a constraint $C(X)$ – a constraint function identical to predicate $C(T, \tau)$. Function $C(T, \tau)$ can be directly transformed to $C(X)$; node and path variables found in X replace τ, nodes and edges of T (n_1, n_2, n_3, e_1, and e_2 in the book example) appear as constants in $C(X)$.

For example, $c_4(X) := (\text{datatype}(n_2) = \text{datatype}(x_{n_2}))$ is a constraint responsible for ensuring that the 'title' node and its match have the same datatype.

Rule-3. The objective function $\Delta(T, \tau)$ is formalized in P using the objective function $\Delta(X)$ – a function identical to $\Delta(T, \tau)$.

Rule-4. Template schema graph T is constant in P, i.e., for two different schema graphs T_1 and T_2, two different COP problems must be declared. As already indicated, T is represented through constants in $C(X)$ and $\Delta(X)$.

For the schema matching problem, the specification of P is now complete.

$X = (x_{n_1}, x_{n_2}, x_{n_3}, x_{p_1}, x_{p_2})$
$D = (N_R, N_R, N_R, \mathcal{L}_R, \mathcal{L}_R)$
$C = \{IC(X), C(X)\}$
$\Delta(X) = $ as defined in the approximation phase (see Sec. 3.3)

4.3 The Benefits of Using COP Framework

The benefit of formalizing a schema matching problem as a COP is that a schema matching problem can now be regarded as a combinatorial optimization problem with constraints. COP problems have been largely investigated and many [non]exhaustive techniques for efficient solving have been proposed [11, 10]. Branch and bound, clustering methods, simulated annealing, tabu search, to name a few, can be investigated and adopted to schema matching problems represented as COPs. Important issues that influence the efficiency, e.g., variable ordering, value ordering, constraint simplification are also discussed in the COP framework.

In Bellflower, we are currently investigating the combination of clustering methods and the branch and bound algorithm for efficient search space traversal.

5 Related Research

Schema matching attracts significant attention as it finds application in many areas dealing with highly heterogeneous data. A survey by Rahm and Bernstein [12] identifies *semantic query processing* as an application domain where schema matching is used as a part of query evaluation. This is similar to how we use schema matching in Bellflower.

Representatives of automated schema matching systems include COMA [5], Cupid [9], and LSD [6], to name a few. These systems formalize only the behavior of the objective function, or use no problem formalization at all. The COP framework and the approach that we have used in the formalization can be used to complement the existing partial formalisms to a complete problem specification. For our approach, we found inspiration in the work of Bergholz [2]. Bergholz addresses the problem of querying semistructured data and provides a formal specification in the form of a constraint satisfaction problem. In his work, querying is treated as strict database querying. Structural relaxations (e.g., matching an edge to a path) have to be accounted for by the user, and specified in the query. Ranking of results is not supported. As such, his formalism is not suitable for describing a semantic schema matching problem.

To come to a full specification of a schema matching problem, we touch several areas. First, we model semantic matching. In [8] a different way to model semantic mappings and to reason about these is given. Second, we model XML schemas as a graph data structure. This is similar to how most other systems model schemas, e.g., Cupid [9]. Finally, we use the constraint optimization problem framework [10] as a base for the formalization.

6 Conclusion

In this paper, we have described an approach to formally specify semantic XML schema matching problems. The formalism is developed to support research related to a large scale schema matching system – Bellflower.

We gave a model of semantic matching followed by the approximations for describing a semantic problem in a syntactic domain. Finally, the constraint optimization framework was identified as a suitable framework for capturing all the declarative syntactic components of the problem.

With this formalism, the goal of this part of our research (see Fig. 1) was achieved: a clear and unambiguous specification of the problem – a good starting point for the exploration of efficient algorithms for solving.

We are currently investigating the combination of clustering methods and the branch and bound algorithm to achieve efficient schema matching in a large scale schema matching application.

References

[1] R. Bartak. Constraint programming: In pursuit of the holy grail. In *Proceedings of the Week of Doctoral Students (WDS)*, pages 555–564, June 1999.
[2] A. Bergholz and J. C. Freytag. Querying Semistructured Data Based on Schema Matching. *Lecture Notes in Computer Science*, 1949, 2000.
[3] P. A. Bernstein, S. Melnik, M. Petropoulos, and C. Quix. Industrial-strength schema matching. *SIGMOD Rec.*, 33(4):38–43, 2004.
[4] H. Do, S. Melnik, and E. Rahm. Comparison of schema matching evaluations. In *Proceedings of the 2nd Int. Workshop on Web Databases*, 2002.
[5] H. H. Do and E. Rahm. COMA — A system for flexible combination of schema matching approaches. In P. A. Bernstein et al., editors, *Proc. Intl. Conf. VLDB 2002*. Morgan Kaufmann Publishers.
[6] A. Doan. *Learning to Map between Structured Representations of Data*. PhD thesis, University of Washington, 2002.
[7] B. He and K. C.-C. Chang. A holistic paradigm for large scale schema matching. *SIGMOD Rec.*, 33(4):20–25, 2004.
[8] J. Madhavan, P. A. Bernstein, P. Domingos, and A. Y. Halevy. Representing and reasoning about mappings between domain models. In *Proc. Conf. (AAAI/IAAI-02)*, pages 80–86.
[9] J. Madhavan, P. A. Bernstein, and E. Rahm. Generic schema matching with cupid. In *Proceedings of the 27th International Conference on Very Large Data Bases(VLDB '01)*, pages 49–58, Orlando, Sept. 2001. Morgan Kaufmann.
[10] K. Marriott and P. J. Stuckey. *Programming with Constraints: an Introduction*. MIT Press, 1998.
[11] Z. Michalewicz and D. B. Fogel. *How to Solve It: Modern Heuristics*. Springer Verlag, December 1999.
[12] E. Rahm and P. A. Bernstein. A survey of approaches to automatic schema matching. *VLDB Journal: Very Large Data Bases*, 10(4):334–350, Dec. 2001.
[13] E. Rahm, H.-H. Do, and S. Mamann. Matching large xml schemas. *SIGMOD Rec.*, 33(4):26–31, 2004.
[14] M. Smiljanić, M. van Keulen, and W. Jonker. Defining the XML Schema Matching Problem for a Personal Schema Based Query Answering System. Technical Report TR-CTIT-04-17, Centre for Telematics and Information Technology, Apr. 2004.

Evolving XML Schemas and Documents Using UML Class Diagrams*

Eladio Domínguez[1], Jorge Lloret[1], Ángel L. Rubio[2], and María A. Zapata[1]

[1] Dpto. de Informática e Ingeniería de Sistemas,
Facultad de Ciencias. Edificio de Matemáticas,
Universidad de Zaragoza. 50009 Zaragoza. Spain
{noesis, jlloret, mazapata}@unizar.es
[2] Dpto. de Matemáticas y Computación. Edificio Vives,
Universidad de La Rioja. 26004 Logroño. Spain
arubio@dmc.unirioja.es

Abstract. The widespread use of XML brings new challenges for its integration into general software development processes. In particular, it is necessary to keep the consistency between different software artifacts and XML documents when evolution tasks are carried out. In this paper we present an approach to evolve XML schemas and documents conceptually modeled by means of UML class diagrams. Evolution primitives are issued on the UML class diagram and are automatically propagated down to the XML schema. The XML documents are also automatically modified to conform to the new XML schema. In this way, the consistency between the different artifacts involved is kept. This goal is achieved by using an intermediate component which reflects how the UML diagrams are translated into the XML schemas.

1 Introduction

XML [17] is increasingly used as a standard format for data representation and exchange across the Internet. XML Schema [16] is also the preferred means of describing structured XML data. These widespread uses bring about new challenges for software researchers and practitioners. On the one hand, there is a need for integrating XML schemas into general software development processes. The production of XML schemas out of UML models [1,8,14] or the binding of XML schemas to a representation in Java code [7] are examples of the relationships between XML and development processes. On the other hand, XML documents (and, in particular, XML schemas) are not immutable and must change over time for various varied reasons, as for example widening the scope of the application or changes in the requirements [15].

In these circumstances, it seems highly valuable to have a framework where XML evolution tasks can be performed while ensuring that consistency between

---

* This work has been partially supported by DGES, project TIC2002-01626, by the Government of La Rioja, project ACPI2002/06, by the Government of Aragón and by the European Social Fund.

the different artifacts involved (documents, models, code) is kept. The general objective of our research is to obtain such a complete framework. As a step in this direction, in this paper we present our approach in order to evolve UML–modeled XML data (XML schemas and documents) by means of applying evolution operations on the UML class diagram.

This work relies on our own scaffolding architecture, presented in [4,5], that contributes to the achievement of a satisfactory solution to analogous problems in the database evolution setting. One of the main characteristics of this architecture is an explicit translation component that allows properties of traceability and consistency to be fulfilled when evolution tasks are carried out. In the present paper we use this architecture as a framework to perform XML evolution activities and, in particular, we explain with a certain degree of detail the algorithms associated to that translation component.

The remainder of the paper is as follows. In section 2, we present an overview of our architecture for evolution. Section 3 is devoted to the algorithm for translating a UML class diagram into an XML schema while section 4 deals with the algorithm for propagating changes from the UML class diagram to the XML schema and XML documents. In section 5 we review related work and finish with the conclusions and future work.

2 Evolution Architecture Overview

As it is said in the introduction, the scaffolding of our approach is constituted by an architecture we presented in [4,5] applied within a database evolution setting. Although the architecture has been proven within this setting, it was designed with the aim of being independent of any particular modeling technique. This fact has allowed us to apply the same architectural pattern to the XML context.

The architecture is shaped along two dimensions. On the one hand, the different artifacts of the architecture are divided into three abstraction levels which fit with the metamodel, model and data layers of the MOF metadata architecture [11]. On the other hand, the architecture is also layered on the basis of several structures that model different development phases. More specifically, the architecture includes a *conceptual component*, a *translation component*, a *logical component* and an *extensional component*. We will describe briefly the meaning and purpose of each component (see [4,5] for details).

The *conceptual component* captures machine–independent knowledge of the real world. For instance, in the case of database evolution, this component would deal with entity–relationship schemas. In the XML evolution approach proposed in the present paper, the conceptual component deals with UML class diagrams modeling the domain. The *logical component* captures tool–independent knowledge describing the data structures in an abstract way. In database evolution, this component would deal with schemas from the relational model, as for instance by means of standard SQL. In the case of XML evolution, the logical models univocally represent the XML schemas. The *extensional component* captures tool dependent knowledge using the implementation language. In databases, it would deal with the specific database in question, populated with data, and expressed in the SQL of the DBMS of choice. Within the XML context, the textual structure of data is represented using XML Schema and the data are specified in textual XML documents conforming to an XML schema. One of the main contributions of our architecture is the *translation component*, that not only captures the existence of a transformation from elements of the conceptual component to other of the logical one, but also stores explicit information about the way in which concrete conceptual elements are translated into logical ones.

More specifically, the way of working of our architecture within the XML context is as follows: given a UML class diagram representing a data structure, it is mapped into a XML schema applying a translation algorithm. XML documents conforming to the resultant XML schema can be created. For various reasons, the data structure may need to be changed. In this case, the data designer must issue the appropriate evolution transformations to the conceptual UML diagram. The existence of the translation component allows these changes to be automatically propagated (by means of the propagation algorithm) to the other components. In this way the extensional XML schema is changed, and consequently the XML documents are also changed so as to conform them to the new XML schema.

3 Translation Algorithm

There are several papers [8,14] where the generation of XML schemas from UML class diagrams is proposed. Paper [8] proposes a generation based on transformation rules and in Table 1 we offer a summary of this approach.

Table 1. Rules for generating XML schemas from UML schemas

UML block	XML item(s)
class	element, complex type, with ID attribute, and key
attribute	subelement of the corresponding class complex type
association	reference element, with IDREF attribute referencing the associated class and keyref for type safety (key/keyref references)
generalization	complex type of the subclass is defined as an extension of the complex type of the superclass

Our goal is not only the generation of the XML schema but also the automatic management of its evolution. For this purpose, we have defined an intermediate component which allows us to maintain the traceability between the UML and XML schemas.

In order to deal with this intermediate component, we have enriched the notion of transformation by developing the notion of *translation rule*. The translation rules are used inside the *translation algorithm*. When this algorithm is applied to the UML class diagram it produces not only the XML schema but also a set of elementary translations stored in the intermediate component. An elementary translation is the smallest piece of information reflecting the correspondence between the UML elements and the XML items.

elementary_translation			
elem_transl_id	type	conceptual_element	logical_item
1	ETT20	employee.name	name element of employeeType type
2	ETT20	employee.department	department element of employeeType type
3	ETT25	employee	idEmployee attribute of employeeType type
4	ETT60	-	key of employee element of complexType of root element
5	ETT01	employee	employee element of complexType of root element
6	ETT05	employee	employeeType complexType
7	ETT00	enterprise	enterprise root element

Fig. 1. Elementary translations after applying the translation to our running example

```
<xsd:schema xmlns:xsd="http://www.w3.org/2001/XMLSchema"> <xsd:complexType name="employeeType">
  <xsd:element name="enterprise">                            <xsd:sequence>
    <xsd:complexType>                                          <xsd:element name="name"
      <xsd:sequence>                                             minOccurs="1" maxOccurs="1"/>
        <xsd:element name="employee" type="employeeType"       <xsd:element name="department"
          minOccurs="0" maxOccurs="unbounded"/>                  minOccurs="0" maxOccurs="1"/>
      </xsd:sequence>                                          </xsd:sequence>
    </xsd:complexType>                                         <xsd:attribute name="idEmployee"
    <xsd:key name="keyEmployee">                                 type="xsd:ID" use="required"/>
      <xsd:selector xpath="employee"/>                       </xsd:complexType>
      <xsd:field xpath="@idEmployee"/>                     </xsd:schema>
    </xsd:key>
  </xsd:element>
```

Fig. 2. Initial extensional XML schema for our running example

Translation rule. We have defined our translation rules taking the transformation rules proposed in [8] as a starting point. Each translation rule basically includes procedures for creating the XML items of the XML schema enriched with procedures for creating the elementary translations. For example, a translation rule for classes defines, among other things, the name of the XML element into which each class is translated as well as the elementary translations to be added to the translation component.

Translation algorithm. This algorithm takes as input conceptual building block instances of the UML schema and creates 1) the elementary translations 2) the logical elements of the *logical XML schema* and 3) the *extensional XML schema*. More details about the translation algorithm can be found in [4].

As we can see, in our setting an XML schema admits two different views. In the first, the XML schema is an instance of the metamodel for XML and each item of the XML schema is an instance of a metaclass of the XML metamodel. In the second view, it is a sequence of characters encoding tree–structured data following rules specified by the XML standard. From now on, when we refer to the first view, we use the term *logical XML schema* while for the second view we use the term *extensional XML schema*.

Example. We consider a UML schema of a company where there is a class employee with attributes name and department. When we apply the translation algorithm to this UML schema, we obtain the elementary translations shown in Figure 1, the corresponding items of the logical XML schema (not shown in this paper) and the initial extensional XML schema shown in Figure 2. For example, inside this algorithm, when the translation rule for classes is applied to the class *employee*, some of the obtained results are: the name of the XML element for the class *employee* is also *employee* (as can be seen in line 5 in Figure 2) and the elementary translation numbered 5 in Figure 1 is added to the translation component. This elementary translation reflects the fact that the class *employee* is translated into the element *employee* of the root element.

4 Propagation Algorithm

The propagation algorithm propagates changes made in the UML schema to the XML schema and XML documents. It is split into propagation subalgorithms for the intermediate, for the logical and for the extensional levels. In this paper, we briefly describe the first two subalgorithms while concentrating on the latter because this subalgorithm is responsible for the evolution of the extensional XML schema and documents.

Propagation subalgorithm for the intermediate and logical levels. In order to change automatically the XML schema and the XML documents, the data designer issues appropriate evolution primitives to the UML diagram. These primitives are basic operations such as addition or deletion of modeling elements (class, attribute, association), transformation of an attribute into a class and so on.

For example, to transform the attribute `employee.department` into a class, the primitive `attribToClass('employee.department')` is executed. This transformation (1) adds to the UML class diagram a `department` class described by the attribute `department`, (2) adds a binary association `employee has department` and, (3) deletes the attribute `employee.department`.

The conceptual changes are the input for the propagation subalgorithm for the intermediate level, which updates the elementary translations of the intermediate component to reflect these changes. After applying this subalgorithm in our running example, the resulting intermediate component is shown in Figure 3 where the elementary translation number 2 has been deleted and the elementary translations from 8 to 18 have been added.

The information about the changes performed in the intermediate component is the input for the propagation subalgorithm for the logical level, which changes the logical XML schema by triggering a set of procedures. Let us see a general description of the procedures which are executed for the `attribToClass` primitive:

(a) **addType**. Creates a new type in the logical XML schema.
(b) **addRootChildElement**. Creates a new child element of the root element.
(c) **addAttributeForType**. Adds a new attribute to a type.
(d) **addKey**. Adds a key to an element of the root type.
(e) **emptyElement**. A nested element is transformed into a non–nested element.
(f) **addKeyref**. Creates a new keyref.

Propagation subalgorithm for the extensional level. This subalgorithm (see sketch in Table 2) takes as input the changes produced in the logical XML

elementary_translation				
	elem_transl_id	type	conceptual_element	logical_item
	1	ETT20	employee.name	name element of employeeType type
	2	ETT20	employee.department	department element of employeeType type
	3	ETT25	employee	idEmployee attribute of employeeType type
	4	ETT60	-	key of employee element of complexType of root element
	5	ETT01	employee	employee element of complexType of root element
	6	ETT05	employee	employeeType complexType
	7	ETT00	enterprise	enterprise root element
	8	ETT20	department.department	department element of departmentType type
	9	ETT25	department	idDepartment attribute of departmentType type
	10	ETT60	-	key of department element of complexType of root element
	11	ETT01	department	department element of complexType of root element
added elementary translations	12	ETT05	department	departmentType complexType
	13	ETT02	binaryAssociation employee has department	department element of employeeType type
	14	ETT21	department	idDepartment attribute of department element of employeeType type
	15	ETT75	multiplicity constraint 0..1	minOccurs and maxOcurrs in the department element of employeeType type
	16	ETT75	multiplicity constraint 0..*	-
	17	ETT65	exists constraint exist1	-
	18	ETT65	exists constraint exist2	keyref from employee to department

Fig. 3. Elementary translations after applying the attribToClass primitive to our running example

Table 2. Sketch of the propagation subalgorithm for the extensional level

```
INPUT: Set of operations on the logical XML schema
OUTPUT: Set of XSLT stylesheets to be applied to the old extensional XML
schema and to the XML documents
For each operation o of the INPUT
  If the operation o is to add on the logical metaclass metaclass_i and
     the conceptual evolution primitive is concept_primit_{i1} then
```
$XML\_sch_{i11};$
```
     ...
```
$XML\_sch_{i1r_1};$
$XML\_doc_{i1r_1+1};$
```
     ...
```
$XML\_doc_{i1n_1};$
```
  endif
  If the operation o is to add on the logical metaclass...
endfor
```

schema and updates the extensional XML schema as well as the XML documents in order to reflect these changes.

In order to do such updates, each change of the logical XML schema triggers one or more XSLT stylesheets which, on the one hand, change the extensional XML schema and, on the other hand, change the XML documents to conform to the new extensional XML schema. The XML stylesheets are executed by procedures of which we distinguish two kinds: the XML_sch* procedures execute stylesheets that act on the extensional XML schema and the XML_doc* procedures execute stylesheets that act on the XML documents. Every procedure has been designed to maintain the consistency between the XML documents and the XML schema.

In our running example, the changes in the logical XML schema produced by the procedures (a) to (f) mentioned above, as applied to our running example, are the input for this subalgorithm. For these changes, the algorithm executes

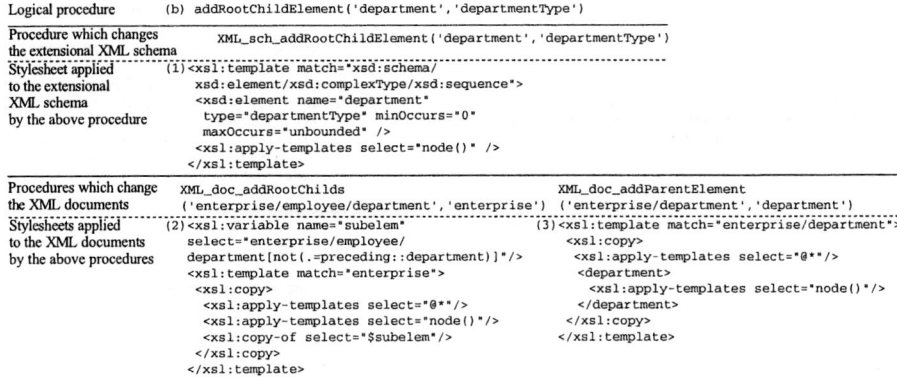

Fig. 4. XML stylesheets applied to the extensional XML schema and to the XML documents after adding a new element to the root element in our running example

the corresponding XML_sch* or XML_doc* procedures, which apply their XML stylesheets. In total, five schema stylesheets and four document stylesheets are applied. An example of the applied stylesheets for the logical procedure (b) is shown in Figure 4, where the identity template as well as the headers have been omitted. Let us explain the meaning of each procedure triggered by the changes made by the (b) procedure.

XML_sch_addRootChildElement(element:string, type:string)

Precondition: The type exists in the XML schema.

Semantics: Modifies the extensional XML schema in order to add to it a new element in the sequence of the complex type of the root element. The type of the new element is `type`.

Effect in the running example: Generates and executes on the extensional XML schema the stylesheet (1) of Figure 4. As a result, the element `department` is added to the extensional XML schema (see sixth line in Figure 5).

XML_doc_addRootChilds(d:xpath_expression,rootelement:string)

Precondition: d is an xpath expression of the form $rootelement\backslash element_1\backslash...\backslash element_n$ and $element_n$ is a terminal element.

Semantics: Copies each node of the node set defined by the xpath expression d as a child of the root node. Moreover, there are no two nodes among the just copied nodes with the same value.

Effect in the running example: Generates and executes on the XML documents the stylesheet (2) of Figure 4.

XML_doc_addParentElement(d:xpath_expression,element_name:string)

Precondition: d is an xpath expression of the form $rootelement\backslash element_1\backslash...\backslash element_n$

Semantics: Each node of the node set defined by the xpath expression d is included as a content of a new element node with the name element_name.

```
<xsd:schema xmlns:xsd="http://www.w3.org/2001/XMLSchema">   <xsd:complexType name="employeeType">
 <xsd:element name="enterprise">                             <xsd:sequence>
  <xsd:complexType>                                           <xsd:element name="name" minOccurs="1"
   <xsd:sequence>                                              maxOccurs="1"/>
    <xsd:element name="employee" type="employeeType"          <xsd:element name="department"
     minOccurs="0" maxOccurs="unbounded"/>                     minOccurs="0" maxOccurs="1">
    <xsd:element name="department" type="departmentType"       <xsd:complexType>
     minOccurs="0" maxOccurs="unbounded"/>                      <xsd:attribute name="idDepartment"
   </xsd:sequence>                                               type="xsd:IDREF" use="required"/>
  </xsd:complexType>                                           </xsd:complexType>
  <xsd:key name="keyEmployee">                                </xsd:element>
   <xsd:selector xpath="employee"/>                          </xsd:sequence>
   <xsd:field xpath="@idEmployee"/>                          <xsd:attribute name="idEmployee"
  </xsd:key>                                                  type="xsd:ID" use="required"/>
  <xsd:key name="keyDepartment">                            </xsd:complexType>
   <xsd:selector xpath="department"/>                       <xsd:complexType name="departmentType">
   <xsd:field xpath="@idDepartment"/>                        <xsd:sequence>
  </xsd:key>                                                  <xsd:element name="department"
  <xsd:keyref name="ref1" refer="keyDepartment">              minOccurs="1" maxOccurs="1"/>
   <xsd:selector xpath="./employee/department"/>            </xsd:sequence>
   <xsd:field xpath="@idDepartment"/>                        <xsd:attribute name="idDepartment"
  </xsd:keyref>                                               type="xsd:ID" use="required"/>
 </xsd:element>                                             </xsd:complexType>
                                                          </xsd:schema>
```

Fig. 5. Final extensional XML schema (in bold, modified parts from the initial extensional XML schema)

There is a new element for each node of the node set. The xpath expression for the new nodes will be $rootelement\backslash element_1\backslash ...\backslash element\_name\backslash element_n$

Effect in the running example: Generates and executes on the XML documents the stylesheet (3) of Figure 4.

In Figure 5 we can see the final extensional XML schema that is obtained after applying the XML schema stylesheets generated by the procedures triggered by the (a) to (f) procedures.

We have implemented our approach with Oracle 10g Release 1 and PL/SQL. In particular, we have used the DBMS_XMLSCHEMA package and its CopyEvolve() procedure. This procedure allows us to evolve XML schemas registered in the Oracle XML DB database in such a way that existing XML instance documents continue to be valid.

5 Related Work

There exist in the literature various proposals for managing the evolution of XML documents, [15] being the most sound proposal since it provides a minimal and complete taxonomy of basic changes which preserve consistency between data and schema. The problem with these proposals is that the data designer has to perform the evolution changes working directly with the XML documents, so that (s)he is concerned with some low-level implementation issues [14].

Like other authors [1,3,8,14], we advocate using a conceptual level or a platform independent level for XML document design. However, we also consider that the possibility of performing evolution tasks at a conceptual level is advisable, since it allows the data designer to work at a higher degree of abstraction. The problem is that, to our knowledge, the approaches that propose a conceptual modeling language for data design, generating the XML documents automatically, do not take into account evolution issues [8,14]. Furthermore, the authors that deal with evolution tasks at a conceptual level do not apply them for the specific case of XML documents [6]. For this reason, as far as we are aware, our proposal is the first framework including a conceptual level for managing XML document evolution tasks.

With regard to other evolution frameworks that consider a conceptual level [6,9], most of these are proposed for the specific database evolution field. The main challenge of these proposals is to maintain the consistency between models of different levels that evolve over time. We tackle this problem, as [6] does, by ensuring the traceability of the translation process between levels. But, although the traceability of transformation executions is a feature required in several proposals (see, for example, QVT [12]), there is no agreement about which artifacts and mechanisms are needed for assuring this traceability [13,18]. In [6] the traceability is achieved storing the sequence (called history) of operations performed during the translation of the conceptual schema into a logical one. In this way the mappings affected by the changes can be detected and modified, whereas the rest can be reexecuted without any modification. The main difference between this approach and ours is the type of information stored for assuring traceability. Whereas in [6] the idea is to store the history of the process performed (probably with redundancies), in our case the goal of the elementary translations is to reflect the correspondence between the conceptual elements and the logical ones, so there is no room for redundancies.

6 Conclusions and Future Work

The main contribution of this work is the presentation of a framework for managing XML document evolution tasks. This framework includes a conceptual level and a logical one, and the consistency between them is kept ensuring the traceability of the translation process between levels. More specifically, we have described, by means of an example, the component that reflects the correspondence between conceptual and logical elements. For this purpose, elementary translations that reflect the relations between the conceptual elements and the logical ones and that facilitate evolution tasks are used. Furthermore the propagation algorithm which guarantees the consistency between the XML schema and documents has been explained.

There are several possible directions for future work. Our solution has been implemented using a particular tool, while approaches such as MDA [10] promise the future development of general model–driven tools that will provide further automatized support to evolution tasks. Because of that we will work on approaching our solution to these other model–driven proposals. In particular, the specification of the transformations involved in our proposal by means of a unified transformation language such as it is demanded in the QVT request for proposal [12] is a goal for further development. Besides, the present proposal takes a forward maintenance perspective, and how to apply our ideas for a round–trip perspective [2] remains an ongoing project. Another direction is how to apply the architecture to other contexts, such as, for example, for managing the binding of XML schemas to a representation in Java code [7].

References

1. M.Bernauer, G. Kappel, G. Kramler, Representing XML Schema in UML – A Comparison of Approaches, in N. Koch, P. Fraternali, M. Wirsing, Martin (Eds.) *Web Engineering - ICWE 2004* LNCS 3140, 2004, 440–444.
2. P. A. Bernstein, Applying Model Management to Classical Meta Data Problems, *First Biennial Conference on Innovative Data Systems Research- CIDR 2003.*
3. R. Conrad, D. Scheffner, J. C. Freytag, XML Conceptual Modeling Using UML, in Alberto H. F. Laender, Stephen W. Liddle, Veda C. Storey (Eds.) *Conceptual Modeling - ER 2000* LNCS 1920, 2000, 558–571.
4. E. Domínguez, J. Lloret, A. L. Rubio, M. A. Zapata, Elementary translations: the seesaws for achieving traceability between database schemata, in S. Wang et al, (Eds.), *Conceptual modeling for advanced application domains- ER 2004 Workshops*, LNCS 3289 , 2004, 377–389.
5. E. Domínguez, J. Lloret, M. A. Zapata, An architecture for Managing Database Evolution, in A. Olivé et al. (eds) *Advanced conceptual modeling techniques- ER 2002 Workshops*, LNCS 2784 , 2002, 63–74.
6. J.M. Hick, J.L. Hainaut, Strategy for Database Application Evolution: The DB-MAIN Approach, in I.-Y. Song et al. (eds.) *ER 2003*, LNCS 2813, 291–306.
7. *Java Architecture for XML Binding (JAXB)*, available at http://java.sun.com/xml/jaxb/.
8. T. Krumbein, T. Kudrass, Rule-Based Generation of XML Schemas from UML Class Diagrams, in Robert Tolksdorf, Rainer Eckstein (Eds.), *Berliner XML Tage 2003* XML-Clearinghouse 2003, 213–227
9. J. R. López, A. Olivé, A Framework for the Evolution of Temporal Conceptual Schemas of Information Systems, in B. Wangler, L. Bergman (eds.), *Advanced Information Systems Eng.- CAiSE 2000*, LNCS 1789, 2000, 369–386.
10. J. Miller, J. Mukerji (eds.), MDA Guide Version 1.0.1, Object Management Group, Document number omg/2003-06-01, May, 2003.
11. OMG, *Meta Object Facility (MOF) specification*, version 1.4, formal/02-04-03, available at http://www.omg.org, April, 2002.
12. OMG, *MOF 2.0 Query / Views / Transformations RFP*, ad/2002-04-10, available at http://www.omg.org, 2002.
13. B. Ramesh, Factors influencing requirements traceability practice, *Communications of the ACM*, 41 (12), December 1998, 37-44.
14. N. Routledge, L. Bird, A. Goodchild, UML and XML schema, in Xiaofang Zhou (Ed.), *Thirteenth Australasian Database Conference, 2002*, 157–166
15. H. Su, D. Kramer, L. Chen, K. T. Claypool, E. A. Rundensteiner, XEM: Managing the evolution of XML Documents, in K. Aberer, L. Liu(Eds.) *11th Intl. Workshop on Research Issues in Data Engineering*, IEEE 2001, 103-110.
16. W3C XML Working Group, *XML Schema Parts 0–2 (2nd ed)*, available at http://www.w3.org/XML/Schema#dev.
17. W3C XML Working Group, *Extensible Markup Language (XML) 1.0 (3rd ed)*, available at http://www.w3.org/XML/Core/#Publications.
18. W. M. N. Wan-Kadir, P. Loucopoulos, Relating evolving business rules to software design, *Journal of Systems Architecture*, 50 (7), july 2004, 367-382.

Building XML Documents and Schemas to Support Object Data Exchange and Communication

Carlo Combi[1] and Giuseppe Pozzi[2]

[1] Università di Verona, strada le Grazie 15 I-37134 Verona, Italy
carlo.combi@univr.it
[2] Politecnico di Milano, P.za L.da Vinci 32 I-20133 Milano, Italy
giuseppe.pozzi@polimi.it

Abstract. The exchange of data between heterogeneous database systems is becoming a key issue in several application domains. XML is emerging as the standard mean for data exchange over the web. As for object oriented databases storing complex information, it is important to be able to exchange both objects and object schemas. In this paper we propose two approaches for translating database objects into XML documents which are both human readable and suitable for system based queries, thus preserving object semantics. Both approaches have been validated by a running prototype.

1 Introduction

Object-Oriented Database Management Systems (OODBMS) have been present since almost two decades. In order to achieve a common standard on the features of the DBMSs from different vendors, the Object Database Management Group (ODMG) has defined ODMG 3.0, a standard, which aims at defining features concerning interoperability among OODBMSs and platform independence [5].

ODMG clearly identified that information interchange among heterogeneous systems is a key issue. XML, defined and standardized by the World Wide Web Consortium W3C over the last years, is emerging as the language for exchanging information over the web for several kinds of applications, as data intensive web sites, distributed database systems, workflow systems, and information systems [2,4]. XML gained attention also as a non-proprietary, standard language for representing data: several proposals were made of native XML database systems and, more generally, of XML query languages as XPATH and XQUERY [7].

In order to achieve XML-based information exchange between OODBMS and other heterogeneous systems, some different requirements must be considered together: i) allow one to migrate, possibly altogether, both object (instance) and class (schema) information; ii) allow one to perform suitable object-based queries on the produced XML documents; iii) allow a human reader to *comfortably* and with *high reliability* access exchanged (XML) information.

Thus, it could be convenient to provide a standard way to transfer data from an OODBMS to an intermediate application and to a web server. This standard way is provided by a translation mechanism receiving the schema of an object-oriented database comprising its inheritance relationships, possibly in ODL (the standard language proposed in [5] to describe the schema of an object database), its data, and writing all of them into an XML file. Several translation mechanisms can be defined, each implementing a specific format for the XML file, prioritizing some aspects or some others. Last but not least, the readability from humans and the capability of directly querying the produced XML document can be considered as important prioritizing aspects.

At the best of our knowledge, even though the problem of translating heterogenous web data received wide attention from the database community [1,2,8,11], related work on the specific topic is quite few. One contribution is from the ODMG standard [5], which defines the Object Interchange Format OIF: unfortunately, OIF allows one to export the state of a database but does not provide any mean to export the schema of the database. The importing system has to know the schema of the database by other means. Another contribution comes from Bierman [3], which proposes the use of XML to define both the schema of the database and the related state. This approach, however, does not consider how to deal with inheritance among classes and interfaces. In both the approaches [3,5], *human readability* of the produced documents is not considered, as they propose a *syntactic* approach where different objects and classes are translated through fixed constructs, which embed schema-dependent features (as the class name, the attribute names and values, and so on).

This paper describes some criteria that can be defined in translating the structure and the contents of an object database into an XML document, considering all the above requirements. According to these criteria, two complementary approaches, called "divide and link" and "all in one", were defined and implemented by a running prototype.

The structure of the paper is as follows: Section 2 introduces a motivating example. Section 3 provides some basic concepts and terminology about ODL and XML. Section 4 considers the two main approaches defined. Section 5 concludes the paper and sketches out pros and cons of the proposed translation approaches.

2 A Motivating Example

As a motivating example, we consider a database whose UML-like schema [5] is depicted in Figure 1. A simple arrow describes an Is_A relationship: the interface Person specializes in the interface TaxPayer. Beyond the attributes of Person, which are Name, Surname, and Address, TaxPayer has the attribute SSN. A bold-faced arrow describes the extend relationship: the first defined class is Student, inheriting attributes from the interface TaxPayer which, in turn, inherits from the interface Person. The attribute of Student is StudentId. The class CollegeStudent inherits from Student and adds the attribute College. Finally, the class PhDStudent specializes the class CollegeStudent by adding the attributes ThesisTitle and ThesisAdvisor.

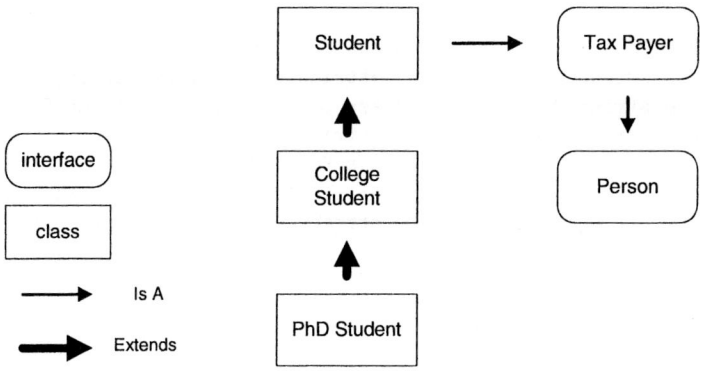

Fig. 1. Schema of a simple database with the interfaces Person, TaxPayer, and the classes Student, CollegeStudent, and PhDStudent

3 Background: ODL and XML

This Section provides a short summary of both ODL and XML, and defines appropriate terms used throughout the paper.

3.1 ODL

ODL is a standard language from ODMG 3.0 to describe the structure, with the inheritance relationships, of an object database. Most of the OODBMS vendors try to adhere to the standard and to gain import/export facilities through it.

In ODL (Object Definition Language) a *specification* defines the external features of a type, i.e. those abstract features that can be seen from outside and do not relate to the programming language of the OODBMS. An *implementation* defines the internal aspects of the type, and it is strictly bound to the programming language of reference: one type may have one implementation for every programming language. An *interface* specifies the abstract behavior of a type, regardless of its implementation. A *representation* is a data structure derived from the abstract state. A *method* is a body of a procedure, derived from the abstract behavior and implemented according to the bound programming language. A *property* is an attribute of a type defined either by a data structure or by a method, or even by a relationship among types. Finally, a *class* is a set of properties accessible to users and a set of behaviors which define the operations allowed over the class itself.

In ODL the *state* inheritance among *classes* (Extends relationship) must be *simple*, while subtyping between *interfaces* and subtyping between *interfaces* and *classes* can be *multiple*. According to ODMG 3.0, an interface is not allowed to have instances, even though it defines types and can be involved into relationships. Interfaces are thus used to enable classes to inherit from them.

In Figure 1, the Extends relationship enables the superclass to inherit the state (and the behavior) of the subclass: on the other hand, the Is_A relation-

```
interface Person {                    class Student: TaxPayer {
  attribute string Name;                attribute string StudentId;}
  attribute string Surname;           class CollegeStudent extends Student {
  attribute string Address;}            attribute string College;}
                                      class PhDStudent extends CollegeStudent {
interface TaxPayer: Person {            attribute string ThesisTitle;
  attribute string SSN;}                attribute string ThesisAdvisor;}
```

Student:
OId: S1, Name: John, Surname: Smith, Address: Boston, SSN: 480840, StudentId: 591951

OId: S2, Name: Ted, Surname: Alloy, Address: Waltham, SSN: 683563; StudentId: 794674

CollegeStudent:
OId: CS1, Name: Bob, Surname: McKnee, Address: Salem, SSN: 544233, StudentId: 655344, College: Van der Bilt

PhDStudent:
OId: PhDS1, Name: Lucy, Surname: Spencer, Address: Hamerst, SSN: 23111, StudentId: 34222, College: Van der Bilt, ThesisTitle: Computer Architectures, ThesisAdvisor: J. von Neumann

Fig. 2. ODL specification (schema) and objects (instances) for the motivating example database

ship enables interfaces and classes to inherit the behavior only, not including the state. A query selecting instances of the class **Student** whose name is "Bob" returns *also* instances of the classes **CollegeStudent** and **PhDStudent** whose name is "Bob". Figure 2 depicts the database schema of Figure 1 in ODL along with some instances. ODL provides also collection types: *set, bag, list, array, dictionary* [5].

3.2 XML and XSD

XML is a standard language from W3C to describe semistructured data. An XML document is a sequence of elements delimited by tags: any element may have subelements. The document requires a compulsory root element. An element may have attributes. To describe the structure of XML documents, the W3C defined the XML Schema (XSD), which provides both a standard collection of types and XML constructs to build complex elements [6].

When designing the schema of an XML document through an XSD document, the scope of the element definition is a vital topic: it must consider the accessibility of element specification to allow import of data from other components, reuse of elements even inside the same schema, impact over other documents If changes are applied. Several criteria can be followed [6]: the *Russian doll* criterium assumes that any element in nested into a higher level element, and that there is a topmost element including the entire structure: this criterium provides a low readability by a human, while includes a discrete protection over data since only the topmost element is exposed. Additionally, component reuse is extremely difficult. The *salami slice* criterium spreads the several elements over small segments: human readability and component reuse are encouraged by this approach whose drawback is the time needed to look for a data item inside several segments. Finally, the *Venetian blind* criterium provides a good compromise among the two previous approaches: according to this criterium, the components are defined as types with a global scope and are used subsequently when elements are instantiated.

4 Translation Approaches

When dealing with an object database, we may decide to export its schema only; we may also want to export the content of the database, too. In the first case, a simple approach consists of defining an XML element for each ODL construct. For example, the ODL definition of the interface Person is translated by the element <interface name="Person">...</interface>.

The more interesting case is related to the exchange of both database structure and contents. In this case, we require that the obtained XML document is easily readable by a human; at the same time, we want to allow the user to directly query the obtained document, maintaining the possible object hierarchies.

To do that, instead of a syntactic approach as in [5,3], we propose a *semantic* approach to the XML-based exchange of object databases: indeed, the human readability of the produced XML documents is obtained by considering and highlighting the specific schema and content of the exchanged object database; moreover, the human readability must be reached, by considering at the same time the fact that the produced XML document can be directly queried through specific XML languages as XPATH or XQUERY, preserving the correspondence between objects and classes, as in the original object database.

As for *human readability*, instead of using fixed constructs for every class, object, or attribute, respectively, our semantic approach is based on the definition of suitable XML elements for each specific object: a database object is translated into an element, having the name of the class the given object belongs to. Attributes (as well as operations with no input arguments) of an object are translated as nested elements of the element corresponding to the given object. Atomic attributes are simple (string) elements, while complex attributes (i.e., references to another object) are translated as elements pointing to a suitable complex element (representing the referred object). Suitable XML attributes are introduced to manage relations between objects and element identities.

In general, when performing a data and schema export of an object database through XML, two documents are generated: i) an XML document which describes the state of the database or of the selected data, and ii) an XSD document which defines types and element structures for the above document.

As for *direct queries* on XML documents, some issues arise when there are inheritance hierarchies: indeed, in this case, we have to consider that an object could belong to more than one class, and thus it should correspond to several elements having different names; moreover, several object attributes should be replied as subelements of different elements, corresponding to different classes of a class hierarchy. As an example, the object CS1 of class **CollegeStudent** should correspond to one element `CollegeStudent` and also to one element `Student`, being an instance both of the class **CollegeStudent** and of the class **Student**.

According to these observations, several different approaches can be defined to convert the database objects to an XML document: each of them should however allow to manage in a proper way queries involving objects belonging to a class hierarchy. In other words, the extent of each class must be correctly represented in the produced XML document. Moreover, we will try to avoid redundancies for elements corresponding to both objects and object attributes.

In the following, we focus on two original, specific approaches:

a. "divide and link": this approach subdivides properties and operations along the hierarchy line of inheritance. Any information related to a data item is linked via suitable attributes which are reachable from the most specialized element which is in the **lowest level** of the hierarchy;
b. "all in one": this approach is complementary to the previously considered one. Any information related to an instance is maintained in the element related to the **most specialized** class.

Both defined approaches described in this paper follow the **Venetian blind** style for the definition of the XSD document related to the converted objects.

4.1 The *Divide and Link* Approach

By the "divide and link" approach, inherited properties and operations are placed at the element of the **topmost level** of hierarchy, i.e. at the least specialized level. Instances of most specialized elements link to instances at a higher level in the hierarchy via suitable attributes. As an example, Figure 3 depicts the XML code derived from the database objects of Figure 2.

In Figure 3, the two instances of **Student**, S1 and S2, are defined along with their properties. Information about the only instance of **CollegeStudent**, i.e. the object having Old CS1 in Figure 2, are divided into different elements: the first element `Student` having attribute `id SCS1` contains properties of **CollegeStudent** inherited from the class **Student**; the element `CollegeStudent` having attribute `id CS1` contains the genuine properties of **CollegeStudent**. Information about the only instance of **PhDStudent** PhDS1 are divided among the instances of its superclasses and the real instance of **PhDStudent** PhDS1: SPhDS1 includes the properties of the object PhDS1 inherited from **Student**, CSPhDS1 includes the properties of the object PhDS1 inherited from **CollegeStudent**. If we want to obtain all the properties of the object PhDS1, we have to follow the links from the element having attribute `id PhDS1` to the element having attribute `id CSPhDS1`, and from CSPhDS1 to SPhDS1.

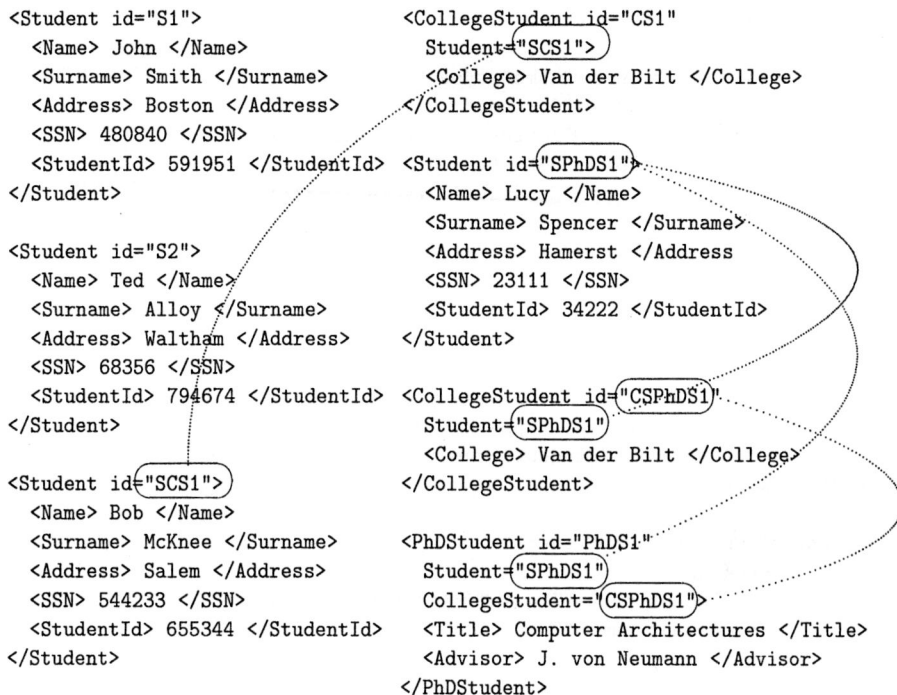

Fig. 3. XML code for the database of Figure 2 according to the "divide and link" approach

In general, the approach provides a suitable element for each object of a given class: queries on objects of a class are performed directly on the XML code.

The attribute id, whose values are automatically generated, allows one to follow the link to join data about a single instance of the most specialized class with data that are spread over several instances of the object hierarchy. For an element of a specialized class, suitable attributes are defined: attributes have the name corresponding to the linked element and refer to the elements corresponding to the same object along the class hierarchy. For example, the element with id PhDS1, which corresponds to an instance of the most specialized class, refers to the element with id SPhdS1 through the attribute Student, and to the element with id CSPhDS1 through the attribute CollegeStudent. It is worth observing that also the element with id CSPhDS1 has the attribute Student referring to the element with id SPhdS1: the use of more attributes, i.e. SCSPhdS1 and SPhDS1, to join data makes access to data more immediate: each element has all the attributes linking to the elements corresponding to more general classes.

As we described, elements corresponding to properties are contained into different elements corresponding to (super)classes on the class hierarchy; links must be followed to reach them. This names the approach "divide and link".

```xml
<xs:complexType name="Student">
    <xs:sequence>
        <xs:element name="Name" type="string"/>
        <xs:element name="Surname" type="string"/>
        <xs:element name="Address" type="string"/>
        <xs:element name="SSN" type="long"/>
        <xs:element name="StudentId" type="long"/>
    </xs:sequence>
    <xs:attribute name="id" type="xs:ID"/>
</xs:complexType>

<xs:complexType name="CollegeStudent">
    <xs:sequence>
        <xs:element name="College" type="string"/>
    <xs:attribute name="id" type="xs:ID"/>
    <xs:attribute name="Student" type="xs:IDREF"/>
</xs:complexType>

<xs:complexType name="PhDStudent">
    <xs:sequence>
        <xs:element name="ThesisTitle" type="string"/>
        <xs:element name="ThesisAdvisor" type="string"/>
    </xs:sequence>
    <xs:attribute name="id" type="xs:ID"/>
    <xs:attribute name="Student" type="xs:IDREF"/>
    <xs:attribute name="CollegeStudent" type="xs:IDREF"/>
</xs:complexType>

<xs:element name="Student" type="Student"
        minOccurs="0" maxOccurs="unbounded"/>
<xs:element name="CollegeStudent" type="CollegeStudent"
        minOccurs="0" maxOccurs="unbounded"/>
<xs:element name="PhDStudent" type="PhDStudent"
        minOccurs="0" maxOccurs="unbounded"/>
```

Fig. 4. XSD code for the database of Figure 2 according to the "divide and link" approach

The final step is that of defining the structure of elements with the same name as their respective types, and specifying the allowed cardinality. The XSD code automatically derived from the ODL code of Figure 2 is depicted in Figure 4.

Interfaces in the Divide and Link Approach. To complete our analysis, we must consider how interfaces defined in ODL can be translated in the "divide and link" approach. Being the interface in ODMG related to the specification of abstract behavior, the translation in XML does not consider any kind of attributes for interfaces; we focus only on the management of objects belonging to instances.

```
<xs:element name="Person" maxOccurs="1">
    <xs:complexType>
        <xs:attribute name="Student" type="xs:IDREFS"/>
    </xs:complexType>
</xs:element>
<xs:element name="TaxPayer" maxOccurs="1">
    <xs:complexType>
        <xs:attribute name="Student" type="xs:IDREFS"/>
    </xs:complexType>
</xs:element>
```

Fig. 5. XSD code for the interfaces of Figure 2 according to the "divide and link" approach

In this direction, an element corresponding to an interface is assigned the attributes that allow one to link elements corresponding to objects which share the considered interface. A possible alternative could be to insert into the element corresponding to the interface also the subelements corresponding to the (abstract) attributes of the interface.

4.2 The *All in One* Approach

In the "all in one" approach, which is complementary to the "divide and link", all the properties of an object are stored in the element corresponding to the most specialized class, i.e. the **bottommost level** of the inheritance hierarchy. To enable elements corresponding to superclasses to access data of subclasses, some links need to be defined. As an example, let us consider Figure 6, which depicts the XML code related to the database of Figure 2. The approach must preserve the concept that instances of a subclass (CollegeStudent) are instances of the superclass (Student), too. In this direction, an empty element Student has been defined with an attribute CollegeStudent: the same has been applied for CollegeStudent with an attribute PhDStudent. These attributes refer to the elements corresponding to objects of more specialized classes. In general, to preserve hierarchies, an attribute with the name of every subclass is defined in the element corresponding to the superclass.

In Fig. 6, S1 and S2, instances of Student, are described along with their properties: as these instances do not specialize in other subclasses, their XML code for the "all in one" approach is exactly the same as their respective XML code in the "divide and link" approach. Let us now consider the instances of the subclasses that specialize the class Student. All the information about the only instance of CollegeStudent CS1 are included into the element CollegeStudent: consequently, elements corresponding to properties inherited from Student are included into CollegeStudent. Similarly, information about the only instance of PhDS1 are included into the element PhDStudent: as above, the elements corresponding to properties inherited from Student, as well as the elements corresponding to properties inherited from CollegeStudent, are included into

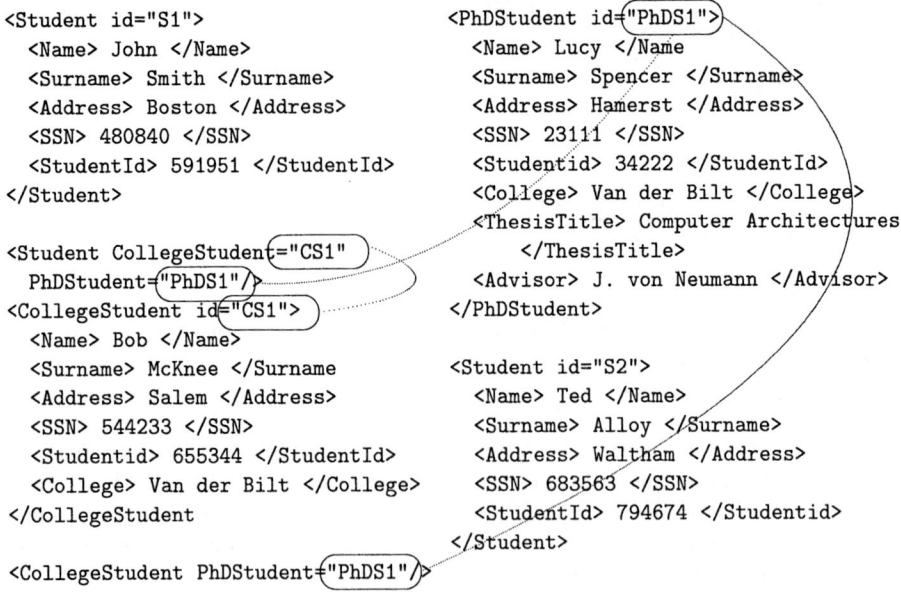

Fig. 6. XML code for the database of Figure 2 according to the "all in one" approach

PhDStudent. To complete the description, we have to specify that both the elements CollegeStudent and PhDStudent represent specialized instances of Student: this is done by the XML empty element <Student CollegeStudent="CS1" PhDStudent="PhDS1"/>. We also have to specify that the element PhDStudent represents a specialized instance of CollegeStudent, too: this is done by the XML empty element <CollegeStudent PhDStudent="PhDS1"/>.

In fact, if we want to perform a query over all the instances of Student, we have to consider the plain instances of Student and all the specialized instances of Student itself, i.e. the instances of CollegeStudent and of PhDStudent. Similarly, to perform a query over all the instances of CollegeStudent, we have to consider the plain instances of CollegeStudent and all the specialized instances of CollegeStudent itself, i.e. the instances of PhDStudent.

We recall that the attributes CollegeStudent and PhDStudent are of type IDREFS and are optional, as they are used only by the empty elements to reference elements representing objects of subclasses. As we described, properties are all stored in the most specialized class: this names the approach "all in one".

Interfaces in the All in One Approach. To complete our analysis, we consider how interfaces defined in ODL can be translated in the "all in one" approach. In the "all in one" approach, we must refer not only to the classes which directly inherit from the considered interface, as in the previous approach: we also have to consider all the class hierarchy inheriting from a given interface (Figure 7).

```
<xs:element name="Person" maxOccurs="1">
    <xs:complexType>
        <xs:attribute name="Student" type="xs:IDREFS"/>
        <xs:attribute name="CollegeStudent" type="xs:IDREFS"/>
        <xs:attribute name="PhDStudent" type="xs:IDREFS"/>
    </xs:complexType>
</xs:element>
<xs:element name="TaxPayers" maxOccurs="1">
    <xs:complexType>
        <xs:attribute name="Student" type="xs:IDREFS"/>
        <xs:attribute name="CollegeStudent" type="xs:IDREFS"/>
        <xs:attribute name="PhDStudent" type="xs:IDREFS"/>
    </xs:complexType>
</xs:element>
```

Fig. 7. XSD code for the elements corresponding to interfaces of Figure 2 according to the "all in one" approach

5 Concluding Remarks

In this paper we proposed two different approaches to translate ODL schema and objects into XML documents, preserving the semantics of objects into the corresponding elements, and providing XML documents which can be directly queried. Semantics of objects are preserved through a translation which produces human readable code via schema dependent elements.

The first approach, namely "divide and link", features an immediate access (through single elements) to properties defined for a class, while access to properties of a subclass requires to join paths by suitably defined attributes, introducing a computational overhead whenever a query is performed.

The "all in one" approach differs as all information about one object are immediately available in one single element with no intermediate identifiers to join data from instances of different classes. On the other hand, some instances of superclasses must be found through the references contained in the attribute values of empty elements associated to every superclass: e.g., some instances of **Student** can be found starting from the elements corresponding to instances of the subclasses **CollegeStudent** and **PhDStudent**.

As a proof-of-concept, the two approaches have been implemented by a prototype developed in the **Java** programming language of the "Java 2 standard edition". Among the OODBMSs compliant to the ODMG standard [9], we chose the **Orient Just Edition - OJE -** by Orient Technologies [10].

Acknowledgements. We are grateful to Fabio De Prà for designing and implementing the running prototype.

References

1. Abiteboul S., Cluet S., Milo T.: *Correspondence and Translation for Heterogeneous Data*. IEEE Int. Conf. on Database Theory 1997: 351-363
2. Ahmad U., Hassan M. W., Ali A., McClatchey R., Willers I.: *An Integrated Approach for Extraction of Objects from XML and Transformation to Heterogeneous Object Oriented Databases*. CoRR cs.DB/0402007: (2004)
3. Bierman G.M.: *Using XML as an Object Interchange Format*, Dept. of Computer Science, Univ. of Warwick 2000, also available as http://research.microsoft.com/%7Egmb/Papers/oifml.ps
4. Carey M. J., Kiernan J., Shanmugasundaram J., Shekita E. J., Subramanian S. N.: *XPERANTO: Middleware for Publishing Object-Relational Data as XML Documents*, Proc. of Very Large Data Bases Int. Conf., 2000: 646-648
5. Cattell R.G.G., Barry D., Berler M., Eastman J., Jordan D., Russell C., Schadow O., Stanienda T., Velez. F.: *The Object Database Standard: ODMG 3.0*, San Francisco: Morgan Kaufmann, 2000
6. Gulbransen D.: *Special Edition Using XML Schema*, Indianapolis: Pearson Education, 2002
7. Harold E.R., Means W.S.: *XML in a nutshell*, Sebastopol: O'Reilly, 2002
8. Milo T., Zohar S.: *Using Schema Matching to Simplify Heterogeneous Data Translation*, Proc. of Very Large Data Bases Int. Conf., 1998: 122-133
9. ODMG compliance list, http://www.odmg.org/odmg/compliancelist.htm
10. OrienTechnologies, http://www.orientechnologies.com/
11. Pottinger R., Bernstein P.A.: *Merging Models Based on Given Correspondences*, Proc. of Very Large Data Bases Int. Conf., 2003: 826-873

Intensional Encapsulations of Database Subsets via Genetic Programming

Aybar C. Acar and Amihai Motro

Department of Information and Software Engineering,
George Mason University, Fairfax, VA

Abstract. Finding intensional encapsulations of database subsets is the inverse of query evaluation. Whereas query evaluation transforms an intensional expression (the query) to its extension (a set of data values), intensional encapsulation assigns an intensional expression to a given set of data values. We describe a method for deriving intensional representations of subsets of records in large database tables. Our method is based on the paradigm of genetic programming. It is shown to achieve high accuracy and maintain compact expression size, while requiring cost that is acceptable to all applications, but those that require instantaneous results. Intensional encapsulation has a broad range of applications including cooperative answering, information integration, security and data mining.

1 Introduction

The problem of finding intensional encapsulations of database subsets has attracted considerable interest for almost two decades. Essentially, intensional encapsulation of data is the *inverse* of query evaluation. Whereas query evaluation substitutes an intensional expression (the query) with its extension (a set of data values), intensional encapsulation assigns an intensional expression to a given set of data values.

The original application of intensional encapsulation was in *cooperative answering systems*, proactive systems that help users achieve their retrieval goals efficiently. The common term for the method was *intensional answering*, and the idea was to respond to database queries with concise expressions that describe, as accurately as possible, the usual (extensional) answers to these queries. The user would thus receive two complementary responses: the usual answer, and a compact description of the answer. For example, a query about the employees who earn over $80,000 would be answered extensionally by the appropriate set of employees, and intensionally by an expression such as "all the engineers, except John, but also Mary".

This paper describes a novel method for generating intensional encapsulations using the paradigm of genetic programming. Given a set of database records, intensional expressions are generated that attempt to "cover" the given set. These expressions are evolved and recombined with each other until a satisfactory result is obtained. The attributes and attribute values used in these expressions are selected using a Bayesian approach that uses the probability distributions of the attribute values in the database.

The advantage of using genetic programming is that it does not require any semantic information about the content of the database, the meaning of its attributes, and so on. In comparison with other methods that are "blind" to semantics, genetic programming offers much more precision. Genetic programming is especially adept at finding intensional encapsulations for sets with small disjuncts (e.g., a set of records containing all engineers and also Mary), where more traditional approaches like decision trees tend to generalize and neglect the exceptions.

Any method for intensional encapsulation is subject to three performance measures. The first measure is *accuracy*: How well does the intensional expression obtained represent the given set. This is interpreted as the *similarity* of two sets: the given set, and the extension of the intensional expression. We adopt a common measure of set similarity, which is the harmonic mean of the relative containments of each set in the other set. Our experiments achieved mean accuracy of 94.6%. Clearly, compact intensional encapsulations are preferred as they are more comprehensible and more likely to be meaningful to the application. Our second performance measure is therefore *conciseness*. Our measure for conciseness is comparative: Our experiments begin with sets that are themselves generated by intensional expressions. We then compare the complexity of the discovered intension with the complexity of the *a priori* intension. In 90.4% of the experiments, conciseness has either remained the same or has actually improved. The third performance measure is *time*: How much effort is spent in obtaining acceptable encapsulations. Genetic programming processes are measured by "generations", and the mean number of generations required was 2.33. Using a desktop computer of modest specifications, a 10 MB database required under 4 seconds on average; for a 100 MB database the average was around 60 seconds. We believe that these initial results prove the viability of our methods, particularly for classes of applications that do not require instantaneous responses.

Our methodology is described in Section 3. Section 4 details our experiments. Summary and conclusions are given in Section 5. We begin with a brief review of related work.

2 Background

The two main subject areas of this paper are genetic programming and intensional encapsulation. The authors are not aware of any previous work that combined these two areas. Hence this section briefly reviews each of these areas separately.

Genetic programming has developed over the last two decades as a local-optimization method for generating simple computer programs that provide solutions for "black-box problems"; i.e., problems that seek to find the correct output for given input, without the need for a general algorithm. The extent to which a program can achieve the correct mapping of its input to the required output defines its *fitness* to the problem. In this process, initial programs are modified and combined with each other to generate "offspring programs", in an attempt to find programs that achieve even higher fitness. This evolution process terminates when a program is obtained that performs above a certain threshold of fitness.

Genetic programming has been used to some extent in data mining. In some cases researchers have preferred genetic programming as a classification method in place of or along with more traditional methods such as decision trees [3]. A more complete treatment of genetic programming and genetic algorithms in data mining can be found in [4].

The problem of finding compact descriptions for database subsets received considerable attention in the last two decades. The problem is usually framed in the context of cooperative query systems [8], and the idea is to annotate answer sets provided by a database system with compact descriptions that provide additional insight and interpretation to these sets. Borrowed from logic, the terms *intension* and *extension* are used in the database literature to describe, respectively, the definition of a database predicate (e.g., a query, a view, or a constraint), and the population of database items that satisfy the predicate (the answer to a query, the materialization of a view, or the values conforming to the constraint). Hence, these compact descriptions have been termed *intensional answers*. The term implies, however, that the process is applicable only when the given set has been generated by an *a priori* query, whereas it is just as useful when the given set is entirely *ad hoc*. We therefore adopt the more general term *intensional encapsulations*.

This problem has been tackled in different database models, including relational databases, logic databases, and databases that utilize concept taxonomies. Some methods find encapsulations that are purely intensional, whereas others also incorporate extensional information into their encapsulations; some methods find encapsulations that characterize the extensions *perfectly* (i.e., the extensions of the discovered intensions are identical to the original extensions), whereas other methods only find *applicable* characterizations (i.e., they only characterize subsets of the given extensions); by their nature, encapsulations of query extensions may need to be updated when the underlying database changes, yet some methods derive their intensional expressions from data-independent information (e.g., from database constraints), indeed thus providing equivalent formulations of the original queries. A survey of a large number of intensional answering methods may be found in [7]. Of particular relevance is [9], where two key quality aspects of intensional descriptions, accuracy and conciseness, are discussed, and their often conflicting nature is observed.

In addition to cooperative answering, intensional encapsulations have other practical uses. They are related to data mining in that it too seeks to derive an underlying explanation from a given collection of data. In the area of information integration, newly discovered information is assigned intensional descriptions, as part of a system that automatically incorporates new sources into a virtual database [2]. In the area of database security, intensional encapsulations may be used to analyze the set of records that have been delivered to a user over a period of time, to determine whether the user has surreptitious intents [1].

3 Methodology

We assume that the data is stored in a relational database, and we shall adopt the terminology and conventions of relational databases. We assume a single database table, denoted R, and a *target* set of records $T \subseteq R$; i.e., T is the set of records of R for which an encapsulated description is sought.

Our method creates an initial population of intensional expressions (indeed, they are *queries* against the table R), and evolves this population until one or more of these queries performs satisfactorily (i.e., with acceptable accuracy). Let Q_i denote a query of this population, and let $P_i \subseteq R$ denote its extension in R; i.e., $Q_i(R) = P_i$. The accuracy of Q_i is measured by the similarity of the sets P_i and T. Perfect accuracy is achieved when $P_i = T$.

The process begins with the generation of a set of random queries Q_i. These arbitrary queries are fully correct queries on the table R that are synthesized from primitives that have been previously adopted. The judicious selection of these primitives and their combination into queries will be discussed later.

Next, each query in the initial population is evaluated and a *fitness* value is computed. Fitness is defined as the similarity of the query's extension P_i and the target set T. The measure to be used will be discussed later, but for now we assume that it is a value between 0 and 1, where 0 denotes complete disjointness of the sets and 1 denotes their complete overlap.

The queries with the highest fitness are then bred with each other using either direct combination, crossover or mutation, to generate a new population of queries. This new generation is then evaluated in the same manner as its predecessor, and the evaluation is used to produce yet a newer generation of queries. Typically, this evolutionary process gradually increases the mean fitness of its population. The process is halted once a member of the current population achieves satisfactory fitness. Satisfactory fitness is defined with a similarity threshold. This threshold may be fixed, or it may depend on the sizes of R and T. This iterative process is illustrated in Figure 1. As there is no guarantee that the process will converge, it will in practice be stopped if fitness does not improve within a given number of generations. In such cases the process will only be able to derive intensional encapsulations of limited accuracy.

As common in genetic programming, the individuals of the population are represented as trees. Since in this application the individuals are queries, the trees correspond to standard relational algebra expressions. In these trees, leaf nodes correspond to selection operators and internal nodes correspond to set operations. The queries we consider invovle four operations in total: selection, union, intersection and set difference. We focus here on the construction of selections, as the other three operators do not involve a choice of parameters.

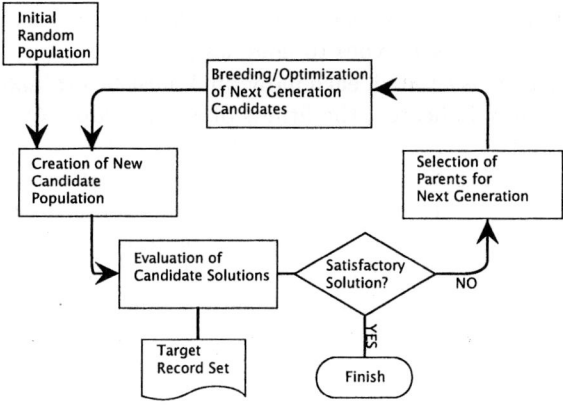

Fig. 1. Overview of the Method

The creation of a new selection operation (either in the generation of the initial population, or in subsequent evolutionary cycles) involves two separate decisions: First, an attribute A is chosen, then appropriate limiting values (either a single value a for an equality selection, or a pair of values a_1 and a_2 for a range selection) are adopted. The choice of A assumes simply that the attributes of R are distributed uniformly (i.e., all the attributes have equal probability of being chosen). Once A has been chosen, the limiting values are adopted in accordance with the type of A. The choice of limiting values is important, as judicious choices will promote good initial fitness and will increase the chance of early convergence. We begin by describing the choice of the limiting value a when the attribute A is nominal.

For each attribute A of R we define a random variable X_A whose range is the domain of A.[1] The limiting values are chosen from the domain of A according to the distribution of X_A. Intuitively, if a value v occurs frequently in the attribute A in the target set T, then it would be wise to begin with a selection $A = v$, as it may be expected that the records thus selected will have a good fit with T. The distribution of X_A is defined with a Bayesian approach. We observe that

$$p(r \in T \mid A = v) = \frac{|\sigma_{A=v}(T)|}{|\sigma_{A=v}(R)|}$$

Namely, the probability that an arbitrary record r is in T, given the property that its attribute A has the value v, is the proportion of records with this property that are included in T. This value is normalized to define the probability distribution of X_A:

$$p(X_A = v) = \frac{P(T \mid v)}{\sum_k p(T \mid V_k)}$$

---

[1] If the domain of A is not available, we use the *active* domain; i.e., the set of values of attribute A in the present instance of R.

We handle numerical and textual attributes in a manner similar to nominal attributes, by reducing these types to nominal attributes.

Once a population is created, each individual must be evaluated to determine its fitness. As already indicated, the fitness of an individual Q_i is the similarity of its extension $Q_i(R) = P_i$ to the target set T.

To define set similarity, we note that the identity of two sets A and B is defined $A = B$ if and only if $A \subseteq B$ and $B \subseteq A$. Consequently, a reasonable approach to set similarity is to measure the *extent* to which each set is contained in the other. The extent to which A is contained in B may be taken as the fraction $\frac{|A \cap B|}{|B|}$. Similarly, the extent to which B is contained in A is $\frac{|B \cap A|}{|A|}$. These fractions range between 0 (total disjointedness) and 1 (total containment). When both fractions are 1, the sets are identical; when either one is 0 (the other is then 0 as well), the sets are disjoint.[2]

For the purpose of fitness, these two measures must be combined into one. Note that when P_i is compared with T, $\frac{|P_i \cap T|}{|T|}$ measures the extent to which the generated expression covers the given set (i.e., its ability to avoid "false negatives"). Similarly, $\frac{|P_i \cap T|}{|P_i|}$ measures the extent to which the generated expression is covered by the given set (i.e., its ability to avoid "false positives"). As we have no preference of one error type over the other, we shall fuse the two measures symmetrically. A well-accepted symmetric fusion of these two measures is their *harmonic mean*. The harmonic mean of two numbers x_1 and x_2 is $2\frac{x_1 \cdot x_2}{x_1 + x_2}$. Substituting $\frac{|P_i \cap T|}{|T|}$ and $\frac{|P_i \cap T|}{|P_i|}$ for x_1 and x_2, our measure of fitness is:

$$2 \frac{|P_i \cap T|}{|P_i| + |T|}$$

This measure preserves the properties that (1) it is between 0 and 1, (2) it is 0 if and only if the two sets are disjoint, and (3) it is 1 if and only if the two sets are identical. Since the target set T is assumed non-empty, it is well-defined.

In genetic programming the two most common methods of selecting individuals with higher fitness are *fitness-proportional* selection and *tournament* selection [5]. In the former, individuals are selected with probability proportional to their fitnesses. In the latter, groups of 3 or 7 individuals are randomly selected and the individual with the highest fitness in each group is selected. In either case, the selection process repeats a number of times equal to the population size to obtain the parents for the new generation. Notice that several copies of the individuals with highest fitness are likely to be added to the parent pool whereas the lowest ranking individuals will have a lower chance at breeding.

Of these two methods we shall use tournament selection with groups of 7. The choice in this case is neither easy nor absolute. However, the fact that tournament selection is easier to implement and easier to parallelize is a major advantage. Also, as with all local search methods, genetic programming tends to converge as it proceeds. This is seen as diminished variation between individuals

---

[2] In information retrieval these measures are known as precision and recall.

in the later generations. In such situations, tournament selection is more likely to select for breeding the individuals with the highest fitness values.

Once a pool of parent individuals has been selected, the next generation of individuals is created using three operations: direct combination, mutation and crossover. Each operation requires two individuals and in turn creates two new children. The next generation does not necessarily comprise new individuals only. A random portion of the parents may be injected into the new mix without any alteration. In our experiments, 10% of the individuals of each generation were comprised of unmodified parents from the preceding generation. The remaining 90% were modified. The modifications are the fairly standard operations of *mutation* and *crossover* as explained in [5]. In addition, we use a third operation called direct combination where two parents are combined into two new larger trees using randomly selected root nodes.

We mentioned in the introduction the benefit of concise intensional encapsulations. Conciseness is not an intrinsic consideration in our methodology; namely, our genetic programming process does not include conciseness in its measure of fitness. Of the three breeding operations, mutation tends to create shorter expressions, direct combination tends to create longer expressions, and crossover tends to keep lengths unchanged. Overall, however, since the increase due to direct combination is on the average larger than the reduction due to mutation, the complexity of expressions tends to increase with generations. In an effort to control this increase, we begin with concise individuals; indeed, the initial generation comprises individuals that are single node each (simple selections).

Once the new generation has been generated, the cycle is repeated as shown in Figure 1. The process terminates when "the best of the new generation" exceeds a prespecified threshold fitness, or a prespecified number of generations pass without an improvement in the best fitness attained. In either case, the individual with the best fitness is adopted.

As we shall observe in the next section, our search process is dominated by the time required for database access. To alleviate this problem, we *cache* intermediate database results. Recall that the leaves of each query tree are selection operators. These are executed in the database, and the results are stored in memory as efficient bit vectors. Thereafter, all subsequent set operations in a particular tree are done in memory, thus avoiding any additional database access. This optimization resulted in substantial improvement.

4 Experimentation

Our methodology was implemented as a prototype and tested on a variant of the TPC-H [10] benchmark database. The original TPC-H relations were projected and joined, resulting in a relation having 24 attributes, 12 of which were nominal, 9 were numerical and 3 were textual. The TPC-H benchmark can generate databases of arbitrary size. Relations of size 10 MB and 100 MB were synthesized to study the scaling of our methodology.

The target sets of records (the sets of records for which encapsulations were sought) were generated by means of queries. Each query was composed by selecting random attributes and random values for those attributes assuming equal probabilities. The query trees were generated with the Probabilistic Tree Creation (PTC2) algorithm [6]. This algorithm can generate random queries of precisely defined size. One of the factors examined in the experiments was the effect of the complexity of the generating query on the accuracy of the encapsulation, and queries ranging from single selection predicates to 5-selection predicates were used. These queries were evaluated on the database, and the extensions retrieved were given to our system as targets. Throughout the experiment, the size of the population was kept at 40. This size was determined after some experimentation. A lower population size of 20 required far too many generations to converge; a higher population size of 60 required more time per generation, without giving substantially better results. For each of the two databases, and for each of the 5 complexity levels, 200 queries were attempted. Altogether, the experiment was repeated 2,000 times. Termination was controlled by setting the fitness threshold to 0.99, and the maximal number of generations to 3.

As explained, the target record sets were generated by random queries. Another acceptable approach would have been to generate random record sets directly. There are three reasons for our choice. First, in many applications (e.g, cooperative answering, or security), the target sets are indeed generated by queries. Second, as we shall see, these *a priori* intensional expressions are used in the evaluation of the effectiveness of the system with respect to conciseness. Finally, using *a priori* intensional expressions guarantees the existence of at least one encapsulation with perfect accuracy for each given target set.

The first measure of performance that we consider is accuracy. Accuracy measures the similarity of the given target set and the extension of the encapsulation obtained at the end of the search process; i.e., it is the fitness of the final result. Recall that fitness values are between 0 and 1. The mean accuracy achieved in the entire set of experiments was 94.6%. Moreover, in over half of the experiments the system found the perfect encapsulation. The complexity of the query that generated the target set seems to have a significant effect on the success of the system. More complex targets resulted in a noticeable decrease in the accuracy of the encapsulations. The mean accuracies for targets of different complexity is shown in Table 1.

Our measure for conciseness of an intensional expression is the number of nodes in the tree that represents it. Determining the effectiveness of the system with respect to conciseness is not straightforward. Our approach has been to *compare* the conciseness of the discovered encapsulation to that of the generating intensional expression (which, of course, is unknown to the system). Overall, in 90.4% of the experiments the system generated intensional encapsulations that were as least as concise as the *a priori* expressions (in 73.1% of the experiments conciseness remained the same, in 17.3% it actually improved). Only in 9.6% of the experiments, the discovered encapsulations were less concise. Like accuracy, conciseness too declined as the complexity of targets increased. Table 1 breaks down the comparative conciseness rates according to the complexity of the targets.

Table 1. Accuracy and Conciseness by Target Complexity

Complexity (Selections)	Mean Accuracy	% Less Concise	% Equally Concise	% More Concise
1	0.998	1.21	98.79	N/A
2	0.969	2.34	84.21	13.45
3	0.950	9.03	78.61	12.36
4	0.928	17.84	56.48	25.68
5	0.877	17.56	47.52	34.92

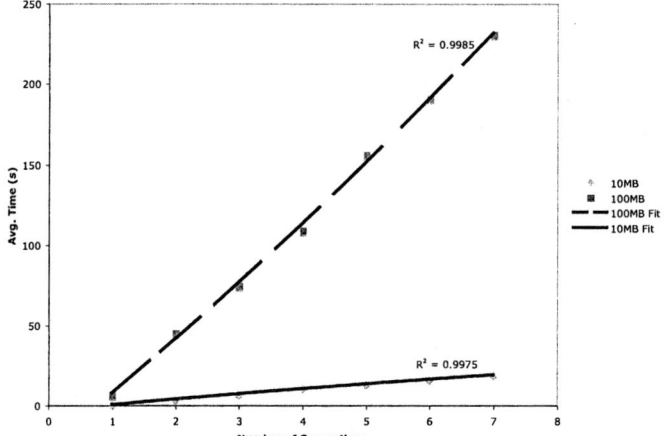

Fig. 2. Time Requirement *vs.* Number of Generations

The third measure of performance that we consider is time. Predictably, the primary bottleneck for the system is database management; in particular, the disk input and output activity. As discussed earlier, genetic programming processes are measured by the number of generations required for the process to converge. The mean number of generations required was 2.339. This information, along with the time required per generation, gives the average time required for an experiment. The average time for the 10 MB database was 3.76 seconds, and the average for the 100 MB database was 61.32 seconds. The relationship of the average experiment time with respect to number of generations is shown in Figure 2.

5 Conclusion

We described a novel approach to the well-known problem of finding intensional encapsulations of database subsets, based on the paradigm of genetic programming. In experiments, our method performed very well *qualitatively*; i.e., with respect to both accuracy and conciseness. Its *time* performance may be considered acceptable for all applications that do not require instantaneous results (its performance for moderate size databases may be considered acceptable even for real-time applications).

Indeed, the time performance achieved may be considered surprisingly good, given the general opinion of genetic programming as a solution method of low efficiency. This accomplishment is largely due to the fact that the programs we handle, namely queries, are very specialized, with restricted contexts and relatively small search spaces. In addition, our judicious choice of selection predicates promoted more rapid convergence of the evolutionary process. Furthermore, by caching solutions in memory, we were able to reduce database access substantially and thus contain the time required for each generation. Combined, the reduction in the number of generations required and efficient processing of each generation, resulted in this reasonably good performance. We observe that our method lends itself to parallelization, and we estimate that by increasing the database power (e.g., by using a cluster of database servers), further and considerable improvements may be achieved.

References

1. Acar, A. C. and A. Motro. Why is this User Asking so Many Questions? Explaining Sequences of Queries. In *Proceedings of the 18th Annual IFIP WG 11.3 Working Conference on Data and Applications Security*, pages 159–176, Kluwer, 2004.
2. Berlin, J. and A. Motro. Autoplex: Automated Discovery of Contents for Virtual Databases. In *Proceedings of COOPIS-01, Sixth IFCIS International Conference on Cooperative Information Systems, Lecture Notes in Computer Science No. 2172*, pages 108–122, Springer, 2001.
3. Carvalho, D. R. and, A. A. Freitas. A Hybrid Decision Tree/Genetic Algorithm for Coping with the Problem of Small Disjuncts in Data Mining. In *Proceedings of the 2000 Genetic and Evolutionary Computation Conference*, pages 1061–1068, Morgan Kaufmann, 2000.
4. Freitas, A. A. A Survey of Evolutionary Algorithms for Data Mining and Knowledge Discovery. In *Advances in Evolutionary Computing: Theory and Applications*, pages 819-845, Springer, 2003.
5. Koza, J. R. *Genetic Programming: On the Programming of Computers by Means of Natural Selection.* MIT Press, 1992.
6. Luke, S. Two Fast Tree-creation Algorithms for Genetic Programming. *IEEE Transactions on Evolutionary Computation*, 4(3):274–283, IEEE, 2000.
7. Motro, A. Intensional Answers to Database Queries. *IEEE Transactions on Knowledge and Data Engineering*, 6(3):444-454, IEEE, 1994.
8. Motro, A. Cooperative Database Systems. *International Journal of Intelligent Systems*, 11(10):717–732, Wiley, 1996.
9. Shum, C. D. and R. Muntz. Implicit Representation for Extensional Answers. In *Proceedings of the Second International Conference on Expert Database Systems*, pages 497–522, Benjamin Cummings, 1988.
10. Transaction Processing Performance Council. TPC Benchmark H Rev. 2.1.0. *Technical Report*, TPC, 2002.

Preferred Skyline: A Hybrid Approach Between SQLf and Skyline

Marlene Goncalves and María-Esther Vidal

Universidad Simón Bolívar, Departamento de Computación, Apartado 89000,
Caracas 1080-A, Venezuela
{mgoncalves, mvidal}@usb.ve

Abstract. The World Wide Web (WWW) is a great repository of data and it may reference thousands of data sources for almost any knowledge domain. Users frequently access sources to query information and may be interested only in the top k answers that meet their preferences. Although, many declarative languages have been defined to express WWW queries, the problem of specifying user preferences and considering this information during query optimization and evaluation remains open. Most used query languages, such as SQL and XQUERY, do not allow specifying general conditions on user preferences. For example, using the SQL ORDER BY clause one can express the order in which the answer will appear, but the user must be aware of filtering the tuples that satisfy their preferences. Skyline and SQLf are two extensions of SQL defined to express general user preferences. Skyline offers physical operators to construct a Pareto Curve of the non-dominated answers. Skyline may return answers with bad values for some criteria and does not discriminate between the non-dominated answers. On the other hand, SQLf gives the best answers in terms of user preferences, but it may return dominated answers. Finally, the skyline operator evaluation time is higher than SQLf. We proposed a hybrid approach, Preferred Skyline, integrating skyline and SQLf to produce only answers in the Pareto Curve with best satisfaction degrees. We report initial experimental results on execution time and answer precision. They show that Preferred Skyline consumes less time than Skyline and its precision is higher than SQLf.

1 Introduction

The World Wide Web (WWW) is a great repository of data and it may reference thousands of data sources for almost any knowledge domain. Constantly, new data sources are published, increasing dramatically the size of the WWW.

Users frequently access sources in order to query information and may be interested only in answers that satisfy their preferences. Electronic commerce is an example of this type of searching, where users express their preference criteria in terms of the quality of services/products.

Although, many declarative languages have been defined to express WWW queries, the problem of specifying user preferences and considering this information during query optimization and evaluation remains open. On one hand, most used query languages, such as SQL (Structured Query Language) [1] and XQUERY [17], do not allow to specify general conditions on user preferences. For example, one can express the order in which the answer of a SQL query will be produced by using the ORDER BY clause. However, to choose the ones that satisfy the user preferences, a filter process must be run on the top of the answer. This process becomes more complex when user criteria involve three or more conditions.

Skyline [9] and SQLf [5] are two SQL extensions to express user-preferences. Skyline orders the answers of a query in terms of several criteria and outputs the set of points that are not dominated by any other point in the dataset. This set is called skyline or first stratum in the Pareto curve. SQLf is an approach defined to express fuzzy queries; user preferences are defined as utility functions. These functions are used to compute the membership degrees of the tuples in the answer of a fuzzy query.

The SQLf query algorithm is based on the Derivation Principle. Following the Derivation Principle a fuzzy query is rewritten into a regular query called derived query. The derived query evaluation time is lower than fuzzy query processing, which is the main problem for fuzzy databases [4]. For the best of our knowledge, there have not defined fuzzy query optimization and evaluation techniques. On the other hand, a naive skyline evaluation is excessively expensive and efficient physical operators have been defined. SFS (Sort Filter Skyline) [9] is an efficient algorithm that allocates skyline answers in a *window*; tuples in the answer are chosen from the input table, which is sorted in terms of the user-preference attributes.

The main objective of skyline algorithms is to efficiently identify optimal results in the space of solutions that meet the multiple user criteria. The solution of a multi-objective optimization problem is referred to as the Pareto curve [14]. A Pareto curve has an exponential number of points and it may be impossible to build this curve in reasonable time. For this reason, algorithms find approximations to Pareto optimal. Skyline identifies the first point in an approximation of the Pareto curve. Elements in the first point, are non-dominated by any other element. An element dominates another element if it is no worse in all criteria, and better in at least one criterion. SQLf may return dominated elements and may not identify all the non-dominated. Filtering dominated answers in SQLf will allow one to find better answers in terms of user preferences. On the other, Skyline can return answers with bad values for some criterion, i.e., it identifies the answers with better values in at least one criterion and worse values in the rest. Finally, Skyline does not discriminate between the non-dominated answers and SQLf does discriminate them in terms of a user-defined predicate.

We propose a hybrid approach, Preferred Skyline, integrating Skyline and SQLf in order to produce only answers in the Pareto Curve that satisfy user criteria. We report initial experimental results on execution time and answer precision. Our initial results show that Preferred Skyline consumes less time than Skyline and its precision is higher than SQLf.

2 Background and Related Work

Kung et al. proposed the first Skyline algorithm in [13], referred to as the maximum vector problem and it is based on the divide & conquer principle. Progress has been made as of recent on how to compute efficiently such queries in a relational system and over large datasets [2][9][16]. In [2], the Skyline operator is introduced. They proposed two algorithms: a block-nested loops style algorithm (and variations) and a divide-and-conquer approach derived from work in [13][16]. In [16], an algorithm that uses specialized indexing for Skyline evaluation is introduced. In [9], a general Skyline algorithm was developed and it is based on the "block-nested loop" algorithm of [2] that is faster, pipelinable and more amenable.

On the other hand, several efforts have been made by different authors in order to provide flexible querying database systems. Bosc and Pivert [5] have proposed SQLf, a fuzzy-set-based SQL extension. In [11][12] SQLf2 and SQLf3 are defined as an SQLf extension with the features of SQL2 and SQL3. There are some query processing mechanism [3][4][6][7] and the most relevant is derivation principle [6][7] because it has a less cost.

2.1 Skyline Query Language

An operator, named Skyline, is defined in [2]. In Fig. 1, SQL is extended with a SKYLINE OF clause.

```
SELECT <attributes> FROM <relations> WHERE <conditions>
    GROUP BY <attributes> HAVING <conditions>
SKYLINE OF a₁ [min|max|diff],…, aₙ [min|max|diff]
```

Fig. 1. A proposed skyline operator for SQL

A SKYLINE OF clause body represents a list of attributes or Skyline dimensions used to rank the dataset. Each dimension can be an integer, float, or a date and may be annotated with the directives: min, max and diff. Mix and max indicate minimum or maximum values and the diff directive defines the interest in retaining the best choices with respect to every distinct value of the attribute. Finally, if none directive is stated, max is the default.

SFS (Sort-Filter-Skyline) [9] is an efficient algorithm that improves the performance of a skyline time computation. First, this algorithm sorts the input table and then, it passes over the sorted tuples to identify the ones that are non-dominated. The main disadvantage of this approach is that it first needs to order the input table and then, scan it to check the dominance relationship.

2.2 SQLf Query Language

One remarkable effort in the creation of flexible querying system for relational databases is SQLf [5]. Fuzzy queries involve fuzzy terms (atomic predicates, modifiers, connectors, comparators and quantifiers) whose semantic is user and context depended. Fig. 2 shows an SQLf basic query block.

```
      SELECT <attributes> FROM <relations>
WHERE <fuzzy conditions> WITH CALIBRATION [n|α|n.α]
```

Fig. 2. SQLf basic block

An SQLf query answer corresponds to the tuples in the Cartesian product of the relations in the FROM clause that satisfy the fuzzy condition. These tuples consist of the attributes in the SELECT clause. Some fuzzy logical expressions can be used with user-defined terms and predefined operators in the WHERE clause. A tolerance is specified in the CALIBRATION clause and indicates the condition to be satisfied by the best tuples. The process to identify the best tuples is called calibration. Two calibration types have been proposed: Quantitative and Qualitative. In case of Quantitative calibration, a maximum number "n" of answers is obtained. On the other hand, tuples whose membership value is greater or equal to "α" are produced if the calibration is Qualitative.

An efficient SQLf evaluation mechanism is based on the Derivation Principle [6][15]. The Derivation Principle Strategy attempts to keep low the number of row access in fuzzy query processing by means of the distribution of the α-cut over conditions involved in the fuzzy query. It derives a regular SQL query whose result contains the rows satisfying the fuzzy query with a degree value of at least α. This principle may be used for the evaluation of fuzzy queries avoiding the scanning of the whole database. A derived necessary condition is a basic concept in the Derivation Principle application. It is a regular condition that expresses the α-cut of a fuzzy condition. It is denoted by: $DNC(<fuzzy\ condition>, \geq, \alpha)$.

Consider the following example to illustrate the Derivation Principle. Suppose *location* is a relation with an attribute *priority* and, *BestZone* is a fuzzy predicate on *priority* domain that measures the *goodness* of a zone. Fig 3 presents the definition of the *BestZone* function. The query: *Find those locations in best areas with a tolerance level of 0.5* is expressed using SQLf as follows:

```
SELECT * FROM location WHERE priority = BestZone
                WITH CALIBRATION 0.5
```

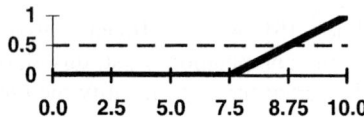

Fig. 3. *BestZone* predicate definition by means of its membership function. We remark the satisfaction 0.5 that is used as a threshold in the example.

First, applying the Derivation Principle, the derived necessary condition: $DNC(priority = BestZone, \geq, 0.5) = Priority \geq 8.75)$ is obtained. Since, the *BestZone* fuzzy function indicates that all the locations whose priority values is greater or equal to 8.75 will have a membership value equal to 0.5, then, the initial query is translated into the following:

```
SELECT * FROM location WHERE priority ≥ 8.75.
```

3 Motivating Example

Consider the following relational table that represents a restaurant guide: Guide(idRest,Reviewer,AvegPrice,QService,QFood,QPlace).

A restaurant is described by an identifier (idRest), the reviewer name (Reviewer), the average of the dish price (AvegPrice), and three values between 1 to 30 that measure the quality of the service (QService), the quality of food (QFood) and the quality of the place (QPlace), respectively.

Suppose the top K restaurants will receive an award, so tuples in table Guide must be ranked in terms of the values of: QService, QFood, QPlace and AvegPrice. A restaurant can be postulated for the award if and only if there is no other restaurant with lower average price and better quality of service, food and place. To nominate a restaurant, one must identify the set of all the restaurants that are not dominated by any other restaurant in terms of these criteria. Winners will be selected among nominates in terms of the top K values of an overall preference that combines values of the previous attributes weighted by a confidence degree in the reviewer decision.

Skyline and SQLf are two extensions of SQL language that could be used to identify the winners from table Guide. However, none of them will provide the set of winners and post-processing will be needed to filter the winners.

Skyline offers a set of operators to build an approximation of a Pareto curve (strata) or set of points that are not dominated by any other point in the dataset (skyline or first stratum). Thus, by using Skyline, ones could just obtain the nominated restaurants.

On the hand, SQLf will allow referees to implement a score function and filter some of the winners in terms of this function. In order to choose winner restaurants, SQLf computes the score to each tuple without checking dominance relationship between tuples in the dataset. Finally, also top K query approaches rank a set of tuples according to some provided functions and do not check dominance relationship.

Although solutions produces by either SQLf or top K queries, will correspond to winners, some nominates may not be considered and in consequence some winner may not be identified [8].

To identify the set of all the winners, a hybrid approach that combines the goodness of Skyline and SQLf or top K will be needed.

In this paper, we propose a Preferred Skyline approach that filters among an approximation of the Pareto curve, the points that meet user preference criteria the most.

4 Preferred Skyline

Preferred Skyline is a hybrid approach between Skyline and SQLf, that offers the best points of the first stratum or skyline of Pareto Curve based on a quantitative or qualitative calibration.

We define its basic block as in Fig. 4. A Preferred Skyline query answer corresponds to the tuples on the Cartesian product of the relations in the FROM clause that are non dominated by any other tuple according to fuzzy skyline criteriaand whose score on a fuzzy condition function, is greater or equal than α.

A tuple t is dominated by a tuple t', if and only if, t' is better than t as in the score function as in all fuzzy skyline criteria. If "n" is specified in the WITH CALIBRATION clause, the n best skyline tuples with the highest score are returned.

```
SELECT <attributes> FROM <relations>
       WHERE <fuzzy_conditions>
SKYLINE OF <fuzzy_skyline_criteria> WITH CALIBRATION [n|αln,α]
```

Fig. 4. SQLf basic block

We have implemented Preferred Skyline as a two steps process that combines SQLf and Skyline. In the first step, tuples in the input tables are filtered using the SQLf Derivation Principle-based algorithm. Then, in the second step, the SFS algorithm identifies non-dominated tuples. Dominated tuples are computed in terms of the fuzzy criteria and the fuzzy predicates calculated in the previous step. Note that this implementation is sound but it may not complete, i.e., there may be some non-identified nominates.

Preferred Skyline algorithm has a (worst-case) complexity of $O(m(\log m)^{d-2})$, where "m" the number of points identified in the first step, and "d" the number of skyline dimensions [13]. The Preferred Skyline time complexity bound is based on the time complexity bounds of SQLf algorithms and Skyline. First, the SQLf Derivation Principle algorithm requires to scan a subset of the input that meets the fuzzy predicates. Then, running time reflects the database access time plus tuple processing time. The database access time is "c_1" times "m" with "c_1" a constant, "m" the number of returned points, "n" the number of points in the data set, m ≤ n. The tuple processing time is "c_2" times "m" with "c_2" a constant. A time complexity bound to compute the fuzzy set is $O(m)$ [15]. This previous filtering reduces Skyline algorithm time. The Skyline algorithm running discards solutions that are not better across all the criteria and are produced by SQLf. The running time of Skyline algorithms can be very high and it can be shown that the best Skyline algorithm to compute an approximation of a Pareto curve has a (worst-case) complexity of $O(n(\log n)^{d-2})$, with "n" the number of points in the data set and d the number of dimensions [13].

5 Initial Experimental Study

We compare the quality of the answers produced by Preferred Skyline, Skyline and SQLf, and their performances. We implemented following three algorithms: the basic SFS algorithm without optimizations [9], the Principle-Derivation-based algorithm [4] and Preferred Skyline as the combination of the previous ones. All the algorithms were implemented in PL/SQL and Swi Prolog and executed on a single processor machine: Intel 866-MHz PC with 512-MB main memory and an 18-GB disk running Red Hat Linux 8.0. In this initial study, we run experiments over synthetic databases.

5.1 Experiment 1: Quality of Preferred Skyline wrt SQLf and Skyline

We study the quality of the answers identified by Preferred Skyline, Skyline, SQLf with respect to the top K answers (TopK). We run nine medium and large queries. Queries represented in SQLf, Skyline and Preferred Skyline languages were defined over the same table and attributes. SQLf queries were randomly generated and characterized by the following properties: (a) there was only one table in the FROM clause; (b) attributes in the fuzzy predicates were randomly chosen among the table attributes using a uniform distribution; (c) base fuzzy predicates were defined on the basis of the fuzzy predicate minimum which is defined in Fig. 5; (d) a fuzzy condition in the WHERE clause was a conjunction of five or nine base fuzzy conditions and (e) the quality calibration was 0.75. Skyline queries had the following properties: (a) there was only one table in the FROM clause; (b) the Skyline directive was min. Preferred Skyline queries had the SQLf query properties plus the Skyline directive min. The size of the table varied between 100,000 and 1,000,000 tuples. Each tuple had ten integer values in the range from 1 to 30 and one string value. Each tuple was randomly generated following a uniform distribution.

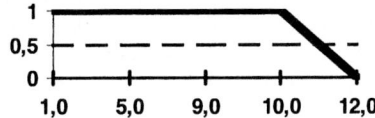

Fig. 5. *Minimum* predicate definition by means of its membership function

In Table 1, we report the following results for the nine randomly generated queries.

— The average number of tuples in the answers produced by Preferred Skyline, Skyline and SQLf.
— The average number of additional tuples identified by SQLf and Skyline with respect to Preferred Skyline.

In Table 1 we can observe that for queries with five fuzzy conditions SQLf returns many additional tuples either for the small or large database. Almost all of these tuples are dominated. This may be because first the SQLf preference criteria are based on Fuzzy Logic and they are more relaxed than Boolean criteria and second, SQLf does not able to check the dominance relationship directly. On the hand, Skyline only returns the tuples in the skyline, i.e., non- dominated tuples, and in consequence, it is more precise.

Finally, for queries with nine fuzzy conditions, SQLf returns few or none additional tuples in all cases. SQLf is more precise maybe because the fuzzy condition criteria are more selective. However, Skyline returns more tuples, many of them have bad values in some criteria. In consequence, Skyline answers are less precise.

Table 1. Small database and five dimensions

Database	Dimensions	Preferred Skyline	SQLf	Skyline	SQLf Additional Tuples	Skyline Additional Tuples
Small	5	40	505	107	465	67
Large	5	32	7850	39	7818	7
Small	9	7	7	8350	0	8344
Large	9	126	166	18311	40	18185

5.2 Experiment 2: Performance of Preferred Skyline wrt SQLf and Skyline

We report time evaluation for nine randomly generated queries expressed by using Preferred Skyline, Skyline, SQLf languages. A fuzzy condition in the WHERE clause is either a conjunction of one, five or nine base fuzzy conditions. The rest of the parameters are set as in experiment 1.

First, we suppose that SQLf queries's execution time is lower than Skyline's because Skyline requires to find all tuples while, SQLf just needs to identify a subset of them. This is because a query that filters the tuples that do not satisfy the tolerance is obtained as result of the application of the Principle of Derivation.

In Fig. 6 we report the effect of the number of criteria in the performance of Skyline, SQLf and Preferred Skyline. Criteria are referred as Skyline dimensions or fuzzy conditions. Time units are seconds and the results are normalized by means of log function. We can observe the following:

a) The processing time for SQLf decreases as the number of fuzzy conditions increases. This may be because the conditions became more selective and the number of filtered tuples decreases.

b) There is not correlation between Skyline evaluation time and the number of dimensions. However, we can observe that the Skyline time increases as the number of tuples in the skyline increases. For all dimensions, Skyline time is higher than the SQLf time. It may be because Skyline scans all the tuples and checks the dominance relationship. For nine dimensions, the skyline is the largest set and the Skyline time is the highest.

c) Similar to the SQLf behavior, the Preferred Skyline evaluation time decreases as the number of dimensions increases. Moreover, the Preferred Skyline evaluation time is lower than Skyline's and higher than the SQLf's. This may because the Preferred Skyline constructs the Pareto curve on top of the set of tuples produced by the SQLf, instead of considering the whole initial set of tuples.

In Fig. 7 we report the effect of the database size on the Skyline, SQLf and Preferred Skyline evaluation time. We can observe that the processing time for Skyline, SQLf and Preferred Skyline decreases as the size of the database increases. Moreover, the Preferred Skyline evaluation time is lower than Skyline's and higher than the SQLf's.

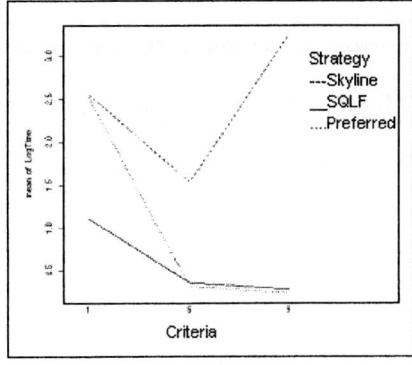 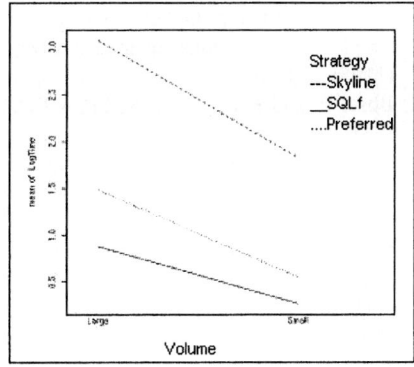

Fig. 6. Dimension-Strategy Interaction Influence in Time for Basic Block Queries

Fig. 7. Volume-Strategy Interaction Influence in Time for Basic Block Queries

6 Conclusions

We have defined a new approach called Preferred Skyline that integrates Skyline and SQLf approaches and returns the best answers of the skyline (first stratum).

We study the performance and quality of Preferred Skyline wrt. Skyline and SQLf. The initial experiments show that Preferred Skyline is more precise than either Skyline and SQLf and its evaluation time is lower than Skyline's and higher than SQLf's. On the other hand, Preferred Skyline may not identify some relevant answers. Additionally, Preferred Skyline is not able to produce just the top k answers when the skyline cardinality is greater than k.

In order to improve the Preferred Skyline and reduce its limitations, it should be extended with the capabilities of finding possible answers in the following strata or next points in the Pareto curve. Necessary probe criteria are needed to ensure that only the required query condition evaluations are performed. In addition, to efficiently evaluate Preferred Skyline queries, a physical operator and cost model must be defined and incorporated into an existing database management system. In the future, we plan to define physical Preferred Skyline operators, their cost models and integrate them into PostgreSQL database management system.

References

1. ANSI X3. "American National Standard for Information Systems: Database Language SQL". American National Standards Institute, NY, (1986), 135.
2. Börzsönyi, S., Kossmann, D. and Stocker, K. "The skyline operator". Proceedings of International Conference on Data Engineering, (2001), 421-430.
3. Bosc, P. and Brisson, A. "On the evaluation of some SQLf nested queries". Proceeding International Workshop on Fuzzy Databases and Information Retrieval, (1995).

4. Bosc, P. and Pivert, O. "On the efficiency of the alpha-cut distribution method to evaluate simple fuzzy relational queries". Advances in Fuzzy Systems-Applications and Theory, (1995), 251-260.
5. Bosc, P. and Pivert, O. "SQLf: A Relational Database Language for Fuzzy Querying". IEEE Transactions on Fuzzy Systems 3, 1 (Feb 1995).
6. Bosc, P. and Pivert, O. "SQLf Query Functionality on Top of a Regular Relational Database Management System". Knowledge Management in Fuzzy Databases (2000), 171-190.
7. Bosc, P., Pivert, O. and Farquhar, K. "Integrating Fuzzy Queries into an Existing Database Management System: An Example". International Journal of Intelligent Systems 9, (1994), 475-492.
8. Chang, K. and Hwang, S-W. "Minimal Probing: Supporting Expensive Predicates for Top-k Queries". Proceedings of the ACM SIGMOD Conference, (Jun 2002).
9. Chomicky, J., Godfrey, P. Gryz, J. and Liang, D. "Skyline with Presorting". Proceedings of 19th International Conference on Data Engineering, (Mar. 2003).
10. Florescu, D., Levy, A., Manolescu, I., Suciu, D. "Query Optimization in the Presence of Limited Access Patterns". Proceedings of the ACM SIGMOD Conference, 1999.
11. Goncalves, M. and Tineo, L. "SQLf: Flexible Querying Language Extension by means of the norm SQL2". The 10th IEEE International Conference on Fuzzy Systems 1, (Dec. 2001)
12. Goncalves, M. and Tineo, L. "SQLf3: An extension of SQLf with SQL3 features". The 10th IEEE International Conference on Fuzzy Systems 1, (Dec. 2001)
13. Kung, H. T., Luccio, F. and Preparata, F. P. "On finding the maxima of a set of vectors". Journal of the ACM, 22 (4), 1975.
14. Papadimitriou, C. H. and Yannakakis, M. "Multiobjective Query Optimization". Proc. ACM SIGMOD/SIGACT Conf. Princ. Of Database Syst. (PODS), Santa Barbara, CA, USA, May 2001.
15. Pivert, O. "Contribution à l'Interrogation Flexible de Bases de Données: Expression et Évaluation de Requêtes Floues". Thèse de Doctoract, Université de Rennes I, France, 1991.
16. Preparata, F. P. and Shamos, M. I. "Computational Geometry: An Introduction". Springer-Verlag, 1985.
17. XQUERY 1.0: An XML Query Language. Available at http://www.w3.org/TR/xquery

Resolution of Semantic Queries on a Set of Web Services

Jordi Paraire, Rafael Berlanga, and Dolores M. Llidó

Departamento de Lenguajes y Sistemas Informáticos,
Universitat Jaume I de Castelló
al068285@alumail.uji.es, {berlanga, dllido}@lsi.uji.es

Abstract. In this article, we present an approach to executing semantic queries on a set of domain-related Web services. The aim of this architecture is to obtain information from the available Web services, by mapping inputs and outputs of the Web service methods into concepts of an ontology defined in OWL (Ontology Web Language). For this purpose, we extend OWL-S to assign concepts and their contexts to the inputs and outputs of the methods, so that each method parameter is annotated without ambiguity. The paper also presents a graph-based data structure in which all the information needed for the semantic composition of annotated Web services is stated. Finally, we show how this data structure is used to solve semantic queries over the Web services.

1 Introduction

In the next generation of the Web, named Semantic Web, numerous semantically annotated resources will be available for both software agents and users. These semantic annotations rely on ontologies consensuated by different communities and user domains. The current contents of the Web should migrate towards this new space. However, so far only small web sites and well-structured information sources (e.g. relational databases) have been annotated, and usually these annotations are manually done. Semi-automatic and automatic mechanisms are emerging, though their results are not completely satisfactory yet.

Recently, the semantic annotation of Web services is getting a great interest in the database community. As a result, different languages (OWL-S [1], DAML-S [5]) and tools (ASSAM [7], METEOR-S [3]) have been proposed. The main motivation of these languages is the semantic composition of Web services [4], although they are also being used for the discovery of interesting Web services, enhancing current catalogue services based on UDDI [13]. In the near future, we will have available hundreds of thousands of semantic Web services providing huge amounts of data. However, semantic Web services cannot relate their contents, as they are conceived as isolated data-providers. In this way, the effective exploitation of all these services requires new mechanisms and tools for discovering, querying and composing them.

In this work we present an approach to the migration and exploitation of Web services in the Semantic Web. We have adopted OWL-S [1] to semantically annotated Web services. Moreover, we have extended it to allow expressing ontology contexts so that concepts and properties associated to methods can be disambiguated. For the querying and semantic composition of web Services, we propose a new semantic data structure that allows us to know which service methods can be composed to solve the user queries according to the ontology.

The paper is organised as follows. Section 2 introduces a motivating example with several web Services annotated with a common ontology. Section 3 describes some related works. Section 4 introduces the definition of context and how it is included in OWL-S specifications. Section 5 presents the proposed semantic data structure as well as the algorithms to generate it. Section 6 defines what a semantic query is and how they are solved by using the semantic data structure. Finally, Section 7 gives some conclusions and future work.

2 Motivating Example

Nowadays there are numerous Web services that provide different functionalities, which run the gamut from on-line data streams (e.g. weather forecast servers) to conversion methods (e.g. translators, unit converters, etc). However, these services are isolated elements that do not relate their contents. By working in cooperation they could provide much more interesting information to the end users and software applications. Semantic annotation of web Services is a first step towards service interoperability. This is done by means of a reference ontology, and must associate each service element (methods and their input/output parameters) to a concept or property of the ontology.

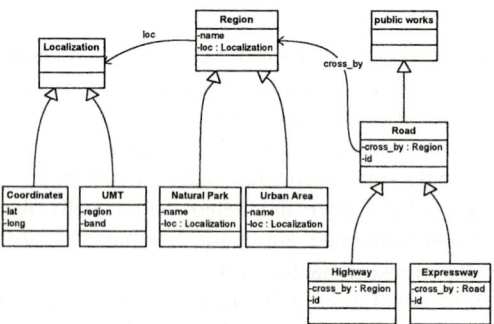

Fig. 1. Ontology required for our Web services examples

Our motivating example consists of four web Services (see Table 1). These services provide information about Natural Parks, geographic information about regions and roads, and unit converters. Notice that each service method is described by its name, input and output parameter types (at syntactic level), which is the information contained in the WSDL (Web Service Definition Language) specification.

Next step in our approach consists of semantically annotating these methods by using the proposed OWL-S extension. Figure 1 shows graphically how the concepts are related in the ontology. It is worth mentioning that we do not only indicate the ontology concept associated to each web service element, but also its context, that is the neighbour elements of the associated concepts. These contexts are described in Section 4 as ontology paths.

Finally, over these semantically annotated Web services, users can specify semantic queries such as "which roads cross a given Natural Park", "where is located a given Natural Park" and "how many regions are covered by a Natural Park". Notice that the resolution of all these queries require the cooperation of several web Services, and that this cooperation is guided by the query.

Table 1. Annotated Web services for the running example

Web Service 1 –Natural Parks	
string **getToponym**(int, string)	From the coordinates UTM of a natural park we obtain toponym of this one.
[int, string] **getLocation**(string)	It gives the UTM coordinates of a natural park from its name.
Web Service 2 –Geographic Regions and their classification	
[float,float] **Coordinates**(string)	Given the name of a region it gives back the coordinates of this one.
string **Type**(string)	It gives back the type of region passed as input parameter.
array[string] **regionsByType**(string)	It gives back all the regions of the type passed as input parameter.
Web Service 3 –Roads by Region	
array[string] **getRegs**(string)	It gives back a vector with all the regions crossed by the road passed as input parameter.
Web Service 4 – Conversion between coordinates	
[int, string] **CoordToUMT** (float, float)	It transforms coordinates into latitude and longitude to coordinates in UTM format.
[float, float] **UMTToCoord** (int, string)	It transforms coordinates UTM to coordinates into latitude and longitude format.

3 Related Work

Within the Semantic Web research area two main projects can be outlined, namely: DAML-S [5, 6] and WSMF (Web Service Modelling Framework) [7]. DAML-S is intended to describe the semantics of Web services and their negotiation processes, whereas WSMF proposes a complex intermediary architecture between agents that combine the different data models and invocation methods of Web services. Due to the complexity of both project proposals, their results are still emerging, and their main outcome is the specification of a language for the semantic annotation of Web services.

The most accepted language to describe semantically Web services is OWL-S 1.0. OWL-S is a language that extends the initial proposal of DAML-S [1], to add semantics to Web services. It uses RDF (Resource Description Framework), and it defines what the service is, the service model, and how to access the service.

On the other hand, WSMF evolves to WSMO (Web Service Modelling Ontology) [7], whose main difference with OWL-S is that the architecture plays an important role, and that a formal logic is used to represent the ontology axioms.

The semantic annotation of Web services is currently made manually, although there exist different approaches for the semi-automatic annotation of WSDL specifications, amongst them we outstand ASSAM [7, 8, 9] and Meteor-S [3]. ASSAM uses machine learning techniques, whereas Meteor-S uses structural measures and lexical similarity.

WSDF (Web Service Description Framework) [2] is a framework that not only provides the representation language for the Web services, but also an execution model for them. In this framework, it is required that the client and the server provide an association within their local structures, and a domain ontology at design time.

For the semi-automatic composition of Web Services, there exist several works that apply reasoning techniques. For example, [10] uses the algorithms proposed by DAML-S MatchMaker, [11] uses first-order logic of the OWL-S descriptions, and [12] applies Problem Solving Methods (PSM) to model semantic Web services.

In our work, we propose a new method for the semantic composition of Web services that is guided by query user specifications. It takes as input a set of already semantically annotated Web services, to construct a semantic composition graph over which execution plans are built accordingly to user queries. In this way, this new approach is intended to bridge the gap between semantic annotations and execution models for web Services.

4 Semantic Annotation of Web Services

OWL-S is a language defined in order to help in the next four tasks: the automatic discovery, the automatic invocation, the interoperation and composition, and the automatic monitoring of Web services execution. In our approach, we focus on the profile Service-Profile, the semantic descriptions of the methods defined in the service and its parameters [1].

OWL-S defines relations between the methods described in WSDL and the concepts of an ontology. This type of association presents an ambiguity problem, as a concept can appear in different relations in an ontology or even in different ontologies, representing different semantic contexts.

To solve this problem, we propose extending OWL-S to define both the associated concept and its context. This is achieved by the inclusion of a new property in the OWL-S "process:parameterType" label, as follows:

```
< process:parameterType rdf:resource =
"http://www.myontology.org/onto#Region"
owlws:path = "/Road/cross_by/Region/{name}">
```

For the sake of simplicity, we regard an ontology as a tuple $(C,R,is\text{-}a)$, where C is the set of concepts (classes), R is the set of concept relations (properties), and $is\text{-}a$ is a partial order over C that represents the concepts taxonomy. In this way, an ontology can be also viewed as a graph where nodes are concepts and edges are properties or is-a relations. Although this is a very simplified representation of an ontology, it is sufficient for the aim of this work.

To define ontology contexts, we use ontology paths. An ontology path is an alternate sequence of concepts and properties that begins at a specific concept and that ends at a target node of the ontology (usually an atomic type or literal). Optionally, paths can group several target nodes to account for complex data types. The syntax of paths is defined in BNF as follows:

```
Path  ::= /class-name/Path2  |  /class-name
Path2::=            property-name        Path         |
         {Target-node,…,Target-node}
Target-node::=atomic-type  |  literal  |  property-name
```

5 Obtaining the Semantic Composition Graph (SCG)

In this section a new semantic structure is introduced to analyze Web service composition for query resolution. The structure consists of a directed labeled graph, whose vertices represent contexts, and whose edges represent Web services methods and abstract relations between contexts.

The directed labeled graph consists of a set of vertices V, a set of edges E and a set of labels. An edge is defined by a triple, $e \in E$ where $e=\langle x,y,l \rangle$ such that $x,y \in V$ and $l \in L$ the set of labels associated to an edge. The edge e is composed by a target $t(e)=x$, a source vertex $s(e)=y$ and a label $l(e)=z$.

The set of labels is defined as $L=\left(L_{method} \cup L_{is\_a} \cup L_\lambda\right)$, where L_{method} represents the set of WS method identifiers, L_{is_a} represents the generalization relations between contexts, and L_λ denotes the set of auxiliary labels to relate method parameters and their contexts. Each WS method L_{method} is identified by the Web service name and the method name, for example "WS1:getToponym".

We define the set of edges as $E=\left(E_{method} \cup E_{is\_a} \cup E_\lambda\right)$, where E_{method} represents the set of edges that refers to concrete WS methods and their parameters, E_{is_a} represents the set of edges that refers to generalization relationships given by the ontology, and E_λ represents the set of edges that refers to generic relationships between contexts.

We define the set of vertices as the set $V=\left(V_{context} \cup V_{and} \cup V_{generator}\right)$, where $V_{context}$ represents the ontology contexts, V_{and} represents the set of nodes that are required to join multiple input parameters of methods, and $V_{generator}$ represents the set of nodes that are required to state empty input parameters of methods. The context associated to a vertex $v \in V$ is denoted as $c(v)$.

A SCG for a set of web services have the following properties:

- **Reachability**: A vertex is reachable depending on its type. Thus, a vertex from $V_{context}$ is reachable if there exists some edge pointing at it, a vertex from $V_{generator}$ is always reachable, and a vertex from V_{and} is reachable if all the vertex pointing at it via some method edge are also reachable.

- **Specialization**: A vertex v_1 specializes another vertex v_2 if $\exists e = \langle v_1, v_2, l \rangle$ such that $v_1, v_2 \in V_{context}$ and $l \in L_{is\_a}$. This property is transitive.

5.1 Creating the Semantic Composition Graph

The generation of a semantic composition graph consists of the following stages:

1. **Creating the vertices.** In this stage all the possible contexts that appear in the ontology are created. Each context will have associated a graph vertex. Contexts are generated by applying the following algorithms:

    ```
    Algorithm ClassContexts(Class, context, Contexts):
        For each property of Class do
            If property has as range another class Class2 then
                newContext = context·"/"·property·Class2
                Contexts.append(newContext)
                ClassContexts(Class2, newContext, Contexts)
            Else
                Contexts.append(context·"/{"·property·"}")

    Algorithm OntologyContexts(Ontology):
        Contexts=[]
        For each class in Ontology:
            ClassContexts(class,"/"+class,Contexts)
        Return Contexts
    ```

2. **Adding context generalization edges.** In this stage, we add all the necessary edges of type is_a between context vertices that can be directly related through the generalization relationship is_a of the ontology. For example, if $c(v_1) = $"/Region" and $c(v_2) = $"/Natural Park" the $(v_1, v_2, \text{is-a}) \in E_{is\_a}$

3. **Inferring implicit information from the ontology.** An is_a edge is created between two context vertices v_1 and v_2 whenever the $c(v_2)$ is suffix of $c(v_1)$. The edge's source is the node whose context contains the suffix v_1. Formally, if $\exists x, y \in V_{context}, suffix(c(y), c(x))$ then $(x, y, \text{is-a}) \in E_{is\_a}$. For example, if $c(v_1) = $"/Region" and $c(v_2) = $"/Road/cross/Region", then $(v_1, v_2, \text{is-a}) \in E_{is\_a}$.

4. **Adding edges based on the input and output parameters of methods.** These parameters are defined in the OWL-S specification, and our extension relates the inputs and the outputs to concepts and their contexts. Table 2 describes the vertices that must be created based on the number of input parameters and the number of concepts that can be associated to the output parameter.

5. **Inferring implicit information in the ontology and OWL-S files.** If a Web service method relates properties of a same class, and this class is specialized by other classes, this method can be also applied to the specialized classes. Formally, if we have $v_1, v_2, v_3, v_4 \in V_{context}$, $e_1 = \langle v_1, v_2, z_1 \rangle$ where $z_1 \in L_{method}$, $e_2 = \langle v_3, v_1, z_2 \rangle$

and $e_3=\langle v_4,v_2,z_3\rangle$ where $z_2,z_3 \in L_{is\_a}$ and both $c(v_1), c(v_2)$ have a common prefix then we add the edge $e_4=(v_3,v_4,z_1)$ to E_{method}. Figure 2 shows the generated edges for some methods of the Web services in Table 1.

6. **Pruning isolated vertices.** For each vertex that is not connected with any other one through a method edge, it is pruned from the SCG.

Table 2. Vertices and edges creation for Web service methods

Method	1 input parameter	N input parameters	No input parameters
1 output concept	$\langle x,y,l\rangle \in E_{method}$ $x,y \in (V_{context})$	$\{\langle x_1,y,l\rangle ...\langle x_n,y,l\rangle\} \subseteq E_{method}$ $\langle y,z,\lambda\rangle \in E_\lambda$ $\{x_1...x_n,z\} \subseteq (V_{context})$ $y \in (V_{and})$ $\lambda \in (L_\lambda)$	$\langle x,y,l\rangle \in E_{method}$ $x \in (V_{generator})$ $y \in (V_{context})$
M output Concepts	$\{\langle x,y_1,l\rangle ...\langle x,y_m,l\rangle\} \subseteq E_{method}$ $x \in (V_{context} \cup V_{generator})$ $\{y_1...y_m\} \subseteq (V_{context})$	$\{\langle x_1,y,l\rangle ...\langle x_n,y,l\rangle\} \subseteq E_{method}$ $\{\langle y,z_1,\lambda_{n+1}\rangle ...\langle y,z_m,\lambda_{n+m+1}\rangle\} \subseteq E_\lambda$ $\{x_1...x_n,z\} \subseteq (V_{context})$ $y \in (V_{and})$	$\{\langle x,y_1,l\rangle ...\langle x,y_m,l\rangle\} \subseteq E_{meth}$ $x \in (V_{generator})$ $\{y_1...y_m\} \subseteq (V_{context})$

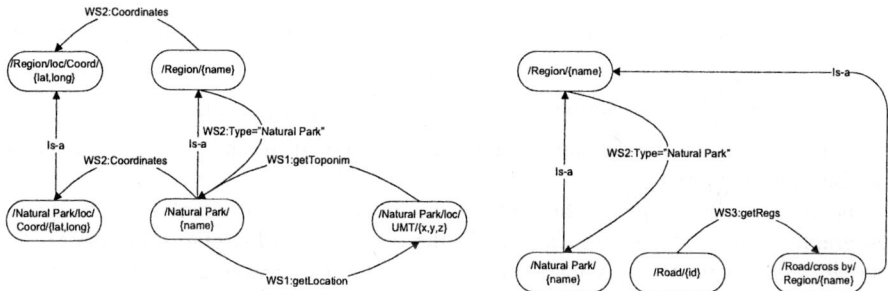

Fig. 2 – 3. Sub-graphs of a Semantic Composition Graph

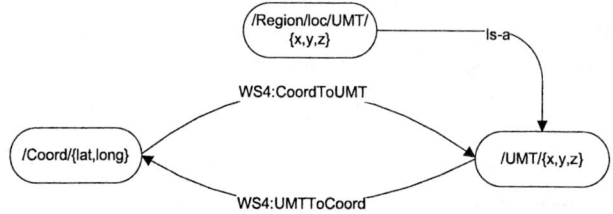

Fig. 4. Sub-graph of a Semantic Composition Graph

6 Resolution of Queries in the Semantic Composition Graph

In this section, we describe the resolution of queries by using the SCG previously described. This process consists of two main steps, namely: the query definition, and the generation of an execution plan for the query. It must be pointed out that in this paper we do not concern with the actual execution of a query since it falls out of the scope of the paper.

6.1 Query Definition

A query q is defined as the pair $q=(S, t)$, where S is a set of ontology path instances and $t \in V_{context}$ is the target vertex. The result set of query is a set of ontology instances for the target context of t.

A query $q=(S, t)$ is well-formed if we can find a minimal sub-graph $G_q=(V_q, E_q, L_q)$ of the SCG such that all its vertex are reachable, $t \in V_q$, and for all instance i in S, there exists a vertex $v \in V_q$ with the same context than the instance i.

6.2 Execution Plan

The execution plan of a query is the sequence of execution actions necessary to obtain the result set of the query. We distinguish two types of execution actions: the execution of a method with one or zero input parameters and the execution of a method with more than one input parameter. For the former, we define a simple transaction T_S as a triple $t=(x_1, m, x_2)$ where x_1 and x_2 are two context variables (i.e. variables whose domains are instances of the corresponding context). For the latter, we define a complex transaction T_C as $t = \langle (x_1,\cdots,x_n),m,(y_1,\cdots,y_m) \rangle$, such that $x_1,...,x_n$ are context variables for the input parameters of method m, and $y_1,...,y_m$ are context variables for the output ones.

The query execution plan is built by traversing the query sub-graph G_q. The query sub-graph G_q is a tree, so we can obtain the query execution plan transversing G_q following the levels by applying At each level of G_q we have to apply the following rules to sets of vertices at the same level:

- $v \in V_{and}$: the transaction $t = \langle (x_1,\cdots,x_n),m,(y_1,\cdots,y_m) \rangle$ is added to the execution plan, where $x_1,...,x_n$ are context variables associated to the vertices that are connected to v with edges whose label is m, and $y_1,...,y_m$ are context variables associated to the vertices that are connected to v with λ edges.

- $e \in E_{is\_a}$: these edges have no effects in the query execution plan.

- $e \in E_{method}$: the transaction (x_1, m, x_2) is added to the execution plan, where $l(e) = m$, x_1 is a variable with context $c(s(e))$ and x_2 is a variable with context $c(t(e))$.

Now, we can define an execution plan as an ordered sequence of transaction sets $\left[\left(t_1^1...t_n^1\right) \prec ... \prec \left(t_1^l...t_k^l\right)\right]$ with the order relation $\prec$, where $\left(t_1^i...t_n^i\right)$ refers to all the transaction of the vertices belonging to the level i of the query sub-graph G_q.

The following examples show the creation of execution plans:

Query 1: Get the longitude-latitude coordinates of a region with UMT={21,A} (See figure 4)

Query=({"Region/loc/UMT={21,A}","/Coord/{lat,long}")
Sub-graph:

$E_{is\text{-}a}$={(/Region/loc/UMT/{region,band}, /UMT/{region,band}, is-a)}
E_{method}={(/UMT/{region,band},/Coord/{lat,long},WS4:<u>UMTToCoord</u>)}

Execution plan: {(V/UMT/{region,band},WS4:<u>UMTToCoord</u>,V/Coord/{lat,long})}

Query 2: Get the name of the Natural Parks crossed by road B-7 (See figure 3)

Query=({"/Road/id =B-7","/Natural Park/name/{string}")
Sub-graph:
$E_{is\text{-}a}$ = {(/Road/cross by/Region/{name}, /Region/ {name}, is-a),
 (/Natural Park/{name}, Region/ {name}, is-a)}
E_{method}={(/Region/{name }, /Natural Park/{name}, WS2:<u>Type</u>),
 (/Road/{id}, /Road/cross by/Region/{name}, WS3:<u>getRegs</u>)}

Execution plan: {(V1/Road/{id},WS3:<u>getRegs</u>,V2/Road/cross by/Region/{name}),
 (V2/Road/cross by/Region/{name},WS2:<u>Type</u>,V3/Natural Park/{name})}

7 Conclusions

The main aim of this work is to take profit from a large set of semantically annotated Web services to obtain new information from their cooperation. We have adapted the language OWL-S for the semantic annotation of Web services according to a given ontology, and we have extended it to enhance the semantic description of method parameters including ontology contexts. In this way, the use of method parameters is disambiguated. The main contribution of the paper is a novel Semantic Composition Graph (SCG), which relates ontology contexts with Web service methods. With a SCG we can specify semantic queries and their possible execution plans, which find automatically the necessary semantic compositions between different Web service methods.

We are implementing this approach in Java, and we plan to evaluate this tool over the Web service collection of ASSAM [8]. Future work also regards the inclusion of time and resource-based constraints that can be published along with the Web services. In this way, we can take into consideration these constraints to find optimal query execution plans over the proper composition sub-graphs. Finally, we also plan to adopt an execution model such as BPEL4WS, to perform properly the generated query execution plans.

Acknowledgements. This work has been partially funded by the CICYT project with number TIC2002-04586-004-3

References

1. D. Marti. OWL-S: Semantic Markup for Web Services: The OWL Services Coalition. http://www.daml.org/services/owl-s/1.0/owl-s.pdf
2. A. Eberhart. Ad-hoc Invocation of Semantic Web Services, Proceedings of the IEEE International Conference on Web Services. San Diego, California, USA, July 2004.
3. A. Patil, S. Oundhakar and K. Verna. METEOR-S Web Service Annotation Framework. (2004). In Proceedings International WWW Conference, New York, USA.
4. Ruoyang Zhang. ONTOLOGY-DRIVEN WEB SERVICES COMPOSITION TECHNIQUES. Thesis.(2004) webster.cs.uga.edu/~ruoyan/thesis1.ppt
5. A. Ankolekar, M. Burstein, J. Hobbs, O. Lassila, D. Martin, D. McDermott, S. McIlraith, S. Narayanan, M. Paolucci, T. Payne, and K. Sycara, "DAML-S: Web Service description for the Semantic Web," in Proceedings of the First International Semantic Web Conference (ISWC 2002), pp. 348–363, 2002.
6. K. Sycara, M. Paolucci, A. Ankolekar, and N. Srinivasan, "Automated discovery, interaction and composition of semantic web services," Journal of Web Semantics, vol. 1, no. 1, December 2003.
7. A. Heß, N. Kushmerick (2004) Iterative Ensemble Classification for Relational Data: A Case Study of Semantic Web Services. Accepted for the 15th European Conference on Machine Learning (ECML 2004)
8. A. Heß, E. Johnston, N. Kushmerick (2004). ASSAM: A Tool for Semi-Automatically Annotating Semantic Web Services. Submitted to the 3rd International Semantic Web Conference (ISWC 2004)
9. A. Heß, N. Kushmerick. (2004) Machine Learning for Annotating Semantic Web Services. AAAI Spring Symposium Semantic Web Services, 2004.
10. E. Sirin, J. A. Hendler, B. Parsia: Semi-automatic Composition of Web Services using Semantic Descriptions. WSMAI 2003: 17-24
11. S. Narayanan, S. McIlraith (2002). Simulation, Verification and Automated Composition of Web Services, Eleventh International World Wide Web Conference (WWW2002).
12. A. Gómez-Pérez, R. González-Cabero, and M. Lama . Papers from 2004 AAAI Spring Symposium. ISBN 1-57735-198-3. A Framework for Design and Composition of Semantic Web Services.
13. http://www.uddi.org

Detecting Semantically Correct Changes to Relevant Unordered Hidden Web Data

Vladimir Kovalev and Sourav S. Bhowmick

School of Computer Engineering,
Nanyang Technological University, Singapore
assourav@ntu.edu.sg

Abstract. Current proposals for XML change detection use structural constraints to detect the changes and they ignore semantic constraints. Consequently, they may produce *semantically incorrect* changes. In this paper, we argue that the semantics of data is important for change detection. We present a semantic-conscious change detection technique for the hidden web data. In our approach we transform the unordered hidden web query results to XML format and then detect the changes between two versions of XML representation of the hidden web data by extending X-Diff, a published unordered XML change detection algorithm. By taking advantage of the semantics, we experimentally demonstrate that our change detection approach runs up to 7 times faster than X-Diff on real life hidden web data and always detect changes that are semantically more correct than those detected by existing proposals.

1 Introduction

Data in the hidden web can change any time and in any way. These changes are reflected on the results of the queries posed on the hidden web. Hence the problem of detecting and representing changes to hidden web data in the context of such query results is an important problem. Let us illustrate with an example.

Consider the AutoTrader.com which is one of the largest car Web sites with over 1.5 million used vehicles listed for sale by private owners, dealers, and manufacturers. The search page is available at http://www.autotrader.com/findacar/index.jtmpl?ac_afflt=none. Figures 1(a) and 1(b) represent snapshots of results returned for searching for *Jaguar* cars on 2nd and 5th July, 2003 respectively. The results are presented as a list of cars. Each result contains car details such as Model, Year, Price, Color, Seller, Vehicle Identification Number (VIN), etc. Given the query results and our understanding of its semantics, we may wish to state the following constraints. First, the VIN in the results uniquely identifies a particular car entity. Note that VIN may not be present for some results. However, if it exists then it will not be removed from the subsequent versions of query results involving the particular car. Second, the year of manufacturing and the model of each car do not get modified in different versions. That is, a "mercedes" cannot be updated to "jaguar" or if the manufacturing year of a car is "2001" then it cannot be modified to "2002" or

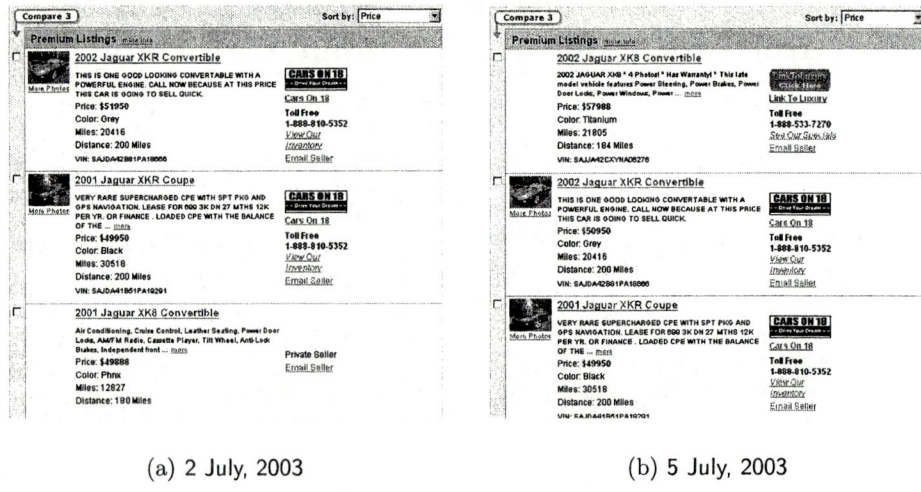

(a) 2 July, 2003 (b) 5 July, 2003

Fig. 1. The results of searching for *Jaguar* cars

any other year in the subsequent versions. Similarly, the `seller` attribute of a car does not get modified in different versions for the same car entity. Furthermore, as underlying information related to the *Jaguar* cars has changed during this time period, the query results in Figure 1(b) contain the relevant changes that have occurred between 2nd July, 2003 and 5th July, 2003. Particularly, the first car in Figure 1(b) has been inserted, the last car in Figure 1(a) has been deleted, and the price of the first car in the older version has been updated from "$51950" to "$50950" during this period.

In this paper, we consider the problem of detecting the above types of changes automatically taking structural as well as a broad class of semantic constraints into account. Note that our goal is to detect and represent the changes that are relevant to a user's query, not any arbitrary change to the hidden web data. Also, we assume that the hidden web query results are unordered.

In our approach, we do not directly compare the two versions of hidden web query results (Figures 1(a) and 1(b). This is because hidden web data is HTML-formatted and every hidden web site generates it in its own fashion. Thus it becomes extremely difficult and cumbersome to develop a generalized technique that can be used for change detection to the hidden web data. Consequently, it is important to develop a technique for transforming the hidden web data to a more structured format so that we can develop such generalized technique for the hidden web data. Hence, the hidden web query results are transformed into XML format before they are used for change detection.

Since there are several recent efforts in the research community to develop change detection algorithms for XML documents [1,5], an obvious issue is the justification for designing a separate algorithm for detecting changes to the XML representation of hidden web data. We argue that although such algorithms will clearly detect syntactically correct changes, they fail to detect *semantically correct* changes. For example, these algorithms may detect that the model of a car element has been updated from "mercedes" to "jaguar". However, this is semantically incorrect! We elaborate on this further in Section 2.

We have developed a semantic-conscious change detection algorithm called HW-DIFF to address the above issue. As we assume the query results to be unordered, we have extended *X-Diff* [5], a published unordered XML change detection algorithm to implement HW-DIFF using Java. *To the best of our knowledge, this is the first approach that address an important limitation of state-of-the-art XML change detection algorithms by making them semantic-conscious.* Our experimental results on four real data sets show that the HW-DIFF detects more semantically correct changes compared to the X-Diff algorithm. Furthermore, it runs up to 7 times faster than X-Diff due to the exploitation of semantic constraints.

2 Related Work

XyDiff [1] is designed for detecting changes in ordered XML documents. X-Diff [5] is designed for computing the deltas for two unordered XML documents. However, these algorithms in many cases produce *semantically incorrect* changes. Let us illustrate this limitation with a simple example. Figure 2(a) shows the old and new versions of an XML document. The results returned by X-Diff and XyDiff are depicted in Figures 2(b). Observe that both the algorithms detect that the Make of the first car is updated from *Jaguar* to *Mercedes*. However, in reality the car whose Make is *Jaguar* definitely cannot be updated to *Mercedes*. Hence, the results generated by X-Diff and XyDiff are semantically incorrect. The correct types of changes that should be detected here are *deletion* of the first car element in Figure 2(a)(i) and *insertion* of a new car (the first car element in Figure 2(a)(ii)). HW-DIFF address this limitation by extending an existing algorithm (X-Diff) with semantic constraints. By incorporating such semantic

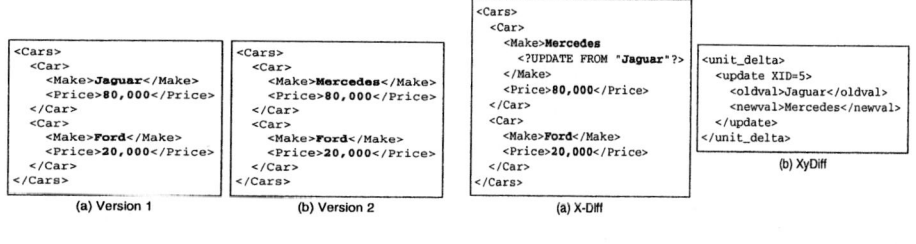

(a) Sample documents (b) Edit scripts

Fig. 2. Change detection

knowledge in a general-purpose change detection algorithm, we can dramatically decrease the number of matching possibilities between the two versions of the document and increase the performance of the algorithm. Hence, HW-DIFF shows better response time compared to X-Diff.

3 Semantic Constraints in Hidden Web Query Results

In this section, we present the semantic constraints in hidden web query results that are captured in the XML representation of the query results using HW-STALKER [2,3].

Identifier: Some elements in a set of query results can serve as a unique identifier for the particular result, distinguishing them from other results. For example, the VIN uniquely characterizes every Car in the query results from a car database. These elements are called *identifiers*. In this work we assume that the *identifier*, being assigned to a particular query result, does not change for this result through different versions of the query results. However, it is possible for the *identifier* to be missing in a result. Also, if an *identifier* is specified (not specified) for a result in the initial version of the query results or when the result appeared for the first time, then it will remain specified (not specified) throughout all versions, until the result is deleted. This reflects the case for most web sites we have studied. HW-STALKER allows specifying only one *identifier* for each result. As each result is transformed into a subtree in the XML representation of the hidden web query results, the *identifier* of a particular node in the subtree is modeled as an XML attribute with name Id and the *identifier* information as value. We now illustrate with an example the usefulness of the *identifiers* in change detection.

Reconsider the query results in autotrader.com. Figure 3 shows partial XML trees of the results in Figure 1. The Car nodes in T_1 and T_2 have child attributes with name Id and value equal to the VIN. Intuitively, if we wish to detect the changes between the two versions of the query results, then we can match the

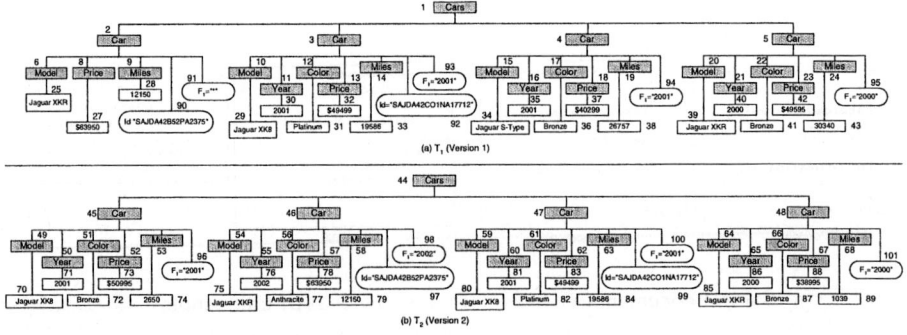

Fig. 3. Partial XML trees of results in Figures 1

`Car` nodes between two subtrees by comparing the `Id` values. For instance, the node 2 in T_1 matches the node 46 in T_2 and the node 3 in T_1 matches the node 47 in T_2 (same `VIN` values). However, the nodes 2 and 3 do not match the node 45 as it does not have any *identifier* attribute.

Facilitator: One or more elements in the result of the hidden web query result set can serve as non-unique characteristics for distinguishing the results from one another. This is particularly important when the results do not have any *identifier* attribute. Two results that have the same characteristics (same attribute/value pair) can be matched with each other. While results that have different characteristics can not be matched with each other. Examples of types of such characteristics are: the `Year` or `Model` of a `Car` node in the query results from car trading site. These non-unique elements are called *facilitators*. Note that these elements may not identify a result (entity) uniquely. But they may provide enough information to identify results that do not refer to the same entities.

We allow specifying any number of *facilitators* on a node. The *facilitators* are denoted by node attributes with names $F_1, F_2, \ldots, F_n$ for all n *facilitator* attributes specified for a particular node. If a node does not have a *facilitator* attribute (the subelement may be missing) then the *facilitator* value is set to "*". Note that the *facilitator* attribute for a node can appear in any version of the query results, but once it appears we assume that it will not disappear in the future versions. As we never know which *facilitator* may appear for a node in the future, a node with missing *facilitator* attribute should be matched with nodes having *facilitators*. The reader may refer to [3] for guidelines the user may follow to choose *facilitators*. In [4], an algorithm is discussed for automatic discovery of facilitators from hidden web data.

Reconsider the Figure 1. We can find several candidates for *facilitators*, i.e., `Color`, `Year`, or `Model`. However, based on the semantic constraints introduced in Section 1, it is reasonable to use the `Year` or `Model` as the *facilitator*. Figure 3 shows the *facilitators* for various nodes. There is one *facilitator* specified: the `Year` as an attribute with name F_1 for every `Car` node. Note that if a `Car` node does not have an subelement `Year` then F_1 is set to "*". Now let us match the node 45 in T_2 with all the nodes in T_1. Observe that node 45 does not have a `VIN`. Therefore, it cannot match with nodes 2 and 3. Hence we do not need to compare node 45 with these nodes. Using F_1 we also observe that the node 45 cannot match with node 5 as the facilitators do not match. We can see that the node 45 only matches node 4 in T_1 as it does no have any `VIN` and its $F_1=$"2001". However, this is not sufficient information to confirm whether these two nodes represent the same car entity. But if we use both the `Year` and `Model` as facilitators then we can answer this question by comparing the `Model` of node 45 with that of node 4. As the `Model` of nodes 4 and 45 are not identical, we can say that these nodes do not represent the same car entity. Thus, we can state that the node 45 is inserted in T_2 as none of the car entities in T_1 matches the car entity described by node 45.

4 Change Detection

4.1 HW-Signature

In order to detect the changes between two trees, we first need to find a matching of corresponding nodes in the two trees. Obviously, matching every node in the first tree to every node in the second tree is an inefficient solution. In X-Diff, this problem is addressed by using the concept of *node signature* [5]. The node signature compares not only the node *type* (text, element, and attribute nodes) and the node *name* (e.g., car and price nodes) of two nodes, but also their ancestors to determine the nodes that are to be matched. It is obtained by concatenating the names of all its ancestor with its own name and type. However, this notion of signature ignores semantic constraints embedded in the data. Hence, we extend the definition of signature in X-Diff by incorporating the semantic constraints associated with the hidden web query results. We call this extended notion of signature as *HW-signature*. Hereafter, in this paper signature refers to the X-Diff version of node signature and HW-signature refers to the signature used in HW-DIFF.

The HW-signature imposes semantic constraints by adding the notion of *identifiers* and *facilitators* in the definition of signature. It is used later in our change detection algorithm HW-DIFF to facilitate the process of matching nodes between the trees representing different versions of the hidden web query results. It not only reduces the number of nodes that are to be matched to one another, but also facilitates more semantically accurate matching compared to the signature.

We first introduce the notion of *HW-node signature* which is one of the basic component of HW-signature. The *HW-node signature* of a node is concatenation of the name of the node and its *identifiers* and *facilitators* (if any).

Let us define some terms for our exposition. Given a node x in the DOM tree T, let $Type(x)$ and $Name(x)$ be the node type of x and the node name of x (including the attributes) respectively. Also, if node x contains *identifiers* and *facilitators* then let $IdValue(x)$ and $FValue(F_i, x)$ be the values of the *identifier* and the *facilitator* attribute F_i of x respectively. Then,

Definition 1. [HW-node Signature] *Suppose x is an element node and $\mathcal{F}$ be a set of facilitator attributes on x. Then the **HW-node signature** is defined as follows: $HW-node(x) = Name(x)[Id(x)][Fac(x)]$ where (1) $[Id(x)] = /Id/IdValue(x)$ if identifier attribute is defined for node x, otherwise $[Id(x)]=\emptyset$; (2) If $\mathcal{F} \neq \emptyset$ then $[Fac(x)] = [F_1(x)][F_2(x)]\ldots[F_n(x)]$ where $[F_m(x)] = /F_m/FValue(F_m,x)$ $\forall$ $1 \leq m \leq n$ and $F_m \in \mathcal{F}$. Otherwise, $[Fac(x)] = \emptyset$.* ∎

For example, consider the two trees in Figure 3. Based on the above definition, $HW-node(3)=$Car/Id/AJDA42C01NA17712/F_1/2001 and $HW-node(52)=$Price.

Definition 2. [HW-Signature] *Let x be an element node. Then $HW\text{-}Signature(x)=/HW\text{-}node(x_1)/HW\text{-}node(x_2)/\ldots/HW\text{-}node(x_n)/*

$HW\text{-}node(x_1)/Type(x)$, where x_1 is the root of T, $(x_1,x_2,\ldots,x_n,x)$ is the path from x_1 to x. If x is a text node, then $\mathbf{HW\text{-}Signature(x)}=/HW\text{-}node(x_1)/HW\text{-}node(x_2)/\ldots/HW\text{-}node(x_n)/Type(x)$. ∎

Definition 3. [**HW-node Equality**] *Let x and y be the element nodes in T_1 and T_2. Let I_x and I_y be the identifiers of x and y. Let $\mathcal{F}_x$ and $\mathcal{F}_y$ be sets of facilitators of x and y respectively and $|\mathcal{F}_x|=|\mathcal{F}_y|$. Let $P=\{(F_{x1},F_{y1}),(F_{x2},F_{y2})\ldots(F_{xk},F_{yk})\}$ be the set of pairs of facilitators such that $F_{xi}\in\mathcal{F}_x$, $F_{yi}\in\mathcal{F}_y$, $FValue(F_{xi},x)\neq$ "*", and $FValue(F_{yi},x)\neq$ "*" $\forall\ 1\leq i\leq k$. Then $\mathbf{HW\text{-}Node(x)}=\mathbf{HW\text{-}Node(y)}$ iff (1) signature(x)=signature(y); (2) $IdValue(x)=IdValue(y)$; and (3) If $|P|\neq\emptyset$ then $FValue(F_{xi},x)=FValue(F_{yi},y)$, $\forall\ 1\leq i\leq |P|$.* ∎

In Figure 3, $HW\text{-}node(3)=HW\text{-}node(47)$, but $HW\text{-}node(2)\neq HW\text{-}node(47)$ as they have Id attributes with different values. Note that for all nodes that have a facilitator F where $FValue(F,x)=$ "*" the last condition in the above definition is ignored. That is, only first two conditions are sufficient for HW-node equality.

Definition 4. [**HW-signature Equality**] *Let x and y be element nodes in trees T_1 and T_2 respectively. Let x_1 be the root of T_1 and $(x_1,x_2,\ldots,x_n,x)$ is the path from x_1 to x. Let y_1 be the root of T_2 and $(y_1,y_2,\ldots,y_n,y)$ is the path from y_1 to y. Then, $\mathbf{HW\text{-}signature(x)}=\mathbf{HW\text{-}signature(y)}$ iff $Type(x)=Type(y)$ and $HW\text{-}node(x_i)=HW\text{-}node(y_i)\ \forall\ 1\leq i\leq n$.* ∎

Observe that the above definition of HW-signature equality combines the criteria of matching nodes by their signatures and matching nodes based on the semantic constraints in the hidden web data. If two nodes have identical HW-signatures then they have identical signatures. However, the inverse is not always true.

4.2 Minimum Cost Matching

In this section we introduce the notion of matching. Formally,

Definition 5. [**Matching**] *A set of node pairs (x, y), M, is called a **matching** from tree T_1 to tree T_2 iff (1) $\forall\ (x,y)\in M$, $x\in T_1$, $y\in T_2$, HW-signature(x)=HW-signature(y); (2) $\forall\ (x_1,y_1)\in M$, $(x_2,y_2)\in M$, $x_1=x_2$ iff $y_1=y_2$ (one-to-one); (3) Given $(x,y)\in M$, suppose x' is the parent of x, y' is the parent of y, then $(x',y')\in M$ (preserving ancestor relationships).* ∎

Observe that the notion of matching is defined in the same way as in [5]. The key difference is in Criteria (1): we use the HW-signature as basic criterion for matching nodes instead of signature as used in X-Diff. Criteria (2) and (3) in this definition prevent children being matched if their ancestors are not matched. These criterion reflect the integrity of XML segments.

Based on a matching M from T_1 and T_2, we can generate an *edit script*. It can be shown using the same method as in [5] that there is a *minimum-cost matching* that corresponds to a *minimum-cost edit script*. Note that we use the same notion of minimum cost edit script as defined in [5] except for that fact that instead of using the signature, we use the notion of HW-signature. Observe that every matching in our approach is also a matching in X-Diff. However, the inverse is not always true. Thus, the X-Diff approach always has equal or more number of matchings compared to our approach. As a particular matching defines a particular edit script, the X-Diff approach chooses the minimum-cost edit script from more number of scripts compared to our approach.

4.3 Algorithm HW-Diff

The algorithm HW-DIFF takes as input the old and new versions of the XML representation of the hidden web query results D_1 and D_2. It returns as output the edit script E for transforming D_1 to D_2. As the algorithm is an extension of the X-Diff algorithm, it can be best described by the following three phases. Note that we do not present the pseudocode here as it is similar to X-Diff except that we use the HW-signature instead of the signature to match nodes.

Phase 1: Parsing and Hashing Phase: In this step, the algorithm parses the input XML documents to trees, and assigns the HW-signatures to each node and computes the XHash values [5] for all the nodes in both trees. After this step, the algorithm checks if the two trees are equivalent by comparing the XHash values of the roots.

Phase 2: Matching Phase: In this step, the algorithm generates the *minimum-cost matching* between two trees by computing the editing distances between the nodes with equal HW-signatures on each level of the trees, going from the leaf nodes to the root nodes. The steps for computing the *minimum-cost matching* in our approach are the same as the steps of computing it for the X-Diff algorithm except that we only compute distances between the nodes with equal HW-signatures instead of equal signatures. As the number of nodes with equal HW-signatures is always less or equal to the number of nodes with equal signatures, the number of distances between the nodes to be calculated in the X-Diff approach is equal or more than the number of distances to be calculated using the HW-DIFF approach. These two numbers are identical only when there are no *facilitators* or *identifiers* specified in the query results.

Phase 3: Edit Script Generation Phase: In this phase, we generate a minimum-cost edit script for changes to the hidden web data based on the minimum cost matching found in the matching phase. This step is similar to X-Diff.

5 Performance Evaluation

We have implemented HW-Diff using Java. All the experiments have been performed on a Pentium 4 CPU 2.4 GHz with 512 MB of RAM. We used Microsoft Windows 2000 Professional as operating system. We use the data from the following four hidden web sites for our experiments: AutoTrader.com, Amazon.com, IMDb.com, and CiteSeer.org. We generated a data set for the experiments based

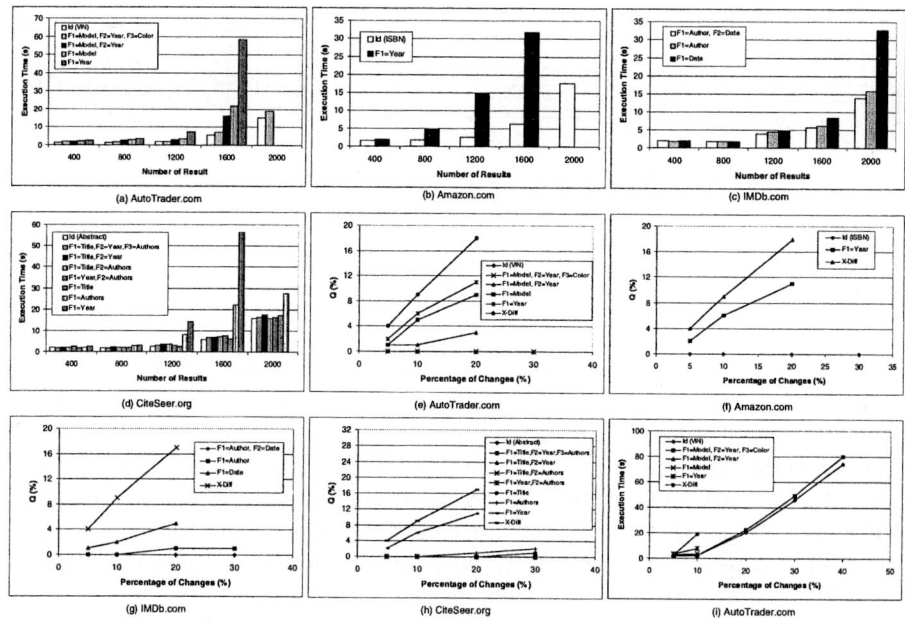

Fig. 4. Performance study

on the results of a set of queries. We created a data set containing files with 400, 800, 1200, 1600, and 2000 results for each site. We monitored these sites for a period of 6 months and archived the query results for our change detection process. We also implemented a program that generates semantically meaningful changed versions of these files with 5%, 10%, 20%, 30%, and 40% of changes of all three types of changes (insert, update, and delete) equally distributed. Note that in this experimental set up and data set, the Java implementation of X-Diff (downloaded from www.cs.wisc.edu/~yuanwang/xdiff.html) cannot detect the changes when the percentage of change is more than 20% due to lack of memory (`java.lang.outofmemory.error`). For some data set it cannot detect the changes when more than 10% data has changed. Similar situation arises for HW-DIFF if there are too many equal values for the facilitators.

Execution Time vs Semantic Attributes: Our first experiment is to evaluate the affect of the selection of attributes in the query results as *identifiers* and *facilitators* on the change detection time. We applied HW-DIFF to the data with different combinations of attributes selected as the *facilitators* and the *identifier*. We used the data set described above with 10% changes. Figures 4(a) to 4(d) show the results for different hidden web sites. HW-DIFF demonstrates best performance when we use the *identifier* attribute. If no *identifier* attribute can be modeled for a particular result set then several *facilitator* attributes help us to achieve similar performance. Observe that for small sets of query

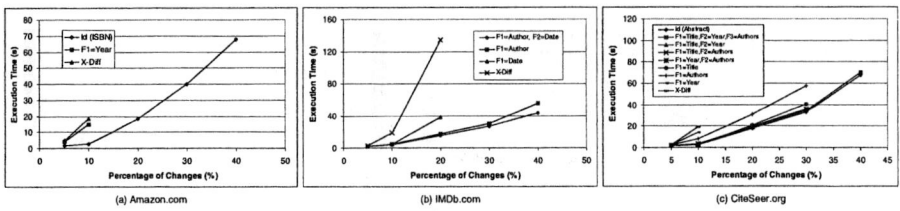

Fig. 5. Performance study (Contd.)

results, the execution time is almost the same and is actually defined by the parsing time. However, as the result size increases, sometimes a single *facilitator* attribute results in significant increase in the change detection time compared to other attributes due to the frequent appearance of results having identical values for this attribute in the sample data. For example, Figure 4(a) shows that if we only use the `Year` of the `Car` as *facilitator* attribute then the change detection time increases significantly, but not so much when we select the `Model` as *facilitator* attribute. This is because more number of cars in the two versions of the query results have the same manufacturing `Year` compared to the number of cars having the same `Model`.

Semantic Incorrectness of Changes: This experiment evaluates the *semantic incorrectness* of the changes detected by HW-DIFF compared to X-Diff. Let N be the total number of results in the change detection delta file D. Let M of these results contain semantically incorrect changes. Then, the *semantic incorrectness* of changes (denoted as Q) is defined as $Q = \frac{M}{N} \times 100\%$. As in the previous experiment, we applied HW-DIFF to the data with different combinations of attributes selected as the *facilitators* and the *identifier*. The data for X-Diff is same but without any *facilitators* or *identifier*. For each web site, we used the data set with 800 results and 5%, 10%, 20%, 30%, and 40% changes. Figures 4(e) to 4(h) show the results for the different hidden web sites. As in the previous experiment, HW-DIFF demonstrates best performance when the *identifier* attribute is used. In this case the semantic incorrectness is reduced to 0% for all cases. If no *identifier* attribute can be modeled for a particular result set then several *facilitator* attributes help us to achieve similar performance. For example, for `AutoTrader.com` the combination of `Model`, `Year`, and `Color` helps to achieve similar performance. Observe that for all cases HW-DIFF outperforms X-Diff as far as detection of the number of semantically correct changes. In fact, the number of incorrect changes detected by X-Diff approximately equals the number of changes in the document for all the cases. Also observe that even though single *facilitator* attribute leads to increase in detection of semantically incorrect changes, it is still less than X-Diff for the given sites.

Execution Time vs Percentage of Changes: Our last experiment measures the execution time on different percentage of changes. For each web site, we used the data set with 1200 results and 5%, 10%, 20%, 30%, and 40% changes.

Figures 4(i) and 5 show the results for different hidden web sites. The affects of the *identifiers* and *facilitators* are the same as the previous two experiments. Observe that for all the sites HW-DIFF outperforms X-Diff (up to 7 times) especially when the percentage of changes is more than 10%.

6 Conclusions

In this paper, we presented a technique to detect semantically correct changes to the hidden web query results. Our work is motivated by the problem that existing change detection algorithms do not exploit the semantic constraints of the data. In our approach, the unordered hidden web query results are transformed to XML format using the HW-STALKER algorithm [2] and then detect the changes between the two versions of XML representation of the hidden web query results. We propose an algorithm HW-DIFF that extends X-Diff, a published change detection algorithm for unordered XML, by incorporating the semantic constraints associated with the data. HW-DIFF detects more semantically correct changes compared to X-Diff and runs up to 7 times faster than X-Diff for the given data set.

References

1. G. COBENA, S. ABITEBOUL, A. MARIAN. Detecting Changes in XML Documents. In *ICDE* , San Jose, 2002.
2. V. KOVALEV, S. S. BHOWMICK, S. MADRIA. HW-STALKER: A Machine Learning-based Approach to Transform Hidden Web Data to XML. In *DEXA*, Zaragoza, Spain, 2004.
3. V. KOVALEV, S. S. BHOWMICK, S. MADRIA. HW-STALKER: A Machine Learning-based System for Transforming QURE-Pagelets to XML. To appear in *Data and Knowledge Engineering Journal (DKE)* , Elsevier Science, 2005/2006.
4. V. KOVALEV, S. S. BHOWMICK. Mining Facilitators and Identifiers from Hidden Web Query Results. *Technical Report* , CAIS-06-2005, 2005.
5. Y. WANG, D. DEWITT, J-Y CAI. X-Diff: A Fast Change Detection Algortihm for XML Documents. *ICDE* , India, 2003.

Design for All in Information Technology: A Universal Concern

Jenny Darzentas[1] and Klaus Miesenberger[2]

[1] Department of Product and Systems Design Engineering,
University of the Aegean, Ermoupolis, Syros, 84100 Greece
jennyd@aegean.gr
[2] University of Linz,
Institut Integriert Studieren, Altenbergerstrasse 69, A-4040 Linz
klaus.miesenberger@jku.at

Abstract. The concept of Design for All is not well understood, and the issues of accessibility and inclusion are often relegated to specialists and dedicated conferences. This paper introduces the concept of Design for All dispelling some of the misunderstandings that surround it, and situating it within the Information Technology context, as distinct from wider considerations such accessibility in the built environment. Some of the reasons for undertaking Design for All are discussed, and, making use of the analogy of the printed book, the paper then shows how Design for All in combination with Information technologies are enablers in the widest sense of the term. Finally, it is noted that Design for All is a process, not a product, and while there are people who specialise in eAccessibility, the research agenda demands more involvement from information technologists of all kinds. These are issues that concern us all, in our roles as designers and implementers of information technology, as well as in our role as consumers of information and participants in the Information Society.

1 Introduction

The term 'Design for All' is a deliberate attempt to describe the meaning of what has been called variously, 'Universal Design' in the USA, 'Inclusive Design' in Britain and Ireland, 'Barrier-free Design' in Germany, and uses the qualifier 'accessible' to describe products, systems and services where consideration has been given to their use by all sorts of users, in all sorts of circumstances. Put another way, it is an attempt to consider diversity, not just in the population, but also in the scope and nature of the interaction, and the contexts of use.

Design for All has been misunderstood in various ways. There are those who view it as a euphemism for 'Design for the Disabled'. In this view, it as understood as designing products and systems for a small minority and requiring specialist knowledge on the part of the design team, such as rehabilitation engineers, physiotherapists, and lately, accessibility experts, etc. It is true that the history of Design for All has its roots in the Universal Design movement, which in the beginning concerned itself primarily with the built environment. The coining of the term, 'Universal Design' in the late 1970's is attributed to the late Ron Mace, an architect who, as a polio victim and a wheelchair user, was one of the best known champions for the design of products and environments to be usable by all people, to the greatest extent possible, without the need for adaptation or specialised design. Speaking at a conference, in 1998, just before his untimely death, he noted that: *"Universal design seeks to encourage attractive, marketable products that are more usable by everyone. It is design for the built environment and consumer products for a very broad definition of users".*[1] This is an important aspect of Design for All: to become part of mainstream design practice, rather than design for a niche market of 'the disabled' and making special accommodations for them.

Another misconception attributed to Design for All is to concentrate on the 'universal' and interpret it as meaning 'one-size-fits-all'. Nothing could be further from the truth. Design for All, in the information and communication technologies (ICT) context, is a graded concept. It allows for:

- The design of information society technology, products, services and applications, which are demonstrably suitable for most of the potential users without any modification
- Design of products, which are easily adaptable to different users (i.e. by incorporating adaptable or customisable user interfaces)
- Design of products which have standardised interfaces, capable of being accessed by specialised user interaction devices. [1]

A useful diagram to compare this with is shown below in Figure 1. This represents all users of ICT equipment and services as a pyramid with human abilities along the vertical axis, from good at the bottom to very poor at the top. There is a wide base containing those who can access all services and devices directly. Above that is a smaller section containing those who can access equipment and services only with some form of (simple) adaptation (e.g. getting up very close to read a display, memorising a sequence of actions, marking smartcards so as to know which way to insert them, etc.). Above this is a still smaller section containing those who need some form of assistive technology to access equipment and services (e.g. supplementary large display for visually impaired people, special keyboard for blind or motor impaired people, extra amplification for hearing impaired people, etc.). At the apex of the pyramid are those people who can only access services and devices with the assistance of another person. The goal of Design for All therefore is to push the boundary between 'Those who can use all' and 'With adaptation' as far up as possible.

The problem with the misconceptions concerning Design for All is that unless they are explicated, they can serve as arguments against it or even lead to design that favours one disability while causing new problems for other disabilities. For instance, a design requirement that caters to the needs of visually impaired, - replace a visual alert with an acoustic one -, does conflict with the needs of the hearing impaired. Designing for All means finding solutions that cater to all, in this case if possible leaving both the visual and accoustic modalities, and perhaps including in addition

---

[1] See biographical sketch at http://adaptiveenvironments.org/accessdesign/profiles/ mace_text. php

some other sensory alert, such as tactile one, like the vibrating alerts now available as standard in most mobile phones. Alongwith this should go the ability to have the choice of modalities, and the functionality that allows a user to switch between them, or to turn them off completely. It is important to remember that there are no stereotypes, elderly people have both visual and hearing impairments, users may find themselves in a dark and noisy environment and thus temporarily deaf and unable to see well. Since we cannot cater *a priori* to the user group, nor to the context of use of a device, then the richer the alternatives, the more likely it is to find something to cover every need.

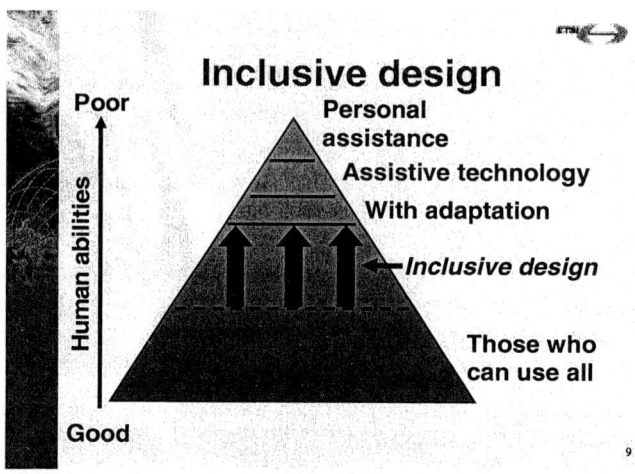

Fig. 1. The Usability Pyramid (Nordby 2003)[2]

2 What Motivates Design for All?

Having cleared up some of the misconceptions about Design for All, the question to answer is what motivates it? Broadly speaking there are four groups of reasons, to do with ethics, demographics, commercial considerations and finally, legislation.

2.1 Ethics

With regard to ethics, Design for All considers the right of all citizens to equal opportunities, especially in terms of the right to education and employment. There is a well understood interdependence between these two: poor education equals poor employment prospects. Lack of education results in lack of knowledge and skills needed to become employable. A less considered, but also important part of education is the acquisition of social skills, e.g. how to communicate and be sociable, that are essential to the workplace. The web is becoming the new societal platform where

---

[2] See presentation materials from the CEN, CENELEC, ETSI "Accessibility for All" Conference, 2003 available at http://www.etsi.org/cce/proceedings/ppt/6_2%20nordby%20visualsupport.ppt

people can provide, share, search and locate information, as well as conduct community activities. Excluding anyone from this new platform is ethically inappropriate and unacceptable.

Ironically, the Internet has brought tremendous advantages to just those people whose impairments or situations prevented them from participating in activities such as shopping in more traditional ways. These may be people who are functionally impaired, or people who are homebound, such those caring for invalids or looking after small children. For these people simple everyday activities like a visit to the shops needs advance planning and arrangements and dependence upon others. For many disabled or socially excluded people, technological advances have given them the means to communicate with the world, and also to unite. The Internet and the support it offers for activities such as shopping, banking, voting, entertainment, and education, not to mention the lifelines provided by various online communities, have opened up opportunities that were not possible for these people before. With these communication channels these groups are also able to make their needs heard.

The Equal Opportunities Ethic, whose pedigree stretches back through the civil rights movement and the 1948 Bill of Human Rights[3], is also in line with the new world view, which moves away from an emphasis on the individual to a more communal, collaborative approach in which social justice is at least as important as individual well being. With regard to disability, there is also the trend to move from a medical model of disability to a social model of disability. That is to say, to consider that it is not individual limitations, of whatever kind, which are the cause of problems, but society's failure to provide appropriate services and adequately ensure the needs of disabled people are fully taken into account in its social organisation [2].

These trends are particularly relevant in the context of the Information Society. As the world goes online, services in their traditional form are no longer so readily available, and indeed some are being phased out. Unless all efforts are made to ensure that accommodations are made where necessary and that access to systems is available for all, there will be a further exacerbation of the 'haves and have-nots'. It is then a prime concern to focus on ways of supporting access and preventing social exclusion.

2.2 Demographics

The motivation for Design for All does not rest on ethical considerations alone. A powerful argument in its favour is that of present day demographics. It is widely acknowledged [3] that people are living longer. Advances in medicine and living conditions in the developed world[4] mean that more people are able to survive what would have been previously fatal conditions. Many of these people have functional impairments, either as a result of their conditions or simply as a result of their advanced age. With increased life expectancy, the ratios of abled to disabled and

---

[3] See for a historical perspective http://www.design.ncsu.edu:8120/cud/univ_design/udhistory.htm

[4] See an interesting perspective from less developed nations on Design for All in Balaram, Singanapalli (2002), Universal Design Education and Development. in: Universal Design, 17 Ways of Thinking and Teaching, Christopher, Jon (Ed.), Husbanken, Norway (p.316).

elderly are changing. Current estimates for the United States are that 20 percent suffer from some kind of disability.

Furthermore, the aging population is growing inexorably, outnumbering the birthrate. In 2050, the world population above 60 years of age will be around 2 billion, out of an estimated 8 billion. The predictions for the UK (which shares with the rest of the Europe a falling birthrate) are that by 2020, almost half the adult population will be over 50, with the over 80's being the most rapidly growing sector. With age comes an increasing divergence of physical capability. Some employees' working lives are curtailed simply because they can no longer do jobs they used to do. This costs companies large sums in premature medical retirement. This lessens the numbers of people in the workforce, and increases the numbers reliant upon pensions. The burden predicted by actuaries is already the root of discussions in most European Union member states about reducing benefits and pensions, and raising the retirement age. Yet some of this is avoidable. Some workers could remain in employment and productive, were accommodations made for them.

With regard to the over 80's, the use of information technologies like email have already been shown to improve quality of life and break the present pattern of isolation [4], while other experiments in healthcare telematics [5] have helped them to maintain their independence. A crucial factor has been catering to the needs of these users, whose requirements are related to the characteristics of their being elderly [6].

2.3 Commercial Incentives

Closely linked to these demographics are commercial incentives. Now in the middle of the first decade of the new millennium, the oldest of the 'Baby Boomers'[5], the most numerous generation in humanity's history, are approaching retirement age. Born and bred in the consumer society, they have a completely different attitude toward the 'third age'. With life expectancy commonly increasing to ranges that have been described as the 'older old' (80-85+ years), the 'younger old' (65 +) find themselves retired, free of family commitments, and in some industries there is a projection that the bulk of their customer base may soon be made up of such people with money and leisure time to spend. In support of this, according to [7], they currently hold 80% of the UK's wealth and buy 80% of all top of the range cars, 80% of cruises and 50% of skincare products. In view of this, Fiat is actively targeting elderly drivers (the over 65s) in its design of vehicle information systems, i.e. the systems for navigation, security, comfort and entertainment. They have found that including features to overcome certain constraints, nearly always increases the usability for everybody [8].

Yet still, many products continue to be designed to appeal to the younger generation and, it seems, ignore the expanding older market sector. Consequently, large sections of the population are being excluded by industry attitudes. In a paper written in 2000, investigating industry attitudes to Design for All, Keates et al. [9] reported that of the FTSE 100 companies (the 100 largest companies trading on the London Stock Exchange) only 37% aim to produce products for the over-50's; 31% take end-user age into consideration when designing a new product or service; 29%

---

[5] Baby boomers refer to those people born between 1946-64.

agreed that aging will affect how they run as companies; and only 18% employ significant numbers of over-50's.

Complementing this research, it appears there is also a problem with marketing. Design for All is still not perceived as marketable. Companies shy away from advertising their products as such and appear still to be obsessed with young people. To continue with examples from the mainstream car industry, Ford makes no secret that the Focus is their most accessible car, and that many of the ideas for its design came from taking into consideration the needs of older people[6], yet this is not emphasized in their marketing campaigns. The same is true of the Renault's Twingo, while the Opel Agila show in their advertising how the car may vary its internal seating arrangements. This is a definite advantage for less agile elderly passengers and passengers with wheelchairs, but elderly and mobility impaired users are not depicted in the advertising. In advertisements for the Ferrari Enzo nowhere does it mention that it has been designed targeting the older driver. In fact, it has wider seats to accommodate more ample figures and has had its door height adjusted to lessen the need to bend (ageing) knees. Thus it seems that Design for All is associated with "do good-ing" and that 'worthiness', it is not an image that sells. This is perhaps an argument for why Design for All must be firmly divorced from its image of 'Design for the Disabled', and shown its ethical base does not reside in acts of charity, but in a firm belief that it serves the community as a whole, making life more comfortable for everybody.

However, change could be happening. The above examples show that the vehicle industry is interested[7]. There are also the changes in the way businesses project their image to their customers. In today's environment corporate social responsibility has increasingly become fundamental in building trust and reputation with the clients and consumers they do business with. In this context, the experience of 'closed doors' can have a negative influence on the way people perceive even the most reliable companies and the strongest brands. Companies that adopt a socially responsible approach to business typically do so to protect or improve their reputation, and because they believe it will financially benefit their business. Many computer linked industries[8] are taking seriously the effort to make it part of their corporate social responsibility profile to show a commitment to Design for All.

Design for All would seem to make good business sense. Incorporating accessibility features from the outset in the design of products and systems is much less expensive than retrofitting. Many techniques and methods introduced by Design for All show benefits, in terms of improving usability for disabled and non disabled users alike, and thus expanding the customer base. However, there are not as yet many clear examples of this, since the metrics are not easily come by. It is hard to for companies to undertake before and after studies, or to measure the effort to make the product or service accessible. A similar situation has been faced by Human Computer Interaction HCI personnel for many years, but fortunately, an emerging breed of consumer is demanding accountability in matters of usability. Thus presently it is

---

[6] Some simulation testing was done at UK's Loughborough University, using their Third Age Suit. http://www.lboro.ac.uk/taurus/simulation3.htm

[7] Note that although the examples given here refer to the ergonomics of the cars, Fiat and Toyota at least are interested in the in-vehicle telematics.

[8] Microsoft, IBM, Sun amongst many others

probably fair to say that companies that display a commitment to Design for All do so because they believe it means a greater access to potential markets, a better corporate image, eliminates costly retrofitting but also reduced risk of action under disability discrimination legislation. Legislation is the fourth in the group of reasons for doing Design for All.

2.4 Legislative and Regulatory Concerns

One of the more cogent reasons for doing Design for All has come from the introduction of a growing raft of legislative and regulatory measures concerning the accessibility of information (content) and information systems, some of the most well known being the Amercicans with Disabilities Act (ADA)[10] in the States and the Disability Discrimination Act in the UK (DDA)[11]). Under these types of legislation some very expensive litigation has taken place, and high profile cases, such as the highly publicised Maguire v Sydney Organising Committee of the Olympic Games (SOCOG) [12].

The effect of globalisation has meant as well that practices in one country are followed closely by large communities based worldwide. Although the States led the way in this type of legislation, other countries are not far behind, while products and systems, if they are to be marketed globally, need to conform to the legislation in each country. This has led to a search for guidelines and standards to be used by designers to ensure their companies' products and systems are not liable for any infringements of the law.

At the same time, following the example set by the US section 508 [13], to encourage the practice of Design for All in the European Union (EU) the two directives (2004/17 and 2004/18) [14] relating to public procurement will require that *"whenever possible, public authorities must take into account accessibility for people with disabilities and design for all requirements, and include technical specifications in the contract documents"*. Member states are required to transpose this into national legislation by the end of 2006. Currently work is underway[9] looking at the harmonisation of eAccessibility requirements to be used in the public procurement of ICT products and services and the requirements for policy implementation in this field [15]. With this 'carrot and stick' approach, and backed up by much work in the area of standards to support the legislation [16, 17 18, 19] these legislative and regulatory concerns are powerful arguments in the service of Design for All.

3 Design for All and Information Technology

That Information and Communication Technologies (ICT) have permeated every area of modern life is well recognised. What is not so well understood is that these technologies can offer almost unlimited potential for people with disabilities and other people suffering from functional limitations. This lack of understanding is because mainstream research and development has concentrated on the non existent 'average

---

[9] Projects such as eInclusion@EU see www.einclusion-eu.org and Web Accessibility Benchmarking Cluster www.wabcluster.org

user' rather than a diversity of users. This potential is mainly based on the flexibility, the multimedia and multimodality that these technologies can provide to answer varying needs of interaction between human and computer. Most traditional information 'tools' were based on one or, more recently, several fixed modalities of interaction, e.g. books, radio. The design of the tools prescribed the way in which they could be accessed and handled.

The book, for example, represents one of the most important tools of modern science and society. Yet it is based on a visual style of presentation and a specific style of handling, that is, page turning. This style of interaction is fixed and immanent to the tool. This interface proved to be an efficient and usable design for hundreds of years -one we are still unable to relinquish- for there is still nothing to replace it. Figure 1 depicts the book, with is content, handling and presentation layer built in to the medium.

Fig. 2. Inflexible Medium: The Book

The 'interface' of this 'tool' is responsible for many of the problems known collectively nowadays as 'print disabilities'. People who are unable to use the visual presentation (e.g. people with vision problems) or the specific handling (e.g. people with mobility and manipulation problems) are put at a disadvantage. The more books or printed materials became a standard the more people were expected to use them, and printed materials became a prerequisite for many essential activities including studying and working. For people with print disabilities the inflexibility of the interface meant exclusion.

The contribution of the invention of the printing press was to increase the availability of written materials. Several centuries later, the invention of braille and other tactile reading systems partially helped those who were vision impaired but its expense and bulk limited its usefulness. In the twentieth century, radio and recordings have also helped the vision impaired, but these too have been limited by expense. It is now, in the twentieth century that the computer has given us the means of creating a new world of access to information.

The analogy of the book is useful to understand how it is possible to unwittingly build exclusion into the tools we develop and use [20,21]. In addition it helps to illustrate what modern ICT can change in this context. The means of presentation and the modalities of handling are no longer bound to a certain tool; they are independent and may be adapted to the needs of users. It is possible to use many different ways to access digital documents. At the time a document is accessed, the presentation style and the handling modalities can be selected, according to the needs of different users. This shows the integrating power of ICT. All users, including those with disabilities, may decide upon the way they want to access the document. Figure 3 shown below, shows how the content and be accessed by different presentation and handling methods.

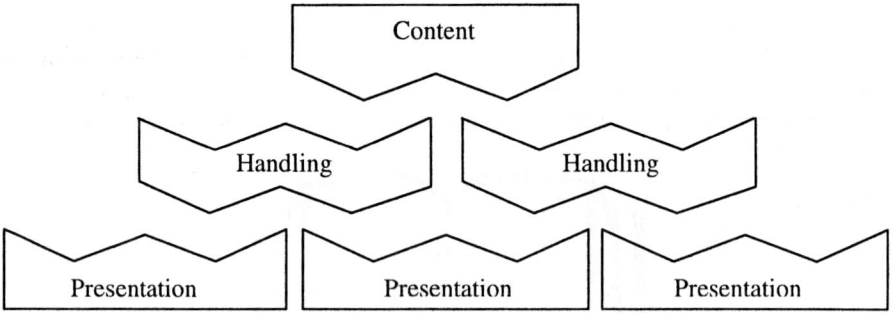

Fig. 3. The flexibility of ICT

Using the example of documents also facilitates understanding that this flexibility, based on multimedia and multimodality is universal as the technologies are 'document' based. That is, they use different levels of descriptions of functionalities and interfaces at a meta level which enable a very flexible interface to almost any system or device using ICT. The application of ICT combined with HCI methodologies to almost any part of daily life makes ICT a universal integrating technology as the interaction may be customised to devices optimised to users' needs, including those with disabilities. Some of these specialised devices are known as Assistive Technologies (AT).

3.1 Design for All and the Role of Assistive Technologies

To refer to the usability pyramid shown in Figure 1, the AT are towards the apex of the triangle, and they belong in the pyramid as ways to offer possibilities of access, when combined with ICT and HCI, even to those with severe disabilities. AT provides extra handling and/or presentation layers, bridging the gap between the standard interface and these users' needs. Some examples of AT for those with print difficulties, are screen readers or voice browsers for the visually impaired. This enables them, for instance, to read newspapers that have web equivalents to the paper copy version. Speech synthesizers vocalise the material on the screen for these readers[10]. Alternate input devices permit persons with motor impairments to operate a computer and to move through the text without having to hold a book or turn pages. Examples of these are numerous, and include combinations of software and hardware,

---

[10] Users who are not familiar with speech synthesizers find the robotic voice off puting, but those who are experts can actually speed them up and understand the output,- an aural equivalent of speed reading.

such as a switch or a pointing device (hardware) that can be used to select symbols on an onscreen keyboard (software).

Now with such flexibility to hand, it is possible to avoid discrimination. This was previously out of the question when no alternatives for presentation and handling existed. It also means that the definition of disabilities can be rephrased. It is not exclusively a question of individual limitations, it is more and more a question of the design of tools and systems to leverage an individual's abilities and provide suitable interfaces to products, systems and services.

While respecting the continuing need for assistive technologies for specialised cases such as refreshable Braille displays, or signing avatars, or highly individualised products for particular users, Design for All also sees AT as a source of inspiration [22]. Designers can look to AT and gain insight into how to provide better products and systems for all. As an example, website designers wanting to make an accessible application, studied and used screen readers in order to better understand how information can be structured when it is auditory, as opposed to visual, since most website design is primarily visual [23]. There are many occasions when solutions for the disabled have provided solutions to problems faced by other sections of the population. An interesting list of mainstream products that were originally designed to overcome disabilities includes the TV remote control, the phonograph, the typewriter, to name but a few[11]. Users of assistive technologies that become mainstream benefit from better support and from having these products moved from the expensive 'niche' market to cheaper mass production. This of course has to be traded off against loss of customisation [24].

As technologies continue to converge and we are seeing the emergence of whole new interaction paradigms, such Brain to Computer Interaction (BCI) manipulating the computer with brainwaves [25] Some implants may allow users (abled and disabled) to interact with applications in a more direct way, bypassing the need for some 'handling' layers.

3.2 Design for All and the Web Accessibility

Practically all Information Technology discussion will involve the Internet, and Design for All too is tied up with issues of Web Accessibility, since the interface to many of the new systems and services is the web. It is displacing traditional sources of information and interaction, like schools, libraries, print materials, discourse of the workplace, and lately government services. Some of the traditional resources were accessible, some not. It also means the dissemination channels are changing, and information can come straight to the user, via desktop or laptop computers; PDAs and mobile phones, etc. No one can afford to remain outside it, and no one needs to.

The Web is the fastest-adopted technology in history, and for people with disabilities, it is sometimes a "mixed blessing". Some of the most common examples of practices that cause problems are the following:

---

[11] A collection of such examples, mostly to do with telecommunications devices, is at http://ideal-group.org/ecc

- Unlabelled graphics, undescribed video, poorly marked-up tables, lack of keyboard support or screen reader compatibility, (causes problems to those with vision impairments)
- Lack of captioning for audio, proliferation of text without visual signposts, (causes problems to those with hearing difficulties)
- Lack of keyboard or single-switch support for menu commands, (causes problems to people with motor difficulties)
- Lack of consistent navigation structure, overly complex presentation or language, lack of illustrative non-text materials, flickering or strobing designs on pages, causes problems to people with cognitive or neurological disabilities.

Attention to these details improves the design of the application for other users, especially leveraging the multimodality of content and giving support for visual, auditory and tactile access [26]. Using the terms introduced above in the book analogy, this means there are handling and presentation options to suit a variety of devices, of situations of use, and of personal needs. The devices may be mobile phones with small display screens, Web-TV, kiosks. The context of use include situations where there is low bandwidth making images slow to download; noisy environments where it is difficult to hear the audio; screenglare where it difficult to see the screen, driving a car or operating other machinery where eyes and hands are "busy". These situations are variously encountered by people in the workplace, while travelling, while enjoying themselves. There are also situations where some modes of interaction are not socially acceptable, such as talking on the mobile phone in the theatre, etc.

The presentation layer can be multimodal. Redundant text/audio/video can support different learning styles, low literacy levels, and second-language access. That is, when the same content is expressed in different modalities, the combination of two or more can reinforce understanding. As an example, many second language users are more proficient in aural than written language. An audio version of onscreen text helps comprehension. Presentation is also influenced by structure. At this level, style sheets can support more efficient page transmission and site maintenance, the captioning of audio files supports better machine indexing of content and retrieval of content, the text in the captions being used to conduct searches of video archives. Similarly, the ALT tag (the tag used to describe a graphic on a web page) can be leveraged to provide the search engines more meaningful content to work with. On a graphics rich web site, there may be very little text for the search engine spiders to use to analyse the site. However a relevant alt tag attached to each image means that the search engines will read them as textual content, and the web site will show up in relevant searches. Of course, it also means that pages make sense to people who are using text browsers, or who have turned off the graphics in the interests of speedy downloading.

There are many resources available with information on all sorts of aspects of accessibility of websites and of information and communications technology[12]. The

---

[12] Include Project Web Accessibility in Mind, http://ww.webaim.org; Dive into Accessibility http://www.driveintoaccessibility.org; INCLUDE project website http://www.stakes.fi/include/

most well known are those from the W3C's Web Accessibility Initiative (WAI)[13] and in particular their Web Content Accessibility Guidelines. At present, version 2 of these guidelines is being developed. They are organised around four principles of accessibility:

- that content must be perceivable,
- that interface elements in the content must be operable,
- that content and controls must be understandable, and
- that content must be robust enough to work with current and future technologies).

Each of these principles is accompanied by guidelines to further explicate them. As can be seen the principles are at a descriptive level which is to aid design, not dictate it. Accessibility is part of Design for All, and Design for All is a process, not a product. What is needed is the application of the principles to methodologies from HCI [27].

4 Design for All: A Research Agenda

Design for All and eAccessibility leverage the integrating power of ICT and HCI, a potential which is well understood by those working in the area, but which needs to be integrated into mainstream research and development. Design for All and eAccessibility still remain at the level of principles and lack a coherent theory which could guide development and application. Four possible research domains are:

1. *From Assessment to the Specification of Profiles*: Research is needed on new ways of interacting and communication based on 'extreme' user interaction abilities and describing, defining and specifying them as the basis for HCI. Coherent concepts and methods are required for how to specify the abilities and needs of users with disabilities to guide mainstream design of interfaces towards accessibility. These fundamentals should help to develop guidelines and support (tools) for the design process.
2. *Non Classical Interfaces*: AT providing innovative, improved and more efficient ways of interaction with the standard HCI for people with disabilities. Based on the profiles defined, research is needed on new possibilities of AT and therefore of non classical user interfaces for extreme users. These new devices would provide new means of interaction and principles on how to design the HCI so that AT can interact seamlessly with it.
3. *Systems, Services, Context Awareness and Semantics*: Bringing ICT and 'intelligence' into the environment increases the possibilities of overcoming problems of people with disabilities. These new possibilities might be considered elaborate alternatives for the mainstream but for people with disabilities they enable an independent life. Research in this domain should explore the potential of new technologies for disabled and elderly people and should guarantee that guidelines for accessibility are incorporated already at an early stage into this domain.

---

[13] W3C Web Accessibility Initiative (WAI): http://www.w3.org/WAI/ W3C WAI Web Content Authoring Guidelines 1.0 http://www.w3.org/TR/WAI-WEBCONTENT/ W3C WAI Web Content Authoring Guidelines, 2.0 http://www.w3.org/TR/WCAG20/

4. *Changes in the Context of Application – socio-economic, social and ethical. Impacts of 'Technology for all'*: Research on how these new approaches change the social, economical and ethical context of disability in the context of an aging population. Areas such as the lack of awareness and education in ICT/HCI domains in the area of care and service provision of people with disabilities and elderly people should be addressed [28]. The economical, social and ethical implications should be discussed.

Design for All as an 'early adopter' addresses topics which are still underestimated in their impact for the individual and society as a whole. A holistic approach oriented towards finding the fundamentals for 'eAccessibility' and 'Design for All' is still needed. In an aging society this research could form the basis for a series of application oriented activities for strengthening this economic sector.

5 Conclusions

This paper began with a definition and explanation of the term Design for All. It is perhaps here the place to include the latest term from the EU: "eInclusion". This means ensuring that in the Information Age, with the broadening of the population of information users, and the increase in the availability, type, functionality and content of new products and services, and of access devices and technologies, there is something to suit everyone, and no one is left out. This will only come about as a result of designing mainstream products and services to be accessible by as broad a range of users as possible. It also means that designers must be instilled with a Design for All culture[14]. This term widens the net to include all sorts of activities, including training in eskills and enhancing digital literacy for users. What it means for us as designers and implementers is that we have to play our part in disabling disablement and enabling enablement[15], remembering that we are designing for "our future selves"[16]. However, as designers and implementers our task has less to do with the 'demographic push' of the aging populations, but on the 'technology pull' represented by the new possibilities and opportunities in the Information Age.

References

1. European Design for All and eAccessibility Network (EDeAN): http://www.e-accessibility. org/design-for-all.htm
2. Oliver, M.: The politics of Disablement, Macmillans 1990
3. World Health Organisation (WHO): Life in the 21st Century, A Vision for All, World Health Report 1998, http://www.who.int/whr/1998/en/whr98_en.pdf

---

[14] This was a goal of the IDCnet project (Inclusive Design Curriculum Network) www.idcnet.org

[15] This was the main theme of a recent conference: see VALID Value in Design: disabling disablement, enabling enablement: Cumulus 2003 Conference in Latvia, 8th -10th May see http://cumulus.artun.ee/themes.html

[16] Phrase coined by Roger Coleman and also the title of a conference: Design for our Future Selves (March 1992) see http://www.hhrc.rca.ac.uk/events/daevents.html

4. White, H., McConnell, E., Clipp, E., Branch, L., Sloane, R., Pieper, C., & Fox, T.: A randomized controlled trial of the psychosocial impact of providing Internet training and access to older adults. Aging and Mental Health, 6(3), 213–221, 2002.
5. Himanen, M.: The Smart Home for Keeping Up the Life Style of the Old Ages. Proceedings of ICADI, – Advancing Technology and Services to Promote Quality of Life. 2003
6. Gregor, P., Newell, A.F., Zajicek, M.: Designing for Dynamic Diversity - interfaces for older people ASSETS 2002, ed. J. A. Jacko pp.151-156, 2002
7. Walker, D.: Live fast, die old BBC News September 2004 http://news.bbc.co.uk/1/hi/magazine/3659996.stm
8. Coda, A., Damiani, S., Montanari, R. In-vehicle telematic systems HMI for elderly Drivers in Universal Access in HCI: Towards an Information Society for All ed Stephanidis, C. pp 788-792, 2001
9. Keates S, Lebbon C, Clarkson PJ (2000) Investigating industry attitudes to Universal Design. Proceedings of RESNA 2000, 276-278 available at http://rehab-www.eng.cam.ac.uk/papers/lsk12/resna2000/
10. Americans with Disabilities Act (ADA) http://www.usdoj.gov/crt/ada/adahom1.htm
11. Disability Discrimination Act (DDA) see http://www.disability.gov.uk/dda/
12. Sloan, M. Web Accessibility and the DDA, Journal of Information, Law and Technology, vol 2 2001 available at http://www2.warwick.ac.uk/fac/soc/law/elj/jilt/2001_2/sloan/
13. 508 of the Rehabilitation Act: www.section508.gov
14. Directive 2004/18/EC of the European Parliament and of the Council of 31 March 2004 on the coordination of procedures for the award of public works contracts, public supply contracts and public service contracts http://europa.eu.int/smartapi/cgi/sga_doc?smartapi!celexapi!prod!CELEXnumdoc&lg=en&numdoc=32004L0018&model=guichett and Directive 2004/17/EC of the European Parliament and of the Council of 31 March 2004 coordinating the procurement procedures of entities operating in the water, energy, transport and postal services sectorshttp://europa.eu.int/smartapi/cgi/sga_doc?smartapi!celexapi!prod!CELEXnumdoc&lg=en&numdoc=32004L0017&model=guichett
15. International Workshop on Accessibility Requirements for Public Procurement in the ICT Domain http://europa.eu.int/information_society/policy/accessibility/regulation/pubproc_ws_2004/a_documents/procurement_conference_report_fin%20nocover.pdf
16. Engelen, J. The work of the eAccessibility experts group, (2003) http://www.etsi.org/cce/proceedings/6_1.htm
17. Rosenbrock,K.H. (2003) The Role of Standards Organizations in ACCESSIBILITY for ALL, powerpoint presentation from CEN/CENELEC/ETSI Conference, Accessibility for All 2003 http://www.etsi.org/cce/proceedings/ppt/1
18. CENELEC (2003) eAccessibility brochure http://www.cenelec.org/Cenelec/Code/Frameset.aspx
19. British Standards Institute (BSI) BSI 7000-6 BS7000-6 Guide to managing inclusive design available at http://www.bsi-global.com/index.xalter
20. Miesenberger, K., Feyerer, E., Wohlhart, D.: ICT and Assistive Technologies in Teachers Education and Training, in: Miesenberger, K., Klaus, J., Zagler, W. (eds): Computers Helping People with Special Needs - 8th International Conference, ICCHP, Linz, Austria, July 2002, Proceedings, Springer Heidelberg, 2002
21. Miesenberger, K.: 'equality = e-quality' 'design for all' und 'accessibility' als Grundlage für eine demokratische, offene und inklusive Gesellschaft, in: Feyerer, E.; Pammer, W. (Hrsg.): Qual-I-tät und Integration, Beiträge zum 8. PraktikerInnenforum, Universitätsverlag Rudolf Trauner, Linz 2004

22. Darzentas J S (2003). Design for All: Designing for Diversity. In: Kameas A, Streitz N (eds), Tales of the Disappearing Computer, pp.165-176. Patras, Greece: CTI Press.
23. Regan, B. Accessibility and design: a failure of the imagination Proceedings of the 2004 international cross-disciplinary workshop on Web accessibility (W4A) Pages: 29 – 37, 2004
24. 24. Harwin, W.S. Niche Product Design, a new model for Assistive Technology, Proceedings of the 3rd TIDE Congress (1998) http://www.stakes.fi/tidecong/832Niche.htm
25. 25. Wolpawa,J.R., Birbaumerc, N, McFarlanda, D.J., Pfurtschellere, G., Vaughan, T.M. Brain–computer interfaces for communication and control, Clinical Neurophysiology 113 (2002) 767–791 http://www.andrew.cmu.edu/user/jker/bcireview.pdf
26. Signore, O.: Culture across Cultures: a Quality Challenge - Experts Meeting on European Cultural Heritage on the Web – 2001, available from http://www.w3c.it/papers/cultureAcrossCultures.pdf
27. Stephanidis, C. (1999). Designing for all in the Information Society: Challenges towards universal access in the information age. ERCIM ICST Research Report http://www.ics.forth.gr/hci/files/ICST_Report.pdf
28. Darzentas J S, Darzentas J (2003). Teaching Design for All in Critical Motivations and New Dimensions. In: Proceedings of 2nd Educational Design Conference, ICSID (International Council of Societies of Industrial Design), pp. 69-73. Hannover, Germany: IF International Forum Design GmbH.

An Efficient Scheme of Update Robust XML Numbering with XML to Relational Mapping[*]

Hyunchul Kang and Young-Hyun Kim

School of Computer Science and Engineering, Chung-Ang University,
Seoul, 156-756, Korea
hckang@cau.ac.kr, yhkim@dblab.cse.cau.ac.kr

Abstract. Despite the emergence of XML as a standard for data exchange on the Web, XML update processing has received little attention. One of the issues that need to be addressed in XML update processing is the *update robustness* of the *XML numbering scheme* employed for efficient containment query processing. In this paper, we propose an efficient update robust XML numbering scheme. It works for both ordered and unordered XML data and fits well in *XML to relational mapping*. The proposed scheme was implemented with a relational database as the XML stores. The experimental results showed that our scheme is more efficient than the previous one.

1 Introduction

Since the emergence of XML as a standard for data exchange on the Web, research on efficient management of XML data has been actively conducted. The *XML numbering* (also called *node numbering or labelling*) schemes have received hot attention in recent years [2,4,5,7,8,10-12]. When an XML document is stored, some numbers could be assigned to its elements. Such numbering is employed to efficiently process *containment queries* for which identifying the *structural relationship* among the elements is needed. These numbers represent the *ancestor-descendant* and *parent-child relationship* among the elements, playing a key role in *structural query processing*.

In a popular XML numbering scheme where an XML document is modelled as a node-labelled ordered tree, each node is assigned four numbers, *(docid, begin : end, level)*. Docid is document identifier. The begin:end pair or *range* is assigned by the *preorder traversal* of the tree where the begin value determines the total order of the tree nodes in the preorder traversal. Level is the level of the node in the tree. For example, for the XML document in Fig. 1a, its tree representation excluding the text with the assigned begin:end pairs is in Fig. 1b. Given two nodes x and y, x is an ancestor of y iff $docid(x) = docid(y)$ and $begin(x) < begin(y) \leq end(y) \leq end(x)$. That is, the begin:end range of x (ancestor) contains that of y (descendant). With an additional condition, $level(y) = level(x)+1$, x is the parent of y.

This *range-based* XML numbering scheme with minor variations for the end value assignment has been widely adopted in investigating XML query processing

---

[*] This work was supported by the Ministry of Information and Communication of Korea through the research grant of IITA.

[1,3,11,12]. However, none of those work considered *XML update*. One of the issues that need to be addressed in XML update processing is the *update robustness* of the XML numbering scheme employed for containment query processing. With insertions and deletions of elements, the structural change occurs in the document, and even a small update could cause the most of such numbers for the updated XML document to be renumbered. As such, the XML numbering scheme which avoids renumbering altogether or as much as possible against updates is desirable. Such scheme is called *update robust, durable,* or *persistent*.

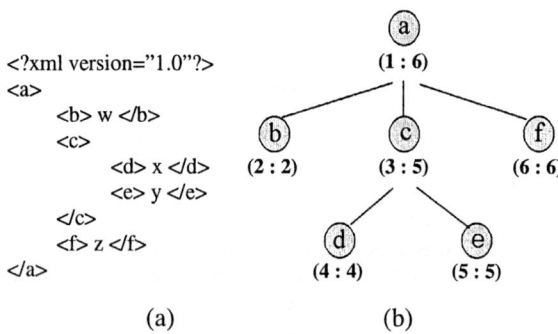

Fig. 1. Example XML Document & Numbering

In this paper, we propose an efficient update robust XML numbering scheme. It is range-based, and above all, very simple while not undermining the structural query processing power at all. It works for both ordered and unordered XML data and fits well in *XML to relational mapping* which is now a very popular vehicle for XML storage and retrieval. The rest of this paper is organized as follows. Section 2 surveys the related work. Section 3 proposes our numbering scheme. Section 4 gives some concluding remarks with the summary of implementation and performance evaluation.

2 Related Work

The first update-conscious XML numbering scheme which is range-based was proposed in [7]. It employs *sparse* numbering for future insertions, and the begin:end range assignment is different from the one shown in Fig. 1b. The begin:end range is replaced by *order : size* pair. Its meaning is as follows (see Fig. 2 for an example) [1]:

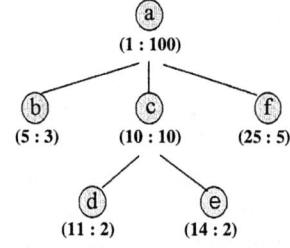

- For node y and its parent x, $order(x) <$ $order(y)$ and $order(y) + size(y) \leq order(x) + size(x)$. It means that the range [$order(x)$, $order(x) + size(x)$] contains the range [$order(y)$, $order(y) + size(y)$].

Fig. 2. Numbering Scheme of [7]

- For two sibling nodes x and y, if x is the predecessor of y in preorder traversal, $order(x) + size(x) < order(y) + size(y)$.

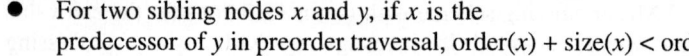
 we do not explicitly mention the docid as well as the level as in Fig. 1b for the ease of explanation.

Thus, for two given nodes x and y, x is an ancestor of y iff order(x) < order(y) ≤ order(x) + size(x). Thus, this scheme has the same structural query processing power as that of Fig. 1b.

The potential of update robustness of the numbering scheme of [7] was explored in [4]. Nine different cases in inserting a node into an XML tree were identified, and for each of them, the conditions among the order:size pairs of the involved nodes that should be met after insertion were presented. For two consecutive nodes X and Y of the tree in preorder traversal, Y can either be (i) the first child of X, (ii) the next sibling of X, or (iii) the next sibling of node A which is ancestor of X (see Fig. 3 without inserted node B). When a new node Z is inserted between X and Y, there are similarly three cases between X and Z, and also three cases between Z and Y, leading to a total of nine possibilities. For example, if Z is inserted as the first child of X, then the aforementioned conditions after insertion are as follows:

1. Y becomes the first child of Z: order(X) < order(Z) < order(Y) and order(Y) + size(Y) ≤ order(Z) + size(Z) ≤ order(X) + size(X).
2. Y becomes the next sibling of Z under X: order(X) < order(Z) and order(Z) + size(Z) ≤ order(Y).
3. Y becomes the next sibling of an ancestor of Z: order(X) < order(Z) and order(Z) + size(Z) ≤ order(X) + size(X).

Other cases are omitted. Initially, the order:size values are assigned as integer with appropriate *gaps* between the order values of the consecutive nodes. When some insertion occurs, the reserved integers are used such that the conditions like the above should be met. When all the integers are used up in a certain gap, the *floating-point numbers* are employed. The problem with this scheme is that it needs to search the stored XML document for the order:size values involved, which may be time-consuming depending on the tree topology involved. Besides, when the XML source is stored in a relational database, the translation of the requested XML insertion into SQL counterpart is very complicated.

In [2], a scheme of *quartering* a begin:end range or the gap between two consecutive ranges with the floating-point numbers to accommodate insertions was proposed. This scheme is to support XML updates in XRel system [11] where the begin:end values are assigned with the byte counts of the XML document. Therefore, the problem with this scheme is that incorrect node numbers are supposed to be generated after insertions, and it needs to pay some cost to fix it. To provide a correcting function, the update records need to be logged.

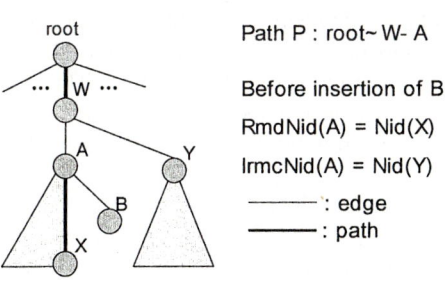

Fig. 3. Insertion of Leaf Element B

An alternative approach to update robust XML numbering is *prefix-based* one [5,8,10]. In this approach, the node label is a *bit string* and for two nodes x and y, x is an ancestor of y iff the bit string of x is a prefix of that of y. In [5], a prefix labeling scheme was proposed where for a node x whose label is denoted as $L(x)$, its first child is labeled as L(x)0, the second as L(x)10, the third as L(x)110, and the *i*-th $(1...1)^{i-1}0$. An improved scheme where the size of the bit string assigned to the nodes is reduced was proposed in [8]. Similar scheme that uses a variant of Dewey encoding scheme was proposed in [10]. The main problems with prefix-based schemes are two-fold: (1) The assigned labels are of variable size which could be usually too long, leading to difficulties in space-efficient implementation. (2) They cannot efficiently handle updates to the ordered XML documents.

3 The Proposed Update Robust XML Numbering Scheme

In this section, we propose our novel update robust XML numbering scheme which is range-based. The most distinctive advantage of our scheme is its *simplicity* in the sense that unlike all the previous schemes surveyed in the previous section, the popular numbering scheme of Fig. 1b which was devised without the consideration of updates is used while (1) not undermining the structural query processing power at all and (2) processing efficiently all types of XML updates from simple to complex ones regardless of whether the document is unordered or ordered. Another advantage is that XML update operations can be simply mapped to SQL. These advantages mean that our proposal could be easily incorporated into the existing XML query processing engines to support updates as well that were developed without the consideration of updates with the popular numbering schemes like the one in Fig. 1b especially when its underlying XML storage is based on a relational DBMS.

3.1 Imaginary Rightmost Child

The begin:end pair in our scheme is denoted as *Nid* (node identifier) and *RmdNid* (*rightmost descendant* node identifier) pair. Fig. 1b shows the (Nid:RmdNid) pairs assigned in the preorder traversal of the tree.[2] Intuitively speaking, for node *n*, RmdNid(*n*) is the identifier of the rightmost descendant node of *n*. But its formal definition is slightly different from such intuition because of insertions and deletions of the nodes. Another key number associated with each node which is *not* explicitly stored is *IrmcNid* (*imaginary rightmost child* node identifier). Intuitively speaking, for node *n*, IrmcNid(*n*) is the value that would have been assigned as the Nid to the imaginary rightmost child node of *n* in the preorder traversal of the tree. This number plays the key role in our update robust numbering scheme though it is *not* explicitly stored. Fig. 4a is Fig. 1b augmented with IrmcNid in boldface (i.e., the third number).

Definition 1 [IrmcNid and RmdNid]. For node *n*, IrmcNid(*n*) is the identifier of the immediate successor node of *n*'s rightmost descendant in the preorder traversal of the XML tree if one exists. Otherwise, IrmcNid(*n*) is the identifier of the imaginary rightmost child of the root. RmdNid(*n*) is some value *z* such that $x \leq z <$ IrmcNid(*n*) where *x* is the identifier of the rightmost descendant node of *n*. □

---

[2] In Fig. 1b, we assumed that Nid's are monotonically increased by 1 in the preorder traversal starting at 1 from the root. In general, however, the numbering could be *sparse*, leaving some *gaps* between consecutive nodes for future insertions.

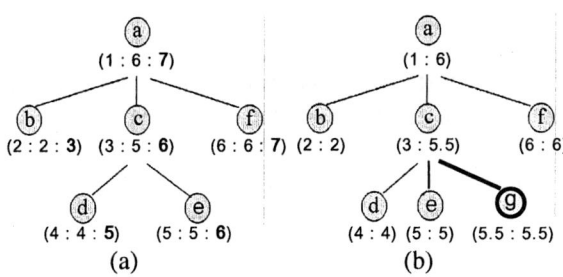

Fig. 4. Nid, RmdNid, IrmcNid

For example, RmdNid(c) and IrmcNid(c) in Fig. 4a are 5 and 6, respectively. c's rightmost descendant is e and e's immediate successor in the preorder is f. Thus, IrmcNid(c) = Nid(f) = 6, and Nid(e) ≤ RmdNid(c) < IrmcNid(c) (i.e., 5 ≤ RmdNid(c) < 6). RmdNid(e) and IrmcNid(e) are also 5 and 6, respectively. The rightmost descendant of every leaf node is itself. Thus, IrmcNid(e) = Nid(f) = 6, and Nid(e) ≤ RmdNid(e) < IrmcNid(e) (i.e., 5 ≤ RmdNid(e) < 6). For a or f in Fig. 4a, no immediate successor of their rightmost descendants (i.e., f) in the preorder exists. In that case, the Nid of the imaginary rightmost child of the root which is 7 in the initial assignment of the Nid's in Fig. 4a is employed. Thus, IrmcNid(a) and IrmcNid(f) are both 7.

Lemma 1. For node n in XML document D, IrmcNid(n) = minimum {Nid(m)'s for all nodes m such that Nid(m) > RmdNid(n), IrmcNid(root)}. □

3.2 XML Update Processing

Now let us consider XML updates. We first deal with the insertion of a leaf element to an unordered document. Modification of the text, deletion/insertion of an arbitrary subtree both to unordered and to ordered documents are treated next.

Insertion of a Leaf. Suppose leaf element <g> v </g> is inserted as a child of c in the XML document of Fig. 1. Node c has already two children d and e. As such, in inserting node g, its position matters. For ease of explanation, let us now assume that the XML document is an *unordered* one, and as suggested in [9], the new element is inserted as the *rightmost* child. Such an insertion requires renumbering the Nid's of some nodes in the document if the preorder is to be kept. In our XML numbering scheme, however, all the current Nid's remain unchanged, Nid(g) and RmdNid(g) are assigned, and just *local adjustments* on the relevant RmdNid's take place. Fig. 4b shows the result of g's insertion. 5.5 were assigned to both Nid(g) and RmdNid(g). Accordingly, RmdNid(c) was adjusted to 5.5. As a result, the preorder is kept. These were done as follows:

1. IrmcNid(c) is computed as the *minimum* of Nid(n)'s for all nodes n such that Nid(n) > RmdNid(c).
2. Both Nid(g) and RmdNid(g) are set to x = (RmdNid(c) + IrmcNid(c))/2.
3. Let y be RmdNid(c), and for all nodes n along the path from the root to c such that RmdNid(n) = y, RmdNid(n) is set to x.

We call this procedure *XInsAdjust*. Note that IrmcNid(c) is computed first because it is *not* the one stored. Now let us apply XInsAdjust to an arbitrary XML document. We assume that for every node n of an XML document, RmdNid(n) was *initialized* to the identifier of the rightmost descendant node of n. Then, the properties that hold with XInsAdjust can be stated in the following Lemmas (refer to Fig. 3), leading to Theorem 1. All the proofs are omitted for the interest of space.

Lemma 2. Consider path P whose target node is A in XML document D where the Nid's have been assigned in the preorder. Suppose leaf element B is inserted as the rightmost child of A and XInsAdjust is done. Then, the following holds:

(1) RmdNid(A)- < Nid(B) < IrmcNid(A)- where $x(A)$- dnotes A's x before insertion,
(2) RmdNid(B) = Nid(B) □

Lemma 3. Consider path P whose target node is A in XML document D where the Nid's have been assigned in the preorder. Suppose leaf element B is inserted as the rightmost child of A and XInsAdjust is done. Then, for each node C that appears along path P *including* A such that RmdNid(C)- = RmdNid(A)-, RmdNid(C) = Nid(B). □

Theorem 1. Consider path P whose target node is A in XML document D where the Nid's have been assigned in the preorder. Suppose leaf element B is inserted as the rightmost child of A and XInsAdjust is done. Then, the Nid's of all the nodes in D including B remain in the preorder without renumbering the Nid's at all. □

Initial Assignment of Nid's and Gap Split. For the *initial* assignment of Nid's to the nodes of an XML tree, at least two parameters, R and G, need to be given as the Nid of the root and as the *gap* between two consecutive Nid's in the preorder traversal, respectively (In Fig. 1b, $R = G = 1$.) G need not be static for all the two consecutive Nid pairs. For the pairs that expect more insertions than others, large G is desirable, whereas for those expecting little insertions, small G will do. Such *dynamic gap control* in the initial assignment of Nid's would be possible when the schema of XML documents (e.g., DTD or XML Schema) is available and/or the patterns of document versioning (or evolution) is known a priori. Nid and RmdNid should be of type *real* because the Nid of the inserted leaf B could be selected from the gap between RmdNid(A) and IrmcNid(A) as a floating-point number where node A is the parent of B. It is desirable to maintain Nid and RmdNid as integers or as real numbers with a small number of fractional digits. For example, the calculation (RmdNid + IrmcNid)/2 in XInsAdjust could be refined to $\lfloor$(RmdNid + IrmcNid)/2$\rfloor$ to truncate the fractional part unless it gets equal to RmdNid.

More fundamental issue here is how the gap is to be *consumed* for insertions. The calculation (RmdNid + IrmcNid)/2 in XInsAdjust results in balanced split of the given gap. More sophisticated gap consumption through *unbalanced gap split* when the information on the expected insertion patterns is available is desired in order to accommodate more insertions in a gap. These issues are beyond the scope of this paper where static gap and balanced gap split are assumed.

Performance Issues. One performance issue in XInsAdjust is how efficiently IrmcNid(n) is computed where n is the parent of the leaf to be inserted. When an *indexing* of nodes on Nid is provided, IrmcNid(n) is easily obtained if RmdNid(n) is given without accessing the nodes to check their Nid's and/or RmdNid's at all. Just the index search is necessary as follows: (1) The index entry whose Nid value is equal to RmdNid(n) is located. (2) The Nid value of its immediate successor entry is IrmcNid(n) if one exists. (3) Otherwise (that is, if the located entry in (1) is the one with the maximum Nid value), IrmcNid(n) is returned as RmdNid(root) + G where G is the gap between two consecutive nodes as mentioned in the previous paragraph. For this latter case, we need to maintain the up-to-date RmdNid(root) in a designated place. Another issue is how efficiently the RmdNid's affected due to the insertion at node n are searched to be adjusted. The nodes whose RmdNid's need adjustment are confined in a path from the root to n (refer to Lemma 3). Among them, only those nodes m such that RmdNid(m) = RmdNid(n) before the insertion are the targets for adjustment. They could be easily found when an indexing of nodes on RmdNid is provided.

Insertion of a Leaf into an *Ordered* XML Document. Ordering support is important for many XML applications. The procedure XInsAdjust described above can be easily extended to deal with insertions into the ordered documents. There are three cases for ordered insertions. For element A, new leaf element B can be inserted (1) as the rightmost child of A, (2) at the right of some designated child of A, say C, but not as the rightmost one, and (3) as the leftmost child of A at the left of the former leftmost, say C. The first case was already dealt with for unordered documents. XInsAdjust that needs to be exercised for the other two cases is very similar to that for the first case, and in fact simpler because the adjustment of RmdNid's is *not* necessary. In the second and the third cases, both Nid(B) and RmdNid(B) are set to (RmdNid(C) + IrmcNid(C))/2 and to (Nid(A) + Nid(C))/2, respectively.

Insertion of a *Subtree*. As for inserting a subtree t consisting of n nodes as a rightmost subtree of node p, a series of leaf element insertions will complete the job. The root of t is inserted first as the rightmost child of p, and then the root's leftmost child is inserted as the rightmost child of the root, and so on. However, such a procedure suggested in the previous work is tedious. More efficient method is to treat t as an independent XML tree tobe numbered, inserting it *as a whole* in the following two steps: (1) The *initial assignment* of Nid's to the nodes of t is done with R = RmdNid(p)+k and $G = k$ where k = (IrmcNid(p)–RmdNid(p))/(n+1) while their RmdNid's are also assigned accordingly. (In other words, n numbers, k_1, ..., k_n where k_1 = RmdNid(p)+k , k_n = IrmcNid(p)–k , and $k_i = k_{i-1}+k$, are generated by dividing the gap between RmdNid(p) and IrmcNid(p) into n+1 segments, and these are assigned to the nodes of t as their Nid's in the preorder traversal.) (2) For all the nodes q along the path from the root to p such that RmdNid(q) = RmdNid(p) before insertion of t, RmdNid(q) is adjusted to IrmcNid(p)–k. Meanwhile, inserting t *not* as the rightmost subtree of p can be done similarly and in a simpler way. (Refer to the cases of order-sensitive insertion.)

Deletion and Modification. Contrary to the insertion, adjustment of RmdNid against the deletion of a subtree or the modification of the text to keep the Nid's in the preorder is *not* necessary. As for modification, the structure of the XML document remains intact, and thus, it is obvious that no adjustment is needed. As for deletion, though it causes structural change in the document, skipping adjustment does not damage the preorder of the Nid's nor correct functioning of further updates against the same document due to the flexible definition of IrmcNid and RmdNid in Definition 1.

3.3 XML Update to SQL Mapping

When XML documents are stored in a relational database with our numbering scheme, the processing of XML updates should be expressed in SQL. In this section, we show that generation of such SQL expressions is very feasible. To simply convey how such XML to relational mapping is accomplished, we assume that only *one* unordered XML document D is stored in a *single* table as in the Edge table approach proposed in [6] where attributes are treated the same as elements. Below, such a single table is called *XMLOneTab*, and presumed to consist of columns Nid, TagName, Npath, Text, ParentNid, and RmdNid. Each node of D is mapped to a tuple of XMLOneTab. For path P whose target node is A and leaf element B, say <b> xyz </b>, to insert B as the rightmost child of A, the following three SQL statements are generated and executed in that order where *:irmcnid*, *:tname*, *:npath*, and *:text* are the host variables:

SELECT min(Nid) **INTO** :irmcnid **FROM** XMLOneTab
WHERE Nid > (**SELECT** RmdNid **FROM** XMLOneTab **WHERE** Npath = 'P')

INSERT INTO XMLOneTab
  SELECT (RmdNid+:irmcnid)/2, :tname, :npath, :text, Nid, (RmdNid+:irmcnid)/2
  FROM XMLOneTab **WHERE** Npath = 'P'

UPDATE XMLOneTab **SET** RmdNid = (RmdNid+:irmcnid)/2
WHERE RmdNid = (**SELECT** RmdNid **FROM** XMLOneTab **WHERE** Npath = 'P')
    AND Npath **NOT LIKE** 'P/%'

The SELECT statement is to compute IrmcNid(A). It is assumed that the imaginary rightmost child of the root is also stored as a tuple of XMLOneTab with proper Nid value. Another assumption is that the inner subquery returns just one instance of A. It is not a strong assumption when it comes to XML update as shown in [9]. (Usually, there would be more predicates in addition to Npath = 'P' in the inner WHERE clause to uniquely designate the target of update.) If that is not the case, however, a slight extension with the stored procedures will do. As for the aggregate function *min*(Nid) in the SELECT clause, an experiment revealed that it was quickly computed only through accessing the B^+ tree index on Nid rather than accessing and sorting all the tuples satisfying the outer WHERE clause.

    The INSERT statement is to insert a tuple for newly inserted element B where the host variables are assigned as :irmcnid = IrmcNid(A), :tname = 'b', :npath = 'P/b',

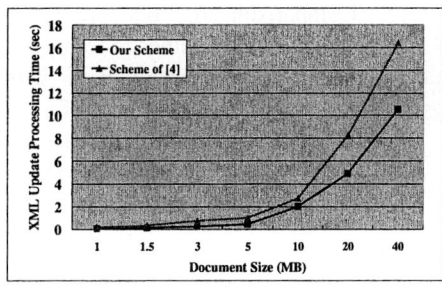

Fig. 5. Time for Element Insertion with Increase of XML Document Size

and :text = '*xyz*'. It fetches the tuple for node *A* by giving condition Npath = '*P*' in the WHERE clause, comes up with the tuple for node *B*, and insert it.

The UPDATE statement is to adjust the RmdNid's affected by the insertion of node *B*. The second condition, Npath NOT LIKE '*P/%*', in the outer WHERE clause is to exclude *A*'s descendants for adjustment. Only those nodes along path *P* inclusive of *A* might be affected as far as RmdNid is concerned (refer to Lemma 3 and Fig. 3).

The SQL statements to delete a subtree or to modify the text of a leaf into *new_value* are the followings where *P* is the path to the root of the subtree to be deleted or the path to the leaf whose text is to be modified:

DELETE FROM XMLOneTab **WHERE** Npath = 'P' OR Npath **LIKE** 'P/%'
UPDATE XMLOneTab **SET** Text = 'new_value' **WHERE** Npath = 'P'

4 Concluding Remarks

In this paper, we proposed an efficient scheme of update robust XML numbering, which is range-based. Compared with other range-based numbering schemes in the literature [2,4,7], our scheme is the most efficient in the sense that (1) it is the *simplest* to handle updates while providing the same structural query processing power, (2) it is the *easiest* in mapping XML updates to SQL.

As proof of concept, our numbering scheme with relational mapping was implemented with Oracle 9*i* in Java on Windows 2000 Server. The relational table schema for XML storage and structural query processing was based on XRel [11] with its begin:end pair replaced by our Nid:RmdNid pair. To compare the performance of our scheme with a previous one, we also implemented the scheme of [4]. Fig. 5 shows the average times for random insertion of a leaf element into the DBLP document assumed to be unordered as the *size* of the document increases. It was revealed that our scheme is less sensitive to the size of the document to be updated than that of [4]. Fig. 6 shows the average times for inserting a leaf element into the catalog document generated in XBench and assumed to be unordered as the *level* of the node under which the insertion is made increases. Since the height of the DBLP document tree is too short for such an experiment, we switched to the catalog document whose tree could be of up to 8 levels. Random insertions of leaves were made at each of level 3 through 7. It was shown that our scheme outperformed that of [4] at every level.

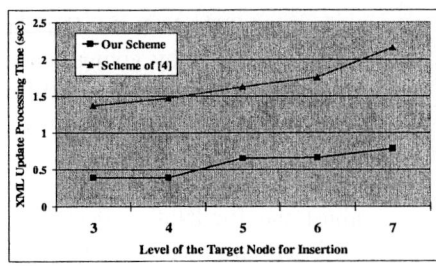
Comparison of our scheme with prefix-labeling schemes in terms of space and update processing time with the same and fixed number of bits for Nid:RmdNid pair and for the bit string (in prefix-labeling) of each node is currently under way.

Fig. 6. Time for Element Insertion at Different FLevel of XML Document

References

1. Al-Khalifa, S. et al.: Structural Joins: A Primitive for Efficient XML Query Pattern Matching. Proc. Int'l Conf. on Data Engineering (2002) 141-152
2. Amagasa, T. et al.: QRS: A Robust Numbering Scheme for XML Documents. Proc. Int'l Conf. on Data Eng. (2003) 705-707
3. Bruno, N. et al.: Holistic Twig Joins: Optimal XML Pattern Matching. Proc. ACM SIGMOD Int'l Conf. on Management of Data (2002) 310-321
4. Chien, S. et al.: Storing and Querying Multiversion XML Documents using Durable Node Numbers. Proc. 2nd Int'l Conf. on Web Information Systems Eng. (2001) 232-241
5. Cohen, E. et al.: Labeling Dynamic XML Trees. Proc. of ACM Int'l Symp. on PODS (2002) 271-281
6. Florescu, D., Kossmann, D.: Storing and Querying XML Data Using an RDBMS. IEEE Data Eng. Bulletin, Vol. 22. No. 3. (1999) 27-34
7. Li, Q., Moon, B.: Indexing and Querying XML Data for Regular Path Expressions. Proc. Int'l Conf. on VLDB (2001) 361-370
8. Lu, J. and Ling, T.: Labeling and Querying Dynamic XML Trees. Proc. APWeb. (2004) 180-189
9. Tatarinov, I. et al.: Updating XML. Proc. ACM SIGMOD Int'l Conf. on Management of Data (2001) 413-424
10. Tatarinov, I. et al.: Storing and Querying Ordered XML Using a Relational Database System. Proc. ACM SIGMOD Int'l Conf. on Management of Data (2002) 204-215
11. Yoshikawa, M. et al.: XRel: A Path-Based Approach to Storage and Retrieval of XML Documents Using Relational Databases. ACM Trans. on Internet Technology, Vol. 1, No. 1. (2001) 110-141
12. Zhang, C. et al.: On Supporting Containment Queries in Relational Database Management Systems. Proc. ACM SIGMOD Int'l Conf. on Management of Data. (2001) 425-436

On Maintaining XML Linking Integrity During Update

Eric Pardede[1], J. Wenny Rahayu[1], and David Taniar[2]

[1] Department of Computer Science and Computer Engineering, La Trobe University,
Bundoora VIC 3083, Australia
{ekpardede, wenny}@cs.latrobe.edu.au
[2] School of Business Systems, Monash University
Clayton VIC 3800
David.Taniar@infotech.monash.edu.au

Abstract. It is a fact that XML update has become more important with the rise of XML Database usage. How update operations affect XML documents needs to be investigated further. In this paper we propose a methodology to accommodate update without violating the XML document's constraints. The constraints maintained are those that are defined using XML linking language: *xlink* and *xpointer*. This language, which is standardized by W3C, is used to provide referential purpose among XML documents or nodes.

Since XML link is embedded as an attribute in an XML instance, our proposal can be used for schema-less documents and for instance-based reference. We propose a set of functions that perform checking mechanisms before updates. The proposed method can be implemented in various ways, and in this case we use XQuery language.

1 Introduction

XML update is a considerably new research for semi-structured data community. There was a perception that XML document does not need frequent update [1]. However, due to the dynamic nature of the web application, we have witnessed a growing number of XML documents that require regular update.

XML update methodologies have been discussed in a few works [1, 11]. Moreover, the researches on constraints preservation during update operations are even fewer. [7] discussed the issues on capturing semantic constraints during XML update. However, it is applicable to schema-based XML documents.

Unfortunately, very frequently we have to store schema-less XML document in our database repository. Furthermore, for some cases –even to the XML with schema- the constraints are not schema-based but more likely to be instance-based.

In this paper we aim to propose a methodology to update XML document without schema bound. The methodology will preserve the referential integrity constraint that exists through some XML linking technologies: *XML Linking Language (XLink)* [14] and *XML Pointer Language (XPointer)* [15].

After the introduction, in section 2 we will discuss the motivation for this work. Section 3 provides basic information regarding the XML linking technologies. Section 4 proposes the methodologies for the update operations insertion, deletion and replacement. In section 5 we provide some analysis of the work including our contributions and limitations. Finally our work will be concluded in section 6.

2 Motivation

XML document is a collection of information that is structured in a tree of nodes. Most of the time, we find an XML node contains information that is not explicitly stated in that particular node. The actual information is stored in another resource and the former node just refers to that resource. The different location between the two sources has raised the issues of referential integrity. How the reference links between the sources are maintained becomes a crucial task.

We have been familiar with the concept of primary and foreign keys since the early era of relational model. The excellent support of referential integrity in this data model is the strength that has given RDB an important position in the database communities. Since then, any emerging data model requires referential integrity maintenance support as a basic requirement. It also applies for the XML data model that has been mentioned as the new era of data format in the database communities.

The common way of referential integrity implementation in XML data model is *ID/IDREF* or *key/keyref*. For update, some XML database products use ID/IDREF to maintain the referential integrity [3, 4, 5, 9, 10]. Another approach uses key/keyref and embeds the referential integrity maintenance in XML query language [7]. Despite the contribution and usability, there is a limitation to these approaches. The system needs to know the ID/IDREF and key/keyref through a schema before it can employ the rules. There are two main cases where the current approaches will not work.

- **XML documents without schema.** The non-schema-based XML document is mostly used by the document-side of the XML community [1]. Even though the XML document is rarely structured, its elements can refer to other sources and thus referential integrity is still necessary.

    For example, it is unlikely to store the following XML with a schema. Inside one element, there is a link that refers to another source. If we need to update the document that affects these link types, the referential integrity might be violated.

    ```
    <Article title="Linking Language in XML Document">
      <firstchapter>
        <para> This work is the continuation of our previous work on
        <article (!--link to another source)> Referential Mechanism in
        XML Data Model </article>. Our main interest………<para>
    ..</firstchapter>..</Article>
    ```

- **Instance-based reference instead of schema-based.** In this case, the same element of two instances that are validated by a schema refers to different sources. Thus, identifying the reference through IDREF/keyref will not be correct. For example, the following schema-based XML document cannot use the IDREF/keyref because the reference links are instance-based. The element authors actually refer to different sources type.

```
<Book title="Database Systems" (!--put link to Amazon website--)>
   <author (!--a link to "author" doc-->Margo Channing</author>
   <author>Eve Harrington</author>
   <author (!--a link to a personal site--> Addison DeWitt</author>
..<publisher>XML Publishing</publisher>
</Book>
```

These two cases can be implemented by using XLink and XPointer. The links will be embedded as attributes to a specific element. In these attributes we identify the source to be referred. We will briefly explain this technology in the section 3.

To the best of our knowledge, there is no work that has discussed the maintenance of these links after an update operation. [6] highlights three different XML update strategies. None of them has preserved various constraints (including referential integrity) of the updated XML document. [7] has attempted to answer the limitations. However, the latter work is only applicable for schema-based constraints. Therefore, in this work we intend to further develop these previous works by investigating the schema-less XML document constraint maintenance during update.

3 XML Linking Technologies

Linking in XML allows users to create a complexly structured network of distributed resources [17]. W3C has been working on two important linking standards, namely XLink and XPointer. While the former has been released as a recommendation [14], the latter is still a candidate for recommendation [15].

XLink is used to describe complex associations between resources identified using Unified Resource Identifiers (URI). Sometimes XLink has added XPointer component for more detailed reference.

XPointer, which is built on the *XML Path Language* (*XPath*) [13], is used as the basis for the fragment identifier for any URI reference that locates a resource [2]. The fragment may be a single XML element or a collection of elements. The only limitation is that the resources must be an XML Document. An example of the links is shown as follows. It has an XPointer embedded in a simple XLink.

```
<Article xmlns:xlink="http://www.w3.org/1999/xlink/namespace/"
   title="Linking Language in XML Document">
   <firstchapter>
      <para> (!--.........--) our previous work on <article
      xlink:href="Article2.xml#xpointer(title('Referential Mechanism in
      XML Data Model'> Referential Mechanism in XML Data Model
      </article>. Our main interest.........</para>
..</firstchapter>
</Article>
```

We can associate a link in XML with directed labeled graph. The resources are the vertices and the link itself is the edge of the graph. Based on the vertices we can classify the links into three types (see Fig.1): (i) a link between two resources in the same collection, (ii) a link between two resources in the same database, but from different collection and (iii) a link between two resources from different database.

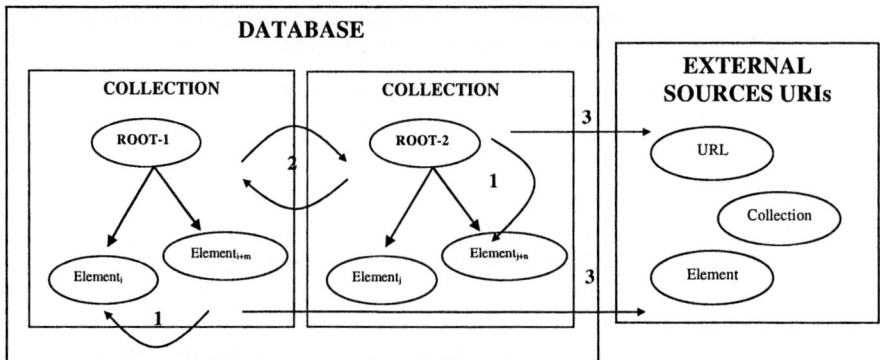

Fig. 1. XML Link Classification based on the Vertices

Among different links, it is hard to maintain the persistent reference using link type 3. There are current content management systems that contain modules for checking external links regularly. However, it usually draws a high overhead cost and manual intervention and thus, is not desirable [17].

The information about the links can be stored into separate database called *linkbase*. Every time the XML document is processed, the linkbase will be loaded. In our work, we aim to utilize the linkbase not only to store the links but also as a look up reference before an update operation. By doing so, we can prevent broken links in our XML documents. An example of a linkbase is shown below.

We can separate the linkbase into two: *internal linkbase* and *external linkbase*. In the latter, we will not have control on the content and therefore some mechanisms that monitor the changes in the content might be required.

```
<?xml version="1.0"?>
<IntLinkBases>
  <Xref xlink:type="xlink:extended"
        xmlns:xlink="http://www.w3.org/1999/xlink">
    <SOURCE xlink:type="locator"
            xlink:href="Article1.xml#xpointer(//article('Referential
        Mechanism in XML Data Model'))" xlink:label="src"/>
    <DESTINATION xlink:type="locator"
            xlink:href="Article2.xml#xpointer[@title='Referential Mecha-
        nism in XML Data Model'])" xlink:label="dest"/>
    <GO   xlink:type="arc" xlink:from="src" xlink:to="dest"/>
  </Xfref>  <!-- More References -->  </IntLinkBase>
```

4 Proposed Methodology

Next, we propose the methodologies for different updates. The aim is to preserve the integrity constraints in the updated documents. The constraints are specified in the linking language attributes of the document. Each operation will have unique checking functions. These functions are generic methods that can be implemented in different ways. In this work we use XQuery as the standard language for XML Database [16].

Finally, to register the links in this work we use a simplified form of linkbase. The linkbase here contains *only* the destination of every link found in our XML document. We do not record the source of the links. Registering full linkbase components, especially with XQuery, is a considerably costly work. Furthermore, we can still check referential integrity by ensuring that the destination of every link is valid.

4.1 Methodology for Insertion

The first update operation is for attribute insertion (see Fig.2). For attribute target, we start checking whether it is a link attribute. If it is a link, our proposed method checks the link destination. For internal link, we check whether the actual destination already exists in our database.

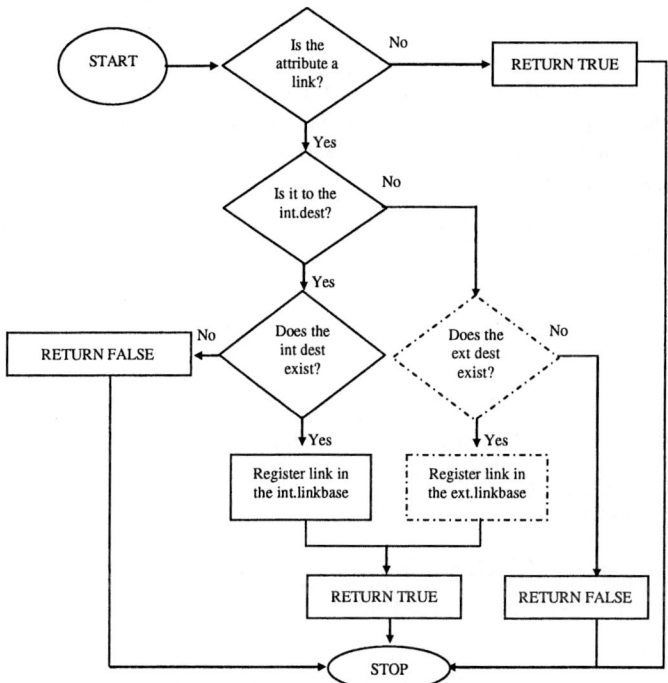

Fig. 2. Checking Function for Insertion

If the link attribute contains a valid link, we need to register it in one of our linkbases. Internal linkbase keeps the links to any source inside our database. On the other side, if the link refers to an external source, we register it in the external linkbase. Note that at this stage we do not perform checking for external destination and thus, in the figure it is shown in dotted lines.

This function will return either TRUE or FALSE value. The former indicates that we can proceed with the insertion. The latter indicates that we need to cancel the insertion. In another words, we use the restricted mechanism.

Now we have proposed a methodology for attribute insertion, what would happen if the target is element(s), which can contain link attribute?

There are two solutions for this problem. First, we propose another checking mechanism for element insertion. However, this option has a potential problem. For instance let us say, we want to insert a group of elements (node 1 to 10). Element in node 1 has a link attribute which refers to element in node 9. When we validate this link attribute, it will return false because the destination does not exist. Hence, we do not select this option.

The second option is the simpler solution. We will insert all the element(s) without any link checking. Once it is done, we insert the attribute links using checking mechanism in fig. 2. The weakness of this option is the additional overhead to separate the attribute link from the element(s). However, this overhead will only be significant if the size of insertion is high. In addition, to get a higher integrity data, some overhead is inevitable.

Finally, to implement the method in fig. 2 we propose to use XQuery. The first function *CheckFromLink* below checks whether the attribute is a link or not. If it is, it checks the destination and whether it exists. The second function, *InsertIntLink*, is called by the *CheckFromLink* if the destination of internal link exists. This second function registers the link in our linkbase.

```
FUNCTION CheckFromLink ($dbName, $docName, $parentName, $attName, $att-
ValueNew) RETURN BOOLEAN
  {LET $linkOutDoc=doc($attValueNew)
      $target:=$dbName.doc($docName)//$linkOutDoc

  RETURN
    IF $attName='xlink'
      THEN (IF contains($attValueNew, $dbName)
            THEN (IF exists ($target)
                  THEN InsertIntLink($dbName,$docName,$attValueNew)
                  ELSE FALSE}
            ELSE TRUE}
      ELSE TRUE}

FUNCTION InsertIntLink ($dbName, $docName, $attValueNew) RETURN BOOLEAN
  {FOR $intLink in $dbName.doc($docName)/linkbase/internal
    UPDATE $intLink{INSERT <linkTo>$attValueNew</linkTo>}
  RETURN TRUE}
```

The following example illustrates the use of our checking function when we want to insert a link attribute in an element. In this example we want to insert the link attribute to "Author.xml#xpointer[@id='MC12']" in the element "Book.xml/author". When we call the *CheckFromLink* function, the link will be registered inside the internal linkbase.

```
FOR $g IN myDatabase.document("Book.xml")/Book[@title="Database System"]
    $p IN $g/Author[1]
LET $attname := xlink
    $attvalue := Author.xml#xpointer[@id='MC12']
UPDATE $p{
WHERE CheckFromLink("myDatabase", "Book.xml", "Author", "xlink",
"Author.xml#xpointer[@id='MC12']")
        UPDATE $p{
            INSERT new_att ($attname, $attvalue)}}
```

4.2 Methodology for Deletion

The main concern for deletion is to avoid deleting a target that is referred by other node(s). In our methodology, we perform the checking to the linkbase before any deletion. If any internal source actually refers to the target node, we have to cancel the deletion. If the deletion can be performed, we also need to remove all links to the targeted node from the linkbase.

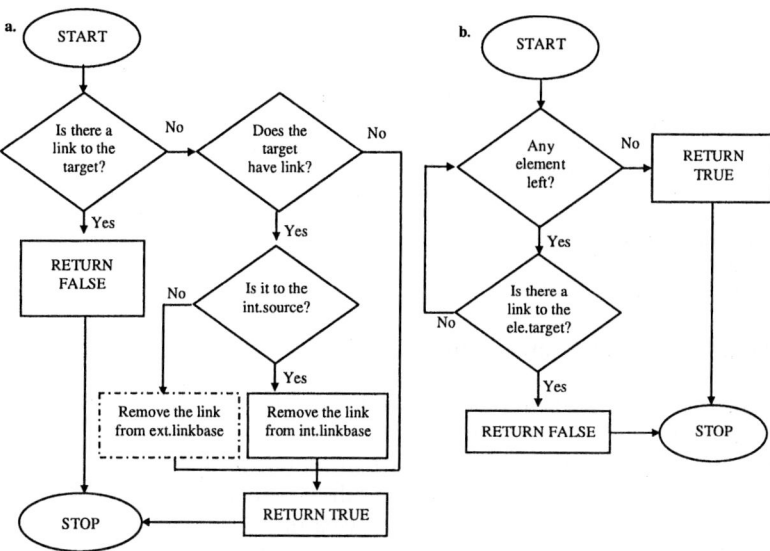

Fig. 3. Checking Function for Deletion

The checking function is shown in flow chart below (see Fig. 3). Fig.3a is the process for attribute deletion and Fig.3b is for the element deletion. As in insertion, checking of attribute link during element deletion is not desirable. However, we still need to separately check the element deletion, because an element might be specified as a destination in the linkbase. If the target is element(s), we suggest removing the attribute links attached in the element(s) before start deleting the element(s).

Using XQuery, we propose three functions below. The first function *CheckToLink* checks whether the attribute is being referred. It also checks if the attribute is a link to another internal destination. If it is, the second function, *DeleteIntLink* is called to remove the link from the linkbase. The final function, *ChecktoLinkEle* checks whether the element is being referred in the linkbase.

```
FUNCTION CheckToLink ($dbName, $docName, $parentName, $attName, $attVal-
ueOld) RETURN BOOLEAN
  {FOR $intLink in $dbName.doc($docName)/linkbase/internal
   LET $target := $intLink[linkTo =
          $dbName.$docName//$parentName#xpointer
          ($attName('$attValueOld'))][1]
 RETURN
   IF not exists ($target)
     THEN (IF $attName = 'xlink')
```

```
            THEN (IF contains ($attValueOld, $dbName)
                 THEN DeleteIntLink($dbName, $docName, $attValueOld)
                 ELSE TRUE)
            ELSE TRUE)
        ELSE FALSE}

FUNCTION DeleteIntLink ($dbName, $docName, $attValueOld)
  {FOR $intLink IN $dbName.doc($docName)/linkbase/internal
   LET $target := $intLink[linkTo = $attValueOld][1]
       UPDATE $intLink{
          DELETE $target}
   RETURN TRUE}

FUNCTION CheckToLinkEle  ($dbName,    $docName,   $parentName,   $eleName)
RETURN BOOLEAN
  {FOR $intLink in $dbName.doc($docName)/linkbase/internal
   LET $target := $intdest[linkTo =
            $dbName.$docName//$parentName#xpointer($eleName)]
   RETURN
       IF not exists ($target)
          THEN TRUE
          ELSE FALSE}
```

4.3 Methodology for Replacement

A replacement can be seen as a deletion followed by an insertion. Therefore, the previous processes can be utilized. Before a replacement, we need to check the linkbase. If the old target is referred by another internal source, we have to cancel the replacement. Otherwise, we have to check whether the new target has a link. Depending on the existence of the referred source, we replace the old link direction with the new direction in the linkbase. These processes are applicable to attribute replacement. For element(s), the process will be the same as in Fig.3b because we still assume that insertion of new element(s) will have to be separated by its attribute insertion.

Using XQuery, we propose two additional functions, *CheckFromToLink* and *ReplaceIntLink*. The first function checks whether the old attribute is not being referred and the new attribute has a valid point to which to link. The second function performs the replacement operation in the internal linkbase. Due to the page limitation, we have not shown the flow chart and the XQuery functions for this update operation.

5 Discussions

In any kind of database, having persistent references is important for integrity purpose. Specifically for XML, persistent references also avoid ubiquitous broken links and invalid search engine results [17]. The current solution is done by regularly checking the broken links and manually rectifying any that are found. This of course requires a considerable effort. Our aim in this work is to avoid the broken links in the first place by checking before updating a document.

In this paper we propose the methodologies for updating XML documents. They aim to maintain the referential integrity embedded in the XLink. We differentiated the method based on the update type into three operations: deletion, insertion, and replacement. For implementation, we apply the query language XQuery not only because it is the most complete W3C-standardized language [12], but also because it is used by most NXD products [3, 4, 5, 8, 9, 10].

Our methodology makes the following contributions, compared to current practices.

a. We use XLink and XPointer for referential purposes instead of ID/ IDREF or key/keyref. While the latter approach is more suitable for database community of the XML user, the usage of linking language is appealing to both database and document communities. Our proposed solution can answer the needs for link maintenance in schema-less XML or instance-based link in XML document

b. We classify the XLink based on the source and the target, and subsequently make classification of link database, linkbase. The more organized database can help the management of XLink and XPointer

c. Our checking mechanisms avoid the possibility of database anomalies after XML update. The anomalies can be created for example by inserting a non-valid link or deleting a referred link. It is noted that in current practice, there is no mechanism that stops users inserting an internal link to a non existence node, etc. These practices will become the potential integrity problems.

Despite our contribution, this work also has some limitations that give room for improvement in the future. First, the use of linkbase in this work is simplified. While the standard linkbase [17] can cover the source, destination and the link between both, our method only automates the storing of the destination. Despite this limitation however, the information of a destination is sufficient for referential integrity checking.

Second, our mechanisms only check links in the internal linkbase. There are a few reasons behind this decision. First, we cannot ensure that the links from our database to external source will always be valid because they are beyond our control. There are current content management systems that contain modules for checking external links regularly. However, they usually draw a high overhead cost and manual intervention and thus, are not desirable. Second, this might be based on a strategic reason such as in the case of commercial purpose [17]. Third, linking to external resources is still a questionable practice to be considered because it might involve some property right issue.

The last issue is that we do not know how the links are to be interpreted and presented. As it is mentioned in [2], in this area of XML the W3C is far ahead of the rest of the world. No concrete implementations of any of the specifications exist yet. Even though the standard is unlikely to change, the adoption has been slow so far. Therefore the implementations may differ from the standards and the standards may have to be reworked [17]. The implementation so far will be application-dependent.

6 Conclusion

We propose checking methodologies to preserve the referential integrity during an update of XML. The proposal checks the references that are implemented by using

XLink and its subsequent XPointer. Since these reference mechanisms do not require a schema, our methods can be used in schema-less XML documents as well as in instance-based reference in XML documents.

We propose a set of checking functions that are triggered before the actual update takes place. The checking functions check the destination of the link, register or remove the link in the database, and perform other operations before deciding whether the update can be proceeded or not. For implementation we apply the methodology into XQuery as the recent standard for XML query language.

Our methodologies avoid the referential integrity violation that can be caused by updating the XML links inside an XML document. These methods have added some new functionality to the current XML data management practice and they are usable both for database and document communities.

References

1. Bourett, R.: XML and Databases. http://www.rpbourret.com/xml/XMLAndDatabases.htm, (2003)
2. Holzner, S. *Real World XML*, New Riders Publishing, Indianapolis, (2003)
3. Ipedo.: Ipedo XML Database, http://www.ipedo.com/html/products.html, (2004)
4. Jagadish, H. V., Al-Khalifa, S., Chapman, A., Lakhsmanan, L. V. S., Nierman, A., Paprizos, S., Patel, J. M., Srivastava, D., Wiwattana, N., Wu, Y., Yu, C.: TIMBER: A native XML database. VLDB Journal, Vol. 11, No. 4. (2002) 279-291
5. Meier, W.M.: eXist Native XML Database. In Chauduri, A.B., Rawais, A., Zicari, R. (eds): XML Data Management: Native XML and XML-Enabled Database System. Addison Wesley (2003) 43-68
6. Pardede, E., Rahayu, J.W. and Taniar, D.: Preserving Aggregation Semantic Constraints in XML Document Update. LNCS 3306 (2004) 229-240
7. Pardede, E., Rahayu, J.W. and Taniar, D.: Preserving Conceptual Constraints during XML Updates, to appear in International Journal of Web Information Systems (2005)
8. Robie, J.: XQuery: A Guided Tour. In Kattz, H. (ed.): XQuery from the Experts. Addison Wesley (2004) 3-78
9. SODA Technology.: SODA. http://www.sodatech.com/products.html, (2004)
10. Software AG.: TAMINO, Number One in XML Management. http://www1.softwareag.com/corporate/products/tamino/default.asp, (2004)
11. Tatarinov, I., Ives, Z.G., Halevy, A. Y., Weld, D. S.:Updating XML. *ACM SIGMOD* (2001) pp.413-424
12. Vlist, E. V-D.: XML Schema, O'Reilly, Sebastopol (2002)
13. W3C, XML Path Language, http://www.w3.org/TR/xpath/, Nov 1999
14. W3C, XML Linking Language, http://www.w3.org/TR/xlink/, Jun 2001
15. W3C, XML Pointer Language, http://www.w3.org/TR/xptr/, Aug 2002
16. W3C: XQuery 1.0:An XML Query Language. http://www.w3.org/TR/xquery, Oct 2004
17. Wilde, E., Lowe, D.: XPath, XLink, XPointer, and XML – A Practical Guide to Web Hyperlinking and Transclusion, Addison Wesley, Boston, (2002)

On the Midpoint of a Set of XML Documents

Alberto Abelló[1], Xavier de Palol[1], and Mohand-Saïd Hacid[2]

[1] Dept. de Llenguatges i Sistemes Informàtics, U. Politècnica de Catalunya
[2] LIRIS- UFR d'Informatique, U. Claude Bernard Lyon 1

Abstract. The WWW contains a huge amount of documents. Some of them share the subject, but are generated by different people or even organizations. To guarantee the interchange of such documents, we can use XML, which allows to share documents that do not have the same structure. However, it makes difficult to understand the core of such heterogeneous documents (in general, schema is not available). In this paper, we offer a characterization and algorithm to obtain the midpoint (in terms of a resemblance function) of a set of semi-structured, heterogeneous documents without optional elements. The trivial case of midpoint would be the common elements to all documents. Nevertheless, in cases with several heterogeneous documents this may result in an empty set. Thus, we consider that those elements present in a given amount of documents belong to the midpoint. A exact schema could always be found generating optional elements. However, the exact schema of the whole set may result in overspecialization (lots of optional elements), which would make it useless.

1 Introduction

The web is a powerful medium for human communication and dissemination of information. Consequently, the web has become a popular knowledge base, where people add documents (private, educational and organizational) and navigate through its content. The rapid growth of information makes it sheer impossible to find, organize, access and maintain the information as the users require. For scalability reasons, one important aspect consists in distilling those documents and extract valuable knowledge from them. There exist multiple formats for information sources, ranging from unstructured data to highly structured. The term semi-structured data has emerged to describe data that has some structure but neither regular, nor known a-priori to the system. It is precisely for this reason that semi-structured documents are self-describing.

The importance of knowing the structure (or schema) of a set of documents has been largely described in the literature. For example, [BGM04] outlines its importance on integrating and analyzing structure of the WWW. On the other hand, [ABS00] points out that a known structure would also facilitate the storage and encourage queries. It is key to improve the access methods to the data, thus availing query optimization and data interchange among companies.

Here we consider a certain kind of semi-structured data, in particular, XML documents. XML has been adopted as standard for data interchange, availing the integration of heterogeneous information sources. A *well-formed* XML document is a document that conforms to the XML syntax rules in [W3C04] (roughly, markups nest properly and attributes are unique). Moreover, a *valid* XML document is a document that is *well-formed* and also conforms to the rules of its DTD. A DTD contains the declarations that provide a grammar for a class of documents. It determines the *element*s and *attribute*s that appear in a document, i.e., the name, type and constraints on every *element* and *attribute*.

As defined in [W3C04], an XML document primarily consists of a nested hierarchy of *element*s with a single root. *Element*s can contain character data (concepts) and *child element*s, in both cases the *element* can have *attribute*s. *Child element*s consist either of a *sequence* list of *element*s or a *choice* list of *element*s. The standard states that *element*s in a *sequence* must be ordered.

The *choice* construct in a DTD indicates that one, and only one, *element* in the *choice* list of contents should appear in the document. The *choice* construct is the key to find a perfect typing. In the rare case that all the documents belong to the same class and use the same terms, the *choice* construct is not needed to find a perfect typing. Otherwise, in a grammar that lacks the *choice* construct we cannot find a common schema, so we have to approximate it. If we use the *choice* construct, finding the schema is reduced to find the best grammar expression for each *element* (for example following a normal form like [AGW01]), so that all *element*s in the document belong to the corresponding grammar. Nevertheless, a perfect schema, one DTD that is followed by all the documents, may arise an overspecialization problem. Some works have overcome overspecialization by using clustering techniques to approximate typing [NAM98, SPBA03]. Such approximated schemas are called inexact schemas in [Wid99].

We aim at finding a common schema for a set of correct semi-structured documents. We take an inexact approach based on the resemblance of documents, thus using the structure similarity among the documents under study. We call this common schema the midpoint. We use the resemblance family of functions in [BGM04], which take into account extra *element*s both in the document and in the DTD. We could then redefine *valid* XML document as a document whose resemblance to its DTD is above a given threshold. The main contribution of this paper is the characterization of the midpoint in terms of a resemblance function and offer an efficient algorithm to obtain it. Although our approach deals with DTDs, it also applies to XML schemas.

The structure of the paper is as follows. In the next section we review the work related with our method. Section 3 presents the formalization of XML into Description Logics that we propose. Section 4 characterizes the midpoint. Section 5 shows an efficient algorithm to obtain the midpoint. Finally, section 6 gives the general conclusions and points out our future work.

2 Related Work

Several authors worked on the generation of DTDs from XML data. A relevant result is [NAM98], which explains how we can get a well structured schema (i.e. not a DTD) approximating the documents. [JOKA02] describes an implementation of an algorithm to generate a DTD followed by an XML document. [SPBA03] classifies the documents in different classes and gets one DTD per class of documents. This is a good solution if there are a few classes with not many documents or *elements* each. However, it may result in lots of different classes or optional *elements* for every class, if we are dealing with a huge amount of heterogeneous documents.

[NAM98] pays attention to inexact schemas, outlining that the size of a perfect typing may be the order of the data set, prohibiting its use for query optimization and interfaces. Therefore, we are not searching a perfect typing but a human-friendly, computationally-tractable, and graphically-representable approximation. To this end, we should use some kind of resemblance or distance. The first option would be tree edit distance (like in [BdR04]), but it results in high complexity (see [ZS89]). Therefore, the most promising option is structure similarity. [NAM98] uses Manhattan distance (i.e. the number of different descendants/ancestors of two *elements*). [BB95] shows different more elaborate resemblance measures. Among those, [SPBA03] uses $\frac{|elem(d_1) \cap elem(d_2)|}{max(|elem(d_1)|,|elem(d_2)|)}$, while in [BGM04] $\frac{|elem(d_1) \cap elem(d_2)|}{|elem(d_1) \cap elem(d_2)| + \alpha \cdot |elem(d_1) \setminus elem(d_2)|, \beta \cdot |elem(d_2) \setminus elem(d_1)|)}$ is used. We took this last measure, because it is more general, and allows to distinguish lack of *elements* in one side or another.

3 Formalizing XML Documents by Means of DL

As we can see in [ABS00], an XML document uses to be thought as a rooted tree. A rooted tree is an acyclic graph $(\mathcal{N},\mathcal{E})$, that has no more than one root. $\mathcal{N}$ is a set of nodes and $\mathcal{E}$ a set of edges. An edge e is an ordered pair of nodes (n_{source}, n_{target}). A node is a leaf, if it is not the source of any edge in $\mathcal{E}$. Along this paper we will use Description Logics (DL) notation to formalize those trees.

Since we only take into account *element* tags (not contents), we are not actually interested in XML documents, but in a restricted class of DTDs that can be automatically generated from one XML document. We assume that we have a pseudo-*DTD* exactly matching each document. These are obtained just parsing documents and eliminating data (leaving *element* tags). Thus, a pseudo-*DTD* does not contain *choice*, nor *unnumbered repetitions*, nor *optional elements*, nor *any*. The problem tackled in this paper is that of finding a true-*DTD* from a set of pseudo-*DTD*s. From here on, we will use the term *DTD* for the pseudo-*DTD*s, and "midpoint" for the true-*DTD*.

Regarding XML attributes, they could be used to match different *element* tags. For example, "<a ID='Id1'>" could be identified with "<b ID='Id1'>" in spite of the different tag name. Nevertheless, that is not the aim of this paper. Representing the information either as an attribute or a child is just a design decision. Thus, from here on, without loss of generality, we will consider XML *attributes* as XML *child elements* without further nesting structure.

As stated in [W3C04], *child elements* are ordered. Order is an important characteristic for documents. However, in databases unordered data can be pro-

document 1: <a><b><c>Hello</c></b><d><e>Bye</e></d></a>
document 2: <a><b></b><d></d></a>
document 3: <a><d><e>Bye</e></d></a>
document 4: <a><d><e>Bye bye</e></d></a>

$dtd_1 = \exists a.(\exists b.\exists c.\top \sqcap \exists d.\exists e.\top)$
$dtd_2 = \exists a.(\exists b.\bot \sqcap \exists d.\bot)$
$dtd_3 = \exists a.\exists d.\exists e.\top$
$dtd_4 = \exists a.\exists d.\exists e.\top$

element: C (concept)
child element: $\exists r.C$ (existential quantification)
sequence: $\sqcap$ (conjunction)
PCDATA or String: $\top$ (top)
EMPTY: $\bot$ (bottom)

Fig. 1. DL representation of an XML document

cessed more efficiently, so it uses to be considered in that way (for example in DOM and SAX). Therefore, we will assume that order is not relevant for us.

We will consider a set of documents as a knowledge base, which comprises two components, i.e. TBox (the terminology, we could recognize it as the schema) and ABox (the assertions about individuals, or instances). As explained in [BCM+03], the TBox contains concepts, and to define a formal semantics of the logic we use an interpretation $\mathcal{I}$. An interpretation is a pair $[\Delta^{\mathcal{I}}, \cdot^{\mathcal{I}}]$, where $\Delta^{\mathcal{I}}$ is the domain (a non-empty set), and $\cdot^{\mathcal{I}}$ is an interpretation function that assigns to every atomic concept A a set $(A^{\mathcal{I}} \subseteq \Delta^{\mathcal{I}})$ and to every atomic role r a binary relation $(r^{\mathcal{I}} \subseteq \Delta^{\mathcal{I}} \times \Delta^{\mathcal{I}})$. Inductively, this is extended to non-atomic concepts as follows (C and D are concepts, and r is a role):

$$\bot^{\mathcal{I}} = \emptyset$$
$$\top^{\mathcal{I}} = \Delta^{\mathcal{I}}$$
$$(C \sqcap D)^{\mathcal{I}} = C^{\mathcal{I}} \cap D^{\mathcal{I}}$$
$$(\exists r.C)^{\mathcal{I}} = \{a \in \Delta^{\mathcal{I}} \mid \exists b. \, (a,b) \in r^{\mathcal{I}} \wedge b \in C^{\mathcal{I}}\}$$

As exemplified in figure 1, we will represent a *document* or piece of document by a concept "C". An unordered *sequence* of pieces of documents will be represented by a conjunction "$C \sqcap D$". Data types (i.e. *PCDATA* and *string*) will be represented by the top concept "$\top$", while an empty *element* (i.e. *EMPTY*) will be represented by bottom concept "$\bot$". Finally, *children* will be represented by means of existential quantification "$\exists element.C$". Actually, existential quantification allows the presence of more than one *element* of the same kind. Nevertheless, as stated before, we do not consider such repetitions. Our formalization allows the usage of DL algorithms like "Subsumption" and "Least Common Subsumer":

Subsumption (also known as "Query Containment" in other areas and noted "$C \sqsubseteq D$", if C is subsumed by D) shows whether one concept is more general than another (i.e. one set contains the other for all interpretations). For example, $dtd_1 \sqsubseteq dtd_3$.

$$C \sqsubseteq D \Leftrightarrow \forall \mathcal{I} : C^{\mathcal{I}} \subseteq D^{\mathcal{I}}$$

Least Common Subsumer ("LCS" from here on) results in the subsumer of a set of concepts that is subsumed by any other subsumer of the set of documents. LCS uses to be applied to learning from examples, and bottom-up construction of knowledge bases. For example, $lcs(dtd_2, dtd_4) = \exists a.\exists d.\top$.

$$L = lcs(C_1, .., C_n) \Leftrightarrow \forall i : C_i \sqsubseteq L \wedge \not\exists D : (\forall i : C_i \sqsubseteq D \wedge D \sqsubseteq L)$$

4 Characterization of the Midpoint

Given a set of DTDs, we would like to find the DTD that has the maximum number of common *elements* wrt the set, at the same time that minimizes the *elements* being in the DTD not in the documents and those in the documents not in the DTD. We will call such DTD the midpoint of the set. In order to characterize the midpoint, we will use the resemblance family of functions used in [BGM04].

$$r : (DTD, setOfDTDs) \mapsto [0,1]$$

$$r(C, E) = \frac{w_c(C, E)}{w_c(C, E) + \alpha \cdot w_p(C, E) + \beta \cdot w_m(C, E)} \quad for\ \alpha, \beta \in \mathbb{R}^+$$

By instantiating α and β we get the concrete function we would like to use (notice that only if $\alpha = \beta$ the resemblance will be symmetric). Positive real values can be assigned to these parameters, weighting the importance of finding plus (*elements* in some DTD that do not appear in the midpoint) and minus (*elements* in the midpoint that do not appear in some DTD) *elements* respectively. The function relies now on three simpler ones that obtain the size of common, plus, and minus *elements*.

$$w_c(C, E) = \sum_{dtd \in E} size(lcs(C, dtd))$$
$$w_p(C, E) = \sum_{dtd \in E} (size(dtd) - size(lcs(C, dtd)))$$
$$w_m(C, E) = \sum_{dtd \in E} (size(C) - size(lcs(C, dtd)))$$

Any result in this paper does not depend on how we compute the size of a DTD. We only impose that the size of a DTD is smaller than the size of adding an *element* to that DTD. Therefore, from here on, in the examples we will assume that every *element* contributes to the size of a DTD with one unit independently of its position in the document. For example, $size(dtd_1) = 5$ and $size(dtd_2) = size(dtd_3) = 3$. A general, more complex and accurate algorithm for obtaining the size of a DTD is given in [BGM04].

$$r(\exists a.\exists d.\top, \{dtd_2, dtd_3\}) = \frac{2+2}{(2+2)+\alpha \cdot (1+1)+\beta \cdot (0+0)} = \frac{4}{4+4}$$
$$r(\exists a.\exists d.\exists e.\top, \{dtd_2, dtd_3\}) = \frac{2+3}{(2+3)+\alpha \cdot (1+0)+\beta \cdot (1+0)} = \frac{5}{5+2+3}$$
$$r(\exists a.(\exists b.\top \sqcap \exists d.\top), \{dtd_2, dtd_3\}) = \frac{3+2}{(3+2)+\alpha \cdot (0+1)+\beta \cdot (0+1)} = \frac{5}{5+2+3}$$
$$r(\exists a.(\exists b.\top \sqcap \exists d.\exists e.\top), \{dtd_2, dtd_3\}) = \frac{3+3}{(3+3)+\alpha \cdot (0+0)+\beta \cdot (1+1)} = \frac{6}{6+6}$$

Fig. 2. Example of multiple midpoints

At this point, it is also important to notice that there may exist more than one DTD maximizing the resemblance (i.e. more than one midpoint). For example, let be $\alpha = 2$ and $\beta = 3$. In this case, as we can see in figure 2, four different DTDs result in the same resemblance to $\{dtd_2, dtd_3\}$. Since this is the maximum resemblance, we can choose the midpoint of $\{dtd_2, dtd_3\}$ among those four DTDs. Theorem 1 states that one of the possible midpoints of the set can be obtained by a conjunction of LCS of the documents. Due to lack of space, proofs have been omitted.

Theorem 1. it Given a set of DTDs $E = \{dtd_1,...,dtd_n\}$, and being B_i branches of the form $\exists r_{B_i}^1.\exists r_{B_i}^2...\exists r_{B_i}^{l_i}.\top$ with $l_i \geq 1$

$$\exists S_1,...,S_p \in \mathscr{P}(E) : \forall B_1,...,B_q : r(\bigcap_{i=1..q} B_i, E) \leq r(\bigcap_{j=1..p} lcs(S_j), E)$$

Lemma 1. *There exists a DTD of the form $\bigcap_{k=1..p} lcs(S_k)$ maximizing the resemblance, so that $\forall 1 \leq i,j \leq p : (S_i \not\subseteq S_j)$.*

Corollary 1. *There exists a DTD of the form $\bigcap_{k=1..p} lcs(S_k)$ maximizing the resemblance, so that $p \leq \binom{|E|}{\lfloor\frac{|E|}{2}\rfloor}$*

5 Obtaining the Midpoint of a set of DTD

First of all, it is important to notice that depending on the values of α and β there are some trivial cases (as shown in table 1). If $\alpha = 0$, we do not mind having extra *element*s in the DTDs wrt the midpoint. Therefore, among the multiple solutions to the problem, we find $\exists element.\top$ (where "element" is the most frequent root *element* in the documents). If $\beta = 0$, we do not mind having extra *element*s in the midpoint wrt every individual DTD. Therefore, $\bigcap_{dtd \in E} dtd$ is among the solutions. Both equaling zero means that just by matching some *element*s in some DTD we get maximum resemblance (i.e. $\forall w_c \neq 0 : \frac{w_c}{w_c + 0w_p + 0w_m} = 1$). Thus, from here on, we will only consider the non-trivial case $\alpha \neq 0$ and $\beta \neq 0$.

This section shows the possibility of finding a midpoint just based on the appearances of each *element* in the set of documents. The first question to answer is how we could know whether the point in the search space we are treating is better than another candidate or not. Surprisingly, it is not necessary to get all plus and minus *element*s. By theorem 2, we know that all we need is the number of common *element*s between each of both DTDs and the set of DTDs E.

Theorem 2. it To decide whether the resemblance of a DTD C against a set of DTDs is better than that of another DTD C', it is only necessary to consider the common *element*s (neither plus, nor minus).

Table 1. Trivial cases on finding a midpoint

Midpoint	$\beta = 0$	$\beta \neq 0$
$\alpha = 0$	any	$\exists element.\top$
$\alpha \neq 0$	$\bigcap_{dtd \in E} dtd$	?

Proof. Let be $r(C, E) \geq r(C', E)$ ("s" stands for "size" if necessary).

$$\frac{w_C(C, E)}{w_C(C, E) + \alpha \cdot w_p(C, E) + \beta \cdot w_m(C, E)} \geq \frac{w_C(C', E)}{w_C(C', E) + \alpha \cdot w_p(C', E) + \beta \cdot w_m(C', E)}$$

$$\frac{\sum_{d \in E} s(lcs(C, d))}{\sum_{d \in E} s(lcs(C, d)) + \alpha \cdot \sum_{d \in E}(s(d) - s(lcs(C, d))) + \beta \cdot \sum_{d \in E}(s(C) - s(lcs(C, d)))}$$
$$\geq \frac{\sum_{d \in E} s(lcs(C', d))}{\sum_{d \in E} s(lcs(C', d)) + \alpha \cdot \sum_{d \in E}(s(d) - s(lcs(C', d))) + \beta \cdot \sum_{d \in E}(s(C') - s(lcs(C', d)))}$$

$$(\sum_{d \in E} s(lcs(C, d)))(\sum_{d \in E} s(lcs(C', d)) + \alpha \cdot \sum_{d \in E}(s(d) - s(lcs(C', d))) + \beta \cdot \sum_{d \in E}(s(C') - s(lcs(C', d))))$$
$$\geq (\sum_{d \in E} s(lcs(C', d)))(\sum_{d \in E} s(lcs(C, d)) + \alpha \cdot \sum_{d \in E}(s(d) - s(lcs(C, d))) + \beta \cdot \sum_{d \in E}(s(C) - s(lcs(C, d))))$$

$$(\sum_{d \in E} s(lcs(C, d)))(\alpha \cdot \sum_{d \in E} s(d) + \beta \cdot \sum_{d \in E} s(C')) \geq (\sum_{d \in E} size(lcs(C', d)))(\alpha \cdot \sum_{d \in E} size(d) + \beta \cdot \sum_{d \in E} size(C))$$

$$\frac{\sum_{d \in E} size(lcs(C,d))}{\alpha \cdot \sum_{d \in E} size(d) + \beta \cdot |E| \cdot size(C)} \geq \frac{\sum_{d \in E} size(lcs(C',d))}{\alpha \cdot \sum_{d \in E} size(d) + \beta \cdot |E| \cdot size(C')} \qquad \square$$

Once we know that it is only necessary to compare the common *elements*, the next question is how we could improve the resemblance. By lemma 2, we know that if adding a branch to the midpoint improves resemblance, all branches appearing the same number of times also improve it independently of their sizes. We may have thought that we have a set of possible improvements to check. Nevertheless, the branches with the same number of appearances do not generate alternative solutions, but all together belong to the same solution.

Lemma 2. *If adding a branch b to a concept increases its resemblance to the set, adding all branches appearing in the same number of DTDs than b will also improve its resemblance.*

Proof. Let be $C \sqsubset C'$ and $r(C, E) \geq r(C', E)$.

$$\frac{\sum_{d \in E} size(lcs(C, d))}{\alpha \cdot \sum_{d \in E} size(d) + \beta \cdot |E| \cdot size(C)} \geq \frac{\sum_{d \in E} size(lcs(C', d))}{\alpha \cdot \sum_{d \in E} size(d) + \beta \cdot |E| \cdot size(C')}$$

$$\frac{\sum_{d \in E}(size(lcs(C', d)) + (size(lcs(C, d)) - size(lcs(C', d))))}{\alpha \cdot \sum_{d \in E} size(d) + \beta \cdot |E| \cdot (size(C') + (size(C) - size(C')))} \geq \frac{\sum_{d \in E} size(lcs(C', d))}{\alpha \cdot \sum_{d \in E} size(d) + \beta \cdot |E| \cdot size(C')}$$

$$\frac{\sum_{d \in E} size(lcs(C', d)) + \sum_{d \in E}((size(lcs(C, d)) - size(lcs(C', d))))}{\alpha \cdot \sum_{d \in E} size(d) + \beta \cdot |E| \cdot size(C') + \beta \cdot |E| \cdot (size(C) - size(C'))} \geq \frac{\sum_{d \in E} size(lcs(C', d))}{\alpha \cdot \sum_{d \in E} size(d) + \beta \cdot |E| \cdot size(C')}$$

Which is true if and only if

$$\frac{\sum_{d \in E}((size(lcs(C, d)) - size(lcs(C', d))))}{\beta \cdot |E| \cdot ((size(C) - size(C')))} \geq \frac{\sum_{d \in E} size(lcs(C', d))}{\alpha \cdot \sum_{d \in E} size(d) + \beta \cdot |E| \cdot size(C')}$$

Since $C \sqsubset C'$ and it does not matter in which DTD the *elements* appear, but whether they appear or not, then $\frac{\sum_{d \in E}((size(lcs(C,d)) - size(lcs(C',d))))}{\beta \cdot |E| \cdot ((size(C) - size(C')))}$ can be seen as $\frac{\#appearance \cdot size(newElement)}{\beta \cdot |E| \cdot size(newElement)}$. Therefore, either adding an *element* or not does not depend on the size of the *element*, but on the number of times it appears in the DTDs. Thus, if adding an *element* is worthwhile, so it is adding any other *element* appearing the same number of times. $\square$

Finally, in corollary 2, we show that *elements* appearing more times result in higher improvement of resemblance. As a special case of this, if an *element* improves resemblance, its parents improve resemblance even more. Thus, before adding an *element* to the result, all its parents should have been added (which otherwise could not have been avoided).

Corollary 2. *Independently of its size, a branch b_1 appearing k_1 times in E improves the resemblance more than another b_2 appearing k_2 times if $k_1 > k_2$.*

Proof. Since, $k_1 > k_2$, then $\frac{k_1}{\beta \cdot |E|} > \frac{k_2 \cdot size(b_2)}{\beta \cdot |E| \cdot size(b_2)}$. Therefore, if b_2 improved the resemblance (i.e. we know that $\frac{k_2}{\beta \cdot |E|} \geq \frac{\sum_{d \in E} size(lcs(C,d))}{\alpha \cdot \sum_{d \in E} size(d) + \beta \cdot |E| \cdot size(C)}$), then b_1 improves it even more: $\frac{k_1}{\beta \cdot |E|} \geq \frac{\sum_{d \in E} size(lcs(C,d)) + (k_2 \cdot size(b_2))}{\alpha \cdot \sum_{d \in E} size(d) + \beta \cdot |E| \cdot size(C) + (\beta \cdot |E| \cdot size(b_2))}$ □

```
WDTD := ∅;
foreach dtd ∈ E do
    foreach branch ⊒ dtd do if [branch, k] ∈ WDTD
        then WDTD := WDTD \ {[branch, k]} ∪ {[branch, k + 1]};
        else WDTD := WDTD ∪ {[branch, 1]};
    endif; endforeach;
endforeach;
M := ⊤; m := | E |;
while ( m/(β·|E|) ≥ Σ_{dtd∈E} size(lcs(M,dtd)) / (α·Σ_{dtd∈E} size(dtd) + β·|E|·size(M)) )
    foreach branch ∈ getSubsetByWeight(WDTD, m) do
        M := M ⊓ branch;
    endforeach;
    m := m − 1;
endwhile;
```

Fig. 3. Algorithm based on appearance

From these theorems, we infer that we can build the midpoint of a set of DTDs from ⊤, by iteratively adding the most frequent *element* in the set of DTDs. Firstly, as we can see in figure 3, we build a weighted DTD (i.e. WDTD), whose contents are $\bigsqcap_{dtd \in E} dtd$, where each piece of branch is weighted depending on its number of appearances in the set of DTDs. Once we have the weight of each branch, we take the maximum possible weight (i.e. $| E |$) and check if it would improve resemblance from ⊤ (i.e. *PCDATA*) to the set of DTDs. If this maximum weight improves the resemblance, we add all branches having such weight to the result and get the next weight smaller than that. We loop adding another subset of branches while their weight improves resemblance.

The first phase of the algorithm is really cheap in terms of complexity. Taking into account that the number of possible children of an *element* should be small, building the weighted tree is linear in the number of *elements* in the set of documents, because we can find a piece of branch in "WDTD" just searching the children of the previous piece of branch we modified/added to "WDTD" (assuming a deep first search of the document we are treating). Regarding the second phase of the algorithm, all calls to "getSubsetByWeight" can be done in linear time in the number of different *elements*, if we kept the *elements* with the same weight in a list. Therefore, the space we need is linear in the number of different *elements* (not counting repetitions), while the time is also linear in the number of *elements* in the set of documents (counting repetitions).

$$WDTD = \{[\exists a.\top, 4], [\exists a.\exists b.\top, 2], [\exists a.\exists b.\exists c.\top, 1], [\exists a.\exists d.\top, 4], [\exists a.\exists d.\exists e.\top, 3]\}$$

$$M_0 = \top \qquad \qquad \frac{4}{4\beta} \geq 0$$
$$M_1 = \exists a.\exists d.\top \qquad \frac{3}{4\beta} \geq \frac{8}{14\alpha + 2 \cdot 4\beta}$$
$$M_2 = \exists a.\exists d.\exists e.\top \qquad \frac{2}{4\beta} \geq \frac{11}{14\alpha + 3 \cdot 4\beta}$$
$$M_3 = \exists a.(\exists b.\top \sqcap \exists d.\exists e.\top) \qquad \frac{1}{4\beta} < \frac{13}{14\alpha + 4 \cdot 4\beta}$$

Fig. 4. Candidate DTDs generated during the execution

If we run this algorithm on the DTDs in figure 1, it would result in the "WDTD" in figure 4 (each 2-upla consists of a branch and the number of documents that contain it). Thus, in the first loop, condition evaluates true (for $\alpha = \beta = 1$, and every *element* contributing by one to the size), and we add the branches appearing four times. Since it still evaluates true, we add those appearing three times, and eventually twice. Since the condition evaluates false for weight equal one, the corresponding branch does not belong to the solution.

$$WDTD = \{[\exists a.\top, \{dtd_1, dtd_2, dtd_3, dtd_4\}], [\exists a.\exists b.\top, \{dtd_1, dtd_2\}], [\exists a.\exists b.\exists c.\top, \{dtd_1\}],$$
$$[\exists a.\exists d.\top, \{dtd_1, dtd_2, dtd_3, dtd_4\}], [\exists a.\exists d.\exists e.\top, \{dtd_1, dtd_3, dtd_4\}]\}$$
$$M = lcs(dtd_1, dtd_2) \sqcap lcs(dtd_1, dtd_3, dtd_4) = \exists a.(\exists b.\top \sqcap \exists d.\exists e.\top)$$

Fig. 5. Obtaining the sets of documents that generate the midpoint

Obtaining the sets of documents that generate the midpoint (see theorem 1) a posteriori (once we know the midpoint) is easy with a small modification of the algorithm. All we need is that "WDTD" keep the set of the documents that contain every branch instead of just a counter of them. Thus, it is trivial to see that the conjunction of the LCS of the documents containing the leafs of the midpoint result in the midpoint. Figure 5 shows how it results in our example.

6 Conclusions and Future Work

Along this paper, we have studied the possibility of approximating the schema (DTD) of a set of XML documents. Based on a given measure of resemblance, we are able to find one midpoint of the set. This midpoint has been characterized in terms of conjunction of Least Common Subsumers of the documents. Moreover an efficient algorithm has also been presented to obtain it. The obtained resemblance may be improved by considering optional *elements* (eventually reaching the perfect typing).

As future work, we plan to deal with the problem of matching tag names, where ontologies can be used. The presence of optional elements in the schema may lead to the identification of equivalent tags from different sources.

Acknowledgements

Our work has been partially supported by the Spanish Research Program PRONTIC and FEDER under project TIC2002-00744.

References

[ABS00] S. Abiteboul, P. Buneman, and D. Suciu. *Data on the Web - From Relations to Semistructured Data and XML.* Morgan Kaufmann, 2000.

[AGW01] J. Albert, D. Giammarresi, and D. Wood. Normal Form algorithms for extended Context-Free Grammars. *Theoretical Computer Science*, 267(1-2):35–47, 2001.

[BB95] V. Batagelj and M. Bren. Comparing resemblance measures. *Journal of Classification*, 12(1):73–90, 1995.

[BCM+03] F. Baader, D. Calvanese, D. McGuinness, D. Nardi, and P. Patel-Schneider, editors. *The Description Logic Handbook.* Cambridge University Press, 2003.

[BdR04] U. Boobna and M. de Rougemont. Correctors for XML Data. In *Proc. of 2nd Int. XML Database Symposium (XSYM'04)*, volume 3186 of *LNCS*, pages 97–111. Springer, 2004.

[BGM04] E. Bertino, G. Guerrini, and M. Mesiti. A matching algorithm for measuring the structural similarity between an XML document and a DTD and its applications. *Information Systems*, 29(1):23–46, March 2004.

[JOKA02] J-S. Jung, D-I. Oh, Y-H. Kong, and J-K. Ahn. Extracting Information from XML Documents by Reverse Generating a DTD. In *Proc. of the EurAsia-ICT 2002*, volume 2510 of *LNCS*, pages 314–321. Springer, 2002.

[NAM98] S. Nestorov, S. Abiteboul, and R. Motwani. Extracting schema from semistructured data. In *Proc. ACM SIGMOD Int. Conf. on Management of Data (SIGMOD 1998)*, pages 295–306. ACM, 1998.

[SPBA03] I. Sanz, J. M. Pérez, R. Berlanga, and M. J. Aramburu. XML Schemata Inference and Evolution. In *Proc. of 14th Int. Conf. on Databases and Expert Systems Applications (DEXA'03)*, volume 2736 of *LNCS*, pages 109–118. Springer, 2003.

[W3C04] W3C. *Extensible Markup Language (XML) 1.0*, 3rd edition, February 2004.

[Wid99] J. Widom. Data Management for XML: Research Directions. *IEEE Data Engineering Bulletin*, 22(3):44–52, 1999.

[ZS89] Z. Zhang and D. Shasha. Simple Fast Algorithms for the Editing Distance Between Trees and Related Problems. *SIAM Journal on Computing*, 18(6):1245–1262, 1989.

Full-Text and Structural XML Indexing on B^+-Tree

Toshiyuki Shimizu[1] and Masatoshi Yoshikawa[2]

[1] Graduate School of Information Science, Nagoya University
shimizu@dl.itc.nagoya-u.ac.jp
[2] Information Technology Center, Nagoya University
yosikawa@itc.nagoya-u.ac.jp

Abstract. XML query processing is one of the most active areas of database research. Although the main focus of past research has been the processing of structural XML queries, there are growing demands for a full-text search for XML documents. In this paper, we propose XICS (XML Indices for Content and Structural search), novel indices built on a B^+-tree, for the fast processing of queries that involve structural and full-text searches of XML documents. To represent the structural information of XML trees, each node in the XML tree is labeled with an identifier. The identifier contains an integer number representing the path information from the root node. XICS consist of two types of indices, the COB-tree (COntent B^+-tree) and the STB-tree (STructure B^+-tree). The search keys of the COB-tree are a pair of text fragments in the XML document and the identifiers of the leaf nodes that contain the text, whereas the search keys of the STB-tree are the node identifiers. By using a node identifier in the search keys, we can retrieve only the entries that match the path information in the query. Our experimental results show the efficiency of XICS in query processing.

1 Introduction

The efficient processing of XPath [1] or XQuery [2] queries is an important research topic. Since the logical structure of XML is a tree, establishing a relationship between nodes such as parent-child or ancestor-descendant is essential for processing the structural part of queries. For this purpose, many proposals have been made such as structural joins, indexing, and node labeling [3,4,5,6,7,8].

In the last few years, the XML full-text search has emerged as an important new research topic [10,11]. However, efficient processing of XML queries that contain both full-text and structural conditions has not been studied well. In this paper, we propose XICS (XML Indices for Content and Structural search), which aims at high-speed processing of both full-text and structural queries in XML documents. An important design principle of our indices is the use of a B^+-tree. Because the B^+-tree is widely used in many database systems, building indices on a B^+-tree rather than creating a new data structure from scratch is an important design choice from a practical point of view. Several indices for XML documents using a B^+-tree have already been proposed. For example, XISS [3] is a node index approach on a B^+-tree. XISS is flexible in that the basic unit to be indexed is a node; however, to process a query, the query needs to be decomposed to a node unit, and then intermediate results need to be joined. The XR-Tree [4] is another tree-structured index for XML documents. In an XR-Tree, nodes in XML documents are labeled and stored in an extended B^+-tree index.

These indices efficiently preserve the ancestor-descendant or parent-child relationship between nodes; however, they do not take full-text searches into consideration. Recently, an indexing approach compatible with a full-text search for XML documents that integrates structure indexes and inverted lists was proposed in [14], which uses element names or keywords as a search key of indices. In our approach, to accelerate both the structures and full-text searches of XML documents, we constructed a B^+-tree in which the search keys are a pair of text fragment t and the node identifier of the leaf node which contains t. The node identifiers consist of two parts: a path identifier that indicates the path from the root node and the Dewey-order among sibling nodes sharing the same path identifiers. Search keys are first sorted by text fragments; hence, the index entries that contain the same text are clustered in the index. In such a cluster, entries representing nodes that have the same structure are clustered together. We call this type of index a COB-tree (COntent B^+-tree). We can answer XPath queries involving both structure and contents specifications such as "//title[contains(.,'XML')]" , which needs a join operation in the case of [14], by traversing the COB-tree only once.

A COB-tree is not suitable for processing structural queries such as "//title", because entries in a COB-tree are first sorted by text. Therefore, we constructed another type of B^+-tree called an STB-tree (STructure B^+-tree). In an STB-tree, the above-mentioned node identifiers are used as search keys. An important observation about an STB-tree is that entries are not clustered by element name. This is because path identifiers do not, in general, cluster nodes having the same element names. To manage this problem, we have developed a *search-key mapping* technique in which index entries are sorted by the lexicographical order of the reverse path (the element path from the node upward to the root node) and not by the path identifier itself. Reverse paths are effective in processing XPath queries that include "//". When searching, the index is traversed by mapping the reverse path to the path identifiers. By employing the *search-key mapping* technique, entries relevant to the nodes that have the same tag name are clustered in the index; hence, a query such as "//title" can be processed efficiently.

XICS consists of a COB-tree and an STB-tree. In general, when processing an XPath query having the *contains()* function, we can filter nodes using the text conditions or the structural conditions in the query. The use of the XICS can accelerate both types of filtering. We have implemented a COB-tree and an STB-tree using GiST [12]. The experimental results show the effectiveness of XICS.

2 PSP: A Node Labeling Scheme

In this section, we explain our node labeling scheme using the XML document shown in Figure 1. Figure 1 is a tree representation of an XML document. The ovals, triangles, rhombi, and strings in the rectangles represent element nodes, attribute nodes, text nodes, and text values, respectively.

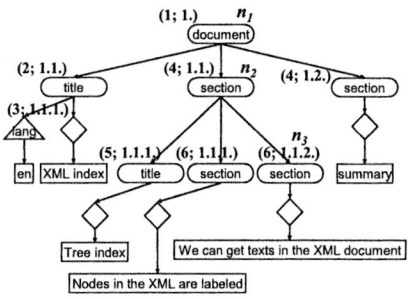

Fig. 1. Tree representation of sample XML document

Table 1. Correspondence of path and path identifier

Path	Path Identifier
/document	1
/document/title	2
/document/title/@lang	3
/document/section	4
/document/section/title	5
/document/section/section	6

Node labeling schemes play an important role in XML query processing, and thus many studies [3,8] of them have been made. A widely used node identifier is a pair of *preorder* and *postorder*, which can uniquely reconstruct the topology of an XML tree. However, such node identifiers do not convey element names or path information. It is important to obtain such information easily from a node identifier in order to quickly obtain the nodes corresponding to path expressions in the query. Therefore, we have designed a node labeling scheme in which node labels contain a *path identifier*. A path identifier identifies the path from the root node to a node. Table 1 shows an instance of path identifiers assigned to the paths in the XML document in Figure 1. In general, we cannot uniquely distinguish the nodes in an XML document only by path identifier. For example, the two nodes corresponding to "/document/section" in Figure 1 have the same path identifier. Therefore, we have introduced the *Sibling Dewey Order* to preserve order information among sibling nodes. The Sibling Dewey Order of the root node is 1. The Sibling Dewey Order of a non-root node n is a concatenation of the Sibling Dewey Order of the parent of n and the sibling order of n among siblings assigned the same path identifiers.

We call a pair of a path identifier and a Sibling Dewey Order a *PSP (Path Sibling Pair)*. Nodes are uniquely identified by a PSP. For example, with reference to the path identifiers in Table 1, each node in Figure 1 is labeled by a PSP $(x; y)$, where x denotes a path identifier, and y denotes a Sibling Dewey Order. For example, the path from the root node to node n_3 is "/document/section/section", so the path identifier is 6 Furthermore, node n_3 is the second sibling among the sibling nodes with the same element name. Therefore, the Sibling Dewey Order of the node n_3 becomes 1.1.2. because the Sibling Dewey Order of the parent node n_2 is 1.1. and the sibling order of n_3 is 2.

The nature of PSP makes it possible to identify the nodes at the instance level and to easily verify the parent-child or ancestor-descendant relationship between nodes. We can quickly obtain the path relationship between two nodes by referring to the inclusive relationship of the paths corresponding to the path identifiers. Note that the table storing the correspondence between paths and path identifiers is small enough to be kept in the main memory. Once a path relationship among nodes is verified, the instance level parent-child or ancestor-descendant relationship is verified by the subsequence matching of the Sibling Dewey Order. The PSP compactly conveys useful information for processing queries efficiently.

3 Index Construction

We propose two kinds of indices on a B^+-tree: A *COB-tree (COntent B^+-tree)* and an *STB-tree (STructure B^+-tree)*. The search keys in a COB-tree are the pairs of the text fragment and the PSP of the node in which the text appears, which is used for processing a query that involves both the text and structure of the XML document. The search keys in an STB-tree are the PSP of all element nodes and attribute nodes, which is used for processing queries that only involve the structural information of the XML documents.

3.1 Text in COB-Tree

To answer full-text searches and keep phrase information, we use the suffix texts of a text in an XML document as the text in the search key of a COB-tree. For example, the suffix of "Nodes in the XML are labeled" are as follows:

```
Nodes in the XML are labeled    XML are labeled
in the XML are labeled          are labeled
the XML are labeled             labeled
```

Pairs of each of the suffix texts and the PSP of the node that contains the suffix text make up the search keys of a COB-tree. However, keeping all phrase information in the index increases the index size. Therefore, we decided to keep only the words that were needed to distinguish the phrase from other phrases. For example, when we refer to Figure 1, for the suffix "the XML are labeled" of the text "Nodes in the XML are labeled", we keep only the first three words "the XML are" as these are enough to be distinguished from the suffix "the XML document" of the text "We can get texts in the XML document". Even if the search phrase is longer than a matching text in the index, we can narrow down the candidate nodes to only one.

3.2 Search-Key Mapping

We must pay attention to the order of the keys, since the cost can be minimized by retrieving adjacent leaf pages of a B^+-tree. If we sort the path identifiers

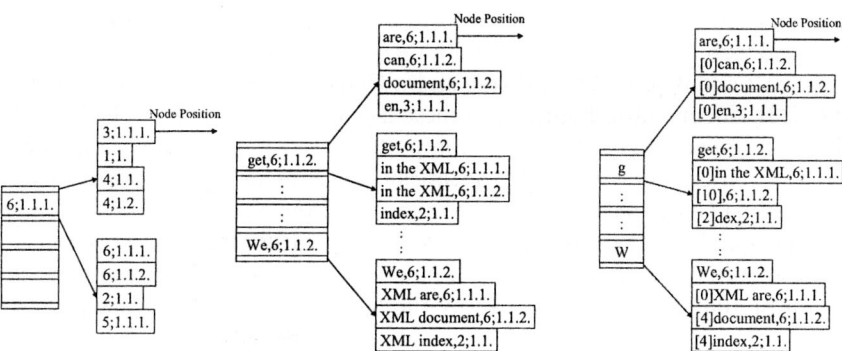

Fig. 2. STB-tree   **Fig. 3.** Normal COB-tree   **Fig. 4.** Prefix-Diff COB-tree

in Table 1 simply by their value, there is almost no meaning to the order. In general, it is difficult to meaningfully assign a unique value to the path. For example, when we process the query "//title", the path identifiers corresponding to the path are expected to be clustered in the B^+-tree. However, if we sort the path identifiers simply by value, the path identifiers corresponding to the path "//title", which are 2 and 5 in the running example, are generally dispersed in one or more leaf pages in the B^+-tree.

To overcome this problem, we propose *search-key mapping*, in which the key order is determined not by the key itself but by the value transformed when using information about the key (mapping information). Table 1 is used to retrieve the correspondence between path and path identifier in the following example. When we process a query that contains "//", such as "//title", the path identifiers 2 and 5 are expected to be clustered in the index. When such a case is considered, it is appropriate to order the path identifiers based on the reverse path of the corresponding path in the B^+-tree. That is, in this example, when we use "\" as a delimiter of the reverse path steps, we prepare mapping information such as "document\" for 1, "title\document\" for 2, "@lang\title\document\" for 3, and so on. Then, the order of the path identifiers is determined based on the lexicographical order of the corresponding reverse path. In this example, the order of the path identifier using the mapping information is 3 <1 <4 <6 <2 <5. Generally, the mapping information is small enough compared with XML documents, and we can retain it in the main memory. Therefore, ordering with mapping information can be done very fast.

Entries corresponding to the nodes with the same tag name are clustered in one location in the index, so we can process the XPath query containing "//" efficiently. Furthermore, since the Sibling Dewey Order is ordered by comparing the value of sibling numbers from the root node, the ordering of the key in an STB-tree is determined first by the path identifiers, using mapping information, and then by the Sibling Dewey Order when the path identifiers are equal. The ordering of the key in a COB-tree is determined first by the text and then by the same method as in an STB-tree when the texts are equal. The above approaches permit the clustering of index entries corresponding to the nodes with the same path in addition to the nodes that contain the same suffix text.

Figures 2 and 3 show an STB-tree and a COB-tree respectively, constructed for the XML document in Figure 1. In these figures, the delimiter of the text and the PSP is ",", and the delimiter of the path identifier and the Sibling Dewey Order is ";". We set $L = 3$, which is a threshold for the maximum phrase length of the text in a COB-tree to reduce the index size from a practical point of view. For simplicity, the indices in Figures 2 and 3 are constructed so that one page can contain a maximum of four entries; however, in actual indices, one page can contain over 100 entries and in this way the height of the B^+-tree is kept low.

3.3 Prefix-Diff COB-Tree

The size of a search key should be small in a B^+-tree. The search key of a COB-tree includes text, and if the phrase length of the text is long, the size of the search key becomes large.

To cope with this problem, we pay attention to the fact that the texts in the search keys contained within the leaf node pages of a COB-tree are ordered lexicographically, and the texts that begin with the same phrase are clustered. We compress the text in the search key by keeping only i) the length of the common prefix with the previous search key; and ii) the following character string after the common prefix. This compression can rebuild the text information in a COB-tree losslessly and reduce the size of search keys. The first search key in a leaf node page must keep the whole original text; however, the other search keys can use the above-described compression technique.

When we search in a COB-tree, the entries are retrieved by a node page block from a disk, and when we search a text in the leaf node page, texts in the search keys are rebuilt first. On the other hand, in the internal node page of a COB-tree, the search key can only be a text, or a text and a PSP pair that is enough to determine which pointer to the child node page should be followed as Prefix B-trees [15].

We call a COB-tree with the above compression a *Prefix-Diff COB-tree*. We call a COB-tree without compression a *Normal COB-tree* when we need to distinguish them. Figure 4 shows a Prefix-Diff COB-tree. The texts of the search keys in the leaf node pages in Figure 4 are compressed. For example, the compressed text "[8]document" of the search key "[8]document,10;1.1.2." indicates that the original text is the same as the text in the previous search key up to the eighth character followed by the different text "document".

4 Query Processing

XPath queries [1] can be processed by traversing XICS and retrieving entries relevant to the nodes corresponding to the query.

Those queries that consist of a path information only can be processed by traversing an STB tree only once. We call such queries *simple path queries*. On the other hand, those queries that have a *contains()* function for the target node can be processed by traversing a COB-tree only once. We call these kinds of queries *full-text queries*. Simple path queries and full-text queries are the basic units of queries. *Composite queries* which have one or more predicates for the nodes in the path of a query are first decomposed into these basic units. We explain the query processing algorithms first for simple path queries and full-text queries and then for composite queries.

In this section, we show some examples of processing XPath queries for the XML document in Figure 1. We use Table 1 to retrieve the correspondence between the path and the path identifier included in the PSP of a node.

4.1 Simple Path Queries

A simple path query has the form $s_1l_1s_2l_2\ldots s_kl_k$, where each s_i is "/" or "//" and l_i is a tag name. In this case, we first get the path identifiers that correspond to this path. If either s_i is "//", the multiple path identifiers are possibly retrieved. Then, we traverse the STB-tree with the path identifiers using *search-key mapping*. An example of simple path query process is as follows:

- **//title**
  The path identifiers corresponding to this path are 2 and 5. When traverse in the STB-tree and retrieve entries that have a path identifier between 2 and 5, we can retrieve entries with search keys "2;1.1." and "5;1.1.1.". The result of this query is the node positions of the "title" node included in each entry. This query can be processed efficiently because the two entries are clustered in the index by the *search-key mapping* technique.

4.2 Full-Text Queries

A full-text query has the form $s_1l_1s_2l_2\ldots s_kl_k[contains(.,'text')]$. In this case, we traverse the COB-tree using the text in the query. The structure information of the query is also checked with the traversal. An example of full-text query processing is as follows:

- **//section/title[contains(., 'Tree')]**
  We traverse the COB-tree using the text "Tree" and the structural information "//section/title", and retrieve the corresponding entries with search key "Tree,5;1.1.1.". We can get the position of the "title" node by following the pointer of this search key.

4.3 Composite Queries

A composite query has the form $s_1l_1[Pred_1]s_2l_2[Pred_2]\ldots s_kl_k[Pred_k]$, where $Pred_i$ is either a simple path query or a full-text query. In this case, the query can be processed by first decomposing the query to "$s_1l_1Pred_1$", "$s_1l_1s_2l_2Pred_2$", ..., "$s_1l_1s_2l_2\ldots s_kl_kPred_k$", and "$s_1l_1s_2l_2\ldots s_kl_k$", and then joining each result. An example of composite query processing is as follows:

- //section[title[contains(.,'Tree')]]

    We first decompose this query into q_1="//section/title[contains(.,'Tree')]" and q_2="//section". Then the entry with the search key "Tree,5;1.1.1." in the COB-tree is retrieved as a result of the query q_1, and the entries with search keys "4;1.1.", "4;1.2.", "6;1.1.1.", and "6;1.1.2." in the STB-tree are retrieved as a result of the query q_2. By joining these PSP labels, we know "5;1.1.1." and "4;1.1." are under a parent-child relationship, and we can get the position of the target "section" node by following the pointer of "4;1.1.".

5 Experiments

We implemented XICS and examined its effectiveness. We used GiST (Generalized Search Tree) [12] for the implementation of B$^+$-tree indices. We used the XML documents provided by the INEX Project [13].

We compared XICS with the method proposed in [14], which is compatible with full-text searches using inverted lists on tag names and keywords. We experimented with these inverted lists indexed by a B$^+$-tree. In the rest of the paper, we call the method proposed in [14] *Integration*. We applied a Prefix-Diff approach to the indices except for the STB-tree, and we set $L = 1$ as the threshold L for the maximum phrase length in the COB-tree, because *Integration* does not support phrase searches.

5.1 Index Size

In the experiment on index size, we created and used four kinds of XML document sets, changing the total size of the XML documents.

Figure 5 shows the size comparison of an STB-tree and an inverted list on tag names of *Integration*, and Figure 6 shows the comparison of a COB-tree and an inverted list on keywords. Each index size is nearly proportional to the size of the XML document set. XICS is about 1.4 times larger than *Integration*.

5.2 Query Processing Time

We examined the query processing time with XICS and *Integration* using the XPath queries in Table 2. We used the whole INEX document set (about 495 MB) in the experiment on query processing. Table 3 shows the processing time of these queries.

A join operation between the query text position and the target node position is needed in *Integration* (Q_3, Q_4, Q_5 and Q_6). Furthermore, a join operation for specifying the sibling number in a query is needed in *Integration* (Q_6). On the other hand, in the case of XICS , we need a join operation when the query is a composite query (Q_4 and Q_5). Since join processing is not the focus of our current study, we did not use any special approach in the join operations. The join operation time depends on the join algorithm. Table 4 shows the index traversal time excluding the join operation time.

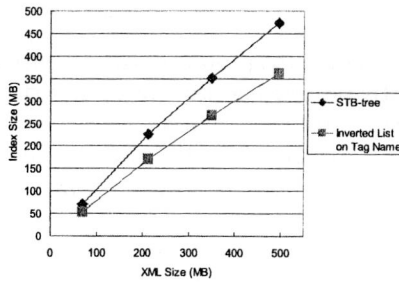

Fig. 5. Size comparison of STB-tree and inverted list on tag names

Fig. 6. Size comparison of COB-tree and inverted list on keywords

Table 2. XPath queries for comparison with *Integration*

	XPath
Q_1	/books/journal/title
Q_2	//sec/st
Q_3	//article/fm/abs/p[contains(., 'software')]
Q_4	//article[contains(./fm/abs/p, 'software')]
Q_5	//sec[contains(./st, 'animation')]
Q_6	//bdy/sec[1]/st[contains(., 'XML')]

Table 3. Execution time(time in milliseconds)

	XICS	Integration
Q_1	78	65
Q_2	410	1037
Q_3	79	19040
Q_4	278	21450
Q_5	332	3649
Q_6	68	46611

Table 4. Index traversal time(time in milliseconds)

	XICS	Integration
Q_1	78	65
Q_2	410	1037
Q_3	79	5137
Q_4	188	446
Q_5	321	510
Q_6	68	1658

XICS achieved an execution time up to 685 times faster than *Integration* with an exception for Q_1. In the case of Q_1, the "title" nodes in the XML document set were very few, and the path information in the search keys of our indices was not so significant. However, in general, we can traverse our indices efficiently by using the path information in the search keys and only retrieve the entries that match the path information in the query. For that reason, we can restrict nodes in the join operation and reduce the whole processing time.

In XICS, we can use the Sibling Dewey Order to specify the sibling number, and we don't need any join operations for it. In general, we need costly join operations to specify the sibling number in other approaches including *Integration*.

6 Conclusions

In this paper, we proposed using XICS to accelerate the process of XPath queries. XICS is based on a B^+-tree and can efficiently process queries that involve structural and full-text searches of XML documents. We particularly concentrated on texts in XML documents and constructed a COB-tree using PSP that contained path information from the root node and the text fragments in the XML document. In addition, we constructed an STB-tree for processing structural queries. *Search-key mapping* enables the efficient processing of a query containing "//". We proposed a compression method in the COB-tree and built a Prefix-Diff COB-tree. We then showed the processing steps for an XPath query using XICS. The experiment results show that XICS is about 1.4 times larger than *Integration*. Paying this slight increase in the cost of the index size, XICS outperforms *Integration* up to 685 times in terms of search time.

Future works include: a more appropriate choice of PSP, a pointer in the leaf pages of the B^+-tree, ordering that is not based on the reverse paths in *search-key mapping*, improvement of the join operation, introduction of data statistics and query workloads, and consideration of document updates.

References

1. W3C, XPath 1.0, http://www.w3.org/TR/xpath, 1999.
2. W3C, XQuery 1.0, http://www.w3.org/TR/xquery/, 2005.
3. Q. Li and B. Moon, "Indexing and Querying XML Data for Regular Path Expressions," In *VLDB*, pp.361–370, September 2001.
4. H. Jiang, H. Lu, W. Wang, and B. C. Ooi, "XR-Tree: Indexing XML Data for Efficient Structural Joins," In *ICDE*, pp.253–264, March 2003.
5. H. Wang and X. Meng, "On the Sequencing of Tree Structures for XML Indexing," In *ICDE*, pp.372–383, April 2005.
6. R. Goldman and J. Widom, "Dataguides: Enabling query formulation and optimization in semistrucutred databases," In *VLDB*, pp.436–445, August 1997.
7. B. Cooper, N. Sample, M. J. Franklin, G. R. Hjaltason, and M. Shadmon, "A Fast Index for Semistructured Data," In *VLDB*, pp.341–350, September 2001.
8. X. Wu, M. L. Lee, and W. Hsu, "A Prime Number Labeling Scheme for Dynamic Ordered XML Trees," In *ICDE*, pp.66–78, March 2004.
9. B. C. Hammerschmidt, M. Kempa, and V. Linnemann, "A selective key-oriented XML Index for the Index Selection Problem in XDBMS," In *DEXA*, 2004.
10. W3C, XQuery 1.0 and XPath 2.0 Full-Text Use Cases, http://www.w3.org/TR/xmlquery-full-text-use-cases/, April 2005.
11. S. Amer-Yahia, C. Botev, and J. Shanmugasundaram, "TeXQuery: A Full-Text Search Extension to XQuery," In *WWW*, pp.583–594, May 2004.
12. J. M. Hellerstein, J. F. Naughton, and A. Pfeffer, "Generalized Search Trees for Database Systems," In *VLDB*, pp.562–573, September 1995.
13. INitiative for the Evaluation of XML Retrieval (INEX), http://inex.is.informatik.uni-duisburg.de/2005/.
14. R. Kaushik, R. Krishnamurthy, J. F. Naughton, and R. Ramakrishnan, "On the Integration of Structure Indexes and Inverted Lists," In *SIGMOD*, June 2004.
15. R. Bayer and K. Unterauer, "Prefix B-trees," *ACM Trans. on Database Systems*, vol.2, no.1, pp.11–26, March 1977.

XML-Based e-Barter System for Circular Supply Exchange

Shuichi Nishioka[1], Yuri Yaguchi[2], Takahiro Hamada[1], Makoto Onizuka[1], and Masashi Yamamuro[1]

[1] NTT Cyber Space Laboratories, NTT Corporation,
1-1 Hikari-no-oka, Yokosuka-Shi, Kanagawa, 239-0847 Japan
{nishioka.shuichi, hamada.takahiro, onizuka.makoto, yamamuro.masashi}@lab.ntt.co.jp
[2] Graduate School of Environment and Information Sciences, Yokohama National University 79-7 Tokiwadai, Hodogaya-ku, Yokohama-Shi, Kanagawa, 240-8501 Japan
yaguchi@arislab.ynu.ac.jp

Abstract. A key function for any barter service is to detect circular exchanges in which all demands and supplies of a circle of users are satisfied. We call the demand and supply of a user his queries and data, respectively. The problem of finding a circular exchange is to detect directed cycles in an exchange graph where an edge connects one user's supply to another user's supply that satisfies the first user's demand. Our contributions to solving this problem are two-fold; 1) a process model of constructing an exchange graph, and 2) two cycle detection algorithms that can find all possible directed cycles. Our model processes an incoming user's queries and data across the stored users' data and queries, respectively, by combining database query processing and stream data processing. The algorithms are extensions of depth-first search (DFS) and Strongly-Connected-Component search (SCCS). Experiments show that our enhanced version of SCCS outperforms the enhanced version of DFS by factors ranging from 23 to 132.

1 Introduction

Real world matching services including barter[5] and job mediation have recently been developed for Internet use. Barter involves the exchange of user's supplies without money payment. If user A's supply matches user B's demand and vice versa, they can exchange their supplies. For example, user A's supply is a television made in Japan, and his demand is not more than three portable music players, at the same time, user B's supplies are five portable music players, and his demand is an audio visual set made in Japan. We call this a two-party exchange.

If trades are restricted to two-party exchanges, there will be few successful candidates. Our challenge is to efficiently find all combinations that yield multiple-party (circular) exchanges. Each combination consists of a set of users whose supplies satisfy their demands. Consider, for example, the combination

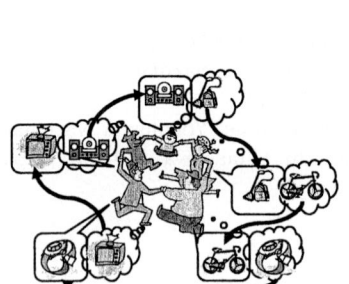

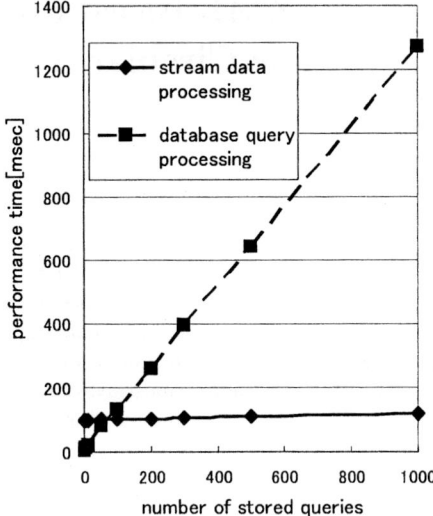

Fig. 1. Circular supply exchange

Fig. 2. Results of preliminary experiment

consisting of three users (A, B, C). The supplies are exchanged as follows. User A gets user B's supply, user B gets user C's supply, and user C gets user A's supply. This exchange is called circular supply exchange in this paper, see Fig.1.

A barter system on the Internet (e-barter system) must manage a large and complex set of information: data and queries. Data is the metadata of the supply a user is willing to exchange. A query expresses what the user wants to swap his supply for. The e-barter system processes the set to find a valid trade combination (VTC) when a new user inputs data and queries. The naive approach to finding a VTC is as follows. First, the system executes database query processing using the new queries, and outputs the data matches. For each match, the system then evaluates the corresponding query against the new data. This approach is impractical due to its excessive cost. Fig.2 shows a preliminary experiment of the naive approach and of stream data processing. This experiment used 1.3 KB of data, and the result at each point in Fig.2 represents a performance of processing the data against the stored queries resulting one query matches. The x-axis in Fig.2 shows the number of stored queries, and the y-axis shows the response time (msec). The dotted line shows the performance achieved by database query processing, and indicates that the performance degrades with the number of stored queries. By contrast, the solid line shows the performance achieved by stream data processing, and indicates that the response time is almost constant regardless of the number of stored queries. Therefore, stream data processing is more efficient in evaluating stored queries than database query processing.

Our first contribution is an efficient process model for the e-barter system that combines database query processing and stream data processing. It proceeds as follows. When a user inputs data and queries, the e-barter system processes the incoming query on the stored data and gets the matched data (database query processing). At the same time, the system processes the incoming data on the stored queries and gets the matched queries (stream data processing). The system then finds cycles among the matched data and queries. The method of detecting cycles is considered to be an operation conducted on directed graph $G(V, E)$ that consists of vertices V and edges E. Each vertex corresponds to a user's supply, and an edge connects one user's supply to another user's supply that satisfies the first user's demand.

We design the e-barter system to output all the detected cycles so that a user can choose his favourite one. Our second contribution is efficient methods to detect all cycles in directed graph G. They are enhancements of depth-first search (DFS) and Strongly-Connected-Component search. DFS maintains vertex state using three values. Strongly-Connected-Component of directed graph G is a maximal set of vertices $U \subseteq V$ such that every pair of vertices u and v in U are reachable from each other. This means that Strongly-Connected-Component inherently includes cycles.

This paper is organized as follows. Sec.2 overviews XML-based e-barter systems and explains our process model. Sec.3 presents two methods that can detect cycles in a directed graph. We implement the methods and compare their performance in Sec.4. Sec.5 describes related work. Conclusions and future directions are presented in Sec.6.

2 XML-Based e-Barter System

The procedure of e-barter consists of following functions: Registration of User, Supplies and Demands, Match (detect VTC as depicted in Fig.1), Negotiation (support negotiation among users after they have been selected as VTC members by the system), Bill (charge for trade expense, user registration fee, service use fee and transportation expense and so on), Ship (support supply delivery when convenient), and Security (protect the private information of users through user authentication at system log-in, the registration of supplies and supply transportation). We focus on the Match function and use XML data (data described using XML) and XPath expression as data and query, respectively.

Fig.3 shows the architecture of the proposed XML-based e-barter system. The Match function is implemented by Cycle Detect Engine, XML Filter Engine and XML Search Engine. Hereafter, we detail the data model and process model for Cycle Detect Engine.

2.1 Data Model

We define the data model for Cycle Detect Engine as $\{(user_k, \{data_l\}, \{query_m\})\}$ $(1 \leq k, l, m)$. This indicates that each user has a set of data and queries. Each *user*, *data* and *query* has unique ID: uID, dID, qID. We use a two-layer data model (Fig.4). The supply layer consists of vertices as *data* and set of *queries*,

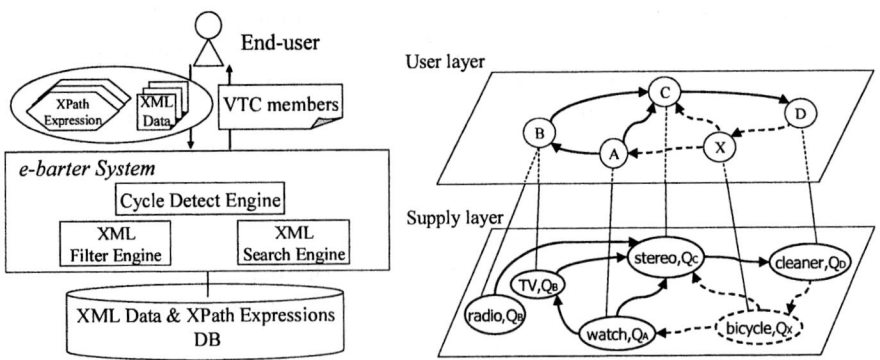

Fig. 3. Architecture of XML-based e-barter system

Fig. 4. Data model

and directed edges as the results of evaluating the *queries*. The user layer consists of vertices as *users* and directed edges projected from the supply layer. The solid lines between the two layers indicate the relations of *user* and *data*.

In the case of Fig.4, the user layer manages four users (A, B, C, D), and the supply layer manages five supplies *(watch, TV, radio, stereo, cleaner)*. For example, user B owns a radio and a TV. The vertices *(radio* and *TV)* in the supply layer are associated with user B's queries (Q_B). The directed edges in the supply layer, from *radio* and *TV* to *stereo*, indicate the result of evaluating Q_B. The directed edge in the user layer, from B to C, is projected from the two directed edges in the supply layer.

2.2 Process Model

We propose an effective process model for Cycle Detect Engine. Here, we call the following process incremental search (*IncrementalSearch*(uID, {dID}, {qID})). Incremental search detects circular exchanges in the stored data and queries, when a new user inputs data and queries. In detail, it processes the incoming data and queries by database query processing and stream data processing. Next, it inputs the results of the two processes to the supply layer in Fig.4, and then detects VTCs. *IncrementalSearch* receives three inputs : uID indicates a new user, {dID} indicates the set of his supplies, and {qID} indicates the set of his queries. It returns the VTCs.

IncrementalSearch(uID, {dID}, {qID})
1   u = userLayer.createVertex (uID)
2   for each $d \in$ {dID}
3   supplyLayer.createVertex (d, {qID}, u)
4   {$d_{matched}$} = gotMatchedData ({qID}, D)
5   for each $d \in$ {dID}

```
6       supplyLayer.createEdges (d, {d_matched})
7    for each d ∈ {dID}
8       {q_matched} = getMatchedQuery (d, Q)
9       for each q ∈ {q_matched}
10         u' = locateUser(q)
11         d_referred = getDataFromUser (u')
12         supplyLayer.createEdge (d_referred, d)
13   cycles = supplyLayer.cycleDetect ()
14   results = userLayer.projectEdges (cycles)
15   return results
```

Line 1 constructs a new vertex u using uID to the user layer. Lines 2-3 create each new vertex ($d \in \{dID\}$), which includes user's demand ($\{qID\}$), in the supply layer, and create a relation between user u in the user layer and data d in the supply layer. Line 4 executes database query processing by evaluating queries $\{qID\}$ on stored data D and gets the results $\{d_{matched}\}$. Lines 5-6 create new directed edges from data d to each data in $\{d_{matched}\}$ in the supply layer. Lines 7-12 execute stream data processing by passing each data d across stored queries Q. In detail, line 8 gets the results ($\{q_{matched}\}$). Lines 9-11 locate user u' (who inputted $q_{matched}$) using each $\{q_{matched}\}$, and select data $d_{referred}$ from the u'. Line 12 creates a new directed edge from each data in $\{d_{referred}\}$ to data d. Line 13 detects cycles in the supply layer. Line 14 projects detected cycles from the supply layer to the user layer. Line 15 returns the resulting VTCs.

In the case of Fig.4, user X inputs the data of bicycle and a set of queries (Q_x). The dotted directed edges from *bicycle* indicate the results of lines 4-6, and the dotted referenced edge to *bicycle* indicates the result of lines 7-12. The results at line 13 are three cycles : {*bicycle, stereo, cleaner*}, {*bicycle, watch, stereo, cleaner*} and {*bicycle, watch, TV, stereo, cleaner*}. Finally, Cycle Detect Engine projects the results to user layer and returns three VTCs : $\{X, C, D\}$, $\{X, A, C, D\}$, $\{X, A, B, C, D\}$.

3 Methods of Detecting Cycles

This section introduces two methods (Enhanced Depth-First Search and Enhanced Strongly-Connected-Component Search) for Cycle Detect Engine. They are extensions of two well-known algorithms[1]: Depth-First Search (DFS) and Strongly-Connected-Component (SCC) Search. We start by listing the symbols used in the algorithms in Table1.

3.1 Enhanced Depth-First Search(EDFS)

DFS, which maintains vertex state using three values : "empty", "accessed" and "search finished", is not enough to locate all cycles because there can be plural

Table 1. Nomenclature

symbol	explanation
$G(V, E)$	a directed graph G having vertices V and edges E
G^T	transpose of G
$d[u]$	first time to discover $u(\in V)$
$f[u]$	search finish time involving all edges of u
$\pi[v]$	predecessor of $v(\in V)$
$time$	a global variable for timestamping
$status$	function to change vertex status
$Adj[u]$	u's adjacency list

cycles in a graph, such as in the supply layer in Fig.4 [1]. Therefore, we enhance the access method of "backtracks" to allow the state of each vertex to have another possible value, "once accessed". When we backtrack to a vertex whose state is "accessed", we change it to "once accessed". We call the enhanced algorithm EDFS and describe it below.

```
EDFS(G)
1   for each u ∈ V[G]
2     do status[u] ← "empty"
3        π[u] ← NIL
4   time ← 0
5   for each u ∈ V[G]
6     if status[u] = "empty"
7        then DFS-Visit'(u)
```

```
DFS-Visit'(u)
1   status[u] ← "accessed"
2   time ← time + 1
3   d[u] ← time
4   for each v ∈ Adj[u]
5     if status[v] = "empty" or "once accessed"
6        then π[v] ← u
7           DFS-Visit'(v)
8           status[u] ← "once accessed"
9   status[u] ← "search finished"
10  f[u] ← time ← time + 1
```

Lines 1-3 set the state of all vertices to "empty" and initialize their π fields to NIL. Line 4 resets the global time counter. Lines 5-7 check each vertex in V in turn and, when an "empty" vertex is found, visit it using $DFS\text{-}Visit'$. Every time $DFS\text{-}Visit'$ is called in line 7, vertex u becomes the root of a new track. When $DFS\text{-}Visit'$ returns, each vertex u has been assigned discovery time $d[u]$ and finishing time $f[u]$.

For each call of $DFS\text{-}Visit'(u)$, line 1 changes the status of u to "accessed", and line 2 increments the global variable $time$. Line 3 sets the discovery time $d[u]$ to the current time. Lines under 4 examine each vertex v adjacent to u. Lines 5-7 recursively visit v if its status is "empty" or "'once accessed'". Line 8 changes the status of u to "once accessed" to show that backtrack has been executed. Finally, after all edges from u have been explored, lines 9-10 change the status of u to "search finished", increment the global timer, and record the finish time in $f[u]$.

---

[1] DFS can search for a cycle that includes the first accessed vertex from a directed graph, but it can't search for all cycles from the directed graph in the supply layer of Fig.4.

If vertex *bicycle* is added in Fig.4, the result of $EDFS$ contains three cycles : {*bicycle, watch, TV, stereo, cleaner*}, {*bicycle, watch, stereo, cleaner*} and {*bicycle, stereo, cleaner*}. A part of the access track is as follows. Starting from vertex *bicycle*, when we explore the edge from vertex *cleaner* to *bicycle*, we find the state of *bicycle* is "accessed", and detect the first cycle {*bicycle, watch, TV, stereo, cleaner*}. Next, we execute backtrack from *cleaner* until the accessed vertex becomes *bicycle*. When the vertex *watch* is accessed in backtrack, we find it has an another edge : *watch* → *stereo*. We then temporarily stop processing backtrack and execute $DFS\text{-}Visit'$. If vertex *bicycle* is accessed from *cleaner*, we detect the second cycle {*bicycle, watch, stereo, cleaner*}. Similarly, we execute $DFS\text{-}Visit'$ again, and access vertex *bicycle* through backtrack. This yields the third cycle {*bicycle, stereo, cleaner*}.

3.2 Enhanced Strongly-Connected-Component Search(ESCCS)

ESCCS detects cycles by finding SCCs then detecting all cycles from SCCs. According to the SCC definition, any vertex, u or v, in the SCC that is reachable from any other means that SCC contains more than one cycle. [1] proves that $SCCS(G)$ correctly computes the strongly connected components of a directed graph. Therefore, the problem of detecting all cycles in G is reduced to the one of detecting those in the SCCs of G. That is, when all SCCs are computed, the scope of the process of detecting all cycles lies inside each SCC, which has fewer vertices than G. Our proposed method uses this characteristic.

The algorithms of Strongly-Connected-Component Search ($SCCS(G)$) and Enhanced Strongly-Connected-Component Search($ESCCS(G)$) are as follows.

$SCCS(G)$
step1 call $DFS(G)$ to compute finish time $f[u]$ for each vertex u
step2 compute G^T
step3 call $DFS(G^T)$, but in the main loop of DFS, consider the vertices in order of decreasing $f[u]$ (as computed in step1)
step4 output the vertices of each group in step 3 as a separate strongly connected component

$ESCCS(G)$
step1 call $SCCS(G)$ to compute all SCCs in G
step2 detect cycles from each SCC which has more than one vertex
step3 output the cycles in step 2

Procedure $SCCS(G)$ works as follows[1]. Step1 processes $DFS(G)$, and creates a list of vertices in ascending order of $f[u]$. $DFS(G)$ indicates that we input directed graph G to the Depth-First Search algorithm. Step2 calculates the transpose of G. Step3 processes $DFS(G^T)$ using the last vertex in the list calculated in step1 of $SCCS(G)$. Step4 outputs the group consisting of the vertices whose status is "search finished". Each group in step3 is an SCC.

Procedure $ESCCS(G)$ works as follows. Step1 searches all SCCs in G. Step2 detects all cycles in each SCC calculated in step1. In detail, step2 checks the number of vertices in each SCC. When it is more than one, step2 detects all cycles. The entire process is repeated until each SCC has been examined.

When we apply the above-mentioned $ESCCS(G)$ to the graph of the supply layer of Fig.4, the result of step 1 at $ESCCS(G)$ contains one SCC, which has all vertices except the radio vertex. Therefore, the computational complexity of step2 at $ESCCS(G)$ is almost as the same as that of EDFS except for the omission of the vertex radio access. In general, the difference in the number of accessed vertices between $EDFS$ and $ESCCS$ depends on the number of vertices in SCC. If SCC has fewer vertices than G, it is more effective in detecting cycles.

3.3 Implementation

For both algorithms (EDFS and ESCCS), we found it was expensive to compute distinct cycles. Therefore, we implement this function by clustering the cycles according to their length first and then the set signature[2,3]. For implementation efficiency, we used a nested hash map: (key : $Length$, object : (key : $Signature$, object : $cycles$)). For each cycle, the signature is calculated by the exclusive disjunction of vertex ID.

4 Evaluation

This section describes the test data (graph) used in the evaluation and assesses the performance of our cycle detecting algorithms for incremental search at the supply layer.

4.1 Setup

We created two sets of graphs: *graph set1* and *graph set2*. Both sets assume that the number of users equals the number of vertices (8000 - 10000). That is each user registers one supply. While both sets have the same number of edges (10000), they differ in terms of the number of edges from each vertex. In detail, each vertex of *graph set1* has either one or two referencing edges, while graph set2 has a randomly set number of edges. In other words, the result of evaluated XPath expressions contains one or two matches (*graph set1*) or a random number (*graph set2*).

4.2 Experiments

We implemented EDFS and ESCCS using Java (J2SE 1.5.0). The environment of the experiments was [CPU]: Pentium III 1.2G Hz, [RAM]: 1.0GB and [OS]: Windows 2000 Professional.

We measured the number of edge traverses and the response time of detecting cycles (line 13 at *IncrementalSearch*) when we inputted the trial data to each graph set and detected the cycles. In detail, the trial data consisted of one vertex, representing data, with several referencing and referenced edges, representing queries results. We randomly generated thirty trial data and entered them into the system ten times for each data. We counted the number of edge traverses and measured the averaged time taken over the ten trials. The results are shown in Fig.5 (EDFS) and Fig.6 (ESCCS). In both figures, the x-axis shows the number of edge traverses and the y-axis shows the response time [sec].

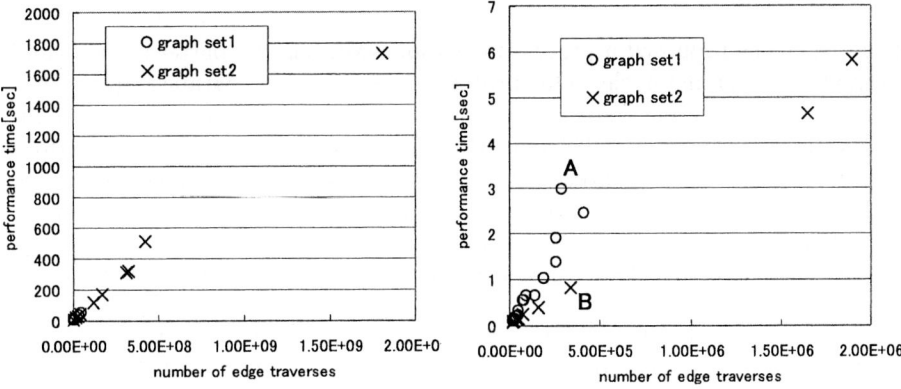

Fig. 5. EDFS results   **Fig. 6.** ESCCS results

4.3 Discussion

We draw two interesting observations from Fig.5 and Fig.6.

The first is that ESCCS is faster than EDFS, between 23 times and 132 times faster. This characteristic is due to the difference in the number of vertices accessed (edge traverses) between EDFS and ESCCS. EDFS recursively accesses all vertices and edges (G), whether they compose cycles or not. ESCCS accesses each vertex and edge twice for searching SCC ($\subseteq G$), and then accesses all vertices and edges in each SCC. The experimental results show that ESCCS is more efficient than EDFS, because ESCCS effectively reduced the redundant accesses to vertices and edges.

The second is that the response times of ESCCS and EDFS scale against the number of edge traverses, regardless of the kind of graphs. We note that Fig.6 exhibits some exceptional points that don't depend on the number of edge traverses. These are because they have so many cycle candidates that it takes some time to differentiate them. For example, at point A in Fig.6, there are nineteen times more detected cycles (13645) than at point B (691).

5   Related Work

[5] proposes a process algebra for e-barter based on microeconomic theory. It restricts the search domain to the region a user belongs to. When no candidate is detected, the search domain is expanded stepwise. Focusing on the search step, [5] doesn't describe any methods for implementation.

[6] proposes a process algebra that can handle both transaction and shipping costs. We will design a complete *e-barter system* by employing these costs.

[4] proposes an algorithm to search for cycles in a graph that consists of more than k vertices. It assumes a static graph which is quite different from the assumption of dynamic graphs presented in this paper for incremental search.

6 Conclusions

This paper has proposed a process model for XML-based e-barter systems and methods of detecting cycles. Our process model combines database query processing with stream data processing, and constructs an exchange graph. We introduced two methods, ESCCS and EDFS, for detecting all possible cycles. Both employ a model that uses directed graphs where an edge connects one user's supply to another user's supply that satisfies the first user's demand. Our methods are enhancements of the algorithms, DFS and Strongly-Connected-Component. We also measured their response times, and the results showed the effectiveness of ESCCS.

Our future tasks include the following: further evaluating the enhanced Strongly-Connected-Component search method using different data sets, and considering other methods of detecting cycles after searching SCCs.

References

1. Thomas H. Corman, Charles E. Leiserson, Ronald L. Rivest, and Clifford Stein. *Introduction to Algorithms.* MIT Press, 2001.
2. Christos Faloutsos and Stavros Christodoulakis. Signature files: an access method for documents and its analytical performance evaluation. volume 2, pages 267–288. ACM Press, 1984.
3. Christos Faloutsos and Stavros Christodoulakis. Description and performance analysis of signature file methods for office filing. volume 5, pages 237–257. ACM Press, 1987.
4. Harold N. Gabow and Shuxin Nie. Finding a long directed cycle. In *Proceedings of the fifteenth annual ACM-SIAM symposium on Discrete algorithms*, pages 49–58. Society for Industrial and Applied Mathematics, 2004.
5. Natalia Lopez, Manuel Nunez, Ismael Rodriguez, and Fernando Rubio. A formal framework for e-barter based on microeconomic theory and process algebras. In *Proceedings of the Second International Workshop on Innovative Internet Computing Systems*, pages 217–228. Springer-Verlag, 2002.
6. Natalia Lopez, Manuel Nunez, Ismael Rodriguez, and Fernando Rubio. A multi-agent system for e-barter including transaction and shipping costs. In *Proceedings of the 2003 ACM symposium on Applied computing*, pages 587–594. ACM Press, 2003.

Context-Sensitive Complementary Information Retrieval for Text Stream

Qiang Ma[1] and Katsumi Tanaka[1,2]

[1] National Institute of Information and Communications Technology,
3-5 Hikaridai, Seika-cho, Soraku-gun, Kyoto 619-0289, Japan
qiang@nict.go.jp
[2] Graduate School of Informatics, Kyoto University
Yoshida Honmachi, Sakyo, Kyoto, 606-8501, Japan
tanaka@dl.kuis.kyoto-u.ac.jp

Abstract. With constant advances in information technology, more and more information is available and users' information needs are becoming more diverse. Most conventional information systems only attempt to provide information that meets users' specific interests. In contrast, we are working on ways of discovering information from the viewpoints of both interest and necessity. For example, we are trying to discover complementary information that provides additional knowledge on the users' topics of interest, not just information that is similar to the topic. In previous work, which was based on extracting topic structures from closed-caption data, we proposed methods of searching for information to complement TV program content; that is, to provide users with more detailed information or different viewpoints. In this paper, we focus on the features of text streams (closed-caption data, etc.) and propose a method for context-sensitive retrieval of complementary information. We modified our topic-structure model for content representation and consider the "context" of a text stream in searching for complementary information. The "context" of the text stream is considered to be a series of topic structures. Based on such kind of context, we propose methods of searching for complementary information for TV programs, including query-type selection, query modification, and computation of the degree of complementarity. The experiment results showed that, comparing to our previous methods, the context-sensitive method could provide more additional information and avoid information overlap.

1 Introduction

Increasing amounts of information are available and our information needs and means of gathering information are becoming more diverse and differentiated than in the past. We can acquire information from different viewpoints or detailed information by integrating information derived from different types of media.

To find similar information to a given example, QBE (Query By Example)[7] and its variants are effective and well-known methods. Unlike the conventional QBE method, which requires the user to specify an example in explicit detail, Henzinger et al. [1] proposed a method for finding similar information to a TV program by dividing closed-caption data into segments according to a fixed duration, and using each segment as an

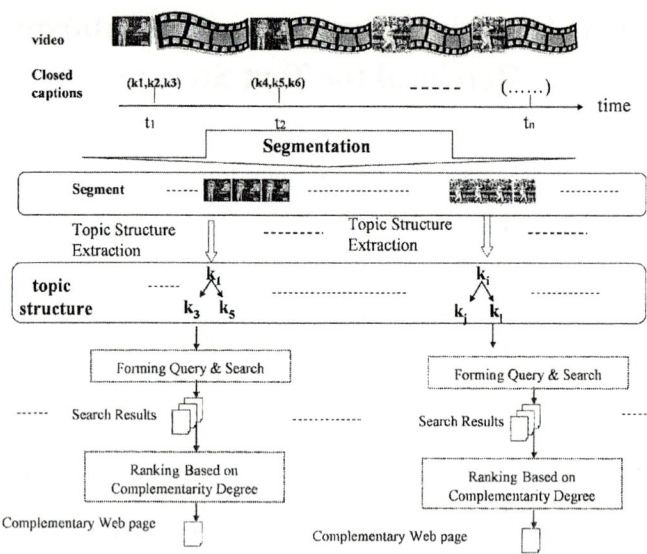

Fig. 1. Complementary information retrieval

example to form a query. These methods are very efficient for searching for information that is similar to the given example. However, in many cases, we want additional information or information from different viewpoints. Although similar information retrieved by conventional methods may contain some additional information, the goal of these methods, i.e., searching for similar information, limits their effectiveness in finding complementary information.

The issue of information complementation is important for acquiring balanced and detailed information. To use an analogy, we need information from different viewpoints to provide a balanced diet, and we also want to enjoy a delicious banquet of detailed information on topics that interest us. In our previous work[2, 3, 4], as one approach to information complementation, we proposed a novel method of providing complementary information based on searching for complementary Web pages to augment the content of a TV program.

Figure 1 shows the processing flow of our method for retrieving complementary information. First, we analyze the closed captions of a TV program to extract the topic structure (keyword graph). The TV program is segmented using the closed captions and a pre-constructed co-occurrence relationship dictionary. Then we conduct an Internet-based search for (candidate) complementary Web pages using structured queries generated on the basis of the topic structure. The Web pages that are retrieved are re-ranked according to their degree of complementarity; this concept is used to estimate the extent to which each page complements the TV program.

In this paper, we propose a context-sensitive method for retrieving complementary information that is an improvement on our previous method. Here, "context" denotes the stream of previous topic structures. Based on comparisons between the context and the current topic structure, we propose methods for forming structured queries automatically, including query-type selection and query modification. We also propose a method of computing the degree of complementarity according to the results of this comparison. Basically, the degree of complementarity is computed based on the comparison of two topic structures, which are represented as a weighted DAG (directed acyclic graph). As the experiment results showed, the context-sensitive method is capable of providing additional information and avoiding information overlap.

The remainder of this paper is organized as follows. Section 2 describes the topic-structure model. In Section 3, we describe our method for retrieving complementary information, including selecting the query type, modifying queries, and computing the degree of complementarity. The results of an evaluation of the method are shown in Section 4 and in Section 5 we present our conclusion and plans for future work.

2 Topic Structure

2.1 Topic Structure

We call an event or activity a "topic". To represent the "topics" described in a video or a Web page, this study uses the concept of topic structure. In contrast to TDT[6] and TopicMap[5], which use "topic structure" (or "topic") to denote the relationship between information resources, we use the topic structure (keyword graph) to represent the content of Web pages, TV programs, etc.

Intuitively, a topic structure consists of a pair of subject and content terms. The subject terms are centric keywords that play a title role on a Web page (or video) and the content terms play a supporting (or describing) role. Both subject and content terms appear in Web pages or videos. Our concept of topic structure is defined as follows:

$$
\begin{aligned}
topic &:= '('\ S, C\ ')' \\
S &:= '\{'\ (subject-term|topic)^+\ '\}' \\
C &:= '\{'\ (content-term|topic)^+\ '\}' \\
subject-term &:= keyword \\
content-term &:= keyword
\end{aligned}
\tag{1}
$$

where "|" stands for "or" and "+" means that the element(s) appears more than once. A keyword should only occur once in a topic structure.

The subject and content terms are extracted by using tf (term frequency) and the co-occurrence relationship between two terms. In short, if a keyword has high rates of co-occurrence with other keywords and its term frequency is higher than that of other keywords, it is considered to be the subject term. Of the remaining keywords, those that have a high co-occurrence relationship with the subject terms have a high probability of being content terms.

When the words w_1 and w_2 co-occur frequently within a topic corpus, we say that the two words have a strong co-occurrence relationship and that their co-occurrence rate is high. In this paper, we estimate the co-occurrence rate $cooc(w_i, w_j)$ between the words w_i and w_j using the following function.

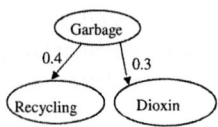

Fig. 2. Example of topic graph

$$cooc(w_i, w_j) = \frac{df(\{w_i, w_j\})}{df(\{w_i\}) + df(\{w_j\}) - df(\{w_i, w_j\})} \quad (2)$$

where $df(\{w_i\})$ is the number of topics containing the word w_i within a pre-specified topic corpus, and $df(\{w_i, w_j\})$ is the number of topics containing both w_i and w_j.

2.2 Topic Graph

A topic structure can be represented as a weighted connected DAG that has at least two vertices, one standing for the subject term and one for the content term. Here, we call this type of graph a topic graph.

The topic graph $G(t)$ of the topic structure, t, is defined as follows:

$$G(t) = (V, E) \quad (3)$$

where V is a vertex set which represents the keywords within t. $E(\subseteq V \times V)$ is a directed-edge set. The directed edge $e = (u, v)$ represents the subject-content relationship between the keywords u and v. $\|V\| \geq 2, E \neq \emptyset$. The weight of the edge is computed by the weight function, $w : E \to R$. Figure 2 shows an example of a topic graph.

In our current work, we use the height and width of a topic graph to represent the level of detail and breadth of the information. That is, if the topic graph is very high, it may describe the topic in detail. Similarly, if it is very wide, it may describe the topic from many perspectives with a high content coverage. From this viewpoint, we define the distance between two vertices as follows:

$$d(u, v) = (1 - cooc(u, v)) \cdot \frac{min(tf(u), tf(v))}{max(tf(u), tf(v))} \quad (4)$$

where $tf(u)$ stands for the term frequency of u and $cooc(u, v)$ denotes the co-occurrence relationship of u and v. Moreover, if $e = (u, v) \in E$, $d(u, v)$ is the weight of e.

Based on the distance between the two vertices, we compute the height of a topic graph to be the shortest path from the root node to the leaf node. Here, the root node and leaf node denote nodes that have no parent and child nodes, respectively.

We assume that the distance of root (leaf) nodes stands for the broadness of the topic and the breadth of perspectives (or viewpoints). Hence, at first, we compute the distances of root nodes, and leaf nodes, respectively. Then, we select the bigger one as the width of that topic graph. Below are details of the procedure used to compute the distance, D, of root nodes (or leaf nodes) N.

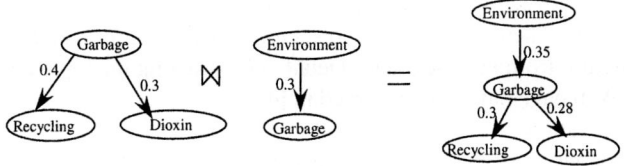

Fig. 3. Example of joining

1. Let a temporal node set $M = \emptyset$; $D = 0$.
2. Select a node n from N; $N = N - \{n\}$, $M = M + \{n\}$.
3. Compute and select the smallest distance $d(m, n')$, where $m \in M$ and $n' \in N$.
4. $M = M + \{n'\}$, $N = N - \{n'\}$, $D = D + d(m, n')$.
5. If $N = \emptyset$, go to 9.
6. Compute and select the smallest distance $d(m', n'')$, where $m' \in M$ and $n'' \in N$.
7. $M = M - \{m'\} + \{n''\}$, $N = N - \{n''\}$, $D = D + d(m', n'')$.
8. Go to 5.
9. Output D and then stop.

2.3 Topic-Structure-Based Joining

To represent the integration of related content, we define the joining of two topic structures. The joining of the two topic structures, t and t', means that their topic graphs are united, producing a connected DAG.

$$t \bowtie t' = \begin{cases} G(t) \cup G(t'), & \text{if } G(t) \cup G(t') \text{ is a connected DAG.} \\ \phi, & \text{others} \end{cases} \quad (5)$$

where $G(t)$ and $G(t')$ stand for the respective topic graphs of t and t', and ϕ stands for null. In addition, $t \bowtie \phi = \phi$. The weight of each edge is re-computed by its weight function. An example of joining is shown in Figure 3.

In this definition, we restricted the result of joining to a connected DAG. That is, the result of joining two topic structures is also a single topic structure. The "connected" condition restricts the two topic graphs to having the same vertex (keyword). The "DAG" condition prevents the introduction of cycles to avoid confusion between keyword roles. If the joining of two topic structures is not ϕ, we say that the two topic structures are joinable. Two Web pages that include joinable topic structures complement each other.

3 Context-Sensitive Retrieval of Complementary Information

Complementary information retrieval consists of three phases:

1. Topic Structure Extraction
   As mentioned above, we extract the topic structure based on tf and the co-occurrence

relationship between keywords. However, a video or Web page may describe more than one topic. Therefore, we need to segment these examples and then extract the topic structure from each segment. Details of extracting the topic structure from a video or Web page have been reported in [4].

2. Query Generation

   In our previous work, we assumed that topic structures extracted from a given example were independent of each other and queries were formed by using each extracted topic structure directly. Since there are four types of queries[3], users must specify their preferred query type in advance.

   If the given example is a video such as a TV news program, the extracted topic structures may be related to each other and we need to take into account their co-relationships when forming a query. That is to say, we consider the topic structures extracted from the video as a topic-structure stream and assume that the previous related topic structures provide the context for the current one. Here, the related topic structures denote a sub-stream of topic structures whose members can be joined with the current topic structure. Based on using this kind of context, we propose a method for automatically forming queries including query-type selection and query modification.

3. Web Retrieval and Re-ranking Based on Degree of Complementarity

   We search for complementary Web pages by issuing a query to a search engine (Google, etc.) and then re-rank the search results based on the degree of complementarity. Basically, we compute the degree of complementarity based on a comparison between the topic graphs of a retrieved Web page and the given example. However, depending on the type of query, we use different methods for computing the degree of complementarity; that is, the degree of complementarity is also context-sensitive. The details are described later.

3.1 Context of Topic-Structure Streams

As mentioned before, we regard the topic structures extracted from a video as a stream and extract previous related topic structures (sub-stream) to provide the context of the current topic structure. That is, the previous related topic-structure stream, which is the context for the current topic structure, consists of joinable topic structures of the current one. In fact, the context is also a topic structure and can be represented by a topic graph, which we call a context graph.

Suppose that the topic structure stream is $T = t_0 t_1 t_2 \cdots t_{i-1} t_i$ and the current topic structure is t, the context graph $C(t_i)$ of t_i is therefore defined as follows:

$$C(t_i) = t_i \bowtie t_{i-1} \bowtie \ldots \bowtie t_j \neq \phi \qquad (6)$$

where, $t_i \bowtie t_{i-1} \bowtie \ldots \bowtie t_j \bowtie t_{j-1} = \phi;\ j \geq 1;\ t_0 = \phi$.

3.2 Query Generation

In our current work, since the result of joining two joinable topic structures may provide supplementary information on the original ones, we assumed that the complementary information for a given example should contain some topic structures that could be joined with the one given. From this viewpoint, we defined four kinds of queries called CD (Content Dependent), SD (Subject Dependent), CB (Content Broadening), and SB (Subject Broadening), respectively.

CD and SD queries are based on a joining where the subject terms in one topic structure appear as the content terms in the other. This type of joining adds more details to the original information. SB and CB queries are based on a joining where two topic structures have the same subject or content terms. This type of joining can broaden the coverage of information.

Suppose the topic structure t of a given example is $(\{s_1, s_2, c_1, c_2, c_3\}, \{(s_1,c_1),(s_1,c_2),(s_1,c_3),(s_2,c_1),(s_2,c_2),(s_2,c_3)\})$. "intitle" and "intext" mean the following terms are the respective subject and content terms of a topic structure contained in a retrieved Web page. "∧" and "∨" stand for "logical AND" and "logical OR", respectively. "¬" means "logical NOT". CD, SD, CB, and SB queries are defined as follows:

1. CD Query: $(intitle:c_1 \land c_2 \land c_3) \land (\neg(intext:s_1 \lor s_2))$
2. SD Query: $(intext:s_1 \land s_2) \land (\neg(intitle:c_1 \lor c_2 \lor c_3))$
3. SB Query: $(intext:c_1 \land c_2 \land c_3) \land (\neg(intitle:s_1 \land s_2))$
4. CB Query: $(intitle:s_1 \land s_2) \land (\neg(intext:c_1 \land c_2 \land c_3))$

For each query, we call the latter part starting from ¬ (e.g., $\neg(intext:s_1 \lor s_2)$) the negative condition part and the former (e.g., $(intitle:c_1 \land c_2 \land c_3)$) the positive condition part. For CB and SB queries, using the negative condition enables us to exclude Web pages containing the same topic structure as the one given. Similarly, for CD and SD queries, the negative condition excludes Web pages containing a topic structure that would result in ϕ if they were joined.

The positive (negative) condition parts of CD, SD, CB, and SB queries consist of only subject terms (or content terms) for a given topic structure. Therefore, these queries are called node-type queries. In contrast, we also define an edge-type query in which the positive (or negative) condition part consists of pair of subject and content terms, i.e., edge of topic graph. An edge-type query is formed as follows:

$$(intitle:s_1\ intext:c_1) \land (\neg(intitle:s_2\ intext:c_3))$$

where, s_1, c_1, s_2, c_3 are slected with the following conditions.

$$\sum_{i=1}^{3}(cooc(s_1,c_i) - cooc(s_2,c_i)) \geq 0$$
$$cooc(s_1,c_1) = max(cooc(s_1,c_1), cooc(s_1,c_2), cooc(s_1,c_3))$$
$$cooc(s_2,c_3) = max(cooc(s_2,c_2), cooc(s_2,c_3))$$

Using an edge-type query, we can search a Web page that contains the same subtopic as the given example but is not the same as the given example. The Web page may describe a different story[6] about an event and may provide contextual information for the given example[4]. Often, Web pages searched for using edge-type queries may provide detailed information from different perspectives. Hence, we call an edge-type query DB query, i.e., a detailing and broadening query.

3.3 Forming a Query

Generally, we use current topic graphs to form queries. However, as we mentioned before, since a topic structure may appear more than once in the stream, we may generate the same query and get the same search results. This may provide overlapping information and conflict with our goal of searching for additional information. To resolve this situation, we propose a mechanism for deciding the query type and modifying the query using the context graph.

In contrast to our previous work in which a user needed to pre-specify the query type, we now select the query type by comparing the current topic graph with its context graph.

- $(H(C(t_i)) - H(t_i)) - (W(C(t_i)) - W(t_i)) > \theta$, i.e., the difference in height is greater than the difference in width. Because the context (previous content) provided more detailed information, we generate SB and CB queries to search for information that broadens the viewpoint of the example given. Here, t_i and $C(t_i)$ denote the current topic graph and its context graph, respectively, and H and W stand for the height and width of the topic graph, respectively. $\theta(> 0)$ is a pre-specified threshold.
- if $(W(C_{t_i}) - W(t_i)) - (H(C_{t_i}) - H(t_i)) > \theta$, we form CD and SD queries to search for more detailed information.
- if $-\theta \leq (H(C_{t_i}) - H(t_i)) - (W(C_{t_i}) - W(t_i)) \leq \theta$, we form a DB (edge-type) query.

If we still get the same result after selecting the query type based on the context graph, we can try using the context graph to form the query instead of the current one. However, intuitively, the context graph may contain more nodes than the current one. Therefore, we need to extract the query graph used to form the query from the context graph. Like our topic structure extraction method[2], a keyword that has high term frequency and co-occurrence relationships with the other terms, will be selected as the subject term of the query graph. Of the remaining keywords, those that have a strong co-occurrence relationship with the pre-extracted subject terms will be selected as the content terms of the query graph.

3.4 Degree of Complementarity

For a given topic structure, we can formulate five types of queries as described above, and for each query, we may acquire more than one Web page. To select the one that is most complementary, we use the notion called complementarity degree to re-rank the retrieved Web pages. Basically, the degree of complementarity is computed by comparing topic graphs. Depending on the query type, there are three different methods for computing the degree of complementarity. Here, we suppose the current topic graph is t and the topic graph of the retrieved page is t'.

- If the query type consists of CD and SD queries, the degree of complementarity is computed as follows to estimate the level of detail provided by the retrieved Web page.

$$comple(t, t') = H(t \bowtie t') - H(t)$$

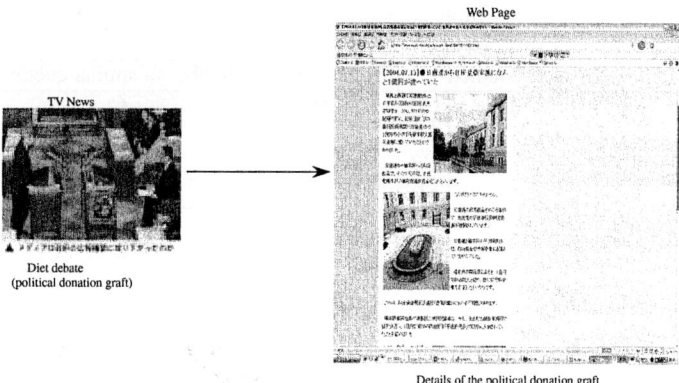

Fig. 4. Example of search result

- If the query is a CB or SB query, the degree of complementarity is computed as the difference in width, which denotes the broadness.

$$comple(t, t') = W(t \bowtie t') - W(t)$$

- If the query is a BD query, we compute the degree of complementarity as the difference in area, which represents both broadness and level of detail.

$$comple(t, t') = H(t \bowtie t') * W(t \bowtie t') - H(t) * W(t)$$

As mentioned above, a Web page may describe more than one topic. In other words, a Web page can be represented as a set of topic structures. Let the topic-structure set of a retrieved Web page p be $\{t_1, t_2, ..., t_n\}$. Let the current topic structure extracted from the text stream be t. The degree of complementarity of p is then computed as follows:

$$com(p) = \sum_{i=1}^{i=n} comple(t, t_i) \qquad (7)$$

where $com(p)$ stands for the degree to which page p complements t.

The Web page p that has the highest degree of complementarity ($com(p)$) within the search results is selected as the complementary Web page for the current topic. In addition, we also take into account the rankings returned by Google. For instance, if two Web pages have the same degree of complementarity, we will select the one ranked higher by Google as the complementary Web page.

4 Experiment

We used closed-caption data for one day of NHK News 7 to test our method of retrieving context-sensitive complementary information and compared it with our previous method, which does not consider the context of topic-structure streams.

Table 1. Results of experiment

Experiment Method			Precision Ratio	Number of similar queries
Non-Context Mode		CD	0.452	6
		SD	0.50	3
		CB	0.474	3
		SB	0.528	6
Context-Sensitive Mode		O2C	0.529	1
		C2O	0.583	2

We built a co-occurrence relationship dictionary on a collection of topics constructed from closed captions (in Japanese) from NHK News 7 programs from Sep. 2002 to Dec. 2004. We used ChaSen (http://chasen.aist-nara.ac.jp/) for Japanese morphological analysis and used only nouns as keywords for further processing. To exclude stop words, we built a stop-words dictionary that contains 593 terms in English and 347 terms in Japanese.

We extracted 39 topic structures from the closed-caption data using the method described previously [3]. Each extracted topic structure contained two subject and three content terms, such as ($\{s_1, s_2, c_1, c_2, c_3\}$, $\{(s_1, c_1), (s_1, c_2), (s_1, c_3), (s_2, c_1), (s_2, c_2), (s_2, c_3)\}$). We implemented the queries defined above using Google's structured search options, such as "intitle", "intext", "allintitle", and "allintext".

We carried out the following two experiments.

1. Context-sensitive complementary information retrieval: We formed a query for each extracted topic structure according to its context, and ranked the retrieved Web pages based on the degree of complementarity. The top-ranked Web page was considered the most complementary Web page.

   We generated queries in the following two ways.
   - O2C (Origin to Context) method: Generally, we formed a query by using the current topic structure extracted from the closed captions. However, if the same query had appeared before, we used its context to form the query instead of the original topic structure.
   - C2O (Context to Origin) method: We formed a query by using the context of the current topic structure. We modified the query by using the current topic structure if the same query had appeared before.
2. Non-context complementary information retrieval: For each topic structure, we formed CD, SD, CB, and SB queries and searched for potentially complementary Web pages using Google. Then, we ranked the Web pages returned by Google based on their degree of complementarity and selected the top-ranked one as the most complementary Web page.

We selected the relevant results from the search results of the above methods from two points of view: a relevant page should provide detailed information on the TV program or describe it from a different perspective. Figure 4 shows an example of a relevant result (complementary Web page). On the left is a TV program reporting a Diet debate on graft relating to political donations and on the right is a Web page describing the issue in detail.

As shown in Table 1, compared to our previous method, using the context-sensitive method improved the precision ratio. In particular, compared to using CD, SD, CB, and SB queries in the non-context retrieval mode, the C2O method improved the precision ratio by 13.1, 8.3, 10.9, and 5.5 points, respectively. In the non-context retrieval mode, the CD, SD, CB, and SB methods produced six, three, three, and six queries that were similar[1], respectively. In contrast, the C2O and O2C methods produced one and two queries that were similar, respectively. Overall, the context-sensitive method improved the precision ratio for retrieval of complementary information and avoided overlapping search results.

5 Conclusion

In this paper, we extended our topic structure model and proposed a context-sensitive method for retrieving complementary information for text streams. The "context" of a text stream is the related topic-structure stream for the current content. By using this kind of context, we proposed methods for selecting and modifying queries, and for computing the degree of complementarity when searching for complementary information. The experiment results showed that our context-sensitive method provided additional information and avoided information overlap.

Further studies on mechanisms for complementary information retrieval and evaluation are necessary. For instance, although we consider the context of a text stream, which is the input data, the same queries still appear. We plan to further investigate the context of search results, i.e., output data, to improve our method of retrieving context-sensitive complementary information.

References

[1] Monika Henzinger, Bay-Wei Chang, Brian Milch, and Sergey Brin. Query-free news search, *Proc. of WWW2003* (2003).
[2] Qiang Ma and Katsumi Tanaka. Topic-structure-based complementary information retrieval for information augmentation, *Proc. of APWeb2004, LNCS3007*, pp. 608-619 (2004).
[3] Qiang Ma and Katsumi Tanaka. Topic-structure-based query-free web retrieval mechanism for information integration of Web and TV programs (in Japanese), *IPSJ Transactions on Databases, Vol. 45, No. SIG 10 (TOD23)*, pp. 18-36 (2004)
[4] Qiang Ma, Akiyo Nadamoto and Katsumi Tanaka. Complementary information retrieval for cross-media news contents, *Proc. of ACM MMDB 2004*, pp. 35-44 (2004).
[5] TopicMap.org. http://www.topicmap.org (2005).
[6] Charles L. Wayne. Multilingual topic detection and tracking: Successful research enabled by corpora and evaluation, *Proc. of LREC2000*, pp. 1487–1494 (2000).
[7] M. Zloof. Query-by-example: A data base language, *IBM Systems Journal, 16, 4*, pp. 324–343 (1977).

---

[1] Here, if the positive condition parts of two queries are the same, we say they are the similar query.

Detecting Changes to Hybrid XML Documents Using Relational Databases

Erwin Leonardi, Sri L. Budiman, and Sourav S. Bhowmick

School of Computer Engineering, Nanyang Technological University, Singapore
{pk909134, assourav}@ntu.edu.sg

Abstract. Recent works in XML change detection have focused on detecting changes to ordered or unordered XML documents. However, in real life XML documents may not always be *purely ordered* or *purely unordered*. It is indeed possible to have both ordered and unordered nodes in the *same* XML document (such documents are called *hybrid* XML). In this paper, we present a technique for detecting the changes to hybrid XML documents. In our approach, old and new versions of XML documents are first stored in a relational database. Then, the *order learning module* is used to determine the *node types* in hybrid XML. The change detection module then uses the knowledge of node types to detect the changes by issuing SQL queries. Our experimental results show that our approach produces better *result quality* compared to existing approaches.

1 Introduction

Detecting changes to XML data is an important research problem. Recently, a number of techniques for detecting the changes to XML data have been proposed. XMLTreeDiff [3] and XyDiff [2] are main-memory algorithms for detecting the changes in *ordered* XML documents. In an *ordered* XML, both the parent-child relationship and the left-to-right order among siblings are important. Wang et al. proposed X-Diff [10] for computing the changes to *unordered* XML documents. In *unordered* XML, the parent-child relationship is significant, while the left-to-right order among siblings is not important. All these algorithms suffer from scalability problem as they fail to detect changes to large XML documents due to lack of memory. In [1,4,5], we have addressed this scalability problem by detecting changes to ordered and unordered XML using the relational database system. Note that all these techniques assume that the ordered or unordered characteristics of XML documents are known ahead of time and they can either be *purely* ordered or *purely* unordered but not both.

Our analysis of different real life XML documents has revealed that XML documents may not always be *purely ordered* or *purely unordered*. It is indeed possible to have both ordered and unordered nodes in the *same* XML document. We call such documents as *hybrid XML*. Let us illustrate this with an example. Suppose we have two versions of an XML document represented as a tree as depicted in Figure 1. Observe that the nodes "authors" and "chapters" are ordered and nodes "books" and "book" are unordered. In one hand, if we consider

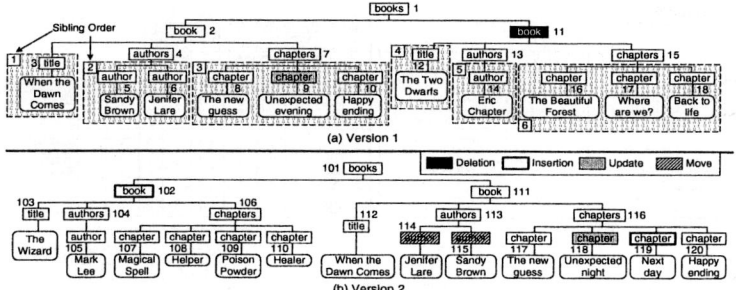

Fig. 1. Two Versions of Hybrid XML

this document as purely ordered XML, then movement of "book" or "books" nodes in different versions will be inaccurately detected as changes by XyDiff and XMLTreeDiff. On the other hand, if we consider this XML document as unordered XML, then we will not be able to detect movement among siblings of the nodes in the subtrees rooted at "authors" node or "chapters" node using X-Diff. For example, we will fail to detect the movement of the child nodes of node 113. Consequently, we need an approach to accurately detect the changes to such hybrid XML documents.

In this paper, we present a technique for detecting the changes to hybrid XML documents. This is part of our change detection system called XANDY (**X**ml en**A**bled cha**N**ge **D**etection s**Y**stem) that we are currently building. The main difference between our approach and the previous approaches is that our approach is able to detect the changes accurately on *hybrid* XML documents, while other approaches focus either on ordered or unordered XML documents. To the best of our knowledge, currently, there is no published approach for detecting the changes to hybrid XML documents.

2 Order Learning Module

In order to detect the changes to hybrid XML, we first must determine automatically the ordered and unordered nodes by analyzing the changes to a set of consecutive versions of a hybrid XML document. We use the following two heuristics to facilitate identification of ordered nodes: (1) Let node x be the ith child of node p in version v_1. Then, if x is moved from the ith to the jth position in version v_2 where $j \neq i$ then p is an ordered node. (2) Let $x_1, x_2, \ldots, x_k$ be a set nodes inserted as children of node p in versions $v_1, v_2, \ldots, v_m$. Let n be the number of nodes that are not inserted as right-most or left-most child of p where $0 < n \leq k$. Then p is an ordered node if $n/k \geq \tau$ where τ is called the *order threshold*.

Figure 2(a) depicts the algorithm that is used to find the type of the nodes in the hybrid XML documents. Given a sequence of consecutive versions of a hybrid

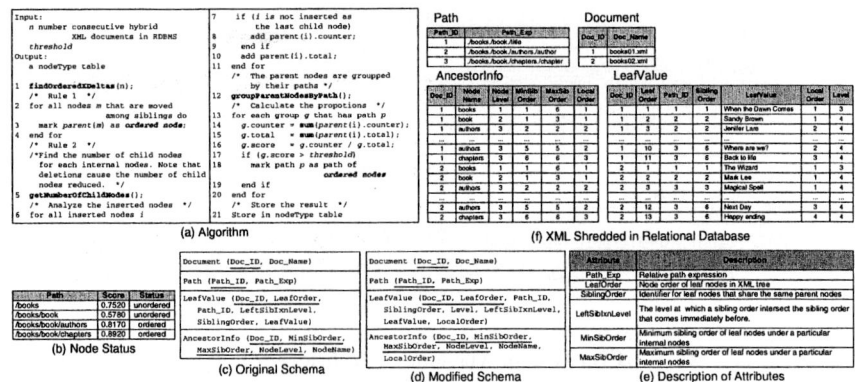

Fig. 2. Algorithm *findingNodeType*, SUCXENT Schemas, and XML data in RDBMS

XML document stored in RDBMS and the *order threshold*, the *findingNodeType* algorithm first detect the changes to these XML documents (line 1). As we need to know whether there are moved nodes, the algorithm uses an ordered change detection algorithm [7] to detect the changes. Next, the algorithm analyzes the moved nodes that are moved among their siblings from the changes (Rule 1, lines 2-4). If node m is moved among it siblings, then the $parent(m)$ is marked as ordered nodes. Next, the algorithm starts analyzing the inserted nodes (Rule 2, lines 5-20). The algorithm calculates the number of child nodes of the internal nodes (line 5). Note that it also considers the deletions. Hence, a deletion of a child node shall reduce the number of child nodes by one. The next step is calculating the number of inserted nodes that are not inserted as last child nodes (lines 6-20). The parent nodes of the inserted nodes are grouped by their node names (line 12). Then, the algorithm calculates the proportion of number of insertions occurred at the positions other than the last position and total number of insertions to a particular internal node (lines 13-20). If this proportion is greater than *order threshold*, then all internal nodes that have the same path as the path of this particular node are considered as ordered nodes. Finally, the result will be stored in the nodeType table (Figure 2(b)).

3 Finding Best Matching Subtrees

In this section, we discuss how to find the most similar subtrees in tree representations of the two versions. Given the old and new versions of a hybrid XML document and the node type information (output from the order learning module), we store both documents in the relational database by using extended version of the SUCXENT schema [8]. The schema is depicted in Figure 2(c). The extended SUCXENT schema is depicted in Figure 2(d). Figure 2(e) depicts the semantics of the attributes. Figure 2(f) depicts the relations containing two shredded XML documents in Figure 1 (partial view only).

We now introduce some definitions that we shall be using to explain algorithm for detecting the best matching subtrees. Let $L(T_1)$ and $L(T_2)$ be two sets of the leaf nodes in T_1 and T_2 respectively. Let $name(\ell)$, $level(\ell)$, and $value(\ell)$ be the node name, node level, and textual content of a leaf node ℓ respectively. Then ℓ_1 and ℓ_2 are **matching leaf nodes** (denoted as $\ell_1 \leftrightarrow \ell_2$) if $name(\ell_1) = name(\ell_2)$, $level(\ell_1) = level(\ell_2)$, and $value(\ell_1) = value(\ell_2)$, where $\ell_1 \in L(T_1)$ and $\ell_2 \in L(T_2)$. The matching leaf nodes are classified into two types: *fixed matching leaf nodes* and *shifted matching leaf nodes*. The *fixed matching leaf nodes* are ones whose positions among their siblings are not changed. The *shifted matching leaf nodes* are ones whose positions among their siblings are changed due to the insertions or deletions of their siblings, and changes of their positions among theirs siblings. Note that only the leaf nodes that are the child nodes of the ordered nodes can be classified into these two types of matching leaf nodes. Next, we define *matching sibling orders*.

Let so_1 and so_2 be two sibling orders in T_1 and T_2 respectively. Let $P = \{p_1, p_2, \ldots, p_x\}$ and $Q = \{q_1, q_2, \ldots, q_y\}$ be two sets of leaf nodes, where $\forall p_i \in P$ have the same sibling order so_1, and $\forall q_j \in Q$ have the same sibling order so_2. Then so_1 and so_2 are the **matching sibling orders** (denoted by $so_1 \leftrightarrow so_2$) if $\exists p_i \, \exists q_j$ such that $p_i \leftrightarrow q_j$ where $p_i \in P$ and $q_j \in Q$. After determining the matching sibling orders, we are able to find the *possible matching internal nodes* at which the *possible matching subtrees* are rooted. Informally, the *possible matching subtrees* are the subtrees in which they have at least one matching sibling orders. Note that the subtrees in T_1 are possible to be matched to more than one subtrees in T_2.

Formally, let $I(T_1)$ and $I(T_2)$ be two sets of the internal nodes in T_1 and T_2 respectively. Let S_1 and S_2 be two subtrees rooted at nodes $i_1 \in I(T_1)$ and $i_2 \in I(T_2)$ respectively. Let $name(i)$ and $level(i)$ be the node name and node level of an internal node i respectively. S_1 and S_2 are the **possible matching subtrees** if the following conditions are satisfied: 1) $name(i_1) = name(i_2)$, 2) $level(i_1) = level(i_2)$, and 3) $\exists P \, \exists Q$ such that $P \leftrightarrow Q$ where $P \in S_1$ and $Q \in S_2$. We only consider matching subtrees in the same level for the same reason as in [10]. Next, we determine the *best matching subtrees* from a set of possible matching subtrees. Consequently, we have to measure how similar two possible matching subtrees are. This is done by *similarity score*.

The **similarity score** $\Re$ of two subtrees t_1 and t_2 as follows. (a) If t_1 and t_2 are the unordered nodes, then $\Re(t_1, t_2) = \frac{2|t_1 \cap t_2|}{|t_1 \cup t_2|}$. (b) If t_1 and t_2 are the ordered nodes, then $\Re(t_1, t_2) = \frac{2|A|+|B|}{|t_1 \cup t_2|}$ where $|t_1 \cup t_2|$ is the total number of leaf nodes of subtrees t_1 and t_2, $|t_1 \cap t_2|$ is number of matching leaf nodes, and $|A|$ and $|B|$ are numbers of nodes of fixed and shifted matching leaf nodes in t_1 and t_2 respectively ($A \cap B = \emptyset$). The similarity score has a value between 0 and 1. Based on the similarity score, we are able to classify the matching subtree into three types: 1)$\Re(t_1, t_2) = 1$. This happens if they are identical except for the orders among siblings (for the child nodes of unordered nodes), and identical (for the child nodes of ordered nodes). 2)**Unmatching Subtrees** ($\Re(t_1, t_2) = 0$). We say two subtrees are unmatching if they are totally different. 3)**Matching Subtrees**

$(0 < \Re(t_1, t_2) < 1)$. The matching subtrees have some parts in the trees that are corresponded each other.

Definition 1. *Let $t \in T_1$ be a subtree in T_1 and $P \subseteq T_2$ be a set of subtrees in T_2. Also t and $t_i \in P$ are possible matching subtrees $\forall\ 0 < i \leq |P|$. Then t and t_i are the **best matching subtrees** (denoted by $t \backsim t_i$) iff $(\Re(t, t_i) > \Re(t, t_j))\ \forall\ 0 < j \leq |P|$ and $i \neq j$.*

3.1 Algorithm

The algorithm for determining the best matching subtrees is depicted in Figure 3(a). Given two XML trees T_1 and T_2 shredded in a relational database as shown in Figure 2(f), the similarity score threshold (say θ=0.2000), and the orderedNodes set (say "/books/book/authors" and "/books/book/chapters"), the *findBestMatchingSubtree* algorithm starts finding the matching best subtrees by checking the root nodes of T_1 and T_2 (lines 1-3, Figure 3(a)). If they have different names, then both XML documents are considered as different. Consequently, the delta only consists of a deletion of T_1 and an insertion of T_2. Otherwise, the algorithm finds the *matching sibling orders* (line 4, Figure 3(a)). The SQL query for retrieving the matching sibling order can be found in [6]. The results are stored in the TempSO table (Figure 4(b)) whose attributes are depicted in Figure 4(a).

Next, the *findBestMatchingSubtree* algorithm determines the deepest level *max-Level* of the root nodes of subtrees in T_1 and T_2 (line 5, Figure 3(a)). For each level *curLevel* starting from level *maxLevel* to the level of the root nodes of the trees (level=1), the algorithm starts by finding the best matching subtrees (lines 6-10, Figure 3(a)). First, the algorithm finds the *possible matching internal nodes* (line 7, Figure 3(a)). The SQL query shown in Figure 3(b) is used to retrieve the *possible matching internal nodes*. NodeType is used to indicate whether an internal nodes is an ordered node (NodeType="1") or an unordered node (NodeType="0"). Figure 3(c) depicts the SQL query to set the node type for ordered nodes. "ORDEREDNODES" in lines 7 and 11 are a set of ordered nodes. We store the results in the Matching table whose attributes are depicted in Figure 4(a). The Matching table of T_1 and T_2 is depicted in Figure 4(c).

The next step is to maximize the similarity scores of the possible matching internal nodes at level *curLevel* at which the possible matching subtrees are rooted (line 8, Figure 3(a)) since we may have some subtrees and sibling orders at (*curLevel*+1) in T_1 that can be matched to more than one subtrees and sibling orders in T_2 respectively, and vice versa. The *maximizeSimilarityScore* algorithm is similar to the Smith-Waterman algorithm [9] for sequence alignments. Due to the space constraints, we do not present the *maximizeSimilarityScore* algorithm here. The readers may refer to [6]. Next, the algorithm shall delete the corresponding tuples of the best matching subtrees if their similarity score is less than the specified threshold θ.

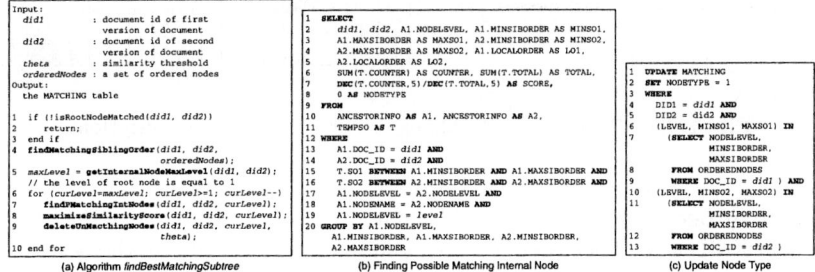

Fig. 3. Algorithms and SQL Queries

4 Detecting the Changes

We are now ready to detect different types of changes in the hybrid XML by issuing a set of SQL queries. The types of changes are detected sequentially as in the discussion. The formal definitions of types of changes can be found in [6].
Insertion of Internal Nodes. Intuitively, the inserted internal nodes are the internal nodes that are in the new version, but not in the old version. Hence, they must not be the root nodes of the best matching subtrees as they are in both versions. The SQL query depicted in Figure 5(a) (*did1* and *did2* refer to the first and second versions of the document respectively) detects the set of newly inserted internal nodes. Consider the example in Figure 1. We notice that the subtree rooted at node 102 in T_2 is inserted. The inserted internal nodes are retrieved by the SQL query depicted in Figure 5(a) and are stored in the INS_INT table as shown in Figure 6(a). The semantics of attributes of the INS_INT table are depicted in Figure 7(a).
Deletion of Internal Nodes. We can use the same intuition to find the deleted internal nodes that are in T_1, but not in T_2. The deleted internal nodes can be detected by slightly modifying the SQL query depicted in Figure 5(a). We replace the "*did2*" in line 7 with "*did1*". The "MINS02" and "MAXS02" in line 9 are replaced by "MINS01" and "MAXS01" respectively. In the example shown in Figure 1, we observe that the subtree rooted at node 11 in T_1 is deleted. The deleted internal nodes are stored in the DEL_INT table as shown in Figure 6(b).
Insertion of Leaf Nodes. The *new* leaf nodes are only available in the second version of an XML tree. These new nodes should be either in the *best matching subtrees* or in the newly *inserted subtrees*. Consider the Figure 1. The leaf nodes 103, 105, 107, 108, 109, and 110 belong to the newly *inserted subtree* rooted at node 102. The leaf node 119 is also inserted in the new version but it is contained in the best matching subtree rooted at node 116. Note that this subtree is not newly inserted one. The SQL query shown in Figure 5(b) is used to detect the inserted leaf nodes that are in the newly inserted subtrees. The inserted leaf nodes that are in the matching subtrees are detected by using the SQL query shown in Figure 5(c). The result of the queries is stored in the INS_LEAF table as shown in Figure 6(c). Note that the highlighted tuples in Figure 6(c) are actually updated leaf nodes. However, they are detected as inserted nodes.

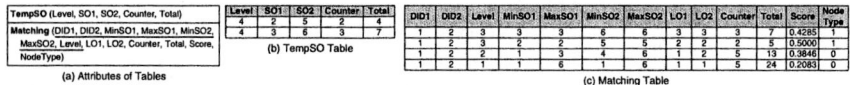

Fig. 4. The TempSO and Matching Tables, and Table Description

Deletion of Leaf Nodes. The *deleted* leaf nodes are only available in the first version of an XML tree. These deleted nodes should also be either in the *best matching subtrees* or in the *deleted subtrees*. Consider the Figure 1. The leaf nodes 12, 14, 16, 17, and 18 belong to the *deleted subtree* rooted at node 11. We also use two SQL queries for detecting these two types of deleted leaf nodes. These SQL queries are generated by slightly modifying the queries in the Figures 5(b) and (c). We replace "INS_INT" in line 4 in Figure 5(b) with "DEL_INT". We also replace the "*did2*" in line 6 in Figure 5(b) and in lines 8 and 20 in Figure 5(c) with "*did1*". The "*did1*" in line 16 in Figure 5(c) is replaced by "*did2*". We also replace "MINSO2" and "MAXSO2" in lines 10 and 21 in Figure 5(c) with "MINSO1" and "MAXSO1" respectively. The "MINSO1" and "MAXSO1" in line 18 in Figure 5(c) are replaced by "MINSO2" and "MAXSO2" respectively. Figure 6(d) depicts the result of the queries which is stored in the DEL_LEAF table. Note that the highlighted rows are actually updated leaf nodes which are detected as deleted leaf nodes.

Content Update of Leaf Nodes. Intuitively, an updated node is available in the first and second versions, but its value is different. Update operations on the leaf nodes depend on the node types of their parents. If the parent nodes are ordered nodes, then update operations on the leaf nodes can be classified into *absolute updates* and *relative updates*. In the *absolute update*, the node's position in the DOM tree is not changed, but the value has changed. In the *relative update* operation, the absolute position as well as the value of the node has changed due to insert/delete/move operations on other nodes. Otherwise, we only have one kind of update operation. We detect the updated leaf nodes by using the INS_LEAF and DEL_LEAF tables in which the inserted and deleted leaf nodes are stored respectively. In addition, we also need to use the Matching table in order to guarantee that the updated leaf nodes are in the matching subtrees. Note that we only consider the update of the content of the leaf nodes. Similar to [10], the modification of the name of an internal node is detected as a pair of deletion and insertion.

We are able to detect the absolute update operations by using the DID1, DID2, Level, SiblingOrder, LocalOrder, Path_Id, and Value attributes of the INS_LEAF and DEL_LEAF tables. For the matching internal nodes in the Matching table, we use DID1, DID2, Level, MinSO1, MaxSO1, MinSO2, and MaxSO2 attributes. The SQL query for detecting the absolute update operations is shown in Figure 5(d). The relative update operations can be detected by modifying the SQL query in Figure 5(d). "D.LOCALORDER = I.LOCALORDER" in line 13 is replaced by "D.LOCALORDER != I.LOCALORDER". The updated nodes that are the child nodes of the unordered nodes can be found by using the SQL query in Figure 5(e). Note that after each type of update operation detected, we need to delete the

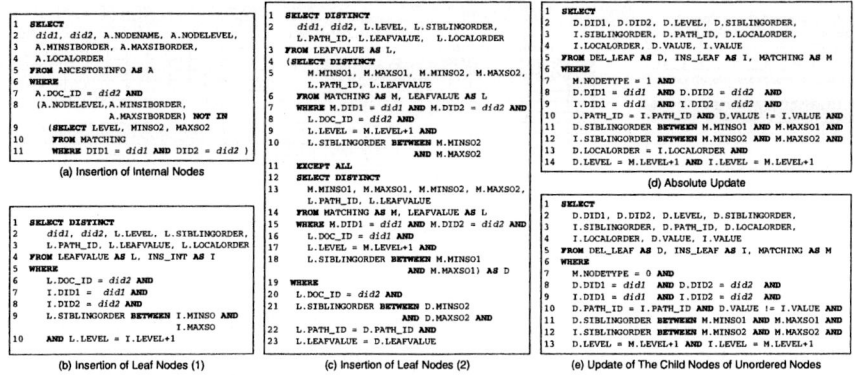

Fig. 5. SQL Queries for detecting the changes

updated nodes detected as deleted and inserted leaf nodes. The updated leaf nodes of the example in Figure 1 are shown in Figure 6(e) (the UPD_LEAF table).

We observe that the result of the SQL queries for detecting the relative updated nodes and the updated child nodes of the unordered nodes may not be correct result in some conditions as follows. First, there are more than one updated leaf child nodes under the same unordered nodes. Second, there are the deleted/inserted and updated leaf nodes occurred under the same unordered nodes. Therefore, we need to correct the result by using the *updateCorrector* algorithm. The algorithm of the *updateCorrector* function is similar to the one in [5]. Due to the space constraint, we do not present the algorithm in this paper. The readers may refer to [6].

Move Among Siblings. The naive approach of detecting the movement is to check whether or not the local order of the node has changed. However, this approach may lead to the detection of *non-optimal* deltas in certain situations. We illustrate this with a simple example. Suppose we have two versions of XML trees as depicted in Figure 7(b). The node $e2$ with value "New" is a newly inserted node. If we do not consider this newly inserted node during the move detection process, then we may detect that the nodes $e2$ with values "C" and "D" are moved among their siblings since they have different local order values in the old and new versions. Hence, the detected delta consists of two move operations and an insert operation. To overcome this problem, we simulate the insertions and deletions occurring under the same parent before detecting the moved nodes.

We observed that a deletion of node a, that has local order equal to k, will decrease the local orders of its siblings, that have local order greater than k, by one. Another observation is that an insertion of node b to be the k-th child of a parent node p will increase the local orders of the child nodes of node p, that have local order greater than or equal to k, by one. Note that we are not interested in the changes on the local orders because of insertions/deletions of its sibling nodes. Hence, we need to determine the nodes that are *really* moved among their siblings. We are able to determine these moved nodes by using the

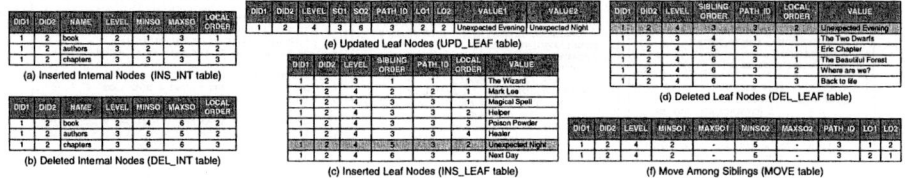

Fig. 6. Detected Delta

above observations for simulating the insertions/deletions of sibling nodes that affect on the local orders. Due to the limitation of space, we do not present the algorithm in this paper. The algorithm can be found in [6]. The moved nodes of the example in Figure 1 are shown in Figure 6(f) (the MOVE table).

5 Performance Study

We have implemented XANDY-H entirely in Java. The implementation and the database engine were run on a MS Windows 2000 Professional machine having Pentium 4 1.7 GHz processor with 512 MB of memory. The database system was IBM DB2 UDB 8.1. Appropriate indexes on the relations are created. We used a set of synthetic XML documents based on SIGMOD DTD (Figure 7(c)). We generated the second version of each XML document by using our own change generator. We distributed the percentage changes equally for each type of changes. XANDY has three variants: XANDY-U [5] for unordered XML, XANDY-O [7] for ordered XML, and XANDY-H for hybrid XML. We compared the performance of these three variants. We also compared our approach to X-Diff[10] and X-Diff-O (The option "-o" of X-Diff is activated so it calculates the minimum editing distance in finding the matchings.). Note that despite our best efforts (including contacting the authors), we could not get the Java version of XyDiff [2].

Result Quality. In this experiment, we study the effect of the percentage of changes on the *result quality* by using "Sigmod-03" data set. We set "authors" as the ordered node. A series of new versions are generated by varying the percentage of the changes from "3%" to "30%". The number of nodes involved in the deltas is counted for each approach. The number of nodes in the optimal XDeltas is compared to the one detected by the different approaches. The ratios are plotted in Figure 8(a). We observed that XANDY-H is able to detect the

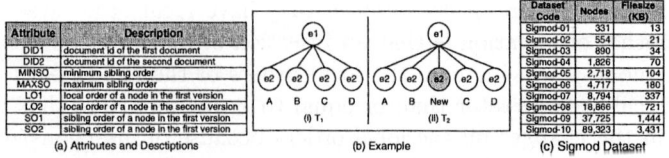

Fig. 7. Example Move among Siblings and Data sets

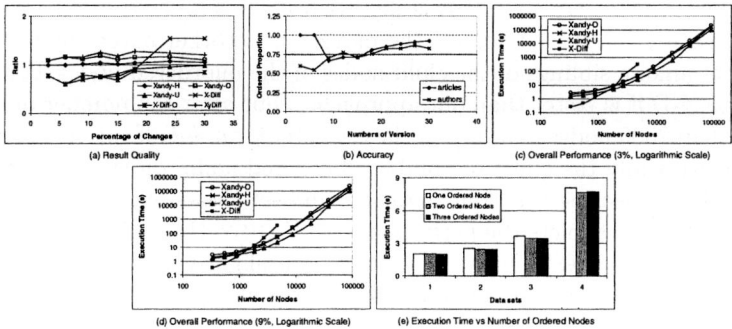

Fig. 8. Experimental Results

optimal or near optimal deltas. The ratios of XANDY-O and XyDiff are always greater than 1. This is because the movements among siblings of the child nodes of unordered nodes are detected as changes. In XANDY-H, such changes are not detected. The ratios of XANDY-U and X-Diff-O are always less than 1. This is because the unordered approaches do not detect the movements among siblings of the child nodes of ordered nodes. The ratio of X-Diff is less than 1 if the percentage of changes is less than "20%". Otherwise, it is greater than 1. This is because X-Diff does not calculate the minimum editing distance. Therefore, X-Diff may detect as a deletion of a subtree if it is changed significantly.

Accuracy of Learning Module. We generate 30 versions of a hybrid XML document based on SIGMOD DTD. The first version has 645 nodes. We set nodes "articles" and "authors" as ordered nodes, and τ is set to "0.75". Figure 8(b) depicts the accuracy of the learning module. The ordered proportion of "articles" is equal to 1 and detected as ordered nodes for the first 6 versions. The insertion of node "article" only occurs once. This insertion does not happen at the last position. After analyzing more than 18 versions, the learning module determines nodes "articles" and "authors" as ordered nodes as the ratios are greater than τ. The accuracy of the learning module depends on the changes occur in the XML documents. The learning module may fail to detect the ordered nodes in certain cases. For example, node "authors" is not detected as an ordered node if there is no occurrence of the move operation and the insertions occurred at the positions other than the last position rarely happen.

Execution Time vs. Number of Nodes. The percentages of changes are set to "3%" and "9%" and the threshold θ is set to "0.0" which shall give us the upper bound of the execution time. We set "authors" as the ordered node. Note that X-Diff is unable to detect the changes on the XML documents that have over 5000 nodes due to lack of the main memory. Figures 8(c) and (d) depict the overall performance of our approach. XANDY-U is faster than XANDY-H and XANDY-O. This is because XANDY-U does not distinguish between fixed and shifted leaf nodes. That is, XANDY-U uses a simple SQL query to find the matching leaf nodes, while XANDY-H and XANDY-O use two SQL queries that are more complex than the one used by XANDY-U. XANDY-H is slightly faster than XANDY-O in most cases. This is because XANDY-O detects the movement to other parent nodes and the movement among siblings of the child nodes of the unordered nodes. For smaller data sets, X-Diff is faster than our approaches, but after the number of nodes is greater than 2500 nodes, our approaches is faster than X-Diff (up to 40 times).

Next, we study the effect of number of ordered nodes on the performance of XANDY-H. We use the first four data sets and set the percentage of changes to "3%". Figure 8(e) depicts the performance of XANDY-H for different numbers of ordered nodes. The performance of XANDY-H is slightly affected by the number of the ordered nodes as the difference of the execution time is only up to 5%.

6 Conclusions

This paper is motivated by the fact that real life XML documents may not always be purely ordered or purely unordered. It is indeed possible to have both ordered and unordered nodes in the *same* XML document. We call such documents as *hybrid* XML. In this paper, we present a technique for detecting the changes to hybrid XML documents using relational databases. Our experimental results show that our approach generates better result quality compared to existing approaches. Also our approach is more scalable than existing main-memory algorithms and up to 40 times faster than X-Diff.

References

1. Y. CHEN, S. MADRIA, S. S. BHOWMICK. DiffXML: Change Detection in XML Data. *In DASFAA*, 2004.
2. G. COBENA, S. ABITEBOUL, A. MARIAN. Detecting Changes in XML Documents. *In ICDE*, 2002.
3. CURBERA, D. A. EPSTEIN. Fast Difference and Update of XML Documents. *In XTech*, 1999.
4. E. LEONARDI, S. S. BHOWMICK, S. MADRIA. Detecting Content Changes on Ordered XML Documents Using Relational Databases. *In DEXA*, 2004.
5. E. LEONARDI, S. S. BHOWMICK, S. MADRIA. XANDY: Detecting Changes on Large Unordered XML Documents Using Relational Databases. *In DASFAA*, 2005.
6. E. LEONARDI, SRI L. BUDIMAN, S. S. BHOWMICK. Detecting Changes to Hybrid XML Documents by Using Relational Databases. *Technical Report, CAIS, Nanyang Technological University, Singapore*, 2005. http://www.cais.ntu.edu.sg/~erwin/docs/
7. E. LEONARDI, S. S. BHOWMICK. XANDY: Detecting Changes on Large Ordered XML Documents Using Relational Database. *Technical Report, CAIS, Nanyang Technological University , Singapore*, 2004. http://www.cais.ntu.edu.sg/~erwin/docs/
8. S. PRAKASH, S. S. BHOWMICK, S. MARDIA. SUCXENT: An Efficient Path-based Approach to Store and Query XML Documents. *In DEXA*, 2004.
9. T. F. SMITH AND M. S. WATERMAN Identification of common molecular subsequences. *Journal Molecular Biology* 147:195-197, 1981.
10. Y. WANG, D. J. DEWITT, J. CAI. X-Diff: An Effective Change Detection Algorithm for XML Documents. *In ICDE*, 2003.

An Index-Based Method for Timestamped Event Sequence Matching*

Sanghyun Park[1], Jung-Im Won[1], Jee-Hee Yoon[2], and Sang-Wook Kim[3]

[1] Department of Computer Science,
Yonsei University, Korea
{sanghyun, jiwon}@cs.yonsei.ac.kr
[2] Division of Information Engineering and Telecommunications
Hallym University, Korea
jhyoon@hallym.ac.kr
[3] College of Information and Communications
Hanyang University, Korea
wook@hanyang.ac.kr

Abstract. This paper addresses the problem of timestamped event sequence matching, a new type of sequence matching that retrieves the occurrences of interesting patterns from a timestamped event sequence. Timestamped event sequence matching is useful for discovering temporal causal relationships among timestamped events. In this paper, we first point out the shortcomings of prior approaches to this problem and then propose a novel method that employs an R^*-tree to overcome them. To build an R^*-tree, it places a time window at every position of a timestamped event sequence and represents each window as an n-dimensional rectangle by considering the first and last occurrence times of each event type. Here, n is the total number of disparate event types that may occur in a target application. When n is large, we apply a grouping technique to reduce the dimensionality of an R^*-tree. To retrieve the occurrences of a query pattern from a timestamped event sequence, the proposed method first identifies a small number of candidates by searching an R^*-tree and then picks out true answers from them. We prove its robustness formally, and also show its effectiveness via extensive experiments.

Keywords: Event sequence, indexing, similarity search.

1 Introduction

A *sequence database* is a set of data sequences, each of which comprises an ordered list of symbols or numeric values [1]. *Similar sequence matching* is an operation that finds sequences similar to a query sequence from a sequence database [1,2,5,8]. During the past decades, many useful techniques have been proposed for similar sequence matching [1,2,4,5,6,7,9,11,12,16].

---

* This work was partially supported by Korea Research Foundation Grant funded by Korea Government (MOEHRD, Basic Research Promotion Fund) (KRF-2005-206-D00015), by the ITRC support program(MSRC) of IITA, and by the research fund of Korea Research Foundation with Grant KRF-2003-041-D00486.

Event	Timestamp
⋮	⋮
CiscoDCDLinkUp	19:08:01
MLMSocketClose	19:08:07
MLMStatusUp	19:08:20
⋮	⋮
MiddleLayerManagerUp	19:08:37
TCPConnectionClose	19:08:39
⋮	⋮

Fig. 1. Example of a timestamped event sequence in a network environment

Wang et al. [14] defined a new type of similar sequence matching that deals with timestamped event sequences. To exemplify this type of matching, let us examine an event management system in a network environment. Here, items, each of which is a pair of (event type, timestamp), are sequentially added into a log file in their chronological order whenever special events arise. Figure 1 shows a sequence of items in a log file.

In such environment, the queries to identify *temporal causal relationships* among events are frequently issued as follows [14]: "Find all occurrences of CiscoDCDLinkUp that are followed by MLMStatusUp within 20±2 seconds as well as TCPConnectionClose within 40±3 seconds."

In reference [14], they call a sequence of items as in Figure 1 a *timestamped event sequence* T, and regard the above query as a query sequence $Q = \langle(\text{CiscoDCDLinkUp}, 0), (\text{MLMStatusUp}, 20), (\text{TCPConnectionClose}, 40)\rangle$ with 2 as a tolerance for the interval between CiscoDCDLinkUp and MLMStatusUp and 3 as a tolerance for the interval between CiscoDCDLinkUp and TCPConnectionClose. Then, the above query is converted to the problem of *timestamped event sequence matching* which is to retrieve from T all subsequences, possibly *non-contiguous*, that are matched with Q. Since a non-contiguous subsequence can be an answer in timestamped event sequence matching, previous methods proposed for similar sequence matching are not appropriate for this new problem.

Reference [14] tackled the problem and proposed a method that employs a new index structure called an *iso-depth index*. This method uses the concept of a *time window*, a contiguous subsequence whose time interval is not larger than ξ, a *window size* determined by a user for indexing. The method extracts a time window from every possible position of a timestamped event sequence, and builds a trie [13] from a set of time windows. Then, it creates *iso-depth links*, which connects all items equally apart from the first items of their time windows, by referencing the trie via a depth-first traversal. This index structure enables to directly jump to a qualified descendent node without traversing the tree, and thus provides the capability to support efficient matching of non-contiguous event subsequences. In this paper, however, we point out two problems of this method as follows.

1. This method performs well when a query specifies the exact values for the time intervals between the first and the following events in a query sequence (i.e., the tolerance of 0). When the tolerance is larger than 0, however, it has to access multiple chains of iso-depth links for each event specified in a query sequence. Thus, the performance of the method becomes worse as the tolerance gets larger.
2. When constructing the iso-depth index from a trie, the method assigns a sequential ID to each node of the trie in a depth-first fashion. Such IDs are not changeable once the iso-depth index has been built [14]. Therefore, the method is not appropriate for dynamic situations where events continuously arrive into a sequence.

We identified that the above two problems are mainly due to the structural characteristics of an iso-depth index. Based on this identification, we propose a novel method that replaces it with a multidimensional index. Our method places a time window on every item in a timestamped event sequence. Next, it represents each time window as a rectangle over n-dimensional space by considering the first and last occurrence times of each event type. Here, n is the total number of disparate event types that may occur in a given application. Because there may be a quite large number of rectangles extracted from an event sequence, it builds an R*-tree [3], a widely-accepted multidimensional index, for indexing them. When n is large, we apply a grouping technique to reduce the dimensionality of an index. To retrieve the occurrences of a query pattern from a timestamped event sequence, the proposed method first identifies a small number of candidates by searching an R^*-tree and then picks out true answers from them. We verify the robustness and effectiveness of the proposed method.

2 Problem Definition

In this section, we define the notations necessary for further presentation and formulate the problem of timestamped event sequence matching.

Definition 1: Timestamped event sequence T

T, a timestamped event sequence, is a list of pairs of (e_i, t_i) $(1 \leq i \leq n)$ defined as follows.
$$T = \langle (e_1, t_1), (e_2, t_2), ..., (e_n, t_n) \rangle$$
where e_i is an event type and t_i is the timestamp at which e_i has occurred. Also, a pair of (e_i, t_i) is referred to as the ith item of T. The number of items in T is denoted as $|T|$. The time interval between the first and the last events, i.e., $t_n - t_1$, is denoted as $\|T\|$. The ith item of T is denoted as T_i, and its event type and timestamp are denoted as $e(T_i)$ and $ts(T_i)$, respectively. A non-contiguous subsequence T' is obtained by eliminating some items from T. Hereafter, we simply call a non-contiguous subsequence a subsequence. We also assume that all the items are listed in the ascending order of their timestamps, i.e., $t_i \leq t_j$ for $i < j$. ■

Definition 2: Query pattern QP

QP, a query pattern, consists of an event list EL and a range list RL defined below.

$$QP.EL = \langle e_1, e_2, ..., e_k \rangle$$
$$QP.RL = \langle [min_1, max_1], [min_2, max_2], ..., [min_k, max_k] \rangle$$

Each element e_i in EL expresses the ith event, and each element $[min_i, max_i]$ in RL denotes the time range within which e_i has to occur following the first event. $|QP.EL|$ is the number of events ($=k$) in $QP.EL$, and $\|QP\|$ is the time interval covered by QP, which is $max_k - min_1$. Also, $QP.EL_i$ is the ith event in $QP.EL$. ∎

Definition 3: Matching of subsequence T' and query pattern QP

Given T' and QP, they are considered to be matched if the following three conditions are all satisfied.

- **Condition 1:** $|T'| = |QP.EL|$
- **Condition 2:** $e(T'_i) = QP.EL_i$ for all i ($=1, 2, ..., |T'|$)
- **Condition 3:** $min_i \leq ts(T'_i) - ts(T'_1) \leq max_i$ for all i ($=1, 2, ..., |T'|$)

∎

Definition 4: Timestamped event sequence matching

Timestamped event sequence matching, shortly event sequence matching, is the problem of retrieving from an event sequence T all subsequences T' that are matched to a query pattern QP. ∎

3 Proposed Method

This section proposes a new indexing method that overcomes the problems of aforementioned approaches, and suggests an algorithm that uses the proposed indexing method for event sequence matching.

3.1 Indexing

The proposed index construction algorithm is given in Algorithm 1. To support efficient event sequence matching, we first build an empty R*-tree (Line 1). The dimensionality of the tree is equal to the number of disparate event types that can occur in a target application. Next, we extract a time window at every possible position of an event sequence (Line 3). The maximum value of the time intervals covered by query patterns of a target application is used as ξ, the size of a time window. Let DW denote the time window extracted at the ith position of T. Then, we construct a rectangle from DW (Line 4) and insert it into the

Algorithm 1: Index construction.

Input : Event sequence T
Output : R*-tree I

1 $I :=$ createEmptyRstarTree();
2 **for** $(i=1; i \leq |T|; i++)$ **do**
3 $\quad$ $DW :=$ extractTimeWindow(T, i);
4 $\quad$ $DR :=$ constructDataRectangle(DW);
5 $\quad$ insertRectangle(I, DR, i);
6 return I;

R*-tree using i as its identifier (Line 5). Finally, we return the R*-tree containing all rectangles (Line 6).

Let $E = \{E_1, E_2, ..., E_n\}$ denote a set of n disparate event types. The rectangle from the time window DW is expressed as $([min_1, max_1], [min_2, max_2], ..., [min_n, max_n])$. Here, min_i ($i = 1, 2, ..., n$) denotes the difference between $ts(DW_1)$ and $first\_ts(E_i)$ where $ts(DW_1)$ is the timestamp of the first item of DW and $first\_ts(E_i)$ is the timestamp of the first occurrence of event type E_i in DW. Similarly, max_i denotes the difference between $ts(DW_1)$ and $last\_ts(E_i)$ where $last\_ts(E_i)$ is the timestamp of the last occurrence of event type E_i in DW. We assign $\|DW\|$ to both min_i and max_i when there are no instances of event type E_i in DW.

In practice, we maintain multiple R*-trees in order to reduce the search space before starting an index search. More specifically, we insert the rectangle for the time window DW into an R*-tree I_j when the first item of DW is of event type E_j. Therefore, the proposed index structure consists of n R*-trees, $I_1, I_2, ..., I_n$, and an index table. The index table consists of n entries, each of which points to the root node of the corresponding R*-tree. Since the index table is not large in most cases, it is kept in main memory.

3.2 Event Sequence Matching

As explained in Section 2, a query pattern QP with k events has the following format: $QP.EL = \langle e_1, e_2, ..., e_k \rangle$, $QP.RL = \langle [min_1, max_1], [min_2, max_2], ..., [min_k, max_k] \rangle$. This query pattern requires that the events should occur in the order of $e_1, e_2, ..., e_k$, and there should be an event e_i within the time range of $[min_i, max_i]$ after the occurrence of the first event e_1. The event sequence matching algorithm that uses the proposed index structure is given in Algorithm 2.

We first construct a query rectangle from a given query pattern (Line 2). The minimum and maximum values of each dimension of a query rectangle are obtained from the corresponding time ranges specified in a query pattern.

Algorithm 2: Event sequence matching.

Input : Query pattern $QP = (\langle e_1, ..., e_k \rangle, \langle [min_1, max_1], ..., [min_k, max_k] \rangle)$,
Target index I, Event sequence T
Output : Set of answers A

1 $A := \{\}$;
2 $QR :=$ constructQueryRectangle(QP);
3 $C :=$ findOverlappingRectangles(I, QR);
4 **for** *(each identifier $id \in C$)* **do**
5 $\quad$ **if** *(isTrueAnswer(T, id))* **then**
6 $\quad\quad$ addAnswer(A, id);
7 return A;

---

1. If there are no time ranges specified for the event type E_i in a query pattern, then the range of the ith dimension becomes $[0, \xi]$.
2. If there is only one time range specified for the event type E_i in a query pattern, then the minimum and maximum values on that time range become the minimum and maximum values of the ith dimension, respectively.
3. If there are more than one time range specified for the event type E_i in a query pattern, then the time range with the smallest interval determines the range of the ith dimension.

After constructing the query rectangle from a query pattern, we search the multi-dimensional index I for the rectangles overlapping with the query rectangle (Line 3). As mentioned in Section 3.1, each query pattern has an associated R*-tree according to the type of its first event. Therefore, the search is performed only on the R*-tree dedicated to the type of e_1. Its location is obtained by looking up the index table. The post-processing step begins after obtaining a set of candidate rectangles from the index search. Using the identifier of each candidate rectangle, this step reads the event sequence to verify whether the candidate actually matches the query pattern (Line 5). Only the candidate rectangles which are actually matched with the query pattern are added into the result set (Line 6) and then returned to the user (Line 7). The theorem in [10] shows that the proposed matching algorithm retrieves without false dismissal [1,5] all time windows containing subsequences matched with a query pattern.

3.3 Dimensionality Reduction

The proposed index becomes very high dimensional when n is large. To prevent the problem of *dimensionality curse* [15] in this case, we apply *event type grouping* that combines n event types into a smaller number, say m, of event type groups. The composition of m groups from n event types enables the proposed n-dimensional index to be m-dimensional. Such event type grouping, however,

Algorithm 3: Event type grouping.

Input : Set of n event types $E = \{E_1, E_2, ..., E_n\}$, Event sequence T, Number of desired event type groups m
Output : Set of m event type groups G

1. Using T, compute the distance of every pair of event types;
2. Construct a complete graph with n nodes and $n(n-1)/2$ edges;
3. Attach a unique label to each node using the integer values from 1 to n. The node labeled with the integer i represents the event type E_i;
4. Attach a weight to each edge. The distance between E_i and E_j is used as a weight of the edge connecting the node i and the node j;
5. **while** *the number of components in the graph is greater than m* **do**
   $\lfloor$ Remove from the graph the edge with the largest weight;
6. Extract G, a set of m event type groups, from m components;
7. Return G;

tends to enlarge the rectangles to be stored in the index, lowering a filtering ratio in searching. Therefore, in this paper, we suggest a systematic algorithm (See Algorithm 3) that performs event type grouping with the least enlargement of the rectangles. For this algorithm, we define a distance metric [10] that measures the degree of enlargement incurred by merging each pair of event types.

4 Performance Evaluation

4.1 Experimental Environment

For the experiments, we generated synthetic event sequences with various $|T|$ and n values. The event types were generated uniformly within the range of $[1, n]$, and their interarrival times followed an exponential distribution. We used queries with 3 event items as a standard query pattern. We submitted 100 queries for an individual experiment and computed their average elapsed time. The machine for the experiments was a personal computer with a Pentium-IV 2GHz CPU, the main memory of 512 MB, and the operating system of Windows 2000 Server.

We compared the performances of the following three methods: (1) The first one is the proposed method using a 5-dimensional R^*-tree with the page size of 1KB. (2) The second one is the sequential-scan-based method. (3) The third one is the method based on an iso-depth index.

4.2 Results and Analyses

While fixing the size of the time window at 50, the first experiment compared the proposed index and the iso-depth index in terms of the index size. Figure 2 shows their sizes with increasing data set sizes and different numbers of event types. The X-axis is for the number of items in the event sequence, and the Y-axis is

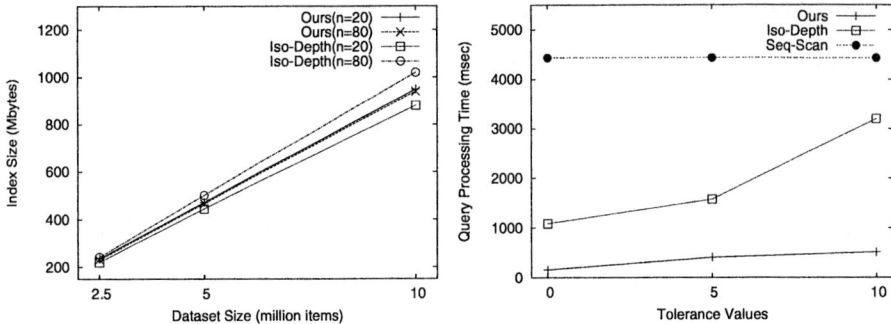

Fig. 2. Sizes of the proposed index and the iso-depth index with increasing data set sizes and different numbers of event types

Fig. 3. Query processing times of the three methods with various tolerance values of query patterns

for the index sizes when the event sequence has 2.5 million items (20M bytes), 5 million items (40M bytes), and 10 million items (80M bytes), respectively.

As clearly shown in the figure, both the proposed index and the iso-depth index grow linearly as the data set increases. It is also evident that the number of event types increases the size of the iso-depth index conspicuously but does not affect much the size of the proposed index due to event type grouping.

The second experiment compared the query processing times of the three methods with various tolerance values of query patterns. The data set had 20 event types and 5 million items, and the size of the time window was 50. The tolerance values were set 0% (=0), 10% (=5), and 20% (=10) of the time window size. The result is shown in Figure 3. The X-axis is for the tolerance values and the Y-axis is for the query processing times.

Since the sequential-scan-based method reads the entire event sequence in any cases, its query processing time does not change much with the tolerance values. On the contrary, the query processing times of our method and the iso-depth index increase conspicuously as the tolerance value grows. This is because both methods have to access more portions of the indexes when the tolerance value becomes larger. As compared with the sequential-scan-based method, our method is about 11 and 8.6 times faster when the tolerance values are 5 and 10, respectively. As compared with the iso-depth index, our method is about 3.9 and 6.3 times faster when the tolerance values are 5 and 10, respectively.

The third experiment compared the query processing times of the three methods with various data set sizes. The size of the time window was 50, and the tolerance value of query patterns was 5 (i.e., 10% of the time window size). The number of event types was 20 at first and then 80. The result is shown in Figure 4. The X-axis is for the number of items in the event sequence and the Y-axis is for the query processing times.

The result shows that the query processing times of all three methods increase linearly with the data set sizes. The query processing time of the sequential-scan-

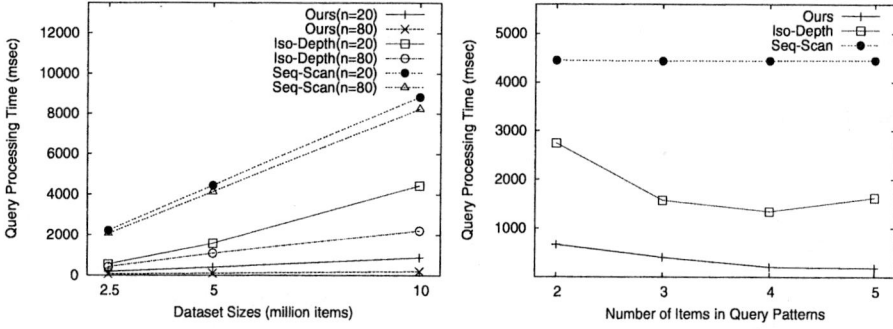

Fig. 4. Query processing times of the three methods with increasing data set sizes and different numbers of event types

Fig. 5. Query processing times of the three methods with various numbers of event items in query patterns

based method does not change much with the number of event types. However, the query processing times of our method and the iso-depth index decrease when the number of event types increases from 20 to 80. This is because both methods generate a smaller number of candidates as the number of event types grows. As compared with the sequential-scan-based method and the iso-depth index, our method performs about 40.9 times and 10.9 times faster, respectively, when the data set has 10 million items and 80 event types.

The fourth experiment compared the query processing times of the three methods with various numbers of event items in query patterns. The data set had 20 event types and 5 million data items. The size of the time window was 50 and the tolerance value was 5. The result is shown in Figure 5.

The query processing time of the sequential-scan-based method does not change much with the number of events in query patterns. However, the query processing times of our method and the iso-depth index decrease when the number of events in query patterns increases. This is because both methods produce a smaller number of candidates as query patterns have more events inside. Especially in our method, the query rectangles become smaller when the query patterns have more events inside, which significantly reduces the number of candidates retrieved by the index search.

5 Conclusions

Timestamped event sequence matching is useful for discovering temporal causal relationships among timestamped events. In this paper, we have proposed a novel method for effective processing of timestamped event sequence matching. According to the performance results, the proposed method shows a significant speedup by up to a few orders of magnitude in comparison with the previous ones. Furthermore, the performance improvement becomes bigger (1) as tolerance ranges get larger, (2) as the number of event types increases, (3) as a data set grows in size, and (4) a query sequence gets longer.

References

1. R. Agrawal, C. Faloutsos, and A. Swami, "Efficient Similarity Searchin Sequence Databases", *In Proc. Int'l. Conf. on Foundations of Data Organization and Algorithms*, FODO, pp. 69-84, 1993.
2. R. Agrawal, K. Lin, H. S. Sawhney, and K. Shim, "Fast Similarity Search in the Presence of Noise, Scaling, and Translation in Time-Series Databases", *In Proc. Int'l. Conf. on Very Large Data Bases*, VLDB, pp. 490-501, Sept. 1995.
3. N. Beckmann, H. Kriegel, R. Schneider, and B. Seeger, "The R*-tree: An Efficient and Robust Access Method for Points and Rectangles", *In Proc. Int'l Conf. on Management of Data*, ACM SIGMOD, pp. 322-331, 1990.
4. K. K. W. Chu and M. H. Wong, "Fast Time-Series Searching with Scaling and Shifting", *In Proc. Int'l. Symp. on Principles of Database Systems*, ACM PODS, pp. 237-248, May 1999.
5. C. Faloutsos, M. Ranganathan, and Y. Manolopoulos, "Fast Subsequence Matching in Time-series Databases", *In Proc. Int'l. Conf. on Management of Data*, ACM SIGMOD, pp. 419-429, May 1994.
6. D. Q. Goldin and P. C. Kanellakis, "On Similarity Queries for Time-Series Data: Constraint Specification and Implementation", *In Proc. Int'l. Conf. on Principles and Practice of Constraint Programming*, CP, pp. 137-153, Sept. 1995.
7. S. W. Kim, S. H. Park, and W. W. Chu, "An Index-Based Approach for Similarity Search Supporting Time Warping in Large Sequence Databases", *In Proc. Int'l. Conf. on Data Engineering*, IEEE ICDE, pp. 607-614, 2001.
8. Y. S. Moon, K. Y. Whang, and W. K. Loh, "Duality-Based Subsequence Matching in Time-Series Databases", *In Proc. Int'l. Conf. on Data Engineering*, IEEE ICDE, pp. 263-272, 2001.
9. S. Park, W. W. Chu, J. Yoon, and C. Hsu "Efficient Searches for Similar Subsequences of Different Lengths in Sequence Databases", *In Proc. Int'l. Conf. on Data Engineering*, IEEE ICDE, pp. 23-32, 2000.
10. S. Park, J. Won, J. Yoon, and S. Kim, "An Index-Based Method for Timestamped Event Sequence Matching", Technical Report, Yonsei University, 2004.
11. D. Rafiei and A. Mendelzon, "Similarity-Based Queries for Time-Series Data", *In Proc. Int'l. Conf. on Management of Data*, ACM SIGMOD, pp. 13-24, 1997.
12. D. Rafiei, "On Similarity-Based Queries for Time Series Data", *In Proc. Int'l. Conf. on Data Engineering*, IEEE ICDE, pp. 410-417, 1999.
13. G. A. Stephen, *String Searching Algorithms*, World Scientific Publishing, 1994.
14. H. Wang, C. Perng, W. Fan, S. Park, and P. Yu, "Indexing Weighted Sequences in Large Databases", *In Proc. Int'l Conf. on Data Engineering*, IEEE ICDE, pp. 63-74, 2003.
15. R. Weber, H.-J. Schek, and S. Blott, "A Quantitative Analysis and Performance Study for Similarity Search Methods in High-Dimensional Spaces", *In Proc. Int'l. Conf. on Very Large Data Bases*, VLDB, pp. 194-205, 1998.
16. B. K. Yi and C. Faloutsos, "Fast Time Sequence Indexing for Arbitrary Lp Norms", *In Proc. Int'l. Conf. on Very Large Data Bases*, VLDB, pp. 385-394, 2000.

Time Parameterized Interval R-Tree for Tracing Tags in RFID Systems[*]

ChaeHoon Ban[1], BongHee Hong[2], and DongHyun Kim[3]

[1] Kyungnam College of Information & Technology, Korea
chban@kit.ac.kr
[2] Pusan National University, Korea
bhhong@pusan.ac.kr
[3] Dongseo University, Korea
pusrover@dongseo.ac.kr

Abstract. For tracing tag locations, the trajectories should be modeled and indexed in a radio frequency identification (RFID) system. The trajectory of a tag is represented as a line that connects two spatiotemporal locations captured when the tag enters and leaves the vicinity of a reader. If a tag enters but does not leave a reader, its trajectory is represented only as a point captured at entry. Because the information that a tag stays in a reader is missing from the trajectory represented only as a point, it is impossible to find the tag that remains in a reader. To solve this problem we propose the data model in which trajectories are defined as time-parameterized intervals and new index scheme called the Time Parameterized Interval R-tree. We also propose new insert and split algorithms to enable efficient query processing. We evaluate the performance of the proposed index scheme and compare it with the R-tree and the R*-tree. Our experiments show that the new index scheme outperforms the other two in processing queries of tags on various datasets.

1 Introduction

RFID is a labeling method in which electronic tags are attached to physical objects and identified when they enter and leave the vicinity of antenna connected to a device known as a reader. There are many applications for RFID systems, such as automated manufacturing, inventory tracking and supply chain management, that need to trace trajectories as well as monitor present locations of the tags[7].

A spatiotemporal index can be constructed for tracing trajectories of tags because they move continuously like moving objects. As the moving objects report periodically their locations while moving, an index can be constructed with trajectories represented as the lines by connecting spatiotemporal locations[3][5][6]. A similar index for tags can be constructed with spatiotemporal locations captured when tags move between readers.

---

[*] This work was supported by the Regional Research Centers Program(Research Center for Logistics Information Technology), granted by the Korean Ministry of Education & Human Resources Development.

There are index methods, namely the 3D R-tree[3], the 2+3 R-tree[5] and the HR-tree[6] for moving objects. The 3D R-tree is the 3-dimensional version of the R-tree[1] in which the third dimension corresponds to time. 2+3 R-tree constructs two kinds of indexes; one presents positions as points and the other represents past trajectories as lines. The HR-tree maintains R-trees for each timestamp; it performs well for objects that change locations infrequently.

The problem with using any of the above index schemes for tags is that tags that enter a reader but do not leave cannot be found in the index. The trajectory of a tag is represented as a line by connecting two spatiotemporal locations captured when the tag enters and then leaves the vicinity of a reader. If a tag enters but does not leave a reader, its trajectory is represented only as a point captured at entry. Because the information that a tag stays in a reader is missing from the trajectory represented only as a point, it is impossible to find the tag that remains in a reader. Therefore, trajectory of the tag should be treated differently in the index.

In this paper, we propose a data model of tag's trajectory and an index scheme in order to solve the problem. Trajectories of tags are represented as time-parameterized intervals whose lengths are dependent on time. Although a tag may only be reported when entering a reader, it is still possible to process queries because its trajectory is represented not as a point but as a time-dependent line. For the time-parameterized intervals we propose a new index scheme called the TPIR-tree(Time Parameterized R-tree) and algorithms of insert and split for processing query efficiently. We also evaluate the performance of the proposed index scheme and compare it with the previous indexes.

The remainder of the paper is structured as follows. The next section reviews previous research on indexing methods for moving objects. Section 3 identifies the problem with previous indexes. Section 4 proposes the data model using time-parameterized intervals for solving the problem. Section 5 suggests the new index scheme and the method of processing queries. We also propose new insert and split algorithms in order to process queries efficiently. Section 6 implements the TPIR-tree and shows its superiority over the other indexes. Finally, section 7 presents a summary of this paper and indicates areas of possible future work.

2 Related Work

There are the index methods, namely the 3D R-tree[3], the 2+3 R-tree[5] and the HR-tree[6] for the moving objects which have similarities to tags. The 3D R-tree is a simple extension of the original R-tree[1] and treats time as third dimension. Because particular applications, such as multimedia objects authoring, involve objects that do not change their location through time, no dead space is introduced by their three dimensional representation. However, this approach creates empty space and high overlaps in the index when used for moving objects.

The 2+3 R-tree uses two R-trees, one for two-dimensional points and the other for three-dimensional lines. The two-dimensional points represent the current spatial information about the data points and the three-dimensional lines would represent historical information. It is important to note that both trees may need to be searched, depending on the time point with respect to which the queries are posed. Moreover, both trees require updating when new data is inserted.

The HR-tree maintains the R-trees for each timestamp. Different index instances are created for different transaction timestamps. However, common paths are stored only once, to save disk space, because they are shared between structures. The performance in processing queries with this method is poor because large numbers of nodes are created for moving objects that frequently change their positions.

3 Problem Definition

We introduce the RFID system in this section and describe the events generated by tag movements. We also define the trajectory of the tag, and discuss problems with using previous index schemes.

3.1 Environment

The RFID system consists of tags, readers and a host server. Tags, which are attached to moving objects such as containers and pallets, move between readers in this system. Readers, placed in specific positions, are able to identify tags within associated interrogation regions and record their spatiotemporal locations. As a tag enters the interrogation region, the *Enter* event occurs and the reader reports the event. When a tag leaves the region, the *Leave* event occurs and the reader reports the event [7].

The tags in the RFID system have similar characteristics to the moving objects. Moving objects continuously change their positions. Tags also change their positions as they enter and leave the readers. Therefore, the index method for moving objects can be applied to trace the trajectories of tags.

In previous indexes for moving objects, the trajectory is represented as a line by connecting two spatiotemporal locations. For example, the moving object reporting its location (x_i, y_i) at time t_i and then (x_{i+1}, y_{i+1}) at t_{i+1} has the trajectory presented as the line $\overline{(x_i, y_i, t_i), (x_{i+1}, y_{i+1}, t_{i+1})}$ mapped in 3-dimensional space whose axes are spatial location, x, y and time, t.

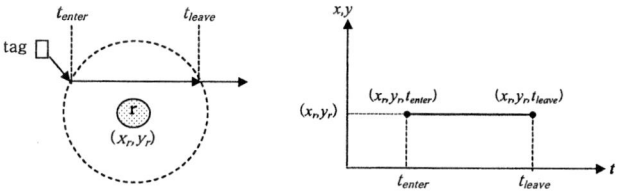

Fig. 1. Trajectory of tag

Similarly, we can represent trajectories of tags as a line captured when tags enter and leave a reader. Notice that the spatial locations of moving objects are their actual locations, but for tags, the locations are those of readers that identify them. We define the trajectory of the tag as follows. We denote x, y, t as the axes of 3-dimensional space, x_r and y_r as spatial location of the tag's reader, and t_{enter} and t_{leave} as the times of *Enter* and *Leave* events.

Definition 1: a tag's trajectory $tr_{tag} = \{(x,y,t) \in R^3 \mid x = x_r, y = y_r, t_{enter} \leq t \leq t_{leave}\}$

For example, let us assume that the *Enter* event occurred at time t_{enter} and the *Leave* event occurred at time t_{leave} as shown in Fig 1. If the reader r is located at (x_r, y_r), a spatiotemporal location of (x_r, y_r, t_{enter}) is captured at the *Enter* event, and (x_r, y_r, t_{leave}) is captured at the *Leave* event. The trajectory of the tag is the line that connects these coordinates.

3.2 The Problem of Representing the Trajectory

If a tag enters but does not leave a reader, a spatiotemporal location is only reported for the entry. Because the information that a tag stays in a reader is missing from the trajectory represented only as a point, it is impossible to find that tag. Let t_{now} be the present time, t_{enter} be time of the *Enter* event, and t_{leave} be the time of the *Leave* event. If $t_{enter} \leq t_{now} < t_{leave}$, then the reader only reported the location of tag at its entry time. Since its trajectory is not complete, having only single point, the entry location, we cannot find the trajectory of a tag that remains within a reader's interrogation region.

This situation is illustrated in Fig 2. Assume that the tag entered the reader r_1 at time t_0 and left at t_2. According to the Definition 1, the trajectory tr_1 from t_0 to t_2 is generated as shown in Fig. 2-(b), and inserted into the index. However, if the tag entered r_2 at time t_1 but did not leave, the leave time of the tag is null in the r_2. Since t_{leave} is null, tr_2 is inserted as a point. The region query, R_1, is used to find trajectories in r_1 and r_2 at certain time as shown in Fig. 2-(b). The query processor in processing R_1 searches the index and generates the candidate set. The candidate set of R_1 could include tr_1 but not tr_2, since tr_2 does not overlap with R_1. It should be required to deal with trajectories that have only entry times.

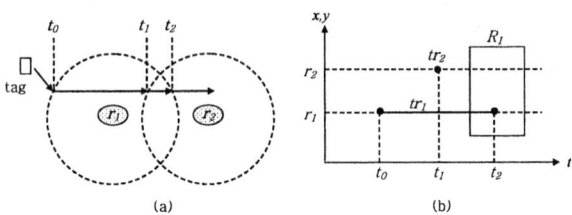

Fig. 2. Problem resulting from staying of a tag in a reader

The basic idea to solve this problem is the time-parameterized intervals. The time-parameterized interval means its time-length is dependent on time. Although a tag reported only *Enter* event, it is possible to process queries because its trajectory is represented as a time-dependent line. In this paper, we propose the data model of time-parameterized interval for trajectories of tags, and the index scheme. We also evaluate the performance of the proposed index scheme compared with the previous indexes.

4 Time-Parameterized Interval Data Model for Tags

The time-parameterized interval, which we call tp-interval, is created when a tag enters a reader. As time changes, the tp-interval changes its value in the time-domain. In the following definitions, we denote tid, x, y, t as axes of 4-dimensional space, to as an identification of a tag, x_r and y_r as spatial location of the tag(reader), t_{enter} as time of Enter event, and $f(t)$ as a function of t.

Definition 2: Time-parameterized interval = $\{(tid,x,y,t) \in R^4 \mid tid = to, x = x_r, y = y_r, t_{enter} \leq t \leq f(t)\}$.

When a tag enters a reader, the tp-interval is created and $f(t)$ is t_{now}, present time that continuously changes. The time-length of the tp-interval is $t_{enter} \leq t \leq t_{now}$, which also change continuously because of t_{now}. Since the trajectory of a tag which enters but does not leave is represented as a time-dependent line, it is possible to process queries when $t_{enter} \leq t_{now} < t_{leave}$. When the tag leaves the reader, the $f(t)$ is changed to t_{leave} and time-length of the tp-interval is $t_{enter} \leq t \leq t_{leave}$. It is also possible to process queries when $t_{now} \geq t_{leave}$.

An example using the tp-intervals is shown in Fig. 3. Assume that a tag enters a reader at t_{enter} and leaves at t_{leave} as shown in Fig. 3-(a). For $t_{enter} \leq t_{now} < t_{leave}$, the trajectory of the tag is the tp-interval whose time-length is $[t_{enter}, t_{now}]$ because it entered but did not leave, as shown in Fig. 3-(b). For $t_{now} \geq t_{leave}$, the trajectory of tag is the tp-interval whose time-length is $[t_{enter}, t_{leave}]$ because it has left the reader in Fig. 3-(c). As we defined trajectories of tags as the tp-interval, it is possible to process queries always.

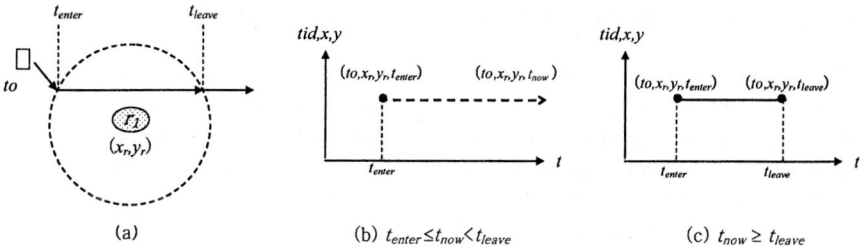

Fig. 3. An example illustrating the tp-interval

The queries retrieve all tp-intervals within specific regions. There are several queries in RFID systems. In the following, we denote $[a^\vdash, a^\dashv]$ as a projection onto a coordinate axis.

Type 1: FIND query: Q = $(tid, [t^\vdash, t^\dashv])$ returns the location(s) of tag tid at $[t^\vdash, t^\dashv]$.
Type 2: LOOK query: Q = $([x^\vdash, x^\dashv], [y^\vdash, y^\dashv], [t^\vdash, t^\dashv])$ returns the set of tags in specific location $[x^\vdash, x^\dashv], [y^\vdash, y^\dashv]$ at $[t^\vdash, t^\dashv]$.
Type 3: HISTORY query: Q = (tid) returns all location(s) of tag tid.
Type 4: WITH query: Q = $(tid, [t^\vdash, t^\dashv])$ returns identifiers of tags located in the same place with tag tid at $[t^\vdash, t^\dashv]$.

The tp-intervals are mapped in 4-dimensional space, unlike trajectories as defined in Definition 1. The representation of the tp-interval with *tid* as another axis allows more efficient processing of FIND, HISTORY and WITH queries. Because *tid* is required as another the parameter, we employ *tid* as the forth dimension of the data space.

5 Time Parameterized Interval R-Tree

In this section we describe the TPIR-tree(Time Parameterized Interval R-tree) for the trajectories of tags. We first define the data structure and the search algorithm used in the index for tp-intervals defined in section 4. We also propose new insert and split algorithms that take advantage of the characteristics of tp-intervals for efficient query processing.

5.1 Data Structure

A leaf node in the TPIR-tree contains entries that are tp-intervals of the form <*MBB*>. The *MBB* is a 4-dimensional minimal boundary box which is the form of <*tid, x, y,* $[t^{\vdash}, t^{\dashv}]$>, instead of <$[tid^{\vdash}, tid^{\dashv}], [x^{\vdash}, x^{\dashv}], [y^{\vdash}, y^{\dashv}], [t^{\vdash}, t^{\dashv}]$> because the identification and spatial location cannot be changed at $[t^{\vdash}, t^{\dashv}]$. If a tag enters a reader but does not leave, then the tp-interval of the form <*tid, x, y, t_{enter}, now*> is inserted. We call it the now interval and denote it *nowI*. If a tag enters and leaves, the tp-interval of the form <*tid, x, y, t_{enter}, t_{leave}*> is inserted. We call it the fixed interval and denote it *fixedI*.

A non-leaf node contains entries of the form <*child-pointer, state, MBB*>, where *child-pointer* is the pointer to a child node, *state* is the entry type and *MBB* is a 4-dimensional minimal boundary box. The *state* of entry is classified as either *fixedEntry* or *nowEntry*.

A *fixedEntry* is an entry whose child node contains only *fixedEntry*s or *fixedI*s. We construct the *MBB* of a *fixedEntry* in the same manner as previous schemes where it is represented as two 4-dimensional points that contain all the entries in the child node.

A *nowEntry* is an entry whose child node contains more than one *nowEntry* or *nowI*. If we construct a *MBB* whose end-time is *now* because of a *nowI* or a *nowEntry* in its child node, the time-length of the *MBB* continues to increase. It leads to useless of insert and split polices based on area criterion. Therefore we construct the *MBB* of a *nowEntry* with the reported points in its child node. At the leaf-1 level, the reported points include both the entry and exit points of *fixedI*(s), but only entry point(s) of *nowI*(s). At the upper level of leaf-1, we construct *MBB*s which cover all entries in the child node. As we use this scheme, *nowI* and *nowEntry*s should be extended when processing queries. We will describe it in the next clause.

Let us assume that there are the *fixedI*s and *nowI*s in 4-dimensional space in Fig. 4-(a). The leaf node, R2, contains three *fixedI*s in its *MBB*, as shown in Fig. 4-(a). R2 is a *fixedEntry* in the parent node, R1, because its entries are all *fixedI*s in Fig. 4-(b). R3 is a *nowEntry* because it contains one *fixedI* and two *nowI*s, and its *MBB* covers the *fixedI* and start points of each *nowI*. In the same manner, R4 and R1 are both *nowEntry*s in their respective parent nodes.

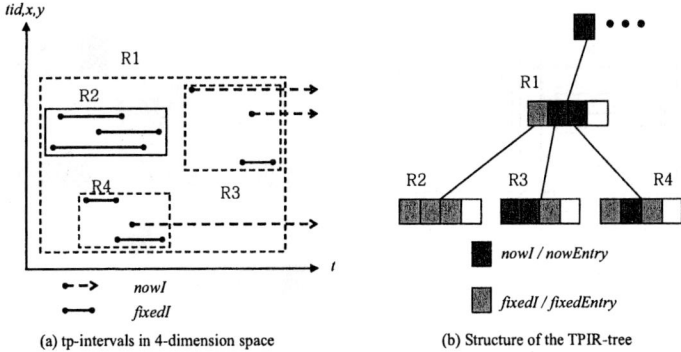

Fig. 4. An example of the TPIR-tree

5.2 The Search Algorithm

The search algorithm descends the tree from the root in the similar manner to the R-tree search. However, the TPIR-tree examines differently dependent on types of nodes, unlike previous method. Until leaf nodes are found, we examine *fixedEntry*s whose *MBB* intersect a query region. In the case of *nowEntry*s, we extend its *MBB* to *now*, and then determine whether it intersects the query region because *MBB* is represented with the start point of *nowI*. After leaf nodes are found, we examine *fixedI* and *nowI* to obtain the query results. The search algorithm is as follows.

```
TPIR_Search( root, q )
TPIR_S1 Set N to be the root
TPIR_S2 If N is a leaf
         for each entry e
             if e = fixedI  AND  e∩q then return e
             else if e = nowI  AND  e_extend ∩ q then return e
        else
         for each entry e
             if e = fixedEntry  AND  e∩q then TPIR_Search( e, q )
             else if e = nowEntry  AND  e_extend ∩ q then TPIR_Search( e, q )
         endif
```

Fig. 5. The search algorithm

Assume that the TPIR-tree is constructed as shown in Fig. 6. The node R1 is examined because it intersects the query directly. R3 is then examined because it intersects the query region after its *MBB* is extended. Finally, all entries in R3 are examined and then the *nowI* is the result because it intersects the query after it is extended.

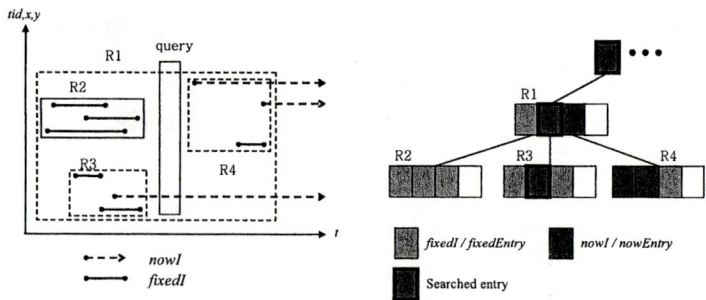

Fig. 6. An example using the search algorithm

5.3 The Insert Algorithm

The insertion process is considerably different than the procedure in the R-trees[1][2]. The insertion strategy for the R-tree is based on the least area enlargement criterion. This leads to high overlap and inefficient query processing because it does not consider that the *nowEntry* is extended when processing query. In the following, we define *Local Fixed MBB(LFMBB)* to calculate area enlargement in order to consider characteristic of *nowEntry* in the TPIR-tree.

Definition 3: *LFMBB* of the *nowEntry* is *MBB* whose end time is fixed to the maximum time of entries in the node.

Table 1. Area enlargement for entries. Area( ) is a function to calculate area. *MBB'* or *LFMBB'* means *MBB* or *LFMBB* which includes inserted interval

Inserted interval	Chosen entry to insert	Area enlargement
fixedI	*fixedEntry*	Area(*MBB'*) - Area(*MBR*)
	nowEntry	Area(*LFMBB'*) - Area(*LFMBB*)
nowI	*fixedEntry*	Area(*LFMBB'*) – Area(*MBB*)
	nowEntry	Area(*LFMBB'*) - Area(*LFMBB*)

```
TPIR_Insert( root, I )
TPIR_I1 Set N to be the root
TPIR_I2 If N is a leaf
           return N
        else
           Choose the entry e by least new area enlargement. Resolve ties by least overlap enlargement.
              If I = nowI and chosen e = fixedEntry then  e.state = nowEntry
           endif
        endif
TPIR_I3 Set N to be the childnode pointed to by the childpointer of e and repeat from TPIR_I2
```

Fig. 7. The insert algorithm

As shown in Table 1, the method for calculating area enlargement depends on the types of inserted intervals and entries. When *fixedI* is inserted, the area enlargement of *fixedEntry* follows same method of previous algorithm, but that of *nowEntry* uses *LFMBB*. In case of inserting *nowI*, we use *LFMBB* and the *MBB* of *fixedEntry* because it changes its state to *nowEntry* after inserting *nowI*. *nowEntry* is the same as inserting *fixedI*. The insert algorithm is as follows.

5.4 The Split Algorithm

When a node overflows, previous methods use margins to choose a split-axis, and then split the node by minimizing the overlap. This leads to high overlap and inefficient query processing because previous methods do not allow the extension of *nowEntry* and *nowI* when a query processes. In the following, we define *Local Fixed nowI(LFnowI)* for splitting nodes more efficiently.

Definition 4: *LFnowI* is the *nowI* whose end point is fixed to the maximum time of all entries in the leaf node.

In the TPIR-tree, a leaf node is split using the previous method with *fixedI* and *LFnowI*, which is from *nowI*. A non-leaf node is also split using the previous method with the *MBB* of a *fixedEntry* and the *LFMBB* of a *nowEntry*. After splitting the node, states of entries in its parent nodes should be changed and the split is propagated to the root. The split algorithm is as follows.

```
TPIR_Split($N_{old}$, $N_{new1}$, $N_{new2}$)
If $N_{old}$ is leaf node then
    change all nowIs to LFnowIs in $N_{old}$ and invoke $R^*$_Split($N_{old}$, $N_{new1}$, $N_{new2}$)
    set state of entries which indicate $N_{new1}$ and $N_{new2}$ in the parent node
else
    change all MBBs of nowEntrys to LFMBBs in $N_{old}$ and invoke $R^*$_Split($N_{old}$, $N_{new1}$, $N_{new2}$)
    set state of entries which indicate $N_{new1}$ and $N_{new2}$ in the parent node
endif
```

Fig. 8. The split algorithm

6 Performance Comparison

We compare TPIR-tree with the R-tree and the R*-tree using varied sets of data and queries. Well-known and widely accepted RFID datasets for experimental purpose do not exist. Due to this lack of real data, our performance evaluation consists of experiments using synthetic datasets. We develop the Tag Data Generator(TDG) based on the Generate Spatio-Temporal Data(GSTD)[4]. The TDG creates trajectories of tags with various distributions, and allows the user to generate a set of time-parameterized line segments from a specified number of tags. We use five sets of FIND and LOOK query windows with a range of 2, 5, and 10% of the total range with respect to each dimension. Each query set includes 1,000 query windows.

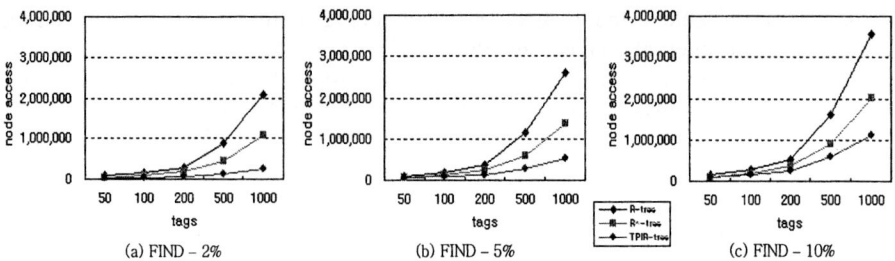

Fig. 9. FIND queries – 2%, 5%, 10%

Fig. 9 shows the number of total node accesses for various FIND queries and datasets. Each tag reports 1,000 *Enter* and *Leave* events; the type of distribution is Gaussian. The TPIR-tree outperforms both the R-tree and the R*-tree, and the gaps in the results between the indexes increased with the number of tags.

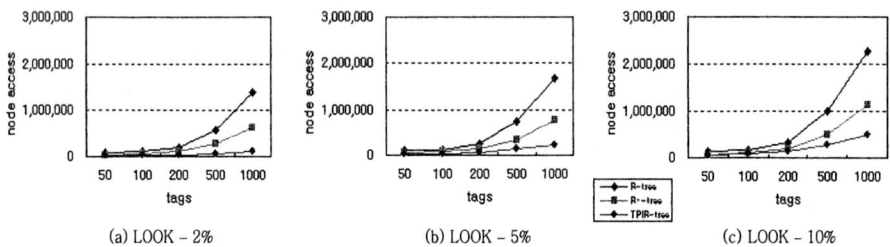

Fig. 10. LOOK queries – 2%, 5%, 10%

Fig. 10 shows the number of total node accesses for various LOOK queries and datasets. The number tag reports and the distribution of dataset is same as for the FIND experiments. The TPIR-tree also outperforms both the R-tree and the R*-tree and the relative gaps in performance increase with the number of tags. The FIND query accesses more nodes than the LOOK query does because the FIND query has zero extent at spatial dimension x and y but the LOOK query has zero extent at identification dimension *tid*.

7 Conclusions and Future Work

An index for trajectories of tags can be constructed using the scheme of moving objects because of their similarity. That index scheme cannot, however, deal with tags that remain in the vicinities of readers.

To solve this problem, we defined the trajectory of the tag using the time-parameterized interval. The time-parameterized interval is a trajectory whose time-length depends on time. Although a tag may only report *Enter* event, it is still possible to process queries because the trajectory is represented as a time-dependent line.

We suggested new index scheme called the TPIR-tree based on the time-parameterized intervals and defined data structures for the tree. To process the query more efficiently, we suggested new insert and split algorithms that use area calculations for entries.

We developed TDG based on the GSTD for synthesizing datasets. Using these datasets, we carried out an extensive performance evaluation of the TPIR-tree, and compared it with the R-tree and the R*-tree. The experiments show that the TPIR-tree outperforms both the R-tree and R*-tree for FIND and LOOK queries.

Future work will include the refinement of the insert and split algorithm. Novel queries, such as the combined and nearest neighborhood queries, deserve further research.

References

1. A. Guttman, "R-trees: A dynamic index structure for spatial searching", In Proc. ACM SIGMOD, pp.47-54, 1984.
2. N. Beckmann and H. P. Kriegel, "The R*-tree: An Efficient and Robust Access Method for Points and Rectangles", In Proc. ACM SIGMOD, pp.332-331, 1990
3. Y. Theodoridis, M. Vazirgiannis and T. Sellis, "Spatio-Temporal Indexing for Large Multimedia Applications", ICMCS, pp.441-448, 1996
4. Y. Theodoridis, J. R. Silva and M. A. Nascimento, "On the Generation of Spatiotemporal Datasets", SSD, Hong Kong, LNCS 1651, Springer, pp.147-164, 1999.
5. M. A. Nascimento, J.R.O. Silva and Y, Theodoridis,"Evaluation of Access Structures for Discretely Moving Points.",In Proc. of the Intl. Workshop on Spatiotemporal Database Management (STDBM'99), pp. 171-188. Edinburgh, UK, Sep/99.
6. M. A. Nascimento and J.R.O. Silva, "Towards historical R-Trees.", In Proc. of the 1998 ACM Symposium on applied Computing, pages 235-240, February 1998.
7. K. Romer, T. Schoch, F. Mattern and T. Dubendorfer,: Smart Identification Frameworks for Ubiquitous Computing Applications. Pervasive Computing and Communications Proceedings of the First IEEE International Conference(2003) 256-262

Efficient Algorithms for Constructing Time Decompositions of Time Stamped Documents

Parvathi Chundi[1], Rui Zhang[1], and Daniel J. Rosenkrantz[2],*

[1] Computer Science Deptartment, University of Nebraska at Omaha, Omaha, NE
{pchundi, rzhang}@mail.unomaha.edu
[2] Computer Science Department, SUNY at Albany, Albany, NY 12222
djr@cs.albany.edu

Abstract. Identifying temporal information of topics from a document set typically involves constructing a time decomposition of the time period associated with the document set. In an earlier work, we formulated several metrics on a time decomposition, such as size, information loss, and variability, and gave dynamic programming based algorithms to construct time decompositions that are optimal with respect to these metrics. Computing information loss values for all subintervals of the time period is central to the computation of optimal time decompositions. This paper proposes several algorithms to assist in more efficiently constructing an optimal time decomposition. More efficient, parallelizable algorithms for computing loss values are described. An efficient top-down greedy heuristic to construct an optimal time decomposition is also presented. Experiments to study the performance of this greedy heuristic were conducted. Although lossy time decompositions constructed by the greedy heuristic are suboptimal, they seem to be better than the widely used uniform length decompositions.

1 Introduction

Discovering temporal information such as trends of topics from time stamped documents has gained significant attention recently [5,6,7,11,12,13]. Mining for temporal information typically involves constructing a time decomposition of the time period associated with the document set. The time period is broken into a sequence of consecutive subintervals of equal length, each of which contains zero or more documents from the document set. Significant topics/keywords for each subinterval, which is called its *information content*, is computed by applying simple *measure functions*, such as term frequency or document frequency, to the subset of documents in that subinterval. The trend of a topic is simply the sequence of measure function values in each of the subintervals of the time decomposition.

A natural time decomposition that can be constructed for a given document set is to construct a subinterval in the decomposition for each distinct time stamp

* Research supported by NSF Grant CCR–0105536.

from the document set. We call such a decomposition the **shortest interval decomposition** of the document set. Although the shortest interval decomposition is simple to construct, it may contain too many subintervals, and therefore may contain too much noise. Other time decompositions can be constructed by merging consecutive subintervals of the shortest interval decomposition into a single subinterval, thereby reducing noise. Such decompositions may result in losing/increasing the significance of keywords, which we call **information loss**. This merging may produce subintervals whose lengths (i.e.; number of subintervals from the shortest interval decomposition) may be different, resulting in higher values of **variability**.

In [8,9], we formulated the problem of given a document set, constructing an optimal decomposition that satisfies one or more constraints. We presented dynamic programming based algorithms to construct time decompositions that satisfy user specified constraints on size, information loss, and variability. Experimental results were provided showing that optimal lossy decompositions are better at capturing temporal information and information content of the underlying document set, as compared to decompositions with equal length subintervals.

The dynamic programming approach to computing optimal lossy decompositions is expensive, especially for large document sets. Moreover, any lossy time decomposition construction requires access to the information loss values of all of the subintervals of the time period of the document set. Given a document set D, let T_D denote the time period of D, n denote the number of subintervals in the shortest interval decomposition of T_D, and m denote the total number of keywords in D that are significant in some subinterval of T_D. Using the algorithms from [9], computing information loss values takes time $O(n^3 m)$ for arbitrary measure functions, constructing an optimal lossy decomposition subject to a single constraint s on size takes time $O(n^2 s)$, and computing an optimal lossy decomposition with two constraints, say one on size s and another on variability v takes time $O(n^3 s/v)$.

In this paper, we design improved algorithms for computing the information loss values, and study greedy heuristics to reduce the time taken for constructing lossy time decompositions. The contributions are as follows:

- An efficient and parallelizable algorithm is presented for computing information loss values for all of the $n(n+1)/2$ subintervals of the time period of the document set, that runs in time $O(n^2 m)$ for any measure function.
- A novel loss computation algorithm specifically for count measures is given that further reduces the time to $O(nm+n^2)$ (and in practice is $O(nm)$).
- An efficient greedy heuristic for computing a lossy time decomposition is presented. It take constraints on size s and variability v as input and generates a time decomposition in time $O(ns)$ that satisfies the constraints.
- The performance of the greedy heuristic is evaluated by constructing time decompositions of various sizes for two measure functions. By comparing these decompositions with the corresponding optimal decompositions, one can conclude that the decompositions constructed by the greedy heuristic are suboptimal in nature; i.e.; in most cases, these decompositions have a

higher information loss. On the positive side, these suboptimal decompositions are still better (i.e.; less information loss) than the currently popular decompositions with equal length subintervals.

The rest of the paper is organized as follows. Section 2 presents some preliminary definitions. Section 3 presents efficient algorithms for computing loss values. Section 4 outlines a greedy heuristic for constructing time decompositions. Section 5 discusses experimental results. Section 6 discusses related work, and Section 7 concludes the paper.

2 Preliminaries

A *time point* is an instance of time with a given *base granularity*, such as a second, minute, day, month, year, etc. A *time interval* is a sequence of one or more consecutive time points. The **length** of a time interval T, denoted $|T|$, is the number of time points within T. We use $T_{x,y}$ to denote a subinterval that includes the xth time point through the yth time point of the time period.

A **decomposition** Π of a time interval T, is a sequence of subintervals $T_1, T_2, \ldots T_k$, such that T_{i+1} immediately follows T_i for $1 \leq i < k$, and T equals the concatenation of the k time intervals, which we write as $T = T_1 * T_2 * \ldots * T_k$. Each T_i is called a **subinterval** of Π. The **size** of decomposition Π is the number of subintervals q in Π. The time interval associated with decomposition Π is denoted as $T(\Pi)$. The **shortest interval decomposition** Π_S of a time interval T is the decomposition with $|T|$ subintervals, one for each time point within T. Each subinterval within Π_S is called a **base interval**.

A decomposition Π_U of a time interval is a **uniform length decomposition** if each subinterval in Π_U contains the same number of time points. For example, the shortest interval decomposition is a uniform decomposition where each interval contains a single time point.

Given two decompositions Π_1 and Π_2 of a time interval T, we say that Π_1 is a **refinement** of Π_2 if every subinterval of Π_1 is covered by some subinterval of Π_2. Decomposition Π_1 is a **proper refinement** of Π_2 if Π_1 is a refinement of Π_2 and Π_1 and Π_2 are not identical.

We now describe the relationship between time stamped documents and time points, intervals and decompositions. Consider a finite set of documents D where each document has a *time stamp* denoting its time of creation or publication. To map these documents to the time domain, we identify a time stamp in a document with a time point. (This implies that time stamps in all documents in D have the same base granularity. If not, or if the time stamps are too fine-grained, we assume that all time points can be converted to an appropriate base granularity.) Given a decomposition, each document is assigned to the subinterval in the decomposition that contains its time stamp.

Given a keyword w and a document set D, a **measure function** f_m computes a value $f_m(w, D)$. We assume that this value is a nonnegative real number. We also assume that if w does not appear in D, then $f_m(w, D) = 0$. We refer to v as a **measure function value** or as a **significance value**. Depending on the characteristics of a given measure function f_m, a keyword w may need to have a high measure function value (at or above a specified threshold) or a low measure function value (at or below a threshold) for it to be deemed significant.

The **information content** of a document set D for a given measure function f_m and a threshold $\alpha \in R^+$ is the set of keywords w appearing in D such that $f_m(w, D) \geq \alpha$ (or in some cases at most α). The *information content* of a time interval T, denoted as $I_\alpha(T, f_m)$, is the information content of the document set assigned to it. The **information content** of a decomposition $\Pi = T_1 * \ldots * T_k$, denoted as $I_\alpha(\Pi, f_m)$, is $\bigcup_{i=1}^{k} I_\alpha(T_i, f_m)$.

Note that $I_\alpha(\Pi, f_m)$ is not necessarily equal to $I_\alpha(T(\Pi), f_m)$. ($T(\Pi)$ is the time interval associated with the decomposition Π.) In fact, the information content of different decompositions of the same document set may be different, both in terms of the cardinality and contents of the keyword set [10]. To compare different decompositions of a document set, a measure based on loss of information was introduced in [8]. Given a time interval T_i, let $T_{i1} * T_{i2} * \cdots * T_{iq}$ be the time points in T_i. We define the **information loss** (μ_j) between the information contents of T_i and a time point T_{ij} ($1 \leq j \leq q$) to be the size of the symmetric difference between $I_\alpha(T_i, f_m)$ and $I_\alpha(T_{ij}, f_m)$. Then, the information loss of T_i, denoted by $\mu(T_i)$, is defined to be $\sum_{j=1}^{q} \mu_j$. The information loss of a decomposition is the sum of information losses for each of its subintervals. A decomposition $\Pi(T)$ of a time interval T is **lossy** if its information loss is nonzero.

3 Computing Loss Values

Any computation of a lossy time decomposition of a given document set involves computing the information loss of a given subinterval. A straightforward algorithm for computing the loss value for all subintervals of the time period associated with a document set can be described as follows. Given a subinterval $T_{x,y}$ of T_D, the time period of the document set, the loss computation involves computing the μ_z value for each z where $x \leq z \leq y$. Computing μ_z involves computing the symmetric difference between the information contents of subintervals $T_{x,y}$ and $T_{z,z}$. This will take at most time $O(m)$ where m is the number of distinct keywords in the document set. the information loss of subinterval $T_{x,y}$ is $\sum_{x \leq z \leq y} \mu_z$ which takes $O(nm)$ time to compute where n is the number of time points in T_D. There are $O(n^2)$ subintervals in T_D. Therefore, the above algorithm takes $O(n^3 m)$ time to compute all loss values.

In this section, we present two algorithms to improve the running time of the loss computation. The first algorithm works for any measure function, whereas the second algorithm works only for count measure functions.

3.1 Efficient Loss Value Computation

We now describe an efficient loss computation technique that is applicable to an arbitrary measure function. The input to the algorithm is the information contents of each of the $n(n+1)/2$ subintervals of T_D, and the output is the information loss of each of these subintervals.

We assume that each keyword is assigned an id, with id h referring to keyword w_h. We assume that the information content $I_\alpha(T_{x,y}, f_m)$ of each of the $n(n+1)/2$ subintervals $T_{x,y}$ is available as a sorted list of the values of h such that keyword w_h is in $I_\alpha(T_{x,y}, f_m)$. We denote this sorted list as $\hat{I}_{x,y}$.

For each subinterval $T_{x,y}$ and keyword w_h, define $C_{x,y}(w_h)$ to be the number of base intervals within $T_{x,y}$ such that w_h is significant for that base interval, i.e., the number of lists $\hat{I}_{z,z}$ containing h, where $x \leq z \leq y$. The function $C_{x,y}$ will be represented as a list $\hat{C}_{x,y}$ consisting of the pairs $\langle h, C_{x,y}(w_h)\rangle$ such that $C_{x,y}(w_h) \geq 1$, sorted on h. The value $\mu(T_{x,y})$ can be computed as $(y-x+1)$ times the number of words in $\hat{I}_{x,y}$, minus the sum of $C_{x,y}(w_h)$ over the words w_h in $\hat{I}_{x,y}$, plus the sum of $C_{x,y}(w_h)$ over the words w_h on the list $\hat{C}_{x,y}$ but not on the $\hat{I}_{x,y}$. Note that given the two sorted lists $\hat{I}_{x,y}$ and $\hat{C}_{x,y}$, the value $\mu(T_{x,y})$ can be computed in time $O(m)$.

For each starting time point x, the algorithm computes $\hat{C}_{x,y}$ and $\mu(T_{x,y})$ for increasing values of y, $x \leq y \leq n$. To start, $\hat{C}_{x,x}$ is constructed from $\hat{I}_{x,x}$, and $\mu(T_{x,x})$ equals zero. Given a list $\hat{C}_{x,y}$, this list can be transformed into the list $\hat{C}_{x,y+1}$ in time $O(m)$ by doing a merge–like simultaneous scan of the list $\hat{C}_{x,y}$ being transformed, and the list $\hat{I}_{y+1,y+1}$.

Since there are $O(n^2)$ intervals, and the time per interval is $O(m)$, the overall time for the algorithm is $O(n^2m)$. The running time can be further improved by parallelizing the algorithm. For each x, the loss values of all subintervals starting at time point x can be treated as an independent subproblem that can be scheduled on a separate processor. This parallel computation of loss values requires n processors and $O(nm)$ time.

3.2 Loss Value Computation for the Count Measures

In an earlier paper [9] we described an $O(n^2m)$ algorithm to compute all loss values for a count measure function. A count measure f_{mc} is a measure function that has the property that for each keyword w and document set D, $f_{mc}(w, D) = \sum_{d \in D} f_{mc}(w, d)$. In this paper, we provide an $O(nm + n^2)$ algorithm. An important concept in reducing the time complexity of the loss computation is to identify all minimal length intervals, which we call **critical intervals**, in which a keyword is significant. Formally for a count measure function f_{mc}, interval $T_{x,y}$ is critical for keyword w_h if and only if the following two conditions both hold: (1) $f_{mc}(w_h, Docs(T_{x,y})) \geq \alpha$ and (2) Either $y = x$ or $f_{mc}(w_h, Docs(T_{x,y-1})) < \alpha$ and $f_{mc}(w_h, Docs(T_{x+1,y})) < \alpha$.

Note that if $T_{x,y}$ and $T_{x',y'}$ are distinct critical intervals for w_h, then $x < x'$ if and only if $y < y'$. Consequently, the critical intervals for a given keyword are totally ordered by their starting time, or equivalently, by their ending time.

Recall that n is the number of time points in $\Pi_S(T_D)$, and m is the number of distinct keywords in the document set D. We assume that a list L_z of keywords and their measure function values for each time point $z \in \Pi_S$ is available. That is, $L_z = \langle h, f_{mc}(w_h, Docs(T_{z,z})) \rangle$ such that $f_{mc}(w_h, Docs(T_{z,z})) > 0$. The starting point of the computation is the set of lists L_z. We assume that each keyword appears on at least one list, i.e. each keyword has a nonzero measure function value for at least one time point.

The algorithm uses several two-dimensional arrays for book keeping, as follows:

- $Critical(x, y)$ ($1 \le x \le y \le n$) is the number of keywords for which interval $T_{x,y}$ is critical.
- $A_{ss}(x, y)$ ($x < y$) is the number of keywords for which there exists an x' such that $T_{x,x}$ and $T_{x',y}$ are consecutive critical intervals.
- $D_{iis}(x, y)$ ($x < y$) is the number of keywords w_h for which there exists a $y' > x$ and an x' such that $T_{x,y'}$ and $T_{x',y}$ are consecutive critical intervals for w_h.
- $N_{iis}(x, y)$ for $y > x$ is the number of keywords that are not significant for $T_{x+1,y}$ and are not significant for $T_{x,x}$, but are significant for $T_{x,y}$. $N_{iis}(x, x)$ is zero. $N_{iis}(x, y) = N_{iis}(x, y-1) + Critical(x, y) - D_{iis}(x, y)$.
- $N_{is}(x, y)$ for $y > x$ is the number of keywords that are not significant for $T_{x+1,y}$, but are significant for $T_{x,x}$ (and consequently are significant for $T_{x,y}$). $N_{is}(x, x)$ is the number of keywords that are significant for $T_{x,x}$. $N_{is}(x, y) = N_{is}(x, y-1) - A_{ss}(x, y)$.
- $N_{ss}(x, y)$ for $y > x$ is the number of keywords that are significant for both $T_{x+1,y}$ and $T_{x,x}$ (and consequently are significant for $T_{x,y}$). $N_{ss}(x, x)$ is zero. $N_{ss}(x, y) = N_{ss}(x, y-1) + A_{ss}(x, y)$.
- $NumSignificant(x, y)$ is the cardinality of $I_\alpha(T_{x,y}, f_{mc})$. $NumSignificant(x, y) = NumSignificant(x+1, y) + N_{iis}(x, y) + N_{is}(x, y)$.
- $Mu(x, y)$ is $\mu(T_{x,y})$. $Mu(x, y) = Mu(x+1, y) + N_{iis}(x, y)*(y - x + 1) + NumSignificant(x+1, y) + N_{is}(x, y) * (y - x) - N_{ss}(x, y)$.

We first compute, for each keyword w_h, an ordered list I_h of time points and measure function values for which the value is nonzero, by scanning all the lists L_z from $z = 1$ to n. Each constructed list I_h consists of all pairs $< z, f_{mc}(w_h, Docs(T_{z,z})) >$ such that $f_{mc}(w_h, Docs(T_{z,z})) > 0$.

Next, from each list I_h, an ordered list of the critical intervals for keyword w_h is constructed. This construction can be done in time proportional to the number of entries in list I_h, by using a two pointer scan of I_h. One pointer is used to identify the starting point x of a critical interval, and the other pointer is used to identify the ending point y of that critical interval. The time required is $O(n)$ for each of the m lists, for a total of $O(nm)$ time.

Next, by scanning the lists of critical intervals, the arrays $Critical$, A_{ss}, and D_{iis} are constructed in $O(nm)$ time.

The algorithm constructs $Mu(x, y)$ for each ending point y using the above collection of arrays. Due to space limitations, the details of the algorithm are omitted. The algorithm runs in time $O(nm + n^2)$. For all practical purposes, $m >> n$. Therefore, the running time in practice is $O(nm)$.

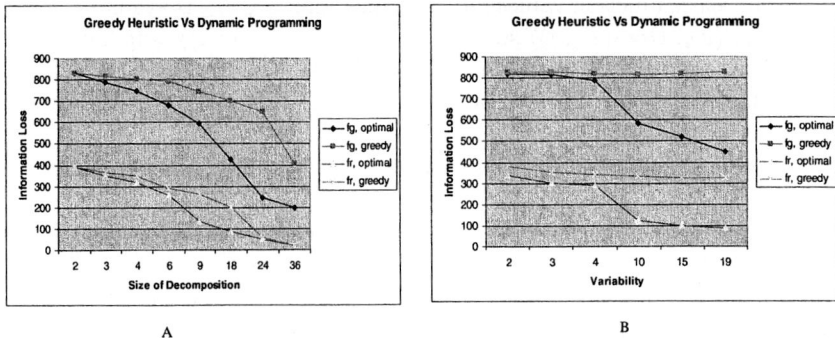

Fig. 1. Greedy Heuristic Vs Optimal Decompositions

4 Greedy Algorithm for Time Decompositions

Here we consider the problem of constructing a minimal loss time decomposition for a given document set, subject to a constraint s on the size of the decomposition, and possibly an additional constraint v on variability. The dynamic programming algorithms from [8,9] produce an optimal decomposition, but are slow because they operate in a bottom–up manner, systematically constructing optimal solutions for subintervals of increasing size. The greedy heuristic presented here reduces the running time by taking a top–down approach, and making a sequence of irrevocable decisions in constructing a decomposition. However, the constructed decomposition is not necessarily optimal. We assume that the heuristic is given as input constraint s and possibly constraint v, and has available to it the loss value $\mu(x, y)$ for each subinterval $T_{x,y}$ in the time period T_D of the given document set

Given a subinterval $T_{x,y}$, we define a **split** of $T_{x,y}$ as the replacement of $T_{x,y}$ by two subintervals $T_{x,z}$ and $T_{z+1,y}$. We define the **benefit** of the split as $\mu(T_{x,y}) - \mu(T_{x,z}) - \mu(T_{z+1,y})$. A positive benefit corresponds to an improvement, since the information loss is lowered, but the benefit might be zero or negative.

The greedy heuristic starts with a decomposition consisting of the single subinterval T_D, and repeatedly refines it until the constraint on the size is violated. At each step of the heuristic, given a current decomposition Π_k of size k, the heuristic constructs a decomposition of size $k + 1$ by choosing a subinterval from Π_k, and splitting it. The split chosen is the one with maximum benefit among all possible splits of the subintervals of Π_k. (Ties are broken arbitrarily). If a constraint on variability is specified, only those splits that would not violate the variability constraint are considered.

The process of refining the current decomposition stops when the size of the current decomposition is s, the size constraint. Note that at each refinement step, the information loss of the decomposition might potentially increase (if the maximum benefit at that step is negative). Therefore, during the sequence of refinements, the decomposition whose information loss is minimal is kept track of, and this decomposition is returned as the final answer. The algorithm entails s steps, each of which can be done in time $O(n)$, for a total time of $O(ns)$.

5 Experiments

In this section, we describe the results from some preliminary experiments conducted on a document set containing news articles from the Reuters-21578 collection, published during March 11th - 13th, 1987. There are 1678 news articles in the data set. For our experiments, the base granularity for the Reuters set was chosen to be an hour to avoid having a sparse distribution of the data. Using this base granularity, the Reuters data had 72 subintervals in its shortest interval decomposition.

The data set was cleaned using a standard procedure that involved removing XML/SGML tags and stop words. Each article was then broken into a sequence of stemmed keywords. In order to construct time decompositions, information content and loss values for all subintervals were first computed. We defined two measure functions for computing the information content. Measure function f_r assigned each keyword the ratio of the number of occurrences of the keyword to the total number occurrences of keywords in the data set as its measure function value and α was set to 0.01.

Measure function f_g first filtered keywords in each subset of documents by considering only those that occur in at least two documents in the subset. Let W_g denote the set of such keywords. Function f_g then computed the measure function value for each keyword w as the ratio of number of occurrences of w to the total number of occurrences of all keywords in W_g. And, $\alpha = 0.01$.

We computed several decompositions of various sizes for both of the measure functions using the dynamic programming based method and the greedy heuristic outlined in the previous section. To evaluate the effectiveness of the greedy heuristic, we conducted two sets of experiments.

In the first set, the information loss of decompositions constructed by the greedy heuristic was compared with the information loss of same size/variability

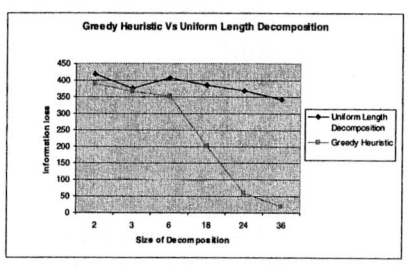

Measure Function f_r Measure function f_g

Fig. 2. Greedy Heuristic Vs Uniform Length Decompositions

decompositions computed by the dynamic programming method. Figure 1 illustrates the results. The X-axis in Figure 1A shows the size of a decomposition and the Y-axis shows the amount of information loss. The top two plots in Figure 1A compare the performance of the greedy heuristic and the dynamic programming method for f_g. The bottom two plots show the comparison for f_r. For both measure functions and for all sizes, the decompositions computed by the greedy heuristic have more information loss than the same size decompositions computed by the dynamic programming method. Figure 1B shows the comparison for the variability metric. In Figure 1B, the X-axis contains variability values and the Y-axis contains information loss. For a fixed decomposition size (18), we computed several decompositions with different values of variability. Again, the top two plots in Figure 1B show the information loss values for f_g, whereas the bottom two plots are for f_r. In both cases, the information loss of decompositions with 18 intervals constructed by the greedy heuristic is always higher than for a decomposition of the same size and variability constructed by the dynamic programming method.

In the second set of experiments, we compared the information loss of decompositions computed by the greedy heuristic with uniform decompositions of the same size. Figure 2 shows the result for measure functions f_r and f_g. In these plots, the X-axis contains the size of a decomposition and the Y-axis contains the amount of information loss. It is clearly seen from this figure that decompositions constructed by the greedy heuristic have less information loss than the same size uniform length decompositions in almost all cases.

6 Related Work

Temporal analysis of topics occurring in time-stamped documents is an active area of research. Much of this work constructs simple decompositions where each subinterval is a day long [11,12,13] or a year long [5,6]. These references are more focused on identifying potential topic keywords and the beginning of trends than on constructing optimal time decompositions or variability.

In the context of mining time series data, a number of methods for segmenting, indexing, and querying of such data have been studied [1,4,2,3], plus references too numerous to cite. However, not much attention has been paid to time series data computed from time stamped documents.

7 Conclusions

This paper details several algorithms for more efficient construction of optimal time decompositions of time stamped documents. The loss computation outlined here improves the running time by a factor of n in general, and by a factor of n^2 for count measures, where n is the number of time points in the time period of the document set. We also outlined an efficient greedy heuristic for computing minimal loss time decompositions of the document set. Experimental results show that the decompositions constructed by the greedy heuristic, although suboptimal in nature, have lesser information loss when compared to uniform length decompositions.

References

1. R. Agrawal, C. Faloutsos, and A. Swami, "Efficient Similarity Search In Sequence Databases", *Proc. of the 4th International Conference of Foundations of Data Organization and Algorithms*, 1993, 69-84.
2. M. Vlachos, M. Hadjieleftheriou, D. Gunopulos, and E. Keogh, "Indexing Multi-Dimensional Time-Series with Support for Multiple Distance Measures", *Proc. of the 9th ACM SIGKDD International Conference on Knowledge Discovery and Data Mining*, 2003, 216-225.
3. E. Keogh, S. Chu, D. Hart, and M. Pazzani, "An Online Algorithm for Segmenting Time Series", *Proc. of the IEEE International Conference on Data Mining*, 2001, 289-296.
4. G. Das, D. Gunopulos, and H. Mannila, "Finding Similar Time Series", *Principles of Data Mining and Knowledge Discovery*, 1997, 88-100.
5. B. Lent, R. Agrawal, and R. Srikant, "Discovering Trends in Text Databases", *Proc. of the 3rd International Conference on Knowledge Discovery and Data Mining (KDD)*, 1997, 227-230.
6. S. Roy, D. Gevry, W. M. Pottenger, "Methodologies for Trend Detection in Textual Data Mining", *Proc. of the Textmine 2002 Workshop*, SIAM Intl. Conf. on Data Mining, 2002.
7. J. Allan, V. Lavrenko, D. Malin, and R. Swan, "Detections, Bounds, and Timelines: UMass and TDT-3", *Proc. of the 3rd Topic Detection and Tracking Workshop*, 2000.
8. P. Chundi and D. J. Rosenkrantz, "Constructing Time Decompositions for Analyzing Time Stamped Documents", *Proc. of the 4th SIAM International Conference on Data Mining*, 2004, 57-68.
9. P. Chundi and D. J. Rosenkrantz, "On Lossy Time Decompositions of Time Stamped Documents", *Proc. of the ACM 13th Conference on Information and Knowledge Management*, 2004.
10. P. Chundi and D. J. Rosenkrantz, "Information Preserving Decompositions of Time Stamped Documents", *Submitted to the Journal of Data Mining and Knowledge Discovery*.
11. R. Swan and J. Allan, "Automatic Generation of Overview Timelines", *Proc. of the 23rd Annual International ACM SIGIR Conference on Research and Development in Information Retrieval*, 2000, 49-56.
12. R. Swan and J. Allan, "Extracting Significant Time Varying Features from Text", *Proc. of the 8th International Conference on Information and Knowledge Management*, 1999, 38-45.
13. R. Swan and D. Jensen, "TimeMines: Constructing Timelines with Statistical Models of Word Usage", *Proc. KDD 2000 Workshop on Text Mining*, 2000.
14. J. Himberg, K. Korpiaho, H. Mannila, J. Tikanmki, and H.T.T. Toivonen, "Time series segmentation for context recognition in mobile devices", *Proc. of the IEEE International Conference on Data Mining*, 2001, 203 - 210.

Querying by Sketch Geographical Databases and Ambiguities

Fernando Ferri[1], Patrizia Grifoni[1], and Maurizio Rafanelli[2]

[1] IRPPS-CNR, via Nizza 128, 00198 Roma, Italy
fernando.ferri@irpps.cnr.it, patrizia.grifoni@irpps.cnr.it
[2] IASI-CNR, viale Manzoni 30, 00185 Roma, Italy
rafanelli@iasi.cnr.it

Abstract. This paper presents GSQL (Geographical Sketch Query Language), a sketch-based approach for querying geographical databases based on the GeoPQL query language. Geographic information is intrinsically spatial and can be conveniently represented using a bi-dimensional space. Graphical User Interfaces and Visual Languages can be used to satisfy this need. However, the growing availability of sketching tools (PDA, digital pens, etc.) enables a more informal and natural user interaction. Sketch based interaction is very effective. Each user can easily sketch his/her geographical query by drawing it, erasing and modifying its parts and highlighting the query target. A query is the expression of the configuration of the expected result. Sketch recognition and query interpretation (and solution of their ambiguities) starts from a context-independent approach and uses the characteristic application domain information. Context-independent sketch interpretation uses spatial and temporal information related to the sketching process. Context-dependent sketch interpretation uses geographic domain information to solve the remaining ambiguities and correctly interpret the drawing and query. An analysis of the ambiguities characterising object sketching in the geographic application domain and their possible solutions are presented herein. Each query identifies the set of geographical objects involved and the target; the query interpretation must unambiguously identify the set of its results.

1 Introduction

Communication technologies and digital tools, with ever greater differences in use and modes of communication, are developing beyond desktop use only to human-computer interaction through PDA, mobile phone, graphic tablet, digital pen, smart pad, and so on. Sketching is a simple, intuitive and natural approach for defining and communicating a new idea. There is thus important and growing interest in digital pens and their use for sketching. Cognitive scientists have highlighted the relevance of sketching for external representation of objects, concepts and relationships to communicate with computers and digital tools. Digital pens assist users in drawing sketches by adopting a more human-oriented approach, in contrast with the machine oriented approach of communications.

The interest in using sketches to communicate information, particularly in a geographic domain, is mainly related to the intrinsic spatial nature of both the sketch and the geographic information. In fact, sketching is particularly suitable for expressing spatial concepts and relations, and communication is mainly based on a graphical approach. The development of visual languages [1][2][3] over the last ten years has already simplified human-computer interaction. In [4][5] are proposed examples of sketch-based geographical query languages. This paper presents an evolution of the Geographical Pictorial Query Language GeoPQL [6]: the Geographical Sketch-based Query Language (GSQL). However, using sketches to interact requires interpretation and resolution of their ambiguities. Sketches are characterised by vagueness, incompleteness and ambiguity. Ambiguities may be produced by various factors, such as the variability of hand-drawn input, different interpretations of the same input and "noise" introduced by the drawing tool. Each sketch consists of a sequence of strokes. A stroke is a trajectory from the point that the pen tip begins to touch the tablet and the point where it is removed from the tablet. Strokes define (according to different contexts) different primitive shapes. In sketch-based interfaces several different recognition and ambiguity management needs can be considered. Some applications manage only few types of graphical objects, such as sketch-based geographical query languages or sketch-based diagrammatic systems and query languages.

This paper proposes some considerations on sketch interpretation [7] in the geographic domain, starting from a general approach combining context-independent and context-dependent interpretations. The context is defined by complex information on the application domain, the interaction tool and the user's skill in drawing sketches. In particular, context-independent sketch interpretation uses spatial and temporal information related to the sketch and drawing process. However, involving the application domain information requires analysis of all bi-dimensional configurations of graphical objects, their matching with the GeoPQL operators and the various ambiguous situations. Sketch interpretation is based on drawing behaviour in different contexts. One behaviour type is characterised by the objectives and features common to all users, while another is related to the specific context in which the sketch was drawn, taking account of complex information on the application domain, the interaction tool, and the user's skill in drawing sketches.

In the following section, sketch ambiguity is presented and discussed. Section 3 presents the Geographical Sketch based Query Language and, section 4 concludes the paper.

2 Ambiguity Related to Sketch-Based Queries for Geographical Data

Configurations of spatial objects and their definition and discussion are analysed in a bi-dimensional space. Sketches are characterised by vagueness, incompleteness and ambiguity [8][9]. Ambiguity can produce a mismatch with a given interpretation. The information provided by the sketch may thus be insufficient for its unequivocal interpretation. Ambiguities may also be caused by noise from tools and sensors, or by co-termination failure (where pen strokes do not meet at their end point) [10]. It is therefore essential to solve ambiguities caused by sketching.

Each geographical query can be expressed by Symbolic Graphical Objects, represented by points, polylines and polygons. Figure 1A gives an example of ambiguity in a geographic domain. The sketch can have at least two interpretations, as shown in Figures 1B and 1C. If the user's goal is to sketch a river passing through a region, the correct interpretation is shown in Figure 1C.

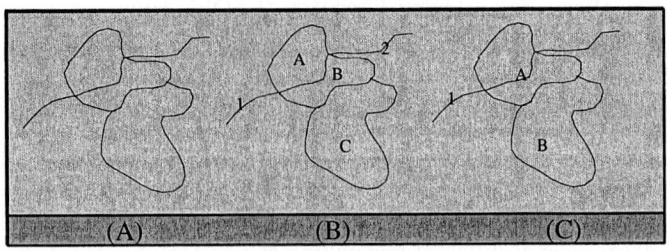

Fig. 1. A sketch and some possible interpretations

Ambiguities in the sketch may be resolved using different approaches (which may be integrated):

- from the user's specification of the correct interpretation;
- by considering both the sketch and the actions performed in drawing it, to obtain the correct interpretation independently of the context;
- by considering the application domains and a significant set of sketch models for each domain.

These approaches can be opportunely combined. Context-independent behaviours and drawing strategies are usually related to space and time, and their related drawing behaviours are generally applicable to sketch interpretation. A non-exhaustive set of behaviours and drawing strategies (related to spatial and temporal concepts) follows: • the user draws a number of strokes • each stroke represents a closed shape (triangle, rectangle, regular and irregular polygons), a polyline or a point, each sequence of strokes represents a closed shape or polyline, • each closed shape, polyline and point is one of the sketch's simple or complex objects, • the user generally finishes drawing one object before beginning a second, • the user draws a complex object starting from its outer parts, and continues by specifying its details, • the user draws different objects in a sketch in accordance with a spatial contiguity (tending to begin a new object near the previous one).

The sketch's spatial aspects are interpreted by considering its spatial information in order to distinguish its elementary components - closed shapes, polylines and points - and identify the spatial relationships between them. However, temporal aspects play an important role in the correct interpretation of a sketch. In this paper temporal aspects concern both the temporal analysis of stroke sequences drawn and re-drawn (possible erasing and re-drawing a part of the sketch). In fact, as well as the spatial relationship, it is important to consider the temporal relationship between strokes and components in the sketch. This enables identification of graphical components with a close temporal relationship. These are obtained by combining the elementary components by considering spatial aspects, and are thus more complex than these elements. They could be considered as the graphical components the user actually wants to draw, although they do not comprise the sketch's simple or complex objects.

Each component can be characterised temporally by a set of time intervals: that is, the intervals in which the component was drawn. For example in Figure 2A, consisting of two strokes (represented in Figure 2B), the two closed shapes (Figure 2A) can be characterised by the time intervals presented in Figures 2C and 2D.

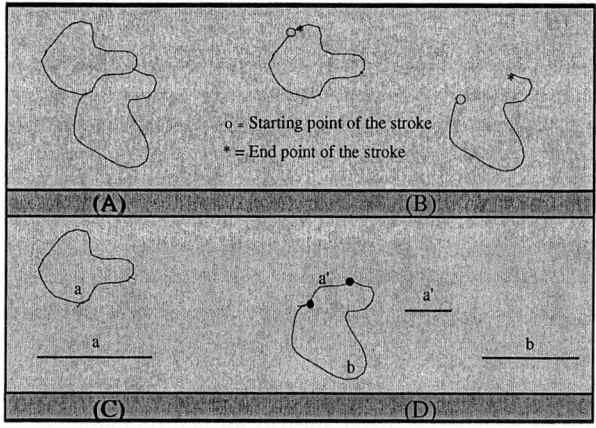

Fig. 2. Sketch temporal information

Temporal information can be very useful in identifying the user's goals. In fact, people tend to draw all of one component or graphic object before moving on to another. This important criterion can be used in two ways to enable the sketch's correct interpretation:

- by minimising the total number of breaks between intervals for all components; i.e. by drawing each component as a stroke (preferably) without interruption.
- by minimising the total waiting time (of breaks) between intervals for all components; i.e. each series of strokes refers to only one component. This is very important if the user prefers to draw a component through a series of strokes. This minimisation can also be applied to recognise complex objects.

Context is often very useful to correctly interpret and disambiguate the sketch. The context may consider a set of operational variables influencing user drawing strategies and behaviours (application domain, information devices, interaction tools, user goals etc.).

We now consider the geographic application domain. The three configurations in Figure 3 represent some typical ambiguous situations, which can be solved using this context.

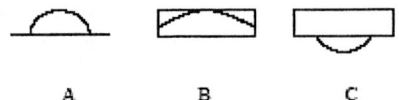

Fig. 3. Three configurations representing typical ambiguous situations

There are two possible interpretations of Figure 3A: the first considers the sketch as being formed by two polylines, where one has its boundary intersecting the other. The second considers the sketch as a polygon with a polyline touching the polygon. Tests with users have demonstrated that they tend to draw the polygon before the polyline when defining a spatial relationship between the two, and thus the second interpretation can be excluded. Three interpretations are possible for Figure 3B: the first considers the sketch as being formed by a polygon, containing a polyline whose boundaries and one internal point touch the polygon's boundaries. The second considers the sketch as formed by a polygon and two touching polylines whose boundaries are the boundaries of the polygon, and which have a point in common. The third interpretation considers the sketch as formed by three polygons.

In this case too, the last interpretation can be excluded: two polygons are not usually drawn by splitting a polygon in this context (the user focuses on two different areas instead of splitting one area in two of them). However choosing between the first and second interpretation is very complex, and use of temporal information is not very effective.

Figure 3C can be interpreted: i) as a polygon and a polyline whose boundaries touch the polygon boundaries, ii) as formed by two polygons. In this case temporal information is not relevant for the interpretation as the sketch could be drawn with just two strokes.

To solve the ambiguities with Figures 3B and 3C the context could be used to consider not the user's behaviour during the drawing of the sequence, but the frequency of the configuration in the context of the geographical query. With this approach, for Figure 3C the configuration with two touching polygons is more frequent than the other, and must thus be considered as the most probable interpretation.

3 The Geographical Sketch Based Query Language (GSQL)

Geographical Sketch based Query Language (GSQL) provides the user with a sketch based extension of the GeoPql query language. GSQL (like GeoPql) enables the user to specify queries using *Symbolic Graphical Objects (SGO)*. Each SGO is represented by a point, polyline or polygon. Here, the elements "set of points", "set of polylines" and "set of polygons" are considered as equivalent to a single SGO "point", "polyline" or "polygon. This means that the current version of GSQL is unable to satisfy constraints on the cardinality of a sgo (its cardinality is always 1) or the orientation of a polyline, and that some operators are used to "select" SGOs which satisfy the relationship in which the operator is an element, rather than to obtain the "result" of the operation. It is possible to assign a semantic to each SGO, linked to the different kinds of information (layer) in the geographical database, and to impose constraints on both the SGO's attributes and its spatial position. GSQL involves geometric, topological and metric operators. Obviously each layer can be represented in a query by an SGO with the same geographical objects: point, polyline and polygon. All geographical objects in a layer have the same type. Both GeoPQL and GSQL have the geographical operators: G-union (Uni) and G-difference (Dif); topological operators: G-disjunction (Dsj), G-touching (Tch), G-inclusion (Inc), G-crossing (Crs), G-pass through (Pth), G-overlapping (Ovl), G-equality (Eql), G-alias (Als) and G-any (Any); and metric operator: G-distance (Dst). The symbols used for the symbolic operators are ←—→ for the G-distance operator and ← "relation name" → for the G-any and G-alias operators, (where "relation name" is *Any* or *Alias*).

Geo-any allows elimination of undesired constraints and if a Geo-any relationship is defined between a pair of SGOs, this means that no constraint exists between them. In contrast, Geo-Alias allows representation of more than one relationship (in OR) between a pair of SGOs. In fact, a graphical representation does not allow, for example, a pair of polygons that are both disjoined and overlapped. The focal question treated in this paper is more complex than the sketch-recognising problem previously introduced. The query language that we propose must be able to express both the query's objects and its target. It must also give an unambiguous interpretation of the Symbolic Graphical Objects. To recognise points, poly-lines and polygons in the sketches drawn by the user, connect each one with a corresponding geographical layer, and intercept relationships among Symbolic Graphical Objects, the sketch understanding process considers both:1) context-independent characteristics (using spatio-temporal information) and 2) application domain characteristics (connecting theSGOs with geographic database layers, verifying the existing SGO relationships, etc.). Each identified object must be coupled with a label and the absence of conflicts between them must be verified. Labels therefore play a very important role in resolving ambiguities during query interpretation, although they are unable to resolve all ambiguities. Section 3.1 gives some examples of ambiguities that can be resolved only by a correct user drawing strategy or by a dialogue between the user and system. The query's target must be highlighted. Some poly-line type SGOs are not connected with the layers, as they represent the following operators: G-distance, G-alias and G-any. For example, Figure 4 gives a pictorial representation of the query "Find all regions which are *passed through* by a river or (alternatively) *include* a lake".

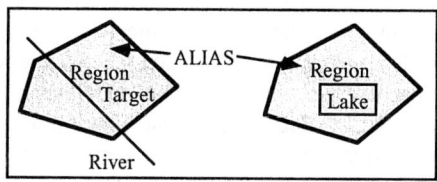

Fig. 4. A query example

Figure 5A shows a pictorial representation of the query "Find all regions which are *passed through* by a river and *overlap* a forest, *and in which the forest is disjoined from the river*". By introducing the G-any operator, Figure 5B gives the query "Find all regions which are *passed through* by a river and *overlap* a forest". The G-Any operator allows visual representation of the need to remove relationships (in this case: *the forest is disjoined from the river*) between a pair of SGOs (in this case: *forest and river*). As with the previously cited examples and considerations, each SGO must be connected by a label to a geographical layer or to one of G-distance, G-alias and G-any. Finally, the SGO identfying the query's target must be highlighted.

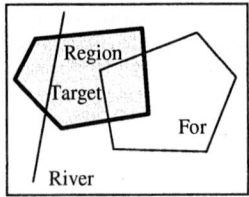 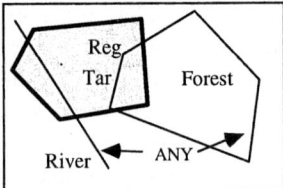

Fig. 5. A second query example

Each query is defined by drawing the Symbolic Graphical Objects involved in the query, writing labels associated with the SGO and highlighting the query target. Some parts of the sketch may be common to two or more objects. During the sketching process the common parts of the different objects must be re-drawn. If one poly-line p1 is completely contained in another p2, re-drawing p1 over p2 enables identification of p1's start point and end points, and two different labels must be written according to the layers connected with the poly-lines (labels and SGOs can be drawn in any order). Finally the target must be highlighted: the query is now specified.

3.1 Analysis of Ambiguities in Sketching Geographical Queries

The different SGO configurations for editing queries must be analysed to solve all ambiguities arising from the sketch interpretation. An analysis of the ambiguities of sketched objects in a bi-dimensional space is presented below (Table 1).

The analysis starts from configurations involving two points (*pp* in Table 1). If points have different spatial coordinates (*ppA1* configuration), they are distinguishable and the drawing does not produce any ambiguity. If they have the same spatial coordinates (*ppB1* configuration), the different objects are un-distinguishable, however they must have two labels associated with two layers (of point type).

This enables resolution of the ambiguity. However this kind of ambiguity cannot always be resolved. In fact a third point near two points with the same spatial coordinates could make it impossible to resolve the ambiguity. In fact, the user might draw the three points and write the three labels in such a way that the system is unable to distinguish the isolated point's label from those of the superimposed points, such as in Figure 6. Here, the point labels are: Town, Spring and Power Station and the query also includes a polygon with the label Region. In this query, it is unclear how to associate the three labels Town, Spring and Power Station with the two points: Any sequence in the point and label drawing process is possible. When points and labels are drawn, the user must specify the query's target.

Table 1. Different Symbolic Graphical Object configurations

pp	A) · · (1) B) · (1)
pl	A) · ⌐ (1) B) ⌐ (1) C) ⌐ (1)
pa	A) · □ (1) B) □ (1) C) □ (1)
ll	A) ⋈ (1) B) h (1) h (2) C) ⋎ (1) ⋎ (2) ⋈ (3) ⋈ (4) ⋈ (5) ⋈ (6) D) ⋈ (1) ⊥ (2) E) ∧ (1)
la	A) ⊐ (1) B) ☒ (1) ⊡ (2) ⊡ (3) ⊡ (4) ⊐ (5) ⊡ (6) ⊡ (7) ⊡ (8) ⊡ (9) ⊡ (10) C) ⊐ (1) ⊐ (2) ⊐ (3) ⊐ (4) □ (5) D) ⊐ (1) ⊐ (2) ⊐ (3) ⊐ (4) ⊐ (5) ⊐ (6)
aa	A) ⊡ (1) B) ⊡ (1) ⊡◇ (2) C) ⊡ (1) ⊡ (2) D) ⊡ (1) ⊡ (2) ⊡ (3) E) ⊡ (1)

Before analysing other configurations we introduce some general hypotheses. A problem in the interpretation of polylines and polygons is that they can consist of one or more (undetermined) strokes, and obviously two strokes touching at one or both ends could be interpreted as two different polylines or one only (Figure 7).

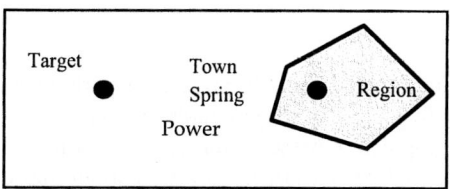

Fig. 6.

Here too, labels giving the number, type (of the pointed layer) and position of polylines and polygons play an important role in resolving ambiguities. In Figure 7, the presence of two labels establishes that the two strokes refer to different polylines.

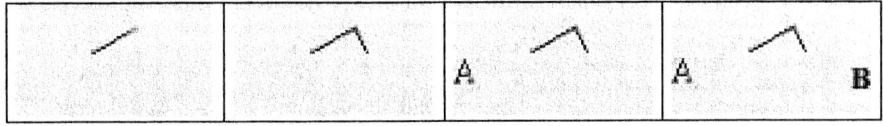

Fig. 7.

By using layer information, the different configurations between point-polyline, and point-polygon can be made unambiguous.

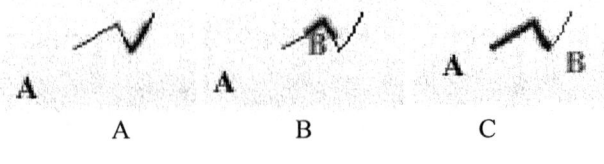

A B C

Fig. 8.

Let us now consider configurations involving two polylines (ll). Polylines also have problems deriving from their superimposition in the sketch. If two or more polylines are superimposed, the number of SGOs involved depends on the number of labels. Strokes, spatial and temporal information are also very important in distinguishing the SGO involved. For example in Figure 8 the retracing of part of the sketch is highlighted by bold lines. However in Figure 8A only one polyline can be associated with the label, independently of the number of strokes and retracings. In Figures 8B and 8C, the presence of two labels allows the retracing to be associated with the second label. However, if the user draws Figure 8B or 8C with more than two strokes and/or retracings, it may be difficult to correctly distinguish the two polylines. In this case spatial and temporal information can help to associate strokes and retracings with polylines. These considerations are also applicable to the other configurations in Table 1.

4 Conclusions

The development of multimodal tools is producing particular interest in interactive sketching, particularly for querying of geographical databases. Geographic data has a spatial nature, whose graphical representation can be considered as more intuitive for users. Sketches have the advantages of familiarity and an improovement of usability. However, interpretation and resolution of their ambiguities is necessary. The sketch understanding process interprets ambiguities by: i) taking account of drawing actions independently of the context; ii) considering application domain knowledge of ambiguities in sketching geographical queries. However, some ambiguities may remain unsolved, requiring the user to specify all necessary information for their correct intepretation.

References

1. D. Papadias, T. Sellis "A Pictorial Query-by-Example Language" Journal of Visual Languages and Computing, Vol.6, N.1, pp. 53-72, 1995.
2. S. Kaushik, E.A. Rundensteiner "SVIQUEL: A Spatial Visual Query and Exploration Language" 9th Intern. Conf. on Database and Expert Systems Applications - DEXA'98, LNCS N. 1460, pp. 290-299, 1998.
3. Calcinelli D., Mainguenaud M. "Cigales, a visual language for geographic information system: the user interface" Journal of Visual Languages and Computing, Vol. 5, N. 2, pp. 113-132, 1994.
4. Meyer B. "Beyond Icons: Towards New Metaphors for Visual Query Languages for Spatial Information Systems" First Intern. Workshop on Interfaces in Database Systems, Springer-Verlag Publ., pp.113-135, 1993.
5. Blaser A.D. and Egenhofer M. J. (2000). A Visual Tool for Querying Geographic Databases, *Proc. ACM AVI 2000*, ACM Press, 211-216.
6. F. Ferri, F. Massari, M. Rafanelli. "A Pictorial Query Language for Geographic Features in an Object-Oriented Environment". Journal of Visual Languages and Computing, Vol. 10, N. 6, pp. 641-671, Dec. 1999.
7. Ferri F., and Grifoni P. (2003). Vectorization of Graphical Components in Sketch-Based Interfaces. *Databases in Networked Information Systems*, Lecture Notes in Computer Science, Vol. 2822 Springer Verlag, 231-244.
8. Mussio P., Bruno N. and Esposito F. (1994). Image interpretation and ambiguities, *Human and Machine Vision: Analogies and Divergiencies*, Cantoni V. (eds), Plenum Press.
9. Scrivener S.A.R, Ball L.J. and Tseng W. (2000). Uncertainty and sketching behaviour, *Design Studies*, 21(5), 465-481.
10. Mahoney J.V. and Fromherz M. P. J. (2002). Three main concerns in sketch recognition and an approach to addressing them, *AAAI Spring Symposium on Sketch Understanding*, 105-112.

Foundations for Automated Trading — It's the Information That Matters

John Debenham

Faculty of IT, University of Technology, Sydney, Australia
debenham@it.uts.edu.au
http://www-staff.it.uts.edu.au/~debenham/

1 Extended Abstract

Business relationships, and the sense of trust that they embody, provides an environment in which trade may be conducted with confidence. Trading involves the maintenance of effective relationships, and refers to the process of: need identification, partner selection, offer-exchange, contract negotiation, and contract execution. So we use the term in a sense that includes the business of e-procurement. Of particular interest are: the selection of trading partners, the development of trading relationships, and the negotiation and execution of contracts in the context of a relationship.

The potential value of the e-business market — including e-procurement — is enormous. Given the current state of technical development it is surprising that a comparatively small amount of automated trading is presently deployed.[1] The technologies we refer to are first *multiagent systems*, and second the theory of competitive interaction. As a discipline, multiagent systems dates back to around 1975 when it was referred to as *distributed artificial intelligence*. The problems of building and deploying autonomous, intelligent agents are far from resolved but the technology has considerable maturity. The theory of competitive interaction, *game theory*, that principally dates back to the 1920s, has been developed mainly by the microeconomic community, and more recently also by the multiagent systems community in the area of *agent-mediated electronic commerce*.

Why is it then that virtually no automated trading takes place?

2 Multiagent Systems and Virtual Institutions

The value to automated trading of multiagent systems technology [1] that provides autonomous, intelligent and flexible software agents is self-evident. Of particular significance are the Belief-Desire-Intention [2] deliberative architectures that accommodate proactive planning systems [3]. Virtual Institutions are software systems composed of autonomous agents, that interact according to

---

[1] Auction bots, and automated auction houses do an important job, but do not automate trade in the sense described here.

predefined conventions on language and protocol and that guarantee that certain norms of behaviour are enforced. This view permits agents to behave autonomously and take their decisions freely up to the limits imposed by the set of norms of the institution. An important consequence of embedding agents in a virtual institution is that the predefined conventions on language and protocol greatly simplify the design of the agents. A Virtual Institution is in a sense a natural extension of the social concept of institutions as regulatory systems that shape human interactions [4].

3 Game Theory and Decision Theory

Game theory tells an agent what to do, and what outcome to expect, in many well-known negotiation situations, but these strategies and expectations are derived from assumptions about the internals of the opponent. In 1928 John von Neumann — sometimes referred to as the father of the modern computer — published the seminar paper [5], and some years later, with Oscar Morgenstern, the well known monograph [6]. Game theory now claims an impressive list of Nobel prize-winners. [7] is an excellent introduction to the area. *Bargaining* is one-to-one negotiation, and provides the only setting in which multi-issue negotiation may take place with an open issue set. *Auctions* address one-to-many negotiations. *Exchanges* and *clearing houses* address many-to-many negotiations. [8] discusses the relative merits of bargaining, auctions and exchanges.

Bargaining. Game theoretic analyses of bargaining are founded on the notion of agents as utility optimisers in the presence of both complete and incomplete information about the agent's opponents. The work of John Nash, [9], popularised in the movie A Beautiful Mind, is an early seminal contribution to bargaining — the "Nash Bargaining solution" — the significance of this work to automated trading is explored in [10]. Other fundamental contributions include the Rubinstein analysis of alternating offers bargaining [11], together with many others who have contributed to this now well-established area [12].

Under some circumstances bilateral bargaining has questionable value as a trading mechanism. Bilateral bargaining is known to be inherently inefficient [13]. [14] shows that a seller is better off with an auction that attracts $n+1$ buyers than bargaining with n individuals, *no matter what* the bargaining protocol is. [15] shows that the weaker bargaining types will fare better in exchanges leading to a gradual migration. These results hold for agents who aim to optimise their utility and do limit the work described here.

Auctions. There is a wealth of material on the theory of auctions [16] originating with the work of William Vickrey [17]. Fundamental to this analysis is the central role of the utility function, and the notion of rational behaviour by which an agent aims to optimise its utility, when it is able to do so, and to optimise its expected utility otherwise.

The design of auction mechanisms has been both fruitful and impressive — where rational behaviour provides a theoretical framework in which mechanism performance may be analysed. A notable example being the supremely elegant *Generalised Vickrey* mechanism [18] that builds on a mechanism proposed by Theodore Groves [19]. Game theory also leads to prescriptive results concerning agent behaviour, such as the behaviour of agents in the presence of hard deadlines [20]. The general value of game theory as a foundation for a prescriptive theory of agent behaviour is limited both by the extent to which an agent knows its own utility function, and by its certainty in the probability distributions of the utility functions (or, *types*) of its opponents.

Exchanges. Exchanges are institutions that cater to many potential buyers and sellers. Exchange mechanisms are known as *double auction mechanisms* [21]. These mechanisms either clear continuously or at discrete time steps. Institutions that use discrete double auctions are sometimes known as *clearing houses* or *call markets*.

An exchange mechanism has to do two things: first to match buyers and sellers and second to determine the terms for settlement. There are two general frameworks: first when the exchange clears at a uniform, non-discriminatory price, and second when traders are paired up, perhaps in an attempt to achieve Pareto optimality, and each pays a different price. If the clearing price is the mean of the marginal bid and the marginal ask then the mechanism is known as a *half double auction*. [22] describes a truth-telling, dominant strategy, single-issue, uniform-price mechanism that, somewhat reminiscent of the Vickrey auction, determines the clearing price as the mean of the lowest unsuccessful ask and highest unsuccessful bid. However that mechanism is not Pareto efficient, and trade can be lost, although this defect becomes less significant as the number of traders increases. There is no perfect mechanism. [23] discusses convergence for single issue exchanges, and assumes that the buyers' and sellers' preferences are complementary — i.e.: what is preferred by one is not preferred by the other. [24] approaches the problem of clearing multi-item, combinatorial exchanges using preference elicitation.

In addition to capital markets, exchanges are applied to creative applications such as trading risk, generating predictions and making decisions [25]. As a means of generating predictions, exchanges have demonstrated extraordinary accuracy. [26] analyses this phenomenon and suggests that marginal traders who are motivated primarily to make a profit submit limit orders, close to the trading price. Exchanges act as an "intelligence lens" that focusses the best information that the traders have on the clearing price. For example, [27] describes the predictions by the Iowa Electronic Markets of the winner of the 1988 US presidential election that were within 0.2% of what occurred.

Decision Theory. Classical decision theory consists of a set of mathematical techniques for making decisions about what action to take when the outcomes of the various actions are not known [28]. An agent operating in a complex environment is inherently uncertain about that environment; it simply does not have enough information about the environment to know either the precise current state of the environment, nor how that environment will evolve [29]. Here utilities provide a convenient means of encoding the *preferences* of an agent. Notable sub-areas of decision theory are Markov decision processes and Bayesian networks [30].

4   Automating the Trading Process

An inherent difficulty in e-business negotiation — including e-procurement — is that it is generally multi-issue. Even a simple trade, such as a quantity of steel, may involve: delivery date, settlement terms, as well as price and the quality of the steel. Most of the work on multi-issue negotiation has focussed appropriately on one-to-one bargaining — for example [31], [32]. There has been rather less interest in one-to-many, multi-issue auctions — [33] analyses some possibilities — and even less work on multi-issue exchanges, despite the size of the e-procurement market that typically attempts to extend single-issue, reverse auctions to the multi-issue case by post-auction haggling.

Fundamental to game theory and decision theory is the central role of the *utility function*, and the notion of *rational behaviour* by which an agent aims to optimise its utility, when it is able to do so, and to optimise its expected utility otherwise. On the surface the utility function seems reasonable — it is simply a representation on some scale of the agent's preferences. It is hard to argue *ex post* against the notion of utility. "Why did you cross the road?" — "Ah your utility function was ...". One difficulty with reducing our assessment of a situation to a single number is that it blurs two important aspects: the information that we have and our degree of belief in it. For example, in valuing a simple object it may be more realistic to construct a probability distribution across a possible evaluation domain where the probabilities represent that strength of belief that that evaluation is correct, than to reduce a valuation to a single value. If I buy a loaf of bread to make a sandwich then part of the value of the loaf to me is in what the remainder of the loaf may, perhaps, be used for in future.

One important feature of negotiation that game theory fails to capture is that negotiation is an *information exchange process* as well as an *offer exchange process*. If I make you an offer then I am telling you what I *am* prepared to pay, if I refuse an offer that you have made to me then I am telling you what I am *not* prepared to pay. This exchange of information reduces the uncertainty in an agent's model of its opponent. So the *value* of information here is the extent to which it reduces that uncertainty.

Information is primitive to the negotiation process. It is valuable in its own right — *its the information that matters*. Everything that an agent knows with certainty or otherwise, including its utility, will have been derived from its information. So if an agent is to benefit from trading other than by good fortune then he must have information that differs from other agents. The uniqueness of an agent's information is achieved in three ways: first, an agent may simply know something that others do not, second, an agent may attach levels of belief to its information that differ from the levels determined by others, and third, an agent may rate the importance, or relevance, of its information to the trading process in a way that differs from others.

> "As a general rule, the most successful man in life is the man who has the best information" — Benjamin Disraeli [twice British prime minister, for the second time in 1874 at the age of 70].

The fundamental significance of information to the trading process raises the question of whether the foundations for automated trading should rest first on information theory, and then perhaps, for those agents that are able to derive a utility function, on game theory or decision theory.

5 Information Theory

Claude Shannon is credited with establishing the basis for information theory [34] in the 1940s, which is now a well-developed branch of science in its own right [35]. Information theory may be applied to the analysis of data compression and data channel capacity, but that is not all. The ideas in it: uncertainty, the value of information, and the simplest way of expressing information are powerful tools. *Entropy*[2] is a measure of uncertainty. The value of *information* is then measured as the expected reduction in uncertainty that knowing that information brings.

Information theory incorporates some powerful logical tools. Consider the problem of estimating the probability distribution $\{p_i\}_{i=1}^{N}$. If nothing is known about these probabilities then E.T. Jaynes proposed [36] that the correct estimate is to choose the distribution with maximum entropy: $p_i = \frac{1}{N}, i = 1, \ldots, N$. E.T. Jaynes proposes that the *maximum entropy distribution* "is uniquely determined as the one which is maximally noncommittal with regard to missing information" [36], and that it "agrees with what is known, but expresses 'maximum uncertainty' with regard to all other matters, and thus leaves a maximum possible freedom for our final decision to be influenced by the subsequent sample data" [37][3]. Suppose further that we have a set of M linear constraints then

---

[2] The following informal justification of the definition of entropy may be found in many elementary books on information theory. It is included here for completeness. Let A be an event, and let p_A be the probability that A will occur, and the function $h : [0,1] \to \Re_+$ a measure of the *uncertainty* in A, $h(p_A)$. Suppose that events A and B are independent of each other, then the function h should satisfy the property that: the uncertainty in the event "A and B" is the uncertainty in event A plus the uncertainty in event B: $h(p_A \times p_B) = h(p_A) + h(p_B)$. It is natural to require h to be a continuous, decreasing function on $[0, 1]$ — and so the function h should have the form: $h(p) = -C \log p$. Setting $C = 1$ and using logarithms to base 2: $h(p_A) = -\log p_A$. Given a random variable X that takes discrete values $\{x_i\}_{i=1}^{n}$ with probabilities $\{p_i\}_{i=1}^{n}$. The *entropy*, $\mathbb{H}$, of the random variable X is the expectation of the distribution $\mathbb{E}(\{h(p_i)\}_{i=1}^{n}) = -\sum_i p_i \log p_i$. So the entropy of a random variable is the *expected reduction in uncertainty* by knowing its true value.
[3] This basic idea is not new and is often associated with William of Ockham [1280 1349] and referred to as "Occam's Razor" [38] although the idea goes back at least to Aristotle.

the *principle of maximum entropy* is to choose the distribution with maximum entropy that satisfies all of the constraints. It may be shown that the maximum entropy principle yields the set that "could have been generated in the greatest number of different ways consistent with the data", and so it is in a sense the "most likely". [39] shows that the maximum entropy principle encapsulates common sense reasoning. Entropy-based inference is particularly useful in negotiation as it enables complete probability distributions to be constructed from a modest amount of observations — i.e.: the actions of the opponent. Maximum entropy inference assumes that what the agent knows is "the sum total of the agent's knowledge, it is not a summary of the agent's knowledge, it is all there is" [39]. This assumption referred to as Watt's Assumption [40]. So if knowledge is absent then it may do strange things. If the knowledge base is expressed in first-order logic, then issues that have unbounded domains — such as price — can only be dealt with either exactly as a large quantity of constants for each possible price, or approximately as price intervals. The representation chosen will effect the inferences drawn and is referred to as representation dependence [41]. Entropy-based inference is particularly suited to automated trading where it enables inferences to be drawn on the basis of sparse but reliable information [42].

6 Information-Based Agents for Automated Trading

Information-based agents attempt to fuse the negotiation with the information that is generated both by and because of it. To achieve this, they draw first on ideas from information theory rather than game theory. An information-based agent decides what to do — such as whether to bid in an auction — on the basis of its information that may be qualified by expressions of degrees of belief. It uses this information to calculate, and continually re-calculate, probability distributions for that which it does not know. One such distribution, over the set of all possible deals, expresses its belief in the acceptability of a deal. Other distributions attempt to predict the behaviour of its opponents — such as what they might bid in an auction. These distribution are calculated from the agent's information and beliefs using entropy-based inference. An information-based agent makes no assumptions about the internals of its opponents, including whether they have, or are even aware of the concept of, utility functions. It is purely concerned with its opponents' behaviour — what they do — and not with assumptions about their motivations.

The Information Principle. An information-based agent's information base contains only observed facts — in the absence of observed facts, he may speculate about what those facts might be. For example in competitive negotiation, an opponent's utility, deadlines, and other private information will never be observable — unless the opponent is foolish. Further, the opponent's motivations (such as being a utility optimiser) will also never be observable. So in competitive negotiation an opponent's private information is "off the agent's radar" — an information-based agent does not contemplate it or speculate about it.

A trading agent is driven by its *needs* — it negotiates with the *aim* of satisfying these needs. So it has an evaluation function that evaluates any outcome against the extent to which it has satisfied its various needs. Given an outcome and a set of needs, the value of such a function is a probability distribution over the agent's evaluation space. Unlike the game-theoretic approaches, this space does *not* represent the agents preferences — it simply represents the agent's beliefs of the extent to which an outcome satisfies its needs.

Valuing Information A chunk of information is valued only by the way that it alters an agent's world model M^t, at time t, that here consists of a number of probability distributions: $M^t = \{P_i^t\}_{i=1}^n$ that are derived from the agent's information at time t: $\mathcal{I}^t$, so we write $M^t = M(\mathcal{I}^t)$. Suppose that the agent receives a string of messages, $X_{(u,t)}$, between time u and time t. The *value* of the information in $X_{(u,t)}$ is the resulting decrease in entropy in the distributions $\{P_i^t\}_{i=1}^n$. That is: $\mathbb{I}(X_{(u,t)} \mid M^u) = \sum_{i=1}^n \mathbb{H}(P_i^u) - \sum_{i=1}^n \mathbb{H}(P_i^t)$. This values the information *as information*, and *not* as the utility that it may perhaps generate.

Information Revelation. An agent's *negotiation strategy* is a function $S : M^t \to \mathcal{A}$ where $\mathcal{A}$ is the set of actions that send messages to its opponent. These messages give valuable information to the opponent about herself. In an infinite-horizon bargaining game where there is no incentive to trade now rather than later, a self-interested agent will "sit and wait", and do nothing except, perhaps, to ask for information. Once an agent is motivated to act she may wish to give the opponent the impression that she is "acting fairly". One way to achieve this is to aim to reveal information to the opponent that approximately equates in value to the value of the information received. This strategy may contribute to establishing a sense of *trust*. Various bargaining strategies, both with and without breakdown, are described in [43], but they do not address this issue. Our agent here assumes that its opponent's reasoning apparatus mirrors its own, and so is able to estimate the change in opponent's entropy as a result of sending a message x to her: $\mathbb{I}(\{x\} \mid M_{\text{op}}^t)$. Suppose that the agent receives a message y from her opponent and observes an information gain of $\mathbb{I}(\{y\} \mid M^t)$. Suppose that she wishes to respond with a message, z, that will give her opponent expected "equitable information gain":

$$z = \left\{ \arg\max_z \text{val}(z, \nu) \geq \alpha \mid \mathbb{I}(\{z\} \mid M_{\text{op}}^t) \approx \mathbb{I}(\{y\} \mid M^t) \right\}$$

where $\text{val}(z, \nu)$ is an evaluation function that estimates the strength of the agent's belief in the proposition that "accepting z will satisfy her need ν", and α is a threshold constant. So $\text{val}(\cdot)$ generalises the notion of utility. The "equitable information gain" strategy generalises the simple-minded alternating offers strategy.

Trust. [44] describes models of *trust* that are built on information theory. In the context of negotiation, trust represents a general assessment on how 'serious' an agent is about the negotiation process, i.e. that his proposals 'make sense' and he is not 'flying a kite', and that he is committed to what he signs. A lack of trust may provoke agents to breakdown negotiations, or to demand additional guarantees to cover the risk of potential defections. Therefore, in any model of trust the central issue is how to model expectations about the actual outcome at contract execution time.

Contracts, when executed, may, and frequently do, yield a different result to what was initially signed. Goods may be delivered late, quality may be (perceived) different from the contract specification, extra costs may be claimed, etc. So the outcome is uncertain to some extent, and trust, precisely, is a measure of how uncertain the outcome of a contract is. Naturally, the higher the trust in a partner the more sure we are of his or her reliability. Trust is therefore a *measure of expected deviations of behaviour* along a given dimension, and in many cases for a given value (region) in that dimension (e.g. I might trust you on low-priced contracts but not on high-priced ones). In this sense, the higher the trust the lower the expectation that a (significant) deviation from what is signed occurs. Two components may somehow be combined to describe our trust in an opponent:

- Trust as *expected behaviour*. Consider a distribution of expected contract executions that represents the agent's "ideal" in the sense that it is the best that she could reasonably expect an opponent to do. This distribution will be a function of the opponent, the agent's trading history with the opponent, anything else that she believes about the opponent, and general environmental information including time — denote all of this by e, then $\mathbb{P}_I^t(b'|b,e)$ denotes for all commitments, b, by an opponent, the ideal expectation of what the opponent will actually do, b', where $b' \in B(b)$ the set of all things that could reasonably be expected to occur following the commitment b. Trust is the relative entropy between this ideal distribution, $\mathbb{P}_I^t(b'|b,e)$, and the distribution of the observation of expected actual contract executions, $\mathbb{P}^t(b'|b)$. That is, *trust* for the single commitment b is: $1 - \sum_{b' \in B(b)} \mathbb{P}_I^t(b'|b,e) \log \frac{\mathbb{P}_I^t(b'|b,e)}{\mathbb{P}^t(b'|b)}$. If $\mathbb{P}^t(b)$ is the probability of the agent signing a contract with the opponent that involves the commitment b then the *trust* that the agent has in her opponent is: $1 - \sum_{b \in B} \mathbb{P}^t(b) \left[\sum_{b' \in B(b)} \mathbb{P}_I^t(b'|b,e) \log \frac{\mathbb{P}_I^t(b'|b,e)}{\mathbb{P}^t(b'|b)} \right]$.
- Trust as *consistency* in expected acceptable contract executions, or "the lack of expected uncertainty in those executions that are better than the contract specification". The *trust* that an agent has on an opponent with respect to the fulfilment of a commitment b is: $1 + \frac{1}{B^*} \cdot \sum_{b' \in B(b)} \mathbb{P}_+^t(b'|b) \log \mathbb{P}_+^t(b'|b)$ where $\mathbb{P}_+^t(b'|b)$ is the normalisation of $\mathbb{P}^t(b'|b)$ for those values of b' for which $\text{val}(b',\nu) > \text{val}(b,\nu)$ and zero otherwise, and B^* is a normalisation constant. Given some b' that the agent does not prefer to b, the trust value will be 0. Trust will tend to 0 when the dispersion of observations is maximal. And, as a general measure of the agent's *trust* on her opponent we naturally use the normalised negative conditional entropy of executed contracts given signed contracts: $1 + \frac{1}{B^*} \sum_{b \in B} \sum_{b' \in B(b)} \left[\mathbb{P}_+^t(b',b) \log \mathbb{P}_+^t(b'|b) \right]$.

7 It's the Information That Matters

All interaction reveals information about the sender to the receiver. A trading agent's information base contains only observed facts. An opponent's utility, deadlines, and other private information, will never be observable, and so are not considered. Information theory provides the theoretical underpinning that enables an informed trading agent to value, manage and trade her information.

References

1. Wooldridge, M.: Multiagent Systems. Wiley (2002)
2. Georgeff, M., Pell, B., Pollack, M., Tambe, M., Wooldridge, M.: The beliefdesireintention model of agency. In Muller, J., Singh, M.P., Rao, A.S., eds.: Proceedings of the 5th International Workshop on Intelligent Agents V : Agent Theories, Architectures, and Languages (ATAL-98), Springer-Verlag: Heidelberg, Germany (1999) 110
3. Ghallab, M., Nau, D., Traverso, P.: Automated Planning : Theory and Practice. Morgan Kaufmann (2004)
4. Arcos, J.L., Esteva, M., Noriega, P., Rodrguez, J.A., Sierra, C.: Environment engineering for multiagent systems. Journal on Engineering Applications of Artificial Intelligence 18 (2005)
5. von Neumann, J.: Zur theorie der gesellschaftsspiele. Mathematische Annalen (1928) 295 320
6. Neumann, J., Morgenstern, O.: Theory of Games and Economic Behavior. Princeton University Press (1944)
7. Rasmusen, E.: Games and Information: An Introduction to Game Theory. 3rd edn. Blackwell Publishers (2001)
8. Vulkan, N.: The Economics of E-Commerce. Princeton University Press (2003)
9. Nash, J.: Equilibrium points in n-person games. Proceedings of the National Academy of Sciences (1950) 48 49
10. Rosenschein, J.S., Zlotkin, G.: Rules of Encounter. The MIT Press, Cambridge, USA (1994)
11. Osborne, M., Rubinstein, A.: A Course in Game Theory. The MIT Press (1994)
12. Muthoo, A.: Bargaining Theory with Applications. Cambridge UP (1999)
13. Myerson, R., Satterthwaite, M.: Efficient mechanisms for bilateral trading. Journal of Economic Theory 29 (1983) 121
14. Bulow, J., Klemperer, P.: Auctions versus negotiations. American Economic Review 86 (1996) 180194
15. Neeman, Z., Vulkan, N.: Markets versus negotiations. Technical report, Center for Rationality and Interactive Decision Theory, Hebrew University, Jerusalem (2000)
16. Klemperer, P.: The Economic Theory of Auctions : Vols I and II. Edward Elgar (2000)
17. Vickrey, W.: Counterspeculation, auctions and competitive sealed tenders. Journal of Finance (1961) 8 37
18. Varian, H.: Mechanism design for computerized agents. In: Proceedings Usenix Workshop on Electronic Commerce. (1995) 1321
19. Groves, T.: Incentives in teams. Econometrica 41 (1973) 617 631
20. Sandholm, T., Vulkan, N.: Bargaining with deadlines. In: Proceedings of the National Conference on Artificial Intelligence (AAAI). (1999)

21. Friedman, D.: The double auction market institution: A survey. In Friedman, D., Rust, J., eds.: The Double Auction Market: Institutions, Theories and Evidence. Addison-Wesley, Reading, MA (1993) 3 26
22. Preston McAfee, R.: A dominant strategy double auction. Journal of Economic Theory 56 (1992) 266 293
23. Rustichini, A., Satterthwaite, M., Williams, S.: Convergence to efficiency in a simple market with incomplete information. Econometrica 62 (1994) 1041 1063
24. Smith, T., Sandholm, T., Simmons, R.: Constructing and clearing combinatorial exchanges using preference elicitation. In: proceedings AAAI Workshop on Preferences in AI and CP: Symbolic Approaches, AAAI (2002) 87 93
25. Kambil, A., Heck, E.V.: Making Markets: How Firms Can Design and Profit from Online Auctions and Exchanges. Harvard Business School Press (2002)
26. Forsythe, R., Rietz, T., Ross, T.: Wishes, expectations and actions: A survey on price formation in election stock markets. The Journal of Economic Behavior and Organization 39 (1999) 83 110
27. Varian, H.: Effect of the internet on financial markets. (1998)
28. Raiffa, H.: Decision Analysis: Introductory Readings on Choices Under Uncertainty. McGraw Hill (1997)
29. Raiffa, H.: Negotiation Analysis: The Science and Art of Collaborative Decision Making. Harvard U.P. (2002)
30. Bernardo, J., Smith, A.: Bayesian Theory. John Wiley and Sons, Inc. (2000)
31. Faratin, P., Sierra, C., Jennings, N.: Using similarity criteria to make issue tradeoffs in automated negotiation. Journal of Artificial Intelligence 142 (2003) 205237
32. Fatima, S.,Wooldridge, M., Jennings, N.R.: An agenda-based framework for multiissue negotiation. Artificial Intelligence 152 (2004) 1 45
33. Debenham, J.: Auctions and bidding with information. In Faratin, P., Rodriguez-Aguilar, J., eds.: Proceedings Agent-Mediated Electronic Commerce VI: AMEC. (2004) 15 28
34. Shannon, C.: A mathematical theory of communication. Bell System Technical Journal 27 (1948) 379 423 and 623 656
35. Cover, T., Thomas, J.: Elements of Information Theory. Wiley Series in Telecommunciations. John Wiley and Sons, Inc. (1991)
36. Jaynes, E.: Information theory and statistical mechanics: Part I. Physical Review 106 (1957) 620 630
37. Jaynes, E.: Prior probabilities. IEEE Transactions Systems Science and Cybernetics 4 (1968) 227 241
38. William of Ockham: Summa logicae, Paris (1448)
39. Paris, J.: Common sense and maximum entropy. Synthese 117 (1999) 75 93
40. Jaeger, M.: Representation independence of nonmonotonic inference relations. In: Proceedings of KR96, Morgan Kaufmann (1996) 461472
41. Halpern, J.: Reasoning about Uncertainty. MIT Press (2003)
42. Golan, A., Judge, G., Miller, D.: Maximum Entropy Econometrics: Robust Estimation with Limited Data. Financial Economics and Quantitative Analysis. John Wiley and Sons, Inc. (1996)
43. Debenham, J.: Bargaining with information. In Jennings, N., Sierra, C., Sonenberg, L., Tambe, M., eds.: Proceedings Third International Conference on Autonomous Agents and Multi Agent Systems AAMAS-2004, ACM (2004) 664 671
44. Sierra, C., Debenham, J.: An information-based model for trust. In: Proceedings Fourth International Conference on Autonomous Agents and Multi Agent Systems AAMAS-2005, ACM Press, New York (2005)

Intensional Query Answering to XQuery Expressions

Simone Gasparini and Elisa Quintarelli

Dipartimento di Elettronica e Informazione, Politecnico di Milano
Piazza Leonardo da Vinci, 32 — 20133 Milano (Italy)
{gasparini, quintarelli}@elet.polimi.it

Abstract. XML is a representation of data which may require huge amounts of storage space and query processing time. Summarized representations of XML data provide succinct information which can be directly queried, either when fast yet approximate answers are sufficient, or when the actual dataset is not available. In this work we show which kinds of XQuery expressions admit a partial answer by using association rules extracted from XML datasets. Such partial information provide intensional answers to queries formulated as XQuery expressions.

1 Introduction

The eXtensible Markup Language (XML) [12] was initially proposed as a standard way to design markup languages to represent, exchange and publish information on the Web, but its usage has recently spread to many other application fields.

XML is a rather verbose representation of data, which may require huge amounts of storage space and query processing time. In [2] several summarized representations of XML data are proposed to provide succinct information and be directly queried. In particular, the notion of *patterns* is introduced as abstract representations of the constraints that hold on the data and for (possibly partially) answering queries, either when fast (but approximate) answers are required, or when the actual dataset is not available or it is currently unreachable.

In this work we show which kinds of queries admit a partial answer by means of association rules extracted from XML datasets by using data mining techniques.

In particular, once a XML dataset has been analyzed by a miner tool and a set of association rules has been extracted, we investigate how to transform an XQuery expression to be applied to the original XML dataset, in order to apply it to the set of rules previously extracted. In this way we provide an approximate intensional answer.

An intensional answer to a query substitutes the actual data answering the query (the extensional answer) with a set of properties (in our work, with a set of association rules) characterizing them [11]. Thus, intensional answers are in general more synthetic than the extensional ones, but usually approximate.

In order to achieve our goal, an intuitive and effective language is needed to query the extracted knowledge.

We focus on XQuery, the standard XML query language introduced by the W3C [13]. In particular, we propose the fragment of XQuery expressions that can be used to retrieve useful information from the extracted sets of association rules. Such useful information can provide intensional answers to queries formulated as XQuery expressions. In [7] we have focused also on a graph-based language, and in particular on XQBE [3], because the user could (visually) express a query without taking care about the details of the language really used to query the document. In this way, the overall querying process appears completely transparent to the user: if the actual dataset is not available, the intensional (approximate) answer will be automatically provided by querying the rule set.

The paper is organized as follows. Section 2 summarizes the different types of patterns proposed in [2] and briefly describes how to represent them in a graph-based formalism. In Section 3 we propose some examples which show the set of queries we can manage with our approach and how to transform XQuery expressions in order to retrieve intensional information about XML documents; the formalization of the transformation process is in [7]. Previous work is discussed in Section 4, while conclusions and possible lines for future work are presented in Section 5.

2 Patterns for XML Documents

The summarized representations introduced in [2] are based on the extraction of association rules from XML datasets. Association rules describe the co-occurrence of data items in a large amount of collected data [1] and are usually represented as implications in the form $X \Rightarrow Y$, where X and Y are two arbitrary sets of data items, such that $X \cap Y = \emptyset$. In the XML context, a data item is a pair *(data-element,value)*, e.g. (Conference,Pods). The quality of an association rule is usually measured by means of *support* and *confidence*. Support corresponds to the frequency of the set $X \cup Y$ in the dataset, while confidence corresponds to the conditional probability of finding Y, having found X and is given by $sup(X \cup Y)/sup(X)$.

In [2] patterns are classified in two orthogonal ways. The first classification refers to the precision with which the pattern represents the dataset: a) an *exact* pattern expresses a property which holds on *any* instance of the dataset. Thus exact patterns represent *constraints* (e.g. functional dependencies between schema elements by means of schema patterns). For example, the name and the edition of a conference identify the location where the conference has taken place. b) A *probabilistic* pattern holds only on a given (large) fraction of the instances in the dataset. It is a weak constraint on the dataset, characterized by a quality index describing its reliability. For example, with a confidence of 0.9 the name of a conference identifies its main topics.

The second classification dimension corresponds to the different summarization levels of the represented information. *Instance* patterns are expressed on the instances of the dataset. In this paper they are used to summarize the content of a XML dataset by means of the most relevant (frequent) association rules holding on the dataset. As proposed in [2], association rules are extracted by using mining algorithms; in particular, to define the concept of transaction a *transaction root* (i.e. an appropriate element of the considered XML document) is selected. A transaction is then defined as a collection of pairs *(element tag,content)* or *(attribute name,value)*, where *element tag* (or *attribute name*) is the name of an element (or attribute) rooted in the transaction root

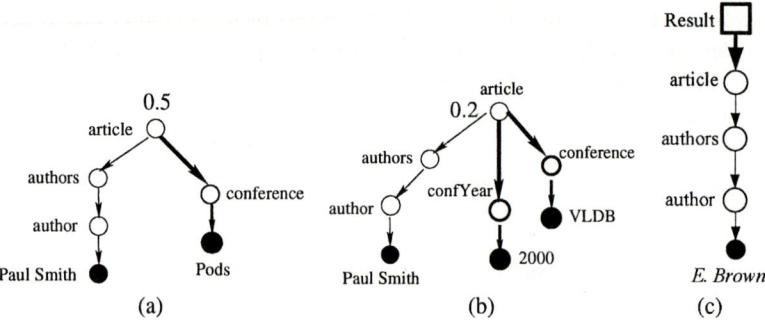

Fig. 1. Three instance patterns

and is defined as a complete sub-path from the root to the element. The quality index of the pattern is the confidence of the rule.

We use previously extracted association rules to derive an approximate answer to an XQuery expression, without requiring to actually access the dataset to compute the answer. The answer may contain a subset or a superset of the required information, depending on the form of the query and of the considered instance patterns.

In this work we focus our attention on (probabilistic) instance patterns. An example of instance pattern is the following: with a confidence of 0.8 the author *Paul Smith* has a publication to at least an edition of the conference *ICDT*.

In [2] a tree-based representation of patterns, which is formalized by means of the language GSL, is proposed as well.

For example, the instance pattern (a) of Figure 1 represents the association rule stating that with a confidence of 0.5 Paul Smith had a publication to any edition of the Pods conference. In the graphical version of patterns we represent nodes with circles (black filled circles represent the content of leaf elements or the value of attribute) and indicate the confidence of the instance pattern on the root of the graph. Thin lines are used to represent the body of the association rule, whereas thick lines represent the head of a rule. A more complex instance pattern expressing an association rule with more than one path in the thick part of the tree (i.e., in the association rule head), is depicted in Figure 1.(b). The rule states that with a confidence of 0.2 Paul Smith had a publication to the conference VLDB 2000. Note that here the confidence is associated to the conjunction of the two conditions in the head of the instance pattern.

3 Experimental Setup

In [7] the set of queries which can be considered to obtain approximate answers by using instance patterns is introduced. For the sake of space, in this work we present our idea only by examples.

For our first experiments we have used a dataset based on a slight variation of the SIGMOD Record XML Document [10]. The document reports information about Conference Proceedings; Listing 1.1 reports a XML fragment of the document itself.

```
<articles>
    <article year"2001">
        <volume>30</volume>
        <number>2</number>
        <month>June</month>
        <conference>ACM SIGMOD International Conference on Management of Data</conference>
        <date>May 21 - 24, 2001</date>
        <location>Santa Barbara, California, USA</location>
        <title articleCode="302001">Securing XML Documents ...</title>
        <authors>
            <author authorPosition="01">E. Brown</author>
            <author authorPosition="02">L. Baines</author>
        </authors>
        <indexTerms>
            <term>XML</term>
            <term>Security</term>
            <term>XQuery</term>
            <term>Theory</term>
        <indexTerms>
    </article>
    ...
</articles>
```

Listing 1.1. A portion of the sample document inspired to the SIGMOD Record [10]

```
<?xml version="1.0" encoding="UTF-8"?>
<!ELEMENT RuleSet (AssociationRule+)>
<!ELEMENT AssociationRule (RuleBody, RuleHead)>
<!ATTLIST AssociationRule
    support CDATA #REQUIRED
    confidence CDATA #REQUIRED>
<!ELEMENT RuleBody (item+)>
<!ELEMENT RuleHead (item+)>
<!ELEMENT item (ItemName, ItemValue)>
<!ELEMENT ItemName (#PCDATA)>
<!ELEMENT ItemValue (#PCDATA)>
```

Listing 1.2. The DTD of the document reporting the extracted association rules set

Starting from this dataset, we perform a mining process to extract association rules. Most of the proposed algorithms for mining association rules [1], [8] consider a collection of transactions, each containing a set of items. In our examples, we have associated each transaction to an `article`, thus, we have extracted association rules describing information about the elements which characterize articles (e.g. `author`, `title`, etc.).

In order to retrieve intensional answers from the set of extracted association rules, we store them in a XML document. Listing 1.2 reports the relevant Document Type Definition (DTD) we use to represent the rule set. We partially take inspiration from the PMML (Predictive Model Markup Language) standard model proposed by the Data Mining Group [5], which describes statistical and data mining models. Our model, however, is simpler and easier to query, i.e. it requires a less complex XQuery expression to formulate a query. For example, a portion of the valid XML document representing some association rules, which have been extracted from the dataset based on the SIGMOD Record XML Document, is shown in Listing 1.3.

```
<ruleSet>
    <AssociationRule support="0.2" confidence="0.8">
        <RuleBody>
            <item><ItemName>author</ItemName><ItemValue>E. Brown</ItemValue></item>
        </RuleBody>
        <RuleHead>
            <item><ItemName>term</ItemName><ItemValue>XML</ItemValue></item>
        </RuleHead>
    </AssociationRule>
    ...
</ruleSet>
```

Listing 1.3. A sample fragment of the XML document of the rule set extracted from the sample document of Listing 1.1

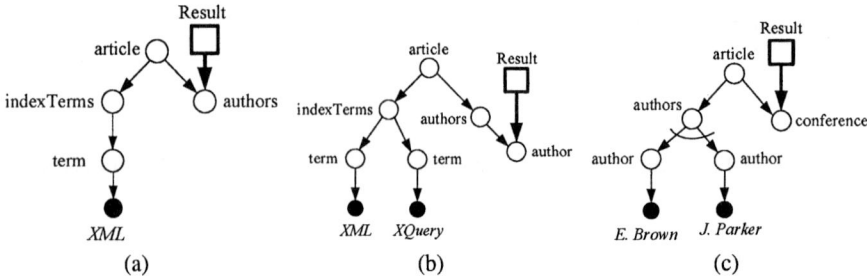

Fig. 2. (a) GSL visual representation of query $Q2$; (b) GSL visual representation of query $Q4$; (c) GSL visual representation of query $Q5$;

In the following we analyze the kinds of queries described in [7] that admit a partial answer by using association rules extracted from XML datasets.

3.1 Queries with Conditions on Content Nodes

Let us consider the first kind of query with conditions on a content node; i.e. queries imposing a restriction on the value of an attribute or on the content of a leaf element of an XML dataset. An example is the query $Q1$ "*List all the information about the articles published by E. Brown*", which contains a condition on the name of an author. The GSL representation is depicted in Figure 1.(c). An XQuery expression for this query is:

```
<result> {
for $article in doc("document.xml")//article
where $article/authors/author/text() = "E. Brown"
return $article }
</result>
```

The above expression can be run on any XQuery engine to get the extensional answer to $Q1$. In order to get an intensional answer from the extracted rule set, we have to transform the original XQuery expression.

For the query $Q1$, according to the DTD for the extracted association rules described before (Listing 1.2), the XQuery expression should be modified as follows:

```
<result> {
  for $article in doc("RuleSet.xml")//AssociationRule
  where $article[RuleBody[item[ItemName="author" and ItemValue="E. Brown"]]]
  return $article }
</result>
```

This expression returns all the association rules that have an item named `author` in the body of the rule, whose value is `E. Brown`. The changes required (underlined in the listing) to query the rule set affect the name of the document to examine (from now on we suppose that the rule set is stored in a XML file named `RuleSet.xml`), the item in the `for` clause, which has to be `AssociationRule`, and the expression in the `where` clause, modified to select only those rules having an item in the body with the same name of the `author` element.

Similarly, to get the association rules that satisfy the condition in the head of the rule, `RuleBody` has to be replaced with `RuleHead` in the `where` clause. A more generic query that looks for interesting information about `E.Brown` both in the body and in the head can be expressed as follows:

```
<result> {
  for $article in doc("RuleSet.xml")//AssociationRule
  where $article//item[ItemName = "author" and ItemValue = "E. Brown"]]
  return $article }
</result>
```

By using the XPath expression `//item`, the `where` clause selects all the association rules which have an item named `author` in the body or in the head of the rule and whose value is `E. Brown`.

Let us consider now the query that retrieves information about a node which is not a direct ancestor of the constrained content node. An example of this kind of query is the query *Q2*: *"List all the authors who wrote articles about XML"*. Figure 2.(a) shows how it can be graphically represented in GSL. Like *Q1*, the source part matches all the `author` having the term `XML` among the index terms of their published articles; the query result will contain all these authors. The XQuery expression is:

```
<result> {
  for $article in doc("document.xml")//article
  where $article/indexTerms/term/text() = "XML"
  return $article/authors/author }
</result>
```

In order to inquire the extracted rule set, the above XQuery expression needs the following transformations:

```
<result> {
  for $article in doc("RuleSet.xml")//AssociationRule
  where $article/RuleBody/item[ItemName = "term"]/ItemValue= "XML"
  return $article[RuleHead/item[ItemName = "author"]] }
</result>
```

The expression returns all the association rules that have an item `term` with required value in the body and has an item `author` in the head, such as the rule relating the author E. Brown and the index term XML in the rule set listed in Listing 1.3. The changes that are required are similar to the ones for query *Q1*, but in this case also a filter on the returned `$author` variable is introduced in order to select only those association rules which contain the item `author` in the head of the rule. In a similar way, by swapping

RuleHead and RuleBody in these expressions, the rules with term in the head and author in the body can be obtained.

The GSL language used to represent XML patterns and the extraction process of association rules make no distinction between elements and attributes of XML dataset since the main aim is to find relationships among elementary values of XML documents. However this choice can be easily tackled transparently to the user, as the following example demonstrates. Let consider the query *Q*3 with condition on the value of an attribute: "*List all the conference held in 1996*". An XQuery expression of *Q*3 is:

```
<result> {
  for $article in doc("document.xml")//article
  where $article/@year = 1996
  return $article/conference }
</result>
```

Due to the mining process, we loose the distinction between elements and attribute and so we have to transform the above expression simply by considering in the same way attributes and elements. Thus the XQuery expression to query the rule set becomes:

```
<result> {
  for $article in doc("RuleSet.xml")//AssociationRule
  where $article/RuleBody/item[ItemName = "year"]/ItemValue= "1996"
  return $article[RuleHead/item[ItemName = "conference"]]}
</result>
```

The expression returns all the rules relating year in the body and conference in the head.

3.2 Queries with AND-Conditions on Content Nodes

Let us now focus on query with AND-conditions on the content nodes. As an example, consider query *Q*4: "*List all the authors who have published articles about XML and XQuery*" (see Figure 2.(b) for the visual representation). A related XQuery expression is:

```
<result> {
  for $article in doc("document.xml")//article
  where $article/indexTerms/term/text() = "XML"
  and $article/indexTerms/term/text() = "XQuery"
  return $article/authors/author }
</result>
```

In order to provide intensional answer to *Q*4 by querying the extracted rule set, the expression has to be modified in the following way:

```
<result> {
  for $article in doc("RuleSet.xml")//AssociationRule
  where $article/RuleBody/item[ItemName = "term"]/ItemValue= "XML"
  and $article/RuleBody/item[ItemName = "term"]/ItemValue= "XQuery"
  return $article[RuleHead/item[ItemName = "author"]]}
</result>
```

This XQuery expression returns all the association rules satisfying both the conditions on the term in the body of the rule and having an item author in the head.

3.3 Queries with OR-Conditions on Content Nodes

Another type of query to consider is the one with two or more OR-conditions. An example of this kind of query is *Q*5: "*List all the conference attended by J. Parker or

E. Brown" (see Figure 2.(c) for the graphical representation. The arc between the two edges represents a disjunctive condition). The equivalent XQuery expression is:

```
<result> {
 for $article in doc("document.xml")//article
 where $article/authors/author = "J. Parker"
 or $article/authors/author = "E. Brown"
 return $article/conference }
</result>
```

In order to query the rule set, we carry out the following adjustments:

```
<result> {
 for $article in doc("RuleSet.xml")//AssociationRule
 where $article/RuleBody/item[ItemName = "author"]/ItemValue= "J. Parker"
 or $article/RuleBody/item[ItemName = "author"]/ItemValue= "E. Brown"
 return $article[RuleHead/item[ItemName = "conference"]]}
</result>
```

Applying this XQuery expression to the rule set, we obtain all the association rules having an item `conference` in the head and satisfying the OR-conditions about both `author` elements in the body of the rule.

3.4 Queries with Element Values

Finally let us consider the query that lists all the different values of a content node. An example is the query *Q6* "*List all the authors who wrote an article, sorting in a lexicographic order*". A relevant XQuery expression can be:

```
<result> {
 for $author in doc("document.xml")//author
 order by $author/text() ascending
 return <author> {$author/text()} </author>}
</result>
```

The above expression should be modified to query the rule set as it follows:

```
<result> {
 for $author in doc("RuleSet.xml")//item[ItemName="author"]/ItemValue
 order by $author/text() ascending
 return <author> {$author/text()} </author>}
</result>
```

This XQuery expression selects all the association rules having an item `author` in the body or in the head of the rule and returns the content of the retrieved `author` elements, lexicographically sorted. This type of query requires a slight adjustment in the expression of the `for` clause to filter the appropriate item in the rules.

4 Related Works

The problem of providing intensional answers by means of integrity constraints has been initially addressed in [11] in the relational databases context. In this work we extend the approach to graph-based probabilistic patterns and XML documents. We starts from the results published in [2], where several summarized representations of XML data are proposed to provide succinct information: the notion of patterns is introduced as abstract representations of the constraints that hold on the data and a graph-based representation of patterns is proposed as well. In particular, instance patterns are represented by the most frequent association rules and are effectively extracted from XML documents by using data-mining algorithms (e.g. by using Apriori). Some preliminary ideas on the possibility to use such instance patterns to provide intensional answers to user's queries are sketched. In this work we extend the result of [2] in order to apply the proposed approach to the XQuery language and we identify some classes of queries that admit an approximate answer by using previously extracted association rules.

Another two works which present a framework to discover association rules in large amounts of XML data are [4, 6].

In [4] the authors introduce a proposal to enrich XQuery with data mining and knowledge discovery capabilities by introducing association rules for native XML documents and a specific operator for describing them. They formalize the syntax and an intuitive semantics for the operator and propose some examples of complex association rules. No algorithm for mining such complex rules is proposed, thus, we have decided to start from the results in [2] and use, as a first step, very simple association rules in order to partially answer to XQuery expressions.

In [6] a template model to specify XML-enabled associations to be effectively mined is presented. In our opinion our work differs from [4, 6] because we do not focus on the problems of representing and extracting complex association rules from XML documents, instead we work on the possibility to use and manipulate the extracted knowledge (at the moment we mine instance patterns by using the Apriori algorithm) in order to give partial and approximate answers to XQuery expressions. As a future work we may consider the method described in [6] to improve the performance of the mining process and to be able to consider also more complex association rules on XML document.

5 Conclusion and Future Work

In this work we have shown how to use association rules to provide intensional answers and obtain approximate information about XML documents. In particular, we have explained which kinds of XQuery expressions admit an approximate answer and how to transform them in order to query previously mined association rules.

We have built a first prototype environment implemented in Java and is mainly composed of two components. The first one visualizes the DTD of a XML document in a graph-based representation. The user chooses the items to include in the process of extraction of association rules by indicating also where to apply stemming, stopwords, and discretization procedures. The native XML document is then transformed in order to be processed by the Apriori algorithm. The second component stores the output of the miner into a MySQL database. To conclude, a graphical interface gives to the user the possibility to query the extracted knowledge by using some classes of queries and more in particular by providing values for few parameters that are then used to automatically compose SQL queries to be applied to the MySQL database of rules. We are now adapting the tool in order to transform the output of the miner into a XML document. Another component under development uses the Saxon [9] engine to apply an XQuery expression either to the original XML document or to the extracted set of rules.

As an ongoing work we are formalizing the degree of approximation (and the time performance) of our approach in answering queries and studying how to combine constraints and association rules to improve the precision of intensional answers. We are also considering extensions of the XQuery fragment proposed in this work that admit partial answers.

Acknowledgment

We like to thank Letizia Tanca for the very useful comments on this work and Elena Baralis and Paolo Garza for the precious collaboration in the setting foundations of this research.

References

1. R. Agrawal and R. Srikant. Fast algorithms for mining association rules in large databases. In *Proceedings of the 20th International Conference on Very Large Data Bases*, pages 487–499. Morgan Kaufmann Publishers Inc., 1994.
2. E. Baralis, P. Garza, E. Quintarelli, and L. Tanca. Answering queries on XML data by means of associations rules. In *Current Trends in Database Technology*, volume 3268. Springer-Verlag, 2004.
3. D. Braga and A. Campi. A graphical environment to query XML data with XQuery. In *Proc. of the Fourth International Conference on Web Information Systems Engineering (WISE'03)*, pages 31–40. IEEE Computer Society, 2003.
4. D. Braga, A. Campi, M. Klemettinen, and P.L. Lanzi. Mining association rules from XML data. In *Proc. of the 2003 ACM Symposium on Applied Computing*, volume 2454, pages 21–30. Lecture Notes in Computer Science, 2002.
5. Data Mining Group. PMML 2.1 – DTD of association rules model. http://www.dmg.org.
6. L. Feng and T. Dillon. Mining XML-Enabled Association Rules with Templates. In *Proc. of the Third International Workshop on Knowledge Discovery in Inductive Databases*, volume 3377, pages 66–88. Lecture Notes in Computer Science, 2004.
7. S. Gasparini and E. Quintarelli. Intensional Query Answering to XQuery expressions. Technical Report 2005.21, Politecnico di Milano. http://www.elet.polimi.it/upload/quintare/Papers/GQ05-Report.pdf.
8. Jiawei Han, Jian Pei, and Yiwen Yin. Mining frequent patterns without candidate generation. In *2000 ACM SIGMOD Int. Conference on Management of Data*, pages 1–12. ACM Press, 2000.
9. M. Kay. Saxon – the XSLT and XQuery processor. http://saxon.sourceforge.net/, 2004.
10. P. Merialdo. SIGMOD RECORD in XML. http://www.acm.org/sigmod/record/xml, 2003.
11. A. Motro. Using integrity constraints to provide intensional answers to relational queries. In *Proceedings of the 15th International Conference on Very Large Data Bases*, pages 237–246. Morgan Kaufmann Publishers Inc., 1989.
12. World Wide Web Consortium. Extensible Markup Language (XML) 1.0, 1998. http://www.w3C.org/TR/REC-xml/.
13. World Wide Web Consortium. XQuery: An XML Query Language, 2002. http://www.w3C.org/TR/REC-xml/.

Optimizing Sorting and Duplicate Elimination in XQuery Path Expressions

Mary Fernández[1], Jan Hidders[2], Philippe Michiels[2,★],
Jérôme Siméon[3,★★], and Roel Vercammen[2,★]

[1] AT&T Labs Research
[2] University of Antwerp
[3] IBM T.J. Watson Research Center

Abstract. XQuery expressions can manipulate two kinds of order: *document order* and *sequence order*. While the user can impose or observe the order of items within a sequence, the results of path expressions must always be returned in document order. Correctness can be obtained by inserting explicit (and expensive) operations to sort and remove duplicates after each XPath step. However, many such operations are redundant. In this paper, we present a systematic approach to remove unnecessary sorting and duplicate elimination operations in path expressions in XQuery 1.0. The technique uses an automaton-based algorithm which we have applied successfully to path expressions within a complete XQuery implementation. Experimental results show that the algorithm detects and eliminates most redundant sorting and duplicate elimination operators and is very effective on common XQuery path expressions.

1 Introduction

XML is an inherently ordered data format. The relative order of elements, comments, processing instructions, and text in an XML document is significant. This *document order* makes XML an ideal format to represent information in which the order is semantically meaningful. For instance, document order can be used to represent the order in which sentences are written in a book, to represent the order of events in the report of a surgical procedure, and to represent the order in which events occurred in a log file. In addition to document order, XQuery 1.0 [3] also provides expressions to impose or access order within a sequence of items. This *sequence order* can be used for dealing with order in the traditional SQL sense. For instance, an XQuery expression can sort a sequence of persons based on their salary and order a sequence of log messages based on their size. Because of the importance of document order for many applications, the semantics of XPath requires that every intermediate step in a path expression return

---

★ Philippe Michiels and Roel Vercammen are supported by IWT – Institute for the Encouragement of Innovation by Science and Technology Flanders, grant numbers 31016 and 31581.
★★ Jérôme Siméon completed part of this work while at Lucent Technologies – Bell Labs.

its result in document order and without duplicates. Uniformly sorting and removing duplicates after each step, however, is expensive, therefore eliminating these operations when they are provably unnecessary can improve performance while preserving the required XPath semantics.

This work is motivated by our earlier theoretical results [11] in which we propose an efficient automaton-based approach to decide whether or not a path expression, evaluated *without* intermediate sorting and duplicate-removal operations returns a result in document order and/or without duplicates. However, this technique permits duplicates in the intermediate results, which can have a deleterious effect on performance, because all subsequent steps in the path expression are evaluated redundantly on each duplicate node. Furthermore, the presented automaton could not be used for path expression with intermediate sorting and duplicate removal operations. In this paper, we present a similar automaton-based solution to the problem of inferring document order and no duplicates in path expressions, but we do so in the context of a complete XQuery 1.0 implementation and we solve all the above problems.

Our contribution is complementary to the research on special-purpose algorithms that support a small subset of the XPath language, in particular, steps (i.e., axis, name-test pairs) in straight-line paths [1] or trees [4]. Such algorithms use specific indices for efficient evaluation of straight-line paths and trees, and they typically do not require any intermediate sorting or duplicate elimination operators. *None* of these algorithms, however, support the complete XPath language, which permits applying arbitrary predicates to any step and querying relative document order. Moreover, each algorithm has its own limitation, such as applying to a subset of XPath axes, prohibiting wildcards, among others. Such limitations make applying these algorithms difficult in a complete XQuery implementation, which interleaves path expressions with other expressions. In contrast, our technique applies to path expressions anywhere they occur within the complete XQuery language, making it directly applicable in industrial-strength implementations.

The paper is organized as follows. In Section 2, we introduce the problem of detecting ordered and duplicate-free results in XQuery path expressions and apply our approach to an example. Section 3 describes our automaton algorithm that computes the ordered and duplicate-free properties. Insufficient space prevents presentation of all the algorithm's details. The interested reader is referred to the compete algorithm and supporting proofs in a companion technical report [6] and to the algorithm's implementation in the Galax engine [1]. Section 4 describes how our algorithm is implemented in the Galax engine. In Section 5, we report the results of applying our algorithm, called DDO, to benchmark queries. We conclude with a summary of related research in Section 6.

2 Motivating Example

In this section, we present a simple path expression applied to the document in Fig. 1 to illustrate the problem of removing unnecessary sorting and duplicate-

---
[1] http://www.galaxquery.org

removal operations and our solution to this problem in XQuery. This document conforms to the partial DTD in Fig. 1, which describes Java classes and packages[2]. The tree representation of the document depicts a part of the JDK with four packages (p) and six classes (c). Integer subscripts denote document order.

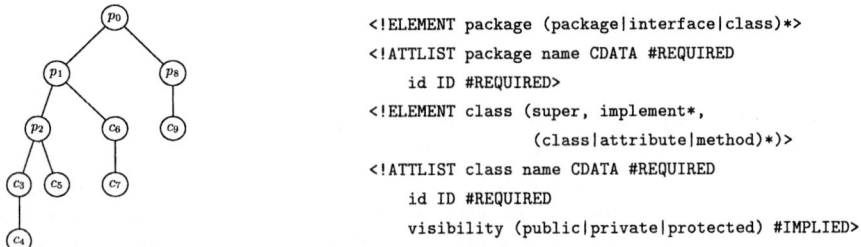

Fig. 1. A tree representation of java classes and packages and its partial DTD

XPath queries can be applied to this document to discover interesting *code smells* (i.e., typical patterns indicating bad design), compute software metrics, specify refactorings, etc. For example, the following query returns all inner classes inside XML packages[3] (there are 67 such classes in JDK 1.4.2):

$jdk/desc-or-self::package[@name="xml"]/desc::class/child::class

In order to explain the DDO optimization on this example, we first need a notion of an *evaluation plan*. We use the XQuery Core language [5] as a simple kind of evaluation plan. The XQuery Core is easy to understand by anyone familiar with XQuery, but it also happens to be a good representation on which to apply the DDO optimization. We start with the evaluation plan obtained by applying the normalization rules in [5] to the given XQuery expression. For instance, if we simplify the previous path expression by omitting the predicate on the second step then the corresponding (simplified) XQuery core expression is shown in Fig. 2 (a).

```
distinct-docorder(
    for $fs:dot in distinct-docorder(
        for $fs:dot in distinct-docorder(
            for $fs:dot in $jdk
            return desc-or-self::package
        ) return desc::class)
    ) return child:class
)
              (a)
```

```
docorder(
    for $fs:dot in distinct-docorder(
        for $fs:dot in (
            for $fs:dot in $jdk
            return desc-or-self::package
        ) return desc::class)
    ) return child:class
)
              (b)
```

Fig. 2. Tidy (a) and duptidy (b) evaluation plan for the (simplified) example query.

Each step is evaluated with respect to an implicit *context node*, which is bound to the variable $fs:dot[4]. The distinct-docorder function sorts its in-

---

[2] This DTD is only a small part of the DTD we use for storing the Java Standard Library (JDK) into an XML format which is an extension of JavaML[2].
[3] Note that the attribute name of a package is not the fully qualified name of the package and hence there are several packages with name "xml".
[4] The fs namespace stands for "Formal Semantics".

put in document order and removes duplicates. We call such evaluation plans *tidy*, because they maintain document order and duplicate-freeness throughout evaluation of the path expression. Tidiness guarantees that the plan always yields the correct result. Moreover, intermediate results cannot grow arbitrarily large, because duplicates are always eliminated. Tidy evaluation plans, however, are rather expensive to evaluate. An alternative to tidy evaluation plans are *sloppy* evaluation plans resulting from the approach in [11], in which there are *no* intervening sorting or duplicate-removal operators between the steps of an evaluation plan and the distinct-docorder operator is only applied to the final result. We call such evaluation plans *sloppy*. Although the sloppy approach is simple and often effective, it does not always lead to the most efficient evaluation plan and, in particular, it sometimes causes an exponential explosion of the size of intermediate results. In this paper, we show how the sloppy approach can be extended such that it can handle evaluation plans in which there are sorting and duplicate-removal operations applied to intermediate results and can precisely determine which of these operations can or cannot be removed safely. Evaluation plans that are the result of this new approach are called *duptidy* evaluation plans.

3 The DDO Optimization

In this section, we present in detail the DDO algorithm for deciding the ord (in document order) and nodup (contains no duplicates) properties. We also describe how this information can be used to optimize the evaluation plan.

To make reasoning easier, we introduce a concise and more abstract notation for evaluation plans in which they are represented as lists of axes and sorting and duplicate-elimination operations. The symbols in Table 1 denote the axes. The σ denotes a sorting operation (docorder) and δ denotes the linear-time removal of duplicates in a sorted sequence (distinct). The function distinct-docorder is written in the abstract evaluation plan as the composition of docorder and distinct. For example, the original query evaluation plan of Section 2 is rep-

Table 1. Axis names and symbols

Axis Name	Axis Symbol	Axis Name	Axis Symbol
child	$\downarrow$	parent	$\uparrow$
descendant	$\downarrow^+$	ancestor	$\uparrow^+$
descendant-or-self	$\downarrow^*$	ancestor-or-self	$\uparrow^*$
following	$\rightarrow\!\!\!\rightarrow$	preceding	$\leftarrow\!\!\!\leftarrow$
following-sibling	$\dot\rightarrow$	preceding-sibling	$\dot\leftarrow$

resented by the abstract evaluation plan $\downarrow^*; \sigma; \delta; \downarrow^+; \sigma; \delta; \downarrow; \sigma; \delta$. The abstract evaluation plan is read from left to right, where each symbol denotes a step in the computation. If we omit certain operations from an evaluation plan, then the corresponding steps in the abstract notation are omitted. For example, the optimized (duptidy) query evaluation plan of Section 2 is denoted by $\downarrow^*; \downarrow^+; \sigma; \delta; \downarrow; \sigma$.

We make two assumptions: (1) an abstract evaluation plan is always evaluated against a single node (in our example, this is p_0 which is bound to $jdk) and (2) the evaluation of the axis functions against a single node always yields a sequence sorted in document order without duplicates. Under these two assumptions, the two evaluation plans above are equivalent in that they always yield the *same* final result. Moreover, the sizes of the intermediate results after each axis and any following σ and δ are also always the same, i.e., the intermediate results never contain duplicates.

The computation of a minimal duptidy evaluation plan corresponds to the following decision problem: given an abstract evaluation plan in which each axis step is followed by $\sigma; \delta$, determine the maximal sets of σs and δs that can be removed such that the resulting evaluation plan applied to any XML document (1) yields the same result as that of the original evaluation plan, and (2) for each step expression, the input is duplicate-free. The second abstract evaluation plan satisfies these constraints. This problem can be reduced to the problem of deciding for a given abstract evaluation plan whether its result is always sorted in document order and whether its result is always without duplicates. We denote these properties by ord and nodup, respectively. Formally, the property ord (nodup) holds for an abstract evaluation plan q if for any node n in any XML document, the result of applying q to n is in document order (duplicate free). We denote this fact as q : ord (q : nodup).

The algorithm for deciding ord and nodup is based upon inference rules that derive the ord and nodup properties. Ideally, we would like inference rules of the following form: if the abstract evaluation plan q has certain properties, then $q; s$ (with s an axis symbol, σ or δ) also has certain properties. Such rules provide an efficient way to derive the ord and nodup properties. For example, for σ and δ, the following rules hold:

$$\frac{}{q; \sigma : \text{ord}} \qquad \frac{q : \text{ord}}{q; \delta : \text{nodup}} \qquad \frac{q : \text{ord}}{q; \delta : \text{ord}}$$

The problem of inferring ord and nodup can be solved by introducing auxiliary properties and inference rules. To illustrate this, we present a small subset of the relevant properties and inference rules here. We refer the reader to the technical report [6] for the the complete set of inference rules and their proofs.

The auxiliary property no2d (for "no two distinct") holds for an abstract evaluation plan if its result never contains two distinct nodes. If no2d and nodup both hold, then there is always at most one node in the result, which implies that each extension of evaluation plan with one axis step is ord and nodup. Because of its importance, the conjunction of no2d and nodup is referred to as the max1 property, i.e., q : max1 iff q : no2d and q : nodup.

Another auxiliary property is lin (for "linear"), which holds for an abstract evaluation plan if it always holds that all two distinct nodes in the result have an ancestor-descendant relationship. The lin property is interesting, because if it holds, then the parent axis preserves the nodup property:

$$\frac{q : \text{lin}, \text{nodup}}{q; \uparrow : \text{nodup}}$$

Properties such as no2d and lin are called *set properties* because they only restrict the set of nodes in the result and do not refer to the sequence order or the presence of duplicates. Obviously, σ and δ preserve these properties since they do not change the result set. Another interesting characteristic of these properties is that they can be lost after one or more child axes, but are recovered if followed by the same number of parent axes. For example, if q : lin then it follows that $q; \downarrow; \uparrow$: lin, $q; \downarrow; \downarrow; \uparrow; \uparrow$: lin, $q; \downarrow; \downarrow; \downarrow; \uparrow; \uparrow; \uparrow$: lin, et cetera. The fact that a certain property π (re)appears after i parent steps is itself an interesting property and denoted by π_i. We also use the notation $\pi_{\leq j}$ as a shorthand for the conjunction of $\pi_0, \ldots, \pi_j$.

From the inference rules, we can construct a deterministic automaton that decides whether ord and/or nodup hold for abstract evaluation plans. The automaton serves two purposes: It is used to prove completeness of the inference rules for ord and nodup, and it provides an efficient algorithm for deciding these properties, which serves as the foundation for an implementation. For the completeness proof we refer the reader to technical report [6]. The automaton is described as an infinite state machine, but it can be shown that the automaton can be described by a one-counter machine and therefore permits an algorithm that operates in linear time and logarithmic space.

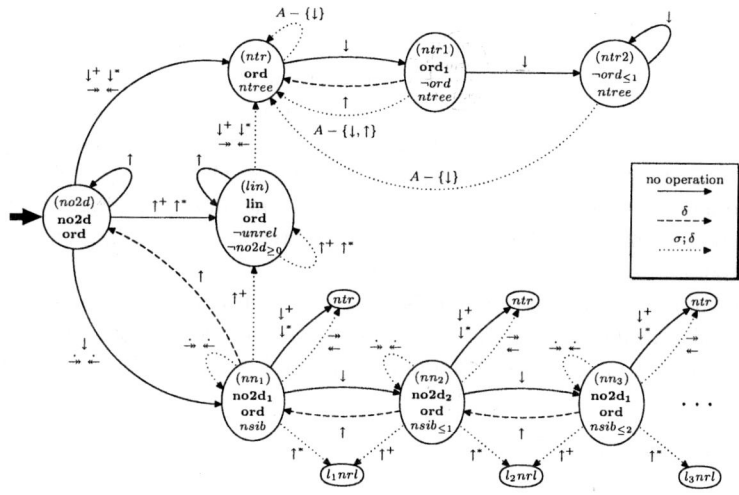

Fig. 3. Initial fragment of the duptidy automaton

Fig. 3 contains a small fragment of the complete automaton, which can be found in the technical report [6]. The initial state is the left-most state labeled *(no2d)*. The regular states contain a name (between brackets) and a list of properties that hold evaluations plans that end in this state[5] that hold . The smaller

---

[5] Note that no state contains the nodup property, because it holds trivially for all duptidy evaluation plans.

states that contain a single name with no brackets denote states for which the transitions are given in another fragment. For all regular states, a transition is given for each axis and this transition is indicated as either a solid arrow to indicate that no σ or δ is required after this step, a dashed arrow to indicate that δ is required or a dotted arrow to indicate that $\sigma;\delta$ is required. An edge labeled with $A - \{\uparrow, \downarrow\}$ indicates transitions for all axes except $\uparrow$ and $\downarrow$. It can be shown that if we construct an evaluation plan with the σs and δs as prescribed by this automaton then it is a minimal duptidy evaluation plan.

4 Implementation

We have implemented our algorithm, as well as the tidy and sloppy approaches, in the Galax XQuery engine. Galax is a complete implementation of the XQuery 1.0 specifications [3] and relies on a simple, well-documented architecture.

In our context, normalization introduces operations to sort by document order and remove duplicates after each path step, resulting in an expression that is tidy as defined in Section 3.

The DDO optimization is applied during the query-rewriting phase. As explained in Section 3, the max1 property is required by the DDO automaton's start state. There are two ways to infer max1. If static typing is available and enabled then the max1 property is derived precisely from the cardinality of the type computed for each subexpression. Static typing, however, is an optional feature of XQuery, and few implementations support it. Implementations that do not support static typing can use a simple static analysis to derive max1. For example, the fn:doc and fn:root functions, the fs:dot variable, and all variables bound by for expressions always have the max1 property. Our algorithm starts whenever the max1 property is derived and injects <u>distinct</u> operators when intermediate results may contain duplicates and <u>docorder</u> when the final result may be out of order.

The final rewritten expression is passed to the compiler, which constructs a compiled evaluation plan for the expression and passes it to the evaluation phase. Compilation and query planning are outside the scope of this paper.

5 Experimental Results

To evaluate the impact of the proposed techniques, we conducted several experiments, the goals of which are to show that the DDO optimization is effective on common queries, and that the new *duptidy* automaton is an improvement over the *sloppy* automaton presented in [11]. The section is organized accordingly. All experiments have been conducted using our Galax implementation.

The first set of experiments include the familiar XMark benchmark [13] suite, applied to documents of various sizes. XMark consists of twenty queries over a document containing auctions, bidders, and items. The queries exercise most of XQuery's features (selection, aggregation, grouping, joins, and element construction, etc.) and all contain at least one path expression. Of the 239

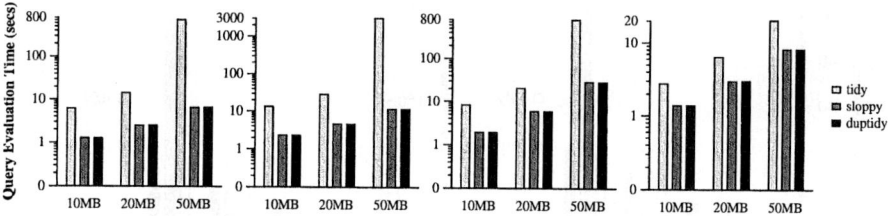

Fig. 4. The impact of the DDO-optimization for XMark queries 6, 7, 14 and 19, respectively, evaluated against input documents of size 10MB, 20MB and 50MB

distinct-docorder operations in all the normalized XMark queries, only three docorder operations remain after the DDO optimization.

Our optimization has the biggest impact on queries with more complex path expressions such as 6, 7, 14 and 19. Fig. 4 shows the increased impact[6] of the DDO optimization on the evaluation times of these queries as the input document increases from 10 to 50 MB. On a 20 MB document we see that Query 6 runs 5.75 times faster with the optimization and Queries 7, 14 and 19 show speedups of more than two to six times. All these queries use of the descendant-or-self axis frequently, which typically yields large intermediate results that are expensive to sort. These queries show also a bigger speedup for larger input documents. For example, the speedup for Query 7 grows from 5.79 times for a 10 MB document 10 MB to over 6 times for 20 MB to 265.33 times (!) for 50 MB. This is not surprising, because in Query 7, the evaluation time is dominated by the unnecessary sorting operations. If more nodes are selected, the relative impact of these sorting operations on the evaluation time increases.

For most of the XMark benchmark suite in Fig. 4, the sloppy approach is as effective as the duptidy approach, because none of the path expressions in these benchmarks generate duplicates in intermediate steps. For some queries, however, the sloppy technique scales poorly in the size of the path expression. This is caused by duplicate nodes in intermediate results; if duplicates are not removed immediately, subsequent steps of the path expression are applied redundantly to the same nodes multiple times. Moreover, if subsequent steps also generate duplicates, then the size of intermediate results grows exponentially. The two graphs in Fig. 5 show the results for path expressions of the form $(*//)^n*$ with $n = 1, 2, 3, 4$ applied to 52 MB and 169 MB documents, respectively. The evaluation time increases exponentially in the number of // steps with the sloppy approach. This shows that the duptidy approach combines the scalability in the size of the document of the sloppy approach with the scalability in the size of the path expression of the tidy approach. One may argue that this problem may only occur sporadically, but when it does, the impact on performance will very likely be unacceptable.

---

[6] Note that the Y-axes on the graphs are plotted in log scale.

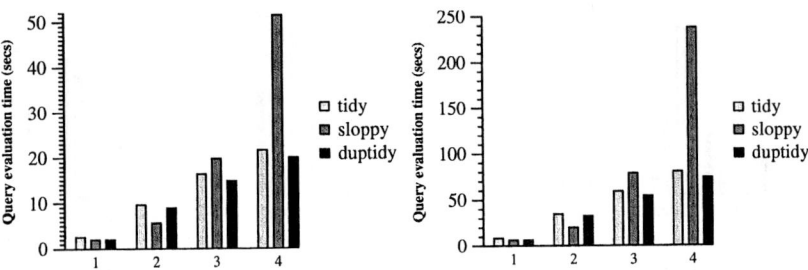

Fig. 5. Comparison of the evaluation times for the *tidy*, *sloppy* and *duptidy* approaches on the `descendant-or-self` queries for input documents of 52 MB and 169 MB

6 Related Work and Discussion

Numerous papers address the semantics and efficient evaluation of path expressions. Gottlob et al [7] show that naive implementations are often unnecessarily unscalable. Many papers deal with sorting and duplicate elimination, which is a strong indication of the importance of this problem. Avoiding duplicate elimination and sorting is particularly important in streaming evaluation strategies [12]. Helmer et al [10] present an evaluation technique that avoids the generation of duplicates, which is crucial for pipelining steps of a path expression. Grust [8,9] proposes a similar but more holistic approach, which uses a preorder and postorder numbering for XML documents to accelerate the evaluation of path location steps in XML-enabled relational databases. By pruning the context list, the generation of duplicates and out-of-order nodes in the intermediate results is avoided, clearing the way for full pipelining. The same holds for the similar *structural join* algorithms [1] that also can compute step expressions efficiently and return a sorted result. Finally, there are also algorithms like *holistic twig joins* [4] that compute the result of multiple steps at once.

Most of this work, however, supports narrow subsets of path expressions. In contrast, our techniques apply to path expressions in the complete XQuery language. Note that the DDO optimization does not impede the above optimizations and, in fact, opens the way for a broader search space for optimizing the query evaluation plan.

Aside from that, the completeness of our approach ensures optimal results for a considerable part of the language. More precisely, it removes a maximal amount of sorting and duplicate-elimination operations from normalized path expressions under the restriction that we only allow duptidy evaluation plans. Summarizing, the DDO optimization is a relatively simple technique that finds a solution that is optimal in a certain theoretical sense and that is hard to improve upon without using more involved cost-based techniques.

In future work, we will continue to improve logical rewritings early in the compilation pipeline as well as implement more sophisticated evaluation strategies later in the compilation pipeline. Currently, the DDO optimization is limited to path expressions within XQuery, but we plan to extend the technique to all of XQuery. Simple improvements include propagating properties computed within a path expression to subsequent uses of the expression, e.g., `let`-bound variables, across function calls, etc., and using static typing properties (e.g., `max1`) not just for the head of the path expression, but for intermediate steps. As part of ongoing research we plan to implement efficient axis-evaluation strategies, such as pipeline-enabling algorithms, which are enabled by the DDO optimization.

References

1. S. Al-Khalifa, H. V. Jagadish, N. Koudas, J. M. Pate, D. Srivastava, and Y. Wu. Structural joins: A primitive for efficient XML query pattern matching. In *ICDE 2002*.
2. G. J. Badros. JavaML: a markup language for Java source code. In *Proceedings of the 9th international World Wide Web conference on Computer networks : the international journal of computer and telecommunications networking*, pages 159–177. North-Holland Publishing Co., 2000.
3. S. Boag, D. Chamberlin, M. F. Fernández, D. Florescu, J. Robie, and J. Siméon. XQuery 1.0: An XML query language, W3C working draft 12 november 2003, Nov 2003. http://www.w3.org/TR/2003/WD-xquery-20031112/.
4. N. Bruno, N. Koudas, and D. Srivastava. Holistic twig joins: optimal XML pattern matching. In *SIGMOD 2002*.
5. D. Draper, P. Fankhauser, M. Fernández, A. Malhotra, K. Rose, M. Rys, J. Siméon, and P. Wadler. XQuery 1.0 and XPath 2.0 formal semantics, W3C working draft, Feb 2004. http://www.w3.org/TR/2004/WD-xquery-semantics-20040220/.
6. M. Fernández, J. Hidders, P. Michiels, J. Siméon, and R. Vercammen. Automata for Avoiding Unnecessary Ordering Operations in XPath Implementations. Technical Report UA 2004-02, 2004. http://www.adrem.ua.ac.be/pub/TR2004-02.pdf.
7. G. Gottlob, C. Koch, and R. Pichler. Efficient algorithms for processing XPath queries. In *VLDB 2002*.
8. T. Grust. Accelerating XPath location steps. In *SIGMOD 2002*.
9. T. Grust, M. van Keulen, and J. Teubner. Staircase join: Teach a relational DBMS to watch its (axis) steps. In *VLDB 2003*.
10. S. Helmer, C.-C. Kanne, and G. Moerkotte. Optimized translation of XPath into algebraic expressions parameterized by programs containing navigational primitives. In *WISE 2002*.
11. J. Hidders and P. Michiels. Avoiding unnecessary ordering operations in XPath. In *DBPL 2003*.
12. F. Peng and S. S. Chawathe. XPath queries on streaming data. In *SIGMOD/PODS 2003*.
13. A. R. Schmidt, F. Waas, M. L. Kersten, M. J. Carey, I. Manolescu, and R. Busse. XMark: A benchmark for XML data management. In *VLDB 2002*. http://monetdb.cwi.nl/xml/.

SIOUX: An Efficient Index for Processing Structural XQueries

Georges Gardarin and Laurent Yeh

PRiSM Laboratory, University of Versailles,
78035 Versailles, France
{georges.gardarin, Laurent.Yeh}@prism.uvsq.fr
http://www.prism.uvsq.fr

Abstract. XML DBMSs require new indexing techniques to efficiently process structural search and full-text search as integrated in XQuery. Much research has been done for indexing XML documents. In this paper we first survey some of them and suggest a classification scheme. It appears that most techniques are indexing on paths in XML documents and maintain a separated index on values. In some cases, the two indexes are merged and/or tags are encoded. We propose a new method that indexes XML documents on ordered trees, i.e., two documents are in the same equivalence class is they have the same tree structure, with identical elements in order. We develop a simple benchmark to compare our method with two well-known European products. The results show that indexing on full trees leads to smaller index size and achieves 1 to 10 times better query performance in comparison with classical industrial methods that are path-based.

1 Introduction

Since XML has been proposed as a standard exchange format by the W3C, many database systems have been developed to store and retrieve XML documents. Most systems are supporting XPath queries and move towards supporting full XQuery, including XPath, FLWR expressions, and full-text search queries. Traditionally, database research distinguishes structure query from content query. Structure queries are dealing with hierarchical traversals of XML trees, i.e., processing path expressions in XPath queries. Content queries are searching for combinations of keywords and values in XML elements, i.e., processing the predicates in XPath queries. In modern XML servers, content search integrated with structure search must be efficiently performed.

The support of structure and content queries require efficient indexing of XML documents. Much research has been carried out to propose and evaluate efficient indexing techniques. Traditionally, document-indexing systems were based on inverted lists giving for each significant keyword the document identifiers with the relative offsets of the keyword instances. With XML most queries are searching for elements rather than for full documents; thus, inverted lists are referencing elements rather than full documents. However, numerous element identifiers may lead to large index difficult to manage.

Most XML indexing methods focuses on structural index giving for a given label path the list of nodes reachable from this path. We describe most of the methods in the next section of this paper. They differ in node identifier generation, label path encoding, selection of useful paths to index (e.g., defined through templates or most frequently used). Most methods are dealing efficiently with XPath queries, but have difficulties with twig queries, i.e., queries with multiple branching paths. We propose a method indexing on label trees rather than on label paths. The method is very effective with documents of irregular schemas, with XPath and twig queries. Notice that the idea of using complex structures (i.e., trees or graphs) as index entries has also been exploited for indexing graphs with frequent sub-graphs [21], but it is the first time full graph-indexing is applied in an XML repository and demonstrated effective in such a context.

Thus, in this paper, we first propose a new method called SIOUX founded on a tree-based indexing approach. The method maintains enriched structural summaries without full references to database nodes. The structural summary of a document is called a treeguide. It is an ordered tree similar to a DTD structure; thus, it keeps element order but shrinks repetitive successive elements in one. Two documents are in the same equivalence class if they have the same treeguide.

The fundamental idea of the method is to index documents by sequences of paths rather than by paths. It results from the observation that path order is generally meaningful (for example, most articles starts with a title and finishes with a conclusion, not the reverse). Moreover, keeping precise structural guides avoid memorizing node identifiers as they can be computed from the treeguide for a query path expression. Furthermore, for twig queries searching for ordered tree structure, path-based index leads to many false drops, which is not the case with tree-based index.

The remaining of this paper is organized as follows. Section 2 gives a short overview of some indexing schemes. In section 3, we describe the SIOUX indexing method founded on tree-based indexing. In section 4, we introduce the algorithms for processing XPath and twig queries. In section 5, we propose a simple benchmark for evaluating the SIOUX indexing method in comparison of Xyleme and X-Hive. The benchmark is run on the three systems and gives rather promising results for the SIOUX method.

2 Overview of XML Indexing Schemes

In this section, we present an overview of XML indexing methods. A lot of research work has been done to index XML. Most approaches are based on path indexing, i.e., two nodes are in the same index entry if they have a common incoming label path. We propose a classification of such approaches.

2.1 Survey of Indexing Schemes

Structure query requires an efficient method to determine what nodes are parents or children of a given set of nodes. This can be done by performing structural joins on the edge (node, label, node) relation encoding the document structure [9], by traversing the document composition graph that is maintained when document are inserted [10],[17],[7], or by using clever numbering schemes for node identifiers [8],[14], [15]. Another problem with structure queries is that regular expressions are used extensively. Thus, label paths may be partial, including simple (*) or recursive (//) wildcards. This may lead to recursive structural joins or navigations in entire XML data graphs. Notice that structural joins and numbering schemes may also be used to check ancestor and descendant relationships, thus helping in solving regular expressions.

To overcome these difficulties, structural summaries of XML document collections have been proposed. Dataguides extended with node references were first introduced in Lore [16]. The structural index is in general quite large as every database node is referenced within the index. Several path index structures as T-indexes [17], APEX [6], A(k) indexes [12], D(k) indexes [4] tried to reduce the index size by indexing only useful paths. Such paths can be determined by specific patterns (T-indexes) or by selecting the most frequently used paths in queries (APEX) or by restricting the path length to k [12] in a dynamic way based on the query load [4]. The Fabric index [7] avoids referencing all nodes by encoding paths of terminal nodes (leaves) and storing them in a balanced Patricia trie. However, this approach requires extensions to maintain path order and to perform partial matching of tags.

Numbering schemes have been implemented for example in Xyleme, a successful native XML DBMS [1]. Two schemes are possible: pre and post-order numbering of nodes (a node identifier is a triple pre-traversal order, post-traversal-order, level) and hierarchical addressing of nodes (a node identifier is the compaction of its rank at each level). In both cases, determining if a node is an ancestor or a parent of another is simply done by comparing the identifiers. Xyleme manages a value and structure mixed index giving the node identifier of each label and of each keyword. In addition, for each XML collection, Xyleme maintains a generalized DTD, i.e., the set of paths with cardinalities. Solving an XPath expression is mostly done through index accesses, i.e., determining for each label and keywords in the XPath the relevant nodes identifiers and intersecting them. The method is quite efficient, but as with the others, the index references all database nodes. It is managed in main memory, which implies that some applications require large main memory.

A more sophisticated numbering scheme based on positional representation of XML elements has been extensively worked out to answer efficiently queries in which elements are related by a tree structure, namely twig queries. Node identifiers are of the form (DocId, LeftPos : RightPos, LevelNum). Twig queries are decomposed in elementary path expressions that are more or less independently solved by navigations or index traversals. Multiple efficient join algorithms have been proposed to join the intermediate results in an efficient way [3] [22] [2]. Others propose to encode XML data trees and twig queries into sequences to transform the problem in sub-sequence matching [19] [18] [11].

2.2 Classification of Indexing Schemes

XML indexing techniques can be presented in a classification hierarchy as portrayed in Figure 1. The first level classifies methods according to the technique used for resolving hierarchical path expressions. Methods using graph traversal maintains some form of dataguide, i.e., an index of all rooted paths. Fabric used an encoding of all paths stored in a Patricia trie that can be explored using text search. Methods based on a numbering scheme require an additional index containing at least one entry per label (often merged with the value index); this index is the starting point of the search to get lists of identifiers that can be compared. Notice that the classified indexing techniques use labels and often label paths as index entries, which makes index large in general. All index forget about path orders and number of occurrences. Furthermore, most methods except Fabric have difficulties with intensive updates, either to maintain index entries or identifiers.

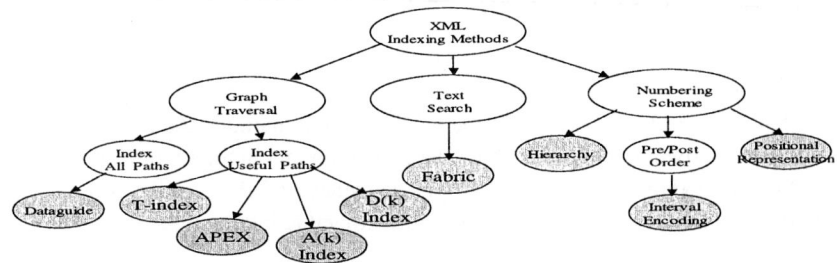

Fig. 1. XML Indexing Method Classification

3 The Sioux Indexing Method

In this section, we describe our new indexing scheme coupling a structure index and a value index. The structure index is based on a treeguide, a finer data structure than dataguide: index entries are ordered label trees rather than label paths. The value index is an inverted list with entries determined by a thesaurus.

3.1 The Structural Index

The structural index defines equivalent classes of documents, one class for each XML tree structure existing in the database. The structure is called a treeguide.

Definition 1: Treeguide. Let x be an XML document. The treeguide TG(x) is the ordered tree that: (i) Includes exactly every label paths in x and no more. (ii) Generates the XML document structure when traversed in preorder.

More formally, let p, p1 and p2 be label paths; p1 is before p2 (denoted p1<p2) if the path p1 is traversed before p2 in depth first traversal. Two documents x and y are in the same equivalence class iff:

(1) $\forall p1 \in x \, \exists \, p \in y : (p=p1)$
(2) **if** $p1, p2 \in x$ and (p1<p2) **then** $\exists \, p1 \in y \, \exists \, p2 \in y: (p1<p2)$

That means x and y have the same treeguide.

Notices that a treeguide differs from a dataguide as label paths in different orders are distinguished; also, it is not an index but a document structure, with no reference to data. For simplicity, we consider only trees although the definition could be extended to graphs with cycles (for encoding references). Attributes in documents are processed as elements, but the order of attributes is irrelevant. To deal with attributes as elements, we include them as the last children of the node they are attached to and we order them by alphabetical order.

As mentioned above, the treeguide is the core of our indexing scheme, which index documents and not nodes.

Definition 2: Treeguide Index. Let C be a collection of XML documents $x_1, x_2, \ldots x_n$. A treeguide index simply gives for each different treeguide of the document collection the list of documents x_i having this treeguide.

A treeguide index shall implement efficiently the following functions:

- Retrieve a given treeguide if it exists.
- Retrieve all documents of a given treeguide.
- Add a given document x_{n+1} in the collection and maintain the index.
- Delete a given document x_i from the collection and maintain the index.
- Find all documents satisfying a given sequence of XPaths in the collection.
- Identify easily document nodes to join with value index on identifiers.

3.2 The Value Index

To accelerate value search (exact match, less or greater predicates, keywords, phrase match, etc.), we use a classical inverted list scheme. Keywords in a text are determined through a simple thesaurus, implemented as a table. For each keyword appearing as element or attribute value, the value index gives the document id, the identifier of the element in the document treeguide, and the offset of the keyword in the element. The value index is organized as a B-tree.

Definition 3: Value Index. The value index is a mapping giving for each keyword the list of document identifiers with the node identifiers and relative addresses of elements containing the keyword.

3.3 Implementation of the Treeguide Index

As explained above, the treeguide index keeps the mapping between treeguides and documents. The structure has to be efficient, compact, and extensible. We divide the mapping in two steps: (i) mapping Treeguides (TG) to treeguide identifiers; (ii) mapping treeguide identifiers (TGI) to XML objects.

All treeguides are integrated in a union tree as exemplified in Figure 2. This global treeguide structure (GTG) is optimized. It is a graph in which: (i) A node represents an XML element or attribute of one or more treeguides. (ii) An edge represents either a parent / child (down edge) or a preceding / following sibling relationship (next edge) in at least one treeguide. To reduce the size of the union graph, the lists of nodes at a given level in the union tree are merged together in sequence order in such a way that the total list be minimum in number of entries. Thus, all nodes at a given level are linked together, but identifiers distinguish treeguides as explained below

Nodes are labeled with the corresponding element name or attribute name prefixed by @. To be able to retrieve a treeguide, nodes belonging to a treeguide are marked with the corresponding treeguide identifier. In other words, the set of treeguide identifiers a node belongs to is added to its label (e.g., book: 1,2,3). The order of element nodes in each treeguide is preserved at each level. The GTG can be updated by inserting nodes at existing levels or at a new bottom level.

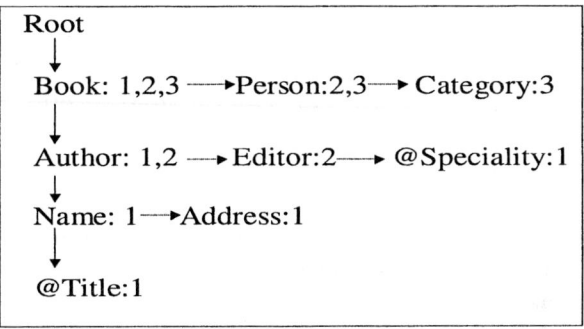

Fig. 2. Example of GTG

To extract a TG of given identifier TGI from the GTG, a simple procedure consists in traversing the tree and extracting all nodes of identifier TGI with the corresponding edges. The advantage of the proposed structure is to make possible the factorization of nodes at the same level in all TG. If a node exists for a given TG at a given level, the cost to represent it for another TG is just an identifier (an integer indeed). The GTG is thus a structure whose number of nodes in worst case is the number of elements and attribute in the database. Notice that if a TGI appears in a node, all its ancestors shall contain this TGI as a TG containing a path contains also all its sub-paths.

To map a treeguide identifier to an XML object, we use a simple indexed table called MAP_TGI. The entry number in the table corresponds to the TGI. TGI are integers allocated from 1 to N; when a TG is deleted, the TGI is marked free for latter allocation to a new treeguide.

4 Query Processing with Treeguide Indexes

In this section, we present the main query processing algorithms using treeguides indexes. We first introduce the XPath query-processing algorithm using the treeguide index and the value index. Next, we discuss twig query processing.

4.1 Resolving XPath Expressions

We consider queries of the form:

    for $V **in** <forest> **where** ($V/XPath$_1$)* **return**($V/XPath$_2$)*

XPath$_1$ are filtering expressions and XPath$_2$ are projection expressions. XPath can be as general as defined in W3C XPath version 2. For simplicity and shortness, we consider only conjunctive queries, but disjunctions could be supported easily in WHERE clauses. An example of such a query is given below:

```
for $B in collection("Books") where
$B/Book/Author[contains(.,"John") and /Address/City=
"Paris" and ../Category="Computer"]//Company
return $B/Book/Author/@Speciality
```

The required label paths are:

{/Book/Author/@Speciality; /Book/Author/Address/City; /Book/Author; /Book/Category; /Book/Author//Company}.

Such a query is indeed a twig query as XPaths have a common root, but we first use it to illustrate processing of independent XPath queries. The evaluation process can be divided in three steps: (i) Determine the TGI that verifies the structural constraints. (ii) Compute the relevant element references. (iii) Extract the response elements in main memory.

Determination of relevant treeguides. This step consists in extracting from all regular path expressions in the query the label paths that are mandatory for the query, as done above for the example query. From the set of label paths, a simple search in the GTG of all TGs including these label paths returns the relevant treeguide identifiers. The algorithm for determining the relevant TGIs simply searches each path expression in the GTG. For each, it collects all the instances and returns the list of all TGIs corresponding to the end-path nodes. Wildcards (*, //) have to be included in the search for retrieving children or descendants of a given name. Expanded path expressions in which wildcards are replaced by effective label paths are inserted in the set of required label paths in place of path expressions with wildcards, so as to memorize effective paths. Positional predicates ([]) are also included in label paths. To search a label path in the GTG, we use an extension of the tree pattern-matching algorithm [13].

Computation of relevant element references. This step first transforms the set of relevant TGIs in document identifiers plus node identifiers; second, it applies the value index to determine precisely the document nodes to retrieve. Going to the MAP_TGI table, we first determine a set of relevant references of documents with the required TG. Each label path is then encoded as a node identifier by prefix traversal of the TG. Finally, we obtain a set of document identifiers with a set of identifiers of elements in these documents. This is the result of the structural search. If the result is empty, the query has an empty answer.

Otherwise, the value search is used to restrict the list of results, if any. Using the value predicate in the query, we access the value index. For each value, we read the corresponding entry and filter its content with the node identifier. Doing the intersection of all sub-entries, we obtain a set of document identifiers with a set of hierarchical addresses of elements in these documents. This gives the result of the value search.

The two sets of document identifiers are intersected, which yields the final result of this step, with the associated expanded path expressions and hierarchical addresses.

Extraction of the relevant elements. The last step consists in loading in main memory the response elements whose precise addresses (document and element identifiers) have been retrieved in the previous step. If certain predicates have not been checked yet, a final loading of the necessary element value and a final check are required. The addresses of the elements are included in the result list of the previous step. Notice that the only required portion of documents to access as results refer precisely to those elements. This requires an object manager capable of accessing directly an element in a document, which is done through an element index managed at beginning of each document.

4.2 Resolving Ordered Tree Pattern Queries

A tree pattern query or twig query searches for a labeled tree in XML documents. It is essentially a complex selection predicate on both structure and content of an XML document. Most proposed algorithms to solve twig queries works with AND and sometimes with OR connectors for sibling nodes [11].

We can handle such queries by searching for the covering paths, then union or intersect the retrieved identifiers. We can also search directly for all treeguides satisfying the relevant tree patterns in the GTG and intersect the retrieved identifiers. The search is simply another application of a simple variation of the search algorithm of [13]. In general, with AND connector linking Path1 and Path2, both order Path1, Path2 and Path2, Path1 have to be considered.

Notice that we can efficiently handle THEN connector, as treeguides are ordered tree. For example, we could handle efficiently the query in slightly extended XQuery:

```
for $B in collection("Books") where
$B/Book/Author[contains(.,"John") and /Address/City=
"Paris" then ../Category="Computer"] then //Company
return $B/Book/Author/@speciality
```

5 Benchmarking Sioux Versus Xyleme and X-Hive

To demonstrate the validity of the SIOUX method, we compared our system with two industrial systems, namely Xyleme [1] and X-Hive [20] that implement efficient path-based indexing. The three systems were set on a Pentium Centrino 1,6 GHz with 1 Giga of RAM under Linux. Measures concern mainly the query execution time and the size of the structure index that is in the core of our approach.

5.1 The Data Sets

As most proposed benchmark have fixed collection schema, we develop our own mini-benchmark with some varying schemas. We consider three data sets whose characteristics are given in table 1. We used the ToXgene tool to generate XML documents varying on characteristics described by the four columns of table 1. The A set holds 300 documents with the same structure. The B and C sets experiment with a larger variety of schemas (22 various structures for the C set) as indicated. Set B and C contain two totally different subsets of schema. In each subset, schema varies on a few tags.

Table 1. The data sets

	# of documents	# of different schemas	Average elements / doc	Maximum depth	Average Size in bytes
Set A	300	1	10	3	1504
Set B	750	18	11	3	436
Set C	1500	22	13	3	1132

5.2 Size of Indexes

In general, due to the opacity of the implementation of industrial systems, it is difficult to compare index sizes. However, as the results below show, the index size necessary to index one document proves that our solution is economic in disk storage. The sizes found with industrial products are of others order of magnitude; this is probably because they use hash tables or other block allocation techniques. Thus, surprising sizes are given in table 2.

Table 2. Size of the structure index in bytes

	Xyleme		Xhive		SIOUX	
	Structure index size	Cost per doc.	Structure index size	Cost per doc.	Structure index size	Cost per doc.
Set A	1501319	5004,39	1158748	3876,94	6263	20,87
Set B	1635788	2181,05	2903830	3875,41	9390	12,5
Set C	1859045	1239,36	5612791	3745,60	15771	10,5
1 doc of A	5001		3878		4163	

Measures of Xyleme are captured directly using a DBMS API. To index only one document, we measure an initial index size of 141176 bytes, which suggests an allocation of fixed blocks for the index.

For X-Hive, no API is available to get the size of the index structure. To get results, we measure the disk memory delta when creating the index and also the main memory delta. We observe no variation on disk, but an important memory variation. As we can observe in table 2, this variation is proportional to the number of documents indexed.

The results are quite encouraging for Sioux. They demonstrate: (1) For SIOUX, an average cost of 11.29 bytes to index each document that contains an average of 12 elements. Thus, the cost of one element is less than 1 byte. (2) Using the GTG structure, indexing 300 documents (Set A) of identical schemas cost almost no more than indexing one document. At the opposite, Xyleme and Xhive index all the nodes, which also explain the gap with our approach. (3) Considering the index size for only one document, table 4 (last line) shows that the cost for the three indexes are quite similar.

5.3 The Queries

We experiment query processing with five typical queries:

1. Query on structure. It projects the documents on an XPath fully specified.

   (Q1) **for** $col **in** collection("catalog"), $b **in** $col/catalog/book **return** $b

2. Twig query on structure. Two paths with same root are searched and qualifying leaves are returned.

   (Q2) **for** $col **in** collection("catalog"), $b **in** $col/catalog/book, $p **in** $col/catalog/price **return** <items> <b>{$b}</b> <p>{$p}</p> </items>

3. Query on structure with non fully specified path (wildcard).

   (Q3) **for** $col **in** collection("catalog"), $p **in** $col//price **return** $p

4. Query on attribute. It is a projection on an attribute fully specified.

   (Q4) **for** $col **in** collection("catalog"), $cur **in** $col/catalog/book/price/@currency **return** $cur

5. Query on text value. It is a selection on a textual element containing a given value.

   (Q5) **for** $col **in** collection("catalog"), $b **in** $col/catalog/book, $a **in** $b/author **where** contains($a, "Rosmarie") **return** $b

The results are given in table 3.

Table 3. XQueries execution time in ms

XQuery	Xyleme	X-Hive	SIOUX
Q1 for A/B/C	36.2/76.2/150	12/12.6/ 390.7	3/4/19
Q2 for A/B/C	47.4/97.5/189	14,4/27.7/461.1	3/4,4/19.3
Q3 for A/B/C	13.9/17.3/31.7	7.5/13/23.7	2/5/14
Q4 for A/B/C	13.1/15.5/29.6	12.8/20.5/397	3/5/13
Q5 for A/B/C	2.2/2.7/6.2	2.4/2,5/ 6,6	4/3/7.5

The first four queries focus on the structure of documents, and the last query focuses on the structure and on a constant value contained in one of the elements. As with the B and C sets, documents have different schemas, the queries extracts a subset of the documents that constitute the solution. The queries have been run for the three systems on a same machine ten times; average execution times are reported in ms.

For the first four queries and for a given dataset, the SIOUX execution times are roughly the same. This can be explained by the fact that the XPaths are processed on the GTG structure to find directly the relevant documents. All the documents with the same structure are processed only one time, in contrast with the other approaches.

Finer measures of our method show that more than 95% of the time is mainly used for the extraction of the XML returned fragments from the originally stored documents (projection).

The second query exhibits a twig path search. No more processing time is paid for Sioux. For the others system, the increase in time can be explained by a second scan of the index or by a join processing. For the last case, the constant value is very selective for the three systems. We assume that the value index access and the result construction times are quite similar. That may mean that we should optimize the value index search and result construction algorithms. In case of larger collections of documents, the reduced size of our index should make SIOUX behave well. In summary, this simple benchmark demonstrates that our approach achieve equal or better performance for simple and twig XPath queries, with a factor up to 10.

5 Conclusion

In this paper, we survey the multiple methods proposed for indexing XML. Most methods indexes on document paths with node identifiers. Then, we introduce SIOUX, a new indexing method that we implemented in a native XML repository. SIOUX indexes documents with ordered structural trees. It separates the structure index and the value index, but unifies both for computing node identifiers satisfying a given predicate. The key of SIOUX is an efficient ordered tree-matching algorithm based on an optimized structure for maintaining the union schema of all documents, with associated references to documents.

A simple but covering various types of query benchmark has been run to demonstrate that SIOUX is more efficient for structure query than two existing products. For value query, it is equivalent with the current implementation. The most benefit for SIOUX comes from its ability to solve twig queries with branching paths through simple tree search in the database schema.

Although XML indexing is a well-visited topic with a lot of contributions, we believe that there is still room in this domain, notably for supporting complex queries including text queries and for extending the index structures to parallel systems and peer-to-peer query processing. We believe also that there exists a large discrepancy between published methods with often convincing performance evaluations on paper and real commercial systems as we saw them during our benchmark. This is a problem for research, which should devise methods easy to implement, as it is the case for SIOUX.

References

1. Serge Abiteboul, Sophie Cluet, Guy Ferran, Marie-Christine Rousset: The Xyleme project. Computer Networks 39(3): 225-238 (2002).
2. S. Al-Khalifa, H. V. Jagadish, N. Koudas, J. M. Patel, D. Srivastava, and Y. Wu. Structural joins: A primitive for efficient XML query pattern matching. In Proceedings of the IEEE International Conference on Data Engineering, 2002.
3. N. Bruno, N. Koudas, and D. Srivastava. Holistic twig joins: Optimal xml pattern matching. In Proc. Of ACM SIGMOD, 2002.

4. Q. Chen, A. Lim, and K. W. Ong. D(k)-index: An adaptive structural summary for graph-structured data. In Proc. of SIGMOD, 2003.
5. S.-Y. Chien, Z. Vagena, D. Zhang, V. J. Tsotras, and C. Zaniolo. Efficient structural joins on indexed xml documents. In Proc. of VLDB, 2002.
6. Chin-Wan Chung, Jun-Ki Min, Kyuseok Shim: APEX: an adaptive path index for XML data. SIGMOD Conference 2002: 121-132
7. Brian Cooper, Neal Sample, Michael J. Franklin, Gísli R. Hjaltason, Moshe Shadmon: A Fast Index for Semistructured Data. VLDB 2001: 341-350
8. P. F. Dietz: Maintaining order in a linked list. In ACM Symposium on Theory of Computing, pages 122--127, 1982.
9. D. Florescu, D. Kossmann: Storing and Querying XML Data using an RDMBS. IEEE Data Eng. Bull. 22(3): 27-34 (1999)
10. R. Goldman, J. Widom: DataGuides: Enabling Query Formulation and Optimization in Semistructured Databases. VLDB 1997: 436-445
11. Haifeng Jiang, Hongjun Lu, Wei Wang, Beng Chin Ooi: XR-Tree: Indexing XML Data for Efficient Structural Joins. ICDE 2003: 253-263
12. R. Kaushik, P. Shenoy, P. Bohannon, and E. Gudes. Exploiting slocal similarity for indexing paths in graph-structured data. In Proc. of ICDE, 2002.
13. Pekka Kilpeläinen: Tree Matching Problems with Applications to Structured Text Databases , PHD Dissertation, University of Helsinki, 1992.
14. Yong Kyu Lee, Seong-Joon Yoo, Kyoungro Yoon, P. Bruce Berra: Index Structures for Structured Documents. Digital Libraries 1996: 91-99
15. Quanzhong Li, Bongki Moon: Indexing and Querying XML Data for Regular Path Expressions. VLDB 2001: 361-370
16. Lore, a DBMS for XML http://www-db.stanford.edu/lore/
17. Tova Milo, Dan Suciu: Index Structures for Path Expressions. ICDT 1999: 277-295
18. P. R. Rao and B. Moon. Prix: Indexing and querying xml using prufer sequences. In Proc. of ICDE, 2004.
19. H. Wang, S. Park, W. Fan, and P. S. Yu. ViST: A dynamic index method for querying xml data by tree structures. In Proc. of ACM SIGMOD, 2003.
20. X-Hive/DB: Advanced XML data processing and storage. www.x-hive.com
21. Xifeng Yan, Philip Yu, Jiawei Han: Graph Indexing: A Frequent Structure-based Approach, SIGMOD 2004: 335-346.
22. C. Zhang, J. Naughton, D. DeWitt, Q. Luo, and G. Lohman. On supporting containment queries in relational database management systems. In Proc. of SIGMOD, 2001.

Searching Multi-hierarchical XML Documents: The Case of Fragmentation*

Alex Dekhtyar, Ionut E. Iacob, and Srikanth Methuku

Department of Computer Science, University of Kentucky
{dekhtyar, eiaco0}@cs.uky.edu, smeth2@uky.edu

Abstract. To properly encode properties of textual documents using XML, multiple markup hierarchies must be used, often leading to conflicting markup in encodings. Text Encoding Initiative (TEI) Guidelines[1] recognize this problem and suggest a number of ways to incorporate multiple hierarchies in a single well-formed XML document. In this paper, we present a framework for processing XPath queries over multi-hierarchical XML documents represented using fragmentation, one of the TEI-suggested techniques. We define the semantics of XPath over DOM trees of fragmented XML, extend the path expression language to cover overlap in markup, and describe FragXPath, our implementation of the proposed XPath semantics over fragmented markup.

1 Introduction

XML documents are required, by definition, to be well-formed. At the same time, it has been known for some time that text has a multi-hierarchical structure [2]. Features from different hierarchies can have *overlapping scopes*. Two key markup hierarchies for encoding text, physical text organization (pages, lines) and chapter-paragraph-sentence-word structure will produce overlapping markup any time a word is split into two lines, a sentence starts in the middle of one line and ends in the middle of another, or a paragraph starts on one page and ends on the next. Use of additional feature hierarchies, only accentuates the problem. Many prominent examples arise from image-based encodings of manuscripts (Figure 1), where, in addition to folio-line and sentence-word structures, we are also interested in encoding manuscript condition (damages), visibility of text under different lighting conditions, and paleographic information (e.g., which scribe wrote which portions of the manuscript).

The significance of multihierarchical document-centric markup and its proper management has been recognized by the TEI community fairly early [2,1]. Two problems need to be recognized and addressed: (a) storage and representation and (b) querying and retrieval. TEI Guidelines (P4)[1] propose a number of solutions to the first problem. Among them is markup fragmentation, a technique that breaks the overlapping conflicts by fragmenting one of the conflicting XML elements to the degree that allows proper nesting. Fragmentation allows to represent multihierarchical markup in a

---

* The work of the first author has been supported in part by NSF grant ITR-0219924 and the NSF grant ITR-0325063. Second author's work has been supported in part by NEH grant RZ-20887-02.

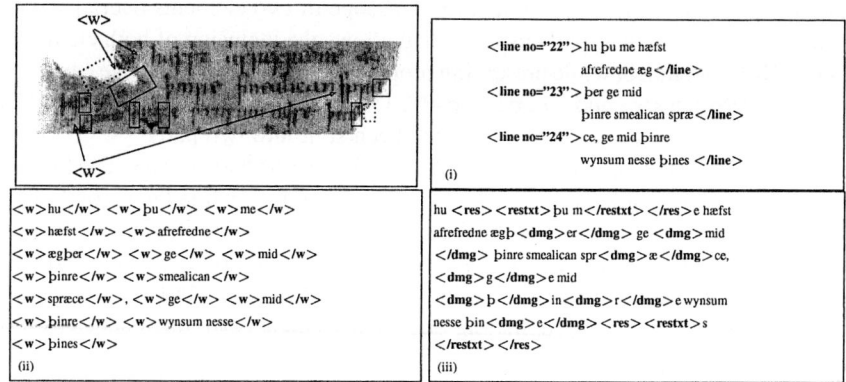

Fig. 1. A fragment of King Alfred's Boethius manuscript folio [3], the corresponding text, and different XML encodings

single XML document. However, this comes at a price. Fragmented XML documents are no longer easy to query using traditional XML query languages such as XPath. In fact, certain queries, easily expressible in XPath over regular XML documents, cannot be expressed in XPath over fragmented XML. While fragmentation is used by a large number of humanities scholars to represent overlapping markup in their encodings, there is nor available formalism, neither appropriate software for querying such encodings in a convenient, consistent, and domain-independent manner.

In this paper, we resolve this problem by providing the semantics of the XPath queries over fragmented XML documents. Because XPath is not expressive enough for querying multihierarchical markup, we enhance it with new features, which, in particular, capture overlapping content for elements from different hierarchies. Our contributions are summarized as follows: (i) we formally define multiple hierarchies for XML documents with markup fragmentation (Section 3); (ii) we give new semantics for computing XPath axes for fragmented XML documents with multiple hierarchies (Section 4); (iii) we propose and implement efficient algorithms for computing XPath axes for XML documents with fragmentation; (iv) we present some preliminary experimental results (Section 5).

2 Overlapping Markup in Text Encoding

Overlapping markup occurs in a large number of text encoding tasks. Figure 1 shows a fragment of a tenth century Old English manuscript [3] and the encodings of this fragment in three different markup hierarchies: physical location, sentence structure and condition. Features from these three hierarchies overlap: <rstxt> (restored text) overlaps <w> in line 22; the word *ægþer* is split between lines 22 and 23 and the word *spræce* is split between lines 23 and 24.

TEI Guidelines (P4)[1] suggest a number of ways for representing multihierarchical markup in a single document. In this paper, we consider one such solution, fragmentation, which works as follows. Whenever the scope of two elements overlaps, one of the elements is broken into parts in a way that allows the inclusion of both elements in the same XML document while preserving proper nesting. For example, one can resolve the conflict between `<w>` and `<line no="23">` elements as shown in Figure 2 Here, the original element `<w>spræce</w>` had been split into two parts: `<w id="W1" next="W2">spræ</w>` and `<w id="W2" prev="W1">ce</w>`. The first fragment nests properly inside the `<line no="23">` element, while the second - inside the `<line no="24">` element. The fact, that these two are the fragments of a single word, rather than two separate words is facilitated by the use of id, prev and next attributes for `<w>` which form a double-linked list of fragments. Markup fragmentation is a simple way of combining conflicting markup in a single XML document. However, [1] leaves open the question of querying the data stored in fragmented form.

```
<line no="23">þer ge mid þinre
   smealican
<w id="W1" next="W2">spræ</w></line>
<line no="24"><w id="W2"
   prev="W1">ce</w>, ge mid þinre
   wynsum nesse þines </line>
```

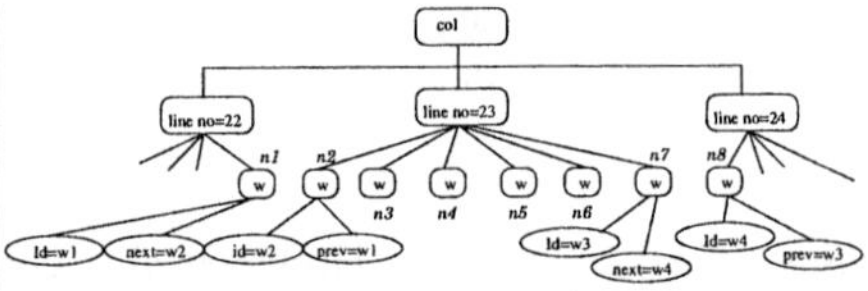

Fig. 2. Fragmentation and the DOM tree for fragmented markup

Example 1. Figure 2 shows a (part of the) DOM tree of the document that uses fragmentation to include `<line>` and `<word>` elements. Consider the following query: *Find all words that are located completely in line 23.*

For a non-fragmented XML document, we can convert this request into XPath: `/descendant::line[@no="23"]/descendant::w`.

When applied to the DOM tree in Figure 2, this expression evaluates to the nodeset $\{n2, n3, n4, n5, n6, n7\}$. However, this is **not** the right answer to the original information request — nodes $n2$ and $n7$ represent fragments of words, not complete words, in line 23. Thus, we need to reformulate the query. The new version is: *Find all `<w>` elements inside the scope of the `<line no="23">` element, such that they are either not fragmented, or all their peer fragments are inside the scope of the `<line no="23">` element.*

This information request cannot be expressed as a single XPath 1.0 query. It states that whether or not a node is included in the answer set is dependent on whether or not other nodes are included in the answer set (in fact, evaluation of this request is equivalent to building a transitive closure for each `<w>` node by following the prev and next links). At the same time, in XPath 1.0, decision on whether to include a node in the answer set is made independent of decisions for other nodes.

We note, however, that while expressing the query above in XPath 1.0 is impossible, there is a simple and straightforward procedure for producing the desired result: search the DOM subtree rooted at `<line no="23">`, and include in the answer set each non-fragmented `<w>` node and all fragmented `<w>` nodes that form a single word. The latter can be determined during a single tree traversal by verifying that once a <w ID="x" next="y"> element (first fragment) is discovered, the matching <w ID ="z" prev="u"> element (last fragment) is also in the scope of <line no="23">.

The example above suggests that the problem is in the fact that the semantics of XPath 1.0 over DOM is incompatible with the semantics of DOM trees for fragmented XML. In the rest of this paper, we show how this can be rectified.

3 Background

We start this section by briefly describing the Document Object Model and the XPath query language for XML together with some notation we use in the rest of the paper.

In Document Object Model (DOM) [4], an XML document is represented as a labeled, unranked tree. We denote by $dom(d)$ the set of nodes in the DOM of d, by $root(d) \in dom(d)$ the root node of d, by $tags(d)$ the set of node labels (tags) in d. In this paper we consider only *element* and *text nodes* in $dom(d)$. We let $type(x)$ to return the type of the argument node: "element" or "text". For a node $x \in dom(d)$ the function $tag(x)$ returns the label of x for element nodes and *null* for text nodes. For two nodes $x, y \in dom(d)$, $x < y$ or $y > x$ denotes that x is before y in the document order[5]. We denote by $ancestor_{DOM}(x)$ the set of *ancestor* nodes of x in DOM. For an element node x we use $scope(x)$ to denote the document content interval from the *start tag* of x to the *end tag* of x.

XPath is a language for addressing parts of an XML document [6]. XPath is used as the means of accessing XML documents in XQuery. It can be used to query XML documents by itself. XPath uses a tree of nodes model to represent an XML document. The main syntactical construction of XPath is *expression* and the nodes of a document are located using the *location path* (a special kind of *expression*). A *location path* is composed of one or more *steps*, at each step a set of nodes is selected based on their relationship (specified in *step*) to each node in a current set of *context nodes*. The node set result of a *step* evaluation is the current set of *context nodes* for the next *step* in the *location path*. The core syntax of XPath can be summarized as follows:
```
locationPath := step₁/step₂/.../stepₙ
step := axis::node-test predicate*
predicate := [expression]
```
The main syntactical construction for a *step* evaluation is *axis*. XPath uses 13 *axes* to address nodes in a document: *ancestor, ancestor-or-self, attribute, child, descendant, descendant-or-self, following, following-sibling, namespace, parent, preceding, preceding-sibling,* and *self*. Formal semantics of XPath axes is given in[6]. The set of nodes from *axis* evaluation is filtered by the *node-test* (basically a node type test or a name test for *element* nodes) and by the *expression*, which is either an location path (evaluated to *true* if the result node set is not empty), or a boolean expression involving functions from the core function library of XPath[6].

3.1 Multiple Hierarchies for XML Documents with Fragmentation

We define a multiple hierarchy over an XML document as a mapping of node names (tags, or elements) onto a finite set of labels (hierarchy names). In any multi-hierarchical document, an element node belongs to a single hierarchy (except for the root node, which belongs to all hierarchies) whereas any text node belongs to all hierarchies. Usually, each hierarchy encompasses a specific set of markup features (e.g., in Figure 1 the three hierarchies are physical position of text, sentence structure and manuscript condition). The key syntactic condition is that document markup restricted to any single hierarchy is *well-formed*. We formally define hierarchies and fragmented XML representations as follows.

Definition 1 (muti hierarchies). *Let H be a set of labels (strings). A multi-hierarchy is a function $\mathcal{H} : tags(d) \rightarrow 2^H$ so that*
(a) if x is the root node or $type(x) =$ "text" then $\mathcal{H}(x) = H$
(b) if x is an element node, not root node, then $\mathcal{H}(x) = \{a\}$ for some $a \in H$.

Definition 2 (fragmented representation). *Let $\mathcal{H}$ be a multi-hierarchy over the set of labels H. Let $d_1, .., d_{|H|}$ be XML documents encoding the same content string S, having the same label for the root node, and with markup from different hierarchies. An XML document d is called a* fragmented XML representation *of $d_1, ..., d_{|H|}$ iff (a) d is well-formed; (b) for each node $x \in d_j$ there exists a set of nodes $\{x_1, \ldots, x_k\}$ all with the same label as x such that $scope(x) = \cup_{1 \leq i \leq k} scope(x_i)$; (c) for any attribute prev or next there exists a unique id attribute with the same value; no id attribute value can appear in two next or two prev attributes.*

Fragmentation allows to store multi-hierarchical markup in a single well-formed document by breaking elements into fragments. Fragments represent the semantics of the original encoding only when combined. For example, <w>spræce</w> is broken into two fragments, <w id="W1" next="W2"> spræ</w> and <w id="W2" prev="W1">ce</w>, but if we are interested in recovering the full word, we must join these two fragments together. Functions $fragments()$ and LMU (Logical Markup Unit), defined below, recover the actual range of the markup corresponding to a given document node by collecting all fragments "related" to the node and constructing the appropriate content respectively.

Definition 3 (fragment). $fragments : dom(d) \rightarrow 2^{dom(d)}$ *is defined recursively: (i) $x \in frag-ments(x)$; (ii) if $y \in dom(d)$ and there exists $z \in fragments(x)$ such that prev or next attribute of y has the same value as the id attribute of z, then $y \in fragments(x)$.*

Basically, the fragments are element nodes, in a double linked list (using *prev*, *next*, and *id* attribute values), which are covering a continuous range of document content.

Definition 4 (logical markup unit). *The* logical markup unit *(LMU) of the markup corresponding to a node x is the set of all text nodes covered by markup corresponding to each node in $fragments(x)$:*
$$LMU(x) := \{t \in descendant_{DOM}(x) \mid type(t) = \text{"text"}\}.$$

Recall that fragmentation is a workaround for representing overlapping markup in a single well-formed XML document. Markup conflicts are not immediately visible within the fragmented XML document, but using LMUs, we can "discover" them: markup are in conflict if their corresponding LMUs overlap.

We slightly abuse notation and use $\mathcal{H}(x)$ in lieu of $\mathcal{H}(tag(x))$ to denote the hierarchy of node x. We say that two document nodes $x, y \in dom(d)$ are in the same hierarchy, denoted $\mathcal{H}(x) \cong \mathcal{H}(y)$ if $\mathcal{H}(x) \subseteq \mathcal{H}(y)$ or $\mathcal{H}(x) \supseteq \mathcal{H}(y)$. We use $dom_{\mathcal{H}(x)} :=$ $\{y \in dom(d) \mid \mathcal{H}(y) \cong \mathcal{H}(x)\}$ to denote the nodes in $dom(d)$ in the same hierarchy as x. It is clear now that the root node and any text node are in the same hierarchy with any other node in a document. The intuition behind this approach is simple: the root node or a text node have no overlapping range with any other logical markup unit.

4 XPath Queries over Multi-hierarchical XML Documents

As suggested in the examples in Section 1, a natural handling of XPath queries over multi-hierarchical XML documents with fragmentation would require each query evaluation result to be expressed as a set of logical markup units. To avoid expensive joins and, most importantly, query reformulation problems, we extend the XPath axis semantics to handle queries for multi-hierarchical XML with fragmentation.

4.1 XPath Axis Semantics for Fragmented Multi-hierarchical XML

The purpose of the new semantics for XPath over fragmented documents is two-fold: (a) restore the proper meaning of XPath axes and (b) extend the expressive power to capture new relationships between nodes from different hierarchies. To achieve (a), we define the semantics of *self, child, parent, descendant, descendant-or-self, ancestor, ancestor-or-self, following-sibling, preceding-sibling, following,* and *preceding* axes over fragmented XML. For goal (b), we define new axes, specific to multi-hierarchical XML documents: *xdescendant, xancestor, preceding-overlapping, following-overlapping,* and *overlapping*. For each Extended XPath axis $\mathcal{X}$, we define the corresponding evaluation function $\mathcal{X} : dom(d) \to 2^{dom(d)}$, where $\mathcal{X}(x)$ evaluates axis $\mathcal{X}$ for the context node x. The evaluation functions for XPath axes are defined as follows:

$$self(x) := fragments(x)$$
$$child(x) := \bigcup_{v \in self(x)} \{y \in dom_{\mathcal{H}(x)}(d) \mid y \in descendant_{DOM}(v) \land$$
$$\neg(\exists z \in dom_{\mathcal{H}(x)}(d) : z \in descendant_{DOM}(v) \land$$
$$z \in ancestor_{DOM}(y))\}$$
$$parent(x) := \{y \in self(z) \mid z \in ancestor_{DOM}(x) \cap dom_{\mathcal{H}(x)}(d) \land$$
$$\neg(\exists v \in dom_{\mathcal{H}(x)}(d) : v \in ancestor_{DOM}(x) \land$$
$$v \in descendant_{DOM}(z))\}$$
$$descendant(x) := \bigcup_{v \in self(x)} \{y \in dom_{\mathcal{H}(x)}(d) \mid y \in descendant_{DOM}(v)\}$$
$$descendant-or-self(x) := self(x) \cup descendant(x)$$
$$ancestor(x) := \{y \in self(z) \mid z \in ancestor_{DOM}(x) \cap dom_{\mathcal{H}(x)}(d)\}$$
$$ancestor-or-self(x) := self(x) \cup ancestor(x)$$
$$following-sibling(x) := \{y \in dom_{\mathcal{H}(x)}(d) \mid y > x \land y \notin self(x) \land$$
$$parent(y) = parent(x)\}$$
$$preceding-sibling(x) := \{y \in dom_{\mathcal{H}(x)}(d) \mid y < x \land y \notin self(x) \land$$
$$parent(y) = parent(x)\}$$
$$following(x) := \{y \in dom_{\mathcal{H}(x)}(d) \mid y > x \land y \notin self(x) \land$$
$$y \notin descendant(x)\}$$
$$preceding(x) := \{y \in dom_{\mathcal{H}(x)}(d) \mid y < x \land y \notin self(x) \land$$
$$y \notin ancestor(x)\}$$

The extended XPath axes are defined below:

$$
\begin{aligned}
xdescendant(x) &:= \{y \in dom(d) - dom_{\mathcal{H}(x)}(d) \mid \forall t \in descendant(y), \\
&\quad type(t) = \text{``text''}(t \in descendant(x))\} \\
xancestor(x) &:= \{y \in dom(d) - dom_{\mathcal{H}(x)}(d) \mid \forall t \in descendant(x), \\
&\quad type(t) = \text{``text''}(t \in descendant(y))\} \\
following-overlapping(x) &:= \{y \in dom(d) \mid \exists t \in descendant(x)(type(t) = \text{``text''} \land \\
&\quad t \in descendant(y)) \land \exists t \in descendant(x) \\
&\quad \forall z \in descendant(y)(type(t) = \text{``text''} \land \\
&\quad t < z) \land \exists t \in descendant(y) \forall z \in descendant(x) \\
&\quad (type(t) = \text{``text''} \land z < t)\} \\
preceding-overlapping(x) &:= \{y \in dom(d) \mid \exists t \in descendant(x)(type(t) = \text{``text''} \land \\
&\quad t \in descendant(y)) \land \exists t \in descendant(x) \\
&\quad \forall z \in descendant(y)(type(t) = \text{``text''} \land t > z) \land \\
&\quad \exists t \in descendant(y) \forall z \in descendant(x) \\
&\quad (type(t) = \text{``text''} \land z > t)\} \\
overlapping(\{x\}) &:= preceding-overlapping(\{x\}) \cup \\
&\quad following-overlapping(\{x\})
\end{aligned}
$$

The following theorems establish the basic properties of the Extended XPath over fragmented XML: (a) all fragments are included in the result of evaluation .and (b) with only one hierarchy present, our definitions are equivalent to those in [6] [1].

Theorem 1. *[7] Let $\mathcal{X}$ be an XPath axis evaluation function for multi-hierarchical XML. Let $x \in dom(d)$ and let $y \in \mathcal{X}(x)$. Then for any $z \in self(y)$, $z \in \mathcal{X}(x)$.*

Theorem 2. *[7] For any XML document with a single markup hierarchy, $|H| = 1$, for any axis $\mathcal{X}$ defined for both XPath and Extended XPath, the evaluation of $\mathcal{X}$ using XPath semantics yields the same results as the evaluation of $\mathcal{X}$ using Extended XPath semantics, for any node in d.*

4.2 Searching XML Documents Using Extended XPath

Let us return to the query from Example 1: *Find all words that are located completely in line 23*. We consider the set of hierarchies shown in Figure 1: "location" (box (i)), "structure" (box (ii)) and "condition" (box (iii)). Because <line> and <w> are in different hierarchies and we want words completely inside lines (relationship represented by the xdescendant axis), the correct Extended XPath expression is: /descendant::line[@no="23"]/xdescendant::w. According to the Extended XPath specifications, the query is evaluated to the node set: $\{n3, n4, n5, n6\}$ (see the DOM tree in Figure 2).

Consider now the following query for the same document: *Find all words that are located partially in line 23*. This query concerns markup overlap. The corresponding Extended XPath query is /descendant::line[@no="23"]/overlapping::w. It evaluates to the node set: $\{n1, n2, n7, n8\}$. To retrieve all words that occur in line 23,

---

[1] The latter result is important from the practical point of view: an Extended XPath processor yields correct results when evaluating XPath expressions for any XML document with a single markup hierarchy.

Algorithm 1: Extended XPath axis evaluation
Input: $N, dom(d)$
Output: N'
$\mathcal{X}$-EVALUATION(N)
(1) $N' = \emptyset$
(2) **foreach** $n \in N$
(3) $\quad N' \leftarrow N' \cup \mathcal{X}(self(n), dom(d))$
(4) **return** N'

Algorithm 2: xancestor
XANCESTOR($n_1, \ldots, n_f, dom(d)$)
(1) $t_1 \leftarrow FTD(n_1)$
(2) $t_2 \leftarrow LTD(n_f)$
(3) $TEMP1 \leftarrow \{x \in self(y) \mid y \in ancestor_{DOM}(t_1) - dom_{\mathcal{H}(n)}(d)\}$
(4) $TEMP2 \leftarrow \{x \in self(y) \mid y \in ancestor_{DOM}(t_2) - dom_{\mathcal{H}(n)}(d)\}$
(5) $N \leftarrow TEMP1 \cap TEMP2$
(6) **return** N

Algorithm 3: xdescendant
XDESCENDANT($n_1, \ldots, n_f, dom(d)$)
(1) $t_1 \leftarrow FTP(n_1)$
(2) $t_2 \leftarrow FTF(n_f)$
(3) $TEMP1 \leftarrow \{x \in self(y) \mid y \in ancestor_{DOM}(t_1) - dom_{\mathcal{H}(n)}(d)\}$
(4) $TEMP2 \leftarrow \{x \in self(y) \mid y \in ancestor_{DOM}(t_2) - dom_{\mathcal{H}(n)}(d)\}$
(5) $TEMP3 \leftarrow \cup_{x \in \{n_1, \ldots, n_f\}} \{y \in (ancestor_{DOM}(x) \cup descendant_{DOM}(x)) - dom_{\mathcal{H}(n)}(d)\}$
(6) $N \leftarrow TEMP3 - (TEMP1 \cup TEMP2)$
(7) **return** N

Algorithm 4: following- overlapping
FOLLOWING-OVERLAPPING($n_1, \ldots, n_f, dom(d)$)
(1) $t_1 \leftarrow FTD(n_1)$
(2) $t_2 \leftarrow LTD(n_f)$
(3) $t_3 \leftarrow FTF(n_f)$
(4) $TEMP1 \leftarrow \{x \in self(y) \mid y \in ancestor_{DOM}(t_1) - dom_{\mathcal{H}(n)}(d)\}$
(5) $TEMP2 \leftarrow \{x \in self(y) \mid y \in ancestor_{DOM}(t_2) - dom_{\mathcal{H}(n)}(d)\}$
(6) $TEMP3 \leftarrow \{x \in self(y) \mid y \in ancestor_{DOM}(t_3) - dom_{\mathcal{H}(n)}(d)\}$
(7) $N \leftarrow (TEMP2 \cap TEMP3) - TEMP1$
(8) **return** N

Fig. 3. Algorithms for evaluation of Extended XPath axes

the following Extended XPath query can be used: `/descendant::w [xancestor::line[@no="23"] or overlapping::line[@no="23"]]`.

4.3 Algorithms for XPath Axis Evaluation

Polynomial time evaluation algorithms for XPath queries, using DOM representation of an XML Document, are given in [8,9]. An algorithm that evaluates XPath axes in linear time (in the size of nodes in the input XML document) is also given in [9]. Similar techniques can be used for evaluating the Extended XPath axes *child, parent, descendant, descendant-or-self, ancestor, ancestor-or-self, following-sibling, preceding-sibling, following,* and *preceding*. The only difference is a node filtering operation, that is, selecting only nodes in a given hierarchy. This can be easily implemented using a *hash* function, so the overall evaluation is still linear. We also point out that evaluation of *self* can be directly carried out using the *id reference* (ID and IDREF) mechanism provided by XML [5] and the DOM API [4].

In Figure 3 we give the algorithms for evaluating *xancestor, xdescendant,* and *following-overlapping*. Note, that the semantics of the Extended XPath axes as described in Section 4.1 is given for *a single* DOM node. In reality, when evaluating an XPath query (see Section 3), at each location step a node set is computed and this node set is used as the the context for the next location step.

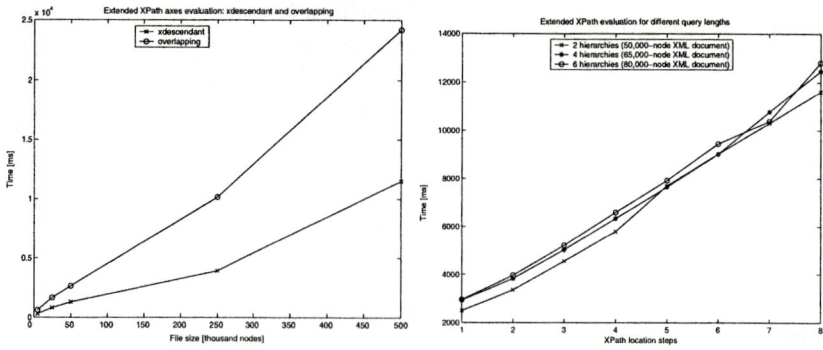

Fig. 4. Results of testing FragXPath

5 Experiments

Using the semantics described in the paper, we have fully implemented and Extended XPath processor for fragmented XML document (*FragXPath*). *FragXPath* **is a main-memory processor**. Below we show the results of a few tests we used to test **FragXPath**. The tests were run on a Dell GX240 PC with 1.4Ghz Pentium 4 processor and 256 Mb main memory running Linux. We generated XML files with multple hierarchies (we use 2,4, and 6 hierarchies). In Figure 4 we report the results of two tests.

The first graph shows the results of testing xdescendant and overlapping axes, which extend traditional XPath, over fragmented XML documents with 4 hierarchies. We used fragmented XML documents with sizes ranging from 50,000 to 500,000 nodes and from 1MB to 45MB size on disk. We used the following Extented XPath queries in our experiments: /descendant::page//overlapping::* and /descendant::page/xdescendant::*.

The second graph shows the dependence of evaluation time on the number of location steps in the query (each query consisted of /overlapping::* location step repeated for 1,2,...8 times) and on files with 2,4, or 6 hierarchies and 50,000, 65,000, and 80,000 nodes respectively. As expected, the graph presented in Figure 4 shows linear time complexity on the query size.

Finally, we compared the work of *FragXPath* with the work of two widely available XPath processors, *Xalan* and *Dom4j* on comparable workloads. While direct comparison of *FragXPath* to XPath processors is not possible – the expressive power of the

Table 1. XPath processors comparison

Processor/Number of steps	1	4	8
$FragXPath$	1208[ms]	1279[ms]	1284[ms]
$Xalan$	1590[ms]	1630[ms]	1632[ms]
$Dom4j$	1336[ms]	1636[ms]	1640[ms]

languages is different, we should expect *FragXPath* to spend about the same time as an XPath processor searching for comparable information in the same DOM tree.

Table 1 shows the times for all three processors for queries consisting of 1, 4, and 8 location steps of the form /descendant-or-self::*. *FragXPath* performs in the same time range as the XPath processors (it is actually faster, but we emphasize, the it is incorrect to say that *FragXPath* works better than *Xalan* or *Dom4j*).

6 Conclusions

Processing of XML with multiple hierarchies has attracted the attention of numerous researchers recently. In [10] we survey the state-of-the-art in the area. Jagadish et al. have considered similar poblem for data-centric XML and proposed the so-called colorful XML to implement multiple hierarchies[11]. In this paper we consider one specific legacy case, stemming from the text encoding community, when XPath semantics needs to be redefined and extended, in order to support efficient querying. Our implementation is faithful to the original XPath semantics, and is immediately applicable to processing queries over the multitude of legacy text encodings prepared using the fragmentation technique. Our current and future work is on considering other legacy cases and also on building a unified framework for processing multihierarchical XML.

References

1. Sperberg-McQueen, C.M., Burnard, L., (Eds.): Guidelines for Text Encoding and Interchange (P4). http://www.tei-c.org/P4X/index.html (2001) The TEI Consortium.
2. Renear, A., Mylonas, E., Durand, D.: Refining our notion of what text really is: The problem of overlapping hierarchies. Research in Humanities Computing (1993) (Editors: N. Ide and S. Hockey).
3. Boethius, A.M.S.: Consolation of philosophy. (Alfred The Great (translator), British Library MS Cotton Otho A. vi) Manuscript, folio 36v.
4. Champion, M., Byrne, S., Nicol, G., Wood, L., (Eds.): Document Object Model (DOM) Level 1 Specification. http://www.w3.org/TR/REC-DOM-Level-1/ (1998) World Wide Web Consortium Recommendation, REC-DOM-Level-1-19981001.
5. Bray, T., Paoli, J., Sperberg-McQueen, C.M., Maler, E., Yergeau, F., Cowan, J., (Eds.): Extensible Markup Language (XML) 1.1. http://www.w3.org/TR/2004/REC-xml11-20040204 (2004) W3C Recommendation 04 February 2004.
6. Clark, J., DeRose, S.: XML Path Language (XPath) (Version 1.0). http://www.w3.org/TR/xpath (1999) W3C, REC-xpath-19991116.
7. Dekhtyar, A., Iacob, I.E., Methuku, S.: Searching Multi-Hierarchical XML Documents: the Case of Fragmentation. Technical Report TR 439-05, University of Kentucky, Department of Computer Science (2005) http://www.cs.uky.edu/~dekhtyar/publications/TR439-05.ps.
8. Gottlob, G., Koch, C., Pichler, R.: XPath query evaluation: Improving time and space eficiency. In: Proceedings of the ICDE, Bangalore, India. (2003) 379–390
9. Gottlob, G., Koch, C., Pichler, R.: Efficient algorithms for processing XPath queries. In: Proc. of VLDB, Hong Kong (2002)
10. Dekhtyar, A., Iacob, I.E.: A Framework for Management of Concurrent XML Markup. Data and Knowledge Engineering **52** (2005) 185–208
11. Jagadish, H.V., Lakshmanan, L.V.S., Scannapieco, M., Srivastava, D., Wiwattwattana, N.: Colorful XML: One Hierarchy Isn't Enough. In: Proc., ACM SIGMOD. (2004) 251–262

Semantic Storage: A Report on Performance and Flexibility

Edgar R. Weippl, Markus Klemen, Manfred Linnert, Stefan Fenz,
Gernot Goluch, and A Min Tjoa

Vienna University of Technology,
A-1040 Vienna, Austria,
weippl@ifs.tuwien.ac.at, klemen@ifs.tuwien.ac.at
http://www.ifs.tuwien.ac.at
http://research.microsoft.com/barc/mediapresence/MyLifeBits.aspx

Abstract. Desktop search tools are becoming more popular. They have to deal with increasing amounts of locally stored data. Another approach is to analyze the semantic relationship between collected data in order to preprocess the data semantically. The goal is to allow searches based on relationships between various objects instead of focusing on the name of objects. We introduce a database architecture based on an existing software prototype, which is capable of meeting the various demands for a semantic information manager. We describe the use of an association table which stores the relationships between events. It enables adding or removing data items easily without the need for schema modifications. Existing optimization techniques of RDBMS can still be used.

1 Introduction

It is commonly known that the amount of digital information increases as people store more information on their Personal Computers. The variety of formats used increases because people store their digital images, emails and faxes they sent and received, and documents they created as well as many files from the Internet. There are several approaches to storing *lifetime's worth of articles, books, ...* which we briefly discuss in Section 4.

The basic idea of our system has the same goal, allowing easy access to all data and information, but differs fundamentally in the approach. We focus on the relationship of various data-objects (such as photos, e-mails, graphics or text files) and events (opening a text file, receiving a phone call, sending an e-mail) rather than relying on the names of these objects for retrieval. Our intent is to allow for more human-like retrieval processes by adding semantic metadata to the data collections. For example, instead of finding a text file based on its name, a semantic search would allow a context-aware query, for instance *I don't know the filename but I know I created it when I was talking to Jim on the phone about a week ago.*

Our prototype (Figure 1) collects raw data from multiple sources such as file events of the operating system or user events from Microsoft Outlook via agents.

On the level of the file system we receive data on which application has accessed (read or written) which file. The user can select which applications or directories to monitor, typically local office applications and user document folders. For instance, we can store that Word.exe has written a specific file document.doc to the disk at a certain time and date. From Microsoft Outlook we can gather information on emails, contacts and calendar items. We also store which computer has been used (to differentiate between laptops and workstations) and the user ID. Additional data collectors are planned that can integrate incoming and outgoing telephone calls (via CTI or serial printer ports) as well as facsimiles, GPS data and EXIF[1] metadata from digital camera images.

Based on the vast amounts of data accumulated, a semantic enrichment engine (SEE) is implemented which uses the data and derives information from it to build semantic databases for human users. Clearly, the usefulness of the whole system depends on the quality, speed and versatility of the semantic database and on the capability of the semantic enrichment engine. In this paper, we will focus on the underlying database schema and propose a database architecture which is the foundation for the semantic analysis. There are certain requirements for such a database:

- *Flexibility:* A database for semantic storage must be highly flexible. It must be able to store heterogenous data from various sources, including e-mail systems, file systems, date books, telephones or GPS modules. Defining new relationships between existing entities will be a common task.
- *Backwards compatibility:* All enhancements to the database must be backwards compatible. Modification of the database schema should occur only rarely.
- *Speed:* The database must perform well due to the high volume of processed data
- *Scalability:* The database design should allow to scale the database up without significant performance loss.

More specifically, our contribution is to:

- Propose a suitable and flexible schema of storing semantic information on relational database engines (Section 3).
- Compare our database schema to other viable approaches (Section 3.1).
- Provide an analysis of performance in comparison to other approaches (Section 3.2).

2 The Problem

Evermore data storage enables people to save virtually their whole life digitally in various file formats or databases — photos, videos, e-mail, address databases etc. Available personal programs to store and manage these files usually offer

---
[1] http://www.exif.org/

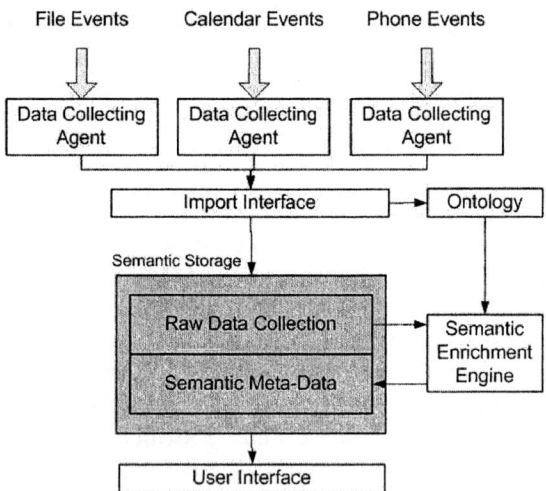

Fig. 1. System architecture: data is collected from different sources and stored in the raw data collection. Subsequently, the semantic enrichment engine (SEE) analyzes the data, adds links between recorded data items and may add additional tables or data items based on the analysis.

searches either via file system hierarchies or via keywords or fulltext search (in case the file contains text data). *Filesystem hierarchies* are not well suited since often precise attributions to a single specific folder are not possible [DEL+00]. *Keywords* are usually either based on the filenames or they need to be typed in manually. Manual keyword input is cumbersome, time consuming and subject to the *Production Paradox* [CR87] — people will simply not do it since they see no immediate advantage. *Fulltext-engines*, on the other hand, are only useful for text-based documents. Integrating photos and music into fulltext-based system is difficult and an area of ongoing research.

Apart from that, people tend to forget names of specific objects. It is often easier to remember the *context* of a situation in which a specific file was created, modified or viewed, especially with regard to a *timeline* ("I remember I just got an e-mail from Mike when I was working on that document"). Semantic enrichment of automated data-gathering processes is a useful tool to complement this human way of thinking in relations rather than thinking in keywords or tags.

Our database schema allows two links to describe the relationship between any two entities — one in each direction. The architecture must also allow to modify the semantic relationships easily and without database schema modifications or reprogramming.

The traditional relational model is considered a basic modeling technique that all computer science students have to know. The model, however, has one important drawback when relationships between already stored data objects need to be modified. Typically, in a semantic information manager we would have to link many different objects, such as e-mails with people, phone calls with

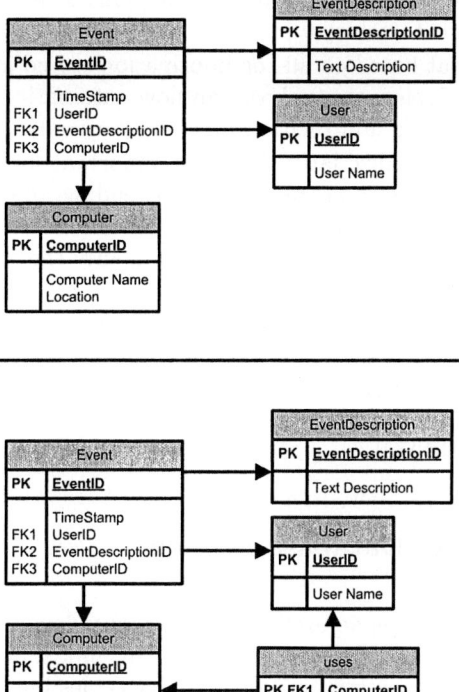

Fig. 2. The upper image shows that for each `event` an `event description`, the `user` who triggered it and the `computer` can be stored. When a new relationship is introduced to record who `uses` a computer the database schema needs to be modified.

numbers etc. This requires many $n : m$ relationships, which are usually realized in modern database systems by introducing a third table which incorporates a $1 : n$ and $1 : m$ relationship. Links between tables are usually realized using foreign keys.

Figure 2 (upper image) shows a simple example using foreign keys. In order to record which user triggered which event on which computer we need the tables `event`, `user` and `computer`. To add a new relationship, e.g. indicating which user is the owner of which computer, we need a new $n : m$ relationship, which would require adding a new table to handle the $1 : n$ and $1 : m$ relation.

Such a database structure would allow to relate any number of objects (documents, e-mails, pictures, date book entries) with events (e.g. creation of a file, responding to email, viewing a picture, changing a date book entry) if all tables and all relationships are known a priori. However, a database containing semantic information is highly volatile with regard to the relationships, which can vary often and extensively. Additionally, since dominant relationships are usually not known a priori, optimizations using cluster functions of the DBMS are extremely difficult to achieve.

Let us assume that based on all the information stored in the system an improved mechanism of semantic analysis can now automatically add descriptions (qualifiers) for events and add relationships automatically.

For instance, if we realize later that it is important for Powerpoint presentations to be associated with people (users) attending an Outlook meeting we would need to add a new table watched to resolve the new $n:m$ relationship. The obvious drawback is that we have to modify the database schema and introduce new indices.

What we were looking for was a way to circumvent these problems using relational databases without being forced to use vendor-specific features not generally supported by SQL standards. We made our system more or less independent from any specific database vendor, so that users can chose to use MySQL, Oracle or MS-SQL[2].

3 The Semantic Database Schema

Our idea, which is based on an architecture of a workflow management software project is to use a relational database, but not to link tables to others *directly* with foreign keys or by using $n:m$ intermediary tables but via a single, generic association or *link table*.

Figure 3 (top image) shows two tables. The table event is used to store all events. The table link is used to create links/association of tupels of different tables to each other.

If the service that records the event is now improved so that it now records also the applications used, a new table is added (Figure 4 (bottom image)). The table *application* stores applications that exist such as Word or Excel. When an event is related to an applications — such as the event save in Word — an entry in the link table is created.

Table 1. Inserting events and links to applications. We assume that (1) application 42 is Word and (2) that the user currently uses computer with the ComputerID 87.

Step	SQL Command
1	INSERT INTO event VALUES (1, currenttime)
2	INSERT INTO event_description VALUES (1, 'save')
3	INSERT INTO link VALUES (1, 'event', 1, 'event_description')
4	INSERT INTO link VALUES (1, 'event', 42, 'application')
5	INSERT INTO link VALUES (1, 'event', 87, 'computer')

---

[2] We are obviously aware of the major differences between these RDBMs but we wanted to develop a system which would allow the user to choose between various databases, depending on the number of users and volume of stored information.

In the classical schema, adding a new table with an $n : m$ relationship to another table (e.g. event) would require adding the table itself an the intermediate table resolving the $n : m$ relationship. Using our approach, only one new table has to be created. Our link table is basically an intermediate table resolving all $n : m$ and $1 : n$ relationships.

Using our approach it is easier to find other tables that a certain table has relationships with. In the classical schema this information is clearly stored in the data dictionary from which all meta information on tables such as foreign key constraints can be retrieved. Data dictionaries, however, are not standardized for all RDBMSs. Therefore, applications need to be modified when using different RDBMSs.

Moreover, using our system it is easily possible to synchronize data from different databases by merely combining all entries from the link table[3].

3.1 Advantages to Other Approaches

We built the prototype of the data collecting agents to work with two different database schemas, one based on $n : m$ intermediary tables and one based on link tables.

Figure 3 shows the main tables of a prototype we built to record events triggered by the file system. For each event the system may record the computer, the location, the application, the involved files and an event description. In addition, parts of the tables required to include Outlook calendar entries (meeting) and contacts (persons) are shown. We omitted many tables as not to make the diagram larger than required to understand the concepts. As previously described, the drawback of this classical approach is that semantic enrichment engine (or other data collecting agents) cannot easily add new tables and relationships.

To avoid this drawback we also used a schema that uses the link table (Figure 4). In this case new relationships can easily be added. Changing an existing $1 : n :$ to $n : m$ relationship needs no changes at all, the same applies to new relationships between two objects which had no prior link. Obviously our approach lacks any constraints on referential integrity or cardinality constraints. While such constraints are certainly important for many applications, it is not essential in our semantic setting. If required we can still implement most constraints by adding customized (functional) constraints on the link table. In an environment which basically allows relating any two objects, referential integrity is not really necessary. In addition it is possible to merge existing databases into one, for instance when merging the events recorded on an employee's desktop and her laptop computer.

In a semantic model, it is difficult to predict the quantity of relationships between the main tables and subsequently the number of intermediary tables. Given a schema with n tables, the number of intermediary tables has an upper bound of $\frac{n \times (n-1)}{2}$, while in our link-based database schema remains constant

---

[3] The IDs that are the primary keys in each table have to be globally unique; this can be achieved by using GUIDs.

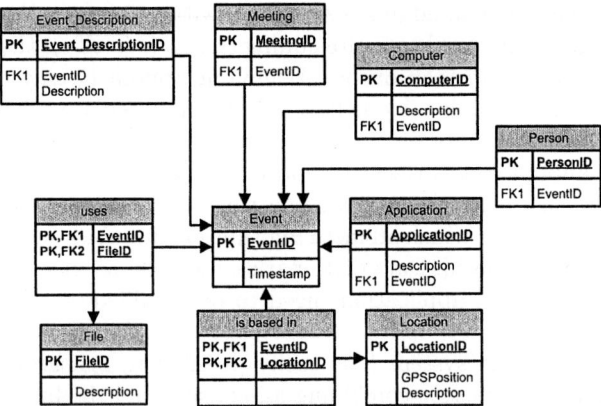

Fig. 3. To store events recorded by the `file data collecting agent` we would need this classical schema; we simplified it by selecting a subset of entities to provide a clear print

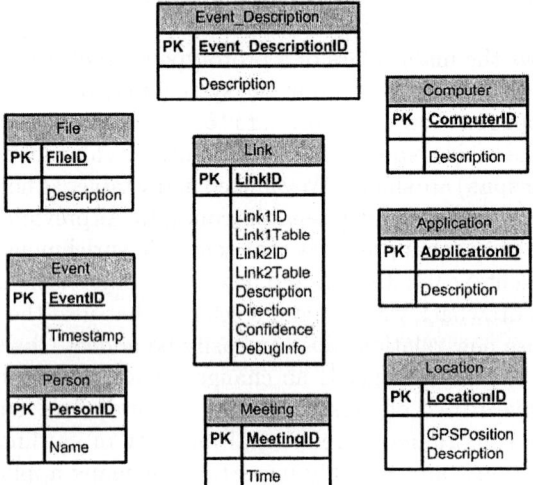

Fig. 4. Instead of using the classical schema (Figure 3) we propose to use this (simplified) schema

with one table. This is an advantage with regard to the complexity and performance of `select` statements and to the overall software complexity.

Since in a semantic setting the number of types of relationships between tables may vary widely, it is difficult to make use of cluster functionality. In our model, the link table is always the most important table, therefore, `clustering` joins with this table will have a significant positive impact on performance which is virtually impossible with traditional approaches without manually tuning the database.

With the link-based approach adding new relationships can be performed within *transactions* whereas schema modifications such as adding new $n : m$ tables are usually performed outside a transaction. Transaction-safe operations are essential because we anticipate many different semantic enrichment engines to work in parallel.

Creating new relationships and deleting existing relationships, both in two directions, should be embedded in a proper transaction procedure. Since in normal operation mode no new tables are added or removed, this is easy to implement. This will ensure that two objects are always linked bi-directionally and removed in pairs.

3.2 Performance Comparison

To test the performance of out database schema on modern databases, we prepared two prototypes, one incorporating a traditional approach and on based on our new architecture on an Oracle 9 database system. Apart from using indeces we did not optimize the database any further - we will do this in our ongoing work on various databases such as SQL Server and MySQL to compare performance and optimization features such as cluster functions. The database was filled with random data. In the traditional design, we created six N:M relationships, each containing 175.000 entries, adding up to 1.050.000 entries. In the new design, we created 1.926.064 entries (our architecture uses two entries to describe a bi-directional relationship) in the link table.

We compared three queries on both systems. Due to the difference of the architecture, the queries would vary between the traditional and the new design.

A typical query – and one we used for comparison (queries 1 and 2) – in the traditional form would look like this:

```
SELECT DISTINCT cl_event_description.description
FROM cl_event_description
INNER JOIN cl_event ON cl_event_description.event_descriptionid
= cl_event.event_descriptionid)
INNER JOIN cl_fileitem ON cl_event.activityid=cl_fileitem.activityid
WHERE description = 'qjdym.pdf'
```

A query with the same effect in the new schema would look like this:

```
SELECT DISTINCT event_description.description FROM event_description
FROM(((link l1 INNER JOIN fileitem ON l1.link1id=fileitem.fileid)
INNER JOIN event ON l1.link2id=event.eventid)
INNER JOIN link l2 ON event.eventid=l2.link1id)
INNER JOIN event_description
ON l2.link2id=event_description.event_descriptionid
WHERE fileitem.description = 'qjdym.pdf'
AND l1.link1table='event_file'
AND l1.link2table='event'
AND l2.link1table='event'
AND l2.link2table='event_description'
```

Table 2. Results of our preliminary performance tests

Query	Classic Design	New Design
1	1.300ms	2.600ms
2	300ms-600ms	15ms-30ms
3	800-900ms	900ms-1.400ms

Query No. 1 was the initial query. Query number two had the same search arguments and was executed immediately after the first, showing a significant better performance due to the database' internal caching strategies. The third query had a different search argument. Our next steps are to perform more elaborate tests; these will also take into account database-vendor specific behavior and optimization potential .

4 Related Work

Vanevar Bush's vision of the Memex [Bus45] has recently become a paper that almost everyone cites when writing about semantically enriched information storage; projects such as Microsoft's *MyLifeBits* [GBL+02] or the *SemanticLIFE* project [AHK+04] build on this vision.

They strive to build a personal digital storage that records all documents, emails, photos, videos, etc. a person works with. MyLifeBits focuses on storing the content in a database; unlike SemanticLIFE it does not strive to semantically enrich the stored data. It seems that MyLifeBits builds on improving search engines and desktop search solutions. The focus of SemanticLIFE seems to be building ontologies and finding new relationships between existing documents.

Haystack [AKS99] — an Open Source system — is a platform to visualize and maintain ontologies. The system is designed to flexibly define interactions and relationships between objects. The focus lies on the quality of the retrieval process.

The main difference between MyLifeBits, SemanticLIFE and our approach is that all the aforementioned systems are built on the concepts of *documents* or *files*. The approach we described relies primarily on events. These events are then related to existing resources and they allow to build more elaborated links between data items. A technical but yet important difference is that we store all data in relational databases that are known to work stably even with huge amounts of data.

5 Conclusion

We proposed an improved way of organizing a database schema so that relationships between tables can easily be added without schema modification. The advantages of our approach are:

1. Relationships can be added without schema modifications. This allows to easily perform operations within transactions.

2. Tables and indices can be clustered to improve the speed of joins with the central link table. In the classical model many $n : m$ relationships exist and it is a priory not clear how to cluster.
3. Our approach allows retrieving relationships from the link table without accessing the data dictionary. Since the data dictionary is vendor specific, the classical approach requires modifying the application for each database system.
4. If n entities exist and $n : m$ relationships are to be established between all entities the number of additional tables is $O(n^2)$, whereas our approach is $O(1)$ Of course this applies only to new relationships, not new tables.

Our prototype is – in the first stept – designed as a single user system where users can choose which content is kept and which is not. An enhanced prototype will also support multi-user environments, which pose additional challenges with regard to security, privacy and collaboration features. We will discuss these aspects in a later paper in detail.

References

[AHK+04] Mansoor Ahmed, Hoang H Hanh, Shuaib Karim, Shah Khusro, Monika Lanzenberger, Khalid Latif, Michlmayr Elka, Khabib Mustofa, Nguyen H Tinh, Andreas Rauber, Alexander Schatten, Nguyen M Tho, and A Min Tjoa. Semanticlife — a framework for managing information of a human lifetime. In *Proceedings of the 6th International Conference on Information Integration and Web-based Applications and Services (IIWAS)*, September 2004.

[AKS99] Eytan Adar, David Karger, and Lynn Andrea Stein. Haystack: Per-user information environments. In *Proceedings of the Conference on Information and Knowledge Management.*, 1999.

[Bus45] Vannevar Bush. As we may think. *The Atlantic Monthly*, 176(7):101–108, 1945.

[CR87] John M. Carroll and Mary Beth Rosson. *Paradox of the active user*, chapter 5, pages 80–111. Bradford Books/MIT Press, 1987.

[DEL+00] Paul Dourish, W. Keith Edwards, Anthony LaMarca, John Lamping, Karin Petersen, Michael Salisbury, Douglas B. Terry, and James Thornton. Extending document management systems with user-specific active properties. *ACM Trans. Inf. Syst.*, 18(2):140–170, 2000.

[GBL+02] Jim Gemmel, Gordon Bell, Roger Lueder, Steven Drucker, and Curtis Wong. Mylifebits: Fulfilling the memex vision. In *ACM Multimedia '02*, pages 235–238, December 2002.

Towards Truly Extensible Database Systems

Ralph Acker[1], Roland Pieringer[1], and Rudolf Bayer[2]

[1] Transaction Software GmbH, Willy-Brandt-Allee 2, D-81829 Munich, Germany
{acker, pieringer}@transaction.de
[2] Institut für Informatik, TU-München, Boltzmannstr. 3, D-85747 Garching, Germany
bayer@informatik.tu-muenchen.de

Abstract. In modern universal database management systems (DBMSs) user-defined data types along with extensible indexing structures try to bridge the gap between standard data-independent DBMS implementations and the requirement of specialized access methods for efficient domain-specific data retrieval, maintenance, and storage. However, these approaches often suffer from restricting the degree of freedom in the implementation and limiting the availability of crucial database features. Due to their design concepts, these extensible indexing frameworks are not intended to be suitable for rapid development and evaluation of research prototypes, as they lack essential generalization, completeness, and depth of their integration into the host DBMS. We discuss the advantages and drawbacks of available extensible indexing techniques and present several methods that can be easily combined into a powerful and flexible framework for storing, indexing, and manipulating domain specific data from any data source. We demonstrate that this framework comprises all properties truly extensible indexing should have. A prototype implementation of this framework was integrated into the relational DBMS Transbase®.

1 Introduction

The demand for modeling structured data coming from a designated application domain introduced user-defined data types into standard DBMSs. To satisfy the need for support of natural operations on these types, user-defined functions were incorporated. Finally, these operations had to be integrated via an extensible indexing framework into the core systems access methods to supplement efficient storage and retrieval functionality. The features of Informix DataBlades, Oracle Data Cartridges, and IBM Extenders, to name the most established ones, are widely known throughout the scientific and industrial community. However, each uses a different approach to open the host system architecture to a certain degree. These frameworks are often found to be either too complex or not flexible enough to cope with the wide range of requirements in domain-specific access methods. Moreover, the available extensible indexing frameworks are clearly not intended to be suitable for rapid development and evaluation of research prototypes. Thus these implementations in the field of database research usually integrate a loosely coupled DBMS via its API or no DBMS at all. Hence, there often exists a broad variety of prototype implementations for closely related research topics where result comparison or transferability is often difficult or impossible.

The implementation of new access paths for DBMSs, native integration of unstructured data types (like XML) or other core extensions usually results in major modifications of the DBMS kernel. Namely, the integration of a new index structure requires changes in the SQL compiler, query plan optimizer, access path layer, cache manager, lock manager, and the physical storage layer. The latter is also likely to affect logging and recovery facilities.

Such changes of the database core system make it very expensive, time consuming, and error prone to implement and test new access methods, user-defined data types, alternative physical data layout models, contiguous data flow from streaming data sources, and external storage approaches such as heterogeneous federated DBMS, external data files, or data on the net.

With the existing approaches, comparison of technologies for applicability in a project or for scientific purposes is only possible with an isolated environment, usually outside a DBMS. For example, Generalized Search Trees (GiST; [1]) offers a generic template for tree-based index implementation. But there is still no industry standard DBMS that thoroughly integrates this framework. On the other hand, there exist frameworks of commercial DBMSs that support integration of new access structures. For example, Oracle Data Cartridges provide DBMS extensibility but are restricted to secondary index integration. Customized primary clustering indexes cannot be integrated with this module. Open source DBMS can be modified in the source code, but do not explicitly provide interfaces to easily integrate new structures without modifying major parts of the kernel code. Such changes are error prone, too.

We will introduce the *AccessManager* specification [2], a new programming interface to several layers of a DBMS kernel. This enables the programmer to add new data structures to the DBMS with a minimum of effort. This is very suitable for rapid development of new access structures and comparison against existing techniques, while having all features of a complete DBMS at hand for representative benchmarking.

This interface is currently being implemented into Transbase® [3], a fully-fledged relational DBMS with a highly modularized architecture.

The remainder of this paper is organized as follows: Section 2 will present a collection of features a truly extensible indexing framework should have. In Section 3 we will provide a brief overview on how these features translate into currently available DBMSs and surveys related work. Section 4 will present our framework and how it achieves the proposed objectives. In Section 5 we give our conclusions as well as an outlook on future work.

2 Motivation

An extensible indexing architecture is a powerful framework that is adaptable to domain-specific requirements of a DBMS application. Its basic purpose is to support natural operations on domain-specific data for efficient storage and retrieval. Both, storage of the data in a primary access path and additional indexes as secondary access paths are available. The query plan optimizer autonomously chooses the best available access path for a query, so access path selection is completely transparent to the user (e.g. in SQL). Additionally, it supports these operations wherever and as thoroughly as possible in all DBMS tasks. That is, all index operations are consistent within their own transactional context. Data integrity is enforced independently, and data and system security is provided through logging and recovery facilities. Multiple operations of concurrent users are processed in parallel, offering locking technology and concurrency control on a reasonably fine granular basis. Intra-query parallelism is available for performance improvements. Indexing methods have direct influence on performance characteristics of the system through their ability of holding required pages in the DBMS data cache.

In spite of these high demands, the implementation itself allows for rapid prototyping and provides sophisticated testing and debugging facilities. It encourages the use of basic software engineering concepts supporting these demands, such as modularization and reuse. So coding complexity is closely dependent on the complexity of the new access structure and its distinctiveness from existing implementations. Built-in access methods of the database system (i.e. B-Tree, UB-Tree [4], and Fulltext) are available as modular components through their exported interfaces. Moreover, the implementation of a new extension itself is made available in this resource pool. Additionally, the host framework provides a rich set of utility functionality for common tasks. System stability and data security is not to be compromised. However, this task conflicts with another, sometimes more important requirement for best possible performance. Portability of indexing implementations is desirable. Finally the indexing framework and the DBMS should provide flexibility to incorporate further requirements that will emerge.

3 State-of-the-Art

Our work focuses on integrating a framework for new access method functionality into the database core. A good survey on how such framework can be integrated into relational DBMSs can be found in [5]. Although methods for thoroughly and well-performing integration are identified, theses approaches are not investigated in detail. Unlike our approach, this work is centered on building extensible indexing on top of the relational interface of the DBMS. A good overview on possible approaches and available techniques on building a DBMS out of components can be found in [6].

In the following we will discuss where existing technology meets the requirements listed above.

Informix DataBlades. The most powerful but highly complex interface for an extensible interface is offered by IBM with its Informix Dynamic Server. The concept of DataBlades [7] allows for extension and modifications on many layers of the host system. User-defined data types and routines add to the functionality. However, the design goal of the Virtual Table Interface (VTI, [8]) and Virtual Index Interface (VII, [9]) was to give the programmer the opportunity to embed external data as 'virtual' tables into the DBMS. Internal storage is a possible option, but it is heavily restricting freedom of implementation. Essential DBMS concepts such as transactional contexts, concurrency, locking, logging and recovery are not commonly supported. They are left to the Blade-developer as an almost unbearable burden.

Oracle Data Cartridges. Since version 8i Oracle offers Data Cartridges as functional extension of their DBMS. Realization and complexity are comparable to Informix DataBlades to a large extent [10], [11]. But only for *internal* data storage much of the available database functionality for extensible indexing is provided. The Oracle Data Cartridge Interface (ODCI) was mainly designed to offer user-defined *secondary* index support. Here every tuple has to be materialized via a row id (RID) lookup in the base table. Therefore this interface exhibits severe deficiencies in its applicability as a universal indexing framework.

IBM DB2 Extender. The most elegant indexing framework with respect to implementation complexity is offered in IBM's DB2 Universal Database system [12], [13]. To build a new index type, a programmer has to provide only four functions that are used as hooks in the actual indexing framework [14]. Although charming, this approach suffers from the fact that at most one B-Tree index is available for indexing and the programmer is limited to the B-Tree index type. Therefore this interface is only suitable for functional indexing.

Open Source Databases. Of course this type of database systems allows (and encourages) every intrusion into the system code. But to the best of our knowledge, they do not offer an explicitly defined, stable, and complete interface for extensible indexing without impact to the entire system. Here the difficulty is to understand the code of the complete DBMS in order to integrate the desired extensions. This obviously results in a tremendous implementation and maintenance effort.

Generalized Search Trees (GiST). This framework [1], [15] defines the minimal common interface required for implementing generalized tree-based indexing structures. It is used mainly for research prototype implementations using *libgist*, a file-based GiST implementation. However, all aspects of a surrounding database system are missing. Although there have been efforts to integrate this framework into a major DBMS, e.g. [16] and [17], these solutions are not widely accepted. Still, the universality [18], [19], [20] of this approach makes the available GiST prototypes interesting for a possible integration into a DBMS via our framework.

The following table shows a comparison of the previously described frameworks, categorized by the database functionality they provide.

Table 1. Features required for an extensible indexing frameworks and applicability in available implementations. Legend: (+) suitable, (-) not suitable

Feature	IBM Informix DataBlades	Oracle Data Cartridges	IBM DB2 Extenders
modularity & reuse	-	-	-
fast prototyping	-	-	+
primary indexes	+	-	-
secondary indexes	+	+	+
external data	+	-	-
internal data	-	+	+
transactions	-	+	+
fine granular locking	-	+	+
logging & recovery	-	+	+
caching	-	+	+
phys. data layout	-	-	-
recent enhancements	-	-	-

This table shows that none of the existing approaches supports the desired database functionality completely. Some features are not supported at all (e.g. caching or physical data layout).

4 Architecture Overview

Our proposed architecture provides modifications on several layers of an arbitrary core DBMS system in order to incorporate an extension framework. Any DBMS implementing this framework can thereby offer extensible indexing. The index modules themselves are portable between host DBMSs without modifications. Figure 1 shows the involved parts of the overall architecture of such a DBMS.

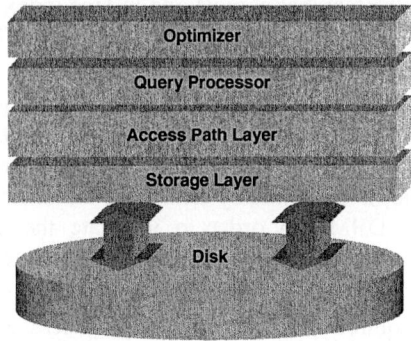

Fig. 1. Strongly simplified model of a classical modularized database system architecture. The query optimizer receives a (usually naive) query execution plan generated from the original SQL query and transforms into a new plan, in order to minimize I/O and CPU costs. This is done, e.g. by consulting information on alternative access paths (indexes) from the DBMS data dictionary. The query processor then carries out the execution plan by interpreting the plan like a computer program. Thereby it utilizes the access path layer, e.g. B-Tree indexes for efficient access. These indexes then retrieve the data from the page-oriented storage layer where the actual disk I/O takes place.

Since the main goal is to maximize performance, our design will use native *dynamic libraries* as primary access path *driver*. This is also the core package for an index extension. Each driver has to export a unique name and a subset of functions to be specified later. The exported functions must follow strict naming conventions, however they accept and return generic structures by reference.

Alternatively, a driver may be written completely in *Java*, implementing the required Java interface definition and made available as Java archive to the system. The core system provides all native facilities required to invoke the Java code. Naturally, the second variant suffers from some loss of performance, however, programming in Java is considered easier and more robust, and therefore safer for the overall system stability. Thus using Java is an appropriate alternative for implementing an index driver. The presence of these two alternatives for implementing access methods leaves the decision to the developer to opt for maximum performance versus better stability through reduced programming complexity.

An access path manager validates the conformity of a new driver, i.e. existence of required interfaces and basic function tests. After successful completion, the manager adds the driver to a pool of available structures, which resides in the data dictionary of the host DBMS. There the driver waits to be invoked either through the query processor or another driver. In the following we will discuss how these extensions interact with the database modules.

SQL Compiler. The DDL extension appointed to create or drop an external index type is:
```
CREATE [PRIMARY|SECONDARY] INDEXTYPE
   <indextype> USING <dynamic library>;
DROP INDEXTYPE <indextype>;
```
Here <indextype> is the unique name that is also exported by the driver. The following modified DDL statements serve to use a specific index type as a new primary or secondary index:
```
CREATE [<indextype>[(<indexspec>)]] TABLE
   <relname> (<fieldspeclist>);
CREATE [<indextype>[(<indexspec>)]] INDEX <idxname> ON
   <relname> (<fieldnamelist>);
```
This is the original SQL CREATE TABLE or CREATE INDEX statement when the optional *indextype* sections are omitted. The *indextype* can be enriched by an optional *indexspec* string literal passed to the index module, e.g. to distinguish between several internal modes. No further SQL extensions are required for using external index modules.

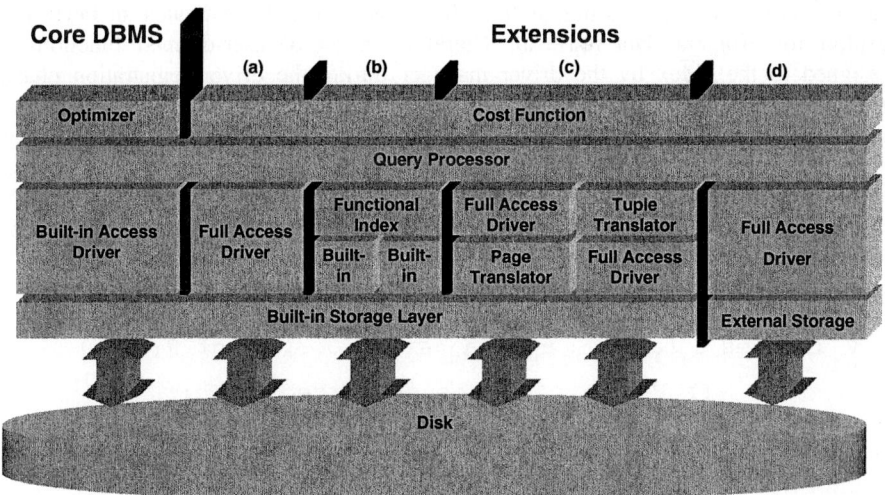

Fig. 2. Overall system architecture. (a) represents a complete index implementation. (b) is a lean functional index implementation relying on two built-in access layers. (c) shows translator layers that convert data structures between representations. (d) shows an indexing and storage package that transport data around the built-in storage layer into an external file.

The subset of interfaces implemented by the driver defines where it can be applied. Any driver may offer *tuple-oriented* or *page-oriented* interfaces, i.e. an index selectively reads pages (or blocks) from the DBMS storage subsystem and returns tuples to the query processor. An example of the call stack of such an implementation is depicted in Figure 2a. Here the driver makes direct use of the internal storage layer for persistent storage. Alternatively, a driver may also be based on another index structure, e.g. the built-in B-Tree index. Then it simply passes its callers tuple-oriented requests to the underlying tuple-oriented layers. Only those interfaces actually need implementation that modify the data to be passed through. This allows for very lean functional index implementation as exemplified in Figure 2b. Here two built-in indexes (e.g. B-Trees) are utilized. If an alternative data layout is required within the pages, an additional component can be inserted into the stack. It appears as page-oriented storage layer to its caller while the component itself is based on the system's page-oriented storage layer. Such a layer can be used to translate between alternative page layouts. This and the analogous tuple translator layer that translates between some access path's internal tuple representation and the representation required by the query processor are shown in Figure 2c. Figure 2d depicts a fully independent storage layer that stores data outside the database, in this example into external files, but also over the network on a remote system (e.g. another DBMS). A driver including an external storage module requires the most complex implementation, because also logging and recovery facilities have to be provided by the driver. Locking and caching can be supplied by the host DBMS if the data can be broken down into cache frames

Query Plan Optimizer. This module is responsible for the index selection. Therefore all information on possible access paths must be available at optimizing time. This information is stored in the DBMS data dictionary, which is maintained via DDL statements as presented earlier. It must be apparent which predicates an index can exploit for efficient data retrieval. Therefore, a set of user-defined functions is assigned to the index by the driver manager during the driver registration phase. Additionally to the function name itself, the optimizer evaluates mappings of common SQL infix notation to supported comparison operators of indexing modules, e.g. *equals* (=), *lt* (<), *like* etc. An optional cost function can be used to choose the best access path for situations where multiple access paths exist for a given predicate. The following algorithm generates an appropriate query execution plan for accessing relation $R(a_0,...,a_n)$ while applying predicate $P(a_{P0},...,a_{Pm})$, $a_{Pi} \in \{a_0,...,a_n\}$ and a projection $\pi(a_0,...,a_n)$:

```
∀ indexes I_i(a_i0,...,a_ik), a_ij ∈ {a_0,...,a_n} of R:
     If P(a_P0,...,a_Pm) is supported by I_i:
          calculate cost(R,I_i,P,π)
choose I_i with minimum costs.
materialize if π(a_0,...,a_n) ⊄ {a_i0,...,a_ik}.
```

Query Processor. The query processor itself is not aware that external indexing is used, although it directly controls the data flow during query execution time by invoking access layer interfaces and thereby retrieves tuples. It passes and expects tuples to be delivered in the internal tuple representation. The physical data layout of access path implementations below is completely transparent.

Access Layer. The most extensive interfaces are used during run-time in the access layer module. Required routines have to cover the creation (*IndexCreate()*) and deletion (*IndexDrop()*) of a new access path. For index maintenance at least the interfaces *IndexInsert()* for insertion of new tuples and *IndexDelete()* for delete operations are required. For efficient update operation support, a driver may also export an optional *IndexUpdate()* routine. Access paths have to be initialized with *IndexOpen()* before first use. *IndexClose()* does the cleaning up. An index structure is informed about transactional state transitions via the *IndexBeginTA()*, *IndexPrepareTA()*, *IndexCommitTA()*, and *IndexRollbackTA()* callbacks. An access layer must guarantee query atomicity for insert, update, and delete operations. Therefore the *IndexSavepointDefine()* and *IndexSavepointApply()* facilities must be provided. This interface family is required to prepare, maintain and use undo information on internal structures in case of aborted DML operations and complete transaction rollbacks. The main task of ensuring data integrity can be entrusted to the storage layer. Finally, *IndexScanOpen()*, *IndexScanNext()*, and *IndexScanClose()* are required for the actual data retrieval as well as for positioning for deletes and updates.

Storage Layer. For storing data externally or for using another physical page layout, an access module exports a page-oriented interface to its caller. It has to implement the storage layer interface rather than the access layer interface. In detail, these are routines for table storage maintenance *StoreCreate()*, *StoreOpen()*, *StoreClose()*, and *StoreDrop()*. New pages are created with *PageAlloc()* and removed with *PageDelete()*. A page is fetched into the DBMS cache and held there using *PageFix()*. In this phase synchronized read/write operations on this page are conducted. If a page is not needed anymore, *PageUnfix()* releases it into the cache LRU stack, where it is held until the caching strategy swaps it out.

The internal page structure itself is not predefined, except a short page header that has to be common for all page instances. This is provided by a template. The bulk of the page layout remains free. Each page is marked to belong to a certain segment type. Transactional control and query flow facilities, that are routed through by the access layers, are also mandatory: *StoreSavepointDefine()*, *StoreSavepointApply()*, *StoreBeginTA()*, *StorePrepareTA()*, *StoreCommitTA()*, and *StoreRollbackTA()*.

It should be noted, that using internal storage greatly relieves an access method programmer from highly complex tasks, such as concurrency control, logging, and recovery. By specifying the required lock type for reading, altering or exclusively locking the page with *PageFix()*, page consistency is guaranteed by the storage layer. The access path structure itself has only to maintain and apply undo information concerning its internal state when reacting on changes of the transactional context.

Using external storage in the presence of transactional consistency means that the module has to supply concurrency control, logging, and recovery wholly by itself. Further, it implies the need for 2-phase commits as two independent systems have to guarantee transactional atomicity. However, such an external data store can safely be used read-only without need for these concepts. Data consistency can also be guaranteed by exclusive locking, which is easier to implement, but always at the expense of reduced concurrency.

Utilities. Tasks that are likely to occur repeatedly in index extensions programming are compiled into a utility library. Examples for such utilities are construction of tuple structures from value representation and vice versa along with comparison operations on tuple structures. The utility library also provides a sophisticated sort operation and temporary storage of vast sets of tuples.

Depending on the purpose of a layer either the access layer or the storage layer has to be implemented. More precisely, a simple functional index has only to "route" these calls through to the access layer below. Only modifications on the data that is passed through is required, i.e. in functional indexes this is the extension of the tuple by some calculated value to be used as index key. This correlates the complexity of our framework immediately with the complexity of the problem to be solved. Additionally the modularity allows for a good rate of reuse.

5 Conclusions

We have presented a design concept for a generalized extensible indexing structure to be implemented into an arbitrary modularized relational DBMS. We have shown that this approach suits the demands for common applicability to extensible indexing requirements. No other available DBMS offers such functionality to a comparable extent. In spite of the necessity for more advanced features for commercial and scientific use, little effort on improving those systems has recently been made.

From the presented design concept arises the specification of a framework to be integrated into any relational DBMS. This specification is currently available as Public Review Version [2].

A reference implementation of this specification was integrated into the Transbase® relational DBMS. Built-in indexing structures of this DBMS and index module prototypes are available to be used as reusable components for extensible indexing. The indexing extensions are fully transparent on SQL level. Concurrency control and recovery facilities are handled by the systems storage layer, if not required otherwise.

Preliminary performance tests prove that the framework itself inducts little or no performance overhead. Comparisons between different index types are not presented here, as the benefits arising from a certain index type is always related to the specific application. Still the ability of choosing the optimal index structure for a certain application with this framework obviously holds a tremendous performance potential.

Future work will cover the integration of additional indexing structures as well as the extension of the framework with new advanced concepts for improved module integration and better adaptivity to new fields of application.

References

1. Hellerstein J. M., Naughton J. F., Pfeffer A.: Generalized Search Trees for Database Systems. Proc. 21st Int. Conf. on Very Large Databases: 562-573, 1995
2. Transaction Software, Access Manager Specification, Transaction Software GmbH, Public Review Version 0.9, June 10, 2005, http://www.transaction.de/service/downloadcenter/whitepapers/

3. Transaction Software, Transbase System Guide, Transaction Software GmbH, Version 6.2, October 20, 2004, http://www.transaction.de/service/downloadcenter/documentation/
4. Bayer R.: The Universal B-Tree for multidimensional Indexing. Technical University of Munich, TUM-I9637, 1996
5. Kriegel H.-P., Pfeifle M., Pötke M., Seidl T.: The Paradigm of Relational Indexing: A Survey, Proc. 10th GI-Conf. on Database Systems for Business, Technology, and the Web (BTW'03), Leipzig, Germany. GI-Edition Lecture Notes in Informatics, P-26: 285-304
6. Dittrich K. R. (ed), Geppert A. (ed), Component Database Systems, Morgan Kaufmann 2000
7. Ubell, M.: The Montage Extensible DataBlade Achitecture, Proc. 1994 ACM SIGMOD Int. Conf. on Management of Data, Minneapolis, Minnesota, May 24-27, 1994
8. IBM Corp.: IBM Informix Virtual-Table Interface, Version 9.4, IBM Corp., Part No. CT1TDNA, March 2003
9. IBM Corp.: IBM Informix Virtual Index Interface, Version 9.4, IBM Corp., Part No. CT1TCNA, March 2003
10. Oracle Corp.: Oracle Database SQL Reference, 10g Release 1 (10.1), Oracle Corp., Part No. B10759-01, December 2003
11. Oracle Corp.: Oracle9i Data Cartridge Developers Guide, Release 2 (9.2), Oracle Corp., Part No. A96595-01, March 2002
12. IBM Corp.: DB2 SQL Reference, Version 8, IBM Corp., Part Number: CT17RNA, 2002.
13. IBM Corp.: DB2 Spatial Extender User's Guide and Reference, Version 8, IBM Corp., Part Number: CT19HNA, 2002
14. Stolze, K., Steinbach, T.: DB2 Index Extensions by example and in detail, IBM Developer works DB2 library, December 2003
15. The GiST Indexing Project, http://gist.cs.berkeley.edu
16. C. Kleiner, U. W. Lipeck: OraGiST - How to Make User-Defined Indexing Become Usable and Useful. In Proc. 10th Conf. on Database Systems for Business, Technology, and the Web: 26.-28.2.2003, Leipzig, LNI P-26, GI, Bonn, 2003, 324–334
17. Döller, M. Enhancement of Oracle's Indexing Capabilities through GiST-implemented Access Methods, Technical Report No TR/ITEC/02/2.09, University Klagenfurt - ITEC Institute, April 2002
18. Kornacker M.: High-Performance Extensible Indexing. Proc. 25th Int. Conf. on Very Large Databases (VLDB): 699-708, 1999
19. Kornacker, M., PHD Thesis: Access Methods for Next-Generation Database Systems. University of California at Berkley, 2000
20. Kornacker M., Mohan C., Hellerstein, J. M.: Concurrency and Recovery in Generalized Search Trees. SIGMOD Conference 1997: 62-72

Transaction Management with Integrity Checking

Davide Martinenghi and Henning Christiansen

Roskilde University, Computer Science Dept.,
P.O.Box 260, DK-4000 Roskilde, Denmark
{dm, henning}@ruc.dk

Abstract. Database integrity constraints, understood as logical conditions that must hold for any database state, are not fully supported by current database technology. It is typically up to the database designer and application programmer to enforce integrity via triggers or tests at the application level, which are difficult to maintain and error prone. Two important aspects must be taken care of. 1. It is too time consuming to check integrity constraints from scratch after each update, so simplified checks before each update should be used relying on the assumption that the current state is consistent. 2. In concurrent database systems, besides the traditional correctness criterion, the execution schedule must ensure that the different transactions can overlap in time without destroying the consistency requirements tested by other, concurrent transactions. We show in this paper how to apply a method for incremental integrity checking to automatically extend update transactions with locks and simplified consistency tests on the locked elements. All schedules produced in this way are conflict serializable and preserve consistency in an optimized way.

1 Introduction

When an update transaction is executed on a database, it is important to ensure that database consistency is preserved and that the transaction produces the desired result, i.e., its execution is not affected by the execution of other, possibly interleaved transactions. A common view in concurrent database systems is that a transaction executes correctly if it belongs to a schedule that is conflict serializable, i.e., equivalent to a schedule in which all the transactions are executed in series (not interleaved). Several strategies and protocols, such as two-phase locking and timestamp ordering, have been established that can dynamically enforce conflict serializability. Locking is the most common practice for concurrency control; however, maintaining locks is expensive and may limit the throughput of the database, as locks actually reduce the concurrency of the accesses to the resources. Another aspect of correctness is determined by the semantic requirements expressed by integrity constraints (ICs). ICs are logical formulas that characterize the consistent states of a database. Integrity maintenance is a central issue, as without any guarantee of data consistency, answers to queries become unreliable. A full check of consistency often requires polynomial time wrt the size of the database, which is usually too costly. We therefore need to simplify the ICs into specialized checks that can be executed more efficiently at each update, employing the hypothesis that the initial database state was consistent. To optimize run-time performance, these tests should be generated at database design time and executed before potentially offensive updates, in order to avoid rollback operations completely. This principle, known as *simplification* of ICs, has been long known and recognized [14], but *ad hoc* techniques are still prevalent. The two main approaches are triggers, at the database level, and hand-coding of tests, at the application level. By their procedural nature, both methods have major disadvantages, as they are prone to errors, require advanced programming skills and have little flexibility wrt changes in the database schema. This suggests a need for automated simplification methods. Although a few, standard principles exist [2], none of them has prevailed in current database systems. In this paper we refer to a simplification procedure [3] based on transformations that produce simplified ICs already at design time; these are necessary and sufficient conditions for consistency that can be tested prior to the execution of updates. Due to space constraints, we restrict updates to tuple additions and deletions and disregard aggregates in ICs. We focus on the interaction between integrity checking and locking policies; we present a method that uses the simplified ICs not only to ensure consistency of each individual update transaction, but also to determine the minimal amount of database resources to be locked in order to guarantee the correctness of all legal schedules.

The paper extends the results presented in [12] and is organized as follows. We review existing literature in the field in section 2. Simplification of ICs is introduced in section 3, while the results concerning its application to database locking are explained and exemplified in section 4. Further discussion on the applicability of the method and concluding remarks are provided in section 5.

2 Related Works

Simplification of ICs is an essential optimization principle for database consistency checking. We emphasize, furthermore, the importance of identifying a violation to be introduced by an update before it is executed, so that inconsistent states are completely avoided. Several approaches to simplification do not comply with this requirement, e.g., [14,11,5,8]. Other methods, e.g., [10], provide pre-tests that, however, are not proven to be necessary conditions; in other words, if the tests fail, nothing can be concluded about consistency. Integrity checking is often regarded as an instance of materialized view maintenance: integrity constraints are defined as views that must always remain empty for the database to be consistent. These approaches use update propagation techniques to perform the task in an incremental way. However, they typically require "immediate" view maintenance (i.e., after each step in a transaction, which is more costly) or, if "deferred" maintenance is allowed, then additional overhead is needed (e.g., to avoid the *state bug*). We refer to [9] for a survey of these methods. Triggers' reactive behavior has been used since [1] for integrity enforcement without, however, semantically optimizing the triggering condition. Semantic optimization of triggers was introduced in [4], where, however, only single updates are allowed. For these reasons, none of the above methods is well-suited for concurrent database transactions. As for locking, the literature is rich in methods aimed at the correctness of concurrently executed transactions. The most common protocol is two-phase locking, but others have been proposed, e.g., [16]. All these methods depend on the implicit assumption that each single transaction preserves consistency when executed alone [6], which, thus, entrusts this responsibility to the designer of the transactions. We present, instead, an integrated approach to automatically obtain this combined with locking, so that the designer need only concentrate on the declarative specification of integrity constraints.

3 A Simplification Procedure for Integrity Constraints

3.1 Preliminaries

We describe our proposal in the function-free first-order language DATALOG extended with default negation (DATALOG$^\neg$) and assume familiarity with the notions of *terms* ($t, s, \ldots$), *variables* ($x, y, \ldots$), *constants* ($a, b, \ldots$), *predicates* ($p, q, \ldots$), *atoms*, *literals*, *formulas* and (definite) *clauses*. We characterize a database as a set of non recursive clauses that we divide in three classes: the *extensional database* or set of *facts*, the *constraint theory* (CT) or set of ICs, and the *intensional database* or set of *rules* [7]. We can disregard the intensional database, as, without recursion, the CT and database can be transformed in equivalent ones that do not contain any intensional predicates [2]. By *database state* we refer to the extensional part only. We further assume that every clause is *range restricted*, i.e., each variable in it appears in a positive database literal in the body. The truth value of a closed formula F, relative to a database state D, is defined as its evaluation in D's standard model [15] and denoted $D(F)$.

Definition 1 (Consistency). *A database state D is consistent with a CT Γ iff $D(\Gamma) = true$.*

The simplification method we describe here can handle general forms of update, but, for reasons of space, we limit our attention to sets of additions and deletions.

Definition 2 (Update). *An update $U = U^+ \cup U^-$ is a non-empty set of additions U^+ and deletions U^-. An addition is a ground atom and a deletion a negated ground atom. The reverse of an update U, denoted $\neg U$, contains the same elements as U but with the roles of additions and deletions interchanged. The additions and deletions of an update are required to be disjoint, i.e. $U^+ \cap \neg U^- = \emptyset$. The notation D^U, where D is a database state, is a shorthand for $(D \cup U^+) \setminus \neg U^-$.*

Updates can also contain *parameters* (written in boldface: **a**, **b**, ...), that are placeholders for constants. In this way we can generalize updates into update *patterns* and simplify ICs for classes of updates, rather than specific updates.

For example, the notation $\{p(\mathbf{a}), \neg q(\mathbf{a})\}$, **a** a parameter, indicates the class of updates that add a tuple to the relation p and remove the same tuple from the relation q. We refer to [3] for further discussion about parameters.

3.2 Semantic Notions

We characterize the semantic correctness of simplification with the notion of conditional weakest precondition, i.e., a test that can be checked in the present state but indicating properties of the new state, further optimized with the hypothesis that the present state is consistent.

Definition 3 (Conditional weakest precondition). *Let Γ, Δ be CTs and U an update. A CT Σ is a Δ-conditional weakest precondition (Δ-CWP) of Γ wrt U whenever $D(\Sigma) = D^U(\Gamma)$ for any database state D consistent with Δ.*

In definition 3, Δ will typically include Γ and perhaps further properties of the database that are trusted. All CWPs of the same CT wrt the same update are in an equivalence class called conditional equivalence.

Definition 4 (Conditional equivalence). *Let Δ, Γ_1, Γ_2 be CTs; then Γ_1 and Γ_2 are conditionally equivalent wrt Δ, denoted $\Gamma_1 \stackrel{\Delta}{\equiv} \Gamma_2$, whenever $D(\Gamma_1) = D(\Gamma_2)$ for any database state D consistent with Δ.*

To find a simplification means then to choose among all the Δ-conditionally equivalent CWPs according to an optimality criterion that serves as an abstraction over actual computation times. We then introduce the notion of resource set, i.e., a portion of the Herbrand base $\mathcal{B}$ (the set of all ground atoms) that affects the semantics of a CT: the smaller the resource set, the better the CWP.

Definition 5 (Resource set). *A subset $\mathcal{R}$ of the Herbrand base is a resource set for a CT Γ whenever $D(\Gamma) = D'(\Gamma)$ for any two database states D, D' such that $D \cap \mathcal{R} = D' \cap \mathcal{R}$. If, furthermore, Γ admits no other resource set $\mathcal{R}' \subset \mathcal{R}$, $\mathcal{R}$ is a minimal resource set for Γ.*

Proposition 1. *For any CT there exists a unique minimal resource set.*

We indicate the minimal resource set of a CT Γ as $\mathcal{R}(\Gamma)$ and in the following we shall omit the word "minimal". For example, the resource set $\mathcal{R}(\{\leftarrow f(c,y) \wedge y \neq d\})$ is $\{f(x,y) \mid x = c \wedge y \neq d\}$. For an update U, the notation $\mathcal{R}(U)$ refers to the set of ground atoms occurring in U.

A CWP is independent of the atoms of the update upon which it is calculated.

Proposition 2. *Let Γ, Δ be CTs, U an update and Σ a Δ-CWP of Γ wrt U. Then $\mathcal{R}(\Sigma) \cap \mathcal{R}(U) = \emptyset$.*

We define an optimality criterion that selects the CWPs with the smallest resource sets.

Definition 6 (Optimality). *Given two CTs Δ and Σ, Σ is Δ-optimal if there exists no other CT $\Sigma' \stackrel{\Delta}{\equiv} \Sigma$ such that $\mathcal{R}(\Sigma') \subset \mathcal{R}(\Sigma)$.*

Different optimality criteria can be defined for CTs. For example, another natural choice is a syntactic order based on the number of literals: the optimal theories are those with the minimal count. It is possible to find examples where the optimal CTs found according to these criteria (minimal resource set, minimal number of literals) differ. However, it should be made clear that they can serve only as approximative comparisons of execution times, which may vary highly in different database state. ICs are simplified as to provide best choices that apply to *any* database state, and we must rely on the query optimizers embedded in standard RDBMSs to take into account state information such as the size of each relation. For example, a syntactically minimal query does not necessarily evaluate faster than an equivalent non-minimal query in all database states; the amount of computation required to answer a query can be reduced, for instance, by adding a join with a very small relation. In the remainder of the paper we stick to the criterion of definition 6, as this proves useful for locking purposes (see section 4.3).

Syntactic notions, such as subsumption, can be used to define a simplification procedure that, for an input CT Γ and update U, produces a CWP of Γ wrt U, indicated as $\mathsf{Simp}^U(\Gamma)$; we refer to the implementation given in [3].

Example 1. Consider a database relation f containing child-father entries and the CT $\Gamma = \{\leftarrow f(x,y) \wedge f(x,z) \wedge y \neq z\}$, meaning that no child can have two different fathers. The simplification wrt the update pattern $U = \{f(\mathbf{a},\mathbf{b})\}$, where $\mathbf{a}$ and $\mathbf{b}$ are parameters, is $\mathsf{Simp}^U(\Gamma) = \{\leftarrow f(\mathbf{a},y) \wedge y \neq \mathbf{b}\}$, which indicates that the added child $\mathbf{a}$ cannot already have a father different from $\mathbf{b}$.

4 Locks on Simplified Integrity Constraints

4.1 Transactions

The notion of transaction includes, in general, write as well as read operations on database elements. We identify a database element (or *resource*) with a ground atom of the Herbrand base, and a write operation adds or removes such an atom from the database state. A transaction is always concluded with either a commit or an abort; in the former case the executed write operations are finalized into the database state, in the latter they are cancelled. We omit, for simplicity, the indication of abort and commit operations in transactions and consider the execution of a transaction concluded and committed after its last operation.

Definition 7 (Transaction). *A transaction T is a finite sequence of operations $\langle T^1, \ldots, T^n \rangle$ such that each step T^i is either a $\mathsf{read}(e_i)$ or a $\mathsf{write}(e_i)$ operation on a database element e_i.*

A schedule is a sequence of the operations of one or more transactions.

Definition 8 (Schedule). *A schedule σ over a set of transactions $\mathcal{T}$ is an ordering of the operations of all the transactions in $\mathcal{T}$ which preserves the ordering of the operations of each transaction. A schedule is* serial *if, for any two transactions T' and T'' in $\mathcal{T}$, either all operations in T' occur before all operations of T'' in σ or conversely. A schedule which is not serial, for $|\mathcal{T}| > 1$, is an* interleaved *schedule.*

A schedule executes correctly wrt concurrency of transactions if it corresponds to the execution of some serial schedule, according to definition 9 below.

Definition 9 (Conflict serializability). *Two operations in a transaction are conflicting iff they refer to the same database element and at least one of them is a* **write** *operation. Two schedules are* conflict equivalent *iff they contain the same set of committed transactions and operations and every pair of conflicting operations is ordered in the same way in both schedules. A schedule is* conflict serializable *iff it is conflict equivalent to a serial schedule.*

Checking conflict serializability can be done in linear time by testing the acyclicity of the directed graph in which the nodes are the transactions in the schedule and the edges correspond to the order of conflicting operations in two different transactions.

4.2 Extended Transactions

In the update language discussed in section 3, the updates consist of **write** operations on database elements, where the elements are the tuples of the database relations. These operations are known and do not depend on previous **read** operations. Furthermore, an update does not contain conflicting operations, as the sets of additions and deletions are disjoint. Therefore we can, for the moment, restrict our attention to write transactions, i.e., sequences of non-conflicting **write** operations. In order to be able to map back and forth between write transactions and updates, we also indicate for each **write** if it is an addition or a deletion (using a $\neg$ sign on the database element).

Definition 10 (Write transaction). *For a given update U, any sequence T, of minimal length, of* **write** *operations on all the literals in U is a* write transaction *on U. Given a write transaction T, we indicate the corresponding update as $\overline{T}$.*

Example 2. The possible write transactions on an update $U = \{p(a), \neg q(a)\}$ are $T_1 = \langle \text{write}(p(a)), \text{write}(\neg q(a)) \rangle$ and $T_2 = \langle \text{write}(\neg q(a)), \text{write}(p(a)) \rangle$. Conversely, $\overline{T_1} = \overline{T_2} = U$. □

In the following we shall indicate the i-th element of a sequence S with the notation S^i. For a given write transaction T of size n and a database state D, the notation D^T refers to the database state $(\ldots((D^{\{T^1\}})^{\{T^2\}})\cdots)^{\{T^n\}}$. The same notation applies to schedules over write transactions. Clearly, $D^T = D^{\overline{T}}$ for any write transaction T, while for a schedule σ the notation $D^{\overline{\sigma}}$ is not allowed, as σ might contain conflicting operations, i.e., σ cannot be mapped to an update $\overline{\sigma}$.

Proposition 3. *Let T be a write transaction, Γ a CT, D a database state consistent with Γ and let Σ be a CWP of Γ wrt $\overline{T}$. Then $D^T(\Gamma) = true$ iff $D(\Sigma) = true$.*

Proposition 3 indicates that a write transaction executes correctly if and only if the database state satisfies the corresponding CWP. This leads to the following notion of simplified write transaction.

Definition 11 (Simplified write transaction). *Let T be a write transaction, Γ a CT and D a database state. The simplified write transaction of T wrt Γ and D is $\langle\rangle$[1] if $D(\Sigma) = \text{false}$ and T if $D(\Sigma) = \text{true}$, where Σ is a CWP of Γ wrt $\overline{T}$.*

Obviously, the execution of a simplified write transaction is always correct.

Corollary 1. *Let T be a write transaction and Γ a CT. Then, for every database state D consistent with Γ, $D^{T_S}(\Gamma) = \text{true}$, where T_S is the simplified write transaction of T wrt Γ and D.*

In order to determine a simplified write transaction, the database state must be accessed. We can therefore model the behavior of a scheduler that dynamically produces simplified write transactions by starting them with read operations corresponding to the database actions needed to evaluate the CWP. Checking a CT Γ corresponds to reading all database elements that contribute to the evaluation of Γ, i.e., its resource set. The effort of evaluating a CT can then be expressed by concatenating ($\circ$) the sequence of all needed read operations with the (simplified) write transaction. To simplify the notation, we indicate any minimal sequence of read operations on every element of a resource set $\mathcal{R}$ as Read($\mathcal{R}$); in section 4.3 we shall use a similar notation for lock (Lock($\mathcal{R}$)) and unlock (Unlock($\mathcal{R}$)) operations.

Definition 12 (Simplified read-write transaction). *For a CT Γ, a write transaction T and a database state D, any transaction of the form*

$$T' = \text{Read}(\mathcal{R}(\Sigma)) \circ T_S$$

is a simplified read-write transaction of T wrt Γ and D, where T_S is the simplified write transaction of T wrt Γ and D, and Σ is a CWP of Γ wrt $\overline{T}$. The execution of T' is legal iff T_S starts at D.

A schedule executes legally if all its transactions do. For a schedule σ containing read operations, we write D^σ as a shorthand for D^{σ_w}, where σ_w is the sequence that contains all the write operations as in σ and in the same order, but no read operation. Note that a legal schedule over simplified read-write transactions is not guaranteed to execute correctly.

Example 3. [1 continued] Let us consider the transactions $T_1 = \langle f(bart, homer)\rangle$ and $T_2 = \langle f(bart, ned)\rangle$. Any schedule σ over T_1, T_2 yields an inconsistent database state, i.e., $D^\sigma(\Gamma) = \text{false}$ for any state D, because *bart* would end up having (at least) two different fathers. We therefore consider schedules over the simplified read-write transactions corresponding to T_1 and T_2. Suitable CWPs of Γ wrt $\overline{T}_i$, $i = 1, 2$, are given by Simp by instantiating the parameters with the actual constants in the parametric simplification found in example 1:

$$\Sigma_1 = \text{Simp}^{\overline{T}_1}(\{\Gamma\}) = \{\leftarrow f(bart, y) \wedge y \neq homer\}$$
$$\Sigma_2 = \text{Simp}^{\overline{T}_2}(\{\Gamma\}) = \{\leftarrow f(bart, y) \wedge y \neq ned\}.$$

---

[1] The empty sequence.

In this way a schedule such as

$$\sigma_1 = \text{Read}(\mathcal{R}(\Sigma_1)) \circ \langle \text{write}(f(bart, homer)) \rangle \circ \text{Read}(\mathcal{R}(\Sigma_2)) \circ \langle \text{write}(f(bart, ned)) \rangle$$

would not be a legal schedule over simplified read-write transactions, because in the database state after the last Read, Σ_2 necessarily evaluates to *false*. However it is still possible to create legal schedules leading to an inconsistent final state. Consider, e.g., the following schedule:

$$\sigma_2 = \text{Read}(\mathcal{R}(\Sigma_1)) \circ \text{Read}(\mathcal{R}(\Sigma_2)) \circ \langle \text{write}(f(bart, homer)), \text{write}(f(bart, ned)) \rangle.$$

At the end of the $\text{Read}(\mathcal{R}(\Sigma_2))$ sequence, T_1 has not yet performed the write operation on f, so Σ_2 can evaluate to *true*, but the final state is inconsistent. □

4.3 Locks

The problem pointed out in example 3 is due to the fact that some of the elements in the resource set of a CWP of a transaction T were modified by another transaction before T finished its execution. In order to prevent this situation we need to introduce locks. A lock is an operation of the form lock(e) where e is a database element; the lock on e is released with the dual operation unlock(e). A transaction containing lock and unlock operations is a *locked transaction*. A scheduler for locked transactions verifies that the transactions behave consistently with the locking policy, i.e., database elements are only accessed by transactions that have acquired the lock on them, no two transactions have a lock on the same element at the same time and all acquired locks are released. The two-phase locking (2PL) protocol requires that in every transaction all lock operations precede all unlock operations; all 2PL transactions are conflict serializable.

We can now extend the notion of simplified read-write transaction with locks on the set of resources that are read at the beginning of the transaction and on the elements to be written.

Definition 13 (Simplified locked transaction). *For a CT Γ, a write transaction T and a database state D, any transaction of the form*

$$T' = \text{Lock}(\mathcal{R}(\Sigma)) \circ \text{Read}(\mathcal{R}(\Sigma)) \circ \text{Lock}(\mathcal{R}(\overline{T}_S)) \circ T_S \circ \text{Unlock}(\mathcal{R}(\overline{T}_S) \cup \mathcal{R}(\Sigma))$$

is a simplified locked transaction of T wrt Γ and D, where T_S is the simplified write transaction of T wrt Γ and D, and Σ is a CWP of Γ wrt $\overline{T}$. The execution of T' is legal iff T_S starts at D.

Any legal schedule over simplified locked transactions is guaranteed to be correct. For such a schedule σ, we write D^σ as a shorthand for D^{σ_w}, where σ_w is the sequence that contains all the write operations as in σ and in the same order, but no read, lock or unlock operation.

Theorem 1. *Let Γ be a CT and D a database state such that $D(\Gamma) = true$. Given the write transactions $T_1, \ldots, T_n$, let T'_i be the simplified locked transaction of T_i wrt Γ and the state D_i reached after the last Lock in T'_i, for $1 \leq i \leq n$. Then any legal schedule σ over $\{T'_1, \ldots, T'_n\}$ is conflict serializable and $D^\sigma(\Gamma) = true$.*

The result of theorem 1 describes a transaction system in which all possible schedules execute correctly. However, the database performance can vary dramatically, depending on the chosen schedule, on the database state and on the waits due to the locks. For this reason, we observe that if the CWPs in use in the simplified locked transactions are minimal according to the resource set criterion, then the amount of locked database resources is also minimized, which increases the database throughput. It is not possible to obtain a minimal simplification *in all cases*, as query containment (which is in general undecidable) and simplification can be reduced to one another. Anyhow, any good approximation of an ideal simplification procedure, i.e., one which might occasionally contain some redundancy, will be useful as a component of an architecture for transaction management based on our principles. For example, the procedure of [3] produced optimal results for non-recursive databases in all examples we tested.

5 Discussion

The proposed approach describes a schedule construction policy that guarantees conflict serializability and correctness, which are essential qualities in any concurrent database system. There are several evident improvements wrt previous approaches. Firstly, it complies with the semantics of deferred integrity checking (i.e., ICs do *not* have to hold in intermediate transaction states), as opposed to what transaction transformation techniques for view maintenance typically offer. Secondly, it features an early detection of inconsistency — before the execution of the update and without simulating the updated state — that allows one to avoid executions of illegal transactions and subsequent rollbacks. This requires the introduction of locks, whose amount is, however, minimized and, in the case of well designed transactions, often null. Consider, e.g., a referential IC and an update that inserts both the referencing and the referenced tuple: no lock and no check are needed with our approach, whereas an (immediate) view maintenance approach would require two checks. Experiments were run with the help of a prototype of the simplification procedure [13], and implemented as stored procedures, on the ICs described in [17], that include rather large sets of complex ICs. An initial comparison with the simplification method of [17][2], has shown that we can save up to 75% of the execution time upon illegal transactions, whereas the performance is similar when the transactions are legal. We also stress that complex ICs, such as arbitrary functional dependencies, beyond key and foreign key constraints, are necessary to capture the semantics of complex scenarios[3].

The presented approach can be further refined in a number of ways. For example, we have implicitly assumed *exclusive* locks so far; however, a higher degree of concurrency is obtained, without affecting theorem 1, by using *shared* locks on $\mathcal{R}(\Sigma)$ and *update* locks on $\mathcal{R}(\overline{T}_S)$ in definition 13. Besides, to achieve serializability, a so-called *predicate lock* (PL) needs to be used on the condition given by the simplified ICs; as is well-known, PLs require a high computational

---

[2] Shown by its authors to perform better than previous approaches, such as [11].
[3] However, in some cases, they may be a symptom of a badly designed schema.

effort and, implementation-wise, are approximated as *index locks*. To this end, performance is highly improved by adding an index for every argument position occupied by an update parameter in a database literal in the simplified ICs. Finally, we note that, although the introduced locks may determine deadlocks, all standard deadlock detection and prevention techniques are still applicable. For instance, an arbitrary deadlocked transaction T can be restarted after unlocking its resources and granting them to the other deadlocked transactions.

References

1. S. Ceri and J. Widom. Deriving production rules for constraint maintainance. In D. McLeod, R. Sacks-Davis, and H.-J. Schek, editors, *16th International Conference on Very Large Data Bases*, pages 566–577. Morgan Kaufmann, 1990.
2. U. S. Chakravarthy, J. Grant, and J. Minker. Foundations of semantic query optimization for deductive databases. In *Foundations of Deductive Databases and Logic Programming*, pages 243–273. Morgan Kaufmann, 1988.
3. H. Christiansen and D. Martinenghi. Simplification of database integrity constraints revisited: A transformational approach. In M. Bruynooghe, editor, *LOP-STR'03*, volume 3018 of *LNCS*, pages 178–197. Springer, 2004.
4. H. Decker. Translating advanced integrity checking technology to sql. In *Database integrity: challenges and solutions*, pages 203–249. Idea Group Publishing, 2002.
5. H. Decker and M. Celma. a slick procedure for integrity checking in deductive databases. In P. Van Hentenryck, editor,*ICLP '94*, pages 456–469.MIT Press,1994.
6. H. Garcia-Molina, J. D. Ullman, and J. Widom. *Database Systems. The complete book*. Prentice-Hall, 2002.
7. P. Godfrey, J. Grant, J. Gryz, and J. Minker. Integrity constraints: Semantics and applications. In *Logics for Databases and Information Systems*, pages 265–306. Kluwer, 1998.
8. J. Grant and J. Minker. Integrity constraints in knowledge based systems. In H. Adeli, editor, *Knowl. Eng. Vol II, Applications*, pages 1–25. McGraw-Hill, 1990.
9. A. Gupta and I. S. Mumick (eds.). *Materialized Views. Techniques, Implementations, and Applications*. MIT Press, 1999.
10. L. Henschen, W. McCune, and S. Naqvi. Compiling constraint-checking programs from first-order formulas. In H. Gallaire, J. Minker, and J.-M. Nicolas, editors, *ADT'88*, volume 2, pages 145–169. Plenum Press, New York, 1984.
11. J. W. Lloyd, L. Sonenberg, and R. W. Topor. Integrity constraint checking in stratified databases. *JLP*, 4(1):331–343, 1987.
12. D. Martinenghi. Optimal database locks for efficient integrity checking. In *ADBIS (Local Proceedings)*, pages 64–77, 2004.
13. D. Martinenghi. A simplification procedure for integrity constraints. http://www.dat.ruc.dk/~dm/spic/index.html, 2004.
14. J.-M. Nicolas. Logic for improving integrity checking in relational data bases. *Acta Informatica*, 18:227–253, 1982.
15. U. Nilsson and J. Małuzyński. *Logic, Programming and Prolog (2nd ed.)*. John Wiley & Sons Ltd, 1995.
16. K. Salem, H. Garcia-Molina, and J. Shands. Altruistic locking. *ACM Trans. Database Syst.*, 19(1):117–165, 1994.
17. R. Seljée and H. C. M. de Swart. Three types of redundancy in integrity checking: An optimal solution. *Data & Knowledge Engineering*, 30(2):135–151, 1999.

An Optimal Skew-Insensitive Join and Multi-join Algorithm for Distributed Architectures

Mostafa Bamha

LIFO - CNRS, Université d'Orléans, B.P. 6759, 45067 Orléans Cedex 2, France
bamha@lifo.univ-orleans.fr

Abstract. The development of scalable parallel database systems requires the design of efficient algorithms for the join operation which is the most frequent and expensive operation in relational database systems. The join is also the most vulnerable operation to data skew and to the high cost of communication in distributed architectures.

In this paper, we present a new parallel algorithm for join and multi-join operations on distributed architectures based on an efficient semi-join computation technique. This algorithm is proved to have *optimal complexity* and *deterministic perfect load balancing*. Its tradeoff between balancing overhead and speedup is analyzed using the BSP cost model which predicts a negligible join product skew and a linear speed-up. This algorithm improves our *fa_join* and *sfa_join* algorithms by reducing their communication and synchronization cost to a minimum while offering the same load balancing properties even for highly skewed data.

1 Introduction

The appeal of parallel processing becomes very strong in applications which require ever higher performance and particularly in applications such as: data-warehousing, decision support and OLAP (On-Line Analytical Processing). Parallelism can greatly increase processing power in such applications [7,1]. However parallelism can only maintain acceptable performance through efficient algorithms realizing complex queries on dynamic, irregular and distributed data. Such algorithms must be designed to fully exploit the processing power of multi-processor machines and the ability to evenly divide load among processors while minimizing local computation and communication costs inherent to multiprocessor machines. Join is very sensitive to the problem of data skew which can have a disastrous effect on performance [6,4,13,10,9,15,8] due to the high costs of communications and synchronizations in distributed architectures [4,5,2].

Many algorithms have been proposed to handle data skew for join operations [13,10,9]. Such algorithms are not efficient for many reasons:

- the presented algorithms are not scalable (and thus cannot guarantee linear speedup) because their routing decisions are generally performed by a coordinator processor while the other processors are idle,
- they cannot avoid load imbalance between processors because they base their routing decisions on incomplete or statistical information,

– they cannot solve data skew problem because data redistribution is generally based on hashing data into buckets and hashing is known to be inefficient in the presence of high frequencies.

In this paper we present a new parallel join algorithm called Osfa_join (Optimal symmetric frequency adaptive join algorithm) for Shared Nothing machines (i.e architectures where memory and disks are distributed). This algorithm has optimal complexity, perfect balancing properties and supports flexible control of communications induced by intra-transaction parallelism. The Osfa_join algorithm is based on an optimal technique for semi-joins computation, presented in [5], and on an improved version of the redistribution algorithm of sfa-join [4] which efficiently avoids the problem of attribute value- and join product skews while reducing the communication and synchronization costs to a minimum.

This algorithm guarantees a perfect balancing of the load of the different processors during all the stages of the data redistribution because the data redistribution is carried out jointly by all processors (and not by a coordinator processor). Each processor deals with the redistribution of the data associated to a subset of the join attribute values, not necessarily its "own" values.

The performance of Osfa_join is analyzed using the scalable and portable Bulk-synchronous parallel (BSP) cost model [14]. It predicts a negligible join product skew and a linear speed-up, independently of the data and of the (shared nothing) architecture's bandwidth, latency and number of processors.

2 PDBMS, Join Operations and Data Skew

Join is an expensive and frequently used operation whose parallelization is highly desirable. The *join* of two tables or relations R and S on attribute A of R and attribute B of S is the relation, written $R \bowtie S$, containing the pairs of tuples from R and S for which $R.A = S.B$. The semi-join of S by R is the relation $S \ltimes R$ composed of the tuples of S which occur in the join of R and S. Semi-join reduces the size of relations to be joined and $R \bowtie S = R \bowtie (S \ltimes R) = (R \ltimes S) \bowtie (S \ltimes R)$.

Parallel join usually proceeds in two phases: a redistribution phase by join attribute hashing and then sequential join of local table fragments. Many such algorithms have been proposed. The principal ones are: *Sort-merge join, Simple-hash join, Grace-hash join* and *Hybrid-hash join* [12]. All of them (called hashing algorithms) are based on hashing functions which redistribute relations so that tuples having the same attribute value are forwarded to the same node. Local joins are then computed and their union is the output relation. Their major disadvantage is to be vulnerable to both *attribute value skew* (imbalance of the output of the redistribution phase) and *join product skew* (imbalance of the output of local joins) [13,11]. The former affects immediate performance and the latter affects the efficiency of output or pipelined multi-join operations.

To address the problem of data skew, we introduced fa_join algorithm in [3,6], to avoid the problem of AVS and JPS. However, its performance is suboptimal when computing the join of highly skewed relations because of unnecessary redistribution and communication costs. We introduce here a new parallel algorithm called Osfa_join (Optimal symmetric frequency adaptive join algorithm) to perform such joins. Osfa_join improves on the sfa_join algorithm introduced in [4] by its optimal complexity by using a new approach for semi-joins computation introduced recently in [5]. Its predictably low join-product and attribute-value skew make it suitable for repeated use in multi-join operations. Its performance is analyzed using the scalable BSP cost model which predicts a linear speedup and an optimal complexity even for highly skewed data.

3 Data Redistribution: An Optimal Approach

In this section, we present an improvement of the algorithm sfa_join [4] called Osfa_join (*Optimal symmetric frequency adaptive join algorithm*) with an optimal complexity. The major difference between sfa_join and Osfa_join lies in the manner of computing semi-joins. We point out that, for semi-joins computation, sfa_join algorithm broadcasts the histograms $Hist_i(R \bowtie S)_{i=1..,p}$ to all processors. Thus, each processor has a local access to the whole histogram $Hist(R \bowtie S)$ to compute local semi-joins. This is not, in general, necessary. In the Osfa_join algorithm, the semi-joins computation is carried out in an optimal way without this stage of broadcast using the techniques presented in [5].

We first assume that relation R (resp. S) is partitioned among processors by horizontal fragmentation and the fragments R_i for $i = 1,..,p$ are almost of the same size on every processor, i.e. $|R_i| \simeq \frac{|R|}{p}$ where p is the number of processors. In the rest of this paper we use the following notation for each relation $T \in \{R, S\}$:

- T_i denotes the fragment of relation T placed on processor i,
- $Hist(T)$ denotes the histogram[1] of relation T with respect to the join attribute value, i.e. a list of pairs (v, n_v) where $n_v \neq 0$ is the number of tuples of relation T having the value v for the join attribute,
- $Hist(T_i)$ denotes the histogram of fragment T_i,
- $Hist_i(T)$ is processor i's fragment of the histogram of T,
- $Hist(T)(v)$ is the frequency n_v of value v in relation T,
- $\|T\|$ denotes the number of tuples of relation T, and
- $|T|$ denotes the size (expressed in bytes or number of pages) of relation T.

In the following, we will describe Osfa_join redistribution algorithm while giving an upper bound on the BSP execution time of each phase. The $O(...)$ notation only hides small constant factors: they depend on the implementation program but neither on data nor on the BSP machine parameters.

Our redistribution algorithm is the basis for efficient and scalable join processing. It proceeds in 4 phases:

Phase 1: Creating local histograms

Local histograms $Hist(R_i)_{i=1,...,p}$ (resp. $Hist(S_i)_{i=1,...,p}$) of blocks R_i (resp. S_i) are created in parallel by a scan of the fragment R_i (resp. S_i) on processor i

---

[1] Histograms are implemented as balanced trees (B-tree): a data structure that maintains an ordered set of data to allow efficient search and insert operations.

in time $c_{i/o} * \max_{i=1,...,p} |R_i|$ (resp. $c_{i/o} * \max_{i=1,...,p} |S_i|$) where $c_{i/o}$ is the cost to read/write a page of data from disk. In principle, this phase costs:

$$Time_{phase1} = O(c_{i/o} * \max_{i=1,...,p}(|R_i| + |S_i|)),$$

but in practice, the extra cost for this operation is negligible because the histograms can be computed on the fly while creating local hash tables.

Phase 2: Local Semi-joins computation

In order to minimize the redistribution cost and thus the communication time between processors, we then compute the following local semi-joins: $\widetilde{R_i} = R_i \ltimes S$ (resp. $\widetilde{S_i} = S_i \ltimes R$) using proposition 2 presented in [5] in time:

$$Time_{phase2} = O\Big(\min\big(g*|Hist(R)| + \|Hist(R)\|, g*\frac{|R|}{p} + \frac{\|R\|}{p}\big) + \max_{i=1,...,p} \|R_i\|$$
$$+ \min\big(g*|Hist(S)| + \|Hist(S)\|, g*\frac{|S|}{p} + \frac{\|S\|}{p}\big) + \max_{i=1,...,p} \|S_i\| + l\Big),$$

where g is BSP communication parameter and l the cost of a barrier of synchronisation [14].

We recall (cf. to proposition 1 in [5]) that, in the above equation, for a relation $T \in \{R, S\}$ the term $\min\big(g*|Hist(T)| + \|Hist(T)\|, g*\frac{|T|}{p} + \frac{\|T\|}{p}\big)$ is time to compute $Hist_{i=1,...,p}(T)$ starting from the local histograms $Hist(T_i)_{i=1,...,p}$ and during semi-joins computation, we store an extra information called $index(d) \in \{1, 2, 3\}$ for each value $d \in Hist(R \bowtie S)$ [2]. This information will allow us to decide if, for a given value d, the frequencies of tuples of relations R and S having the value d are greater (resp. lesser) than a threshold frequency f_0. It also permits us to choose dynamically the probe and the build relation for each value d of the join attribute. This choice reduces the global redistribution cost to a minimum.
In the rest of this paper, we use the same threshold frequency as in fa_join algorithm [3,6,4], i.e. $f_0 = p * log(p)$. For a given value $d \in Hist(R \bowtie S)$,

- the value $index(d) = 3$, means that the frequency of tuples of relations R and S, associated to value d, are less than the threshold frequency. $Hist(R)(d) < f_0$ and $Hist(S)(d) < f_0$,
- the value $index(d) = 2$, means that $Hist(S)(d) \geq f_0$ and $Hist(S)(d) > Hist(R)(d)$,
- the value $index(d) = 1$, means that $Hist(R)(d) \geq f_0$ and $Hist(R)(d) \geq Hist(S)(d)$.

Note that, unlike hash-based algorithms where both relation R and S are redistributed, we will only redistribute $R \ltimes S$ and $S \ltimes R$ to perform the join operation $R \bowtie S$. This will reduce communication costs to a minimum.
At the end of this phase, on each processor i, the semi-join $\widetilde{R_i} = R_i \ltimes S$ (resp. $\widetilde{S_i} = S_i \ltimes R$) is divided into three sub-relations in the following way:

$$\widetilde{R_i} = \widetilde{R'_i} \cup \widetilde{R''_i} \cup \widetilde{R'''_i} \quad \text{and} \quad \widetilde{S_i} = \widetilde{S'_i} \cup \widetilde{S''_i} \cup \widetilde{S'''_i} \quad \text{where:}$$

---

[2] The size of $Hist(R \bowtie S)$ is generally very small compared to $|Hist(R)|$ and $|Hist(S)|$ because $Hist(R \bowtie S)$ contains only values that appears in both relations R and S.

- All the tuples of relation $\widetilde{R'_i}$ (resp. $\widetilde{S'_i}$) are associated to values d such that $index(d) = 1$ (resp. $index(d) = 2$),
- All the tuples of relation $\widetilde{R''_i}$ (resp. $\widetilde{S''_i}$) are associated to values d such that $index(d) = 2$ (resp. $index(d) = 1$),
- All the tuples of relations $\widetilde{R'''_i}$ and $\widetilde{S'''_i}$ are associated to values d such that $index(d) = 3$, i.e. the tuples associated to values which occur with frequencies less than a threshold frequency f_0 in both relations R and S.

Tuples of relations $\widetilde{R'_i}$ and $\widetilde{S'_i}$ are associated to high frequencies for the join attribute. These tuples have an important effect on attribute value and join product skews. They will be redistributed using an appropriate redistribution algorithm to efficiently avoid both AVS and JPS. However the tuples of relations $\widetilde{R'''_i}$ and $\widetilde{S'''_i}$ (are associated to very low frequencies for the join attribute) have no effect neither on AVS nor JPS. These tuples will be redistributed using a hash function.

Phase 3: Creation of communication templates

The attribute values which could lead to attribute value skew (those having high frequencies) are also those which may cause join product skew in standard algorithms. To avoid the slowdown usually caused by attribute value skew and the imbalance of the size of local joins processed by the standard algorithms, an appropriate treatment for high attribute frequencies is needed.

3.a To this end, we partition the histogram $Hist(R \bowtie S)$ into two sub-histograms: $Hist^{(1,2)}(R \bowtie S)$ and $Hist^{(3)}(R \bowtie S)$ in the following manner:

- the values $d \in Hist^{(1,2)}(R \bowtie S)$ are associated to high frequencies of the join attribute (i.e. $index(d) = 1$ or $index(d) = 2$),
- the values $d \in Hist^{(3)}(R \bowtie S)$ are associated to low frequencies of the join attribute (i.e. $index(d) = 3$),

this partition step is performed in parallel, on each processor i, by a local traversal of the histogram $Hist_i(R \bowtie S)$ in time:

$$Time_{3.a} = O(\max_{i=1,\ldots,p} \|Hist_i(R \bowtie S)\|).$$

3.b Communication templates for high frequencies

We first create a communication template: the list of messages which constitute the relations' redistribution. This step is performed jointly by all processors, **each one not necessarily computing the list of its own messages, so as to balance the overall process.**

Processor i computes a set of necessary messages relating to the values d it owns in $Hist_i^{(1,2)}(R \bowtie S)$. The communication template is derived from the following mapping, its intended result. For relation $T \in \{\widetilde{R'}, \widetilde{S'}\}$, tuples of T are mapped to multiple nodes as follows:

if $\big(Hist(T)(d) \quad mod(p) = 0\big)$ **then**

    each processor j will hold : $block_j(d) = \frac{Hist(T)(d)}{p}$ of tuples of value d.

else

  begin

    - Pick a random value j_0 between 0 and $(p-1)$

    - **if** (processor index j is between j_0 and $j_0 + (Hist(T)(d) \quad mod(p))$) **then**

      the processor of index j will hold a block of size : $block_j(d) = \lfloor\frac{Hist(T)(d)}{p}\rfloor + 1$

    else

      processor of index j will hold a block of size : $block_j(d) = \lfloor\frac{Hist(T)(d)}{p}\rfloor$.

  end.

where $\lfloor x \rfloor$ is the largest integral value not greater than x and $block_j(d)$ be the number of tuples of value d that processor j should own after redistribution of the fragments T_i of relation T.

The absolute value of $Rest_j(d) = Hist_j(T)(d) - block_j(d)$ determines the number of tuples of value d that processor j must send (if $Rest_j(d) > 0$) or receive (if $Rest_j(d) < 0$).

For $d \in Hist_i^{(1,2)}(R \bowtie S)$, processor i owns a description of the layout of tuples of value d over the network. It may therefore determine the number of tuples of value d which every processor must send/receive. This information constitutes the communication template. Only those j for which $Rest_j(d) > 0$ (resp. < 0) send (resp. receive) tuples of value d. This step is thus completed in time : $Time_{3.b} = O(\|Hist^{(1,2)}(R \bowtie S)\|)$.

The tuples associated to low frequencies (i.e. tuples having $d \in Hist_i^{(3)}(R \bowtie S)$) have no effect neither on the AVS nor the JPS. These tuples are simply mapped to processors using a hash function and thus no communication template computation is needed.

The creation of communication templates has therefore taken the sum of the above two steps :

$$Time_{phase3} = Time_{3.a} + Time_{3.b} = O(\max_{i=1,..,p} \|Hist_i(R \bowtie S)\| + \|Hist^{(1,2)}(R \bowtie S)\|).$$

Phase 4: Data redistribution

4.a Redistribution of tuples having $d \in Hist_i^{(1,2)}(R \bowtie S)$:

Every processor i holds, for every one of its local $d \in Hist_i^{(1,2)}(R \bowtie S)$, the non-zero communication volumes it prescribes as a part of communication template : $Rest_j(d) \neq 0$ for $j = 1,..,p$. This information will take the form of *sending orders* sent to their target in a first superstep, followed then by the actual redistribution superstep where processors obey all orders they have received.

Each processor i first splits the processors indices j in two groups : those for which $Rest_j(d) > 0$ and those for which $Rest_j(d) < 0$. This is done by a sequential traversal of the $Rest_{..}(d)$ array.

Let α (resp. β) be the number of j's where $Rest_j(d)$ is positive (resp. negative) and $Proc(k)_{k=1,..\alpha+\beta}$ the array of processor indices for which $Rest_j(d) \neq 0$ in the manner that :

$$\begin{cases} Rest_{Proc(j)}(d) > 0 & for \quad j = 1,..,\alpha \\ Rest_{Proc(j)}(d) < 0 & for \quad j = (\alpha+1),..,\beta \end{cases}$$

A sequential traversal of $Proc(k)_{k=1,..\alpha+\beta}$ determines the number of tuples that each processor j will send. The sending orders concerning attribute value d are computed using the following procedure:

$i := 1; \quad j := \alpha + 1;$
while $(i \leq \alpha)$ **do**
    begin
        * n_tuples=min($Rest_{Proc(i)}(d), -Rest_{Proc(j)}(d)$);
        * order_to_send(Proc(i),Proc(j),d,n_tuples);
        * $Rest_{Proc(i)}(d) := Rest_{Proc(i)}(d) -$ n_tuples;
        * $Rest_{Proc(j)}(d) := Rest_{Proc(j)}(d) +$ n_tuples;
        * **if** $Rest_{Proc(i)}(d) = 0$ **then** $i := i+1$; **endif**
        * **if** $Rest_{Proc(j)}(d) = 0$ **then** $j := j+1$; **endif**
    end.

---

of complexity $O(\|Hist^{(1,2)}(R \bowtie S)\|)$ because for a given d, no more than $(p-1)$ processors can send data and each processor i is in charge of redistribution of tuples having $d \in Hist_i^{(1,2)}(R \bowtie S)$.

For each processor i and $d \in Hist_i^{(1,2)}(R \bowtie S)$, all the orders order_to_send($j,i,...$) are sent to processor j when $j \neq i$ in time $O\left(g * |Hist^{(1,2)}(R \bowtie S)| + l\right)$.

In all, this step costs: $Time_{4.a} = O(g * |Hist^{(1,2)}(R \bowtie S)| + \|Hist^{(1,2)}(R \bowtie S)\| + l)$.

4.b Redistribution of tuples with values $d \in Hist_i^{(3)}(R \bowtie S)$:

Tuples of relations $\widetilde{R_i'''}$ and $\widetilde{S_i'''}$ (i.e. tuples having $d \in Hist_i^{(3)}(R \bowtie S)$) are associated to low frequencies, they have no effect neither on the AVS nor the JPS. These relations are redistributed using a hash function.

At the end of steps 4.a and 4.b, each processor i, has local knowledge of how the tuples of semi joins $\widetilde{R_i}$ and $\widetilde{S_i}$ will be redistributed. Redistribution is then performed, in time: $Time_{4.b} = O(g * (|\widetilde{R_i}| + |\widetilde{S_i}|) + l)$.

Phase 4, has therefore taken the sum of the above two costs:

$$Time_{phase4} = O(g * \max_{i=1,..,p}(|\widetilde{R_i}| + |\widetilde{S_i}| + |Hist^{(1,2)}(R \bowtie S)|) + \|Hist^{(1,2)}(R \bowtie S)\| + l),$$

and the complete redistribution algorithm costs:

$$Time_{redist} = O\Big(c_{i/o} * \max_{i=1..p}(|R_i| + |S_i|) + \min\big(g*|Hist(R)| + \|Hist(R)\|, g*\frac{|R|}{p} + \frac{\|R\|}{p}\big)$$

$$+ \max_{i=1..p}\|R_i\| + \max_{i=1..p}\|S_i\| + \min\big(g*|Hist(S)| + \|Hist(S)\|, g*\frac{|S|}{p} + \frac{\|S\|}{p}\big)$$

$$+ g*(|\widetilde{R_i}| + |\widetilde{S_i}| + |Hist^{(1,2)}(R \bowtie S)|) + \|Hist^{(1,2)}(R \bowtie S)\| + l\Big). \quad (1)$$

We mention that, we only redistribute the semi-joins $\widetilde{R_i}$ and $\widetilde{S_i}$. Note that $|\widetilde{R_i}|$ (resp. $|\widetilde{S_i}|$) is generally very small compared to $|R_i|$ (resp. $|S_i|$) and $|Hist(R \bowtie S)|$ is generally very small compared to $|Hist(R)|$ and $|Hist(S)|$. Thus we reduce the communication cost to a minimum.

4 Osfa_join : An Optimal Skew-insensitive Join Algorithm

To perform the join of two relations R and S, we first redistribute relations R and S using the above redistribution algorithm at the cost of $Time_{redist}$ (see equation 1 in previous section).

Once the redistribution phase is completed, the semi-joins $\widetilde{R_i}$ (resp. $\widetilde{S_i}$) are partitioned into three disjoint relations as follow: $\widetilde{R_i} = \widetilde{R'_i} \cup \widetilde{R''_i} \cup \widetilde{R'''_i}$ (resp. $\widetilde{S_i} = \widetilde{S'_i} \cup \widetilde{S''_i} \cup \widetilde{S'''_i}$) as described in phase 2.
Taking advantage of the identities:

$$R \bowtie S = \widetilde{R} \bowtie \widetilde{S} = (\widetilde{R'} \cup \widetilde{R''} \cup \widetilde{R'''}) \bowtie (\widetilde{S'} \cup \widetilde{S''} \cup \widetilde{S'''})$$
$$= (\widetilde{R'} \bowtie \widetilde{S''}) \cup (\widetilde{R''} \bowtie \widetilde{S'}) \cup (\widetilde{R'''} \bowtie \widetilde{S'''})$$
$$= (\widetilde{R'} \bowtie \widetilde{S''}) \cup (\widetilde{R''} \bowtie \widetilde{S'}) \cup (\widetilde{R'''} \bowtie \widetilde{S'''})$$
$$= (\bigcup_i \widetilde{R'_i} \bowtie \widetilde{S''}) \cup (\bigcup_i \widetilde{R''} \bowtie \widetilde{S'_i}) \cup (\bigcup_i \widetilde{R'''_i} \bowtie \widetilde{S'''_i}). \qquad (2)$$

Frequencies of tuples of relations $\widetilde{R'_i}$ (resp. $\widetilde{S'_i}$) are by definition greater than the corresponding (matching) tuples in relations $\widetilde{S''_i}$ (resp. $\widetilde{R''_i}$). Fragments $\widetilde{R'_i}$ (resp. $\widetilde{S'_i}$) will be thus chosen as *build* relations and $\widetilde{S''_i}$ (resp. $\widetilde{R''_i}$) as *probe* relations to be duplicated on each processor. This improves over fa_join where all the semi-join $S \ltimes R$ is duplicated. It reduces communications costs significantly in asymmetric cases where both relations contain frequent and infrequent values.

To perform the join $R \bowtie S$, it is sufficient to compute the three following local joins $\widetilde{R'_i} \bowtie \widetilde{S''}$, $\widetilde{R''} \bowtie \widetilde{S'_i}$ and $\widetilde{R'''_i} \bowtie \widetilde{S'''_i}$ (cf. equation 2). To this end, we first broadcast the fragments $\widetilde{R''_i}$ (resp. $\widetilde{S''_i}$) to all processors in time:

$$Time_{step.a} = O(g * (|\widetilde{R''}| + |\widetilde{S''}|) + l).$$

Local joins $\widetilde{R'_i} \bowtie \widetilde{S''}$, $\widetilde{R''} \bowtie \widetilde{S'_i}$ and $\widetilde{R'''_i} \bowtie \widetilde{S'''_i}$ could be done in time:

$$Time_{step.b} = c_{i/o} * O\Big(\max_{i:1,..,p}(|\widetilde{R'_i}| + |\widetilde{S''}| + |\widetilde{R'_i} \bowtie \widetilde{S''}|) + \max_{i:1,..,p}(|\widetilde{R''}| + |\widetilde{S'_i}| + |\widetilde{R''} \bowtie \widetilde{S'_i}|)$$
$$+ \max_{i:1,..,p}(|\widetilde{R'''_i}| + |\widetilde{S'''_i}| + |\widetilde{R'''_i} \bowtie \widetilde{S'''_i}|)\Big)$$
$$= c_{i/o} * O\Big(\max_{i:1,..,p}(|\widetilde{R'_i} \bowtie \widetilde{S''}| + |\widetilde{R'_i} \bowtie \widetilde{S''}| + |\widetilde{R''} \bowtie \widetilde{S'''_i}|)\Big). \qquad (3)$$

The equation 3 holds due to the fact that the join size is at least equal to the maximum of the semi-joins sizes.
The cost of the local join computation is thus the sum of the two costs above:

$$Time_{local-join} = Time_{step.a} + Time_{step.b}$$
$$= O(g * (|\widetilde{R''}| + |\widetilde{S''}|) + c_{i/o} * \max_{i:1,..,p}(|\widetilde{R'_i} \bowtie \widetilde{S''}| + |\widetilde{R''} \bowtie \widetilde{S'_i}| + |\widetilde{R'''_i} \bowtie \widetilde{S'''_i}|) + l).$$

The global cost of the join of relations R and S using Osfa_join algorithm is the sum of redistribution cost with local join computation cost. It is of the order:

$$Time_{Osfa\_join} = O\Big(c_{i/o} * \max_{i=1,..,p}(|R_i| + |S_i|) + \max_{i=1,..,p}\|R_i\| + \max_{i=1,..,p}\|S_i\| + l$$

$$+ \min\left(g * |Hist(R)| + \|Hist(R)\|, \; g * \frac{|R|}{p} + \frac{\|R\|}{p}\right)$$
$$+ \min\left(g * |Hist(S)| + \|Hist(S)\|, \; g * \frac{|S|}{p} + \frac{\|S\|}{p}\right)$$
$$+ g * (|\widetilde{R_i}| + |\widetilde{S_i}| + |Hist^{(1,2)}(R \bowtie S)|) + \|Hist^{(1,2)}(R \bowtie S)\|$$
$$+ g * (|\widetilde{R''}| + |\widetilde{S''}|) + c_{i/o} * \max_{i:1,\dots,p}\left(|\widetilde{R'_i} \bowtie \widetilde{S''}| + |\widetilde{R''} \bowtie \widetilde{S'_i}| + |\widetilde{R'''_i} \bowtie \widetilde{S'''_i}|\right).$$

The join of relations R and S using the Osfa_join algorithm, avoid JPS because the values which could lead to attribute value skew (those having high frequencies) are those which often cause the join product skew. This values are mapped to multiple nodes so that local joins have almost the same sizes. It avoids thus, the slowdown usually caused by attribute value skew and the imbalance of the size of local joins processed by the standard algorithms. We recall that, the redistribution cost is minimal because redistribution concerns only tuples which are effectively present in the join result.

Note that, the size of $\widetilde{R''}$ (resp. $\widetilde{S''}$) est generally very small compared to the size of the join $\widetilde{R''} \bowtie \widetilde{S'_i}$ (resp. $\widetilde{R'_i} \bowtie \widetilde{S''}$) and the size of local join on each processor i, $|\widetilde{R'_i} \bowtie \widetilde{S''}| + |\widetilde{R''} \bowtie \widetilde{S'_i}| + |\widetilde{R'''_i} \bowtie \widetilde{S'''_i}|$, have almost the same size $\simeq \frac{|R \bowtie S|}{p}$.

Remark: Sequential join processing of two relations R and S requires at least the following lower bound: $bound_{inf_1} = \Omega\left(c_{i/o} * (|R| + |S| + |R \bowtie S|)\right)$.
Parallel processing with p processors requires therefore: $bound_{inf_p} = \frac{1}{p} * bound_{inf_1}$. and Osfa_join algorithm has *optimal* asymptotic complexity when:

$$|Hist^{(1,2)}(R \bowtie S)| \leq c_{i/o} * \max(\frac{|R|}{p}, \frac{|S|}{p}, \frac{|R \bowtie S|}{p}) \qquad (4)$$

this is due to the fact that, the local joins results have almost the same size and all the terms in $Time_{Osfa-join}$ are bounded by those of $bound_{inf_p}$. This inequality holds, if we choose a threshold frequency f_0 greater than p (which is the case for our threshold frequency $f_0 = p * log(p)$).

5 Conclusion

In this paper, we have introduced the first parallel join algorithm with **optimal complexity** based on an efficient semi-join algorithm introduced in [5] and on a "symmetric" sub-set replication technique allowing to reduce the communication costs to the minimum while guaranteeing near perfect balancing properties. The algorithm Osfa_join is proved to have an optimal complexity even in the presence of highly skewed data. Its predictably low join product skew makes it suitable for multi-join operations.

The performance of this algorithm was analyzed using the BSP cost model which predicts a linear speedup. The $O(\dots)$ notation only hides small constant factors: they depend only on the implementation but neither on data nor on the BSP machine. Our experience with the join operation [4,6,3,2] is evidence that the above theoretical analysis is accurate in practice.

References

1. M. Bamha, F. Bentayeb, and G. Hains. An efficient scalable parallel view maintenance algorithm for shared nothing multi-processor machines. In *the 10th International Conference on Database and Expert Systems Applications DEXA'99*, LNCS 1677, pages 616–625, Florence, Italy, 1999. Springer-Verlag.
2. M. Bamha and M. Exbrayat. Pipelining a skew-insensitive parallel join algorithm. *Parallel Processing Letters*, Volume 13(3), pages 317–328, 2003.
3. M. Bamha and G. Hains. A self-balancing join algorithm for SN machines. *Proceedings of International Conference on Parallel and Distributed Computing and Systems (PDCS)*, pages 285–290, Las Vegas, Nevada, USA, October 1998.
4. M. Bamha and G. Hains. A skew insensitive algorithm for join and multi-join operation on Shared Nothing machines. In *the 11th International Conference on Database and Expert Systems Applications DEXA'2000*, LNCS 1873, 2000.
5. M. Bamha and G. Hains. An efficient equi-semi-join algorithm for distributed architectures. In *the 5th International Conference on Computational Science (ICCS'2005). 22-25 May, Atlanta, USA*, LNCS 3515, pages 755–763, 2005.
6. M. Bamha and G. Hains. A frequency adaptive join algorithm for Shared Nothing machines. *Journal of Parallel and Distributed Computing Practices (PDCP)*, Volume 3, Number 3, pages 333-345, September 1999.
7. A. Datta, B. Moon, and H. Thomas. A case for parallelism in datawarehousing and OLAP. In *Ninth International Workshop on Database and Expert Systems Applications, DEXA 98*, IEEE Computer Society, pages 226–231, Vienna, 1998.
8. D. J. DeWitt, J. F. Naughton, D. A. Schneider, and S. Seshadri. Practical Skew Handling in Parallel Joins. In *Proceedings of the 18th VLDB Conference*, pages 27–40, Vancouver, British Columbia, Canada, 1992.
9. K. A. Hua and C. Lee. Handling data skew in multiprocessor database computers using partition tuning. In *Proc. of the 17th International Conference on Very Large Data Bases*, pages 525–535, Barcelona, Catalonia, Spain, 1991. Morgan Kaufmann.
10. M. Kitsuregawa and Y. Ogawa. Bucket spreading parallel hash: A new, robust, parallel hash join method for skew in the super database computer (SDC). *Very Large Data Bases: 16th International Conference on Very Large Data Bases, August 13–16, Brisbane, Australia*, pages 210–221, 1990.
11. V. Poosala and Y. E. Ioannidis. Estimation of query-result distribution and its application in parallel-join load balancing. *In: Proc. 22th Int. Conference on Very Large Database Systems, VLDB'96, pp. 448-459, Bombay, India*, September 1996.
12. D. Schneider and D. DeWitt. A performance evaluation of four parallel join algorithms in a shared-nothing multiprocessor environment. In *Proceedings of the 1989 ACM SIGMOD International Conference on the Management of Data, Portland, Oregon*, pages 110–121, New York, NY 10036, USA, 1989. ACM Press.
13. M. Seetha and P. S. Yu. Effectiveness of parallel joins. *IEEE, Transactions on Knowledge and Data Enginneerings*, 2(4):410–424, December 1990.
14. D. B. Skillicorn, J. M. D. Hill, and W. F. McColl. Questions and Answers about BSP. *Scientific Programming*, 6(3):249–274, 1997.
15. Joel L. Wolf, Daniel M. Dias, Philip S. Yu, and John Turek. New algorithms for parallelizing relational database joins in the presence of data skew. *IEEE Transactions on Knowledge and Data Engineering*, 6(6):990–997, 1994.

Evaluation and NLP[1]

Didier Nakache[1,2], Elisabeth Metais[1], and Jean François Timsit[3]

[1] CEDRIC /CNAM: 292 rue Saint Martin - 75003 Paris, France
[2] CRAMIF: 17 / 19 rue de Flandre - 75019 Paris, France
[3] Réanimation médicale CHU Grenoble INSERM U578 - 38043 Grenoble, France
datamining@wanadoo.fr, metais@cnam.fr,
jf.timsit@outcomerea.org

Abstract. F-measure is an indicator which has been commonly used for 25 years to evaluate classification algorithms in textmining, based on precision and recall. For classification and information retrieval, some prefer to use the break even point. Nevertheless, these measures have some inconvenient: they use a binary logic and don't allow to apply a user (judge) assessment. This paper proposes a new approach for evaluation. First, we distinguish classification and categorization from a semantic point of view. Then, we introduce a new measure: the K-measure, which is an overall of F-measure, and allows to apply user requirements. Finally, we propose a methodology for evaluation.

Keywords: evaluation, measure, classification, categorization, NLP.

1 Introduction

Natural language processing produces many algorithms for classification, clusterisation and information retrieval. The performance of these algorithms is computed from several measures, like precision and recall. To make the reading of performance easier, [Van Rijsbergen 79] created a synthetic measure: the F-measure, which is a combination of these two indicators. Today, needs are diversified, problems are more complex, but we have kept the same indicator for 25 years [Sparck Jones 2001]. Is this use still justified? Without renouncing to existing scales, how to integer new needs? In several domains, like in medicine, some users may consider that a medium result is a bad, or inappropriate, result. So, we had to find an indicator able to answer this problem, without losing qualities of existing measures.

To do this, we introduce our paper by precising the main concepts: evaluation, classification, categorization, and information retrieval. We will propose a definition for each one (section 2). Section 3 presents the state of the art for evaluation and main indicators. Finally, after having analyzed the F-measure properties (section 4), we will propose a new approach for evaluation, adapted for each case, and allowing to integrate user's requirements (section 5).

---

[1] This work is partially financed by MENRT for the RNTS Rhea project.

2 Etymology and Definitions

Terms 'classification' and 'clusterisation' have different histories and origins. No scientific definition could be found, except in Webster dictionary which gives two meanings for the word classification: 'taxonomy' and .... category.

According to the history of these two terms and their current meaning, **we propose to define classification** as being action of arranging a whole set into hierarchical or ordered structure, in existing classes or not, or the result of this action, and **clusterisation** as being action (or its result) of grouping elements with common characteristics. Nevertheless, in a classification, it will be possible to quantify or valorize the difference between proposition and requirement. We can consider an answer as being partially true, and associate a metric to the difference. Finally, **information retrieval** is different from classification and categorization by a great set of enabled answers (potentially infinite), by missing of referential, and often obligation of human evaluation. Classical application could be a web crawler, or AI answers to a request. With so many different tasks, evaluation methods and indicators can be different.

3 State of the Art

3.1 What Is Evaluation?

Evaluation consists in measuring the difference between an expected result and the final result. No metric is associated, but we use to generate a number between 0 and 1 without unity. Some elements are very subjective and can't be automated. Tefko Saracevic [Saracevic 70] insists on the main role of judge.

3.2 Indicators and Measures: Toward the F Measure

A system can answer to a request according to the following model:

	Pertinent	Not pertinent	Total
Found (or proposed)	a	B	a+b
Not found (or not proposed)	c	D	c+d
	a+c	b+d	a+b+c+d=N

From this contingency table, NLP community computes several distances:

precision = $a/(a+b)$, recall = $\frac{a}{a+c}$, pertinence= $\frac{a+d}{a+b+c+d}$, error = $\frac{b+c}{a+b+c+d}$,

fallout= $\frac{b}{b+d}$, silence = $\frac{c}{a+c}$, specificity = $\frac{d}{b+d}$, noise = $\frac{b}{a+b}$, overlap = $\frac{a}{a+b+c}$ and generality = a/N

Finally, 4 single measures (a, b, c, d) generate 10 basic indicators, themselves combined to generate other measures. In most of the cases, we only use precision

and recall. From these different measures, several synthetic indicators have been created, but the most famous is the F-Measure from [Van Rijsbergen 79]:
F-Measure = ((1+ß²)*Precision*Recall) / ((ß²*Precision)+Recall), with usually ß² = 1
It can be noticed that this measure doesn't take pertinence into consideration and is binary: an answer is "good" or "not good".

4 Analysis of F-Measure

First, we have demonstrated that the F-measure is a harmonic average of precision and recall. Then, we have observed its properties. When precision has the same value as recall, we get: Precision = Recall = F1-measure. Therefore, the result is comprehensive and we try to maximize it by maximization of both precision and recall (like for 'Break Even Point' approach). Indeed, it would be difficult to evaluate an algorithm which would have a good precision and a bad recall (or reverse).

Let's compute harmonic mean M of precision P and recall R: $\frac{2}{M} = \frac{1}{P} + \frac{1}{R}$ so $\frac{2}{M} = \frac{P+R}{P*R}$, and $\frac{M}{2} = \frac{P*R}{P+R}$. Finally, we get: $M = \frac{2*(P*R)}{P+R} = F1$

We notice that F1-measure is a harmonic mean of precision and recall. Nothing can justify this choice from a mathematical point of view. Nevertheless, harmonic mean has an interesting property which is: the result strongly decreases when only one of its components decreases. At the opposite, it grows strongly when the parameters are both high. This property is interesting because it would give a low result for algorithms which would improve precision or recall exclusively in prejudice of the other one.

We can demonstrate that property for the F1-measure: we have F1=2*P*R/(P+R), with precision=P and recall=R. Let's have S=P+R and D=P-R. Our problem becomes: how to improve F-measure when S increases (so precision AND recall are high) and D is minimized (keeping precision and recall closed). We have:
$S^2 - D^2 = (S+D)(S-D) = (P+R+P-R) \times ((P+R)-(P-R)) = 2P \times 2R = 4PR$

And finally: $F1 = \frac{2*P*R}{P+R} = \frac{S^2 - D^2}{2S} = \frac{S}{2} - \frac{D^2}{2S}$; that's the reason why F-measure is improved when S increases, and decreases when D increases. If one of the components is low, the resulting mean is low too. The Fn measure has another interesting property: it allows to modify importance of precision or recall.

5 Proposition of New Indicator: Toward K-Measure

In section 1, we tried to define classification and distinguish it from categorization and information retrieval. Now, we are going to find a new measure, with more possibilities for evaluation.

Case of Categorization

After analysis of F-measure, we found a formula which could integrate those needs and introduce **K-Measure**, based on F-measure:

K-Measure = $(1+ß^2)*(Precision*Recall)^\alpha / ((ß^2*Precision)+Recall)$

First, we can see that if $\alpha=1$, then K-measure is equal to F-measure. If $\alpha=1$ and $ß^2=1$, we get the usual F1-measure. So, the K-measure is a generalization of the F-measure. This is particularly useful because we can keep the history. Now, let's see properties when $ß^2=1$, and α parameter is varying with values 1, 1.2, and 1.6:

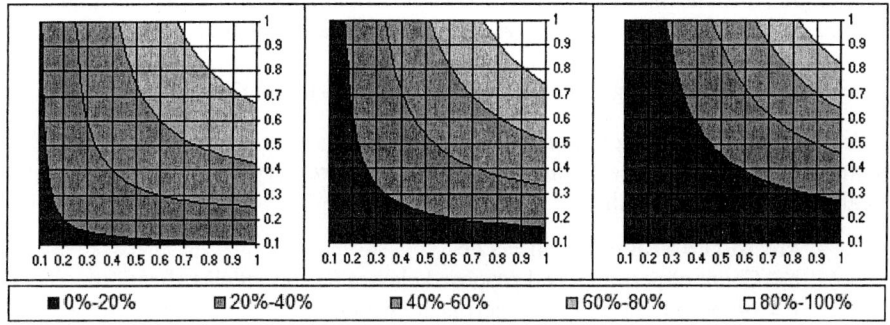

Fig. 1. Evolution of K measure when only α parameter is varying

We notice that when α parameter increases, the requirement level increases too. For example, if precision=recall=0.4, F-measure = 0.4, and k-measure = 0.13 with $\alpha=1.6$ (three times less). This result will be considered as bad, while F-measure considers it as medium. So, we can formalize a requirement level, just increasing α parameter.

We can observe that favor precision or recall is preserved, by increasing β parameter. And finally, we can use both parameters α and β:

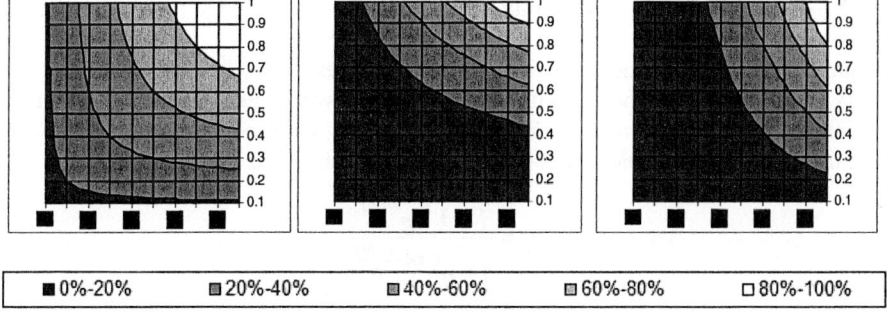

Fig. 2. Values of K-measure for ($\alpha=1$; $\beta=1$), ($\alpha=2$; $\beta=0.2$), ($\alpha=2$; $\beta=5$)

In conclusion, K-measure has very interesting properties for evaluation:
- It is an overall of F measure which keeps its properties,
- It allows to express a judge requirement level,
- It can as well represent a Break Even Point approach when $\alpha = 0.5$.

It is a formula of convergence, and an overall of different approaches used nowadays.

Case of Classifications

As proposed in section 1, a classification distinguishes from categorization because we can use a distance measure between classes. [Budanitsky 2001] demonstrated that best measure of semantic distance was Jiang and Conrath measure:

$$d = Dist_{jc}(c1:c2) = 2 \log(p(lso(c1:c2))) - (\log(p(c1)) + \log(p(c2)))$$

with lso(c1 :c2)= largest common group.
If we call 'd' that distance (with d=1 when classes are very far), then precision and recall can be defined like this:

Precision = a / B et Recall = a / c,
a = Count of pertinent and proposed classes (= correct classification),
B= proposed class but not pertinent: we consider the distance 'd' with the nearest correct class. Then compute (1-d) to have B near 1 when distance is weak,
c = Count of not proposed and pertinent classes.

It is then possible to use K-measure.

Case of Information Retrieval (IR)

Information retrieval is different from classification and categorization because of the large number of possible answers. Example of classical application would be a web crawler.

To find a good indicator, we started from the score used by [Voohrees 2003] $\frac{1}{Q}\sum_{i=1}^{Q}\frac{n}{i}$, where n represents the number of good answers in range i, Q is the number of questions. To represent a requirement level (for example: "I want that good answers are in the first 30, because it is the length of a web page", we need to modulate the initial Boolean and linear approach by integrating a sigmoid function. After empirical researches, we could find a coefficient W_i which solves our problem:

$$W_i = \frac{1 + e^{(l-k)}}{1 + e^{(-k \times (\frac{N-i+1}{N}) - l))}}$$

With k and l, two parameters (default values are k=15, and l=0.7), N represents the number of answer, and i the range of the answer.

Let's see the properties of that equation when k and l are varying (in our example, we have N=273)

K=15, l=0.7

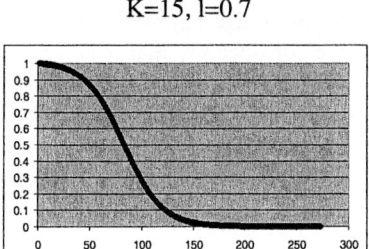

We can see that if the required answer doesn't appear in top 50, the score is strongly down, and quite null if higher than 150. The l parameter moves inflexion point (right and left), and k changes the slope.

The two parameters allow generating any requirement level. This score favor fact of giving good answers in first. To compute final indicator, we just multiply weight by pertinence. For automatic computing, we can use a Boolean approach: 1 for a good answer, otherwise 0. But for human evaluation, each judge can give a percentage. Global evaluation indicator becomes:

$$D\text{ Mesure} = \frac{\sum_{i=1}^{N} \text{Pertinence}_i * w_i}{\sum_{i=1}^{N} w_i} = \frac{\sum_{i=1}^{N} \text{Pertinence}_i * \frac{1+e^{(l-k)}}{1+e^{\left(-k*\left(\frac{N-i+1}{N}\right)-l\right)}}}{\sum_{i=1}^{N} \frac{1+e^{(l-k)}}{1+e^{\left(-k*\left(\frac{N-i+1}{N}\right)-l\right)}}}$$

For automatic computing, we can use a Boolean approach: 1 for a good answer, otherwise 0. But for human evaluation, each judge can give a percentage.

This evaluation indicator is interesting because it allows:

- To represent requirement level,
- To be able to evaluate otherwise than with 0 and 1,
- To control requirements.

6 Conclusion

In this paper, we first defined classification and categorization. In the first case, we were able to measure the distance between classes, but not in second case as it is binary. The F-measure, which was created 25 years ago, has been established as a standard for evaluation. Since then, the needs evolutes but not evaluation. Analysis of F-measure helps us to create a new measure: K-measure, an overall of F-measure able to integrate requirements. We demonstrate how to use k-measure for classification as well as to integrate the distance between the results. Finally, we propose a new measure for information retrieval which enhances finding good answers first and allow the expression of needs.

K-measure provides the following advantages: a meta measure of convergence between Van Rijsbergen's F-measure and Joachims's break even point. It has mathematical properties which allow to create a synthetic indicator from any other measure. Finally, it allows to integrate the judge approach of Saracevic and to formalize the required levels. Therefore, we consider say that it is a measure which converges the three approaches without modifying any of their properties.

In our future works, we will experiment these measures, particularly their impacts on classical measures.

Acknowledgements

We would like to thank:

- Professor Jacky AKOKA and the Cedric laboratory - CNAM (Conservatoire National des Arts et Métiers) and
- Pierre KEBAILI and Jacques TONNER (CRAMIF : Caisse Régionale d'Assurance Maladie d'Ile de France)

for supporting us.

Bibliography

[Budanitsky 2001] A. Budanitsky and G. Hirst : "Semantic distance inWordNet: An experimental, application-oriented evaluation of five measures" Department of Computer Science Univ. of Toronto

[Saracevic 70] Tefko Saracevic, "Introduction to Information Science", 111-151. New York: R.R. Bowker, 1970. Chap. 3 : The concept of "relevance" in information science: A historical review.

[Sparck Jones. 2001] K. Sparck Jones. "Automatic language and information processing: Rethinking evaluation". Natural Language Engineering, 7(1):29–46. 2001

[Van Rijsbergen 79] K. Van Rijsbergen, "Information Retrieval", (2nd Ed.) Butterworths, London. www.dcs.gla.ac.uk/Keith/Preface.html

[Voorhees 2003] E. M. Voorhees : "Evaluating the Evaluation: Edmonton", May-June 2003. Main Papers , pp. 181-188. Proceedings of HLT-NAACL 2003

Movies Recommenders Systems: Automation of the Information and Evaluation Phases in a Multi-criteria Decision-Making Process

Michel Plantié[1], Jacky Montmain[1,2], and Gérard Dray[1]

[1] LGI2P, Laboratoire de Génie informatique et d'ingénierie de la production,
EMA Site EERIE –parc scientifique Georges Besse, 30035 – Nîmes, France
[2] URC EMA-CEA - Site EERIE –parc scientifique Georges Besse,
30035 – Nîmes, France
{Michel.plantie, Jacky.Montmain, Gerard.Dray}@ema.fr

Abstract. The authors' interest is focused on advanced recommending functionalities proposed by more and more Internet websites w.r.t. the selection of movies, e-business sites, or any e-purchases. These functionalities often rely on the Internet users' opinions and evaluations. A « movie-recommender » application is presented. Recommender websites generally propose an aggregation of the user's evaluations critics according to different relevant criteria w.r.t. the application. The authors propose an Information Processing System (IPS) to collect, process and manage as automatically as possible these opinions or critics to support this multi criteria evaluation for recommendation. The RS (Recommender System) firstly proposes information extraction techniques in order to classify the available users' critics w.r.t. the criteria implied in the evaluation process and to automatically associate numerical scores to these critics. Then multicriteria techniques are introduced to numerically evaluate, compare and rank the competing movies the critics are reported to. Finally the RS is presented as an interactive Decision-Making Support System (DMSS) relying on a sensibility analysis of the movies ranking. A particular attention is paid to the automation of the information phase in the decision-making process: movie comments cartography according to users' evaluation criteria and attribution of a partial score to each critic considered as the expression of a value judgment in natural language.

1 Problematic Introduction

The impact of Information and Communication Sciences and Technologies is a kernel factor in developing our modes of organization, if not our societies. The economist and Nobel prizewinner H.A.Simon introduced the term of decisional computer sciences [20]. Regardless of how humans are involved in systems nowadays, the systems are so complex that increasingly intricate and inescapable dynamic Information Processing Systems (IPS) are bound to emerge [21]. The aim of such an IPS is to develop models and methodologies that are predominantly compatible with cognitive modes used by human beings when confronted to complex decisions. In particular, in the

Simon's Human Sciences viewpoint, the different phases of a decision-making process (DMP) don't appear as a linear sequence but as a process with multiple possible cognitive loops. Thus, Intelligence (information), design (representation) and choice (selection) phases are necessarily overlapped in a looped DMP contrarily to the sequential Operational Research viewpoint [22].

The 1990s proved this viewpoint right. Indeed, in the 1990s, there has been an explosion of information technologies, and thus of choices a person faces. Individuals cannot hope to evaluate all available choices by themselves unless the topic of interest is severely constrained. When people have to make a choice without any personal knowledge of the alternatives, a natural course of action is to rely on the experience and opinions of others. We seek recommendations from people who are familiar with the choices we face, who have been helpful in the past, whose perspective we value, or who are recognized experts [24].Today increasing numbers of people are turning to computational Recommender Systems (RS) [4]. Emerging in response to the technological possibilities and human needs created by the World Wide Web, these systems aim to mediate, support, or automate the everyday process of sharing recommendations [24].Different types of RS are available on the web. We propose to give a brief synthesis in the next paragraph.

During the last few years, RSs have merged to help users in their quest for relevant and personalized information in more and more vast corpus. Several techniques are used to design such systems. The most widespread of them is the "Collaborative Filtering" (CF) [7][10]. The CF deals with the users' preferences w.r.t. the selection of given items (books, movies, etc.). It enables to achieve clusters of users who have expressed similar tastes. To each user, the CF associates a neighbourhood of users who have tastes in common with him. The CF can then propose to a user all the items his neighbourhood has previously appreciated and selected as a recommendation.

A second common approach is the "Content-Based Filtering" (CBF). Applications mostly concerns the selection of documents [14][10]. In that case, the CBF deals with the characteristics, the properties of the documents and propose to the user documents that have similar characteristics or properties to those he has already consulted. The goal is therefore to find semantic neighbouring documents. For several years now, many research studies in the natural language processing (NLP) and the text-mining communities provide relevant tools for this issue [17][6][8][1]. These systems are based on statistic and semantic representations of documents.

RSs have been implemented in several domains on the web. Recommendation of e-business sites has been a privileged application domain [18][19][13]. However users still hesitate to take for granted the RS propositions. Recommendations lack credibility because they are considered as a means of hidden advertising. So a new generation of RS sites has merged: they are based upon the gathering and management of users' feedback experiences. This experience feedback from web users is better accepted in the context of recommendation. Our RS system belongs to this category.

Nevertheless the data gathering and management in RS is often a daunting task because not enough supported. For example, the "expert" user must firstly give his opin ion in natural language (NL) and then he is generally compelled to provide with a score (precise values, stars, etc.) consistent with the content of his experience feedback in NL. This score is essential to perform any further numerical evaluation in a recommendation perspective but the consistency checking between it and the NL report isn't supported at all. Furthermore, the evaluation of the compared items (products, services, etc.) generally relies on several criteria and thus necessitates the reiteration of the previous step for each dimension of the evaluation issue! All these « manual » and repetitive tasks have a deterrent effect upon the voluntary "expert" users! We propose to automatically orchestrate these fastidious steps.

As a singular (but representative) case of study, we focus on movie selection support systems, the "movie recommenders" [15][4]: many web sites offer movie advises and evaluations to film lovers looking for a movie on Internet. The NL feedback experience is here the film critic. The critics are picked up either in specialized journals or written down by the RS's users. Scores are associated to the movies' critics. Generally a purely qualitative value is required for this partial score. Imprecise values like stars are also often used, a star representing a bounded interval of scores. Assigning a score to a critic is a delicate and subjective task. However, this redundancy represents a genuine asset in the framework of RS [4]. Indeed, the RS provides its customers with very synthetic pieces of information through these scores: they enable to provide the RS's users with the ranking of the competing movies and any other aggregated indicators such as average scores upon the film buffs' critics. Nevertheless, the webmasters of the RS sites recommend themselves: "... I recommend you to prefer the critic in NL when available rather than to mere synthetic scores..."The critic in NL is a rhetorical element that elucidates and legitimates the afferent score. Indeed, human beings often use reasoning on real numbers (precise or not, reliable or not), thus the critic must be the symbolic transcription of the score. This transcription is a rather tedious and difficult task because subjectivity is inherent to the user's evaluation. For example the meaning of a star can differ from one user to another.

Furthermore, movies are generally evaluated through several criteria (script, actor, cast, production, music...). Thus, a score assigned to a critic is a partial evaluation of the movie w.r.t. a given criterion. The global score attributed to a movie then corresponds to the aggregation of its partial scores w.r.t. each criterion. Until recently, the most common aggregation tool, which is used in multi-criteria decision-making, is the weighted arithmetic mean, as it is the case in many recommender systems [4]. Movies are then ranked according to the aggregated scores they have been assigned. The recommendation principle underlying our RS is based on coupling a base of NL critics and an information fusion system based on multi criteria techniques. All these steps will be succinctly described, but this paper is only focused on the automated transcription procedure that enables to attribute a partial score to a critic in NL and on the critics mapping w.r.t. the set of criteria proposed by the RS.

Section 2 describes the automatic critic/score transcription. Section 3 explains the automated mapping of the critics w.r.t. the set of criteria established by the RS. Section 4 presents the complete processing of the critics in the evaluation, comparison and selection processes implied in the movies RS.

2 Critic-Score Transcription

The first step in our critics processing is how to automatically extract scores from collected movie critics. The score reflects the value judgment expressed in NL in the critic. In this paper we only deal with qualitative scores: the comments and critics will be classified either "positive" or "negative". The automated critic/score transcription consists in the following steps:

- Construction of a movie critics database with the labels "positive" and "negative",
- Extraction of all the lemmatized words from the critics database with the Synapse analyser [23].
- The list of these lemmatized words is the support of our text representation: each critic can thus be represented as a Boolean vector whose each coordinate is a Boolean that expresses the presence or not of the corresponding lemmatized keyword in the critic,
- Classification by supervised machine learning: we have realized a cross-validation campaign to classify the "critics' vectors" in two classes: positive (P) and negative (N). The principle is to build-up several learning sets on already labelled movie critics and then to calculate the associated decision trees who will then be used as classifiers,
- Analysis of the trees' size and their consistency.

Each of these steps is described in the following subsections.

2.1 Decision Trees

We use a decision tree classification method. The basic ideas of classification with decision trees are:

- In a decision tree, each node corresponds to an attribute different from the class (in our case a lemmatized keyword of the critic's representation vector) and each arc is associated to a possible value of this attribute (a Boolean here). A tree leaf specifies the expected class for the records described by the attributes path from the root to the leaf.
- In a decision tree, each node should be associated with an attribute different from the class one and that presents the highest informational degree among the attributes that haven't been already considered in the path from the root (this property defines a good decision tree).
- For example, entropy is used to measure the information quantity hold by a node (This notion has been introduced in the Shannon information theory),

In our problematic, the decision tree is build up by machine learning on the P-N—labelled critics database.

2.2 A Finalized Representation

The [1][6][8][17] references present several approaches usable in the documents classification framework. These approaches are focused on representing a knowledge domain and not dedicated to a specific processing of textual information. They are intended to be "multiple uses". Here, the philosophy of our modelling method is of different nature, the genericity of the model is left off in favour of the information processing: the aim of the processing is unique, i.e. finding a representation able to optimize critics classification in one of the a priori identified class (here P or N class). The idea is then indexing the critics in accordance with the most discriminative lemmatized words for the considered classes. Thus, in our approach the entire critics' corpus representation is guided right from the beginning by the unique processing objective set up by the goal.

2.3 Knowledge Database

Our tests have been done on a knowledge database filled up with cinema movie critics coming from a set of Internet websites. In a first experiment, we have asked to a small group of film lovers, so called "the experts" of this experiment, to classify these critics in two different categories: "positive" (P) or "negative" (N). In our implementation, we used 176 cinema movie critics where: 88 critics were labelled as negative, 88 as positive.

2.4 Complete Key Words Extraction

A lemmatization with the commercial Synapse analyser is firstly carried out over the whole critics database [23]. Thus, the words coming from the same family but different only on gender or in numeral attribute, are gathered on one unique lemma. Definite and indefinite articles are discarded. The corpus includes of this lemmatized 10765 lemmatized words. A vector representation is associated to the corpus: the higher the frequency of the lemmatized word, the lower its coordinate. Each critic is then represented by a vector in which the ith coordinate is the frequency in the critic of the ith most frequent lemmatized word in the learning corpus.

2.5 Cross Validation Campaign

We have used the CART method to compute the decision trees [9]. The Figure 1 shows an example of a decision tree used for the classification process. This example illustrates the movie RS domain. The test performed at each node of the tree node tells whether or not a specific word is present in the text for a specific movie critic. To calculate which word should be tested at each node a supervised machine learning procedure is performed: The word associated to a node is computed so as to minimize at this node a measure of the mixing degree of each class. In our case we use the well known "Gini" function described in the CART method [9].

We then proceed to a supervised machine learning. Since the size of the knowledge base (176 critics) is quite small, we have used the cross validation procedure. We have constructed 10 sets of 176 texts. Each of these sets uses 160 texts to compute the decision trees and 16 texts for evaluation. The 160 texts are equally distributed in the two categories, i.e. 80 texts for each category P-N. In the same way the 16 texts are distributed in 8 texts by category P-N.

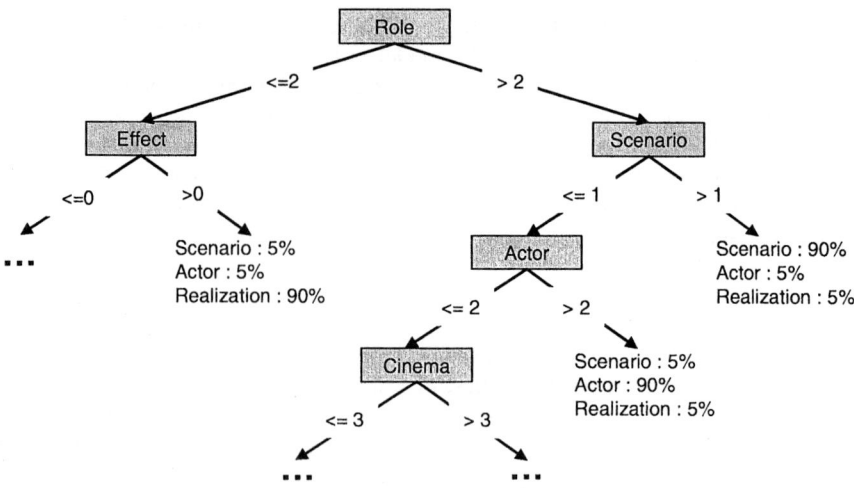

Fig. 1. A Decision Tree Example

2.6 Performances Estimation Method

To evaluate the learning results, we use F_β^i score [16]:
$$F_\beta^i = \frac{(\beta^2+1)\pi_i \rho_i}{\beta^2 \pi_i + \rho_i} \quad (1)$$

F_β^i is founded on precision and recall measures.

In our study β=1 providing the same weight to precision and recall defined as:

$$\rho_i = \frac{TPi}{TPi+FNi}, \pi_i = \frac{TPi}{TPi+FPi} \quad (2)$$

TPi, FPi, FNi, respectively define for a class $i=P,N$ the well classified items (i classified as i), the wrong classified items (j classified as i) and the omitted items (i classified as j). Precision π_i for a class i is the proportion of selected items that are correct. Recall ρ_i for a class i is the proportion of target items that were selected.

2.7 Performances Estimation for Positive/Negative Evaluation Experiment

Table 1. F_β^i values for the 10 training sets and the (P) and (N) categories

set	1	2	3	4	5	6	7	8	9	10
F_1^P	0.78	0.77	0.82	0.88	0.77	0.67	0.84	0.62	0.75	0.75
F_1^N	0.71	0.84	0.80	0.88	0.76	0.71	0.77	0.74	0.75	0.75

The results are satisfying since the average for the $F_\beta^{'i}$ values is more than 76%.

2.8 Quality of the Calculated Decision Trees

The cross validation campaign produced ten decision trees. These trees must now be compared in order to verify the homogeneity of the corresponding ten classifiers. In particular, we can verify that the keywords implied in the 10 trees are approximately the same and that the trees structures are similar.

The number of words in a tree goes from 19 at minimum to 31 at maximum. That means that the number of keywords necessary to index the critics in the score transcription application is a drastic and efficient reduction of the initial representation space constituted by the 10765 words of the corpus! Over the set of the 10 computed trees, the total number of words used is less than 80. The representation space necessary to the classification task is then limited and allows us to plan light calculations processes. In addition, words common to the entire ten trees amount to 20% of the total number of words in each tree.

Our method allows selecting "a posteriori" the space representation adapted to the intended goal, the most fitted to the problem and the most efficient in compute time. Furthermore this representation is not "purely" statistic: the different paths of the decision tree represent the semantic features of the corpus. The classification process introduces by itself semantic highlights.

These results allow us to use our method as a means to get automatic scoring of opinions expressed in natural language. Although the scores are purely qualitative in this version, we plan to set up 4 categories: "positive", "very positive", "negative" and "very negative". The rejected critics are categorized as neutral.

3 Criteria Evaluation

In the last section we have seen that the system is able to automatically attribute a score to a critic written in natural language. In our general presentation of the movie recommenders, we have focused our attention on the fact that the critics are related to n evaluation criteria (script, actors, image, music, etc.). It is then necessary to adapt the previous transcription "critic to score" for each dimension of the evaluation.

A score relative to one given criterion is said to be a partial score. Extending the automated transcription described in section 2 to partial scores necessitates extracting fragments from the critics that are related to the evaluation criteria. We describe this mapping procedure in the following.

In a second experiment, we have proposed our experts to split up the critics in text fragments w.r.t. the evaluation criteria of the RS. Each fragment is classified in one of the three classes, i.e. the three criteria: "Script" (C1) or "Actor" (C2) or "Movie Direction" (C3). In our implementation, we use 192 fragments from 144 cinema movie critics. 64 fragments are attributed to each criterion.

We have constructed 10 sets of 192 fragments. Each of these sets uses 174 fragments to compute the decision trees, and 18 fragments for evaluation. The 174 fragments are equally distributed in the three criteria, i.e. 58 fragments for each criterion. In the same way the 18 texts are distributed in 6 texts by criterion.

3.1 Performances Estimation for Criteria Classification Experiment

Table 2. F_β^i values for the 10 training sets and three categories

set	1	2	3	4	5	6	7	8	9	10
F_1^{C1} : Script		0.62	0.86	0.80	0.83	0.73	0.83	0.62	0.55	0.55	0.75
F_1^{C2} : actor		0.3	0.92	1.00	0.83	0.83	0.91	0.83	0.91	0.91	0.74
F_1^{C3} : movie Direction	0.73	0.67	0.86	0.67	0.42	0.77	0.36	0.57	0.57	0.64

The results are quite satisfying since the average for the F_β^i values is more than 73%.

3.2 Homogeneity for Criteria Classification Experiment

The number of words in a tree goes from 32 at minimum to 41 at maximum. This representation reduction is rather drastic compared to the 5314 words of the corpus of this second experiment. The number of common words in all the trees is 12: it represents 29,3 % up to 37,5% of the total number of words in one tree. The total number of words used in the ten trees is only 82. As stated in the first experiment, the representation space necessary to the classification task is quite limited and relevant. Each path from the top to a leaf of the tree represents a multi-word co-occurrence [6]. This notion of co-occurrence is to be related to semantic features of documents representation. There's something more than statistics in the text analysis.

4 The Recommendation System

We give in the following a very short description of the complete movie RS as described in [4]. The main goal of this section is to show the interest and role of the previous calculations in the complete RS processing. Sections 2 and 3 have automated the mapping of critics w.r.t. a set of criteria and the association of partial scores to them. These partial scores are then used in a multi criteria quantitative evaluation of movies. Multi criteria aggregation (MCA) is the basis of movies evaluation and ranking in RSs. However, aggregation in RSs is usually reduced to its simplest form: average ratio or for the better weighted average ratio. We have proposed aggregation operators with richer semantics allowing to model different aggregation strategies for evaluation [5]. In this paper and for the sake of understanding, we have made up our mind to carry on the presentation with the weighed average operator as an illustration of the multi criteria analysis in the RS. The global score of a movie is thus a weighted average (WA) of the partial scores obtained for each evaluation criterion. The weights define the decisional strategy but the way they are determined is not discussed in this paper. Furthermore, several critics are available w.r.t. a given couple (movie, criterion). It means that a first aggregation has to be processed to aggregate the partial scores w.r.t. this couple. A simple arithmetic average is considered in this paper for this first aggregation level. A *grid evaluation* (figure 1) of the movies candidates according to a set of criteria is at the origin of the decision support functionalities. The basic idea of movies evaluation refers to collective choice theory, identifying the criteria as voters whose votes are the critics (the value judgments they convey), and the movies as candidates for election. The scores embodied in the critics and assigned in the grid allow the differing intensities of voter preferences to be taken into account: each vote is an evaluation of a movie i with respect to a criterion j. The overall score of a movie corresponds to the aggregate of partial preferences obtained for each criterion, and can thus be equated with a criteria-driven election procedure.

The score associated to the critic corresponds to a degree of satisfaction that is converted into a color code ranging from non-satisfaction (red) to complete satisfaction (green), and which may take any intermediate value (depending on the granularity of the classifier described in section 2).

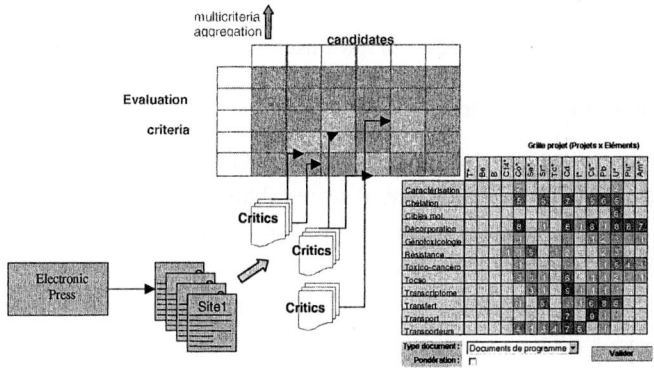

Fig. 2. Multicriteria evaluation for movie critics

The evaluation process for the film lovers group is showed in Fig. 2. As soon as a critic is put in the knowledge base, it is first automatically mapped on the evaluation grid in a criteria line for a film column with the classification technique described in section 3. A score is then automatically attributed to the mapped critic through the transcription critic/score in section 2. Then the average scoring is computed in the cell where the critic has been mapped. The movie evaluation corresponding to the critic is automatically computed with the WA operator. $WA(X_k) = \sum_{j=1}^{n} \lambda_j x_k^j$ where WA is the weighed average, λ_j the weight for criterion j, x_k^j the score for movie k w.r.t. criterion j and n is the number of criteria.

4.1 Argumentation

For the considered aggregation operator, the best movie, noted X_1 is then obtained. By definition we have: $\forall i, WA(X_1) \geq WA(X_i)$. We have shown in [12] how it's possible to automatically extract the most outstanding critics from the knowledge base, i.e. the main discursive items that explain this ranking. The calculation details are given in [2][3] for more complex operators than WA ones. The basic idea of the algorithms is to rewrite any mathematical entity necessary to the argumentation function as a ranked sum of criterion rating contributions to this mathematical entity (it corresponds to an interpretation of the relative importance of criteria in terms of marginal contributions). For example, in the case of the WA operator, the reasons for which movie X_1 is preferred to movie X_i, is got by rewriting formula $WA(X_1)-WA(X_i)$ as:

$$WA(X_1) - WA(X_i) = \sum_{j=1}^{n} \lambda_j . (x_1^j - x_i^j) = \sum_{j=1}^{n} Contribution(criterion\ j).$$

Then, the most significant contributions are selected through order of magnitude reasoning. It provides the most determinant criteria $\{j^*\}$ in the choice of X_1 rather than X_i: justification is the basis of recommendation [3]. When the criteria $\{j^*\}$ have been identified, the RS can then select the bets critics in the grid cells (1, $\{j^*\}$) and the worst ones in the grid cells (i, $\{j^*\}$) in the knowledge base to elucidate the choice in natural language for the RS user.

4.2 Reliability of the Classification

Now consider the reliability of the classification for the film lover and customer of the RS. Let's write x_i the vector of the partial scores obtained by movie X_i.

To define the decisional risk, i.e. the reliability of the recommendation, we propose to measure it according to a distance notion between movie X_1 and movie X_i, founded on the L_1 norm and including the concept of improvement effort [4]:

$$d(\mathbf{x}_1, \mathbf{x}_i) = \min \left\| \vec{\delta}_1^i \right\|_{l_1} / WA(\mathbf{x}_i + \vec{\delta}_1^i) = WA(\mathbf{x}_1)^{\ 1}$$

The risk notion introduced is quite different of a conventional probabilistic one and is more in line with a sensitivity analysis of the movies ranking to any external information disturbance. Thus on the basis of this distance, we define the decisional risk notion as the expression r associated with the movie classification stability defined as follows: $r = 1 - \min_{\substack{i=1..p \\ i \neq 1}} \dfrac{d(\mathbf{x}_1, \mathbf{x}_i)}{n}$ where p is the number of competing movies.

Thus, the lower the distance between X_1 and its challengers, the more sensitive the ranking and the less reliable the selection of X_1: indeed a "small quantity of information" (i.e. few but relevant critics) could be sufficient to modify the movies ranking. We consider that we are able to make a decision when the risk is going under a fixed threshold C_r. This threshold defines the decision acceptability in this scheme. The calculus of $d(\mathbf{x}_1, \mathbf{x}_i)$ gives the least effort to provide (in the sense of norm L1) in order that the evaluation of X_i should be at least equal to the one of X_1. This calculus enables to determine the criteria on which X_i should (be) improve(d) first in order to improve as much as possible its overall score. In other words the expression $d(\mathbf{x}_1, \mathbf{x}_i)$ provides the criteria where X_i must necessarily progress to reach X_1 with a minimal effort. Thus, the RS provides the film lovers with the sensitive or critical dimensions

---

[1] When the aggregation operator is a WA this optimization problem is a mere simplex.

of the evaluations. The RS manager can also use this kind of information to relevantly complete his knowledge base with corresponding additional critics [5].

Through the concept of risk and acceptability of the decision, we have defined a reaction feedback loop upon the content of the critics knowledge base used for the movies evaluation. Pointing out only the most relevant movies and criteria for which additional critics should be of great interest modifies the selection process dynamics. The management of the RS is thus represented as a control loop: the risk accompanying the decision is the controlled variable and is strongly linked to the entropy of the knowledge base managed by the RS. Each of the three phases—Intelligence, Design, Choice—of the decision-making process is identified to a function of the control loop: actuator, process and regulator. This viewpoint thus proposes a way the iterative cognitive phases—Intelligence, Design and Choice—which represent the Simon's Human Sciences vision of the decision process, can be represented in a control theory framework. The cognitive loop of the Simon's model of DMP, we evoked in the introduction, is seen as a control loop on the decisional risk, itself related to the entropy of the critics corpus.

5 Conclusion

We have developed a Decision Making Support System combining both text-mining techniques for the information phase and multi criteria analysis techniques for the justification and selection phases of movies in a RS. This movies RS approach supports the idea of cognitive automation of collective decision-making process: the Simon's cognitive and descriptive model of decision-making process is here interpreted in a cybernetic framework . Our RS is a synthetic tool to automate or to strongly support the information, evaluation, comparison, and selection steps in the web-recommenders problematic. This paper is focused on the automatic transcription from critics into scores. This step associated with an automatic critics mapping procedure produce a complete automation of the information phase implied in the collective DMP implied in the RS. In this kind of DMP (Simon's IPS model), the information phase plays a major role and that's why its automation is an essential step in the RS. Exhaustive cognitive automation, as proposed in this paper, is probably (and hopefully!) a utopian aim but should represent one ideal for the Computer Science and Process Control Theory communities in the era of numerical networks. Indeed knowledge acquisition and processing in always greater corpus are probably a more crucial problem to achieve the « righteous » decision than the search of an apparently optimal decision that relies on many modeling hypotheses and simplifications. That's what Simon pointed out in 1947[21]!

References

1. Abramowicz, Witold and Piskorski, Jakub, (2003). Information Extraction from Free-Text Business Documents, Effective Databases for Text & Document Management, p 12-23, IRM Press, Hershey, USA.
2. Akharraz, A., Montmain, J., Mauris, G (2002a). A project decision support system based on an elucidative fusion system. *Fusion 2002*, Annapolis, Maryland, USA.

3. Akharraz, A., Montmain, J., Mauris, G (2002b). Fonctionnalités explicatives d'un système de fusion de connaissances collectives par intégrale de Choquet 2-additive. *LFA'2002*, Montpellier, France.
4. Akharraz, A. , Montmain, J., Mauris, G (2004). Elucidation and risk expressions of a movie recommendation based on a multi-criteria aggregation with a Choquet integral. *IPMU 2004, 10th International Conference on Information processing and Management of uncertainty in Knowledge-Based Systems*, Genova, Italy..
5. Akharraz, A., Montmain, J., Mauris, G. (2004). A cybernetic modeling of a multi-criteria decision process in organization. *EURO XX , 20th European Conference on Operational Research*, Rhodes, Greece.
6. Besançon, R. and M. Rajman (2000). Le modèle DSIR : une approche à base de sémantique distributionnelle pour la recherche documentaire. Revue *TAL'2000*, n°41(2), pp. 1-27
7. Breese, J.S., Heckerman, D., Kadie, C., Empirical analysis of predictive algorithms for collaborative filtering. *Proceedings of the 14th Conference on Uncertainty in Artificial Intelligence*, Madison, USA, pp. 43-52.
8. Chauché, J. (1990). Détermination sémantique en analyse structurelle : une expérience basée sur une définition de distance. *TA Information*, **31**(1), pp 17-24.
9. (Crawford et al., 1991) Crawford, S., Fung, R, Appelbaum, L., Tong, R. (1991). Classification trees for information retrieval, *Actes du 8th International workshop Machine Learning*, Northwestern university, Illinois.
10. Herlocker, J.L., Konstan, J.A., Borchers, A., Riedl, J. An algorithmic framework for performing collaborative filtering. *Proceedings of the Conf. on Research and Development in Information Retrieval*, Berkeley, California, USA.
11. Lang K. (1995). NewsWeeder: Learning to filter netnews. Machine Learning. *Proceedings of the Twelfth International Conference*, Lake Tahoe, California.
12. Montmain, J., Akharraz, A. and Mauris, G. (2002). Knowledge management as a support for collective decision-making and argumentation processes. *IPMU'2002*, Annecy, France.
13. Montmain, J., Denguir, A., Mauris, G. (2005). How deriving benefits from expert advices to make the right choice in multi-criteria decisions based on the Choquet integral? European workshop on the Use of Expert Judgement in Decision-Making, Aix-en-Provence, France.
14. Pazzani, M., Muramatsu, J., Billsus, D., Identifying interesting web sites. *Proceedings of the Thirteenth National Conference on Artificial Intelligence*, Portland, Oregon.
15. Perny, P., Zucker, J-D. (2001). Preference based search and machine learning for collaborative filering : the "film-conseil" movie recommender system. *Information, Interaction, Intelligence*, **1**(1), pp.9-48.
16. Van Rijsbergen, C.J. (1979). *Information Retriaval*, Butterworths, London 1979, 2° edition. http://www.dcs.gla.ac.uk/Keith/Preface.html.
17. Salton G. The SMART Retrieval System – *Experiments in Automatic Document Processing »*, Prentice Hall, Englewood Cliffs, NJ,1971.
18. Schafer J.B., Konstan J., Riedl J. (1999). Recommender Systems in E-Commerce. *Proceedings of the ACM'1999 Conference on Electronic Commerce,* Denver,Colorado, USA.
19. Schafer, J.B., Konstan, J., Riedl, J. (2001). E-Commerce Recommendation Applications. *Journal of Data Mining and Knowledge Discovery*, Vol. 5 Nos. 1/2, pp. 115-152.
20. Simon, H.A. (1977). The new science of management decision. *Prentice Hall*, New Jersey.
21. Simon, H. A. (1983). Administration et processus de décision. (trad. (Simon, 1947). *Économica*, Paris.
22. Simon, H.A. (1997). Models of bounded rationality. *MIT Press*, Cambridge Massachusetts.
23. Synapse analyzer : http://www.synapse-fr.com
24. Terveen, L., Hill, W. (2001). Beyond recommender systems : helping people help each other. In HCI in the milenium, J. Caroll, ed., Addison-Wesley, pp 1-21, 2001.

On Building a DyQE - A Medical Information System for Exploring Imprecise Queries

Dennis Wollersheim and Wenny J. Rahayu

Department of Computer Science and Computer Engineering, La Trobe University,
Melbourne, Australia
{dewoller,wenny}@cs.latrobe.edu.au

Abstract. This paper sets out DyQE, a dynamic query expansion information retrieval system implemented in the medical domain, aimed at exploring imprecise queries. DyQE enhances standard query and result set navigation through integration with dynamic taxonomy and broad query expansion. The query expansion rules are sourced from a fine grained evaluation of data retrieval-based query expansion. DyQE offers both a concise representation of a broad subject area, and a wide variety of interesting links to related subject areas.

1 Introduction

The amount of computer searchable information in the world is broadening, deepening, and diversifying. This increased supply is matched and driven by an increase and broadening of demand; non experts are encroaching on the experts turf, and lowering the average expertise of a searcher. These factors drive the enhancement of search.

Traditionally, information retrieval (IR) has been focused on targeted search, the retrieving of discrete answers from known questions. The user has a question, the system has an answer, IR is the process of matching them up. Targeted search models the interface between search and human as discrete and clean. Search is treated as a standalone tool, which facilitates implementation and evaluation.

On the other hand, targeted IR is not so useful when dealing with questions and answers which are less precise. The imprecise realm is better served by exploratory approaches to knowledge discovery, with a concomitant increase in user involvement. While imprecise search has elements in common with targeted search, there are also places where the targeted search tools do not serve it well. The basic desiderata of targeted search, correct answers and precise questions, are often missing from imprecise search.

1.1 Imprecise Query

Imprecise query is defined to be a query which does not precisely specify the information need, and cannot retrieve documents which will satisfy the user. While most queries contain both precise and imprecise elements, here we focus on the latter. This area has been neglected because it is difficult to retrieve something that is not specified. Too, it requires interaction with the user, something difficult both to do and to evaluate. Even given these impediments, we argue that there exist resources which increase the usefulness of IR to imprecise query.

Imprecise query (IQ) is not a new phenomenon; in the real world, few queries are entirely precise. IQ is an important topic because the forces which drive it are increasing. Imprecise query originates with users who cannot sufficiently describe what they are looking for. This can be due to either lack of knowledge of the field, or lack of knowledge of self. The domain knowledge deficiency is driven by a number of factors. Information is becoming more complex, interconnected, and abundant, and the user base is broadening.

Targeted search tools handle imprecise query poorly. There is an expectation that the user will themselves read through the results, recognising and extracting more precise search terms. This is a valid goal, as recognition memory is much more powerful than recall [1]. The problem is that the onus is on the user to reformulate and resubmit their original query. As imprecise query is characteristic of relatively inexperienced and often less confident users, this step can lead to an aborted search process, which clearly does not fulfil the user's information need.

Purely automatic solutions for imprecise query are untenable, because by definition, an imprecise query does not contain sufficient information. We will need to involve the user in the solution process, but the user is not well served by a linear list of results. Instead, it would be more useful to identify and summarise the semantic space around such a query, and allow the user to navigate it, using recognition in place of recall.

In DyQE, we use query expansion to explore the semantic space surrounding imprecise query, and use dynamic taxonomy (DT) to deal with the result sets. The next section introduces DT, while DT's full integration into DyQE will be described in Section 4.

1.2 Dynamic Taxonomy

Dynamic Taxonomy (DT) [2, 3] is a browsing framework which provides classification and filtering tools to organise the browse process. It was designed to use the structure found in a simple taxonomy to enhance user IR, using a combination of simple query expansion and interactive result set modification.

While query expansion summarises the semantic area surrounding a result set, dynamic taxonomy summarises the result set itself, by displaying the hierarchy containing those concepts. Users can also navigate the metadata based hierarchy, choosing terms, and obtaining document sets that are categorised under these terms, or terms subsumed by these terms. By the inclusion of these subcategories, DT performs simple, strictly hierarchical expansion of chosen query terms.

The entailing oversupply of documents that results from such a query expansion is handled by both query preview of search results (showing the number of subsumed documents), and via the zoom operator, which provides dynamic filtering of the result set.

A problem with a metadata browser is that of index term overload. DT reduces index complexity in two ways. Firstly, it displays a hierarchical view of the index term set, allowing complexity to be hidden under higher level terms. Secondly, the aforementioned zoom operator dynamically reduces the term set.

The zoom operation reduces the term set by filtering it against the document base. In response to a request to zoom on a index phrase, the system prunes the taxonomy, retaining only the taxonomic elements which categorise the set of text atoms which are also categorised by the zoom phrase. More importantly, any terms in the taxonomy that do not either directly or indirectly classify the remaining text atoms are pruned. This effectively filters the term set against the set of documents that contain the term (or subsumptions thereof). After a zoom, other retrieval operations act on the reduced taxonomy, and successive zooms add further constraints.

2 Building DyQE

DyQE is composed of query expansion rules, and a dynamic taxonomy browsing structure. This section details the construction of each of these elements.

2.1 Query Expansion

When faced with the standard text retrieval result of an imprecise query, the user has few options other than scanning the result set, or reformulating the query; DyQE uses query expansion techniques to give the user clickable avenues of exploration, providing a concise summary of the semantic area around a query.

Query expansion (QE) is an information retrieval tool where words related to a query are added back into the query, and the query rerun. Query expansion addresses an oft-characterised problem; a query is made up of words, but the query terms are not used in the relevant documents. The information need is not specified by the query words. It is an unsolved problem; even Google, the state of the art in commercial information retrieval, does minimal query expansion [4].

Query expansion has been widely explored, but mostly from a simple text retrieval perspective. Our work brings two novel elements to QE by looking at the problem from a data retrieval perspective: direct evaluation, and direct retrieval.

By using direct evaluation, we characterise high relevance medical query expansions using the process shown in Figure 1. First, the documents from the Ohsumed test collection (1) [5] are categorised (2) using the UMLS [6] concepts, resulting in a set of concept identified documents (3). A similar process takes place with the Ohsumed test queries (4,5).

After data preparation, we judge the various query expansion algorithms. For each concept identified query (9), we expand it using one of a set of expansion algorithms. In the evaluation step (12), the expanded query set (11) is matched against the relevant document concept set (7), leading to a success measure for this query and expansion algorithm. By generalising these measures, we arrive a set of rules for generating the high quality medical query expansions for user by DyQE.

Within the DyQE framework itself, we also use identified document concepts as handles for directly retrieving documents, both from DyQE queries, and from the query expansions generated from these queries.

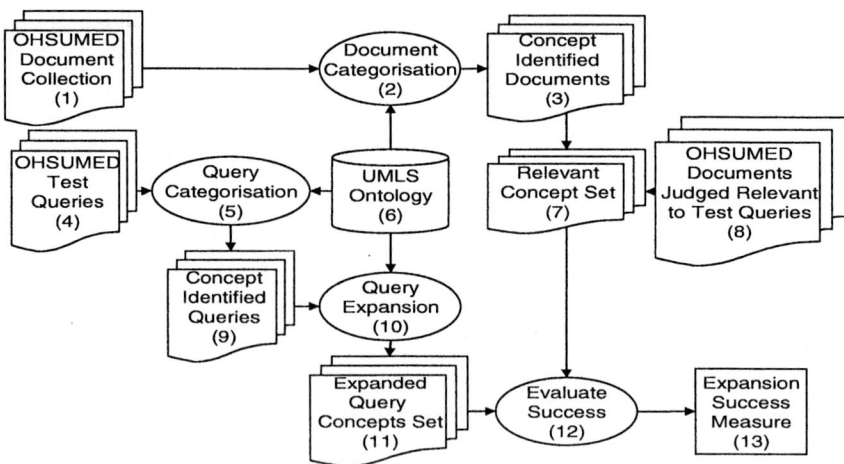

Fig. 1. Generate and directly evaluate query expansion algorithms using UMLS ontology and Ohsumed document test collection

2.2 Dynamic Taxonomy

Figure 2 shows the DT building process for use in DyQE. The subsumption hierarchy is extracted from UMLS based on the identified concepts from the categorised Therapeutic Guidelines documents.

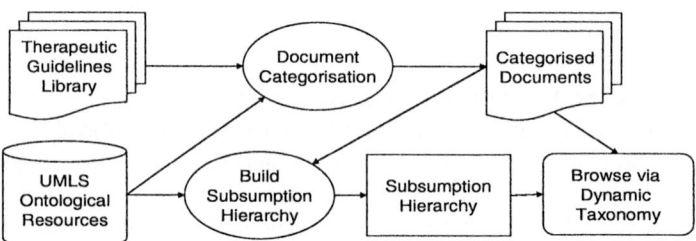

Fig. 2. Dynamic taxonomy build process

3 DyQE Conceptual Framework

The DyQE interface facilitates structured exploration of the semantic space surrounding a query. While this system still offers the standard 'enter query, browse results' paradigm, it integrates this with both a dynamically generated list of high relevance query expansions, and a dynamic taxonomy summarisation index structure. Once the user has entered a query, the query is parsed, and from this, three sets of links are generated:

- the standard document fragments, similar to that retrieved by a text retrieval algorithm,
- a dynamic summarisation structure, outlining the corpus section that is described by the query terms, and
- a set of high relevance query expansions, describing the nearby semantic space.

This functionality is instantiated in the following manner. In preparation, we experimentally determine the characteristics of the most useful query specific ontological relationships, as described above. These characteristics are then used by DyQE to generate high relevance expansions based on the current query. Because there are numerous such relationships, we also provide a dynamic taxonomy based browser, which gives the user both signposts as to the current semantic location, and categorisation tool for the surfeit of results.

Dynamic taxonomy is designed to do subsumption based query expansion and taxonomic summarisation of results. DyQE extends DT's original expansion scheme, combining the highest precision query expansions with taxonomic based browsing. Adhoc query expansion fits cleanly into the dynamic taxonomy framework as merely another way to move in the hierarchy, providing the ability to change the current browse focus to a closely related concept.

DT has a unique set of features, combining query expansion and summarisation using the same subsumption hierarchy. Subsumption is very functional, being comprehendible, recognisable and definable, with these qualities making it useful for summarisation. It provides the user with markers as to their current browse location, and prevents confusion. Simple subsumption provides good location cues, but it is limited as a query expansion tool, representing only a single class of relationship.

Browsing itself can be cumbersome, as web surfing testifies. In practice, browsing is often preceded by a query. For example, when using a reference book, we often look up a primary index word, then scan sub headings. In the web, searching is a very important modality. The functionality of DT can be greatly enhanced by the addition of a query facility, and so our work also grafts query onto dynamic taxonomy.

Original DT involves traversal of a contiguous area of semantic space. Even with the addition a query facility, providing the equivalent of a semantic 'goto', navigation is still limited to three possible directions: move in (specialise), move out (generalise), or alter query and jump again. It is difficult to jump "nearby" without having a good knowledge of the domain, and, as searching becomes more widespread, this domain knowledge tends to become relatively more rare. This is especially the case in the medical field, where there is a high demand for knowledge, and a vast amount of available knowledge.

Often, this domain vocabulary knowledge, and consequent refined search skill, come from familiarisation with the literature, that same literature that is represented by the documents at and around the current search point. Query preview, query expansion, and dynamic summarisation together can provide a summary of this fine grained background domain knowledge, *in the context of the current query*. This provides the user with both a summary of the necessary domain knowledge, and pointers to elements in the nearby semantic neighbourhood. This provides much power to the user, exactly what is necessary to deal with imprecise query.

4 System Architecture

Our prototype is based on the original dynamic taxonomy structure. By this we mean that it is built around a subsumption tree hierarchy, allowing browsing by traversal, and the ability to zoom in on a query concept. Dynamic taxonomy has two base functions: query expansion via a subsumption based hierarchy, and results summarisation via that same hierarchy. This work extends the former component, allowing expansion via other highly productive link sets, and the latter, by allowing other forms of categorisation.

While DT implicitly displays all nodes subsumed by the current browse focus, we extend this, by offering and allowing the choice of one of a set of expansions to replace the current focus. In effect, we offer a small sideways semantic jump to a slightly different region of the semantic space. This acts in a similar fashion to this is the "related word" feature of thesauri.

DyQE extends DT's categorisation through the display of applicable query expansions. At any time, DyQE displays a list of current possible query expansions, based on 1) the current focus concept, 2) the original query type, and 3) the current zoom level, corresponding to the current subset of the document collection. This latter point comes about because the expansions are filtered, similar to the term filtering done on the DT hierarchy, against the document collection the remains accessible at the current zoom level.

As the user traverses the hierarchy, they are presented with the expansion alternatives related to the current browse focus; it both gives them a picture of their semantic neighbourhood, and allows them sideways movement, instead of merely up and down the hierarchy. The offered query expansions provide an idiosyncratic summary of document content at the current zoom level. In another light, these links are a continuing set of "have you seen this?" type links, allowing for opportunistic connections.

In dynamic taxonomy, navigation is via the traversal of a tree. We supplement this navigation through dynamic query expansion, with the source for the query expansions following the tree traversal focus. As the tree traversal focus changes, a secondary panel displays the most likely relevant set of expansions for this node, given the above criteria. At any time, the user can select one of these expansions, which causes the current focus to be replaced with the chosen expansion. Additionally, as the focus changes, a third panel containing summaries of the document categorised by the focus concept are displayed.

Figure 3 shows a summary of the results arising from DyQE actions. There are 3 basic actions: subsumption based browsing, query expansion, or entering query text (1). The internal results from these actions are shown in (2), and the visible results are displayed in (3).

5 Implementation

We base our implementation of DyQE on the Therapeutic Guidelines (TG) medical guideline collection [7]. We identify concepts and generate a subsumption hierarchy for the TG information using the process described in [8]. The query expansion rules are generated using the system described in [9]. We store the raw HTML text, the identified concepts, and the subsumption hierarchy in an Oracle database. The DyQE browser itself is written in the Java programming language.

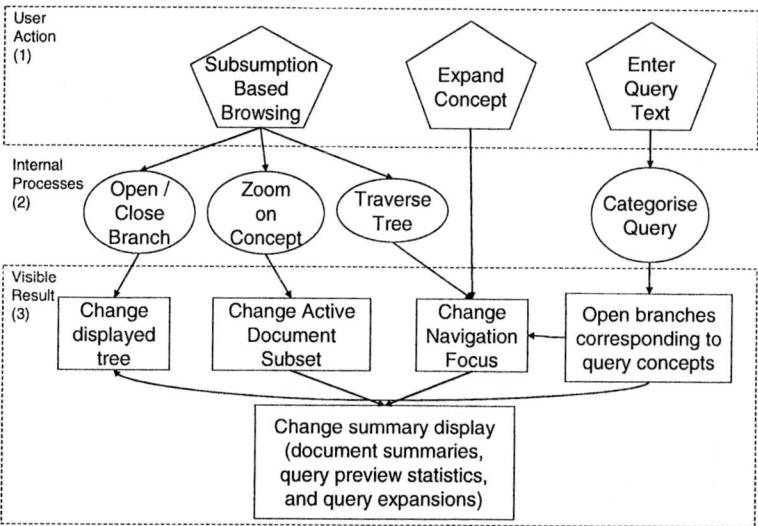

Fig. 3. Schematic of possible user actions, resulting internal processes, and visible results for the DyQE system

DyQE has three broad categories of user action: query expansion, text query, and browsing. Browsing involves traversal of the subsumption tree, with the added possiblity of zooming in on a query concept.

The DyQE screen layout can be seen in Figure 4. On the top left, there is box for entering a query. To the right of this are the control buttons: search, zoom, undo, redo, and goto next query concept. The last thing on this line are the concept representing the current zoom level of the document base.

The remainder of the screen is divided into 4 boxes. The upper left box contains the dynamic taxonomy structure. This is arranged as a treeview, containing both the names of the taxonomic concepts, and the number of documents classified by this concept. Below this are a list of query expansion choices, in increasing semantic distance order. The top right box contains a list of document summaries, chosen by the currently focused taxonomic term. Clicking on one of these summaries fills the bottom right box with the full text of the summarised document.

System operation is as follows. At any time, there is one active concept which has the focus in the taxonomic tree. When the root concept has the focus, the summary panels are empty, but at all other times, the document fragments displayed in the summary panel, and the expansion displayed in the expansion panel, are related to the currently active taxonomic concept.

In typical usage, the user will enter an imprecise query in the query box. The system identifies the medical concepts in the query, opens up the dynamic taxonomy at all of these concepts, and zooms in on each of the concepts. Navigation focus is then located at the first query concept, and as a result, the fragments related to that concept are displayed. At this point, due to the implicit zoom, the taxonomy panel displays a summary of the document set that is classified by the concepts in the query.

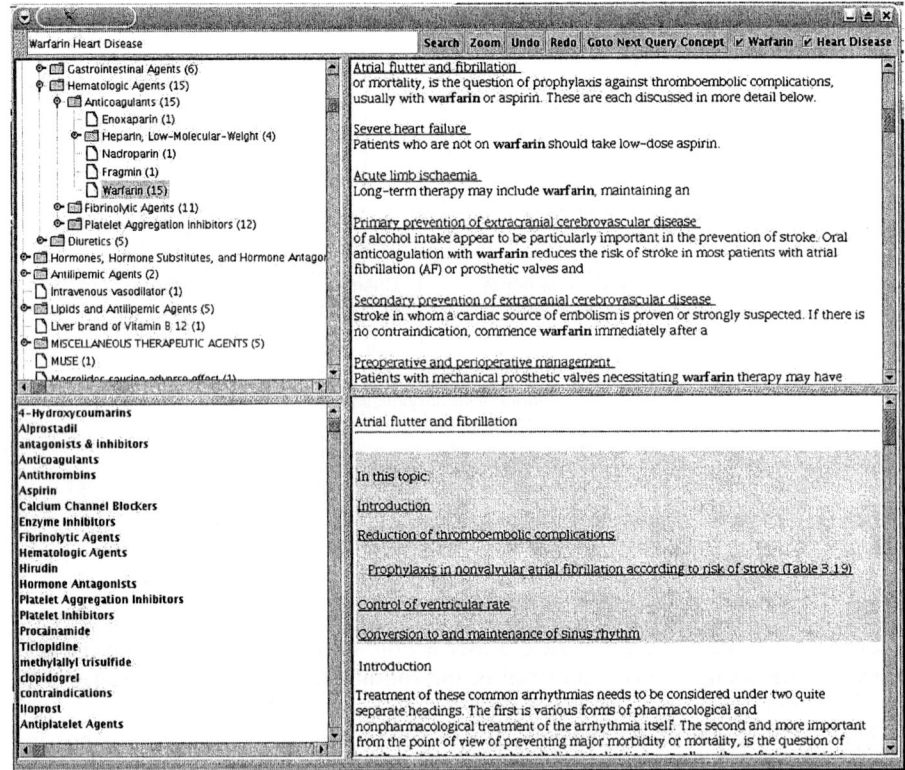

Fig. 4. DyQE screen layout

The taxonomy panel has largely standard DT function. Options include zoom, movement in and out (corresponding to specialisation and generalisation), and the opening and closing of branches. The only difference is the feature of dynamic focus movement, which happens due to outside events. One such event is the choosing of a query expansion.

Potential query expansions are displayed in the query expansion box. Expansions offered are displayed in order of relevance. When the user chooses a query expansion, this changes the focus of the taxonomy pane (with corresponding change of retrieved document fragments). If user wishes, they can then zoom on the found expanded term.

There are five control buttons; Undo, Redo, Zoom, and FocusNextQueryConcept. Undo and redo apply to the last action, with undoable actions including change of focus, zoom, entering of a query concept, and clicking on query expansions or hyperlinks. FocusNextQueryConcept is active when there is a multiple concept query, and it moves the focus to the next query concept. In the example, the user entered the query 'warfarin heart disease', and the two query concepts 'warfarin' and 'heart disease' were identified and zoomed in the query tree. Because the initial query concept was 'warfarin', FocusNextQueryConcept moves the query focus to 'heart disease'.

6 Discussion

The hypothesis of this paper is that query expansion can be usefully integrated into dynamic taxonomy, extending both retrieval and query preview capabilities. To evaluate this, we will build such a system, and do proof by demonstration [10].

We will evaluate our system on two levels: feasibility of design, and usability of functionality. With regards to the former, we address the feasibility of designing a system with a selected feature set. We specify a desired general feature set, and then evaluate how the system implements these features. We want the following features:

1. orientation tools which keep the user informed of their current position in the semantic space,
2. query preview tools, motivating continued searching,
3. user control enhancement, and
4. multiple modality searching

The second evaluation we perform relates to functional usability. This is more complex than design feasibility, because functional usability exists only in relationship with a user. Where design feasibility looks at implementation details, functional usability looks at task fulfilment. Here, we answer the question, does the system provide functionality for user. Because of this, our questions are more general; instead of looking at specific implementation details, we focus on the system's functionality in relationship to tasks that are not fulfilled by standard IR systems. Our evaluation of this feature will consist of broad areas of functionality, and show examples of where the prototype provides such functionality.

In the area of functional usability, medical query based browser should fulfil the following criteria:

1. answer typical medical questions which are difficult to answer with standard retrieval methods,
2. be accessible to users with little domain knowledge,
3. have ability to provide interesting views of the data, and
4. provide serendipitous access to related results.

Feasibility of design is supported by visual features which keep the user oriented and motivated, including the text summaries, the query preview elements, and the subsumption hierarchy and query expansions related to the current zoom level and focus concept. These visual features are buttressed by action tools, such as undo and redo buttons, and a variety of search modalities, such as integrated query/browse, hyperlink driven result sets, and both subsumption and query expansion based browsing.

The functional usability criteria is met because of the rich interface. The implementation of multiple access modalities, with many hyperlinks, provides broad easy access to the corpus, with many opportunities for recognition. The variety of access modalities provides interesting, query centred views of the corpus.

7 Conclusion

This system is an overall advance in the area of exploration of results arising from an imprecise query. It fulfils our original goal, providing tools to explore the semantic area around an imprecise query. When the user recalls search terms, they can enter queries. If the user wants to search using recognition, they can do so in either a top down fashion, browsing the ontologically based taxonomy, or bottom up in a document centred fashion, through zooming in on the document concepts.

These exploration options are supported by a multitude of passive signposts, showing the user both their position in the taxonomic hierarchy, in the query expansion space, and in the document space. These signposts are also hyperlinks, allowing the user to go and investigate further, following their interest. The interface is highly responsive, enticing the user to continue exploring. The screen is very live; clicking on almost any part of it leads to some action. This is not an entirely good thing, with the potential for user confusion. The 'back' button is a concession to this problem.

This paper sets out and evaluates an innovative information exploration tool useful for imprecise query. This system is implemented in the medical field, and the techniques can be ported to other domains.

References

1. Mulhall, E.F., Experimental studies in recall and recognition. American Journal of Psychology, 1915. 26(2): p. 217-228.
2. Sacco, G., Dynamic taxonomies: a model for large information bases. IEEE Transactions on Knowledge & Data Engineering, 2000. 12(3): p. 468-79.
3. Sacco, G.M., Conventional taxonomies vs. Dynamic Taxonomies. 2002, Dept. Computer Science, Univ. Torino.
4. Sherman, C. (2002, May 22, 2002). Google's Gaggle of New Goodies. Retrieved 3 August, 2004, from http://searchenginewatch.com/searchday/article.php/2159971
5. Hersh, W.R., et al., A performance and failure analysis of saphire with a medline test collection. Journal of the American Medical Informatics Association, 1994. 1(1): p. 51-60.
6. UMLS. (2004). UMLS Website. Retrieved 20 Nov 2004, from http://www.nlm.nih.gov/research/umls/
7. Therapeutic Guidelines Ltd, eTG Complete. 2002, Melbourne, Australia: Therapeutic Guidelines Ltd.
8. Wollersheim, D. and W. Rahayu. Implementation of Dynamic Taxonomies for Clinical Guideline Retrieval. in International Conference on Medical Informatics. 2001. Hyderabad, India: Institute of Public Enterprise.
9. Wollersheim, D. and W. Rahayu. An Algorithm For Finding Effective Query Expansions Through Failure Analysis Of Word Statistical Information Retrieval. in ISCIT 2003. 2003. Songkhla, Thailand: Prince of Songkhla University.
10. Nunamaker, J., Chen, Minder and Purdin, Titus D.M., Systems Development in Information Systems Research. Journal of Management Information Systems, 1991. 7(3): p. 89 - 106.

A Proposal for a Unified Process for Ontology Building: UPON[*]

Antonio De Nicola[*], Michele Missikoff[*], and Roberto Navigli[**]

[*] Istituto di Analisi dei Sistemi ed Informatica
Consiglio Nazionale delle Ricerche
Viale Manzoni, 30 – 00185 Roma
{denicola, missikoff}@iasi.cnr.it
[**] Dipartimento di Informatica
Università di Roma "La Sapienza"
Via Salaria, 113 – 00198 Roma
navigli@di.uniroma1.it

Abstract. Ontologies are the backbone of the Semantic Web, a semantic-aware version of the World Wide Web. To the end of making available large-scale, high quality domain ontologies, effective and usable methodologies are needed to facilitate the process of Ontology Building. Many of the methods proposed so far only partly refer to well-known and widely used standards from other areas, like software engineering and knowledge representation. In this paper we present UPON, a methodology for ontology building derived from the Unified Software Development Process. A comparative evaluation with other methodologies, as well as the results of its adoption in the context of the Athena Integrated Project, are also discussed.

1 Introduction

Ontologies, i.e. semantic structures encoding concepts, relations and axioms of a given domain, are the backbone of the Semantic Web (Berners-Lee et al., 2001), a semantic-aware version of the World Wide Web. Ontologies allow the web resources to be semantically enriched. This is a pre-condition to provide new, advanced services over the web, such as the semantic search and retrieval of web resources.

Unfortunately the community has not yet reached a consensus on one or more standard methods for building large-scale ontologies. For this reason, in this paper we propose a method derived from a well-established software engineering process, the Unified Software Development Process (Jacobson et al., 1999).

Along this line, we present UPON, a novel approach to large-scale ontology building that takes advantage of the Unified Process (UP). As a result, on one side, the adoption of the UP and the Unified Modeling Language (UML) makes ontology building an easier task for modellers familiar with these techniques. On the other side, we show how well each phase of ontology building fits in the UP, thus guiding the process of ontology development through a number of consolidated steps.

---

[*] This work is partially supported by the Interop NoE and Athena IP, 6th European Union Framework Programme.

UPON is aimed at supporting the work of the ontology engineers, that we classify as knowledge engineers (KE) and domain experts (DE). Even though automatic ontology learning methods allow ontology engineers to significantly speed up the ontology building process, the automatically generated ontology always requires an additional manual validation and integration. Therefore, a manual procedure is still necessary to guide the process of releasing the final ontology.

The paper is organized as follows: in Section 2 we present our approach to ontology building. Section 3 discusses previous work in this area and provides a two-fold evaluation of UPON, the first by comparison with others methodologies, and the second in the context of the Athena Integrated Project[1]. In particular, using UPON, an eProcurement ontology was built with the support of AIDIMA[2], a research and development association, dedicated to technology and innovation transfer to the Spanish woodworking and furniture sector. Finally, in Section 4 we provide conclusions and future work.

2 UPON: Unified Process for Ontology Building

In this section we present UPON (Unified Process for ONtology building), an incremental methodology for ontology building. The process we propose stems its characteristics from the Software Development Unified Process, one of the most widespread and accepted methods in the software engineering community, and uses the Unified Modeling Language (UML) to support the preparation of all the blueprints of the ontology project. UML has been already shown to be suitable to this end (Guizzardi et al., 2002), confirming its nature of rich and extensible language.

What distinguishes the UP and UPON from the other processes, respectively for software and ontology engineering, is their *use-case driven, iterative and incremental* nature.

UPON is *use-case driven* in that it aims at producing an ontology with the purpose of serving its users, both humans and automated systems (e.g. semantic web services, intelligent agents, etc.). User interactions take place through *use cases* that drive the exploration of all aspects of the ontology.

The nature of the process is *iterative* because each activity is repeated possibly concentrating on different parts of the ontology being developed, but also *incremental*, since at each cycle the ontology is further detailed and extended.

Following the UP, in UPON we have cycles, phases, iterations and workflows. Each cycle consists of four phases (*inception, elaboration, construction* and *transition*) and results in the release of a new version of the ontology. Each phase is further subdivided into iterations. During each iteration, five workflows (described in the next subsections) take place: *requirements, analysis, design, implementation* and *test*. Workflows and phases are orthogonal in that the contribution of each workflow to an iteration of a phase can be more or less significant: early phases are mostly concerned with establishing the requirements (identifying the domain, scoping the ontology, etc.), whereas later iterations result in additive increments that eventually bring to the

---

[1] "Advanced Technologies for Interoperability of Heterogeneous Networks and their Application", Integrated Project 507849, 6th EU FP - http://www.athena-ip.org
[2] http://www.aidima.es/aidima

final release of the ontology (Fig. 1). Notice that, as illustrated in the figure, more than one iteration may be required to complete each of the four phases. This scheme follows faithfully the Unified Process. In addition, as shown in the figure, the domain expert provides his contribution in the early workflows and partially during the *Test* while the knowledge engineer is mostly focused on the *Design* and *Implementation*.

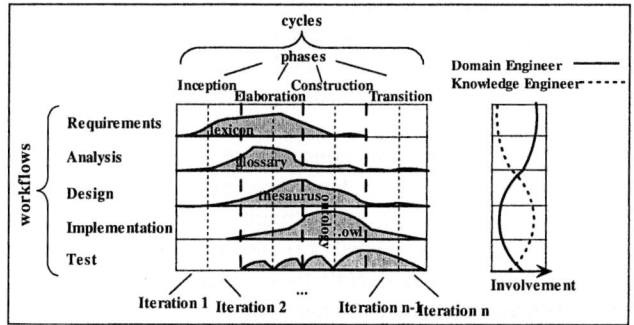

Fig. 1. The UPON Framework

The first iterations (*inception phase*) are mostly concerned with capturing requirements and partly performing some conceptual analysis. Neither implementation nor test is performed. During subsequent iterations (belonging to the *elaboration phase*) analysis is performed and the fundamental concepts are identified and loosely structured. This may require some design effort and it is also possible that the modellers provide a preliminary implementation in order to have a small skeletal blueprint of the ontology, but most of the design and implementation workflows pervade iterations in the *construction phase*. Here some additional analysis could be still required aiming at identifying concepts to be further added to the ontology. During the final iterations (*transition phase*), testing is heavily performed and the ontology is eventually released.

The incremental nature of UPON requires first the identification of the relevant terms in the domain, gathered in a lexicon; then the latter is progressively enriched with definitions, yielding a glossary; adding to it the basic ontological relationships allows a thesaurus to be produced, until further enrichments and a final formalization produces the sought reference ontology.

In the following subsections each ontology workflow is described in detail, with the help of a practical example.

2.1 The Requirements Workflow

Requirements capture is the process of specifying the semantic needs and knowledge to be encoded in the ontology. The essential purpose of this workflow is to reach an agreement between the modellers, the knowledge engineers, and the final users (Jacobson et al., 1999), represented by the domain experts.

During the first meetings, knowledge engineers and domain experts establish the guidelines for building the ontology. The first goal is the identification of the objectives of the ontology users. To this end, it is necessary to: (i) determining the domain of interest and the scope, and (ii) defining the purpose. These objectives are achieved by: (iii) writing a storyboard, (iv) creating an application lexicon, (v) identifying the competency questions, and (vi) the related use cases.

(i) Determining the domain of interest and the scope. Delimiting the domain of interest is a fundamental step to be performed (Uschold and King, 1995), aiming at focusing on the appropriate fragment of reality to be modelled. If the domain is huge, one or more sub-domains may also be determined.

The domain we used to validate the UPON methodology is *eBusiness*. In particular, we focused on *eProcurement*, the *business-to-business* (*B2B*) purchase and sale of goods and services over the Internet.

Defining the scope of the ontology consists in the identification of the most important concepts to be represented, their characteristics and granularity. Defining a scope means making a set of ontological commitments, bringing some part of the domain into focus at the (required and expected) expense of blurring other parts. These ontological commitments are not incidental: they provide a guidance in deciding what aspects of the domain are relevant and what to ignore.

Following Guarino et al. (1994), the ontological commitment can be seen as "a mapping between a language and something which can be called an ontology". This allows one to preliminarily identify terms as representatives of ontology concepts.

Usually at this stage modellers have only a vague idea of the role each concept will play, i.e., their semantic interconnections, within the ontology. If necessary, they can annotate these ideas for further development during subsequent iterations.

In the *eProcurement application*, the ontology chiefly concerns all the processes and the interactions between a buyer and a supplier (e.g., exchange of business documents like an *invoice* or a *purchase order*).

(ii) Defining the purpose (or motivating scenario). The reason for a new ontology, its intended uses, and the kinds of users must be established. In the *eProcurement application*, the goal of the ontology is to provide a better understanding of the domain of interest and be a support for semantic interoperability between two legacy systems. In particular, we envisage three basic uses of the developed ontology:

- search and retrieval of semantically enriched documents;
- ontology-based reconciliation of data messages exchanged between a buyer and a supplier in business transactions;
- ontology-based reconciliation of business processes between two different business partners (e.g. the steps in a purchasing activity).

(iii) Writing a storyboard. In this step the domain expert is asked to write a panel or series of panels of rough sketches outlining the sequence of all the activities that defines a particular scenario. This storyboard can be also used to extract the terminology of the domain expert.

(iv) Creating the *application lexicon*. This task can be supported by using some automatic tools to extract knowledge from documents, such as OntoLearn (Navigli and Velardi, 2004).

(v) **Identifying the competency questions.** Competency questions are questions an ontology must be able to answer (Gruninger and Fox, 1995). They are identified through interviews with domain experts, brainstorming, an analysis of the document base concerning the domain, etc. The questions do not generate ontological commitments, but are used during the test workflow to evaluate the ontological commitments that have been made. The usage of competency questions is more appropriate when the ontology will be used for querying and discovering resources rather than for reconciliation.

(vi) **Use-case identification and prioritization.** UPON proposes to take competency questions into account through use-case models. A *use-case model* serves as a basis to reach an agreement between the users (i.e., who require the ontology) and the modellers, and contains a number of *use cases*. In the context of ontologies, use cases correspond to knowledge paths through the ontology to be followed for answering one or more competency questions. Although they are to be specified during the analysis and design workflows, it is necessary to *prioritize* and *package* (i.e. group) them during requirements. The result will help dictate which use cases the team should focus on during early iterations, and which ones can be postponed.

The outcome of the Requirements Workflow is a set of documents, including those resulting from the above steps, to be extended during subsequent iterations.

2.2 The Analysis Workflow

The conceptual analysis consists of the refinement and structuring of the ontology requirements identified in previous section. The ontological commitments derived from the definition of scope are extended, by reusing existing resources and through concept refinement.

Considering reuse of existing resources: Identification of relevant terms (domain lexicon). The description of this activity adheres to the view of linguistic ontology (Gómez-Pérez et al., 2004) in which concepts, at least the lower and intermediate levels, are anchored to texts, i.e. they have a counterpart in natural language.

Reuse concerns internal legacy resources as well as external resources requiring possible refinements and extensions, like interviews, documents, standards, glossaries, thesauri, computational lexicons and available ontologies.

In the *eProcurement application* the domain experts considered the following *eBusiness* standards: ebXML (http://www.ebxml.org), RosettaNET (http://www.rosettanet.org), and OAGIS (http://www.openapplications.org). The analysis of these standards comprises 2614 elements (140 from ebXML, 1873 from RosettaNET, 600 from OAGIS). A statistical analysis was done in a corpus of documents of reference to identify frequently used terms to be included in the domain lexicon. The domain experts decided to include, in this lexicon, all the terms present in at least two standards (e.g. Price, Currency, TransportMode, etc.). Other terms were included only after approval from a wider panel of experts. After this activity, the domain lexicon contained 83 terms.

Modelling the application scenario using UML diagrams. The goal of this activity is to model the application scenario and better specify the Use Case Diagrams, drawn in the requirement workflow, with the aid of Activity and Class Diagrams. The reason to use UML is that it represents the scenario in a shared language, that allows domain experts (especially business people) to perform this activity without the support of the knowledge engineer.

Building the glossary. A first version of a glossary of concepts of the domain of interest has to be built merging the application lexicon (from the domain experts) and the domain lexicon (from the existing resources). Considering the scope of the two lexicons we can organize all the concepts in two major areas: the intersection area and the disjoint area (see Fig. 2). As done with the analysis of existing resources, it is possible to use a similar "inclusion policy": the glossary should include all the concepts coming from the intersection area and, after the domain experts approval, the ones from the disjoint area. Then domain experts should agree on the definition of concepts. It is very important that the concepts are defined according to precise references or mentioning the author of that definition.

2.3 The Design Workflow

The refinement of entities, actors and processes identified in the analysis workflow, as well as the identification of their relationships, is performed during the design workflow. The design of the ontology follows the OPAL methodology (Missikoff and Taglino, 2002).

Categorising the concepts according to the *OPAL* methodology (Actor, Process, Object). Each concept can be further enriched with the identification of a top-level "category" for the defined concept (e.g. *entity* for Product, *process* for Purchase Order Issuing, *actor* for Purchasing Unit, etc.).

These "categories" include the major ontological categories, according to proposals of top ontologies, such as (Sowa, 1999), or meta-ontologies (Uschold and King, 1995). We adopted the *OPAL* methodology.

Refining the concepts and their relations. At this stage, the gradual and incremental passage from terms to concepts is made clear by the formal definition of relations between sets of synonyms identified in the previous phase.

As a first structuring step, concepts can be organized in a taxonomic hierarchy through *generalization* (the *kind-of* or *is-a* relation). Three main approaches are known in the literature (Uschold and Gruninger, 1996): *top-down* (from general to particular), *bottom-up* (from particular to general) and *middle-out* (or *combined*). The combined approach consists in finding the salient concepts and then generalizing and specializing them. This approach is considered to be the most effective because concepts "in the middle" tend to be more informative about the domain.

The resulting taxonomy can finally be extended with other relations, i.e., *part-of* and *association*. The outcome of this step is a UML *class diagram*, using *generalization (IsA)*, *aggregation (Part-Of)* and *association* relations. A UML association relation can be labeled with a predicate and allows to represent all the relations needed for the ontology to be built.

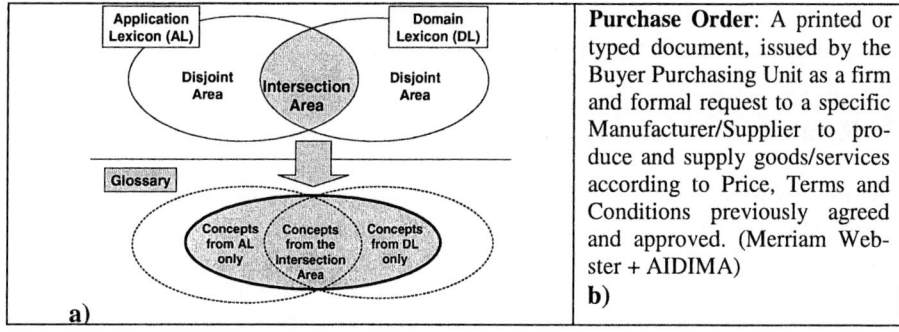

Fig. 2. a) Activity of glossary building. b) One of the concepts included in the *eProcurement* glossary with its definition.

2.4 The Implementation Workflow

The purpose of this workflow is to formalize the ontology in a language and to implement it in terms of components. Components implement concepts from the design workflow and follow the established grouping into packages (i.e. ontology portions). *Use-case prioritization* from the requirements workflow and *packaging* from all the previous workflows allow component engineers to work on different parts of the ontology to be integrated at subsequent iterations.

Components can be written down in a variety of languages and notations. The adoption of a certain formalism is appropriate as long as it conveys the appropriate expressiveness and it allows an easy reuse within the community. As a result of a long standardization effort, the Ontology Web Language (OWL: http://www.w3.org/TR/owl-features) is the main candidate for encoding an ontology to be used on the Semantic Web. The outcome of this workflow is the implementation model, including packages of implemented components.

For instance, in the *eProcurement* domain, concepts can be packaged in two groups: the ones concerning internal activities, performed inside a business organization (e.g. *Purchase Requisition Form, Evaluating Purchase Request, ...*), and the ones concerning interaction activities, performed between two different business organizations (e.g. *Purchase Order, Issuing Purchase Order*).

2.5 The Test Workflow

The test workflow allows to verify that the ontology correctly implements its requirements. UPON envisages two kinds of test. The first concerns the coverage of the ontology over the application domain. In particular, the domain expert is asked to semantically annotate the UML diagrams, representing the application scenario, with the ontology concepts. This test is more appropriate for ontologies to be used for the ontology-based reconciliation of messages and business processes. The second concerns the competency questions and the possibility to answer them by using concepts in the ontology. For instance, in the *eProcurement application* such a test gives a positive result, since it is possible to answer to the question *"What are the documents that a company receives before a Purchase Order?"* using the ontology concepts

Request For Quotation, Processing RFQ, Sending RFQ. This test is more appropriate for ontologies to be used for discovery and search of web resources.

3 Related Work and Evaluation

The first contributions to ontology building methods are due to Gruber (1993), Gruninger and Fox (1995), Uschold and King (1995), Uschold and Gruninger (1996), constituting the basis for many subsequent proposals. Gruber's seminal work discusses some basic ontology design criteria (clarity, coherence, extendibility, minimal encoding bias and ontological commitment). Gruninger and Fox (1995) provide a skeletal methodology for ontology building, while a method based on competency questions is presented by Uschold and King (1995).

A complete ontology development process, *METHONTOLOGY*, is proposed by Fernández et al. (1997). The process is composed by the following phases: specification, conceptualization, formalization, integration, implementation, maintenance. Its life cycle is based on evolving prototypes and specific techniques peculiar to each activity. Other activities, like control, quality assurance, knowledge acquisition, integration, evaluation and documentation are carried out simultaneously with the ontology development activities.

With a strong emphasis on knowledge maintenance and management, Sure et al. (2004) propose *On-To-Knowledge*, an ontology development process consisting of five main phases: feasibility study, kick-off, refinement, evaluation, application and evolution. Each phase consists of a number of sub-steps.

Other approaches, often tied to industry or research projects, include the methods used for building *CyC*, *SENSUS*, and *KAKTUS* (OntoWeb deliverable, 2002). A complete overview of ontology building methods is provided by Corcho et al. (2003).

We provide a two-fold evaluation of the proposed approach. First, we provide a comparative evaluation with respect to the methodologies introduced above. Second, we briefly describe our experience in using the process in building an ontology of *eProcurement* for the Athena Integrated Project.

In order to evaluate a number of different ontology building processes, Fernández and Gómez-Pérez (2002) present a framework based on the comparison with respect to the IEEE 1074-1995 standard for software development life cycle. Here we integrate UPON into the evaluation framework in order to assess it with respect to the other proposals.

The IEEE standard, applied to ontologies, distinguishes three kinds of processes: *project management processes*, concerning the creation of a project management framework for the entire ontology life cycle; *ontology development processes*, including a *pre-development* process (an environment study and a feasibility study), a *development* process (requirements, design, implementation) and a *post-development* process (installation, operation, support, maintenance and retirement of an ontology); *integral processes*, required to complete ontology project activities.

Because of its nature, UPON does not deal with project management processes and pre/post development activities, while this is a major benefit of the On-To-Knowledge approach. On the other side, the adoption of UPON does not require any learning curve for domain experts using UML and the Unified Process, because it is just an adaptation of the UP to ontology building. This is an advantage also over the adoption of METHONTOLOGY, that roughly covers the same development processes as UPON. Furthermore, an extension of the UP, the *Enterprise Unified Process* (Nalbone et al., 2004), is being developed with the aim of taking project management and all the other pre/post development activities into account. In the future we will consider the extension of UPON to these other aspects.

Another big advantage of UPON over the other methodologies is that diagramming, documentation and versioning can be performed with the aid of a variety of tools specialized for UML, like Rational Rose, Microsoft Visio, etc.

UPON was applied in the context of the Athena Project for building an ontology of *eProcurement*. Despite its preliminary stage, both domain experts and modellers expressed their appreciation. The developed ontology consists of 23 actors, 21 processes, 14 objects and 83 attributes, complex and atomic. Though it may seem a "small ontology", it is appropriate for the given purposes. In particular it allows the semantic annotation of the main business documents (e.g. the purchase order and the invoice) used in a purchasing transaction.

4 Conclusions and Future Work

In this paper we presented UPON, an ontology building methodology based on the Unified Process. Ontology building is different from developing a software system, but we showed that the basic phases are the same and some diagrammatic specifications can be used for each phase of the lifecycle of both software systems and ontologies.

The strength of the approach lies in the UP being a highly scalable and customizable framework. It can indeed be tailored to fit a number of variables: the ontology size, the domain of interest, the complexity of the ontology to build, the experience and skill of the project organization and its people. Furthermore, the modellers can decide to adapt the scheme presented here for one of the methodologies derived from the UP (like the Rational Unified Process).

In a future work, we would like to provide a more detailed evaluation of the process with respect to the other proposals as well as an analysis of how to adapt cross-phase activities to the needs of ontology building. In describing UPON, some aspects of the UP, like interfaces, architectures, activity diagrams etc., have been neglected for the sake of space.

Finally, an important aspect is the possibility of assessing the quality of an ontology built with the UPON methodology. This issue is currently under elaboration and will be presented in the next future.

References

1. T. Berners-Lee, J. Hendler, O. Lassila (2001). The Semantic Web. *Scientific American*, may 2001.
2. O. Corcho, M. Fernández, A. Gómez-Pérez (2003). Methodologies, tools and languages for building ontologies. Where is the meeting point? *Data & Knowledge Engineering*, 46.

3. M. Fernández, A. Gómez-Pérez, N. Juristo. (1997) METHONTOLOGY: From Ontological Art towards Ontological Engineering. *Symposium on Ontological Engineering of AAAI*. Stanford, California.
4. M. Fernández, A. Gómez-Pérez (2002). Overview and analysis of methodologies for building ontologies. *The Knowledge Engineering Review*, **17**(2).
5. A. Gómez-Pérez, M. Fernández-Lopez, O. Corcho (2004). *Ontological Engineering*, Springer-Verlag, London.
6. T. R. Gruber (1993). A Translation Approach to Portable Ontology Specification. *Knowledge Acquisition* **5**, pp. 199-220.
7. M. Gruninger and M. S. Fox. Methodology for the Design and Evaluation of Ontologies, Proc. of *Workshop on Basic Ontological Issues in Knowledge Sharing* in IJCAI 95, Montreal, Canada, 1995.
8. N. Guarino, M. Carrara, P. Giaretta (1994). Formalizing Ontological Commitments. In *Proceedings of AAAI 94*, volume 1, pp. 560-567.
9. G. Guizzardi, H. Herre, G. Wagner (2002). Towards Ontological Foundations for UML Conceptual Models. *1st International Conference on Ontologies, Databases and Application of Semantics*, Irvine, California, USA.
10. I. Jacobson, G. Booch, and J. Rumbaugh (1999). *The Unified Software Development Process*. Addison Wesley, USA.
11. M. Missikoff, F. Taglino (2002). Business and Enterprise Management with SymOntoX. 1st International Semantic Web Conference, Sardinia, Italy.
12. R. Navigli, P. Velardi (2004). Learning Domain Ontologies from Document Warehouses and Dedicated Websites, *Computational Linguistics* 30(2), MIT Press, June.
13. J. Nalbone, M. Vizdos, M. Ambler. *Adopting the Enterprise Unified Process*. White paper, Ronin International Inc., 2004.
14. *OntoWeb Deliverable 1.4: A Survey on Methodologies for Developing, Maintaining, Evaluating and Reengineering Ontologies* (2002). http://ontoweb.aifb.uni-karlsruhe.de/About/Deliverables/D1.4-v1.0.pdf
15. J. Sowa (1999). *Knowledge Representation: Logical, Philosophical and Computational Foundations*. Brooks/Cole, USA.
16. Y. Sure, S. Staab, R. Studer (2004). On-To-Knowledge Methodology (OTKM). *Handbook on Ontologies*, Springer, pp. 117-132.
17. M. Ushold, and M. Gruninger: Ontologies: Principles, Methods and Applications. *Knowledge Engineering Review*, 11(2) (1996).
18. M. Uschold and M. King: Towards a Methodology for Building Ontologies. Proc. of Workshop on Basic Ontological Issues in Knowledge Sharing in IJCAI 1995, Montreal, Canada (1995).

Transforming Software Package Classification Hierarchies into Goal-Based Taxonomies[*]

Claudia Ayala[1] and Xavier Franch

Universitat Politècnica de Catalunya
08034 Barcelona, Catalunya, Spain
{cayala, franch}@lsi.upc.edu

Abstract. Software package selection is an activity that plays an increasingly crucial role in the delivery of software systems. One of its main open issues is how to structure the knowledge about the software marketplace and in particular how to know which types of packages are available and which are their objectives. Profit and non-profit organizations of any kind use to arrange these types into categories in a hierarchical form. However, the rationale behind the proposals found is often confusing and therefore their usefulness is hampered. In this paper we propose the use of taxonomies for structuring this knowledge. Our taxonomies are goal-driven, which means that we provide a rationale for the decisions taken. The leaves of the taxonomies are the types of packages available in the market, whilst the intermediate nodes are categories that group them when closer relationships are found. The proposed taxonomies are not defined from the scratch but applying the appropriate transformation rules to some departing classification available. We define the syntactic form of the rules and also their applicability conditions as properties on the involved goals. We apply them to a particular case, a taxonomy for business applications.

1 Introduction

The amount of software packages [1, 2] available on the market is growing more and more. This tendency is due both to the increasing adoption of component-based software technologies by the community, and to the continuous creation of new communication and marketing channels that bridge the gap between providers and consumers of those products. Therefore, there is an increasing need for organizing the available types of software packages to achieve more efficient and reliable selection processes.

As a response to this need, profit and non-profit companies, organizations and teams have arranged this knowledge by defining categories of services, products and knowledge, usually structured in a hierarchical form [3-14]. Regardless of their comprehension, completeness, and scope, all of these proposals share a common characteristic that may be considered as a drawback: they present a hierarchy of items without a clear rationale behind. The categorization relies on experience, knowledge, and observation but they rarely use knowledge engineering and requirements engineering techniques to classify the enclosed items. Sometimes, the meaning of a

---

[*] This work has been partially supported by the Spanish MEC project TIN2004-07461-C02-01.
[1] C. Ayala's work has been partially supported by a FI grant (Catalan government).

particular category is not clear without further examining the items, especially if it is absolutely unknown to the user. As a result, the understanding, use, evolution, extension, and customization of the categorization proposal may be difficult.

The purpose of this paper is to present an approach for solving this drawback. Our proposal is based on the use of goals to provide semantics to the nodes of existing ad-hoc classification hierarchies. Then, we may define the process of taxonomy construction as the repeated application of transformation rules over the nodes of the source hierarchy. These transformations must satisfy some completeness and correctness conditions with respect to the involved goals which will be presented here. For illustration purposes, we apply these rules to a case study.

2 A Process for the Construction of Software Package Taxonomies

The transformation of an unstructured classification into a goal-based taxonomy can be roughly divided into two steps. Firstly, we apply techniques for discovering goals in the departing classification hierarchy; examples are the GBRAM method [15], built on top of the Inquiry Cycle approach [16], and decision trees building algorithms such as C4.5 [17] and CART [18] for expressing goals as a combination of classifiers values. Secondly, we rearrange the hierarchy to make it correct and complete by applying repeatedly transformation rules.

In the rest of the paper we focus on the second step of the process. In other words, we consider that the goal discovery process will be covered by existing techniques as those mentioned above. For defining formally the transformation rules, we first state the notions of taxonomy and goal and we define what a correct and complete taxonomy is. These two notions will induce naturally a process to apply the transformation rules in a comfortable order that guarantees termination while being expressive enough.

A *goal-oriented taxonomy* T is a tree over a domain. As such, we need predicates and functions shown in table 1.

Table 1. Predicates and functions over taxonomies

Belongs(T, A): the element A belongs to T	*Parent*(T, A, B): A is parent of B in T
Leaf(T, A): A is a leaf in T	*Root*(T, A): A is the root of T
Children(T, A): returns the set of children of A in T	
Successors(T, A): returns the set of successors of A in T	*Goal*(A): goal of node A
Ancestors(T, A): returns the set of ancestors of A in T	*Name*(A): name of node A

Goals are defined over a set $X = \{x_k\}_n$ of independent variables that characterize the taxonomy. *Goal satisfaction* is defined by means of assignment to the variables, therefore for each assignment $ass = (x_1 \leftarrow v_1, \ldots, x_n \leftarrow v_n)$, the expression $sat_{ass}(G)$ yields true if the goal G evaluates to true for this assignment, otherwise false. Throughout the rest of the paper we use the predicates on goals with the meaning and abbreviations showed in table 2.

Table 2. Predicates, semantics and abbreviations used over goals

Predicate or function	Semantics	Abbrev
impliesGoal(G, H): the goal G implies the goal H	$\forall ass: sat_{ass}(G) \Rightarrow sat_{ass}(H)$	$G \Rightarrow H$
soft-impliesGoal(G, H): the goal G implies the goal H for some assignment whilst the reverse is not true	$\exists ass: sat_{ass}(G) \Rightarrow sat_{ass}(H) \wedge \neg\exists ass: sat_{ass}(H) \Rightarrow sat_{ass}(G)$	$G \overset{\pm}{\Rightarrow} H$
disjointGoals(G, H): goals G and H are mutually exclusive	$\forall ass: \neg\, sat_{ass}(G) \wedge sat_{ass}(H)$	$\neg G \wedge H$
equivGoals(G, H): goals G and H are equivalent	$\forall ass: sat_{ass}(G) = sat_{ass}(H)$	$G \equiv H$
emptyGoal(G): goal G is never satisfied	$\forall ass: \neg\, sat_{ass}(G)$	$G = \varnothing$
$F = $ *diffGoals*(G, H): obtain the difference of goals G and H	$\forall ass: sat_{ass}(G) \wedge \neg\, sat_{ass}(H) \Leftrightarrow sat_{ass}(F)$	$G - H$
$F = $ *unionGoals*(G, H): obtain the union of goals G and H	$\forall ass: sat_{ass}(G) \vee sat_{ass}(H) \Leftrightarrow sat_{ass}(F)$	$G \cup H$
$F = $ *intersectGoals*(G, H): obtain the intersection of goals G and H	$\forall ass: sat_{ass}(G) \wedge sat_{ass}(H) \Leftrightarrow sat_{ass}(F)$	$G \cap H$
UnionGoalsExt($\{G_k\}_n$), *intersectGoalsExt*($\{G_k\}_n$) are extensions to a set of goals (used quantified)		

A goal-oriented taxonomy T is said to be correct and complete if it satisfies the conditions below. C1 ensures that decomposition of software package types is well-formed, C2 that the taxonomy provides a unique way for classifying software packages and C3 that software packages can always be classified using the taxonomy:

C1. *Parent-child correctness*. The goal of each node is implied by its parent goal:

$\forall X$: belongs (T, X): [$\forall Y$: Y$\in$ children(T, X): Goal(X) $\Rightarrow$ Goal(Y)]

C2. *Siblings correctness*. The goals of siblings are disjoint:

$\forall X, Y$: X $\neq$ Y $\wedge$ belongs (T, X) $\wedge$ belongs(T, Y) $\wedge$

($\exists A$: belongs (T, A): parent(T, A, X) $\wedge$ parent(T, A, Y)): $\neg$ Goal(X) $\wedge$ Goal(Y)

C3. *Completeness*. The goals of siblings cover altogether the goal of their parent:

$\forall X$: belongs (T, X) $\wedge \neg$ leaf(T, X): [Goal(X) $\equiv \cup Y$: Y$\in$children(T, X): Goal(Y))]

Given these correctness and completeness notions, we can define a process for rearranging a goal-oriented taxonomy: first we remove conflicts among parents and children to ensure C1, next we detect and solve conflicts among siblings to ensure C2 and afterwards we complete the taxonomy identifying new nodes that fulfill the parent goal to ensure C3. We add a fourth step, once we have a correct and complete goal-oriented taxonomy, to tailor the result to the particular (and subjective) taste of the designer with respect to level of detail. Transformation rules are used in each step to progress towards the result.

3 A Set of Transformation Rules for Manipulating Taxonomies

In this section we present the transformation rules that are used when restructuring taxonomies. Taxonomy manipulation is goal-based taking into account the properties of correctness and completeness of taxonomies stated in section 2. There are 8 transformation rules that are applied into the 4 identified steps; some rules apply to more than one step. Some of the rules may take slightly different forms, and we have therefore some different variations of the basic idea which are given different names. The rules are specified by pre and postconditions using the predicates and functions on taxonomies and goals introduced in section 2; in postconditions, the expression *x@pre* stands for the value of *x* before applying the rule. Due to lack of space, the predicates on the form of the tree are not written explicitly, they can be easily inferred from Fig. 1, which shows graphically the transformation rules. In each step we assume as invariants the conditions Ci (see section 2) that have been ensured in the previous step that must be considered implicitly as part of the preconditions and postconditions of the rules that apply in this step. Last, we get rid of renamings, we assume that every rule has the right to change the name of the involved nodes for legibility.

3.1 Transformation Rules in Step 1

When a node B is found such that its goal is not implied by its parent's goal, we have basically two options: to move B to another part of the taxonomy T or else to remove it. We introduce therefore two rules, *Reallocation* and *Removal*.

R1. Reallocation(T, A, B, X) Changes the current position of B (and its successors), because its goal violates C1 with respect to its parent's goal A. The new parent position will be X.
- *Precondition*: $\neg\, Goal(A) \Rightarrow Goal(B)$

There are several variations of reallocation, each refining slightly this initial contract:
- B's goal is implied by some other node X's goal in the taxonomy T, which is the destination of the reallocation. We call this variant *Strict Reallocation* and it is characterized by the fact that its precondition is further enlarged:

R1.1. Strict Reallocation(T, A, B, X).
- *Precondition*: $\neg\, Goal(A) \Rightarrow Goal(B) \land Goal(X) \Rightarrow Goal(B)$

- B's goal is not implied by any other node's goal in the taxonomy T, but there is a relationship with node X's goal, which is the destination of the reallocation. We represent this relationship by the concept of soft implication ($\pm\Rightarrow$, see section 2). In this case, we have three more subcases:

  a) X's goal is left as it is, which means that we need further rules to be applied on X and B to reach a correct state. In other words, this reallocation is just a first move in a multi-rule movement. We call this *Unfinished Reallocation*.

R1.2. Unfinished Reallocation(T, A, B, X).
- *Precondition*: $\neg\, Goal(A) \Rightarrow Goal(B) \land Goal(X) \pm\Rightarrow Goal(B)$
---

  b) X's goal is enlarged, to capture the part of B's goal that is not implied. Of course, this increment of satisfaction must be propagated to all X's ancestors. This variant is called *Enlarged Reallocation*.

R1.3. Enlarged Reallocation(T, A, B, X).
- *Precondition*: $\neg\, Goal(A) \Rightarrow Goal(B) \land Goal(X) \pm\Rightarrow Goal(B)$
- *Postcondition*: $Goal(X) = Goal@pre(X) \cup Goal(B)\; \land$
  $\forall Y \in ancestors(T, X): Goal(Y) = Goal@pre(Y) \cup Goal(B)$
---

c) B's goal is narrowed, to discard the part of the goal that is not implied by X's goal. Of course, this narrowing must be propagated to all B's successors. Thus, we obtain the *Narrowed Reallocation*.

R1.4. Narrowed Reallocation(T, A, B, X).
- *Precondition*: $\neg\,\text{Goal}(A) \Rightarrow \text{Goal}(B) \wedge \text{Goal}(X) \not\Rightarrow \text{Goal}(B)$
- *Postcondition*: $\text{Goal}(B) = \text{Goal@pre}(B) \cap \text{Goal}(X) \wedge$
  $\forall Y \in \text{successors}(T, X): \text{Goal}(Y) = \text{Goal@pre}(Y) \cap \text{Goal}(B)$

In the case of removal, in this step we consider a special case of the general *Removal* rule, called *Hard Removal* (for distinguishing it from the type of removal introduced later) that is applied when the node is not related neither to its parent goal, nor to other nodes, nor the overall taxonomy goal.

R2. Removal (T, A, B). Deletes the B node (and its successors) from the taxonomy T.

R2.1. Hard Removal (T, A, B)
- *Precondition*: $\neg\,\text{Goal}(A) \Rightarrow \text{Goal}(B)$

3.2 Transformation Rules in Step 2

When some siblings $\{C_k\}_n$ that are children of A are found such that their goals are not disjoint, we have basically three options:

- To remove repeatedly until no overlapping exists, applying the *Soft Removal* rule such that an element B of these $\{C_k\}_n$ (and its successors) is removed each time.

R2.2. Soft Removal(T, A, B).
- *Precondition*: $\exists C: \text{parent}(T,A,C): \text{Goal}(B) \wedge \text{Goal}(C)$

- To merge them to hide the overlapping part applying a particular case of the Merge rule, called *Inclusive Merge*.

R3. Merge (T, A, $\{C_k\}_n$, B). Merges the nodes $\{C_k\}_n$ into one called B. The new node's goal is the union of siblings' goals. The children of the merged nodes become children of the new goal. It is important to stand out that these new children are in fact siblings and so new conflicts may arise, to be dealt with later in step 2.
- *Postcondition*: $\text{Goal}(B) = \cup\, k: 1 \leq k \leq n: \text{Goal}(C_k)$

R3.1 Inclusive Merge(T, A, $\{C_k\}_n$, B)
- *Precondition*: $\cap\, k: 1 \leq k \leq n: \text{Goal}(C_k) \neq \emptyset$

- To keep them extracting the common part applying the *Split* rule. This rule has a slightly difficult contract. It takes the common part of the set of siblings $\{C_k\}_n$ and makes a new node B with it. In the precondition, we must make sure that C1 is not violated after applying the rule. This could happen if for some child of some of the involved nodes, its goal is not implied neither by its current parent after the operation, nor by the new node; in other words, the goal of the child could be partially covered by the old and new nodes.

R4. Split (T, A, $\{C_k\}_n$, B).
- *Precondition*: $\cap\, k: 1 \leq k \leq n: \text{Goal}(C_k) \neq \emptyset \wedge$
  $\forall X \in \text{children}(T, C_k): \text{Goal}(X) \Rightarrow (\cap\, k: 1 \leq k \leq n: \text{Goal}(C_k)) \vee$
  $(\cap\, k: 1 \leq k \leq n: \text{Goal}(C_k)) \Rightarrow \text{Goal}(X)$

- *Postcondition*: Goal(B) = ∩ k: 1 ≤ k ≤ n: Goal(C_k) ∧
  ∀k: 1≤ k ≤ n: Goal(C_k)= Goal(C_k)@pre −Goal(B) ∧
  ∀k: 1 ≤ k ≤ n: ∀X∈ children@pre(T, C_k):
  (Goal(B) ⇒ Goal(X)) ⇒ parent(T, B, X) ∧
  (Goal(C_k) ⇒ Goal(X)) ⇒ parent(T, C_k, X)

3.3 Transformation Rules in Step 3

Step 3 is oriented to reach the state C3. When the decomposition of a node is such that its children do not cover its goal, the only behavior that applies is to create new nodes covering the part of goal left. Thus, we only can to apply the *Identification* rule adding as preconditions the incompleteness of parent's goal and that the new node's goal will not violate the states C1 and C2 ensured in the two previous steps.

R5. Identification(T, A, B). Inserts a new node as child of an existing one whose goal is not fully covered by its children's goals. The new node's goal must not violate neither C1 nor C2.
- *Precondition*: Goal(A) ⇒ Goal(B) ∧
  (∀X: X∈ children(A): ¬Goal(X) ∧ Goal(B)) ∧
  ¬ (Goal(A) ≡ ∪ X: X∈ children(A): Goal(X))

3.4 Transformation Rules in Step 4

Step 4 just restructures the taxonomy once it has been proven correct with the aim of leveraging the incoming taxonomy. In a few words, the rationale for changing the form of a correct taxonomy is:

- a leaf A is too abstract (i.e., its attained goal is too coarse-grained, mixing different concepts) and should be decomposed into $\{C_k\}_n$ nodes to add detail. Thus, *Division* rule should be applied:

R6. Division(T, A, $\{C_k\}_n$). Breaks a node A into several descendants. Relationships among the new nodes' goals and the divided node's goal shall ensure that C1, C2 and C3 are preserved.
- *Precondition*: ∀k: 1 ≤ k ≤ n: Goal(A) ⇒ Goal(C_k) ∧
  ∀j, k: 1 ≤ j < k ≤ n: ¬(Goal(C_j) ∧ Goal(C_k)) ∧
  Goal(A) ≡ ∪ k: 1 ≤ k ≤ n: Goal(C_k)

- the children of a node A do not really add value to the taxonomy and must be either removed applying *Pruning* rule or merged (the variant used in this step is called *Non-inclusive Merge* a weaker version of the merge of step 2):

R7. Pruning(T, A). Eliminates the children (and all its successors) of an intermediate node A.

R3.2 Non-inclusive Merge (T, A, $\{C_k\}_n$)
- *Postcondition*: Goal(B) = ∪ k: 1 ≤ k ≤ n: Goal(C_k)

- the conceptual gap among a node A and some of its children is too wide, resulting in a too flat hierarchy, and an intermediate node with a new goal must be introduced using *Abstraction rule*:

R8. Abstraction(T, A, {C_k}$_n$, B). Creates a new node B as parent of a set of existing ones {C_k}$_n$, which becomes child of their parent A. The new node's goal is the union of the goals of the nodes in the set. The children of the merged nodes become children of the new goal.
- *Postcondition*: Goal(B) = $\cup$ k: $1 \leq k \leq n$: Goal(C_k)

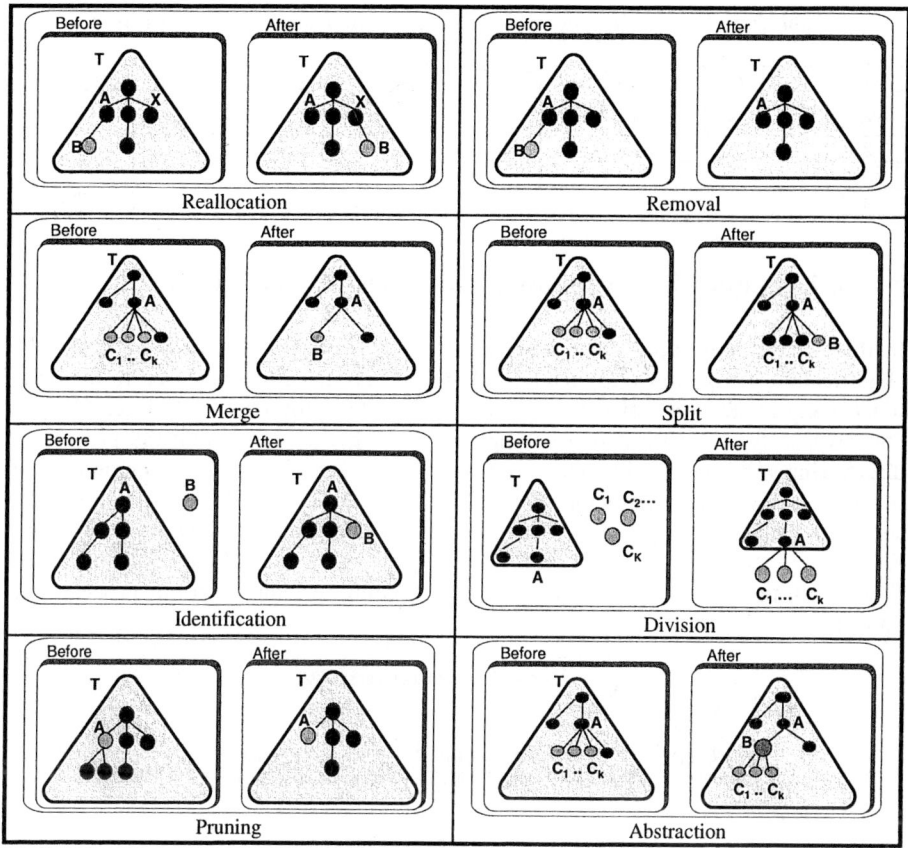

Fig. 1. Set of Transformation Rules

3.5 Final Remarks

As a summary, table 3 presents the transformation rules according to the step in which they can be used. It is not difficult to demonstrate both the correctness of the rules and the termination of each step. For correctness, it can be shown that, at each step, the rules preserve the conditions that apply. Our style in writing the rules (preconditions, postconditions, and invariants) makes these proofs easier. For termination, we can define metrics whose value is not incremented by the application of the rules. For step 1, the metrics counts the number of pairs parent-child that violate the goal implication rule. Each rule applied decrements by 1 or does not modify the value. For step 2, it is not so easy because individual merges can generate more conflicts among children than the one that is being solved; therefore, we need a more elaborated metrics in which not just the number but also the position at the tree (more precisely, the level) is taken into account. For step 3, and identification either decrements by 1 or does not modify the metrics' value. Step 4 has not an invariant to be ensured, so we do not need termination condition, the step may finish at any moment.

Table 3. Summary of transformation rules and their applicability to the 4 steps

Step	Reallocation	Removal	Split	Merge	Identification	Division	Pruning	Abstraction
1	R1.1, R1.2, R1.3, R1.4	R2.1						
2		R2.2	R3	R4.1				
3					R5			
4				R4.2		R6	R7	R8

4 An Example: A Taxonomy for Business Applications

In this section, we apply our goal-based transformation rules for restructuring the classification of Business Applications (BA) –i.e. products that are used in the daily functioning of all types of organizations worldwide– proposed by Gartner [3]. We only expose the process of rearranging the hierarchy, assuming that the process of discovering goals and binding them to the departing classification has been performed before. We focus on a particular part of the original Gartner BA classification, the subtree bound to Supply Chain Management (see Fig. 2). Due to lack of space, we leave one of its nodes (Supply Chain Planning) out of our study. We complement the figure with the goals of the nodes that we are going to manage in our process (see table 4).

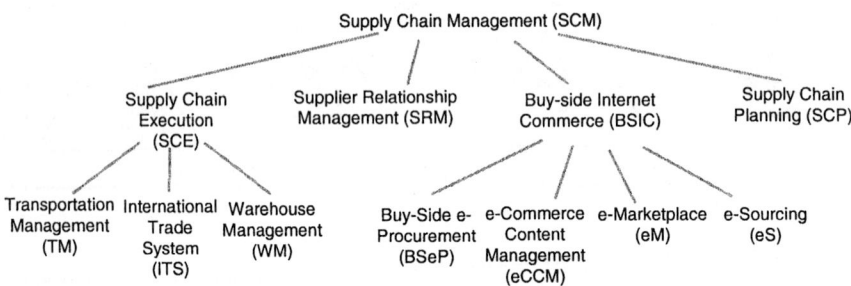

Fig. 2. An excerpt of the BA Gartner classification

Taking into account the form of the tree and the attached goals, table 5 summarizes the goal-based reasoning and transformation rules applied in each step of our example, whilst Fig. 3 shows the taxonomy after each of the 4 steps. The relationships among goals that violate some condition are stated in the second column. The other two columns state the rule that is applied at every moment. The relationships among goals require knowledge on the domain, enough as to discern for instance that in the first step we discover that the goal of SCE is not oriented to automate business processes, such that we can infer that G(SCE) does not imply G(ITS).

Table 4. Goals boud to some nodes of the BA taxonomy

Node Names	Goal Attained
Supply Chain Management (SCM)	To encompass the process of creating and fulfilling demands of the market for goods and services, mainly in 2 categories: execution and planning
Supply Chain Execution (SCE)	To manage relationships with the supplier (sourcing and procurement), and manufacture and logistics aspects
Transportation Management (TM)	To manage all freight deliver activities across the enterprise
International Trade Systems (ITS)	To automate the import/export business process
Warehouse Management (WM)	To manage the operation of a warehouse or distribution center
Supplier Relationship Management (SRM)	To manage enterprise interactions with the organizations that supply goods and services that are used.
Buy-Side Internet Commerce (BSIC)	To manage the internet by-side commerce
eCommerce Content Management (eCCM)	To address how to take unstructured product content and create and manage structured data on internet

Table 5. Transforming the original Gartner classification into a goal-based taxonomy

Step	Goal Reasoning		Rule Applied
1	¬G(BSIC) ⇒ G(eCCM)	2.1	Hard Removal(BA, BSIC, eCCM)
	¬G(BSIC) ⇒ G(eM)	2.1	Hard Removal(BA, BSIC, eM)
	¬G(BSIC) ⇒ G(BSeP) ∧ G(SRM) ⇒ G(BSeP)	1.1	Strict Reallocation(BA, BSIC, BSeP, SRM)
	¬G(BSIC) ⇒ G(eS) ∧ G(SRM) ⇒ G(eS)	1.1	Strict Reallocation(BA, BSIC, eS, SRM)
	¬G(SCM) ⇒ G(BSIC)	2.1	Hard Removal(BA, SCM, BSIC)
	¬G(SCE) ⇒ G(ITS)	2.1	Hard Removal(BA, SCE, ITS)
2	G(SCE) ∩ G(SRM) ≠ ∅	3.1	Inclusive Merge(BA, SCM, {SCE, SRM})
3	¬ (G(SCE) ≡ G(BSeP)∪G(eS)∪G(WM)∪G(TM)) Left goals: Manufacturing Management (MM), Not-eProcurement (eP), Not-eSource (NeS)	5 5 5	Identification(BA, SCE, MM) Identification(BA, SCE, NeP) Identification(BA, SCE, NeS)
4	Logistics Management (LM) Sourcing (S) Procurement (P) Supplier Interactions(SI)	8 8 8 8	Abstraction(BA, SCE, {WM, DM}), creates LM Abstraction(BA, SCE, {eS, NeS}), creates S Abstraction(BA, SCE, {eP, NeP}), creates P Abstraction(BA, SCE, {S, P}), creates SI

We have rearranged the whole Gartner BA taxonomy. It originally had 96 nodes, 78 were leafs (i.e., types of software packages) and just 18 intermediate nodes. The longest path from the root to a leaf was of length 6 (just one, and two of length 5), whilst the maximum width was 10 siblings (average width 4,33). Our process resulted in a taxonomy of 188 nodes, 120 of them leafs. The tree changed its form, with a longest path of length 8 (in fact, 16 paths of this length and 21 of length 7) and 7 siblings at most (average width 3,18). As a result, not only we provided rationale for the taxonomy, but also we let it well-suited for our main purpose, to use it for software package selection, with better defined ways to reach a leaf (i.e., a type of software package) from the root having less alternatives to consider at each step.

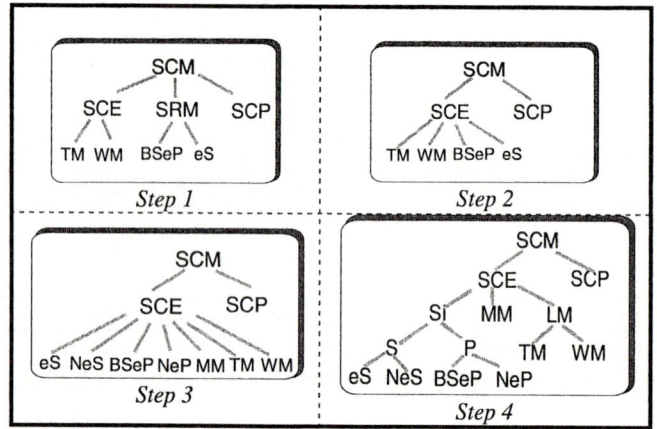

Fig. 3. The 4-Step Taxonomy construction process applied to an excerpt of the BA case

5 Conclusions

In this paper we have presented a proposal for building taxonomies that arrange the existing myriad of software packages into categories. The proposal is build upon the notion of goal.

We have identified 8 transformation rules specified by contracts that are used along a 4-phase process to manipulate an existing departing taxonomy to obtain the target one. As a result, and this is the main contribution of our work, we obtain a high-quality taxonomy in which the rationale for the classification is very clear and correctness and completeness are ensure by construction. As far as we know, this rationale distinguishes our approach of other taxonomy proposals as the ones mentioned in the introduction.

This work is a continuation of [19], in which we just presented a taxonomy in the form of decision tree for business application. In this paper we have improved our proposal by making it domain-independent, by defining precisely the rules and the process to use them, and by using the more general notion of goal instead of classifier (as done in decision trees).

We have demonstrated the feasibility of our approach in one of the most populated and critical fields of the software package marketplace (business applications). In particular, we have solved some problems observed in the departing hierarchy: categories whose reason-to-be was not clear, categories that were not defined precisely (as a consequence, their granularity was not always adequate); categories that overlapped; the criteria for decomposing categories was never declared and often was not evident, making hard the use of the hierarchy; levels of abstraction were different at different parts of the hierarchy; and so on.

Different actors may benefit from our approach:

- Software consultant companies offering assessment for business automation may structure their services better.
- Medium- and large-size companies with their own IT department may be more confident on their own selection.
- Software engineers which usually carry out package selection may structure better their knowledge and may aim at a better return of investment.

References

1. D. Carney, F. Long. "What Do You Mean by COTS? Finally a Useful Answer". *IEEE Software*, 17 (2): 83-86, March/April 2000.
2. B. Craig Meyers, P. Oberndorf. *Managing Software Acquisition*. SEI Series in Software Engineering, 2002.
3. Gartner Inc. web page. www.gartner.com, last accessed February 2005.
4. Forrester Research Inc. web page. www.forrester.com, last accessed February 2005.
5. ComponentSource web page. www.componentsource.com, last accessed February 2005.
6. Genium Software Development web page. http://www.genium.dk/index.xml, last accessed February 2005.
7. INCOSE web page. www.incose.org, last accessed February 2005.
8. ITPapers web page. www.itpapers.com, last accessed February 2005.
9. eCOTS web page. www.ecots.org, last accessed February 2005.
10. IT product guide web page. http://productguide.itmanagersjournal.com, last accessed February 2005.
11. CBSE web page. www.cbsenet.org/pls/CBSEnet/ecolnet.home, last accessed Feb. 2005.
12. E. Arranga. "Cobol Tools: Overview and Taxonomy". *IEEE Software*, 17(2): 59-61, 2000.
13. R. Glass and I. Vessey, "Contemporary Application-Domain Taxonomies". *IEEE Software*, 12(4): 63-76, 1995.
14. SWEBOK web page. www.swebok.org, last accessed February 2005.
15. A.I. Antón. "Goal-Based Requirements Analysis". In *Proceedings 2nd IEEE International Conference on Requirements Engineering* (ICRE), Colorado Springs (USA), 1996.
16. C. Potts, K. Takahashi, A.I. Antón. "Inquiry-Based Requirements Analysis". *IEEE Software*, 11(2), March 1994.
17. J.R. Quinlan. *C4.5: Programs for Machine Learning*. Morgan Kauffman, 1993.
18. L. Breiman, J.H. Friedman, R.A. Olshen, C. J. Stone. *Classification and Regression Trees*. Belmont, CA: Wadsworth International Group, 1984.
19. J.P. Carvallo, X. Franch, C. Quer, M. Torchiano. "Characterization of a Taxonomy for Business Applications and the Relationships Among Them". In *Proceedings of 3rd International Conference on COTS-Based Software Systems* (ICCBSS), LNCS 2959, 2004.

Approximations of Concept Based on Multielement Bounds[*]

Jianjiang Lu, Baowen Xu, Dazhou Kang, Yanhui Li, and Peng Wang

Dep.of Computer Science and Engineering, Southeast University,
Nanjing 210096, China
Jiangsu Institute of Software Quality, Nanjing, 210096, China
bwxu@seu.edu.cn

Abstract. Ontology-based information system can increase the precise and recall of information retrieval and filtering on the Web but faces the problem of Ontology heterogeneity. The approximate information filtering approach rewrites queries with their approximations to suit specific ontology-based information sources. The core of the approach is to find approximations of concepts. The current methods find least upper bounds and greatest lower bounds of a concept and then use them to get upper and lower approximations of the concept. However, they consider the bounds only containing separate concepts, so the quality of approximations is not very acceptable. This paper defines multielement least upper bounds and multielement greatest lower bounds that contain not only separate concepts but also disjunctions or conjunctions of concepts. It can be proved that the approximations based on them can be better approximations of concepts than the current methods.

1 Introduction

Information retrieval is one of the most basic and important services on the Web. The classic techniques based on keywords are unable to exploit the semantic knowledge within documents and hence cannot give precise answers to queries [1]. Ontology-based information systems can retrieval pages that refer to precise semantics but not ambiguous keywords, and can greatly increase the precision and recall of queries [2]. However, different information systems may use different ontologies, and have the problem of heterogeneity: a query may be expressed in the vocabulary of one ontology, but the information system may use another ontology and cannot answer the query because the two ontology are heterogenous [3]. There are two approaches to solve the problem: one is to combine the two ontologies by Ontology merging or mapping [4]; the other is to rewrite the query. This paper focuses on query rewriting approaches.

---

[*] This work was supported in part by the NSFC (60373066, 60303024), National Grand Fundamental Research 973 Program of China (2002CB312000), and National Research Foundation for the Doctoral Program of Higher Education of China (20020286004).

Query rewriting approaches rewrite a query to an equivalent query expressed in the vocabulary of another ontology in order to suit specific ontology-based information sources. Since often no perfectly corresponding query exists, or the expense of finding it is unacceptable, it requires rewriting a query to an approximate query. One of the approaches is approximate information filtering [5] based on concept subsumption in Ontology. The core of approximate information filtering is finding approximations of concepts. The current methods use conjunction of the least upper bounds of a concept as the upper approximation of the concept, and use disjunction of the greatest lower bounds as the lower approximation. But the quality of the approximations is not very acceptable in many cases, because they only focus on one-to-one concept subsumption relations between ontologies [6].

In this paper, we consider the subsumption relations between concepts and disjunction or conjunction of concepts. Our idea is to add disjunctions and conjunctions into the least upper and greatest lower bounds to get multielement bounds. The results of the work shows the idea is feasible and effective. The paper is organized as follows: Section 2 introduces the background and basis. Section 3 presents the definitions of multielement least upper bounds and multielement greatest lower bounds; then proves that the approximations based on them be better than the current methods; it also gives the definitions of the simplified bounds to increase efficiency.

2 Approximate Information Retrieval

The ontology-based information systems [7] classifies the pages, documents or any other pieces of information items into classes referring to concepts in the relevant ontology. Then, it can identify and rank information items based on user's query requirements with respect to concepts in an ontology. It can be also called concept-based.

Definition 1 (Concept-based information source). *Information source is a set of information items e.g. web pages, documents. If every information item in an information source S has been classified into one or more concepts in an ontology $\mathcal{O}$, i.e. the information items are individuals in $\mathcal{O}$, then S is called a concept-based information source with respect to ontology $\mathcal{O}$. Let the concepts in ontology $\mathcal{O}$ form the set $T = \{C_1, C_2, \ldots, C_n\}$. $C_i^{\mathcal{I}(S)}$ means the set of information items in S classified into C_i. Top concept $\top$ and bottom concept $\bot$ are special concepts. For any S and $\mathcal{O}$, $\top^{\mathcal{I}(S)}$ contains all the information items in S, and $\bot^{\mathcal{I}(S)} = \emptyset$.*

There are subsumption relations between concepts. Let C, D be concepts, $C \sqsubseteq D$ means C is subclass of D. We assume that all information sources S are compatible with concept subsumption [2], i.e. $C \sqsubseteq D \rightarrow C^{\mathcal{I}(S)} \subseteq D^{\mathcal{I}(S)}$.

Every Boolean expression of concepts is a concept query, and it can be interpreted as the set of information items which should be in the answer of the query.

Definition 2 (Concept query). *A concept query is an expression on the set of concept names in an ontology, and are called query for short. For any query Q, $Q^{\mathcal{I}(S)}$ is the answer to Q in information source S. Let $\mathcal{O}$ be an ontology and its concept set be T. In any information source S, a query with respect to $\mathcal{O}$ can be define as:*

1. *every concept name in T is a query, and the answer to C is $C^{\mathcal{I}(S)}$;*
2. *if Q_1 and Q_2 are queries, then $Q_1 \wedge Q_2$, $Q_1 \vee Q_2$ are queries, and $(Q_1 \wedge Q_2)^{\mathcal{I}(S)} = Q_1^{\mathcal{I}(S)} \cap Q_2^{\mathcal{I}(S)}$, $(Q_1 \vee Q_2)^{\mathcal{I}(S)} = Q_1^{\mathcal{I}(S)} \cup Q_2^{\mathcal{I}(S)}$;*
3. *if Q is a query, then $\neg Q$ is also a query, and $(\neg Q)^{\mathcal{I}(S)} = T^{\mathcal{I}(S)} - Q^{\mathcal{I}(S)}$.*

There are subsumption relations between queries [8].

Definition 3 (Query subsumption). *Query subsumption is a transitive and reflexive relation. Let Q, R be concept queries, R subsumes Q ($Q \sqsubseteq R$) if $Q^{\mathcal{I}(S)} \subseteq R^{\mathcal{I}(S)}$ in any information source S. Q and R are equivalent queries ($Q \equiv R$) if $R \sqsubseteq Q$ and $Q \sqsubseteq R$; R properly subsumes Q ($Q \sqsubset R$) if $Q \sqsubseteq R$ but not $R \sqsubseteq Q$; $Q \sqsubseteq \bot$ if $Q^{\mathcal{I}(S)} = \emptyset$ in any S.*

There are heterogeneity problems in concept-based information systems. Let the ontology of the user (who asks a query) be $\mathcal{O}_1$ and the ontology of the system (who answers the query) be $\mathcal{O}_2$, T be the set of concepts in $\mathcal{O}_2$. Generally, the system is only able to answer queries with respect to T. So it needs to rewrite the user's queries to equivalent queries with respect to T. However, many of them may not have such equivalent queries, or it is impossible to find them in an acceptable time. Approximate queries are often needed [9].

Let Q be a query with respect to $\mathcal{O}_1$, R be its approximate query with respect to $\mathcal{O}_2$. The recall and precision of approximations [2] can be defined as:

$$\mathrm{recall}(Q, R) = \frac{|Q^{\mathcal{I}(S)} \cap R^{\mathcal{I}(S)}|}{|Q^{\mathcal{I}(S)}|} ; \tag{1}$$

$$\mathrm{precision}(Q, R) = \frac{|Q^{\mathcal{I}(S)} \cap R^{\mathcal{I}(S)}|}{|R^{\mathcal{I}(S)}|} . \tag{2}$$

If $\mathrm{recall}(Q, R) = 1$ in any S, we say R is complete; if $\mathrm{precision}(Q, R) = 1$ in any S, we say R is correct. We can use subsumption relations between queries to find such approximations. A query Q^u is called a upper approximation of the query Q if $Q \sqsubseteq Q^u$; and Q^l is called a lower approximation of Q if $Q^l \sqsubseteq Q$. The upper approximations are complete, and the lower approximations are correct.

A concept or query may have several upper or lower approximations of different qualities. The precision and recall decides the quality of approximations [9]. The approximations with higher precision and recall are better. Subsumption relations between approximations can be used to compare the quality of the approximations.

- Let R_1, R_2 be upper approximations of Q with respect to $\mathcal{O}_2$, if $Q \sqsubseteq R_1 \sqsubseteq R_2$, then it has $\mathrm{precision}(Q, R_1) \geq \mathrm{precision}(Q, R_2)$, and $\mathrm{recall}(Q, R_1) = \mathrm{recall}(Q, R_2) = 1$, so R_1 is better than R_2 as the upper approximation, then we can say R_1 is closer to Q than R_2.

– Let R_1, R_2 be lower approximations of Q with respect to $\mathcal{O}_2$, if $R_1 \sqsubseteq R_2 \sqsubseteq Q$, then it has recall$(Q, R_1) \le$ recall(Q, R_2), and precision$(Q, R_1) =$ precision$(Q, R_2) = 1$, so R_2 is better than R_1 as the lower approximation, then we can say R_2 is closer to Q than R_1.

It is impossible to find and record approximations of all queries. A feasible method is to rewrite queries according to the approximations of concepts. Firstly, find approximations of all the concepts in $\mathcal{O}_1$ with respect to $\mathcal{O}_2$ and record the results; this process can be done offline. Hereafter, when getting a query with respect to $\mathcal{O}_1$, rewrite it to a new query with respect to $\mathcal{O}_2$ according to these results; this process should be carried out online [6].

The process is based on the fact that any query expressions can be rewritten to an equivalent form in which negations only apply to concept names using the following equations: $\neg(Q_1 \wedge Q_2) = \neg Q_1 \vee \neg Q_2$ and $\neg(Q_1 \vee Q_2) = \neg Q_1 \wedge \neg Q_2$. Let $\mathcal{O}_1, \mathcal{O}_2$ be two ontologies, T be the set of concepts in $\mathcal{O}_2$, for any concept C in $\mathcal{O}_1$, C^+ and C^- are the upper and lower approximations of C with respect to T. If Q is a concept query with respect to $\mathcal{O}_1$, we can easily get the upper or lower approximations of Q with respect to T: let Q' be the equivalent form of Q in which negations only apply to separate concept names,

1. for any concept name C in Q', if C is not applied by a negation, then replace C with its upper approximation C^+; if C is applied by a negation, then replace C with its lower approximation C^-. The result query is the upper approximation of Q respect to T.
2. for any concept name C in Q', if C is not applied by a negation, then replace C with its lower approximation C^-; if C is applied by a negation, then replace C with its upper approximation C^+. The result query is the lower approximation of Q respect to T.

Then the key problem is how to find approximations of each concept C in $\mathcal{O}_1$ with respect to $\mathcal{O}_2$. The current methods compute approximations of concepts with least upper bounds and greatest lower bounds of concepts [5].

Definition 4 (Least upper bounds). *The least upper bounds of C with respect to T is a set of concepts in T, notated as* $\text{lub}^T(C)$, *and it has:*

$$\forall D \in \text{lub}^T(C) \rightarrow C \sqsubseteq D ; \tag{3}$$
$$\forall A \in T, C \sqsubseteq A \rightarrow \exists B \in \text{lub}^T(C), B \sqsubseteq A . \tag{4}$$

Definition 5 (Greatest lower bounds). *The greatest lower bounds of C with respect to T is a set of concepts in T, notated as* $\text{glb}^T(C)$, *and it has:*

$$\forall D \in \text{glb}^T(C) \rightarrow D \sqsubseteq C ; \tag{5}$$
$$\forall A \in T, A \sqsubseteq C \rightarrow \exists B \in \text{glb}^T(C), A \sqsubseteq B . \tag{6}$$

The upper and lower approximations of a concept can be easily defined as:

$$A^{T+}(C) = \top \wedge \bigwedge_{A_i \in \text{lub}^T(C)} A_i ; \qquad (7)$$

$$A^{T-}(C) = \bot \vee \bigvee_{B_i \in \text{glb}^T(C)} B_i . \qquad (8)$$

Since all concepts in $\text{lub}^T(C)$ subsumes C, the conjunction of them is also subsumes C. Since C subsumes all concepts in $\text{glb}^T(C)$, C also subsumes the disjunction of them. Therefore, $A^{T+}(C)$ is an upper approximation of C with respect to T; $A^{T-}(C)$ is a lower approximation of C with respect to T.

The quality of the approximations of concepts is the most important factor in approximate information filtering. Unfortunately, the quality of $A^{T-}(C)$ and $A^{T+}(C)$ is not very acceptable in many cases. In concept set T, the superclasses of C may be much larger than C and the subclasses of C may be much smaller than C. They often cause lowquality approximations. In the worst cases, if C has no subclass or superclass in T, then $A^{T-}(C)$ always returns the empty set and $A^{T+}(C)$ returns the full set [7]. Concept sets and concept hierarchies of two ontologies are often disparate that there are few such subsumption relations, the worst cases are not rarely happened.

Subsumption relations between concepts and disjunction or conjunction of concepts can be used to compute better approximations. For example, let A, B be concepts in T,

- If there are no concept in T subsumes C, then $A^{T+}(C) = \top$. $C \sqsubseteq A \wedge B$ are also impossible. However, it may has $C \sqsubseteq A \vee B \sqsubset \top$, so $A \vee B$ is a upper approximation of C and it is better than $A^{T+}(C)$.
- If C does not subsume any concept in T, then $A^{T-}(C) = \bot$. It cannot has $A \vee B \sqsubseteq C$. However, it may has $\bot \sqsubset A \wedge B \sqsubseteq C$, so $A \wedge B$ is a lower approximation of C and it is better than $A^{T-}(C)$.

We consider adding these disjunctions and conjunctions to least upper bounds and greatest lower bounds. Since the bounds then contain not only separate concepts, we call them multielement least upper bounds and multielement greatest lower bounds. Using the multielement bounds can get better approximations.

3 Multielement Bounds

We will formally define the multielement least upper and multielement greatest lower bounds of concepts. In order to increase readability, we introduce several notations: let $\mathcal{O}_1, \mathcal{O}_2$ be two ontologies, C be a concept in $\mathcal{O}_1$, T be the set of all concepts in $\mathcal{O}_2$. If $E = \{D_1, D_2, \ldots, D_i\}$ is a set of concepts in T, then E is called a i-concept-set in T, $|E| = i$. We define $\check{E} \doteq D_1 \vee D_2 \vee \ldots \vee D_i$ be the disjunction of all concepts in E. $\check{E}$ is called a i-concept-disjunction in T. If $|E| = 1$, let $\check{E} = D_1$; if $|E| = 0$, let $\check{E} = \top$. We also define $\hat{E} \doteq D_1 \wedge D_2 \wedge \ldots \wedge D_i$ be the conjunction of all concepts in E. $\hat{E}$ is called a i-concept-conjunction in

T. If $|E| = 1$, let $\hat{E} = D_1$; if $|E| = 0$, let $\hat{E} = \bot$. We specify D be a concept in T, E, F be concept-sets in T, $\check{E}, \check{F}$ be corresponding concept-disjunctions in T, and $\hat{E}, \hat{F}$ be the corresponding concept-conjunctions in T.

3.1 Multielement Least Upper Bounds

The definition of multielement least upper bounds is similar to least upper bounds, but the members of bounds expand to concept disjunctions from separate concepts.

Definition 6 (Multielement least upper bounds). *The multielement least upper bounds of C with respect to T is a set of concept-disjunctions in T, notated as* $\mathrm{mlub}^T(C)$, *if the following assertions hold:*

$$\forall \check{E} \in \mathrm{mlub}^T(C) \rightarrow C \sqsubseteq \check{E} ; \tag{9}$$

$$\forall F \subseteq T, C \sqsubseteq \check{F} \rightarrow \exists \check{E} \in \mathrm{mlub}^T(C), \check{E} \sqsubseteq \check{F} . \tag{10}$$

The first assertion ensures each member of $\mathrm{mlub}^T(C)$ subsumes C. The second ensures any concept-disjunctions that subsumes C also subsumes at least one member of $\mathrm{mlub}^T(C)$. Notice that $\mathrm{mlub}^T(C)$ may not be unique for certain C and T.

We define

$$\mathrm{MA}^{T+}(C) = \top \wedge \bigwedge_{\check{E}_i \in \mathrm{mlub}^T(C)} \check{E}_i . \tag{11}$$

It is an upper approximation of C with respect to T. We compare it with the $\mathrm{A}^{T+}(C)$ from the current approach by Eq.7. Since subsumption relations between approximations can be used to compare the quality of the approximations, we use the following theorem to prove that $\mathrm{MA}^{T+}(C)$ is better than $\mathrm{A}^{T+}(C)$.

Theorem 1. *Let $\mathcal{O}_1, \mathcal{O}_2$ be two ontologies; T be the set of concepts in $\mathcal{O}_2$. For any concept C in $\mathcal{O}_1$,*

$$C \sqsubseteq \mathrm{MA}^{T+}(C) \sqsubseteq \mathrm{A}^{T+}(C) \tag{12}$$

Proof. We prove $C \sqsubseteq \mathrm{MA}^{T+}(C)$ and $\mathrm{MA}^{T+}(C) \sqsubseteq \mathrm{A}^{T+}(C)$ respectively:

From Eq.9, for any $\check{E}_i \in \mathrm{mlub}^T(C)$, it has $C \sqsubseteq \check{E}_i$. So for any information source $\mathcal{S}$ and information item x, if $x \in C^{\mathcal{I}(\mathcal{S})}$, then for any $\check{E}_i \in \mathrm{mlub}^T(C)$, $x \in \check{E}_i^{\mathcal{I}(\mathcal{S})}$; so, $x \in \bigcap_{\check{E}_i \in \mathrm{mlub}^T(C)} \check{E}_i^{\mathcal{I}(\mathcal{S})} = (\mathrm{MA}^{T+}(C))^{\mathcal{I}(\mathcal{S})}$. Therefore, it has $C^{\mathcal{I}(\mathcal{S})} \subseteq (\mathrm{MA}^{T+}(C))^{\mathcal{I}(\mathcal{S})}$, from Definition 3, we can get that $C \sqsubseteq \mathrm{MA}^{T+}(C)$.

For any information source $\mathcal{S}$ and information item x, if $x \notin (\mathrm{A}^{T+}(C))^{\mathcal{I}(\mathcal{S})}$, then because $\bigcap_{D_i \in \mathrm{lub}^T(C)} D_i^{\mathcal{I}(\mathcal{S})} = (\mathrm{A}^{T+}(C))^{\mathcal{I}(\mathcal{S})}$ from Eq.7, there must exist at least one $D \in \mathrm{lub}^T(C)$ that $x \notin D^{\mathcal{I}(\mathcal{S})}$; from Eq.3, it has $C \sqsubseteq D$, then from Eq.10, there exists $\check{E} \in \mathrm{mlub}^T(C)$ that $\check{E} \sqsubseteq D_i$; since $x \notin D^{\mathcal{I}(\mathcal{S})}$, so it has $x \notin \check{E}^{\mathcal{I}(\mathcal{S})}$, and then $x \notin \bigcap_{\check{E}_i \in \mathrm{mlub}^T(C)} \check{E}_i^{\mathcal{I}(\mathcal{S})} = (\mathrm{MA}^{T+}(C))^{\mathcal{I}(\mathcal{S})}$. Therefore, for any information source $\mathcal{S}$ and information item x, if $x \notin (\mathrm{A}^{T+}(C))^{\mathcal{I}(\mathcal{S})}$, then $x \notin (\mathrm{MA}^{T+}(C))^{\mathcal{I}(\mathcal{S})}$, i.e. $(\mathrm{MA}^{T+}(C))^{\mathcal{I}(\mathcal{S})} \subseteq (\mathrm{A}^{T+}(C))^{\mathcal{I}(\mathcal{S})}$; then we can get that $\mathrm{MA}^{T+}(C) \sqsubseteq \mathrm{A}^{T+}(C)$ from Definition 3.

This theorem shows that $\mathrm{MA}^{T+}(C)$ is better than $\mathrm{A}^{T+}(C)$. Therefore, the multielement bounds are effective in finding better approximations than the original bounds.

There may be many multielement least upper bounds of C with respect to T. Most of them may contain many redundant members: if $\check{E}$ and $\check{F}$ are in the bounds, and it has $\check{E} \sqsubseteq \check{F}$, then removing $\check{F}$ from the bounds cannot breach the assertions in Definition 6, and it has $\check{E} \wedge \check{F} = \check{E}$, so from Eq.11, we can get that $\check{F}$ is redundant in computing the upper approximation. The redundancy will increase the size of the expression of approximation, thereby reduce the efficiency. In order to remove the redundancy, we define the simplified multielement least upper bounds.

Definition 7 (Simplified multielement least upper bounds). *Let $\mathcal{O}_1$, $\mathcal{O}_2$ be two ontologies; C be a concept in $\mathcal{O}_1$; T be the set of concepts in $\mathcal{O}_2$. $\mathrm{slub}^T(C)$ is called the simplified multielement least upper bounds of C with respect to T, if it is the multielement least upper bounds of C with respect to T, and for any $\check{E} \in \mathrm{slub}^T(C)$ the following assertions hold:*

$$\neg \exists F \subseteq T, C \sqsubseteq \check{F} \sqsubset \check{E} ; \tag{13}$$

$$\neg \exists \check{F} \in \mathrm{slub}^T(C), \check{F} \equiv \check{E} ; \tag{14}$$

$$\neg \exists F \subseteq T, (\check{F} \equiv \check{E}) \wedge (|F| < |E|) . \tag{15}$$

We add the three assertions to remove redundancy. The first one ensures that the members of the bounds are least in subsumption hierarchy: there is no disjunction of concepts that is between C and any member of the bounds; the second one ensures that only one of multiple equivalent disjunctions can be selected in the bounds; the third one ensures that the selected one is minimal in length.

Theorem 2. *Let s_1 be simplified multielement least upper bounds of C with respect to T, for any s_2 that are multielement least upper bounds of C with respect to T, it has $|s_1| \leq |s_2|$.*

Proof. Let s_1, s_2 be nonempty sets as a presupposition. Since s_1 are multielement least upper bounds of C with respect to T, from Eq.9, for any $\check{E} \in s_1$, it has $C \sqsubseteq \check{E}$. Since s_2 are also multielement least upper bounds of C with respect to T, then from Eq.10, for any $\check{E} \in s_1$, there exists $\check{F} \in s_2$ that $\check{F} \sqsubseteq \check{E}$.

Assume $|s_2| < |s_1|$, then using the pigeonhole principle, we can get that there must exists two different members of s_1, $\check{E}_1$ and $\check{E}_2$, satisfying $\check{F}_1 \sqsubseteq \check{E}_1$ and $\check{F}_1 \sqsubseteq \check{E}_2$, where $\check{F}_1$ is a member of s_2, and it has $C \sqsubseteq \check{F}_1$. Since s_1 is simplified multielement least upper bounds of C with respect to T, from Eq.13, it cannot has $C \sqsubseteq \check{F}_1 \sqsubset \check{E}_1$ or $C \sqsubseteq \check{F}_1 \sqsubset \check{E}_2$. Therefore, it must have $\check{F}_1 \equiv \check{E}_1 \equiv \check{E}_2$. Then for $\check{E}_1 \in s_1$, there exists $\check{E}_2 \in s_1$ that $\check{E}_1 \equiv \check{E}_2$; from Eq.14, we can get that s_1 are not simplified multielement least upper bounds of C with respect to T. It comes an contradiction. Therefore, the assumption of $|s_2| < |s_1|$ is false. Then it must have $|s_1| \leq |s_2|$.

Theorem 2 shows that simplified multielement least upper bounds have the least number of members as the multielement least upper bounds of C with respect to T. Using simplified multielement least upper bounds can reduce the size of the expression of upper approximations of concepts and increase efficiency.

3.2 Multielement Greatest Lower Bounds

The definition of multielement greatest lower bounds is similar to greatest lower bounds, but the members of bounds expand to concept conjunctions from separate concepts.

Definition 8 (Multielement greatest lower bounds). *The multielement greatest lower bounds of C with respect to T is a set of concept-conjunctions in T, notated as $\mathrm{mglb}^T(C)$, if the following assertions hold:*

$$\forall \hat{E} \in \mathrm{mglb}^T(C) \to \hat{E} \sqsubseteq C ; \tag{16}$$

$$\forall F \subseteq T, \hat{F} \sqsubseteq C \to \exists \hat{E} \in \mathrm{mglb}^T(C), \hat{F} \sqsubseteq \hat{E} . \tag{17}$$

The first assertion ensures each member of $\mathrm{mglb}^T(C)$ is subsumed by C. The second ensures any concept-conjunctions subsumed by C is also subsumed by at least one member of $\mathrm{mglb}^T(C)$. Notice that $\mathrm{mglb}^T(C)$ may not be unique for certain C and T.

We define

$$\mathrm{MA}^{T-}(C) = \bot \lor \bigvee_{\hat{E}_i \in \mathrm{mglb}^T(C)} \hat{E}_i . \tag{18}$$

It is an lower approximation of C with respect to T. We compare it with the $\mathrm{A}^{T-}(C)$ from the current approach by Eq.8. Since subsumption relations between approximations can be used to compare the quality of the approximations, we use the following theorem to prove that $\mathrm{MA}^{T-}(C)$ is better than $\mathrm{A}^{T-}(C)$.

Theorem 3. *Let $\mathcal{O}_1, \mathcal{O}_2$ be two ontologies; T be the set of concepts in $\mathcal{O}_2$. For any concept C in $\mathcal{O}_1$,*

$$\mathrm{A}^{T-}(C) \sqsubseteq \mathrm{MA}^{T-}(C) \sqsubseteq C \tag{19}$$

Proof. We prove $\mathrm{MA}^{T-}(C) \sqsubseteq C$ and $\mathrm{A}^{T-}(C) \sqsubseteq \mathrm{MA}^{T-}(C)$ respectively:

From Eq.16, for any $\hat{E}_i \in \mathrm{mglb}^T(C)$, it has $\hat{E}_i \sqsubseteq C$. For any information source $\mathcal{S}$ and information item x, if $x \in (\mathrm{MA}^{T-}(C))^{\mathcal{I}(\mathcal{S})}$, then for any $\hat{E}_i \in \mathrm{mglb}^T(C)$, it has $x \in \hat{E}_i^{\mathcal{I}(\mathcal{S})}$; since $\hat{E}_i \sqsubseteq C$, so $x \in C^{\mathcal{I}(\mathcal{S})}$. Therefore, $\mathrm{MA}^{T-}(C))^{\mathcal{I}(\mathcal{S})} \subseteq C^{\mathcal{I}(\mathcal{S})}$, from Definition 3, we can get that $\mathrm{MA}^{T-}(C) \sqsubseteq C$.

For any information source $\mathcal{S}$ and information item x, if $x \in (\mathrm{A}^{T-}(C))^{\mathcal{I}(\mathcal{S})}$, then because $\bigcup_{D \in \mathrm{glb}^T(C)} D^{\mathcal{I}(\mathcal{S})} = (\mathrm{D}^{T-}(C))^{\mathcal{I}(\mathcal{S})}$ from Eq.8, there must exist at least one $D \in \mathrm{glb}^T(C)$ that $x \in D^{\mathcal{I}(\mathcal{S})}$; from Eq.5, it has $D \sqsubseteq C$, then from Eq.17, there exists $\hat{E} \in \mathrm{mglb}^T(C)$ that $D \sqsubseteq \hat{E}$; since $x \in D^{\mathcal{I}(\mathcal{S})}$, so it has $x \in \hat{E}^{\mathcal{I}(\mathcal{S})}$, and then $x \in \bigcup_{\hat{E}_i \in \mathrm{mglb}^T(C)} \hat{E}_i^{\mathcal{I}(\mathcal{S})} = (\mathrm{MA}^{T-}(C))^{\mathcal{I}(\mathcal{S})}$. Therefore, for any information source $\mathcal{S}$ and information item x, if $x \in (\mathrm{A}^{T-}(C))^{\mathcal{I}(\mathcal{S})}$, then $x \in (\mathrm{MA}^{T-}(C))^{\mathcal{I}(\mathcal{S})}$, i.e. $(\mathrm{A}^{T-}(C))^{\mathcal{I}(\mathcal{S})} \subseteq (\mathrm{MA}^{T-}(C))^{\mathcal{I}(\mathcal{S})}$; then we can get that $\mathrm{A}^{T-}(C) \sqsubseteq \mathrm{MA}^{T-}(C)$ from Definition 3.

This theorem shows that $\mathrm{MA}^{T-}(C)$ is better than $\mathrm{A}^{T-}(C)$ as the lower approximation of C with respect to T. Therefore, the multielement bounds are effective in finding better approximations than the original bounds.

Most of multielement greatest lower bounds may also contain many redundant members: if $\hat{E}$ and $\hat{F}$ are in the bounds, and it has $\hat{F} \sqsubseteq \hat{E}$, then removing $\hat{F}$ from the bounds cannot breach the assertions in Definition 8, and it has $\hat{E} \vee \hat{F} \equiv \hat{E}$, so from Eq.18, we can get that $\hat{F}$ is redundant in computing the lower approximation. The redundancy will increase the size of the expression of approximation, thereby reduce the efficiency. In order to remove the redundancy, we define the simplified multielement greatest lower bounds.

Definition 9 (Simplified multielement greatest lower bounds). *The simplified multielement greatest lower bounds of C with respect to T, notated as* $\mathrm{slub}^T(C)$, *is the multielement greatest lower bounds of C with respect to T, and for any $\hat{E} \in \mathrm{slub}^T(C)$, the following assertions hold:*

$$\neg \exists F \subseteq T, \hat{E} \sqsubset \hat{F} \sqsubseteq C ; \tag{20}$$

$$\neg \exists \hat{F} \in \mathrm{slub}^T(C), \hat{F} \equiv \hat{E} ; \tag{21}$$

$$\neg \exists F \subseteq T, (\hat{F} \equiv \hat{E}) \wedge (|F| < |E|) . \tag{22}$$

The three assertions remove redundancy. The first one ensures that the members of the bounds are greatest in subsumption hierarchy: there is no conjunction of concepts that is between C and any member of the bounds; the second one ensures that only one of multiple equivalent conjunctions can be selected in the bounds; the third one ensures that the selected one is minimal in length.

Theorem 4. *Let s_1 be simplified multielement greatest lower bounds of C with respect to T, for any s_2 that are multielement greatest lower bounds of C with respect to T, it has $|s_1| \leq |s_2|$.*

Proof. It can be proved in the same way as Theorem 2.

Theorem 4 shows that simplified multielement greatest lower bounds have the least number of members as the multielement greatest lower bounds of C with respect to T. Using simplified multielement greatest lower bounds can reduce the size of the expression of lower approximations of concepts and increase efficiency.

4 Conclusion

This paper presents new defined multielement least upper bounds and multielement greatest lower bounds for approximate information retrieval. The bounds contain not only separate concepts but also disjunctions or conjunctions of concepts. The approximations based on them are better approximations of concepts than the current method. We define the simplified bounds to increase efficiency at last. How to find the simplified bounds correctly and quickly is the future work. In fact, the approximations based on multielement bounds are the closest approximations if negations cannot be used in approximation expressions.

How to find the closest approximations containing negations is the future work. Concept-based information retrieval only use concepts in Ontology. However, relations in Ontology are also important in information retrieval and facing heterogeneous problems. It is required to extend approximate information retrieval to deal with queries containing relations. Finding the closet approximations of concepts does not mean that then we can get the closest approximations of queries [6]. A framework of the whole process of approximate information retrieval in heterogeneous systems should solve this problem.

References

1. Shah, U., Finin, T., Joshi, A., Cost, R.S., Mayfield, J.: Information Retrieval on the Semantic Web. In: the 10th International Conference on Information and Knowledge Management. McLean: ACM Press (2002) 461–468
2. Tzitzikas, Y.: Collaborative Ontology-based Information Indexing and retrieval. Doctoral Dissertation, Heraklion (2002)
3. Visser, P.R.S., Jones, D.M., Bench-Capon, T.J.M., and Shave, M.J.R.: An analysis of ontological mismatches: Heterogeneity versus interoperability. In AAAI 1997 Spring Symposium on Ontological Engineering, Stanford, USA (1997)
4. Wache, H., Vogele, T., Visser, U., *et al*: Ontology-based integration of information—a survey of existing approaches. In: IJCAI Workshop on Ontologies and Information Sharing. California, AAAI Press (2001) 108–117
5. Stuckenschmidt, H.: Approximate information filtering with multiple classification hierarchies. International Journal of Computational Intelligence and Applications, **2(3)** (2002) 295–302
6. Akahani, J., Hiramatsu, K., and Satoh, T.: Approximate Query Reformulation based on Hierarchical Ontology Mapping. International Workshop on Semantic Web Foundations and Application Technologies (SWFAT-2003) (2003)
7. Stuckenschmidt, H.: Ontology-Based Information Sharing in Weakly Structured Environments. PhD thesis, AI Department, Vrije Universiteit Amsterdam (2002)
8. Goasdoué, F., Rousset, M.C.: Answering Queries using Views: a KRDB Perspective for the Semantic Web. ACM Transactions on Internet Technology, **4(3)** (2004) 255–288
9. Chang, C., Garcia-Molina, H.: Approximate query mapping: Accounting for translation closeness. The VLDB Journal, **10(2-3)** (2001) 155–181

Query Expansion Using Web Access Log Files[1]

Yun Zhu and Le Gruenwald

The University of Oklahoma, 200 Falgar Street, Norman, OK 73019, USA
{zhujulie, ggruenwald}@ou.edu
http//www.cs.ou.edu/~database/faculty.htm

Abstract. Query Expansion has long been recognized as one of the effective methods in solving short queries and improving ranking accuracy in traditional IR research. Many variations of this method have been introduced throughout the past decades; however, few of them have incorporated web log information into the query expansion process. In this paper, we propose an expansion technique that expands document content at the initial index stage using queries extracted from the web log files. Our experimental results show that even with a minimal amount of real world log information available and a professionally cataloged knowledge structure to aid the search, there is still a significant improvement in using our query expansion method compared to the conventional query expansion ones.

1 Introduction

With the explosive growth of the World Wide Web, many web sites are providing web interfaces for users to access their databases. Thus, it is becoming increasingly important to find an optimum retrieval system suitable for such applications. Compared to the conventional full text retrieval systems, the web-interfaced retrieval systems face additional obstacles and opportunities that need to be addressed.

One of the well known problems posed to the web search systems is that web users tend to enter very short query terms, generally two to three keywords per query [11]. With the paucity of query terms, it is much more likely to have the word mismatch scenario where query terms do not match any keywords in a relevant document. Although these web-based search systems encounter the severe word mismatch problem, they also have an additional piece of information available that can be exploited for search purposes – web access log files recording user activities when they access the web site.

For decades, many studies in IR have tried to address the short query problem. One of the most recent and effective approaches is query expansion [5]. This technique involves expanding and reweighing query terms and reforming query results based on the expanded query. The source for term expansion is typically derived from user feedback, or documents assumed to be relevant to the original query or knowledge structure such as thesaurus. Although this technique has been

---

[1] This work was partially supported by the National Library of Medicine, Grant No. 1 G08 LM007877-01 and 1 G08 LM008054-01.

shown to be effective [5, 18], few studies have so far explored its application in web search and incorporation of web log information. The only experiment that utilizes log information was limited to expansion term selection [8]. However, there are more areas in the retrieval process where log information can be applied.

In this paper, we propose a new query association and expansion method that utilizes web log information to the full extent. By applying log mining techniques, we are able to expand the document contents with query terms entered by the users. We then perform expansion search based on the expanded document contents. Our query expansion method achieves good improvement compared to conventional expansion techniques even when there is professionally cataloged knowledge structure to aid the search and only a minimal amount of log information available.

2 Related Works

The concept of query expansion was originated in the 1970's [12] where user feedback is applied not only to the reweighing of terms, but also to the expansion of search terms for further retrieval improvements. The basic idea of this technique is that each time the system retrieves a set of documents based on a user's query, a set of extra terms is then selected from the relevant documents identified by the user, then finally a new query is formed with the selected terms and a new search is performed. This process can be carried out iteratively, and it is expected that the more iterations it goes through, the more number of relevant documents will be retrieved. Although this technique has been shown to be effective [13, 16], the requirement for users' constant feedback on relevance is not appealing.

Throughout the years, many variations of query expansion techniques have been introduced. They can be categorized into three main groups: manual query expansion [4], query expansion based on the complete document collection [5, 6, 7, 9] and query expansion based on local analysis [2, 17, 18] (also referred to as *Relevance Feedback* or *Pseudo Relevance Feedback*). The manual query expansion involves users' judgment on which terms to select for expansion. This technique is rarely implemented because studies have shown that it does not improve search results effectively [4]. The basic idea for query expansion based on the complete document collection is to study the correlation between terms in the documents and identify the relationships between terms throughout the collection. This technique usually involves the manual or automatic building of a thesaurus type knowledge structure to aid the search. Unfortunately, building such a knowledge structure is extremely expensive, and has not achieved any significant improvements in experiments [5]. The third group, query expansion based on local analysis, assumes that the top n documents retrieved based on users' original queries are always relevant, thus the expansion terms are selected via studying the correlations between the terms within those n documents. This technique dismisses users from any form of input, and has shown improvements in many studies, especially in the experiments from TREC [5, 18].

Recently, there have been two interesting studies on applying alternative pseudo relevance feedback techniques to web search and both have achieved significant improvement. The first study by Billerbeck and others [3] utilizes a query association technique, which relates a historical query term with the top n ranked documents retrieved using the Okapi ranking formula [13,18]. At the end of the process, each document is represented by a surrogate file formed by a set of query terms associated with it. The surrogate files then become the base for the initial document retrieval and term selection. The retrieval based on the expanded query is later performed on the original document collection. The basic idea is that queries are usually well thought out descriptions of what the users are looking for, so the surrogate files formed by those queries are well defined abstracts of the document, and thus improving the final search results. The researchers claimed an improvement of 18-20% over the conventional expansion approach. Although this technique has achieved promising results, there are several issues that need further improvement. First, the initial formation of the surrogate files uses a ranking formula to identify the association, thus the reliability of the surrogate files depends on how perfect the ranking formula is, and it does not reflect the true desire of the users. Second, this technique requires a complete query set that is appropriate for the document collection; otherwise, the quality of the surrogate files will not be good enough to improve the search.

The second study aims at improving query expansion using web log information [8]. The researchers developed a probabilistic term selection and reweighing function that determines expansion terms not only on their original weight, but also on the probability of both the terms and the document appearing together in a user session. The motivation behind this technique is that the researchers believed the correlations between the query terms and documents extracted from a web log are valuable user feedback and more reliable than the pseudo relevance feedback. The experiment results showed a substantial improvement over the pseudo relevance feedback approach. However, examining their formula closely, we have found that if a term does not appear in the content of a document, then no matter how relevant that term is to the document, it will always be assigned a zero probability for that document. That is to say, the formula does not capture the terms that are deemed relevant by the users, but do not appear in the document contents. Furthermore, this technique also requires a web log that has sufficient document coverage and content coverage from the queries; otherwise, the system will not be able to obtain any term for expansion.

3 Log-Based Association Expansion

The Log-based Association Expansion approach we propose in this paper is aimed at eliminating the limitations of the two approaches discussed in Section 2. In our approach, we extract associations between users' queries and documents from the web log, which is a more reliable source of user feedback compared to query association. We then make full use of these extracted associations by not only applying them to expansion term selection, but also to original document content expansion. The process can be broken down into two phases: document expansion by web log mining and query expansion retrieval. Their detailed descriptions are as follows:

Phase 1. Document Expansion by Web Log Mining – The system expands document contents with associated query terms extracted from the web log using a mining algorithm.

In this phase, the system first parses the web log and extracts the information such as IP addresses, timestamps, document IDs and search keywords entered. The IP addresses and timestamps are then used to identify user sessions. This paper uses a 30 minutes timeout to identify the sessions – an approach that has been considered in the literature as a default approach for session identification [19].

The system then runs a mining algorithm on the extracted information to identify the associations between query terms and documents. We implemented a mining algorithm (shown in Figure 1) inspired by the Apriori data mining technique [1] which uses a user-defined minimum support threshold (min_sup) to identify frequent item sets (a set of items the frequency of each is equal to or higher than min_sup). Here frequency refers to the number of sessions in which a query-document pair appears together. The first part of the algorithm (lines 1 to 5) is aimed at identifying frequent query-document pairs. It first obtains the frequency for each pair, and if the frequency is higher than or equal to min_sup (line 4), every term in the query is added to the document with the corresponding frequency. The algorithm then handles non-frequent query-document pairs (lines 6 to 9): if the query term exists in the document, it is also added to the document. The assumption is that the single threshold value might have left out relevant query terms that have not yet accumulated enough frequency, thus by adding terms that exist in the documents, we partially salvage relevant terms with low frequencies without risking adding irrelevant terms.

Fig. 1. Mining algorithm for the association identification

```
1 For each document d_i and query q_i
2     Count frequency n as the number of sessions where d_i and q_i
3     appear together
4     If (n/total_session_count>=min_sup)
5         Add every term x_j in q_i to d_i for n times
6     Else
7         For each x_j in q_i that was not added to the document
8             If (x_j appears in d_i )
9                 Add x_j to d_i for 1 time
```

At the end of this web log mining process, we obtain a set of documents expanded by users' query terms. There are several advantages for this addition. First, the query terms and associations identified by the process are a true reflection of user's judgment on relevance feedback and, therefore, are more reliable than the associations created by a ranking algorithm. Second, the process adds terms to the original document rather than building a separate file out of query terms. This not only enables the early use of log information in the web development stage, but also ensures the full coverage of document contents where there is none or incomplete log information available for the document. Third, by adding query terms within the frequent item set to the document, we are able to capture terms that might not exist in the document, yet relevant to the document contents. The web log mining process should be repeated periodically when a sufficient amount of log information has been accumulated.

Phase 2. Query Expansion Retrieval – When a user's query Q arrives, the system performs query expansion search based on the expanded document derived from Phase 1. The query expansion search process is carried out in the following steps:

a. Initial Retrieval Based on Q – The system uses Formula (1) to measure each document's score W with respect to Q, and retrieves a set of documents ordered by their scores from the highest to the lowest. This formula is a modified version of the Okapi formula [13], where the values of the parameters are with respect to the expanded document rather than the original document. For each document, the formula sums the weight (w_i) for each term that appear in both the document and the query Q and adjust the weight with a normalizing factor. The documents are then ranked according to the result in descending order. It is worth noting that both w_i and W are inherently influenced by the query terms added in the expanded document. Basically, terms that reflect users' desire is more likely to have a higher weight in the document, and documents containing those terms are more likely to obtain higher scores when there is a match between the terms in the document and the query terms.

$$W = \sum_{i \in d \cap q} w_i \times \frac{TF(k_1+1)}{K+TF} \quad (1)$$

where d is the set of terms in the expanded document, q is the set of terms in the query Q, TF is the number of times the term appears in the expanded document, $w_i = \log \frac{(N-n+0.5)}{(n+0.5)}$ when relevant information (documents known to be relevant) is not available, $w_i = \log \frac{(r+0.5)(N-n-R+r+0.5)}{(R-r+0.5)(n-r+0.5)}$ when relevant information is available, R is the number of relevant expanded documents, r is the number of relevant expanded documents containing the term, N is the number of expanded documents, n is the number of expanded documents that contain the term, $K = k_1((1-b)+b\frac{DL}{AVDL})$, DL is the length of the expanded document, $AVDL$ is the average length of the expanded documents in the given collection, and b, k_1 are tuning constants usually set to 0.75 and 1.2, respectively.

b. Expansion Term Selection – The system selects expansion query terms from the set of terms within the top n documents (denoted as T) derived from step a. During this step, each term i within T is weighted using Formula (2).The terms with the highest weights and do not belong to the original query are selected to form a new query.

$$\ln(\sum_{i \in T} w_i + 1) \quad (2)$$

c. Expanded Search and Result Sets Merging – Using Formula (1), the system performs another search based on the new query derived from step b. Then it combines the retrieved document set with the original document set derived from step a. In order not to overpower the new query results with the original query, we use formula (3) to obtain the weight for each of the document in the final result set:

$$W_{orig} + \alpha \cdot W_{new} \qquad (3)$$

where W_{orig} is the document weight based on the original query, W_{new} is the document weight based on the new query, and α is a value from 0 to 1 to adjust the influence of the new weight on the result. The final result set is displayed in the decreasing order of document weights.

Our technique differs from Billerbeck's [3] in that we expand each document with queries extracted from the web log instead of building a new surrogate file based on associations. We believe our technique uses a more reliable source for query expansion because web logs give a true reflection of users' judgments. Comparing with Cui's [8], which also utilizes web logs, our technique expands the usage of log information in that it is not only applied to expansion term selection, but also to document contents expansion at the initial phase. Thus web log information influences every step of the expansion process starting from the first retrieval based on the user's original query. Furthermore, our web mining technique also enables the addition of new and related terms to the document contents. Another advantage of our technique is that it can be implemented even when there is not enough log information available, and still fine-tunes the search performance, while the other approaches would not be able to produce any query expansion terms.

4 Experiments

4.1 Test Data Collection

Our document collection comes from a real world web site – HEAL (Health Education Assets Library) [10]. The web site hosts over 36,000 multimedia files for medical professionals. These multimedia files are organized using metadata tables that textually describe every aspect of the files, and web user interfaces are provided for users to search these files through the metadata tables. The document length for each description ranges from 2 words to 314 words. In order to improve the search performance, special medical catalogers assign each file to the MeSH (Medical Subject Headings) tree [12] and additional keywords table. All the techniques implemented in the experiments are aided by the MeSH tree and keyword tables.

The log access files were collected from the web site server from May 2002 to June 2004. Due to the fact that this web site is relatively new, the number of visits is incomparable to other popular web search sites. Among these log files, we were only able to identify 4,747 sessions that contain search, clicking or downloading activities. Compared to over four million sessions in Cui's experiments [8], our log information is extremely limited.

We used 50 queries to conduct the experiments. These 50 queries were selected by the medical professionals and researchers who have used the HEAL system out of 100 queries randomly generated from the log activities. The average length of those queries is 1.6 words. The relevance judgment was conducted by the medical professionals on a 2,000 experiment document collection, which was also randomly selected from the 36,000 files in the database. These 2,000 files form the test collection for retrieval effectiveness testing. The term weights are assigned based on the complete database collection rather than the test collection.

4.2 Experiment Setup

All the formulas used in the experiments have been listed in Section 3. During these experiments the following retrieval techniques and test runs are studied on the same test collection for comparison purposes:

1. FreqCase – This search system uses Formula (1) to perform document retrieval and no expansion process or relevant information is involved.
2. LogCase – This is a variant of our proposed Log-based Association Expansion search system. It searches on the expanded documents using the algorithm from FreqCase.
3. ExpCase – This search system is the conventional query expansion search. In this paper, this approach has the same process as our Log-based Association Expansion, except that no log information was added.
4. ExpLogCase – This is our proposed Log-based Association Expansion search system described in Section 3. The system utilizes validated search terms and expansion search process to perform the search.
5. CuiCase – This is the test run for Cui's probabilistic query expansion using query logs [8].

Due to the limited amount of real world log activities, we have generated simulated log activities to study the effect of abundant and correct log activities on the performance of the above search systems. The simulated log activities were created via randomly selecting relevance feedback from the medical professionals' relevance judgments, and inserting them for a random number of times (ranging from 2-7 times) into the extracted log information. The following are the test runs using the simulated log information:

6. LogCaseSim – This is a test run for LogCase with simulated web logs.
7. ExpLogCaseSim – This is a test run for ExpLogCase with simulated web logs.
8. CuisCaseSim – This is a test run for CuiCase with simulated web logs.

Apart from the above test runs, we also tried test runs for Billerbeck's query expansion using query association [3]. Unfortunately, the association creation process was not successful due to the fact that there are insufficient historical queries to form proper surrogate files for each document. For this experiment, we have also tested exhaustively on dynamic parameter value settings to identify the ones that yield the best combination of search accuracy and response time. These values are 0.000632, 6, 2 and 1/3 for min_sup, number of top ranked documents for expansion, number of terms selected for expansion and α, respectively.

5 Experiment Results

For the experiments, we used the precision for the first 10, 20, 30, 40 and 50 documents retrieved (denoted in Table 2 as p@10...p@50), the average precision for the first 50 files retrieved (denoted as Avg. P) the recall for the first 300 documents retrieved (denoted as Recall 300), and Average 11-point interpolated Recall-Precision (denoted as avg. 11-RP) as the evaluation metrics [2].

Table 2. P@10, 20, 30, 40, 50, Average Precision, Average 11-point precision, and recall 300

	p@10	p@20	p@30	p@40	p@50	Avg. P	Vs. FreqCase	Avg. 11-RP	Recall (300)
FreqCase	0.6220	0.5460	0.4713	0.4055	0.3560	0.4802	-	0.3299	0.4364
LogFreqCase	0.6900	0.6300	0.5687	0.5070	0.4560	0.5703	0.1878	0.4426	0.6065
ExpCase	0.7020	0.6370	0.5780	0.5160	0.4680	0.5802	0.2083	0.4804	0.6875
ExpLogCase	0.7200	0.6560	0.5987	0.5455	0.4940	0.6028	0.2555	0.5161	0.7381
CuiCase	0.6360	0.5770	0.5120	0.4605	0.4212	0.5213	0.0857	0.3922	0.5882
logFreqCaseSim	0.8580	0.7830	0.7120	0.6470	0.5972	0.7194	0.4983	0.6314	0.7780
ExpLogCaseSim	0.8480	0.7710	0.7100	0.6450	0.5928	0.7134	0.4857	0.6688	0.8615
CuiCaseSim	0.6380	0.6110	0.5820	0.5360	0.5008	0.5736	0.1945	0.5048	0.7769

From Table 2, we can see that for the first 50 files retrieved, all of the non-simulation runs gained significant improvement over the FreqCase in terms of Avg. P. Among them, LogFreqCase outperformed FreqCase by 18%. This shows that user log information can greatly improve the retrieval performance. Furthermore, such improvement can be further enhanced when query expansion is applied. Our technique, ExpLogCase, had the highest precision value for all the first N files retrieved, and gained 25% and 5.7% over FreqCase and LogFreqCase.

The Avg.P value for CuiCase is the lowest among all the non-simulation runs. It underperformed by 15% compared to ExpLogCase. There are several factors contributing to such low performance. First, the term selection in Cui's approach relies heavily on the web query logs, and the limited amount of logs available in this experiment affects the quality of expansion terms. Second, as mentioned earlier, Cui's approach missed out query terms that are relevant to the document but did not appear in the document. Our technique captures such terms, thus resulting in a better performance. Third, for this particular test data set, the vector space ranking algorithm in CuiCase underperforms by 5.5% in terms of Avg.P compared to the probabilistic model implemented in our technique. All the simulated runs experienced 20% to nearly 50% improvements in terms of Avg.P (See Table2) over the FreqCase. However, CuiCaseSim's Avg.P value was 24% lower compared to LogFreqCaseSim. This shows that our technique outperforms Cui's even when there is sufficient log information.

We also analyzed the test runs using the average 11-interpolated precision (Table 3). The test run for the proposed technique, ExpLogCase, again outperformed all the others. It had a 56%, 31%, 16.6% and 7.4% improvement over FreqCase, CuiCase, LogFreqCase and ExpCase, respectively. Furthermore, its simulated test run – ExpLogCaseSim outperformed LogFreqCaseSim and CuiCaseSim by 5.9% and 32%.

Table 3. Comparison Analysis for Average 11-point precision

	Vs. FreqCase	Vs. LogFreqCase	Vs. Expcase	Vs. LogFreqCaseSim	Vs. CuiCase	Vs. CuiCaseSim
FreqCase	-	-	-	-	-	-
LogFreqCase	0.3416	-	-	-	0.1286	-
ExpCase	0.4561	0.0853	-	-	0.2249	-
ExpLogCase	0.5643	0.1660	0.0743	-	0.3159	-
CuiCase	0.1888	-0.1139	-	-	-	-
logFreqCaseSim	-	-	-	-	-	0.2507
ExpLogCaseSim	-	-	-	0.0592	-	0.3247
CuiCaseSim	-	-	-	-	-	-

These figures show that overall, the expansion techniques outperform the non-expansion ones. Our technique, ExpLogCase, outperforms all the other techniques in terms of precision for the first 50 files retrieved, recall 300 and average 11-point precision even in situations where there is a very limited amount of extracted query associations available.

6 Conclusions

Various expansion retrieval techniques have explored retrieval effectiveness using original documents and rely on historical queries or surrogate files for further expansion. We have proposed a technique that incorporates the use of web log activities in improving information retrieval from the initial index term weighing stage. Our technique is robust enough to handle situations when not enough log activities are available. Our experiment has shown that the Log-base Association Expansion approach can achieve significant improvements using log information and outperforms similar approaches. Thus we can conclude that using log activities at the initial stage of expansion search does improve web search.

In future, we plan to further investigate the effect of the amount of log activities on the readjustment of various parameters in our technique. We also plan to study the efficiency and tradeoff between the initial log mining process and its impact on term weight readjustment and how often the term scores should be readjusted.

References

1. Agrawal, R., Imielinski, T., Swami, A.:Mining Association Rules Between Sets of Items in Large Databases. ACM SIGMOD, (1993) 1 – 10
2. Baeza-Yates, R., Ribeiro-Neto, B.:Modern Information Retrieval (Chapter 3).Addison Wesley, ACM Press, NY, (1999)
3. Billerbeck B., Scholer F. Williams H.E., Zobel, J.:Query Expansion using Associated Queries. CIKM, (2003) 2 – 9

4. Brajnik, G. Mizzaro, S., Tasso, C.: Evaluating User Interfaces to Information Retrieval Systems: A Case Study on User Support. ACM SIGIR, (1996) 128 – 136
5. Carpineto, C. Mori, R.D., Romano, G., Bigi, B.: An Information-Theoretic Approach to Automatic Query Expansion. ACM Transaction on Information Systems, 19(1) (2001) 1 - 27
6. Carpineto, C., Romano, G.: Effective Reformulation of Boolean Queries with Concept Lattices. FQAS 98, Roskilde, Demark, (1998) 83 – 94
7. Cooper, J.W., Byrd., R.J.: Lexical Navigation: Visually Prompted Query Expansion and Refinement. In Proceedings of the 2nd ACM International Conference on digital Libraries, (1997) 237 – 246
8. Cui, H., Wen, J.R., Nie, J.Y., Ma, W.Y.: Probablistic query expansion using query logs. The Eleventh International World Wide Web Conference, ACM, May, (2002) 325 – 332
9. Grefenstette, G.: Explorations in Automatic Thesaurus Discover. Kluwer Academic Publisher, MA, (1994)
10. HEAL: http://www.healcentral.org, accessed on June 7th, 2005
11. Jensen, B.J., Sprink, A., Scaracevic, T.: Real life, real users and real needs: A study and analysis of users' queries on the Web. Information Processing and Management. 36(2) (2000) 207 – 277
12. MeSH: http://www.nlm.nih.gov/mesh/meshhome.html, accessed on June 7th, 2005
13. Robertson, S.E., Walker, S.: Okapi/Keenbow at TREC-8. TREC-8, (1999) 151 – 162
14. Salton, G.: The SMART retrieval system (Chapter 14). Prentice- Hall, Englewood Cliffs, NJ., (1971)
15. Sparck Jones, K.: Experiments in relevance weighting of search terms. Information Processing and Management. 15 (1979) 133 – 144
16. Sparck Jones, K.: Search term relevance weighing given little relevance information. Information Processing and Management. 35 (1979) 30 – 48
17. Sparck Jones K., Walker S., Robertson, S.E.: A Probabilistic Model of Information Retrieval: Development and Comparative Experiments Part 1. Information Processing and Management, 36 (2000) 779 – 808
18. Sparck Jones K., Walker S., Robertson, S.E.: A Probabilistic Model of Information Retrieval: Development and Comparative Experiments Part 2. Information Processing and Management, 36 (2000) 809 – 840
19. Srivastava, J., Cooley, R., Deshpande, M., Tan, P.N.: Web Usage Mining, Discovery and Applications of Usage Patterns from the Web Data. SIGKDD Explorations, 1(2), (2000) 12 – 23

An XML Approach to Semantically Extract Data from HTML Tables*

Jixue Liu[1], Zhuoyun Ao[1], Ho-Hyun Park[2], and Yongfeng Chen[3]

[1] School of Computer and Information Science, University of South Australia
jixue.liu@unisa.edu.au
[2] School of Electrical and Electronics Engineering, Chung-Ang University
hohyun@cau.ac.kr
[3] Faculty of Management, Xian University of Architecture and Technology
chenyf@xauat.edu.cn

Abstract. Data intensive information is often published on the internet in the format of HTML tables. Extracting some of the information that is of users' interest from the internet, especially when large number of web pages need to be accessed, is time consuming. To automate the processes of information extraction, this paper proposes an XML way of semantically analyzing HTML tables for the data od interest. It firstly introduces a mini language in XML syntax for specifying ontologies that represent the data of interest. Then it defines algorithms that parse HTML tables to a specially defined type of XML trees. The XML trees are then compared with the ontologies to semantically analyze and locate the part of table or nested tables that have the interesting data. Finally, interesting data, once identified, is output as XML documents.

1 Introduction

The World Wide Web has become more and more important as a knowledge resource. The information in the web is often published on web pages in a language called HTML, namely Hyper Text Markup Language [9]. In particular, data intensive information is often published in a construct called a HTML table. The users of the web access the information by using a browser to search through pages and tables to locate interested items. This traditional way of information extraction is time consuming when large numbers of pages and vast volumes of data need to be collected. For example, it is almost impossible to access all pages on the internet for recent prices of computer parts. For this reason, it is desirable to develop efficient and reliable technologies to semantically extract interesting information from the internet. At the same time, the degree of automation and the semantic accuracy of the technologies are critical to fulfill the desire. This motivates the research of investigating techniques for extracting information from HTML tables in this paper.

---

* This research was supported by the international join research grant of the IITA (Institute of Information Technology Assessment) foreign professor invitation program of the MIC (Ministry of Information and Communication), Korea.

Information extraction from HTML tables appears in two different types. One type of extraction uses an **extraction schema** or **ontology** as a query containing requirements of data of interest (called interesting data). The schema is then used to test whether the data in a HTML table satisfies the requirements. The data that meets the requirements becomes interesting data and is extracted and stored [6,12]. We refer to this type of extraction as **data extraction**. Another type of extraction does not use extraction ontologies. Instead, it aims to extract structures and types of web pages and tables on the web pages [4,11], which we refer to as **structure and type understanding**. In this paper, we concentrate on the problem of automatic *data extraction* from HTML tables.

HTML is a language for information presentation on web pages and does not have mechanisms to represent the semantics of the information it presents. At the same time, flexible HTML grammar and the use of the HTML table construct for positioning information rather than presenting data records pose a number of challenges and issues for data extraction [6,12,13]. Some of these are explained as the followings.

- The use of synonyms (e.g., car and motorcar), abbreviations (e.g., kilometers and km), hypernyms (vehicle for car), and hyponyms (sports-car for car) for table headings makes it hard to use pure string matching to find interesting columns in tables;
- Tables are not only used to present structured data like the one in Figure 1, but also used to position information like menus and pictures in place. This makes the identification of the tables that contain interesting data a big challenge;
- When tables are in a nested structure, not only the table at the top level but also all the nested tables need to be analyzed to locate the ones that contain the data of interest.
- The row span and the column span constructs of HTML tables and especially nested tables require table handling techniques to use complex processes. As shown in Figure 1, the code of the author column behind the table can be row spans and columns spans and it can also be nested tables. All possible options are expected to be handled properly.

Because of these challenges table processing needs to analyze tables as a whole, including names, types, and structures etc., against the extraction ontology, not just table headings as done in some work as we now summarize.

A number of work has been done in the area of information extraction from web pages and HTML tables [6,12,3,10,8,13,14,7]. Work such as [5,4] emphasizes on understanding web pages to extract common structures of the pages for wrapper writing purposes. Work like [11,7,13] focuses on understanding tables and the types used in the tables, which is on a more detailed level than web page understanding. Work on data extraction (using a template or an ontology) include [1,6,12,10,8,13,14] but the one that is close to our work is [6]. The work in [6] uses a relational schema as a template (although synonyms are considered) and deals with nested tables by heuristics. In contrast, we propose an ontology language that can represent hierarchic structures of ontologies. In addition, our

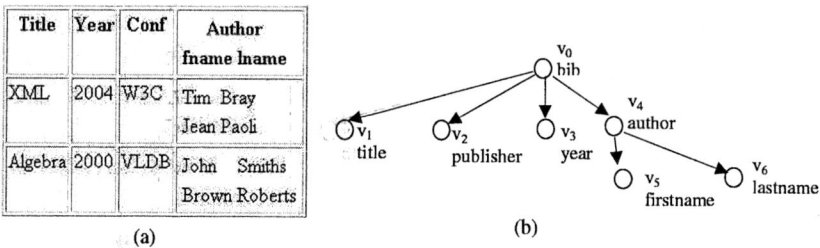

Fig. 1. A motivation example and an o-tree

approach handles nested tables not by heuristics but by comparing the structures of an ontology and the structure of an XML tree to identify tables of interest, which means a real semantic method, as detailed in the following.

The main contributions of our approach are outlined as follows.

1) We define a mini language for specifying extraction ontologies. The syntax of the language is in XML [2] which is widely accepted as a language for data exchange. The basic construct of the language is an element, a name for which data will be extracted. The language also has other constructs to support the specification of synonyms, hypernyms, hyponyms, multiplicity, and conditions on data values. An element is allowed to have child elements which means generally an ontology is a hierarchy. An ontology specified in this language defines what data an application expects to get. The ontology also works as a schema for the output of extraction.

2) We define a model to represent tables on a HTML page. The model is a specific XML tree model and node types of *table*, *row*, and *cell* are defined for the nodes of the tree alongside some other attributes. This model, as it is a tree structure, can naturally represent nested tables no matter how many levels of nesting are on the web page. A tree of this model is called content tree. An algorithm is defined to parse any HTML page to a content tree.

3) Algorithms are defined to compare an ontology and a content tree to obtain a mapping tree which states which node in the content tree is for which element in the ontology. The comparison involves two sub types: element name comparison and value testing. Element name comparison is to compare an element name with a cell value of the content tree and to find a table heading that matches the element. Because this is not always successful, then the second type of comparison, value testing, is to test specifically defined characteristic symbols and value conditions to identify a possible heading for the element. These two types of comparison do not give full semantics and there is a final step to check parent-child relationships to make sure that the mapping tree indicate a similar structure as the ontology.

4) Finally an algorithm is defined to extract data from a content tree based on the mapping obtained from the previous step. The data extracted appears as XML elements.

We start the presentation by introducing the mini-language for ontologies.

2 Language for Specifying Extraction Ontology

In this section, we define a mini language for specifying extraction ontologies. The extraction ontologies then work as queries. Data in HTML tables will be parsed and analyzed and interesting data that satisfies the requirements of the queries will be retrieved as instances of the queries.

The basic constructs of the language are EMPTY [2] XML elements and attributes. A general format of this is $< elementname[\ attribute = "value"] >$ where the part in the square brackets is optional and can be repeated for multiple times. An XML element corresponds to a **concept** in an ontology and the element name is the same as the concept name. The optional attributes of the element specify the variations and the conditions of the concept. An element can have some child elements which correspond to child concepts of the concepts. This means that the language allows the definition of ontologies with a hierarchical structure. The optional attributes of an element we define for an element include syn, hyp, $symb$, $mult$, and $cond$. The attribute syn contains a set of synonyms separated by comma ',' of the element name. For example, if the element name is $mileage$, then the value of syn would be $syn = "odometer, kilometer, km"$. The attribute hyp contains a set of hypernyms (generalizations of the element name) and hyponyms (specializations) separated by ','. For example, if the element name is car, then there would be $hyp = vehicle, sports\text{-}car$. $symb$ is an attribute to store characteristic symbols or strings to identify the value type of the element. For example, if the element name is $cost$, then the dollar sign $ helps identity the column for $cost$. Note that these characteristic symbols are only helping to confirm a reasoning but not decisive. The attribute $mult$ defines the number of occurrences of the element under its parent and it takes a symbol between " $+$ " and " $*$ " which are defined in the XML Recommendation [2]. If $mult$ does not appear in an element, then the multiplicity of the element is $'+'$. Finally $cond$ is an attribute containing a logic condition which is extended to allow regular expressions to be put in the boolean function $expr(regular\text{-}expr)$. For example, for an $color$ element, the attribute appears as $< color\ cond = "expr(*blue*)" >$ to mean color contains blue. Following is an example showing the use of the mini language in an extraction ontology for bibliography.

```
<bib syn="references", hyp="publication,article"/>
   <title syn="rubric" hyp="name"/>
   <publisher hyp="company" mult="*"/>
   <year syn="yr" hyp="time" condi= ">=2003"/>
   <author syn="writer"/>
       <firstname syn="fn,forename" hyp="name"/>
       <lastname syn="familyname" hyp="name"/>
   </author>
</bib>
```

An ontology defined in this language can be mapped into a tree, called an **o-tree**, which will be used for semantic analysis in the next a few sections. Each node of the tree has a unique id, usually using v_i, and a label of an element in the ontology. We use $elem(v_i)$ to return the element name on node v_i and use attributes as $syn(v_i)$, $hyp(v_i)$, and $condi(v_i)$ to return the corresponding attribute values of v_i. This is also applicable to other types of trees presented later.

3 Parse HTML Tables to XML Tree

In this section, we propose an algorithm to parse HTML tables into XML trees. The result of parsing is an XML tree which will be used for semantic analysis in the following section. We choose to parse the HTML tables on a web page to an XML tree, not other models, because an XML tree is a natural representation of hierarchically structured information like that contained in HTML tables. In contrast to [7] where the nested table model lacks modelling power and some special constructs are employed to improve it, our use of XML modelling is sufficient for representing the information in nested HTML tables.

We note that there are many tools on the internet like Altova XMLSpy and Stylus Studio XML IDE that convert HTML pages to XML documents, but this type of conversion is simply takes HTML tags as XML tags and HTML contents as text nodes of XML and there is no real structure conversion. In contrast, our work involves fundamental structure conversion which will enable us to conduct semantic analysis.

We now propose a **c-tree** (stands for Content tree) algorithm. The output of the algorithm is a c-tree which is defined to represent both the structures and the contents of the HTML tables on a web page with row spans and column spans normalized. The tree has four types of nodes, a *root* node, some *table* nodes, *row* nodes, and *cell* nodes. The *root* node represents the web page and therefore whether a page contains tables or not, it always has a root node. Other types of nodes correspond to tables and rows and columns of the tables. When a cell contains other tables, which is a very common case with regard to the use of tables, a *table* node is created under the *cell* node for each of the nested tables. This causes c-trees nested under c-trees.

Each node of a c-tree has a unique ID and a label among *root*, *table*, *row* and *cell*. The label of the root node is always *root*. The child nodes of the root are all labelled with *table*. The child nodes of a *table* node are all labelled with *row* and the child nodes of a *row* node with *cell*. A node also has a position number. The *root* node's position number is always 0 and all other nodes' positions are relative to that of their parent. Thus the k-th cell in row j of table i means that the position number for the corresponding table node is i, position number of the row node is j and the position number of the cell node is k. If a node is a *cell* node, it also has a value which is the content of the cell in the HTML table. Note that this value can be either a column heading of the table or a data value in a row of the table. At this stage of parsing, we have no way to know which type it belongs to. For *cell* nodes, there are optional attributes, $rspan = n$ and $cspan = m$ (only one appears on each node), to mean if the cell has a span. These two attributes are used to normalize the c-tree at the end of the algorithm. After the normalization, the two attributes are undefined.

An XML Approach to Semantically Extract Data from HTML Tables   701

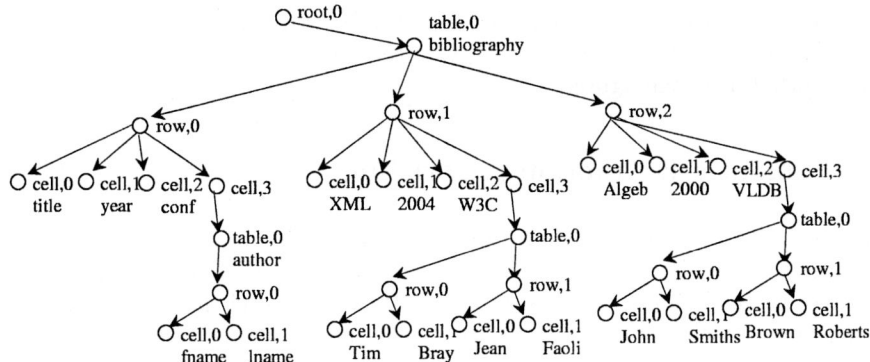

Fig. 2. c-tree of bibliography

We define functions for a node for the ease of references. Given a node v, function $posi(v)$ returns the position number of the node. Function $val(v)$ returns the value of v. If v is not a *cell* node, $val(v)$ returns *null*. Function $elem(v)$ returns the label of v. Function $chil(v)$ returns the set of all child nodes of v.

Algorithm 3.1 (c-tree)
```
Input: a HTML page
Do:(A) - parsing
   (1) create a root node v_r
   (2) for each < table > on the page create a node under v_r with the label
   table and the position number being the sequential number of the table among
   all non-nested tables on the page.
   (3) for each < tr > of the table, create a node under the table node with
   the label row and the position number being the sequential number of the
   row among all the rows of the table.
   (4) for each < td > or < th > of the row, create a node under the row
   node, with the label cell, the position number being the sequential number
   of the cell among all cells of the row, and the value being the content
   of the cell.
   (5) if < table > is found within a cell, create a table node under the cell
   with the position number being the sequential number of the table among
   all the tables in the cell. Then the parsing moves to Step (3).
   (B) - normalizing
   (1) if a cell has the rspan attribute and the cell position number k, make
   duplicates of the cell node and insert a duplicate to position k under
   each of the sibling row nodes covered by the span and adjust the position
   numbers on the cell nodes of the siblings.
   (2) if a cell has the cspan attribute, make duplicates of the node s.t.
   the number of duplicates is the same as the number of the spanned columns,
   insert the duplicates after the node, and adjust the position numbers.
Output: the c-tree v_r
```

Figure 2 shows a c-tree converted from the HTML document for Figure 1(a). In the figure, position numbers are put after the labels of nodes. All node IDs are omitted from the figure.

4 Semantic Extraction Algorithms

In this section, we propose algorithms that semantically analyze a c-tree for interesting data. The algorithms are complicated in three main aspects. Firstly, because of the use of tables in positioning information such as menus and advertizements on web pages, the tables on a web page may not contain interesting data. Even if they do, the locations of the tables that contain interesting data can be any where on a page. Secondly accurately analyzing tables and locating interesting data should not only rely on the success of keyword matching between an o-tree and a c-tree, but also on the success of structure matching. In other words, we want the relationships of elements in an o-tree to be matched with a similar structure in a c-tree. It is this second point that makes our work different from that of [6] which uses heuristics to trim unrelated tables without considering relativeness of data in the tables to the elements in the o-tree. Finally, the algorithm should be able to run in both strong mode and weak mode. By **strong mode**, it means that the structure of interesting data has to exactly match the structure of the o-tree. For example with strong mode and the o-tree in Figure 1, the data for $fname$ and $lname$ has to be in a table nested in the table containing data for $title$ and $Year$. In comparison, **weak mode** does not require an exact structure match. In this mode, a c-tree containing data in nested tables can be matched to an o-tree that has only one level or a c-tree containing data in one table can be matched to the multiple levels of an o-tree.

In the rest of this section, we firstly define a structure called a **mapping tree** which represents the relationship between a c-tree and an o-tree. Then we define a function to compare a $table$ node in a c-tree with a node in an o-tree and this function is critical to building a mapping tree. After this, we define a criteria to judge whether a mapping has been found between a c-tree and an o-tree. If a mapping tree is found, data needs to be extracted from the content tree. So we define an algorithm to output data in XML format. Finally we define the overall control algorithm of the analysis.

We define a mapping tree to return the result of a successful match. A mapping tree is created out of a duplicate of an o-tree by removing attributes syn and hyp of the nodes in the duplicate and adding two attributes $hmap$ and $vmap$ to each node in the duplicate. The attribute $hmap$ will be used to store a position path when a heading match (defined in next paragraph) is found for the element. The attribute $vmap$ will be used to a position path when a value match is found for the element. Here a **position path** shows the type of nodes that contain the information for an element and is defined to be a sequence of position numbers on the path from the root node to a node in a c-tree. For example in Figure 2, 0.0.0.3.0.0.1 is a position path that uniquely identifies the type of nodes containing data for the element $lname$.

We define a function called *compare* which takes three arguments, a mapping tree m, a non-leaf node o of an o-tree, and a *row* node r of a c-tree. The function compares the children of o to the children of r to find a match between a child x of o and a child y of r. y is a **heading match** of x if $val(y) = elem(x)$ or $val(y)$ is contained in $syn(x)$ or $hyp(x)$, and y is a **value match** of x if $symb(x)$ is in $val(y)$. The function is defined for the strong mode and the weak mode separately. In the strong mode, the leaf nodes of o are compared with the leaf nodes of r and the non-leaf nodes of o are compared with the nested tables in r. In the weak mode, the descendents of o are used for comparison. At the same time, any descendents of o that have not got a match are compared with the nested tables of r. This function is an important part of our approach that performs semantic checks when comparison is conducted.

```
/* m is a mapping tree, o is an o-tree, and r is a row node */
m-tree compare(m,o,r){ // for strong mode
   for each x in child(o),
      if x is a leaf node,
         for every leaf y in r, compare elem(x) to val(y) to find a
            heading (value) match for x
         if a heading (value) match is found, set the position path of y
            to hmap (vmap) attribute of the node in m
            that corresponds to x.
      else
         for every non leaf y in r and for each table child z of y and
            for each row child w in z, compare(m,x,w);
}
m-tree compare(m,o,r){ // for weak mode
   for each x in desc(o),
      compare x to the value of each child y of r to find a heading
         (value) match for x
      if a heading (value) match is found, set the position path of y
         to the hmap (vmap) attribute of the node in m
         that corresponds to x.
      if x is not a direct child of o, set the position path of the
         immediate table ancestor of y to hmap of the immediate
         parent of x.
      if x has children that do not have a match and y has table
         children,
         for each table node w of y and for each row node z of w,
            compare(m,x,z);
   return m;
}
```

We define a **criteria** to test whether a mapping has been **found** in a mapping tree. A mapping is found if for the mapping tree all of the followings are true: (1) the attribute *hmap* or the attribute *vmap* of every node is set with a value except for those with $mult =' *'$; (2) all position paths of *hamp* and *vmap* of all nodes are distinct; (3) if the node v of the mapping tree has children, then the position path p on v has to be the precedence of the position path of all v's children. For all other cases, the mapping is not a possible mapping. We note that Point (3) of the criteria checks whether the mapping for a sub o-tree is from one nested table. If not, the mapping is not found. If a mapping has been found, we say that the mapping tree is **complete**.

In the following, we define an algorithm that extracts data of interest from a c-tree with the mapping of a mapping tree.

```
/* v_t a table node, v_m a mapping tree */
xml-document dataOutput(v_m, v_t){
    make a duplicate of v_t and all its ancestors.
    label the node v_t by elem(v_m).
    for each x in desc(v_m), label all nodes
        reached by hmap(x) (or vmap(x)) with elem(x).
    remove all nodes with the cell label.
    remove all row nodes that make any of conditions in condi false.
    collapse the tree by moving all children of a row node to its parent
        and remove the row node.
    remove the ancestors of v_t.
    return v_t.
}
```

The following algorithm controls the comparison of an o-tree to all tables of a c-tree to locate the table containing interesting information.

Algorithm 4.1 (analysis)

```
Input: a c-tree v_c, a o-tree v_o, and a mapping tree v_m
Do: For each table tree child v_t of v_c
        call m = compare(v_m, v_o, v_t);
        if m is complete, output XML document dataOutput(v_m, v_t)
        else if v_t has table descendents at the cell level, move these table
            descendents to v_c and remove this table node from v_c.
        else remove the table node
        goto the next table child of v_c
Output: a set of XML documents.
```

Discussion. The above algorithms work for the cases where the table containing interesting data has headings or characteristic symbols. There are other cases where the heading of a table is on the left or a table does not have headings. For the first case, a controlled transformation between row nodes and cell nodes of the content tree will make the above algorithms applicable. In the second case, extra information such as sample data need to be used. Because of the space limit, we leave out these algorithms in this paper. Also because of the space limit, we leave out performance discussion of our approach.

5 Conclusions

In this paper, we proposed a way of using XML modelling to semantically analyze HTML tables and extract data of interest. We introduced a mini language in XML syntax to specify ontologies representing the data of interest. This language has considered factors of synonyms, hyper- and hypo- names, symbolic characteristics of values and conditions on the data to be extracted. We then defined algorithms that parse HTML tables to a specially defined type of XML trees, semantically analyze the trees to locate the part of table or nested tables that have the interesting data, and to extract and output interesting data. The further work of this research is to study the transformation of $c-trees$ so that tables with headings on the left side can be recognized. At the same time, sample documents need to be incorporated in the algorithms to make the recognition of tables without headings possible.

References

1. Terje Brasethvik and Jon Atle Gulla. Natural language analysis for semantic document modeling. *DKE*, 38(1):45–62, 2001.
2. Tim Bray, Jean Paoli, and C. M. Sperberg-McQueen. Extensible markup language (xml) 1.0. *http://www.w3.org/TR/1998/REC-xml-19980210*, 1998.
3. Valter Crescenzi, Giansalvatore Mecca, and Paolo Merialdo. Roadrunner: Towards automatic data extraction from large web sites. *VLDB*, pages 109–118, 2001.
4. Valter Crescenzi, Giansalvatore Mecca, and Paolo Merialdo. Roadrunner: automatic data extraction from data-intensive web sites. *SIGMOD Conference*, page 624, 2002.
5. Valter Crescenzi, Giansalvatore Mecca, Paolo Merialdo, and Paolo Missier. An automatic data grabber for large web sites. *VLDB*, pages 1321–1324, 2004.
6. David W. Embley, Cui Tao, and Stephen W. Liddle. Automatically extracting ontologically specified data from html tables of unknown structure. *ER*, pages 322–337, 2002.
7. Irna M. R. Evangelista Filha, Altigran Soares da Silva, Alberto H. F. Laender, and David W. Embley. Using nested tables for representing and querying semistructured web data. *CAiSE*, pages 719–723, 2002.
8. J. Hammer, H. Garcia-Molina, J. Cho, R. Aranha, and A. Crespo. Extracting semistructured information from the web. *Proceedings of the Workshop on Management of Semistructured Data*, 1997.
9. HTML-Working-Group. Hypertext markup language (html). *W3C - http://www.w3.org/MarkUp/*, 2004.
10. Wai Lam and Wai-Yip Lin. Learning to extract hierarchical information from semi-structured documents. *CIKM*, pages 250–257, 2000.
11. Kristina Lerman, Lise Getoor, Steven Minton, and Craig A. Knoblock. Using the structure of web sites for automatic segmentation of tables. *SIGMOD Conference*, pages 119–130, 2004.
12. Kristina Lerman, Craig A. Knoblock, and Steven Minton. Automatic data extraction from lists and tables in web sources. *Automatic Text Extraction and Mining workshop (ATEM-01), IJCAI-01, Seattle, WA - http://www.isi.edu/ lerman/papers/lerman-atem2001.pdf*, 2001.
13. Seung-Jin Lim and Yiu-Kai Nag. An automated approach for retrieving hierarchical data from html tables. *CIKM*, pages 466–474, 1999.
14. Stephen Soderland. Learning to extract text-based information from the world wide web. *KDD*, pages 251–254, 1997.

Automatic Generation of Semantic Fields for Resource Discovery in the Semantic Web

I. Navas, I. Sanz, J.F. Aldana, and R. Berlanga

Departament de Llenguatges i Sistemes Informátics,
Departament de Ingenieria y Ciencia de los Computadores,
Universitat Jaume I, E-12071 Castellón. Spain
{berlanga, isanz}@uji.es
Computer Languages and Computing Science Department,
Higher Technical School of Computer Science Engineering,
University of Málaga 29071 Málaga, Spain
{ismael, jfam}@lcc.uma.es

Abstract. In this paper we present and evaluate two approaches for the generation of Semantic Fields, which are used as a tool for resource discovery in the Semantic Web. We mainly concern ourselves with semantic networks that describe their interests and resources by means of ontologies. Semantic Fields are intended to help users to locate these resources by specifying a brief description (also as an ontology). We propose two ways to automatically build Semantic Fields. The first one is used in the KREIOS approach, which is based on the pre-computation of distances between all the ontology pairs. The second one is based on a fast incremental clustering algorithm, which groups together similar ontologies as they are published. These groups constitute a pre-computed set of Semantic Fields.

Keywords: Resource discovery, similarity of ontologies, query distribution.

1 Introduction

Information in the Web has grown very quickly. Now, the semantics of the information on the web is becoming explicit. Ontologies provide a formal representation of the real world by defining concepts and relationships between them. In order to provide semantics to web resources, instances of such concepts and relationships are used to annotate them. These ontology-based annotations of resources are the foundation of the Semantic Web.

As the amount of annotated resources is continuously increasing, finding relevant resources according to their semantics becomes a crucial and urgent problem to be solved. To enable information processing and content retrieval in distributed environments like the Semantic Web with lots of ontologies, it is necessary to define appropriate techniques to organize all these ontologies. Thus, if we are able to find the relevant ontologies for a given request, we will provide a solution to both resource retrieval and query distribution problems.

This paper presents two discovery methods for finding relevant resources related with domain ontologies. The discovery methods are based on the concept of *Semantic Field*, which is a group of interrelated ontologies that can be relevant for a given information request. The first method relies on both semantic distance and ontology neighborhood to build Semantic Fields, whereas the second method relies on the concepts of ontology similarity and document clustering. While the first method is devised for specific and personalized Semantic Field building, the second one is intended to produce generic ontology groups according to their domains.

As an example of the practical usage of Semantic Fields, consider a peer-to-peer network of heterogeneous resources, which are described using a variety of ontologies (usually called a Semantic Overlay Network [5]). Semantic fields can be used to group together similar ontologies and, accordingly, related resources. This provides several advantages: better management (the network self-organizes) and better performance (queries can be routed to relevant groups of resources). Note that, in such a scenario, resources can enter and leave the network at any moment, and so do their semantic descriptions. This requires the system to respond incrementally to such changes.

The paper is organized as follows: Section 2 details the problem of ontology clustering; Section 3 discusses how to measure ontology distances, including the KREIOS and OntoCluster approaches; Section 4 presents the evaluation of both approaches; Section 5 introduces a discussion about the obtained results, followed by some conclusions and future work in Section 6.

2 Ontology Clustering

The problem of finding similar resources to a given query is similar to the task of Information Retrieval (IR), where the system retrieves the most relevant documents to a query. As in IR, the Cluster Hypothesis can also be applied to semantic descriptions. This states that documents relevant to the same queries tend to be more similar to each other than to non-relevant ones. This hypothesis has produced numerous clustering methods and algorithms for classifying documents. Broadly speaking, most of these algorithms are intended to calculate document groups in such way that the intra-similarity of each group is maximized, whereas the inter-similarity between groups is minimized. In [15] we can find a revision of the main document clustering algorithms.

In our scenario, it is also necessary that the Semantic Fields (ontology groups) are dynamically generated. That is, whenever a new ontology is published, existing groups must be updated accordingly. Hence, only incremental clustering algorithms can be applied for maintaining Semantic Fields. The most popular incremental clustering algorithms are based on the single-pass and multi-pass strategies (e.g. K-means). All these algorithms rely on the concept of *centroid*, which allow comparing each incoming document to each existing group. However, for Semantic Fields, the concept of *centroid* seems rather artificial, and it is not clear neither its meaning nor the way it could be updated.

To the best of our knowledge, no clustering algorithm specific for ontologies has been proposed. Most of the related works are focused on defining semantic similarity measures between ontologies to improve merging and schema matching tasks. As earlier mentioned, ontology clustering can be a very useful tool for instance retrieval, query distribution and matchmaking. Some recent works like [1,3,10,11] apply clustering algorithms to build global schemas for a large set of heterogeneous XML documents. In these works, structural similarity functions are defined to asses when two XML documents can be assigned to a same DTD or XML-schema. In [1,11], fast incremental algorithms are proposed to update incrementally the global schemas, whereas in [3,10] hierarchical non-incremental algorithms are applied. However, nowadays there not exists a study about which clustering algorithms can be used for these tasks and which are appropriate for each kind of applications.

3 Ontology Distances

As it can be noticed in the previous section, the computation of Semantic Fields requires either an ontology distance function or a ontology similarity function. Much work on the computation of ontology distances stems from the ontology alignment problem. This problem consists of finding mappings between concepts and relations of two different ontologies. Some of these works are adaptations of database schema matching mechanisms (e.g. CUPID, CLIO, COMA [7], etc.) earlier developed in the database community. More recently, several works have been proposed to use edit distances to calculate in a more flexible way such schema mappings (e.g. [12,13]). All these approaches only regard the structural aspects of the schemata. Although several approaches exist for calculating conceptual semantic distances within a thesaurus like WordNet [2], they cannot be directly used to compare two different ontologies. Recently, some works (e.g. [4,14]) propose different similarity criteria for comparing two ontologies, regarding their linguistic as well as their structural aspects.

COMA [7] is a schema matching system developed as a platform to combine multiple matchers in a flexible way. It provides a large spectrum of individual matchers that can work on automatic mode or with reuse of previously found mappings. The use of COMA in our approach has two main advantages: it is possible to obtain COMA for research studies, and it can be extended with simple matchers (e.g. semantic matchers) improving results of this tool.

In a first approach we use the COMA framework in automatic mode, although it could make use of manual mappings previously published in the network to get better matching results. COMA is a framework that can apply sets of matching algorithms to relational schemas and XML documents. It also provides a set of matchers that perform syntactical and structural matching processes. However we needed to match ontologies, described with OWL, so we developed a new class for COMA Framework (OWLToModel) that transforms a OWL ontology into a directed graph that COMA can deal with.

c1/c2	c(2,1)	c(2,2)	c(2,3)	c(2,4)	c(2,5)	c(2,6)	c(2,7)	c(2,8)	c(2,9)	c(2,10)	c(2,11)	Max
c(1,1)	0	0	0	0	0	0	0	0	0	0	0	0
c(1,2)	0	0	0	0	0	0	0	0	0	0	0	0
c(1,3)	0.615	0	0	0	0	0	0	0	0	0	0	0.615
c(1,4)	0	0	0	0	0.964	0	0	0.978	0	0	0	0.978
c(1,5)	0	0	0	0	0	0	0	0	0.76	0	0	0.76
c(1,6)	0	0	0	0.54	0	0	0	0	0	0	0	0.54
c(1,7)	0	0	0	0	0	0	0	0	0	0	0.82	0.82
Max	0.615	0	0	0.54	0.964	0	0	0.978	0.76	0	0.82	

Fig. 1. Mappings Table for two ontologies using COMA

Then, using distances returned by COMA, we can obtain a matrix of semantic distances between terms for each pair of ontologies. With this matrix, the Partial Semantic Affinity (PSA) between two ontologies O_1 and O_2 can be computed as follows:

$$PSA(O_1, O_2) = \frac{\#Concepts(O_1)}{\sum_{c \in concepts(O_1)} \max(mappings(c, O_2))}$$

PSA represents the relation between the number of concepts of the source ontology (PSA is not symmetric) and the number of similar concepts of both ontologies. Thus, when the compared ontologies are the same, PSA gets its maximum value 1.

Finally, we define Semantic Affinity (SA) between these two ontologies as follows,

$$SA(O_1, O_2) = SA(O_2, O_1) = \min(PSA(O_1, O_2), PSA(O_2, O_1))$$

Let us see an example of calculating semantic affinity between two ontologies. In this case the first ontology has 7 nodes (classes and properties are considered nodes), and the second ontology has 11 nodes. Figure 1 shows the mappings table (similarity values between pair of nodes that are returned by COMA), in which we have included the maximum value for each row and column. The reason for using this value is that, we consider that each node of one ontology can be matched with one node of the other ontology. Thus, a node is matched with the node that has the maximum similarity with it.

3.1 The KREIOS Approach

The first proposed method is based on the key idea that Semantic Fields evolve dynamically depending on the application perspective. Thus, the perspective changes because of application decisions, such as the ontology used, expected size of the Semantic Field, precision needed, response time or user queries. In a first approach we take into consideration that Semantic Fields depend on the ontology that the application chooses and a set of parameters defined by it.

Making use of only one parameter, the affinity range, we can state Semantic Field expected size and precision. Thus, if we make use of small values we will have smaller and more precise semantic fields. However, if we define high affinity range values, semantic fields will be greater and not very useful.

Let O be the selected ontology, R the affinity range, and $\{O_i/i \in (1..n)\}$ previously published ontologies, we formally define a Semantic Field (SF) as

$$SF(O, R) = \{O_i / SA(O, O_i) \leq R\}$$

Semantic Fields can be enhanced by providing further information about the *sub-domains* where each published ontology can be ascribed [9]. A sub-domain can be represented as the set of relevant concepts for a particular application. With this information, semantic distances can be calculated more precisely. However, this is not the focus of this paper, in which we compare two methods without sub-domain information.

In this way, we make use of ontology selection, the entry point and affinity range to test our approach. When an application defines the entry point (connected to an ontology), the application-based Semantic Field will only depend on the affinity threshold, so that it only selects ontologies with semantic affinity lower than this threshold.

3.2 The OntoCluster Approach

The OntoCluster approach builds Semantic Fields by clustering together related ontologies, according to a given similarity measure. The algorithm is based in the application of a Representative-Based (RB) clustering technique in a distributed context. In RB clustering, objects are grouped based on the similarity to one or more members of the group (the "representatives") and not a centroid. The resulting clusters correspond to Semantic Fields.

Let $RepSet(SF)$ be the set of ontologies from a Semantic Field SF that are the cluster representatives, and $sim(O_1, O_2)$ a similarity function that compares two ontologies O_1 and O_2. Then, a Semantic Field can be formally defined as follows:

- $\forall O_i \in SF, \exists O_r \in RepSet(SF), sim(O_i, O_r) \geq \beta_{sim}$
- $\forall O_i \in SF, \nexists O'_r \in RepSet(SF'), SF' \neq SF, sim(O_i, O'_r) \geq \beta_{sim}$
- $\forall O_r \in RepSet(SF), \nexists O'_r \in RepSet(SF), sim(O_r, O'_r) > \beta_{rep}$

Notice that the configuration of clusters relies on two parameters, β_{sim} and β_{rep}. The first parameter controls the homogeneity of the clusters: for all members, the similarity to some representative is always greater than β_{sim}. In contrast, β_{rep} is the *minimum* similarity between representatives within a group; this allows a certain heterogeneity within Semantic Fields. Thus, the set of representatives plays the role of a semantic contour for its corresponding Semantic Field. It is worth mentioning that there does not exist a unique set of representatives for a given cluster, and it will depend on the applied clustering algorithm. In this work, we have used an adaptation of the algorithm presented in [11], in which ontologies are encoded as sets of maximal paths, and which has been designed to work on a fully distributed scenario like P2P networks.

In OntoCluster Semantic Fields are created incrementally. When a new ontology is published in the network, all the current representatives are notified. In general, if the similarity between a representative and the new ontology is high enough, the new ontology is added to the representative's cluster. Note that several, more complex, cases are possible:

- The new ontology may become a cluster representative, if its similarity to some other representative in the group is smaller than β_{rep}.
- The new ontology may be close to representatives in more than one cluster. This will usually lead to cluster reorganization.
- If the ontology is not close enough to any existing cluster, it becomes a new cluster and it is its unique representative.

As in other document clustering algorithms, OntoCluster relies on the concept of *similarity* instead of that of distance.

Regarding the directed graph derived from an ontology O expressed in OWL, we represent it as the set of non-recursive maximal paths, denoted $Paths(O)$. Besides, the elements of each path are normalized so that usual suffixes (e.g. plurals, past tenses, etc.) are removed. We then define the similarity function between two ontologies as follows:

$$pathSim(p_1, p_2) = \frac{|elements(p_1) \cap elements(p_2)|}{max(|elements(p_1)|, |elements(p_2)|)}$$

$$partial\_sim(O_1, O_2) = \frac{\sum_{p_i \in Paths(O_1)} max_{p_j \in Paths(O_2)}(pathSim(p_i, p_j))}{|Paths(O_1)|}$$

$$sim(O_1, O_2) = sim(O_2, O_2) = \frac{partial\_sim(O_1, O_2) + partial\_sim(O_2, O_1)}{2}$$

where the function *elements* returns the set of elements of the given path, *pathSim* returns the similarity between two paths, *partial_sim* gives the average similarity between the best pairwise matches of O_1's paths against O_2. Finally, *sim* is the symmetric function that returns the average between the two partial similarities.

4 System Evaluation

We have studied the clustering effectiveness using as input data a set of semantically annotated descriptions of web services [8]. The data set consists of 116 ontologies representing a variety of very heterogeneous resources [1]. We have manually identified 14 Semantic Fields from this data set. The quality of the system-generated Semantic Fields have been evaluated with traditional information retrieval measures, namely: precision, recall and F1 measure. Given a

---

[1] http://moguntia.ucd.ie/repository/datasets/

system-generated field F_i and a manual group G_j, these measures are defined as follows:

$$Precision(F_i, G_j) = \frac{|F_i \cap G_j|}{F_i}$$

$$Recall(F_i, G_j) = \frac{|F_i \cap G_j|}{G_j}$$

$$F1(F_i, G_j) = \frac{2 \cdot Precision(F_i, G_j) \cdot Recall(F_i, G_j)}{Precision(F_i, G_j) + Recall(F_i, G_j)} = \frac{|F_i \cap G_j|}{|G_j| + |F_i|}$$

To define a global measure for all the groups, firstly each manual group must be mapped to the system-generated group that maximizes the measure. This mapping function is defined as follows:

$$\sigma(G_j) = \arg max_{\forall F_i} \{measure(F_i, G_j)\}$$

Then, the overall measure can be calculated by either macro-averaging or micro-averaging these mappings. For example, the micro and macro averages for F1 are calculated as follows:

$$micF1 = 2 \cdot \frac{\sum_{i=1}^{N_o} |G_i \cap F_{\sigma(G_i)}|}{\sum_{i=1}^{N_o} |G_i| + |F_{\sigma(G_i)}|}$$

$$macF1 = 2 \cdot \frac{1}{N_o} \cdot \sum_{i=1}^{N} F1(F_{\sigma(G_i)}, G_i)$$

Here N_o is the total number of ontologies of the data set.

Additionally, in order to measure the average quality of all the generated Semantic Fields (not only the best matches), we also calculate the macro- average of F1 over the inverse mappings, formally:

$$\sigma^{-1}(F_i) = \arg max_{\forall G_j} \{F1(F_i, G_j)\}$$

$$macF1^{-1} = 2 \cdot \frac{1}{N_o} \cdot \sum_{i=1}^{N} F1(F_i, G_{\sigma^{-1}(F_i)})$$

In Figure 2 we show the results obtained for some well-known hierarchical-agglomerative clustering algorithms. Remember that these algorithms cannot be applied to a real scenario since they are not incremental. We include them as the baseline systems of the evaluation. We indicate between parenthesis the optimal threshold of each algorithm to obtain the best groups. It can be concluded that the best algorithm for this data set is the average-link one, although due to the high number of generated clusters (second column) it gets a slightly low value for the inverse $F1$ (last column) with respect to the complete-link algorithm.

Regarding the proposed approaches for Semantic Field generation, Figure 3 shows the optimal results (between parenthesis we indicate the best values for

Algorithm	#SF	micF1	macF1	Prec.	Recall	$F1^{-1}$
Single-link (0.35)	37	0.490	0.450	0.377	0.7024	0.493
Complete-link (0.30)	27	0.536	0.462	0.500	0.5746	0.535
Average link (0.1)	81	0.581	0.531	0.500	0.6922	0.526

Fig. 2. Results for the baseline clustering algorithms

Approach	#SF	micF1	macF1	Prec.	Recall	$F1^{-1}$
KREIOS ($radius = 3$)	115	0.604	0.564	0.5426	0.6824	0.5673
OntoCluster (sim) ($\beta_{sim} = 0.5, \beta_{rep} = 0.6$)	52	0.643	0.580	0.5255	0.8283	0.6884

Fig. 3. Results for the proposed approaches

the systems parameters). It must be pointed out that in OntoCluster, optimal parameters have been estimated by analysing the distribution of pairwise similarities for a sample of ontologies.

As can be noticed, both approaches clearly overcome the results obtained for the baseline systems. It must be pointed out that the KREIOS approach generates as many clusters as ontologies are. This is because queries can be fetched from any entry point of the network, and therefore the system must calculate a Semantic Field for each one. As a consequence, this produces lower values in the inverse $F1$.

5 Discussion

The previous results show that both approaches perform relatively well on a real set of ontologies. However, we think that much work must be done to improve the semantic distance functions as well as semantic similarity criteria to obtain acceptable system precisions.

The main advantage of KREIOS is that it builds dynamically the Semantic Fields according to the given query. However it has to calculate the matrix of distances between each pair of ontologies. In a network with a high number of incoming ontologies this is a drawback, and the cost of maintaining such a matrix is high $O(N_o^2)$. However, if each new ontology calculates its similarity with published ontologies, the cost for this node will be $O(N_o)$ (although the global cost is $O(N_o^2)$). On the other hand, the distribution of queries is very efficient since the system just has to retrieve from the matrix the nodes that are near the query.

Regarding the OntoCluster approach, it obtains the best results for most of the evaluation measures. However, unlike the KREIOS approach, Semantic Fields are incrementally constructed and maintained independently of the user queries. This makes the distribution of queries difficult whenever the involved ontologies are located in different Semantic Fields. An advantage of OntoCluster is that the group representatives allow fast cluster updating as well as an efficient query distribution based on Super-Peers. Notice that just the group representatives that are similar to the query are selected, and these representatives distribute the query among the group members.

6 Conclusions

In this paper we have introduced the concept of *Semantic Field* as a means of discovering resources in semantic networks. Given a query, each network node is able to locate the ontologies that are semantically related to it, and then to bring the query to their corresponding nodes.

We have presented two clustering methods that automatically generate these Semantic Fields. One method, KREIOS, is based in the concept of semantic neighborhood given a semantic distance between ontologies. The second method, OntoCluster, is based on a representative-based clustering algorithm, which builds a partition of the network ontologies into a set of semantically-related groups. Both clustering algorithms work incrementally and in a totally distributed way (i.e. they do not assume the existence of any central network node in which to perform the ontology clustering algorithm).

The results of Section 4 show that the two presented approaches perform relatively well on a real set of ontologies. However, we think that much work must be done to improve the semantic distance functions as well as semantic similarity criteria to obtain an acceptable system precision. Thus, we are working on including other matchers (Semantic Matchers) in the COMA Framework in order to improve the mappings obtained in automatic mode. On the other hand, the affinity measure could be improved introducing the sub-domain parameter, that is, choosing a set of relevant concepts for each application. Finally, we are studying the possibility of combining both approaches, and how it can affect the cluster quality.

Acknowledgements. This work has been supported by the MCyT grant TIC2002-04586-C04-04/03. We would like to thank Do Hong-Hai and Dr. Erhard Rahm of the University of Leipzig for their help with COMA Framework and to Maria del Mar Roldán García for her discussions about ontology affinity measures.

References

1. Bertino, E. Guerrini, G., Mesiti, M.: A Matching Algorithm for Measuring the Structural Similarity between an XML Document and a DTD and its Applications. Information Systems 29(1), Pag. 23–46, 2004.
2. Budanitsky, A., Hirst, G.: Semantic Distance in WordNet: An Experimental, Application-oriented Evaluation of Five Measures. Workshop on WordNet and Other Lexical Resources, NAACL-2000. Pittsburgh, 2001.
3. Dalamagas, T., Cheng, T., Winkel, K-J., Sellis, T.: A methodology for clustering XML documents by structure. Information Systems. In Press.

4. Doan, A., et al.: Learning to Match Ontologies on the Semantic Web. VLDB Journal 12(4), Pag. 303–319, 2003.
5. Crespo, A., Garcia-Molina,H.: Semantic Overlay Networks for P2P Systems. Technical report, Computer Science Department, Stanford University, 2002.
6. Giunchiglia, F., Shvaiko, P., Yatskevich M.: S-Match: an Algorithm and an Implementation of Semantic Matching. In Proceedings of the First European Semantic Web Symposium, ESWS 2004 ,Heraklion, Crete, Greece, 2004.
7. Hong-Hai, D., Erhard, R.: COMA - A System for Flexible Combination of Schema Matching Approaches, Proc. 28th Intl. Conference on Very Large Databases (VLDB), Hongkong, 2002.
8. Hess,A., Johnston, E., Kushmerick, N.: ASSAM: A Tool for Semi-automatically Annotating Semantic Web Services. International Semantic Web Conference, Hiroshima, 2004.
9. Navas, I., Roldán, M.M., Aldana, J.F.: Kreios: Towards Semantic Interoperable Systems. ADVIS 2004, Pag. 161–171, 2004.
10. Lee, M., Yang, L., Hsu, W., Yang, X.: XClust: clustering XML schemas for effective integration. In Proc. CIKM 2002, Pag. 292–299, 2002.
11. Sanz, I., Pérez, J.M, Berlanga, R., Aramburu, M.J.: XML Schemata Inference and Evolution. DEXA 2003, Pag. 109–118, Praga, 2003.
12. Euzenat, J., Valtchev, P.: Similarity-Based Ontology Alignment in OWL-Lite. ECAI 2004, Pag. 333–337, Valencia, 2004.
13. Maedche, A., Staab, S.: Measuring Similarity between Ontologies. EKAW 2002, Pag. 251–263, Siguenza, 2002.
14. Rodriquez, M.A., Egenhofer, M.J.: Determining Semantic Similarity Among Entity Classes from Different Ontologies. IEEE Transactions on Knowledge Data Engineering 15(2), Pag. 442–456, 2003.
15. Salton, G.: Automatic Text Processing. Addison-Wesley, 1989.
16. Yang, B., Garcia-Molina, H.: Comparing Hybrid Peer-to-peer systems. In Proc. of the 27th International Conference on Very Large Data Bases, Rome, Italy, 2001.

JeromeDL - Adding Semantic Web Technologies to Digital Libraries

Sebastian Ryszard Kruk[1], Stefan Decker[1], and Lech Zieborak[2]

[1] Digital Enterprise Research Institute,
National University of Ireland, Galway, Ireland
`firstname.lastname@deri.org`
[2] Main Library, Gdansk University of Technology, Gdansk, Poland
`zieborak@pg.gda.pl`

Abstract. In recent years more and more information has been made available on the Web. High quality information is often stored in dedicated databases of digital libraries, which are on their way to become expanding islands of well organized information. However, managing this information still poses challenges. The Semantic Web provides technologies that are about help to meet these challenges.

In this article we present JeromeDL, a full fledged open-source digital library system. We exemplify how digital library content management can benefit from the Semantic Web. We define and evaluate browsing and searching features. We describe how the semantic descriptions of resources and users profiles improve the usability of a digital library. We present how digital libraries can be interconnected into one heterogeneous database with use of semantic technologies.

1 Introduction

Increasing investment in research and development as well as the trend to produce more and more written information are challenges for Digital Libraries. Metadata - one of the main cornerstones of the Semantic Web - has been used in libraries for centuries. E.g., tree-structured classifications schemes used to coordinate materials on the same and related subjects lead to the hierarchical organization of catalogs. The catalog approach to manage resources has been successfully adapted in on-line directories like Yahoo! or the Open Directory Project. Since more and more information becomes available also a number of search engines have emerged. Even the search engines utilizing algorithms like PageRank[1] still seem to not always find the high quality information we desire.

The Semantic Web effort continues to explore the usage of metadata on the Web, and comes up with additional ways how to manage resources. Semantically annotated content of the digital library's database can be retrieved by new properties. These properties interlink different resources and provides new meaningfull information to the existing fulltext and bibliographic descriptions.

In this paper we present JeromeDL, an open-source digital library, and exemplify which parts of JeromeDL benefit from the Semantic Web.

2 Architecture of Digital Library and the Semantic Web

The JeromeDL[1] architecture[5] is an instantiation of the architecture presented in [2] with special focus on the exploitation of the Semantic Web based metadata (RDF, FOAF, and ontologies). The main components of the JeromeDL system consists of:

- **resource management:** Each resource is described by the semantic descriptions according to the JeromeDL core ontology. Additionally a fulltext index of the resource's content and MARC21, and BibTeX bibliographic descriptions are provided. Each user is able to add resources via a web interface. To satisfy the quality of delivered content, each resource uploaded through the web interface has to be approved for publication. The administrative interface for librarians (JeromeAdmin) allows to manage resources and associated metadata (MARC21, BibTeX and semantic annotations) as well as to approve user submissions.
- **retrieval features:** JeromeDL provides searching and browsing features (see section 4.1) based on Semantic Web data.
- **user profile management:** In order to provide additional semantical description of resources[4], scalable user management based on FOAF (see section 3.2) is utilized.
- **communication link:** Communication with an outside world is enabled by searching in a network of digital libraries. The content of the JeromeDL database can be searched not only through the web pages of the digital library but also from the other digital libraries and other web applications. A special web services interface based on the Extensible Library Protocol (ELP)[8] (see secion 4.2) has been developed.

3 Semantic Description of Resources in Digital Libraries

There are several approaches to constructing the resource description knowledge base for digital libraries. Conventional catalogs and fulltext indexes are just the most popular examples. In addition one can use bibliographic descriptions like MARC21 or BibTeX. MARC21 consists of few keywords and free text values, without a controlled vocabulary. Therefore machines are not able to utilize much of a MARC21 description.

Text values are not enough to support machine based reasoning.

To perform more intelligent interactions with readers, the knowledge base must be equipped with semantics. The concept of ontology introduced by the Semantic Web is a promising path to extend Digital Library formalisms with the meaningfull annotations. Not exploiting existing standards in Digital Libraries would be a waste of resources. Therefore it is important to introduce ontologies to the digital libraries domain. The ontologies have to be compatible with already existing bibliographic description formalisms.

---

[1] JeromeDL - e-Library with Semantics: http://www.jcromcdl.org/

3.1 JeromeDL Core Ontology

The main purpose of the bibliographic ontology is to *annotate* resources. There is no need to completely capture and formalize the content of the resources. The JeromeDL Core ontology (see Fig. 1) requires only a high level core, which is used to capture the essence of bibliographic annotation. This corresponds to the notion of an upper level ontology, as e.g., discussed in [7] for Digital Libraries. The upper level ontology for JeromeDL aims at compatibility with existing standards. So a good starting point for building an ontology for bibliographic description is DublinCore Metadata.

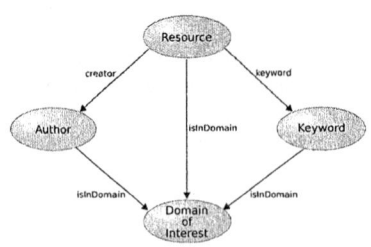

Fig. 1. JeromeDL core ontology

WordNet[2] was a potential candidate as a part of the JeromeDL core ontology. However, some properties defined for the keyword concept in the JeromeDL core ontology are not accessible within the WordNet ontology.

Resources may also be described in BibTeX and MARC21 format. The MarcOnt Initiative[3] is aiming to extend the MARC21 with ontological information. The annotation information is available in RDF format, and can be easily combined with other information. In JeromeDL this feature of RDF is exploited to connect resource information with social networking information and user profiles.

3.2 Semantic Social Collaborative Filtering for Digital Libraries

A classic library requires its users to identify themselves in order to be able to assign a resource (e.g., a book) to a reader. Digital resources in the Internet are often easily duplicable and often a reader does not have to identify himself before viewing specific content, with the exception of restricted resources. However, a reader of a Digital Library can benefit in many ways from the identification.

Registered readers are able to annotate, evaluate and classify resources stored in the JeromeDL database. Electronic bookmarks are popular on the WWW. Everyone can organize already examined resources the way he perceives the world. To identify categories a reader is interested in information on previously read books, electronic bookmarks, annotated resources and highly evaluated resources, are automatically collected. Each resource is described by some categories. Based on the collected categories JeromeDL identifies the categories a reader is interested in (see Fig. 2).

On-line communities introduced the idea of online social networking [9] as a way to interconnect members of a community at give community members a way to explore the community.

---

[2] http://www.cogsci.princeton.edu/~wn/
[3] MarcOnt Initiative: http://www.marcont.org/

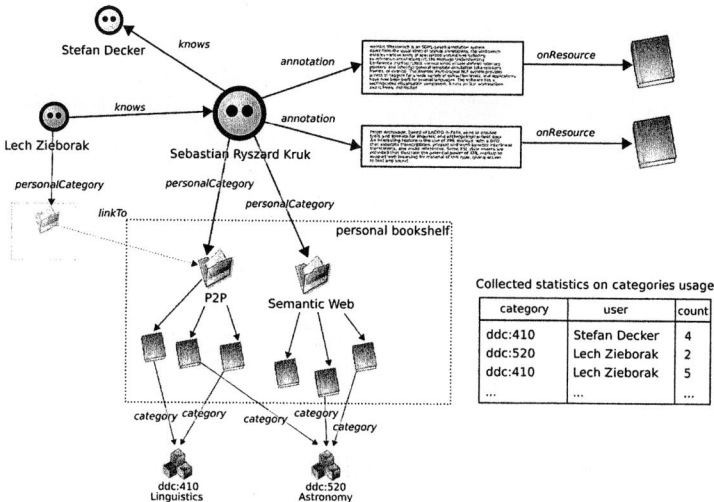

Fig. 2. The user's profile in JeromeDL

To manage the users' profiles in the JeromeDL system the FOAFRealm[4][3] library is used. It provides a semantic social collaborative filtering[4] features to resource retrieval. The FOAF based representation of user-profiles enables one to interlink FOAF-profiles with arbitrary other metadata, such that user profiles and social network information can be exploited automatically in searches.

The users of the JeromeDL are able to browse bookmarks of their friends and link some folders (categories) into their own structure. Readers can also state how much their interests are similar to their friends. Later on each of categories created by the reader have a unique ACL (access control list) that defines which friends are able to see or use the content of this category. The ACL entries are based on the distance and similarity level between issuer of the category and the user that is willing to read the content of this category.

3.3 Interconnecting Heterogeneous Ontologies

The multiplicity of different types of descriptions used in a digital library system can cause many problems when trying to interconnect them. Legacy bibliographic formats, such as MARC21, Dublin Core or BibTeX may take a form of binary file, text file with specific formatting or (if we are lucky) XML or RDF file. To take advantage of information which they contain, an framework must be created to manage and translate between different metadata.

Description of resource's structure, different bibliographic metadata (MARC21, BibTeX, DublinCore), user profiles and access control lists are hard to manage. The semantic description of resources provides a unified way to make the different types or even distributed metadata interoperable.

---

[4] FOAFRealm project: http://www.foafrealm.org/

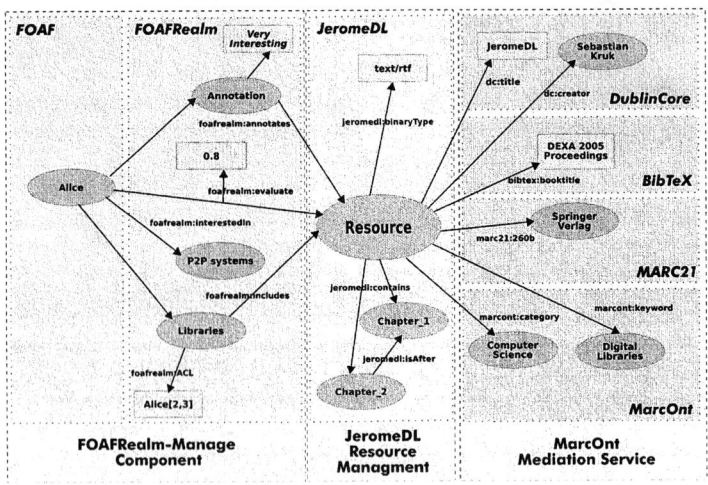

Fig. 3. Components and ontologies in JeromeDL

JeromeDL uses additional libraries to cope with the multiplicity of metadata being managed. Figure 3 represents the overview of ontologies and components used in JeromeDL to annotate resources. FOAFRealm-Manage component is responsible for use management based on FOAF and semantic social collaborative filtering. MarcOnt Mediation Service enables to describe resources with legacy bibliographic descriptions like MARC21 or BibTeX translated into MarcOnt ontology. It is possible to generate the legacy metadata description of a resource from existing semantic one. JeromeDL resource management handles descriptions of structure (e.g. chapters) and content of resources in RDF. And RDF-based object consolidation makes it possible to provide a semantically enhanced retrieval features (see section 4).

Transforming description of resource in legacy format such as MARC21 to semantic description requires few steps. An example flow of transforming MARC21 description to MarcOnt semantic description would be: (1) Parse a binary MARC21 file and create a MARC-XML file. (2) Transform a MARC-XML file to a MARC-RDF file using XSLT. (3) Transform a MARC-RDF graph to a MarcOnt semantic description.

The third step represents the most difficult task - translating one RDF graph into another one, using a different vocabulary. In other words - it requires specifying a set of rules, where a single rule identifies existence of one set of triples as a requirement of creating another set of triples. Translating MarcOnt semantic descriptions back into specified legacy format requires going in other direction on the same way. To perform translations between RDF graphs RDF Translator[5] has been used.

---

[5] RDF Translator: http://rdft.marcont.org/

4 Semantically Enhanced Resources Retrieval in Digital Library

4.1 Query Processing in JeromeDL

To initially find resources a search over the complete content of JeromeDL is possible. The search algorithm of JeromeDL consists of three major steps. Each step requires different metadata sources that describe resources in specific ways:

step A – the first step is the fulltext index search on the resources' contents and users' annotations on resources,
step B – the next step is the bibliographic description search consisting of MARC21 and BibTeX formats,
step C – the last step finally is a user-oriented search with semantics, based on the semantic description of the resources and information about most interested categories (regarding the user that issued the query).

Query Object. When issuing a query to JeromeDL a reader has to submit a query object (see example Fig. 4), usually using an HTML-form.

Each query contains several entries which state what information the search algorithm should look for in the resource description. The reader can choose from Dublin Core Metadata, MARC21-based and BibTeX-based properties. A special property that indicates the content of the resource is additionally provided. Each property contains the list of possible values, that the reader expects to find in the description of the resource. The user can specify which values are required and which are prohibited. Additionally each value may have a ranking value specified, so results containing a desired value are higher ranked. It is possible to define a maximum distance between words consiting the phrase value.

Result Object. A result object (see example Fig. 5) contains the information about the resources that have been found and additional information on the query process that has been executed. Each of the resources is described with: the URI of the resource, title and authors, categorizations and keywords, summary – digest, information on the type of the resource (like XSL:FO, SWF, an antique book's page scans), and the ranking of the resource in this result set. Additionally some debugging information and history of the query processing is included in the result object.

Semantically Enhanced Search Algorithm. The search algorithm with semantics implemented in the JeromeDL system[5] processes the query object according to the flow described earlier and returns a set of result objects.

JeromeDL's search algorithm was designed based on the following requirements:

- The query should return resources where descriptions do not directly contains the required values.

IsSemanticQuery	true	
IsConjunction	false	
property	name="keywords"	
	value=P2P(*mustExists*)	
	value="Semantic Web"	
	(*ranking*=10)	
property	name="category"	
	value=AI(*mustNotExists*)	
...		
fulltext	value="semantic routing"	
	(*proximity*=4)	

resource	**uri**=http://jeromedl.org/show?id=...
	title="EDUTELLA: A P2P ...
	author="Wolfgang Nejdl, ...
	categories=[distributed systems, ...]
	keywords=[P2P, RDF]
	summary="Metadata for the WWW ...
	bookType=pdf
	hits=3
...	
info	"... *semantic web* is to general ...
...	

Fig. 4. The search query object

Fig. 5. The search result object

- The meaning of values provided in the query should be resolved in the context of users' interests.

These goals can be achieved by combining fulltext search as well as searching the bibliographic description and semantic descriptions of resources. The semantically enabled search phase includes query expansion based on the user's interests.

Bibliographic Descriptions. To provide support for legacy bibliographic description formats like MARC21 or BibTeX a digital library system needs to utilize the information provided by these descriptions.

RDF Query Templates. In the last phase (phase C) of the search process the RDF query is performed. Since reader has no knowledge on the actually representation of the semantical description of resources. The literals provided in the query object are translated into the paths queries, based on the predefined ontology.

Semantically Enabled Query Expansion. If the size of the result set is outside the predefined range <MIN, MAX>, the query expansion procedure is called[5].

The information about the readers' interests and semantic descriptions of the resources is exploited to tailor the result set. Unnecessary resources are removed. Previously omitted resources are added to result object. All entries in result object are ranked according to user's interests.

The query expansion is performed iteratively. The decision which property to choose for the query expansion in an iteration depends on the number of the results received from the previous iteration.

Extrapolated Profile. When a reader has just registered to the JeromeDL system the profile information is incomplete. JeromeDL is *extrapolating user profiles* by asking for friends, whose profile is used to extrapolate the readers profile. During the search process the search engine is able to exploit categories defined by the reader's friends.

4.2 Searching in a Distributed Digital Libraries Network

A recent trend in digital libraries is to connect multiple digital libraries to federations where each digital library to able to search in other digital libraries systems. JeromeDL supports federated digital libraries by providing a communication infrastructure for a distributed network of independent digital libraries (L2L) similar to communication in a P2P network. Utilizing XML encoded query and result objects enabled building a SOAP based protocol prototype - Extensible Library Protocol (ELP)[8]. The use of Web Services for building the P2P network of digital libraries will enable connecting JeromeDL in the future to the ongoing projects like OCKHAM[6].

The idea of the ELP is to allow communication in the heterogeneous environment of digital libraries. Each library has to know about at least one other digital library, so it could connect to the L2L network. Each query is processed across the minimal spanning tree of the L2L network.

The minimal requirement imposed on the digital library is to support at least the DublinCore Metadata. If two digital libraries describe the resources with semantics, like JeromeDL system, the communication between them is automatically upgraded to the semantic description level. It allows to use the search algorithm with semantics in the L2L communication.

5 Evaluation of the Search Algorithm with Semantics

The aim of the search algorithm presented in the previous section is to reflect the readers' expectations and to reduces the time required to find the specified resources in JeromeDL. An evaluation of the search algorithm needs to cover the computable effectiveness measures and users' satisfactory level. The quality of retrieval features in JeromeDL depends on user oriented resource description (FOAFRealm-manage component) and bibliographic description (JeromeDL resource management, MarcOnt mediation service).

The semantic social collaborative filtering supported by FOAFRealm has been evaluated in [4]. It has been assumed that high quality information is collected by experts. The results of experiments revealed that each user can find an expert on particular subject within 7 hops in social network graph.

In order to measure the improvement of effectiveness of the semantic enabled search algorithm[5], the database of the prototype system has been filled with 100 resources. After a little time of browsing 50 queries have been processed with and without the semantic query expansion phase. To evaluate the gain in effectiveness produced by the semantic phase of the semantic searching process, tree metrics have been calculated: precision, recall and waste [11].

The results have shown that the semantic query expansion phase in the search algorithm improves the results by 60% compared to the search process without the semantic (user-oriented tailoring) phase.

---

[6] OCKHAM: http://www.ockham.org/

6 Future Work

The evaluation of the JeromeDL search algorithm revealed that the results depend strongly on the semantic parts of resources' descriptions. That leads to the conclusion that better quality of the semantic description will result in higher effectiveness of the searching process.

Definition of Evaluation Experiment for the Search Algorithm. The JeromeDL search algorithm utilizes tree types of information: (1) implicit descriptions, including semantic description; (2) descriptions provided by readers: annotations, personal bookshelves, history of usage; (3) information about relations between readers.

To evaluate the whole search subsystem of JeromeDL, we propose a staged experiment, that would cover all aspects of usability. In each experiment performed the efficiency measures: precision, recall and waste[11] are computed.

The database of JeromeDL system is filled with a mass of resources and MARC21 and BibTEX descriptions translated to MarcOnt ontology Readers perform some browsing in the categories that are interesting to them. **Experiment 1:** Readers are querying the system two times: with and without the query expansion with semantics. With the knowledge on the database content of the digital library, learned during the browsing part, they calculate the metrics: precision, recall and waste of each query result. **Experiment 2:** Readers register to the JeromeDL system and continue browsing its content, annotating some resources and creating personal bookshelves. Later on, readers performs the queries once again, computes the metrics and compares them to the metrics obtained from Experiment 1. **Experiment 3:** Each reader indicates his friends registered in the JeromeDL system. Readers provides ACLs to the categories in their personal bookshelves and links categories created by their friends into their own personal bookshelves. Readers performs the queries for the last time and compares the results with the previous experiments.

Building Network of Federated Libraries. The work started by the Library of Congress on MARC21-based web services allows to expect that these technology will also enable communication with ELP-based digital libraries. To simplify the use of the distributed environment of digital libraries the current work initiates connects the L2L network to e-Learning environments[6], on-line communities and P2P networks.

To overcome the problems that can arise in the P2P network of digital libraries (called L2L networks), semantic routing algorithms can be applied. Possibilities include HyperCuP[10] and categorization based multicasting. That would also improve scalability of the L2L network by limiting the required bandwidth in the nodes.

7 Conclusions

In this paper we presented JeromeDL, a digital library that deploys Semantic Web technology for user management and search. The FOAF vocabulary is used to gather information about user profile management, and semantic descriptions are utilized in the search procedure. JeromeDL is actively deployed in several installations and is continually enhanced with semantic features. JeromeDL is implemented in Java and available under an open-source license. Parties interested in setting up JeromeDL are invited to join our library P2P network.

References

1. S. Brin and L. Page. The anatomy of a large-scale hypertextual Web search engine. *Computer Networks and ISDN Systems*, 30(1–7):107–117, 1998.
2. J. Frew, M. Freeston, N. Freitas, L. L. Hill, G. Janee, K. Lovette, R. Nideffer, T. R. Smith, and Q. Zheng. The alexandria digital library architecture. In *Proceedings of the Second European Conference on Research and Advanced Technology for Digital Libraries*, pages 61–73. Springer-Verlag, 1998.
3. S. R. Kruk. Foaf-realm - control your friends' access to the resource. In *FOAF Workshop proceedings*, http://www.w3.org/2001/sw/Europe/events/foaf-galway/papers/fp/foaf_realm/, 2004.
4. S. R. Kruk and S. Decker. Semantic social collaborative filtering with foafrealm. In *submitted to ISWC*, 2005.
5. S. R. Kruk, S. Decker, and L. Zieborak. Jeromedl - a digital library on the semantic webgi-. In *submitted to ODBASE*, 2005.
6. S. R. Kruk, A. Kwoska, and L. Kwoska. Metadito - multimodal messanging platform for e-learning. In *International Workshop on Intelligent Media Technology for Communicative Intelligence*, pages 84–87. Polish-Japanese Institute of Information Technology, PJIIT - Publishing House, 2004.
7. C. Lagoze and J. Hunter. The abc ontology and model. *Journal of Digital Information*, 2(2), 11 2001.
8. M. Okraszewski and H. Krawczyk. Semantic web services in l2l. In T. Klopotek, Wierzchon, editor, *Intelligent Information Processing and Web Mining*, pages 349–357. Polish Academy of Science, Springer, May 2004. Proceedings of the International IIS: IIPWM'04 Conference held in Zakopane, Poland, May 17-20, 2004.
9. I. O'Murchu, J. G. Breslin, and S. Decker. Online social and business networking communities. In *Proceedings of the Workshop on the Application of Semantic Web Technologies to Web Communities*, Valencia, Spain, August 2004. 16th European Conference on Artificial Intelligence 2004 (ECAI 2004).
10. M. Schlosser, M. Sintek, S. Decker, and W. Nejdl. Ontology-based search and broadcast in hypercup. In *International Semantic Web Conference*, Sardinia, http://www-db.stanford.edu/ schloss/docs/HyperCuP-PosterAbstract-ISWC2002.pdf, 2002.
11. P. C. Weinstein and W. P. Birmingham. Creating ontological metadata for digital library content and services. *International Journal on Digital Libraries*, 2(1):20–37, October 1998. ISSN: 1432-5012 (Paper) 1432-1300 (Online).

Analysis and Visualization of the DX Community with Information Extracted from the Web

F.T. de la Rosa, M.T. Gómez-López, and R.M. Gasca

Departamento de Lenguajes y Sistemas Informáticos, Universidad de Sevilla
{ffrosat, mayte, gasca}@lsi.us.es

Abstract. The aim of the present work is the graphical representation of the structures of a specific knowledge area with data extracted from the Web. Recent Internet development has facilitated access to these new resources and has contributed towards the creation of new disciplines which are aimed at taking full advantage of these resources. The main obstacles to this exploitation are their location and processing. This paper defines a generic architecture which solves the problems of processing these resources by combining techniques of extraction, analysis and visualization of data. Specifically in this work we will automatically explore two of the most important structures which define the DX community: the subjects within the community which generate the greatest interest and its social network. Graphical representations are presented to facilitate the analysis of this community.

1 Introduction

Knowledge extraction or knowledge discovery of the resources available on the Internet is one of the fastest growing areas of research in the scientific community, involving areas such as: Webmining, Cybermetrics, Webometrics, Natural Language Processing (NLP), etc. The aim of this work is to implement architecture to perform this task automatically. The transformation of information into knowledge is understood as a "non-trivial extraction of implicit, previously unknown, and potentially useful information from data" [1]. To this end, the architecture has needed the integration of techniques belonging to different areas, notably: Information Extraction, Information Recovery, Scientometrics, Visualization Techniques and Graph Theory Techniques.

The present work is focused on analyzing two of the most important structures which define a community of researchers: the social network and the thematic areas. In order to carry out this analysis, knowledge of the bibliography of the community is necessary. This information enables both the social network to be analyzed through its co-authorship, as well as the application of the techniques of the co-words and NLP to analyze their thematic areas. As an illustrative example of these techniques, a study applied to the DX community is included in this work. For this reason the web pages with the bibliography of the DX workshops since 1997 to 2003 have been downloaded and semi-automatically annotated with NLP techniques.

Although co-authorship and co-word techniques can seem applicable to only the bibliographic information, they have major potential for those systems which can be modeled as a graph where the nodes are entities (words, web pages, enterprises, etc), and where the edges provide information about the existing relationships between the different entities (joint occurrence, reference, friendship, etc). For example, the co-authorship technique can be used to analyze the relationships produced between members of a discussion forum or between company employees, and the co-word technique allows the analysis of the subjects dealt with in any corpus of documents or field with textual information.

As described in previous work [2], it is necessary to use tools which focus on information from various perspectives in order to create new knowledge from the increasing quantity of information the systems offer. The construction of these perspectives should be guided by our aims or information requirements. For this reason, an architecture is suggested which fulfills our information requirements through the adequate modeling of these networks. For example, for the problem of the analysis of the structures of the DX community, an expert does not have the same information requirements as a new researcher. The expert would be interested in the search for similar authors or emergent lines of research in the same field, whereas a inexperienced researcher would want to discover which subjects are involved and the names of the most influential and relevant authors. Moreover, a company with the intention of obtaining some competitive advantage, would have completely different requirements to others. For example, this company could be interested in looking for experts collaborating on joint projects or in finding out the interests of the researchers of its competitors.

As we have seen, the range of information requirements is very wide and the quality of information under analysis is very large and diffuse, and is sometimes only available from the Internet, as in the case of the communications of the DX community. Development of applications is necessary in order to provide us with automatic selection of desired information.

In order to demonstrate the architecture and techniques used in this work which solve these problems, the article has been divided into the following sections: in Section 2 the developed architecture is described, in Section 3 the process of clearing errors from the extracted data is detailed, and in the Sections 4 and 5 the techniques used to analyze the structures of the DX community are laid out using different visual representations to show its social network and thematic areas. Finally, conclusions are presented in Section 6.

2 Architecture

In previous work [3], an architecture was presented, which integrated all the necessary processes to discover knowledge, from the extraction of information to the processing of analysis and visualization. In Figure 1 the different phases of the architecture can be observed. The architecture has been applied to summarize press articles containing information extracted from different digital newspapers and to analyze the structures of different scientific communities from the bibliographic database DBLP. In both cases the architecture uses a crawler/wrapper to extract the information [4]. One of the most interesting features of the architecture is the decoupling of the process of information extraction from the treatment of the data extracted (analysis and visualization). This has been obtained by making use of a Semistructured Database (SSDB). In this work, the architecture has been enriched by introducing new modules which enable NLP techniques to be used to extract information from heterogeneous web pages, errors in the extracted data to be corrected, and a visual representation of these data to be obtained. For this

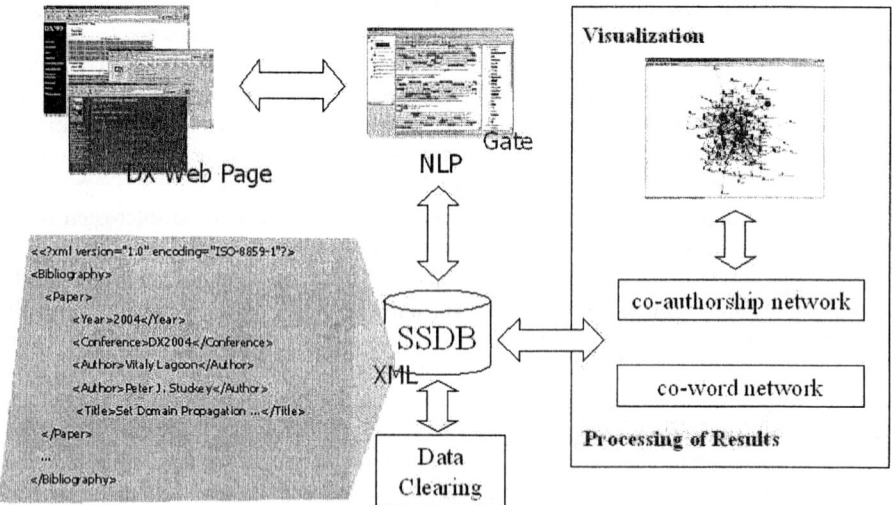

Fig. 1. System Architecture

reason, the architecture has been applied to a more complex problem: the exploration of knowledge areas.

Following the architecture, web pages of the different DX workshops have been annotated by NLP techniques. The information gathered from the different workshops has been stored in an SSDB, which is recovered information from the authors, articles and titles. The titles have also been annotated with its Noun Phrases (NP) which are groups of words that can function as subjects or objects in sentences.

Once the information has been extracted, three processes have to be carried out to obtain the visualization of the information. The first process consists of filtering the authors and the erroneous NP data. For the filtering of these data a data clearing tool is developed which allows the search for and elimination of the errors. In Section 3 it is described in more detail.

Once the SSDB has been filtered of errors, two processes are developed in the phase of processing and analysis, to calculate the co-authorships and co-word networks. Finally, these networks are visually analyzed. In order to carry out the visual analysis task, a tool assists the user in the development and exploration of new perspectives of these networks. The processes of analysis and visualization of the networks will be described in a detailed way in Sections 4 and 5.

3 Data Clearing

After the information extraction of the DX communications, the authors and NP identifiers must be normalized. Some identifiers are synonymous (in that they identified different forms but referred to the same author or NP). For example *"Rafael Ceballos"* is an identifier synonymous to *"R. Cevallos"* and *"model-based diagnostics"* is synonymous to *"Model-based Diagnosis"*. This process of elimination of errors is known as Data Clearing and in [5] a revision of Data Clearing techniques can be found.

A tool has been developed in order to eliminate these errors which calculates several measures of similarity between pairs of identifiers (in this case, strings). The goal of this tool is to enable the user to select synonymous identifiers. For this reason, the tool shows sets of pairs of identifiers, ordered according to their similarity. In the great majority of cases the identifiers with a high similarity are similar identifiers, although not always. From these selections, the tool forms groups of synonymous identifiers, which afterwards are replaced by a single representative identifier. By default this identifier is the most frequent, although the user can change it for another existing or new identifier. This process is totally automatic except for the selection of the pairs.

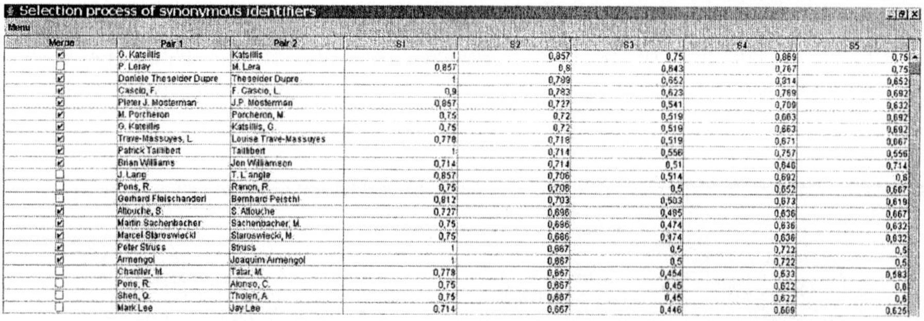
Selection process of synonymous identifiers

Menu

Merge	Pair 1	Pair 2	S1	S2	S3	S4	S5
✓	G. Katsillis	Katsillis	1	0,857	0,75	0,869	0,75
	P. Leray	M. Lera	0,857	0,8	0,643	0,767	0,75
✓	Daniele Theseider Dupre	Theseider Dupre	1	0,789	0,652	0,814	0,652
✓	Cascio, F.	F. Cascio, L.	0,9	0,783	0,623	0,769	0,692
✓	Pieter J. Mosterman	J.P. Mosterman	0,857	0,727	0,541	0,709	0,632
✓	M. Porcheron	Porcheron, M.	0,75	0,72	0,519	0,663	0,692
✓	G. Katsillis	Katsillis, G.	0,75	0,72	0,519	0,663	0,692
✓	Trave-Massuyes, L.	Louise Trave-Massuyes	0,778	0,718	0,519	0,671	0,667
✓	Patrick Taillibert	Taillibert	1	0,714	0,556	0,757	0,556
✓	Brian Williams	Jon Williamson	0,714	0,714	0,51	0,646	0,714
	J. Lang	T. L'angle	0,857	0,706	0,514	0,692	0,6
	Pons, R.	Ranon, R.	0,75	0,706	0,5	0,652	0,667
	Gerhard Fleischanderl	Bernhard Peischl	0,812	0,703	0,503	0,673	0,619
✓	Allouche, S.	S. Allouche	0,727	0,696	0,485	0,636	0,667
✓	Martin Sachenbacher	Sachenbacher, M.	0,75	0,696	0,474	0,636	0,632
✓	Marcel Staroswiecki	Staroswiecki, M.	0,75	0,686	0,474	0,636	0,632
✓	Peter Struss	Struss	1	0,667	0,5	0,722	0,5
✓	Armengol	Joaquim Armengol	1	0,667	0,5	0,722	0,5
	Chantler, M.	Tatar, M.	0,778	0,667	0,454	0,633	0,583
	Pons, R.	Alonso, C.	0,75	0,667	0,45	0,622	0,6
	Shen, Q.	Tholen, A.	0,75	0,667	0,45	0,622	0,6
	Mark Lee	Jay Lee	0,714	0,667	0,446	0,609	0,625

Fig. 2. Selection process of synonymous identifiers, ordered by the metrics **s2**

The measures of similarity used in this tool are based on the algorithm of the *Longest Common Subsequence (LCS) of two Sequences*, a technique of dynamic programming and with polynomial complexity. In our case the sequences were the characters of each of the identifiers or NP. The definitions of the metrics used are:

$$s1 = \frac{|lcs(x,y)|}{\min(|x|,|y|)}; \quad s2 = \frac{2*|lcs(x,y)|}{|x|+|y|}$$

$$s3 = \frac{|lcs(x,y)|^2}{|x|*|y|}; \quad s5 = \frac{|lcs(x,y)|}{\max(|x|,|y|)} \tag{1}$$

$$s4 = 0.33*s1 + 0.33*s2 + 0.33*s3$$

In these definitions $lcs(x,y)$ is the algorithm which calculates the LCS of the identifiers x and y, and the cardinal represents the length of the identifiers. It is also possible to use other measures of similarity between chains, such as the *Levenshtein distance* or *edit distance* of polynomial cost $O(n*m)$ and this measure is less sensitive to the permutation of words in the chains, as for example in the case *"Rafael Ceballos"* and *"Ceballos, R."*. The *LikeIt distance*, [6], with $O(n+m)$ cost, is appropriate to compare strings of large size (n and m are the lengths of both strings).

Our process has been incorporated into the architecture and its use in different SSDB has been very effective, since the number of pairs of words with a high percentage of similarity is scarce and in only a few minutes a user can decide which pairs of identifiers are synonymous. In Figure 2 the selection process offered by the tool can be observed.

Although the calculation of the measures of similarity for all the pairs of identifiers in the treated SSDB is reasonable, this calculation is considered to be very costly in a very large SSDB. As future works, we suggest using the contextual information that these networks offer us, to improve the efficiency of the algorithm, as well as to automate the process of decision making, by using clustering techniques.

4 Co-authorship Networks

Once data have been cleared, a process is developed to calculate the co-authorship and later the social network is represented. The aim of this technique is the representation of the "invisible colleges" formed in separate established fields of

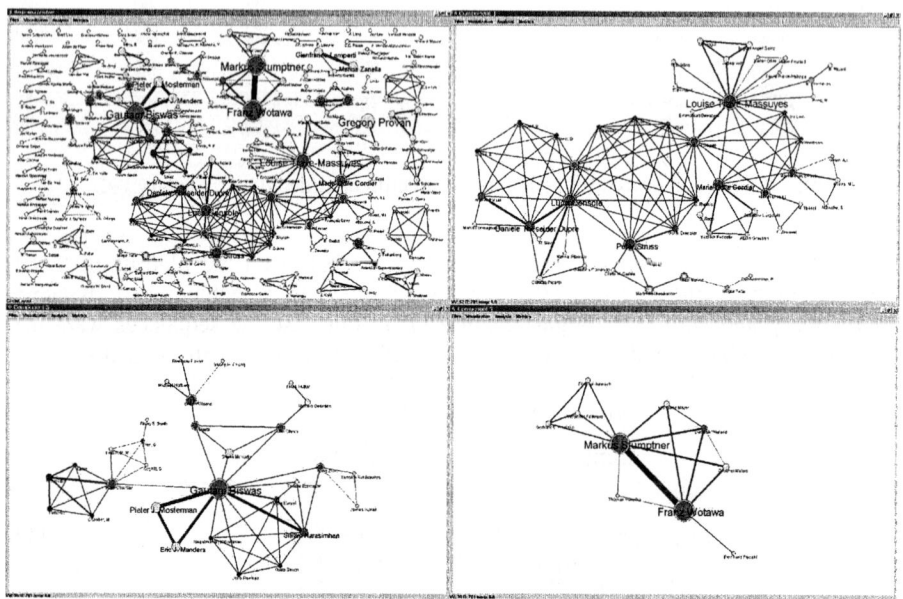

Fig. 3. Co-authorships network of DX community

research. In previous work, [7], the *invisible colleges* are defined as researchers circles influenced by a few researchers of high productivity. There are several metrics to represent the *invisible colleges* through the relationships between the authors: metrics based on *co-citation* [8], metrics based on the *sociometric centrality* and metrics based on the *geodesic distance* [9].

The most appropriate technique to represent the *invisible colleges* from the available data is the *sociogram* [10]. Therefore the impact of the authors and the co-authorship among authors will be used as metrics and are defined as:

$$\text{impact}(w_i) = \#Appearencess\ in\ papers\ titles \quad (2)$$

$$\text{coocurrences}(w_i, w_j) = \#\ Ocurrences\ of\ the\ words\ w_i\ and\ w_j\ in\ papers\ titles \quad (3)$$

where a_i and a_j represent two different authors and # represents the number of publications or collaborations. For a revision of co-authorship visual techniques [11] can be consulted.

With regard to the algorithm for the distribution of the nodes on the screen, the Kamada-Kawai algorithm [12] has been used. The colour of each node indicates the importance of author. This importance is calculated with de PageRank algorithm [13]. Other example of co-authorships networks is presented in the annex.

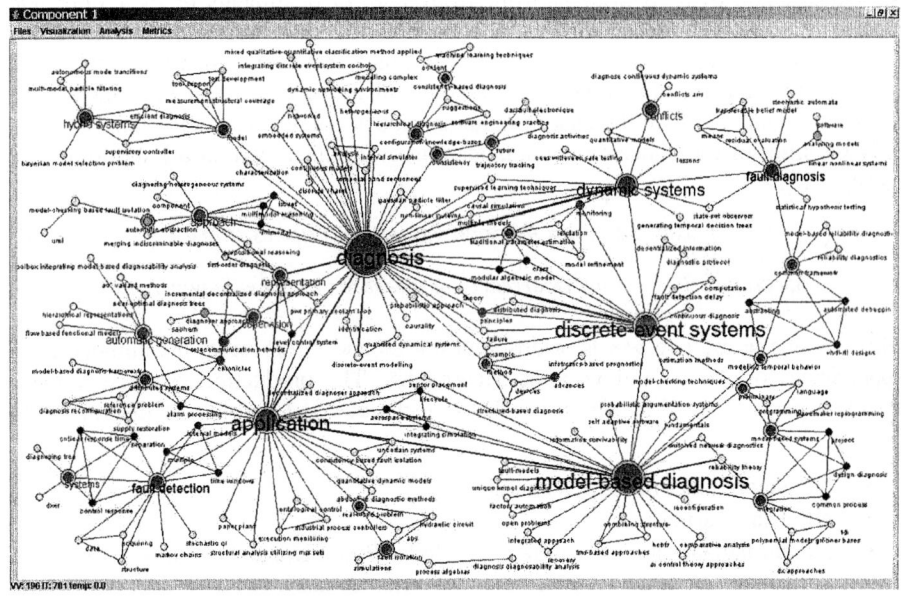

Fig. 4. Co-word network of DX community

The visual analysis of the co-authorship network of the DX community presents of the following features:

1. The network is fragmented into one large, two medium sized and very large number of smaller clusters of authors.
2. The most connected authors in the large cluster are P. Dague, L. Console, L. Trave-Massuyes and P. Struss. This is the kernel of the DX community.
3. The medium sized clusters have G. Biswas, M. Stumptner and F. Wotawa as main researchers.
4. In the smaller clusters, there are several clusters whose size is 5 or 7 authors, however the majority of clusters are composed of one, two or three components.

5 Co-word Network

The aim of the technique of the co-word is the identification of focuses or centers of interest, as well as the relationships that exist between them. These focuses or centers of interest are equivalent to the thematic areas dealt with by the DX community. Our goal is to produce a series of maps from the information obtained with this technique, which deepen the understanding of the thematic structure of the DX community. This technique has been analyzed widely in [14,15,16] and in [17], where we can find the description of a tool, Leximap, which uses this methodology together with techniques of Natural Language Analysis (NLA). The foundations of the technique are based on the construction of a co-word network from a set of documents or their titles and summaries. The co-word network is composed of nodes that represent the terms and of edges whose weights represent the co-occurrences between two words. Unlike the traditional technique, in this work it is assumed that the most frequent terms are the most important, owing to the lack of redundancies in the data available data (we have only the titles of the collected communications). The metrics used are the following ones:

$$\text{impact}(w_i) = \#Appearencess\ in\ papers\ titles \quad (4)$$

$$\text{coocurrences}(w_i, w_j) = \#\ Ocurrences\ of\ the\ words\ w_i\ and\ w_j\ in\ papers\ titles \quad (5)$$

where w_i and w_j are two words or different tokens and # represents the number of w_i appearances or the w_i and w_j joint occurrences. The production process of these thematic maps also differs from the classic technique and consists of the following phases:

- NP annotation with NLP techniques.
- NP data clearing.
- NP normalization. For example, "A Model-Based Diagnosis Framework:" is normalized as "a model-based diagnosis framework".
- NP stop word elimination. For example, "a model-based diagnosis framework" is normalized as "model-based diagnosis framework"
- Co-word networks construction.

The visual analysis of the co-word network of the DX community presents the following features:

1. The main subject of this community is the diagnosis and an important subsubject is the model-based diagnosis.
2. The types of the system to be diagnosed are discrete, dynamic and hybrid systems.
3. The most important applications of the work are related with car subsystems, telecommunication networks, aerospace systems, distributed systems and fault detection in industrial systems.
4. The methods used in the DX community are related to artificial techniques where the consistency-based and abductive methods stand out.

6 Conclusion and Future Works

In this paper, two important conclusions can be highlighted. First, the resources available on the Internet can be exploited automatically when an adequate architecture is developed. The architecture presented in this paper holds all the necessary processes to analyze and view the information extracted from the Internet. We name this type of architecture *Internet Knowledge Summarization, Analysis and Visualization (iK-SAV)*.

The second conclusions, is the existence of uses for the visual analysis techniques in the development of interactive applications, thereby facilitating the tasks of the final user and the exploration of the research community.

In this case, the DX community has been analyzed and its social network and subject network is represented.

With respect to possible future work, we expect to expand the range of analysis that our tool covers. We intend to implement clustering algorithms which allows the construction of hierarchical maps and which facilitates the exploration of networks. It would also be necessary to improve the application so that the visualization of more complex networks is possible where there are different types of mixed entities. Furthermore, filtering could be carried out by means of the attributes stored in the entities and/or relationships.

Acknowledgements

This work has been funded by the Ministerio de Ciencia y Tecnología of Spanish (DPI2003-07146-C02-01) and the European Regional Development Fund (ERDF/ FEDER).

References

1. W. J. Frawley, G. Piatetsky-Shapiro and C.J. Matheus. Knowledge Discovery in Databases: An Overview. In: G. Piatetsky-Shapiro and C.J. Matheus. Knowledge Discovery in databases, pages 1-27, MIT press, 1991
2. Bent Hetzler and Paul Whitney and Lou Martucci and Jim Thomas. Multi-faceted Insight Through Interoperable Visual Information Analysis Paradigms. In: Proceedings {IEEE} Symposium on Information Visualization 1998.

3. F. de la Rosa T., Rafael M. Gasca, Carmelo Del Valle, Rafael Ceballos: Arquitectura de un Crawler para Extraer las Estrcturas y Contenidos de Recursos Electrónicos. JISBD 2002: 259269
4. Thomas Kistler and Hannes Mariais. WebL – A Programming language for the Web. Computer Networks and IDSN Systems (Procceding of the WWW7 Conference). Volume 30. pages 259270. Elsevier.1998.
5. E. Rahm and H.H. Do. Data Clearing: Problems and Current Approaches. IEE Bulletin of the Technical Commitee on Data Enginnering. 23(4), 2000
6. S. R. Bus, And P. N. Yianilos, A bipartite matching approach to approximate string comparison and search, NEC Research Institute Technical Report, 1995.
7. Derek J. de Solla Price. Little Science, Big Science. Columbia Univ. Press, New York, 1963.
8. Henry Small. Co-citation in the scientific literature: a new measure of the relationship between two documents. Journal of the American Society for Information Sciences 24, pp.265-269, Jul-Aug 1973.
9. José Luis Molina, Juan M. Muñoz Justicia y Miquel Domenech. Redes de publicaciones científicas. Un análisis de la estructura de coautorías. Revistas Hispano Americana para el Análisis de Redes Sociales. Vol1. 2002
10. Moreno, J. L. (1934). Who shall survive? New York: Beacon Press.
11. Chen, C. Mapping Scientific Frontiers: The Quest for Knowledge Visualization. Springer. 2003
12. Tomihisa Kamada and Satoru Kawai: An algorithm for drawing general indirect graphs. Information Processing Letters 31(1):7-15, 1989
13. Page, L. and Brin, S. (1999). "The Anatomy of a Large-Scale Hypertextual Web Search Engine".
14. 14. Callon, M., Law, J., and Rip, A. Mapping the dynamics of science and technology: Sociology of science in the real world. London: Macmillan. 1986
15. Callon, M., Courtial, J.P. y Laville, F. Co-Word analysis as a tool for describing the network of interactions between basic and technological research: the case of polymer chemistry. Scientometrics, 1991, vol. 22, n°1, p. 155-205.
16. Coulter, N., Monarch, I. & Konda, S. Software engineering as seen through its research literature: A study in co-word analysis. Journal of the American Society for Information Science, 49(13), 1206-1223. 1998
17. Ira A. Monarch. Information Science and Information Systems: Converging or Diverging? 2000. http://www.slis.ualberta.ca/cais2000/monarch.htm

Annex. Co-Authorships of Journal of Software Engineering and Databases kernel

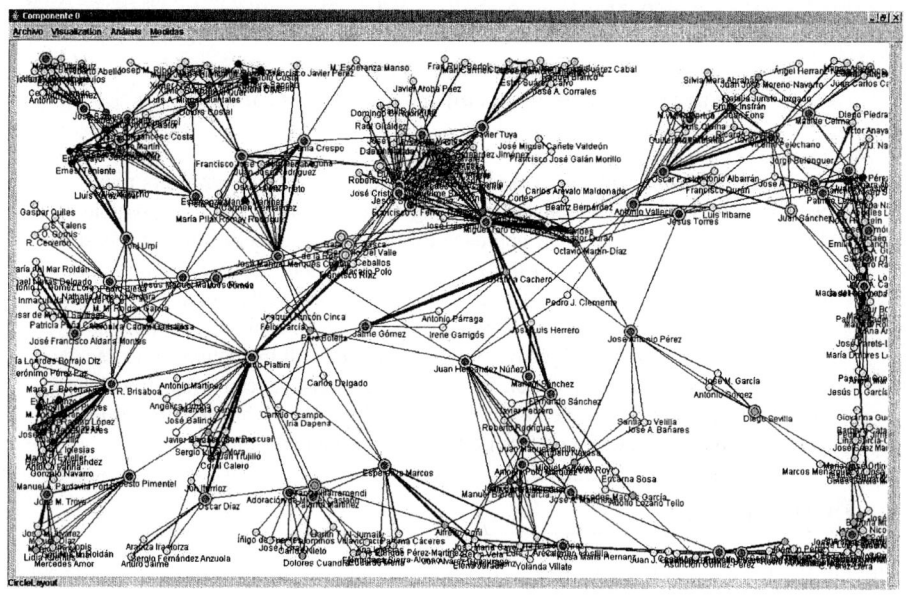

Learning Robust Web Wrappers*

B. Fazzinga, S. Flesca, and A. Tagarelli

DEIS, University of Calabria
{bfazzinga, flesca, tagarelli}@deis.unical.it

Abstract. A main challenge in wrapping web data is to make wrappers robust w.r.t. variations in HTML sources, reducing human effort as much as possible. In this paper we develop a new approach to speed up the specification of robust wrappers, allowing the wrapper designer to not care about detailed definition of extraction rules. The key-idea is to enable a schema-based wrapping system to automatically generalize an original wrapper w.r.t. a set of example HTML documents. To accomplish this objective, we propose to exploit the notions of extraction rule and wrapper subsumption for computing a most general wrapper which still shares the extraction schema with the original wrapper, while maximizes the generalization of extraction rules w.r.t. the set of example documents.

1 Introduction

The human-oriented HTML format is the major container of information on the Web. While there are still reasons to believe that this supremacy will last in the immediate future, specific informative contents can be effectively extracted from HTML pages by exploiting wrapper programs. Once information has been extracted, a common approach is to encode such information into a machine-readable format, such as XML.

Generally, a wrapper consists of a set of extraction rules which are used both to recognize relevant contents within a document and provide a semantic description of the extracted contents. Several wrapping technologies have been recently developed: we mention here *DEByE* [8], *W4F* [16], *XWrap* [9], *RoadRunner* [2], and *Lixto* [1].

Although the schema of the required information, i.e. *extraction schema*, should be carefully defined at the time of wrapper generation, most existing wrapper design approaches focus mainly on how to specify extraction rules. Indeed, such approaches ignore potential advantages coming from the specification and usage of the extraction schema. For instance, a schema-based wrapper is more likely to be capable of recognizing and discarding irrelevant or noisy data from extracted documents, thus improving the extraction accuracy.

Two preliminary attempts of exploiting extraction schema have been recently proposed [11,6]. In [11], where a heuristic, user driven approach to extraction rule refinement is proposed, the adopted tree-like schema is not able to express alternative subexpressions. In [6], DTD-style extraction rules exploiting enhanced content models are used in both learning and extracting phases.

A new wrapping approach which profitably combines extraction rules and extraction schema has been proposed in [3]. Here, the authors define a clean declarative

---

* Work supported by a MIUR grant under the project "GeoPKDD - Geographic Privacy-aware Knowledge Discovery and Delivery", 2004.

wrapper semantics, and introduce the notion of (preferred) extraction models for source HTML pages w.r.t. a given wrapper. The approach has been implemented in the *SCRAP (SChema-based wRAPper for web data)* system, which is designed for extracting data from HTML documents and modeling them as an XML document.

Designing and maintaining wrappers may require labor-intensive and error-prone tasks, since high human involvement is needed. In particular, a main challenge in wrapping web data is to make wrappers robust w.r.t. variations in HTML sources, reducing the need for wrapper maintenance. Indeed, if extraction rules are too specific, frequent wrapper updates must be accomplished to reflect even minimal differences from the original web page layout. Among recent works which address the problem of repairing, or maintaining wrappers, [10] is a schema-guided wrapping approach which proposes a maintenance solution based on assumptions on features of the extracted data. More precisely, syntactic and hypertextual features and annotations of extracted data items are assumed to be preserved after page variations and then exploited to recognize the desired information in the changed pages and induce new rules.

In this paper we develop a new approach to speed up the specification of robust wrappers. The starting point is an initial wrapper associated with a set of example HTML documents to be wrapped. The wrapper designer does not need to care about detailed specification of extraction rules. Indeed, possible redundancy in the initial wrapper can be overcome by exploiting the notions of extraction rule and wrapper subsumption. This enables the wrapping system to automatically generalize the initial wrapper. We propose an algorithm for computing a most general wrapper, that is a new wrapper which still shares the extraction schema with the original wrapper, while eliminates redundant conditions from extraction rules.

2 SCRAP in a Nutshell

In this section we give an overview of the SCRAP wrapping system, focusing on the underlying concepts of *schema-based wrapper* and *XPath extraction rules*.

A *wrapper* is defined on the basis of: *i)* the desired, user-specified schema of the information to be extracted, and *ii)* a set of extraction rules.

Extraction schema reflects what a user requires to extract from a source page. As the SCRAP output is an XML document, the schema is typically represented by a DTD. DTDs easily allow the extraction of information with multi-value attributes (operator +), missing attributes (operator ?), and variant attribute permutations (operator |).

As in most of the earlier approaches (such as [14,1]), the extraction of desired information proceeds in a hierarchical way by exploiting a tree model for HTML documents, i.e. HTML parse trees. Each extraction rule applies to a sequence of nodes of an HTML parse tree, providing a sequence of node sequences. A wrapper associates the root element e_r of the DTD with the root of the HTML parse tree to be processed, then it recursively builds the content of e_r by exploiting the extraction rules to identify the sequences of nodes that should be extracted.

Definition 1 (Wrapper). *Let El be a set of element names, $\mathcal{D}$ be a DTD defining element names in El, $\mathcal{R}$ be a set of extraction rules, and $w : El \times El \mapsto \mathcal{R}$ be a function*

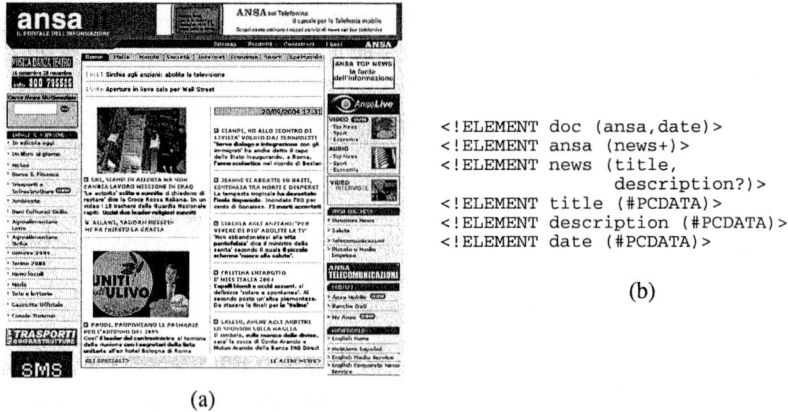

Fig. 1. (a) Example *ANSA* page from www.ansa.it, and (b) the associated extraction schema

associating each pair of element names $e_i, e_j \in El$ with a rule $r \in \mathcal{R}$. A wrapper is defined as $\mathcal{WR} = \langle \mathcal{D}, \mathcal{R}, w \rangle$.

A clean declarative semantics for SCRAP wrappers has been defined in [3]. Roughly speaking, this semantics specifies that a portion of page is extracted if valid pieces can be extracted w.r.t. the right content models according to the extraction schema.

Example 1. Suppose that a user would like to extract significant information about news from the *ANSA* Italian News Agency site. A portion of the page displayed in Fig.1(a) is identified as a news if it contains nested items that can be recognized to be title and description (if available). The date of the last page change has to be also extracted. A simple DTD describing the desired extraction schema is reported in Fig.1(b).

The SCRAP system, whose architecture is depicted in Fig. 2, consists of two major components, namely a *Wrapper Engine* and a *Wrapper Generator* toolkit. The Wrapper Generator (WG) provides tools for defining the extraction schema and the set of extraction rules for a target HTML document:

- The Schema Editor (SE) allows the designer to graphically build the structure of target information in the form of a DTD.
- The Extraction Rule Generator (ERG) provides a visual wizard which guides the designer through the specification of wrapping rules. Given a source HTML page and the extraction schema as inputs, the designer is able to perform the following main steps for each extraction rule to be newly created: selects the right pair of elements according to the schema, highlights a portion on the current source page to find the location path of a representative instance of the target rule, adds extraction filters and restrictive conditions. We shall detail in Section 2.1 how extraction rules are composed and used in SCRAP.

The Wrapper Engine (WE) encloses a running environment which is essentially devoted to: evaluate the extraction rules against the target HTML page, compute a preferred extraction model conforming to the extraction schema, and build an XML document containing the extracted data. Further details about the WE can be found in [3].

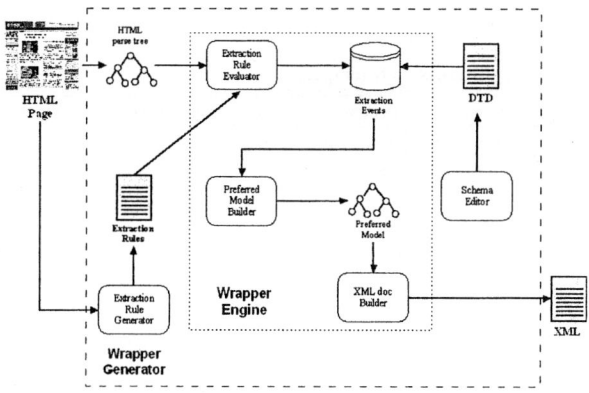

Fig. 2. The SCRAP architecture

2.1 XPath Extraction Rules

Our wrapping approach in principle does not rely on any particular form of extraction rules, that is any preexisting kind of rules can be easily plugged in. However, to devise a complete specification of wrapper in SCRAP, an effective implementation of extraction rules based on XPath [17] has been provided.

The primary syntactic construct in XPath is the *expression*. The main kind of expression is called *location path*, which consists of a sequence of location steps separated by symbol '/' and exhibits the following form: $axes_1 :: node\_test_1[predicate_1]/ .../axes_n :: node\_test_n[predicate_n]$. The evaluation of each location step provides a sequence of nodes that is possibly used as the context for the next step. In this work, we focus on a subset of XPath language related to child and descendant axes.

A key role in XPath extraction rules is played by XPath predicates. An *XPath predicate* takes a *context* sequence, i.e. a sequence of nodes, as input and applies an XPath expression to yield a *target* sequence of sequences of nodes. Indeed, an XPath atom $\$c : lp \twoheadrightarrow \$t$ is formed by an XPath expression lp and two variable names, input binding ($\$c$) and output binding ($\$t$), which are respectively associated to the context and the target sequence.

XPath predicates are the basis of extraction filters which, in turn, define extraction rules. An *XPath extraction filter* is a pair $\langle tp, \mathcal{P} \rangle$, where tp is an XPath atom and $\mathcal{P}$ is a conjunction of atoms, referred to as *condition atoms*, which act as filtering conditions on $\$t$. The application of an XPath extraction filter $f = \langle tp, \mathcal{P} \rangle$ to a sequence $s = [n_1, \ldots, n_k]$ of nodes yields a sequence of node sequences $f(s) = [s_1, \ldots, s_h], h \leq k$, such that: *1)* $s_i < s_j$, for each $i < j$, *2)* each s_i belongs to the result of the application of the XPath expression to context s, *3)* each s_i satisfies $\mathcal{P}$.

Atoms in $\mathcal{P}$ allow the specification of conditions which reflect structural and content constraints to be satisfied from subsequences in $f(s)$. In principle, $\mathcal{P}$ may be formed by both XPath and built-in atoms. The latter are particularly important as they capture the needs of the designer for evaluating complex structural relations between elements, or for manipulating regular expressions in order to extract specific substrings within text elements. Table 1 sketches the features of the main predicates used in SCRAP.

Table 1. Major types of extraction and condition predicates in SCRAP

Predicate Type	Arguments	Description
XPath Predicate	expr, context	Returns the result of evaluation of **expr** applied to the **context**
After, Before	context, e_s, e_t	Returns the elements e_t placed after (resp. before) e_s w.r.t. the **context**
TextHandler	regexpr, context	Returns the result of evaluation of **regexpr** applied to the **context**

Besides XPath extraction filters, SCRAP rules may also use filters which specify restrictive constraints on the size of the extracted sequences. In particular, we consider two kinds of *external filters*. The *absolute size condition* filter as specifies bounds (min, max) on the size of a node sequence s, that is $as(s)$ is true if $min \leq size(s) \leq max$. The *relative size condition* filter rs specifies policies $\{minimize, maximize\}$, that is, given a sequence S of node sequences and a sequence $s \in S$, $rs(s, S)$ is true if rs = minimize (resp. rs = maximize) and there not exists a sequence $s' \in S, s' \neq s$, such that $s' \subset s$ (resp. $s' \supset s$).

An *XPath extraction rule* is defined as $r = \langle EF, as, rs \rangle$, where $EF = f_1 \vee \ldots \vee f_m$ is a disjunction of extraction filters, as and rs are external filters. For any sequence s of nodes, the application of an XPath extraction rule $r = \langle EF, as, rs \rangle$ to s yields a sequence of node sequences $r(s)$, which is constructed as follows. Firstly, we build the ordered sequence $EF(s) = [s_1, \ldots, s_k] = \cup_{i=1}^{m} f_i(s)$, that is the sequence obtained by merging the sequences produced by each extraction filter $f_i \in EF$ applied to s. Secondly, we derive the sequence of node sequences $S' = [s_{i1}, \ldots, s_{ih}], h \leq k$, by removing from $EF(s)$ all the sequences $s_i \in EF(s)$ such that $as(s_i)$ is false. Finally, we obtain $r(s)$ by removing from S' all $s_{ij} \in S'$ such that $rs(s_{ij}, S')$ is false.

3 Generalizing Wrapper Definition

The visual specification of wrappers has been proved to be one of the most effective ways of designing rule-based wrappers [1]. The extraction schema comes into aid to further simplify the wrapper design process. However, wrapper designing is often too tight in the specification of extraction rules, causing the wrappers to be sensitive to even small changes in the source HTML page. Moreover, redundant conditions can be also specified in the extraction rules, due to an improper combined usage of schema and extraction rules. For instance, it may happen that the extraction rule for a book requires the presence of an emphasized heading, corresponding to the book title, while the extraction rule for the book title selects all the emphasized headings. Removing the above constraint from the book extraction rule makes wrapper maintenance easier, since changes in book title layout only require to be reflected in the title extraction rule.

In the following we introduce a framework for generalizing wrappers. The notion of generalization is meant as a specific-to-general learning task, being an original wrapper and associated extraction examples the specific starting point, and most general wrappers entailing those examples the ending point. However, differently from other wrapper learning approaches [4,5,7,14], we do not need to perform a time-consuming marking process on example documents, since the original wrapper is able to mark them.

3.1 Extraction Rule and Wrapper Entailment

Let $\mathcal{WR}$ be a wrapper and d be an HTML document. We denote with $xdoc = \mathcal{WR}(d)$ the XML document extracted by $\mathcal{WR}$ w.r.t. d. Moreover, given a set $\mathcal{S} = \{d_1, \ldots, d_n\}$ of HTML documents, the application of $\mathcal{WR}$ to $\mathcal{S}$ yields a set $\mathcal{X} = \{xdoc_1, \ldots, xdoc_n\}$ of XML documents. We now provide suitable definitions of containment for XML elements and documents, as they play a basic role in the notion of wrapper entailment.

Definition 2 (Element containment). *Let e_1 and e_2 be two XML elements having respectively $s' = [n'_1, \ldots, n'_k]$ and $s'' = [n''_1, \ldots, n''_h]$ as child sequences. We say that e_1 is contained in e_2 ($e_1 \subseteq e_2$) if and only if they have the same element name and there exists a subsequence $s''_k = [n''_{i1}, \ldots, n''_{ik}]$ of s'', such that $n'_j \subseteq n''_{ij}, \forall j \in [1..k]$.*

Definition 3 (Document containment). *Let $xdoc_1$ and $xdoc_2$ be two XML documents having respectively root elements e_{r_1} and e_{r_2}. We say that $xdoc_1$ is contained in $xdoc_2$ ($xdoc_1 \subseteq xdoc_2$) if and only if $e_{r_1} \subseteq e_{r_2}$.*

The relation of entailment between two generic wrappers lies essentially on a comparison, in terms of containment, between the corresponding extracted documents.

Definition 4 (Wrapper entailment). *Let $\mathcal{WR}_1 = \langle \mathcal{D}_1, \mathcal{R}_1, w_1 \rangle$ and $\mathcal{WR}_2 = \langle \mathcal{D}_2, \mathcal{R}_2, w_2 \rangle$ be wrappers and $\mathcal{S}$ be a set of HTML documents. $\mathcal{WR}_2$ entails $\mathcal{WR}_1$ w.r.t. $\mathcal{S}$ ($\mathcal{WR}_2 \models_{\mathcal{S}} \mathcal{WR}_1$) if and only if $\mathcal{WR}_1(d) = \mathcal{WR}_2(d), \forall d \in \mathcal{S}$, and $\mathcal{WR}_1(d) \subseteq \mathcal{WR}_2(d), \forall d \notin \mathcal{S}$.*

Before introducing the notion of rule entailment, we need to briefly explain how containment between node sequences is here intended. Given two node sequences $s' = [n'_1, \ldots, n'_k]$ and $s'' = [n''_1, \ldots, n''_h]$, we say that s'' contains s' ($s' \subseteq s''$) if and only if there exists a subsequence $s''_k = [n''_{i1}, \ldots, n''_{ik}]$ of s'' such that $n'_j = n''_{ij}, \forall n'_j \in s'$.

Definition 5 (Extraction rule entailment). *Let r_1 and r_2 be two extraction rules, $\mathcal{S}$ be a set of HTML documents, and s be any node sequence of $d \in \mathcal{S}$ which makes sense the application of both r_1 and r_2. r_1 entails r_2 ($r_1 \models r_2$) if and only if for each $d \in \mathcal{S}$ and for each sequence $s'' \in r_2(s)$, there exists a sequence $s' \in r_1(s)$ such that $s'' \subseteq s'$.*

Property 1. *Let $\mathcal{WR}' = \langle \mathcal{D}, \mathcal{R}', w' \rangle$ and $\mathcal{WR}'' = \langle \mathcal{D}, \mathcal{R}'', w'' \rangle$ be two wrappers, with $|\mathcal{R}'| = |\mathcal{R}''| = k$, and $\mathcal{S}$ be a set of HTML documents. $\mathcal{WR}'' \models_{\mathcal{S}} \mathcal{WR}'$ if $r''_i \models r'_i$, $\forall i \in [1..k]$.*

3.2 Extraction Rule and Wrapper Subsumption

The notions presented in the previous section are sufficiently general to be applied to wrappers defined on extraction schemas which are not necessarily equivalent. However, the main assumption of the schema-based wrapping approach is that extraction schema is well specified and unlikely to change, therefore we shall consider wrappers sharing the same schema with an original wrapper. A further assumption is that of dealing with non-recursive schemas [3]. Viewed in this respect, we seamlessly approximate wrapper entailment by exploiting the notion of *subsumption* [13] to define an efficient algorithm for wrapper generalization.

As it is usual in traditional logics, subsumption between literals and clauses is strictly related to the existence of substitutions, i.e. mappings of terms to variable symbols. In order to adapt standard subsumption to our setting, subsumption between extraction rules and wrappers, which in turn need to resort to the notions of equality and containment for XPath predicates, must be suitably defined. Unfortunately, XPath containment revealed to be computationally expensive in the general case [12,15]. It is worth emphasizing that XPath expressions within XPath predicates can be represented by the formalism of tree patterns [12]. This result suggests us to consider a limited form of containment for XPath, namely *containment by homomorphism*: homomorphism containment between two tree patterns p, q ($p \preceq q$) is equivalent to the problem of finding a *homomorphism* from q to p. A homomorphism h from a pattern q to a pattern p is a total mapping from the nodes of q to the nodes of p, such that:

- h preserves node types, that is if the type of a node in q is an element name then the corresponding node in p must have the same element name, whereas if the type of the node in q is any one (i.e. wildcard) then nothing is required for the corresponding node in p;
- h preserves structural relationships, that is, given two nodes v and u of q, we have that: *1)* if v is a child of u then $h(v)$ must be a child of $h(u)$ in p, or *2)* if v is a descendant of u then $h(v)$ must be either a child or a descendant of $h(u)$.

Given two XPath atoms $a = \$c_a : lp_a \rightarrow \$t_a$ and $b = \$c_b : lp_b \rightarrow \$t_b$, $a \preceq b$ if and only if $\$c_a = \$c_b$, $\$t_a = \$t_b$ and $lp_a \succeq lp_b$. If a and b are condition (non-XPath) atoms, we say that $a \preceq b$ if a is equal to b. Moreover, if A and B are two conjunctions of extraction and condition atoms, we say that $A \preceq B$ if and only if for each atom a in A there exists an atom b in B such that $a \preceq b$.

Definition 6 (Extraction rule subsumption). *Let $r = \langle EF = \{f_1 \vee \ldots \vee f_m\}, [min, max], \_\rangle$ and $r' = \langle EF' = \{f'_1 \vee \ldots \vee f'_m\}, [min', max'], \_\rangle$ two extraction rules. We say that r' subsumes r ($r' \vdash r$) if and only if:*

1. *for each f'_i in EF' there exists an f_j in EF such that $f'_i \vdash f_j$.*
2. *$[min', max'] \supseteq [min, max]$.*

We say that a filter $f'_i = \langle tp'_i, \mathcal{P}'_i \rangle$ subsumes a filter $f_j = \langle tp_j, \mathcal{P}_j \rangle$ ($f'_i \vdash f_j$) if and only if there exists a substitution θ such that $tp'_i \theta \preceq tp_j$ and $\mathcal{P}'_i \theta \preceq \mathcal{P}_j$.

Definition 7 (Wrapper subsumption). *Given two wrappers $\mathcal{WR}_1 = \langle \mathcal{D}, \mathcal{R}_1, w_1 \rangle$ and $\mathcal{WR}_2 = \langle \mathcal{D}, \mathcal{R}_2, w_2 \rangle$, $\mathcal{WR}_2$ subsumes $\mathcal{WR}_1$ ($\mathcal{WR}_2 \vdash \mathcal{WR}_1$) if and only if, for each pair of elements names e_1, e_2 in $\mathcal{D}$, $w_2(e_1, e_2) \vdash w_1(e_1, e_2)$.*

4 Computing Most General Wrappers

A wrapper $\mathcal{WR}'$ is said to be a *most general generalization* of $\mathcal{WR}$ (for short, most general wrapper) if $\mathcal{WR}' \vdash \mathcal{WR}$ and, for each wrapper $\mathcal{WR}'' \neq \mathcal{WR}'$, $\mathcal{WR}'' \vdash \mathcal{WR}$ and $\mathcal{WR}' \vdash \mathcal{WR}''$. The computation of a most general wrapper substantially needs to search for a wrapper which maximizes the generalization of extraction rules, while still correctly extracts data from a given set of source documents.

For this purpose, an appealing idea is that of defining atomic steps of generalization over extraction rules and their basic components. Given an extraction rule r, the generalization result consists of a set of new rules each obtained by applying one atomic step of generalization to r.

4.1 Generalization Steps

Let $r = \langle EF = \{f_1 \vee \ldots \vee f_m\}, as, \_\rangle$ and $r' = \langle EF' = \{f'_1 \vee \ldots \vee f'_m\}, as', \_\rangle$ be two extraction rules. r' is derived from r, denoted with $r \to r'$, if and only if there exists an atomic *step of generalization* which satisfies one, and only one, of the following conditions:

1. there exist $f_j = \langle tp_j, \mathcal{P}_j \rangle$ and $f'_j = \langle tp'_j, \mathcal{P}'_j \rangle$, with $f_j \neq f'_j$, and $f_i = f'_i, \forall i \in [1..m], i \neq j$, such that:
   (a) $p' \preceq p$, where $p = tp_j$ (resp. $p' = tp'_j$) or $p \in \mathcal{P}_j$ (resp. $p' \in \mathcal{P}'_j$), and p, p' are XPath atoms;
   Moreover, given two XPath atoms $p = \$c : lp \twoheadrightarrow \$t$ and $p' = \$c' : lp' \twoheadrightarrow \$t'$, $p' \preceq p$ holds if and only if lp includes lp' ($lp' \succeq lp$), that is lp' can be derived from lp through one of the following operations:
     - removal of one predicate step or a whole step (that is not the last one) (e.g.//a//b → //b, /a[f] → /a, /a[/b//c] → /a[//c]),
     - replacement of one child axis with descendant one (e.g. /a → //a),
     - replacement of one node test, which does not belong to last step, with the wildcard symbol (e.g. //a/b → //*/b);
   (b) there exists a condition atom $p \in \mathcal{P}_j$ such that $\mathcal{P}'_j = \mathcal{P}_j - p$;
   (c) there exists a substitution θ such that $\mathcal{P}'_j \theta \preceq \mathcal{P}_j$ and:
     - $\theta = x/c$, such that $c \in \mathcal{C}(\mathcal{P}_j), x \in \mathcal{V}(\mathcal{P}'_j)$, or
     - $\theta = x/y, x/z$ such that $y, z \in \mathcal{V}(\mathcal{P}_j), x \in \mathcal{V}(\mathcal{P}'_j)$,
   where $\mathcal{C}(\mathcal{P})$ and $\mathcal{V}(\mathcal{P})$ denote the set of all symbols of constant and variable, respectively, appearing in atoms in $\mathcal{P}$;
2. $as' = [min\text{-}1, max]$, or $as' = [min, max\text{+}1]$, or $as' = [min, \infty]$.

Starting from an extraction rule r it is possible to generate all rules r' which subsume r by applying a finite number of atomic generalization steps, as stated by the following theorem.

Theorem 1. *Let r and r' be two extraction rules. If $r' \vdash r$ then there exists a sequence of extraction rules $r_0, \ldots, r_n$ such that $r_0 = r$, $r_n = r'$, and $r_{i-1} \to r_i, \forall i \in [1..n]$.*

4.2 The Algorithm of Wrapper Generalization

Fig. 3 sketches the main phases of an algorithm which takes a wrapper and a set of example source documents as input and computes a most general wrapper. Function **generalize** computes the set of all extraction rules that can be obtained by applying atomic generalization steps. Furthermore, we remark that, for any newly generalized wrapper $\mathcal{WR}'$, $\varphi(w, r, r')$ returns a function w' defined as follows:

- $w'(e_i, e_j) = r'$ for each $(e_i, e_j) \in El \times El$ such that $w(e_i, e_j) = r$, and
- $w'(e_i, e_j) = w(e_i, e_j)$ otherwise.

```
Input: A wrapper WR = ⟨D, R, w⟩, a set S = {d₁,..., dₙ} of example HTML documents.
Output: A most general wrapper w.r.t. WR and S.
Method:
  let X = {xdoc₁,..., xdocₙ} be the set of XML documents extracted by applying WR on S;
  MW := WR;
  repeat
     NW := ∅;                          /* the set of generalized wrappers at the current step */
     let MW = ⟨D, R, w⟩;
     for each r ∈ R do
        R' := generalize(r);
        for each r' ∈ R' do
           WR' := ⟨D, R − {r} ∪ {r'}, φ(w, r, r')⟩;
           if (valid(WR', X, S))
              NW := NW ∪ {WR'};
     if (NW ≠ ∅)
        MW := selectWrapper(NW);
  until (NW = ∅)
  return MW;
```

Fig. 3. The MostGeneralWrapper algorithm

Function valid verifies that the set $\mathcal{X}' = \{xdoc'_1, \ldots, xdoc'_n\}$ of XML documents extracted by a new wrapper $\mathcal{WR}'$ from the set $\mathcal{S}$ is such that $xdoc'_i = xdoc_i, \forall\, i \in [1..n], xdoc'_i \in \mathcal{X}', xdoc_i \in \mathcal{X}$. Finally, function selectWrapper non-deterministically chooses a wrapper from the set NW of general wrappers. The algorithm iterates until no generalized wrapper can be generated.

It easy to see that the MostGeneralWrapper algorithm works in exponential time w.r.t. the size of the initial wrapper, since evaluating a wrapper requires exponential time w.r.t. the size of the wrapper itself. However, an interesting characterization of the complexity of this algorithm is given in terms of the number of performed generalization steps.

Theorem 2. *Let $\mathcal{WR}$ be a wrapper. The MostGeneralWrapper algorithm correctly computes a most general generalization of $\mathcal{WR}$ performing at most $O(a + t + s + \sum_{i=0}^{n}(2 \times c_i + v_i + h_i))$ atomic steps of generalization, where:*

- *a is the number of XPath location steps using the child axis appearing in XPath atoms of $\mathcal{WR}$,*
- *t is the number of XPath location steps not using a wildcard as node test appearing in XPath atoms of $\mathcal{WR}$,*
- *s is the number of XPath location steps appearing in XPath atoms of $\mathcal{WR}$,*
- *n is the number of filters in $\mathcal{WR}$ and, for each filter f_i in $\mathcal{WR}$, c_i and v_i are, respectively, the number of constant and variable occurrences in f_i while h_i is the number of condition atoms in f_i.*

5 Conclusions and Future Work

We addressed the problem of learning robust web wrappers, i.e. wrappers which are resilient to changes in source HTML pages. In particular, we proposed a wrapper generalization approach that permits to speed-up the specification of robust wrappers, since the wrapper designer does not need to care about detailed specification of extraction rules. Indeed, only an initial "correct" wrapper is needed, then redundant conditions can be removed exploiting the notions of extraction rule and wrapper subsumption. We provided formal definitions of wrapper and extraction rule entailment and subsumption, and developed an algorithm for non-deterministically computing a most general generalization of the initial wrapper.

Future work will be devoted to the definition of preference rules that enable the wrapping system to find the best possible generalization. A further promising research path is to investigate complex generalization tasks, such as the combination of two or more existing wrappers.

References

1. R. Baumgartner, S. Flesca, and G. Gottlob. Visual Web Information Extraction with Lixto. In *Proc. 27th VLDB Conf.*, pages 119–128, 2001.
2. V. Crescenzi, G. Mecca, and P. Merialdo. RoadRunner: Towards Automatic Data Extraction from Large Web Sites. In *Proc. 27th VLDB Conf.*, pages 109–118, 2001.
3. S. Flesca and A. Tagarelli. Schema-Based Web Wrapping. In *Proc. ER 2004, 23rd International Conference on Conceptual Modeling*, pages 286–299, 2004.
4. D. Freitag and N. Kushmerick. Boosted Wrapper Induction. In *Proc. 17th AAAI Conf.*, pages 577–583, 2000.
5. C.-H. Hsu and M.-T. Dung. Generating Finite-State Transducers for Semistructured Data Extraction from the Web. *Information Systems*, 23(8):521–538, 1998.
6. D. Kim, H. Jung, and G. Geunbae Lee. Unsupervised Learning of mDTD Extraction Patterns for Web Text Mining. *Information Processing and Management*, 39(4):623–637, 2003.
7. N. Kushmerick, D. S. Weld, and R. Doorenbos. Wrapper Induction for Information Extraction. In *Proc. 15th IJCAI*, pages 729–737, 1997.
8. A. H. F. Laender, B. A. Ribeiro-Neto, and A. S. da Silva. DEByE - Data Extraction By Example. *Data & Knowledge Engineering*, 40(2):121–154, 2002.
9. L. Liu, C. Pu, and W. Han. XWRAP: An XML-Enabled Wrapper Construction System for Web Information Sources. In *Proc. 16th ICDE*, pages 611–621, 2000.
10. X. Meng, D. Hu, and C. Li. Schema-Guided Wrapper Maintenance for Web-Data Extraction. In *Proc. 5th ACM Intl' Workshop on Web Information and Data Management*, pages 1–8, 2003.
11. X. Meng, H. Lu, H. Wang, and M. Gu. Data Extraction from the Web Based on Pre-Defined Schema. *JCST*, 17(4):377–388, 2002.
12. G. Miklau and D. Suciu. Containment and Equivalence for an XPath Fragment. In *Proc. 21st PODS*, pages 65–76, 2002.
13. S. Muggleton and L. De Raedt. Inductive Logic Programming: Theory and methods. *Journal of Logic Programming*, 19/20:629–679, 1994.
14. I. Muslea, S. Minton, and C. Knoblock. Hierarchical Wrapper Induction for Semistructured Information Sources. *Autonomous Agents and Multi-Agent Systems*, 4(1/2):93–114, 2001.
15. F. Neven and T. Schwentick. XPath Containment in the Presence of Disjunction, DTDs, and Variables. In *Proc. 9th ICDT*, pages 315–329, 2003.
16. A. Sahuguet and F. Azavant. Building Intelligent Web Applications Using Lightweight Wrappers. *Data & Knowledge Engineering*, 36(3):283–316, 2001.
17. World Wide Web Consortium – W3C. XML Path Language 2.0, 2003.

Control-Based Quality Adaptation in Data Stream Management Systems

Yi-Cheng Tu[1], Mohamed Hefeeda[2], Yuni Xia[1], Sunil Prabhakar[1], and Song Liu[1]

[1] Purdue University, West Lafayette, IN 47906, U.S.A.
[2] Simon Fraser University, Surrey, BC, Canada

Abstract. Unlike processing snapshot queries in a traditional DBMS, the processing of continuous queries in a data stream management system (DSMS) needs to satisfy quality requirements such as processing delay. When the system is overloaded, quality degrades significantly thus load shedding becomes necessary. Maintaining the quality of queries is a difficult problem because both the processing cost and data arrival rate are highly unpredictable. We propose a quality adaptation framework that adjusts the application behavior based on the current system status. We leverage techniques from the area of control theory in designing the quality adaptation framework. Our simulation results demonstrate the effectiveness of the control-based quality adaptation strategy. Comparing to solutions proposed in previous works, our approach achieves significantly better quality with less waste of resources.

1 Introduction

The past few years have witnessed the emergence of applications such as network monitoring, financial data analysis, location-based services, and sensor networks in which information naturally occurs in the form of continuous data streams. These applications do not fit in the data model and querying paradigm of traditional Database Management Systems (DBMSs). Data stream management systems (DSMSs) such as Aurora [1], STREAM [2], and TelegraphCQ [3] are built for data management and query processing in the presence of multiple, continuous, and time-varying data streams. Instead of being stored in advance on disks, streaming data elements arrive on-line and stay only for a limited time period in memory. Consequently, a DSMS has to handle the data elements before the buffer is overwritten by new incoming data elements.

Processing of data streams brings great challenges to DBMS design for two major reasons. First, stream data are continuously generated in large volumes by external sources such as a sensor network. Second, the data are often collected from remote sites and are prone to loss and delay in most cases. From the applications point of view, queries to data streams are also different from those against traditional data. While snapshot queries (e.g. *show me the current room temperature*) are mainstream in traditional DBMSs, persistent queries that output results periodically (e.g. *show me the temperature readings every 5 minutes*) are very common in data stream applications. Unlike those in a traditional DBMS, queries in a DSMS can be processed with various levels of timeliness, data reliability, and precision [4,5]. For example, the above query can be rewritten as *every 5 minutes return the temperature readings that are collected no longer than 5 seconds ago*. Here the extra parameter of "5 seconds" represents a requirement on data freshness. We call such parameters the *quality* of the query, much like QoS parameters in multimedia applications. Quality support for queries is a critical issue in DSMS design as it is directly related to user satisfaction.

Quality guarantees for multiple streams/queries in a DSMS are difficult to maintain due to limitations of the physical resources and fluctuations in the application's behavior. A data stream system could contain a large number of streams and continuous queries. Quality will degrade when the system is overloaded. Even with careful admission control, fluctuations of resource availability (e.g. bandwidth variations of a network link) and application resource usage (e.g. bursty traffic) may still cause temporary overloading that interferes with the proper processing of queries. To deal with such variations, the DSMS needs to automatically adjust the quality of individual queries (*adaptation*) at runtime. For example, in case of overloading, data tuples can be discarded to save costs for query processing (*load shedding*). In considering quality adaptations, we always have to answer the following two questions:

1. *When to perform adaptation?*
2. *What is the ideal magnitude of adaptation?*

In this paper, we propose an approach that answers these two questions.

Streaming data are intrinsically dynamic with respect to the arrival patterns [6]. As an example, Figure 1 shows the traces of real TCP traffic recorded from a cluster of web servers. Note the number of packet arrivals per unit time fluctuates within the range of [120, 450] and no obvious period can be observed. Furthermore, the processing costs of data tuples are also difficult to predict. As a result, estimation of instantaneous and future resource consumption could easily fail. Thus, reservation-based QoS-provisioning strategies [7] may not be applicable to DSMSs. This opens great opportunities for optimization towards an autoconfiguring DSMS that smartly adjusts quality levels of streams in response to fluctuations of system status and input rates.

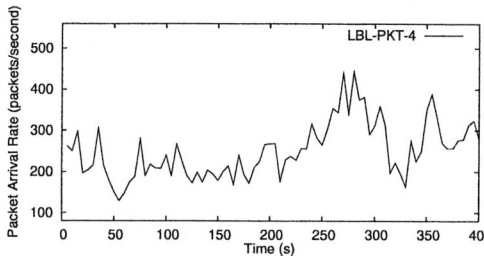

Fig. 1. Fluctuations in the arrival rate of real TCP traffic

In this paper, we propose a solution that is derived from classical control theory to address the above challenge. We formulate quality adaptation in DSMS as a feedback control problem. Despite the difficulties of modeling the DSMS behavior, we utilize well-established tools provided by control theory to estimate the model and develop formulas to make adaptation decisions based on the derived model. The unpredictable traffic pattern and processing cost are modeled as disturbances to the control loop. We present experimental results that demonstrate the validity of our method. To the best of our knowledge, this is the first work that applies control theory to data stream management research. Our ongoing research shows that the control-based approach may also be useful in a broader range of topics in database research.

2 Related Work and Our Contribution

Current works in DSMS study strategies to maximize quality parameters such as query precision [8] and loss tolerance [1]. Little attention has been paid to quality adaptation. Research that is most closely related to our work is QoS-aware load shedding introduced in the context of the Aurora project [5]. In Aurora, a load shedding roadmap (LSRM) is constructed to determine the target and amount for adaptation. LSRM generates a list of possible shedding plans and sorts them by their expected returns in CPU cost. The amount of shedding is given by a fixed percentage P that is obtained empirically. At runtime, the amount of load shedding increases by P as long as there is overloading. In [9], load shedding strategy that minimizes the loss of accuracy of aggregation queries in DSMS is discussed. The use of feedback control is inspired by the work of Lu *et al* [10], which deals with the problem of real-time scheduling.

The major contribution of this work lies in its improvement on current research on load shedding [5,9] in the following aspects: (i) In previous works, adaptation (shedding) decisions depend heavily on steady-state estimates of data traffic and processing costs. The fluctuations in data arrival are regarded negligible. Therefore, adaptation does not work well on fluctuating/bursty data inputs. Our control-based approach explicitly takes these uncertainties into account. (ii) The magnitude of adaptation (e.g., percentage of load to shed) is determined using simple rules of thumb. As a result, adaptation is often imprecise: its magnitude can either be insufficient (undershoot) to achieve desirable quality or over-killing (overshoot) that leads to waste of resources. Furthermore, system tuning is tedious due to the use of rules of thumb. Our solution allows us to analytically tune the controller to achieve guaranteed performance.

3 The DSMS Model

We follow a push-based data stream query processing model (Fig 2), which is a generalization of those of STREAM [2] and Aurora [1]. Streams (S1 – S3) are generated in remotely-located devices and sent to the DSMS via a network. Upon arriving at the DSMS, each data tuple from a stream is processed by several database *operators* chained as a pipeline. The pipelines are called *query plans*, which are formed by the DSMS for active queries. For example, query

Q1 involves a join operation (O1) between S1 and S2, followed by a selection operation (O3). Execution of operators are controlled by a resource *scheduler*. In this model, we do not dictate a specific policy for the scheduler. Our quality adaptation framework works for arbitrary scheduling policies. Before being selected for processing, data tuples are kept in waiting queues (q1 – q4) for the operators. Various system resources including CPU [5], memory [11], and network bandwidth [12] could be the bottleneck in DSMS query processing under different situations. In this paper, we concentrate on CPU usage. Each operator O_i has an estimated CPU cost denoted as c_i.

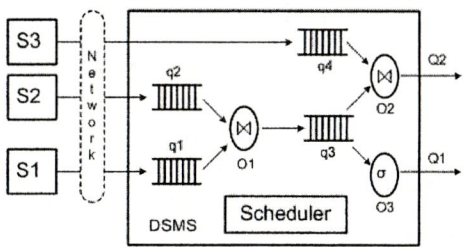

Fig. 2. System model of a typical DSMS

Depending on the applications we are interested in, the selection of quality parameters varies. In this research, we concentrate on *tuple delays* (i.e. time elapsed between the generation and the end of processing of a tuple) as we believe this is the most critical quality for many applications. Specifically, we allow users to choose their delay requirements from a set of discrete values. A violation of tuple delay requirement is called *deadline miss*. We control deadline misses by regulating the system load (*load shedding*). A trivial strategy to maintain low deadline miss ratio would be shedding a large fraction of the load at all times. However, high data loss due to load shedding is also undesirable therefore the problem becomes how to control deadline misses with less data loss.

4 The Control-Based Quality Adaptation Framework

Feedback control refers to the operation of manipulating system behavior by adjusting system input based on system output (feedback). A well-known example is the cruise control of automobiles. The central idea of feedback control is the feedback control loop, which consists of the following components (Fig 3): (i) *Plant*, which is the system to be controlled; (ii) *Monitor*, which periodically measures the status of the plant; (iii) *Controller*, which compares the current status of the plant sensed by the monitor versus the desired status that is set beforehand. The difference between the current status and the desired status is called *error*. The function of the controller is to map the error to an appropriate control signal that is sent to the actuator; (iv) *Actuator*, which adjusts the behavior of the plant in proportion to the control signal.

Control theory provides tools (e.g., Root locus) to efficiently design mappings from the error to the control signal. Furthermore, under the effects of environmental fluctuations, control theory allows us to choose and tune the controller parameters in order to: (i) guarantee system stability, (ii) provide theoretical bounds on the system outputs, (iii) eliminate or bound the error in the steady state, and (iv) adjust the settling time, which is the time needed for the system to reach the steady state. These features distinguish the feedback control approach from *ad hoc* solutions that use rules of thumb. Readers interested in more details on control theory are referred to [13].

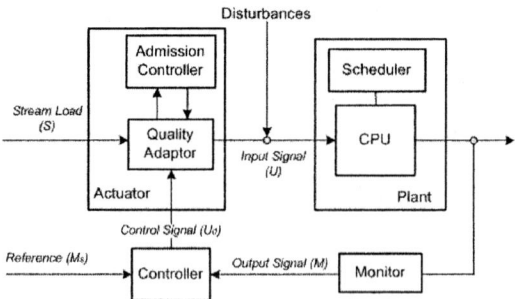

Fig. 3. The control-based quality adaptation framework

4.1 The Feedback Control Loop

Figure 3 also shows the architecture of the proposed control-based quality adaptation framework. The plant is the DSMS, a central part of which is the CPU and its scheduler. Plant status is monitored periodically and output signals are sent to the controller. The monitor is a simple component in this case since the output signal is a variable maintained by the scheduler. We use the Deadline Miss Ratio (M), which is the fraction of tuples that miss their processing deadlines, as the output signal. The fluctuations of data arrival rate and the inaccuracy in CPU cost estimation of operators are modeled as disturbances to the system.

The actuator is divided into two parts: the *Admission Controller* and the *Quality Adaptor*. The former decides whether new streams can be accommodated by the system while the latter adjusts each stream to control the load on the CPU. We use a unitless quantity, CPU utilization (U), to represent the load on CPU. U is defined as the total CPU time needed to process all the data tuples that arrive within one unit time. Note U is the input signal to the plant. The quality adaptor is implemented as a load shedder, which drops tuples from the admitted streams to reduce the load on the CPU. The percentage of tuples to drop (i.e., the shed factor) is determined by the controller, while choosing the victim tuples to drop depends on the implementation of the load shedder itself. We adopt the simplest load shedding strategy: choosing victim tuples randomly. This strategy is not optimized for global utility as streams and queries may have different priorities. A strategy that takes these differences into account is called semantic adaptation [5]. We plan to investigate the complications of adopting semantic adaptation in our control-based paradigm in the future.

The feedback control loop works as follows: a desired deadline miss ratio M_s is specified by the system administrator. The monitor measures the output signal M at the end of every sampling period. The controller compares M to M_s and generates the control signal: the amount of load that needs to be shed. For convenience, we define the control signal (U_d) to be the percentage of load that needs to be kept. In other words, $1 - U_d$ is the shedding factor. The controller then sends the load change U_d to the actuator. Clearly, the generation of input signal U_d is the key point in this loop and will be discussed in Section 4.2. Intuitively, U and M are positively related: when U increases, the load put on the CPU also increases therefore more deadline misses occur.

4.2 Controller Design

Now we describe how the input signal is generated by the controller. First we denote $M(k)$ and $U(k)$ as the output and input of the plant at the k-th sampling period. We start the controller design by constructing a dynamic model for the plant. Unlike mechanical systems, our DSMS is not likely to be modeled using known laws of nature. Fortunately, modern control theory provides *system identification* techniques [14] to estimate the model of complex systems. The idea is to model the plant as a difference equation with unknown parameters. For example, the DSMS could be modeled by the following difference equation:

$$M(k) = a_1 M(k-1) + a_2 M(k-2) + b_1 U(k-1) + b_2 U(k-2) \quad (1)$$

where a_1, a_2, b_1, b_2 are system-specific parameters. Then we can determine the order and parameters of the above difference equation experimentally. Specifically, we subject the DSMS of interest with synthetic traffic loads (with white noise) and measure the output. By doing this for a number of iterations we obtain the parameters using Least Square Estimation [14]. The open loop model shown in Eq (1) can be converted into a transfer function in z-domain:

$$G(z) = \frac{M(z)}{U(z)} = \frac{b_1 z + b_2}{z^2 - a_1 z - a_2}. \quad (2)$$

We use a standard Proportional-Integral (PI) [13] controller to compute the input signal as the following:

$$U(k) = U(k-1) + g\big((M_s - M(k)) - r(M_s - M(k-1))\big) \quad (3)$$

where g, r are controller constants. The transfer function of the PI controller is $C(z) = \frac{g(z-r)}{z-1}$. To finish the controller design, we have the following closed loop transfer function:

$$T(z) = \frac{C(z)G(z)}{1 + C(z)G(z)}. \quad (4)$$

As mentioned earlier, the major advantage of the control-based approach over the rules-of-thumb method is that we can analytically tune the controller to achieve guaranteed performance in terms of stability, steady state error, maximum overshoot, and convergence time. In our case, we can use well-known techniques such as Root Locus (available in MATLAB) to tune controller parameters (g and r) based on Eq (4).

Since the quantity $U(k)$ obtained from Eq (3) is the desirable load injected into the plant, we have $U_d(k) = U(k)/S(k)$ where $S(k)$ is the real load generated by the streams at period k. Unfortunately, $S(k)$ is unknown when we calculate $U_d(k)$. We could use $S(k-1)$ to estimate $S(k)$.[1]

Setting sampling period. The length of sampling period has profound effects on controller design and is a compromise between performance and cost. A general rule is to set the sampling frequency to be as least twice of the signal frequency [13], which is the frequency of fluctuations in streams in our system.

4.3 Admission Controller

To avoid the situation of running a large number of queries all under high data loss ratio, we use an admission controller (AC) to help protect the system from unexpected high loads. The AC checks if a newly registered stream can be served by the system given the current load. For a new stream T_i, the theoretical admission condition is:

$$U + h_i r_i \leq U_s \qquad (5)$$

where h_i and r_i are the per-tuple cost and arrival rate of T_i, respectively. The target utilization U_s is generated empirically based on M_s [10]. The practical value of the above admission condition is limited for two reasons: (i) U only reflects the current load situation of the system; (ii) both h_i and r_i are unknown when the stream first registers. We remedy the above conditions as follows: we first make estimations of the the requested utilization by taking a moving average of current and historical data. For example, at the k-th control period, an estimation (U_e) of U can be written as

$$U_e(k) = \gamma U(k) + (1-\gamma)\frac{1}{a}\sum_{i=k-a}^{k-1} U(i), \ (0 < \gamma < 1)$$

Then we can use an optimistic admission controller such as $U_e(k) < U_s$. In applying this optimistic condition, we assume the cost of one single stream is small compared to the total CPU capacity. Even if we make a bad decision at the AC, the control loop will provide a second chance to correct this decision.

5 Experimental Results

To validate our idea of using feedback control for quality adaptation in DSMSs, we implement a control loop as shown in Fig 3 on a data stream simulator. The core of the simulator is a CPU scheduler based on the Earliest Deadline First (EDF) policy. One of the nice features of this policy is that it has a *utilization bound* of 1.0 for both periodic and sporadic tasks [15], meaning there will be (asymptotically) zero deadline misses if utilization (U) is lower than 1.0. In our simulator, we set the target deadline miss ratio M_s to 0, this is the same as to set a target utilization U_s (the same U_s in Eq (5)) to anything smaller than 1.0. We set U_s to be 0.9 in our experiments.

---

[1] We can show by analysis that this has very little impact on the performance of the controller. We have to skip the analysis due to space limitations.

We define four classes of processing delays: 250ms, 500ms, 1s, and 2s. The monitoring cycle is 5 seconds if not otherwise specified. System identification and analytical tuning of the PI controller (details skipped) suggest we set the g and r values to 0.5 and 0.3, respectively. We test our quality framework with both synthetic and real-world stream data. For the synthetic data, we generate streams with update arrival times following the exponential distribution and the b-model [6]. For real-world data, we use the *LBL-PKT-4* dataset from the Internet Traffic Archive (http://ita.ee.lbl.gov/index.html) that contains traffic traces extracted from web servers. The queries to the stream data are simulated in a manner that is similar to Babcock *et al.* [11].

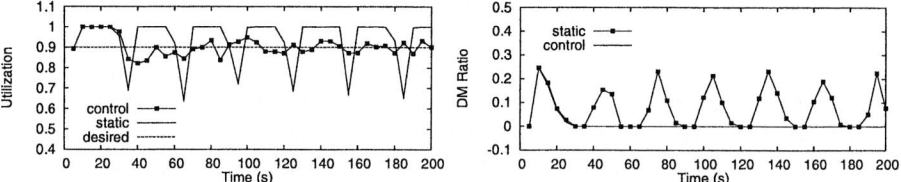

Fig. 4. Utilization and deadline misses by different load shedding strategies

We compare the performance of our control-based method with that of a *static load shedding* strategy similar to the approach in Aurora. The latter uses a rule of thumb in determining U_d: its shed factor is updated in increments of a *base factor* (0.1 unless specified otherwise). Figure 4 shows the results of both shedding methods using the same set of data streams generated with Poisson arrival pattern. The total load of the streams is about 1.4, simulating a constant overloading situation. The control-based strategy converges to a stable state at about 35 seconds and the errors afterwards are kept within ±10% of the desired value. On the contrary, the static shedding strategy shows a zigzag pattern in the achieved utilization with an error range significantly larger than that of the control-based method. As a result, its deadline miss ratio reaches about 20% periodically while there are almost no deadline misses in the control-based experiment.

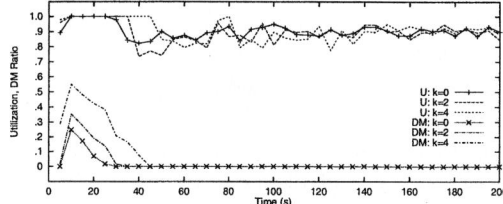

Fig. 5. Performance of control-based load shedding strategy under different precisions of cost estimation

We also investigate the response of our adaptation scheme to imprecise per-tuple cost estimations (Figure 5). We introduce uncertainties to the costs by selecting the real costs of each query iteration randomly from a range around the profiled value. For example, the '$k = 2$' treatment in Figure 5 chooses a cost value for each tuple from the range $[0.5h, 1.5h]$ where h is the profiled CPU

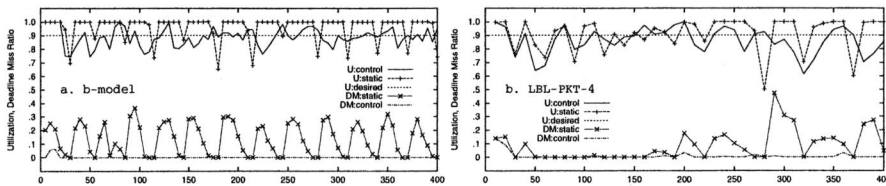

Fig. 6. Performance of different load shedding strategies under different bursty traffic patterns. a. Synthetic b-model traffic; b. real TCP traffic.

cost. This range for the case of '$k = 4$' is set to be wider ($[0.1h, 4.1h]$) and the profiled cost h is not even the mathematical expectation of all the possible values. Our quality adaptation strategy handles the incorrect cost estimations well. Comparing to the original experiment where all costs are precisely profiled ('$k = 0$'), the system achieves the same level of stability. The only difference is that the time used to converge to the stable status is longer as uncertainty on costs increases. In other words, the system 'learns' the real value of costs gradually. For all three cases, deadline miss rates are almost zero for most of the time although more can be observed before convergence.

To test system performance under the disturbance of bursty data arrivals, we run experiments with the b-model data and real TCP trace (Fig 1). The resource utilization data (Fig 6) are obviously less smooth than those in Fig 4 as more undershoots can be observed. The undershoots become more serious as the traffic gets more bursty. The control-based strategy performs better in reducing overshoots when compared with static shedding. This is further supported by the deadline miss ratio measured: deadline miss events are abundant in static shedding while very few are observed in control-based shedding. Control-based shedding shows less undershoot than static shedding in both Fig 6a and Fig 6b.

6 Conclusions and Future Work

This paper presents the first attempt to use a proportional-integral controller to solve a practical problem - auto adaptation of stream qualities - in DSMSs. We argue that continuous queries in DSMSs are quality-critical in terms of timeliness, reliability, and precision. We propose a quality adaptation framework that emphasizes maintaining low levels of deadline misses. A common practice for DSMSs to overcome excessive incoming requests is load shedding, which is made difficult by the bursty data input and imprecise tuple processing cost estimation. We use a feedback control loop to dynamically adjust load under such uncertainties. Compared to previous work, the control-based approach leads to significantly better quality with less waste of resources.

We are currently in the process of implementing a quality controller in a real DSMS. This involves modeling and controlling more complex systems than the one described in this paper. Furthermore, we are investigating the possibilities of using control theory to solve other database problems such as data replication and dynamic resource allocation.

References

1. Carney, D., Çetintemel, U., Cherniack, M., Convey, C., Lee, S., Seidman, G., Stonebraker, M., Tatbul, N., Zdonik, S.: Monitoring Streams - A New Class of Data Management Applications. In: Procs. of the 28th VLDB Conf. (2002) 84–89
2. Arasu, A., Babcock, B., Babu, S., Datar, M., Ito, K., Motwani, R., Nishizawa, I., Srivastava, U., Thomas, D., Barma, R., Widom, J.: STREAM: The Stanford Stream Data Manager. IEEE Data Engineering Bulletin **26** (2003) 19–26
3. Chandrasekaran, S., Deshpande, A., Franklin, M., Hellerstein, J., Hong, W., Krishnamurthy, S., Madden, S., Raman, V., Reiss, F., Shah, M.: TelegraphCQ: Continuous Dataflow Processing for an Uncertain World. In: Proceedings of 1st CIDR Conference. (2003)
4. Olston, C., Jiang, J., Widom, J.: Adaptive Filters for Continuous Queries over Distributed Data Streams. In: Proceedings of ACM SIGMOD '03. (2003) 563–574
5. Tatbul, N., Çetintemel, U., Zdonik, S., Cherniack, M., Stonebraker, M.: Load Shedding in a Data Stream Manager. In: Proceedings of the 29th VLDB Conference. (2003) 309–320
6. Zhang, M., Madhyastha, T., Chan, N., Papadimitriou, S., Faloutsos, C.: Data Mining Meets Performance Evaluation: Fast Algorithms for Modeling Bursty Traffic. In: Proceedings of the 18th ICDE Conference. (2002) 507–516
7. Nahrstedt, K., Steinmetz, R.: Resource Management in Networked Multimedia Systems. IEEE Computer **28** (1995) 52–63
8. Arasu, A., Babcock, B., Babu, S., Datar, M., Rosenstein, J., Ito, K., Nishizawa, I., Widom, J.: Query Processing, Resource Management, and Approximation in a Data Stream Management System. In: Procs. of 1st CIDR Conf. (2003)
9. Babcock, B., Datar, M., Motwani, R.: Load Shedding for Aggregation Queries over Data Streams. In: Procs. of ICDE Conf. (2004)
10. Lu, C., Stankovic, J., Tao, G., Han, S.: Feedback Control Real-Time Scheduling: Framework, Modeling, and Algorithms. Journal of Real-Time Systems **23** (2002) 85–126
11. Babcock, B., Babu, S., Datar, M., Motwani, R.: Chain: Operator Scheduling for Memory Minimization in Data Stream Systems . In: Proceedings of ACM SIGMOD '03. (2003) 253–264
12. Cheng, R., Kalashnikov, D., Prabhakar, S.: Evaluating Probabilistic Queries over Imprecise Data. In: Proceedings of ACM SIGMOD '03. (2003) 551–562
13. Franklin, G.F., Powell, J.D., Workman, M.L.: Digital Control of Dynamic Systems. Edison-Wesley, Massachusetts (1990)
14. Paraskevopoulos, P.N.: Modern Control Engineering. Marcel Dekker, New York (2002)
15. Abdelzaher, T., Sharma, V., Lu, C.: A Utilization Bound for Aperiodic Tasks and Priority Driven Scheduling. IEEE Trans. on Computers **53** (2004) 334–350

Event Composition and Detection in Data Stream Management Systems

Mukesh Mohania[1], Dhruv Swamini[2], Shyam Kumar Gupta[2], Sourav Bhowmick[3], and Tharam Dillon[4]

[1] IBM India Research Lab, I.I.T., Hauz Khas, New Delhi
[2] Dept of Computer Science and Engg, I.I.T. Delhi, Hauz Khas, New Delhi
[3] Nanyang Technological University, Singapore
[4] Faculty of Information Technology, University of Technology Sydney, Australia

Abstract. There has been a rising need to handle and process streaming kind of data. It is continuous, unpredictable, time-varying in nature and could arrive in multiple rapid streams. Sensor data, web clickstreams, etc. are the examples of streaming data. One of the important issues about streaming data management systems is that it needs to be processed in real-time. That is, active rules can be defined over data streams for making the system reactive. These rules are triggered based on the events detected on the data stream, or events detected while summarizing the data or combination of both. In this paper, we study the challenges involved in monitoring events in a Data Stream Management System (DSMS) and how they differ from the same in active databases. We propose an architecture for event composition and detection in a DSMS, and then discuss an algorithm for detecting composite events defined on both the summarized data streams and the streaming data.

1 Introduction

The data in Data Stream Management System (DSMS) is delivered continuously, often at well defined time intervals, without having been explicitly asked for it [9, 10]. The data needs to be processed in near real-time, as it arrives because of one or more of the following reasons – it may be extremely expensive to save the raw streaming data to disk; the data is likely to represent real-time events, like intrusion detection and fault monitoring, which need to be responded to immediately. Another major challenge handling streams is because of their delivery at unreliable rates, the data is often garbled, and they have limited processor resources. It is likely to be subjected to *continuous queries (CQ)* – which need to be evaluated continuously as data arrives, in contrast to the *one-time queries,* which are evaluated once over a point-in-time snapshot of the data set. The streaming data being infinite in size, and if the need for storage be, it has to be summarized or aggregated [11].

Active functionality [1, 2] in a database enables automatic execution of operations when specified events occur and particular conditions are met. Active databases enable important applications, such as alerting users that a certain event of importance has occurred, reacting to events by means of suitable actions, and controlling the invocation of procedures. Most of the research efforts on incorporating this functionality have focused on active capabilities in the context of relational database systems [2]. However, due to the nature of streaming data, pointed out earlier, active functionality cannot be easily incorporated on DSMS. Old aggregated data needs to be referred to, from time to time, for events evaluation and prove very expensive if the system was to make a disk access for the same each time. Also, the system would be required to handle detection of events on streaming data in real-time which is not an issue dealt with in case of traditional databases.

In this paper, we deal with the problem of referencing the old data to respond to user-specified events in real time. As stated in [6], certain applications require reference to data, not only when it arrives, but also after it is summarized (or aggregated). The work illustrates a monitoring application for which access to the entire historical time series is required. Similarly, for event detection in streaming databases, there could be a need to use the past data for evaluation of events. Consider the field of financial data, where the value of various stocks keeps changing continuously. A user may be interested in re-computation of DowJones Average when any two of IBM, GE or Boeing stock prices change by 1% in an hour during the day. Assuming that the aggregation of the data is done every 10 minutes, the system would be required to compare the values to past data. As another example, consider the problem of monitoring constraints on the data, as declared by the user. They could be of the following types – referential integrity (foreign key), primary key, domain constraints etc. For example, consider two relation schemas R_1 and R_2, such that the attributes of R_1 reference to relation R_2. As new data arrives for R_1, it would be required to check it against attribute values of R_2 to ensure data integrity. This information would have to be retrieved from the disk, which would be very time-expensive. Our performance results show that events (primitive or composite) in DSMS can be detected from the data streams and/or from the aggregated data in near real-time.

Initial work on active databases and time-constraints data management was carried out in the HiPAC project [1]. In this project, an event algebra has been proposed, called SNOOP [3], for defining the primitive and composite events. In [5], the authors propose a real-time event detection method for multi-level real-time systems. There are many other systems, such as ODE[4], SAMOS [12], and Sentinel, address event specification and detection in the context of active databases, however, they differ primarily in the mechanism used for event detection. The *Aurora* [10] builds up a new data processing system exclusively for stream monitoring applications. It provides with a large number of stream operators to work with, from simple stream filters to complex windowing and aggregation operators. The core of the system consists of a large network of triggers. The *OpenCQ* [7] and *NiagaraCQ* [8] systems support continuous queries for monitoring persistent data sets over a wide-area network. OpenCQ uses a query processing algorithm based on incremental view maintenance, while NiagaraCQ addresses scalability in number of queries by using techniques for grouping continuous queries for efficient evaluation.

The rest of the paper is organized as follows. The event model is outlined in Section 2. The system architecture is proposed in Section 3. The event composition and detection in the proposed system is described in Sections 4. The experimental results are discussed in Section 5. Finally, we conclude the paper in Section 6.

2 Event Syntax

An event is defined as a tuple: <event type, event_life_time, event_occ_time, attribute list>. *Event type* defines the name of events which share a common system defined meaning specified by the *eid*. *Event-life-time* is the time for which the occurrence of this event is of importance and *event-occ-time* is the time at which the event occurs. *Attribute list* is a flat list of typed values which carry further information about the event.

An event E (either primitive or composite) is formally being defined as a function from the time domain onto the boolean values, True and False.

$E : T \rightarrow \{\text{True, False}\}$

given by E = True *if an event of type E occurs at time point t,* False *otherwise*. The following operators are used in our system for composing primitive events.

There are two kinds of events defined – primitive and composite. The most common primitive events involve modifications to the data that occur through commands like *insert, delete, update,* etc. in relational database systems and through method invocations in object-oriented database systems. Temporal events are the other type of frequently used primitive events. More advanced systems allow the user to register compositions of such primitive events too. As mentioned above, lot of work has been dedicated to evolve event algebras that would capture the necessary compositions of events and their efficient detection. Figure 1 gives the BNF syntax of the composite event used in our system; the consequent sub-sections will describe the operators and their semantics, followed by the strategy adopted for event detection in the system. We adopt SNOOP [4] as an *Event Specification Language (ESL)* that allows specification of database, temporal, explicit and composite events.

---

composite_ev ::= <element_ev><event_op><composite_ev><time_constraint>

element_ev ::= <primitive_ev> | <atomic_condition_ev>

primitive_ev ::= <basic_update_ev> | <temporal_ev>

time_constraint ::= **till***<absolute_time> |* **in***<time_span>*

atomic_conditon_ev ::= <attribute_name><composite_op><value>

basic_update_ev ::= <db_op> | <ext_signals>

temporal_ev ::= <abs_time> | <interval_time> | <rel_time>

event_op ::= AND | OR | ANY | SEQ | NOT | A | P

db_op ::= UPDATE | INSERT | DELETE

time_span ::= n **seconds** *| n* **minutes** *| n* **hours** *| n* **days**

Fig. 1. BNF syntax of Event Algebra

3 System Description

In this section, we describe the proposed architecture of the event composition and detection in a data stream management system as shown in Figure 2. The detection of events is done by two separate monitoring routines, by *Event Checker* on streaming (queued) data and by *Trigger Messenger*, database inbuilt triggers on summarized data. The data is first buffered in the queue and then summarized/aggregated using application specific algorithms after a fixed interval of time or after a specified number of data points have arrived. The summarized information is then inserted into the persistent storage of the system, marked as *DB2* in the figure. When a new event is defined, the *event parser* sends the correct event definitions to the *event manager* to be stored for later retrievals.

3.1 Event Manager

The event manager stores the structural information of the events specified by the user. An *Event Specification Language* is used that allows specification of database, temporal, explicit and composite events. In our system implementation, we define events using SNOOP as event algebra [3].

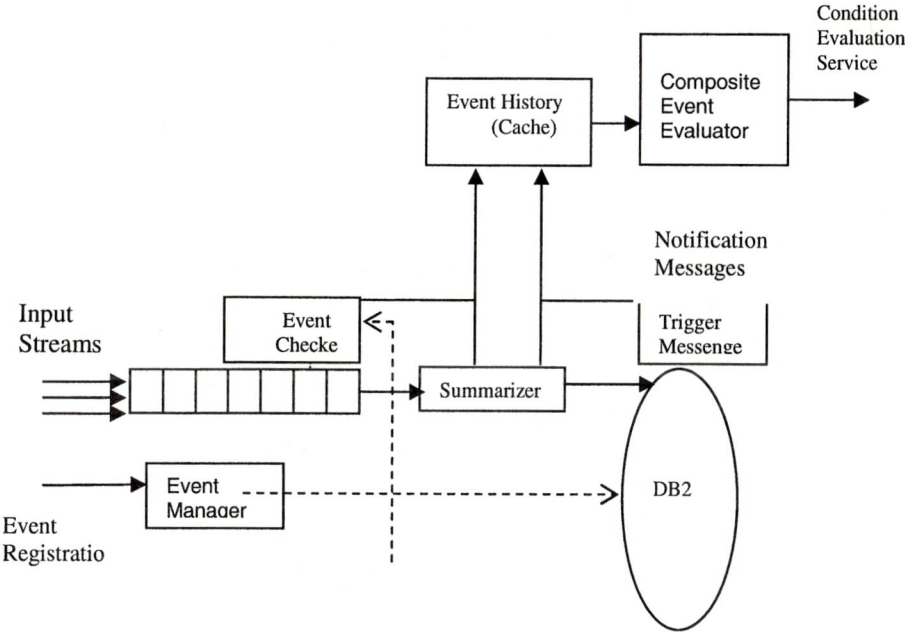

Fig. 2. Architecture of Event Composition and Detection in DSMS

When a new event is registered with the system, the event definition is extracted and corresponding event handler is initialized. If the component(s) of the event is already known to the system as triggering event(s), then the new event subscribes to it and if it is known as a triggering event, then the corresponding mechanisms for its detection are initialized in the *Event Checker* and triggers are set in *DB2*. The structural information of the event is also sent to *Composite Event Evaluator* where the occurrence of the composite events will be detected.

3.2 Data Summarization

The streaming data from the application is initially buffered in the *Data Queue* and then data is summarized. The data summarization can be time-based or data-based, i.e. it could be done after fixed intervals of time or after the arrival of a fixed number of data points in the stream. For example, a stock market may record the average value of stocks after every 10 minutes, irrespective of the number of times the value changes in that period, or the average of every 20 values can be stored. The definition of data summarization can be seen as computing materialized views. These views are then incrementally maintained as new data is summarized.

Considerable amount of work has been done in developing techniques for data reduction and synopsis construction – *sketches, random sampling, histograms, wavelets* to name a few [7, 9, 11]. Gilbert et al. have proposed QuickSAND: Quick Summary and Analysis of Network Data which builds compact summaries of network traffic data called *sketches* based on random projections. These sketches are much smaller in size and respond well to trend-related queries or to features that stand out of data. Network data can also be summarized incrementally at multiple resolutions to answer point queries, range queries and inner product queries using SWAT [11]. Gibbons and Matias have proposed two sampling based summary statistics of data – concise samples and counting samples. These are incremental in nature and more accurate compared to other techniques. The samples were actually created to provide approximate answers to hot list queries. The data summarization techniques are application-specific and hence the system would choose them according to the type of data that it must deal with. The technique selected should be such that the summary created should be amenable to answering queries and take only permissible amount of processing memory.

3.3 Event Cache

Monitoring is a continuous activity and lasts for a long period of time. For any monitoring system, there would be an upper bound on its memory requirements. If the system was to go on saving information about all event occurrences or partially completed events, the available memory space would be soon exhausted. Such situations can arise from very simple kind of events. Consider the event defined $E_1;E_2$ i.e. trigger is raised every time event E_2 occurs after event E_1 has occurred. It could happen that there are multiple occurrences of E_1 before a E_2 occurs. The system should not go on saving all these occurrences of E_1 blindly, but make use of some policy for the same to discard the irrelevant ones.

To deal with the problem of memory usage, we define an event-life time for every event, after which the event is considered *dead* for future consideration. This time must be user-defined, else the system-default is taken. Other solutions for the same could be to store only the recent-most occurrence of the event type, rejecting the older, valid occurrences or to permit one occurrence in one solution only. Whereas the former would function in a similar fashion as using the *recent parameter context* described in [3], the latter will not solve the problem in cases such as the example above.

When a cache entry is made with a new event, time for its removal from the cache is determined using the following equations:

$t_{life} = t_{occ} + time\_span$ OR $t_{life} = abs\_time$

The cache makes periodic scans of the event entries for clean-up actions and removes events with older t_{life} than the present system time.

4 Event Detection

This section deals with the specific strategies adopted by the system for event detection. The steps involved are detection of the primitive events, collection of all occurring events, composition of the same to detect complex events and de-registration of events which are not of interest any longer. We describe below all the steps in detail one by one.

4.1 Basic Event Detection

When a user registers a new event with the system, the following actions take place:
- *Assignment of a unique event identifier (eid)*
  - A new event registered with the system is assigned with an eid. The eid is used to identify this class of events in future.
- *Parsing of the event*
  - The Event Parser reads and parses the new event registered and decomposes it to sub-events such that each of them is a primitive event.
- *Update of events monitoring routines*
  - The sub-events are also assigned eids and sent to event monitoring routines *DB2* and *Event Checker* for monitoring data for their occurrence.

Monitoring applications could be hardware monitoring or software monitoring or hybrid of the two. Our monitoring technique is strictly a software monitoring system thus saving on cost and assuring portability across different platforms. Disadvantages are that since no special hardware is being dedicated to the process, it would be sharing the resources with the rest of the system.

The event recognition is done by dedicated monitoring routines at two levels – low level recognition and high-level recognition. The low level event recognition involves detection of primitive events and high-level handles detection of composite events. A special monitoring component – *Event Checker* is responsible for monitoring events in the new, arriving data, whereas the events on the summarized data are checked by setting appropriate *triggers* on the database. *Composite Event Evaluator (CEE)* is dedicated for high-level event recognition once the primitive events are detected. Events are detected on the summarized as well as on the streaming data.

- *Events on summarized data*

We make use of inbuilt triggers in the database to detect events on the summarized data. This is called *Synchronous monitoring* of events since an event occurrence is communicated explicitly to and in synchronization with the user. The triggers are installed on the data columns or objects of interest as specified in the sub-events.

- *Event on streaming data*

For monitoring the arriving data for events, we make use of *system-controlled polling* with system-defined interval where the system checks for the occurrence of the event every interval-time. We detect the events of interest by comparing two snapshots generated by two different polling time points, find out the changes i.e. the inserts, deletes and updates that have taken place.

4.2 Event Notification

The occurrence of primitive events needs to be reported to the *CEE* for detection of composite events. The event is packed with t_{occ}, t_{life} and specified attributes into a packet and sent to the *Event Cache* using message queues. Databases like *DB2* have inbuilt support for message queues (*Websphere Message Queues*) which can be exploited directly. The arrival of the events at the *Cache* needs to be co-ordinated since they would be coming from two asynchronous sources – *database* and *Event Checker*. This can be done by either setting priorities or by using semaphores to enforce mutual exclusion while writing to the *Event Cache*.

The events information is picked up by *CEE* from the *Cache* for subsequent evaluation of composite events. The details about the composition of events are given in the next sub-section. The cache must only keep information about relevant events, which would contribute to event detection in future. Each event is marked with a timestamp indicating the time when it occurred. With the knowledge of the validity interval of an event, which is either user specified or system specific, the old events are removed from the cache.

4.3 Composition of Summarized and Streaming Data Events

Event Algebra provides the necessary expressive power and allows composition of events. Composite events, though more complex in nature, are more useful to the user. The *Composite Event Evaluator* stores the structural information of the registered composite events as well as the data-structures needed to describe the different event-types. The approach taken for event composition is different from earlier works of Ode [4] and SAMOS [12]. SAMOS defines a mechanism based on Petri Nets for modeling and detection of composite events for an OODBMS. They use modified colored Petri nets called SAMOS Petri Nets to allow flow of information about the event parameters in addition to occurrence of an event. It seems that common sub-expressions are represented separately leading to duplication of Petri Nets. Also the use of Petri nets limits the detection of events in chronicle context only. Ode used an extended finite automaton for the composite event detection. The extended automaton makes transitions at the occurrence of each event like a regular automaton and in addition looks at the attributes of the events and also computed a set of relations at the transition. The definition of 'AND' operator on event histories does not seem to produce the desired result; the automaton for the operator constructed according to the specification given by [5] does not seem to reach an accepting state. Since most of the operators in Ode are defined in terms of the 'AND' operator, it makes their semantics also questionable.

We use event trees to store the structure of registered composite events. The composing primitive events are placed at the leaves of the tree whereas the internal nodes represent the relevant operators. The information about the occurrences of primitive events is injected at the leaves and flows upwards. The advantages of using event trees over the previously mentioned methods is that in case of common sub-events, event trees can be merged together and hence reduce storage requirements. For example, let events be A::= E0 AND (E1;E2), B::= (E1;E2) OR E3 and C::= E2;E3. Clearly E1;E2 is common to events A and B and hence their trees can be coalesced. Also, the event trees can be used to detect events in all four parameter contexts.

There could be two distinct ways of keeping the event trees – as a single, consolidated structure for all events, or as specialized graphs, one for each event. A single event graph minimizes on redundancy but makes garbage-collection difficult. Specialized graphs carry an overhead due to multiple copies of the structure but make garbage collection very simple. There are advantages and disadvantages to both and the choice would depend on the application. The choice of the kind of tree used for storage would depend on the application and resources available. The algorithm followed for composite evaluation using event trees is given in Figure 3.

As mentioned earlier, the system must also carry out *garbage collection* to prevent the system from getting clogged with semi-composed events. Hence, a validity interval must be associated with each composite event, either user-specified or system-defined.

ALGORITHM Composite Event Detection
  Construct an event graph for each rule with nodes as operators and leaves as primitive events. The primitive event nodes are the source and the rule nodes are sinks. Edges are from constituent events to composite event.

  For each occurrence of a primitive event
      Store its parameter in the corresponding terminal node 't';
      activate_terminal_node(t);

  PROCEDURE activate_terminal_node(n)
    For all rule-ids attached to the node 'n'
        signal event;
    For all outgoing edges i from 'n'
        propagate parameters in node 'n' to the $node_i$ connected by edge i
        activate_operator_node($node_i$);
    Delete propagated entries in the parameter list at 'n'

Fig. 3. Algorithm for event detection using event trees

4.4 Deregistration of Events

After some time, the user may no longer wish to be notified of certain events. Hence arises the need for facility of deregistration of events – removal of the event structure from the *CEE*. If the event was a primitive one, then it requires a check if any other event is subscribed to it. If not, then the event can be removed from the triggers of the database and from the monitoring routines, else only the subscribing information will be notified.

5 Performance Results

The system was tested for simulated real-time click-stream data using web logs from IIT-CSE web-site (www.cse.iitd.ernet.in). The *access_log* from the web server was used to create continuous messages from *dataGenerator.java*. The *Threads.java* calls the Event Manager which allows user to register events that have to be monitored for. The information about the events registered is also sent to the Receiever, which form the event trees for event composition. It goes on to set the corresponding triggers on the DB2 and set monitoring routines from them which would check for the events on the queued data. As and when an event is detected on either of these, a message is sent to *Receiver.java* about the same. The Receiver maintains the event trees and computes the events following the receipt of sub-events and notifies the user on detection of any registered events.

The system was registered with 20 composite events and tested on a month log data. The number of events missed vs. the window size (number of tuples after which summarization is done), was plotted. There was a slight degradation in the accuracy of detecting events, with the change in window-size from 50,70 to 100. The miss rate went up from 0.68% to 0.693% which is almost ignorable. However, this was accompanied with reduction in memory space used by the database. The following Figure 4 depicts the same.

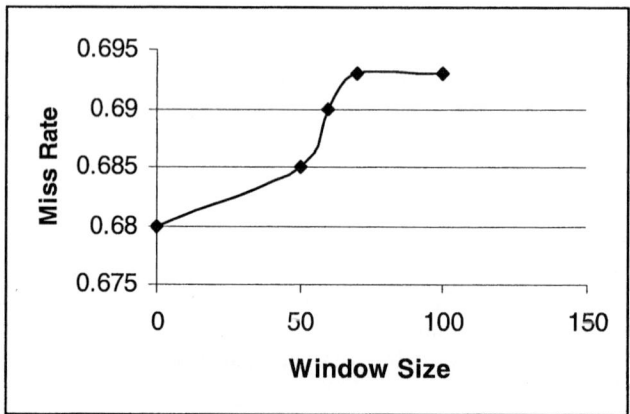

Fig. 4. Miss Rate (of events) vs. Window Size used for summarization

6 Conclusions

This paper has described an architecture and algorithms for detecting composite events in a data stream management system. These events can trigger active rules defined over data streams for making the system reactive. These rules are triggered based on the events detected on the data stream, or events detected while summarizing the data or combination of both. Integration of active rules in data stream management system is important in many real-time applications, such as monitoring a single portfolio that has equities from several stocks exchanges, monitoring the fraud transactions, etc. In this paper, we have described the event model considered in our system implementation and discuss the functionalities of each component of the architecture. We have discussed the various approaches for summarizing the data and then how to notify the events, if generated from this summarization to the composite event evaluator for composing the events. We have done some experiments to measure the miss rate of these events with respect to the varying window size. We have observed that the miss rate is almost negligible as we increase the window size.

References

1. S. Chakravarthy et al. HiPAC: A research project in active time-constrained database management – final technical report. Technical Report XAIT-89-02, Reference Number 187, Xerox Advanced Information Technology, July 1989.
2. U. Schreier, H. Pirahesh, R. Agarwal, and C. Mohan. Alert: an architecture for transforming a passive DBMS into an active DBMS. In *Proc. of the 1991 Intl. Conf. on Very Large Data Bases,* pages 469-478, Sept. 1991.
3. S. Chakravarthy and D. Mishr. Snoop: An Expressive Event Specification Language for Active Databases. *University of Florida CIS Tech. Report,* Sept. 1991.
4. N. Gehani, H. V. Jagadish, and O. Shumeli. Composite Event Specification in Active Databases: Model and Implementation. In Proc. *18th International Conference on Very Large Data Bases,* pages 100-111, Vancouver, Canada, 1992.
5. S. Chakravarthy, V. Krishnaprasad, E. Anwar, and S. K. Kim. Composite Events for Active Databases: Semantics Contexts and Detection. In *20th International Conference on Very Largee Databases (VLDB94),* pages 606-617, September 1994.
6. P. Bates. Debugging Heterogeneous Distributed Systems Using Event-Based Models of Behavior. *ACM Transactions on Computer Systems,* 13(1):1-31, February 1995.
7. L. Liu, C. Pu, and W. Tang. Continual queries for internet scale event-driven information delivery. *IEEE Trans. On Knowledge and Data Engineering,* 11(4):583-590, Aug. 1999.
8. J. Chen, D. J. DeWitt, F. Tian, and Y. Wang. NiagaraCQ: A scalable continuous query system for internet databases. In *Proc. of the 2000 ACM SIGMOD Intl. Conf. on Management of Data,* pages 379-390, May 2000.
9. S. Babu and J. Widom. Continuous queries over data streams. *ACM SIGMOD Record,* 2001(3):109-120.
10. D. Carney, U. Cetinternel, M. Cherniack, C. Convey, S. Lee, G. Seidman, M. Stonebraker, N. Tatbul, and S. Zdonik. Monitoring streams – a new class of data management applications. In *Proc. 28th Intl. Conf. on Very Large Data Bases,* Hong Kong, China, August 2002.
11. Bulut and A. K. Singh. SWAT: Hierarchical stream summarization in large networks. In *IEEE International Conference on Data Engineering,* page to appear, 2003.
12. S. Gatziu and K. Dittrich, 'Events in an Active Object-Oriented Database', In Proceeding of the 1st International Workshop on Rules in Database Systems, Springer-Verlag, pages 23-39, 1994.

Automatic Parsing of Sports Videos with Grammars

Fei Wang[1], Kevin J. Lü[2], Jing-Tao Li[1], and Jianping Fan[1]

[1] Institute of Computing Technologies, Chinese Academy of Sciences,
100080 Beijing, P.R. China
{feiwang, jtli}@ict.ac.cn
[2] Brunel University, UB8 3PH Uxbridge, U.K.
kevin.lu@brunel.ac.uk

Abstract. Motivated by the analogies between languages and sports videos, we introduce a novel approach for video parsing with grammars. It utilizes compiler techniques for integrating both semantic annotation and syntactic analysis to generate a semantic index of events and a table of content for a given sports video. The video sequence is firstly segmented and annotated by semantic event detection with domain knowledge. A grammar-based parser is then used to identify the structure of the video content. Meanwhile, facilities for error handling are introduced which are particularly useful when the results of automatic parsing need to be adjusted. As a case study, we have developed a system for video parsing in the particular domain of TV diving programs. Experimental results indicate the proposed approach is effective.

1 Introduction

Digital videos have become more and more popular and the amount of digital video data has been growing significantly. As a result, efficient processing of digital videos has become crucially important for many applications. Most of current video systems are still unable to provide the equivalent functions, like "table of contents" or "index" which are available for a textbook, or for locating required information. Because manual video annotation is time-consuming, costly and sometime can be a painful process, various issues of content-based video analysis and retrieval have been intensively investigated recently [1, 2]. The key problem that needs to be resolved is that of automatically parsing videos, in order to extract meaningful composition elements and structures, and to construct semantic indexes.

This study is concerned with the automatic parsing of sports videos. As a great favorite of a large audience over the world, sports videos represent an important application domain. Usually, a sports game has a long period, but only part of it may need to be reviewed. For example, an exciting segment from a one-hour diving competition may only last a few seconds – from jumping from the springboard to entering the pool. It's discouraging to watch such a video by frequently using the time-consuming operations of "fast-forward" and "rewind". Thus, automatic parsing of sports videos is highly valued by users, for it not only helps them to save time but also gives them with the pleasing feeling of control over content that they watch [3]. Moreover, efficient tools are also useful to professional users, such as coaches and athletes, who often need them in their training sessions.

The task of sports video parsing is similar to creating an index and a table of contents for a textbook, which encompasses two subtasks:

1) Extracting index entries based on semantic annotation;
2) Constructing a comprehensive structure hierarchy based on content structural analysis.

Most related previous work on sports videos has its focus on semantic annotation with shot classification [4, 5], highlight extraction [6, 7], and event detection [5, 8-10]. A video shot is referred to as an unbroken sequence of frames recorded from a single camera, and usually it is the basic unit in video processing. Based on domain-specific feature extraction, such as color, edge, and motion, Neural Networks [4] and Support Vector Machines [5] were used to classify shots into predefined categories. In order to extract the most interesting segments or highlights of a sports video, the method based audio-track analysis [6] and the method by modeling user's excitement [7] were proposed separately. However, the lack of exact semantics is the main drawback in those approaches. The end users will almost always like to interact with high-level events, such as a serve in tennis, or a goal in soccer. In [8], several high-level events in tennis videos were detected by reasoning under the count-line and player location information. In [9], they first determined candidate shots in which events are likely to take place by extracting keywords from closed caption streams, and then those candidates were matched and selected with example image sequences of each event. Both the rule-based approach [5] and the statistical-based approach [10] were used to infer high-level events by employing context constraints of sports domain knowledge. Although significant progress has been made on automatic semantic annotation, it is still hard to obtain sufficient accuracy when handing the vast amount of video content in real environment.

Structural analysis is another important issue, which has been mentioned in the literature [11, 12]. However, their approaches are restricted to segmenting fundamental units such as serve and pitch in tennis, play and break in soccer. In [13], a general-purpose approach was proposed which does not require an explicit domain model. It adopts the time-constraint clustering algorithm to construct a three-layer structure, i.e., shot, group and scene. However, such an unvarying structure representation is not suitable for sports videos owing to the lack of the ability to model various game structures. Thus, none of the existing work is capable of recognizing the hierarchical game structures of sports videos.

The aim of this paper is to introduce a novel approach to integrate both semantic and structural analysis for sports videos parsing with grammars. Different from other systems in the literature, we suggest that sports videos could be treated as languages, where the sport video parsing system is analogous to a compiler. Our system consists of three procedural steps: basic unit segmentation, semantic annotation and syntax analysis. Firstly, the raw video stream is segmented into basic units, which are equivalent to words in a language. Although there exist different units, such as shots, sub-shots, or other predefined segments, we treat the shot as the basic unit due to it's ubiquity in video analysis. Secondly, each basic unit is annotated during semantic analysis. This step detects semantic events and assigns tokens indicating these events to the basic units. Finally, we utilize context-free grammars to represent the content inter-structures of sports videos, because the grammars provide a convenient means for encoding the external rules into the application domain with a parse tree. Based on the grammars, we employ the syntax analysis to identify a hierarchical composition of the video content. Meanwhile, with the use of the grammars, our system would be able to identify misinterpreted shots and to detect errors since automatic analysis based on low-level features cannot provide 100% accuracy. To our best knowledge, this study is the first attempt to integrate semantic annotation and syntactic analysis for parsing sports videos. Experimental results show that our system is effective and easy to use. Although we only demonstrate parsing diving competition videos as a case study in this paper, the framework can also be applied to other sports videos.

The rest of the paper is organized as follows. Section 2 presents our approach to modeling sport videos. This is followed by a framework for automatic parsing of TV diving programs in Section 3. Experimental results are reported in Section 4. Section 5 concludes the paper.

2 Modeling Sports Videos

In many types of sports broadcasting, one can have the following two interesting observations. First, each sports game can be represented in a tree structure. For example, a tennis game is divided first into sets, then games and serves. A diving game contains several rounds, and there are some plays in each round. In order to facilitate user access, efficient techniques need to be developed to recognize the tree structure from raw video data.

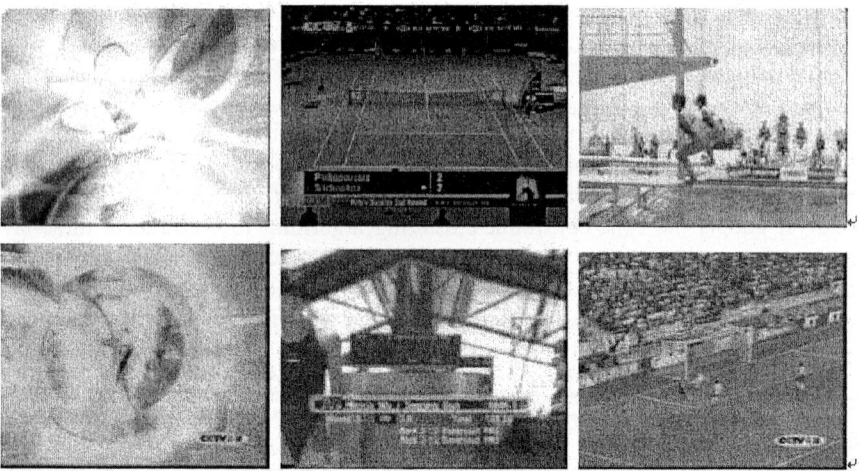

Fig. 1. Examples of events in sports videos: (a) replay events, (b) state events, and (c) target events

Second, there are a number of repetitive domain-specific events in sports videos, which are meaningful and significant to users. These events can be classified into three groups: *replay events, state events* and *target events* (see Fig. 1). In sports videos, interesting events are often replayed in slow motion immediately after they occur. We call the replay segments as *replay events*. *State events* occur when the game state is changed, such as score. Because they typically indicate the beginning and the end of structural units, *state events* are highly correlated with the game structure. Finally, *target events* represent specific objects and their motions in a game, such as shots in soccer games or dives in diving competitions.

Due to a wide variety of video content, it is almost impossible to provide a versatile method of event detection, which is able to bridge the gap between the low-level features and the high-level semantics. Thus, we have devoted a great deal of attention to the application context. Based on our observations from sports videos, we reveal that:

(1) Replay events typically are sandwiched between specific shot transitions;

(2) State events are usually accompanied with superimposed captions, which are overlapped on the video in the production process to provide information about the situation of the game;

(3) In target events, motion introduced by objects and cameras is much active.

Based on the above observations, sports video parsing is similar to language processing which is based on dictionaries and grammars. In the scope of sports videos, the dictionary that we use to annotate shots is a set of domain-specific events, and the grammar is a set of rules represented in the form of the tree structure.

3 A Framework for Parsing Sports Videos

In this section, we first introduce a framework which provides the system overview and then discuss the related algorithms for semantic and structural analysis. To show the merit of our approach, we develop a system for parsing TV diving programs as a cast study.

3.1 Overview

The purpose of this framework is to parse a sport video to construct a semantic index and a table of contents based on events. Through the use of the index and the table of contents, users will be able to position specific video contents which they are looking for. The proposed system, which is a compiler-like, is composed of three phases: shot detection, semantic annotation and syntactic analysis. Fig. 2. shows the flowchart of the framework.

First, the raw stream is segmented into a sequence of shots by using automatic shot boundary detection techniques. A number of algorithms have been proposed for this purpose and we implemented a histogram-based approach, which achieves a satisfactory performance for both abrupt and gradual shot transitions [14].

Second, shots are recognized as tokens based on semantic event detection. Each event is associated with a token. For example, the token "d" represents the dive event in diving competitions. After an event is detected, every shot in the event is annotated with the token, which can be used as an event-based index. Different event detection methods can be integrated into our framework. In this paper, three domain-specific approaches are proposed including replay event detection, state event detection and target event detection.

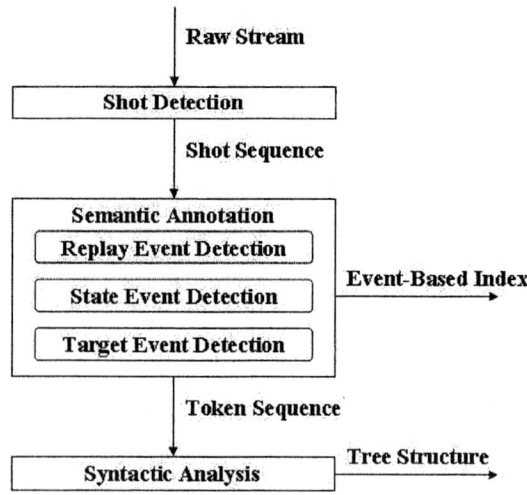

Fig. 2. Architecture of the system

Finally, we use the sequence of tokens to construct a tree structure. Every sport game has its own rules that are the base that the structure that the game needs to follow. Prior to parsing, the syntax of the sports game is described by a context-free grammar. Then we exploit compiler techniques to design a parser. Meanwhile, error detection and recovery procedures are implemented in the syntactic analysis phase.

3.2 Semantic Annotation

In nature, the semantic annotation is the process in which each shot is classified by predefined event models. As stated in Section 2, the events are divided into three categories: replay events, state events, and target events.

Replay events are sandwiched between special shot transitions, which usually contain logos with special editing effects. We have developed a straightforward algorithm for automatic detection of the replay event, which includes the following steps:

1. The pixel-wise intensity distance is measured between the frames in shot boundaries and the example logo images at the region where logos typically appear. If the distance is below an empirically chosen threshold, then the special shot transition is detected;

2. If the interval between two special transitions is in the range of a possible duration for a replay, a replay event is recognized and all shots between the transitions are annotated with the replay event.

State events are normally accompanied by superimposed captions providing important information about the status of the game. In a diving competition, there are three kinds of state events including "ready", "score", and "round end". "Ready" is the event when the player gets ready on the platform or springboard. The superimposed text includes player's name, rank, etc. After that, the player dives into the pool. When the player climbs out the pool, the text box of the score appears which is defined as the event "score". The event "round end" refers to the end of a round associated with a scoreboard. Superimposed text in different state events has different layout and keywords. In our system, the three types of state events can be detected.

First, the text (existing in the form of "text blocks", i.e., a rectangle box that covers a line of text) in each frame is detected and obtained by automatic text detection [15]. Then we measure the similarity between the frame and the example image of the state event. Let $F = \{f1,...,fn\}$ and $G = \{g1,...,gm\}$ denote the text blocks in the frame and the example image respectively. $|f|$ or $|g|$ is the number of pixels in each text block, and $f \cap g$ is the set of joint pixels in f and g. In the matching, the similarity is given by

$$s(F,G) = \frac{\sum_{f \in F}\sum_{g \in G} \tau(f,g) |f \cap g|}{\max(\sum_{f \in F} |f|, \sum_{g \in G} |g|)} \tag{1}$$

where

$$\tau(f,g) = \begin{cases} 1, & \text{if } \min(|f \cap g|/|f|, |f \cap g|/|g|) \geq 0.7 \\ 0, & \text{else} \end{cases}$$

If the similarity is beyond a threshold, the frame would be matched with the state event. We count the matched frames in a shot, and assign the shot with the token of the state event that has the most matched frames. If few frames are matched, the shot doesn't belong to any state event.

As discussed in Section 2, most of the target events can be well characterized by motion. In a diving competition, we are pursuing the "dive" as the target event. In fact, it is one shot, in which an athlete dives into the pool from the platform or springboard. The camera focuses on the athlete, and at the moment of diving, there is a dominant downward camera motion. Therefore, the camera motion can be used as a critical cue.

In the current version of our system, we use a camera motion detector to recognize and model events. For estimating the camera motion between two successive frames, we first calculate motion vectors from block-based motion compensation, and then the vectors are counted to infer the camera motion. Because the camera usually puts athletes at the center of the view in a diving competition, we don't calculate the motion vectors near the center of frames, which could reduce the computational cost as well as the false estimation caused by the front objects (i.e. the athletes).

3.3 Syntactic Analysis

To introduce the syntactic analysis for sports video parsing is essential for three reasons. First, by use it, we can efficiently construct the tree structure based on compiler techniques. Second, by describing the knowledge about the game structures with grammars, we can separate the domain knowledge from the parsing process. Thus, the system is more flexible and can be easily extended. Third, a new facility of error handling can be introduced. It also helps users to locate errors in the results of automatic parsing, which could make the system more friendly and usable.

Table 1. Tokens in a diving game

Token	Category	Semantics
r	replay event	replay segment
b	state event	be ready for a dive
s	state event	score
e	state event	end of round
d	target event	dive
u	undefined shot	undefined shot

Once the sports video is annotated with the tokens by the event detection (see Table 1), we need to identify the structure by the syntactic analysis. The approach used in the syntactic analysis is similar to a language compiler, which builds a parse tree from the input sequence according to the grammar. Here, the stream of tokens produced by the semantic annotation is parsed, and then based on the grammar description to construct the table of contents for a specific game.

We use context-free grammars to describe the syntax of sports games. For example, the tree structure of a diving competition (as shown in Fig. 1) can be expressed as following:

$S \rightarrow R \mid RS$
$R \rightarrow Pe \mid PR$
$P \rightarrow bdrs$

where S is the start symbol, R means a round which consists of P – the play of each diver. We ignore undefined shots as "blanks" between events. If several shots in succession are annotated by the same token, the first one is fed to the parser while the left one is skipped. By elimination of left factoring, the grammar is translated to the LL grammar, and then a predictive parser is used to construct a parse tree.

Because the tokens recognized by automatic semantic annotation may be inaccurate and the actual video content may not be confirmed with the grammar, how to respond to errors is another task of the syntactic analysis. In our system, we introduce a new facility for error handling. It is particularly useful when the results of automatic parsing need to be validated manually. The objectives of our error handling facility includes: (1) to report the error occurrence timely and precisely; (2) to recover from an error for later analysis; and (3) it should not seriously reduce the speed of normal processing. If an error occurs long before it is detected, it is difficult to identify precisely what is the nature of the error. For the viable-prefix property, (i.e. an error is detected at the moment that the prefix of the input cannot be a prefix of any string of the language), the LL method that we used can detect an error as it happens. To recover errors, in general, several strategies have been widely accepted and used, including panic model, phase level, error production, and global correction. The panic model is used for the simplicity and efficiency in our system, where the parser discards the input symbol until a designated set of synchronized tokens is found (delimiters as "e").

4 Experimental Results

Our system has been implemented on a Pentium IV 1.8GHz PC using Java language with Java Media Framework API under Windows 2000. To assess and evaluate the system, we tested it by parsing diving competition videos with the digitization rate 25 frames/sec in MPEG format of 352×288 frame resolution. The videos about 4 hours come from different competitions and stadiums. The ground truth is labeled manually.

The experiments carry two objectives. The first is to evaluate the event detection based on the semantic annotation. The second is to evaluate the performance of the syntactic analysis.

Table 2. Result of semantic annotation on event level

	Replay Event		State Event		Target Event	
	Precision	Recall	Precision	Recall	Precision	Recall
A	100%	100%	100%	93%	70%	75%
B	100%	100%	100%	92%	74%	63%
C	100%	100%	99%	91%	82%	97%
D	97%	99%	99%	79%	69%	81%
Total	99%	100%	99%	87%	74%	81%

The evaluation for semantic annotation is measured by the precision and recall rates for each type of events.

$$precesion = \frac{\text{number of correctly detected events}}{\text{number of detected events}}$$

$$recall = \frac{\text{number of correctly detected events}}{\text{number of events}}$$

From Table 2, our system achieves better performance on replay events and state events than on target events. Comparing contents of these three types of event, we found that target events are generally different from state events and reply events. We believe the reason lies in the large motion variation in the video shots. To enhance the performance, more effective features and more powerful statistical models are required.

In our experiments on diving competitions, high-level structure units beyond shots include play and round. A play is defined as the segment from the event "ready" to the event "score". A round is the interval between the events "round end". Unlike [13], in which the structure that most people agreed with was used as the ground truth of the experiments, our definition and evaluation are more objective. From the results in Table 3, it is observed that the proposed approach never made a false detection, but tended to miss some high-level units. This is because in the grammar-based syntactic analysis, a high-level unit is defined in terms of not only events occurring but also the relations between them. Namely, an event may be missed because some events associated with it are detected wrong. A more powerful strategy of error recovery may resolve this problem.

In Table 4, we assess the ability of error detection in the syntactic analysis. The LL method is able to detect an error as soon as possible. However, it is always difficult to correct the error immediately without manual interruption. In the pane mode of error recovery in our system, the parser recovers itself until a synchronizing token is found. Due to the interval before the parser gets recovered from an error and is ready for detecting the next error, some errors may be missed. In the current system 62% of errors are reported. Considering the simple strategy that we adopted, the results are very encouraging.

Table 3. High-level structure construction results

	Shots	Play			Round		
		Detected	Miss	False	Detected	Miss	False
A	356	34	6	0	4	0	0
B	448	34	6	0	5	0	0
C	673	49	11	0	5	0	0
D	850	50	22	0	6	0	0
Total	2327	167	45	0	20	0	0

Table 4. Error report in the syntactic analysis

	Annotation Error	Reported Error	Missed Error
A	29	22	7
B	28	18	10
C	28	22	6
D	80	40	40
Total	165	102	63

5 Conclusions

In this paper, we have proposed a novel framework for video parsing with grammars. Motivated by the analogies between languages and sport videos, we introduced integrated semantic and structural analysis for sports videos by using compiler principles. Video table of contents and indexes based on events provide users with a semantic way of finding the content in which they are interested. In addition, the grammar enables users to identify errors in the results of automatic parsing, which could make the system more friendly and usable. As a case study, a video parsing system for TV diving programs has been developed.

At present, we are extending this framework to other typical sports videos (i.e., volleyball, tennis, and basketball). The remaining problems are from two challenges: 1) to enhance the event detection, e.g., more audio-visual feature representations and machine learning techniques; 2) to extend the grammar-based parser to handle loose structure patterns like basketball and soccer, where stochastic grammars may be better.

References

1. Ngo, C.W., Zhang, H.J., Pone, T.C.: Recent Advances in Content Based Video Analysis. Int. J. Image and Graphics (2001)
2. Dimitrova, N., Zhang, H.J., Shahraray, B., Sezan, I., Huang, T. Zakhor, A.: Applications of Video-Content Analysis and Retrieval. IEEE Multimedia, Vol. 9, No. 4 (2002)
3. Li, F.C., Gupta, A., Sanocki, E., He, L., Rui, Y.: Browsing Digital Video. Proc. ACM Conference on Human Factors in Computing Systems (2000) 169-176
4. Assfalg, J., Bertini, M., Colombo, C., Bimbo, A.D.: Semantic Annotation of Sports Videos. IEEE Multimedia, Vol. 9, No. 2 (2002)
5. Duan, L.Y., Xu, M., Chua, T.S., Tian, Q., Xu, C.S.: A Mid-level Representation Framework for Semantic Sports Video Analysis. Proc. ACM Multimedia (2003)
6. Rui, Y., Gupta, A., Acero, A.: Automatically Extracting Highlights for TV Baseball Programs. Proc. ACM Multimedia (2000) 105-115
7. Hanjalic, A.: Generic Approach to Highlights Extraction from a Sports Video. Proc. IEEE Int. Conf. Image Processing (2003)
8. Sudhir, G., Lee, J.C.M., Jain, A.K.: Automatic Classification of Tennis Video for High-Level Content-Based Retrieval. Proc. IEEE Int. Workshop on Content-Based Access of Image and Video Databases (1998) 81-90
9. Babaguchi, N., Kawai, Y., Kitahashi, T.: Event Based Indexing of Broadcasted Sports Video by Intermodal Collaboration. IEEE Trans. Multimedia, Vol. 4, No. 1 (2002)
10. Xu, G., Ma, Y.F., Zhang, H.J., Yang, S.Q.: A HMM Based Semantic Analysis Framework for Sports Game Event Detection. Proc. IEEE Int. Conf. Image Processing (2003)
11. Zhong , D., Chang,, S.F.: Structure Analysis of Sports Video Using Domain Models. Proc. IEEE Int. Conf. Multimedia and Expo (2001)
12. Xie, L., Chang, S.F., Divakaran, A., Sun, H.: Structure Analysis of Soccer Video with Hidden Markov Models. Proc. Int. Conf. Acoustic, Speech, and Signal Processing (2002)
13. Rui, Y., Huang, T.S., Mehrotra, S.: Constructing Table-of-Content for Videos. Multimedia Systems, Vol. 7, No. 5 (1999)
14. Lienhart, R.: Comparison of Automatic Shot Boundary Detection Algorithm. Proc. SPIE Storage and Retrieval for Image and Video Databases (1999)
15. Zhong, Y., Zhang, H.J., Jain, A.K.: Automatic Caption Localization in Compressed Video. IEEE Trans. Pattern Analysis and Machine Intelligence, Vol. 22, No. 4 (2002)

Improved Sequential Pattern Mining Using an Extended Bitmap Representation

Chien-Liang Wu, Jia-Ling Koh, and Pao-Ying An

Department of Information and Computer Education,
National Taiwan Normal University,
Taipei, Taiwan 106, R.O.C.
jlkoh@ice.ntnu.edu.tw

Abstract. The main challenge of mining sequential patterns is the high processing cost of support counting for large amount of candidate patterns. For solving this problem, SPAM algorithm was proposed in SIGKDD'2002, which utilized a depth-first traversal on the search space combined with a vertical bitmap representation to provide efficient support counting. According to its experimental results, SPAM outperformed the previous works SPADE and PrefixSpan algorithms on large datasets. However, the SPAM algorithm is efficient under the assumption that a huge amount of main memory is available such that its practicability is in question. In this paper, an Improved-version of SPAM algorithm, called I-SPAM, is proposed. By extending the structures of data representation, several heuristic mechanisms are proposed to speed up the efficiency of support counting further. Moreover, the required memory size for storing temporal data during mining process of our method is less than the one needed by SPAM. The experimental results show that I-SPAM can achieve the same magnitude efficiency and even better than SPAM on execution time under about half the maximum memory requirement of SPAM.

1 Introduction

The problem of mining sequential patterns was first introduced by Agrawal and Srikant in [2]: Given a database of data-sequences, the problem is to find all sequential patterns with a user-defined minimum support, also named frequent sequential patterns. The main challenge of mining sequential patterns is the high processing cost of support counting for large amount of candidate patterns.

Many studies have proposed methods for solving this problem [2, 3, 5, 6, 7]. Among the related works, Apriori-ALL[1], GSP[6], and SPADE[7] algorithms all belong to Apriori-like algorithms. An Apriori-like method finds all frequent items first. By adopting multi-pass approach, the candidate patterns with length l are generated from the frequent patterns with length $(l-1)$ in each iteration. Then the supports of these candidate patterns are checked to discover frequent patterns with length l. The Apriori-like sequential pattern mining methods suffer from the costs to handle a potentially huge set of candidate patterns and scan the database repeatedly. For solving these problems, PrefixSpan algorithm, originated from FreeSpan [4], was proposed in [5]. PrefixSpan was designed based on divide-and-conquer scheme. An elegant recursive method was presented to create projected databases where each one has the same prefix subsequence. By growing local frequent prefix subsequences in each projected database recursively, all the sequential patterns were discovered. Although PrefixSpan prevented from generating unnecessary candidate patterns, the cost of constructing projected databases recursively was a burden when processing large databases.

To further speed up the efficiency of support counting, SPAM algorithm was proposed in [3]. In SPAM, a vertical bitmap representation was created for each item to record its appearing information in a sequence. Then, a depth-first traversal strategy was adopted for generating candidate patterns. By performing bitwise operations on the bitmaps, the supports of candidate patterns were obtained quickly. In addition, an effective pruning mechanism was employed in SPAM to reduce the number of generated candidates. According to its experimental results, SPAM outperformed not only SPADE but also PrefixSpan for large databases. However, the SPAM algorithm is efficient under the assumption that a huge amount of main memory is available such that its practicability is in question.

In this paper, an Improved-version of SPAM algorithm, called I-SPAM, is proposed for mining frequent sequential patterns efficiently. By extending the structures of bitmap data representation, an appearing sequence table is constructed additionally. Based on the modified data representation, several heuristic mechanisms are proposed to speed up the efficiency of support counting further. Moreover, the required memory size for storing temporal data during performing depth-first traversal on the search space is less than the one of SPAM. The experimental results show that I-SPAM can achieve the same magnitude efficiency and even better than SPAM on execution time under about half the maximum memory requirement of SPAM.

The remaining of this paper is organized as follows. We define the related terms for the problem of mining sequential patterns in Section 2. The designed structures of data representation are introduced in Section 3. Then I-SPAM algorithm is developed in Section 4. In Section 5, the experimental results of performance evaluation by comparing I-SPAM with SPAM are reported. Finally, we summarize the contribution of the proposed method and discuss further research issues in Section 6.

2 Preliminaries

The problem of mining sequential patterns was originally proposed by [2]. The following definitions refer to [2, 3, 5, 6].

Let $I=\{i_1, i_2,\ldots, i_n\}$ be the set of all possible **items** in a specific domain. A subset of I is called an **itemset**. A sequence $\alpha = <s_1 s_2 \ldots s_l>$ is an ordered list of itemsets, where s_j is an itemset. Each s_j in a sequence is called an **element** of the sequence and denoted as $(x_1 x_2 \ldots x_m)$, where x_k is an item. For brevity, the brackets are omitted if an element has only one item, i.e., (x) is written as x. The number of instances of items in a sequence α is called the length of the sequence and denoted as $|\alpha|$. A sequence with length l is called an *l*-**sequence**. A sequence $\alpha = <a_1 a_2 \ldots a_n>$ is called a **subsequence** of another sequence $\beta = <b_1 b_2 \ldots b_m>$ and β a **supersequence** of α, denoted as $\alpha \sqsubseteq \beta$, if there exist integers $1 \leq j_1 < j_2 < \ldots < j_n \leq m$ such that $a_1 \subseteq b_{j1}, a_2 \subseteq b_{j2}, \ldots,$ and $a_n \subseteq b_{jn}$.

A **sequence database** S is a set of tuples, where each tuple: [*sid, s*] consists of a sequence, s, and the identification of sequence, *sid*. A tuple [*sid, s*] is said to contain a sequence α, if α is a subsequence of s. $|S|$ denotes the number of sequences in sequence database S. The **support** of a sequence α in database S is the number of tuples in the database containing α, denoted as $sup_S(α)$. Given a positive integer, min_sup, as the **support threshold**, a sequence α is called a **frequent sequential pattern** in database S if $sup_S(α) \geq min\_sup$. Otherwise, the pattern is **infrequent**. The problem of mining sequential patterns is to find all frequent sequential patterns from a sequential database S.

3 Bit Sequence Representation

In our approach, for each sequence α in a sequence database S, a bit sequence table is constructed. In the table, each item X contained in sequence α has a corresponding bit sequence, denoted as $Bit_X(α)$. The length of $Bit_X(α)$ equals the number of elements in α and the first bit of $Bit_X(α)$ is the leftmost bit. If item X is in the j-th element of α, the j-th bit of $Bit_X(α)$ is set to be 1; otherwise, it is set to be 0. The bit sequence tables of all the sequences in sequence database S collectively represent the contents of sequences in the database.

[Example 1]. Consider sequence s_1=<a(cd)ad> shown in Fig. 1(a), which consists of four elements: a, (cd), a, and d. Because item a appears in the 1st and the 3rd elements of s_1, the bit sequence of a in s_1, denoted as $Bit_a(s_1)$, is 1010. Similarly, $Bit_c(s_1)$= 0100 and $Bit_d(s_1)$= 0101 are obtained. The bit sequence tables of all the five sequences in S are constructed as shown in Fig. 1(c).

[Definition 1]. Given a sequence $α=<a_1a_2...a_n>$. If α is contained in a tuple $[s_i, β]$ of the sequence database where $β=<b_1b_2...b_m>$, there must exist integers $1 \leq j_1 < j_2 < ... < j_n \leq m$ such that $a_1 \subseteq b_{j1}, a_2 \subseteq b_{j2}, ...,$ and $a_n \subseteq b_{jn}$. The integer j_n is named a sequential position of α in sequence s_i. The first sequential position of α in s_i is defined to be the minimum value among all the sequential positions of α in s_i. Otherwise, if α is not contained in sequence s_i, the first sequential position of α in s_i is 0.

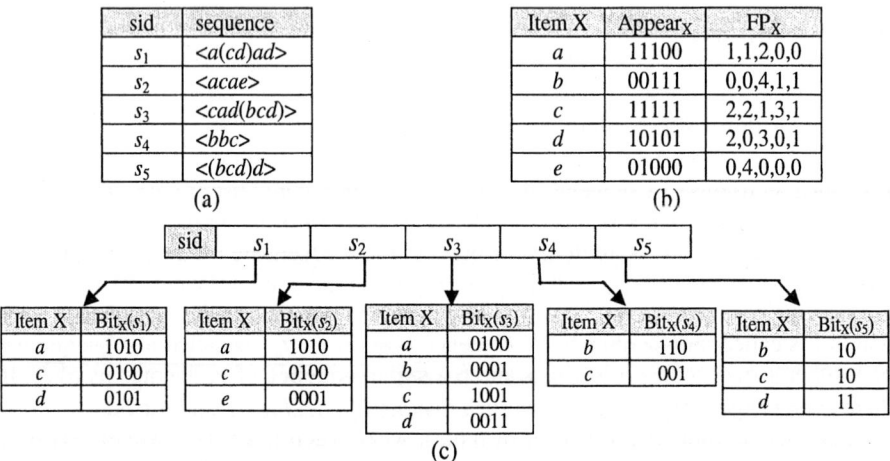

Fig. 1. (a) the sample database S, (b) the appearing sequence table of S, and (c) the bit sequence structure of S

In order to reduce the cost of checking bit sequence tables, an appearing sequence table is constructed in our approach, which is composed of three fields: **item name**, **appearing sequence**, and **first_position sequence**. The appearing sequence of an item X is a bit sequence with length $|S|$, denoted as $Appear_X$, which is used to record whether item X appears in the sequences of database S. If X appears in the i-th sequence of S, the i-th bit in $Appear_X$, denoted as $Appear_X(i)$, is set to be 1; otherwise, it is set to be 0. The first bit is located at the far left of appearing sequence. In addition, for each item X, an integer sequence called first_position sequence, is constructed. The sequence is denoted as FP_X, which consists of $|S|$ nonnegative integers, from left to right, used to record the first sequential positions of $<X>$ in every sequence of the database.

[Example 2]. Consider the example shown in Fig. 1(a). Item d appearing in sequences s_1, s_3, and s_5, thus, $Appear_d$ ="10101" and FP_d = "2,0,3,0,1" are constructed. The whole appearing sequence table of S is shown as Fig. 1(b).

The representation of appearing sequence and first position sequence are applicable to represent the distribution of a sequential pattern contained in the database. For example, pattern $P=<ad>$ is contained in sequences s_1 and s_3. Therefore, $Appear_P$="10100" and FP_P="2,0,3,0,0". Accordingly, if the appearing sequence of a pattern Q is known, the number of bits with 1 in $Appear_Q$, denoted as **1_count**($Appear_Q$), implies the support of Q.

4 I-SPAM Algorithm

In this section, based on the representations of appearing sequences, the strategy for computing the supports of candidate patterns efficiently is introduced. Then the mining process of the proposed I-SPAM algorithm is described.

4.1 Candidate Patterns Generation

According to the monotonic property of frequent patterns, a pattern is possible frequent only if all its subsequences are frequent. Therefore, a candidate pattern is generated by inserting a data item into a pre-known frequent pattern.

Given a data item T in the database, the S-extended method generates a candidate sequence by appending a new element containing itemset {T} after the last element of a sequence α. The generated pattern is named a S-extended sequence of α. On the other hand, an I-extended sequence of α is obtained by inserting a data item T to the last element X of α. These two patterns are named the S-extended and I-extended sequences of α by T, respectively. For example, suppose sequence α=$<aa>$ and b denotes a data item. Then $<aab>$ is the S-extended sequence and $<a(ab)>$ is the I-extended sequence of α by b.

4.2 Support Counting Strategies

The appearing and first_position sequences, introduced in the previous section, are used to speed up the support counting of candidate patterns.

1) Checking S-extended Sequences

Let β denote a S-extended sequence of α by appending a new element containing itemset $\{T\}$ to α. Suppose $Appear_\alpha$ and FP_α are given and the appearing sequence table of the database is constructed. The appearing sequence of the new pattern β, $Appear_\beta$, must have the properties that if bit j has value 1, then the corresponding sequence s_j must contain sequence α and $\{T\}$, and there exists α before T in the sequence. After getting $Appear_\beta$, the support of β is obtained easily. The following strategies are designed to get the appearing sequence of β efficiently by avoiding the non-necessary checking on bit sequence tables as far as possible.

First, the approximation of $Appear_\beta$, denoted as A_Appear_β, is obtained by performing an AND operation on $Appear_\alpha$ and $Appear_T$. Because $1\_count(A\_Appear_\beta)$ is larger than or equal to $1\_count(Appear_\beta)$, β is not possible a frequent pattern if $1\_count(A\_Appear_\beta) < min\_sup$ and it is pruned without needing further checking.

On the other hand, if $1\_count(A\_Appear_\beta) \geq min\_sup$, for those bits in A_Appear_β with value 1, the corresponding sequences have to be checked whether they contain β actually to get $Appear_\beta$. For each bit k in A_Appear_β, if its value is 0, both $Appear_\beta(k)$ and $FP_\beta(k)$ are set to be 0. Otherwise, the values in $FP_\alpha(k)$ and $FP_T(k)$ are compared. If $FP_\alpha(k)$ is less than $FP_T(k)$, it implies the first sequential position of sequence α appearing is before all the occurring of item T in the k-th sequence. In other words, the k-th sequence of S contains the new pattern β and $FP_T(k)$ is the first sequential position that β occurring in this sequence. Therefore, $Appear_\beta(k)$ is set to be 1 and $FP_\beta(k)$ is set to be $FP_T(k)$. Although, it is not necessary that β does not occur in the k-th sequence if $FP_\alpha(k)$ is larger than or equal to $FP_T(k)$. Therefore, the following detailed checking on the bit sequence $Bit_T(k)$ is executed.

A left-shift operation is performed on $Bit_T(k)$ by $FP_\alpha(k)$ bits. If the resultant sequence is non-zero, it means there existing a position where item T located after the first sequential position of α in the k-th sequence. That is, β is contained in the k-th sequence. Let bit h denote the first bit in the resultant sequence with value 1, it indicates the first sequential position of β in the sequence is located h positions after the first sequential position of α. Therefore, $Appear_\beta(k)$ is set to be 1 and $FP_\beta(k)$ is set to be $FP_\alpha(k)+h$. Otherwise, sequence β is not contained in the k-th sequence of S, and both of $Appear_\beta(k)$ and $FP_\beta(k)$ are set to be 0.

The appearing sequence of β, $Appear_\beta$, is obtained after performing the checking for all the bits in A_Appear_β with value 1. Finally, β is certified to be a frequent pattern if $1\_Count(Appear_\beta)$ is larger than or equal to min_sup.

2) Checking I-extended Sequences

Let sequence α be represented as $<\alpha'X>$, where X denotes the last element of α. Besides, let γ denote an I-extended sequence of α by inserting item T to the last element of α. For the appearing sequence of γ, $Appear_\gamma$, if its j-th bit has value 1, sequence α and $\{T\}$ must be contained in the corresponding sequence s_j. Moreover, there exists an element containing both X and $\{T\}$, which is located after α' in the sequence.

Similarly, the approximation of $Appear_\gamma$, denoted as A_Appear_γ, is obtained by performing an AND operation on $Appear_\alpha$ and $Appear_T$. The candidate pattern γ is not possible frequent if $1\_count(A\_Appear_\gamma) < min\_sup$ and it is pruned.

On the other hand, if 1_count(A_Appear$_\gamma$)≥*min_sup*, for those bits in A_Appear$_\gamma$ with value 1, the corresponding sequences have to be checked whether they contain γ actually to get Appear$_\gamma$. For each bit k in A_Appear$_\gamma$, if its value is 0, Appear$_\gamma$ is set to be 0. Otherwise, the values in FP$_\alpha(k)$ and FP$_T(k)$ are compared. If FP$_\alpha(k)$ is equal to FP$_T(k)$, it implies there exists an element within the k-th sequence which contains both {T} and the last element X of α. Besides, the element is located after α' because FP$_{\alpha'}(k)$ < FP$_\alpha(k)$. In other words, the new pattern γ is contained in the k-th sequence of S and FP$_\alpha(k)$ is the first sequential position of γ in this sequence. Therefore, Appear$_\gamma(k)$ is set to be 1 and FP$_\gamma(k)$ is set to be FP$_\alpha(k)$.

However, it is not necessary that γ does not occur in the k-th sequence if FP$_\alpha(k)$ is larger or less than FP$_T(k)$. Therefore, the following detailed checking on the bit sequences Bit$_X(k)$ and Bit$_T(k)$ is executed. First, Bit$_X(k)$ is obtained by performing AND operations on Bit$_{x1}(k)$, Bit$_{x2}(k)$, ..., and Bit$_{xi}(k)$, where x_i is an item in X.

Then, another AND operation is performed on Bit$_X(k)$ and Bit$_T(k)$ to get Bit$_{(X \cup \{T\})}(k)$. If the resultant sequence is non-zero, it indicates that both X and {T} appear in certain element in the k-th sequence at the same time. To make sure there existing such an element located after α', the similar strategy adopted for checking S-extended sequences is applied.

The first sequential position of α (i.e. <α'X>) in the k-th sequence is FP$_\alpha(k)$. It implies, after α' appears, FP$_\alpha(k)$ is the smallest sequential position of X in sequence k. If γ is contained in the sequence, there must exist an element containing both X and {T} whose sequential location is no less than FP$_\alpha(k)$. Therefore, a left-shift operation is performed on Bit$_{(X \cup \{T\})}(k)$ by (FP$_\alpha(k)$-1) bits. If the resultant sequence is non-zero, it implies that such an element exists which is located after α'. That is, γ is contained in the k-th sequence. Let bit h denote the first bit in the resultant sequence with value 1, it indicates the first sequential position of γ in the sequence is located h positions after position (FP$_\alpha(k)$-1). Therefore, Appear$_\gamma(k)$ is set to be 1 and FP$_\gamma(k)$ is set to be (FP$_\alpha(k)$-1)+h. Otherwise, sequence γ is not contained in the k-th sequence of S, and both of Appear$_\gamma(k)$ and FP$_\gamma(k)$ are set to be 0.

The appearing sequence of γ, Appear$_\gamma$, is obtained after performing the checking for all the bits in A_Appear$_\gamma$ with value 1. Finally, γ is certified to be a frequent pattern if 1_Count(Appear$_\gamma$) is larger or equal to *min_sup*.

[Example 3]. Following the running example shown in Fig. 1, suppose min_sup is set to be 2. A sequence α=<ac> is given, and Appear$_{<ac>}$=11100 and FP$_{<ac>}$="2,2,4,0,0" are known. The process for checking whether the S-extended sequence <acd> and I-extended sequence <a(cd)> of <ac> being frequent is described as following.
- Checking S-extended sequence <acd>:
(1) A_Appear$_{<acd>}$= Appear$_{<ac>}$ ∧ Appear$_d$= 10100; 1_Count(A_Appear$_{<acd>}$) ≥ 2, continue.
(2) For the 1st and 3rd bit in A_Appear$_{<acd>}$
   (2-1) A_Appear$_{<acd>}$(1)≠0; FP$_{<ac>}$(1)=2 is not less than FP$_d$(1)=2;
      Get Bit$_d$(1)=0101; Left-shift(Bit$_d$(1)) by 2 bits→0100(non-zero);
      The first bit in the resultant sequence with value 1 is bit 2;
      Therefore, Appear$_{<acd>}$(1) is set to be 1, and FP$_{<acd>}$(1) is set to be FP$_{<ac>}$(1)+2=4.
   (2-2) Check A_Appear$_{<acd>}$(3)≠0; FP$_{<ac>}$(3)=4 is not less than FP$_d$(3)=3;

Get $Bit_d(3)=0011$; Left-shift($Bit_d(3)$) by 4 bits→0000(zero);
Therefore, $Appear_{<acd>}(3)$ and $FP_{<acd>}(3)$ are set to be 0.
(3) For the bit $k=2, 4, 5$ in $A\_Appear_{<acd>}$
 (3-1) Check $A\_Appear_{<acd>}(k)=0$; Therefore, $Appear_{<acd>}(k)$ and $FP_{<acd>}(k)$ are set to be 0.
(4) $Appear_{<acd>}=10000$, $1\_Count(Appear_{<acd>})<2$; Therefore, $<acd>$ is not a frequent pattern.

- Checking I-extended sequence $<a(cd)>$:
(1) $A\_Appear_{<a(cd)>} = Appear_{<ac>} \wedge Appear_d = 10100; 1\_Count(A\_Appear_{<a(cd)>}) \geq 2$, continue.
(2) For the 1st and 3rd bit in $A\_Appear_{<acd>}$
 (2-1) Check $A\_Appear_{<a(cd)>}(1) \neq 0$; $FP_{<ac>}(1)=2$ is equal to $FP_d(1)=2$;
  Therefore, $Appear_{<a(cd)>}(1)$ is set to be 1, and $FP_{<a(cd)>}(1)$ is set to be $FP_{<ac>}(1)=2$.
 (2-2) Check $A\_Appear_{<a(cd)>}(3) \neq 0$; $FP_{<ac>}(3)=4$ is not equal to $FP_d(3)=3$;
  Get $Bit_c(3)=1001$ and $Bit_d(3)=0011$; $Bit_{(cd)}(3)= Bit_c(3) \wedge Bit_d(3)=0001$;
  Left-shift($Bit_{(cd)}(3)$) by (4-1) bits→1000(non-zero);
  Therefore, $Appear_{<a(cd)>}(3)$ is set to be 1, and $FP_{<a(cd)>}(3)$ is set to be ($FP_{<ac>}(3)-1)+1=4$.
(3) For the bit $k=2, 4, 5$ in $A\_Appear_{<acd>}$
 (3-1) Check $A\_Appear_{<acd>}(k)=0$; Therefore, $Appear_{<acd>}(k)$ and $FP_{<acd>}(k)$ are set to be 0.
(4) $Appear_{<a(cd)>}=10100$, $FP_{<a(cd)>}=$ "2,0,4,0,0",
 Check $1\_Count(Appear_{<a(cd)>}) \geq 2$; Therefore, $<a(cd)>$ is a frequent pattern.

4.3 I-SPAM Algorithm

The whole process of I-SPAM Algorithm is described as the pseudo codes shown below, which are similar to the ones of SPAM algorithm. The modified parts include the codes for constructing the bit sequence table and appearing sequence table, and removing infrequent items from the tables. The S-temp$_{<\alpha>}$/I-temp$_{<\alpha>}$ is used to store the candidate items which are possible to construct frequent S-extended/I-extended sequences from sequence α according to the pruning strategy adopted in SPAM algorithm [3]. Initially, for each item $T \in L_1$, S-temp$_{<T>}$ is set to be L_1, and I-temp$_{<T>}$ is assigned the set of items in L_1 and greater than T, respectively. Then procedure M_DFS() is called recursively to perform the process of generating candidates from T and discovering frequent patterns in a depth-first manner.

The significant difference between SPAM and I-SPAM is that the appearing sequences and first_position sequences are used for more efficient support counting to avoid checking bit sequence tables as possible. Moreover, the memory size to retain the appearing and first_position sequences of patterns temporally during executing I-SPAM is less than the one to retain the bitmap sequences of patterns while executing SPAM.

```
Algorithm I-SPAM (Sequence Database S, min_sup)
  For each [sid_i, s]∈ S  /* construct the tables */
    For each element s_j of s
      For each item k∈ s_j
```

```
            If Appear_k(i)==0, set Appear_k(i)= 1;
            Set the j-th bit in Bit_k(i) to be 1;
            If FP_k(i)==0, set FP_k(i)= j;
L_1= ∅ ;
For each item k in appearing sequence table
    If 1_Count(Appear_k)< min_sup, /* remove from the tables */
        For i=1 to |S|
            If Appear_k(i)==1,
                Remove Bit_k(i) from the bit sequence table;
            Remove the tuple [k, Appear_k, FP_k] from appearing
            sequence table;
    Else L_1= L_1 ∪ {k};
For each item T∈ L_1
    S-temp_<T>= L_1;
    I-temp_<T>= {x | x∈ L_1 ∧ x > T by lexicographic order};
    Call M_DFS(T, Appear_T, FP_T, S-temp_<T>, I-temp_<T>).
```

5 Performance Evaluation

In this section, the experimental results on the performance of I-SPAM in comparison with SPAM [3] are reported. All the experiments are performed on a personal computer with 2.4GHz Intel Pentium 4 CPU, 512MB main memory, and running Microsoft Windows XP.

The experiments were performed on synthetic data generated by the IBM synthetic market-basket data generator AssociGen[2]. The inputted parameters AssociGen: D(number of sequences in the dataset), C(average number of elements per sequence), T(average number of items per element), S(average length of potentially frequent sequential patterns), and I(average length of itemsets in maximal potentially frequent patterns) are considered the factors while comparing I-SPAM against SPAM.

5.1 Comparison with Spam on Execution Time

The experimental results on execution time are shown in Fig. 2, where the *min_sup* setting and the parameters used for generating data set are controlled individually in each experiment. For SPAM algorithm, some experimental results are missing from the figures. It means, under the parameter setting, the SPAM algorithm could not be executed properly in the running environment.

First, by varying *min_sup* setting, the execution times of these two algorithms are evaluated on three datasets with various scales(the first is 0.6MB, the second is 1.4MB and the third is 7.9MB). The experimental results are shown in Fig. 2(a), 2(b) and 2(c), respectively. The results show that I-SPAM can achieve the same magnitude efficiency and even better than SPAM on execution time. The primary reason is due to the representation of appearing and first_position sequences, which are used for more efficient support counting to avoid checking the bit sequences as possible. When the *min_sup* setting becomes larger, fewer candidate patterns are generated such that the benefit gained by I-SPAM is reduced. Additionally, the cost for pruning infrequent items from bits sequence and appearing sequence tables by I-SPAM is increasing. Therefore, the execution time of I-SPAM approaches the one of SPAM when *min_sup* is larger than 0.025. However, when *min_sup* is small enough, the execution efficiency of I-SPAM outperforms SPAM about a factor of 1.5. Moreover, SPAM is not executable when performing on large dataset with *min_sup* less than 0.08.

Agreeing with the previous experimental results, the results shown in Fig. 2(d) indicate that I-SPAM outperforms SPAM when the numbers of sequences in the datasets(D) are larger than 5K. For small datasets, checking the bitmap representation directly could be performed very quickly. Therefore, in some cases of small datasets(when D is 3K), the overhead for processing the appearing and first_position sequences outweighs the benefits achieved by these structures, and SPAM runs slightly faster in these situations.

Among the parameters used in AssociGen, as the average number of elements per sequence(C) and the average number of items per element(T) increase, the size of generated synthetic datasets will increase. Therefore, the experimental results shown in Fig. 2(e) and 2(f) indicate the coincident result shown in Fig. 2(d) due to the similar reasons as in the case of increasing the number of sequences in the dataset. Due to page limit, the experimental results on parameters (S) and (I) setting are omitted here.

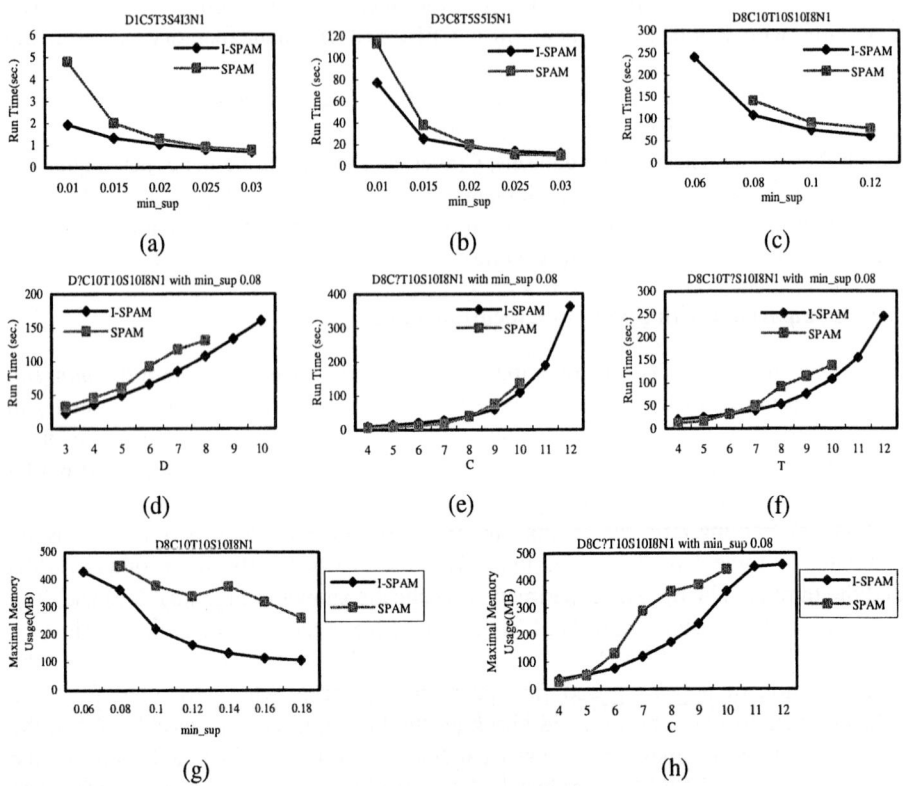

Fig. 2. Experimental results

5.2 Comparison with SPAM on Maximal Memory Usage

The estimated results on maximal memory usage are shown in Fig. 2(g) and 2(h). In the experiment performed on the 7.9MB dataset, Fig. 2(g) shows that the maximal memory requirement of I-SPAM is about half of the one required by SPAM. The primary reason is due to the size of required memory for storing the appearing and first_position sequences of a pattern temporally during executing I-SPAM is less than the one for storing the bitmap sequence of a pattern while executing SPAM. Fig. 2(h) shows the maximal memory requirement of I-SPAM and SPAM by varying the average number of elements per sequence in the datasets, which indicates the similar outcomes.

To summarize the experimental results, in general, I-SPAM has better scalability than SPAM for larger datasets and less *min_sup* setting under the same running environment.

6 Conclusion and Future Works

In this paper, an improved-version of SPAM algorithm, called I-SPAM, for mining frequent sequential patterns is proposed. With the aid of appearing sequence table, more efficient support counting is achieved by avoiding checking the bit sequences as possible.

Moreover, the required memory size for storing the temporal variables is reduced effectively to be less than the one needed by SPAM. The experimental results demonstrate that I-SPAM outperforms SPAM on execution time especially when performed on larger datasets and with smaller *min_sup* setting. Furthermore, the maximal memory requirement is reduced effectively to be about half of the one required for executing SPAM in most cases.

Constraints are essential for many sequential pattern mining applications. In the future, it is worthy our studying on pushing constraints in the mining process of I-SPAM to reduce the explored portion of the search space dramatically.

References

[1] R. Agarwal and R. Srikant. Fast Algorithm for Mining Association Rule in Large Databases. In Proc. 1994 Int. Conf. Very Large DataBases, pp. 487-499, 1994.
[2] R. Agarwal and R. Srikant. Mining Sequential Pattern. In Proc. 1995 Int. Conf. Data Engineering, pages 3-10, 1995.
[3] J. Ayres, J. Flannick, J. Gehrke, and T. Yiu. Sequential PAttern Mining Using A Bitmap Representation. In Proc. 2002 Int. Conf. Knowledge Discovery and Data Mining, 2002.
[4] J. Pei, J. Han, Q. Chen, U. Dayal, and H. Pinto. FreeSpan: Frequent Pattern-Projected Sequential Pattern Mining. In Proc. 2000 Int. Conf. Knowledge Discovery and Data Mining, 2000.
[5] J. Pei, J. Han, B. Mortazavi-Asi and H. Pinto. PrefixSpan□Mining Sequential Patterns Efficiently by Prefix-Projected Pattern Growth. In Proc. 2001 Int. Conf. on Data Engineering , 2001.
[6] R. Srikant and R. Agrawal. Mining Sequential Patterns: Generalizations and Performance Improvements. In Proc. 5th Int. Conf. Extending Database Technology, 1996.
[7] M.J. Zaki. SPADE: An Efficient Algorithm for Mining Frequent Sequences. In Machine Learning Journal, 42(1/2): 31-60, 2001.

Dimension Transform Based Efficient Event Filtering for Symmetric Publish/Subscribe System

Botao Wang and Masaru Kitsuregawa

Institute of Industrial Science, The University of Tokyo,
Komaba 4-6-1, Meguro Ku, Tokyo, 135-8505 Japan
{botaow, kitsure}@tkl.iis.u-tokyo.ac.jp

Abstract. There exists a class of publish/subscribe applications, such as recruitment, insurance, personal service, classified advertisement, electronic commerce, etc., where publisher needs the capability to select subscribers. Such kinds of publish/subscribe applications are called symmetric publish/subscribe system. The existing event matching algorithms designed for traditional publish/subscribe systems (called asymmetric publish/subscribe system) can not be applied to symmetric publish/subscribe systems efficiently.

By extending the existing data model and algorithm, we propose an event matching method for symmetric publish/subscribe system based on dimension transform regarding the query in multidimensional space. An efficient underlying multidimensional index structure is chosen and verified. Our proposal is evaluated in a simulated environment. The results show that, our proposal outperforms the other possible solutions in one or two orders of magnitude. For a typical workload containing one million subscriptions with 16 attributes, an event can be filtered within several milliseconds and the subscription base can be updated within hundreds of microseconds. We can say that our proposal is efficient and practical for symmetric publish/subscribe systems.

1 Introduction

There exists a class of publish/subscribe applications, such as recruitment, insurance, personal service, classified advertisement, electronic commerce, etc., where publisher needs the capability to select subscribers who can receive its publications. Consider the recruitment for example, company is publisher and job seeker is subscriber. For a complete recruitment matching, besides providing with working conditions, the publisher (company) wants to check the information related to the subscriber (job seeker) also. For example, the subscriber is required to be older than 18. Accordingly, the subscriber needs to provide his own information also. Such kinds of systems are called *symmetric* publish/subscribe system. Different from traditional publish/subscribe system (called *asymmetric* publish/subscribe system in this paper), both subscriber and publisher keep information and filtering criteria as shown below.

(S1) Subscription :
Criteria:(Salary > 500) AND (Location = Paris), Information:(Age, 25)
(E1) Event :
Information :(Salary, 400 − 600), (Location, Paris), Criteria: (Age > 30)

In the context of event matching, many event matching techniques [4] [5] [7] [8] [13] [16] [17] have been proposed. The main challenge here is that all above techniques are designed for asymmetric publish/subscribe system. These techniques can not be applied to symmetric publish/subscribe system for three reasons: 1) Predicates are defined and included in event. 2) Not only point data (Location in E1) represented by one constant but also range data (Salary in E1) represented by a pair of constants need to be supported. 3) The frequency of index updating is same as that of event arriving. The new type of event matching techniques for symmetric publish/subscribe system is required.

As far as we know, the symmetric publish/subscribe system is first introduced in [12] without performance evaluation. In this paper, for symmetric publish/subscribe system, we propose and evaluate an efficient event matching method based on a multidimensional index structure MultiLevel Grid File (MLGF) [14] [15] with dimension transform.

The main contributions of this paper are that: 1) Propose an event matching model for symmetric publish/subscribe system, which allows information and criteria to be defined in both event and subscription. The format of information is extended from point format to range format. 2) Extend the dimension transform techniques used in [13] to support event matching for both symmetric and asymmetric publish/subscribe systems. Moreover, different from [13], where UBTree [2] [3] [10] [11] is chosen as its underlying index structure, we propose a more efficient multidimensional index structure MLGF, the performance of event matching can be improved one order of magnitude in almost all cases.

The remainder of this paper is organized as follows. Section 2 defines the event matching model of symmetric publish/subscribe system. Section 3 introduces the main idea of our proposal after analyzing the limitations of the related solutions. Section 4 describes the method of the dimension transform to support event matching of symmetric publish/subscribe system. Section 5 introduces the related work. Section 6 reports experimental evaluation. Finally, conclusions are presented in Section 7.

2 Event Matching of Symmetric Publish/Subscribe System

2.1 Architecture of Symmetric Publish/Subscribe System

The architecture of symmetric publish/subscribe system is shown in Fig.1-a. There event and subscription are "symmetric", and the roles of subscriber and publisher are relative not absolute. While an event arrives, besides matching the event on subscription base, the system inserts the event to event base also.

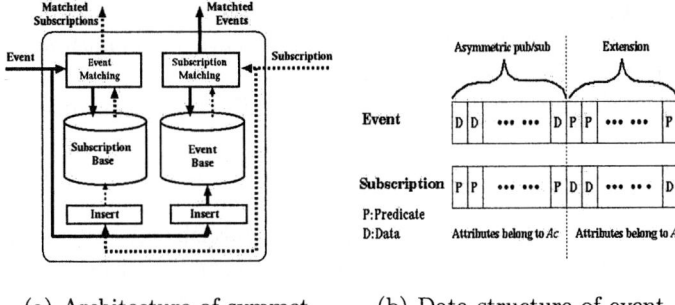

(a) Architecture of symmetric publish/subscribe

(b) Data structure of event and subscription

Fig. 1. The symmetric publish/subscribe system

The frequency of event (subscription) matching operations is same as that of data updating of event (subscription) base. Symmetric publish/subscribe system should support both high rate of event matching and high rate of data updating.

2.2 Data Model of Symmetric Publish/Subscribe System

Schema Attributes. The schema attributes are defined from the view of subscriber. Let Ac, Ai and A denote filtering criteria domain, information domain and publish/subscribe application domain, the schema attribtues are defined as following:

$Ac = \{ac_1, ac_2, ..., ac_g, ..., ac_i\}$ $1 <= i$, $ac_g \in Ac$, $1 <= g <= i$
$Ai = \{ai_1, ai_2, ..., ai_h, ..., ai_j\}$ $0 <= j$, $ai_h \in Ai$, $0 <= h <= j$
$A = Ac \cup Ai$

Event and Subscription. Both event and subscription in symmetric publish/subscribe system consist of filtering criteria and information data as shown in Fig.1-b. Because range data (interval) must be supported and predicate can be represented as an interval also, an event e and a subscription s are defined as conjunctions of intervals in the following formats:

$e = \{(a_1 : EI_{a_1}), ..., (a_k : EI_{a_k}), ..., (a_{i+j} : EI_{a_{i+j}})\}$
$s = \{(a_1 : SI_{a_1}), ..., (a_k : SI_{a_k}), ..., (a_{i+j} : SI_{a_{i+j}})\}$

where $a_k \in A = Ac \cup Ai$, $1 <= k <= i+j$, and EI_{a_k}, SI_{a_k} are the intervals in the application domain respectively. The format of the interval is:

$Ia = [Is_a, Ie_a]$

where $a \in A$, $Is_a, Ie_a \in a$, $Is_a <= Ie_a$. Notice that both predicate and information data are represented by the same interval format here. They are different semantically.

Event Matching. An event pair (a, EI_a) matches a subscription pair (a, SI_a) if EI_a intersects SI_a. An event e satisfies a subscription s if all subscription pairs in s are matched by its corresponding event pairs.

3 Solution Overview

3.1 Limitations of Related Solutions

Compound Algorithm. As far as we know, the symmetric publish/subscribe system was first introduced in [12] without performance evaluation. The events are matched based on two indexes: predicate index (Count algorithm [16] or Handson [7] [8]) built on the data belong to Ac and data index (B+tree) built on the data belong to Ai. The event data is divided into two subsets (Fig.1-b): the data subset belong to Ac and the data subset belong to Ai. The two data subsets are sent to their corresponding indexes and the result subscriptions are obtained by joining two intermediate result sets from two indexes.

The main problem of the Compound algorithm is performance. Both predicate index and data index are a cluster of one-dimensional structures there. As analyized and evaluated in [3] [10] [13] [17], the performance of such kind of clusters is very sensitive to the selectivity of attributes. According to the analyses and evaluation results in [3] [10], it is hard to expect competitive performance with multiple B+trees compared to the multidimensional index structures like UBTree. As introduced in [13] [17], the performances of UBTree-based and RTree-based event matching are three orders of magnitude faster than that of the Count algorithm [16] in most of cases regarding different workloads. Logically, the Count algorithm [16] and the Hanson algorithm [7] [8] have same complexity order for event matching.

Algorithms Based on Multidimensional Indexes. Multidimensional indexes, like UBTree [3] [10] and RTree [6] are feasible for event matching of asymmetric publish/subscribe system as introduced in [13] [17]. The dimension transform is adopted in order to avoid overlaps among the hypercubes corresponding to subscriptions. There the hypercubes in d space are transferred into points in $2d$ space. The point access method used is UBTree.

The problems of [13] [17] are that: 1) The method introduced in [13] can not be applied to symmetric publish/subscribe directly. The reason is that the new data type (range data) and new operation (predicate in event) are newly defined in symmetric publish/subscribe system, and event matching here is an intersection query based on the model (Section 2.2) instead of a point enclosed query [13] which corresponds to asymmetric publish/subscribe system . 2) For the range search based on UBTree which was chosen as the underlying index structure in [13], the number of empty spaces (no data is kept there) becomes larger with increasement of number of dimensions. Skipping the empty space is an expensive memory operation, which can not be neglected in the event matching based on main memory structure.

3.2 Main Idea

The main idea of our solution is stated as: the event matching of symmetric publish/subscribe system is regraded as an intersection query on hypercubes in d space and the intersection query on hypercubes is transformed into a range query on points in 2d space so as to make use of efficient point access methods for event matching.

Different from [13] [17], the dimension transform (to be introduced in Section 4) supports event matching of symmetric publish/subscribe system. Moreover, instead of UBTree, we propose to use a more efficient underlying index structure, MultiLevel Grid File (MLGF) [14] [15]. MLGF is a dynamic, balanced, multidimensional index structure that adapts to nonuniform and correlated distributions. For the details of Multilevel Grid File, please refer to [14] [15].

4 Dimension Transform

4.1 Dimension Transform for Symmetric Publish/Subscribe System

As defined in Section 2.2, both subscription and event are conjunctions of intervals. The method of dimension transform is same for all attributes. In the follows, we introduce the dimension transform method for one attribute. The same intervals
$$EI_a = [EIs_a, EIe_a], SI_a = [SIs_a, SIe_a]$$
defined in Section 2.2 is used here. Given an attribute $a \in A$ with domain size $[Min, Max]$, two new dimensions in a 2d space Dsa and Dea are defined corresponding to starting and ending points.

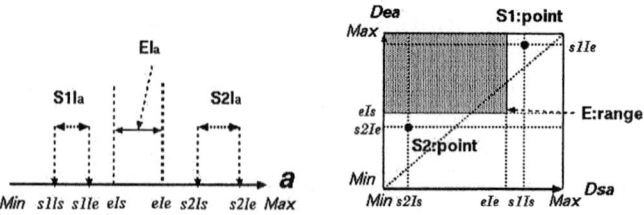

Fig. 2. Dimension Transform

We start from the cases that EI_a doesn't intersect with SI_a, which means the predicate is not matched. As shown in Fig.2, there are only two cases which are represented by two pairs of intervals $(EI_a, S1I_a)$ and $(EI_a, S2I_a)$. Logically, the two cases can be summarized as follows,
$$EIs_a > SIe_a \text{ OR } EIe_a < SIs_a$$
From above expression, we can deduce the expression representing intersection of two intervals:

NOT ($EIs_a > SIe_a$ OR $EIe_a < SIs_a$)
$$\Updownarrow$$
($EIs_a <= SIe_a$ AND $EIe_a >= SIs_a$)
$$\Updownarrow$$
$(EIs_a <= SIe_a <= Max)$ AND $(Min <= SIs_a <= EIe_a)$

If SIs_a and SIe_a are considered as one point in the 2d space, by mapping SIs_a and SIe_a to the newly defined two dimensions Dsa and Dea, one 1d intersection query on hypercubes can be transformed into one 2d range query on points as shown in Fig.2. The range in 2d space is
$$Range : ([Min, EIe_a], [EIs_a, Max])$$
and the point is
$$Point : (SIs_a, SIe_a)$$

5 Related Work

A lot of algorithms related to event matching have been proposed. They are proposed for publish/subscribe systems [1] [5] [9] [13] [16] [17], continuous queries [4] and active databases [7] [8].

Predicate indexing techniques have been widely applied. There, a set of one-dimensional index structures are used to index the predicates in subscriptions. Mainly, there are two kinds of algorithms based on multiple one-dimensional index structures: Count algorithm [16] and Hanson algorithm [7] [8]. The performances of Count algorithm and Hanson algorithm have same complexity order, they differ from each other by whether or not all predicates in subscriptions are placed in the index structures. Meanwhile in [13] [17], the event matching based on multidimensional index structures has been proved to be feasible and efficient compared to the Count algorithm. The conclusions of [13] [17] are the basis of this paper. Hanson algorithm is extended in [5] where subscriptions were clustered according to their equality predicates and mutli-attribute hashing was utilized to find the related clusters. The size of domain can not be too larger for reason of multi-attribute hashing.

The testing networking based techniques [1] [9] initially preprocess the subscriptions into a matching tree. Different from the predicate indexes, [1] and [9] built subscription index trees based on subscription schema. They suffer from the problems of space and maintenance.

Event matching is one critical step of continuous queries. In [4], predicate index was built based on Red-Black tree, there algorithm is similar to bruteforce which scans the total Red-Black tree every time when an event arrives.

All above algorithms are designed for asymmetric event matching, which can not be applied to symmetric publish/subscribe system directly.

6 Evaluation

6.1 Evaluation Environment

Three kinds of solutions have been implemented and compared based on main memory structure: 1) Naive. RTree is used directly for intersection query without dimension transform. 2) Compound. It is an implementation similar to the algorithm proposed in [12]. Different from the original proposal, two indexes for

Table 1. Simulated parameters

Parameter	Value range	Default value
Global parameters		
Number of subscriptions	0-2,500,000	1,000,000
Number of attributes (dimension)	8-64	16
Ratio of attributes belong to Ac to attributes belong to Ai	16:0-0:16	8:8
Ratio of one subscription is matched (selectivity)	0.001-0.05%	0.01%
Parameters related to subscription or event		
Ratio of an attributes to be used to define predicate	0-100%	100%
Ratio of equality predicates to be defined	0-100%	50%
Ratio of point data to be defined	0-100%	50%

predicates and information data kept in subscriptions are two RTrees. 3) Dimension Transform. Two point access methods are chosen: UBTree and MLGF.

The events and subscriptions are created according to a workload specification. The parameters used in the evaluations are tabulated in Table.1 along with their range and default values. For each test, we change one parameter and fix the others with their default values without specific introduction. For each test, the average response time of 1000 inputs is measured.

All the solutions have been implemented in C++. The type of all attributes is short integer. The fanout of UBTree, MLGF tree and R-tree[1] are 200, 20, 10. With these values, because the best response times were obtained in one preliminary test with a workload of 1 million subscriptions and 10 thousands events in a 16d space. The hardware platform is a Sun Fire 4800 workstation with four 900MHz CPUs and 16G bytes memory under Solaris 8.

6.2 Evaluation Results

Performances Related to Event Matching. Fig.3-a shows the scalability on the number of subscriptions. All solutions have good scalabilities here.

Fig.3-b shows the performances with different the numbers of dimensions. Compared to the performance of *Compound*, the performance of *Naive* deteriorates quickly than that of *Compound*. The reason is that the number of dimensions used in *Naive* is double of that used in *Compound* (two RTrees are used). The influence of the number of dimensions on RTree's performance accelerates when the number of dimensions increases. The total number of intermediate results obtained from two indexes of *Compound* has an average value 2789 when dimension number is 8 and an average value 205 when dimension number is 16. That is the reason why its performance seems to upgrade a little when dimension number is 16, because the number of the intermediate results decreases 10 times here. Contrast to our expectation, the performance of MLGF does not changes linearly with the number of dimensions. The main reason is that the selectivity

---

[1] Version 0.62b. http://www.cs.ucr.edu/ marioh/ spatialindex. Only the two parameters related to fanout are changed here. The others are default values.

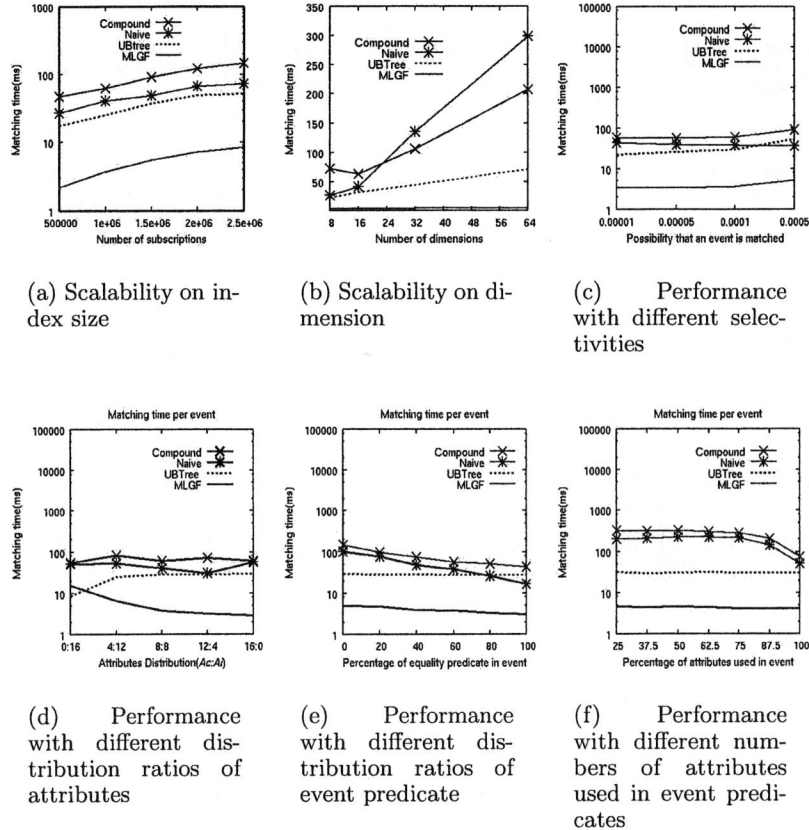

Fig. 3. Performances related to event matching

is fixed by default and the number of candidate objects which were filtered to get final results, decreases with the number of dimensions here.

Fig.3-c shows the performance with different selectivities. Here 1 million subscriptions are used and the number of results for one event matching changes from 10 to 500. Except *Naive*, the time costs of other solutions become larger with the increasement of the selectivity. The reason that *Naive* is relatively stable is that the numbers of candidate objects are on same order of amount.

Fig.3-d shows the influence of attributes distribution related to the numbers of attributes defined in Ac and Ai. "0:16" means the size of Ac is 0 and the size of Ai is 16. Subscriptions consist of information data only and events consist of predicates only. In this case, the event matching of symmetric publish/subscribe is same as a traditional query which is applied on static data (subscriptions). "16:0" means the size of Ac is 16 and the size of Ai is 0. It means that subscriptions consist of predicates only and event consists of information data only, which is similar to asymmetric publish/subscribe. The difference is that the in-

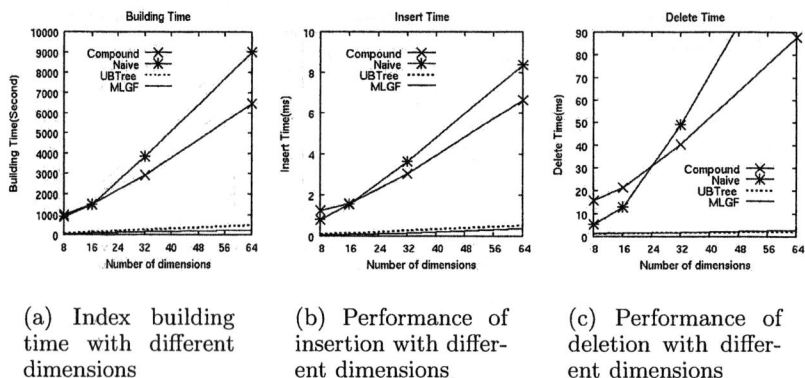

(a) Index building time with different dimensions (b) Performance of insertion with different dimensions (c) Performance of deletion with different dimensions

Fig. 4. Performances related to index updating

formation data kept in the events has format of range data (Section 2.2). In above two cases, *Compound* method creates only one index (predicate or data) same as *naive*, so the performances of them are same. The performance difference between MLGF-based solution and UBTree-based solution becomes larger with increasement of Ac's size. It indicates that MLGF is more suitable than UBTree for both symmetric and asymmetric publish/subscribe system.

Fig.3-e shows that the distribution ratio of different predicates (equality or non-equality) used in the events influences the performance bitterly. Except *UBTree*-based solution, the performances of other solutions become better while the percentage of equality predicates becomes larger. It is a process that the corresponding query changes from intersection query (symmetric publish/subscribe) to point enclosed query (asymmetric publish/subscribe), because equality predicate can be represented in the format of point data.

Fig.3-f shows that the changing of the number of unused attributes in the event predicate only influences the performance of *Compound* and *Naive*. The performances become better for the reason that the more the number of used attributes is, the less the overlap is. But it does not influence the performance of *UBTree* and *MLGF* where dimension transform has been done.

Performances Related to Index Updating. As introduced in Section 2.1, the index of symmetric publish/subscribe system must support high dynamically updating operations. Fig.4-a shows that the index building time based on *UBTree* and *MLGF* increases linearly with the number of dimensions. In contrast, *Compound* and *Naive* deteriorate quickly for the reason of heavy overlaps.

Fig.4-b and Fig.4-c show the performances of insert operations and delete operations respectively. Time costs of *Compound* and *Naive* increase exponentially with the number of dimensions because Rtree is built based on the overlap of spatial objects. The insert operation of *MLGF* is a little faster than that of *UBTree* and the delete operation of *MLGF* is a little slower than that of *UBTree*. The reason is their different partition strategies. Merging two regions of $MLGF$ is a little expensive than merging two nodes of $UBTree$. The time costs of $MLGF$ and $UBTree$ increase linearly with the number of dimensions.

7 Conclusions

In this paper, we have described the event matching problem of symmetric publish/subscribe system and discussed the strategies of applying multidimensional index structures to symmetric publish/subscribe system. The key feature of our solution is that map the intersection query on hypercubes to a range query on points with dimension transform so as the efficient point access method (Multi-Level Grid File) can be utilized for event matching.

Three kinds of solutions based on RTree, UBTree and MLGF, were evaluated and compared with various workloads in a simulated environment. The results show that our proposal outperforms the others in one or two orders of magnitude in almost all cases regarding different workloads. Performance studies show that an event can be filtered within several milliseconds and subscriptions can be updated within hundreds of microseconds for a typical workload containing one million subscriptions with 16 attributes. We can say that our proposal is efficient and practical for symmetric publish/subscribe applications with high rates of incoming events and high rates of data changes.

References

[1] M. K. Aguilera, R. E. Strom, D. C. Sturman, M. Astley, and T. D. Chandra. Matching events in a content-based subscription system. In *The 18th annual ACM symposium on Principles of distributed computing*, pages 53–61, 1999.

[2] R. Bayer. The universal b-tree for multidimensional indexing. Technical Report TUM-I9637, Technische Universitat Munchen, November 1996.

[3] R. Bayer and V. Markl. The ub-tree: Performance of multidimensional range queries. Technical Report TUM-I9814, Technische Universitat Munchen, June 1998.

[4] S. Chandrasekaran and M. J. Franklin:. Streaming queries over streaming data. In *VLDB*, pages 203–214, 2001.

[5] F. Fabret, H. A. Jacobsen, F. Llirbat, J. Pereira, K. A. Ross, and D. Shasha. Filtering algorithms and implementation for very fast publish/subscribe systems. In *SIGMOD*, pages 115–126, 2001.

[6] A. Guttman. R-trees: A dynamic index structure for spatial searching. In *SIGMOD*, pages 47–57, 1984.

[7] E. N. Hanson, C. Carnes, L. Huang, M. Konyala, L. Noronha, S. Parthasarathy, J. B. Park, and A. Vernon. Scalable trigger processing. In *ICDE*, pages 266–275, 1999.

[8] E. N. Hanson, M. Chaabouni, C.-H. Kim, and Y.-W. Wang. A predicate matching algorithm for database rule systems. In *SIGMOD*, pages 271–280, 1990.

[9] A. Hinze and S. Bittner. Efficient distribution-based event filtering. In *Workshops: 1st International Workshop on Distributed Event-Based Systems(DEBS)*, IEEE Computer Society, 2002.

[10] V. Markl. *MISTRAL:Processing Relational Queries using a Multidimensional Access Tecnnique*. PhD thesis, Technische Universitat Munchen, 1999. Published by infix Verlag, St.Augustin. DISDBIS 59, ISBN 3-89601-459-5.

[11] F. Ramsak, V. Markl, R. Fenk, M. Zirkel, K. Elhardt, and R. Bayer. Integrating the ub-tree into a database system kernel. In *VLDB*, pages 263–272, 2000.

[12] W. Rjaibi, K. R. Dittrich, and D. Jaepel. Event matching in symmetric subscription systems. In *Proceedings of the 2002 conference of the Centre for Advanced Studies on Collaborative research*, page 9. IBM Press, 2002.

[13] B. Wang, W. Zhang, and M. Kitsuregawa. UB-Tree based efficient predicate index with dimension transform for pub/sub system. In *DASFAA*, pages 63–37, 2004.

[14] K. Y. Whang, S. W. Kim, and G. Wiederhold. Dynamic maintenance of data distribution for selectivity estimation. *The VLDB Journal*, 3(1):29–51, 1994.

[15] K.-Y. Whang and R. Krishnamurthy. The multilevel grid file - a dynamic hierarchical multidimensional file structure. In *Proceedings of the Second International Symposium on Database Systems for Advanced Applications*, pages 449–459, 1992.

[16] T. W. Yan and H. Garcia-Molina. The sift information dissemination system. *ACM Trans. Database Syst.*, 24(4):529–565, 1999.

[17] W. Zhang. Performance analysis of Ub-tree indexed publish/subscribe system. Master's thesis, Department of Information and Communication Engineering, The University of Tokyo, 2004.

Scalable Distributed Aggregate Computations Through Collaboration

Leonidas Galanis[1] and David J. DeWitt[2]

[1] Oracle USA, 500 Oracle Pkwy, Redwood Shores, CA 94065, USA
leonidas.galanis@oracle.com
[2] University of Wisconsin – Madison, 1210 W Dayton St, Madison, WI 53706, USA
dewitt@cs.wisc.edu

Abstract. Computing aggregates over distributed data sets constitutes an interesting class of distributed queries. Recent advances in peer-to-peer discovery of data sources and query processing techniques have made such queries feasible and potentially more frequent. The concurrent execution of multiple and often identical distributed aggregate queries can place a high burden on the data sources. This paper identifies the scalability bottlenecks that can arise in large peer-to-peer networks from the execution of large numbers of aggregate computations and proposes a solution. In our approach peers are assigned the role of aggregate computation maintainers, which leads to a substantial decrease in requests to the data sources and also avoids duplicate computation by the sites that submit identical aggregate queries. Moreover, a framework is presented that facilitates the collaboration of peers in maintaining aggregate query results. Experimental evaluation of our design demonstrates that it achieves very good performance and scales to thousands of peers.

1 Introduction

Peer-to-Peer (P2P) computing has gained both scientific and social importance recently due to the success of systems such as Freenet [3], Gnutella [6] and Napster [12]. Harnessing P2P technology has the potential to produce systems that combine good scalability with minimal infrastructure cost. P2P systems are designed to start out small and seamlessly evolve to very large distributed systems with thousands of participants. The P2P computing paradigm has inspired many research projects to focus on a large variety of open problems. [15], [16], [22] and [25] provide the basis for low-level location services, otherwise known as Distributed Hash Tables (DHTs). [2], [11] and [18] illustrate how to use DHTs to build distributed file systems. [8] and [5] attempt to process complex queries in large P2P systems. The result has been the emergence of a concept known as data centric networking ([7] and [21]). With the advent of P2P systems, finding interesting data efficiently has become a major focus of research in the networking community.

Aggregate computations on data from distributed data sources constitute an important class of queries. P2P tools promise to make such queries feasible and therefore more frequent. If an aggregate computation is interesting to *multiple* peers in the network, the data sources participating in the computation can expect to receive the same query *multiple* times. Thus a new problem arises: The *many-to-many* query problem (M2M), which places scalability limits on query processing in P2P systems. To better illustrate the M2M problem, consider an application that brings together commodity traders from around the world in a large P2P commodity trading system without a centralized infrastructure. Traders post their sale and bid prices based on information obtained by querying each other. Typically, participants determine their asking price or bid after consulting the maximum bid and minimum sale price for a commodity across all traders. In the absence of a central server, a trader has to query all other traders in order to determine the maximum bid and the minimum sale price. Thus, if m sellers and n bidders are trading on one particular commodity, each trader has to answer $m+n$-1 *identical* queries. Furthermore, the total number of messages that must be exchanged among the participants and the total number of queries executed in the system is $(m+n)\cdot(m+n-1)$. Using a central server instead of a P2P system, each participant would require only 2 queries to retrieve the minimum sale price and the maximum bid, which translates to $2\cdot(m+n)$ messages for $(m+n)$ queries and another $(m+n)$ messages for the $(m+n)$ updates of bids and sale prices. Consequently, any P2P system would still not scale well for this type of application due to the high message traffic and query processing load. On the other hand, a central server can scale by adding additional hardware. The challenge is to make a P2P infrastructure scale gracefully under the M2M query scenario by leveraging existing resources.

This work presents a framework for efficiently processing *many-to-many* aggregate queries over large P2P networks in a scalable fashion. Our approach requires the same number of queries and messages as would be required with a centralized system by leveraging DHT technology and catalog services ([5]). The contributions of this work can be summarized as follows:

- A method for defining the special handling of aggregate computations that follow the *many-to-many* query pattern.
- An efficient query processing strategy that leverages existing P2P technology and allows for scalable processing of *many-to-many* aggregate queries.

Experimental validation of our approach demonstrates its scalability potential and, at the same time, shows the adverse impact of the M2M query problem on P2P applications. We believe that our design opens up new possibilities for novel distributed applications, since distributed aggregation is going to be increasingly essential for efficiently surveying large amounts of distributed data.

The paper is organized as follows: Section 2 outlines the overall system architecture. Section 3 delves into the detailed design of the distributed aggregate computation layer. Section 4 presents the results of the experiments. The paper ends with related work (Section 5) and concluding remarks (Section 6).

2 System Architecture

The software stack on *each* peer consists of four layers: 1) a **Distributed Hash Table** layer (DHT), 2) the **Catalog Service** (CS) layer, 3) the **Aggregate Computation** (ACL) layer, and 4) a query engine with access to the local data. The design does not dictate a specific data model or query language, but all examples will assume XML [24] data sources and XPath [23] queries.

The **DHT** layer is based on existing technology ([15], [16], [22] and [25]). Its purpose is to support the efficient and scalable location of *keys* or *object identifiers* used by the higher-level layers of the system. In essence, DHTs are fully distributed hash tables that employ protocols for efficiently directing requests for specific *keys* to the nodes in the network that are responsible for those *keys*.

The **Catalog Service** (CS) layer is the data discovery tool. Each node employs a CS that, when given an arbitrary Xpath query, locates the relevant data sources. Subsequently, the query only needs to be submitted to a subset of the peers in the distributed system. To provide this functionality, the CS requires that each data source provide a summary of its data in a special form when it joins the distributed system. The CS is based on the framework presented in [5].

The **Aggregate Computation Layer** (ACL) maintains the registered aggregate queries that have been submitted by the various nodes in the P2P network. The ACL is the focus of this paper and its detailed design is presented in Section 3.

3 Distributed Aggregation

Any node can establish special handling of aggregate queries by requesting the creation of an *aggregation point* (AP) if it discovers that it frequently needs to contact a large number of nodes in order to compute an aggregate or if it becomes overwhelmed with large numbers of identical requests that are part of an aggregation computation. The ACL creates an aggregation point when provided with an *activation record* (AR) that contains the following fields:

Aggregate Function: This field determines the aggregate function (*average*, *minimum*, *maximum* etc) that is applied by the peer responsible for the aggregation computation maintenance to the incoming data.

Target Data: This field contains a query that defines the data needed for computing the aggregation. The target element or attribute of the query determines the catalog service peer ([5]) that is the peer that will create and maintain the AP.

Scope: The scope can be either *global* or *local*. Global scope means that the aggregate function should be computed over all peers with relevant data, while local scope computes one value for each peer.

Group By: The *group by* field refines the aggregation by defining on or more aggregate groups (similar to the SQL "group by" construct). Each group is assigned to a node that maintains the aggregate computation for the specific group.

Table 1. Activation Record for the commodity traders example

Aggregate	MAXIMUM	Scope	GLOBAL
Target Data	//bidder/item/current_bid	Group By	//bidder/item/@item_id

An aggregation point corresponds to one or more groups depending on the *group_by* field. Each group is assigned to the *Aggregation Point Host* (APH) that is a node in the P2P network. The APH is selected among the peers in the P2P system based on the activation record. A DHT *key* is computed using all the fields of the AR. This key determines which peer will currently serve as the APH and thus assume responsibility for the aggregate computation.

To illustrate the creation of an activation record, consider again the example of commodity traders. Suppose bidders are peers that post their bids online as XML documents and update them as they trade. The current price a bidder is willing to pay for a commodity item i can be accessed using the path p_{bid} = //bidder/item [@item_id = i]/current_bid. Sellers naturally want to find the bidder with the maximum bid. Thus, if there are a large number of sellers of commodity i, and a large number of bidders, an aggregation point is needed to avoid M2M and make trading more efficient. Table 1 shows what the required activation record looks like. The aggregate function is the *maximum* and the scope is global. The target path is p_{target} = //bidder/item/current_bid. Hence, current_bid is the catalog key that determines the DHT key for catalog information and so the peer that maintains the AR. The group by field is the path $p_{group\_by}(x)$ = //bidder/item/@item_id = x. The p_{group_by} field essentially assigns each traded item to a different DHT key.

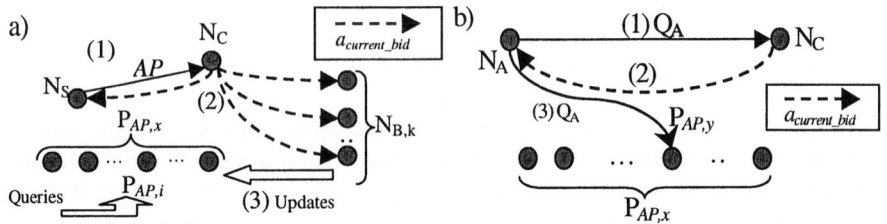

Fig. 1. a) Installation of an Aggregation Point b) Redirection of query Q_A to node $P_{AP,y}$

Under normal operation the catalog service would use *current_bid* to identify the relevant data sources. However, if an *AP* is installed, the mode of query processing changes. Each node uses *Aggregation Key Map* (AKM), which acts as a subscription system that associates catalog keys with their activation records. Fig. 1a outlines the process based on the commodity traders example. Suppose that peer N_S, which hosts sellers of commodity i decides to request the creation of the aggregation point *AP* that is defined by the activation record described in Table 1. The request will be forwarded to the peer N_C that holds catalog information for *current_bid* (step 1). N_C will generate the association $a_{current\_bid}$ = current_bid → $MAX_{GLOBAL}(p_{target}, p_{group\_by}(x))$ and insert it in the AKM. Note that multiple associations for a given key can exist in the AKM and they are selected based on the actual query. Then, N_C forwards $a_{current\_bid}$ to all peers $N_{B,k}$ that host bidders and to N_S (step 2). N_C knows about all such peers since it is hosting catalog information for *current_bid*. Upon receipt of $a_{current\_bid}$ each $N_{B,k}$ is expected to send updates about the current bid for all traded commodities to specific other peers that form the *set of aggregation point hosts* (**APH**) (step 3). The DHT layer, using the information in $a_{current\_bid}$, can uniquely determine each peer in **APH**. For example, for commodity item i, the APH $P_{AP,i}$ is determined by hashing the list (MAX, GLOBAL, p_{target}, $p_{group\_by}(i)$) to retrieve a DHT key k_i. Thus $P_{AP,i}$ becomes the maintainer of the requested aggregation for commodity i. Aggregation responsibility is tied to the key k_i and not to the peer $P_{AP,i}$. This way if $P_{AP,i}$ leaves, the DHT ensures that k_i points to a different peer.

The question that remains is how peers other than N_S find out about the new aggregation points. This turns out to be straightforward since N_C is the *designated* node for all inquiries regarding *current_bid* (Fig. 1b). Thus, any other node N_A which receives a query such as Q_A = MAX(//bidder/item [@item_id = y]/current_bid) will request catalog information from N_C (step 1). N_C will then provide N_A with the association $a_{current\_bid}$ (step 2). Having this information N_A can identify $P_{AP,y}$ as the peer to visit in order to obtain the answer to Q_A (step 3). Furthermore, N_A locally caches $a_{current\_bid}$ and thus only needs to contact N_C once.

The peers in **APH** can become heavily loaded if they are assigned very popular commodities. In this case load balancing is necessary. We have devised a method that deals with high request rates for both queries and updates. Due to space limitations we do not present the load balancing mechanisms. (see [4] for details).

4 Experimental Evaluation

The experiments are based on a *Distributed Commodity Trading* (DCT) scenario derived from [14]. The potential for eliminating the centralized auctioneer and the "fixed time trading rounds" ([14]) is the motivation to realize DCT. In our scenario traders are users of a large P2P network and buy and sell commodities. Each trader interchangeably follows a *seller session* or a *bidder session*. During a seller session the trader queries for the bidder with the maximum bid for one of its commodities and if successful proceeds with the sale. During a bidder session the trader tries to determine a reasonable bid for a commodity by querying the selling prices in the network. Thus, traders constantly query each other, which leads to the manifestation of the M2M problem. Complete description of the scenario is available in [4].

Table 2. Mean measured CPU and Disk service times of a peer running

Query Load	XPath	Catalog Lookups
CPU (ms ± ms)	540 ± 57	34 ± 11
Disk (ms ± ms)	1800 ± 324	75 ± 11

4.1 Experimental Methodology

We use simulation and a prototype system (Sect. 0) to evaluate our architecture. Simulations follow a two-step methodology that combines system measurements with simulation. First measurements were taken from a system that consists of an XPath query engine, a catalog layer and an aggregation layer (Section 0). This system was loaded with both trading data and catalog information. Then workloads of XPath queries, catalog information lookups and aggregate computations were executed and measurements were collected (Table 2), which yields the nominal peer performance ([4]). The XMark benchmark data generator [20] was used to generate about 1GB of data for auctions that have a structure similar to our trading scenario data. Catalog information lookups were measured using 256 MB of catalog data as described in [5]. The system used for measurements was a 2.4 GHz Pentium 4 PC running Linux with an IDE Hard Disk and 512 MB of RAM. To obtain variance across the peers during the simulations in the P2P network the nominal performance is multiplied by a factor that is uniformly distributed between 0.8 and 1.2. The second step involved building a discrete event simulation model using CSIM [1] consisting of nodes interconnected with a DHT. The nodes in the P2P network are modeled as single CPU, single disk workstations using the measurements from the first step. The prototype system experiments used our departmental cluster with 40 nodes similar to the one used for single node measurements.

4.2 Simulation Setup

Simulations for two peer-to-peer and one central server system were implemented. This section describes their characteristics and their basic differences. Both peer-to-peer systems simulate a DHT that is a generic version of Chord [22]. Following the observation made in [8] we did not use a detailed network model, opting instead for a simple delay model where network delays are exponentially distributed with a mean of 50ms. We assumed that network bandwidth was not a limiting factor since only a small amount of data is transferred in each network message. A catalog service as presented [5] is also present on both P2P systems and is used by traders to locate other traders.

The impact of network volatility on a peer-to-peer system depends on the specific DHT implementation. Therefore our experiments examine stable peer-to-peer systems in order to obtain results that are independent of the underlying DHT implementation and demonstrate the raw impact of the Aggregation Layer framework in improving performance.

The first P2P version that utilizes the aggregation layer has two variants: **AL** (Aggregation Layer) and **LBAL**. The difference is that the second variant employs load balancing (**LB**) [4]. The second P2P setup does not have an aggregation layer and comes in two variants **GC** (General Catalog) and **GCI**. **GC** utilizes the catalog service to discover traders, but directs XPath queries to the traders' peers in order to collect data values and compute the maximum bid and the minimum selling price. These XPath queries are issued *simultaneously* to all traders and the aggregate is computed after the results are retrieved. This setup suffers under the M2M query problem. The **GCI** variant utilizes a local index that makes XPath queries for retrieving bids and sale prices as fast as the aggregate computations and catalog information lookups in the variants **AL** and **LBAL**, and is used for a fairer comparison to **AL** and **LBAL**.

The central server system is intended as a reference point for evaluating the performance of the peer-to-peer variants. It consists of an ideal cluster of with as many nodes as the corresponding P2P system. The traders access their accounts from their workstations connected to the Internet, thus experiencing *network delay* for each query and update request. The central server system also comes in two variants: **CS** and **CSI**. The **CSI** variant employs the same fast local index as **GCI**.

4.3 Performance Results

The goals of this section are to determine the extent to which the aggregation layer improves performance and identify those cases where load balancing is required. A very important parameter in all configurations is the number of unique traded items T, which affects both P2P systems similarly. The smaller T is, the larger, on average, is the number of traders for a particular item. The consequence for each node in **GC** and **GCI**, and for each aggregation point in **AL** and **LBAL** is more requests on average.

The first series of experiments involved peer-to-peer networks from 100 to 100,000 nodes. The numbers of bidders and sellers in the P2P network are approximately equal and each node hosts one trader. The number of items assigned to each trader is uniformly distributed between 5 and 15. The popularity of the traded items follows the 80/20 rule (a.k.a. Pareto's principle) observed in many real world settings: 20% of the items are chosen by traders 80% of the time. The centralized versions of the system have exactly the same trader and commodity distributions. The configuration with 10,000 nodes is presented first to demonstrate our key findings when varying the number of unique traded items (commodities).

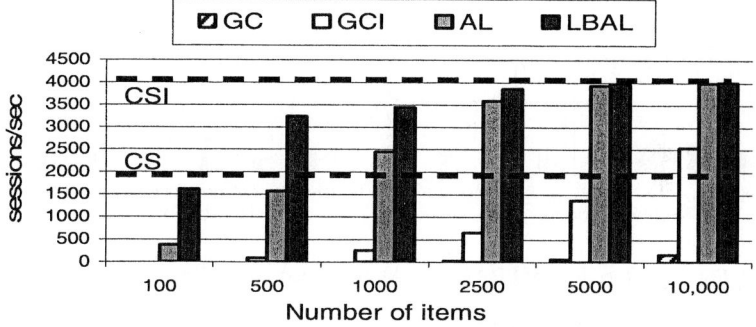

Fig. 2. Seller session throughput for 10,000 nodes

The throughput of seller sessions (Fig. 2) as a function of the different number of items traded is the first set of results presented (relative error at most 1% with 95% confidence). Bidder sessions follow a similar trend [4]. The throughput for **CS** and **CSI** is insensitive to the number of unique traded items (dashed lines). For both P2P systems a small variety of items has an adverse effect as expected. Nevertheless, the impact of a small number of items is more significant on **GC** and **GCI** than on **AL**. For 1000 items, the throughput of **AL** is 9.6 times better than **GCI** while for 10,000 items **AL** is 1.5 times better. At the same time as the number of items decreases, the need for load balancing becomes apparent: for over 2500 items **AL** and **LBAL** have similar performance. In the case of 100 items, however, **LBAL** is over 4 times better than **AL**.

Table 3. Average trader session durations for 10,000 nodes

#items	CS	CSI	GC	GCI	AL	LBAL
100	3.13 s	1.48 s	N/A	N/A	15.60 s	2.04 s
500			N/A	47.1 s	4.09 s	1.84 s
1000			236.1 s	22.9 s	2.61 s	1.79 s
2500			153.4 s	9.2 s	1.73 s	1.58 s
5000			72.0 s	4.41 s	1.56 s	1.52 s
10,000			30.2 s	2.24 s	1.51 s	1.49 s

Table 3 shows the average duration of traders' sessions. Session durations are indicative of the usability of each configuration. Short sessions imply short query response times, which in turn imply more accurate values for minimum sale price and maximum bid. The high session durations for **GC** and **GCI** show that they are not usable. As expected, **LBAL** does a very good job by keeping the duration of sessions below 2 sec. Without load balancing, the average session duration for **AL** with 100 items climbs to 15.6 sec. The throughput and response time numbers show that **GC** is virtually unusable. **GCI** is viable in the 5000 and 10,000 item setups but still lags far behind both **AL** and **LBAL** in terms of system throughput. The absence of data for **GC** (for 100 and 500 items) and **GCI** (for 100 items) was the result of event backlogs in the simulator, which led to high memory image sizes, forcing the simulations to abort.

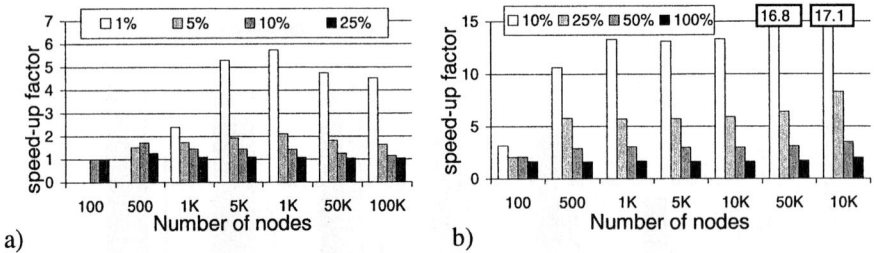

Fig. 3. a) Speed-up of LBAL over AL. b) Speed-up of LBAL over GCI.

While we have obtained results for a variety of network configurations, due to space limitations scalability results are summarized in Fig. 3a and Fig. 3b. Fig. 3a shows the speed-up of **LBAL** over **AL** in trader session throughput. The percentages in the legend denote the number of items in each network as a percentage of the total number of nodes. The graph, in essence, shows which combinations of network size and traded items make load balancing a necessity. For instance, in the 100 node network load balancing is not necessary. In the 500 node network the load balancing benefits are observable. In the larger networks load balancing of aggregate computations becomes a necessity as demonstrated by the achieved speed-up. Let $r = $ *number of unique traded items / number of nodes*. In large networks (number of nodes > 1000) the smaller r is, the larger is the speed-up of **LBAL** over **AL** due to load balancing. These results suggest that if $r \geq 25\%$ the speed-up achieved using load balancing is not significant.

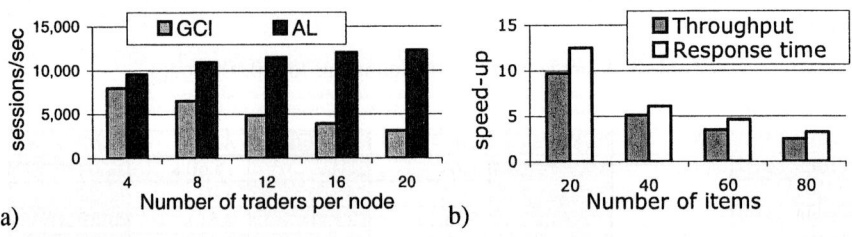

Fig. 4. a) Combined trader throughput for 10,000 nodes, 50,000 unique items and varying number of traders b) Speed-up of PAL over PGC

Fig. 3b shows the trader session throughput speed-up of **LBAL** over **GCI**. The percentages have the same meaning as in Fig. 3a. The percentages are now larger as **GCI** would not work on large networks (>10,000) with a small variety of traded items. **GCI** appears somewhat usable when the number of traded items is large (>50% of total number of nodes): With $r = 50\%$ **GCI** is about two to four times slower than the systems with the aggregation layer (**AL**, **LBAL**). For $r = 10\%$ or 25% **GCI** is clearly not scalable, which is indicated by the increasing speed-up.

Fig. 4a shows how the combined session throughput varies with the number of traders per node in **GCI** and **AL**. The network has 10,000 nodes and 50,000 unique items, which favors **GCI**. While **AL** starts out slightly better than **GCI** it becomes 4 times better (20 traders).

4.4 Prototype Experiments

We implemented a prototype system to confirm the simulation results. The system is written in Java and uses Pastry [16] as the DHT and Berkeley DB XML as the storage and query engine layer, which is accessed through the Java native interface. For the experiment we used 40 machines from our departmental Linux cluster. A trader with 15 commodities, on average, is emulated on each machine. The non-aggregation layer configuration **PGC** corresponds to **GCI** in our simulations and the aggregation layer configuration **PAL** corresponds to **AL**. Due to space constraints we only present Fig. 4b that shows the speedup of trader sessions of **PAL** over **PGC** achieved in the system with 40 nodes and a varying number of unique commodities (items). The aggregation layer achieves significant speed-up in a working prototype system and confirms the simulation results.

5 Related Work

Related work in P2P architectures has been mentioned in Sect.1. Here we present work more closely related to distributed aggregation, which is a relatively new subject in the context of P2P systems. Willow [16] organizes nodes in a single tree. Aggregate computations percolate automatically up the tree whenever there are data changes or new aggregate queries are installed. However, these updates are not instantaneous and converge eventually. The Aggregation Layer presented here follows a best-effort approach by having a flat structure. SOMO [25] similar to our approach layers on top of a DHT and, like Willow, organizes the aggregate computations in a tree. SOMO has a generic gathering procedure that can be programmed to perform aggregate computation. This procedure is invoked periodically, in contrast to the updates and requests to the aggregation points of the Aggregation Layer, which are on demand. The aforementioned projects are a sample of many similar ongoing projects addressing distributed aggregation in P2P systems.

SCRIBE [19] is an application layer multicast publish/subscribe system that uses a PASTRY [16] to define rendezvous points for managing group communication on a specific topic. It uses topic identifiers to assign topics to peers similarly to our use of catalog keys to assign aggregation points to peers. A basic difference between our approach and SCRIBE is that aggregation point hosts do not implement publish/subscribe functionality, and are thus much simpler. Their purpose is to passively collect data and maintain an always up-to-date aggregate. Distributed aggregation methods in [10] presents distributed aggregate computations using gossip-based protocols in P2P networks. Its focus, however, is on how quickly aggregate computations converge to the actual value and not how to facilitate large volumes of aggregate queries over distributed data sets.

6 Conclusions

In this paper we presented the case for the many-to-many query problem that is bound to be a concern in very large distributed systems where queries require data from multiple data sources. Using existing technology we developed a framework that can solve this problem for a broad class of important queries by harnessing the resources of the peers in the distributed system. Our experimental evaluation using both simulations and a real working prototype shows how severe the M2M problem can be and how our architecture efficiently solves it in a P2P environment.

References

1. CSIM Development Toolkit for Simulation and Modeling. http://www.mesquite.com.
2. F. Dabek, M. F. Kaashoek, D. Karger, R. Morris, I. Stoica. Wide-area cooperative storage with CFS. SOSP 2001.
3. FreeNet. http://www.freenetproject.org
4. L. Galanis. Towards a Data-Centric Internet. Ph.D. Thesis. 2004 Univ. of Wisconsin.
5. L. Galanis, Y. Wang, S. R. Jeffery, D. J. DeWitt. Locating Data Sources in Large Distributed Systems. VLDB 2003
6. Gnutella Resources. http://gnutella.wego.com/
7. J. M. Hellerstein. Toward Network Data Independence. SIGMOD Record, Vol. 32, No. 3, Sept. 2003.
8. R. Huebsch, J. M. Hellerstein, N. Langam, B. T. Loo, S. Shenker, I. Stoica. Querying the Internet with PIER. VLDB 2003
9. Kazaa. http://www.kazaa.com.
10. D. Kempe, A. Dobra, J. Gehrke: Gossip-Based Computation of Aggregate Information. FOCS 2003
11. J. Kubiatowicz et al. OceanStore: An Architecture for Global-Scale Persistent Storage. In Proc. ASPLOS 2000.
12. Napster. http://www.napster.com
13. Network Time Protocol (NTP). http://www.ntp.org.
14. E. Ogston, S. Vassiliadis. A Peer-to-Peer Agent Auction. AAMAS'02.
15. S. Ratnasamy, P. Francis, M. Handley, R. Karp, S. Shenker. A Scalable Content-Addressable Network. in Proc. of the 2001 Conference on Applications, Technologies, Architectures, and Protocols for Computer Communications.
16. R. van Renesse and A. Bozdog. Willow: DHT, Aggregation, and Publish/Subscribe in One Protocol. International Workshop on Peer-to-Peer Systems (IPTPS) 2004.
17. Rowstron, P. Druschel, Pastry. Scalable, distributed object location and routing for large-scale peer-to-peer systems. IFIP/ACM Intl. Conference on Distributed Systems Platforms.

18. Rowstron, P. Druschel. Storage management and caching in PAST, a large-scale, persistent peer-to-peer storage utility. SOSP 2001.
19. Rowstron, A. Kermarrec, M. Castro, P. Druschel. Scribe: The design of a large-scale event notification infrastructure. Intl. Workshop on Networked Group Communication 2001.
20. Schmidt, F. Waas, M. Kersten, M. J. Carey, I. Manolescu, R. Busse. XMark. A Benchmark for XML Data Management. VLDB 2002.
21. S. Shenker. The Data-Centric Revolution in Networking. Keynote VLDB 2003.
22. Stoica, R. Morris, D. Karger, M.F. Kaashoek, H. Balakrishnan. Chord: A Scalable Peer-to-Peer Lookup Service for Internet Applications. SIGCOMM 2001.
23. XML Path Language (XPath) 2.0 http://www.w3.org/TR/xpath20/
24. XML Extensible Markup Language. http://www.w3.org/XML.
25. Z. Zhang, S. –M. Shi and J. Zhu. SOMO: Self-Organized Metadata Overlay for Resource Management in P2P DHT. International Workshop on Peer-to-Peer Systems (IPTPS) 2003.
26. Y. Zhao, J. Kubiatowicz, A. Joseph. Tapestry: An Infrastructure for Fault-tolerant Wide-area Location and Routing. UCB Tech. Report UCB/CSD-01-1141.

Schemas and Queries over P2P

Pedro Furtado

DEI /CISUC, Universidade de Coimbra, Polo II, Portugal
pnf@dei.uc.pt

Abstract. Query processing in overlay networks has been receiving significant attention from researchers recently. Such systems offer flexibility and de-centralization. The challenge is to add representation and query capacity in such a networked environment, resulting in a peer-to-peer data management system. The issue of how schemas can be incorporated and queried in p2p while abiding to the de-centralized and flexible philosophy has not been properly handled. In this paper we analyze constructs and strategies to build database-like schemas and process simple queries over those schemas on P2P. For this we describe schema spaces, attribute value locators and data shipment issues. We also engage in experimental work to analyze our proposals using a network simulator to test the strategies with different networked scenarios.

1 Introduction

An overlay network is formed by a subset of the underlying physical network nodes. The connections between overlay nodes are provided by overlay links (IP-layer paths), each of which is usually composed of one or more physical paths. Peer-to-peer systems form such an overlay network that can be used in several applications such as data sharing over thousands of participants in a decentralized and scalable way. One of the major issues in unstructured P2P systems was the poor scalability and unnecessary overhead associated with message flooding that was necessary in order to route messages to nodes. The content-based lookup of DHT-based (structured) P2P systems improves significantly object retrieval efficiency by eliminating the need to flood the system for object location. Examples of structured P2P systems include Chord [11] or CAN[7]. These systems provide simultaneously a very flexible de-centralized networked environment over which more complex data representation and querying constructs than basic file sharing can be implemented. For instance, instead of simply sharing music files by some ID, a database schema representing musicians, songs, records and the like can be setup and queried on the networked environment. Together with querying functionality come schemas in every flavor (semi-structured, XML, RDF, relational or object models). Currently, there is a significant research effort into finding efficient ways of incorporating full data management functionality this context. Although there are other works on querying over P2P, the issue of providing primitives for schemas to be incorporated and queried efficiently within P2P while maintaining the flexibility and de-centralization has been neglected. In order to maintain the flexibility and de-centralization, there should be no super-peers or a one-in-charge architecture, but rather peers and distributed schema requirements that should be met. Our focus is on this subject and on query processing over a distributed relational schema implemented on P2P. In this paper we concentrate on handling the schema and basic querying efficiently. We motivate the need for schema (sub)spaces, as the linear address space of a large DHT-P2P system is inadequate to represent every schema. We propose a simple approach to defining those subspaces, thereof called "Schema Spaces". Schema Spaces should adhere to the P2P decentralized and flexible organization and addressing scheme, while still accommodating different schema requirements. We also discuss constructs to handle basic querying efficiently and evaluate the advantage of such constructs in the experimental section. Without content-based indexing, data can only be retrieved by broadcasting the request. We define how attributes and expressions can be indexed by an attribute value locator (AVL) structure and discuss the advantage of such strategy. We describe how queries are processed and also discuss queries requiring data shipment between nodes. In the experimental section we consider different networked scenarios and test the strategies in those scenarios.

The paper is organized as follows: section 2 discusses related work. Section 3 introduces the architecture of the Peer Partitioned Data Management (PPDM) platform. Schema representation and use is discussed in section 4. In section 5 we discuss efficient query processing. Section 6 contains simulation results and section 7 concludes the paper.

2 Related Work

As we already mentioned in the introduction, structured P2P systems (e.g. CAN [7], Chord [11], Pastry [10]) use some DHT (Distributed Hash Table), whereby object identifiers are hashed onto a corresponding node and location queries are routed into the correct node without flooding. Typical DHT-based structured P2P systems split the key space into zones and assign each zone to a peer. Given an object, the DHT uses a hash function over the object identifier to determine the node where the object or its location information should be. Each peer on the path passes the request to one of its neighbors, which is closer to the destination in the virtual space. This is a location query, whose answer contains the object or the peer identifiers where the object is stored. The requester then retrieves the object from one of the identified peers. This basic routing approach avoids costly message flooding and was designed for typical object sharing applications among peers (e.g. files) in a scalable and flexible fashion. Topology-aware overlay networks can be built using Skipnet [3] and/or the scheme in [6], which uses the distances to landmarks to cluster nodes into locality bins. MAAN [2] and RDFPeers[1] are Multi-Attribute Addressable Networks which extends Chord to support multi-attribute and range queries. Range queries are addressed by mapping attribute values to the Chord identifier space via uniform locality preserving hashing. In [13] tuple attributes are hashed for content-based access. We use similar strategies in our query processor but define an attribute value locator, generalize its use to expressions, describe how queries are processed and test and compare the strategies experimentally. More complex queries have also been dealt with partially in [13] and in PIER [4] using strategies such as parallel hash-join. None of these cited works or others deal effectively with the address space issue in P2P when it is necessary to represent schemas in a flexible way. We do so by offering primitives to define subspaces – schema spaces. We also discuss generic constructs to process basic queries on PPDM and show how those queries are handled given the schema spaces. PPDM also optimizes the processing of "complex" queries involving heavy joining and/or aggregation functionality, but we discuss optimization elsewhere and instead concentrate on basic query handling here.

3 Peer-Partitioned Data Manager - PPDM

Figure 1 provides an overview of the PPDM modules. The P2P Routing and Location module (RL) is responsible for locating an object and for routing messages over the underlying overlay network architecture. The P2P Storage Manager (SM) is responsible for the administration of object persistence. This includes storage, retrieval, replication and migration of objects in response to requests. It uses the Routing and Data Location module (RL) to locate the data. The node manager (NM) is responsible for adding and removing nodes from the system. Finally, the Data Manager (DM) handles schema definition, indexing and querying. Most of these modules are simply part of and managed by the P2P system: "Routing and Data Location (RL)"; "Node Manager (NM)". The "Storage Manager (SM)" module must be able to handle data schemas in nodes containing schemas. Nodes participating in the storage and processing of complex queries are expected to have a simple data management engine (DBE) as part of the storage manager (SM) to handle local data management. The DBE should be able to handle storage, indexing and querying locally. In most of the discussion from now on we assume data is organized in the DBE as relational tuples with a metadata identifying their structure, although other models can be modeled and processed in a similar manner (e.g. RDF and XML). The added data manager module (DM) offers the data management functionality typical of a DBMS on top of the P2P functionality, including definition and querying over schemas.

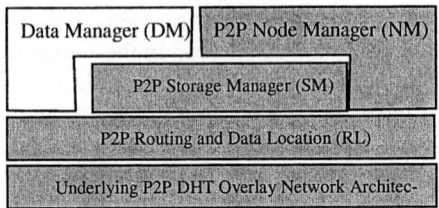

Fig. 1. PPDM Modules

4 Schema Definition and Use

In order to allow multiple schema spaces in an overlay such as Chord [11], there must be a primitive for some node to create a subspace as an overlay network (space). Assuming user x wishes to create a smaller space S2 on a Chord overlay with up to 2^7 nodes to hold some schema, he can issue the command CREATE_ChordSpace("S2",7). A subspace is a space with the added restriction that all nodes in it must belong to a parent space. If such a restriction is to be imposed on

S2, then the parent space must also be indicated: CREATE ChordSpace("S2",7,"S1"). The basic Chord ring requires each node to maintain information on neighbors: the successor list and the finger table. The nodes in the successor list and the finger table pointing at nodes spaced exponentially around the identifier space. Therefore, each node needs to maintain the state of O(log N) neighbors. If a node belongs to the representation of x spaces, it must maintain the state of O(x log N) neighbors. For query processing efficiency, it should also be possible to create spaces with desired locality characteristics. This could be done by specifying which nodes to insert into the space or using automatic topologically-oriented creation of spaces. Internet domain name prefixes (DNS) or the binning strategy of [6] can be used to implement this. The binning strategy uses landmarks to estimate latencies [5, 12] and clusters nodes into bins according to distance order to the landmark set.

We assume a relational model and SQL and concentrate on enabling the representation of any schema through a metadata that defines entities (relations), attributes and relationships between entities (references). Node x as the creator and owner of a schema labelled "Travelling", creates the schema on space Sx: CREATE_Schema("Travelling", Sx). Relations are created using the SQL Data Definition Language, but the creator (an administrator) must indicate the schema where the relation is to be created, storage options and indexing attributes. Storage options define where and how relation tuples should be stored. The layout option specifies whether relations are fully replicated, partitioned or placed in a single location: partition by x (default, the objects will be DHT-hashed into nodes by key x); replicate (the objects will be replicated into all nodes), useful for small immutable (reference) relations; single location (tuples of relation are placed in a single node). For partitioned relations (the default) one attribute should be indicated as hash-key to determine the placement (Partition by x). This attribute determines the clustering into nodes and can be the primary key of the relation or some other attribute. For instance, consider relations flight(fn°, origin, destination, departure, ...) and airport(designation, place, ...). The following example creates relations for these in schema S1. The relation flight is partitioned by fn°. Relation Airport is replicated into all nodes.

>CREATE TABLE flight(...) in schema S1 Partition by fn°;
>CREATE TABLE airport(...) in schema S1 replicate;

5 Querying Schemas

In this section we discuss how generic lookup queries are handled - queries looking for specific objects typically resident in one or a small set of nodes. We also discuss queries involving "data shipment", that is, queries for which it is necessary to ship data between nodes in order to process the query. A basic knowledge of routing strategies is important to follow the discussion. Therefore, we briefly discuss routing and broadcasting in the context of Chord before the remaining discussion.

5.1 Basic Chord Routing and Broadcasting

Chord ([11]) organizes nodes in an identifier circle modulo 2^m, called the Chord ring. The basic Chord ring requires each node to maintain information on neighbours. As discussed in the previous section, finger tables (2^k, k=0,...,log2N-1) allow each node to maintain the state of only O(log N) neighbours. Chord hashes both the key of a data object and a peer's IP address into an m-bit identifier. The keys' identifiers map to peers' identifiers using consistent hashing (i.e. a function succ(id), where id is the identifier for the data object's key). For a lookup query, the object key is hashed and the resulting succ(id) node is sought. The node chooses a finger to hop nearer the succ(id) (e.g. the hop that approximates most to succ(id) node). This process is repeated by the next nodes until the succ(id) node is reached and returns the object to the requester. It is straightforward to see that Chord requires O(logN) routing hops for these location/routing operations. In order to use the routing strategy described above, it is necessary for the object to be indexed by the DHT hash-key, otherwise flooding or broadcasting must be used. The authors of [5] proposed a broadcasting strategy for Chord without flooding or sending more than one message into the same node. A user entity initiates the broadcast by submitting broadcast(info) to a node Q. This node acts as a root to a (virtual) broadcast spanning tree. The spanning tree is built as follows: node Q forwards the message into neighbours with a limit parameter that restricts the forwarding space of a receiving node: broadcast(info,limit). The limit parameter for a forward into Finger[i] is set to Finger[i+1], meaning that each neighbour Finger[i] will forward only within the interval [Finger[i], Finger[i+1][. Finger[i] will therefore not forward into neighbours (fingers) pointing beyond this interval because another neighbour is taking care of forwarding into those nodes. This forwarding is now applied recursively, forming the spanning tree. As all nodes are contacted once, broadcasting has a cost N-1 in number of messages and log N in number of hops (because nodes have a logarithmically decreasing forwarding range). In comparison, unicasting (lookup query) had a cost log N in number of messages and log N in hops.

5.2 Lookup Queries

Consider a query accessing one or more tuples of a relation based on an attribute value. If the attribute is the hash-key, only a single node has to be looked up. This takes up to log N hops (number of Chord hops to reach any node). Otherwise, a broadcast of the query into all the schema space would be necessary to lookup the tuple. Although this also takes up to log N hops (number of Chord hops to reach any node), broadcasting a request generates a large traffic over the network, which potentially degrades the performance of the whole system. A much more efficient and scalable alternative can be found by hash-indexing other attributes into nodes. Content-based access for attributes other than the hash-key or expressions can be implemented using "Attribute Value Locator" (AVL) structures. We define the AVL as an abstract structure (that is, with alternative physical implementations). A simple AVL abstract structure has the format:

$AVL[a_i, rel](v_l, tr_l)$

In this structure, a_i is an attribute or expression on attributes and *rel* is a relation, so that $AVL[a_i, R_j]$ is the structure used for content-based access to attribute/expression a_i of relation R_j. For each tuple of R_j with value v_i for the expression, this structure $AVL[a_i, R_j]$ represents a pair (v_l, tr_l) that is hashed by v_l into a node of the schema space. The parameter tr_l is a reference to the node and rowid of the tuple within the node. An additional "indirection step" is required then to locate the tuples. As an example, suppose an AVL[*destination, flight*] is built. Given a query: SELECT fn° WHERE destination="LONDON", the query processor hashes the value 'LONDON' to obtain the node to lookup the AVL[destination, flight] structure. Then it looks in that node for tuples AVL[destination, flight]('LONDON',tr_i) and uses tr_i to retrieve the tuples satisfying the condition from the corresponding nodes. The following command modifies the relation to include AVLs for origin and destination:

ALTER TABLE flight(...)
   MODIFY origin AVL, destination AVL;

This basic AVL functionality also supports multi-attribute conditions by allowing the specification of expressions and multiple values as v_i instead of single attributes. Lookup queries are processed as follows: consider a lookup query (e_i, v_v) (expression e_i with value v_i). A request is built with (e_i, v_v) and the requester IP;

```
IF lookup value attribute is oid (DHT-hashed)
         route request into lookup node using hash(vi)
ELSE IF there is some AVL indexing the expression
route request into AVL holding node using hash(v)
determine lookup nodes from AVLs
         route request to lookup node(s)
ELSE broadcast request to all nodes
```

The lookup nodes must then get the tuple(s) and return them to the requester:

submit the request query on their DBE
reply to the requester IP with answer(s)

Finally the requester merges the answers to get the final result. Figure 2 summarizes the steps taken:

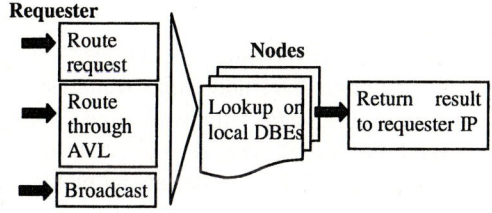

Fig. 2. Flow for Lookup Query

5.3 Queries with Data Shipment

Data shipment concerns queries whose processing requires data shipment between nodes before a final answer can be computed and returned to the requester. This is a typical scenario in distributed databases and may entail a semi-join or shipping all needed attributes from one node into the other one. The main difference in comparison to the simple lookup query is that now the processing of the query requires data to be shipped between nodes. As an example of a query requiring data shipment, consider a pair of relations placed in different nodes. Data has to be forwarded from one node to the other to process a join between them (typical issue in distributed databases):

Node X:
flight(fn°, originAirport, destAirport, departure, ...)
Query:
   select A.place "FROM", B.place "TO", departure from flight F, airport A, airport B
   where F.originAirport=A.airp_id and F.destAirport=B.airp_id;

Node Y:
airport(airp_id, designation, place, ...)

In this case, either the airport relation (part of it) is shipped to node X or flight (part of it) is shipped into node Y to process the query. Both the final query answer and the data that needs to be shipped can be small or very large. The algorithm is similar to the previous one but with an added data shipment step shown in Figure 3.

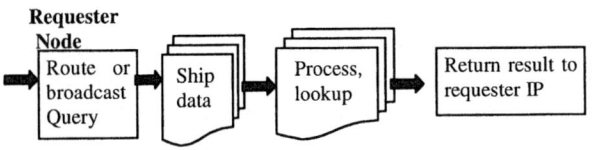

Fig. 3. Flow with Data Shipment

6 Experimental Results

Our objective in this section is to analyze the overheads involved in processing lookup and data shipment queries on the PPDM on a networked environment.

We devised an inter-network with three subnet categories, based mainly on link latency/bandwidth considerations. The objective was to test the constructs considering nodes with varied inter-node "costs": LOCAL - high-speed local network (LAN-like with inter-node latencies of 0.1ms); intermediate "HUBS" - intermediate latency interconnects (inter-node latencies of 1ms); GLOBAL – larger latency interconnections (inter-node la-tencies of 4ms). This is similar to a transit-stub (TS) topology [15] but considering 3 network categories. Inter-node links were also generated following a strategy similar to [15]. The experimental setup was based on the generation of four 100 node hubs linked through the transit network. Each hub harbored five 200 node LANs. From these nodes we generated three node sets by picking nodes randomly: a LOCAL set based on picking nodes from a LAN; a CLOCAL set, by picking nodes from all LANs within a single HUB (cluster of LANs); a GLOBAL set, by picking nodes randomly from all LANs, therefore going through all hubs. The experimental results are based on superimposing a Chord overlay on top of the network simulation. We discuss mostly data exchange time – the time taken to route a query request into lookup nodes and to return the answer. We do not discuss the time taken to process the query in the lookup nodes against their DBE (query engine) because that time would be dependent on the size of the data set and the characteristics of the query engine and indexing structures.

6.1 Simple Lookup

As discussed in section 5, the lookup query involves routing or broadcasting a request through the overlay, processing it and returning the requested data. It is expected to take at most log N hops in Chord (the number of hops needed to reach the destination node), but when AVLs are used to answer the query, there is another indirection step, increasing the time-to-route. Figure 4 (log-scale) shows in solid lines the data exchange time – lookup request plus returning the answer – when the lookup is "direct" (DHT-hashed attribute) and in dashed lines the extra overhead of the indirection step when an AVL is used (-i). The results are shown considering local, clocal or global access with respect to both request and indirection step. The overhead of AVL indirection shown in the figure is not large in absolute terms, although it does introduce a delay especially when the lookup node is near but the AVL hash node is far. Of course the overhead can also increase if the latencies are larger than those used in the experiments (0.1ms local, 1 ms clocal and 4 ms global). The advantage of AVL over flooding or broadcasting is expressed in Figure 5, which shows the amount of traffic generated in our experiments – measured in average number of messages per request - considering 100 requests/millisecond randomly divided by 1k, 10k or 100k nodes. Flooding or broadcasting result in a much larger amount of traffic.

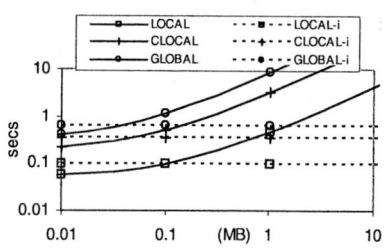

Fig. 4. Simple Lookup (secs) **Fig. 5.** Traffic Brodcast vs AVL

6.2 Data Shipment

In Figure 6 (log-plot) we analyze the time taken to answer a query requiring data shipment. For simplicity we fixed the query result size in 100KB. The times shown concern:

"request" - time to route the request using chord routing, plus time to send the answer back to the requester;

"ship" - time to ship data between processing nodes, measured against the size of the data to be shipped.

Both the request and the data shipment may be local, clocal or global. The corresponding request and shipment times are to be summed to obtain the data exchange time. From this figure we can see that if the sizes of the data that may need to be shipped are relevant, it is important to have latency locality for the schema (local ship), because otherwise the shipment overhead becomes significant when compared to the request overhead (e,.g. in these experiments shipping 100MB over the global network took almost 1000 seconds versus 42 seconds on a local schema).

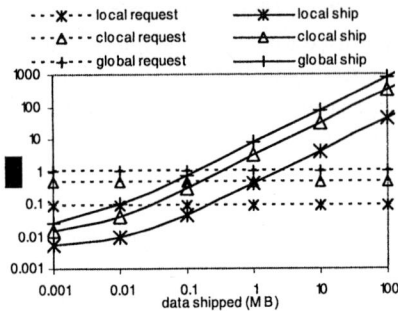

Fig. 6. Request and Shipment Times

Both the request and the data shipment may be local, clocal or global. The corresponding request and shipment times are to be summed to obtain the data exchange time. From this figure we can see that if the sizes of the data that may need to be shipped are relevant, it is important to have latency locality for the schema (local ship), because otherwise the shipment overhead becomes significant when compared to the request overhead (e,.g. in these experiments shipping 100MB over the global network took almost 1000 seconds versus 42 seconds on a local schema).

7 Conclusions

In this paper we have analyzed how to manage schemas and process simple queries efficiently in a flexible P2P environment. We have shown that it should be possible to define subspaces and schemas within those subspaces and analyzed the importance of latency-locality in those schemas. We have also discussed the processing of lookup queries in such environments and proposed an abstract "Attribute Value Locator" structure to support lookup queries on non-hashed attributes or expressions. We have setup a networked simulator experimental environment that was used to test the issues raised by the proposals. We conclude that the discussion and constructs used in the Peer-to-Peer Data Management architecture are useful for handling schema representation and query processing in a networked environment.

References

1. Cai M., M. Frank, J. Chen, and P. Szekely. A Scalable Distributed RDF Repository based on A Structured Peer-to-Peer Network. In Proceedings of the 13th international conference on World Wide Web, New York, NY, USA.
2. Cai M., M. Frank, J. Chen, and P. Szekely. MAAN: A multi-attribute addressable network for grid information services. In 4th Int'l Workshop on Grid Computing, 2003.
3. Harvey N., Michael B. Jones, Stefan Saroiu, Marvin Theimer, Alec Wolman: SkipNet: A Scalable Overlay Network with Practical Locality Properties. USENIX Symposium on Internet Technologies and Systems 2003.
4. Huebsch R. et al. "Querying the Internet with PIER", in VLDB 2003: 321-332.

5. Ng T. E. and H. Zang. Predicting Internet Network Distance with Coordinates-Based Approaches. In the 21st IEEE INFOCOMM, June 2002.
6. Ratnasamy S., Mark Handley, Richard M. Karp, Scott Shenker: Topologically-Aware Overlay Construction and Server Selection. INFOCOM 2002.
7. Ratnasamy S., P. Francis, M. Handley, R. Karp, and S. Shenker. A scalable content addressable network. In ACM SIGCOMM, 2001.
8. RDF Schema: http://www.w3.org/TR/rdf-schema. World-Wide Web Consortium.
9. Ripeanu M., I. Foster, and A. Iamnitchi. Mapping the Gnutella network: Properties of large-scale peer-to-peer systems and implications for system design. IEEE Internet Computing Journal, 6(1), 2002.
10. Rowstron A. and P. Druschel. Pastry: Scalable, decentralized object location, and routing for large-scale peer-to-peer systems. Lecture Notes in Comp.Science, 2218, 2001.
11. Stoica I., R. Morris, D. Karger, F. Kaashoek, and H. Balakrishnan. Chord: A scalable peer-to-peer lookup service for internet applications. In ACM SIGCOMM, 2001.
12. Szymaniak M. et al. "Scalable Latency Estimation", in Intl. Conf. on Parallel and Distributed Systems, ICPADS, Newport Beach, USA, July 2004.
13. Triantafillou P., Theoni Pitoura: Towards a Unified Framework for Complex Query Processing Over Structured Peer-to-Peer Data Networks. HDMS 2003.
14. Zhao B. Y., J. D. Kubiatowicz, and A. D. Joseph. Tapestry: An infrastructure for fault-tolerant wide-area location and routing. Tech. Report CSD-01-1141, UC Berkeley, 2001.
15. E. Zegura, K. Calvert, and S. Bhattacharjee, "How to Model an Internetwork," in Proceedings IEEE Infocom '96, CA, May 1996.

Threshold Based Declustering in High Dimensions

Ali Şaman Tosun

Department of Computer Science,
University of Texas at San Antonio,
San Antonio, TX 78249
tosun@cs.utsa.edu

Abstract. Declustering techniques reduce query response times through parallel I/O by distributing data among multiple devices. Except for a few cases it is not possible to find declustering schemes that are optimal for all spatial range queries. As a result of this, most of the research on declustering have focused on finding schemes with low worst case additive error. Recently, constrained declustering that maximizes the threshold k such that all spatial range queries $\leq k$ buckets are optimal is proposed. In this paper, we extend constrained declustering to high dimensions. We investigate high dimensional bound diagrams that are used to provide upper bound on threshold and propose a method to find good threshold-based declustering schemes in high dimensions. We show that using replicated declustering with threshold N, low worst case additive error can be achieved for many values of N. In addition, we propose a framework to find thresholds in replicated declustering.

1 Introduction

Many emerging database applications including geographical information systems and scientific visualization demand effective storage and efficient retrieval of spatial data In these applications, the data objects are usually represented as two-dimensional vectors, and a correlation between objects is defined by a distance function between corresponding vectors. For example, in GIS, objects can be defined with their coordinates (longitude and latitude) and the distance between them is defined as the geographical distance of the real entities. A common type of query is the range query, where the user specifies an area of interest (usually a rectangular region) and all data points in this area are retrieved. Typical spatial data applications include large data repositories. Therefore, efficient retrieval and scalable storage of large spatial data becomes more important.

Several retrieval structures and methods have been proposed for retrieval of spatial data [17,3,21,13]. Traditional retrieval methods based on index structures developed for single disk and single processor environments are becoming ineffective for the storage and retrieval in multiple processor and multiple disk environments. Since the amount of data is large, it is very natural to use multi-device/disk architectures in these systems. Besides scalability with respect to storage, multi-disk architectures give the opportunity to exploit I/O parallelism during retrieval. The most crucial part of exploiting I/O parallelism is to develop storage techniques of the data so that the data can be accessed in parallel. A common approach for efficient parallel I/O is as follows. The data space is partitioned into disjoint regions, and data is allocated to multiple disks. When users issue a query, data falling into disjoint partitions is retrieved in parallel from multiple disks. This technique is referred to as *declustering* and can be summarized as a good way of distributing data to multiple I/O devices.

To process a range query, all buckets that intersect the query need to be accessed from secondary storage. The minimum possible cost when retrieving b buckets distributed over N devices is $\lceil \frac{b}{N} \rceil$. An allocation policy is said to be *strictly optimal* if no query, which retrieves b buckets, has more than $\lceil \frac{b}{N} \rceil$ buckets allocated to the same device. It is impossible to reach strict optimality for spatial range queries [1] and the lower bound on extra disk accesses is proved to be $\Omega(\log N)$ for N disks even in the restricted case of N-by-N grid [5]. A large number of declustering techniques have been proposed to achieve performance close to the bounds either on the average case [9,19,10,14,16,15,11,4,20,18] or in the worst case [6,2,5,7].

Most of the declustering techniques in the literature assume only one copy of the data. Replication is a well-studied and effective solution for several problems in a database context, especially for fault tolerance and performance purposes. Recently, replicated declustering received a lot of interest. Replicated declustering for spatial range queries with goals of providing *strict optimality* is investigated and it has been shown that using 2 copies it is possible to achieve strict optimality for up to 15 disks and using 3 copies it is possible to achieve strict optimality for up to 50 disks [22,12]. For arbitrary queries it has been shown that using 2 copies b buckets can be retrieved in at most $\lceil \sqrt{b} \rceil$ disk accesses [23] and using design-theoretic scheme [25] with c copies $(c-1)k^2 + ck$ buckets can be retrieved in at most k disk accesses. Schemes for replicated declustering of range queries are proposed in [8]. One of the schemes uses an efficient single copy declustering scheme as the first copy and spreads the second copy uniformly. The well-studied Random Duplicate Allocation (RCA) algorithm chooses disks uniformly at random for storage of buckets. RCA doesn't provide any deterministic bounds but provides a rather nice probabilistic bound. The worst case additive error of RCA is at most 1 with high probability. However, a max-flow algorithm needs to be solved for retrieval of buckets and max-flow algorithms are computationally expensive.

Recently, constrained declustering based on thresholds is proposed for 2-dimensional data [24]. The goal is to maximize the threshold k such that all spatial range queries $\leq k$ buckets are optimal is proposed. Upper bound of threshold is about $\frac{N}{2}$ and threshold algorithm finds schemes with threshold better than $\frac{N}{4}$ in 2 dimensions.

In this paper, we extend constrained declustering to high dimensions. We investigate many issues that arise in high dimensions including construction of

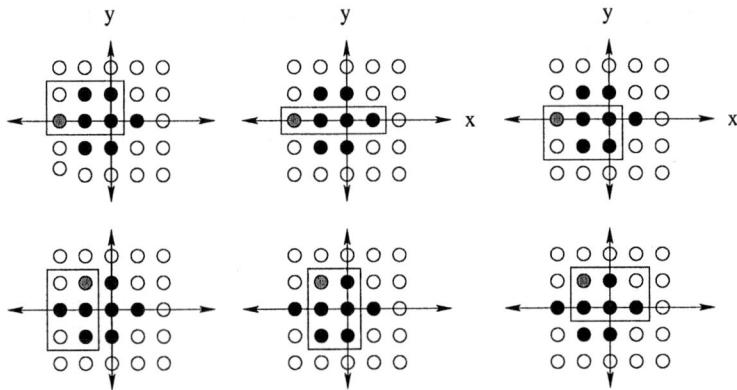

Fig. 1. Example of bound diagram for 6

high dimensional bound diagrams, achievable thresholds in high dimensions and implications for replicated declustering.

The rest of the paper is organized as follows: in section 2 we explain how to construct bound diagrams in high dimensions, in section 3 we discuss implications of high dimensional threshold-based declustering on replicated declustering and we conclude in section 4.

2 High-Dimensional Bound Diagrams

Constrained declustering [24] investigates schemes that maximizes the threshold k such that all spatial range queries with $\leq k$ buckets are optimal. Bound diagrams are introduced to find upper bound on maximum threshold achievable in a 2-dimensional N-by-N declustering system with N disks. Given a threshold value k, the idea is to place as many points as possible in a grid without violating the constraint that any two points appear together in a rectangle (spatial range query) with $\leq k$ buckets. The implication being that to achieve a threshold of k we need to have at least as many disks as the number of points in the bound diagram. There are multiple bound diagrams for a given k. One bound diagram for $k = 6$ is given in figure 1. Each row in the figure shows the rectangles with area ≤ 6 in which the gray point appears with other points. Second row of the figure shows the rectangles for another gray point. Similarly, it can be shown that every pair of points appear together in a rectangle with ≤ 6 elements. White nodes in the figure represents other nodes in the declustered system. This bound diagram has 8 elements. This means to achieve a threshold of 6 at least 8 disks are needed.

We next give bound diagram constructions in high dimensions. We use the notation $\mathbb{Z}$ for the set of integers and bound diagram in d-dimensions is a subset of $\mathbb{Z}_1 \times \mathbb{Z}_2 \times ... \times \mathbb{Z}_d$. Subscript is used to help explain the fact that there are d terms. Our fundamental result is the following theorem. l_1 distance between 2 d-dimensional points x and y is defined as $l_1(x,y) = \sum_{k=1}^{d} |x_k - y_k|$. We use the distance to show that any points appear together in a rectangle with $\leq$ threshold buckets.

Theorem 1. $B(d,a) = \{x | l_1(x,o) \leq a\}$ is a d-dimensional bound diagram with threshold $x(d,a)$ that has $y(d,a)$ elements where

$$x(d,a) = \prod_{k=1}^{2a \bmod d} (\lfloor \frac{2a}{d} \rfloor + 2) \cdot \prod_{k=1}^{d-(2a \bmod d)} (\lfloor \frac{2a}{d} \rfloor + 1) \quad (1)$$

$$y(d,a) = y(d-1,a) + 2 \sum_{k=1}^{a} y(d-1, a-k) \quad (2)$$

Proof: Proof is in 2 steps. In the first step we show that B(d) is a d-dimensional bound diagram with threshold x(d,a) and in the second step we show that B(d,a) has y(d,a) elements.

- **Step 1:** We need show that B(d,a) is a bound diagram with threshold x(d,a). By definition of B(d,a) we now that for points x,y in B we have $l_1(x,o) \leq a$ and $l_1(y,o) \leq a$. By using properties of l_1 distance we have that $l_1(x,y) \leq l_1(x,o) + l_1(o,y)$. Therefore, $l_1(x,y) \leq 2a$.
  We now need to find the threshold for two d-dimensional points that satisfy $l_1(x,y) \leq 2a$. By definition of l_1 distance we get

$$\sum_{k=1}^{d} |x_k - y_k| \leq 2a \quad (3)$$

The smallest hyper-rectangle that includes x and y in it has

$$\prod_{k=1}^{d} (|x_k - y_k| + 1) \quad (4)$$

points in it. We need to find the maximum value of equation 4 subject to constraint given in equation 3 and the fact that all the points have integer coordinates. The value of equation 4 is maximized when the values of $|x_k - y_k|$ for different dimensions are as close to each other as possible (without violating integer constraint). This is achieved when

$$x(d,a) = \prod_{k=1}^{2a \bmod d} (\lfloor \frac{2a}{d} \rfloor + 2) \cdot \prod_{k=1}^{d-(2a \bmod d)} (\lfloor \frac{2a}{d} \rfloor + 1) \quad (5)$$

- **Step 2:** We need to show that B(d,a) has y(d,a) elements. We can do this by using the number of elements in B(d-1,α) where $\alpha = 0..a$. By dividing d-dimensional shape into d-1 dimensional slices the number of elements in B(d,a) can be written as

$$y(d,a) = \sum_{x_d = -a}^{a} y(d-1, a - |x_d|) \quad (6)$$

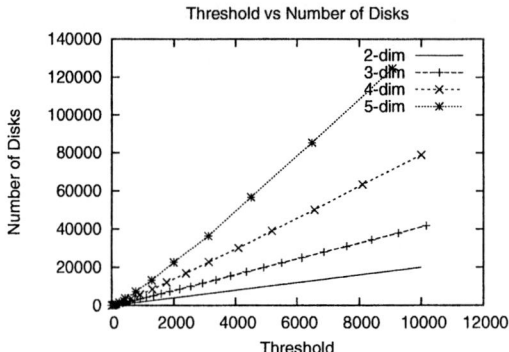

Fig. 2. Number of disks required to have threshold

By definition of B(d,a) x_d can be at most a and at least $-a$ (otherwise $l_1(x,o) > a$).

We can rewrite the above equation as

$$y(d,a) = y(d-1,a) + 2 \sum_{x_d=1}^{a} y(d-1, a-x_d) \qquad (7)$$

Therefore, using the result of d-1 dimensions we can find the number of elements in the bound diagram.

This completes the proof of the theorem. □

The thresholds and number of disks required to have that threshold is given in figure 2. As the number of dimensions increase the minimum number of disks required to have that threshold increases as well.

We next investigate how threshold changes as number of dimensions increase.

Theorem 2. *Let t_d be the maximum achievable threshold in d dimensions and t_{d+1} be the maximum achievable threshold in d + 1 dimensions, then $t_d \geq t_{d+1}$.*

Proof: Proof is by contradiction. Assume that $t_d < t_{d+1}$. By setting the first coordinate in d+1 dimensions to 0, we get a d-dimensional subspace. Therefore, we achieve threshold of t_{d+1} in d-dimensions. This contradicts the assumption that t_d is the maximum achievable threshold in d dimensions. □

Theoretical upper bounds on threshold computed using theorem 1 can be tightened using theorem 2. We next investigate high-dimensional declustering schemes that provide good threshold values. We define *generalized periodic disk allocation* which is high dimensional extension of *periodic disk allocation* given in [12].

Definition 1. *A d-dimensional disk allocation scheme $f(i_1, i_2, ..., i_d)$ is generalized periodic if $f(i_1, i_2, ..., i_d) = (a_1 * i_1 + a_2 * i_2 + ... + a_d * i_d) \mod N$, where N is the number of disks and a_i $i = 1..d$ are constants.*

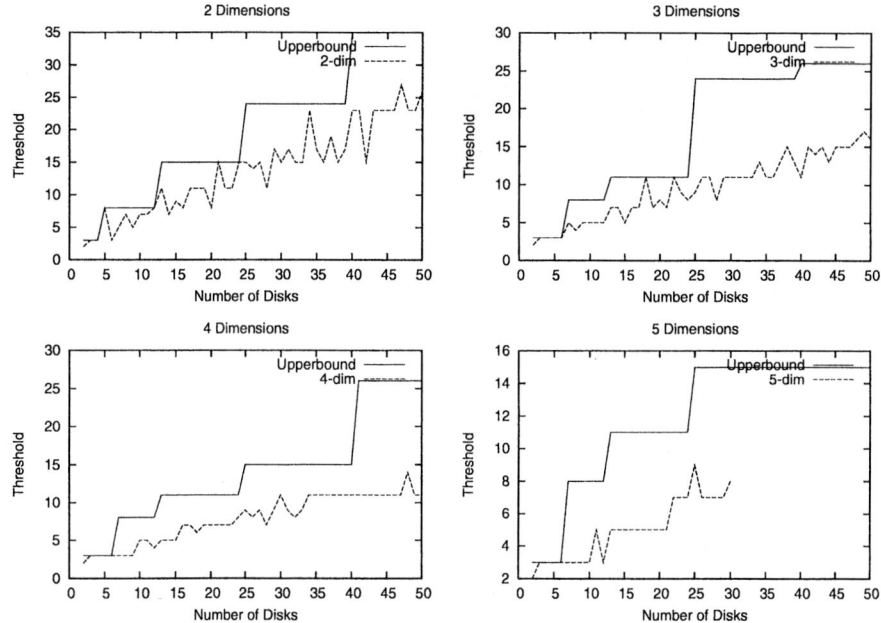

Fig. 3. Thresholds and upper bounds

Using generalized periodic disk allocations we investigated what thresholds are achievable. The results for 2-5 dimensions are given in figure 3. Upper bound is computed using theorems 1 and 2.

Threshold-based declustering produces schemes with low worst-case additive error. For a query which has optimal retrieval cost k and actual retrieval cost m additive error is $m-k$. Worst-case additive error is maximum additive error over all the queries. For 3 and 4 dimensions additive error is given in figure 4. In 3 dimensions additive error is low. In 4 dimensions certain numbers correspond to high additive error. Currently, we are working on a number theoretic explanation of this.

3 Thresholds in Replicated Declustering

Threshold based declustering in high dimensions have many interesting implications provided by the following theorem.

Theorem 3. *Let A be a c-copy replicated declustering scheme in d dimensions with threshold N, an $i_1 x i_2 x ... x i_d$ query ($\lceil \frac{i_1 * i_2 * ... * i_d}{N} \rceil = k$) can be retrieved in $OPT + (m - k)$ worst case cost if the $i_1 x i_2 x ... x i_d$ can be divided into m hyper-rectangles each having $\leq N$ buckets.*

Proof: Assume that we can divide the $i_1 x i_2 x ... x i_d$ hyper-rectangle into m hyper-rectangles each having $\leq N$ buckets. Each of the smaller hyper-rectangles can

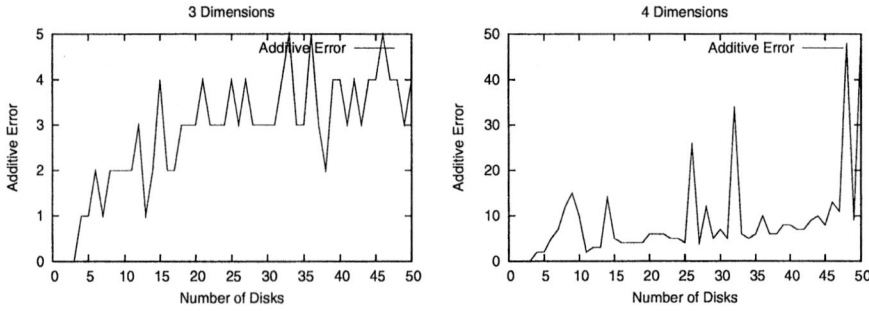

Fig. 4. Worst-case additive error

be retrieved in 1 disk access each. Therefore, All the smaller hyper-rectangles can be retrieved in m disk accesses in total. Since optimal retrieval cost is k. Worst case cost is $OPT + (m - k)$. □

In order to minimize the worst case retrieval cost of a d-dimensional query we need to find the minimum number of hyper-rectangles that the query can be divided where each hyper-rectangle has $\leq N$ buckets. This problem can be solved using dynamic programming. In 2-dimensions the recursive formulation is as given below

$$M[i,j] = min\{ \min_{1 \leq a \leq i-1} \{M[a,j] + M[i-a,j]\} + \min_{1 \leq b \leq j-1} \{M[i,b] + M[i,j-b]\}\}$$

in d-dimensions the recursive formulation is given as

$$M[i_1, i_2, ..., i_d] = \min_{k=1}^{d} \{ \min_{1 \leq x \leq i_k - 1} \{M[..., i_{k-1}, x, i_{k+1}, ...] + M[..., i_{k-1}, i_k - x, i_{k+1}, ...]\}\}$$

The optimal way to divide the query to hyperrectangles each having $\leq N$ buckets can be stored in a table. Each table entry stores the dimension to divide and the size of one of the chunks. For example, in 2 dimensions with N=12. The entry corresponding to 5x5 query would be (1,2) meaning that the query is divided along the first dimension into a 2x5 subquery and a 3x5 subquery. We then use the entry corresponding to 3x5 query to find out how to divide it optimally. Storing such a table improves scheduling since data is precomputed.

Using the recursive formulation we investigated the minimum number of rectangles that a high dimensional hyper-rectangle can be divided such that each hyper-rectangle has at most N buckets. The results for 2-4 dimensions are given in figure 5. The fraction is computed assuming that all i-by-j queries are equally likely. So, in 2 dimensions probability of having a i-by-j query on an N-by-N grid is $\frac{1}{N^2}$. In 3 dimensions, probability of having an i-by-j-by-k query on an N-by-N-by-N grid is $\frac{1}{N^3}$. In 2 dimensions all the queries can be retrieved in worst case cost of OPT+1. In 3 dimensions, for prime numbers, fraction of queries that can be optimally divided into hyper-rectangles is low (optimal is

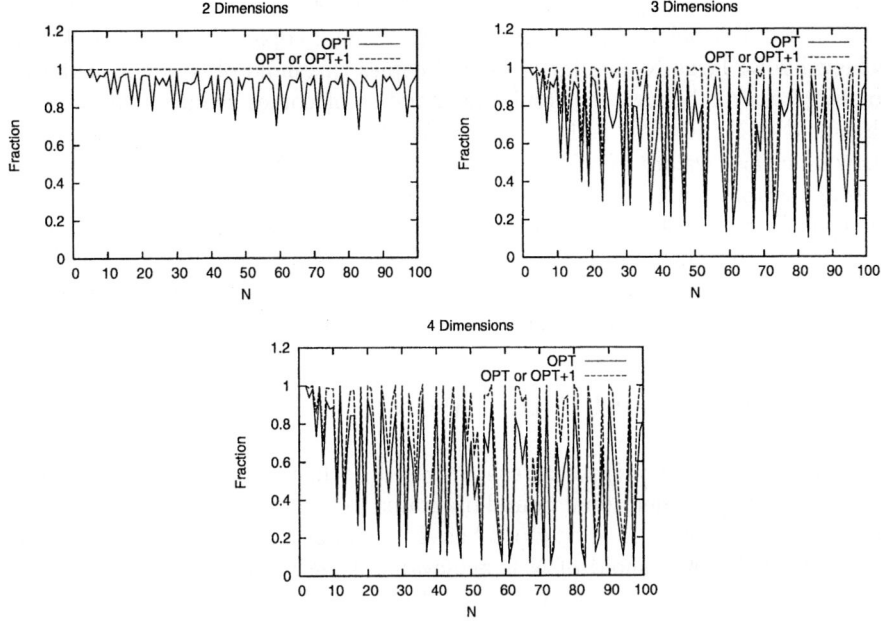

Fig. 5. Fraction of queries that are OPT or OPT+1

k rectangles if $\lceil \frac{ijk}{N} \rceil = k$). Currently, we are working on a number theoretic explanation of this.

We next investigated how to find c-copy replicated declustering schemes in d-dimensions with threshold N. Our approach is based on threshold based declustering. We start with the scheme that achieves the best single copy threshold and use shifted versions as the second or third copy. For each query a bipartite matching problem needs to be solved to find if that query is optimal or not. Since we are only interested in whether threshold of N is achievable or not, we

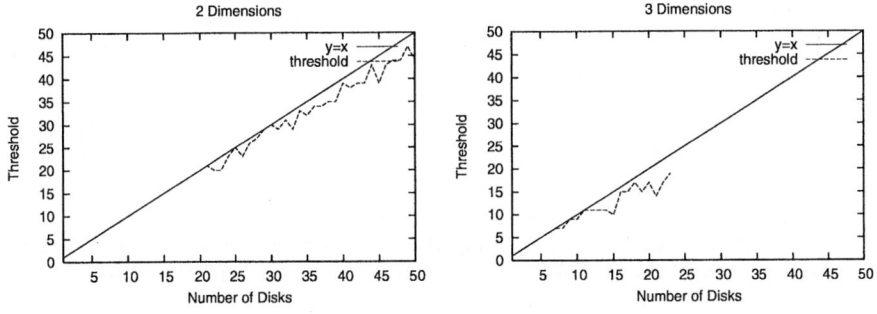

Fig. 6. Thresholds achievable using 2 copies

only perform matching for queries with $\leq$ N buckets. The results using 2 copies for 2 and 3 dimensions is given in figure 6. Using 2 copies threshold of N is not achievable for large N. Similarly, using 3 copies threshold of N is not achievable for large N. We believe the minimum number of copies required to achieve a threshold of N increases as N increases. We have also plotted the line $y = x$ to show how close we are to achieve the threshold N. In 2-dimensions, threshold of N is achievable using 2 copies up to 21 and for a few values larger than 21. In 3 dimensions, threshold of N is achievable up to 11 using 2 copies. The approach we take is somewhat limited and better thresholds are probably possible using other techniques. We only tested queries of size up to and including N, is some cases better thresholds are possible.

4 Conclusions and Future Work

In this paper we investigate threshold-based declustering in high dimensions. We propose high-dimensional bound diagrams to find upper bound on threshold and generalized periodic allocations based technique to find schemes with good threshold. When threshold of N is achievable using replicated declustering, by dividing a large query into hyper-rectangles of size N, worst case results can be derived for larger queries. Using threshold-based declustering as base copy, we propose replication scheme to find replicated declustering schemes with threshold N. Future work includes investigation of upper bound for threshold using multiple copies and derivation of replicated declustering schemes with better threshold values.

References

1. K. A. S. Abdel-Ghaffar and A. El Abbadi. Optimal allocation of two-dimensional data. In *ICDT*, pages 409–418, Delphi, Greece, January 1997.
2. M. J. Atallah and S. Prabhakar. (Almost) optimal parallel block access for range queries. In *Proc. ACM PODS*, pages 205–215, Dallas, Texas, May 2000.
3. N. Beckmann, H. Kriegel, R. Schneider, and B. Seeger. The R* tree: An efficient and robust access method for points and rectangles. In *Proc. ACM SIGMOD*, pages 322–331, May 23-25 1990.
4. S. Berchtold, C. Bohm, B. Braunmuller, D. A. Keim, and H-P. Kriegel. Fast parallel similarity search in multimedia databases. In *Proc. ACM SIGMOD*, pages 1–12, Arizona, U.S.A., 1997.
5. R. Bhatia, R. K. Sinha, and C.-M. Chen. Hierarchical declustering schemes for range queries. In *EDBT 2000*, pages 525–537, Konstanz, Germany, March 2000.
6. C.-M. Chen, R. Bhatia, and R. Sinha. Declustering using golden ratio sequences. In *ICDE*, pages 271–280, San Diego, California, Feb 2000.
7. C.-M. Chen and C. T. Cheng. From discrepancy to declustering: Near optimal multidimensional declustering strategies for range queries. In *Proc. ACM PODS*, pages 29–38, Wisconsin, Madison, 2002.
8. Chung-Min Chen and Christine Cheng. Replication and retrieval strategies of multidimensional data on parallel disks. In *CIKM*, October 2003.

9. H. C. Du and J. S. Sobolewski. Disk allocation for cartesian product files on multiple-disk systems. *ACM Trans. on Database Systems*, 7(1):82–101, March 1982.
10. C. Faloutsos and D. Metaxas. Declustering using error correcting codes. In *Proc. ACM PODS*, pages 253–258, 1989.
11. H. Ferhatosmanoglu, D. Agrawal, and A. El Abbadi. Concentric hyperspaces and disk allocation for fast parallel range searching. In *Proc. ICDE*, pages 608–615, Sydney, Australia, March 1999.
12. Hakan Ferhatosmanoglu, Ali Şaman Tosun, and Aravind Ramachandran. Replicated declustering of spatial data. In 23rd *ACM SIGMOD-SIGACT-SIGART Symposium on Principles of Database Systems*, June 2004.
13. V. Gaede and O. Gunther. Multidimensional access methods. *ACM Computing Surveys*, 30:170–231, 1998.
14. S. Ghandeharizadeh and D. J. DeWitt. Hybrid-range partitioning strategy: A new declustering strategy for multiprocessor database machines. In *VLDB*, pages 481–492, August 1990.
15. S. Ghandeharizadeh and D. J. DeWitt. A performance analysis of alternative multi-attribute declustering strategies. In *Proc. ACM SIGMOD*, pages 29–38, 1992.
16. J. Gray, B. Horst, and M. Walker. Parity striping of disc arrays: Low-cost reliable storage with acceptable throughput. In *Proc. VLDB*, pages 148–161, Washington DC., August 1990.
17. A. Guttman. R-trees: A dynamic index structure for spatial searching. In *Proc. ACM SIGMOD*, pages 47–57, 1984.
18. K. A. Hua and H. C. Young. A general multidimensional data allocation method for multicomputer database systems. In *Database and Expert System Applications*, pages 401–409, Toulouse, France, September 1997.
19. M. H. Kim and S. Pramanik. Optimal file distribution for partial match retrieval. In *Proc. ACM SIGMOD*, pages 173–182, Chicago, 1988.
20. S. Prabhakar, K. Abdel-Ghaffar, D. Agrawal, and A. El Abbadi. Cyclic allocation of two-dimensional data. In *ICDE*, pages 94–101, Orlando, Florida, 1998.
21. H. Samet. *The Design and Analysis of Spatial Structures*. Addison Wesley, Massachusetts, 1989.
22. A. S. Tosun and H. Ferhatosmanoglu. Optimal parallel I/O using replication. In *Proceedings of International Workshops on Parallel Processing (ICPP)*, Vancouver, Canada, August 2002.
23. Ali Şaman Tosun. Replicated declustering for arbitrary queries. In 19th *ACM Symposium on Applied Computing*, March 2004.
24. Ali Şaman Tosun. Constrained declustering. In *International Conference on Information Technology Coding and Computing*, April 2005.
25. Ali Şaman Tosun. Design theoretic approach to replicated declustering. In *International Conference on Information Technology Coding and Computing*, April 2005.

XG: A Data-Driven Computation Grid for Enterprise-Scale Mining

Radu Sion[1], Ramesh Natarajan[2], Inderpal Narang[3], Wen-Syan Li[3], and Thomas Phan[3]

[1] Computer Sciences, Stony Brook University, Stony Brook, NY 11794
sion@cs.stonybrook.edu
[2] IBM TJ Watson Research Lab, Yorktown Heights, NY 10598
nramesh@us.ibm.com
[3] IBM Almaden Research Lab, 650 Harry Rd, San Jose, CA 95120
{narang, wsl, phantom}@us.ibm.com

Abstract. In this paper we introduce a novel architecture for data processing, based on a functional fusion between a data and a computation layer. We show how such an architecture can be leveraged to offer significant speedups for data processing jobs such as data analysis and mining over large data sets.

One novel contribution of our solution is its data-driven approach. The computation infrastructure is *controlled from within the data layer*. Grid compute job submission events are based within the query processor on the DBMS side and in effect controlled by the data processing job to be performed. This allows the early deployment of on-the-fly data aggregation techniques, minimizing the amount of data to be transfered to/from compute nodes and is in stark contrast to existing Grid solutions that interact with data layers mainly as external "storage".

We validate this in a scenario derived from a real business deployment, involving financial customer profiling using common types of data analytics (e.g., linear regression analysis). Experimental results show significant speedups. For example, using a grid of only 12 non-dedicated nodes, we observed a speedup of approximately 1000% in a scenario involving complex linear regression analysis data mining computations for commercial customer profiling.

1 Introduction

As increasingly fast networks connect vast numbers of cheaper computation and storage resources, the promise of "grids" as paradigms of optimized, heterogeneous resource sharing across boundaries [6], becomes closer to full realization. It already delivered significant successes in projects such as the Grid Physics Network (GriPhyN) [9] and the Particle Physics Data Grid (PPDG) [15]. While these examples are mostly specialized scientific applications, involving lengthy processing of massive data sets (usually files), projects such as Condor [5] and Globus [7] aim at exploring "computational grids" from a declared more main-stream perspective.

There are two aspects of processing in such frameworks. On the one hand, we find the computation resource allocation aspect ("computational grid"). On the other hand however data accessibility and associated placement issues are also naturally paramount ("data grid"). Responses to these important data grid challenges include high performance file sharing techniques, file-systems and protocols such as GridFTP, the Globus

Replica Catalog and Management tools [8] in Globus, NeST, Chirp, BAD-FS [16], STORK [4], Parrot [3], Kangaroo [2] and DiskRouter [1] in Condor. The ultimate goal of grids is (arguably) an increasingly optimized use of existing compute resources and an associated increase of end-to-end processing quality (e.g. lower execution times). Intuitively, a tighter integration of the two grid aspects ("computational" and "data") could yield significant advantages e.g., due to the potential for optimized, faster access to data, decreasing overall execution times, increasing associated Quality of Service metrics. There are significant challenges to such an integration, including the minimization of data transfer costs by performing initial data-reducing aggregation, placement scheduling for massive data and fast-changing access patterns, the ability to directly handle data consistency and freshness.

In this work we propose, analyze and experimentally validate a novel integrated data-driven grid-infrastructure in a data mining framework. Computation jobs can now be formulated, provisioned and transparently scheduled from within the database query layer to the background compute Grid. Such jobs include e.g., the computation of analytical functions over a data subset at the end of which the result is returned back in a data layer (either by reference to a specific location or inline, as a result of the job execution). To do so, we designed and implemented a light-weight, minimum overhead grid scheduling and management software, a proof of concept implementation of the data-driven computation scheduling paradigm. The tightly data-layer integrated design presented significant new foundational and implementation challenges in both the data and computational aspects.

On the one hand, apparently, the manipulation of large data sets *from within the data layer* becomes easier. While this is true in principle, it does not come without additional problems to be tackled. Massive parallel data access patterns have the natural potential to result in data processing bottlenecks. This will require mechanisms for automatic smart data placement and replication as part of computation staging. On the other hand, equally challenging we find the (portable) integration of computation scheduling awareness in a traditional data-layer query engine, without the requirement of significant alterations to its core. We achieved this by operating within the boundaries of traditional SQL by providing a set of functional extensions allowing for computation formulation and external grid scheduling. This was important for two reasons: (i) portability with other DBMS (e.g. MySQL), (ii) backwards compatibility with existing applications requiring no major code rewriting to benefit from the grid infrastructure.

Another main design insight behind our implementation is that (arguably) any global grid is ultimately composed of clustered resources at its edge. It is then only natural to represent it as a hierarchy of computation clusters and associated close-proximity data sources. Using our end-to-end solution (data-layer aggregation and compute grid invocation), in our considered application domain (data analysis for predictive modeling) significant speed-ups have been achieved versus the traditional case of data-layer processing.

Using a grid of only 12 non-dedicated nodes, we observed a speedup of approximately 1000% in a scenario involving complex linear regression analysis data mining computations for commercial customer profiling.

Thus, the main contributions of this work include: (i) the proposal, design and implementation of a novel paradigm for grid scheduling from within a relational DBMS data-layer, allowing for speedups to be of impact at the actual relational algebra level, (ii) the use of data-aggregation techniques minimizing transfer overhead and optimizing the trade-off between required data migration costs and actual speed-up benefits, (iii) the design and implementation of a supporting grid management solution and (iv) the experimental evaluation thereof in a commercial customer profiling data analysis scenario.

The paper is structured as follows. Section 2 introduces our main commercial usecase scenario and explores some of the associated data analytics. Section 3 introduces the main solution. Section 4 analyzes system performance and discusses experimental results. Section 5 discusses avenues for further exploration and concludes.

2 Scenario: Real-Time Customer Analytics

Let us now explore an important commonly encountered operation scenario for data mining in a commercial framework that yielded significant cost and speed-up benefits from our solution: a large company (i.e., with a customer base of millions of customers), maintains an active customer transaction database and deploys data mining to better customize and/or optimize its customer-interaction response and associated costs. There are two types of customer interactions, each subject to different types of requirements and response mechanisms, namely (i) incoming ('pull" model) inquiries and (ii) outgoing advertisements ('push" model, see Figure 1). For space reasons, here we are discussing (i).

Incoming inquiries (e.g., over the phone, online) are handled in a real-time or shortnotice manner. There are bounds on response-time (e.g., Human-Computer interaction experiences should feature response times of under 7-8 seconds to be acceptable) [17]

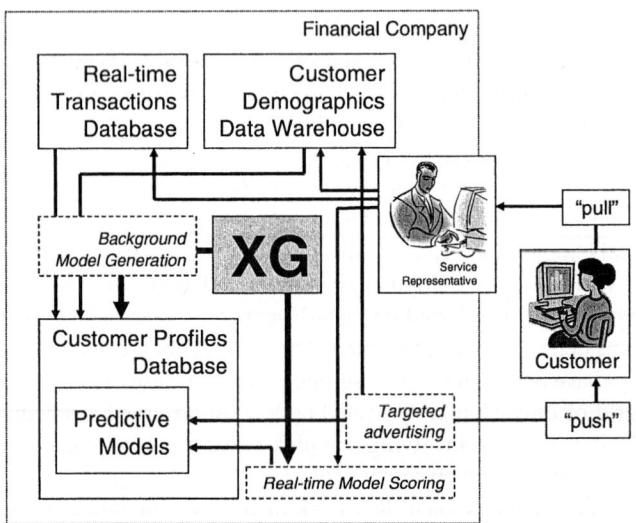

Fig. 1. Push/pull customer interaction scenario.

to be satisfied. Due to their customer-initiated nature, these interactions could be (intuitively) quite valuable, thus additional resources and care should be taken in satisfying real-time and quality aspects. An imprecise but fast initial "pre"-response might be often preferable to an exact but slow one, as it is likely that higher waiting-times would result in a drop in overall customer satisfaction.

The company's response data is based on previously recorded customer "profiles", composed of a history of transactions and a set of related predictive models (e.g. answering questions like "what is the likelihood of this customer to buy a specific product in the next 2 weeks"). Such profiles need to be maintained with sufficient (preferably maximal) accuracy and the associated (predictive) models re- computed periodically or as part of an event- driven paradigm in which associate customer events trigger individual model re- computations. Scalability issues need to be carefully considered and sized to the potentially large number of close-timed events. Higher predictive model accuracy can be attained by enabling speedups in the model computation and then performing these more often and with increasing accuracy constraints (more CPU cycles required). Often, the per-customer nature of profiling naturally allows model generation tasks to be out-sourced to a computation grid, thus providing opportunities for scalability.

In an *incoming* interaction, often the center-point (and likely the most expensive) is processing a function of the immediate input data and the customer predictive models in the stored profile ("model scoring"). Often, also, new models need to be computed on the fly. Because of its real-time nature, and the potential for thousands of simultaneous incoming customer requests, this scenario is extremely challenging. It would benefit from an ability to outsource different simultaneous model scoring tasks to a computation grid.

To understand the size of this problem, let us quantify some of the previous statements. To do so we outline an actual deployment case business scenario for which the orders of magnitude of the values have been preserved. In this scenario, incoming customer calls and online system accesses are event-triggering.

Let us assume a customer base of over 10 million customers. Roughly 0.1% (10k) of them are active at any point in time (interactive and automated phone calls, web access, other automated systems). Preferably, the company response in each and every transaction should be optimally tailored (i.e., through on-demand data mining) to maximize profit and customer satisfaction. On average, only 75% (7.5k) of these active (meta)transactions are resulting in actual data mining tasks and, for each second, only 20% of these task- triggering customers require data mining. To function within the required response-behavior boundary, the company has to thus handle a continuous parallel throughput of 1500 (possibly complex) simultaneous data mining jobs. Achieving this throughput at the computation and data I/O level is very challenging from both a cost and scalability viewpoint.

3 Proposed Solution

Our end-to-end solution comprises several major components: modeling, aggregation and computation outsourcing (in the data layer) and grid scheduling and management (grid layer).

3.1 Data Layer Overview

Designing specifically for data mining over large data sets, requires a careful consideration of network data transfer overheads. As traditional data mining solutions are often based on code directly executed inside the database query processor, these overheads could often be reduced by an initial data aggregation step performed inside the data layer, before outsourcing the more computation heavy model generation tasks.

We propose a design that (i) tightly integrates the grid with the data layer and (ii) hides its management complexity by transparently performing behind the scenes. Our solution allows for dispatching of multiple simultaneous data processing tasks from within the query processor (i.e. SQL level) by performing simple calls through a user defined function (UDF) mechanism. At the completion of these tasks, their results become available within the actual data layer, ready for further processing.

The interaction between the data layer and compute grid is composed of two elements: (a) a grid-data layer interface and (b) data placement/replication mechanisms. Here we detail (a) and briefly outline a design for (b).

Job submission is initiated in the database and forwarded to the main computation grid through a web-service interface exposing the main grid scheduling control knobs. This interaction is enabled by user defined functions (UDF) within DB2. Present in a majority of big-vendor DBMS solutions including DB2 [11], Oracle [14] and SQL Server [13], UDFs are SQL-extensions that allow interaction with host-language functions for performing customized tasks. The UDF concept presents a host of advantages, including the ability to modularize an application, to provide custom functionality not offered within the database, to reuse and share code etc.

The grid scheduler controls are exposed through a webservice interface. Through the XML Extender [12] and its SOAP messaging capabilities, DB2 provides the ability to create UDFs that interact with webservices. This allows the invocation of job submission methods exposed by the schedulers in the compute grid layer (see Figure 2 (a)). This invocation is asynchronous so as to not block the calling thread and to allow actual parallelism in data processing. Incidentally, due to DB2's internal query handling, in this particular case, additional advantages are obtained through the use of the GROUP

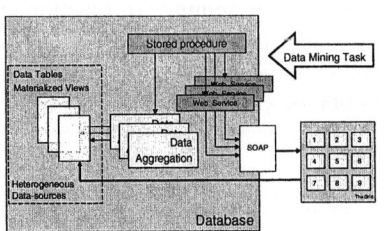
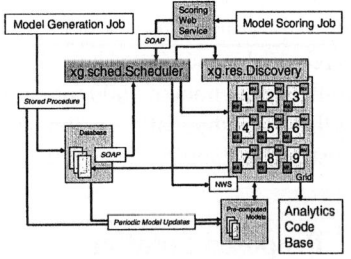

Fig. 2. (a) Data Layer Overview: The grid is leveraged transparently from the data side. Mining tasks can execute normally within the query processor (e.g., as stored procedures). (b) Computation Grid Overview: Single compute grid cluster shown.

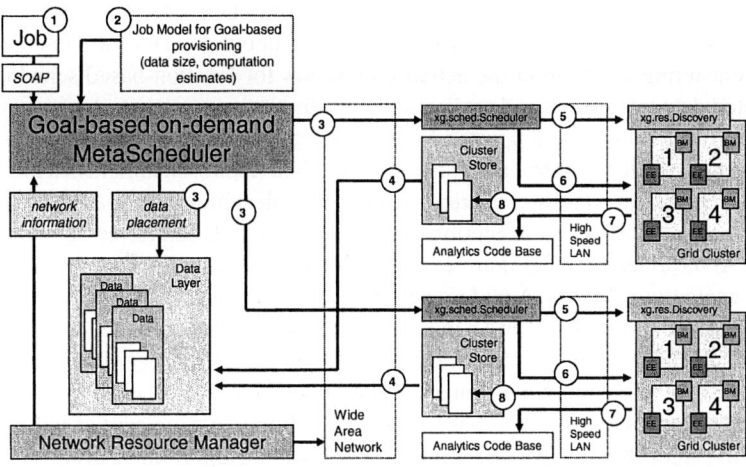

Fig. 3. Both data replication/placement (to cluster stores) and job scheduling in the hierarchical grid infra-structure is to be controlled by a meta scheduler

BY clause which can also benefit from potential SMP (symmetric multi-processor) parallelism behind the scenes.

While extensive details are out of the current scope, for illustration purposes, let us discuss here the following query:

```
SELECT c_id, reg_analysis_grid(reg_agg(c_assets))
FROM customer_tx WHERE c_age < 21 GROUP BY c_id
```

After the initial aggregation step (performed by $reg\_agg()$) the resulting computations are outsourced to the grid (grouped by customer, c_id) through the $reg\_analysis\_grid()$ UDF. This constructs the necessary SOAP envelopes, converts the arguments to a serializable format and invokes the grid scheduler with two parameters for each customer: (i) an URL reference to the external regression analysis code (located in the grid codebase, see Figure 3) and (ii) a reference to the aggregate input data.

There are two alternatives for data transfer to/from the compute grid: *inline* (as an actual parameter in the job submission – suitable for small amounts of input data and close local clusters) and *by-reference* where actual input data sources are identified as part of the job submission – suitable for massive data processing in a global grid. To support the input/output data by reference paradigm, in our design data replication is activated by the meta-scheduler at the grid cluster level, leveraging 'close" data stores and linking in with future data replication/placement mechanisms (e.g., Information Integration [10]) if the data is 'far" (see Figure 3).

3.2 Computation Layer Overview

XG is our experimental grid management solution custom designed for tight data-layer integration. It enables a hierarchical grid structure of individual fast(er)-bus compute clusters (at the extreme just a single machine). This design derived from the insight that (arguably) a majority of grid infra-structures are to be composed of multiple high-speed cluster networks linked by lower speed inter-networks. Designing an awareness of this clustering structure in the actual grid allows for location-based scheduling and associated data integration and replication algorithms.

The grid hierarchy is supported by the concept of a meta-scheduler (Figure 3), a software entity able to control a set of other individual (meta)schedulers in a hierarchical fashion, composing a multi-clustered architecture. Job submission at any entry-point in this hierarchy results in an execution in the corresponding connected subtree (or subgraph). At the cluster level (Figure 2 (b)) a scheduler (xg.sched.Scheduler) is managing a set of *computation nodes*. A node is composed (among others) of an Execution Engine (xg.blade.ExecutionEngine) and a monitor (xg.blade.BladeMonitor).

The scheduler deploys a discovery protocol (BladesDiscovery) for automatic discovery of available compute resources, a polling mechanism (BladesPoller) for monitoring job progress and notifications for job rescheduling (e.g., in case of failures) and a scheduling algorithm for job scheduling. The scheduling algorithm is designed as a plug-in within the scheduler, allowing for different scheduling policies to be hot- swapped. For inter-operability, the schedulers are designed be invoked (e.g. for job scheduling) through a web-service interface. It allows for job submission (with both inline and by-reference data), job monitoring and result retrieval when the persistence of results was requested in the job submission step.

4 Experimental Results

We performed experiments on a grid cluster composed of 70 general purpose 1.2GHz Linux boxes with approximately 256MB of RAM each. The data layer used deployed IBM DB2 ver. 8.2. with the XML Extender [12] enabled.

4.1 Linear Regression Model

We implemented code for linear regression modeling. In order to be able to easily assess *actual* job computation times (required for the next experiments), we first evaluated its behavior to varying input size (number of tuples of the input data set).

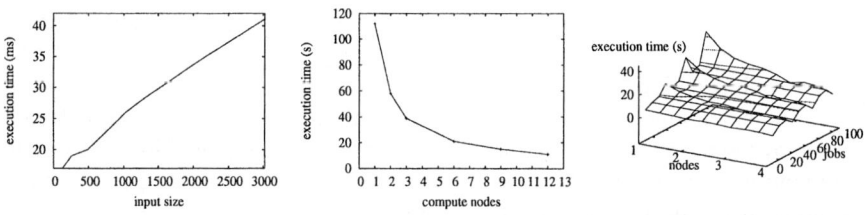

Fig. 4. (a) The considered regression analysis behavior to data input size is virtually linear. (b) Grid speed-up. With increasing number of nodes, the overall execution time decreases naturally. The data points shown are for a job load of 100 jobs with an input size of roughly 90k tuples each. (c) Overall observed execution time with varying number of jobs and grid nodes. Notice the (intuitive) upper-left to lower-right tilt of the surface. The considered input size per job was roughly 30 k tuples.

As can be seen from Figure 4 (a) a naturally linear dependency was observed. The proof-of-concept un-optimized code can handle 73k tuples/sec in the considered setup. We estimate $1-2$ orders of magnitude speed-up in an optimized industry-level version.

This linearity allows the construction of a natural metric evaluating the amount of computation associated with a certain job. In the following we are going to use the term "job size" to denote the amount of input data corresponding to the considered job(s). This metric naturally identifies the amount of CPU cycles a certain job will require and is arguably independent from the speed of the deployed CPU. Another related metric could be defined by a translation to actual MIPS numbers but we feel this would be out of scope and of no additional benefit in this framework.

4.2 Grid Speed-Ups

Once a "job size" metric was established, we proceeded by evaluating the actual speed-ups of the model generation process with increasing number of grid nodes. The mining job load was generated by issuing a GROUP BY query (as described in Section 3.1) that resulted in 100 regression analysis jobs (e.g., one model for each of 100 customers).

In Figure 4 (b) it can be seen that the solution naturally scales. In a scenario with 100 jobs of input size 90k, execution time went down from roughly 112 seconds for one compute node, to about 11 seconds when 12 nodes where deployed.

In Figure 4 (c) the grid speed-up is analyzed from a 3-dimensional perspective. The question answered here is: does the design scale in *both* the number of jobs *and* the number of available compute resources? Noting the upper-left to lower-right tilt of the execution time surface is providing the answer. It basically confirms that as the number of jobs goes up, the implemented scheduling algorithm discovers and utilizes available compute resources properly.

4.3 Overheads

Another question of importance is whether the scheduling and overheads are stable and allow for arbitrary scaling in the number of jobs. In Figure 5 (a) it can be seen that the overall scheduling overhead is linear in the number of jobs, as expected. It averages about 40ms per job in the experimental proof-of-concept Java release. Significant speed-ups can be obtained in an optimized version.

Additionally we observed (see also Figure 5 (a)) a slight, (arguably) insignificant, increase in scheduling times with increasing number of nodes. The causes for this are two fold: (i) resource matching, blade and runtime job monitoring all take additional time, likely directly proportional to the size of the resource pool (i.e., number of nodes in this case) and (ii) we believe a certain "collision" factor (e.g., due to using the same network bus) is also associated with migrating jobs to a larger number of nodes.

Figure 5 (b) shows a result depicting direct inline result transfer overheads for the considered scenario. It can be seen that the behavior is also stable and linear, averaging about 35 ms per job. If the data is passed by reference these overheads are not occurring directly, but are rather hidden in the process of result transfer back to the data sources, directly from the grid to the data layer.

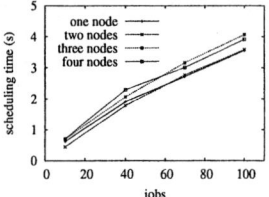 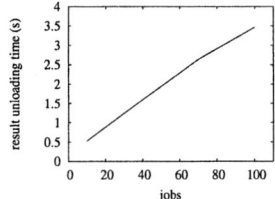 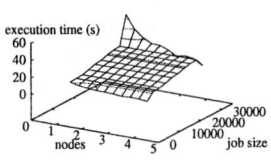

Fig. 5. (a) Overall scheduling overhead is linear in the number of jobs (averaging at about 40 ms per job). There is a very small (increasing) dependency of the number of nodes. The considered input size per job was also roughly 30 k tuples. (b) In the case of inline result transfer, its associated total overhead is (naturally) linear in the number of jobs and, in this scenario averaged 35 ms per job (mainly network costs). The experiment was performed with job input sizes of roughly 30 k tuples. (c) Overall execution time for 100 jobs with varying number of grid nodes and job size ranging from 1500 to 30 k input tuples per job, corresponding to roughly 20 to 400 ms individual times. Observe the natural upper-left to lower-right tilt.

4.4 Scalability

Figure 5 (c) explores whether the solution actually scales for varying job sizes. In other words, what happens if the jobs become so "small" that their execution time is comparable to or even lower than the observed overheads? Does deploying such a solution still make sense? It can be observed that, intuitively, the most benefits are reaped in the case of large jobs. However, the upper-left to lower-right tilt again confirms that overall, the grid scales favorably and execution times are reduced even in the case of multiple small jobs.

5 Conclusions

In this work we introduced a novel architecture for data processing, a functional fusion between a data and a computation layer. We then experimentally showed how our solution can be leveraged for significant benefits in data processing jobs such as data analysis and mining over large data sets.

There are significant open avenues for future research. While in this initial effort we dealt with mostly independently executing jobs, increased capabilities and expression power can be achieved by the integration of a message passing interface solution in the compute grid, allowing jobs to communicate and synchronize. Failure recovery is currently based solely on job re-scheduling to different compute nodes. Check-pointing would increase the ability to better deal with large jobs in a failure-prone environment.

Security is of paramount importance. Privacy-preserving primitives for data processing in (possibly hostile, eavesdropping) compute grid-environments should be addressed and deployed. More-over, it is essential to take resource scheduling to a new level and treat both data placement and computation scheduling as first class citizens. This becomes especially relevant in on-demand environments where a maximal throughput in data and compute intensive application is not possible using current manual data partitioning and staging methods.

Last but not least, we believe *grid-aware query processing* to be an exciting avenue for future research, ultimately resulting in a computation aware grid query optimizer within a traditional DBMS query processor.

References

1. DiskRouter. Online at http://www.cs.wisc.edu/condor/diskrouter.
2. Kangaroo. Online at http://www.cs.wisc.edu/condor/kangaroo.
3. Parrot. Online at http://www.cs.wisc.edu/condor/parrot.
4. STORK: A Scheduler for Data Placement Activities in the Grid. Online at http://www.cs.wisc.edu/condor/stork
5. The Condor Project. Online at http://www.cs.wisc.edu/condor.
6. The Global Grid Forum. Online at http://www.gridforum.org.
7. The Globus Alliance. Online at http://www.globus.org.
8. The Globus Data Grid Effort. Online at http://www.globus.org/datagrid.
9. The Grid Physics Network. Online at http://www.griphyn.org.
10. The IBM DB2 Information Integrator. Online at http://www.ibm.com/software/data/integration
11. The IBM DB2 Universal Database. Online at http://www.ibm.com/software/data/db2.
12. The IBM DB2 XML Extender. Online at http://www.ibm.com/software/data/db2/extenders/xmlext
13. The Microsoft SQL Server. Online at http://www.microsoft.com/sql.
14. The Oracle Database. Online at http://www.oracle.com/database.
15. The Particle Physics Data Grid. Online at http://www.ppdg.net.
16. John Bent, Douglas Thain, Andrea C. Arpaci-Dusseau, Remzi H. Arpaci-Dusseau, and Miron Livny. Explicit Control in a Batch-Aware Distributed File System. In *Proceedings of the First USENIX Symposium on Networked Systems Design and Implementation (NSDI)*, San Francisco, CA, March 2004.
17. Julie Ratner. *Human Factors and Web Development, Second Edition.* Lawrence Erlbaum Associates, 2002.

A Rule System for Heterogeneous Spatial Reasoning in Geographic Information System

Haibin Sun and Wenhui Li

Key Laboratory of Symbol Computation and Knowledge
Engineering of the Ministry of Education,
College of Computer Science and Technology, Jilin University,
Changchun 130012, China
Offer_sun@hotmail.com

Abstract. In this article, we investigate the hybrid spatial reasoning problem in geographic information system, which can be formulated as a hybrid formalism, which combines two essential formalisms in qualitative spatial reasoning: topological formalism and cardinal direction formalism. Although much work has been done in developing composition tables for these formalisms, the previous research for integrating heterogeneous formalisms was not sufficient. Instead of using conventional composition tables, we investigate the interactions between topological and cardinal directional relations with the aid of rules that are used efficiently in many research fields such as content-based image retrieval. These rules are shown to be sound, i.e. the deductions are logically correct. Based on these rules, an improved constraint propagation algorithm is introduced to enforce the path consistency.

1 Introduction

Combining and integrating different kinds of knowledge is an emerging and challenging issue in Qualitative Spatial Reasoning (QSR), content-based image retrieval and computer vision, etc. For an example in Geographic Information System (GIS), Assume that we are given two map layers, we know that region A is north of region B and B overlaps with region C from one layer, and that region C is north of region D from the other. What are the cardinal direction relation and topological relation between regions A and D? Obviously, we need to investigate the reasoning problem with the hybrid system combining topological and directional relations between spatial regions to derive potential spatial relations. The spatial reasoning technique becomes the research focus for it can avoid time-consuming geometric computation. Gerevini and Renz [1] have dealt with the combination of topological knowledge and metric size knowledge in QSR, and Isli et al. [2] have combined the cardinal direction knowledge and the relative orientation knowledge.

To combine topological and directional relations, Sharma [3] represented topological and cardinal relations as interval relations along two axes, e.g., horizontal and vertical axes. Based on Allen's composition table [4] for temporal interval relations, Sharma identifies all of the composition tables combining topological and directional relations. But his model approximated regions with Minimal Boundary Rectangles (MBRs), and if a more precise model (e.g., in this paper) is used, his composition tables will not be appropriate. We base our work on a topological model [7] and Goyal and Egenhofer's model [8].

In this paper, we detail various interaction rules between two formalisms and we also investigate the computational problems in the formalism combining topological and cardinal directional relations.

In the next section, we give the background for this paper. The interaction rules are introduced in section 3, which are used to implement our new path consistency algorithm in section 5 after some definitions and terminologies are prepared in section 4. In section 6, the conclusion is given.

2 Background

We first introduce the two formalisms of topological and cardinal directional relations, respectively. The region considered in this paper is a point-set homeomorphic to a unit disk in Euclidean space $\mathbb{R}^2$.

2.1 Topology Formalism

Topology is perhaps the most fundamental aspect of space. Topological relations are invariant under topological transformations, such as translation, scaling, and rotation. Examples are terms like *neighbor* and *disjoint* [6]. RCC8 is a formalism dealing with a set of eight jointly exhaustive and pairwise disjoint (JEPD) relations, called basic relations, denoted as DC, EC, PO, EQ, TPP, $NTPP$, $TPPi$, $NTPPi$, with the meaning of DisConnected, Extensionally Connected, Partial Overlap, EQual, Tangential Proper Part, Non-Tangential Proper Part, and their converses (see Fig.1). Exactly one of these relations holds between any two spatial regions. In this paper, we will focus on RCC8 formalism.

Randell et al. [7] presented a formalism defining these RCC8 relations by assuming a primitive dyadic relation: $C(x,y)$ read as 'x connects with y'. $C(x,y)$ holds when the topological closures of regions x and y share a common point. The relation $C(x,y)$ is reflexive and symmetric, i.e., $\forall x C(x,x)$ and $\forall xy[C(x,y) \to C(y,x)]$. Using $C(x,y)$, the dyadic relations $P(x,y)$ ('x is part of y'), $PP(x,y)$ ('x is proper part of y') and $O(x,y)$ ('x overlaps y') can be defined as:

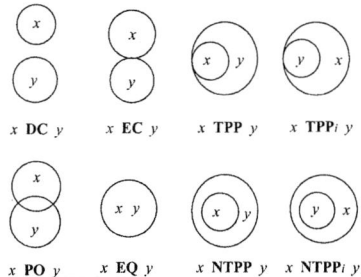

Fig. 1. Two-dimensional examples for the eight basic relations of RCC8

$$P(x,y) \equiv_{def} \forall z[C(z,x) \to C(z,y)],$$
$$PP(x,y) \equiv_{def} P(x,y) \land \neg P(y,x)$$
$$\text{and } O(x,y) \equiv_{def} \exists z[P(z,x) \land P(z,y)],$$

respectively, and then the RCC8 relations are defined as follows.

$$DC(x,y) \equiv_{def} \neg C(x,y) \tag{2.1}$$
$$EC(x,y) \equiv_{def} C(x,y) \land \neg O(x,y) \tag{2.2}$$
$$PO(x,y) \equiv_{def} O(x,y) \land \neg P(x,y) \land \neg P(y,x) \tag{2.3}$$
$$TPP(x,y) \equiv_{def} PP(x,y) \land \exists z[EC(z,x) \land EC(z,y)] \tag{2.4}$$
$$NTPP(x,y) \equiv_{def} PP(x,y) \land \neg \exists z[EC(z,x) \land EC(z,y)] \tag{2.5}$$
$$TPPi(x,y) \equiv_{def} TPP(y,x) \tag{2.6}$$
$$NTPPi(x,y) \equiv_{def} NTPP(y,x) \tag{2.7}$$
$$EQ(x,y) \equiv_{def} P(x,y) \land P(y,x) \tag{2.8}$$

2.2 Cardinal Direction Formalism

Goyal and Egenhofer [8] introduced a direction-relation model for extended spatial objects that considers the influence of the objects' shapes. It uses the projection-based direction partitions and an extrinsic reference system, and considers the exact representation of the target object with respect to the reference frame. The reference frame with a polygon as reference object has nine direction tiles: north (N_A), northeast (NE_A), east (E_A), southeast (SE_A), south (S_A), southwest (SW_A), west (W_A), northwest (NW_A), and same (O_A, i.e., the minimum bounding rectangle) (see Fig.2). The cardinal direction from the reference object to a target is described by recording those tiles into which at least one part of the target object falls. We call the relations where the target object occupies one tile of the reference object *single-tile* relations, and others *multi-tile* relations. We denote this formalism by CDF(Cardinal Direction Formalism) for brevity. It should be noted that Sharma [3] did not consider the kind of *multi-tile* relation and the intermediate relations, i.e., *NW, NE, SE* and *SW*.

Let A be a region. The *greatest lower bound* of the projection of region A on the x-axis (respectively y-axis) is denoted by $inf_x(A)$ (respectively $inf_y(A)$). The *least upper bound* of the projection of region A on the x-axis (respectively y-axis) is denoted by $sup_x(A)$ (respectively $sup_y(A)$). The *minimum bounding*

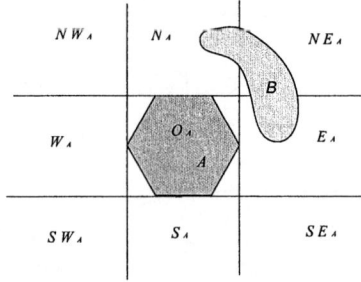

Fig. 2. Capturing the cardinal direction relation between two polygons, A and B, through the projection-based partitions around A as the reference object

box of a region A, denoted by $MBB(A)$, is the box formed by the straight lines $x = inf_x(A)$, $x = sup_x(A)$, $y = inf_y(A)$ and $y = sup_y(A)$. Based on these symbols, Skiadopoulos and Koubarakis [9] formally defined the cardinal directional relations.

$$a\ O\ b \Leftrightarrow inf_x(b) \leq inf_x(a), sup_x(a) \leq sup_x(b), inf_y(b) \leq inf_y(a),$$
$$sup_y(a) \leq sup_y(b) \qquad (2.9)$$
$$a\ S\ b \Leftrightarrow sup_y(a) \leq inf_y(b), inf_x(b) \leq inf_x(a), sup_x(a) \leq sup_x(b) \quad (2.10)$$
$$a\ SW\ b \Leftrightarrow sup_x(a) \leq inf_x(b), sup_y(a) \leq inf_y(b) \qquad (2.11)$$
$$a\ W\ b \Leftrightarrow sup_x(a) \leq inf_x(b), inf_y(b) \leq inf_y(a), sup_y(a) \leq sup_y(b) \quad (2.12)$$
$$a\ NW\ b \Leftrightarrow sup_x(a) \leq inf_x(b), sup_y(b) \leq inf_y(a) \qquad (2.13)$$
$$a\ N\ b \Leftrightarrow sup_y(b) \leq inf_y(a), inf_x(b) \leq inf_x(a), sup_x(a) \leq sup_x(b) \quad (2.14)$$
$$a\ NE\ b \Leftrightarrow sup_x(b) \leq inf_x(a), sup_y(b) \leq inf_y(a) \qquad (2.15)$$
$$a\ E\ b \Leftrightarrow sup_x(b) \leq inf_x(a), inf_y(b) \leq inf_y(a), sup_y(a) \leq sup_y(b) \quad (2.16)$$
$$a\ SE\ b \Leftrightarrow sup_x(b) \leq inf_x(a), sup_y(a) \leq inf_y(b) \qquad (2.17)$$

$a\ R_1 : \cdots : R_k\ b, 2 \leq k \leq 9, \Leftrightarrow$ there exists regions $a_1, \cdots, a_k$ such that
$$a = a_1 \cup \cdots \cup a_k, a_1 R_1 b, a_2 R_2 b, \cdots,$$
$$\text{and } a_k\ R_k\ b \qquad (2.18)$$

3 Interaction Rules Between RCC8 and CDF

The internal operations, including converse and composition, on RCC8 can be found in [10]. The internal operations on CDF have been investigated in [9] and [11]. In order to integrate these two formalisms, we must investigate interaction rules between them. These rules are very useful to improve the spatial reasoning and can be the complement of the present composition tables. The spatial reasoning based on rules is more efficient and extended easily in the future as Sistla et al. [5] indicated.

The notation and representation of these rules are similar to [5], i.e. each rule will be written as $r :: r_1, r_2, \cdots, r_k$, where r is called the head of the rule, which is deduced by the list $r_1, r_2, \cdots, r_k$ called the body of the rule.

To facilitate the representation of the interaction rules, we denote a basic cardinal direction (i.e., single-tile or multi-tile relation) relation by a set SB, which includes at most nine elements, i.e. the nine single-tile cardinal direction relations. For example, a relation $O{:}S{:}SE{:}SN$ (multi-tile relation) can be denoted by $\{O,S,SE,SN\}$. The general cardinal direction relation (i.e., a basic cardinal direction relation or the disjunction of basic cardinal direction relations) can be regarded as a superset GB, whose element is the kind of set SB. So we have the relation: $SB \in GB$. The universal relation is the set $BIN = \{O, N, NE, E, SE, S, SW, W, NW\}$, and the universe, i.e. the set of all possible cardinal relations, is denoted by U.

Now, we present a system of rules for deducing new spatial relations from existing ones.

3.1 Rules for Deducing CDF Relations from RCC8 Relations (RCC8 → CDF)

Assuming that there exists some RCC8 relation between two regions A and B and we want to know the potential cardinal direction relations between them, we show the deduction rules in three cases and give their proofs if necessary.

Case 1 From the RCC8 relation A DC B, we can not specify the CDF relation between them, i.e.,

$$A \; U \; B :: A \; DC \; B, \tag{3.1}$$

where U is the universe of possible CDF relations between two non-empty and connected regions.

This rule is obvious, because the DC relation is the least restricted relation between two regions.

Case 2 Let x denote any relation symbol in $\{EC, PO, TPPi, NTPPi\}$. We have the following rule for each x. Because this rule is difficult to represent, we adopt first-order logic and the notations for CDF.

$$\forall SB \in GB(A, B), O \in SB \; :: \; A \; x \; B \tag{3.2}$$

Proof. According to definitions (2.2), (2.3), (2.6) and (2.7), A and B must have a common part. From B $\subseteq MBB$(B), it follows that A and MBB(B) must have a common part (i.e., A∩MBB(B)≠∅). According to the definitions (2.18) and (2.9), region A must have a part which satisfies the relation O with respect to B. □

Case 3 Let x denote any of the relation symbols in $\{TPP, NTPP, EQ\}$. We have the following rule for each such x.

$$A \; O \; B :: A \; x \; B \tag{3.3}$$

Proof. From the relation A x B, we have A⊆B. Hence A⊆MBB(B). According to the definition (2.9) for CDF relation O, we conclude that the relation A O B holds. □

3.2 Rules for Deducing RCC8 Relations from CDF Relations (CDF → RCC8)

In this section, we will investigate the rules deducing RCC8 relation between any two regions A and B from the CDF relation between them in three cases.

Case 1 Let y denote any relation symbol in $\{DC, EC, PO, TPP, NTPP, EQ, TPPi\}$ (i.e., $\overline{NTPPi}$). We have the following rule.

$$A \; y \; B :: A \; O \; B \tag{3.4}$$

Proof. From the relation A O B and the definition (2.9), we have A⊆MBB(B). we can construct a scenario where A⊆MBB(B) and A y B are simultaneously satisfied. We now prove the relation A $NTPPi$ B is impossible if A O B holds. According to definitions (2.5) and (2.7), it is clear that there must be a part belonging to A which is outside of MBB(B). Hence the CDF relation between A and B must be a multi-tile one according to the definition (2.18). So there is a contradiction. □

Case 2 Let x denote a cardinal direction relation which is a multi-tile relation at least including O and another single-tile relation, for example $\{O{:}N{:}NE\}$. Let y denote the relation set $\{DC,\ EC,\ PO,\ TPPi,\ NTPPi\}$, which means y can be anyone of these relations. We have the rule below.

$$A\ y\ B :: A\ x\ B \tag{3.5}$$

Proof. From the relation x, we know there must be a part of A in MBB(B), and another outside it. So any of the RCC8 relations $\{TPP,\ NTPP,\ EQ\}$ is impossible, because, if so, A will be contained in MBB(B). □

Case 3 Let x denote any of the cardinal direction relations which do not contain O. Another rule can be described as follows.

$$A\ DC\ B :: A\ x\ B \tag{3.6}$$

Proof. This rule is obvious. Because x does not contain relation O, we have A∩MBB(B)=∅. Hence A∩B=∅, it follows A DC B according to definition (2.1) for RCC8 relation DC. □

3.3 Rules for Deducing Relations from the Composition of RCC8 and CDF Relations (RCC8 ∘ CDF)

We will discuss these rules in three cases.

Case 1 Let x denote any of the relation symbols in $\{TPP, NTPP\}$, y any CDF relation and z the induced CDF relation. The rule is described as follows.

$$A\ z\ C :: A\ x\ B, B\ y\ C, \tag{3.7}$$

Where, if y is a single-tile CDF relation, z equals y, and if y is a multi-tile CDF relation, z is any subset of y.

Proof. From A$\{TPP, NTPP\}$ B, We know A⊆B. Hence, if B satisfies a single-tile CDF relation with respect to C, A must also satisfy it. Then it follows that A y C holds. We now consider the situation where y is a multi-tile CDF relation. According to definition (2.18), B can be regarded as consisting of several subregions which satisfy single-tile relations in y with respect to C, respectively. So region A can be one of, or consist several of these subregions. It follows that the relation z can be any subset of y. □

Case 2 This rule is similar to the above except that x is anyone of the relation symbols in $\{TPPi, NTPPi\}$. So we have the relation A⊇B. It follows that the rule can be described as follows.

$$A\ z\ C :: A\ x\ B, B\ y\ C, \tag{3.8}$$

where z is any superset of y, i.e. y is the subset of z.

Case 3 This rule is obvious, so we present it directly.

$$A\ y\ C :: A\ EQ\ B, B\ y\ C \tag{3.9}$$

The rules for deducing RCC8 relations from the composition of RCC8 and CDF relations can be derived by combining the above rules (3.7)-(3.9) and rules (3.4)-(3.6).

3.4 Rules for Deducing Relations from the Composition of CDF and RCC8 Relations (CDF ∘ RCC8)

The rules are presented in three cases as follows

Case 1 Let x denote any single-tile CDF relation and y denote the deduced CDF relation. The rule is described as follows.

$$A \ y \ C :: A \ x \ B, C \ \{TPP, NTPP\} \ B, \tag{3.10}$$

Where, if x is any of the relation symbols in $\{NW, NE, SE, SW\}$, y equals x, and if x is N (respectively S, E or W), y is any subset of $\{NW, N, NE\}$ (respectively $\{SW, S, SE\}$, $\{NE, E, SE\}$ or $\{SW, W, NW\}$).

Proof. To prove the first case, we take the relation NW for example. From the relation C $\{TPP, NTPP\}$ B and definitions (2.4) and (2.5), we have the following ordering relations: $sup_x(C) \leq sup_x(B)$, $inf_x(B) \leq inf_x(C)$, $sup_y(C) \leq sup_y(B)$ and $inf_y(B) \leq inf_y(C)$. From the relation A NW B, we can list the following ordering relations according to its definition (2.13): $sup_x(A) \leq inf_x(B)$ and $sup_y(B) \leq inf_y(A)$.

From the above ordering relations and transitivity of $\leq$, we see that $sup_x(A) \leq inf_x(C)$ and $sup_y(C) \leq inf_y(A)$, which corresponds to the definition (2.13). The proof for NE, SE or SW is similar.

The second case can be proved similarly. □

Case 2 Using the above methods, we can also verify the following rule.

$$A \ y \ C :: A \ x \ B, C \ \{TPPi, NTPPi\} \ B, \tag{3.11}$$

Where, if x is SW (respectively NW, NE or SE), y is any subset of $\{W, SW, S, O\}$ (respectively $\{N, NW, W, O\}$, $\{N, NE, E, O\}$, or $\{E, SE, S, O\}$), and if x is N (respectively S, E or W), y is any subset of $\{N, O\}$ (respectively $\{S, O\}$, $\{E, O\}$ or $\{W, O\}$).

Case 3 Let x denote any CDF relation. This rule is obvious. We just describe it directly as follows.

$$A \ x \ C :: A \ x \ B, B \ EQ \ C \tag{3.12}$$

The rules for deducing RCC8 relations from the composition of CDF and RCC8 relations can be derived by combining the above rules (3.10)-(3.12) and rules (3.4)-(3.6).

3.5 Composite Rules

The advocation of the rules in this section is motivated by such situations where given the relations A N B, B PO C, C N D, what is the relation between A and D? We can not find the answer using the above rules and we should find more powerful rules.

Sharma [3] verified and extended [12]'s inference rule:

$$A \ x \ D :: A \ x \ B, B \ y \ C, C \ x \ D \ .$$

In this paper, we adapt this rule to our model and investigate its properties. Let R denote any of the RCC8 relation symbols in $\{EC, PO, TPP, NTPP, TPPi, NTPPi, EQ\}$, x and y denote any single-tile CDF relation and z denote the deduced CDF relation, respectively. These rules are discussed in three cases.

Case 1
$$A\ z\ D :: A\ x\ B, B\ R\ C, C\ y\ D, \qquad (3.13)$$
where x is N (respectively S, W, or E), y is any of the relation symbols in $\{NW$, N, $NE\}$ (respectively $\{SW, S, SE\}$, $\{NW, W, SW\}$, or $\{NE, E, SE\}$) and then z is any subset of $\{NW, N, NE\}$ (respectively $\{SW, S, SE\}$, $\{NW, W, SW\}$, or $\{NE, E, SE\}$).

Proof. When x is N and y is NW, we have the relations A N B, B R C and C NW D. From A N B and the definition (2.14), we have the following ordering relations: $sup_y(B) \leq inf_y(A)$, $inf_x(B) \leq inf_x(A)$ and $sup_x(A) \leq sup_x(B)$.

From C NW D and the definition (2.13) for relation NW, we have the following ordering relations: $sup_x(C) \leq inf_x(D)$ and $sup_y(D) \leq inf_y(C)$.

From B R C, we know that B∩C≠∅. So let p be an arbitrary point in B∩C. p_x is its x-coordinate and p_y its y-coordinate, respectively. So, p satisfies the following ordering relations. $inf_x(B) \leq p_x \leq sup_x(B)$, $inf_x(C) \leq p_x \leq sup_x(C)$, $inf_y(B) \leq p_y \leq sup_y(B)$ and $inf_y(C) \leq p_y \leq sup_y(C)$.

From the above ordering relations and transitivity of $\leq$, we have the resulting ordering relation $sup_y(D) \leq inf_y(A)$, which means the possible relations between A and D can be A N D, A NW D, A NE D, A $N{:}NW$ D or A $N{:}NE$ D, i.e., all the subsets of $\{NW, N, NE\}$. When y is N or NE, the same result can be derived. Other cases can be proved similarly. □

Using the above methods, we can validate the following two rules.
Case 2
$$A\ z\ D :: A\ x\ B, B\ R\ C, C\ y\ D, \qquad (3.14)$$
where x is any of the relation symbols in $\{NW, NE\}$ (respectively $\{SW, SE\}$, $\{NW, SW\}$, or $\{NE, SE\}$), y is N (respectively S, W, or E) and then z is any subset of $\{x, N\}$ (respectively $\{x, S\}$, $\{x, W\}$, or $\{x, E\}$), i.e., when x is NE and y is N, then z is any subset of $\{NE, N\}$.
Case 3
$$A\ z\ D :: A\ x\ B, B\ R\ C, C\ y\ D, \qquad (3.15)$$
where x is NW (respectively SW, NE, or SE), y equals x, and then z is NW (respectively SW, NE, or SE).

4 Terminologies and Definitions

If every one of the constraints in a Constraint Satisfaction Problem (CSP) involves two variables (possibly the same) and asserts that the pair of values assigned to those variables must lie in a certain binary relation, then the constraint satisfaction problem is called Binary Constraint Satisfaction Problem.

We define an RCC8-BCSP as a BCSP of which the constraints are RCC8 relations on pairs of the variables. The universe of a RCC8-BCSP is the set $\mathbb{R}^2$ of regions anyone of which is a point-set homeomorphic to a unit disk. Similarly we can define CDF-BCSP as a BCSP of which the constraints are CDF relations on pairs of the variables and the universe is the set $\mathbb{R}^2$ of regions anyone of which is a point-set homeomorphic to a unit disk, and RDF-BCSP as a BCSP of which the constraints consist of a conjunction of RCC8 relations and CDF relations on pairs of the variables and the universe is the set $\mathbb{R}^2$ of regions anyone of which is a point-set homeomorphic to a unit disk.

A binary constraint problem with n variables and universe U can be simply viewed as an n-by-n matrix M of binary relations over U: the relation M_{ij} (in row i, column j) is the constraint on $<x_i, x_j>$.

Let M and N be n-by-n matrices of binary relations. We have definitions as follows:

$$(M \circ N)_{ij} = (M_{i0} \circ N_{0j}) \cap (M_{i1} \circ N_{1j}) \cap ... \cap (M_{in-1} \circ N_{n-1j}) = \bigcap_{k<n} M_{ik} \circ N_{kj}.$$

Let $M^2 = M \circ M$.

An n-by-n constraint matrix M is path-consistent if $M \leq M^2$.

M is path-consistent just in case $M_{ij} \subseteq M_{ik} \circ M_{kj}$. We must note that path consistency is the necessary, but not sufficient, condition for the consistency of a BCSP.

5 Path Consistency in RDF-BCSP

To enforce the path consistency in RDF-BCSP, we must consider the interactions between the RCC8 component and CDF component in RDF-BCSP in addition to the internal path consistency in RCC8-BCSP and CDF-BCSP, respectively.

We devise a constraint propagation procedure $Dpc()$ for enforcing path consistency in RDF-BCSP, which is adapted from the path consistency algorithm described in [4]. Our algorithm employs two queues RCC8-Queue and CDF-Queue, which are initialized to all pairs (x, y) of the RCC8-BCSP and CDF-BCSP variables, respectively, verifying $x \leq y$ (the variables are supposed to be ordered). The algorithm removes pairs of variables from the two queues in parallel or in turn. When a pair $\langle X, Y \rangle$ of variables of RCC8-BCSP (respectively CDF-BCSP) is removed from RCC8-Queue (respectively CDF-Queue), firstly the RCC8 (respectively CDF) relation on $\langle X, Y \rangle$ is converted to the CDF (respectively RCC8) relation on $\langle X, Y \rangle$ according to the rules (3.1)-(3.3) (respectively (3.4)-(3.6)). If the resulting CDF (respectively RCC8) relation on $\langle X, Y \rangle$ is different from the original relation on $\langle X, Y \rangle$, the pair of variables will be entered to the CDF-Queue (respectively RCC8-Queue); Then this CDF (respectively RCC8) relation on the pair $\langle X, Y \rangle$ is used to update the CDF (respectively RCC8) relations on the neighboring pairs of variables (pairs sharing at least one variable) according to the prerequisites in the rules provided by section 3. If a pair is successfully updated, it is entered into RCC8-Queue (respectively CDF-Queue), if it is not already there, in order to be considered at a future stage for propagation. This propagation procedure is common with Allen's algorithm, what's different is that the RCC8 (respectively CDF) relation on every pair of variables will be used to refine the relevant relations according to these rules provide by section 3.

The algorithm loops until it terminates if the empty relation, indicating inconsistency, is detected, or if RCC8-Queue and CDF-Queue become empty, indicating that a fixed point has been reached and the input RDF-BCSP is made path consistent.

Theorem 1. *The constraint propagation procedure Dpc() runs into completion in $O(n^3)$ time, where n is the number of variables of the input RDF-BCSP.*

Proof. The number of variable pairs is $O(n^2)$. A pair of variables may be placed in queue at most a constant number of times (8 for a pair of RCC8 variables, which is the total number of RCC8 atoms; and 218 for a pair of CDF variables, which is the total number of CDF basic cardinal direction relations. Every time a pair is removed from queue for propagation, the procedure performs $O(n)$ operations. □

6 Conclusions

In this paper, we have combined two essential formalisms in qualitative spatial reasoning, i.e., RCC8 and cardinal direction formalism. These discussions can be used to solve the consistency problem in Geographic Information System. The modeling and computational problems in Fuzzy QSR should be also interesting.

References

1. A. Gerevini and J. Renz. Combining Topological and Size Constraints for Spatial Reasoning. *Artificial Intelligence (AIJ)*, vol. 137(1-2): 1-42, 2002
2. A Isli, V Haarslev and R Moller. Combining cardinal direction relations and relative orientation relations in Qualitative Spatial Reasoning. Fachbereich Informatik, University Hamburg, Technical report FBI-HH-M-304/01, 2001
3. J. Sharma. Integrated spatial reasoning in geographic information systems: combining topology and direction. Ph.D. Thesis, Department of Spatial Information Science and Engineering, University of Maine, Orono, ME, 1996
4. James F. Allen. Maintaining knowledge about temporal intervals. *Communications of the ACM*, vol. 26(11): 832-843, November, 1983
5. A. Prasad Sistla, Clement T. Yu and R. Haddad. Reasoning About Spatial Relations in Picture Retrieval Systems. In: *20th International Conference on Very Large Data Bases*, pp. 570-581, Morgan Kaufmann, 1994
6. M. Egenhofer. A Formal Definition of Binary Topological Relations. In *Third International Conference on Foundations of Data Organization and Algorithms (FODO)*, Vol. 367, pp. 457-472, Paris, France: Lecture Notes in Computer Science, Springer-Verlag, 1989
7. Randell D, Cui Z and Cohn A. A spatial logic based on regions and connection. In: Nebel B, Rich C, Swartout W, (eds.) *Proc. of the Knowledge Representation and Reasoning*, pp. 165~176, San Mateo: Morgan Kaufmann, 1992
8. R. Goyal and M. Egenhofer. Cardinal Directions between Extended Spatial Objects. *IEEE Transactions on Knowledge and Data Engineering* (to be published), 2000
9. S. Skiadopoulos and M. Koubarakis. Composing cardinal direction relations. *Artificial Intelligence*, vol. 152(2): 143—171, 2004
10. D. A. Randell, A. G. Cohn and Z. Cui. Computing Transitivity Tables: A Challenge For Automated Theorem Provers. In *11th International Conference on Automated Deduction*, pp.786-790, Berlin: Springer Verlag, 1992
11. Serafino Cicerone and Paolino Di Felice. Cardinal directions between spatial objects: the pairwise-consistency problem. *Information Sciences*, vol. 164: 165-188, 2004
12. A. Prasad Sistla, Clement T. Yu, and R. Haddad. Reasoning About Spatial Relations in Picture Retrieval Systems. *International Journal on Very Large Databases (VLDB)*, vol. 3(4): 570-581, 1994

Querying a Polynomial Object-Relational Constraint Database in Model-Based Diagnosis

M.T. Gómez-López, R.M. Gasca, C. Del Valle, and F.T. de la Rosa

Departamento de Lenguajes y Sistemas Informáticos,
Escuela Técnica Superior de Ingeniería Informática, Universidad de Sevilla, Spain
{mayte, gasca, carmelo, ffrosat}@lsi.us.es

Abstract. Many papers related to Constraint Databases (CDBs) theories exist, including proposals that present frameworks for the treatment of constraints as a new data type. Our proposal presents a new way of storing and manipulating constraints as a usual data, and of making queries about the constraint variables derived from an Object-Relational Constraint Database (ORCDB). In this work, the constraints stored in an ORCDB are only polynomial equality constraints. The proposal is based on Gröbner bases, constraint consistency and constraint optimisation techniques. Most works in CDB use spatial-temporal data as a case study, however this work presents an emergent engineering domain, that of fault diagnosis.

1 Introduction

This work is based on the necessity of dicovering new ways of storing constraint information such as spatio-temporal, scientific, medical or engineering data. Current databases have limitations in storing constraint data, due to the finite size of the physical support. Very large databases have delays in retrieving and modifying information. This type of data makes it necessary to find another method to represent constraint data as discrete information.

The main objective of this paper is to present a way of storing and querying constraints and their variables. The constraints are stored as objects in an Object-Relational Constraint Database (ORCDB) using Oracle^{TM} 9.i. This function is indispensable for model-based diagnosis, due to the the lack of solutions creating equivalent systems which depend on the known variables. This paper proposes a solution to the problem of obtaining the constraints of a system, by means of asking about their variables.

In order to obtain new constraints inferred from an ORCDB, four different techniques are used: symbolic techniques, based on Gröbner Bases; constraint optimisation techniques; constraint consistency; and a combination of symbolic and constraint consistency techniques.

Constraint Databases (CDBs) have been specially used in the treatment of spatial-temporal data, however this work demonstrates that other engineering areas also can benefit from using CDBs. For this reason an emergent engineering domain is used, that of fault diagnosis.

This work is organised as follows: Section 2 analyses other previous works. Section 3 presents model-based diagnosis as a case of study. Section 4 analyses the most important techniques to develop the architecture. Section 5 shows the architecture and its most important modules. Sections 6 and 7 present the syntax and functionality for the creation of an ORCDB, insertion of new records into tables and for querying an ORCDB. Finally, some conclusions and future work are presented.

2 Background

Constraint Databases began their development in 1990 with the paper of Kuper, Kanellakis and Revesz [1], and grew out of the research on Datalog [2] and Constraint Logic Programming (CLP).

Many database applications have to deal with infinite concepts such as time and space. However, databases have a finite capacity. The basic idea is that constraints can be used to represent, in a compact way, data that could be very large, or even infinite.

There are other methods for implementing and building prototypes for CDBs, whose main objective is handling spatial-temporal data. The most important approaches are analysed:

- **MLPQ/PReSTO:** This proposal [3] presents a combination of MLPQ (Management of Linear Programming Queries) and PReSTO (Parametric Rectangle Spatio Temporal Object). MLPQ is a system for the management and linear programming query in CDBs. It allows Datalog queries and the addition of operators over linear functions. PREsTO facilitates the performance of relational algebra querying systems that change over time. Although both present similar SQL syntax, they actually use a plane file to store the information and a Datalog query transformation process.
- **DEDALE** [4] is one of the first implementations of CDBs based on linear constraint models. DEDALE provides a language to query CDBs, which allows information to be obtained and uses a graphical interface to show the results. In order to represent the constraints, DEDALE uses the object-oriented paradigm, a more appropriate way to represent complex data. In this approach all the information is stored as objects. The type of data used in DEDALE is the spatial data model and a special module is given for spatial queries.
- **CCUBE:** (Constraint Object-Oriented Database System) [5] is a constraint object-oriented database system. The CCUBE system is designed to be used for the implementation and optimisation of high-level constraint object-oriented query languages. The CCUBE data manipulation language (Constraint Comprehension Calculus) is an integration of constraint calculus for extensible constraint domains within monoid comprehension. CCUBE gives an optimisation-level language for object-oriented queries. The data model for the constraint calculus is based on constraint spatio-temporal (CST)

objects. CCUBE guarantees polynomial time data complexity whose implementation uses the linear programming package CPLEX.

3 Diagnosis: A Motivating Example

Fault detection and identification of faulty components are very important company strategies, due to the economic demand and environment conservation required to remain in competitive markets. Diagnosis allows us to determine why a correctly designed system does not work as is expected and is based here on the monitorization of a system using DX [6] approach [7]. These papers were proposed to identify the discrepancies between the observed and correct behaviour of systems.

In engineering applications the storage of these data and query processing are often overlooked. Other works such as [8] have improved the efficiency in some phases of the model-based diagnosis with CDBs.

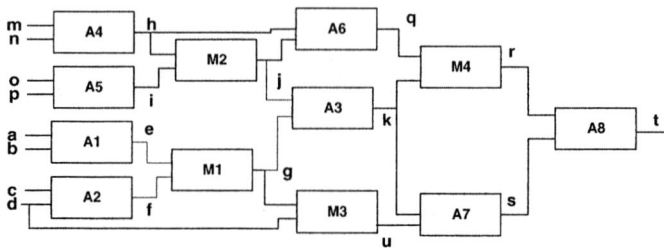

Fig. 1. Diagnosis Example

In this work, a new approach is proposed for querying ORCDBs in order to obtain equivalent systems which can be diagnosed such as the system shown in Figure 1. The example presents a group of components, multipliers (Mi) and adders(Ai), which work together. The use of SQL over constraints makes it possible to obtain several models. These models are compared to the real values in order to perform the diagnosis of the system. The location of sensors defines which variables are observable. Depending on the query, it is possible to know whether a part or the full system works correctly. It is also possible to obtain a group of equivalent constraints by replacing the non-observable variables.

4 Computational Techniques

In order to develop our architecture, four different tools are used. The first tool is the symbolic technique of Gröbner Bases, the second is the use of constraint consistency technique, the third is the constraint optimisation technique, and the last tool is a combination of symbolic and constraint consistency techniques.

4.1 Gröbner Bases

Gröbner bases theory [9] is the origin of many symbolic algorithms used to manipulate multiple variable polynomials. It is a generalisation of Gauss's elimination of multivariable lineal equations and of the Euclides algorithm for one-variable polynomial equations. Gröbner bases have better computational properties than the original system.

Gröbner bases transform a set of polynomial constraints into a standard form. By having the set of equality polynomial constraints in the form $P = 0$, Gröbner bases produce an equivalent system $G = 0$ which has the same solutions as the original.

For our work, there is a function called GröbnerBasis, which calculates Gröbner bases by means of a finite set of polynomial equations and a set of output variables, and those variables to be eliminated.

The signature of GröbnerBasis function is:

GröbnerBasis({Polynomials},{Output Variables},{Unwanted Variables})

4.2 Constraint Consistency and Constraint Optimisation Techniques

The previous problems of engineering can be modelled as Constraint Satisfaction Problems (CSP) [10]. A CSP consists of a finite set of variables, a domain of values for each variable and a set of constraints that restrict the combinations of values of the variables. The aim in a CSP is to determine a value for each variable so that all constraints in the problem are satisfied. Usually, a combination of search with consistency techniques is used to solve these problems. The consistency techniques remove inconsistent values from the domains of the variables during the search. Several local consistency and optimisation techniques have been proposed as ways of improving the efficiency of search algorithms.

The consistency techniques are used as a process to obtain the values of the unknown variables from the known variables, by avoiding the use of symbolic techniques that usually have a higher computational complexity. For the Constraint Consistency techniques (Subsection 7.2), the search is not necessary because the domain of the known variables in the queries has just one value. But constraint optimisation techniques (Subsection 7.3) can have several correct values, so it is necessary to define an objective and the search is necessary. Our proposal takes advantages of all these techniques and dynamically builds CSPs depending on the query. In this work the domain of the integer is the only type used.

5 The Architecture

The main objective of our work is to add an interface to make the use of constraints transparent, by handling *Constraint Type* as a usual type of data. To store constraints, the semantics of SQL has been modified, by changing as less as possible the syntax of the queries. Figure 2 shows the architecture of the system.

The interaction between the user and the system is through the interface CROQL (Constraint Relational Object Query Language). The *Lexical and Syntactic Analysis* module verifies that the query is correct. The *SQL Transformation* module obtains the necessary information to perform the query. The *TypeOfQuery* module decides which technique is necessary, in order to return the solution to the user. Depending on the query, one of the four modules (optimisation, consistency, symbolic or consistency/symbolic technique) is used. It is also possible to query the ORCBD without any modification.

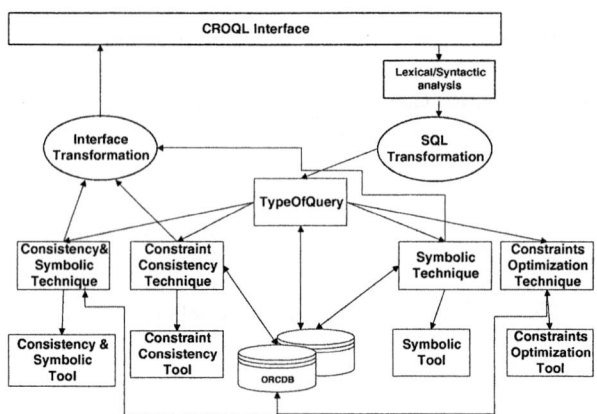

Fig. 2. Architecture of the system

The user of ORCDBs can ask, in a very easy way, about usual types, constraints or variables related to the constraints. The constraints are stored as objects indexed by the variables which contain them, in order to improve the execution time for obtaining the constraints related to some variables. In an OR-CDB it is possible to store the same information because all the information is stored in a relational database. However when the user asks about information related to constraints it is necessary to develop some transformations. In order to clarify when it is necessary to use each part of the architecture, the example shown in Figure 1 is used.

6 Creating an ORCDB and Inserting Information

In this section, it is shown how it is possible to create and fill an ORCDB. Some implementation decisions have been accepted to improve the computational time in the queries, and to make the information versatile. One of the most important advantages of our proposal is to make the utilisation of constraints transparent to the user, therefore a very similar syntax of SQL is kept in CROQL.

6.1 Creating an ORCDB

In order to create an ORCDB the following sentence is used:
    CREATE CONSTRAINTDATABASE <database_name>

In our model, when an ORCDB is created, the tables shown in Figure 3 are created too, in order to improve the computational time for obtaining the constraints related to some variables. These tables allow the identification of each constraint (table *Constraint*), each variable (table *Variable*) and to establish the relations between the constraints and the variables (*Constraint/Variable*), thereby avoiding the study of all constraints.

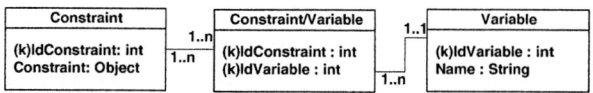

Fig. 3. Tables to index constraints and variables

6.2 Creating a Table in an ORCDB

As our proposal tries to modify SQL syntax as little as possible, the syntax is not modified at all to create a table. The unique change is that it is possible to create constraint fields, where $<$ field_type$_i$ $>$ is *Constraint Type*. In our case, the possible type of constraints is polynomial equality constraints.

For the example shown in Figure 1, the sentence is:
    CREATE TABLE Component (IdComponent Integer, Name String,
    Behaviour Constraint)

6.3 Inserting New Information into the Tables

If a field of a table has been created as *Constraint Type*, it is possible to add constraint information. Our proposal adds the option to of handling the constraint as a usual type, such as *Integer, String, Date* ...

Therefore, if the user tries to add information of an incorrect type to a field, an error will be produced as in a relational database. The checking of the type works as for usual types.

When constraint data is added, indexes are created in the table *Constraint* in order to locate constraints more quickly and efficiently.

The users cannot see the indexes, and these are just used to speed up the queries. These indexes are necessary when constraints are added, and they are created and stored in an implicit way.

In order to store the example shown in Figure 1 in an ORCDB, one query could be:
    INSERT INTO Component (IdComponent, Name, Behaviour)
        VALUES (101, A1, "a + b = e")
The ORCDB after inserting some components is shown in Figure 4.

Component				Constraint			Variable			Constraint Variable	
Id	Name	Behaviour		Id	ConstraintObject		Id	Name		IdCo	IdVar
1	A1	1		1	a+b=e		1	a		1	1
2	A2	2		2	c+d=f		2	b		1	2
3	M1	3		3	e*f=g		3	e		1	3
4	M2	4		4	h*i=j		4	d		2	5
5	A3	5		5	h+g=k		5	c		2	4
6	M3	6		6	d+g=u		6	f		...	...
...	...	...		...	...		...	...			

Fig. 4. Example of tables with stored constraints

7 Querying an ORCDB

This Section describes which part of the system is used depending on the query.

With our methodology, it is possible to query constraint variables, it means querying <field_name> or <field_name>.VariableName, where <field_name> is a *Constraint Type*.

Depending on the query, different parts of the architecture are used:

- If the query involves usual types or constraints stored directly in the ORCDB, but the query does not involve variables, the query is not transformed.
- If the query involves variables from constraints stored in the ORCDB and none one of the variables are instantiated, a symbolic tool is used, as explained in Subsection 7.1.
- If the query involves variables of constraints stored in the ORCDB, where the objective is defined in the query, a optimisation tool is used. This is explained in Subsection 7.3.
- If the query involves constraint variables stored in an ORCDB and some variables are instantiated, there are two possibilities: using consistency techniques, if all the variables are instantiated (Subsection 7.2); or using a combination of symbolic and consistency techniques, if only some variables are instantiated (Subsection 7.4).

7.1 Symbolic Techniques

This part of the architecture is used when none of the variables are instantiated in the query. For this reason, those variables which do not appear in the query but are related to constraints which contain the variables of the query, must be replaced by variables of the query.

An example of a query solved using the symbolic technique is:

SELECT Component.Behaviour.a, Component.Behaviour.b, Component.Behaviour.c, Component.Behaviour.d, Component.Behaviour.u FROM Component

The idea of this process is to determine each *group of related constraints*, which is defined as:

G is a group of related constraints if
$G \equiv \bigcup_i \{c_i\} \mid \forall\ c_i\ \text{VarNoQuery}(c_i) \subseteq \text{VarNoQuery}(G - c_i)$

where c_i is a constraint and VarNoQuery(C) are the variables of the constraints C that do not appear in the query

For the example of Figure 1, the information shown below represents the constraints related to the query, and the variables that do not appear in the query in this form {Component, {VarNoQuery(Component) }}. The actual information is the indexes of constraints and variables, however to show the idea clearly, the names of components and variables are used. The information for our example is: {A1,{e}},{A2,{f}}, {M3,{g}},{A7,{s,k}},{M1,{e,f,g}},{A3,{g,j,k}},{M4,{k,q,r}}

In this case, A1 participates in a *group of related constraints* if e is in another constraint, such as M1. M1 participates in a *group of related constraints* if f and g are in another constraint, such as A2 and M3 respectively. This means that {A1, A2, M3, M1} form a *group of related constraints*. The rest of the constraints do not participate in a *group of related constraints*

In order to use the Gröbner bases, Mathematica^{TM} v.5 is used. For the example, the call to this function is :
GroebnerBasis[{a+b-e, c+d-f, e*f-g, g*d-u}, {a, b, c, d, u}, {e, f, g}]
And the result is: {a*c*d + b*c*d + a*d^2 + b*d^2 - u = 0}

7.2 The Constraint Consistency Tool

When all the variables in the query are instantiated, it is possible to use the module of constraint consistency technique. In this case, all the *groups of related constraints* are instantiated. A constraint is instantiated if it has only one unknown variable which means that all *VarNoQuerys* can be instantiated.

An example of this type of query is:
SELECT Component.Behaviour.u FROM Component
WHERE Component.Behaviour.a=1 AND Component.Behaviour.b=3
AND Component.Behaviour.c=2 AND Component.Behaviour.d=1

Once it is known that this query generates instantiated constraints, a Constraint Satisfaction Problem (CSP) is created in order to infer the value of u. This CSP is created dynamically using the constraints obtained from the ORCDB, the *VarNoQuerys* and the instantiated variables. Figure 5.a shows the CSP for the example.

The result is u= 12. All *VarNoQuery* variables are instantiated, but only u is presented as the solution. The OPL Studio^{TM} [11] is used in order to instantiate the variables.

7.3 The Constraint Optimisation Tool

When a query has several solutions and the user wants to select from among the possible options, the module of optimisation is used. An example of a query that uses this module is:
SELECT MIN(Component.Behaviour.u) FROM Component
WHERE Component.Behaviour.a>=3 AND Component.Behaviour.b>= 1
AND Component.Behaviour.b< 5 AND Component.Behaviour.c>2
AND Component.Behaviour.d<=3 AND Component.Behaviour.d>=0

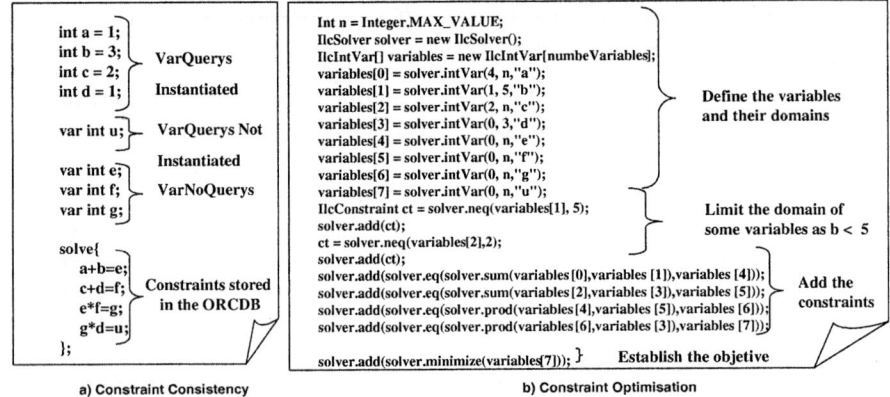

Fig. 5. Examples of CSP

Once it is known that this query generates instantiated constraints, a Constraint Satisfaction Problem (CSP) is created in order to infer the value of u. This CSP is dynamically created by using the constraints obtained from the ORCDB, *VarNoQuery* and the instantiated variables. Figure 5.b shows the CSP associated. JSolver^{TM} [12] is used in order to optimise the constraints.

7.4 The Constraint Consistency and Symbolic Tool

This module of the architecture is used when only some variables are instantiated in the query. In this case, a mixed tool is necessary, in order to propagate and to replace the variables in a symbolic way. This function also is from Mathematica^{TM} v.5. An example of this type of query can be:

SELECT Component.Behaviour.u FROM Component
WHERE Component.Behaviour.a=1 AND Component.Behaviour.d=2

In order to obtain the value of u, the system uses the syntax:

Solve[{Constraints Related to the query},{Out Variables},{VarNoQuery}]

For the example, the call would be:

Solve[$\{a+b == e, c+d == f, e*f == g, g*d == u\}$, $\{u\}$, $\{e, f\}$]

And the result would be: {u = 2 (2 + 2 b + c + b c)}

8 Conclusions and Future Work

This work extends the semantics of SQL, in order to store constraint information as a new data type. The constraints data are indexed in order to improve the computational time. The interaction between the user and the system is transparent to the constraint handler. The system allows the use of polynomial equality constraints, by using four techniques to perform the queries: symbolic, constraint consistency, constraint optimisation and symbolic/consistency techniques.

As future work, we propose extending the domains of variables and constraints. We also suggest an extension to incorporate different types of constraints, not only polynomial equalities. As for as SQL sentences are concerned, it is necessary to offer all the possibilities of standard SQL, such as UPDATE, REMOVE and other types of queries.

Acknowledgements

This work has been partially funded by the Ministerio de Ciencia y Tecnología of Spain (DPI2003-07146-C02-01) and European Regional Development Fund. (ERDF/FEDER).

References

1. G. M. Kuper P. C. Kanellakis and P. Z. Revesz. Constraint query languages. *Symposium on Principles of Database Systems*, pages 299–313, 1990.
2. P. Revesz. Datalog and constraints. *Constraint Databases, G. Kuper et al. eds., Springer-Verlag*, pages 155–170, 2000.
3. P. Z. Revesz, R. Chen, P. Kanjamala, Y. Li, Y. Liu, and Y. Wang. The mlpq/gis constraint database system. In *Proceedings of the 2000 ACM SIGMOD International Conference on Management of Data, May 16-18, 2000, Dallas, Texas, USA*, page 601. ACM, 2000.
4. Stéphane Grumbach, Philippe Rigaux, and Luc Segoufin. The dedale system for complex spatial queries. In *SIGMOD Conference*, pages 213–224, 1998.
5. A. Brodsky, V. E. Segal, J. Chen, and P. A. Exarkhopoulo. The ccube constraint object-oriented database system. In *SIGMOD '99: Proceedings of the 1999 ACM SIGMOD international conference on Management of data*, pages 577–579. ACM Press, 1999.
6. R. Davis. Diagnostic reasoning based on structure and behavior. *In Artificial Intelligence 24*, pages 347–410, 1984.
7. R. Reiter. A theory of diagnosis from first principles. *Artificial Intelligence 32*, 1:57–96, 1987.
8. M. T. Gómez-López, R. Ceballos, R. M. Gasca, and C. Del Valle. Applying constraint databases in the determination of potential minimal conflicts to polynomial model-based diagnosis. In *CDB*, pages 75–89, 2004.
9. B. Buchberger. Gröbner bases: An algorithmic method in polynomial ideal theory. *Multidimensional Systems Theory, N. K. Bose, ed.*, pages 184–232, 1985.
10. Albert Croker and Vasant Dhar. A knowledge representation for constraint satisfaction problems. *IEEE Trans. Knowl. Data Eng.*, 5(5):740–752, 1993.
11. Reference Manual. Ilog opl studio 3.6. April, 2001.
12. Reference Manual. Jsolver 2.1. April, 2003.

A Three-Phase Knowledge Extraction Methodology Using Learning Classifier System

An-Pin Chen[1], Kuang-Ku Chen[2], and Mu-Yen Chen[1]

[1] Institute of Information Management, National Chiao Tung University,
Hsinchu, 300, Taiwan
{apc, mychen}@iim.nctu.edu.tw
[2] Department of Accounting, National Changhua University of Education,
Changhua 50058, Taiwan
Kungku83@ms47.hinet.net

Abstract. Machine learning methods such as fuzzy logic, neural networks and decision tree induction have been applied to learn rules but they may be trapped into local optimal. Based on the principle of natural evolution and global searching, a genetic algorithm is promising in obtaining better results. This article adopts learning classifier systems (LCS) technique to provide a three-phase knowledge extraction methodology, which makes continues and instant learning while integrates multiple rule sets into a centralized knowledge base. This paper makes three important contributions: (1) it represents various rule sets that are derived from different sources and encoded as a fixed-length bit string in the knowledge encoding phase; (2) it uses three criteria (accuracy, coverage, and fitness) to select an optimal set of rules from a large population in the knowledge extraction phase; (3) it applies genetic operations to generate optimal rule sets in the knowledge integration phase. The experiments prove the rule sets derived by the proposed approach is more accurate than other machine learning algorithm.

1 Introduction

Developing an expert system requires construction of a complete, correct, consistent, and concise knowledge base. The knowledge base construction always involves interaction and dialogue between domain experts and knowledge engineers. Therefore, to acquire and integrate multiple knowledge inputs from many experts or by various knowledge-acquisition techniques thus plays an important role in building effective knowledge-based systems [1][2].

Generally, knowledge integration can be though of as a multi-objective optimization problem [15]. Due to the huge searching space, the optimization problem is often very difficult to solve. A genetic algorithm (GA) was usually used to discover a desirable but not necessarily optimal set of rules. The application of a GA in search of an optimal rule set for machine learning is known as Genetic Based Machine Learning (GBML). A well-known GBML architecture is the so-called Learning Classifier Systems (LCS) developed by Holland [4][6]. More recent GBML architectures are the Extended Classifier System (XCS) developed by Wilson [13], Anticipatory Classifier System by Stolzmann [10], and EpiCS by Holme [7].

Our research objective was therefore to employ the XCS technique which can integrate multiple rule sets into one centralized knowledge base effectively. The rest of this paper is organized as follows. We discuss relative GA literatures in Section 2. Section 3 describes the system architecture of the XCS-based model. We then present knowledge encoding methodology in Section 4. Section 5 briefs on how the knowledge extraction methodology for reinforcement. The knowledge integration methodology is explained in Section 6. The experimental results are reported in Section 7. Finally, the conclusion and future work are discussed in Section 8.

2 Preliminaries

In this section we summarize and discuss two alternative ways in which the GA may be applied to LCS. These two methods, Michigan and Pittsburgh approaches, were first described as long ago as 1978 and 1980, respectively.

The first Michigan-style classifier system was Cognitive System One (CS-1) devised by Holland and Reitman [6]. CS-1 maintains a population of classifiers with genetic operations and credit assignment applied at the level of the individual rule. Since CS-1, a large number of alternative credit assignment schemes have been proposed, most notably the bucket-brigade [5] and Q-learning [11][12] for dealing with environments where reward may be infrequent and delayed. These proposed credit assignment schemes have achieved a great deal of success. The GA in a Michigan-style classifier system operates at the level of the individual classifier with selection of parent classifiers for mating based on strengths.

In 1980, Smith published results of an alternative LCS, LS-1, in which the unit of genetic manipulation is a suitably encoded genotype representing a complete set of classifiers [9]. Credit is assigned to complete sets of rules via interaction with the environment. This typifies so called "Pittsburgh"-style classifier systems. The GA in LS-1 operates at different levels: at the highest level, complete rule-sets are selected as the basis for reproduction to generate new rule-sets; at the lowest level individual rules are chosen by the GA to generate new rule.

Clearly the role of the GA in Michigan and Pittsburgh approaches is rather different, and the distinction arises from the difference in level at which the GA is applied. Both approaches, at least in their simplest forms, suffer from distinct, known problems which arise from the different way in which the GA is applied.

3 System Architecture

The system architecture is as shown in Figure 1. The system is an implementation version of the general framework of the Wilson's XCS classifier system. At first, the system initializes the classifier set in which is originally empty and will be covered by new classifiers automatically. Here, we assume that all knowledge sources are represented by rules since almost all knowledge derived by knowledge acquisition (KA) tools or induced by machine learning (ML) methods may easily be translated into or represented by rules. After the next new run of system, the initialization stage will load the learned classifier rule sets to be ready to run.

In the knowledge encoding phase, the system detects the environment states and encodes each rule among a rule set into the condition message of bit-string structure. Then, the system generates the match set from the classifier set which contains the classifiers matched to the condition message. Next, the system products a prediction array according to the prediction accuracy of matched classifiers, and generate an action set. After that, the system determinates the winner action with the highest accuracy, and then executes this winner action against the environment.

In the knowledge extraction phase, the system will gain the rewards from the environment after executing an action, and then makes the process of credit/rewards apportionment to the classifiers in the action set of previous step.

In the knowledge integration phase, the system instantly stars the learning procedure after the process of credit/rewards apportionment for each activity. In the meantime, the system triggers the GA to implement the evolutionary module, i.e., the GA contains selection, crossover, and mutation activities. Finally, it will report the execution performance, and store learning classifier set for the reapplication in the next activity requirements.

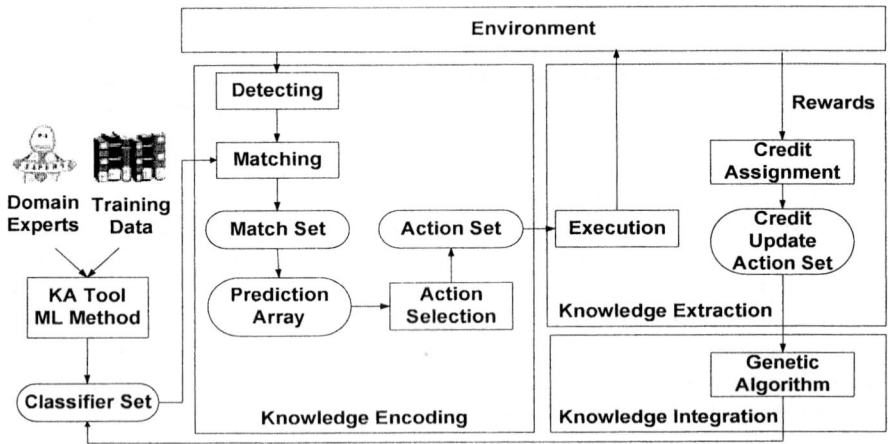

Fig. 1. System Architecture of XCS classifier system

4 Knowledge Encoding Phase

We use a pure binary string to do genetic coding. A classification rule can be coded as one chromosome consists of several segments. Each segment is corresponding to either an attribute in the condition part of the rule or a class in the conclusion part of the rule. Each segment consists of a string of gents that take a binary value 0 or 1. Each gene is corresponding to one linguistic term of the attribute or class. To improve the clarity of the coding, we use a semicolon to separate segments and a colon to separate the IF part and the THEN part.

Here, we use a famous example for deciding what sport to play according to "Saturday Morning Problem" is given to demonstrate the process of encoding representation [8][14]. Three sports {*Swimming, Volleyball, Weight_lifting*} are to decide by four attributes {*Outlook, Temperature, Humidity, Wind*}. The attribute *Outlook* has three possible values {*Sunny, Cloudy, Rain*}, attribute *Temperature* has three possible values {*Hot, Mild, Cool*}, attribute *Humidity* has two possible values {*Humid, Normal*}, and attribute *Wind* has two possible values {*Windy, Not_windy*}. Also, assume that a rule set RS_q from a knowledge source has the following three rules:

r_{q1} : IF (*Outlook* is *Sunny*) and (*Temperature* is *Hot*) THEN *Swimming*;

r_{q2} : IF (*Outlook* is *Cloudy*) and (*Wind* is *Not_windy*) THEN *Volleyball*;

r_{q3} : IF (*Outlook* is *Rain*) and (*Temperature* is *Cool*) THEN *Weight_lifting*;

The intermediate representation of these rules would then be:

r'_{q1} : IF (*Outlook* is *Sunny*) and (*Temperature* is *Hot*) and (<u>*Humidity* is *Humid* or *Normal*</u>) and (<u>*Wind* is *Windy* or *Not_windy*</u>) THEN *Swimming*;

r'_{q2} : IF (*Outlook* is *Cloudy*) and (<u>*Temperature* is *Hot* or *Mild* or *Cool*</u>) and (<u>*Humidity* is *Humid* or *Normal*</u>) and (*Wind* is *Not_windy*) THEN *Volleyball*;

r'_{q3} : IF (*Outlook* is *Rain*) and (*Temperature* is *Cool*) and (<u>*Humidity* is *Humid* or *Normal*</u>) and (<u>*Wind* is *Windy* or *Not_windy*</u>) THEN *Weight_lifting*.

The tests with underlines are dummy tests. Also, r'_{qi} is logically equivalent to r_{qi}, for i = 1, 2, 3. After translation, the intermediate representation of each rule is composed of four attribute tests and one class pattern.

After translation, each intermediate rule in a rule set is ready for being encoded as a bit string. Each attribute test is then encoded into a fixed-length binary string, whose length is equal to the number of possible test values. Each bit thus represents a possible value. For example, the set of legal values for attribute *Outlook* is {*Sunny, Cloudy, Rain*}, and three bits are used to represent this attribute. Thus, the bit string 110 would represent the test for *Outlook* being "*Sunny*" or "*Cloudy*". With this coding schema, we can also use the all-one string 111 (or simply denoted as #) to represent the wildcard of "don't care".

As a result, each intermediate rule in RS_q is encoded into a chromosome as shown in Fig. 2. It should be mentioned that our coding method is suitable to represent multi-value logic with OR relations between terms within each attribute, and the AND relations between attributes. After knowledge encoding, the genetic process chooses bit-string rules for "mating", gradually creating good offspring rules.

	Outlook	Temperature	Humidity	Wind	Sports
r'_{q1}	100	100	# #	# #	100
r'_{q2}	010	# # #	# #	01	010
r'_{q3}	001	001	# #	# #	001

Fig. 2. Bit-String Representation of RS_q

5 Knowledge Extraction Phase

In the knowledge extraction phase, genetic operations and credit assignment are applied at the rule level. In our approach, the initial set of bit strings for rules comes from multiple knowledge sources. Each individual within the population is a rule, and is of fixed length. Good rules are then selected for genetic operations to produce better offspring rules. The genetic process runs generation after generation until certain criteria have been met. After evolution, all the rules in a population are then combined to form a resulting rule set.

5.1 Initial Population

The GA requires a population of individuals to be initialized and updated during the evolution process. In our approach, the initial set of bit strings for rules comes from multiple knowledge sources. Each individual within the population is a rule, and is of fixed length. If all of rule sets have k rules, then the initial population size is k.

5.2 The Strength of a Rule

The strength of the fitness of a rule can be measured jointly by its coverage, accuracy, and relative contribution among all the rules in the population [15]. Let U be the set of test objects. The coverage of a rule derived rule (r_i) is defined as follows:

$$Cg(r_i) = \frac{|\Gamma_{r_i}^U|}{n} \quad (1)$$

Where $\Gamma_{r_i}^U$ is the set of test objects in U correctly predicted by r_i. The n is the number of objects in U. The coverage $Cg(r_i)$ is the relative size of this condition set in the entire object space. Obviously, the larger the coverage, the more general the rule is.

The accuracy of a rule r_i is evaluated using test objects as follows:

$$Ac(r_i) = \frac{|\Gamma_{r_i}^U|}{|\Gamma_{r_i}^U| + |U - \Gamma_{r_i}^U|} \quad (2)$$

$(U - \Gamma_{r_i}^U)$ is the set of test objects in U wrongly predicted by r_i. The accuracy of the rule is the measure indicating the degree to which the condition set is the subset of the conclusion set, or the truth that the condition implies the conclusion. Obviously, the higher the accuracy, the better the rule is.

Since an object may be classified by many rules, we want to measure the contribution of each rule in the classification of each object. If an object is classified correct by only one rule, this rule has full contribution or credit which equals 1. If an object is classified correctly by n rules, these rules should share the contribution, thus each of them has only 1/n contribution. The contribution of a rule is the sum of its contribution to correctly classify each object. The contribution of a rule r_i is defined as follows:

$$Cb(r_i) = \sum_{u \in U} \frac{\Psi(r_i, u)}{\sum_{r_i \in R} \Psi(r_i', u)} \qquad (3)$$

Where $\Psi(r, u) = \begin{cases} 1 & \text{if } u \text{ is correctly classified by a rule } r \\ 0 & \text{otherwise} \end{cases}$

The R is the population of all the rules. The u is a test object in U. The contribution measure captures the uniqueness of the rule. A rule with high contribution is in general less overlapping with other rules. Finally, we integrate all the quality measures into a single fitness function. The fitness of a rule r_i is defined by Equation (4).

$$Fit(r_i) = \left(\left(Ac(r_i) - \frac{1}{L} \right) + \frac{Cg(r_i)}{L} \right) Cb(r_i) \qquad (4)$$

The L is the number of all possible classes. The Ac(r_i) is subtracted by 1/L represents the accuracy of random guessing among L evenly distributed classes. The reason for making this subtraction is that a useful rule should be more accuracy than random guessing. We use 1/L as the weight for the coverage. When there are more classes, the coverage should have less weight because in this situation accuracy will be more difficult to achieve than coverage. Finally, the sum of the net accuracy and the weighted coverage is multiplies by the Cb(r_i) which represents the rule's competitive contribution in the population.

6 Knowledge Integration Phase

Genetic operators are applied to the population of rule sets for knowledge integration. They could create new rules from existing rules. There are two primitive genetic operators: crossover and mutation. The detail operators are described as follows.

The crossover operator exchanges string segments between two parent chromosomes to generate two child chromosomes. Continuing the above example, assume r_1 and r_2 are chosen as the parents for crossover. Assume the crossover point is set on their first and second segments.
Parent 1: (**100**; **100**; ##; ##; 100)
Parent 2: (**010**; **###**; ##; 01; 010)
Child 1: (**010**; **###**; ##; ##; 100)
Child 2: (**100**; **100**; ##; 01; 010)
 The two newly generated offspring rules are then:
Child 1: IF (Outlook is Cloudy) then Swimming;
Child 2: IF (Outlook is Sunny) and (Temperature is Hot) and (Wind is Not_windy) THEN Volleyball.

The mutation operator is randomly changes some elements in a selected rule and leads to additional genetic diversity to help the process escape from local-optimum "traps". As an example, the mutation on the second segment of the r_1 is shown as follows:

Existing: (**100**; **100**; ##; ##: 100).
Mutated: (**100**; **001**; ##; ##: 100) or (**100**; **010**; ##; ##: 100) or (**100**; **011**; ##; ##: 100) or (**100**; **101**; ##; ##: 100) or (**100**; **110**; ##; ##: 100) or (**100**; **111**; ##; ##: 100).

7 Experimental Results

A simple experiment to demonstrate LCS is the 6-bit multiplexer [3]. A Boolean 6-bit multiplexer is composed out of a 6 bit condition part (input) and a 1 bit action part (output). Figure 3 illustrates the 6-bit multiplexer. The first 2 bits of the input determine the binary address (00,01,10,11) which will select 1 of the 4 data lines. The output is determined by the value on the current selected dateline. Figure 4 shows the resulting classifier format for the 6-bit multiplexer. Where msb is the most significant bit and lsb is the least.

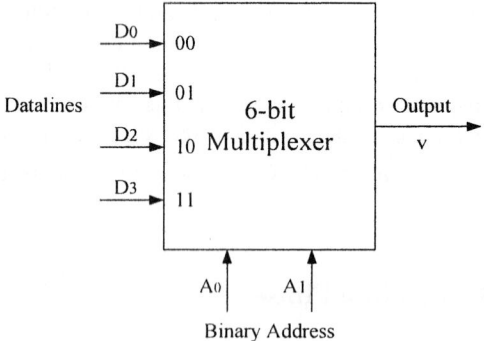

Fig. 3. A 6-bit multiplexer

A_1	A_2	D_0	D_1	D_2	D_3	v
Bit 1	Bit 2	Bit 3	Bit 4	Bit 5	Bit 6	Bit 7
Address msb	Address lsb	Data 00	Data 01	Data 10	Data 11	Data

Fig. 4. The classifier format for 6-bit multiplexer

With our multi-value logic coding method, each input and output has two values "On" and "Off" and thus can be represented by a string of two bits. We use *10* to represent "On", *01* to represent "Off", and # to represent a wildcard "don't care". As an example, (0;1;0;0;1;1) has an output of (0) because the input at data line 01 is 0. The format fir this example is (0;1;0;0;1;1:0). It is clear that the input values of the data lines 00, 10 and 11 in this example are not needed to generate the output. Further, the above case then can be represented as (01;10;01;01;10;10:01). The whole behavior of the 6-bit multiplexer can be summarized in the following eight rules:

Rule 1: (01;01;01;##;##;##:01)
Rule 2: (01;01;10;##;##;##:10)
Rule 3: (01;10;##;01;##;##:01)
Rule 4: (01;10;##;10;##;##:10)
Rule 5: (10;01;##;##;01;##:01)
Rule 6: (10;01;##;##;10;##:10)
Rule 7: (10;10;##;##;##;01:01)
Rule 8: (10;10;##;##;##;10:10)

Since there are 5 binary inputs and 1 binary output, only a total of 64 different cases can be used for training. However, with a possible wildcard, we could have $3^7 = 2187$ different rules. The total number of different rule sets then is 2^{2187}. Due to discover the optimal set of rules form this huge searching space is not an easy task. We use XCS-KI algorithm to learn the rules. To apply our algorithm, the population size is fixed to 200. In each generation, 20% of the population is selected for reproduction. The crossover probability is 0.8, and mutation probability is 0.04. For selecting the replacement candidate, the subpopulation size is 20 and initial fitness is 0.01. The algorithm converges quickly. The optimal set of eight best rules is extracted from the 48th generation. In this experiment, rules extraction of the proposed approach is compared to that of the other classification methods (decision tree, fuzzy decision tree, neural network, and genetic algorithm).The number of rules extracted in each generation is illustrated in Figure 5.

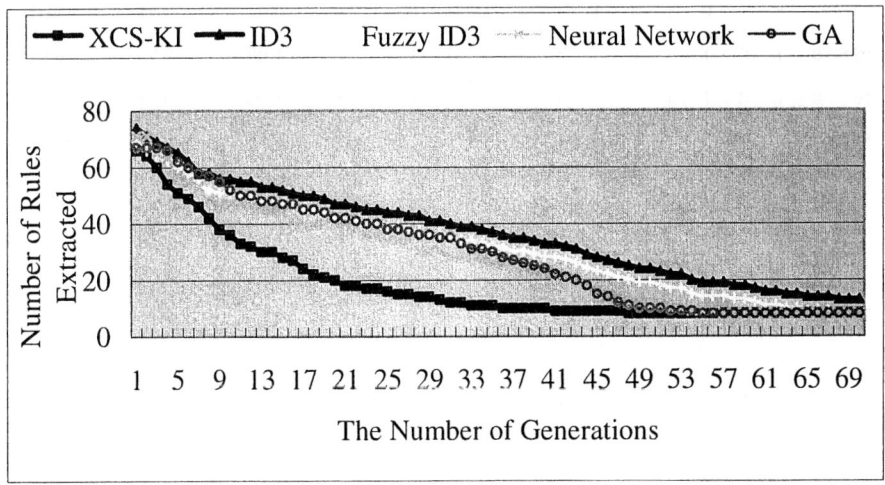

Fig. 5. The evolution process

The optimal set of 8 best rules was extracted form the 48th generation, which 17 other rules that have the highest fitness values shown in Table 1. The 8 rules with * are the best rules extracted from the population. Notice that the two rules with the highest fitness values are the most general rules.

Table 1. The Rules in the 48th generation for the Six-bit Multiplexer Problem

Rule	A$_1$		A$_0$		D$_0$		D$_1$		D$_2$		D$_3$		v		Accuracy	Coverage	Fitness
	On	Off	On	Off	On	Off	On	Off	On	Off	On	Off	On	Off			
1	1	1	1	1	1	1	1	1	1	1	1	1	1	0	0.33	1.00	3.10
2*	0	1	1	0	1	1	0	1	1	1	1	1	0	1	0.99	0.85	2.54
3	1	1	1	1	1	1	1	1	1	1	1	1	0	1	0.45	1.00	2.26
4*	0	1	1	0	1	1	1	0	1	1	1	1	1	0	0.94	0.81	1.87
5	1	1	1	1	1	0	1	0	1	1	1	1	0	1	0.74	0.78	1.81
6	1	1	1	0	1	1	1	0	1	1	0	1	1	0	0.85	0.65	1.72
7*	0	1	0	1	0	1	1	1	1	1	1	1	0	1	0.97	0.74	1.65
8	1	1	1	1	0	1	0	1	0	1	1	1	0	1	0.55	0.67	1.63
9	1	1	0	1	1	0	1	0	0	1	1	1	1	0	1.00	0.25	1.60
10*	1	0	0	1	1	1	1	1	1	0	1	1	1	0	1.00	0.88	1.44
11	1	0	1	1	1	1	0	1	0	1	0	1	0	1	0.68	0.45	1.33
12	1	1	1	0	1	1	1	1	1	1	1	1	1	0	0.77	0.84	1.18
13	0	1	0	1	1	1	1	1	1	0	1	0	1	0	0.71	0.39	1.06
14*	1	0	1	0	1	1	1	1	1	1	0	1	1	0	0.92	0.91	1.01
15*	0	1	0	1	1	0	1	1	1	1	1	1	1	0	1.00	0.93	0.97
16	0	1	0	1	1	1	1	1	1	0	1	1	0	1	1.00	0.52	0.92
17	1	1	1	0	1	1	0	1	0	1	0	1	0	1	0.94	0.63	0.79
18	1	0	1	0	1	1	1	1	1	0	0	1	1	0	0.96	0.41	0.72
19	0	1	1	1	1	1	0	1	0	1	0	1	0	1	0.96	0.82	0.67
20	1	0	1	1	0	1	1	1	0	1	1	0	1	0	0.91	0.83	0.61
21*	1	0	0	1	1	1	1	1	0	1	1	1	0	1	0.99	0.75	0.55
22	1	1	0	1	1	1	1	1	1	1	0	1	0	1	0.99	0.80	0.52
23*	1	0	1	0	1	1	1	1	1	0	1	0	1	0.89	0.78	0.48
24	1	1	1	1	0	1	1	1	1	1	0	1	0	1	0.72	0.23	0.37
25	1	0	1	1	0	1	1	1	0	1	1	0	0	1	0.51	0.81	0.33

8 Conclusion

In this paper, we have shown how the knowledge coding and knowledge integration methodology can be effectively represented and addressed by the proposed XCS-KI algorithm. The main contributions are included: (1) it needs no human experts' intervention in the knowledge integration process; (2) it is capable of generating classification rules that can be applied as well when the number of rule sets to be integrated increases; (3) it uses three criteria (accuracy, coverage, and fitness) to apply knowledge extraction process which is very effective in selecting an optimal set of rules from a large population. The experiments prove the rule sets derived by the proposed approach is more accurate than other machine learning algorithm.

References

1. Baral, C., Kraus, S., and Minker, J.: Combining Multiple Knowledge Bases. IEEE Transactions on Knowledge and Data Engineering, Vol. 3, No. 2 (1991) 208–220
2. Boose, J. H., and Bardshaw, J.M.: Expertise Transfer and Complex Problems: Using AQUINAS as a Knowledge-Acquisition Workbench for Knowledge-based Systems. International Journal of Man–Machine Studies, Vol. 26 (1987) 3–28
3. Goldberg, D.E.: Genetic Algorithms in Search, Optimization, and Machine Learning. Reading, MA, Addison-Wesley (1989)
4. Holland, J.H.: Adaptation in Natural and Artificial Systems. University Press of Michigan, Ann Arbor (1975)
5. Holland, J.H.: Properties of the bucket brigade algorithm. In: Grefenstette, J.J. (Eds.), Proc. First International Conference on Genetic Algorithm and their Applications. Lawrence Erlbaum, Hillsdale, NJ (1985) 1-7
6. Holland, J.H., Reitman, J.S.: Cognitive Systems Based on Adaptive Algorithms. In: Waterman, D.A., Hayes-Roth, F. (Eds.), Pattern directed interference systems. Academic Press, New York (1978) 313-329
7. Holmes, J.H.: Evolution-assisted Discovery of Sentinel Features in Epidemiologic Surveillance, Ph.D. thesis, Drexel University, Philadelphia, PA (1996)
8. Quinlan, J.: Induction of Decision Tree. Machine learning, Vol. 1 (1986) 81–106
9. Smith, S.F.: A Learning System based on Genetic Adaptive Algorithms. Ph.D. Thesis, University of Pittsburgh (1980)
10. Stolzmann, W.: An Introduction to Anticipatory Classifier Systems. Lecture Notes in Artificial Intelligence, Vol. 1813, Springer, Berlin (2000) 175–194
11. Sutton, R. S.: Reinforcement learning architectures for animals. In: Meyer, J. A. and Wilson, S. W (Eds.), Proceedings of the First International Conference on Simulation of Adaptive Behavior. MIT Press, Bradford Books (1991) 288-296
12. Wilson S.W.: ZCS: A Zeroth level classifier system. Evolutionary Computation, Vol. 2, No. 1 (1994) 1-18
13. Wilson S.W.: Rule Strength Based on Accuracy. Evolutionary Computation, Vol. 3, No. 2 (1996) 143-175
14. Yuan, Y., and Shaw, M. J.: Induction of Fuzzy Decision Trees. Fuzzy Sets and Systems, Vol. 69 (1995) 125–139
15. Yuan, Y., and Zhuang, H.: A Genetic Algorithm for Generating Fuzzy Classification Rules. Fuzzy Sets and Systems, Vol. 84 (1996) 1–19

A Replica Allocation Method Adapting to Topology Changes in Ad Hoc Networks

Hideki Hayashi, Takahiro Hara, and Shojiro Nishio

Dept. of Multimedia Eng., Grad. Sch. of Information Science and Tech., Osaka Univ.,
1-5 Yamadaoka, Suita, Osaka 565-0871, Japan
{hideki, hara, nishio}@ist.osaka-u.ac.jp

Abstract. In ad hoc networks, data accessibility decreases due to network divisions. To solve this problem, it is effective that each mobile host creates replicas of data items held by others. In this paper, we assume an environment where mobility and access characteristics of mobile hosts have the locality and propose a method that locally relocates replicas just before a network division occurs.

1 Introduction

Recently there has been increasing interest in *ad hoc networks* that are constructed of only mobile hosts [6,9,10]. In ad hoc networks, network divisions frequently occur due to the movement of hosts. If a network division occurs, mobile hosts cannot access data items held by mobile hosts in another network. In Fig. 1, if the central radio link is disconnected, the mobile hosts on the left-hand side and those on the right-hand side cannot access data items D_1 and D_2, respectively. A key solution is to replicate data items on mobile hosts [1,2,3]. In [1], we proposed three replica allocation methods in ad hoc networks. These methods periodically relocate replicas to mobile hosts based on the access frequency to each data item and the network topology. This time period is called by *relocation period*.

In a real environment, it is more likely that mobility and access characteristics of mobile hosts have the locality. A good example is rescue affairs at disaster sites where the working area is divided into some regions and each region is assigned to some rescuers to streamline work. Each rescuer frequently moves in the assigned region and accesses data items held by rescuers in the same assigned region. If a method proposed in [1] is used and the relocation period is long, data accessibility may decrease because network divisions occur and the replica allocation at that time becomes ineffective. If the relocation period is short, the traffic may increase because the replica relocation unnecessarily occurs in the entire network despite the topology remains unchanged. In this case, an approach in which replicas are locally relocated as needed is more effective than one in which replicas are periodically relocated in the entire network. In this paper, we propose a method that locally relocates replicas held by mobile hosts adapting to topology changes. This method manages the topology information

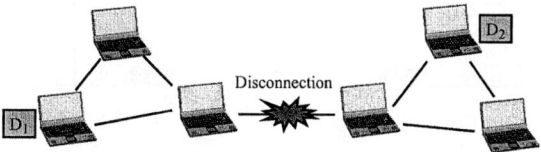

Fig. 1. Network division

on mobile hosts within N hops and the information on data items held by them, and locally relocates replicas when a mobile host detects a situation just before a network division occurs.

The remainder is organized as follows. In Sect. 2, we explain a replica allocation adapting to topology changes. In Sect. 3, we show simulation results to evaluate our proposed method. In Sect. 4, we show related works. Finally, in Sect. 5, we summarize this paper.

2 Replica Allocation Adapting to Topology Changes

In this section, we describe the management of topology information to detect a situation just before a network division occurs and information on data items held by mobile hosts, which is used to relocate replicas. We also explain the replica relocation when a mobile host detects a situation just before a network division occurs.

2.1 Assumptions and Approach

We assume that each mobile host creates up to C replicas of original data items (originals) held by others in its memory space. When a mobile host requests a data item, the request is immediately successful if it holds the original/replica in its memory space. Otherwise, it queries the data item to its *connected mobile hosts*, which are mobile hosts connected with each other by one-hop/multihop links. If one of them holds the original/replica, the request is successful. If none of them hold the data item, the request fails.

In addition, we make the following assumptions:

- The set of all mobile hosts is denoted by $M = \{M_1, M_2, \cdots, M_m\}$.
- The set of all data items is denoted by $D = \{D_1, D_2, \cdots, D_n\}$. The original of each data item is held by a particular mobile host. For simplicity, all data items are same size and are not updated.
- Mobility and access characteristics of mobile hosts have the locality.

2.2 Management of Topology Information

Each mobile host holds the information on neighboring mobile hosts, called *neighbor information*, of others. When each mobile host manages the neighbor information of all mobile hosts, the traffic becomes very large. Thus, each mobile

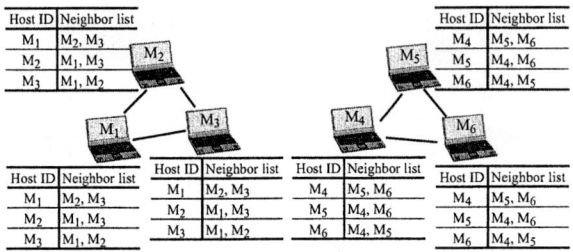

Fig. 2. Neighbor list tables ($N \geq 1$)

Table 1. Packets for managing neighbor list table

Packet name	Elements
Partial update	host ID, (dis)connected host ID, status, TTL(Time To Live)
Batch update	host ID, neighbor list, TTL

host holds the neighbor information of mobile hosts within N hops as a *neighbor list table*. Fig. 2 shows neighbor list tables held by mobile hosts ($N \geq 1$).

This table needs to be updated every time two mobile hosts are (dis)connected. Table 1 shows packets for managing the table. In the partial update packet, "host ID" denotes the host identifier of the host sending the packet, "(dis)connected host ID" denotes the host identifier of the host (dis)connected with the host sending the packet, and "status" shows that the two hosts are (dis)connected. We explain the update operations when M_i and M_j are (dis)connected.

Update operation on connection:

1. M_i inserts the host identifier of M_j into the neighbor list for M_i in its neighbor list table.
2. M_i floods with a partial update packet within N hops in order to update neighbor lists for M_i held by mobile hosts which are originally connected with M_i within N hops. In this packet, status is "Connection (Con)" and TTL is N. When a mobile host receives this packet, it inserts the host identifier of M_j into the neighbor list for M_i and rebroadcasts the packet whose TTL is decremented by 1. This operation is repeated until TTL becomes 0.
3. M_j and mobile hosts which are originally connected with M_j may not know the neighbor information of M_i and mobile hosts which are originally connected with M_i. Thus, M_i sends M_j batch update packets including the neighbor information of mobile hosts which are originally connected with M_i with $n(< N)$ hops. In each packet, TTL is set to $N - n$. M_j inserts the received neighbor information into its neighbor list table and broadcasts the packets whose TTLs are decremented by 1 to its neighbors except for M_i.

M_j also behaves in the same manner as M_i. Fig. 3 shows the update operation of neighbor list tables when M_3 and M_4 in Fig. 2 are connected (N=2). A dotted

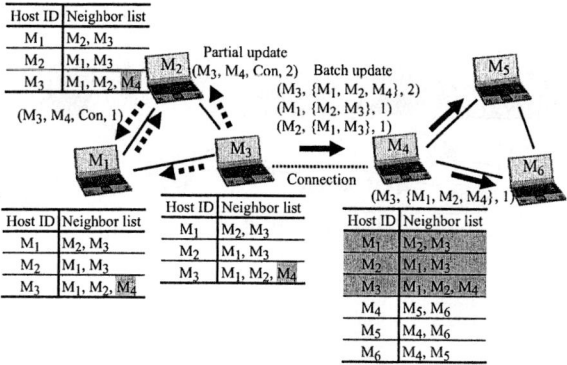

Fig. 3. Update operation of neighbor list tables on connection ($N = 2$)

arrowhead and a solid arrowhead denote transmissions of a partial update packet and a batch update packet, respectively. Elements in parentheses correspond to that of each packet in Table 1. Gray parts denote inserted information.

Update operation on disconnection:

1. M_i deletes the host identifier of M_j and M_i from neighbor lists for M_i and M_j, respectively.
2. M_i checks mobile hosts within N hops from M_i. Specifically, starting from host IDs in M_i's neighbor list, M_i records host IDs of mobile hosts that can be reached within N times' traverse from the starting IDs. After that, M_i deletes neighbor lists for mobile hosts that become more than N hops away.
3. M_i floods with a partial update packet within N hops to update neighbor lists for M_i held by others within N hops. In this packet, disconnected host ID is M_j and status is "disconnection (Dis)." When a mobile host receives this packet, it deletes the host identifier of M_j from the neighbor list for M_i and rebroadcasts the packet whose TTL is decremented by 1. It also deletes neighbor lists for mobile hosts outside N hops in the same manner as M_i.

M_j also behaves in the same manner as M_i. Fig. 4 shows the update operation of neighbor list tables when M_3 and M_4 in Fig. 3 are disconnected ($N = 2$). Gray parts denote deleted information.

2.3 Management of Holding Data Information

Each mobile host holds the information on data items held by others, called *holding data information*, within N hops as a *holding data table*. Holding data tables are updated every time when two mobile hosts are (dis)connected in the same manner as neigbhor list tables. Additionally, they need to be updated every time when replicas are relocated. Table 2 shows packets for managing the table. In the partial update packet, "allocated (discarded) data ID" denotes the data identifier of the data item allocated (discarded) by the host corresponding to

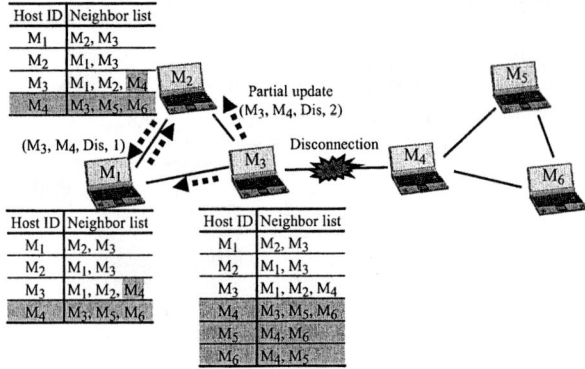

Fig. 4. Update operation of neighbor list tables on disconnection ($N = 2$)

Table 2. Packets for managing holding data table

Packet name	Elements
Partial update	host ID, allocated (discarded) data ID, status, TTL
Batch update	host ID, data ID list, TTL

"host ID" and "status" shows that the data item corresponding to "data ID" is allocated (discarded). In the batch update packet, "data ID list" includes data identifiers of data items held by the host corresponding to "host ID." We explain the update operation when M_i replaces D_k with D_l in its memory space.

Update operation on replica relocation:
1. M_i deletes the data identifier of D_k from the data ID list for M_i and inserts that of D_l into the list.
2. M_i floods with two partial update packets within N hops. In the first packet, discarded data ID is D_k, status is "Discard (Disc)." When a mobile host receives this packet, it discards the host identifier of D_k from the data ID list for M_i. In the second packet, allocated data ID is D_l, status is "Allocation (Alloc)." When a mobile host receives this packet, it inserts the host identifier of D_l into the data ID list for M_i.

Fig. 5 shows the update operation of holding data tables when M_3 replaces D_8 with D_9 ($N = 2$). A rectangle denotes memory space, where a gray and a white ones are for an original and a replica, respectively. A dotted arrowhead denotes transmissions of partial update packets. In each table, gray parts show that the data identifiers of D_8 are replaced with that of D_9.

2.4 Replica Relocation

We assume that a situation just before a network division occurs is a case when a mobile host detects only a single route to a neighbor, i.e., when it cannot

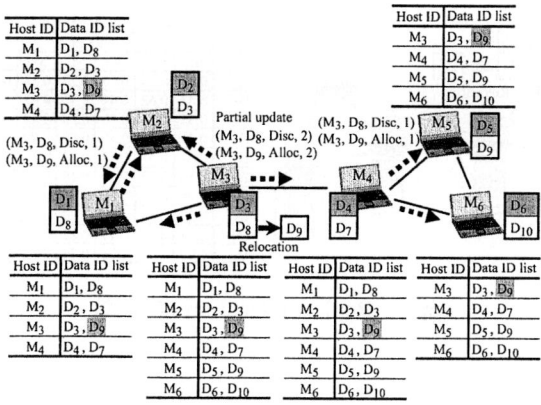

Fig. 5. Update operation of holding data tables on relocating replicas ($N = 2$)

detect a loop including the host and the neighbor. Specifically, starting from a host identifier included in the neighbor lists of the host's neighbor, if the host can reach the host identifier of itself by traversing neighbor list tables, it detects a loop including the host and the neighbor. In Fig. 2, M_3 can detect a loop of $\{M_3 \to M_1 \to M_2 \to M_3\}$. Each mobile host executes the loop detection when updating the neighbor list table. When M_i cannot detect a loop including itself and its neighbor (M_j), replicas are relocated as follows:

1. M_i sends a *relocation message* to M_j. After receiving this message, M_j sends its holding data table to M_i.
2. M_i attempts to detect loops including itself and its neighbor except for M_j. The set of mobile hosts constructing a detected loop is called *relocation group*. If M_i cannot detect any loops, it selects itself as the relocation group. Replicas are relocated in the relocation group.
3. M_i requests data items to M_j as follows:
   (a) M_i calculates the access frequency of the relocation group to each data item held by mobile hosts in the relocation group and that included in the holding data table of M_j. This is calculated as a summation of access frequencies of all hosts in the relocation group to the data item.
   (b) Let C_g denote the maximum number of replicas allocated to mobile hosts in the relocation group. Among C_g data items with the highest access frequencies of the group, M_i requests data items which are included in the holding data table of M_j and are not held by the relocation group.
4. M_j receives these data items from hosts within N hops and transmits them to M_i.
5. M_i determines which mobile hosts allocate each of the requested data items in the relocation group. If there is a mobile host that has free memory space, the requested data item is allocated to the host. Otherwise, if there is replica duplication among mobile hosts, the requested data item is allocated to one of these mobile hosts after eliminating the duplication. If there are no free

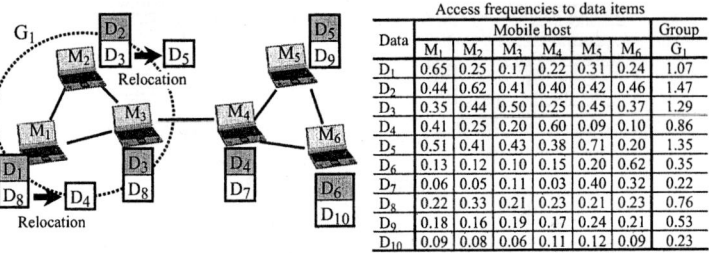

Fig. 6. Replica relocation ($N = 2$)

memory space and no replica duplication, the requested data item is allocated to the mobile host that has a replica with the lowest access frequency of the group after it discards the replica.

Fig. 6 shows that replicas are relocated in group G_1 ($N = 2$) when M_3 cannot detect any loops including itself and M_4. A table shows access frequencies to data items. M_1 replaces D_8 with D_4 and M_2 replaces D_3 with D_5.

3 Simulation Experiments

In this section, we present simulation results to evaluate our proposed method.

3.1 Simulation Model

The number of mobile hosts is 45 and they exist in a size 600 × 600 [m] flatland. The flatland is equally divided into 9 regions. Initially, we assign 5 hosts to each region and randomly determine the position of each host in the assigned region. Each host moves toward the destination at a velocity randomly determined from 0.01 to 1 [m/sec] The destination is selected from positions in the assigned region with probability β (*movement probability inside region*) and positions outside the assigned region with probability $1 - \beta$. If a host moves into a region different from the assigned one, it is newly assigned to the region. When a mobile host arrives at the destination, it pauses for a duration from 0 to 1000 [sec]. The radio communication range of each host is 80 [m].

There are 45 types of data items ($D = D_1, \cdots, D_{45}$) whose size is 1 [MB]. M_i holds D_i as the original. Each host creates up to 7 replicas in memory space. Each host issues access requests for originals held by hosts in the same assigned region (*internal data items*) based on the normal distribution with mean 0.3 and standard deviation 0.01 and for originals held by hosts in the different assigned regions (*external data items*) based on the normal distribution with mean 0.01 and standard deviation 0.0001 at every 10[sec].

In this experiment, the proposed method is compared with the following in [1], where their relocation period is fixed as 50[sec] to avoid the decrease of data accessibility due to topology changes.

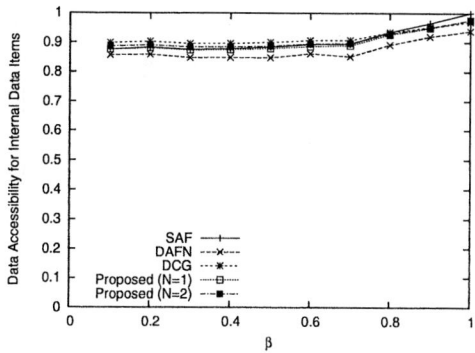

Fig. 7. β and data accessibility for internal data items

SAF (Static Access Frequency): Each mobile host allocates replicas of data items in descending order of its access frequencies.

DAFN (Dynamic Access Frequency and Neighborhood): This method eliminates replica duplication of a data item among neighboring mobile hosts after tentatively allocating replicas with the SAF method.

DCG (Dynamic Connectivity based Grouping): This method creates bi-connected components of mobile hosts as stable groups and allocates replicas of data items in descending order of the group access frequencies without replica duplication in each groups.

We evaluate the following four criteria during 500,000 [sec].

Data accessibility for internal data items: The ratio of the number of successful requests for internal data items to the number of requests for them.

Data accessibility for external data items: The ratio of the number of successful requests for external data items to the number of requests for them.

Data accessibility: The ratio of the number of successful requests for all data items (both internal and external) to the number of requests for them.

Traffic: The summation of products of the total hop count for sending a data item when relocating a replica and its size for all replica relocations.

3.2 Effects of Movement Probability Inside Region

We examine the effects of the movement probability inside region β. Fig. 7, 8, 9, and 10 show the results. Fig. 7 shows that as β increases, in each method, the data accessibility for internal data items increases. This is because mobile hosts in the same assigned region are easily connected. Our proposed method approximately shows the same result as the SAF and DCG methods.

Fig. 8 shows that as β increases, in each method, the data accessibility for external data items decreases because it is difficult for each mobile host to connect with mobile hosts in different regions. The DCG method gives the highest data accessibility for external data items and our proposed method gives the next.

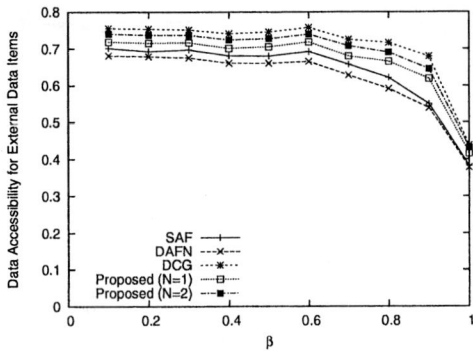

Fig. 8. β and data accessibility for external data items

This is because these methods relocate replicas without replica duplication in each group and mobile hosts can access many kinds of data items. In our proposed method, the higher N gives the higher data accessibility for external data items because replicas can be relocated among mobile hosts in different regions.

Fig. 9 shows that as β increases, in each method, the data accessibility increases. This result is strongly affected by accesses to internal data items because mobile hosts much more frequently access them. The DCG method gives the highest data accessibility and our proposed method gives the next.

Fig. 10 shows that as β increases, in each method, the traffic decreases. This is because mobile hosts nearly always connect with the same hosts. The traffic of our proposed method is much smaller than that in the DAFN and DCG methods because it relocates replicas locally. This result shows that our proposed method can drastically reduce the traffic while the data accessibility is much the same as that in the DCG method.

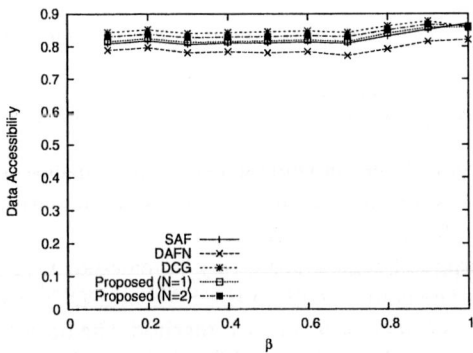

Fig. 9. β and data accessibility

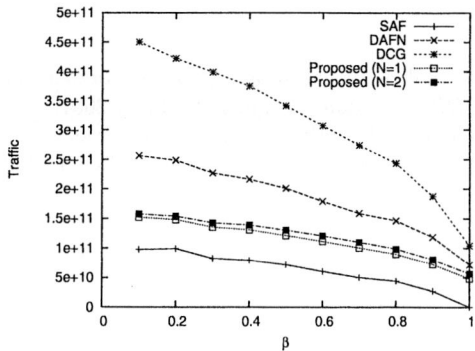

Fig. 10. β and traffic

4 Related Works

In [7,8], the authors proposed methods in which replicas are allocated to a fixed number of mobile hosts which act as servers and the consistency among the replicas is kept based on the quorum system. These methods differ from our proposed method because the authors assume that all replicas are allocated to only mobile hosts with unlimited memory space selected as servers. We assume that replicas are allocated to all mobile hosts with limited memory space.

In [11], the authors proposed a method that predicts when a network division occurs and allocates replicas to mobile hosts before the network division. It differs from ours because they assume a specific mobility model.

5 Conclusions

We proposed a replica allocation method adapting to topology changes. This method manages topology information on mobile hosts within N hops and that on data items held by them, and locally relocates replicas when a mobile host cannot detect a loop including itself and the neighbor. The simulation results showed that this method can improve the data accessibility and reduce the traffic.

As part of our future work, we plan to extend this method in an environment where each data item is updated consulting methods proposed in [4,5].

Acknowledgments. This research was partially supported by The 21st Century Center of Excellence Program "New Information Technologies for Building a Networked Symbiotic Environment" and Grant-in-Aid for Young Scientists (A)(1668005) and for Scientific Research (A)(17200006) of the Ministry of Education, Culture, Sports, Science.

References

1. T. Hara, "Effective replica allocation in ad hoc networks for improving data accessibility," *Proc. of IEEE Infocom'01*, pp. 1568–1576, 2001.
2. T. Hara, "Replica allocation methods in ad hoc networks with data update," *ACM-Kluwer Journal on Mobile Networks and Applications (MONET)*, vol. 8, no. 4, pp. 343–354, 2003.
3. T. Hara, N. Murakami, and S. Nishio, "Replica allocation for correlated data items in ad-hoc sensor networks," *ACM SIGMOD Record*, vol. 33, no. 1, pp. 38–43, 2004.
4. H. Hayashi, T. Hara, and S. Nishio, "Cache invalidation for updated data in ad hoc networks," *Proc. of Int'l Conf. on Cooperative Information Systems (CoopIS'03)*, pp. 516-535, 2003.
5. H. Hayashi, T. Hara, and S. Nishio, "Updated data dissemination for updating old replicas in ad hoc networks," *ACM/Springer Personal and Ubiquitous Computing Journal*, vol. 9, no. 4, 2005, to appear.
6. D.B. Johnson, "Routing in ad hoc networks of mobile hosts," *Proc. Workshop on Mobile Computing Systems and Applications (WMCSA'94)*, pp. 158–163, 1994.
7. G. Karumanchi, S. Muralidharan, and R. Prakash, "Information dissemination in partitionable mobile ad hoc networks," *Proc. of Symposium on Reliable Distributed Systems (SRDS'99)*, pp. 4–13, 1999.
8. J. Luo, J.P. Hubaux, and P. Eugster, "PAN: providing reliable storage in mobile ad hoc networks with probabilistic quorum systems," *Proc. of ACM MobiHoc'03*, pp. 1–12, 2003.
9. M.R. Pearlman, and Z.J. Haas, "Determining the optimal configuration for the zone routing protocol," *IEEE Journal on Selected Areas in Communications*, vol. 17, no. 8, pp. 1395–1414, 1999.
10. C.E. Perkins, and E.M. Royer, "Ad hoc on demand distance vector routing," *Proc. IEEE Workshop on Mobile Computing Systems and Applications (WMCSA'99)*, pp. 90–100, 1999.
11. K. Wang, and B. Li, "Efficient and guaranteed service coverage in partitionable mobile ad-hoc networks," *Proc. of IEEE Infocom'02*, vol. 2, pp. 1089–1098, 2002.

On a Collaborative Caching in a Peer-to-Peer Network for Push-Based Broadcast

Kazuhiko Maeda[1], Wataru Uchida[2], Takahiro Hara[1], and Shojiro Nishio[1]

[1] Graduate School of Information Science and Tech., Osaka University
[2] Network Lab., NTT DoCoMo, Inc.
{k.maeda, hara, nishio}@ist.osaka-u.ac.jp
uchida@netlab.nttdocomo.co.jp

Abstract. In this paper, we propose a new collaborative caching strategy in a push-based broadcast environment where clients construct a peer-to-peer network by connecting with each other. In the proposed strategy, a client takes into account its own access probabilities and information on queries issued by other clients, and caches data items with large benefits of the response time. We confirm that the proposed strategy reduces the average response time by simulation experiments.

1 Introduction

Recently, there has been an increasing interest in research of a push-based broadcast system where a server delivers various data to clients, and they do not send any requests to the server but wait for the data to be broadcast. A key advantage of the push-based broadcast system is a higher throughput for data access from many clients. The push-based broadcast system is used for services where information with high publicity, such as movies, sounds, news, and charts. However, the server has to broadcast many kinds of data in order to satisfy clients' requests. This causes each client to wait data to be broadcast for a long time. To shorten the response time, several strategies for caching broadcast data at clients have been proposed [1,2]. These strategies calculate the benefit of response time from the client's access probability and the time factor (eg, broadcast cycle) of each data item, and cache data items with large benefits. These researches assume that clients have two ways to access data; access their own cache and listen broadcast data.

Today, there has been also an interest in a new type of information sharing called P2P systems [7,8]. In a P2P system, terminals called *peers* construct a logical network (*P2P network*) by connecting with each other. If a peer which wants a certain data item sends an access request (*query*) to its adjacent peers in the P2P network, the query be propagated until the query reaches a peer that holds the requested data item. Then, the data item is delivered to the peer that issued the query. Since each peer behaves in autonomous and distributed ways, this system has high scalability.

In a push-based broadcast system, it is expected that the average response time for data access could be further reduced if clients construct a P2P network and they access requested data not only from the broadcast server and their own cache but also from the P2P network, i.e., other clients' cache. To the best our knowledge there is no conventional work that addresses caching strategies of broadcast data using a P2P network. In this paper, we assume that many clients that receive the push-based broadcast service construct the P2P network, and propose a new caching strategy by which clients collaboratively cache the broadcast data. In the proposed strategy, each client replaces its cache by taking into account not only its own access probabilities but also queries from other clients in order to reduce the average response time in the whole system.

The reminder is organized as follows. We introduce conventional caching strategies in section 2 and describe the system model in section 3. We propose a collaborative caching strategy in section 4, and evaluate it using simulation experiments in section 5. We show some related works in section 6. Finally, in section 7, we summarize this paper.

2 Conventional Caching Strategies

In PIX [1] and PT [2] strategies, it is assumed that clients can access data items from only their own cache or broadcast channel. When a client requests for a certain data item, it checks whether it caches the requested data item. If it does, it can access the item immediately. If not, it waits for the broadcast data item. The response time is the time interval until the data item is broadcast next.

PIX strategy

The algorithm of the PIX strategy is as follows.

1. The PIX value, $K(j) = p_j \cdot y_j$, is calculated by each client for each data item j $(1 \leq j \leq M)$. Here, M is the total number of data items which are broadcast by the server, p_j is the probability that the client accesses data item j, and y_j is the broadcast period of data item j.
2. The client caches γ data items which have the γ highest $K(j)$. Here, γ is the number of data items that the client can cache.

The PIX strategy reduces the response time of data access by caching items which have high access probabilities and long broadcast periods.

PT strategy

The algorithm of the PT strategy is as follow.

1. Every time when each data item, k, is broadcast, the PT values are calculated by each client for data items in the client's cache and data item k. The PT value, L_j, of data item j is calculated by $L_j = p_j \cdot (u_j(Q) - Q)$. Here, Q is the current time and $u_j(Q)$ is the time when data item j is broadcast next.
2. If a data item in the cache gives a lower PT value than L_k, data item j whose PT value is the lowest is replaced by k.

The PT value, L_j, represents the expected value of increase in response time if the client does not have data item j in its cache. The PT strategy compares the increases in response time of data items if they are discarded from the cache, and prefetches data items with larger gains in response time.

3 System Model

Figure 1 shows a system model assumed in this paper. In this system model, peers (clients) can send/receive data items to/from other peers in the P2P network. Each peer can cache a limited number of data items. When a peer wants to access a data item, it chooses a way that gives the shortest response time among the three access methods: accessing the item stored in its own cache, receiving the item from the broadcast, and receiving the item from another peer's cache.

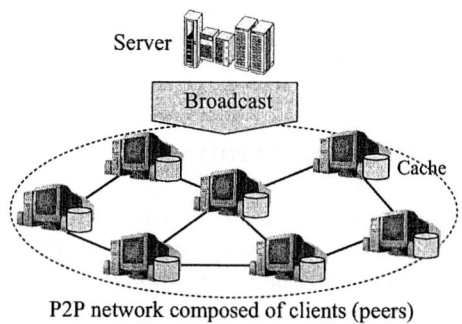

Fig. 1. Assumed environment

In this paper, it is assumed that the response time when accessing an item in its own cache is 0. Thus, if a request issuing peer holds the item in its own cache, it always accesses the cached item. If the peer does not hold, it compares the time remaining until the item is broadcast next with the time that is required to receive the item from another peer in the P2P network. If the former is shorter, the peer waits until the item is broadcast next. The response time when receiving a requested item from the broadcast is the time until the data item is broadcast next. If the latter is shorter, the peer checks whether another peer holds the requested item by using *flooding* [10]. In flooding, a peer issues a query with a certain TTL (Time To Live), and broadcasts the query to all its adjacent peers. If an adjacent peer does not hold the requested item, it re-broadcasts the query to all its adjacent peers, and this repeats until the query reaches a peer that holds the requested item or the logical hop count from the request issuing peer exceeds the TTL. If a peer that holds the requested item is found (in the following, it is denoted that the query "hits"), the peer sends a reply message to the request issuing peer. This message is sent to the request issuing peer through peers that relayed the query on the reverse direction. If the request issuing peer receives some reply messages, it receives the requested data item from the peer with the lowest logical hops. This data transmission is directly performed between the two peers using the physical network. If the query does not hit, the request issuing peer waits until the data item is broadcast next.

We also put the following assumptions:

- The system has a single broadcast server, and peers do not send any access requests to the server, i.e., pure push-based broadcast.
- All data items are of the same size and not updated. It takes one unit of time (one time slot) to broadcast one data item.
- Each peer knows the broadcast program. It can be realized by several ways, e.g., the server periodically broadcasts the program information.
- The delay of query propagation and the time to process a query is ignorable.
- The time to transmit a data item between every pair of peers is the same. We put this assumption for simplicity, but our proposed strategy can be easily extended to adapt an environment where transmission delays differ among peers.

4 Collaborative Caching Strategy

In this section, we propose a new collaborative caching strategy using a P2P network. In order to collaboratively cache data items, peers should know what data items are already cached by other peers and what data items are frequently accessed. However, since there are a huge number of peers in a push-based broadcast system, it is impractical that peers precisely know this information. Our main idea is that each peer guesses this information only using queries from other peers, e.g., arrival rate of query and results of data lookup. The proposed strategy shortens the average response time by determining cache replacement from this guessed information and its own access probabilities. This approach is reasonable because a query propagates only within a certain area determined by the TTL and thus the information guessed from queries indicates what items are cached and frequently accessed by neighboring peers within the TTL.

4.1 Query Information from Other Peers

To guess the above information, in the proposed strategy, each peer classifies queries that the peer issued or received from its neighbors. When a query arrives at a peer, the peer counts the query as one of the following three categories based on the result of looking up. Each of the three categories is counted for each data items.

- *F (Failure) query*: The query that did not hit, i.e., neither the peer nor further peers that the query propagated had the requested data item.
- *S (Success) query*: The query that hit, i.e., among the peer and further peers that the query propagated, at least one peer had the requested data item.
- *C (Connected) query*: The query that hit at the peer and the requested item was downloaded, i.e., the peer had the requested item and actually sent it to the query issuing peer.

Let us suppose a situation in which peer a is adjacent to peers b, c, and d as shown in Figure 2 and only peer d caches data item i. When a query requesting

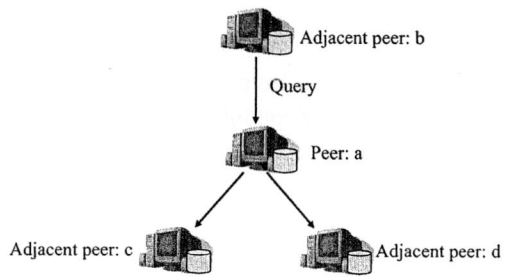

Fig. 2. Query propagation

item i propagates from peer b to peer a, the query is further broadcast to adjacent peers c and d since a does not have i in its own cache. Since only peer d caches item i, it sends a reply message to the query issuing peer via the path dab. From the reply message, peers a and b know that they are on the propagation path of the query that found data item i, and thus, a, b, and d count the query as an S query. If the query issuing peer received data item i from peer d, peer d counts the query as a C query instead of S query.

Here, it should be noted that a query is counted only once even if the same query or its results reached through multiple routes. The priority is given in the order of C, S, and F queries. For example, in the above case, if peer a receives the same query via another route and the TTL of the query is 0, the query cannot reach peer d and thus cannot find a peer that has the requested data item. In this case, while the query can be categorized to both S and F queries at peer a, only S query is counted according to the priority mentioned above.

By categorizing and counting queries, the following facts can be found.

- If a peer counts many F queries for a data item, it is shown that the data item is frequently requested by its neighboring peers including itself, but there is no neighboring peer that caches it.
- If a peer counts many S queries for a data item, it is shown that the data item is frequently requested by its neighboring peers including itself and some peers or itself cache it.
- If a peer counts many C queries for a data item, it is shown that the data item is frequently requested by its neighbors and the item cached by the peer is actually sent to the neighbors.

Increasing rates of the three categories dynamically change every time when a peer replaces its cache. For example, when data item i that is cached by no neighboring peers is frequently requested, many F queries are counted for item i. However, if one of the neighboring peers caches item i, many S queries will be counted at the peers, whereas many F queries had been counted until now.

4.2 Proposed Strategy

The collaborative caching strategy proposed in this paper extends the PIX strategy to take into account data accesses from other peers in the P2P network. The proposed strategy, *C-PIX* (*Collaborative PIX*), calculates the benefits of the expected response time in the entire system when a peer replaces one of the cached data items with the broadcast data item. Based on the calculation, the C-PIX strategy determines the cache replacement.

For data item j in a peer's cache, the expected value of increase in response time in the entire system when the peer discards j from its cache is defined by the following equation:

$$U_j = P_j \cdot y_j/2 + C_j \cdot (y_j/2 - l). \tag{1}$$

We call this *the C-PIX value*. Here, l denotes the time required for sending a data item between two peers, P_j denotes the access probability of item i per unit time, and F_j, S_j, C_j denote the arrival rates of F, S, C queries per unit time.

For broadcast data item k which is not in the peer's cache, the expected value of decrease in response time in the entire P2P network when the peer caches k is defined as the k's C-PIX value, U_k. If $S_k = 0$ at peer A, it is likely that A's neighboring peers do not cache data item k, and peer A and its neighbors have to access k from the broadcast channel. Therefore, for peer A and its neighbors, the expected response time of accessing k is $y_k/2$. On the other hand, if $S_k > 0$ at peer A, at least one neighboring peer caches data item k and peer A can receive the data item from the peer. Thus, the expected response time of accessing k is l. From the above discussions, U_k is expressed by the following equation:

$$U_k = \begin{cases} P_k \cdot y_k/2 + F_k \cdot \alpha_k \cdot (y_k/2 - l) & (S_k = 0) \\ P_k \cdot l + F_k \cdot \alpha_k \cdot (y_k/2 - l) & (S_k > 0). \end{cases} \tag{2}$$

Here, α_k denotes the forecast ratio of F queries that will change to C queries when the peer caches data item k.

When a peer discards data item i from its cache, $\acute{\alpha}_i$ is set as the value of α_i, and then, α_i is changed by the following equation:

$$\alpha_i = x \cdot \acute{\alpha}_i + (1 - x) \cdot C_i / \{F_i + C_i\}. \tag{3}$$

Here, x ($0 \leq x \leq 1$) is the parameter that determines how much the new α_i is influenced by the former one. When x is set to an unnecessary large value, the system cannot sensitively adapt to changes of the environment. It is important to determine an appropriate value of x considering the feature of the system.

In the C-PIX strategy, each peer calculates the C-PIX values for all data items stored in its cache and finds the minimum one, U_m, among them. If U_m is smaller than U_k, item m is replaced with broadcast item k. If the cache replacement occurs, the query counts of F, S, and C queries for the item discarded from the cache and the newly cached item are set to 0.

Now, we define the warmup time, T, that represents the time necessary for receiving enough queries for calculating the C-PIX value after caching a new data item. Until T units of time passes after caching data item i, U_i is calculated not by equation (1) but by the following equation:

$$U_i = P_i \cdot y_i/2 + \acute{F}_i \cdot (y_i/2 - l) \tag{4}$$

Here, $\acute{F}_i$ denotes the value of F_i before caching data item i.

5 Performance Evaluation

5.1 Simulation Environment

It is known that an unstructured P2P network constructed on the Internet follows the *power-law* [6]. Based on this fact, we determined the degree of peer j, d_j, which is the number of j's adjacent peers in the P2P network, by the following equation:

$$d_j = \lfloor w_{max} \cdot r_j^{\mathcal{R}} \rfloor. \quad (\mathcal{R} < 0) \tag{5}$$

Here, r_j denotes the rank of peer j, which is its index in the descending order of outdegree (number of adjacent peers), and w_{max} denotes the maximum number of adjacent peers. For simplicity, we assume $r_j = j$. A network which is constructed by connecting peers at random according to the power-law is called a *PLRG (Power-law Random Graph)*. In our simulations, the number of peers was set to 500 and we used a PLRG network, where $(w_{max}, \mathcal{R})$ is $(240, -0.8)$ as many conventional works did [6]. Here, it is known that $\mathcal{R}$ of the real network is approximately -0.8.

The access probability at each peer was determined based on the Zipf distribution [14], where the following two different distributions were used:

Access distribution 1 (A. D. 1)F
The smaller the identifier of each data item is, the higher the probability that the data item is accessed. The order of access probabilities of data items is the same at all peers. However, the values of the access probability of each data item are not the same among peers but vary a little. Specifically, access probability p_{ji} of item i at peer j was given by the following equation:

$$p_{ji} = \frac{i^{-\theta_j}}{\sum_{k=1}^{M} k^{-\theta_j}}. \tag{6}$$

Here, θ_j is called a Zipf coefficient, and if this is set to a large value, a small number of data items are accessed frequently. In our simulations, θ_j was also determined based on the Zipf distribution by the following equation:

$$\theta_j = \frac{j^{-0.8}}{\sum_{k=1}^{MAX\_PEER} k^{-0.8}}. \tag{7}$$

Here, MAX_PEER denotes the total number of peers.

Access distribution 2 (A. D. 2)F
Every peer has different orders of access probabilities of items. Access probability p_{ji} of item i at peer j was given by the following equation:

$$p_{ji} = \frac{\{(i - h_j + 1) \bmod M\}^{-0.5}}{\sum_{k=1}^{M} k^{-0.5}}. \tag{8}$$

Table 1. Average response time varying x and T (A. D. 1)

T (Time slot) \ x	0.1	0.2	0.3	0.4	0.5	0.6	0.7	0.8	0.9
100	36.7	33.8	31.9	31.5	34.6	42.6	56.8	88.4	168.4
200	29.9	38.0	51.4	69.7	94.4	128.1	180.6	258.8	306.7
300	38.2	53.1	73.0	97.2	129.0	173.1	222.4	259.7	280.0
400	50.5	69.3	93.1	123.0	162.0	193.2	209.9	220.8	218.8
500	48.8	64.2	83.1	106.0	119.9	128.1	132.4	134.9	136.5
600	63.8	91.8	122.1	106.3	205.2	231.6	249.2	263.0	265.2
700	51.7	68.2	89.5	112.9	138.2	165.9	186.9	197.6	193.4
800	44.6	56.7	72.1	88.5	108.9	134.4	161.0	167.3	159.3
900	42.7	53.7	66.8	84.2	106.2	127.1	142.8	144.5	135.5
1000	83.7	92.3	98.2	100.7	101.0	103.2	102.5	102.8	104.7

Here, h_j denotes the item which peer j accesses most frequently. The probability that peer j accesses data item i most frequently (namely, $h_j = i$) was also determined based on the Zipf distribution by the following equation:

$$q_i = \frac{i^{-0.8}}{\sum_{k=1}^{M} k^{-0.8}}. \tag{9}$$

The probability that each peer issues an access request at each time slot was set to 0.1. Therefore, the access frequency of data item i at peer j becomes $P_{ji} = p_{ji} \times 0.1$.

We assumed that the server broadcasts all data items periodically. Initially, data items were cached at each peer according to the PIX strategy. The initial value of α_i for each data item at each peer was set to 1. The total number of data items was set to 1,000, the TTL of each query was set to 3. The download time l of a data item from the P2P network was set to 10 time slots.

Based on the above simulation environment, we evaluated the average response time of the proposed strategy during 300,000 time slots. For the purpose of comparison, we also evaluated the average response times in the cases where peers can receive data items from the P2P network and determine the cache replacement based on the PIX and PT strategies.

5.2 Impact of x and T

In order to determine appropriate values of x and T, we evaluated the average response times of the proposed strategy where x varies from 0.1 to 0.9 and T varies from 100 to 1,000. The maximum number of data items which a peer can cache (cache size) was fixed to 100, and the access probability of each peer was given according to A. D. 1. Table 1 shows the result. A gray part in both tables indicates the minimum value of average response time for each value of T.

From this result, it is shown that two parameters, x and T, are correlated. As T gets smaller, x that gives the shortest average response time gets higher. This is because the proposed strategy determines the cache replacement by guessing what items neighboring peers cache based on received queries and their results. If T is too small, C queries cannot be counted sufficiently since there is not enough time to collect the query information. Therefore, items which are in fact needed from neighboring peers may be judged to be unnecessary, and thus, are discarded from the cache. Moreover, if C queries are not counted sufficiently, α_i decreases as shown in equation (3), and thus, the cached item is discarded in a short time. We can solve this problem by setting x large (see equation (3)).

The shortest response time is given where $x = 0.1$ and $T = 200$ in the simulation environment. Therefore, we use these values in the following simulations.

5.3 Impact of Cache Size

Fig.3 and Fig.4 show the average response times of the proposed strategy and the other two strategies where the cache size varies from 0 to 1000. We applied A. D. 1 in Fig.3, and A. D. 2 in Fig.4.

From these results, the C-PIX always gives the shortest average response time. Moreover the difference in performance is larger when using A. D. 1 than using A. D. 2. When A. D. 1 is used, all peers have the similar access characteristics, and thus, in the PIX and PT strategies, they cache the same items. As a result, they can hardly find requested items in the P2P network. On the contrary, in the C-PIX strategy, each peer determines the cache items by taking into account items cached by neighboring peers. Even when the cache size of each peer is small, this strategy can improve the hit ratio of queries and shorten the average response time.

6 Related Works

P2P systems are classified into two categories; *structured* [11,13] and *unstructured* [3]. Structured systems have precise control over the network topology and locations of data items in the whole network, while unstructured ones do not. Since blind methods such as flooding are used to look up requested data items in unstructured one, they also have a disadvantage that network traffic and looking up delay are larger than structured ones. Instead, unstructured ones have an advantage of being built easily and flexibly. This is because most P2P systems currently in service use unstructured networks for data looking up [7,8]. In this paper, we assumed an unstructured system.

There are many conventional works that address collaborative caching in some research fields such as web caching [5], distributed file systems [4,12], and adhoc network [9]. For example, in the research field of web caching, several strategies in which proxy servers collaboratively cache Web contents. These strategies aim to reduce the network traffic and balance the processing load of Web servers which hold original contents. In one of strategies [5], proxies are hierarchically coupled like DNS (Domain Name System), where the root of the hierarchy is the server which holds original contents. When a client requests contents, it first asks whether the proxy which is responsible to its domain caches them. If not, the request is forwarded to proxies of higher level in the hierarchy. These approaches are similar to structured P2P systems since proxies are hierarchically coupled and data requests are routed based on particular rules, and thus, contrary to our approach.

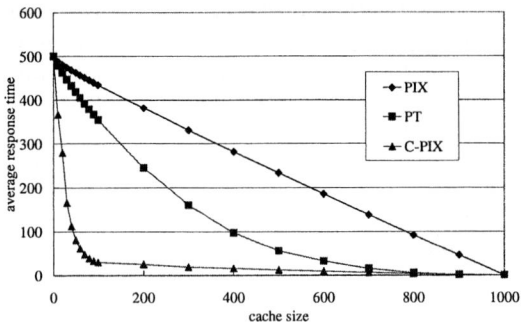

Fig. 3. Cache size vs. average response time (A. D. 1)

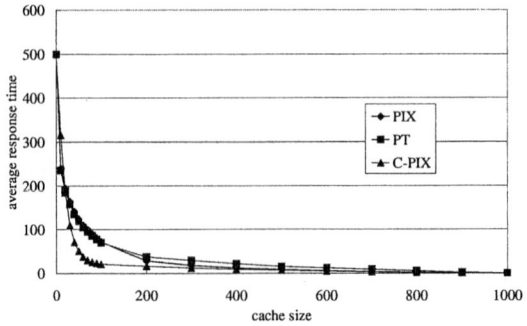

Fig. 4. Cache size vs. average response time (A. D. 2)

7 Conclusion

In this paper, we propose a new caching strategy in a push-based broadcast system where clients compose a P2P network. To reduce the average response time in the entire system, in the proposed strategy, each client autonomously determines cache replacement by taking into account not only its own access probabilities to data items but also queries issued from other peers. From the results of simulation experiments, we confirmed that the proposed strategy, C-PIX, gives better performance than the conventional caching strategies.

The C-PIX strategy is an extension of the PIX strategy which is a typical caching strategy in a push-based broadcast system. We also plan to consider another collaborative caching strategy that is based on the PT strategy.

Acknowledgements

This research was supported by The 21st Century Center of Excellence Program "New Information Technologies for Building a Networked Symbiotic Environment" and Grant-in-Aid for Scientific Research on Priority Areas (16016260) of the Ministry of Education, Culture, Sports, Science and Technology, Japan.

References

1. Acharya, S., Alonso, R., Franklin, M., and Zdonik, S.: Broadcast Disks: Data Management for Asymmetric Communication Environments, Proc. ACM SIGMOD'95, pp. 199–210 (1995).
2. Acharya, S., Franklin, M., and Zdonik, S.: Prefetching from a Broadcast Disk, Proc. ICDE'96, pp. 276–285 (1996).
3. Cohen, E., and Shenker, S.: Replication Strategies in Unstructured Peer-to-Peer Networks, Proc. ACM SIGCOMM'02, pp. 177–190 (2002).
4. Dahlin, M., Wang, R., Anderson, T., and Patterson, D.: Cooperative Caching: Using Remote Client Memory to Improve File System Performance, Proc. Symp. on Operating Systems Design and Implementation, pp. 267–280 (1994).
5. Fan, L., Cao, P., Almeida, J., and Broder, A.: Summary Cache: A Scalable Wide-area Web Cache Sharing Protocol, Proc. ACM SIGCOMM'98, pp. 254–265 (1998).
6. Faloutsos, M., Faloutsos, P., and Faloutsos, C.: On Power-Law Relationships of the Internet Topology, Proc. ACM SIGCOMM'99, pp. 251–262 (1999).
7. FreeNet, <URL:http://freenet.sourceforge.net>.
8. Gnutella, <URL:http://gnutella.wego.com>.
9. Hara, T.: Cooperative Caching by Mobile Clients in Push-based Information Systems, Proc. ACM CIKM'02, pp. 186–193 (2002).
10. Lv, Q., Cao, P., Cohen, E., Li, K., and Shenker, S.: Search and Replication in Unstructured Peer-to-Peer Networks, Proc. Int'l Conf. on Supercomputing, pp. 84–95 (2002).
11. Ratnasamy, S., Francis, P., Handley, M., and Karp, R.: A Scalable Content-Addressable Network, Proc. ACM SIGCOMM'01, pp. 161–172 (2001).
12. Sarkar, P., and Hartman, J.: Efficient Cooperative Caching Using Hints, Proc. Symp. on Operating Systems Design and Implementation, pp. 35–46 (1996).
13. Stoica, I., Morris, R., Karger, D., Kaashoek, F., and Balakrishnan. H.: Chord: A Scalable Peer-to-Peer Lookup Service for Internet Applications, Proc. ACM SIGCOMM'01, pp.149–160 (2001).
14. Zipf, G. K.: Human Behavior and the Principle of Least Effort, Addison-Wesley (1949).

An Efficient Location Encoding Method Based on Hierarchical Administrative District[*]

SangYoon Lee[1], Sanghyun Park[1], Woo-Cheol Kim[1], and Dongwon Lee[2]

[1] Department of Computer Science,
Yonsei University, Korea
{sylee, sanghyun, twelvepp}@cs.yonsei.ac.kr
[2] School of Information Sciences and Technology,
Penn State University, USA
dongwon@psu.edu

Abstract. Due to the rapid development in mobile communication technologies, the usage of mobile devices such as cell phone or PDA becomes increasingly popular. As different devices require different applications, various new services are being developed to satisfy the needs. One of the popular services under heavy demand is the Location-based Service (LBS) that exploits the spatial information of moving objects per temporal changes. In order to support LBS efficiently, it is necessary to be able to index and query well a large amount of spatio-temporal information of moving objects. Therefore, in this paper, we investigate how such location information of moving objects can be efficiently stored and indexed. In particular, we propose a novel location encoding method based on hierarchical administrative district information. Our proposal is different from conventional approaches where moving objects are often expressed as geometric points in two dimensional space, (x, y). Instead, in ours, moving objects are encoded as one dimensional points by both administrative district as well as road information. Our method is especially useful for monitoring traffic situation or tracing location of moving objects through approximate spatial queries.

Keywords: Location-Based Service, Road network, Moving object, Indexing.

1 Introduction

Due to the recent development in mobile communication technologies, the usage of mobile devices such as cell phone or PDA becomes increasingly popular, and novel services are being developed to serve various needs. One of the popular services for mobile devices is the Location-based Service (LBS) that exploits the location information of moving objects (i.e., mobile devices). For instance, the following queries are utilizing the "location" of moving objects: "Find the location of a person with a phone number X.", "What is the nearest Thai restaurant

---

[*] This work was partially supported by Korea Research Foundation Grant (KRF-2004-003-D00302 and KRF-2005-206-D00015).

to a hotel Y?", or "Where is the delivery truck, shipping the TV that I purchased over the Internet?", etc.

The LBS is the service that keeps track of the location information of moving objects per time unit, stores them into databases, and handles users' queries based on the stored location information. The queries used in the LBS can be categorized as spatial (i.e., finding moving objects within some spatial constraints), trajectory (i.e., finding moving paths of objects per some time units), and hybrid (i.e., both spatial and trajectory) queries [9].

In particular, moving objects in the context of LBS have the following challenges: (1) they have high update cost since databases have to update location information as time passes; (2) they have high storage cost since location information is typically multi-dimensional (i.e., object, time, location, etc.); (3) data to handle are large-scale since databases need to maintain temporal data (i.e., past and present); (4) they have high retrieval cost due to the large amount of data. Therefore, it is important to devise an indexing and query processing technique that can handle such a large-scale multi-dimensional spatio-temporal data efficiently.

In this paper, we investigate a data encoding method to enable effective indexing and query processing for such a setting. In conventional approaches (e.g., 3DR-tree [11], HR-tree [5], STR-tree [8], TB-tree [9], and MV3R-tree [10]), the location information of moving objects were expressed as a geometric coordinate (x,y) in two dimensional space. However, instead, we propose to express location information using both *hierarchical administrative district* and *road network* [3][7] in one dimensional space that, we believe, fits better the real world. For instance, if a moving object is in a building with a coordinate of latitude=125.58 and longitude=-37.34, then it can be expressed as a set of fields according to an administrative district such as city, road-name, road-block (e.g., Seoul, Main road, 165). Furthermore, by converting the fields into a binary string that has efficient ways to process queries, we overcome the aforementioned challenges of the LBS.

Our proposed scheme has at least three advantages: (1) it reduces the storage cost and dimensions of index by expressing location information in one dimensional space, instead of two dimensional space. This results in the improved query processing. (2) In real world, moving objects can only follow along the "roads". However, if one expresses location information as geometric coordinates, then one may include spaces where moving objects can never move into, so called *dead space*, incurring storage waste. (3) Since location information is based on the information of the administrative district, the results can be easily converted into address formats that are easier, as answers, for human users to interpret.

2 Proposed Encoding Method of Location Information

In many countries, addresses are often represented as a set of fields such as district name, road name, and location on the road. For example, the address of the City Hall of Seoul, Korea is represented as a triplet of (Seoul, Eulji road, 31).

Similarly, the address of the Natural History Museum of England is (London, Cornwell Road, -), where the third field is null. Exploiting this addressing scheme, one can easily encode the location of a moving object as a one-dimensional binary string. By adding more fields, it is trivial to extend the scheme to be able to support more general addresses. From here forward, to keep the presentation simple, we only focus on the triplet scheme, (district, road, location on road), to represent addresses within a specific country.

The procedure to encode the location of a moving object consists of three steps as follows: (1) obtain the address of the place at which the moving object is located and express it as a triplet, (2) transform each field of the triplet into a binary string, and (3) concatenate the three binary strings into a single binary string. The first and third steps are trivial, and thus we elaborate on the second step.

We first discuss the way to encode districts. For easier illustration, let us consider an imaginary country with 4 counties (A, B, C, D) as a whole and 8 cities (a, b, ..., g) in each county - a total of 32 districts to encode. The simplest encoding method is to use their lexicographical orders. That is, by using 2 bits for county names and 3 bits for city names, one can encode a district as a 5-bit string whose first two bits represent the lexicographical order of its county name and the remaining three bits represent the lexicographical order of its city name. For example, one can express the district "A county a city" as "00 000", the district "A county b city" as "00 001" and "B county a city" as "01 000".

Although this encoding scheme is simple to implement, it does not provide the information about the relative position of districts. For example, let us consider two moving objects, one located at the district "00 000" and the other at the district "00 001". Comparing these two binary strings, one can deduce that the two objects be in the same county but in different city. These two binary strings, however, do not provide any clue as to the relative positions of the two objects.

To overcome these limitation, we propose to use a mapping technique based on space-filling curves such as Z-ordering [6], R-ordering [1], and H-ordering [2]. A space-filling curve is a one-dimensional curve which visits every point within a multi-dimensional space. In order to represent the relative locations of districts more efficiently, we choose Z-ordering among various space-filling curves and modify it to start from the upper left corner rather than the lower left corner as in the original Z-ordering. The detailed algorithm to encode the districts contained in a region is given in Algorithm 1, and an illustrative example is shown in Fig.1.

Compared to the encoding method based on lexicographical orders, the proposed encoding method produces more informative binary strings. Let us consider the two moving objects again, one located at the district "00 000" and the other at the district "00 001". In addition to the facts that the two objects are in the same county but are in different city, we can infer more facts: (1) since the first two bits for cities are all "00", the cities are located at northwest area of the county, and (2) since the last bits for cities are different, the city where the first object is located is north of the city where the second object is located.

Algorithm 1: Mapping administrative districts into binary strings.

1. Compute the central point of each district.
2. Divide the region into two sub-regions, **north** and **south**, so that the numbers of central points in both **north** and **south** are similar.
3. If region **north** has more than one central point, divide it into two sub-regions, **north_east** and **north_west**, so that the numbers of central points in both **north_east** and **north_west** are similar.
4. Do the same for region **south** symmetrically.
5. For each sub-region obtained from Steps 3 and 4, if it contains more than one central point, repeat Steps 2 - 4.
6. Considering the division process undergone, map the central point of each district onto a two-dimensional space.
7. Using a modified Z-ordering, assign a binary string to each district.

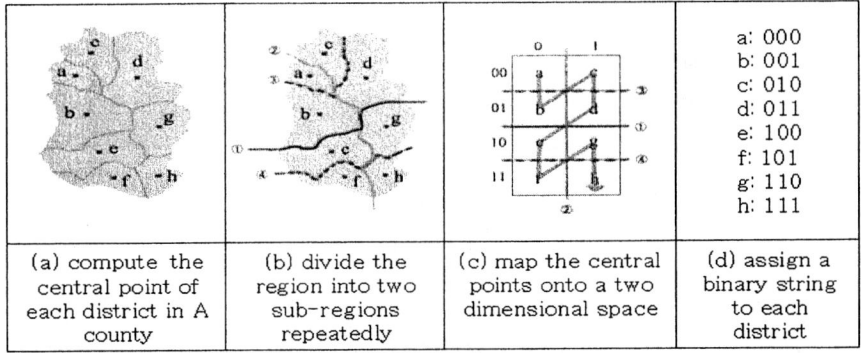

Fig. 1. An example which illustrates how Algorithm 1 works on A county

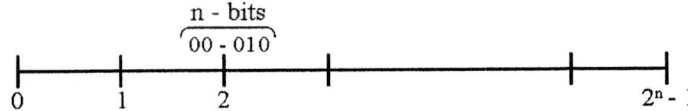

Fig. 2. A road which is partitioned into $2^n - 1$ units of the same size

The algorithm to encode the roads within a district is not much different from Algorithm 1. The changes needed to be made on Algorithm 1 are as follows: (1) every instance of word "district" is to be replaced with word "road", and (2) every instance of word "region" is to be replaced with word "district".

Now let us consider the way to encode the location on road. We first partition the road into $2^n - 1$ units of the same size, and then represent each boundary as an n-bit binary string as shown in Fig.2. Lastly, we choose the boundary nearest from an object and use its binary string as the location of the object on road.

The proposed encoding scheme has the following characteristics: (1) one can find out the *lowest* common administrative district by extracting the longest common prefix of a given set of binary strings, and (2) a district containing a set of lower districts can be represented by the range of binary strings; for example, county "A" in Fig.1 is represented by the range $[00000, 00111]$.

3 System Organization

As shown in Fig.3, our LBS implementation consists of two sub-systems for *population* and *query processing*. The population sub-system is responsible for collecting the information of moving objects and storing it into databases, and the query processing sub-system is in charge of answering to the queries about the moving objects. To support the proposed encoding scheme, in addition, the

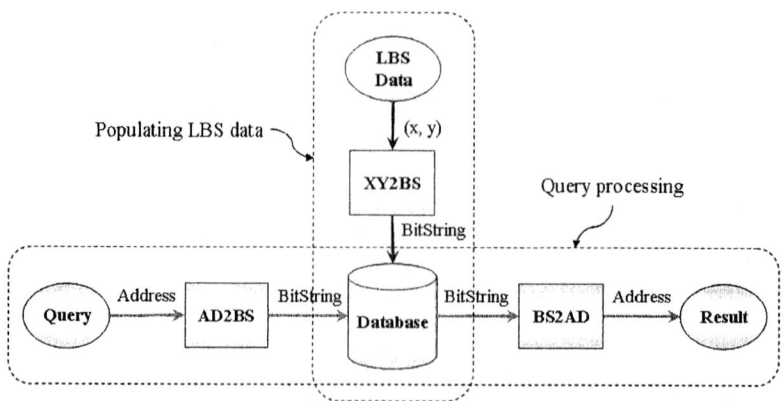

Fig. 3. LBS system which uses the proposed location encoding scheme

Module XY2BS converts a two dimensional coordinate denoting the location of a moving object into the equivalent binary string. To expedite the conversion process, XY2BS maintains an R-tree built from the roads in administrative districts. For a given road R, let bitstring(R) and rectangle(R) denote the binary string of R and the rectangle for the two end points of R, respectively. For each road R in districts, then, the R-tree stores rectangle(R) and bitstring(R) in one of its leaf nodes. Algorithm 2 describes how XY2BS makes use of the R-tree to quickly convert two dimensional points to corresponding binary strings.

It is much more intuitive for users to ask queries using real-life address such as "Seoul, Main road, 100" than using coordinates such as "longitude=-65, latitude=+45". Similarly, it is also preferable to use such real-life address in the query results. Therefore, in our prototype, we assume that both users' queries and query results are in the real address format. Module AD2BS converts this real-life addresses into equivalent binary string representations, and

Algorithm 2: Utilizing an R-tree to quickly convert a two dimensional point, (x, y), into the equivalent binary string.

1. Generate the rectangle $uMBR$ by expanding x to its left and right by uR, and expanding y up and down by uR. $uMBR$ is then expressed as $([x - uR, x + uR], [y - uR, y + uR])$. Here, uR is a system parameter used for determining the nearness of roads from a two dimensional point.
2. Search the R-tree for the roads whose MBRs overlap $uMBR$.
3. From the roads obtained in Step 2, select the road R whose Euclidean distance to (x, y) is the smallest.
4. Project (x, y) onto the road R. Let (x', y') denote the coordinate of (x, y) after the projection.
5. Using the relative position of (x', y') on the road R, calculate the binary string for (x', y').
6. Concatenate bitstring(R) and the binary string for (x', y').

module **BS2AD** converts binary strings back to equivalent real-life addresses. For rapid conversion to binary strings, **AD2BS** maintains a B-tree where district and road names are used as a key and binary strings are stored at leaf nodes. For fast conversion to real-life addresses, **BS2AD** also maintains a B-tree where binary strings are used as a key, and district and road names are stored at leaf nodes.

4 Query Processing

This section describes how our LBS implementation processes typical LBS range and trajectory queries.

4.1 Range Query Processing

Range queries are to find the moving objects within a specific region during a given time interval or to find a set of time intervals during which a specific moving object was within a given region. Let us consider an example query: "Find all cell phone users who have been in b city of A county during the time interval [10 pm, 11 pm]". To answer this query, the system first calls module **AD2BS** to convert the district name (i.e., "A county, b city") to the corresponding binary string. Since there are likely to be more than a single road in the given district, the district name is expressed as a range of binary strings. The system then searches the database using the range of binary strings and the time interval (i.e. [10 pm, 11 pm]) as a query predicate.

4.2 Trajectory Query Processing

Trajectory queries are to retrieve the path on which a moving object has traversed during a given time interval. Let us consider an example query: "Between the time interval [10 pm, 11 pm], where has Sam been moving around?". If the system represents the locations of moving objects as two dimensional geometric points, the answer to such a query consists of a set of line segments and thus can

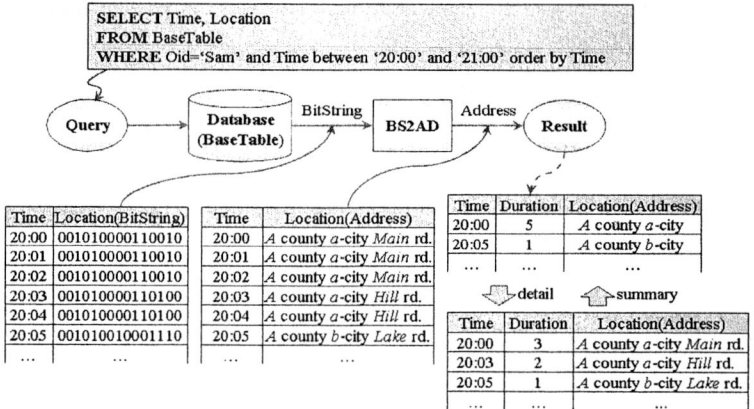

Fig. 4. An example of trajectory query procesing

be meaningfully displayed only on electronic maps. However the answers from the proposed LBS system can be easily converted to real-life addresses and thus can be delivered to users in text or voice format (in addition to being useful on electronic maps as well).

To process trajectory queries, the system first searches the database using the object and time interval information, and then sort the result in ascending order of time as shown in Fig.4. The system then calls module BS2AD to convert the binary strings in the result into the corresponding administrative district addresses, and finally sends out the result in text or voice format to users. When showing the result to users, the system may represent a set of adjacent rows as a single row by extracting their common prefixes. That is, it is feasible that the result is displayed in the unit of 'county' first and, whenever necessary, in the unit of 'city' (similar to the drill-down of OLAP applications)

5 Experiment

To evaluate the effectiveness of the proposed location encoding scheme, we performed experiments with real district and road data of a specific region in Seoul, Korea. The region we used for experiments consists of 2 counties (actually 'gu' in Korea), 46 cities (actually 'dong' in Korea), and 387 roads. We created synthetic moving objects within this region and let them follow the roads in a random fashion for 500 minutes. We then observed their locations every 1 minute. At first the collected data were stored in 3DR-tree as a triplet of (timestamp, x-coordinate, y-coordinate) and then stored in 2DR-tree as a pair of (timestamp, binary string representation of location). Identifiers of moving objects were used as a key and thus stored in leaf nodes of 3DR-tree or 2DR-tree.

We evaluate the effectiveness of the proposed encoding scheme by comparing the 3DR-tree with the 2DR-tree in terms of index size and query processing time.

The machine for the experiments was a personal computer with a Pentium-IV 2.6 GHz CPU, the main memory of 512 MB, and the operating system of Linux Fedora core 3.

5.1 Index Size

While increasing the number of moving objects from 400 to 2,000, we measured the sizes of the 2DR-tree and the 3DR-tree. Since 500 location data were collected from each object, the total number of records stored in the indexes was 200,000 when there were 400 objects and 1 million when there were 2,000 objects. As shown in Table 1, the 2DR-tree which stores the locations in binary string representation consumed about 58% of the storage space spent by the 3DR-tree. Therefore, the reduction ratio of the index size was approximately 42% and this reduction ratio increased slightly when the number of moving objects became 2,000.

Table 1. Sizes of 2DR-tree and 3DR-tree

# of moving objects (Tuples)	Size of 3DR-Tree (KB)	Size of 2DR-Tree (KB)	Reduction ratio (%)
400 (200,000)	10,973	6,393	41.7
800 (400,000)	22,467	12,779	43.1
1200 (600,000)	34,342	19,329	43.7
1600 (800,000)	46,221	25,906	44.0
2000 (1,000,000)	58,218	32,565	44.1

5.2 Query Processing Time

While increasing the number of moving objects from 400 to 2,000, we observed how long it takes for the 2DR-tree and the 3DR-tree to process range queries and trajectory queries. We generated 1,000 queries for each query type and measured the time elapsed to process all the 1,000 queries.

We first performed the two types of range queries: "Find a set of time intervals during which a specific object was in a given *city*" (type 1) and "Find a set of time intervals during which a specific object was in a given *county*" (type 2). As shown in Fig.5, the query processing times of both the 2DR-tree and the 3DR-tree increase linearly as the number of moving objects grows, but the increase ratio of the 2DR-tree is smaller than that of the 3DR-tree. Compared to the 3DR-tree, the 2DR-tree achieved about 98% performance improvement for the queries in type 1 and 67% to 69% improvement for the queries in type 2. Such an improvement seems to be achievable because the proposed scheme reduces the index size significantly and makes search regions become one-dimensional ranges rather than two-dimensional rectangles.

We then performed another two types of range queries: "Find the moving objects which were within a given *city* at any time in the first 250 minutes" (type 3) and "Find the moving objects which were within a given *county* at any time in the first 250 minutes" (type 4). To process these types of range queries, we have to search the index using the rectangles representing the time and location

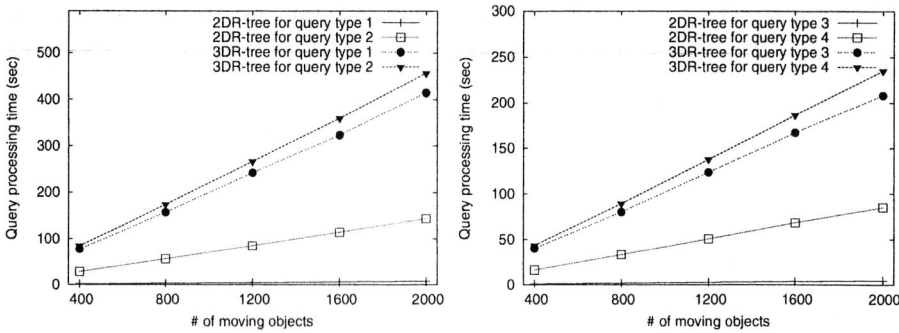

Fig. 5. Elapsed time to process type 1 and type 2 queries

Fig. 6. Elapsed time to process type 3 and type 4 queries

constraints. Remember that the 2DR-tree and the 3DR-tree express locations as one-dimensional binary strings and two-dimensional geometric points, respectively. Therefore, the search regions for the 2DR-tree become two dimensional while the search regions for the 3DR-tree become three dimensional. As shown in Fig.6, the performance improvement of the 2DR-tree becomes larger as the number of moving objects increases. As a result, the 2DR-tree achieved improvement up to 98% for the queries in type 3, and up to 64% for the queries in type 4.

We lastly performed a trajectory query: "Where has a specific object been moving around for the first 250 minutes?" (type 5). To process such a query, we have to traverse down the index using the time constraint. Since traversing the 2DR-tree is more effective than traversing the 3DR-tree in terms of CPU and I/O cost, the 2DR-tree achieved about 44% performance improvement when there were 400 objects and about 41% when there were 2,000 objects.

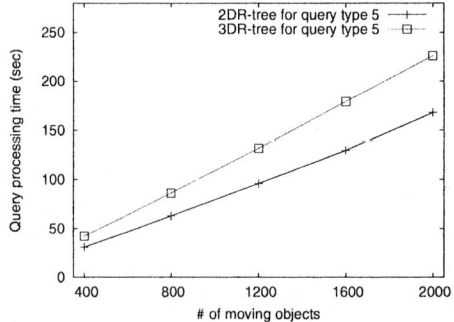

Fig. 7. Elapsed time to process type 5 queries

6 Conclusion

In this paper, we have proposed an effective location encoding method that uses the information in the hierarchical administrative district and the road network of real world. Our method captures moving objects as binary strings in one dimensional space instead of conventional (x, y) coordinates in two dimensional space, and thus can reduce storage cost by upto 44% while improving query processing by 64% to 98%. The benefits of our proposal include: (1) it improves upon previous indexing and query processing algorithms by exploiting binary strings; (2) it is easy to drill-down or roll-up query results in a hierarchical administrative district; (3) since it uses the ontologies of administrative district that are intuitive to human users, it is suitable to display query results as text or voice even without electronic maps.

One of the obstacles of the Location-based Service (LBS) is how to reduce the rapidly increasing spatio-temporal data without sacrificing query performance. To address this problem, we plan to exploit the property that when two binary strings of location information share the same prefix, two corresponding moving objects on the road network must be located in the same administrative district. That is, the location information of moving objects can be further compressed per administrative district by using common prefixes.

References

1. C. Faloutsos, "Gray Codes for Partial Match and Range Queries", IEEE Trans. on Software Engineering, 14(10), pp. 1381-1393, 1988.
2. C. Faloutsos and S. Roseman, "Fractals for Secondary Key Retrieval", In Proc. ACM PODS, pp. 247-252, 1989.
3. S. Gupta, S. Kopparty, and C. Ravishankar, "Roads, Codes, and Spatiotemporal Queries", In Proc. ACM PODS, pp. 115-124, 2004.
4. A. Guttman, "R-trees: A Dynamic Index Structure for Spatial Searching", In Proc. ACM SIGMOD, pp. 47-54, 1984.
5. M. A. Nascimento and J. R. O. Silva, "Towards Historical R-trees", In Proc. ACM Symposium on Applied Computing, pp. 235-240, 1998.
6. J. A. Orenstein and T. H. Merrett, "A Class of Data Structures for Associative Searching", In Proc. ACM SIGACT-SIGMOD Symposium on Principles of Database Systems, pp.181-190, 1984.
7. D. Papadias, J. Zhang, N. Mamoulis, and Y. Tao, "Query Processing in Spatial Network Databases", In Proc. VLDB Conference, pp. 802-813, 2003.
8. D. Pfoser, Y. Theodoridis, and C. S. Jensen, "Indexing Trajectories in Query Processing for Moving Objects", Chorochronos Technical Report, CH-99-3, 1999.
9. D. Pfoser, C. S. Jensen, and Y. Theodoridis, "Novel Approaches in Query Processing for Moving Objects", In Proc. VLDB Conference, pp. 395-406, 2000.
10. Y. Tao and D. Papadias, "MV3R-Tree: A Spatio-Temporal Access Method for Timestamp and Interval Queries", In Proc. VLDB Conference, pp. 431-440, 2001.
11. Y. Theodoridis, M. Vazirgiannis, and T. K. Sellis, "Spatio-Temporal Indexing for Large Multimedia Applications", In Proc. IEEE International Conference on Multimedia Computing and Systems, pp. 441-448, 1996.

Personalized and Community Decision Support in eTourism Intermediaries

Chien-Chih Yu

National ChengChi University, Taipei, Taiwan ROC 11623
ccyu@mis.nccu.edu.tw

Abstract. The rapidly growing web technologies and electronic commerce applications have stimulated the need of personalized and group decision support functionalities in eTourism intermediary systems. The goal of this paper is to propose a functional framework and design process for building a web-based customer-oriented decision support system to facilitate personalized and community tourism services. Major decision support functions include personalized data and model management, information search and navigation, product/vendor evaluation and recommendation, do-it-yourself travel planning and design, community and collaboration management, auction and negotiation, as well as trip tracking and quality control. A system implementation approach as well as a system prototype will also be presented and discussed.

1 Introduction

The fast growth of web technologies and applications in recent years have driven both business and public sectors towards adopting innovative e-commerce (EC) and e-business (EB) models and processes. Innovative business models emerged in the EC/EB domain include e-shop, e-mall, e-auction, e-procurement, e-marketplace, e-communities, e-brokers, e-advertisers, e-trust, value chain integrator, and other commerce-support e-intermediaries [20,25]. Major identified EC characteristics include global markets, 24/7 operations, quick responses, competitive pricing, multimedia and hypermedia information, interactive search and navigation process, personalized and customized services, innovative products and services, push and pull marketing mechanisms, etc. Inevitably, the travel and tourism industries have also faced new challenges that pushed them to adopt more innovative Internet-based strategies and technologies [3,5,12,18,23]. Developing new forms of products, services, systems and processes is considered critical for all participants in the tourism supply chain to survive from severe market competition as well as to sustain competitiveness and profitability. Eventually, the growing EC/EB trends have stimulated the demands of more information-intensive and decision-support functions and services that incorporate personalized needs and preferences in all tourism-related searching, deciding, and booking processes. For example, Puhretmair et al. (2002) indicate an inevitable trend of tourism information systems to offer extended decision-making support in tourist travel planning [14]. Ricci et al. (2002) present a case-based reasoning (CBR) approach for a web-based intelligent travel recommender system to support users in travel-related information filtering and product bundling

[15]. Buhalis and Licata (2002) point out that eTourism is still in its infancy but will be one of the most rapidly expanding industries on-line. They expect future eTourism intermediaries to be capable of fulfilling customer expectations and providing comprehensive and coherent services [1]. Stamboulis and Skayannis (2003) report that there has been a trend to flexibilization of the tourist product by a form of customization [18]. Werthner and Ricci (2004) discuss how EC and Web may change the structure of travel and tourism industries and forge new ways to satisfy consumer needs. More customized and configured tourism-related products and services are expected from the tourism supply chain. They also expect to see tourists playing a more active role in specifying their services and using reverse auction sites, and intermediaries such as Internet travel sites providing new market functionalities that focus on personalized recommendation services for travelers [23]. Yu (2004) present a web-based consumer-oriented intelligent decision support system (CIDSS) for personalized e-services and indicate e-tourism as one of the potential application area. Major application-level functional modules comprised in the CIDSS framework include consumer and personalized management, navigation and search, evaluation and selection, planning and design, community and collaboration management, auction and negotiation, transactions and payments, quality and feedback control, as well as communications and information distributions. [26].

It can be seen that the trend to provide more customized and personalized tourism-related products and services as well as associated decision support functions is quite obvious. Nevertheless, the function and service framework as well as the design and implementation method to efficiently and effectively develop such a desired tourism decision support system have not been well illustrated and sufficiently discussed yet. In the research literature of the travel and tourism domain, the dominant research approach is empirical study that focuses on information and communication technology (ICT) adoption strategies, marketing analysis, business performance, and customer satisfaction [2,4,7,17,19,21,22,24]. As for research in the tourism information system area, most of previous works focused on management-support, destination-oriented, or transaction-based planning and operation functions [6,9,13,16]. Only few have addressed personalization and decision support issues in the e-tourism domain, besides, only partial solutions have been delivered [8,10,14,25]. The lack of comprehensive research efforts regarding the development of personalized and community decision support systems for e-tourism applications is significant. This situation leads to the absence of a clear guidance for the e-tourism industry to embrace innovative EC/EB and Web technologies, to meet customer needs and create business values. On the other hand, current travel and tourism related information systems and websites such as Travelocity, Expedia, Priceline, Trip, and ezTravel, etc mainly provide similar destination information services as well as online reservation and transaction services at similar quality levels. Destination oriented information include destination guides, photo galleries, tour maps, featured events and activities, package deals, traveler tips and advice. Online reservation and transaction services include flight booking, hotel reservation, and car rental etc. Although several web sites such as Amadeus and Abacus provide flight search and connection planning services, no extended personalized and group decision support services have been provided in current web based destination, reservation, and intermediary systems. As for European Commission's efforts on tourism service network, i.e. the FETISH project (www.fetish.t-6.it), current functions focus on supporting travel agencies to access traveler requested services and to integrate them into a convenient service package. The direct and personalized B2C services won't be provided until the B2B functions are fully matured. Therefore, more in-depth research exploration on eTourism issues regarding function and service framework, as well as design and implementation processes of the personalized and community decision support system is strongly demanded.

This paper aims at proposing a necessary function and service framework as well as design and implementation methods for constructing a customer-oriented decision support system for eTourism intermediaries to facilitate the desired tourism related personalized and community decision services. The rest of this paper is organized as follows. The function and service framework is presented is section 2, followed by system design and implementation approaches, as well as an operational prototype in section 3. The final section contains a conclusion.

2 The Function and Service Framework

Adapting Yu's CIDSS framework [26] to specifically take into account the tourism-related personalized and community decision support requirements, the function and service framework proposed for e-tourism intermediaries consists of personalized data and model management, information search and navigation, product/vendor evaluation and recommendation, do-it-yourself (DIY) travel planning and design, community and collaboration management, auction and negotiation, as well as trip tracking and quality control as major functional components. Explanation of corresponding tourism-related decision services are provided below.

Personalized Data and Model Management Services: Services provide in this group allow customers to create and maintain their personal profiles including basic information and personalized travel preferences, as well as evaluation criteria for selecting tourism-related products, services, agents, and vendors. Also included are editing facilities for customers to create personalized travel web pages that equip with subject directories, bookmarks, annotations and notebooks to link and manage frequently accessed tourism resources.

Information Search and Navigation Services: These services provide customers with search and navigational mechanisms to retrieve and browse detailed tourism information such as destinations and events, airline schedules and fares, accommodations and transportations, group packaged tours, as well as relevant news, weathers, maps, travel agencies and tourism suppliers, etc. Customers can also pick and save destinations, attractions, and accommodations in a personal favorite list for future use during the DIY travel planning and design process.

Product/Vendor Evaluation and Recommendation Services: Using decision support services in this group, customers may first specify their needs and preferences by retrieving previously stored data from personal profiles or by directly inserting data through an input screen for a specific instance, and then activate the evaluation process using system default or personalized evaluation criteria. The results are system recommended tourism products and vendors such as package tours and travel agencies that closely match customers' needs and preferences.

Do-It-Yourself Travel Planning and Design Services: Customized and Personalized travel planning and tour design are main functions of this services group. Through interactive steps, customers can specify regions/countries and number of days at the first place, and then design personalized travel plans by picking, bundling, and sequencing chosen destinations, attractions, restaurants and hotels in daily basis.

Community and Collaboration Management Services: The basic community services allow customers to locate people of similar travel interests, to form special tourism interest groups, to set up tourism-related community forums and communication channels, and to share travel experiences and resources. Advanced service functions allow customers to present their personal travel plans to the community, to exchange ideas and collaboratively design alternative trip plans, to vote and select one with highest votes as commonly accepted group trip plans for implementation. Extended supporting services include recommendations of alternative trip plans based on collaborative filtering or CBR techniques.

Auction and Negotiation Services: This group of services provides a dynamic and competitive pricing environment for customers to hold better bargaining positions. The auction services allow customers to issue tourism requests with specified needs and preferences, and then launch reverse auction sessions that call for travel agents, tourism suppliers, and tour operators in the tourism supply chain to bid on the posted individual or group trip plans. The submitted bids are then evaluated according to pre-specified criteria; and those with satisfactory cost/benefit levels are selected as candidates for contract negotiation. The negotiation services allow customers to negotiate terms and contracts with chosen tourism operators.

Trip Tracking and Quality Control Services: This service group provides mechanisms via fixed and mobile devices for group trip members and their families, the travel agents and operators to track in-progress situations during the tour operating period, as well as to make necessary changes for controlling the quality of services.

The proposed e-tourism decision support system also provides transaction and payments services for allowing customers to actually book and issue payments to selected trip plans, or to simply purchase specific tourism products such as tickets or souvenirs. In addition, the communications and information distribution services provide most recent and relevant tourism information for customers' interests, as well as email, online chatting, FAQ, situation reporting channels, feedback and complaint handling functions via wired and/or wireless communication networks.

Through the use of these innovative decision services, customers such as travelers and tourists are able to perform the following personalized and community decision processes.

1. To create and maintain personalized travel objectives, preferences, web pages, and evaluation criteria.
2. To search and navigate tourism-related information such as destinations and accommodations, attractions and features, package tours and travel agencies, etc., as well as to create lists of favorite destinations and accommodations.
3. To activate the evaluation and selection procedure using pre-specified criteria for choosing tourism products and vendors to match their needs with specified satisfaction level.
4. To design personalized travel plans when no existing package tours pass the pre-specified satisfaction level.

5. To find and organize customers of similar interests to exchange ideas and collaboratively design and develop commonly accepted group trip plans.
6. To propose requests and initiate reverse-auction sessions for inviting tourism vendors and services providers to bid on proposed individual and/or group trip plans, as well as to evaluate and select those with best bids as candidates
7. To negotiate terms and contracts with chosen travel agencies and tour operators.
8. To track the progress and control qualities during the tour operations of the contracted trip plans.

Customers can also book selected trip plans and receive new and just-in-time information in pull and push styles. With decision services to this extent, all phases of customers' decision-making process related to tourism and travel matters can be fully supported, and personalization and customization concerns be successfully incorporated. Figure 1 illustrates the proposed framework for personalized and community eTourism decision support functions with backend systems and servers

3 System Design and Implementation

For efficiently and effectively constructing the personalized and community decision support system for e-tourism intermediaries, we use Object-Oriented (OO) modeling approach to represent tourism-related information, decisions, and knowledge in a uniform way. OO conceptual models of specific decision processes are created and integrated to illustrate classes and relationships of all participated market players, products, decision models and knowledge. For instance, in order to carry out the package tour evaluation and recommendation process, classes and relationships of customers, travel agencies, package tours, evaluation models and rules must be identified and presented. Information attributes of a package tour object include tour name, regions/countries, destinations, attractions, tour duration, tour booking price, departure date, tour features, daily trip schedules, and accommodations (with names and ranks), etc. There are reference relationships between package tours objects and

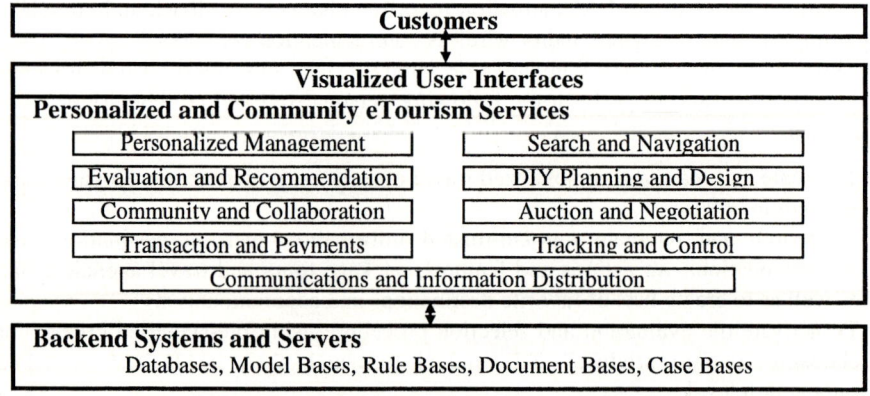

Fig. 1. The functional framework of personalized e-tourism services

customers as well as travel agencies respectively. The travel agencies provide many different package tours to the tourism market, while customers specify their specific needs of package tours for specific instances. A specific set of attributes in the package tour object can be chosen as measurement items of the evaluation model. When specifying their needs and preferences, customers provide values and weights of these measurement attributes as evaluation criteria. Retrieving data of these selected attributes from package tours provided by different travel agencies, and triggering specified tour evaluation rules, scores of every measurement items can be generated. Final matchability scores of these package tours can then be computed based on generated item scores and given weights. Package tours with final scores exceeding the customer specified satisfaction level are presented in a list for further inspection by customers. To be more specific, core objects identified for the package tour evaluation and recommendation decision process include Customer, Travel Agency, Package Tour, Destination, Attraction, Feature, Accommodation, Decision Process, Decision Model, Model Input, Model Output, Decision Knowledge, Knowledge Input, Knowledge Output, Customer Needs Instance, Instance Input, Instance Output, and so on. In this example, the selected instance input elements are Region/Country/Destination Name, Tour Duration, Tour Booking Price, Accommodation Rank, Departure Dates, Feature Names, and associated weights for each input element. Interval and multiple values are allowed for these input elements. The instance output elements include Tour Name, Region/Country, Tour Duration, Tour Booking Price, Accommodation Names and Ranks, Departure Dates, Tour Destinations and Attractions, Tour Features, Daily Trip Schedule, Travel Agency Name, Address, Telephone, Fax, E-mail, and Web Site, as well as the package tour's final Matchability Score. Decision Knowledge, in a simplified case, can be treated as a rule set. The decision process of the package tour evaluation case contains only one decision model and one associated rule set. All desired values of the model and knowledge input elements are obtained from input values of the instance input elements related to customer needs. Figure 2 depicts the OO model that conceptualizes the package tour evaluation and recommendation process; while

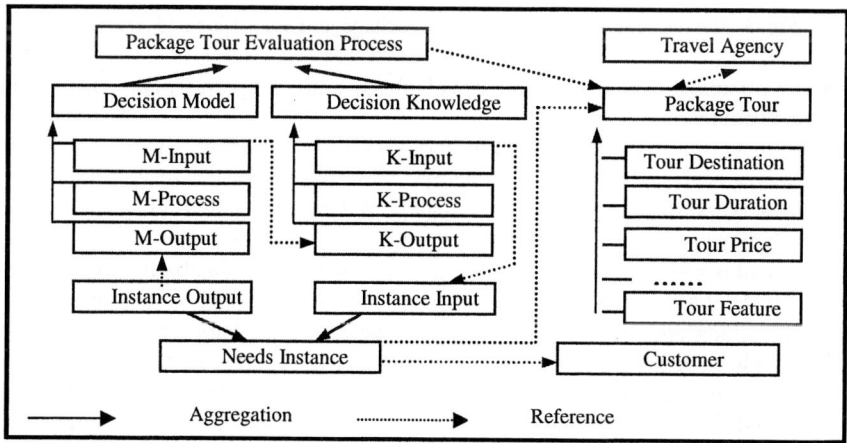

Fig. 2. An OO model for package tour evaluation and recommendation process

Figure 3 shows the evaluation model and associated rule sets. Conceptual modeling of the group trip plan auction and tour operator recommendation process can be conducted in a similar way. As objects of package tour, customer, and travel agency are changed to objects of group trip plan, community, and tour operator, and the attribute items, evaluation criteria and rules are slightly modified, a similar OO model for group trip plan auction and recommendation process can be developed. As for do-it-yourself travel planning and tour design process, the involved objects include Personal Travel Plan, Customer, Destination, Attraction, Feature, and accommodation, and the outcome is a daily schedule of the personalized travel plan. When submitting the personal travel plan to community for developing a group trip plan, or directly to auction session for selecting service providers, attribute values of the personalized travel plan such as plan name, destinations, attractions, features, duration, departure dates, expected price, accommodation rank, etc. must be specified.

SET $T = Sum(T1*W1,...,T6*W6)$
Subject to $Sum(W1,..,W6) = 1$
where T = total score of matchability,
T_i and W_i are value and weight of the ith evaluation criteria, $i = 1,..., 6$

If Trip destination set B belong to the Input destination set A then T1 = "100"
 else T1 = (100-10*(Count(A-B))
If Trip length in days l is within the Input days interval (l1, l2) then T2 = "100"
 else if l < l1 then T2 = 100 − 20*(l1 − l)
 or if l > l2 then T2 = 100 − 20*(l − l2)
If Trip price c is within the Input price interval (c1, c2)
 then T3 = "100"
 else if c < c1 then T3 = 100 − 10*(c1 − c)/5000
 or if c > c2 then T3 = 100 − 20*(c − c2)/5000
IF Accommodation rank a is >= Input accomm. rank a1
 then T4 = "100"
 else T4 = 100 − 20*(a1 − a)
If Departure date d is within the Input date interval (d1, d2)
 then T5 = "100"
 else if if d < d1 then T5 = 100 − 20*(d1 − d)/3
 or if d > d2 then T5 = 100 − 20*(d − d2)/3
If Trip feature set F contains Input feature set F1
 then T6 = "100"
 else T6 = 100 − 100*Count(F1-F)/Count(F1)

Fig. 3. The decision model and rules for package tour evaluation and selection

Eventually, package tours, personal travel plans, and group trip plans share many common attributes.

To facilitate system implementation and operation, we adopt a multi-tier Client-Broker-Server network structure that incorporates client browsers of customers, web resources servers of tourism suppliers, and application servers of intermediaries including information and recommender servers, community and communication servers, auction and negotiation servers, as well as backend database and document servers, model base servers, and knowledge base servers. The e-tourism decision support functions and services are placed in these intermediary application servers that link with backend resources, data, model, and knowledge servers. A prototype system is constructed using Dreamweaver web page authoring tool, Java scripting language, and SQL server database software. Application functions and interfaces, as well as the system embedded model and knowledge computation programs are written and executed as Java programs. The system required database is created and managed using MS SQL server. Multimedia document files such as daily schedules, travel cases, and destination images are stored as separate files but still coded in and managed by the SQL server.

Figure 4 demonstrates several user view pages of the prototype system. Starting from the upper left hand side and continuing as clockwise, the first one is a guide tour page for destination navigation. The second page displays a package tour evaluation form for customers to specify needs and preferences, weights of measurement items and the acceptance level of matchability. The third page is an interactive working zone for designing personalized travel plan in which specific destinations, restaurants, and hotels can be selected and organized in daily bases. When the customer completes the design steps, he can review the final trip schedule in a separate frame and decide whether to stop or to make modifications. The final page shows a submission form for tour operators to place bids on specific trip plans listed in the auction page.

The service framework and prototype system have been proposed to a group of 14 CEOs and CIOs who take an EMBA class related to innovative e-services. And a survey regarding importance, feasibility, and potential effectiveness of the proposed services and system has been conducted after three weeks of focused discussions. The

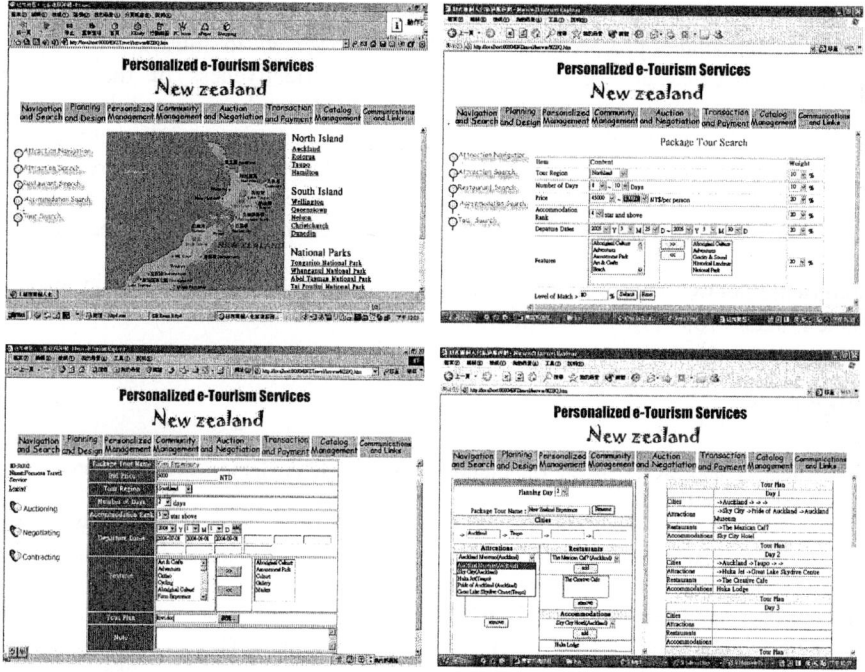

Fig. 4. A destination navigation page, a package tour evaluation page, a DIY travel planning page, and a bid submission page

survey outcome shows that both service functions and the decision support system are well received and highly demanded. Under a five-point scale measurement ranging from 1 to 5 as the very low to very high opinions for response selections, the average scores of total importance and effectiveness are 4.5 and 4.4 respectively. The top three ranked e-tourism services are search and navigation (4.54), evaluation and recommendation (4.21), and DIY travel planning and design (4.21). Moreover, comparing the prototype system to existing tourism web sites, the prototype is trivially the only system capable of providing full personalized and community decision support services to customers in tourism domain.

4 Conclusion

In this paper, we first address the need of personalized decision support services in e-tourism systems, and then present a framework of personalized and community decision support functions and services. Major functional modules of the e-tourism intermediary service system include personalized data and model management, information search and navigation, product/vendor evaluation and recommendation, do-it-yourself travel planning and design, community and collaboration management, auction and negotiation, and trip tracking and quality control. Conceptual object-oriented models are created to represent the information retrieval as well as decision and knowledge computing processes. A system implementation approach is provided and an implemented prototype system is also presented to illustrate the system operation processes as well as to validate the effectiveness of the proposed personalized decision support functions and services. It can be expected that by using the system and services all e-tourism customers, intermediaries, and the entire supply chain can leverage their capabilities and create substantial values. Future research topics include practically implementing the proposed service framework, as well as measuring system performance from both the customer and business perspectives.

Acknowledgment. This research was supported in part by the National Science Council under Project NSC 92-2416-H004-019.

References

1. Buhalis, D. and Licata, M.C.: The Future eTourism Intermediaries. Tourism Management. 23(3) (2002) 207-220.
2. Cai, L., Card, J.A., and Cole, S.T.: Content Delivery Performance of World Wide Web Sites of US Tour Operators Focusing on Destinations in China. Tourism Management. 25(2) (2004) 219-227.
3. Connell, J. and Reynolds, P.: The Implications of Technological Developments on Tourist Information Centres. Tourism Management 20(4) (1999) 501-509.
4. Frew, A.J.: Information and Communications Technology Research in the Travel and Tourism Domain: Perspective and Direction. Journal of Travel Research. 39(2) (2000) 136-145
5. Hjalager, A.M.: Repairing Innovation defectiveness in Tourism. Tourism Management. 23(5) (2002) 465-474.
6. Knoblock, C.: Agents for Gathering, Integrating, and Monitoring Information for Travel Planning. IEEE Intelligent Systems. 17(6) (2002) 63-64.

7. Law, R. and Leung, R.: A Study of Airlines' Online Reservation Services on the Internet", Journal of Travel Research. 39(2) (2000) 202-211.
8. Loban, S. R.: A Framework for Computer-Assisted Travel Counseling. Annals of Tourism Research. 24(4) (1997) 813-834
9. McCormack, J.E. and Roberts, S.A.: Exploiting Object Oriented Methods for Multi-Modal Trip Planning Systems. Information and Software Technology 38(6) (1996) 409-417.
10. Nunez-Suarez, J. et al.: Experiences in the Use of FIPA Agent Technologies for the Development of a Personal Travel Application. In Proceedings of the 4th International Conference on Autonomous Management. (2000) 357-364.
11. O'Keefe, R.M. and Mceachern, T.: Web-Based Customer Decision Support Systems. Communications of the ACM. 41(3) (1998) 71-78
12. Palmer, A. and McCole, P.: The Role of Electronic Commerce in Creating Virtual Tourism Destination Marketing Organizations. International Journal of Contemporary Hospitality Management. 12(3) (2000) 198-204.
13. Proll, B. and Retschitzegger, W.: Discovering Next Generation Tourism Information Systems: A Tour on TIScover. Journal of Travel Research. 39(2) (2000) 182-191
14. Puhretmair, F., Rumetshofer, H., and Schaumlechner, E.: Extended Decision Making in Tourism Information Systems. Lecture Notes in Computer Science, Vol. 2455. Springer-Verlag, (2002) 57-66
15. Ricci, F., Arslan, B., Mirzadeh, N., and Venturini, A.: ITR: A Case-Based Travel Advisory System. Lecture Notes in Artificial Intelligence, Vol. 2416. Springer-Verlag, (2002) 613-627
16. Ritchie, R.J.B. and Ritchie, J.R.B.: A Framework for an Industry Supported Destination Marketing Information System. Tourism Management 23(5) (2002) 439-454.
17. Seddighi, H.R. and Theocharous, A.L.: A Model of Tourism Destination Choice: A Theoretical and Empirical Analysis. Tourism Management. 23(5) (2002) 473-487.
18. Stamboulis, Y. and Skayannis, P.: Innovation Strategies and Technology for Experience-based Tourism. Tourism Management. 24(1) (2003) 33-43.
19. Tierney, P.: Internet-based Evaluation of Tourism Web Site Effectiveness: Methodological Issues and Survey Results. Journal of Travel Research. 39(2) (2000) 212-219.
20. Timmers, P.: Business Models for Electronic Markets. Electronic Markets. 8(2) (1998) 3-8
21. Wang, K.C., Hsieh, A.T., and Huan, T.C.: Critical Service Features in Group Package Tour: An Exploratory Research. Tourism Management 21(2) (2000) 177-189.
22. Wang, Y., Yu, Q., and Fesenmaier, D.R.: Defining the Virtual Tourist Community: Implications for Tourism Marketing. Tourism Management. 23(4) (2002) 407-417.
23. Werthner, H. and Ricci, F.: E-Commerce and Tourism. Communications of the ACM 47(12) 2004 101-105.
24. Wober, K. and Gretzel, U.: Tourism Managers' Adoption of Marketing Decision Support Systems. Journal of Travel Research 39(2) (2000) 172-181.
25. Yu, C.C.: Designing a Web-Based Consumer Decision Support System for Tourism Services, In Proceedings of the 4th International Conference on Electronic Commerce, (2002).
26. Yu, C.C.: A Web-Based Consumer-Oriented Intelligent Decision Support System for E-Services, In Proceedings of the 6th International Conference on Electronic Commerce, (2004) 429-437.

Reengineering the Knowledge Component of a Data Warehouse-Based Expert Diagnosis System

Jean-François Beaudoin[1], Sylvain Delisle[1], Mathieu Dugré[1], and Josée St-Pierre[2]

[1] Département de mathématiques et d'informatique
[2] Département des sciences de la gestion
Institut de recherche sur les PME,
Laboratoire de recherche sur la performance des enterprises,
Université du Québec à Trois-Rivières,
C.P. 500, Trois-Rivières, Québec, Canada, G9A 5H7
Phone: 1-819-376-5011 + 3832
Fax: 1-819-376-5185
{jean-francois_beaudoin, sylvain_delisle, mathieu_dugre, josee_st-pierre}@uqtr.ca
www.uqtr.ca/{~delisle, dsge}

Abstract. We describe the weaknesses of an existing expert diagnosis-recommendation system we have developed for SMEs. In good part, these weaknesses are related to the fact that the system was not implemented with appropriate artificial intelligence techniques. We recently decided to tackle the problem and re-engineered the core of the system with the help of an up-to-date expert system shell. In the process, we revised the formalization and reorganization of the system's expertise and developed a brand new knowledge base. We here describe the new system and the improvements made, and we identify ongoing and future developments.

1 Introduction

In 1999, we developed an expert diagnosis system for small and medium-sized enterprises (**SMEs**), the PDG system [1, 2]. This system is based on a benchmarking approach [3-5] and performs a multidimensional evaluation of a SME's production and management activities, and assesses the results of these activities in terms of productivity, profitability, vulnerability and efficiency. This system is fully operational and has been put to use on actual data from more than 500 SMEs from Canada, USA, and France. By academic standards, it is clearly a successful real-life application [2].

What is peculiar though, especially from a knowledge-based systems perspective, is the fact that although the PDG system is packed with knowledge and expertise on SMEs, it has not been originally implemented with "traditional" symbolic Artificial Intelligence (**AI**) techniques due to lack of time, human and financial resources. Today, we must admit that this implementation decision was not optimal as it is the main cause for certain weaknesses in the system's knowledge component, including its lack of flexibility, difficulty in understanding, and limited capacity for adaptation, improvement and updating.

We are currently working on the development of a second generation PDG system, which we call the PDGII system. Although it is based on the first system, two key components have undergone in-depth reengineering: its database, which has now become a powerful data warehouse, and its knowledge base and reasoning engine, which are being re-designed and re-implemented with symbolic AI techniques [6]. In what follows, we first explain the reasons justifying the development of the new PDGII system and we identify the goals we have set ourselves in this second generation system. Then, the main part of the paper consists in a discussion of the new knowledge-based subsystem: the selected AI techniques and tools, the formalization of the expertise, and the additions and benefits brought along. We also briefly talk about potential future developments in the PDGII system.

Our work takes place within the context of the Research Institute for SMEs. The Institute's core mission is to support fundamental and applied research to foster the advancement of knowledge on SMEs to contribute to their development. Our lab, the LaRePE *(LAboratoire de REcherche sur la Performance des Entreprises*: www.uqtr.ca/inrpme/ larepe/), is mainly concerned with the development of scientific expertise on the study and modeling of SMEs' performance, including a variety of interrelated subjects such as finance, management, information systems, production, technology, etc. All research projects carried out at the LaRePE involve both theoretical and practical aspects, always attempting to provide practical solutions to real problems confronting SMEs, often necessitating in-field studies.

2 Towards the Reengineered Diagnosis System

The initial PDG system was and still is a good diagnosis system [2]. With the use of a lot of data collected from a comprehensive questionnaire filled by an evaluated SME, this system identifies and evaluates the enterprise's weaknesses. Then, relevant recommendations are suggested to help the evaluated SME correct its weaknesses and thus improve its performance. The questionnaire's data are stored in a database (now a data warehouse) and the SAS statistical package is used to perform various statistical calculations. Thereafter, the PDG system imports these statistical data to perform the diagnosis and to produce a detailed evaluation report in which we find the results presented as graphics and texts. The whole system, from the diagnosis program to the report production program, was originally developed with Microsoft Excel. This system is fully functional since 1999 and still produces performance diagnostic reports very much appreciated by SME owners-managers.

However, despite its success and correctness, the original PDG system was out of date with the current state of the art in this kind of system [7-9] and suffered from important gaps and weaknesses that made its functioning, updating, understanding, and evolution rather difficult. The main element of any expert system is a knowledge base in which resides the system's expertise. The fact is that the original PDG system does not have an explicit knowledge base. Indeed, the expertise elements are scattered throughout the Excel programming code and cells. Consequently, it is extremely difficult to find and update expertise elements, even more to ensure that changes will not result in the introduction of unforeseen consequences. The usability and flexibility of the code is reduced dramatically by this weakness. The high coupling between the code and the expertise makes the improvement of the system excessively difficult: this is definitely a major handicap for a good expert system that needs to evolve with our grasp of the application domain, especially in the long run.

Moreover, although the final diagnosis reports produced by the PDG system are of the highest quality, the report production component is not flexible at all. The code associated with the production of the report is intermingled with the code supporting the diagnosis system's expertise. Thus, it is impossible to modify the report without affecting the rest of the PDG system. For example, simply removing, adding, or modifying a graphic in the report involves a considerable programming effort. So, there is a harmful coupling between the diagnosis expert system and the report generation elements, especially those dealing with graphical representations.

Our laboratory is currently working on a brand new PDGII system that will correct these weaknesses. This new SME performance diagnosis system is a complete reengineering of the old system and is built on a solid artificial intelligence basis. Here are the goals we have set ourselves with regard to the knowledge-base component:

- Centralize and formalize all the expertise elements in a flexible and well-structured knowledge base.
- Replace Excel by another programming tool more adapted to our situation and needs.
- Separate the programming code of the diagnosis system from the programming code of the report's graphical representations.
- Encapsulate in a flexible way the various objects involved in a diagnosis so that they will be able to easily support new reports and specific user profiles.
- Revise the graphics production mechanism to support in a flexible way more personalized final reports.
- Devise a structure and mechanism that will save in our data warehouse all the detailed diagnosis results.

3 The New Knowledge-Based Component

3.1 Selecting the Appropriate AI Tool

To implement the new PDGII system, we had to find appropriate, new programming tools. We needed to program the newly reengineered expert system, based on up-to-date AI techniques [6], plus other more conventional (non-AI) elements. As to the main conventional implementation language, we chose Java. Since most of the systems in our laboratory are now programmed in Java, practical considerations motivated this choice. As far as the knowledge-based component is concerned, we needed a capable and efficient tool that would support the creation of a knowledge base and the use of an inference engine. In order to find the best AI tool to suit our needs, we conducted a quite extensive comparative evaluation based on information available on vendor's Web sites and also on several applied AI research papers. We even tested some of these tools on our systems. In the end, the winner was Flex.

Flex [10] is a tool from Logic Programming Associates Ltd (www.lpa.co.uk) and is especially designed for the development of expert systems, including both the knowledge base and the inference engine components. Flex knowledge bases are "frame-based" [11] and they are easy to develop. Flex also has its own inference engine. The knowledge base and the inference rules must be written in the Flex KSL (Knowledge Specification Language) [10]. An important feature of the Flex KSL language is that it is close to English in many ways, so it is easy to use and to understand. Here is an example that illustrates how easy it is to define a frame and an instance of the latter:

frame evaluation_criterion ;
    default description **is** 'Complete the description for the criterion.'

frame benchmark_data ;
    default enterprise_value   **is** _ **and**
    default reference_group_value **is** _ **and**
    default benchmark_value.

frame technological_proficiency **is a** evaluation_criterion ;
    default data1 **is a** benchmark_data **and**
    default data2 **is a** benchmark_data **and**
    default data3 **is a** benchmark_data **and**
    default data4 **is a** benchmark_data .

instance criterion1 **is a** technological_proficiency .

In this example, we can see the use of the inheritance mechanism. We have the **evaluation_criterion** parent frame and its more specialized children frame **technological_proficiency**. The children frame inherits all the attributes of the parent frame, unless otherwise specified. The type of these children attributes is also a frame. So, each attribute of the children frame will be of type **benchmark_data**. Finally, we can see how easy it is to create an instance of the children frame.

We could have specified explicit values for the attributes of the instance **criterion1**, but as it is possible to build Flex procedures in KSL (or even in Prolog), we could also have specified the attributes data by programming, as in:

do criterion1's data1's enterprise_value **becomes** 232.67 .

The Flex inference engine supports both forward and backward chaining. Here is an example showing the simplicity with which one can write a forward chaining rule:

rule benchmark_value_verification
    if S **is an instance of** evaluation_criterion **and**
        S`s data1`s enterprise_value > S`s data1`s reference_group_value
    then S`s data1`s benchmark_value **becomes** 'Enterprise is better' .

In addition to Flex, LPA also offers other interesting and useful tools for the development of AI-based systems. The Flint tool [12] supports the management of uncertainty in an expert system through these AI techniques: fuzzy logic, Bayesian updating, and certainty factors—this is a tool we will reconsider later in the development of our new PDGII system. With yet another LPA tool, the ProData Interface [13], it is possible to use a database from within a Flex-based system. This is an important capability in the PDG system as it must absolutely be able to get access to the data warehouse containing all SME-related data. Another useful LPA tool is the Intelligence Server [14], which allows an external (or foreign) application to connect to a Flex knowledge base and submit requests to it. Consequently, we can create the non-AI subset of the new PDGII system in Java and work with the Flex knowledge base through the Intelligence Server interface.

3.2 System Architecture

We now consider in more detail how the different tools mentioned in Section 3.1 are actually organized in the PDGII system: see Figure 1 below. First of all, there is a Java program acting as the entry point of the system; this program controls the execution of the entire system. A diagnosis editor allows the user to enter essential information and parameters about the configuration of the diagnosis to be produced, such as the evaluated SME's identification, the information for the creation of the reference group (against which the evaluated SME will be compared), the desired diagnosis type, etc. Another important element for the PDGII system is that it is possible, during this configuration phase, to select and modify some expertise elements (via the Intelligence Server interface), such as weights, that will be used for the performance diagnosis. For testing purposes, such flexibility in this configuration phase is quite useful when we want to measure the impact of some parameters on the system's behaviour without making any other changes.

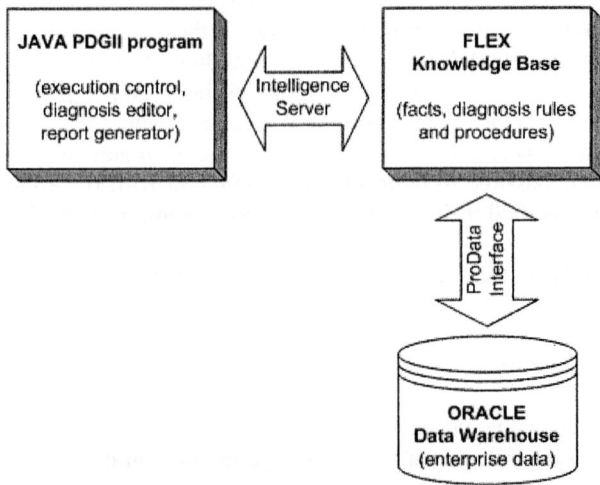

Fig. 1. The PDGII system architecture

It is also possible to select the desired profile for a PDGII diagnosis. We will come back to this later, but let us just say that several different profiles of diagnosis can be created in order to support the evaluation of SMEs from different perspectives. In fact, the knowledge base contains predetermined profiles of PDGII diagnoses. The user simply has to select the one he/she desires. For example, the complete profile consists in the performance evaluation of all activities of an SME. Yet another profile consists in the evaluation of, only, the production and management systems.

Once the diagnosis has been launched, the knowledge base has to communicate with the Oracle data warehouse to download all the relevant SME data. Our data warehouse has been built one year ago [15] and is still the subject of ongoing work. This new data warehouse supports the expert diagnosis system, and is also used in various other research projects on SME data. Communication between the Flex knowledge base and the data warehouse is made possible through the ProData interface. The Flex knowledge base then performs the diagnosis with the help of its facts, rules and procedures. At the end of the diagnosis, the results are first uploaded in the Oracle database (data warehouse) and then used by the report maker from the Java program. At this stage, a report configuration can be specified by the user.

4 Expertise Organization and Formalization

4.1 The Knowledge Base Structure

In the initial version of the PDG system, expertise was scattered throughout the Excel implementation. It was extremely difficult to locate and understand expertise elements, and ensure their safe maintenance. Because of the crucial role played by the PDG system's knowledge component, the finding of a solution to this problem very much influenced the design of the new PDGII system. The initial phase of the reengineering was thus the identification (and understanding) of all the expertise elements dispersed in the original Excel implementation—a difficult and tedious task since the system had been programmed over a period of several years, by different programmers, and supported by essentially no documentation. Then, all expertise elements were verified, centralized, and organized into a well-structured, frame-based Flex knowledge base.

We also wanted this knowledge base to be usable by other systems, not only the PDGII system. So it had to be devised in a relatively generic way. Indeed, throughout the years, our laboratory has built a strong expertise in SME performance evaluation. This expertise has translated into the development of performance evaluation criteria in several key SME-related domains. In fact, an expert system such as the PDGII system would not be possible without these precious criteria belonging to various domains. Thus, we decided to build a knowledge base that could be used by any diagnosis system in our laboratory, not only the PDGII system. A high degree of flexibility and reusability was a goal of the utmost importance in this phase of our work.

Because these SME evaluation criteria are not necessarily specific to the PDGII system, it was important to make this distinction in the knowledge base. Consequently, we organized the knowledge base in two parts. The first part (left-hand side in Figure 2) contains all the expertise that can be used by any of our diagnosis systems, i.e. which is generic and not PDGII-specific. This subset of the knowledge base contains 64 evaluation criteria. The second part (right-hand side in Figure 2) of the knowledge base contains all the expertise elements that are specific to each diagnosis system, such as the PDGII system. Figure 2 illustrates how the knowledge base is organised.

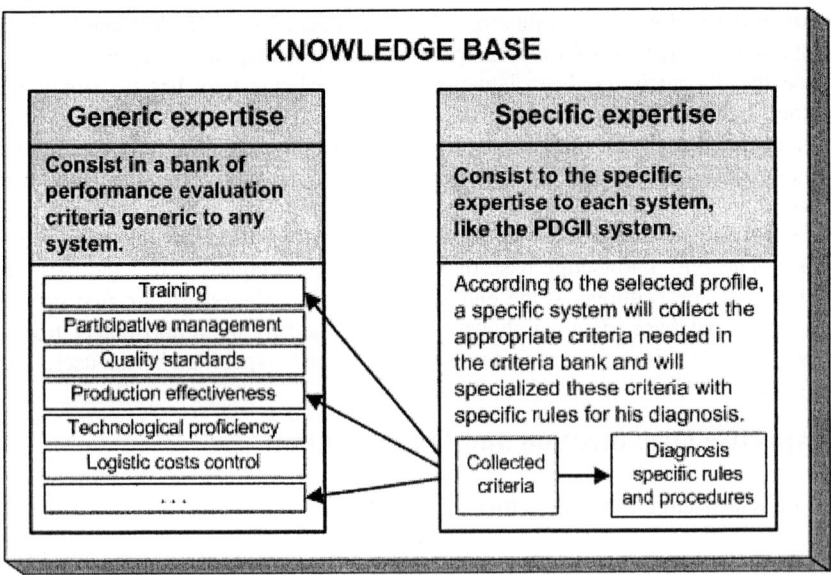

Fig. 2. The expertise general to every diagnosis system appears on the left-hand side, and the expertise specific to each diagnosis system on the right-hand side

Another important concept in the organisation of the knowledge base is the link between the generic and the specific parts. As mentioned before, the PDGII system uses different diagnosis profiles, each defining a specific orientation of the diagnosis performed by the PDGII system. For example, one specific PDGII profile could define a specialized diagnosis of the SME's human resources activities, while another PDGII profile could define the general diagnosis of all activities. Each profile is defined by the evaluation criteria needed to perform the associated diagnosis. Indeed, each profile selects the required criteria in the generic subset of the knowledge base, and then complements these criteria with PDGII-specific knowledge (e.g. PDGII data, PDGII rules, etc.) to allow the computation of the diagnosis in the specific context of the PDGII system.

4.2 Levels of Formalization in the PDGII Expertise

Another major improvement implemented in the PDGII system's knowledge base is the three-level expertise formalization that was carried out. To better understand these levels, let us first take a look at the structure of the PDGII system's diagnosis. The latter performs a performance diagnosis of an evaluated SME in terms of results and management practices in different activity sectors (and business functions), relative to a reference group of similar SMEs. Each activity sector relies on evaluation criteria for a sector-specific diagnosis—these criteria are organized appropriately in the knowledge base as explained in Section 4.1. Figure 3 below presents the three-level PDGII diagnosis structure and the three-level expertise associated with them.

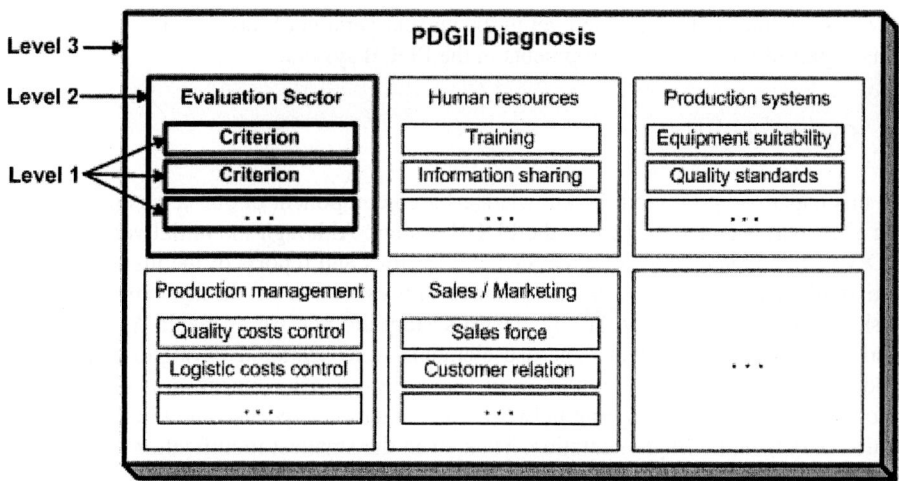

Fig. 3. The PDGII diagnosis system structure and its three-level expertise

The <u>first level</u> corresponds to all the generic and specific evaluation criteria that the PDGII system has selected in the knowledge base, as explained in Section 4.1. These expertise elements include data related to the evaluated SME and the SMEs in the reference group (for benchmarking purposes), and the PDGII-specific rules needed by the relevant criteria. Moreover, this first expertise level also contains all the rules allowing the production of the comments and recommendations on the evaluated SME's performance on the selected criteria. So, all the expertise elements used during the individual evaluation of the criteria of each selected activity sector, according to the active profile, are part of this first expertise level.

The knowledge base's <u>second expertise level</u> corresponds to the expertise on the global evaluation of each activity sector (or business function) of a PDGII diagnosis. Each evaluation criteria of each sector are grouped together to perform this global sector evaluation. Playing a central role among the elements of this second expertise level is the weight of each evaluation criterion relative to its sector. We also find all the rules allowing the global performance diagnosis of each activity sector, and also the rules allowing the identification of the weakest criteria of each sector for the evaluated SME. Once the identification of the weakest criteria of each sector is done, comments and recommendations associated with these criteria are produced with the help of the first expertise level.

The <u>third expertise level</u> of the knowledge base is associated with the global evaluation of all activity sectors of a PDGII diagnosis profile. It corresponds to a complex and sophisticated level of expertise because we must be able to compare and balance different sectors of activity within the evaluated SME, while being able to explain why it does better or worse than its reference group and if this needs attention or action in the near future. Thus, it still is a challenging task for SME performance evaluation experts to find reliable expertise rules to model this kind of global evaluation. At present time, a human expert always revises the evaluation automatically produced by the PDG system at this level. Thus, this third expertise level is not totally implemented yet in the current version of the knowledge base. And this is part of our future developments in the PDGII system.

5 Conclusion

In this paper, we presented the knowledge-based component of our new expert system on SME performance diagnosis, the PDGII system. Although the initial version of the PDG system managed to produce SME evaluations and reports of the highest quality, the implementation rendered maintenance and evolution of the system a daunting task. In particular, the fact that the expert system did not use available AI techniques and tools, and the fact that expertise elements were scattered throughout the Excel code and cells, made any evolution of the system a risky business. Another major problem was the tight coupling between the evaluation expertise and the report generation details in the implementation. Thus, even the smallest modification made to the report produced by the diagnosis system was a great challenge and often led to unforeseen consequences. For all these reasons, and despite the success of the initial version, we made the decision the move along and reengineer the PDG system, leading to the new PDGII system presented here.

Several important improvements were made along the way. The choice of LPA's Flex software for the knowledge-based component of the PDGII system, as well as the use of the Java programming language contributed to adequate integration at the software level, especially in the context of the software architecture of our laboratory. The two main components in our new PDGII system are the data warehouse and the knowledge-based expert system. An important task of expertise organization and formalization was carried out, as explained in Section 4, to regroup the PDG's diagnosis expertise under three different but complementary levels. Moreover, this knowledge base was developed with the goal of explicitly distinguishing generic knowledge (i.e. used in several diagnosis systems) from specific knowledge (i.e. used in only one specific diagnosis system).

Another advantage of the new PDGII system is that the user has a better control over the diagnosis. Indeed, a user has the possibility to configure some expertise elements of the knowledge base during the configuration phase of a diagnosis. The PDGII system has also gained in control and flexibility with the inception of diagnosis profiles that will affect the diagnosis on different activity sectors of the evaluated SME. Profiles also allow the user to obtain personalized evaluation reports. These improvements represent significant benefits both to the end users, i.e. owners-managers, and the PDG development team.

We are currently performing an extensive validation in which we produce, in parallel, the performance diagnosis with both the new PDGII system and the existing PDG system, from the same data. We then make a detailed comparison of the results in order to identify potential bugs in the new system. So far, more than ten full diagnosis comparisons have been made and only minor bugs have been uncovered.

As it has been done for the last ten years, our laboratory continues to develop and formalize its expertise in SME performance evaluation. The new PDGII system makes a significant contribution in that regard. As to future work, the performance diagnosis results saved in our data warehouse will be used for data mining. Also, another important future work item will be the completion of the third level expertise of our knowledge base as presented above.

Acknowledgements

The authors acknowledge the Natural Sciences and Engineering Research Council of Canada and the J.-Armand Bombardier Foundation for their financial support.

References

1. St-Pierre, J. and S. Delisle, *An Expert Diagnosis System for the Benchmarking of SMEs' Performance*. Benchmarking-An International Journal, to appear.
2. Delisle, S. and J. St-Pierre, *Expertise in a Hybrid Diagnostic-Recommendation System for SMEs: A Successful Real-Life Application*. 3029, Lecture Notes in Computer Science, Spinger-Verlag. 2004. pp.807-816. (Winner of the best paper award)
3. St-Pierre, J., L. Raymond, and E. Andriambeloson. *Performance Effects of the Adoption of Benchmarking and Best Practices in Manufacturing SMEs*. in *Conference on Small Business and Enterprise Development*. 2002. The University of Nottingham (UK).
4. Cassell, C., S. Nadin, and M.O. Gray, *The Use and Effectiveness of Benchmarking in SMEs*. Benchmarking: An International Journal, 2001. **8**(3): pp.212-222.
5. Yasin, M.M., *The Theory and Practice of Benchmarking: Then and Now*. Benchmarking: An International Journal, 2002. **9**(3): pp.217-243.
6. Shu-Hsien Liao, *Expert System Methodologies and Applications--A Decade Review from 1995 to 2004*. Expert Systems with Applications, 2005. **28**(1): pp.93-103.
7. Carlsson, C. and E. Turban, *DSS: Directions for the Next Decade*. Decision Support Systems, 2002. **33**(2): pp.105-110.
8. Nedovic, L. and V. Devedzic, *Expert Systems in Finance--a Cross-section of the Field*. Expert Systems with Applications, 2002. **23**(1): pp.49-66.
9. Shim, J.P., et al., *Past, Present, and Future of Decision Support Technology*. Decision Support Systems, 2002. **33**(2): pp.111-126.
10. LPA, *Flex Expert System Toolkit: Flex Reference*. 1996, London: Logic Programming Associates Ltd.
11. Turban, E. and J.E. Aronson, *Decision Support Systems and Intelligent Systems*. 2001: Prentice Hall.
12. LPA, *Flint Reference*. 2004, London: Logic Programming Associates Ltd.
13. PA, *ProData Interface*. 2004, London: Logic Programming Associates Ltd.
14. LPA, *Intelligence Server*. 2004, London: Logic Programming Associates Ltd.
15. Delisle, S., M. Dugré, and J. St-Pierre. *Multidimensional SME Performance Evaluation: Upgrading to Data Warehousing & Data Mining Techniques*. Proceedings of the International Conference on Information and Knowledge Engineering. 2004. Las Vegas, Nevada: CSREA Press.

A Model-Based Monitoring and Diagnosis System for a Space-Based Astrometry Mission

Aleksei Pavlov[1,*], Sven Helmer[2], and Guido Moerkotte[2]

[1] Max-Planck-Institut für Astronomie, Königstuhl 17, 69117 Heidelberg, Germany
pavlov@mpia.de
[2] Fakultät für Mathematik und Informatik, D7, 27, Universität Mannheim, 68131 Mannheim, Germany
{helmer, moerkotte}@informatik.uni-mannheim.de

Abstract. Space-based astrometry missions can achieve an accuracy that has not been possible before (by ground-based observations). However, in order to guarantee this precision, it is of the utmost importance to check the scientific quality of the data constantly. We present a model-based monitoring system, called Science Quick Look, that is able to carry out the preliminary scientific assessment. We have implemented a prototype of the system and show the results of an evaluation.

1 Introduction

Astrometry is the oldest branch of astronomy and deals with the positions, distances, and motions of stars. Apart from providing a reference frame for the observations of astronomers, astrometrical data is important for navigation and guidance systems, accurate time keeping, and supplying astrophysicists with motion and distance data.

We can employ basic trigonometry to find the distance of a far-away object S, e.g. a star, by determining how S appears to move when observed from the two ends of a baseline perpendicular to a line from the baseline's center point to the object. The largest baseline available when looking at stars is twice the distance from the Earth to the Sun, which is approximately 300 million kilometers (see Figure 1). The apparent movement of a star against background stars (which are so far away that their movement is not detectable) is called its parallax. This is the angle marked p in Figure 1. Angles are measured to a precision of arc-seconds. For example, the parallax of the star nearest to our solar system, Alpha Centauri, is 0.75″ (three quarters of an arc-second).

The development of better instruments over time has led to a steady increase in accuracy of the obtained data. Important milestones were the development of astrolabes, sextants, telescopes, radio telescopes, and CCD (charge-coupled device) chips. The latest step was the introduction of space-based astrometry via satellites, which eliminated the blurring effects of the atmosphere. Figure 2 shows the precision that was feasible during different times in history (the values for DIVA and GAIA are predicted).

---

[*] This work was supported by a grant from the Klaus Tschira Foundation (KTS).

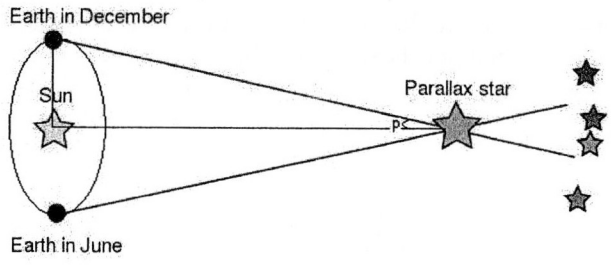

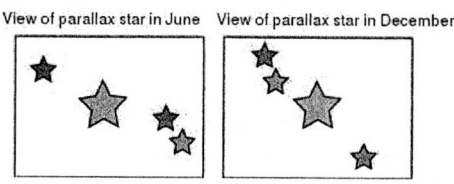

Fig. 1. Parallax of a star

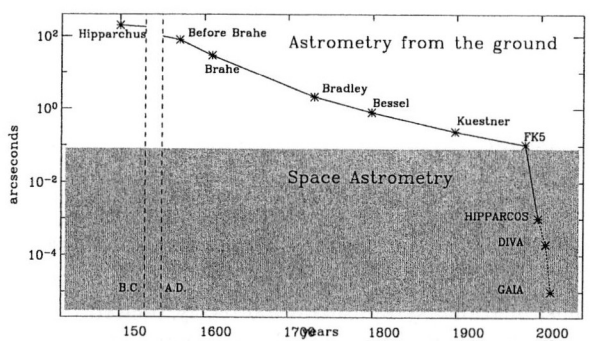

Fig. 2. Precision in arc-seconds over time

The focus of our work was to create a prototype for the monitoring and diagnosis process to assist an operator/astronomer in rapidly assessing the scientific data quality. On the one hand, we needed to generate meaningful statistics and diagnostics that reflect any changes in the system state. On the other hand, we wanted to provide expert advice on possible explanations for any problems. As C.A. Kitts notes in [11], automating the process of monitoring the operability of a spacecraft can augment or replace human decision making and thus increase reaction speeds, reduce errors and mitigate cognitive overload, enhance safety, lower costs, focus analysis and free human reasoning for more complicated tasks. However, in order to automate the monitoring process, we need to compare the data generated by the satellite to reference data. We extract this reference data from a model we developed predicting the behavior of the satellite.

When talking about monitoring operability, we have to distinguish between two different types of faults that can occur. First, we have to check the *housekeeping data*

(HK) and *attitude control system data* (ACS) to keep the satellite in orbit and on its correct course. This job is done by the ground-based space operations center. Second, we may also have faults in the instruments collecting the *scientific data*. Defects in this area do not put the satellite at immediate risk, but they may corrupt the data to such an extent that it becomes worthless for later scientific analysis. For this reason, it is mandatory to constantly analyze the scientific content of the data sent down from the satellite. In order to do this we developed a *Science Quick Look (ScQL)* monitoring framework. For the HIPPARCOS mission [1] (the first and only space-based astrometry mission up to now) the quality check of the scientific data was a very cumbersome task, since it had not been automated. Here we present an approach on how to meet this challenge by building a semi-automated monitoring and diagnosis system for the first time.

We have begun working in the framework of the DIVA project, which aimed at measuring the positions of about 35 million stars with the help of a low-cost satellite. In the meantime, DIVA has been absorbed into the larger GAIA project. At the moment, work done for DIVA is adapted to GAIA.

The remainder of the paper is organized as follows. Section 2 covers the related work. In Section 3 we give an overview of the general design of the ScQL process. The model that our monitoring system is based on is described in Section 4. Section 5 presents our monitoring and diagnosis system, while Section 6 gives a brief evaluation of our work. Section 7 contains concluding remarks.

2 Related Work

For comparing the observed data to our model and drawing conclusions from this, we rely on reasoning systems. In this section we will take a brief look at these systems. The first large group of reasoning systems comprise symptom-based approaches, in which symptoms are directly related to faults. Traditional rule-based systems represent the accumulated experience of experts in the form of empirical associations, i.e., rules that associate symptoms with their underlying faults. Examples for rule-based approaches (which include dictionary-based, tree-based, or use-case-based reasoning) can be found in [2,4,8]. Fault dictionaries are lists of symptom/fault pairs indexed by a description of the symptoms. In order to build such a dictionary, we need a specification on how a system behaves if a certain component is broken. The resulting list of fault/symptom pairs is then inverted to form our dictionary. An example of this technique can be found in [17]. Decision trees are a way to break down complex diagnostic situations hierarchically. This means that we step through a sequence of tests before arriving at a diagnostic solution. See [4] for more details. A relatively recent method is case-based reasoning, in which previously successful solutions are adapted to similar problems. Case-based systems learn by acquiring new knowledge in the form of additional case studies. Examples for these systems can be found in [16].

The second large group of reasoning systems are based on models. Here we do not rely on empirical knowledge about symptoms and faults, but on fundamental knowledge of the considered domain. Davis and Hamscher state some general rules in [4] on how to model the behavior, structure, and failures of a system from the viewpoint of troubleshooting. Qualitative models, as described in [5], are not concerned with exact quantitative values, but describe a system at a high level of abstraction. An example for a qualitative description of a parameter is that its value is increasing, decreasing, or constant. Inc-Diagnose is an algorithm developed by Ng [19] and is based on a formal theory by Reiter for diagnosis [14]. While the approaches described so far emerged from the AI community, there has also been work started from an engineering point of view, like fault detection and isolation (FDI) [3].

One thing that became clear during our study of the literature was that there is no universal method for coping with all possible situations. We favor a model-based approach, in which we can extract diagnostic clues from discrepancies between predicted behavior and observations. This approach is rather natural for a scientist (after all, the users of our system are going to be astronomers), as this is how he or she usually solves scientific problems. There are also some shortcomings of the symptom-based approaches, the main one being that it is difficult to comprehend why a system arrives at a certain conclusion. In contrast to this, a model-based approach rests upon established facts of the domain, rather than relying on empirical knowledge. Also, maintaining the knowledge for complex symptom-based systems is also a challenging task, as small changes in the design may necessitate revisions in a large part of the knowledge base.

3 General Design of Science Quick Look

3.1 Requirements of ScQL

The job of the ScQL is to continuously check the correct operation of the on-board instruments. On the one hand, we have to monitor the hardware, i.e., the optics with its lenses and mirrors, the detectors with their light-sensitive areas (CCD chips), and different supply voltages. On the other hand, we have the software controlling the instruments and their output. In order to make clear what ScQL has to check here, we give a brief description of the modus operandi. The image detection software scans the raw data stream from the CCD array for star-like images. The centroiding algorithm determines the central positions of these images. Knowing this center position, the window cutting algorithm cuts out a small rectangular area around the image. This is done because transmitting the whole output of the CCD array to the ground station would use up too much of the limited data transmission rate. Then we have algorithms for identifying attitude stars. The (on-board) attitude star catalog consists of a collection of reference stars (with known positions). With the help of the reference stars the position of the satellite can be determined more accurately. This has a considerable impact on the quality of the scientific data. Last but not least, let us mention one more algorithm. Due to the rotation of the satellite, the stellar images are moving from the left to the right in the focal plane. To obtain sharp images, the shifting and reading out of the CCDs needs to be synchronized with the current rotation movement of the satellite. This is the job of the clock stroke rate adjustment. ScQL has to verify the validity of the output of all the algorithms described above.

3.2 Parts of the ScQL Process

Schematically, the process of ScQL is composed of three parts: a star transit simulator, monitoring, and diagnosis. All these parts depend heavily on the employed model. Our model takes into consideration the Galaxy, the structure of the satellite, the behavior of the satellite's components, and the scanning strategy of the satellite. The star transit simulation is responsible for describing the predicted behavior of the satellite. It is also used for generating simulated data during the development of the system (as no observed data is available yet). Monitoring produces statistics and derived parameters from observations. These values are compared to predicted ones and if the differences are too large, the system raises alarms. In the diagnosis step the symptoms generated by the monitoring process are related to faults in the system.

3.3 Faults and Residual Generation

We define a fault as a deviation of a parameter from the modeled (nominal) behavior of the satellite. We distinguish between abrupt, incipient, and intermittent faults (see Figure 3).

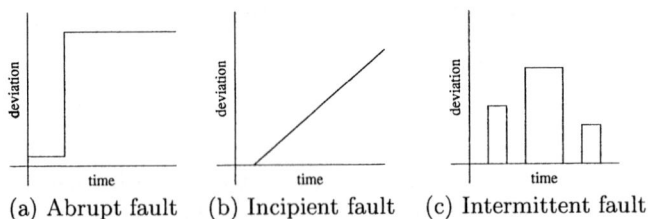

Fig. 3. Typical fault classes

The detection of faults is based on comparing the system parameters computed from observations (measurements) with the values generated by a model of the system. The difference between the two is referred to as a residual signal:

$$r_i(t) = \theta_i(t) - \hat{\theta}_i(i), \qquad 1 \leq i \leq k,$$

where r_i denotes the ith residual, θ_i the ith computed parameter from the measured system output, $\hat{\theta}_i$ the estimated (modeled) i^{th} system output parameter and k the number of residuals. The goal is to generate structured residuals to meet monitoring and diagnosis requirements. Residuals are designed to be equal or converge to zero in the fault-free case ($r_i(t) \approx 0$). A fault is described by the significant deviation of one or more residuals from zero ($\|r_i(t)\| > \eta_i > 0$, where $\eta_i \in \mathbb{R}$ denotes a threshold).

4 Star Transit Model

Before building the actual monitoring and diagnosis system, we had to develop a model for the domain. This is quite complicated, as many parameters and features have to be considered. We can only give a brief overview here, for details see [13].

The two main parts are the simulation of the sky and how it is perceived by the satellite. As we are interested in the nearest stars, our sky is practically equivalent to the Galaxy (see Subsection 4.1). For the satellite, we consider its movement (Subsection 4.2) and the behavior of its instruments (Subsection 4.3).

4.1 Simulation of the Galaxy

Modeling the distribution of the reference attitude stars is not that difficult, as they are chosen in such a way that they are homogeneously distributed throughout the sky. However, as we intend to map a much larger number of stars, we opt for a more realistic multi-component Galaxy model as described by Kharchenko et al. in [9,10]. In this model the Galaxy is viewed as a symmetrical system with respect to its rotation axis and its equatorial plane. The Galaxy is divided up into three parts consisting of the thin disk, the thick disk, and the spheroid. (The spheroid is the central part of the Galaxy, which is surrounded by a disk. The disk is divided into a thick disk, the inner ring around the spheroid, and a thin disk, the outermost, sparsely populated part of the Galaxy.) Within each group we have different density and luminosity (brightness) distributions. For simulating a complete map of the sky – including the positions and magnitudes of stars – we divide it up into 252 subareas and populate these subareas according to functions for spatial and luminosity distributions. For details on these functions see [13].

4.2 Scanning Law

When scanning the sky with a satellite, several conflicting constraints have to be considered [12]. The angle between the observed fields of view and the Sun should be at least 45° in oder to minimize straylight. The inclination of the scans on the ecliptic should be as small as possible because the parallactic effect is parallel to the ecliptic. Also, two successive scans should overlap in order to avoid unobserved regions. For DIVA the scanning law is as follows: the satellite does a complete rotation in 2 hours, the rotation axis moves slowly, circling the Sun in 56 days keeping an angular distance of 45° to the Sun.

4.3 Satellite Instruments and Data

The previous two subsections describe a theoretical view of the part of the universe that is relevant to us. When simulating the behavior of the actual satellite, we have to take into account that its instruments have a limited precision. This is reflected in the generation of the data from the simulated satellite.

The data that is produced by the satellite consists of long ribbons of data pixels. These ribbons are supplied by the CCD chips recording the movement of stars along the focal plane of the satellite. Our simulated data reflects this.

Windows containing star images are cut out and described by the following parameters: k_w, the number of the TDI (time-delayed integration) clock stroke at which the lower left corner is read into the read-out register, m_w the number of the column from which the lower left corner is read, and the type of the window (which also defines its size). Checking the validity of these parameters is one of the most important tasks of ScQL, so we focus on them. Our model currently contains a total of 30 parameters. This number will increase as we incorporate more features into our model.

5 Monitoring and Diagnosis System

5.1 Monitoring

Figure 4 shows the overall architecture of our monitoring system. The topmost layer provides a user of our system with a (graphical) user interface. It is based on IDL (Interactive Data Language) by Research Systems Inc. IDL provides tools for visualization, data analysis, and cross-platform application development [15]. Here, we only employ the user interface part. Below that, we have the Foundation Class Layer (FCL) which was originally developed by Smirnov [18] in order to simplify the creation of applications for the analysis of astronomic data. We adopted and modified the two main parts of the FCL, the Visualizer and the DataForms. The Visualizer provides a lot of easy-to-use widget tools for the visualization of large and complex data sets. DataForms is responsible for collecting the input from the user. On the lowest level, there is the actual ScQL-monitoring. It consists of an EventHandler preprocessing the user input, forwarding it to the component responsible for generating statistics and parameter estimations. In turn, the output of this component is fed into the Visualizer and a component responsible for controlling visualization parameters. The statistics-generating component (which is the most complicated part) is capable of checking the parameters, some of which were mentioned in Section 3.1. For details, interested readers are referred to [13].

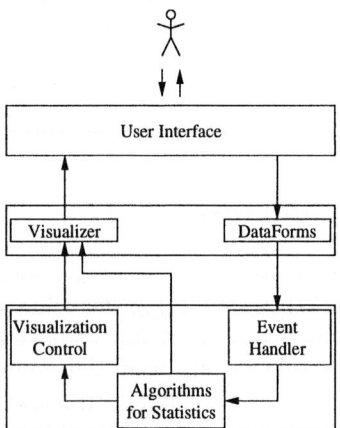

Fig. 4. Architecture of the monitoring system

5.2 Diagnosis

Our current work focuses on the monitoring system, i.e., the diagnosis system is not worked out as elaborately as its monitoring counterpart at the moment. Basically, it consists of a set of 50 rules implemented in COOL (CLIPS Object-Oriented Language). CLIPS (C Language Integrated Production System) is a tool for building expert systems [6,7]. The object-oriented approach of COOL allows us to compose the diagnosis system using modular components, which can be reused later.

6 Short Evaluation of Our Approach

The monitoring system was tested extensively by feeding simulated star transit data into it and generating and evaluating statistics. As an example parameter, we present our evaluation results for the window rate. This parameter tells us how many cut-out windows can be found in a certain period of time in the data stream from the satellite. Figure 5(a) shows how many windows arrive in each three-minute interval. We restrict ourselves to displaying a total elapsed time of two hours and stars with a brightness down to a magnitude of $V = 10.5$ (which corresponds to approximately 1.2 million stars) to keep things legible. The peaks can be explained by the fact that the distribution of the stars is not homogeneous. The density is highest when scanning in the equatorial plane of the Galaxy (the satellite does a full rotation in two hours). Each dot in Figure 5(a) stands for one test run (a total of 50 runs were done in this case). The solid line represents the mean value of all observations.

We now introduced some faults into the simulated data (an abrupt, an incipient, and an intermittent fault) and watched the reaction of the monitoring system. The monitoring system was calibrated with the measurements shown in Figure 5(a). We determined a σ and 3σ interval around the mean value. Figure 5(b) shows the mean window rate as a reference (dash-dotted line at y=0.0). The dotted line is the σ interval and the 3σ interval is the dashed line. The solid line is the residual computed by comparing the (simulated) observation with the expected value. After approximately 60 minutes, we introduced an abrupt fault decreasing the window rate (simulating the malfunctioning of a part of the CCD array). The monitoring system reacted promptly to this event, as the residual signal went over the threshold of 3σ. As a consequence, an alarm was raised.

Figure 5(c) (for an incipient fault after 60 minutes) and Figure 5(d) (for intermittent faults between 20 to 50 and 90 to 110 minutes) show a similar picture. For the incipient fault, an alarm is raised after 60 minutes. The system goes back to normal status for a short time, only to reach a permanent alarm level after 70 minutes. For the intermittent faults the system goes into alarm status for the duration of the faults and reverts back to normal after they are over.

We should mention that during the mission the thresholds will change over time, as we collect more and more information. After half a year of observations,

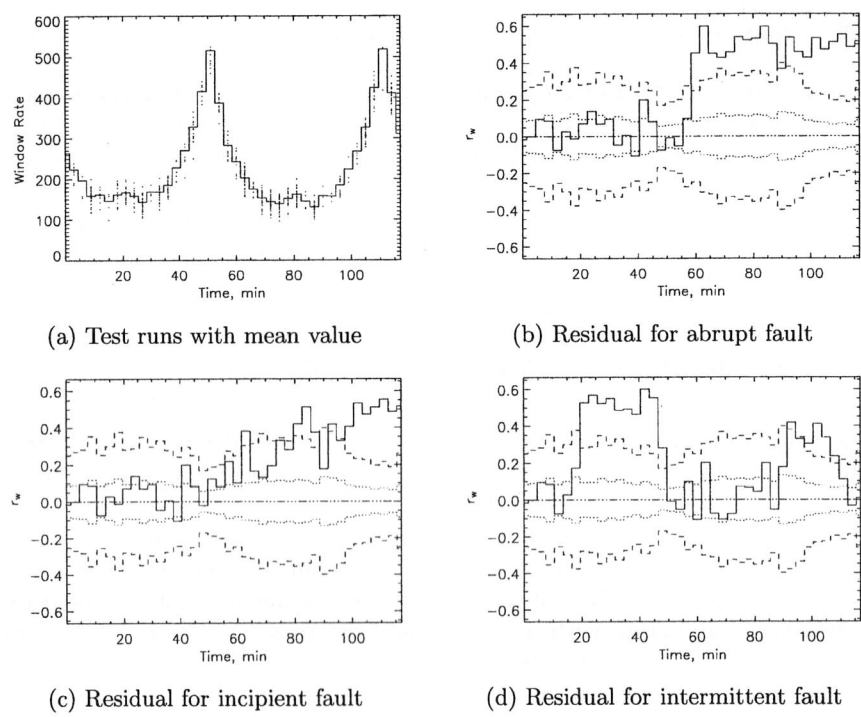

Fig. 5. Window rate

our knowledge about the sky will improve substantially (as we are able to construct a complete sphere). This will allow us to refine our model and determine thresholds that are as close as possible to the nominal case without raising false alarms.

7 Conclusion and Outlook

In order to guarantee a high level of precision when collecting scientific data during a space-based astrometry mission, the quality of the data needs to be checked constantly. The first goal of our work was to study the problem of monitoring scientific data considering the specific characteristics of a astrometry space mission. We decided to build a model-based system, as it is the most appropriate approach in our opinion. At the core of this model is a star transit simulator that mimics the behavior of the satellite and simulates its observations. We also implemented a prototype of a monitoring system that is able to process astronomical data in quasi-real time.

The results of an evaluation of our systems are very promising, so we plan to pursue further studies in this area. First of all, we want to improve the diagnosis part of our system to bring it on par with the monitoring part. Second – as the DIVA project has run out – we will adapt our approach to the next space-based astrometry mission, GAIA, whose satellite will be launched in 2012. The frameworks of DIVA and GAIA are quite similar, due to the fact that the underlying principles of operation and the basic geometry of the measurements are the same. Building a ScQL monitoring system for GAIA has become a lot easier, as an important first step has already been taken in the DIVA project.

References

1. European Space Agency. The Hipparcos and Tycho catalogues. *SP-1200*, 1997.
2. E.M. Awad. *Building Expert Systems: Principles, Procedures, and Applications.* Addison-Wesley Publishing Company, INC., 1996.
3. J. Chen and R.J. Patton. *Robust model-based fault diagnosis for dynamic systems.* Kluwer academic publishers, Boston, 1999.
4. R. Davis and W. Hamscher. *Exploring Artificial Intelligence.* Morgan Kaufmann Publishers, 1988.
5. J. de Kleer. Physics, qualitative. *Articial Intelligence*, 1992.
6. J. Giarratano and G. Riley. *CLIPS Reference Manual.* PWS Publishing Company, Boston, 1998.
7. J. Giarratano and G. Riley. *CLIPS User's Manual Volume II: Objects.* PWS Publishing Company, Boston, 1998.
8. F. Hayes-Roth, D.A. Waterman, and D. Lenat, editors. *Building Expert Systems.* West Publishing Company, 1983.
9. N. Kharchenko, S. Rybka, A. Yatsenko, and E. Schilbach. Predicted star counts and mean parallaxes down to the 23rd magnidute. *Astron. Nachr. 318*, 3:163–171, 1997.
10. N. Kharchenko and E. Schilbach. Program mega: Stellar counts and galactic models. *Baltic Astronomy*, 5:337–356, 1996.
11. C.A. Kitts. A global spacecraft control network for spacecraft autonomy research. *Proceeding of SpaceOps'96: The Forth International Symposium on Space Mission Operations and Ground Data Systems in Munich, Germany*, September 1996.
12. J. Kovalevsky. *Modern Astrometry.* Springer-Verlag Berlin Heidelberg New York, 1995.
13. A. Pavlov. *A Model-Based Monitoring System for Rapid Assessment of Payload and Spacecraft Health/Performance.* PhD thesis, Universität Mannheim, Mannheim, 2005.
14. R. Reiter. A theory of dianosis from the first principles. *Artificial Intelligence*, 32(1):57–95, 1987.
15. Inc. 1994 Research Systems. Idl user's guide. *http://www.rsinc.com/idl/*.
16. R.C. Schank and R.P. Abelson. *Scripts, Plans, Goals and Understanding.* Erlbaum, Hillsdale, New Jersey, US, 1977.
17. J.W. Sheppard and W.R. Simpson. Improving the accuracy of diagnostics provided by fault dictionaries. In *14th IEEE VLSI Test Symposium (VTS '96)*, pages 180–186, 1996.
18. O. Smirnov. Dasha-2:improving visualization and processing of photometric data with idl objects. *Astronomical Data Analysis Software and Systems VIII*, 172:437, March 1999.
19. Hwee Tou Ng. Model-based, multiple-fault diagnosis of time-varying, continous physical devices. pages 9–15, 1990.

An Effective Method for Locally Neighborhood Graphs Updating

Hakim Hacid and Abdelkader Djamel Zighed

Lyon 2 University,
ERIC Laboratory- 5, avenue Pierre Mendès-France
69676 Bron cedex - France
hhacid@eric.univ-lyon2.fr, Abdelkader.Zighed@univ-lyon2.fr

Abstract. Neighborhood graphs are an effective and very widespread technique in several fields. But, in spite of the neighborhood graphs interest, their construction algorithms suffer from a very high complexity what prevents their implementation for great data volumes processing applications. With this high complexity, the update task is also affected. These structures constitute actually a possible representation of the point location problem in a multidimensional space. The point location on an axis can be solved by a binary research. This same problem in the plan can be solved by using a voronoi diagram, but when dimension becomes higher, the location becomes more complex and difficult to manage. We propose in this paper an effective method for point location in a multidimensional space with an aim of effectively and quickly updating neighborhood graphs.

1 Introduction

Nowadays, advances occur in all fields, more particularly in information technologies. The needs of information and data processing are more and more increasing. In addition, information is conveyed by data being in various forms like multimedia data, temporal data, spatial data and the Web. In addition to the data heterogeneity, their significant mass make their processing more difficult.

In front of this situation, store and retrieve multimedia databases is not an easy task. The traditional Database Management Systems (DBMS) are not able to process the new emergent data such as multimedia data. This kind of systems is conceived to manage textual databases. The structure of the data qualified as "complex" is not adequate for these systems. Data structuration enables to center and clean them. Also, this structuration allows solving the performance problem of the data-processing support which can store and process only a limited quantity of information. Starting from this divergence, the concept of complex data was born.

Deal with multidimensional data structuration means deal with the point location problem in a multidimensional space. The point location problem is a key question in the automatic multidimensional data processing. This problem can be described as follows: having a set of data Ω with n items in a multidimensional space $\mathcal{R}^d$, the problem is then to find a way to pre-process the data so that if we have a new query item q, we'll able to find its neighbors within as short as possible time.

In this article, we deal with the point location in a multidimensional space, and this, in order to find an efficient way for optimizing the updating task of the neighborhood graphs. We propose a fast algorithm of a point location in a multidimensional space based on some neighborhood graphs properties. Section 2 presents a state of art on the point location problem, on neighborhood graphs as well as the problematic. Our proposition, based on the search of an optimal hyper sphere, is presented in section 3. Next, we present an illustration example of the method as well as some results. Finally, we conclude and give some future works in section 5.

2 State of Art

Neighborhood search is a significant problem in several fields, it is handled in data mining [8], classification [6], machine learning [5], data compression [13], multimedia databases [10], information retrieval [7], etc. Several works in connection with the neighborhood research in databases exist like [3][18][23].

The point location problem in one-dimensional space can be solved by applying a sorting then a binary search which is rather fast and inexpensive in term of resources with a complexity of $O(n \, log \, n)$ (n corresponds to the number of items). In a two-dimensional space, this problem can be solved by using voronoi diagram [19]. Unfortunately, when the dimension increases, the problem becomes more complex and more difficult to manage. Several methods of point location in a multidimensional space were proposed. We can quote for example the ones based on the points projection on only one axis [11][14][17], or the work based on partial distances calculation between items [2].

As introduced, the objective of the point location is to find a way to preprocess the data so that if we have a new query item, we'll be able to find its neighbors within as short as possible time. One possible way to represent such data structure is a neighborhood graph.

Neighborhood graphs, or proximity graphs, are geometrical structures which use the concept of neighborhood to determine the closest points to another given a query point. For that, they are based on the distance measures [22]. We will use the following notations throughout this paper.

Let Ω be a set of points in a multidimensional space $\mathcal{R}^d$. A graph $\mathcal{G}(\Omega, \varphi)$ is composed by the set of points Ω and a set of edges φ. Then, for any graph we can associate a binary relation upon Ω, in which two points $(p,q) \in \Omega^2$ are in binary relation if and only if the couple $(p,q) \in \varphi$. In an other manner, (p,q) are in binary relation (R) if and only if they are directly connected in the graph $\mathcal{G}$. From this, the neighborhood $\mathcal{N}(p)$ of a point p in the graph $\mathcal{G}$ can be considered as a sub-graph which contains the point p and all the points which are directly connected to it.

Several possibilities were proposed for building neighborhood graphs. Among them we can quote the Delaunay triangulation [19], the relative neighborhood graphs [21], the Gabriel graph [12], and the minimum spanning tree [19]. For illustration, we describe hereafter two examples of neighborhood graphs, relative neighborhood graph (*RNG*) and Gabriel graph (*GG*).

2.1 Relative Neighborhood Graphs

In a relative neighborhood graph $\mathcal{G}_{RNG}(\Omega,\varphi)$, two points $(p,q) \in \Omega^2$ are neighbors if they check the relative neighborhood property defined hereafter.

Let $\mathcal{H}(p,q)$ be the hyper-sphere of radius $d(p,q)$ and centered on p, and let $\mathcal{H}(p,q)$ be the hyper-sphere of radius $d(q,p)$ and centered on q.

$d(p,q)$ and $d(q,p)$ are the dissimilarity measures between the two points p and q. $d(p,q) = d(q,p)$.

Then, p and q are neighbors if and only if the lune $\mathcal{A}(p,q)$ formed by the intersection of the two hyper-spheres $\mathcal{H}(p,q)$ and $\mathcal{H}(q,p)$ is empty [21]. Formally:

$$\mathcal{A}(p,q) = \mathrm{H}(p,q) \cap \mathcal{H}(q,p) \quad Then \ (p,q) \in \varphi \ iff \ \mathrm{A}(p,q) \cap \Omega = \phi$$

Figure 1 illustrates the relative neighborhood graph.

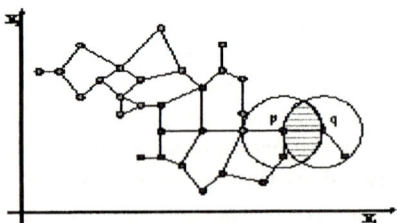

Fig. 1. Relative neighbourhood graph

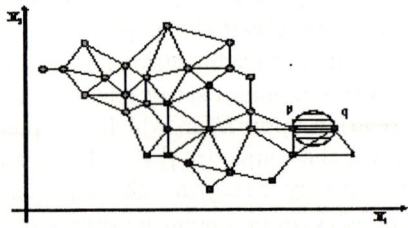

Fig. 2. Gabriel graph

2.2 Gabriel Graph

This graph is introduced by Gabriel and Sokal [12] into a geographical variations measurement concept. Let $\mathcal{H}(p,q)$ be the hyper-sphere of diameter $d(p,q)$ (cf. Figure 2). Then, p is the neighbour of q if and only if the hyper-sphere $\mathcal{H}(p,q)$ is empty. Formally :

$$(p,q) \in \varphi \; iff \; \mathcal{H}(p,q) \cap \Omega = \phi$$

2.3 Neighborhood Graphs Construction Algorithms

Several algorithms for neighborhood graphs construction were proposed. The algorithms which we quote hereafter relate to the construction of the relative neighborhood graph.

One of the common approaches to the various neighborhood graphs construction algorithms is the use of the refinement techniques. In this approach, the graph is built by steps. Each graph is built starting from the previous graph, containing all connections, by eliminating some edges which do not check the neighborhood property of the graph to be built. Pruning (edges elimination) is generally done by taking into account the construction function of the graph or through geometrical properties.

The construction principle of the neighborhood graphs consists in seeking for each point if the other points in the space are in its proximity. The cost of this operation is of complexity $O(n^3)$ (n is the number of points in the space). Toussaint [22] proposed an algorithm of complexity $O(n^2)$. He deduces the RNG starting from a Delaunay triangulation [19]. Using the Octant neighbors, Katajainen [16] also proposed an algorithm of complexity. Smith [20] proposed an algorithm of complexity $O(n^{23/12})$ which is less significant than $O(n^3)$.

2.4 Problems Involved in the Neighbourhood Graphs

Neighbourhood graphs are very much used in various systems. Their popularity is due to the fact that the neighbourhood is determined by coherent functions which reflect, in some point of view, the mechanism of the human intuition. Their use is varied from information retrieval systems to geographical information systems.

However, several problems concerning the neighbourhood graphs are still of topicality and require detailed work to solve them. These problems are primarily related to their high cost of construction and on their update difficulties. For this reasons, optimizations are necessary for their construction and update.

We can consider two possible cases for the neighborhood graphs optimization. The first one is the case where the graph is not built yet, there is a necessity to find an optimal algorithm to build the structure or approximate it in order to have a graph as close as possible to the basic one. The second case is the one where the graph is already built, its rebuilding (with an approximation) can cause an information loss, therefore, it is a question of finding an effective way to update the graph without rebuilding it. In this paper, we are concerned by the second case and we propose an effective method of locally updating the neighborhood graph without having to rebuild it.

3   Neighborhood Graph Local Update

We consider that the neighborhood graph local update task passes by the location of the inserted point (or removed), as well as the points which can be affected by the update. To achieve this, we proceed in two main stages : initially, we determine an optimal space area which can contain a maximum number of potentially closest points to the query point (the point to locate in the multidimensional space). The second stage is done in the aim of filtering the items found beforehand. This is done in order to determine the real closest points to the query point by applying an adequate neighborhood property. This last stage causes the effective updating of the neighborhood relations between the concerned points. The steps of this method are summarized in the followings:

- Lay out the point q in the multidimensional space $\mathcal{R}^d$;
- Seek the first nearest neighbor of q (say p);
- Fix a search area starting from p ;
- Scan the concerned area and update the connections between the items which are there;
- Take the truths neighbors close to q and see if there are exclusions.

The main stage in this method is the search area determination. This can be considered as a question of determining an hyper sphere which maximizes the probability of containing the neighbors of the query item while minimizing the number of items that it contains.

We exploit the general structure of the neighborhood graphs in order to determine the ray of the hyper sphere. We are focusing, especially, on the *nearest neighbor* and the *farther neighbor* concepts. So, two observations in connection with these two concepts seem to us interesting :

- The neighbors of the nearest neighbor are potential candidates neighbors for the query point q.
  From there, we can deduce that:
- All the neighbors of a point are also candidates to the neighborhood of a point to which it is a neighbor.

In order to establish these sets, we determine initially an hyper sphere which maximizes the probability of containing the neighbors of the inserted point, after this, filtering the recovered items to find the partially truths neighbors.

With regard to the first step, determine the ray of an hyper sphere which maximizes the probability of containing the neighbors of the inserted point, this ray is the ray of the sphere including all neighbors of the first nearest neighbor to the query item. We consider this ray as the one formed by the sum of the distances between the inserted point and its nearest neighbor, and the one between the nearest neighbor and its further neighbor. That is, let consider q be the query point and p the nearest neighbor of q with a distance d_1. Let consider X be the further neighbor of p with a distance d_2. The ray SR of the hyper sphere can be expressed as:

$$SR = d_1 + d_2 + \epsilon$$

ϵ is a relaxation parameter, it can be fixed according to the state of the data (their dispersion for example) or by the domain knowledge. In order to avoid the high dimension effects, we fixed experimentally this parameter to 1.

The content of the hyper sphere is processed in order to see whether there are some neighbors (or all the neighbors). The second step constitutes a reinforcement step and aims to eliminate the risk of losing neighbors or including bed ones. This step proceeds so as to exploit the second observation: we take all truths neighbors of the inserted point recovered beforehand (those returned in the first step) as well as their neighbors and update the neighborhood relations between these points. The algorithm hereafter summarizes the various steps of this method.

LocaleUpdate($\mathcal{G}(\Omega,\varphi)$,p)

- $p_x = \{p_i \in \Omega, i = 1, ..., n / ArgMax\ d(p, p_i)\}$
- $N(p_x) = \{p_i \in \Omega, p\ R\ p_i\}$
- $p_y = \{p_i \in N(p_x), p_x \neq p_y / p_y\ R\ p_x \wedge ArgMax\ d(p_x, p_y)\}$
- $SR = d(p, p_x) + d(p_x, p_y) + \epsilon$
- $\Omega'_1 = \{p_i \in \Omega, i = 1, ..., n / ArgMax\ d(p, p_i)\}$
- **For each** $p_i \in \Omega'_1$ **Do** Check if $p\ R\ p_i$ **End For**
- $\Omega'_2 = \{p_j \in \Omega'_1, j = 1, ..., |\Omega'_1| / d(p, p_j) \leq SR\}$
- $\Omega'_3 = \{p_k \in \Omega, p_t \in \Omega'_2, / p\ R\ p_k \vee p_k\ R\ p_t\}$
- **For each** $p_i \in \Omega'_3$ **Do** Check if $p\ R\ p_i$ **End For**
- $\Omega'_4 = \{p_l \in \Omega'_3 / p\ R\ p_j\}$
- Update the neighborhood in Ω'_4
- Return $(\mathcal{G}(\Omega + 1, \varphi'))$

φ': represents the number of new connections after the addition of the query point.

The complexity of this method is very low and meets perfectly our starting aims (locating the neighborhood points in an as short as possible time). It is expressed by:

$$O(2n + n'^2)$$

With

- n : the number of items in the database.
- n' : the number of items in the hyper sphere ($<< n$).

This complexity includes the two stages described previously, namely, the search of the ray of the hyper sphere and the seek of the truths neighbors which are in it and corresponds to the term $O(2n)$. The second term corresponds to the necessary time for the effective update of the neighborhood relations between the real neighbors which is very weak taking into account the number of candidates turned over. This complexity constitutes the maximum complexity and can be optimized by several ways. The most obvious way is to use a fast nearest neighbor algorithm.

4 Illustrations and Experiments

In the followings, we'll illustrate the various steps of the proposed method. Let us consider a relative neighborhood graph for an item set as well as a query point as illustrated on Figure 3. Once the point q situated, it is then necessary to seek its nearest neighbor as well as the further neighbour of this last one. This step is illustrated in Figure 4.

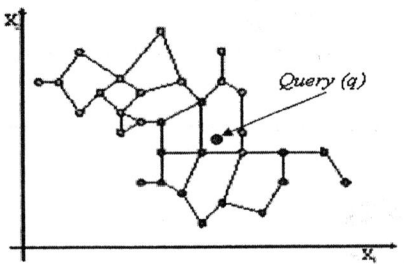

Fig. 3. Query point Position

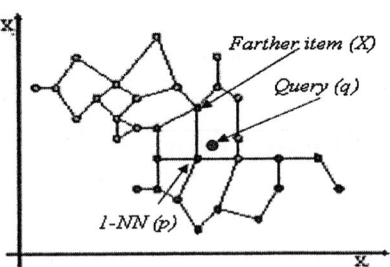

Fig. 4. Parameters determination

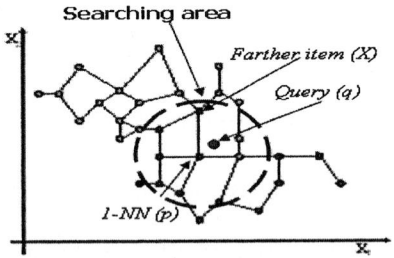

Fig. 5. Seeking of the candidates points

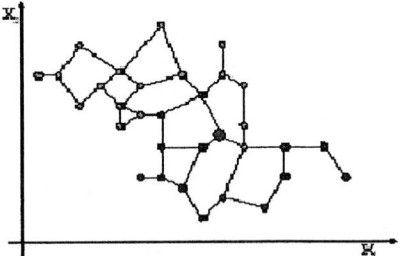

Fig. 6. Effective update

The parameters determined, we can then build the (hyper) sphere which contains all the potentially candidate points and update the relations within the (hyper) sphere like illustrated in Figure 5 and Figure 6 respectively.

To check the utility and the interest of the suggested method, we carried out some tests on various data sets. The principle of these experiments is as follows: We have m data sets $\{S_1, S_2, ..., S_m\}$ with different items count $\{n_1, n_2, ..., n_m\}$, we build a neighborhood graph on each data set and we save the corresponding graph structure of each set which will serve like reference.

Once the reference graphs are built, we take each data set and we again build new graphs using $n - 1$ items. We use then our method in order to insert the remaining item and we calculate the recall on the various built graphs. This operation is repeated on several items on the m data sets.

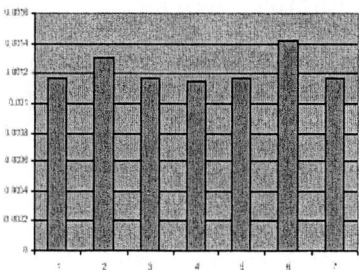

Fig. 7. Recall variations on different data sets

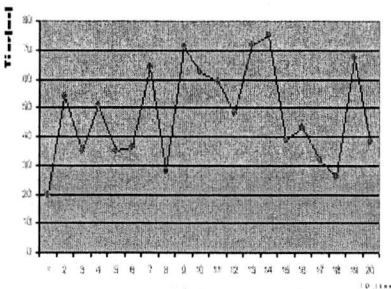

Fig. 8. Time variations on 20 items insertions

We used several data sets for these experiments, for example, Iris [1][9], UCI Irvine [15] and the Breiman's waves [4]. The graphic of Figure 7 illustrates the variation of the recall on various data sets by taking three situations : the recall is calculated on the reference graph, then on the graph with n-1 items and finally after the insertion of the remaining point. The first experiment constitutes our reference. The experiments carrying numbers 2,4,6 were carried out with an item in less and experiments 3,5,7 after the insertion of the remaining item in the corresponding previous experiment. That is, after the insertion of the remaining item, we always find the recall of the reference graph, this means that the method finds the good neighbors of the inserted item into each experiment.

In term of execution time, this last is variable and depends on several parameters among which we can quote primarily the data density. This parameter influences the number of points to take into account in the hyper sphere. A summary is presented in Figure 8 which is a result of locally insertion of 20 points taken arbitrary in a data set containing 5000 items represented in 21 dimensions. The obtained results are interesting (the time is expressed in milliseconds) and answer perfectly to the objectives laid down at the beginning.

5 Conclusion and Future Works

The direct use of the neighborhood graphs is not suitable, because their complexity does not make it reasonable to build them starting from great databases. We proposed in this article an effective method for updating neighborhood graphs locally. This method is based on an intelligent function of point location in a multidimensional space, and on the exploitation of some neighborhood graphs characteristics. The experiments carried out with this method showed its effectiveness. The use of this method can be very beneficial in particular in on line applications.

Like future works, we plan to fix the problem of the relaxation parameter determination by setting up an automatic determination function. This can be done by taking into account some statistical indicators on the data like the dispersion. Also we plan to extend this algorithm in order to make an incremental algorithm for the construction of the neighborhood graphs.

References

1. E. Anderson. The irises of the gaspé peninsula. *Bulletin of the American Iris Society 59*, pages 2–5, 1935.
2. C.-D. Bei and R. M. Gray. An improvement of the minimum distortion encoding algorithm for vector quantization. *IEEE Transactions on Communications 33*, pages 1132–1133, 1985.
3. S. Berchtold, C. Böhm, D. A. Keim, and H.-P. Kriegel. A cost model for nearest neighbor search in high-dimensional data space. In *PODS*, pages 78–86, 1997.
4. L. Breiman, J. H. Friedman, R. A. Olshen, and C. J. Stone. Classification and regression trees. *Wadsworth International Group: Belmont, California*, pages 43–49, 1984.
5. R. S. Cost and S. Salzberg. A weighted nearest neighbor algorithm for learning with symbolic features. *Machine Learning*, 10:57–78, 1993.
6. T. M. Cover and P. E. Hart. Nearest neighbor pattern classication. *IEEE Trans.Inform. Theory*, 13:57–67, 1967.
7. S. C. Deerwester, S. T. Dumais, T. K. Landauer, G. W. Furnas, and R. A. Harshman. Indexing by latent semantic analysis. *JASIS*, 41(6):391–407, 1990.
8. U. M. Fayyad, G. Piatetsky-Shapiro, and P. Smyth. From data mining to knowledge discovery: An overview. In *Advances in Knowledge Discovery and Data Mining*, pages 1–34. 1996.
9. R. Fisher. The use of multiple measurements in taxonomic problems. *Annals of Eugenics*, 7:179–188, 1936.
10. M. Flickner, H. S. Sawhney, J. Ashley, Q. Huang, B. Dom, M. Gorkani, J. Hafner, D. Lee, D. Petkovic, D. Steele, and P. Yanker. Query by image and video content: The qbic system. *IEEE Computer*, 28(9):23–32, 1995.
11. J. H. Friedman, F. Baskett, and L. J. Shustek. An algorithm for finding nearest neighbors. *IEEE Trans. Computers*, 24(10):1000–1006, 1975.
12. K. R. Gabriel and R. R. Sokal. A new statistical approach to geographic variation analysis. *Systematic zoology*, 18:259–278, 1969.
13. A. Gersho and R. M. Gray. Vector quantization and signal compression. *Kluwer Academic, Boston, MA*, 1991.

14. L. Guan and M. Kamel. Equal-average hyperplane partitioning method for vector quantization of image data. *Pattern Recognition Letters*, 13(10):693–699, 1992.
15. S. Hettich, C. Blake, and C. Merz. Uci repository of machine learning databases, 1998.
16. J. Katajainen. The region approach for computing relative neighborhood graphs in the lp metric. *Computing*, 40:147–161, 1988.
17. C.-H. Lee and L. H. Chen. Fast closest codeword search algorithm for vector quantisation. *IEE Proc.-Vis. Image Signal Process*, 141:143–148, 1994.
18. K.-I. Lin, H. V. Jagadish, and C. Faloutsos. The tv-tree: An index structure for high-dimensional data. *VLDB J.*, 3(4):517–542, 1994.
19. F. Preparata and M. I. Shamos. *Computationnal Geometry-Introduction*. Springer-Verlag, New-York, 1985.
20. W. D. Smith. Studies in computational geometry motivated by mesh generation. *PhD thesis, Princeton University*, 1989.
21. G. T. Toussaint. The relative neighborhood graphs in a finite planar set. *Pattern recognition*, 12:261–268, 1980.
22. G. T. Toussaint. Some insolved problems on proximity graphs. *D. W Dearholt and F. Harrary, editors, proceeding of the first workshop on proximity graphs. Memoranda in computer and cognitive science MCCS-91-224. Computing research laboratory. New Mexico state university Las Cruces*, 1991.
23. D. A. White and R. Jain. Similarity indexing: Algorithms and performance. In *Storage and Retrieval for Image and Video Databases (SPIE)*, pages 62–73, 1996.

Efficient Searching in Large Inheritance Hierarchies*

Michal Krátký, Svatopluk Štolfa, Václav Snášel, and Ivo Vondrák

Department of Computer Science, VŠB – Technical University of Ostrava,
17. listopadu 15, 708 33 Ostrava–Poruba, Czech Republic
{michal.kratky, svatopluk.stolfa, vaclav.snasel, ivo.vondrak}@vsb.cz

Abstract. Inheritance hierarchies have become more and more complex according to an enlargement of object-oriented technology. One of the main problems is the effective searching in such hierarchies. More sophisticated algorithms are needed to searching in the data. In this article we present a novel approach to efficient searching in large inheritance hierarchies. The updatable approach employs the multi-dimensional data structures to indexing inheritance hierarchies and effective searching in the data.

Keywords: inheritance hierarchy, indexing inheritance hierarchy, multi-dimensional data structures.

1 Introduction

Inheritance hierarchies have become more and more complex according to an enlargement of object-oriented technology. The *inheritance* is transitive, reflexive, and anti-symmetric relation between types. The idea of constructing the inheritance hierarchy is closely tight with the *polymorphism* and *code reuse* [24] that are the main principles of object oriented technology. Inheritance hierarchy is based on two ideas. The first one, a descendant inherits all operations and attributes of ascendants. The second one, a descendant may be also the ascendant for other descendants. The number of classes has grown rapidly in class hierarchies during the last decade and the searching in such large hierarchies became the area of intensive research interest.

Every algorithm for searching in class hierarchies should satisfy several general requirements, such as the runtime efficiency, space efficiency, and incremental hierarchy modifications. The runtime efficiency requirement means that every algorithm should be very fast and effective. The space efficiency requirement demands small encoding data structures to avoid space overflow. And at last, the incremental hierarchy modifications postulate support for runtime updates of the inheritance hierarchy that do not waste time and space capacity, since they are usually provided during runtime.

---

* Work is partially supported by Grant of GACR No. 201/03/1318.

Many algorithms for encoding inheritance hierarchies have been published, but they solve only the inheritance hierarchy problem. On the other hand, our approach might be also useful for searching of attributes, operations and so on. Due to the fact that our approach is persistent and simply updatable in contrast to the common applied approaches, our method might be also useful in other class hierarchy oriented domains, such as object oriented file systems or persistent object databases.

The key question addressed by this article is whether algorithms for searching in multi-dimensional data may be successfully adapted for inheritance hierarchy problem and searching in this hierarchy. The next section briefly outlines existing encodings of inheritance hierarchies. This is followed by explanation of multi-dimensional approach and discussion about possibilities of this method in Section 3. Multi-dimensional data structures are employed in the novel approach. Therefore some of them are briefly described in Section 4. In Section 5 we put forward experimental results prove the efficiency of our approach. The final section presents our conclusions and discusses a possibility of our future work.

2 State of the Art

The question of encoding inheritance hierarchies has been thoroughly researched over the last few years. According to our research, basic solutions to this problem use heuristic algorithms that are effective and fast only for the relatively small inheritance hierarchies. However, the number of classes (or objects) may rise rapidly to thousands (e.g. inheritance hierarchies of JDK [26] or .NET [19] platforms), millions and more (e.g. object oriented file systems) and such types of heuristic algorithms are not able to satisfy the requirements anymore. This section surveys some of the main encoding algorithms for inheritance hierarchy problem that are used commonly in practice.

Relative Numbering of Nodes

Every node (class from the hierarchy) is numbered by a couple of integers $l(x), r(x)$ (see Figure 1(a)). The hierarchy is traversed by the *depth first search* algorithm from the top and the counter c is incremented for each new node. Current value in the c counter is stored in the $l(x)$ when the node is touched for the first time. When the algorithm leaves the node, current value of c is stored in $r(x)$. The type x is a subtype of the type y if and only if the $l(y) < l(x)$ and $r(x) \leq r(y)$. The information about the number of subclasses may also be obtained from this couple of integers $(r(x) - l(x))$, but if we add incremental modification to this algorithm then this information will be lost. The possibility of incremental modification is allowed if the counter is incremented by the specific number greater than one. New node z may be than added between the two nodes x and y and its $l(z)$ value will be set to $l(y) - l(x)$ and $r(z)$ value will be set to $r(x) - r(y)$.

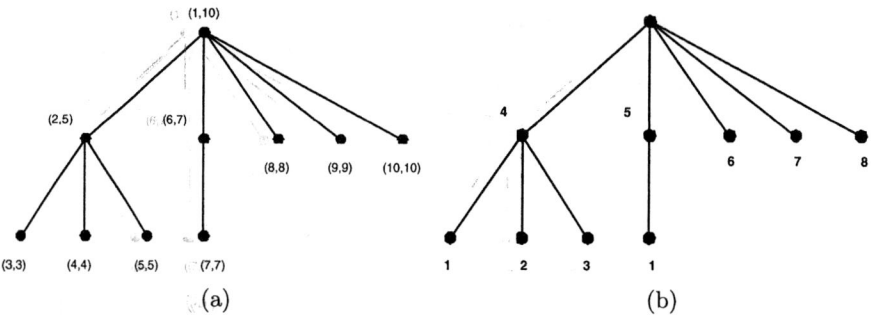

Fig. 1. (a) Relative numbering of nodes. (b) Bit-vector Encoding Caseau

Cohen's Algorithm

Cohen's algorithm was the first widely and practically used technique. All classes in hierarchy are signed by number. The complete path to the root is recorded for every class in the array of its ascendants at the appropriate position. This position depends on the depth of the superclass in the hierarchy. Inheritance testing between classes x and y is provided by the searching of y in the array of class x at the appropriate position of the potential superclass y. The great advantage is the constant time comparison, but the relative small space consumption quickly rise in consequence of hierarchy amount explosion.

Bit-vector Encoding

Caseau [5] introduced the first application of the bit-vector encoding for the inheritance hierarchy encoding problem. The idea of encoding consists of creating the conflict graph, its coloring and bit-vector encoding construction from the colors of nodes. Let C be the chain of classes $x_0, x_1, \ldots, x_l$ of the class hierarchy T. Then *weight* of this chain is equal to $\sum_{i=0}^{l} degree(x_i)$, where $degree(x)$ is the number of direct subclasses of class x. The size of the encoding field is then equal to the maximum of the *weights* of all chains of the hierarchy T (see Figure 1(b)).

Krall, Vitek a Horspool follow the idea of Caseau in [12]. The improvement of algorithm consists in the modification of source hierarchy. Algorithms for graph creation, coloring, and bit-vector encoding remain same.

Caseau, Habib, Nourine a Raynaud have presented the new algorithm for the bit-vector encoding creation from the colored graph in [6]. The *weight* function for the chain C is then $\sum_{i=0}^{l} cmin(degree(x_i))$, where $cmin(n)$ is the minimal number of colors for the encoding of class that has n direct subclasses. The size of the encoding field is then also equal to the maximum of the *weights* of all chains of the hierarchy T. Another approach has been presented by Raynauda and Thierry [23]. The source tree is divided to the two parts (binary tree) and different colors are then associated to both subtrees. This *greedy* algorithm then consists of the following steps. The first one, binary tree T' is created, where every node of this tree is colored. Colors of superclasses are then distributed to the all of its subclasses. Finally, bit-vector encoding is generated.

Tree Based Indexes and Other Solutions
Palacz and Vitek describe in [21] a constant-time subtype test algorithm designed for time and space constrained environments (such as Real-Time Java) which require predictable running times, low space overheads, and dynamic class loading.

There are also many approaches to indexing of tree based structures in our field of the interest. Such type of index is especially applied in object oriented databases (OODB) where inheritance and aggregation hierarchies are the main structures. These indexes, based on e.g. CH-tree [11], CG-tree [10], hcC-tree [25], *class division* [22] and so on, are less or more effective and usually based on some simple structures like B$^+$-trees. Indexing based on triple-node hierarchy [16] or multi key index approach [20] an so on are other solutions to this problem. In survey [3] techniques of OODB are analysed. Although, many techniques have been noticed, we thing that our persistent and updatable approach is useful and usable for indexing inheritance hierarchies and brings new solution to this problem and its application to OODB, object oriented file systems an so on. For example, let us take a solution in the Longhorn operation system called WinFS [18].

3 Multi-dimensional Approach to Indexing Inheritance Hierarchy

In our novel approach we represent an inheritance hierarchy, which is possible to model as a tree, as a set of all the root to leaf paths. Then, such paths are represented as multi-dimensional points and inserted into a multi-dimensional data structure (see Section 4). This novel method brings advantages as follow:

- Queries (we employ the term from database point of view), e.g. descendants of a class are searched, are transformed into queries of multi-dimensional data structures. No heuristics are applied to querying, exact defined point and range queries (see the next Section) are employed.
- Consequently, better complexity is allowed. Classical approaches provide only $O(n)$ complexity. Range query algorithms provide $O(r \times log(n))$ complexity, where r is the number of intersect regions (see Section 4). Our experiments show that the complexity of the approach is better than linear, i.e. the r value is rather low.
- Applied multi-data data structures are persistent [17], therefore we can index large inheritance hierarchies and the querying is the same for large and small one.
- The approach is simply updatable (incremental).

Similar approach was developed for indexing XML data [27] in [13], but no multi-dimensional indexing was not applied to indexing inheritance hierarchy.

3.1 Multi-dimensional Model

Let us have an inheritance tree defined as $T = (V_T, E_T, C_T)$, where V_T is a set of vertexes (nodes) and E_T is a set of edges of the tree. One name of class

$\in C_T$ is assigned to each tree node. From other point of view the tree T may be represented as a set of paths $\mathcal{P}$ – a set of all the root to leaf paths. $p \in \mathcal{P}$, $p = c_0/c_1/\ldots/c_l$, where $c_i \in C_T$ is the name of class, c_0 is the name of root, c_l is the name of leaf class, l is the length of the path p.

Example 1 (A decomposition of inheritance tree into a set of paths).
Let us consider inheritance hierarchy in J2SE 1.4.2 [26]. A part of the hierarchy is depicted in Figure 2. We get the set of paths $\mathcal{P}$ by the decomposition of the tree into all the root to leaf paths. $\mathcal{P} = \{$java.lang.Object/java.awt.GridLayout, java.lang.Object/java.awt.Component/java.awt.Container, java.lang.Object/java.awtPageAttributes$\}$

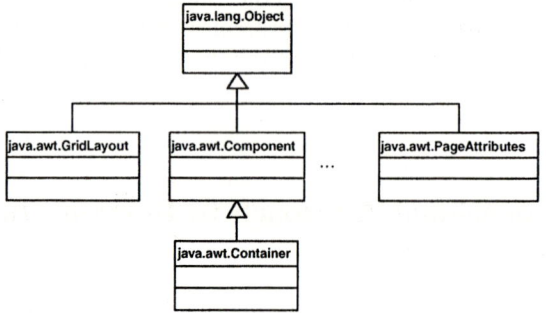

Fig. 2. A part of inheritance hierarchy of J2SE 1.4.2

Such path may be represented as a multi-dimensional point and the point can be indexed by a *multi-dimensional data structure* [4], e.g. UB-tree [1], BUB-tree [7] or R-tree [9]. In Section 4 some of them are briefly described. The employment of such structures satisfies above described advantages. Querying of an inheritance hierarchy is performed by exactly defined point and range queries. Of course, these persistent data structures may be stored in the main memory. On the other hand the indexing of a large collection is possible in contrast to main memory techniques described in Section 2.

Now, we define indices for indexing an inheritance tree in the novel approach.

1. **Term index** - each string value (class names in the case) is stored in the index together with its unique number. We can employ e.g. B-tree [28] to solve the problem. A sophisticated approach [14] would be applied for satisfying a complex term query. For example term query may be defined as a regular expression, e.g. let us take query: "Get all ascendants of class '*Frame'.".
2. **Path index** - a multi-dimensional data structure containing points representing paths of the inheritance tree.

Definition 1 (Multi-dimensional point representing a path).
Let us take a root to leaf path $p \in \mathcal{P}$ in an inheritance tree, $p = c_0/c_1/\ldots/c_l$,

where c_i is the class name. The n-dimensional point representing the path is defined $t_p = (id(c_0), id(c_1), \ldots, id(c_l))$, where $id(c_i)$ is the unique number of string c_i, $n = l + 1$.

Obviously, such paths have not the same length. We need know the dimension of indexed space before indexing of the first point. We can set the dimension to $n = l_{max} + 1$ according to the maximal length of path in the inheritance tree. Points of dimension $< n$ are aligned by blank values (e.g. zero in the case). An overhead of the technique is enormous, therefore we discuss a solution of the problem in Section 3.4.

3.2 Querying of Inheritance Hierarchy

As mentioned the querying is performed by point and range queries. In the case of the point query, input is a multi-dimensional point and the algorithm searches whether the point is/is not contained in the structure. A range query is defined by the n-dimensional box – *query box* – defined by two points and the result contains all points of indexed space in the box.

Definition 2 (Range query).
Let Ω be an n-dimensional discrete space, $\Omega = D^n$, $D = \{0, 1, \ldots, 2^{\tau_D} - 1\}$, and points (tuples) $T^1, T^2, \ldots, T^m \in \Omega$. $T^i = (t_1, t_2, \ldots, t_n)$, τ_D is the chosen length of a binary representation of a number t_i from domain D. The range query RQ *is defined by a* query hyper-box (query window) QB *which is determined by two points* $QL = (ql_1, \ldots, ql_n)$ *and* $QH = (qh_1, \ldots, qh_n)$, QL *and* $QH \in \Omega$, ql_i *and* $qh_i \in D$, *where* $\forall i \in \{1, \ldots, n\} : ql_i \leq qh_i$. *This range query retrieves all points* $T^j(t_1, t_2, \ldots, t_n)$ *in the set* $\{T^1, T^2, \ldots, T^m\}$ *such as* $\forall i : ql_i \leq t_i \leq qh_i$.

The querying of the inheritance hierarchy includes three phases. In the first phase, we get unique numbers of query terms. In the second one, we perform a sequence of range queries (called *complex range query*) in the path index. In the third one, unique numbers of found points are transformed to class names using the term index. Now definitions of complex range queries to querying of an inheritance tree are depicted.

Definition 3 (Complex range query to searching ascendants of a class T).
Let us take an n-dimensional discrete space $\Omega = D^n$ and the name of a class T. All ascendants of the class are found by the complex range query (containing $n-1$ range queries) defined by the n-dimensional points: $(min(D), id(T), min(D), \ldots) :$ $(max(D), id(T), max(D), \ldots), \ldots, (min(D), min(D), \ldots, id(T)) : (max(D), max(D), \ldots, id(T))$.

Definition 4 (Complex range query to searching descendants of a class T).
Let us take an n-dimensional discrete space $\Omega = D^n$ and the name of a class T. All descendants of the class are found by the complex range query (containing $n - 1$ range queries) defined by the n-dimensional points: $(id(T), min(D), \ldots) :$ $(id(T), max(D), \ldots), \ldots, (min(D), \ldots, id(T), min(D)) : (max(D), \ldots, id(T), max(D))$.

Example 2 (Indexing and querying of inheritance hierarchy).
Let us take a part of the inheritance hierarchy in Figure 2. Names of classes java.lang.Object, java.awt.GridLayout, java.awt.Component, java.awt.Container, and java.awt.PageAttributes are inserted into the term index with unique numbers 1, 2, 3, 4, and 5. Since the maximal length of path is 2, dimension of the space $n = 3$. $D = \{0, 1, \ldots, 2^{32} - 1\}$, $max(D) = 2^{32} - 1$, $min(D) = 0$. We get points representing paths $(1, 2, 0)$, $(1, 3, 4)$, and $(1, 5, 0)$ in the inheritance tree. The points are inserted into a multi-dimensional data structure (path index).

Now, we would like to search all sub-classes of the class java.lang.Object. In other words, we want to find all points containing unique number 1 in arbitrary coordinate (except the last coordinate – a leaf has no children). The query is performed by the complex range query: $(1, min(D), min(D)) : (1, max(D), max(D))$ and $(min(D), 1, min(D)) : (max(D), 1, max(D))$. Points $(1, 2, 0)$, $(1, 3, 4)$, and $(1, 5, 0)$ are retrieved in the path index. Now, class names are obtained in the term index.

More, we would like to search all super-classes of class java.awt.Container. We search points containing the value 4 into arbitrary coordinate (except the first one – the root has no ascendants). We create complex range query containing two range queries: $(min(D), 4, min(D)) : (max(D), 4, max(D))$ and $(min(D), min(D), 4) : (max(D), max(D), 4)$. In the case, result includes point (1,3,4) and strings java.lang.Object and java.awt.Component are retrieved in the term index.

Direct ascendant (parent) and descendant (child) are obtained by a modification of above described range queries.

3.3 Update of the Index

Incremental hierarchy modifications postulate support for runtime updates of the inheritance hierarchy that do not waste time and space capacity, since they are usually provided during runtime. Due to the fact our approach employs dynamic data structures, incremental hierarchy modifications are simply possible.

Let us take a class c inherits from class c_{l-1}. The whole path $c_0/c_1/\ldots/c_{l-1}/c$ is represented as the point $(id(c_0), id(c_1), \ldots, id(c_{l-1}), id(c))$. Such point is inserted into the multi-dimensional data structure. Any amount of classes, whole paths and so on are inserted in the same manner. Delete of leaf class is simply. If we would like to delete a non-leaf class (exactly a subtree) we update or delete any amount of points containing classes in the subtree. Let us take out the multi-dimensional data structures provide logarithmic time complexity for insert, update, and delete operations.

3.4 A Characteristic of Inheritance Hierarchy

In Figure 3 we see a characteristic of real inheritance hierarchy from path length frequency point of view. Obviously, most paths have the length one – most of classes have only one ascendant (class Object). We can see paths have very different length. A naive approach is the alignment of points dimension to the maximal dimension, consequently to the maximal length of path. Of course, such naive technique is ineffective due to the overhead of align values. A multi-dimensional forest [14] is a solution of the problem.

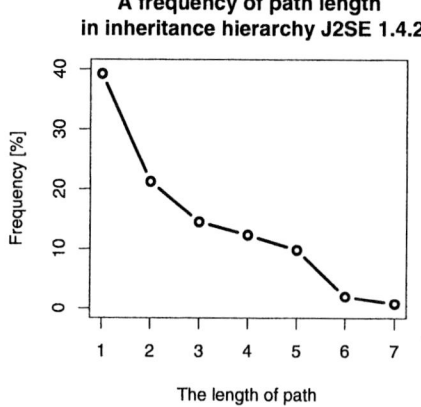

Fig. 3. Frequency of the length of paths for real inheritance hierarchy

The multi-dimensional forest includes variable number of multi-dimensional trees where each of them indexes a space of different dimension. In the case we can create the forest containing three trees indexing spaces of dimension 3, 5, and 8. Therefore the overhead of the structure remains the same for indexing small number of paths with the large length as well. In Figure 3(a) we can see the maximal length of path is 7. Consequently, the number of range queries is 7 ($n - 1$, see Definitions 3 and 4) in the worst case during an execution of the class query. Moreover, the multi-dimensional data structures allow performing the complex range query on the one run in the tree [8].

4 Multi-dimensional Data Structures

Now R-tree, (B)UB-tree, and signature multi-dimensional tree are briefly described. These data structures are employed in our experiments (see Section 5).

R-tree
R-tree [9] is a multi-dimensional data structure based on the hierarchy of *MBBs* (*minimal bounding box*). These MBBs are created around indexed points. Indexed points are inserted into leaf nodes. Super-leaf nodes contain MBBs and other inner nodes contain super-MBBs. Increasing dimension of indexed space brings some influences which decrease the efficiency of querying multi-dimensional

data. These influences are called as *curse of dimensionality* [29]. For example, increasing number of MBBs have non-empty intersection, consequently the large number of tree nodes is read in the secondary storage during query execution. Therefore different variants of R-tree, trying to eliminate the influences, have developed, e.g. R*-tree [2].

UB-tree

Universal B-tree (UB-tree) [1] and its variant Bounding UB-tree (BUB-tree) [7] are multi-dimensional data structures based on the *Z-ordering* and B^+-tree. Z-ordering allows to compute the Z-address for each point of indexed space. The space filling Z-curve is created by ordering points according to their Z-addresses.

Z-regions represent clusters of points in a space, which are close (according to the Z-ordering). In contrast, BUB-tree does not index the *dead space* (part of the space containing no data). A Z-region is stored on a disk page in the (B)UB-tree hierarchy. Z-regions make it possible efficient processing of the range query. Leafs contain indexed points, inner nodes contain Z-regions and (super)Z-regions. In opposite to other multi-dimensional data structures, e.g. *R-tree*, Z-regions of the (B)UB-tree are disjunctive. This fact is very important for higher dimensions when the curse of dimensionality takes place.

Signature R-Tree

The range query used in the multi-dimensional approach is called *narrow range query*. Points defining a query box have got some coordinates the same, whereas the size of interval defined by other coordinates near to the size of space's domain. Notice, regions intersecting a query box during processing of a range query are called *intersect regions* and regions containing at least one point of the query box are called *relevant regions*. We denote their number by N_I and N_R, respectively. Many irrelevant regions are searched during processing of the narrow range query in multi-dimensional data structures. Consequently, a ratio of relevant and intersect regions, so called *relevance ratio* c_R is closed to 0 with the increasing dimension of indexed space.

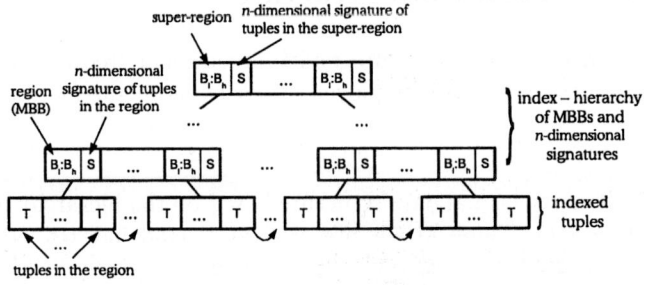

Fig. 4. A structure of the Signature R-Tree

In [15] Signature R-tree data structure was introduced. This data structure enables efficient processing of the narrow range query. Items of inner nodes contain a definition of (super)region and n-dimensional signature of tuples included in the (super)region (see Figure 4). A superposition of tuples' coordinates by operation OR creates the signature. Operation AND is applied to better filtration of irrelevant regions during processing of the narrow range query. Other multi-dimensional data structures (e.g. (B)UB-tree) are possible to extend in the same way.

5 Experimental Results

We have tested our approach to compare it with two basic commonly used algorithms for encoding of inheritance hierarchies. These two encoding algorithms are named Cohen and Numbering. In the Cohen, the set of super-classes is created for all classes and the information about class height in the class hierarchy is used. In the Numbering, relative numbering is created and we also used the non incremental version where the number of subclasses can be easily obtained and used.

It is difficult to compare the different approaches properly, so the reference number of touched classes was chosen. Efficiency was tested for the query, where all subclasses of specified class were searched. The method of indexing was created as implementation independent. It means that class hierarchies were encoded outside the main program that uses them. Such type of testing simulates the efficiency of algorithm applied in some indexing framework. First, the class is searched in the external index and then the query is processed. The number of touched classes is then counted according to the used algorithm. It is obvious, that our algorithm employed a sophisticated index for class names indexing. Such type of indexing was not applied for Cohen and Numbering algorithms. The properties needed for querying according to selected algorithm are searched sequentially. This simulates the real usage of these algorithms. Even without this limitation, these algorithms were not so efficient as our multi-dimensional approach on tested class hierarchies.

The result represented as bar charts shows the average number for all approaches. Subclasses of all classes were searched and the average value was computed. Smaller number means higher efficiency of the algorithm. We can see tests for four inheritance hierarchies in Figure 5. The first hierarchy consists of 14,940 classes, second hierarchy consists of 8,255 classes, third hierarchy consists of 7,071 classes, and fourth hierarchy consists of 3,988 classes. All of them show that our approach is more effective even on the relatively small number of classes. We can see that all multi-dimensional data structures give better results than the conventional methods. The Signature R-tree gives the best results. For example in Figure 5(a) the number of touched nodes is 7.7% of touched nodes for Cohen method and 14.7% for the Numbering compared with the Signature R-tree. The average time of query performance is 0.02s[1]. In the case of Signature

---

[1] The experiments were executed on an Intel Pentium ®4 2.4Ghz, 512MB DDR333.

R-tree the size of index is 2MB for the first hierarchy. Let us compare it with 1.7MB of Numbering index size. We can see the overhead of our approach is not enormous.

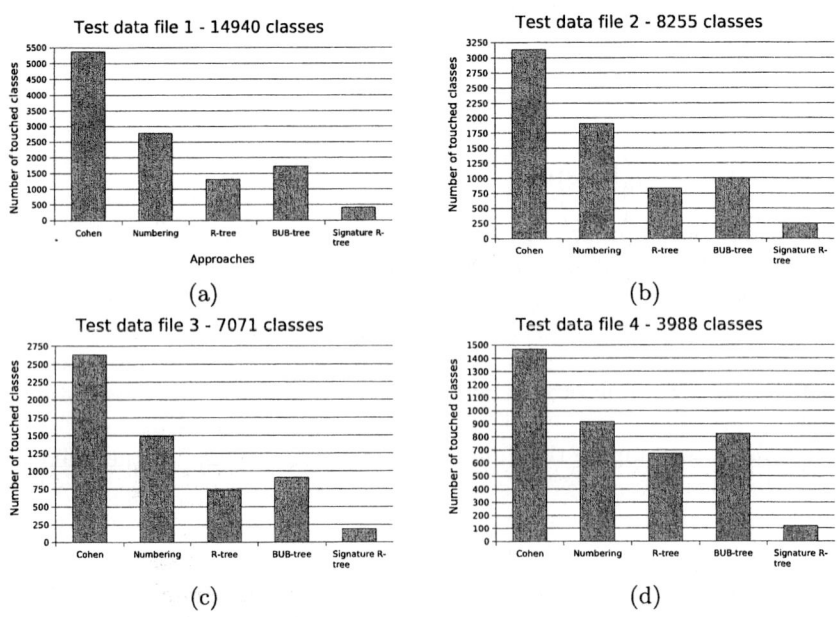

Fig. 5. The number of touched classes

These two basic algorithms (Cohen and Numbering) are not able to satisfy requirements anymore if the amount of classes is higher. These algorithms have linear complexity for such type of query and they were not created for such problem. On the other hand, our approach have been already successfully tested on XML documents with millions of nodes. Since the inheritance hierarchies will grow in the future, we have shown that the new multi-dimensional approach might be one of solutions to this problem.

6 Conclusions

In this paper, we have presented the new approach for searching in large inheritance hierarchies. This approach applies multi-dimensional data structures for indexing of class hierarchies. Inheritance hierarchies are stored and indexed as a set of multi-dimensional points. Querying is then performed by multi-dimensional point and range queries. We have tested our multi-dimensional approach with several structures like R-tree, BUB-tree, and Signature R-tree. Although, our tested hierarchies were relatively small, the efficiency of our approach was proved in comparison tests with other commonly used algorithms. It is important that the our approach is persistent and simply updatable in contrast to the classical approaches.

Our future work will be devoted to the extension of our algorithm and application to other closely connected problems such as object oriented file systems and so on. We would also like to identify other types of queries and test our approach on huge hierarchies.

References

1. R. Bayer. The Universal B-Tree for multidimensional indexing: General Concepts. In *Proceedings of WWCA'97, Tsukuba, Japan*, 1997.
2. N. Beckmann, H.-P. Kriegel, R. Schneider, and B. Seeger. The R*-tree: An effcient and robust access method for points and rectangles. In *Proceedings of the 1990 ACM SIGMOD*, pages 322–331, 1990.
3. E. Bertino, B. Catania, and L. Chiesa. Definition and analysis of index organizations for object-oriented database systems. *Information Systems*, 23(2):65–108, April 1998.
4. C. Böhm, S. Berchtold, and D. Keim. Searching in High-dimensional Spaces – Index Structures for Improving the Performance Of Multimedia Databases. *ACM*, 2002.
5. Y. Caseau. Efficient Handling of Multiple Inheritance Hierarchies. In *Proceedings of ACM Conference on Object-Oriented Programming, Systems, Languages, and Applications, OOP-SLA'93*, pages 271–287. ACM, 1993.
6. Y. Caseau, M. Habib, L. Nourine, and O. Raynaud. Encoding of Multiple Inheritance Hierarchies and Partial Orders. *Computational Intelligence*, 15:50–62, 1999.
7. R. Fenk. The BUB-Tree. In *Proceedings of 28rd VLDB International Conference on Very Large Data Bases, VLDB 2002, Hongkong, China*, 2002.
8. R. Fenk, V. Markl, and R. Bayer. Improving Multidimensional Range Queries of non rectangular Volumes specified by a Query Box Set. In *Proceedings of International Symposium on DWACOS*, 1999.
9. A. Guttman. R-Trees: A Dynamic Index Structure for Spatial Searching. In *Proceedings of ACM SIGMOD 1984, Annual Meeting, Boston, USA*, pages 47–57. ACM Press, June 1984.
10. C. Kilger and G. Moerkotte. Indexing Multiple Sets. In *VLDB'94, Proceedings of the 20th International Conference on VLDB, 1994, Santiago de Chile, Chile*, 1994.
11. W. Kim, K. Kim, and A. Dale. Indexing Techniques for Object-Oriented Databases. *Addison-Wesley*, pages 371–394, 1989.
12. A. Krall, J. Vitek, and R. N. Horspool. Near Optimal Hierarchical Encoding of Types. In *Proceedings of Ecoop'97*, volume 1241 of *LNCS*. Springer–Verlag, 1997.
13. M. Krátký, J. Pokorný, and V. Snášel. Implementation of XPath Axes in the Multi-dimensional Approach to Indexing XML Data. In *Current Trends in Database Technology, DataX, EDBT 2004*, volume 3268 of *LNCS*. Springer–Verlag, 2004.
14. M. Krátký, T. Skopal, and V. Snášel. Multidimensional Term Indexing for Efficient Processing of Complex Queries. *Kybernetika, Journal of the Academy of Sciences of the Czech Republic*, 40(3):381–396, 2004.
15. M. Krátký, V. Snášel, P. Zezula, J. Pokorný, and T. Skopal. Efficient Processing of Narrow Range Queries in the R-Tree. Technical Report ARG-TR-01-2004, Amphora Research Group (ARG), 2004, http://www.cs.vsb.cz/arg/techreports/sigrtree.pdf.

16. F. H.-W. Luk and A. W. Fu. Triple-node Hierarchies for Object Oriented Database Indexing. In *Proceedings of the intl. conference on CIKM '98*. ACM Press, 1998.
17. Y. Manolopoulos, Y. Theodoridis, and V. Tsotras. *Advanced Database Indexing*. Kluwer Academic Publisher, 2001.
18. Microsoft. WinFS, 2004, http://msdn.microsoft.com/data/winfs/.
19. Microsoft. .NET Homepage, 2004, www.microsoft.com/net/.
20. T. A. Mück and M. L. Polaschek. A Configurable Type Hierarchy Index for OODB. *VLDB Journal*, 6(4):312–332, 1997.
21. K. Palacz and J. Vitek. Java Subtype Tests In Real-Time. In *Proceedings of Ecoop'03*, volume 2743 of *LNCS*. Springer–Verlag, 2003.
22. S. Ramaswamy and P. C. Kanellakis. OODB Indexing by Class-Division. In *Proceedings of the 1995 ACM SIGMOD*, volume 24. ACM Press, 1995.
23. O. Raynaud and E. Thierry. A Quasi Optimal Bit-vector Encoding of Tree Hierarchies. Application to Efficient Type Inclusion Tests. In *Proceedings of Ecoop'2002*, Lecture Notes in Computer Science. Springer–Verlag, 2002.
24. J. R. Rumbaugh, M. R. Blaha, W. Lorensen, F. Eddy, and W. Premerlani. *Object–Oriented Modeling and Design*. Prentice Hall, 1991.
25. B. Sreenath and S. Seshadri. The hcC-tree: An Efficient Index Structure for Object Oriented Databases. In *Proceedings of the 20th International Conference on VLDB, 1994, Santiago de Chile, Chile*, pages 203–213, 1994.
26. Sun. Java^{TM} 2 Platform, Standard Edition, v 1.4.2 API Specification, 2003, http://java.sun.com/j2se/1.4.2/docs/api/.
27. W3 Consortium. Extensible Markup Language (XML) 1.0, 1998, http://www.w3.org/TR/REC-xml.
28. N. Wirth. *Algorithms and Data Structures*. Prentice Hall, 1984.
29. C. Yu. *High-Dimensional Indexing*, volume 2341 of *Lecture Notes in Computer Science*. Springer–Verlag, 2002.

Author Index

Abbadi, Amr El 65
Abelló, Alberto 441
Acar, Aybar C. 365
Acker, Ralph 596
Agrawal, Divyakant 65
Aldana, J.F. 706
Al-Radaideh, Qasem A. 105
An, Pao-Ying 776
Ao, Zhuoyun 696
Araki, Tadashi 260
Ayala, Claudia 665

Baïna, Karim 24
Ballegooij, Alex van 55
Bamha, Mostafa 616
Ban, ChaeHoon 503
Bayer, Rudolf 596
Beaudoin, Jean-François 910
Belkhatir, Mohammed 113
Berlanga, Rafael 385, 706
Bhowmick, Sourav S. 134, 395, 482, 756
Bouzguenda, Lotfi 1
Bressan, Stéphane 230
Budiman, Sri L. 482
Burdescu, Dumitru Dan 124

Cheang, Chan Wa 166
Chen, An-Pin 858
Chen, Kuang-Ku 858
Chen, Mu-Yen 858
Chen, Yangjun 207
Chen, Yongfeng 696
Chia, Liang-Tien 134
Chiaramella, Yves 113
Choi, Jae-Ho 290
Christiansen, Henning 606
Chundi, Parvathi 514
Chu, Yang 134
Combi, Carlo 353
Cong, Gao 85
Cornacchia, Roberto 55
Cui, Bin 85

Darzentas, Jenny 406
de la Rosa, F.T. 726, 848
De Nicola, Antonio 655

de Palol, Xavier 441
de Vries, Arjen P. 55
Debenham, John 534
Decker, Stefan 716
Dekhtyar, Alex 576
Delisle, Sylvain 910
DeWitt, David J. 797
Dillon, Tharam 756
Domínguez, Eladio 343
Dray, Gérard 633
Dugré, Mathieu 910

Fan, Jianping 766
Fang, Youlin 34
Fazzinga, B. 736
Fenz, Stefan 586
Fernández, Mary 554
Ferri, Fernando 524
Flesca, S. 736
Franch, Xavier 665
Furtado, Pedro 808

Gaaloul, Walid 24
Galanis, Leonidas 797
Gardarin, Georges 564
Gasca, R.M. 726, 848
Gasparini, Simone 544
Godart, Claude 24
Goluch, Gernot 586
Gómez-López, M.T. 726, 848
Goncalves, Marlene 375
Gong, Zhiguo 166
Grifoni, Patrizia 524
Gruenwald, Le 186, 686
Gupta, Shyam Kumar 756

Hacid, Hakim 930
Hacid, Mohand-Saïd 441
Hamada, Takahiro 461
Han, Peng 95
Hara, Takahiro 868, 879
Hayashi, Hideki 868
Hefeeda, Mohamed 746
Helmer, Sven 920
Hidders, Jan 554

Author Index

Hong, BongHee 503
Hou U, Leong 166
Hsu, Wynne 270

Iacob, Ionut E. 576
Ibrahim, Hamidah 105
Ishikawa, Yoshiharu 145

Jonker, Willem 333

Kang, Dazhou 676
Kang, Hyunchul 421
Kanjo, Daisuke 156
Kato, Ai 260
Kawai, Yukiko 156
Kersten, Martin 55
Keulen, Maurice van 333
Kim, DongHyun 503
Kim, Sang-Wook 493
Kim, Woo-Cheol 890
Kim, Young-Hyun 421
Kitagawa, Hiroyuki 145
Kitsuregawa, Masaru 786
Klemen, Markus 586
Koh, Jia-Ling 776
Kovalev, Vladimir 395
Krátký, Michal 940
Kruk, Sebastian Ryszard 716
Kurokawa, Sayumi 145
Kwon, Dongseop 75

Lee, Dongwon 890
Lee, Mong Li 270
Lee, SangKeun 290
Lee, SangYoon 890
Lee, Sukho 75
Lee, Taewon 75
Lee, You-Ri 310
Leonardi, Erwin 482
Li, Changqing 300
Li, Hanyu 270
Li, Hua-Gang 65
Li, Jianxin 280
Li, Jing-Tao 766
Li, Wenhui 838
Li, Wen-Syan 828
Li, Yanhong 186
Li, Yanhui 676
Ling, Tok Wang 300
Linnert, Manfred 586

Liu, Jixue 696
Liu, Song 746
Llidó, Dolores M. 385
Lloret, Jorge 343
Lu, Jiaheng 300
Lu, Jianjiang 676
Lü, Kevin J. 280, 766
Lyu, Jyh-charn 250

Ma, Qiang 471
Maeda, Kazuhiko 879
Martinenghi, Davide 606
Metais, Elisabeth 626
Methuku, Srikanth 576
Michiels, Philippe 554
Miesenberger, Klaus 406
Minakuchi, Mitsuru 260
Missikoff, Michele 655
Miyamori, Hisashi 176, 260
Moerkotte, Guido 920
Mohania, Mukesh 756
Mondal, Anirban 85
Montmain, Jacky 633
Motro, Amihai 365
Mulhem, Philippe 113

Nakache, Didier 626
Narang, Inderpal 828
Natarajan, Ramesh 828
Navas, I. 706
Navigli, Roberto 655
Nemoto, Jun 44
Ni, Wei 300
Nishio, Shojiro 868, 879
Nishioka, Shuichi 461

Ogawa, Yasushi 260
Onizuka, Makoto 461

Pardedc, Eric 431
Paraire, Jordi 385
Park, Dong-Gue 310
Park, Ho-Hyun 696
Park, Sanghyun 493, 890
Pavlov, Aleksei 920
Phan, Thomas 828
Pieringer, Roland 596
Plantié, Michel 633
Pok, Gouchol 250
Pozzi, Giuseppe 353
Prabhakar, Sunil 240, 746

Quintarelli, Elisa   544

Rafanelli, Maurizio   524
Rahayu, Wenny J.   431, 645
Ray, Indrakshi   14
Rosenkrantz, Daniel J.   514
Rotem, Doron   220
Rubio, Ángel L.   343
Ryu, Keun Ho   250

Sanz, I.   706
Selamat, Mohd Hasan   105
Shen, Jialie   85
Shen, Rui-Min   95
Shimizu, Toshiyuki   451
Siméon, Jérôme   554
Sion, Radu   828
Smiljanić, Marko   333
Snášel, Václav   940
Stanescu, Liana   124
Stejic, Zoran   260
Stockinger, Kurt   220
Stoffel, Kilian   324
Štolfa, Svatopluk   940
St-Pierre, Josée   910
Studer, Thomas   324
Sulaiman, Md Nasir   105
Sun, Haibin   838
Swamini, Dhruv   756

Tagarelli, A.   736
Tan, Kian-Lee   85
Tanaka, Katsumi   156, 176, 260, 471
Tang, Nan   280
Taniar, David   431
Tiang, Tan Boon   230
Timsit, Jean François   626
Tjoa, A. Min   586
Tosun, Ali Şaman   818
Toyama, Motomichi   44
Tu, Yi-Cheng   240, 746

Uchida, Wataru   879

Valle, C. Del   848
Vercammen, Roel   554
Vidal, María-Esther   375
Vondrák, Ivo   940

Wang, Botao   786
Wang, Fei   766
Wang, Heng   34
Wang, Peng   676
Weippl, Edgar R.   586
Wollersheim, Dennis   645
Won, Jung-Im   493
Wong, Kam-Fai   280
Wu, Chien-Liang   776
Wu, Kesheng   220
Wu, Ping   65

Xia, Yuni   746
Xie, Bo   95
Xin, Tai   14
Xu, Baowen   676

Yaguchi, Yuri   461
Yamamuro, Masashi   461
Yang, Dongqing   34
Yang, Fan   95
Yan, Jingfeng   240
Yeh, Laurent   564
Yoon, Jee-Hee   493
Yoon, Young-Jin   290
Yoshikawa, Masatoshi   451
Yu, Byunggu   197
Yu, Chien-Chih   900
Yu, Hailing   65
Yu, Jeffrey Xu   280
Yu, Tian   300

Zapata, María A.   343
Zhang, Jianwei   145
Zhang, Rui   514
Zhu, Yajie   14
Zhu, Yun   686
Zieborak, Lech   716
Zighed, Abdelkader Djamel   930